ANNALS OF COMMUNISM

Each volume in the series Annals of Communism will publish selected and previously inaccessible documents from former Soviet state and party archives in a narrative that develops a particular topic in the history of Soviet and international communism. Separate English and Russian editions will be prepared. Russian and Western scholars work together to prepare the documents for each volume. Documents are chosen not for their support of any single interpretation but for their particular historical importance or their general value in deepening understanding and facilitating discussion. The volumes are designed to be useful to students, scholars, and interested general readers.

The Kirov Murder and Soviet History

Matthew E. Lenoe

Translations by Matthew E. Lenoe

Documents compiled by Mikhail Prozumenshchikov

Yale

UNIVERSITY PRESS

New Haven & London

This volume has been prepared with the cooperation of the Russian State Archive of Contemporary History (RGANI) in the framework of an agreement concluded between RGANI and Yale University Press.

Documents held by the Archive of the President of the Russian Federation (APRF), the Russian State Archive of Contemporary History (RGANI), and the State Archive of the Russian Federation (GARF) are used with permission of these archives.

Published with assistance from the Mary Cady Tew Memorial Fund.

Designed by James J. Johnson and set in Sabon Roman type by The Composing Room of Michigan, Inc. Printed in the United States of America.

Library of Congress Cataloging-in-Publication Data

Lenoe, Matthew E. (Matthew Edward)
  The Kirov murder and Soviet history / Matthew E. Lenoe ; translations by Matthew E. Lenoe.
     p. cm. (Annals of Communism)
  Includes bibliographical references and index.
  ISBN 978-0-300-11236-8 (cloth : alk. paper)
    1. Kirov, Sergei Mironovich, 1886–1934—Assassination. 2. Stalin, Joseph, 1879–1953. 3. Kommunisticheskaia partiia Sovetskogo Soiuza—Purges. 4. Political purges—Soviet Union—History. 5. Political atrocities—Soviet Union—History. 6. Soviet Union—History—1925–1953. I. Title.
  DK268.K5L46 2010
  947.084'2—dc22   2009041252

A catalogue record for this book is available from the British Library.

This paper meets the requirements of ANSI/NISO Z39.48-1992 (Permanence of Paper).

10 9 8 7 6 5 4 3 2 1

Yale University Press gratefully acknowledges the financial support given for this publication by the John M. Olin Foundation, the Lynde and Harry Bradley Foundation, the Historical Research Foundation, Roger Milliken, the Rosentiel Foundation, Lloyd H. Smith, Keith Young, the William H. Donner Foundation, Joseph W. Donner, Jeremiah Milbank, and the David Woods Kemper Memorial Foundation.

Yale University Press is grateful to Vladimir Pavlovich Naumov for his help in conceptualizing this book and contributing to the research at the early stages of this project.

For Eleanor and Simon

Contents

Maps

Acknowledgments

I wish to thank those generous donors who have helped to finance this project, including the supporters of the Annals of Communism series and Hokkaido University's Slavic Research Center, where I was a Foreign Visiting Fellow in 2005–2006. Portions of research for this work I did on summer trips to Moscow paid for by faculty development funds at the University of Arkansas at Little Rock and Assumption College. I also have utilized research funds from the University of Rochester to purchase published document collections and other materials relevant to the book.

I am grateful to Jonathan Brent, executive editor of the Annals of Communism series, for bringing me, a relatively untried scholar, into this exciting project in 2003. Jonathan helped to fund and arrange two of my research trips to Moscow. Throughout the writing process he has been an encouraging and patient editor. I also wish to thank Sarah Miller for shepherding the manuscript through the publication process, and Gavin Lewis for his thorough and sensible copyediting. Vadim Staklo, head administrator for the Annals of Communism series and a scholar in his own right, helped me to coordinate my research with the Russian State Archive of Contemporary History (RGANI) and to understand the Kirov document collection.

This book utilizes many previously unavailable sources, but it is also a synthetic work bringing together arguments and findings from a number of scholars who have worked on the Kirov murder. It relies most heavily on recent groundbreaking scholarship by Alla Kirilina, J. Arch Getty, and Oleg Khlevniuk. Studies by Amy Knight, Robert Tucker, Robert Conquest, Roy Medvedev, and others inform my own reconstruction of Kirov's biography and the Great Terror. William Taubman's recent biography of Nikita Khrushchev is invaluable for understanding the complex political turbulence of "the Thaw." Alvin Coox, now deceased, did extensive work on Genrikh Liushkov's biography. The names of other scholars whose work has informed my own can be found in the notes.

I wish to thank those scholars and archivists who personally helped me with the book. Vladimir P. Naumov provided essential guidance at the outset of the project. Nataliya Georgievna Tomilina, director of RGANI, and Mikhail Yurevich Prozumenshchikov, deputy director, showed me wonderful hospitality in Moscow and helped me to access the documents I needed. Mr. Prozumenshchikov supervised the collection of documents for publication, provided citations for them, and answered my questions about RGANI's Kirov document holdings. I also want to express my appreciation to the RGANI staff who tracked down hundreds of citations and photographs for me.

Irina Zhdanova, a scholar of the Russian revolutionary era, did invaluable research for me in the former Leningrad Communist Party archive (TsGAIPD SPb) on the 1928–1929 political turmoil in Leningrad. Ms. Zhdanova also provided me with fascinating citations on Kirov's image in post-Soviet popular culture. Matthew Payne shared his research on collectivization in Kazakhstan and helped me to understand Kirov's 1934 trip to that republic. Terry Martin pointed me towards a 1927 Commissariat of Justice proposal for emergency tribunals that prefigured the infamous "Law of December 1, 1934" approved by the Politburo following Kirov's assassination. Tatyana Bakhmetyeva went through the diaries of the assassin Nikolaev with me, checking my translations and suggesting a number of important alternative interpretations of ambiguous phrases. David Brandenberger provided me with a copy of the hard-to-find film Soviet film *Velikii grazhdanin*, a Stalinist fictionalization of Kirov's political career in Leningrad. Fujio Ogino of Shoka University in Otaru, Japan, advised me on the Japanese archival system and possible approaches to finding material on Genrikh Liushkov therein. J. Arch Getty suggested that I look in the newly opened Yezhov archive at the Russian State Archive of Social and Political History for materials on Kirov's murder. Getty also helped me to puzzle out the timing of the first interrogation of Milda Draule (the assassin's wife) following the killing. Finally, my thanks go to the anonymous readers for Yale University Press who strongly supported the manuscript.

Scholars who have provided helpful comments on parts of the book manuscript include Haruki Wada, Stephen Bittner, James Harris, David Wolff, Yevgeny Dobrenko, and Mikhail Dolbilov.

It has been a pleasure to spend the last two years of this book project in the History Department at the University of Rochester. My thanks go to my colleagues at Rochester for welcoming me to the department and supporting my work.

I also want to express my appreciation to my former colleagues in the History Department at the University of Arkansas at Little Rock for running their History Institute lecture series for the general public. It was here that I first gave a talk on the Kirov murder, in 1998. Soon after this my dissertation adviser and mentor Sheila Fitzpatrick encouraged me to write a review article on the Kirov assassination. I thank her for suggesting that I pursue the topic, which has proven both fascinating and productive.

Dr. James Ferris, R. W. Rivers, and Jennifer Prutsman-Pfeiffer provided expert analysis of the auto accident in which Kirov's bodyguard Mikhail Borisov died. My thanks to them.

I am indebted to the Russian State Archive of Cinematic and Photographic Documents (RGAKFD), and in particular to director Natalia Kalantarova, for permission to reproduce photographs from the archive's collection. My thanks also go to Alexandra Shilova of Moscow for visiting RGAKFD, selecting the photographs, and arranging permission to publish them.

Chapter 14 was published in a somewhat different form as "Khrushchev Era Politics and the Investigation of the Kirov Murder, 1956–1957," *Acta Slavica Iaponica* 24 (2007): 47–73. Sections of Chapters 11 and 13 appeared in Matthew Lenoe, "Did Stalin Kill Kirov and Does It Matter?" *Journal of Modern History* 74 (June 2002): 352–380. I thank both journals for permission to publish these sections of the book.

My wife Mari Tsuchiya Lenoe helped me to translate materials from the Japanese press on Genrikh Liushkov, including the 1939 article excerpted in the Conclusion. She also read and commented on several book chapters. During intense periods of work on the manuscript, she took over my share of housework and child care, even as she herself worked full-time. I am immensely grateful to her for her support and love.

Note on Translation, Transliteration, and Dates

Soviet official documents tend to include lengthy, convoluted sentences and to use the same words repeatedly. In translating I have often divided one Russian sentence into two or more English ones. Where the same Russian term is repeated in a single sentence I have sometimes translated it with two different English words.

For transliterating the Russian Cyrillic alphabet I have used a modified version of the usual Library of Congress system, to make reading easier for those unfamiliar with the Russian language. Soft and hard signs are not included in the transliterations. In the final position, Library of Congress "ii" and "yi" become "y." Final "iia" becomes "ia," and final "ia" becomes "ya." Initial "E" = "Ye," "Ia" = "Ya," and "Iu" = "Yu." The "ë" ("io") is rendered as "yo," except after "sh," "shch," and "ch" where it appears as "e." For a few well-known personal and place names I have used the common English spelling (e.g. Mikoyan, Zinoviev).

In citations and for Russian wording included to clarify translations, I use the full Library of Congress transliteration system to avoid any ambiguities.

I have found that capitalizing the first letter of every word in the formal names of Soviet bureaucratic institutions results in a very clunky text. In my own commentary (as opposed to the translated documents), therefore, I have often chosen to label such institutions with an uncapitalized generic descriptive term—"the Leningrad Soviet's executive committee," for example, rather than the proper name "Leningrad Soviet Executive Committee."

Before the October Revolution of 1917 Russia used the Julian calendar that Catholic and Protestant Europe abandoned by the end of the eighteenth century. The Bolsheviks soon shifted to the "new" Gregorian calendar. I have tried to use Julian dates ("Old Style") consistently through the date of the October Revolution (October 25, 1917 in the Julian calendar, November 7 in the Gregorian). All dates after that are according to the Gregorian calendar ("New Style").

Note on Soviet Government and Territorial Structures

Readers outside the field of Russian history may be confused by the many Soviet state and party institutions that appear in this book. The government apparatus of the USSR was divided nominally between these two groups of institutions. However, these interpenetrated and contained many of the same personnel. The rough understanding of the time was that party institutions set policy and supervised the state organs, which implemented party decisions.

The party was a pyramidal hierarchy of committees. By the early 1930s the function of the committees was generally to rubber-stamp decisions made by the executive "bureaus" and "secretariats" that committee members nominally elected to carry out day-to-day business. Thus, the most important decisions in the Leningrad Region were made by the bureau and secretariat of the Leningrad regional party committee. Kirov was the senior member of both. In theory all officers were elected. At the bottom of the pyramid, workplace Communist Party committees elected representatives to committees on the next level, and so on, right up to the party's Central Committee. Members of the bureaus and secretariats were also in theory elected by their own party committees. In practice senior officials on upper-level bureaus and secretariats nominated candidates for all important party posts and party committees generally elected these candidates. Already by the early 1920s the most important appointments were made by the executive apparatus of the Central Committee (TsK), which was dominated by Stalin and his fellow members of the TsK bureau (Politburo), Secretariat, and Orgburo.

Party committees above the workplace level generally had "control" organs, which were responsible for monitoring the conduct of party members and disciplining them. Prior to 1934 the highest level control organ was the Central Control Commission (TsKK), which topped a pyramid of subordinate control commissions. In 1934 the control commissions were renamed and reorganized so as to subject them to tighter control by the TsK executive apparatus. The Committee on Party Control (KPK) replaced the Central Control Commission. Lower-level organs were similar renamed "committees on party control." Connected closely to the party control organs was the so-called Workers' and Peasants' Inspectorate (Rabkrin or RKI), which monitored the state apparatus, including economic enterprises, for corruption and incompetence.

Like the party hierarchy, the state hierarchy included committees called soviets. The system of election to the soviets changed in 1936, but prior to that the bottom level was popularly elected. In fact by the early thirties the Communist authorities designated just one candidate for every seat on the soviet, who was invariably elected. The soviets had no effective political power by this date. However, the state executive organs, the "executive committees," which were staffed by Communist officials, did make real decisions.

The Soviet secret police (an alternative description is "state security police") went through a confusing series of renamings and reorganizations. From 1917–1921 they were the Extraordinary Commission (ChK or Cheka), from 1922–1923 the "State Political Directorate" (GPU), and from 1923 to 1934 the Consolidated State Political Directorate (OGPU). In July 1934 the OGPU was subordinated directly to the People's Commissariat of Internal Affairs (NKVD). Although most "state security" functions were transferred to a new NKVD subdivision known as the Main Directorate of State Security (GUGB), most scholars simply identify the secret police from this point as the NKVD. I follow this practice. In 1946 the NKVD was redesignated MVD (Ministry of Internal Affairs). Although the relationship between the "operational" state security departments and the MVD shifted several times during the last years of Stalin's rule, for simplicity's sake I simply refer to the MVD. In 1954 secret police functions were united in the Committee on State Security (KGB) and separated from the MVD. The Russian Federation successor to the KGB is the Federal Security Service (FSB).

For the period of most importance to this book, the early to middle 1930s, the relevant subdivisions of the security police were the Operations Department, the Special Political Department, the Special Department, and the Economic Security Department. Operations handled arrests, guard duty, and similar functions. The Special Political Department monitored and suppressed internal political dissent. The Special Department engaged in counterespionage, seeking to expose foreign spies and their supposed Soviet collaborators. This included operations against foreign embassies and consulates as well as military counterespionage. The Economic Security Department was supposed to combat sabotage and "wrecking" at Soviet factories and other economic enterprises. These departments' functions obviously overlapped. In addition senior security police officers sometimes formed "special" task forces that worked independently of the formal organizational structure.

During the 1920s Soviet authorities changed the administrative units of the USSR. In 1929, at the province level, they replaced the *guberniia* with the *oblast*. Between 1924 and 1929 in rural areas they replaced *uezdy* (analogous roughly to counties in Britain or the United States) with *raiony*. I have translated Soviet territorial divisions as follows (from smallest to largest).

City *raion* = ward.
Rural *raion* = district.
Rural *uezd* = county.
Volost = township.
Guberniia = province.
Oblast = region.
Krai = territory.

From 1921 to 1927 the Central Committee maintained a Central Committee Bureau for the Northwestern Territory (Severo-zapadnoe biuro TsK) with some supervisory authority over several province party committees (Petrograd, Novgorod, Pskov, Murmansk, Cherepovets). In practice this bureau seems to have functioned as a means for the TsK and the Petrograd/Leningrad provincial party committee to manage affairs in the other "northwest" provinces. The bureau was abolished with the shift from the *guberniia* to the *oblast*.

Note on the Documents and Citations

Nearly all of the documents reproduced here were provided to Yale University Press by the Russian State Archive of Contemporary History (RGANI), which in the Soviet era was one of the Communist Party Central Committee's document repositories. The originals of a number of these documents, however, are stored in the Central Archive of the Russian Federation Federal Security Service (TsA FSB RF) or the Archive of the President of the Russian Federation (APRF). They are cited accordingly. Citations to Russian government archives are in the standard Russian format, by collection (*fond,* abbreviated as "f."), inventory (*opis',* "op."), file (*delo,* "d."), folio (*list,* "l."), and verso of a folio (*oborotnaya strana,* "ob."). The single exception is the TsA FSB RF, which uses a different filing system. FSB archive documents are identified by criminal case file (*arkhivnoe ugolovnoe delo,* abbreviated here as "a.u.d."), volume (*tom,* "t."), and page (*list,* "l.").

In a few cases (Kirov's death certificate, for example), I had photocopies of original handwritten drafts for document translations. Generally, however, the documents were available to me in typescript. In the case of the notebooks kept by Leonid Nikolaev, Kirov's assassin, some ambiguities about wording exist. The Soviet security services transcribed Nikolaev's writings, or excerpts thereof, several times. Because Nikolaev's handwriting was hard to decipher in some spots, there are minor discrepancies between different transcriptions. I have not flagged these in the document translations except when they result in versions with substantially different meanings.

The majority of the translated Russian archival documents fall into two groups. The first is documents from criminal case files released by the

KGB to various TsK authorities beginning in 1956. Central to this book are the documents from the initial investigation of Kirov's murder in 1934–1935, which were released by the KGB to the TsK in April 1956. I will address at various points the question of whether the KGB withheld important evidence from this document release.

The second group of translated documents is the reports of the Central Committee and KPK commissions that investigated the Kirov murder and Stalinist repression after Stalin's death. For the Kirov murder the major investigations were in 1956 ("the Molotov commission"), the winter of 1960–1961 ("the Shatunovskaya commission"), the summer of 1961, and 1962 to 1967. Several of these reports include long excerpts from criminal investigative files of the 1930s. In order to distinguish clearly the different chronological layers of evidence in the Kirov case, I have often presented such excerpts as separate documents. In presenting the 1960s reports themselves, I have omitted the excerpts from earlier materials reproduced elsewhere in the book. The reports also tend to repeat one another on important points, and I have excised much of the repetitive material.

Duplicates of many of the documents from the 1934–1935 investigation of the Kirov murder released by the KGB to the TsK in 1956 can be found at the Russian State Archive of Social and Political History in the recently acquired collection of documents from Nikolai Yezhov's personal archive. The Yezhov archive (f. 671) is an important source in its own right for the Kirov murder. Of particular interest is the notebook Yezhov kept in December 1934 and early 1935 on the investigation.

Within translated documents I have placed my own comments in brackets, parenthetical comments from the documents themselves between slash marks, and Russian wording included to clarify translations within parentheses. Where I have omitted material from the original document, I have placed ellipses between brackets. Ellipses without brackets are from the original document itself. In quotations outside actual documents, my occasional omissions of text are without brackets and original parenthetical comments appear within parentheses.

In interrogation records I have included the official titles of interrogators only at their first appearance in the book. Otherwise they are omitted.

Acronyms and Abbreviations

ACP	Azerbaijani Communist Party.
ARC	Azerbaijani Revolutionary Committee. Front organization for the Azerbaijani Communist Party, created in April 1920 to justify the Soviet takeover of the independent Azerbaijani republic.
Cheka	Extraordinary Commission (*Chrezvychainaia komissiia*). State security organ, 1917–1922.
FSB	Federal Security Service (*Federal'naia sluzhba besopasnosti*). State security police of the Russian Federation today. Successor to the Cheka/OGPU/NKVD/KGB.
Gosplan	Central planning organization for the Soviet economy.
GPU	State Political Directorate (*Gosudarstvennoe politicheskoe upravlenie*). Secret police/security service of the Soviet republic, 1922–1923.
GUGB	Main Directorate of State Security (*Glavnoe upravlenie gosudarstvennoi bezopasnosti*). The state security/secret police department of the NKVD from 1934 to 1940.
Gulag	Main Directorate of Camps (*Glavnoe upravlenie lagerei*). Responsible for the administration of concentration camp system. Subordinate to the NKVD from 1934.
Istmol	Youth section of the Leningrad Institute of Party History (*Istoriia molodezhi*).
KGB	Committee on State Security (*Komitet gosudarstvennoi bezopasnosti*). State security service/secret police, 1954–1991.

Komsomol	Communist Youth League (*Kommunisticheskii soiuz molodezhi*).
KPK	Committee on Party Control (*Komitet partiinogo kontrolia*). From 1934 onwards the committee charged with monitoring and disciplining Communists for corruption, moral turpitude, and disruptive behavior. Under tighter TsK control than its predecessor, the TsKK.
MTS	Machine Tractor Station (*Mashinno-traktornaia stantsiia*). These stations rented heavy equipment such as tractors to collective farms from the early 1930s onward. They were important outposts of the party and the state security organs in the countryside.
MVD	Ministry of Internal Affairs (*Ministerstvo vnutrennykh del*). Used in this book to designate the secret police/security service that was a department of the MVD from 1946–1954.
NEP	New Economic Policy (*Novaia ekonomicheskaia politika*). The Soviet government's economic policy of relative decentralization and partial privatization of trade and business, in force from 1921 through 1928. More generally, the relatively "soft" era of Soviet rule during those years.
NKVD	People's Commissariat of Internal Affairs (*Narodnyi kommisariat vnutrennykh del*). In this book used most often to designate the secret police/security service (GUGB) that was a department of the NKVD from 1934–1946.
OGPU	Consolidated State Political Directorate (*Ob'edinennoe gosudarstvennoe politicheskoe upravlenie*). Secret police/security service of the Soviet republic/Soviet Union, 1923–1934.
Orgburo	Organizational Bureau (*Organizatsionnoe biuro*). Executive organ of the Communist Party TsK. Subordinate only to the Politburo.
Osoaviakhim	Society for the Support of the Armed Forces and Aviation-Chemical Defense (*Soiuz obshchestv sodeistviia oborone i aviatsionno-khimicheskomu stroitel'stvu SSSR*). Soviet civil defense organization with attached reserve military formations.

Politburo	Political Bureau (*Politicheskoe biuro*). Highest executive organ of the Communist Party and its TsK.
Rabkrin	Workers' and Peasants' Inspectorate (*Raboche-krestianskii inspektorat*). State analogue to the TsKK/KPK. Rabkrin inspected economic enterprises and local bureaucracies to root out corruption.
Revvoensovet	Military-Revolutionary Council (*Revoliutsionno-voennyi sovet*). Councils including prominent Communists that worked together with Red Army officers in commanding Red Army units.
RKI	*See* Rabkrin.
SD	Social Democratic Party. Used in this book in reference to the Russian Social Democratic Labor Party (*Rossiskaia sotsial-demokraticheskaia rabochaia partiia*), founded in 1889, the precursor to the Soviet Communist Party.
Sovnarkom	Council of People's Commissars (*Sovet narodnykh komissarov*). The initial organ of "Soviet" (read "Bolshevik") dictatorship after the October Revolution. Continued to play an important role on paper in executive decision-making through the 1930s.
SPD	Social Democratic Party of Germany (*Sozialdemokratische Partei Deutschlands*).
SR	Socialist Revolutionary Party. Political party in tsarist Russia supporting the establishment of socialism based on land redistribution and the peasant commune.
TsK	Central Committee of the Soviet Communist Party (*Tsentral'nyi komitet*).
TsKK	Central Control Commission (*Tsentral'naia kontrol'naia komissiia*). Until 1934 the body charged with hearing the cases of and disciplining Communists charged with corruption, squabbling, or moral turpitude. Relatively independent of the TsK compared to its successor, the KPK.
VSNKh	All-Union Council on the National Economy. (*Vsesoiuznyi sovet natsional'nogo khoziaistva*). Central coordinating body for the Soviet economy.

VTsSPS   All-Union Central Council of Labor Unions (*Vsesoiuz-nyi tsentral'nyi sovet professional'nykh soiuzov*).

VVRK   Temporary Military Revolutionary Committee (*Vremen-nyi voenno-revoliutsionnyi komitet*). Emergency committee established in the Astrakhan area by the Bolsheviks in 1919 to battle the Whites.

Archives Cited

APRF   Archive of the President of the Russian Federation (*Arkhiv prezidenta Rossiiskoi federatsii*).

GARF   State Archive of Russian Federation (*Gosudarstvennyi arkhiv Rossiskoi federatsii*).

RGALI   Russian State Archive of Literature and Art (*Rossiiskii gosudarstvennyi arkhiv literatury i iskusstva*).

RGANI   Russian State Archive of Contemporary History (*Rossiiskii gosudarstvennyi arkhiv noveishei istorii*).

RGASPI   Russian State Archive of Social and Political History (*Rossiiskii gosudarstvennyi arkhiv sotsial'noi i politicheskoi istorii*).

TsA FSB RF   Central Archive of the Russian Federation Federal Security Service (*Tsentral'nyi arkhiv Federal'noi sluzhby bezopastnosti Rossiiskoi federatsii*).

TsGAIPD SPb.   Central State Archive of Historic Political Documents, St. Petersburg (*Tsentral'nyi gosudarstvennyi arkhiv istoriko-politicheskikh dokumentov Sankt-Peterburga*).

RGAKFD   Russian State Archive of Cinematic and Photographic Documents (*Rossiiskii gosudarstvennyi arkhiv kinofotodokumentov*).

Introduction

O n December 1, 1934, at about 4:30 P.M. Sergei Kirov, first secretary of the Leningrad Communist Party organization, left
his automobile and walked into the main entrance of the
Smolny Building, the government headquarters for the city. Kirov
planned to spend an hour or so consulting with other city leaders
before addressing a 6 P.M. meeting of Communist activists. Upstairs
prominent Leningrad officials had already gathered to prepare for the
event. Kirov climbed the main stairwell past the first and second
floors, stopping to converse briefly with one or two employees. The security officer responsible for guarding Kirov inside Smolny, Mikhail
Borisov, trailed him by at least one flight, if he was on the stairs at all.

The Smolny Building, where Kirov had his office, exemplified the
dramatic turns and contradictions of Russian history. Under the tsars,
it had housed a school for daughters of the nobility; during the October Revolution it served the Bolsheviks as headquarters, and Lenin
himself lived there for several months. In 1934 Smolny was the administrative heart of the city that gave birth to the revolution. The onetime
aristocratic finishing school was now a symbol of "Soviet Power," the
Communist government that ruled in the name of the workers and
peasants.

The placement of offices inside Smolny reflected the organization of
Soviet Power itself. On the first two floors, offices of the city and regional governments, as well as of the Communist youth organization,
or Komsomol, were open to the general public. Entrance to the third
floor, however, was by Communist Party card. Here were the premises
of the regional and city party committees, where real decisions were

made, then passed downstairs for implementation by the state organs. According to its leaders, the Communist Party was the Soviet avant-garde, supervising and instructing the "laboring masses" as they constructed a modern socialist society. It was the party's special knowledge of history, gained through mastery of Marx's "scientific" theory of history, that justified the dictatorial powers of the leadership, headed by the party Central Committee's first secretary, Joseph Stalin. Kirov, recently appointed a Central Committee secretary himself, was a Politburo member and one of the top dozen or so men in the party.

To bridge the distance between themselves—the avant-garde—and the masses, Communist officials in the 1920s and early 1930s recruited factory workers into the party in large numbers. As Communists these "promotees" (*vydvizhentsy*) benefited from access to white-collar jobs, as well as better apartments, better rations, and superior educational opportunities.[1] Some, such as Nikita Khrushchev and Leonid Brezhnev, climbed eventually to the very summit of the Soviet state hierarchy. Hundreds of thousands of others got an education and made professional or bureaucratic careers, becoming the backbone of the Soviet state by the 1940s. Yet others, thrust into positions for which they had little or no training, failed.

Now, as Kirov walked through the guard post at the entrance to the third floor, one of these failures, an unemployed Communist named Leonid Nikolaev, was about to exit a bathroom down the main hallway. Nikolaev, the son of a cleaning lady and an alcoholic carpenter, had held about a dozen jobs since he joined the party in 1924, during the recruitment campaign that followed Lenin's death. Since his most recent firing in April 1934 he had been unemployed. Nikolaev had come to Smolny seeking a ticket to the 6 P.M. activists' meeting. He carried a briefcase holding some old newspapers, and, in his pocket, a revolver.

As Nikolaev stepped out of the bathroom, he saw Kirov walking towards him, down the main third floor hallway. Turning towards the wall, as if to light a cigarette, Nikolaev let him pass, and then followed. As Kirov turned left, into a smaller side corridor that led to his office, Nikolaev accelerated his steps and came up behind him. He pulled his revolver from his pocket, cocked it, and shot Kirov in the back of his head. The Leningrad party chief died instantly, sprawling forward onto the floor.

For the Communist leadership, the murder in Smolny was traumatic, not just because the victim was one of them but also because the murderer was a Communist and a worker. Something had gone badly wrong, for the party and the proletariat were supposed to be pillars of the regime. The Kirov murder struck straight down to the deepest insecurities of Communist officialdom. In seventeen years of rule, the Bolsheviks had restored order and reconstructed the economy following the chaos of World War I and the Russian Civil War. They had introduced universal public education for the first time in Russian history, placed many ordinary working people in supervisory jobs, made women legally equal to men, and expanded modern industry. They had also ruled with police terror, which increased greatly in the late 1920s, suppressed all open political dissent, confiscated private property, banned most private businesses, and forced the peasants who still made up the majority of the population to work for very little on collective farms managed by the party/state apparatus. As a direct result of forced collectivization more than five million country people died of starvation in 1932–1933.

To invest in modern industry, Bolshevik leaders, beginning in the late 1920s, had forced Soviet factory workers to labor harder for less pay, to the point that they were close to starvation in some cities. While the winners in Soviet society, those among "the masses" who joined the Communist Party and reaped the educational and material benefits, supported the regime, many peasants and even substantial numbers of urban workers were hostile to the new "bosses" (*verkhushka*). There also remained in the USSR millions of people designated by the party as "class enemies"—former priests, ex-tsarist policemen and bureaucrats, onetime businessmen, and the better-off peasants known as kulaks. Stalin and other senior Soviet officials were acutely aware that they had made many enemies. And now a Communist worker, a man who according to government propaganda should have been unquestioningly loyal to the regime, had shot one of the party's top officials.

This book is in large part the story of how one of the greatest mass murderers of modern history, Joseph Stalin, made use of the fear and rage provoked by the Kirov murder to justify the execution or confinement in forced labor camps of millions of innocent people. In the months following the murder, Stalin did all he could to heighten the atmosphere of suspicion and dread that accompanied the killing. He warned of terrorist plots to assassinate the entire Soviet leadership, and proclaimed that no one could be trusted because "enemies" had penetrated the party itself. He focused at first on former "Left" Communists who had opposed his consolidation of power in the 1920s. In

Leningrad thirteen men, mostly former Left sympathizers, were framed, charged with plotting a terrorist attack on Kirov, and executed together with the actual assassin, Leonid Nikolaev. Two of Stalin's most prominent former rivals, Grigory Zinoviev and Lev Kamenev, were tried in January 1935 for "moral complicity" in the assassination and sentenced to long prison terms. Thousands of other former supporters of Zinoviev, Kamenev, and Stalin's exiled archenemy Leon Trotsky were arrested and sent to concentration camps in the winter of 1934–1935.

Following a year and a half of steady repression of former Left Communist opponents as well as the usual "class enemy" suspects, Stalin ramped up the attack on the remnants of the defunct Communist opposition groups. In August 1936 he organized the trial and execution of Kamenev and Zinoviev on charges of conspiring to murder Kirov, Stalin himself, and several other Soviet leaders. Then, in early 1937, the security organs arrested the former leaders of the "Right Deviation," a loose group of Communists who had opposed forced collectivization and Stalin's domination of the party. The most prominent of these men, Nikolai Bukharin and Aleksei Rykov, were put on trial in March 1938 for terrorism, treason, and complicity in Kirov's murder. They were subsequently executed.

By the time of the March 1938 show trial, the Soviet Union was embroiled in a cataclysm of state-sponsored violence. Beginning in late June 1937 Stalin, in an apparent attempt to eliminate any possible source of resistance to his rule, presided over the execution of thousands of senior party officials who had no record of political opposition. Many of these men and women were charged with complicity in Kirov's murder and/or conspiring to kill Stalin himself. The dictator and his closest associates also ran so-called "mass operations" in which the state security forces shot around 700,000 people, deporting or arresting millions more. Many of those arrested died of neglect and abuse in the forced labor camps. While the Kirov murder was not the direct pretext or the real motivation for the mass operations, the atmosphere of dread and hyper-vigilance that Stalin developed around the assassination facilitated them.

Stalin's use of Kirov's death to justify terror led by 1939 to conjectures in the West that he might have ordered the killing himself. Also, chewed-up fragments of rumors from the Soviet Union reached European socialists and fueled such speculation. Over the succeeding decades Western authorities on Soviet affairs and Soviet advocates of de-Stalinization accumulated many bits and pieces of evidence suggesting Stalin's complicity in the crime. By the early 1970s speculation had become certainty for Western scholars such as Robert Conquest and Soviet opponents of Stalinism like Roy Medvedev.[2]

Various narratives of Stalin's conspiracy to murder Kirov evolved, but the majority shared a set of common elements. According to most versions, Stalin ordered the hit on Kirov because the latter had come to represent a relatively moderate faction of the party opposed to state terror. In 1932, the story went, Kirov led a coalition of Politburo members who had rejected Stalin's demand for the execution of oppositionist Mikhail Riutin. At the Seventeenth Party Congress in 1934 some provincial party bosses made a move to replace Stalin with Kirov in the post of first secretary. Stalin had been forced to falsify the voting record of the congress after hundreds of delegates voted against his candidacy to the Central Committee (TsK). Support for Kirov's candidacy, in contrast, was supposed to have been nearly unanimous.

In these accounts Kirov's moderation and Stalin's determination to destroy all potential political opponents were the twin motives behind the murder. Most stories of Stalin's involvement in the crime also included a list of incriminating evidence. The security police (NKVD) supposedly provided Nikolaev with the murder weapon and the pass that enabled him to penetrate Smolny. Before the crime Leningrad police twice (or thrice, or more times) arrested Nikolaev in Kirov's vicinity, divested him of his revolver, and later released him and returned the weapon. On the day after the murder Kirov's bodyguard, Borisov, was mysteriously killed in a "car accident" while NKVD officers were transporting him to an interrogation by Stalin. In fact, went the "Stalin did it" versions of the crime, Borisov was murdered because he was the only eyewitness to the assassination. Observers also found it suspicious that senior officers in the NKVD received relatively light sentences for negligence in guarding Kirov. Some speculated that they were let off easy because they had actually cooperated with central authorities to facilitate the killing.

These became the key elements of the case for Stalin's involvement in the assassination. Today the dictator's leading role in Kirov's murder is a standard part of the popular narrative of the Great Terror of the late 1930s, questioned only by a few academic specialists. The Library of Congress's online exhibit, "Revelations from the Russian Archives," for example, asserts without qualification that Stalin was behind Kirov's assassination. Robert Conquest's 1989 *Stalin and the*

Kirov Murder, Robert Tucker's *Stalin in Power* (1990), and Amy Knight's 1997 book, *Who Killed Kirov?,* all argue strongly that Stalin ordered Kirov's assassination. Simon Sebag Montefiore, the author of a recent popular biography of the dictator, concludes with regard to the killing that "the whiff of (Stalin's) complicity still hangs in the air."[3]

Yet even before the archival gold rush attendant upon the fall of the Soviet Union, a few Western scholars voiced doubts that Stalin had conspired to kill Kirov. Most notably, J. Arch Getty in *Origins of the Great Purges* (1985) questioned the sources on which the received narrative was based. Getty noted that the NKVD defectors and émigrés who reported the various elements of the "Stalin did it" version were in fact passing on third-, fourth-, or more-hand rumors. He cast doubts too on oral history evidence gathered in the late 1950s and early 1960s during Khrushchev's de-Stalinization drive, observing both the investigators' political biases and the length of time elapsed since the crime. Finally, Getty reiterated Adam Ulam's skepticism that Stalin would have resorted to such a risky expedient as political assassination to rid himself of Kirov. The Leningrad party chief, Getty argued, was no moderate rival to Stalin, but a loyal follower of second rank.[4]

The opening of Soviet archives in the early 1990s tended to strengthen Getty's arguments. Two Russian scholars, Alla Kirilina and Oleg Khlevniuk, used newly available documents to debunk many of the received myths about the Kirov assassination. Khlevniuk, while agnostic about Stalin's involvement in Kirov's murder, assembled Central Committee documentation to demonstrate that the Leningrad party chief was never a rival to the Soviet dictator. Kirilina utilized Leningrad archives, Central Committee sources, and her own interviews with surviving witnesses to show that many details of the received narrative were simply false, and to argue that Leonid Nikolaev was probably a lone gunman.[5]

Neither Khlevniuk nor Kirilina is an apologist for Stalin. Khlevniuk has characterized the Soviet system as "totalitarian" and has written document-based studies of Gulag repression and the functioning of the Politburo in the 1930s. Kirilina, who was a researcher at the Leningrad Institute of Party History during the perestroika years, feels nostalgia for certain aspects of the Soviet era, but not for the police repression or the mass terror of the 1930s. She views Stalin as a tyrant who committed mass murder and severely damaged Soviet society.

Her work emphasizes his manipulation of the murder to justify the Terror.

A principal task of this book is to evaluate the received narrative of Stalin's conspiracy to kill Kirov using documents from the archives of the Central Committee. Following Nikita Khrushchev's 1956 "Secret Speech" denouncing the Stalinist terror (at least that part directed against the Communist Party), TsK officials undertook several different investigations of Kirov's murder. The document base for this book derives mostly from those investigations, which utilized KGB files as well as party records. Investigators also took written depositions from eyewitnesses to various moments of the drama and from hundreds of persons reporting rumors and purported eyewitness accounts passed along orally though several intermediaries.

Some of the most important evidence in the Kirov murder case comes from the first days of the original criminal investigation, in early December 1934. The KGB released these top secret files to Central Committee investigators on April 20, 1956.[6] My account of the actual killing is based largely on these documents. The recently opened archive of Nikolai Yezhov, head of the NKVD from late 1936 to 1938, also contains valuable materials from the December 1934 investigation of the killing. Other key evidence has to do with the biography of Nikolaev himself, and comes largely from the April 20, 1956 KGB document release and, via Kirilina, from the Leningrad party archives. Nikolaev's personality and biography have long been obscured by Soviet secretiveness and analysts' focus on the question of Stalin's involvement in the murder. The newly available information permits a much fuller portrait of Kirov's killer than previously possible.

The reader may well ask whether the documents in question are trustworthy. More specifically, did the KGB and party officials seek to exculpate Stalin of responsibility for the Terror? It is vital to understand that the inquiries in question, with the possible exception of work done in 1966–1967, had no such goal. As this book will demonstrate, TsK investigators in 1956–1957 accepted Stalin's responsibility for the Great Terror of the late 1930s and collected evidence exposing it. The probe was top secret and party leaders concealed many of its findings from the general public for fear that disclosure would undermine their authority. But the Khrushchev supporters in charge of the investigation, including KGB chief Ivan Serov, sought to collect as much material as possible incriminating Stalin. This was what Khrushchev wanted, so that he could discredit his political rivals, Stalin's old henchmen Viacheslav Molotov, Lazar Kaganovich, and Georgy Malenkov. This could be done without full public disclosure of the investigation's findings. Khrushchev needed only to reveal them to the highest-ranking members of the party elite.

The 1960–1961 investigation run by the Party Control Committee (KPK) was aimed explicitly at inculpating Stalin in the Kirov murder. Party reformers backing Khrushchev aimed to construct an entirely new history of the Stalin years, in which the dictator and a few of his closest associates were alone responsible for the mass deaths and "distortions of Leninism." This story-line would absolve the Communist Party as a whole of guilt. The 1960–1961 investigation gathered a great deal of evidence that Stalin conspired to kill Kirov, some of which found its way in more or less distorted forms into the received narrative of the assassination. We will evaluate that evidence.

I have chosen to recount the story of Kirov's political career, his murder, and the subsequent investigations in chronological order, and to present most of the evidence in the same way. My decision has to do with the accumulation of many layers of evidence in the assassination case, the most important of which are:

1. Pre-murder documents related to the lives of Kirov and Nikolaev.
2. The materials of the December 1934–January 1935 investigation of the killing.
3. Documents from the renewed "investigation" of the Great Terror years (1936–1939), many of which are witness statements given under torture or the threat of same.
4. Memoirs and commentaries published by Russian émigrés and Soviet defectors during the Great Terror and afterwards.
5. Materials of the 1956–1957 Central Committee inquiry.
6. Materials of the 1960–1961 KPK investigation run by Olga Shatunovskaya.
7. Documents of the KPK investigation that followed Shatunovskaya's, from 1961 through 1967.

The Kirov murder was a political sensation in 1934, and Soviet authorities as well as Western commentators continued to treat it as such right up to the collapse of the USSR. Thus every layer of evidence was deeply influenced by the political landscape in which it was laid down. The Soviet political landscape, contrary to the image many have of a frozen totalitarian monolith, was shifting constantly. Thus, to understand each document one needs to know the political context of its production, the placement of the author or authors in that context, and their motivations. One needs to know what sources the author uses for any factual claims, and what the genealogy of those sources is. One cannot, for example, simply take at face value a claim made in 1990 in the Soviet press that Nikolaev was detained and released three times before the killing. The author of the claim, Olga Shatunovskaya, was apparently relying on her memory of written depositions her investigators gathered in 1960–1961, which in turn were based on very problematic testimony extracted during the Great Terror by NKVD officers bent on building a case incriminating "Rightist" leaders in Kirov's death.[7]

It can be seen from the example above that as layers of evidence accumulated in the Kirov case, so too did distortions, myths, and outright lies. Stalin himself began the process when he insisted that NKVD investigators build a case against former party oppositionists in the days after the killing. During the Great Terror NKVD officers tortured witnesses until they provided testimony supporting fantastic charges of conspiracy against former party leaders. This highly unreliable and self-contradictory body of testimony muddied the waters of the Kirov case to the point that later commentators could not tell up from down. Then, in 1960–1961, KPK investigators intent on creating a usable history of Stalinist terror that would salvage the honor of the party appealed to elderly Communists' sense of duty to the cause when they asked them to "remember" probably mythical events. They also made extensive use of the layer of falsified evidence from the Great Terror.

To understand the evidence, then, and distinguish insofar as possible folklore from fact, a chronological approach is necessary.

Readers may be surprised by the skepticism with which I treat evidence passed on orally through several interlocutors. There are several reasons for this skepticism. First, many of the second-, third-, or more-hand tales relating to the Kirov murder are directly contradicted by documentary evidence. Second, scientific studies have demonstrated that human memory is highly malleable and oral transmission of narratives unreliable. In the 1970s Elizabeth Loftus and others showed that researchers could alter subjects' memories of a sequence of slides showing a car accident by feeding them misleading information after the viewing.[8] More recently Loftus and other researchers have generated false childhood "memories" in adults through repeated interviewing. In these studies approximately one-quarter of research subjects "accepted" the false memories. Studies by Loftus, Goff, and Roediger have also shown that asking people to imagine particular scenarios increases the likelihood that they will later "remember" such scenarios as real "events."[9]

Deponents in the Kirov case in the early 1960s had been exposed to a deluge of bad information about the murder over the course of almost three decades, and there is no doubt that this contaminated many of their memories. For example, at the March 1938 show trial of the "Rightist" leaders, prosecutors put out a highly dubious story that former NKVD chief Genrikh Yagoda had ordered the release of Nikolaev following his detention before the murder. This story made its way into the accounts of testifiers in the early 1960s who could not have had personal knowledge of the order in question.

One mechanism of memory distortion that is highly relevant to evidence on the Kirov murder is so-called "source amnesia." Research by cognitive scientists and neuropsychologists has revealed that neurologically healthy subjects, especially elderly adults, often fail to remember what the source of a particular piece of information was. When this happens, people "become susceptible to various other kinds of memory distortions and illusions." For example, subjects can mistake misinformation given to them later for the memory of an actual event. Source amnesia is almost certainly an important form of memory distortion in the Kirov murder case, with testifiers in the early 1960s forgetting, for example, whether they heard a story from an eyewitness, such as Kirov's deputy in Leningrad, Mikhail Chudov, or from someone else who attributed the story to Chudov.[10]

Recent studies indicate that even adult subjects' memories are susceptible to alteration by leading questions or misinformation given by authority figures, such as policemen and therapists. Most of the evidence in the Kirov case was gathered by police officers or party officials, with the questioner often explicitly taking a particular investigatory and/or political line. Moreover, the written word itself can function as an "authority." In one of Elizabeth Loftus' studies 43 percent of subjects preferred false details in a written narrative of a slide sequence over the actual details of the slides. Consciously or unconsciously these subjects trusted the authority of the printed word over their own experience. Witnesses in the early 1960s reproducing orally transmitted stories about the Kirov murder often cited Nikita Khrushchev's published speeches to party congresses. Many were also no doubt influenced by false accounts of the assassination in the Soviet press during the 1930s.[11]

To the mechanisms of memory alteration listed above, we can add the well-attested distorting effects of increasing age and partisanship.[12] Increasing age must have affected the memories of some witnesses contacted by the Soviet investigative commissions of the late 1950s and 1960s, for many were already in their sixties or seventies. Partisanship too had to influence the memories of those who testified from the 1930s all the way to the perestroika era, for many were participants in the most bitter intra-party struggles.

Yet in spite of the myriad ways in which memories can be distorted, it is also true that some people retain very accurate recall of emotionally loaded or otherwise important events for most of their adult lives. Alice and Howard Hoffman have demonstrated that Howard's memories of his combat service with a U.S. mortar company in World War II were quite accurate and stable more than thirty years after the war's end. The Hoffmans' study suggested that events with a high emotional charge can be filed in a kind of "archival memory," and contingent perhaps on frequent rehearsal, remain in memory for decades.[13] It is important, then, to assess the reliability of individual witnesses by comparing whenever possible their accounts of past events with contemporary documents.

The considerations above apply both to eyewitness reports and to stories passed from one person to another before commitment to paper. But with the second category of testimony ("rumor," "hearsay"), an additional set of difficulties come into play. Readers need only remember the childhood game of "telephone," in which a chain of players transmit a phrase by whispering. At the end of the chain the phrase is most often hilariously distorted. Research, for example the pioneering 1947 study by Gordon Allport and Leo Portman, confirms that narratives passed on orally through several interlocutors undergo drastic changes. Allport and Postman used a simple experimental protocol in which a chain of six to seven interlocutors passed on an observer's description of a projected slide. The "terminal reports" erred substantially with regard to the slide itself and usually differed a good deal from the initial report. Studying the report transcripts, Allport and Postman identified three main types of distortion in rumors—leveling, sharpening, and assimilation.[14]

In leveling many of the details of the story transmitted disappear. Much of the context needed to make sense of the original story melts away. In sharpening other details are emphasized to make the story more dramatic and attention-catching. Assimilation refers to the fact that the sharpened details generally reshape the story in conformity with the values, cultural categories, obsessions, or narrative conventions of the population passing it along. Allport and Postman used a real life example from the summer of 1945, when the visit of a Chinese tourist to a rural Maine town led to widespread rumors of a "Japanese spy" taking photographs of the area (the tourist in fact had no camera).[15] Myriad examples of these sorts of rumor distortions can be found in hearsay stories about the Kirov drama. For example, V. M. Verkhovykh's lone eyewitness claim in 1960 that "122 or 123" delegates voted against Stalin's TsK membership at the Seventeenth Party Congress was soon "sharpened" to "270" or even "more than 300" votes against Stalin.

In addition to the nearly universal patterns of leveling, sharpening, and assimilation, Postman and Allport noted other, less common forms of distortion of oral accounts in transmission. In some cases peripheral details became sharpened to the point that the central theme of the oral report changed. Sometimes transmitters introduced new details into their narrative, generally consistent with the process of assimilation. Postman and Allport also observed an "effort after meaning." Transmitters often strove to make sense of the description of the slide passed on to them, providing a coherent story-line, attributing motives to characters, or assigning causes to events depicted. Time and place errors as well as verbal misunderstandings were fairly frequent.[16]

In evaluating hearsay related to the Kirov murder, I will try to identify potential source stories—the original kernel of truth that might lie at the beginning of the chain of transmission. If a plausible source story attested in documents of the time can be found for a rumor, then we have an explanation for it. For example, Khrushchev-era rumors that a moderate faction in the Politburo had sought to replace Stalin with Kirov may have their origin in Stalin's well-attested effort to promote Kirov to the post of TsK secretary in Moscow. Kirov resisted the move, and it is possible that Stalin's other lieutenants in Moscow, such as Molotov or Kaganovich, did too.

Apart from the general scientific evidence, there are more specific reasons to approach with care testimony about the Kirov murder first recorded in the 1950s and 1960s. These are rooted in Bolshevik political culture and Russia's authoritarian history. Over long centuries of despotic rule Russians had learned to lie to authority, and the TsK investigators in the fifties and sixties represented authority. Overlaying the longstanding Russian suspicion of authority was the culture of Communist politics that developed in the two decades following the October Revolution. In this culture, history served the party leadership. Changes in the party's "general line" might demand changes in historical memory, and it was the duty of party members to accept and support such changes. For the first few years of the 1960s Khrushchev supporters high in the party hierarchy were pressing for a new history of Stalinism, one in which the dictator himself ordered Kirov's death. The status of this new history remained equivocal, but some party members may have felt prompted to provide evidence for it.

A second relevant aspect of Communist political culture was the practice of hysterical denunciation that overwhelmed the party by the late 1920s. This arose in part from the Bolsheviks' prerevolutionary tradition of violent and frequently personal polemics, in part from the party's decision after the revolution to control society by encouraging Soviet subjects to denounce one another, and in part from the insecurity of a minority political party ruling over a restive population and menaced by "capitalist encirclement." Stalin and other politicians cultivated the resulting atmosphere of suspicion for their own profit. During the Great Terror of the late 1930s party members feared for their lives, and this intensified the culture of denunciation. This culture did not die instantaneously with Stalin. It remained an important part of the Soviet political scene.

Many of the depositions and interviews taken by Central Committee and Party Control Committee investigators in the fifties and sixties (the bulk of which were from Communists) vibrated with hysteria, rage, and fear, including those that attacked the dictator. Stalin's Communist denouncers were in the right, and the cause of de-Stalinization was just. But it bears remembering that many had themselves been fanatic Stalinists until the day of their own arrest. Many, indeed, had sent fellow party members, not to speak of non-Communists, to jail or worse. And most had accepted and acted on the principle that the end of constructing Communism justified means that included mass violence, summary trials, and the starvation of millions. When they turned on their former master, they did so with the same fanaticism and hysteria that they had shown in his service. While the broadest outlines of their case against Stalin were correct, the details were not always so.

One more source of distortion in the Kirov evidence was outright lying. This was as true of the Khrushchev era as it was of the Stalin years.

In the fifties and sixties NKVD officers such as P. M. Lobov and V. M. Yakushev, both murderers, told whatever lies were necessary to ingratiate themselves with the party officials who happened to be in front of them at any given moment. Others guilty of lesser crimes, such as P. P. Petrovsky, did the same.

In light of the above, this book will rely first on written documents produced around the time of the events they describe. In spite of some scornful talk about "archival fetishism" in Soviet history, written documents have one important advantage over oral folklore. If not forged, they do not change over time (where relevant, we will discuss the possibility of document forgery). Moreover, large-scale forgery of plausible documents requires a major effort. By contrast, it is the easiest thing in the world to put false oral tales into circulation.

I will also use oral testimony put to paper in the 1950s and 1960s, particularly where it can be partially confirmed with reference to earlier documents, and where the witnesses do not contradict themselves or change their evidence over time. By building one layer of evidence on top of another in chronological order, we will be able to recognize distortions and falsehoods more easily. In particular, we will be able to find and evaluate the original sources for key elements of the received narrative of the Kirov murder.

In pursuing this project I have been fortunate to work with documents earlier scholars did not have access to, including many files of the 1950s and 1960s Central Committee investigations and the recently opened archive of Nikolai Yezhov. Previous historians of the assassination were forced by official secrecy to work with very limited sources. Factual errors in their work were often due to simple lack of information.[17]

At the same time I myself have not had full access to documents on the Kirov murder. The archives of the Federal Security Service (FSB, aka KGB, NKVD, etc.) are effectively closed, although a number of KGB documents on the murder have been released and reliable researchers (such as Yu. I. Sedov) have seen and reported on relevant files. Nevertheless, a complete release of documents could put many questions to rest. Making public the original copies of Leonid Nikolaev's diaries and notes, for example, could essentially solve the case. Researchers who concluded that Nikolaev was a lone gunman apparently had access to the originals of Nikolaev's writings in 1956.[18] A complete release could confirm this version, or upset it. (Just months after this manuscript was completed, one researcher, Tatyana Sukharnikova, was able to see the original copies of Nikolaev's writings. See the Conclusion for a discussion of her findings.)

I had broad, but not complete, access to materials on the Kirov investigations in the archives of the Party Control Committee. Staff members of this archive were helpful and worked hard to support my research. However, they conduct their work within an increasingly restrictive set of Russian laws on the protection of "state security." According to the explanations of a number of Russian archivists I have talked to, laws on the protection of individual privacy also restrict the release of documents related to crimes in the past. The use of such laws to cover up inconvenient or uncomfortable histories is not restricted to the Russian Federation. United States President George W. Bush also substantially tightened access to government records, allowing the indefinite classification of some documents on "national security" grounds.[19] Such restrictions are conducive to abuse of power and falsification of history.

This book synthesizes and depends on much work by other scholars. Although I disagree with a number of their conclusions, I benefited from the sources uncovered by Robert Conquest, Robert Tucker, and especially Amy Knight.[20] Knight's narrative of Kirov's life aided me in organizing my own presentation of his biography. I depended heavily on J. Arch Getty's, Tucker's, and Conquest's reconstructions of the course of events during the Terror.[21] Getty referred me to a key source on the assassination, the newly opened Yezhov archive, and helped me puzzle out the anomalous timing of the first interrogation of Nikolaev's wife (see below, pp. 175–176). The argument that Khrushchev used the investigation of the Kirov murder as a political weapon against Molotov and Kaganovich comes from Getty and Alla Kirilina. My evaluation of various émigré sources, especially the writings of Boris Nicolaevsky, owes much to Getty.[22] I am also indebted to Oleg Khlevniuk's detailed studies of the high politics of the 1930s, and his methods for dealing with hearsay accounts of conflict between Soviet leaders. Khlevniuk deduced the norms of Bolshevik politics from an exhaustive reading of the Central Committee sources and then compared hearsay tales to those norms. He asked what kinds of conflict were routine and what kinds extraordinary.

My greatest debt is to Alla Kirilina, the most knowledgeable scholar in the world on Kirov's killing. I have used evidence gathered by Kirilina in most chapters of this book, and I follow fairly closely her genealogy of evidence in the case. My decision to categorize and analyze the evidence in chronological strata owes something to Kirilina, but much also to popular accounts of serious scholarship on early Christianity, such as L. Michael White's *From Jesus to Christianity* (2004). I was influenced in particular by the rigorous attention analysts of the New Testament and the apocryphal gospels pay to the precise wording and historical context of each document. The efforts of scholars to discern different compositional layers in particular gospels—sections added at different times—also intrigued me.[23]

I have a particular view of what happened in Leningrad in 1934, based on years of reviewing the available evidence. The body of the book is organized around an argument for that view, but I have consciously striven to include all plausible evidence contradicting my case. In the conclusion I will summarize my own understanding of events, but also lay out what I see as the best alternative accounts.

Some may be tempted to accuse me of apologizing for Stalin because I do not take on faith the received narrative that he ordered Kirov's murder. To prevent misunderstandings, I want to make my position clear. I have an intense, personal contempt for despots and authoritarians of all stripes, from Stalin to Mao, from Hitler to Franco, from Rios Montt to Pinochet, Pol Pot, and King Leopold II, Belgian ruler of the "Congo Free State." I am profoundly uninterested in arguments for the "necessity" of dictatorship, mass violence, police repression, torture, indefinite detention and so on, no matter who makes them. Call me unreasonable on this point.

Stalin was one of the deadliest tyrants of world history, and Communism as a system of government was a cruel failure with millions of victims. At the same time I recognize that simply writing off Communism or any other despotism as "evil" is an inadequate response, because it is too easy. By sensationalizing rather than analyzing we miss the motivations and rationale for despotism, and we distance ourselves from it. Thus we miss our own potential need to submit to a hero-leader, our own susceptibility to fear and hatred, and our own capacity for violence. We fail to recognize that despotisms have their origins in needs, fears, and political problems common to all of humanity.

It is near anathema in the profession of history today to talk about "learning lessons" from the past. I confess that this ban has never made sense to me, and so I want to suggest that there are lessons to be drawn from the Kirov murder, and not just to do with the evils of Communism. Like the prosperous democracies of the early twenty-first century, Soviet society was haunted by the fear of terrorism. The assassin Nikolaev, the authorities, and much of the Soviet population understood the Kirov murder as a terrorist attack. Stalin's extraordinary repressions made sense to many Soviet subjects as the only possible response to "terror." As our own governments prosecute a "war on terror" that they have extended far beyond the al-Qaeda organization that massacred three thousand civilians in New York City in 2001, it behooves us to consider carefully the extraordinary actions they have taken. The recently concluded administration of President George W. Bush instituted a number of draconian and illegal policies parallel to Stalin's own measures against "terrorism." While it goes without saying that the Bush administration was not "Stalinist" and did not engage in mass murder of citizens or the dispatch of political dissidents to forced labor camps, its policies posed a serious threat to human rights and the rule of law. They included setting up a system of special military tribunals for accused terrorists, asserting the right to ignore habeas corpus inside the United States, undertaking mass surveillance without warrant of citizens' private communications, using torture (including techniques familiar to the Stalinist secret police) on hundreds of prisoners, launching a bloody war against an Iraqi regime uninvolved in the 2001 massacre, and attacking the domestic political opposition relentlessly as "soft on" or even sympathetic to terrorism. In May 2009 US intelligence officials revealed that Bush's Vice-President Richard Cheney pressured interrogators to repeatedly "waterboard" al-Qaeda suspects until the latter "admitted" to nonexistent connections with Saddam Hussein's regime in Iraq. Cheney wanted the torture to produce the "intelligence" that he and Bush needed to justify the invasion of Iraq. This particular move is strongly reminiscent of the use of torture by Stalin and his secret police to extract false but politically useful "confessions" of terrorist conspiracies.[24]

Courts have voided some of the Bush administration's illegal and unconstitutional policies, and the new administration of President Barack Obama has ended others. However, polling indicates that almost one-half of Americans still believe that torture of "terrorism suspects" is "often" or "sometimes" permissible, regardless not just of moral objections, but also of the many practical problems of using torture to collect information. In short the threat to liberty and individual rights embodied in the "war on terror" did not end with the Bush administration.[25] It is a fact that every modern despotism has thrived on the threat of terrorism, real, exaggerated, or imagined.

Hitler and Franco had their Communist terrorists, the Jacobins had their aristocratic and clerical conspirators, Stalin had his kulaks and capitalist spies. Without such heinous enemies, why would political elites, not to speak of the population as a whole, accept the despot's arbitrary rule?

CHAPTER I

From Kostrikov to Kirov, 1886–1925

After Sergei Kirov's assassination in 1934 Soviet authors and screenwriters turned him into a Bolshevik martyr, the personification of everything truly "Leninist," struck down at the height of his powers. Stalinists and anti-Stalinists alike praised him as "fearless," "bold," "stern," "sympathetic to people," and "tireless"—standard traits of the Socialist Realist "positive hero" in Stalinist novels.[1] All memoir accounts of Kirov's youth and early political career date from after his death, and nearly all appear to be influenced by the martyrology. Furthermore, ironically, commentators in the West who came to see Kirov as a moderate rival to Stalin repeated the Soviet (originally Stalinist) hagiography of Kirov in their portrayals of the Leningrad leader as a sympathetic foil for the dictator.

To get some sense of who Kirov really was, it is best to avoid whenever possible the distortions of the hagiography that followed his death. Some reference to memoirs is unavoidable, particularly for the years prior to 1917. However, this account will stick to the earliest layer of the memoir literature (1934–1935), and, for Kirov's childhood, to his sisters' book, *It Happened in Urzhum: Memories of S. M. Kirov*, written around 1960. Otherwise, the focus will be on documents dating from Kirov's life, including his own speeches, articles, and correspondence.

Sergei Mironovich Kostrikov (Kirov) was born on March 27, 1886 (New Style) in the remote town of Urzhum, Viatka Province, to Yekaterina Kuzminichna Kostrikova and Miron Ivanovich Kostrikov. Urzhum lay in the Viatka River watershed, over two hundred kilometers north of the city of Kazan as the crow flies. Yekaterina came from a family of free peasants made good—her father Kuzma farmed some rented land and ran a small hostel in town. Miron was raised by his mother, Melania Avdeevna, who worked as a maid and nanny.[2]

The Kostrikovs had a hard life. Miron and Yekaterina's first four children died very young. The couple lived in Kuzma's house, and Kuzma expected Miron to help him with the farm. Unfortunately, Miron, who was literate and had clerked in the state forestry service, hated agricultural work. By the time Sergei was born his father was a full-blown alcoholic. Sergei's surviving sisters Anna (born 1883) and Yelizaveta (born 1889) remembered their father with great bitterness in their 1962 memoir. According to them Miron refused to work, drank heavily, beat his wife, and sometimes locked the children out of the house in the snow. Probably soon after 1890 Miron abandoned the family.[3]

In 1893, when Sergei was seven years old, his mother died of tuberculosis. Sergei's grandmother, Melania, then in her late sixties, had to take over the care of her three grandchildren. Unable to support all of them on her three-ruble per month pension as a soldier's widow and her earnings from odd jobs, Melania placed Sergei in an orphanage run by the local zemstvo Society for Charity. (The zemstvos were elected organs of local self-government created during Tsar Alexander II's liberalizing reforms of the 1860s.)[4]

Although Soviet biographies of the Stalin years portrayed Kirov's childhood as poverty-stricken, lonely, and desperate (a synecdoche, indeed, of the deprivation and slavery of Tsarist Russia as a whole), this picture is too bleak. Memoir evidence from Urzhum suggests that friendships with neighbors and former employers helped sustain the Kostrikov family. Melania Avdeevna had served as a nanny in the family of one of the board members of the Society for Charity (V. F. Polner), and this connection helped her secure a place for Sergei at the orphanage. Kirov's sisters in their old age recalled that in 1892, when Anna entered school, former employers of their mother and grandmother contributed money towards tuition and supplies, as did neighbors. The Samartsevs, the Kostrikovs' tenants, aided the family in many ways, and Sergei and his sisters emulated the Samartsev children's educational accomplishments. Alexander Samartsev was Sergei's contemporary and closest childhood friend. Nor was Sergei really separated from his biological family. He visited his sisters and grandmother nearly every Sunday, and they came to see him often at the orphanage.[5]

Kostrikov was a good student at the local Orthodox Church elementary school, and at the Urzhum Municipal School, a kind of junior high where the Society for Charity paid his tuition. In 1901 Aleksandr Sergeevich Raevsky, Sergei's teacher of geography and natural sciences, wrote the earliest available description of Kostrikov, an official school evaluation. He described the boy as "serious, conscientious, aware of his duties . . . distinguished . . . by his completely irreproachable conduct," but overburdened by work at the orphanage.[6]

Upon Sergei's completion of the Municipal School in 1901, Irina Glushkova, head matron of the zemstvo orphanage, petitioned the Society for Charity to fund further education for him. Instructors at the Municipal School supported Glushkova's request, and the Society's board approved it. Kostrikov was to study in the city of Kazan at the Industrial Institute, a newly opened postsecondary school that trained engineers, machinists, and technicians. Russian industry had expanded rapidly in the 1890s and there was an important market for such specialists. Zemstvo board member Polner arranged for Kostrikov to live rent-free in an informal student hostel run in Kazan by his wife's sister Liudmila Gustavovna Sundstrem.[7]

Kostrikov, who by all accounts had been a dutiful, well-behaved child in Urzhum, showed independence and even rebelliousness after he moved to Kazan. In an autobiography written around 1923 as part of the ritual process of accounting for his origins before joining the Communist Party, Kirov wrote of this period that "here (in Kazan) he became a nearly autonomous adult . . . " (It was a convention to write such autobiographies in the third person, to emphasize the author's selflessness and devotion to the Communist cause.) After his first year at the Industrial Institute, Kostrikov left Sundstrem's hostel and rented an apartment with two other boys from the Institute. At the same time Sundstrem left Kazan and closed down the rooming house.[8]

As it turns out, Kostrikov was probably the reason for Sundstrem's abandonment of her hostel. Alla Kirilina reported recently (2004) seeing an archival document indicating that Sergei had "intimate relations" with his landlady (that is, Sundstrem), and the latter gave birth to their daughter. Between Kirov's death and World War II, a group of Soviet filmmakers producing a movie about him uncovered the episode. A September 2, 1936 report by the Party Control Committee (KPK) to Stalin on the firing of the director of Leningrad Films and several subordinates apparently also refers to the filmmakers' discovery of Kirov's illegitimate daughter, calling their research "disgusting" and "counterrevolutionary." Given party leaders' pretense of having no private lives and their puritanical public image, any discussion of the affair in the 1930s or later would have been taboo.[9]

While it was the common assumption in Russia that mothers and not fathers were primarily responsible for children, including children born out of wedlock, Kostrikov's behavior is not particularly creditable. Sundstrem, an older single woman without financial resources, was left to deal with the new child on her own. Kostrikov moved on as if the entire episode had never occurred. As far as is known he never contacted Sundstrem or his daughter again. Obviously his behavior suggests a tendency to evade responsibility. There is also a hint in the whole incident that Kostrikov, perhaps as a result of losing his own mother so early, was especially attracted to mother figures, such as Glushkova and Sundstrem, and was quite capable of charming them by playing the role of dutiful "son." This attraction could sometimes, as in Sundstrem's case, be sexual. At the time of his "intimate relations" with Sundstrem, Kostrikov would have been only fifteen or sixteen years old.

The first documentary evidence that Kostrikov was dissatisfied with the existing structure of Tsarist society comes from his time in Kazan. In the spring of 1903, just before the Easter holidays, Kostrikov wrote to Irina Glushkova's sister, Anastasia, about conditions at the Krestnikov soap and match factory in Kazan, which he had visited as part of his curriculum at the Industrial Institute. He criticized the factory owner for forcing workers to work on holidays, and asked "why just one man is living in luxury, not doing a jot of work, and another knows no rest and lives in terrible deprivation." In November 1903 the Industrial Institute's Academic Council disciplined Kostrikov for refusing to write an essay for a required class in Scripture.[10]

Kostrikov was coming of age during an extraordinarily turbulent time in Imperial Russia. Tsar Nicholas II, who had succeeded his father in 1894, insisted on maintaining the impossible fiction of autocratic rule over a modernizing and diversifying society. His efforts to curtail the powers of the zemstvos, to censor speech in the press, to restrict student political activity at the universities, and to russify non-Russian ethnic groups met with intense opposition from factory workers, students, newly minted professionals in medicine and law, and even the supposedly passive peasantry. From 1898 onward strikes and student protests against the autocracy spread widely. When the government's mishandling of the war with Japan in 1904–1905 culminated in mutinies, peasant rebellions, and a general strike in the Empire's cities, Nicholas was forced to grant his subjects the right to elect a representative assembly, the Duma. In Kazan, student protests began in late October 1903, months before the war with Japan broke out. The immediate cause was the death of an arrested Kazan university student in police custody. Students turned the funeral ceremonies into a protest meeting that the police broke up.[11]

Among educated persons, especially those far from the centers of political power, opposition to the Tsar's absolute rule was so widespread that the police could not hope to contain it. Kostrikov, an impressionable boy from a poverty-stricken background, soaked up the mood. The process may well have begun in Urzhum. In his early 1920s autobiography Kirov wrote that "even in Urzhum he had met political exiles, whose influence he very soon felt. Later, when he visited Urzhum on holidays these acquaintances became more serious and produced definite results—he began to read illegal literature with fair regularity, talked a lot with the exiles, etc. This elementary political education enabled him to make some connections with student revolutionaries in Kazan and, by the time of his graduation from technical school he had become quite a serious revolutionary, with an inclination towards the Social Democrats."[12]

The very last phrase is important. To understand why, a minimal knowledge of some of the revolutionary political parties in early twentieth-century Russia is necessary. First, all political parties in the Empire were technically illegal until after October 1905. But various groups were organizing illegally in the late nineteenth and the first years of the twentieth century, many of them socialist. Among the most prominent socialist parties were the Socialist Revolutionaries, who advocated large-scale redistribution of land to the peasants who made up the majority of the Empire's population. The Socialist Revolutionaries saw the future of Russia in the communal landholding system that still prevailed in many villages. The Social Democrats (SDs), on the other hand, were Marxists who believed that the future held in store a revolution of the proletariat, the urban factory workers, who would take over the government apparatus, confiscate large-scale private property, and create a centrally planned economy. Proletarian dictatorship and a planned industrial economy would lead to an era of unprecedented economic productivity, a fair distribution of wealth, and social harmony. This, in the most general terms, was the Marxist vision of "socialism."

However in 1903 the Social Democratic Party split. To be more precise, leaders of the party in exile fell to squabbling. One faction, which became known as "Bolsheviks" (literally, "those in the majority") wanted a professional party of a few full-time conspirators, with a centralized top-down command system. This faction ultimately became the Communist Party of the Soviet Union. The other, the "Mensheviks" ("those in the minority"), advocated a more loose definition of party membership and a somewhat less authoritarian system of decision-making. The split was as much about personal differences between Vladimir Ilich Ulianov (Lenin), the future Bolshevik leader, and other prominent Social Democrats, such as Yuly Martov, as it was about differing plans for organizing the party. The labels "majority" and "minority" were accidental, corresponding only to the voting at the 1903 party congress where the schism opened. It is also important to note that the split had much more significance for the leaders of the party in exile than for the underground activists living inside Russia. As Adam Ulam, Kirilina, and others have pointed out, Bolsheviks and Mensheviks often cooperated between 1903 and 1917.[13]

At the time Kirov wrote his 1923 party autobiography, he was already a regional leader in the Soviet Union. After coming to power top Bolsheviks were very jealous of their own claims to a leading role in the revolutionary movement, and highly suspicious of alternative revolutionary parties (all of which were effectively illegal by 1921). To further his political career Kirov had good reason to claim Bolshevik allegiance as far back as possible. Thus, it is telling that he wrote only of his "inclination" (*uklon*) towards the Social Democrats in 1904. In other words, Kostrikov was *not* a full-fledged Social Democrat in 1904 (and certainly not a Bolshevik), but a youth with vague revolutionary ideals.

After graduation in the spring of 1904, Kostrikov returned briefly to Urzhum, and then left for the Siberian city of Tomsk. In his political autobiography a decade and a half later, Kirov noted simply that he wanted to continue his education (he could easily have gotten a job as a skilled mechanic at this point if he had wanted to). According to the memoirists Kostrikov aimed to enter the Tomsk Technological Institute. However, entrance required a diploma from a *gimnazia* (an elite liberal arts high school), or passing an exam. Sergei enrolled in night courses in Tomsk, run on a volunteer basis by reform-minded professors, where he could prepare for the test. He found work in a city office as a draftsman.[14]

Through a roommate Kostrikov made contact with underground Social Democratic activists in Tomsk in the fall of 1904. According to his autobiography, Kostrikov soon became involved in "elementary preparatory work" for the SDs, probably meaning teaching elementary "political literacy" in secret to less educated party sympathizers.[15]

Kostrikov's activity was part of a surging anti-Tsarist movement throughout Russia, involving nearly all sectors of society. A congress of zemstvo representatives from all over the Empire met in St. Petersburg in November 1904, calling for government recognition of individual rights and the establishment of a representative assembly. Liberal-minded members of the educated classes began a campaign of public "banquets," modeled on those that preceded the 1848 overthrow of French King Louis-Philippe, to promote these goals. On January 2, 1905 (Old Style) the Far Eastern naval base of Port Arthur fell to the Japanese, and with it the remains of the devastated Russian Pacific Fleet. Defeat undermined the autocracy's standing throughout society. Then, on January 9, 1905 a spark flew into the tinder of revolutionary expectation—soldiers at the Tsar's Winter Palace in St. Petersburg fired on a peaceful demonstration of workers, killing over a hundred people. News of the massacre, "Bloody Sunday," spread rapidly throughout the Empire.

Tomsk university students and underground political parties responded with public demonstrations. On January 12, 1905 student radicals seized control of one of the reform "banquets," turning it into a rowdy protest against the autocracy. Then, on January 18, activists organized a large illegal street demonstration to protest "Bloody Sunday." Some participants came armed. Cossack units and police dispersed the demonstration in serious street fighting, and killed at least one demonstrator, Osip Kononov. Most members of the Tomsk Social Democratic organization were students (as many as three hundred at this time), and the SDs played a major role in organizing the Tomsk protests. Later Bolshevik claims to have led the demonstrations, however, were disingenuous, because Mensheviks dominated the Social Democratic movement in Tomsk.[16]

Soviet historians and memoirists long after Kirov's death presented him as a key organizer of both January demonstrations in Tomsk, and as the leader of a well-organized "militant brotherhood" (*boevaia druzhina*) of armed Social Democratic activists who fought the Cossacks on January 18. These assertions are most likely false. In his autobiography, Kirov wrote simply that he "took part in the organization of an armed demonstration in January 1905." Immediately after Kirov's assassination, Mikhail Popov, a former member of the Tomsk Social Democratic Party Committee, wrote that Kostrikov had been "a member of a subcommittee" charged with organizing the street protest. The exaggerations that developed later fit a general pattern in the hagiography of overstating Kirov's importance in the pre-1917 revolutionary movement as well as in the Bolshevik leadership post-1917.[17]

In the aftermath of the January 18 demonstration, fifty-two professors demanded an end to police attacks on youth, while students at Tomsk University and Tomsk Technological Institute went on strike. Employees struck at some workplaces as well. The dead demonstrator Kononov was turned into a martyr, and his January 30 funeral into another demonstration against the autocracy. Student activists planned to continue the demonstrations, according to Kirov's biographer Sinelnikov, but on February 2, 1905 police arrested over forty of them at a secret organizational meeting. Among the detained was Sergei Kostrikov.[18]

According to a police report of April 9, 1905, Kostrikov refused to give evidence to interrogators and was generally defiant. The dutiful orphan boy had become an enemy of the Tsarist state.[19]

On April 6, 1905, the police in Tomsk released Kostrikov. In his political autobiography Kirov dated his "real revolutionary work" from this point. Based on memoirs and speculation after his death, Soviet historians claimed for him a leading role in the Bolshevik wing of the Tomsk Social Democratic movement in the following months. However, Kirilina points out that documentation from the period is scarce, consisting largely of records of Kostrikov's arrests. Kirov himself did not make extravagant claims later about his leadership role in the revolution of 1905. To quote his autobiography once more: "By and large he engaged in distribution of illegal literature and propaganda, led small study circles, attended worker meetings and so on. He attached himself to the small group of Bolsheviks—the majority of the organization supported the Mensheviks. Then he was co-opted onto the Tomsk Committee of the Russian Social Democratic Workers' Party . . . he ran an illegal printing press. During the revolution of 1905 he worked in Tomsk, and primarily at the Taiga railroad station, where he and Pisarev, who perished in 1905, supervised a strike of railway workers with great success."[20]

Note that in 1923 Kirov did not claim to have been a leader of the

Tomsk Social Democrats or their Bolshevik faction. He did, however, claim that by 1905 he was no longer just a revolutionary "with an inclination towards the Social Democrats" but a Bolshevik. This was in spite of the fact that Mensheviks dominated the Social Democratic organizations in Tomsk, Irkutsk, and Vladikavkaz, where Kostrikov lived and worked between 1908 and 1917.[21] Even assuming that Kostrikov was a confirmed Bolshevik in the prerevolutionary years, he certainly had plenty of experience working closely with Mensheviks, a reality that could have been problematic for him as a party leader in the 1920s and 1930s.

In the summer and fall of 1905 demonstrations against the autocracy, strikes, mutinies, and peasant actions against landlords were spreading throughout the Russian Empire. These culminated in a general strike that paralyzed many cities in October. In Tomsk, Kostrikov was present at a conference of Siberian Social Democratic organizations in June, and participated in the dedication of a monument to the dead standard-bearer Kononov. Sometime in mid to late summer he joined the Tomsk SD committee (which had eleven or so members). He and another SD activist, Pisarev, were dispatched to the Taiga railroad station eighty kilometers from Tomsk to link up with discontented railway workers. When railwaymen all along the Trans-Siberian Railroad struck in October, Kostrikov and Pisarev took part in the strikers' seizure of the Taiga station.[22]

By January 1906 the Tsarist government was regaining control of the situation. After conciliating supporters of constitutional democracy (the so-called Kadet [Constitutional Democratic] party and others), by establishing a representative assembly, Nicholas II and his advisers moved to repress strikers, peasant rebels, and the impromptu revolutionary councils that had arisen in the cities—the soviets. The government declared martial law and military tribunals tried thousands of revolutionaries, executing hundreds. On January 30, 1906 gendarmes arrested Kostrikov during a raid on the apartment of the treasurer of the Tomsk SD organization. Sergei lied to them about his age so that the authorities would process him as a juvenile. He was released on bail in April, reportedly paid by the SD organization of Tomsk acting through a "private person."[23]

Kostrikov was not free for long. In mid-July the gendarmes arrested him once more, along with his comrade Popov and others. Reportedly they were looking for the printing press that the SDs were setting up in a secret chamber under a Tomsk house. Although they did not find it, prosecutors charged Kostrikov under Article 129 of the Russian Criminal Code, which set penalties for persons found guilty of inciting rebellion, sowing "hostility between classes or specific groups of the population," or advocating "the overthrow of the existing civil structure of the state." On February 16, 1907 the Tomsk regional (*okrug*) court sentenced him to one year and four months in prison. The 1907 indictment confirms that Kostrikov was a member of the Tomsk SD committee at the time of his arrest.[24]

The original text of Kostrikov's indictment, however, also exposes further falsifications that Kirov, the party leader, introduced into his life story to make himself appear a more steadfast revolutionary. In his autobiography Kirov exaggerated his prison term, giving it as three years, rather than sixteen months. He also claimed falsely that he had been convicted under Article 126 rather than Article 129. The difference is significant. Article 126 focused on persons guilty of participating in organizations aiming to overthrow the existing state structure by means of violence, and mandated sentences of hard labor for up to eight years. Article 129, under which Kostrikov was in fact convicted, focused on revolutionary propaganda rather than on membership in organizations as such, and penalties were limited to exile or jail terms, except in the case of persons using means "dangerous to the lives of many people."[25]

In June or July of 1908 Kostrikov was released from the Tomsk prison. Very little is known about his life for the next year and a half. He left Tomsk for the city of Novonikolaevsk (today Novosibirsk) to the south and then moved on to Irkutsk in eastern Siberia. In this period he lost touch for good with his family and friends in Urzhum—the last communication his sisters received from him was a brief postcard he wrote on the train to Irkutsk. Kostrikov's final abandonment of his childhood home may have been due to the fact that he was now a convicted political criminal. Contact with him could be risky, both for those contacted and for Kostrikov himself. Indeed, gendarmes raided the Kostrikovs' home in Urzhum in 1907 and investigated Irina Glushkova, the orphanage matron who had almost single-handedly sponsored Sergei's education. A desire to escape his past, perhaps including the daughter Sundstrem bore him, might have also contributed to Kostrikov's abandonment of his home region. He remained in touch by letter with SD comrades in distant cities, and surely he could have found a way to communicate with his family if he had wanted to.[26]

On April 7, 1909 Tomsk police found the illegal SD printing press that Kostrikov had helped set up, reportedly after a traditional Russian masonry stove collapsed into the secret underground chamber. The gendarmes now sought to rearrest him on new charges. However, the fugitive received word in Irkutsk that the police were on his track, and left. In May 1909 he fetched up in Vladikavkaz, a medium-sized administrative city in the North Caucasus region, where he had contacts from his revolutionary work in Tomsk. He adopted the pseudonym Mironov.[27]

After the revolution Kirov was not particularly eager to discuss the details of the next eight years, from 1909 to 1917, which he spent largely in Vladikavkaz. In these years he became well known locally as a journalist for the legal liberal newspaper *Terek* (named after the region where Vladikavkaz was located), and he apparently forsook underground political work. While this was unexceptionable behavior for Social Democrats in those years, from the point of view of Bolsheviks after the revolution it was not something to be proud of. It did not fit the new official narrative in which underground revolutionaries had fought the evil Tsarist state with unflagging determination.

In his party autobiography Kostrikov passed over his years in the North Caucasus very quickly.

> K[irov] ended up in Vladikavkaz. There was no [SD] organization here. Only individual comrades. As a fugitive [literally, "as an illegal"], he worked for a local, legal newspaper. In 1915 he was arrested once again, and was for a time held in Tomsk in connection with the printing press case. He spent a year in jail, and was tried, but was acquitted "for lack of evidence." In fact the reason for acquittal was not "lack of evidence," but because a new era was dawning, the revolution was knocking at the door, and the court could not help but hear it.
>
> By order of the gendarmes he was to go to Narym Region [a remote area of Siberia] but this was not destined to be. He returned to the Caucasus, where the beginnings of an [SD] organization were being laid down. Here he remained until the revolution of 1917.[28]

This passage is remarkable for a number of reasons. First, Kirov does not claim to have undertaken any important underground political activity until 1917. This contradicts later Soviet histories that attempted to portray him as the organizer of an active, if small, Bolshevik organization in Vladikavkaz. Second, he passes over in one sentence his career as a writer for *Terek,* which was the dominant focus of his life from 1909 to 1917. Third, he lies about the date of his second trial in Tomsk, and distorts the results of that trial.[29]

Direct sources from the period of Kirov's residence in Vladikavkaz include his private letters, his articles in *Terek,* at least one internal passport he used, and police and court records. The letters indicate that Kirov remained in touch with Social Democratic comrades, including Mikhail Popov in Siberia and the Serebrennikovs, the couple from the Tomsk SD movement whom he followed to Vladikavkaz. He also seems to have traveled widely in the Caucasus region and in the Empire at large. An internal passport with a false name used by Kostrikov and possibly others has stamps showing visits to Moscow, Astrakhan, Samara Province (on the Volga River), and the Nizhny Novgorod region. Evidence from letters also shows Kostrikov visiting Rostov on Don, near the northeastern shore of the Black Sea, in 1915, probably to see his friend Mikhail Popov, who had just moved there. Articles in *Terek* indicate that he also visited many locales in the Caucasus and North Caucasus regions and went on hiking and mountain-climbing expeditions.[30]

Kirilina concludes that "it is hard to agree with those who assert that Kirov undertook major underground work in Vladikavkaz." She describes how he entered the Serebrennikovs' "social circle," which was not exclusively Social Democratic, but "progressive" in orientation. These were professionals and administrators—"a different layer of society from that in which he grew up . . . educated people, cultured . . . " He went to the theater, met the future Moscow director Yevgeny Vakhtangov, and enjoyed the company of the local intelligentsia. A report from the Tsarist gendarmerie filed just before Kostrikov's arrest in late summer 1911 described him as "sociable," generous with his friends, and something of a dandy. Perhaps the closest to political activism Kostrikov came was teaching in a weekend school for workers.[31]

Kirilina picks out an important aspect of Kirov's personality that Soviet sources were not comfortable with—he was ambitious and upwardly mobile. In Soviet terms he could be (and was) attacked as a "careerist" and a fop. Aristocrats in prerevolutionary Russia would have seen him as a presumptuous social climber.

Kostrikov main business in the years 1909–1917 was writing for *Terek.* This is obvious from the bare fact that he wrote over fifteen hundred separate pieces for the paper. His work covered just about every journalistic genre imaginable, including travel and nature writing, feuilletons, political and social commentary, theater and book reviews, and reporting. Kirilina describes *Terek* as "an ordinary provincial newspaper of bourgeois-liberal leanings: a few articles of liberal character, many advertisements, gossip about local notables, announcements, crime stories." The paper was founded by owner S. I. Kazarov in 1906, upon the introduction of more open press laws after the revolution of 1905. It was a profitable operation with a large circulation for the Russian provinces—over ten thousand.[32]

In a sense, Kostrikov had been preparing for a career as a journalist since his work on the secret SD printing press in Tomsk, supposedly as author of some of their leaflets. At *Terek* he passed rapidly through the standard apprenticeship for Russian newspapermen of the time. Beginning as a copy editor, he moved on to writing short news items for the "Chronicle" section, and then to a full reporter's position. This took all of six months.[33]

Kirilina argues that as a journalist Kostrikov was a "revolutionary democrat." Her conclusion is convincing. Trying to find "Leninist" orthodoxy (as defined by Soviet ideologists decades later) in his articles is anachronistic. He did not issue calls for worker revolution, nor could he have done so without being arrested. His work included sympathetic reporting of strikes in the oil fields near Baku and Grozny, advocacy of mass public education, exposés of the evils of penal servitude, support for women's rights, criticism of the European arms race, and denunciation of World War I profiteering by capitalist "sharks." Closer to home, he wrote on ethnic tensions between non-Slavic mountain peoples (Chechens, Ossetians, and others) and Cossacks, exposed corruption in the local bureaucracy, and covered the poor housing conditions of Vladikavkaz workers. From 1914 through the February 1917 revolution in Russia he avoided criticizing the Tsarist government's conduct of World War I, and he did not challenge the military fervor of the Russian "patriots" supporting the war.[34]

Kostrikov the *Terek* journalist was not a Bolshevik in the post-1917 sense of that term. But neither was he a supporter of "bourgeois" liberal democracy. Indeed, his writings in *Terek* show a clear hostility towards the parties that supported constitutional monarchy (the Octobrists) and liberal republicanism (the Kadets).[35] Like many progressive-minded Russians of his time, Kirov resented the autocracy as antiquated, corrupt, and an affront to human dignity. Like many, he believed that democratic change—the passing of power to ordinary working people—and "socialism" would bring progress. He probably did not have more than a vague idea what "socialism" in practice might mean, and he probably did not ask himself whether the principles of "democracy" and "socialism" might be in some situations be incompatible.

The move to Vladikavkaz did not rid Kostrikov of the gendarmes. In late August or early September 1911, they tracked him down and arrested him at the *Terek* editorial offices on charges related to the illegal printing press he had helped to set up in Tomsk. He was transferred to Tomsk for trial. In mid-March 1912 he was tried and acquitted.[36]

In his political autobiography, Kirov claims that this trial took place in 1915, and that the court acquitted him because of the imminent expectation of revolution. It seems that he did this to obscure another episode that might have been embarrassing for a Bolshevik leader. Memoirs of Kostrikov's lawyer, N. Levin, published in 1935, tell a different story about the acquittal. Levin writes that he chose not to turn the trial into a forum for Kostrikov's revolutionary views ("an 'agitational' case"), which had been a common tactic among anti-Tsarist activists since the legal reforms of the 1860s. Instead he sought to get Kostrikov off using standard legal tactics. Levin demonstrated that the officer who arrested Kostrikov in July 1906 could not recognize him. According to Kostrikov's old Tomsk comrade Popov, Levin also contended that the printing press did not belong to the SD organization at all, but rather to a gang of counterfeiters.[37]

The problem with all of this for the postrevolutionary Kirov was that rather than standing up to denounce the evils of the existing order like a true revolutionary, he had gotten off the hook on "bourgeois" technicalities. Levin reveals his clear understanding of this problem, when he insists that Kirov wanted "a principled defense" but that he convinced him otherwise.[38] Thus Levin protected the revolutionary honor of the now-martyred Kirov. However, it seems quite likely that Kostrikov in 1912 had no objections to a defense based on existing Russian law.

Why did Kirov falsify the date of his trial? It is possible that he believed a 1915 exoneration based on the general revolutionary atmosphere would be more believable to readers than an exoneration on the same grounds in 1912. It is also possible that he felt his lack of political activity in 1915–1916, when revolutionary dissatisfaction was spreading rapidly in the Empire, was awkward. This could be explained away if he was doing jail time.

Probably the best source we have for Kostrikov's inner life for any period is his 1911–1912 jail correspondence with Maria Lvovna Markus, whom he later married. Markus, born probably in 1882, was a secretary in *Terek*'s financial office. Her father, Lev Petrovich Markus, had once studied to be a rabbi but made a living as a watch repairman. Maria Lvovna's two older siblings, Sofia and Yakov, were involved in early revolutionary activity in Tbilisi and St. Petersburg. During the revolution Yakov served as Commissar of Enlightenment in the government of the Terek Republic. He was killed by the Whites in February 1919.[39]

Kostrikov's letters from jail to Maria Lvovna, whom he addressed with the affectionate "Marusia," show him as a young man in love, bearing his isolation by imagining reunion with his beloved. From his tone, it appears that Kostrikov thought of himself as having greater verbal intelligence than Maria, and he was probably right. It was not intelligence, energy, beauty, or accomplishments that drew him to her. It was rather her "simplicity" and her "direct character," her "natural completeness." Sergei compared her in one letter to Varenka Olesova, the heroine of an early (1898) Maxim Gorky story, a simple, healthy, and spirited country girl who the "dry," detached young professor in the tale is unable to love. One might speculate that Maria Lvovna, who was about four years older than Kostrikov and who was by all accounts something of a home body, was a surrogate mother figure for him, just as Glushkova and Sundstrem had been. Throughout their marriage she manifested a fretful concern over his well-being.[40]

Kostrikov shared with Maria Lvovna interests in music, drama, and literature—it appears from his letters that Maria was a musician. Many of the letters deal with drama and fiction they were both familiar with, for example the plays of the Symbolist Leonid Andreev, and Dostoevsky's novels. In Andreev's surreal dramas, which Maria professed not to understand at all, Kostrikov saw a tragic tale of man striving in vain to overcome death and ignorance in an indifferent universe. Kostrikov's sense of tragedy, if he retained it after he became Kirov, conflicted with Bolshevik insistence on "the shining future" of mankind, and may have contributed to his ironic sense of humor, remarked upon by many who met him as a Communist leader.[41]

Kostrikov's comments from jail on Dostoevsky's *The Brothers Karamazov* are also telling. He wrote to Maria that the character of Alyosha, the self-effacing and empathetic brother, appealed to him. Warmed by Alyosha's goodness, he observed, "human souls begin to open themselves up." Then he concluded with an abrupt turn: "This philosophy of 'from the soul' is close to me. But wisdom dictates a different attitude towards people." Before his girlfriend, Kostrikov wanted to claim devotion to the ideals of honesty and empathy between human beings, but he simultaneously disavowed them. In the real world, he concluded, adherence to such ideals was foolish.[42]

In these early letters, Kostrikov comes across as a bright if conventional aspirant to membership in the progressive intelligentsia (he refers to himself with some self-knowledge as a "dilettante"). He litters his correspondence with clichés—"old wine in new skins," "Andreev has not discovered America," "memory, the treasure chest of the past." His ideas, as in his interpretation of Andreev's plays, seem to be entirely derivative. As a party leader in the 1920s and 1930s he was always very adept at reproducing precisely the "Central Committee line" in his speeches. Even his view of life as a heroic but futile struggle with death was a quasi-Nietzschean commonplace among young Russian men with some education.[43]

In spite of his reassurances to Maria that he was a "tough fellow," Kostrikov suffered in jail. Boredom and isolation at times drove him to the edge of madness. During one bad period, he wrote to her that "I want to scream, curse, run to the farthest edge of the world. It is hard, indescribably hard. . . . If only you knew what a torture this idleness is."[44]

Tomsk authorities released Sergei following his acquittal on March 16, 1912. He first took the train to the Urals city of Cheliabinsk to visit his Social Democratic comrade from the 1905 revolution, Mikhail Popov. Moscow, where he hoped to find a job as a journalist, was next on his itinerary. There he stayed with his old friends from the Tomsk revolution, Nadezhda Germogenovna Serebrennikova and her husband, Ivan Fyodorovich Serebrennikov. The couple had moved from Vladikavkaz to Moscow, and once again Sergei wanted to follow them, as he had from Siberia to Vladikavkaz. Kostrikov's extensive correspondence with Nadezhda over the course of two decades suggests strongly that he was in love with her.[45]

The main source for Kostrikov's 1912 visit to Moscow is a letter he penned to Popov in Cheliabinsk. The second city of Imperial Russia tempted and frustrated him. He visited the Kremlin, a number of museums, and the Bolshoi Theater, where he saw the operas *Sadko, Das Rheingold,* and a German production of *Oedipus the King.* The city's cultural life astounded him. To Popov he wrote, "in the provinces, we see neither [real] drama, nor opera, but are forced to satisfy ourselves with sad parodies." But he could not remain in Moscow to enjoy these glories. There was no work in journalism. Kostrikov told his friend, "It is not so simple and easy to accomplish this innocent goal. I visited a literary-artistic circle. I saw nearly all of the big fish in literature and journalism. They all gave me the same answer: it's going to be hard to find anything here—too many of our brothers in the profession."[46]

After almost two weeks in Moscow, Kostrikov headed south for Vladikavkaz. The prospect of returning to a humdrum provincial life depressed him. To Nadezhda Serebrennikova he wrote, from a station en route, "my mood is deadly. . . . I don't want to read—I cannot. I can't sleep. Everything is boredom, ennui, sadness. . . . Ahead is the murk and slime of *Terek*. Is it possible that the newspaper will suck me in and my dream of Moscow will never come true?" Nor did Kostrikov's mood improve upon arrival in Vladikavkaz. "Yesterday," he wrote to Popov, "I returned to my former place of residence. The publisher greeted me with arms spread wide, and even gave me a sloppy kiss. What a kiss! But you know what? To hell with him."[47]

Immediately after his return to Vladikavkaz in mid-April 1912, Kostrikov got a new (false) internal passport, in the name of Dmitry Zakharovich Kornev. The passport was particularly valuable, for it stated that "Kornev" had been exempted from military service. It also gave "Kornev's" family status as "married," to Maria Lvovna Markus. Kostrikov had apparently wed Maria within days of his homecoming. He also chose a new pen-name, publishing over the pseudonym "Kirov" for the first time on April 26, 1912. In later years former employees of *Terek* stated that Kostrikov chose the name "Kir" (Cyrus), a Christian doctor martyred in third-century Egypt, from a calendar of Orthodox saints' days, russifying it with an "-ov." A second story is that "Kirov" was based on the name of the Persian king Cyrus.[48]

The prerevolutionary Kostrikov was of course more complex than the "life-loving," tough but compassionate, iron-willed Bolshevik of the hagiographies. He was an ambitious young journalist of progressive socialist views, who cherished literary pretensions and worked hard. A child of Russia's "rural fastnesses," he longed for the theaters, the music, and the sophistication of the big city. He could be charming and generous with friends, and evidently had an easy way with older women. His ability to please people could only have been strengthened after he was orphaned, when it became a vital survival skill. But Kostrikov's charm covered darker layers of his personality. He had seen death and state oppression up close in Tsarist prisons. He tended to understand human existence as a struggle against heavy odds, with an uncertain outcome. In contrast to the relentless insistence on his eternal "cheerfulness" in most of the Soviet biographies, Kostrikov experienced periods of depression and sleeplessness, and acquaintances sometimes perceived him as somber. The poet Dzakho Gatuev, who worked with Kostrikov at *Terek,* remembered him in 1935 as quiet and even "gloomy."[49] Often Kostrikov reconciled "progressive" optimism with his darker perceptions of life through ironic comments.

Kostrikov tended to take a circumspect attitude in conversation. He did not particularly trust other people (see his comments about Alyosha Karamazov above), and he waited to see what they had to say. He was certainly capable of duplicity and evasion of responsibility, as when he abandoned his child by Sundstrem. Although he became known in party circles as "modest," a good listener, Kostrikov's silences concealed a readiness and ability to manipulate others. Maria Lvovna's sister, Sofia, as enthusiastic a participant in the post-1934 Kirov cult as any, inadvertently but eloquently described this trait: "He had an extraordinary ability to listen to his interlocutor, while steering the conversation in the direction he needed. He didn't like to talk too much."[50] Kirov's reserve, his native intelligence, and his ability to manipulate others inconspicuously all stood him in good stead once he became a party leader.

Revolution in the North Caucasus

In August 1914 Russia embarked on war against Imperial Germany and the Austro-Hungarian Empire. As onetime Minister of the Interior Pyotr Durnovo predicted in February 1914, World War I was catastrophic for the Russian imperial state. Rank-and-file soldiers often fought with determination, and inflicted severe defeats on the Austrian forces in the southern sectors of the front. In the north, however, German troops, who enjoyed a superior supply system and greater artillery support, pressed the Russians out of Poland, Lithuania, and southern Latvia. A flood of refugees moved eastward, overburdening the resources of the Russian state. The rail system proved inadequate to the demands of total war, and transport breakdowns led to food shortages in the cities by the winter of 1916–1917. Military defeats utterly discredited the autocracy in the eyes of most of the population. In February 1917 (Old Style) crowds demanding bread and mutinous military units took over the capital of Petrograd (renamed from the "Germanic" St. Petersburg). Pressed by his generals, who did not wish to send front-line troops into the capital for a bloody fratricidal battle against the revolutionaries, the Tsar abdicated. The so-called Provisional Government, based around liberal leaders from the imperial Duma, took power. In Petrograd and other cities socialists, workers, and servicemen organized soviets to ensure that the Provisional Government did not act against the interests of the common people.

Word of the February Revolution and Tsar Nicholas II's abdication reached towns in the Terek region between March 3 and 5, 1917 (Old Style). The end of the autocracy and the collapse of central authority stimulated an efflorescence of local organizations seeking a share in power, nowhere more than in the North Caucasus. Municipal dumas and other local authorities created Civil Executive Committees to replace the central Tsarist bureaucracy in towns all over the region. In Vladikavkaz socialist activists and workers organized a city Soviet of Workers' Deputies, while military units organized a separate soviet for soldiers. The Terek Cossack Host (a Cossack "host" [*kazache voisko*] was an administrative unit uniting a number of Cossack villages obliged to provide troops for Tsarist military units) established an elective "circle" (*krug*) to replace the leaders appointed by the imperial government. Representatives of the various peoples of the Caucasus mountains (the most numerous being the Chechens) demanded and received places on the Vladikavkaz Civil Executive Committee which assumed responsibility on paper for governing the whole Terek region. Within two months the mountaineers, who had a longstanding rivalry over land with the Slavic Cossacks, would form their own Congress of United Mountain Peoples. In May a meeting of Terek region civil executive committees formally accepted the authority of Mikhail Karaulov, a Cossack leader and former Duma deputy dispatched by the Provisional Government in Petrograd to serve as regional commissar.[51]

In the pages of *Terek* Kirov welcomed the revolution as "patriotic in the best sense of the word," the dawn of a new age of freedom and justice in Russia. He urged workers to cooperate with the Provisional Government as long it "keeps pace with the revolution." (Before Lenin's arrival in Petrograd in April 1917, the Bolshevik leadership in that city, including Stalin, took the same position.) Richard D. King, the closest student of Kirov's activities in 1917–1918, concludes that he also supported the merger of Bolshevik and Menshevik organizations that took place throughout the North Caucasus in the early months of the revolution. In keeping with the mood of the moment, Kirov published a call for Social Democratic unity in *Terek* on March 9 (Old Style). "Comrades," he proclaimed, "the hour has begun when our Party must harmoniously close its mighty ranks in order to take a most resolute part in the great hour of building a new Russia."[52]

The February Revolution was an opportunity for Kirov, who was well known locally as a socialist-leaning journalist, to play a role on a much larger stage than before. On March 5, 1917 he addressed the meeting of the Vladikavkaz Duma session that set up a civil executive committee for the city. By April 1917 he was a member of the city Soviet of Workers' Deputies. It is clear that by this time Kirov self-identified as a Bolshevik. He was elected to the soviet's executive committee (distinct from the Civil Executive Committee established by the Duma), as a Bolshevik representative, along with two other party members, I. Ya. Turygin, and Maria Lvovna's brother Yakov Markus.[53]

For most of the period between February and October 1917, as the Provisional Government lost control of the former Russian Empire, Kirov and the Vladikavkaz Bolsheviks maintained a tenuous alliance with local Mensheviks. This was a simple necessity due to the Social Democrats' weakness in the area. However, the Petrograd Menshevik leaders' decision to join the Provisional Government in May 1917, the growing hostility of local Cossack landholders to the radical town soviets, and the Provisional Government's police offensive against the Bolsheviks following the July Days worker demonstrations in Petrograd convinced Kirov that a right-wing reaction threatened the revolution. On August 9, 1917 he published a declaration of the Vladikavkaz Bolsheviks' opposition to the Provisional Government in *Terek*. He also abused the Mensheviks relentlessly in print in spite of the Terek Bolsheviks' tactical alliance with them.[54]

Kirov, October, and the Terek Republic

Kirov was selected by the Vladikavkaz soviet on October 5, 1917 to serve as its delegate to the Second All-Russian Congress of Soviets, scheduled to meet in Petrograd in late October. He arrived in the capital just in time to witness the Bolshevik seizure of power, timed to present the congress with a fait accompli, on the night of October 24–25, 1917. Contrary to later grandiose claims by Soviet biographers, Kirov did not play any significant role in events. But at the congress, which convened on the evening of October 25, he must have seen Lenin in person for the first time.[55]

Soon after the Congress of Soviets adjourned on October 27, Kirov returned by train to Vladikavkaz. The trip would have taken several days given the disorganization of the rail system. On November 4 (Old Style), he spoke about events in Petrograd to the Vladikavkaz soviet, which had already passed a resolution sympathetic to the October insurrection. He presented the Bolshevik seizure of power as a defensive move against an impending coup by the Provisional Government. He condemned the Mensheviks and Socialist Revolutionaries for supporting that government, which he accused of thirsting "to sink the party of the revolutionary proletariat, soldiers, and peasants in blood." Kirov emphasized the popular nature of the Petrograd insurrection. In conclusion, he led delegates in a cheer for the Second Congress of Soviets and "the Third Great Russian Revolution" (after 1905 and February 1917).[56]

The fact was, however, that the leaders of the Terek Cossack Host, who opposed the Bolsheviks, still dominated the Terek region. Moreover, the Cossacks had worked out a temporary alliance with the Chechens and other mountaineer groups. Out of prudence neither Kirov nor other leaders of the Vladikavkaz soviet called for outright recognition of the Bolshevik government in the months following October. The story of the Grozny soviet in October–November 1917 confirms the wisdom of the course adopted by the Vladikavkaz socialists. On November 3, at the instigation of Bolshevik members, the Grozny soviet voted to recognize the Council of People's Commissars. Cossack commanders responded by demanding that the soviet disband and the Bolshevik-dominated 111th Reserve Infantry Regiment stationed in the city disarm. Menaced by Cossack and Chechen units, leaders of the soviet concluded that resistance was futile. The regiment left for Stavropol, to the northwest, accompanied by thousands of worker refugees from the oil fields around the city. Other refugees headed to the Caspian port of Baku. Chechen soldiers and Cossacks occupied Grozny, although they soon fell to fighting with one another.[57]

The civil conflict in the Terek region after October can be summed up as a three-cornered struggle between the soviets and their mostly urban, socialist sympathizers, the Terek Host, and the mountain peoples. Initially the government of the Terek Host seemed to be in control of the situation, as Cossack leader Mikhail Karaulov successfully conciliated the League of United Mountain Peoples and declared martial law throughout the region. By mid-December, however, the alliance of Cossacks and mountain peoples was breaking down on the ground, particularly around Grozny. Moreover, some Cossacks, influenced by socialist agitators and angered by the reconciliation with the Chechens and the Ingush, rejected Karaulov's leadership, and he was killed by soldiers sympathetic to the Bolsheviks on December 13. As fighting between Slavic elements of the population and the Ingush and Chechens intensified, renegade Cossacks, Slavic peasants, and urban radicals began forming ad hoc "Military-Revolutionary Councils" in towns around the region, largely in self-defense. These groups were not under the authority of the Terek Host and in fact usually opposed it.[58]

At two congresses in January–March 1918, the first in Mozdok, the second in Piatigorsk, representatives of renegade Cossacks, the Ingush mountaineers, the Military-Revolutionary Councils, and socialist-dominated town soviets sought to forge an alternative power center to the Terek Host. Delegates debated the questions of an offensive against the Chechens (a move the Cossacks and other Slav delegates supported), recognition of the central Bolshevik Council of People's Commissars (Sovnarkom), and procedures for electing local governments. Due again to their relative weakness, the Bolsheviks accepted an alliance with other socialist parties, known as the Socialist Bloc, at these congresses. Representatives of the Bloc sought to head off a war between the Slavs and the mountain peoples, in part because they needed the latter as allies against the Terek Host. Kirov, who was a lead speaker for the Bloc, argued eloquently that such a war would only strengthen "the reaction."

With respect to recognition of the Bolshevik central government and the terms for local elections, Kirov played a subtle game. He spoke strongly in favor of Bolshevik election procedures which would exclude businessmen, landowners, and other potentially counterrevolutionary groups from voting. He actively opposed the "four tail" franchise (universal, direct, secret, one-person-one-vote balloting) advocated by moderate socialists and the Ingush delegates. Kirov's stance on the local elections marked him as a convinced Bolshevik. However for pragmatic reasons he led the effort to hold the Socialist Bloc together by delaying recognition of Sovnarkom, a move that Left Bolsheviks such as Andzhievsky of Piatigorsk pushed hard for. When the time was ripe, however, at the very end of the Piatigorsk Congress, Kirov played a central part in persuading the moderate socialists to ac-

Map 1. Kirov's Civil War and After, 1918–1925. Based on V. V. Toche-
nova et al., eds., *Atlas SSSR* (Moscow: Glavnoe upravlenie geodezii i
kartografii SSSR, 1983).

cept the authority of the central Bolshevik government. On March 5, 1918 delegates voted to recognize Sovnarkom. On March 9 the congress announced the formation of the Terek Republic, which was to be a constituent of the Russian Soviet Federation.[59]

The first thing to note about Kirov's role in revolutionary activity in 1917–1918 is that contrary to the claims of later Soviet historians, he was not the most important Bolshevik leader in the Terek region. Samuil Buachidze, Mamia Orakhelashvili, and Yakov Markus, Kirov's brother-in-law, arguably had at least as much authority. Anisimov, the leader of the party in Grozny, and Piatigorsk's Left Bolshevik Andzhievsky, who pushed relentlessly for recognition of Sovnarkom, were also major players.

A second important point has to do with recent Western discussion of Kirov's role in the revolutionary years. King, on whose research the above account of events in the Terek region rests, discerns in Kirov's speeches and actions signs of his "pragmatism" and "relative lack of dogmatism." Kirov, King writes, was an "independent-minded leader," "not the stuff of which minions are made." Amy Knight draws similar conclusions, arguing that Kirov's readiness to compromise with other socialists in the Terek region shows that he was a very different man from "Lenin and Stalin, for whom the very idea of persuasion and conciliation was anathema." These conclusions seem to me to be based on an oversimplified view of Bolshevik political tactics, a selective reading of Kirov's available speeches and writings, and an anachronistic projection of the atmosphere of late 1930s Stalinist conformism back to the chaos and uncertainty of 1917–1918.[60]

Kirov was probably not as personally intolerant as Lenin or as vengeful as Stalin. That said, both Lenin and Stalin used persuasion, conciliation, and compromise as tactical maneuvers in politics. Moreover both were capable of the most calculated pragmatism. Stalin in March 1917 advocated cooperation with both the Mensheviks and the Provisional Government, and Lenin after the October Revolution established what was nominally a coalition government with the Left Socialist Revolutionary Party. As King himself makes clear, Lenin and Stalin both advocated a policy of coalition between disparate revolutionary forces in the Terek region in late 1917. The Bolsheviks were too weak in the area to act otherwise. There is a parallel case on the Pacific coast of the old Russian Empire. In the face of Japanese military power and intense local anti-Bolshevik sentiment, Soviet leaders, including Lenin, accepted the existence of a quasi-independent "Far

Eastern Republic" in this area from 1920 to 1922. The republic's government was a coalition of socialist parties.

In 1917 very few politicians, and certainly not Kirov, could imagine the transformation of the Bolshevik movement into a despotism dominated by a single dangerous "Chief" (*vozhd*). There were, however, strong tendencies in the party that facilitated that transformation. The prerevolutionary Bolsheviks were committed to the total destruction of the existing political, social, and economic order in Russia. They were not democrats in the sense most Americans and Europeans use that word today. They believed in forced expropriation of landowners' and capitalists' wealth and a franchise limited to the have-nots of society—the workers and poorest peasants. In short, they expected to set up a dictatorship of the proletariat. Such a dictatorship would be democratic in the sense that it would defend the objective interests of the common people. In the Bolshevik view this was the only realistic way to destroy the corrupt and backward old order. At the same time, most Bolsheviks believed that the worker and peasant "masses" were not fully "conscious" in a political sense. They would need the leadership and instruction of the better-educated party activists as they established their dictatorship. Kirov shared these inclinations. His writings in *Terek* and his letters suggest that he was a committed opponent of the old autocratic order well before the revolution.[61] He hoped for its total annihilation, although he had no way of knowing when or how that might come. It is true that Kirov, like many provincial Social Democrats with Bolshevik sympathies, did not immediately accept Lenin's April Theses, which demanded that the Bolsheviks struggle against the Provisional Government. But by the summer of 1917 he concluded that that government was an obstacle to revolutionary change. Sooner or later, it would have to give way to the "democratic" dictatorship of the workers and poor peasants, so that an entirely new society could be constructed from the ground up. Kirov's actions in the Terek region from August 1917 onward were oriented towards hastening the arrival of that "democratic" dictatorship. If compromise with Mensheviks and Socialist Revolutionaries was necessary to defeat the counterrevolutionaries in the North Caucasus, he was ready and willing to make it. But it is clear that he saw the Bolsheviks as the party that was truly determined to achieve what he hoped for—the destruction of the old order. From the late spring of 1917 he unequivocally identified himself as a Bolshevik in multiple articles and speeches.

Given the chaotic situation in Russia and their own organizational weakness, the Bolsheviks in 1917–1918 had to be tactically flexible. They were revolutionaries of an authoritarian bent, but they simply did not have the tight discipline that the Communist Party of the Soviet Union would eventually develop. There was no "general line" of the kind that Stalin would enforce beginning in the late 1920s. Even if there had been, communications between Petrograd and the periphery were too sporadic for party leaders to control provincial party members. In this situation one cannot read Kirov's equivocation with regard to Lenin's April Theses or his readiness to compromise with other socialists in the Terek region as evidence of any special independence or tolerance. Kirov stood out rather by his ability to achieve his goals, and the party's, through maneuver, temporary coalition-building, persuasion, and deception. More senior party leaders soon came to value him as a specialist in sorting through the most complex political tangles.

Civil War

In the weeks after the Piatigorsk Congress, local governments throughout the region hastened to recognize the authority of the Terek Republic. However, Cossack acceptance of land redistribution soon dissolved. Cossacks throughout the region rose against demands by the new Terek soviet government that they turn some of their lands over to the mountaineers. By late June 1918 civil war engulfed the region. In response to events in the Terek region and other uprisings, the Moscow government created a single unified North Caucasus Military Region, headed by Commissar Grigory Grigorevich Ordzhonikidze, a veteran Bolshevik from Georgia.[62]

As the situation deteriorated in late May, the Terek Republic's Council of People's Commissars dispatched Kirov to Moscow, the new capital of the Soviet Republic, as the Bolshevik-ruled state was now called, to petition for military aid. Kirov spent more than a month there, negotiating for scarce supplies with central authorities, including Yakov Sverdlov, chairman of the Soviet Republic's Executive Committee, Yelena Stasova, chief secretary of the party's Central Committee, and Joseph Stalin, Commissar for National Minority Affairs. As a Georgian, Stalin had a special interest in the progress of the Bolshevik cause in the Caucasus, and he apparently looked favorably on Kirov's requests for aid. There remains in the archives a note he wrote on May

29, 1918 vouching for Kirov's trustworthiness to the commissariats of military and internal affairs.[63]

In July Kirov left Moscow for the North Caucasus, traveling down the Volga with money and barges loaded with thirty thousand rifles, twenty-five thousand uniforms, and other military supplies for Red Army troops in the North Caucasus. Troops of the White General Denikin controlled railways through south Ukraine and the expedition had to move by boat along the Volga to Astrakhan, where the river flowed into the Caspian Sea, and then across the Kalmyk Steppe. Based on the memoirs of A. V. Vologodsky, cited by Amy Knight, it appears that Kirov got the funds to Piatigorsk, but not the supplies. Stalin, now in command at the Volga city of Tsaritsyn (later Stalingrad, later Volgograd), confiscated some of them, and the rest were transported only as far as Astrakhan, where local Red forces took what remained.[64]

Kirov returned to Moscow in October–November 1918, again to request military supplies. In the capital he participated in the Sixth Congress of Soviets as a delegate for the North Caucasus. He then led a convoy carrying supplies south through the central Volga region, this time by train. While he was en route, however, the military situation changed dramatically. Denikin's forces invaded the North Caucasus from the north, linking up with the Terek Cossacks and routing the Red Eleventh and Twelfth Armies led by Ordzhonikidze. When Kirov arrived at Astrakhan, at the Volga's mouth, in the middle of January 1919, there was no question of proceeding further south. Astrakhan itself was under threat. From the west came Denikin's Volunteer Army; from the east came the forces of General Kolchak, who had just seized control of the anti-Bolshevik republic that dominated Siberia. Should the two forces link up and close the Volga River to Soviet traffic, Bolshevik Moscow would be cut off from important grain and oil supplies from the south.[65]

The Bolsheviks' hold on Astrakhan was perilous. The city soviet was composed of a variety of contending parties, the region was home to many Cossacks hostile to the Soviet government, and supplies of food and military equipment were short. Aside from the Cossacks, many peasants and city inhabitants also disliked "the commissars." Thousands of soldiers from the shattered Eleventh Army were straggling into the city following a winter trek across the Kalmyk Steppe, bringing with them an epidemic of typhus. British naval units on the

Caspian threatened an assault from the sea. E. B. Bosh, chairman of the province's Communist Party Committee, and A. G. Shliapnikov, the former Petrograd metal worker who headed the Military-Revolutionary Council (Revvoensovet) that directed the newly formed Caspian-Caucasus Front of the Red Army, were at loggerheads. In early January 1919 a special Central Committee commission, headed by Ivan Babkin, arrived in the city to deal with the crisis. Even as the commission began its investigation, Soviet authorities crushed an uprising led by former Imperial Army officers (January 12, 1919). Arriving in the midst of this chaos, Kirov was sent to work in the political department of the Caspian-Caucasus Front Staff, which was trying to organize forces to defend Astrakhan.[66]

The Central Committee commission sent Bosh and Shliapnikov back to Moscow. Apparently on Moscow's initiative, party, soviet, and military authorities in Astrakhan decreed the formation in the last days of February 1919 of a Temporary Military Revolutionary Committee (VVRK) with dictatorial powers over the region. Six members, including Kirov, made up the VVRK (which was distinct from the Revvoensovet of the Red Army forces). One of their first actions was to cut rations for the city's population.[67]

Warfare in the Astrakhan area was as brutal as any in the Russian Civil War. Reds and Whites alike executed POWs and civilians, often using cruel methods such as drowning. This was a struggle to the death, with no expectation of clemency on either side. Revolutionary forces treated the city of Astrakhan, which they considered to be full of "enemy elements," almost as a free fire zone. Prior to Kirov's arrival, Lenin ordered Shliapnikov to "do your utmost to catch and shoot Astrakhan's speculators and bribers. We must deal with these sons of bitches in such fashion that they'll remember it for all time." This was a trumpet call for summary executions.[68]

Although Soviet sources blame Cossacks, ex–Imperial Army officers, priests, merchants, and former Tsarist bureaucrats for anti-Soviet sentiment in Astrakhan, even they admit to widespread unrest in the city's factories in early March 1919. The February 27 cut in rations drove workers to desperation, exacerbating preexisting anger at "the arbitrariness of the commissars, their constant threats with their revolvers." Communist agitators, among them Kirov, spoke to many factory meetings, urging workers to bear the deprivations in the name of the war against the imperialist and class enemies. In many places they were answered with shouts of "Down with the Commissars!"

There was open talk of a general strike against the Bolsheviks, set for March 10. On March 7 the VVRK declared martial law in an attempt to head off the strike.[69]

But the strike came off, in spite of the Bolsheviks' efforts. On the morning of March 10 thousands of workers left their jobs and gathered in the streets. Many soldiers of the 45th Rifle Regiment and a company of sappers went over to the side of the strikers. In response the Revvoensovet of the Caspian-Caucasus Front and the VVRK issued a public order signed by Kirov among others that "Ration cards are to be taken immediately from all who refuse to work . . . [those persons] who oppose Soviet Power are to be shot on the spot. . . ." By the early afternoon there was scattered shooting in the city and demonstrators had seized a police station and the premises of a ward party committee. They surrounded the buildings that housed the city's party and military authorities. At 3:30 P.M. the Revvoensovet issued an order over Kirov's signature: "I order the merciless annihilation of the White Guard sons of bitches, using all available means at our disposal."[70]

Eyewitness accounts collected by Socialist Revolutionaries in Berlin in the early 1920s described Communists opening fire on a huge, peaceful workers' meeting with rifles and machine guns. The SR sources, cited by anti-Bolshevik émigré S. P. Melgunov, claimed that around two thousand persons were shot in massacres around the city on that and the following day. By the end of the month, they asserted, the Bolsheviks had executed four thousand people. N. A. Efimov, citing Soviet archives, claims that Bolshevik forces shot fifteen hundred people in the immediate aftermath of the strike and uprising. Soviet sources claim, unsurprisingly but plausibly, that the initial demonstrations were not entirely peaceable. It is clear, at any rate, that inside the city the Bolsheviks were at war with much of the very class they claimed to represent, the proletariat.[71]

Kirov was a full participant in the crushing of the March 1919 uprising in Astrakhan. Through his experience of civil war, he had come to accept that Red Terror was necessary to crush the seemingly implacable "class enemy" and clear the way for construction of a new social order. Summary executions and starvation of noncooperators he endorsed as the tools of victory. At an August 1919 conference of the Astrakhan party organization, he also endorsed the taking of hostages as a method of deterring guerrilla attacks. "If we determine," he said, "that some county or village is helping the White Guardists, then we will simply treat them as enemies of the working class. We will take hostages from the counterrevolutionary villages, and they will answer with their heads for the destruction of railroad tracks. And if we discover that in some village a detachment of White Guardists is being hidden, we will destroy that nest of counterrevolution."[72]

Later Soviet historiography portrayed Kirov as the maximum leader of the defense of Astrakhan, but this paints him too large. Kirilina argues that in the first half of 1919 more important roles were played by Mekhanoshin and Saks, both members of the Revvoensovet; Georgy Atarbekov, head of the Astrakhan Cheka (the secret police) and military police, and Ivan Babkin, the Central Committee special emissary who headed the reorganization of the city administration in January–February 1919. In the summer of 1919, when Denikin's army captured Tsaritsyn and cut Astrakhan off from Moscow, Mikhail Frunze, Valerian Kuibyshev, and Fyodor Raskolnikov, members of the Revvoensovet of the Red Army's newly formed Astrakhan Group, rallied the defense. Kirov was just one of a number of important leaders in the region.[73]

Kirov's authority did increase over the course of the defense of Astrakhan. In the wake of the March 1919 uprising, the Red Army command ordered the re-creation of the Eleventh Army. Kirov was appointed chief of the army's political department, in charge of propagandizing the troops, maintaining their morale, and monitoring potential anti-Soviet sentiment. On May 7 he was promoted to member of the army's Revvoensovet. In the summer of 1919 Kirov became coordinator of all underground activities in the enemy-occupied Caucasus and North Caucasus. One of the more important tasks he supervised was the smuggling of oil out of Baku, occupied by an independent Azerbaijani government hostile to the Bolsheviks. In this capacity Kirov was in regular contact with Anastas Mikoyan, leader of the semilegal Communist organization in Baku and future Politburo member.[74]

Following Denikin's capture of Tsaritsyn on June 30, 1919, Astrakhan again seemed in danger of falling. By August, however, White forces had stalled and Red plans for a counterattack were underway. These were implemented in early November 1919, as the collapse of Kolchak's army and the defeat of Denikin at Orel in central Russia allowed the redeployment of Red Army units to the southeast. On November 12 Soviet forces around Astrakhan opened an offensive aimed at clearing the south Volga of the Whites and retaking the North Caucasus. In less than a week of fighting Bolshevik troops defeated White Cossack forces in the Volga delta, while other Eleventh Army units pushed north towards Tsaritsyn, which fell on January 3, 1920. Eleventh Army forces also advanced south into the North Caucasus, reaching the border of Kirov's own Terek region at the end of November 1919.[75]

In the course of this campaign Kirov made a serious enemy, Yury Pavlovich Butiagin, a onetime friend and former comrade from the Terek Social Democratic movement. In January 1920, Butiagin commanded a Red Army unit operating near Kizliar in the Kalmyk Steppe southwest of Astrakhan. In his capacity as a member of the Eleventh Army Revvoensovet, Kirov got into a heated telephone exchange with Butiagin after the latter ignored orders. Butiagin held a grudge against Kirov after the falling-out. In July 1921, when party members had to exchange their old party cards for new ones as part of a general Communist Party membership screening (a "purge"), Butiagin denounced his former comrade-in-arms to the Central Committee. He accused Kirov of working for a "bourgeois" newspaper (*Terek*) before the revolution, of being a Menshevik, and of political opportunism. Referring to Kirov's activities in 1917–1918, Butiagin noted that "He vacillated and maneuvered for a long period of time." Kirov, Butiagin claimed, had not received a Communist Party card until 1919. He described Kirov as a good talker who did not do serious work: "Comrade Kirov, as an orator, has some popularity with the masses, but he has no longstanding record (*stazh*) of practical party or soviet work, which he is either incapable of undertaking, or carefully evades, limiting himself in the main to speeches at factories and mass meetings." Many of Butiagin's specific accusations were disingenuous. The party did not issue cards at all until 1917, and the prerevolutionary distinction between Bolshevik and Menshevik had been blurred in the provinces. But there was a kernel of truth to the charges. Butiagin was not the last to denounce Kirov as a smooth-talking opportunist.[76]

Conquering the Transcaucasus

During the winter of 1919–1920 Red Army forces in the Caucasus regrouped in preparation for a drive into the North Caucasus and the Transcaucasus, where the newly independent republics of Azerbaijan, Armenia, and Georgia struggled to survive. As a member of the Eleventh Army Revvoensovet, Kirov worked closely with the Cau-

casian Regional Committee of the party and its senior member Ordzhonikidze in planning for the offensive. In February 1920 the Central Committee designated Ordzhonikidze as chairman and Kirov as
vice-chairman of a newly formed bureau for the "restoration" of Soviet authority in the North Caucasus. Also on the bureau were the
Georgian Bolshevik Polikarp ("Budu") Mdivani and Nariman Narimanov, a prominent Azerbaijani socialist. In preparation for the offensive Lenin put Stalin in charge of integrating the Eleventh Army and
other forces into a Caucasian Front. On March twelve units of the new
Front moved south into the North Caucasus region. They entered
Vladikavkaz on March 31, 1920, and Grozny in the first days of April.
Kirov saw Maria Lvovna, who had remained in Vladikavkaz throughout the Civil War, for the first time in almost two years.[77]

In March 1920, as the Eleventh Army moved into the Terek region,
Lenin wrote to Ordzhonikidze of the pressing need to seize Baku, the
capital of Azerbaijan. The Soviet Republic was in desperate need of the
region's oil. In the same note, Lenin also looked forward to Soviet occupation of independent Georgia. In both Azerbaijan and Georgia,
Lenin warned, the Soviets needed to act "diplomatically" and "with
great care" so as to disarm local nationalism and "prepare a strong
foundation for Soviet Power." Nonetheless, he was clearly suggesting
the takeover of sovereign states whose political systems were more
open than that of the young Soviet Republic. On April 8 the Central
Committee formally created a Caucasus Bureau tasked with organizing the Soviet advance into the Transcaucasus. Like the North Caucasus Bureau before it, the Caucasus Bureau was headed by Ordzhonikidze, with Kirov as his deputy. As the appointments suggest,
Ordzhonikidze had become Kirov's political patron. By the fall of
1920, if not earlier, the two also developed a close friendship.[78]

The situation in Baku was very complicated. On most of the territory of the Azerbaijani Republic, Azeris, Muslim peasants speaking a
dialect of Turkish, dominated. In the city and its environs, however,
the populace was more mixed, including large Russian, Russian Jewish, and Armenian communities. Although the Bolsheviks had no support in the Muslim countryside, they did have many backers in Baku,
chiefly among Russians (especially oil workers) and parts of the Armenian population. They had actually won the November 1917 elections to the Constituent Assembly inside the city. In spite of overwhelming support in rural areas, the government of the Azerbaijani
Republic, dominated by the Azeri nationalist Musavat Party, proved

unable to defend Baku due to significant discontent in the city and a full-scale war with neighboring Armenia over the disputed Karabakh region.[79]

From April 26 to 30, 1920 Ordzhonikidze and Kirov coordinated a scenario in which the Azeri Communist Party (ACP) created an Azerbaijani Revolutionary Committee (ARC) in Baku, composed entirely of Azeri Communists. These men were for most part former members of the Hummet Party, a Marxist-leaning party of Azeris. The most prominent was Nariman Narimanov. The entire purpose of the ARC was to give the revolution a "native" Azeri shading that the ACP, whose membership was ethnically mixed, could not project. The ACP and the ARC demanded that the Azerbaijani government accept Red Army occupation troops, while promising that the Soviets would respect Azeri independence. They also sent a formal appeal for assistance to Soviet Russia. The Eleventh Army had in fact already entered Azerbaijan, and a Soviet flotilla anchored off Baku. On the evening of April 27, one hour before the ARC ultimatum expired, the parliament of the Azerbaijani Republic agreed to accept Soviet occupation. The next morning an armored train bearing the first Red Army soldiers rolled into Baku from the north. Two days later, on April 30, 1920, Kirov and Ordzhonikidze made a triumphal entry into the city, posing at the railroad station for a much-reproduced photograph.[80]

Soviet histories used the "invitation" from the ARC and the Red Army's unopposed entry into Baku to portray the takeover of Azerbaijan as peaceful and popular. The reality was otherwise. In Baku the Bolsheviks reneged on their promises to respect Azerbaijani independence and executed prominent members of the nationalist Musavat Party that had dominated the republic's politics. In the countryside Azeri peasants, officials of the old republic, and Azeri as well as ex-Ottoman troops (the Ottomans supported the Azeris on grounds of shared Turkic ethnicity) organized to resist the takeover. Army units of the Azerbaijani Republic defended the region's second largest city, Ganje, from the Red Army in a siege that lasted weeks and concluded with at least a thousand of the loyalists dead. In the northern territory of Zakatala anti-Soviet forces numbering three thousand fought pitched battles with Red Army troops for ten days. According to Audrey Altstadt loyalists resisted the Bolsheviks in every sizeable town in Azerbaijan. Guerrilla resistance continued into 1924.[81]

As early as March 1920, before the occupation of Baku, Ordzhonikidze and Kirov both were eager to push through Azerbaijan and on to Georgia, where the Mensheviks were running the government. In the first days of May, before the organization of Soviet authority in the Azeri countryside had even begun, both men telegraphed Moscow to urge an invasion of Georgia. The pretext for such a move, that pro-Communist uprisings had begun in the republic, was exaggerated. Lenin rejected any invasion for the moment, largely because the Red Army was heavily engaged in Ukraine with Polish forces which had invaded Soviet-occupied territory in the last days of April 1920. Sometime between May 10 and 15 Kirov traveled to Moscow to report on the situation in the Caucasus. There he received a new assignment directly from Stasova and Lenin. Rather than invading Georgia, he would serve as Soviet ambassador to the republic.[82]

Kirov spent the second half of May 1920 preparing for his diplomatic assignment. Officials of the Commissariat of Foreign Affairs, including the commissar himself, Georgy Chicherin, briefed him. He also met with Cheka officials and with Yelena Stasova. On May 31, Kirov had his first documented meeting with Lenin, who gave him final instructions for his Georgia assignment. In his letters to Lenin from the Georgian capital of Tbilisi Kirov adopted a fawning tone. "Your predictions about my work," he wrote, "have been brilliantly confirmed with every step." In another letter he praised Lenin's "outstanding analysis" of the Soviet regime's "relations to backward peoples in capitalist countries."[83]

One of Kirov's tasks during his four months as ambassador to Tbilisi was supporting Bolshevik intelligence operations in Georgia. In pursuit of this assignment, he encountered Lavrenty Beria, a Bolshevik intelligence agent for the Eleventh Army and future head of the Soviet state security police (NKVD). The Georgian government arrested Beria immediately before Kirov's arrival in Tbilisi. Kirov repeatedly petitioned the Georgian authorities for his release, which was finally granted in August 1920. Judging by published documents, Kirov's other main occupation was protesting various alleged violations of the Soviet-Georgian peace treaty by the Georgian government. He complained of the positioning of Georgian forces in the neutral zone along the Terek frontier, of harassment of Soviet representatives in the republic, and of the influx of refugees into Soviet territory from South Ossetia, where Georgian forces suppressed an insurrection in the summer of 1920. However, his correspondence also reveals that the Soviets themselves were fanning the flames of discontent in Georgia. In a letter to Lenin Kirov noted that Georgian authorities were persecuting "even such innocent organs . . . as the branch of the [Soviet] Commissariat of Foreign Trade," inadvertently revealing that there were also less "innocent" Soviet representatives on Georgian soil.[84]

In September 1920 the Moscow authorities reassigned Kirov from Tbilisi, placing him on the commission negotiating a peace treaty with Poland in the Latvian capital of Riga. En route, Kirov stopped in Moscow, where he met with Lenin to discuss his posting after the peace negotiations. His stint in Riga was brief, as the Poles and Soviets signed an armistice on October 12. Although negotiations on a final treaty dragged on until March 1921, the Central Committee transferred Kirov back to his old home in the Terek region upon conclusion of the armistice. He was appointed chairman of the Terek Revolutionary Committee, in effect the governing body for the region. Many of the other prominent local Communists who might have been candidates for the job, including Buachidze, Yakov Markus, and Andzhievsky, had died during the Civil War.[85]

Kirov returned to the Caucasus at a fraught moment for himself and his patron Ordzhonikidze. In the summer of 1920 Communists from among the North Caucasian mountaineers had accused Ordzhonikidze of bullying them, expressing prejudice against the mountain peoples, and protecting corrupt subordinates. A number of senior Communists from the Caucasus region were determined to remove him from his leadership position. They also attacked Kirov. At his September 1920 meeting with Lenin, Kirov complained of the "gossip" which made it "impossible to work in the Caucasus." Lenin assured Kirov that he supported him and Ordzhonikidze, and insisted that both of them must continue to work in the region. In a letter to Ordzhonikidze quoted by Amy Knight, Kirov wrote that "Ilich says that under these conditions it is especially important to have people in the Caucasus who know local customs. I, of course, did not object."[86]

In the meantime, most of the Chechen population had risen against the Soviet authorities. The mountain peoples, including many of the Chechen and Ingush settlements, had fought with Red Army partisans against White Cossacks and Denikin's army in 1918–1920. They greeted the Eleventh Army, which advanced into the region in the spring of 1920, with red banners. However, the Red Army and the Russian Communists who advanced in its train quickly antagonized the mountain peoples. Russians took over local government while Red soldiers, often drunk, abused civilians and seized food stores. Heavy-handed anti-Islamic measures added to the mountaineers' resentment. In August 1920 Chechen leaders meeting in the village of Hotso declared a jihad against the Soviets. The rebellion spread rapidly through what is now western Dagestan and southeastern Chechnya. The Eleventh Army and associated forces did not succeed in putting it down until May 1921, after reportedly losing ten thousand men, or over a quarter of the troops engaged. Chechen casualties, civilian and military, were probably substantially higher. Both sides behaved with great brutality. Soviet soldiers massacred civilians and tortured or executed prisoners. The region was devastated, and famine set in by the spring of 1921. As the de facto head of the government of the Terek region in the winter of 1920–1921 Kirov must have played an important role in the very violent suppression of the Chechen rebellion. At the same time he, Stalin, and Ordzhonikidze worked with native mountaineer Communists to establish a Soviet Mountain Republic in January 1921. Granted substantial autonomy, and with native Communists in leadership positions, this republic was supposed to prove to the mountain peoples that Soviet Power was compatible with their freedom.[87]

Unfortunately, relations between the Communist mountaineer leaders on the one hand, and Ordzhonikidze, Kirov, and Stalin on the other, never went smoothly, even before the establishment of the Soviet Mountain Republic. Ordzhonikidze, who became widely known in the party for his quick temper and intimidation of others with shouting and even blows, antagonized the native Communists. Although he himself was Georgian, Ordzhonikidze was rapidly becoming known for his contempt for local "national minority" Communists (that is Chechens, Georgians, Azeris, etc.) who offered opposition to the centralizing drive of the Soviet state. One of Kirov's important jobs during this period was running interference for his patron's bullying. He was, in effect, the "good cop" to Ordzhonikidze's "bad cop." Immediately upon his arrival back in Vladikavkaz (October 1920) Kirov participated in a meeting of party officials held to discuss the charges against Ordzhonikidze of bullying and corruption. Ordzhonikidze was present, as was Stalin. Kirov rebutted the charges against his patron, calling them "White Guard provocations" and minimizing them as petty quibbling. Trivializing threats and intimidation against lower-ranking party members—here was Kirov's "moderation" in action.[88]

At the time of Stalin's visit to the Caucasus, he and Ordzhonikidze were already preparing for a Soviet invasion of Armenia, a move which Kirov also advocated. Stalin wrote to Lenin in November 1920 warning that the Entente (that is, Britain and France) was planning a "great war" in the Caucasus, using the Georgian Republic as their Trojan horse. (In fact, the British had decided some time before to abandon the Caucasus to Bolshevik conquest.) In light of this "threat," Stalin argued, the Red Army should send more units to the Azerbaijani frontiers with Georgia and Armenia.

Armenia in particular was highly vulnerable to Soviet pressure. Even as the landlocked, impoverished Armenian government was defending itself against Turkish invasion, the Soviet government engaged in peace negotiations with the Turks that threatened the republic's territorial integrity. The Western powers did not or could not provide substantial aid to Armenia. In light of these circumstances the Armenian government on December 2, 1920 accepted a Red Army garrison. After the Bolsheviks broke their promise to allow continued Armenian independence, insurrections broke out against them. These were not suppressed until March 1921.[89]

Stalin, Ordzhonikidze, and Kirov continued to press forward, lobbying Lenin and the Central Committee for authorization to invade Georgia. Lenin, who hoped to sovietize the Menshevik republic without offending Georgian nationalism, was reluctant to take immediate action. In the end Ordzhonikidze and the Caucasus Bureau acted without formal Central Committee sanction, organizing an "uprising" that served as a pretext for a full-scale invasion. On the night of February 11–12, 1921 the Eleventh Army began offensive operations against Georgia. Kirov contributed by organizing units in the Terek region for a trek through the Mamison Pass, hitherto believed to be impassible in winter.[90]

In the early 1920s Kirov had a reputation for knowing "local customs" in the Caucasus, and after his death Soviet publications portrayed him as an important "friend of the nationalities" in the region. It would be a mistake, however, to conclude that Kirov opposed the centralization of authority in Moscow or the use of coercion against recalcitrant "national minority" populations. Influenced by his early contacts with Anastas Mikoyan in Baku, Kirov was one of the first proponents of using front organizations and cultural concessions to co-opt Caucasian nationalism and ensure Soviet domination of the region. By the middle 1920s this had become official Soviet policy towards non-Russian ethnic groups. As described by Terry Martin, it involved the establishment of nominally independent or autonomous "republics" for each group, which would "federate" with the Russian

Soviet Republic. Communist party leaders encouraged these republics to teach the "native" language in schools, staff the bureaucracy with members of the titular ethnic group, and promote "native" culture in various ways. At the same time the Central Committee leadership retained the power to make most meaningful policy decisions. The policy's object was to sustain a Moscow-centered union of Soviet republics without provoking a nationalist backlash in non-Russian areas. The hope was that eventually the "national minorities" would pass through the historical stage of strong identity with their ethnic group and assimilate some kind of internationalist Soviet identity. In spite of certain soft-line aspects, such as the promotion of "native" languages and cadres, the policy was ultimately imperial.[91]

Kirov's involvement in setting up "Soviet Azerbaijan" and the Soviet Mountain Republic does not indicate that he was a soft-liner or an advocate of compromises with Caucasian nationalists, but that he understood the uses of conciliation when mixed with coercion. Although Mikoyan's program was nuanced and took account of local nationalisms, it was ultimately aggressive and dependent for implementation on the Red Army. In 1920–1921 Kirov consistently backed Ordzhonikidze's drive for invasions of Azerbaijan, Armenia, and Georgia, a drive that had Stalin's support. He was instrumental in the "liberation" of Azerbaijan, in propagandizing supposed Menshevik repression in Georgia, and probably in the crushing of the Chechen rebellion. It is important to note that many Bolshevik leaders, including Lenin, accepted the need to adopt soft-line tactics and rhetoric when they were weak or needed popular support. Martin's comments on the distinction between hard-line and soft-line Communist policies are apposite here: "Hard-line policies were the core Bolshevik tasks, whereas soft-line policies were designed to make those policies palatable to the larger population. . . . This did not mean that the [soft-line policies were] insincere or purely decorative, but simply that [they were] a secondary consideration and would be implemented only to the extent [they] did not conflict with hard-line policy goals."[92] That Kirov became known as a persuasive speaker and a practitioner of soft-line forms of contact with the populace (mass meetings and the like) simply does not mean that he was uncomfortable with the use of mass coercion or other hard-line methods. The soft and hard lines were complementary, not contradictory.

Soviet Viceroy in Baku

In March 1921 the Tenth Party Congress elected Kirov a candidate member of the party's Central Committee, a post which placed him among the highest-ranking hundred or so Bolsheviks. His position in the party was, however, threatened by an attack on his patron Ordzhonikidze by delegates who were apparently from the same group of mountaineer Communists that had challenged him in the summer and fall of 1920. According to Mikoyan's memoirs, Ordzhonikidze almost missed reelection to the Central Committee. Stalin and Lenin, however, spoke in his defense, with the latter making a joke out of Ordzhonikidze's bullying, minimizing it as Kirov had done five months earlier in Vladikavkaz.[93]

The Tenth Party Congress took place simultaneously with the mutiny of sailors at the Kronstadt naval base. The sailors, who had once been among the strongest supporters of the Bolsheviks, were inspired by striking workers in Petrograd who demanded legalization of private trade, free elections, freedom of speech, and termination of forced grain requisition from the peasants. Socialist opponents of the Bolsheviks, including the Mensheviks, had some part in leading the strikes. Both the mutiny and the strikes shook Soviet leaders, as they suggested a collapse of the Bolsheviks' original support base, military units and urban workers. Widespread peasant rebellions provoked by the forced grain requisitions added to their anxiety. The Tenth Party Congress sanctioned the suppression of the mutiny by force, but also discussed changes in economic policy, including the legalization of small-scale private trade and replacement of arbitrary grain seizures with a set tax. This became known as the New Economic Policy (NEP).[94]

Provincial party leaders returned from the party congress tasked with explaining the coming change of course to local officials and the Communist rank and file. In early April 1921, Kirov discussed the Kronstadt mutiny, peasant discontent, and the NEP with a meeting of party and labor union activists in Tbilisi. Amy Knight suggests that Kirov was "more candid" than other party spokespersons at this session, admitting to widespread peasant discontent. In fact, as Knight's own account shows, Kirov described events in the same terms that Lenin had used at the party congress. Soviet newspapers might avoid discussion of peasant discontent in print, but at party meetings officials and activists discussed it openly. Kirov was neither more nor less candid than Lenin himself.[95]

In the spring of 1921 Kirov worked with Ordzhonikidze to extend the power of the Caucasus Bureau, and thus the central leadership, in the new Soviet republics of the Transcaucasus. He backed Ordzhonikidze's successful campaign for merger of the region's transport, banking, and trade systems against opposition from some Georgian Communists and from ex-Hummet Azeris, including Narimanov. He also chaired a commission to resolve border disputes between Georgia, Armenia, and Azerbaijan. Kirov and Ordzhonikidze both pressed for Azeri cession of the entire disputed region of Karabakh to Armenia, in spite of widespread opposition from Azeri Communists, again including Narimanov. In the end Kirov and Ordzhonikidze agreed to a compromise in which Karabakh became an autonomous region within Azerbaijan. Narimanov remained unhappy with the settlement.[96]

The centralizing drive of the Caucasus Bureau met with resistance among Communist Azeris, who resented the concessions to Armenians in Karabakh, the free shipment of Baku oil to Russia, Georgia, and Armenia, and the dominance of Russians in the apparatus of the republic's Communist Party. By the summer of 1921, the party in Azerbaijan was in crisis, as supporters and opponents of centralization battled one another. To deal with the crisis, the Central Committee appointed Kirov, who was working in Tbilisi on the Caucasus Bureau, as first secretary of the Communist Party of Azerbaijan. During discussion of the appointment in the Central Committee apparatus, Lenin, Ordzhonikidze, Stasova, and Stalin all backed Kirov's candidacy. In July 1921 he moved to Baku to take on his new assignment.[97]

Kirov's first move was to purge "nationalist" Communists who opposed Ordzhonikidze's and Stalin's centralization campaign. Other Azeri Communists, most notably Narimanov, he would corral and use in an effort to keep the "natives" quiescent. Audrey Altstadt writes that "Kirov was to be the instrument of Ordzhonikidze's and Stalin's influence in Azerbaijan in the wake of conflicts with Narimanov over territorial and economic issues." In August 1921, following a Caucasus Bureau resolution censuring "factionalism" in the Azerbaijan party, Communists guilty of "nationalist deviations" were reassigned to posts outside the Soviet Republic. Then, beginning in October, the party expelled over four thousand members. Sinelnikov's account of both purges indicates that they were primarily directed against Communists "who pressed Russians and Armenians out of local enterprises on the sly," returned lands in Karabakh to previous (Azeri) landlords, and allowed former Musavat nationalists into local government. In other words they were directed against Azeris. The result, as Sinelnikov wrote in 1964, was that "the Baku proletariat, under the party's guidance, once again took its place at the head of the ranks of the laborers of the Transcaucasus, as it had in the prerevolutionary era." In short, Kirov had reasserted the dominance of the Russian city over the Azeri countryside.[98]

Kirov could not or did not effectively promote the official "affirmative action" policy in Azerbaijan. Due to the shortage of educated Azeri cadres, Russian and Armenian prejudice, and Kirov's purges of "nationalists," the recruitment of indigenous officials and party members (*korenizatsiia*) made little headway. Kirov actually presided over a decrease in the percentage of Communists who were Azeris. In 1923 the Azerbaijani Communist Party included 47 percent Azeris, 35 percent Russians, and 12 percent Armenians. Two years later the respective percentages were 43 percent Azeris, 38 percent Russians, and 18 percent Armenians. Under Kirov the Baku oil workers and Russian and Armenian Communist intellectuals remained the bulwark of the Azerbaijani Soviet regime, presiding over a more or less hostile rural Azeri underclass.[99]

Unsurprisingly, Kirov ended up in direct conflict with Nariman Narimanov, who led the "affirmative action" efforts in Azerbaijan. Not only was Narimanov the token Azeri representative on a variety of Transcaucasus-level committees, he also led the campaign to modernize Azeri Turkish by rendering it in Latin rather than Arabic characters. Narimanov made himself particularly inconvenient by his vocal opposition to economic centralization at Azeri expense. To get him out of the way, the Central Committee executive apparatus "promoted" him to the USSR Central Executive Committee in 1923 and called him to Moscow. In late 1923 and early 1924 Narimanov expressed great bitterness towards Ordzhonikidze and Kirov in a report and at least one letter of denunciation to party authorities. According to Amy Knight, Narimanov portrayed Kirov as "Sergo Ordzhonikidze's lackey." He charged him with using force to suppress Islamic religious practice, deceiving Moscow authorities about the extent of anti-Soviet unrest, and usurping the legitimate "Muslim-Communist" revolution. He also complained about the excessive influence of Armenians in the Azeri Communist Party, among them Mikoyan and Levon Mirzoian, a close friend of Kirov's who headed the Baku city organization. Ordzhonikidze, Narimanov charged, had masterminded his transfer to the Central Executive Committee to get him out of the way in Azerbaijan.[100]

Kirov's most important job in Baku was to ensure a steady supply of oil—the region produced roughly half of the Soviet Union's total petroleum output. Indeed Baku oil was a central preoccupation of Kirov throughout his career as a Bolshevik leader. From his management of Caspian smuggling in the summer of 1919 to his battles to ensure adequate shipments of fuel to Leningrad in the early 1930s, Kirov's activities connected with the oil fields around the Azerbaijani capital. Because Soviet biographers of Kirov tend to attribute all economic accomplishments in Baku and then Leningrad to their hero's personal interventions, it is difficult to know just how involved he was in the technical side of the industry during his tenure in Azerbaijan. He certainly had a reputation both in Baku and Leningrad for visiting the point of production to talk with workers. It also seems likely that his technical education in Kazan helped him to understand production issues more deeply than Bolshevik leaders with a humanistic schooling. While Kirov was in charge in Baku, Azneft, the state trust charged with operating the oil fields, expanded the use of rotary drilling (as opposed to obsolete percussion methods), opened up two major new fields, and shifted the motive force for much of the drilling equipment from gasoline-fueled internal combustion engines to electric motors, realizing substantial energy savings. Nevertheless, oil production did not reach the 1913 level until 1927, two years after Kirov had departed for Leningrad. In the meantime consumer-oriented light industries languished for lack of investment. Craft and textile production did not reach pre–World War I levels until 1930.[101]

Kirov's standing in the party rose steadily. He was elected to a mostly ceremonial membership in the USSR Central Executive Committee in December 1922. Four months later, the Twelfth Party Congress made him a full member of the party's Central Committee. In July 1924, the Central Committee Secretariat, headed by Stalin, designated him first secretary of the ACP, confirming a position that he already held in fact. His advance seems to have been due to his administrative skills, his circumspection, especially in relations with superiors, and his ability to pick the winning side in party leadership squabbles, particularly those involving Leon Trotsky, who was eventually to become Stalin's archenemy. In the winter of 1920–1921 Kirov sided with Lenin against Trotsky's plan to militarize Soviet labor unions and subject industrial workers to army-style discipline. Three years later he again fought Trotsky, this time at Stalin's side.[102]

In the fall of 1923 Trotsky and his allies began denouncing openly the trend towards central nomination of party officers (rather than local election), the involvement of the political police in party disputes, and the repression of free discussion within the party. Stalin and his allies (among them Bukharin, Zinoviev, and Kamenev) relying on the support of provincial party secretaries, were able to defeat Trotsky soundly at regional party meetings in December 1923. Ordzhonikidze and Kirov both stood squarely on Stalin's side. On December 17, 1923 Stalin instructed Kirov on the correct line towards Trotsky, namely to condemn his policies but simultaneously insist that other party leaders still needed him in the top echelons of power. It was important for Stalin at this point to present himself to the entire Communist leadership as a reasonable moderate. Kirov followed his instructions to the letter, eliciting from a meeting of Baku party activists on December 21 a resolution condemning the "factionalism" of Trotsky supporters. At the same time he assured the activists that "Trotsky has more than once been capricious with the truth, but this does not mean that he should not be in the Central Committee." In January 1925, during another round of attacks on Trotsky, Kirov again followed Stalin's line exactly, attacking Trotsky's arguments and his supposed factionalism, but averring that he remained a loyal, if misguided, Bolshevik.[103]

By the end of his tenure in Baku, Kirov was a hardened Bolshevik politician, not an idealistic naïf. He had used and then discarded many allies, from the Mensheviks of the Socialist Bloc in the Terek region to Nariman Narimanov in Azerbaijan. He had ordered the execution of striking workers in Astrakhan, participated in the bloody suppression of the Chechen rebellion in 1920–1921, and presided over the pacification of the Azerbaijani countryside. He understood that revolutionary politics were a dirty game. One can only assume that if he still believed in the future of Bolshevik socialism, he saw all of these measures as necessary for its accomplishment—the standard ends-justify-the-means for every sort of authoritarian and militaristic repression.

When Kirov departed Baku at the end of 1925, he left a great deal of resentment behind, even among ACP officials allied with him. Apart from political motives, the locals apparently resented his penchant for living the high life. When the Soviet satirist Aleksandr Zorich visited Baku soon after Kirov's transfer, someone informed him that Maria Lvovna had left behind her two dogs, Ralfik and Bim, and their "nanny," who prepared them special meals and took them on walks. Months after Kirov and Maria Lvovna had gone to Leningrad, the dogs and their caretaker still occupied the Kirov home in Baku, a large mansion owned before the revolution by one of the city's millionaires. Zorich took this information and wrote it up as "Two Dogs," a devastating satire on Maria Lvovna's precious lifestyle in the October 1926 issue of the major journal *Ogonyok*. According to Zorich, the dogs ate dishes prepared by the cook from porcelain bowls that had the ex-millionaire's monogram on them. Maria Lvovna visited them three times from Leningrad at state expense. The third visit was due to Ralfik's being taken ill. "A consulting committee of veterans, canine experts, huntsmen, lovers of nature, and specialists in all things doggy" kept vigil at his death bed. After the animal expired, Maria Lvovna organized what amounted to a state funeral. Although Zorich did not name Kirov or his wife, their identities were quite transparent, as was the implication that they were part of a new Soviet bourgeoisie.[104]

According to Pyotr Chagin (1960), who worked with Kirov in Baku and Leningrad, the satire was inspired by Sultan Efendiev, an Azeri Communist who had supported Kirov and his centralization drive against Nariman Narimanov. In spite of the constant assertions of Kirov's charm and affability in the hagiography, it appears that he provoked dislike even among Azeris who were on his side in the ACP's factional struggles. Although it was a standard tactic in intra-party disputes to charge one's opponents with living in "bourgeois" luxury, there is other evidence confirming that Kirov enjoyed the high life. Many Soviet leaders of the time did, although they did their best to keep their lifestyles hidden from the general population. Zorich's breach of this concealment was a major problem for Kirov.[105]

The "Two Dogs" affair requires a short digression, because Chagin in 1960 claimed that the feuilleton was a Stalin demarche against Kirov, and a sign of serious fulminating hostility between the two. Chagin's evidence is, however, unreliable. Not only does he wrongly identify Efendiev as a "nationalist" Narimanov ally, he also claims that Efendiev and Narimanov both were Stalin's tools simply because they had served with him in the Commissariat of Nationalities during the Civil War years. Chagin also asserts inaccurately that Ordzhonikidze, in his new capacity as head of the Central Control Commission (TsKK), had Zorich "fired from *Pravda*."

The fall of 1926 was a time of vigorous press denunciation of party officials for corruption, high-living, and sexual misbehavior. The TsKK and TsK eventually stepped in to squelch much of this "sensationalistic" coverage. In this atmosphere it is entirely believable that journalists at *Ogonyok* would take aim at Kirov without central orders. Even if Stalin was involved with the publication of "Two Dogs," it is likely that the article was part of his campaign to force Kirov and Ordzhonikidze both to give up for good their positions in the Caucasus and come to the center to strengthen his position against the new "United Opposition" headed by Grigory Zinoviev, Lev Kamenev, and Leon Trotsky (see Chapter 2).[106]

Returning to Kirov's work in Baku, it is undoubtedly true that some of his Russian and Armenian colleagues, such as A. F. Miasnikov and A. P. Serebrovsky, the head of the Azeri state oil company Azneft, found him to be an affable hard worker, a capable detail man, "simple, kind, and accessible."[107] Miasnikov reported in his diary that the first secretary was "a true democrat" who enjoyed going out to the point of production to meet the workers and talk with them. But from another angle, Kirov was something of an operator, a fair-spoken man who was nearly always amiable in face-to-face meetings, but was quite capable of betrayal. He was good at picking the winning side in political conflicts, and at holding his tongue as he waited for the winning side to emerge. In a "bourgeois" society, he might have made a good salesman or lobbyist.

Even Stalin and Hitler had their human sides, and Kirov was certainly not as destructive a personality as either of them. He did not harbor obsessive hatreds, and he was not a sadist in the clinical sense. But he certainly accepted the need to deploy violence against the regime's putative enemies, and he certainly respected Stalin for his "toughness," intelligence, and political acumen. Kirov, like his patron Ordzhonikidze, chose to follow Stalin early, and he stuck with him, whatever his private doubts or fears may have been.

CHAPTER 2

Conquering Leningrad, 1925–1929

In the fall of 1925 a new Communist opposition group challenged the party leaders grouped around Stalin. Led by Politburo members Lev Kamenev and Grigory Zinoviev, the opposition also had the support of Lenin's widow Nadezhda Krupskaya and Commissar of Finance Grigory Yakovlevich Sokolnikov. The Zinovievites' main institutional base was the party organization of Leningrad, which Zinoviev headed. The new oppositionists repeated many of the criticisms leveled by Trotsky and his supporters in 1923–1924, namely that the Soviet leadership was crushing democracy within the party and undermining the living standards of urban workers. They also argued that the Central Committee's NEP policy of allowing peasants to market their products in relative freedom was fostering the development of a dangerous wealthy peasant (kulak) class. There was also a personal dimension to the struggle. Following the death of Lenin in January 1924 party leaders were battling openly for power at the top.[1]

Like Trotsky, Zinoviev also became embroiled in a debate over Stalin's newly coined slogan "socialism in one country." During the years of revolution and civil war Bolshevik leaders had hoped for the world proletarian revolution that Marx had predicted. In fact most assumed that the Russian Revolution would trigger an international revolution. As one result, they anticipated that a Communist Germany would provide the Soviet Union with technological aid and investment from its advanced industrial economy. When this did not happen the Soviet Communists were left alone in a hostile world. The intervention of the Allied powers against the Reds in the Civil War exacerbated their sense of living in a dangerous capitalist encirclement. Stalin's response to this situation was to popularize the slogan "socialism in one country," standing for his claim that in spite of the delay in the world revolution, the Soviets could build a socialist society on their own. Both Trotsky and Zinoviev foolishly haggled with Stalin over nuances, arguing that while the capitalist world order remained intact the USSR could begin but not complete the "construction of socialism." This allowed Stalin to portray both men as "lacking faith in the revolution."[2]

It is quite probable that "socialism in one country" had genuine resonance for Kirov, who had frequently written in *Terek* of the patriotic need to modernize Russia politically, culturally, and technologically. For the prerevolutionary Kirov, the victory of socialism was an integral part of that modernization. Stalin's optimism, his commitment to progress, and his calls for party unity in the name of getting the job done must have attracted him.

At an October 1925 plenum of the Central Committee the Zinovievite leaders criticized Central Committee policies in a major party forum for the first time. They demanded, in vain, that the TsK sanction an intra-party debate on the "soft" regime policy towards the kulaks. After Stalin ally Nikolai Bukharin refused to publish articles by Kamenev or Krupskaya on the peasant issue in *Pravda*, the Zinovievites girded for a fight at the upcoming Fourteenth Party Congress. On November 18 the Leningrad authorities, probably under pressure from the TsK, removed Georgy Safarov from the editorship of *Leningradskaya pravda*, the city's leading party newspaper which had taken openly Zinovievite positions. However, they replaced him with another Zinoviev supporter, Zaks-Gladnev. At the Leningrad provincial party conference held in early December, the rhetoric was heated. Safarov, who still held major posts in the Leningrad party organization, proclaimed, "the kulak is a kulak, and as Lenin taught us, he is a verminous pig (*vrednaia skotina*) of the worst sort."[3]

In spite of the Zinovievites' show of unity at the December Leningrad provincial party conference, there were supporters of the Central Committee inside the Leningrad apparatus. Nikolai Komarov, Stalin's candidate for the Leningrad party's secretariat, was a veteran factory worker who had joined the city's Bolshevik organization in 1909. In debates among the Leningrad leaders in the fall of 1925 S. S. Lobov, Ivan Moskvin, and Nikolai Shvernik, all senior functionaries and veterans of the city's Bolshevik movement, joined Komarov in supporting the Central Committee. There was also dissent lower down the city's Communist hierarchy. A number of party cells (the primary unit of party organization, usually based at a particular workplace) in the Vyborg Ward passed resolutions dissenting from the Zinoviev line in the weeks before the Fourteenth Party Congress.[4]

On December 18, 1925 the congress convened in Moscow, to remain in session through the thirty-first. At the request of forty-three delegates from Leningrad, Zinoviev delivered a "supplementary presentation" to the main Central Committee reports given by Stalin and his close associate Molotov. The Zinovievites stood their ground, although they were badly outnumbered and the audience harassed their speakers with whistles and shouts. In addition to their policy criticisms, they attacked Stalin's domination of party life. Kamenev declared that "We are against the theory of one-man leadership, we are against the creation of a Chief (*vozhd*)." Ivan Petrovich Bakaev, a prominent figure in Leningrad and member of the party's Central Control Commission (TsKK), warned that the growing culture of denunciation inside the party was making frank policy discussions impossible.[5]

Stalin, Bukharin, and their allies mostly played the role of "moderates." They defended the NEP policy of conciliating the middle peasants. They also proclaimed their continued commitment to "collective leadership," denying that Stalin was any kind of Chief. Above all, supporters of the Central Committee charged the Zinovievites with violating the ban on factional activity passed by the Tenth Party Congress in 1921. The oppositionists were schismatics, a threat to party unity. Kirov, who was a delegate to the congress, probably expressed the view of the majority when he said that the Zinovievites were obstructing real work with their hysterical and unnecessary criticisms of the Central Committee. This was a view that Kirov and other Stalin supporters expressed frequently—that they were interested in getting things done, not wasting energy in silly theoretical debates. As Stalin and Kirov both said more than once, "the party is not a discussion club."[6]

On the key resolution to approve the Central Committee's presentation, the congress voted 559 in favor and 65 opposed, with 41 abstentions. Stalin defeated the Zinovievites easily.[7]

On December 24, following the vote on the TsK presentation, more than eighty Leningrad delegates left the congress for their home city. Over the next three days they defended their conduct at the congress before ward and workplace meetings of Leningrad Communists. Most of these meetings passed resolutions calling for "party unity" but simultaneously endorsing the actions of the Leningrad delegation. *Leningradskaya pravda* ran transcripts of speeches by both sides at the party congress, but the newspaper's editorial slant was entirely towards Zinoviev. On December 26 the lead editorial attacked the TsK majority's "kulak deviation" and affirmed that "our delegation was right."[8]

On December 28 the party congress, still in session in Moscow, passed a resolution entitled "Appeal of the Fourteenth Party Congress to the Leningrad Organization." The appeal cited the continuing anti-TsK line of *Leningradskaya pravda* and demanded that the Leningrad organization cease all "discussion" of the party congress's resolutions and fall into line. That night (December 28–29) the TsK ordered the replacement of *Leningradskaya pravda* editor Zaks-Gladnev with TsK supporter Ivan Skvortsov-Stepanov. The following morning a Central Committee delegation arrived in Leningrad to take the fight against Zinoviev inside the city organization. The members included Skvortsov-Stepanov, Mikoyan, Ordzhonikidze, and Kirov. Later in January Molotov, labor union leader Mikhail Tomsky, and Bukharin would all come to Leningrad to battle the Zinovievites.[9]

Leningrad leaders dubbed the TsK delegation the "Savage Division," a term applied during World War I to Tsarist army units recruited from the Caucasian mountain peoples. These troops were supposedly more barbarous than soldiers of European origin. The Leningraders, in short, saw Stalin using his brutal Caucasian cohort— Ordzhonikidze, Mikoyan, and Kirov—to seize their home territory. This was especially galling because Leningrad was the birthplace of both the February and the October revolutions, and the city's leaders included many veteran Bolsheviks from the city's steel and armaments factories. These factories had a quasi-sacred status in party discourse, as incubators of class-conscious proletarian revolutionaries.[10]

According to Molotov, reminiscing in the 1970s, the TsK strategy was to first win over party cells at smaller factories, leaving for last the gigantic Red Putilov armaments and machine plant, on which the Zinovievites had a tight grip. Accounts of the struggle in *Leningradskaya pravda* corroborate Molotov's memory. However, the Central Committee representatives on the first day did aim for a couple of big victories at major party organizations. On the evening of December 29 Kirov, Ordzhonikidze, Mikoyan, and Komarov spoke to a mass meeting of party activists from the mostly proletarian Vyborg Ward, where TsK support was high (except among Communist youth—see below).

They were opposed by Zinovievite speakers including Krupskaya and two high-ranking Leningrad officials, Grigory Yevdokimov and Aleksandr Kuklin. The pro-TsK crowd heckled the opposition speakers, taunting the elderly atheist Krupskaya with shouts of "Hey, Holy Mother!" Mikhail Rosliakov, a planning official in the Leningrad Council on the National Economy, remembered decades later being impressed with Kirov's skill as an orator: "His speech was passionate, full of conviction, inspired." The meeting voted 850–50 in favor of a resolution endorsing the Fourteenth Party Congress resolutions and condemning the Leningrad delegation's actions. The ward's party committee did the same, voting 45–10. In Petrograd Ward, the party committee passed an equivocal resolution, while the larger body of activists endorsed the Central Committee line by a very narrow margin.[11]

After the easy victory in Vyborg, Kirov and his senior colleagues returned to Moscow to prepare a major campaign against Zinoviev. When they came back to Leningrad on the morning of January 5, they took the fight into the trenches—the party cells of small workshops, institutes, and apartment complexes throughout the city. They sought to mobilize lower-ranking Communists against their Zinovievite superiors. Over the next ten days, Kirov spoke at ten major party meetings, and probably attended many more. The struggle was fierce. Kirov himself earned the lasting enmity of many leading Communists in the city, who bestowed upon him the epithets "Gap-tooth" (*karzubyi*) and "Spotty" (*riaboi*, meaning his face was pitted with acne scars). Leningrad activists and lower-level party officials did all that they could to defend their positions in the city. Zinoviev supporters shouted down some Central Committee speakers, and forcibly blocked others from attending party meetings. They confiscated TsK literature and central newspapers from TsK propagandists. There were attempts to prevent pro-TsK Communist cells from assembling. Central Committee forces used the same tactics when they had the physical force on hand to do so. Street fights broke out.[12]

What was Kirov saying to his audiences? One of his speeches reported by *Leningradskaya pravda* was to a conference of chairmen of rural soviet executive committees on January 19. In spite of the "iron encirclement of the imperialist powers," Kirov told the gathering, the Soviet Union had succeeded in rebuilding the economy after the Civil War. Given the USSR's wealth of natural resources and the development of internal markets under the NEP, he said, the capitalist powers'

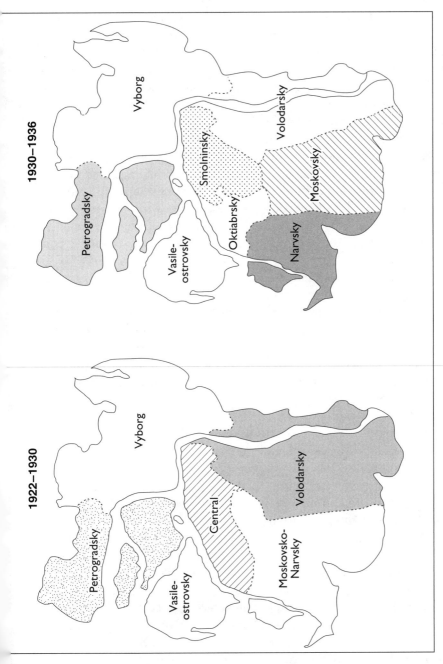

Map 2. Leningrad Wards, 1922–1936. Based on A. V. Kobak et al., eds., "Sankt Peterburg: Entsiklopediia," www.encspb.ru (internet resource based on B. V. Anan'ich et al., eds., *Sankt Peterburg: Entsiklopediia* [Moscow: ROSSPEN, 2004]).

"hopes of crushing us have dimmed." Referring to the prospective victory of allied Nationalist and Communist forces in China's civil war, Kirov assured listeners that "the revolution in the east" would deprive the European imperial powers' "locomotive" of its "coal-car" (that is, the colonies that supplied Europe with raw materials). After giving this upbeat assessment of the Soviet Union's situation, Kirov portrayed the Zinovievite opposition as pessimistic doomsayers. "The opposition," he declared, "says we cannot build socialism in one country. We say we can. The opposition says our industry is state capitalist. We say it is socialist. The opposition says the NEP is a retreat. We say it is a bridge to socialism." Kirov claimed too that the opposition exaggerated the kulak threat, thus undermining the working class's supposed alliance with middle and poor peasants. He concluded with a warning that such deviations were a grave threat to the party, which required unity above all. The newspaper titled Kirov's presentation, "Unity is Our Strength."[13]

Kirov's speech was Central Committee boilerplate. There was nothing original in it. Even the optimism, sometimes supposed to be a Kirov trademark as opposed to Stalin's "gloom," followed closely the general secretary's assessment of the Soviet Union's prospects in the Central Committee's political report to the Fourteenth Party Congress one month earlier. Here Stalin spoke of the "healthy and strengthening stabilization, the growth of our economy," and "the continually growing unity of interest against the common enemy—against imperialism."[14]

As the battle for the party cells went on in the city's factories and offices, the Central Committee plenum, meeting in Moscow following the party congress, fought to impose its will on the Leningrad Province Party Committee. On January 4, the TsK pressured members of the Leningrad committee to fire the Zinovievites Grigory Yevdokimov and Aleksandr Kuklin from their three-man secretariat. The next day Kirov, Tomsky, Molotov, and other TsK representatives, just returned from their brief trip to Moscow, met with officials of the Leningrad organization to nominate a new secretariat. The Leningrad officials rejected the TsK candidates, Kirov and Leningraders N. P. Komarov and Aleksei Badaev. However, they soon agreed to accept a Central Committee override of their decision. On January 7, the Politburo made the expected decision to appoint Kirov, Komarov, and Badaev to the secretariat. Thus Kirov became the leader of the Leningrad party organization.[15]

As Amy Knight and Alla Kirilina have pointed out, Kirov did not want the Leningrad posting. He and Stalin initially agreed that he would take the job for a few months, then return to Baku, a fiction that Kirov maintained until mid-March. Around December 25 he wrote to his wife from the Fourteenth Party Congress. "From the newspapers you'll see that we have a desperate fight going on here at the congress, unlike any we've had before. Read *Pravda* thoroughly and you will be up to speed on events. In connection with this fight, the question has been put here of sending me to work in Leningrad permanently. Today this was spoken of in very, very concrete terms. Obviously, I am categorically opposed. Sergo (Ordzhonikidze) is also against my transfer there. I don't know how this will end."[16]

Kirov's reluctance to go to Leningrad is understandable. He had been in Baku for four years, he knew the ins and outs of Azerbaijani politics, and he had a comfortable life. Now he was being asked to undertake a nasty factional battle for a hostile city. Both he and Ordzhonikidze, who resisted promotion to the Central Control Commission in the fall of 1926, would have preferred to remain party bosses in the Caucasus.[17] Stalin, however, had uses for them in his struggle for power in the center, and his will prevailed. Kirov's apparent dismay at the transfer does not indicate disloyalty to Stalin, although it may suggest a disinclination to do his dirtiest work. In evaluating Kirov's letters to Maria Lvovna, it is also important to remember that she did not want to leave Baku. Kirov was probably at pains to assure her that he did not want to go to Leningrad either, but that higher authorities had forced the issue.

Once in Leningrad, Kirov was caught up in the excitement of battle. His personal letters express a mixture of fatigue and pride. On January 10 he wrote to Ordzhonikidze that "as expected they did not give us a particularly hospitable reception here. Especially as we immediately visited the big factories. . . . We now have a numerical majority of party members. The party collectives are passing resolutions for new ward committee elections, and in a few spots they demand new elections for the provincial committee." Soon after this he wrote to Maria Lvovna that "I'm at meetings every day. Well, the meetings here! There are cells that consist of 1,500–2,000 members [much larger than in Baku]. That's just one cell. Workers, men and women, everywhere. . . . The situation here is desperate, I've never seen anything like it."[18]

By January 16, the TsK forces were in control of the situation. On that day Kirov reported to Ordzhonikidze and Stalin that the party organizations in the Vyborg, Petrograd, Volodarsky, and Moskva-Narva wards had rejected the opposition. The remaining centers of resistance were a few small factories and the big prize, Red Putilov. On January 20 came the culminating confrontation at Putilov, a mass meeting of party members. Speakers for the Central Committee, including Tomsky, Molotov, and Voroshilov, won the day, as the factory's Communists voted to censure the opposition. Glebov-Avilov, former head of the city's labor unions under Zinoviev, decried "the smashing of the Leningrad organization."[19]

Reporting in *Leningradskaya pravda* following the defeat of the Zinovievites revealed where the main centers of opposition to the Central Committee had been. Communist activists had resisted most strongly—not surprising given that they were part of Zinoviev's patronage machine and stood to lose jobs and privileges should he be driven from the city. In particular the Komsomol (Communist Youth League) had fought hard against the Central Committee representatives. This was true throughout the city, but especially in Vyborg Ward, where the Komsomols explicitly rejected the ward party committee's support for the TsK on December 29 or 30.[20] *Leningradskaya pravda* condemned by name V. V. Rumiantsev, the senior Komsomol official under Zinoviev, who was a Vyborger. Another important center of opposition was in Moskva-Narva Ward where the Komsomol committee passed a resolution equivocating on support for the Central Committee as late as February 6.[21]

As the factional battle simmered down, Kirov was exhausted, but also proud of the victory over the opposition and of his new position as leader of the Soviet Union's second city, site of the October Revolution (Figures 1, 2). To Maria Lvovna in Baku he wrote of his "very complex and responsible" work. On February 23 he bragged to his friend Levon Mirzoian, head of the Baku party organization, of the vast size of the Leningrad organization (over 100,000 members) and "the much greater dimensions" of the metropolis. One advantage to work in Leningrad, he claimed, was that the politics of party cliques and factions was simpler than in Baku. "Here everything is clearer, [our] line is better defined, there is less complicated diplomacy. Of course the fight was extraordinarily tough, and . . . in places went as far as physical face-smashing." But now "the entire apparatus is in our hands." Kirov reported that he'd lost his voice and his chest ached as a result of the battle. "I've never had to jabber and fuss anywhere as I have here."[22]

In the first months of 1926 Kirov and other TsK supporters purged the Leningrad organization of the most vocal Zinovievite leaders. A comparison of the provincial party committee election results in December 1925 and February 1926 shows that a number of the most prominent Zinoviev supporters were removed, as well as Zinoviev himself. At this point in the party's history, punishment for oppositionists was generally demotion and/or transfer to remote provincial posts. Expulsion from the party was a relatively harsh penalty. Thus, most of the purged Zinovievites eventually received lower-ranking jobs in the apparatus, or were shipped out to the Far East, Central Asia, Siberia, or other remote locations. Many of those exiled eventually returned to Leningrad.[23]

Leading Zinovievites were also demoted from important central positions. Zinoviev himself remained a full Politburo member for the time being, but Kamenev was bumped from full to candidate membership, and Sokolnikov lost his candidate membership. Stalin had the Politburo enlarged from seven to nine full members. Two of his closest collaborators, Molotov and Voroshilov, along with Mikhail Kalinin, were advanced to full membership. Several Zinovievites, including Kuklin and the former Deputy Commissar of Defense M. M. Lashevich, were expelled from the Central Committee or demoted to candidate status.[24]

From February 10 to 12, 1926 the Twenty-third Conference of the Leningrad party organization convened to formalize the Central Committee's victory. The conference elected new governing bodies, including a new provincial party committee and a new control commission. Politburo member Nikolai Bukharin, head of the All-Union Council on the National Economy (VSNKh) Feliks Dzerzhinsky, and Kirov gave the marquee speeches. Kirov and Bukharin both stressed that the Zinovievite leadership had duped and intimidated the city's rank-and-file Communists. The latter could not be held responsible for the many oppositionist resolutions they had passed in the last days of December 1925.[25] This narrative was probably necessary for the continued functioning of the city's apparatus, which the Central Committee did not have the resources or will to purge thoroughly. The fact, however, was that most of the city party organization had supported Zinoviev, if only because he was their political boss. Kirov would have to deal with this reality.

In his concluding address to the Twenty-third Conference, Kirov focused on the need for unity, calm, and discipline. Avoiding direct mention of the opposition, he clearly aimed to conciliate the many former Zinovievites in the audience. "Today . . . after the difficult troubles that have befallen our Leningrad organization," Kirov told the conference, "we will leave this hall full of the same faith, the same selfless hope in our deepest historical work, we will continue the grand mission that humanity has laid upon our shoulders. . . ."[26]

Besides the former Zinovievites, Kirov had other potential enemies in Leningrad. Those senior Communists in the city who had stood with the Central Committee in the factional fight, such as Nikolai Komarov, Ivan Mikhailovich Moskvin, and G. A. Desov, believed that they deserved to inherit the leadership. These officials were generally Petersburg natives or longtime residents. On February 13, 1926, Kirov wrote to Ordzhonikidze that "yesterday we finished the conference, and thus finished the first phase of our work against the opposition. Today we had the plenum of the provincial party committee, we elected the secretaries, the bureau, and so on. . . . There is some very, very bad news, which is that a new fight is shaping up based on the unbelievable local cliquishness (*mestnichestvo*) here." There was substantial resistance among the "Old Leningraders" to Kirov's leading the city.[27]

To support Kirov in his new post, Stalin made a rare trip to Leningrad in April 1926. On the twelfth and thirteenth of that month he addressed a plenary session of the provincial party committee and a meeting of activists. Kirov needed Stalin's support, and he had to proceed with caution in relations with the veteran Leningraders. This was particularly so because he came from Baku without a "tail" (Rosliakov's term). It was common in the 1920s and early 1930s for party bosses transferred from one bailiwick to another to pull with them an entire raft of loyal subordinates who could be trusted, among other things, not to pass information to the party control organs or the secret police. Kirov did not bring such a group with him to Leningrad. Some months after his arrival, a few transfers from Baku trickled in—for example Pyotr Chagin, onetime editor of the newspaper *Baku Worker,* became editor of Leningrad's *Red Gazette.*[28] But for the most part Kirov would have to build his own connections in the city. As a result, he had to share a great deal of power with the veteran Leningraders, in particular Komarov, who chaired the Leningrad soviet from 1926 to 1929. In these years it is fair to speak of a collective leadership in the city. It was not until after Komarov's expulsion from Leningrad that Kirov became the undisputed leader of the metropolis.[29]

The defeat of the Zinovievites in Leningrad did not squelch doubts about either the NEP or Stalin's growing power. Oppositionists were soon organizing again. By April 1926 Zinoviev and Kamenev allied themselves with Trotsky to press for greater democracy inside the party, rapid industrialization, and a harder line against the kulaks. At April and July 1926 plenary sessions of the Central Committee the oppositionists defended their views. The majority replied with accusations of "factionalism" and stripped Zinoviev of his Politburo membership. To strengthen his position Stalin promoted his Caucasian cohort—Mikoyan, Ordzhonikidze, and Kirov—together with two other associates, Andreev and Kaganovich, to candidate membership in the Politburo. In October 1926 Trotsky was expelled from the Politburo. Following their loss of major leadership positions, the so-called "United Opposition" began an underground campaign to put their views before party cells all over the Soviet Union. This campaign would go on for more than a year before the opposition's final defeat at the Fifteenth Party Congress in November 1927.[30]

Kirov focused on the fight against the United Opposition during his first two years in Leningrad. His letters to Levon Mirzoian in Baku show him obsessed with maintaining vigilance against possible "sallies." On July 12, 1926, just before the opening of the Central Committee plenum, he wrote:

> The overall situation in the party forces one to pay close attention to everything. Our former opposition has not forgotten and cannot forget about Leningrad. They have their calculations, they still have plenty of connections [here], they try to use them, especially recently. This cannot fail to complicate work.
>
> I am now going to Moscow for the plenum. There will be a mountain of news from there. The plenum promises to be a historic one. . . .
>
> How are things in the organization? Vague rumors have reached here about [factional] groupings in Baku. Is that true, and along what lines are these groups forming, if they exist? These are factional times, there's no point in being surprised about it.[31]

In this same letter Kirov commiserated with Mirzoian about the Central Control Commission's reduction of a sentence brought by the Azerbaijani control commission against a group of former Workers' Opposition leaders in Baku. Kirov had argued against senior TsK leaders (including Molotov) that the harsher sentence passed in Baku should stand, but to no avail. In this particular case at least, Kirov and Mirzoian supported a harsher penalty for oppositionists than Stalin's right-hand man Molotov. "Up there on the heights they can see better than we can down here," Kirov commented acidly to Mirzoian.[32]

The political atmosphere in Kirov's Leningrad in 1926–1927 can be gathered from the memoirs of Victor Serge (Kibalchich), a Trotskyite recently returned from a posting abroad with the Comintern. Serge participated in the United Opposition's campaign to propagandize their views at party cell meetings and street demonstrations. From the Central Committee's January 1926 offensive to the Fifteenth Party Congress in late 1927, according to Serge, thuggery and intimidation dominated party politics. When Serge and a fellow oppositionist attempted to present their views to a meeting of their party cell (at the newspaper *Red Gazette*), "activists" shouted them down with cries of "Traitors! Mensheviks! Tools of the bourgeoisie!" When oppositionists organized their own meetings, the Leningrad leaders threatened them with violence. "The Central Committee authorized the 'activists' to break up 'illegal meetings' by force. Squads of husky fellows, ready to beat up anyone on behalf of the Central Committee, were formed in the various districts of the city, and provided with lorries. Concerned for its dignity, the Opposition recoiled from the prospect of fistfighting; meetings were stopped or else held in absolute secrecy."[33]

Serge also reports a wave of suicides and generalized despair during this period among the veteran Communists he knew. Party members who had doubts about the suppression of debate and the growing centralization of power were going into opposition, destroying themselves, or sinking into a silent internal exile. Kirov took another route, that of certainty, sloganeering, and complete identification with the victors. In the fall of 1927 he told a conference of the Petrograd Ward party organization, "if this [opposition activity] had happened under Lenin . . . neither Zinoviev, nor Trotsky, nor Kamenev would have had a political bone left in their body. When they try to represent Lenin as some kind of intra-party liberal, comrades, that is a vile slander of Lenin!" To the delegates at the Fifteenth Party Congress which marked the United Opposition's final defeat, he said, "All who get crossed up, who vacillate, and who doubt, must be left behind in the historical abyss. Our road with you is only forward and only to victory!"[34]

Kirov and the "Right Deviation," 1928–1929

Arguments that Kirov had important doubts about Stalinist policies usually begin with Stalin's crushing of the "Right Deviation," a loose coalition within the party that opposed the extraction of grain from Soviet peasants by force in 1928–1929. Nikolai Bukharin, Aleksei Rykov, and labor union leader Mikhail Tomsky were the key leaders of the Right. In the early 1950s the Menshevik émigré Boris Nicolaevsky became convinced that Kirov too had supported the Right until the summer of 1928. Amy Knight in *Who Killed Kirov* (1999) argued that Kirov had serious questions about forced collectivization and Stalin's domination of the Soviet leadership. He was in short, a kind of proto-Rightist.[35]

It is probably true that Kirov hoped to avoid an open conflict between Stalin and the Right. But so did other loyal Stalinists like Kliment Voroshilov, Sergo Ordzhonikidze, and Yemelian Yaroslavsky. Perhaps also Kirov and other Stalin supporters did not understand at the beginning of the struggle that their leader would go so far as to massive use of force to collectivize the Soviet peasantry. Nonetheless they all followed the Central Committee line as defined by Stalin and actively worked to annihilate the Right.

Whether or not he had sympathies with the Right, it is clear that Kirov had a very difficult time steering the Leningrad organization through the storm of the 1928–1929 conflict. Within the organization several high-ranking party members sympathized with the Right. They viewed Stalin's new course as a dangerous and opportunistic turn towards exactly the Left line of squeezing the peasants advocated by the Trotskyist and Zinovievite oppositions. Pyotr Petrovsky, the editor of *Leningradskaya pravda* until mid-October 1928, was a supporter of the Right. Two of the most articulate spokesmen for the Right at the Central Committee plenums of 1928–1929 were A. I. Stetsky and F. Ya. Ugarov, both prominent party officials from Leningrad. Other important members of the Leningrad party organization, including N. P. Komarov, I. P. Zhukov, G. A. Desov, and A. E. Badaev, seemed to have leaned Right through the summer of 1928, before it became obvious that Stalin's victory was imminent.

The presence of important Rightists inside the Leningrad organization led decades later to speculation that Kirov himself might have been a sympathizer. A more realistic assessment is that Kirov remained a Stalin loyalist throughout the conflict with the Right, although he probably hoped that an open split in the party could be avoided. Kirov behaved in circumspect fashion throughout much of the struggle, in all likelihood because he had to preserve the stability of the Leningrad organization. Maintaining Leningrad as a base of support for Stalin was especially important in the summer and fall of 1928, when the leadership of the Moscow party organization leaned Right. During the months from June to October 1928 Stalin's continued preeminence in the party was under serious threat. By holding Leningrad in line, Kirov played a key role in his victory.

The proximate cause of the split between Stalin and the Right was the employment of compulsion by party/state agents to collect grain from peasants in the winter of 1927–1928. Under the NEP the Soviet government did so by taxation and purchase at government-set prices. Official policy was to motivate peasants to sell grain to state agents and consumer cooperatives by offering attractive prices for it. In the winter of 1927–1928, when government grain procurements fell well below (artificially inflated) expectations, the Central Committee executive apparatus ordered the use of various "extraordinary measures." These included mass mobilization of party members to requisition grain, and charging peasants who could not or would not turn in their harvest with speculation under Article 107 of the Russian Republic criminal code. In practice procurement agents often used force or the threat of force to confiscate grain. As Bukharin and others recognized, the "extraordinary measures" resembled the Bolsheviks' forcible seizure of grain during the Civil War.

Differences between Stalin and Nikolai Bukharin on the long-term use of "extraordinary measures" and the proper means for attacking the kulaks emerged at a Politburo session of February 9, 1928. Bukharin wanted decisive condemnation of "excesses" in grain procurements and argued for "attacking" the kulak with government intervention in markets, not with arrests and property confiscation. The February 9 Politburo session passed a resolution that obscured the serious differences between the two sides with compromise language.[36]

On March 13, 1928 Kirov spoke to a plenum of the regional party committee about the grain procurement crisis of the winter past. Bukharin and other officials skeptical of "extraordinary measures" were emphasizing the roots of the crisis in "objective conditions"— shortages of industrial commodities to sell to peasants and excessively low state prices for grain. The implication was that adjustments in state policies towards the grain market could fix the problem. Kirov briefly acknowledged the "objective conditions," but then went directly on to speak at length about "a particular political phenomenon" in the countryside. In spite of an overall increase in the availability of industrial commodities for sale in rural areas, and better organization of the procurement campaign compared to 1926–1927, Kirov said, flax procurements were far behind the plan (flax was the Leningrad Region's most important cash crop). Why? Because kulaks were hiding flax from the state. Thus, at the very outset of the debate over coercing the peasantry, Kirov took the Stalinist position. He went on to endorse with an anecdote the use of Article 107 against recalcitrant kulaks.

> One has to say in general that in our area the flax has ended up in the hands of the kulak, just as grain has in the grain-growing regions. . . . Comrades from Pskov Province told me how they go up to a kulak and show him the contents of the ever-popular Article 107. This is a very significant argument in the countryside, and quite possibly makes no less of an impression than the work of our propagandists. The fellow immediately jumps to attention, and it turns out that in addition to some stores of flax that are very substantial . . . , he also has serious cash on hand, and not our paper money, but pure silver. . . .
>
> Recently we have devoted ourselves to peaceful constructive work, and in such conditions it is obviously better when everything goes peacefully—smoothly, a minimum of "excesses," and so on. And now it turns out that some cooperative and procurement officials in the countryside are, if not highly dependent on, then in intimate relations with the well-off strata of the countryside. . . .[37]

Kirov warned his audience that a number of rural party workers who had proven "not entirely fit for the job" (that is, had been too soft on the kulaks) had already been transferred and some "will be the object of more thorough special attention from the party organs." The countryside, he asserted "turned out to be better-off than we thought." It was time to shake up "the rural calm and peace." For March 1928, this was quite harsh rhetoric, indicating to listeners that confiscation of peasants' "excess wealth" was the order of the day. Although Kirov could not have known what the precise consequences of his rhetoric would be, he was aggressively pressing activists to threaten force against peasants. His speech presaged the forced collectivization campaign with its deportations, violence, and mass starvation.

There was an incipient division in the Leningrad leadership over the use of "extraordinary methods" against the peasantry. Six weeks after Kirov's presentation on the kulak danger (April 25, 1928) Komarov told another plenary session of the regional committee that the party's "pressure on the countryside" was alienating urban workers with relatives in the villages. This was a clear signal of his skepticism about the use of coercion against the peasants.[38]

At an April plenary session of the party's Central Committee and Central Control Commission, the split was still not quite in the open. Stalin loyalist Anastas Mikoyan opened the plenum with a report on the grain procurement crisis in which he condemned "excesses" and incidents of "disturbingly sadistic" abuse of peasants. However, Mikoyan resisted wholesale condemnation of "extraordinary measures," denied that government procurement targets were inflated, and blamed cooperatives for disorganization and passivity during the procurements campaign. In particular he attacked I. E. Liubimov, head of the Central Union of Consumer Cooperatives (Tsentrosoiuz). Among the speakers who came to Liubimov's defense was A. E. Badaev, chief of the Leningrad consumer cooperatives union. Badaev allowed that cooperatives needed more central coordination of the prices they offered peasants for grain, but argued against turning all procurements over to the state (to Mikoyan's Commissariat of Trade). In defending the cooperatives it could be said that Badaev was taking a kind of proto-Right position. However, too much should not be read into his comments. The outlines of the Stalin-Right split were very unclear and a number of speakers, including Stalin loyalists such as V. Ya. Chubar, also questioned aspects of Mikoyan's presentation.[39]

After the April TsK/TsKK plenum, the Stalin-Right conflict heated up rapidly. The Leningrad organization was involved, with Kirov evidently acting to suppress proto-Rightist activity. According to information reaching Leon Trotsky from Moscow informants in late May or early June of 1928, Aleksandr Slepkov, one of Bukharin's young protégés on the *Pravda* editorial staff, spoke in Leningrad to a small group of activists about the danger of Stalin's new "Left course." Slepkov urged the necessity of an open battle against Stalin. He was supported by A. I. Stetsky, head of the Leningrad party's Agitation and Propaganda (Agitprop) Department. Trotsky claimed that an informer denounced the meeting to Kirov, who then notified "higher-ups," that is to say Stalin or one of his close associates. Soon after this (July 23, 1928) the Central Committee removed Slepkov from his editorial posts at *Pravda* and the central theoretical journal *Bolshevik*.[40]

Another Bukharin "schoolboy" (as the Rightist leader's intellectual protégés in the press were called) who held a key position was Pyotr Petrovsky, editor of *Leningradskaya pravda*. Like Slepkov, he fell victim to Stalin's purge of Bukharin supporters from the press in the summer and fall of 1928. Trouble began in the wake of the April 1928 plenum when *Leningradskaya pravda* published a front-page condemnation of "extraordinary methods" of grain procurement. Then in May the paper ran a transcript of a talk by Stalin at the Institute of Red Professors in Moscow with a key citation from Lenin excised. In the three-line citation, Lenin referred to the peasantry as "the last capitalist class." Although Petrovsky was on vacation at the time of this incident, Stalin held him responsible, and attributed ideological significance to the cut. Petrovsky, Stalin said later, believed that Lenin's views on the peasants were "heretical."[41]

In late June Petrovsky entered into an open polemic with Stalin's lieutenant Molotov in the pages of *Leningradskaya pravda,* evidently as part of a coordinated push-back against Stalin's new "Left course" by Bukharin's "schoolboys." On June 27 the *Red Gazette* ran part of a speech by Molotov (over the transparent anonym "M-ov") entitled "Grain Factories" in which he argued that because voluntary collectivization would proceed slowly, the government should immediately establish giant state farms on virgin lands. Two days later, on June 29, Petrovsky attacked the Molotov piece in an essay in *Leningradskaya pravda* entitled "A Daring Discovery?" In essence, Petrovsky accused Molotov of abandoning Lenin's NEP plan for developing small peasant farming through state sponsorship of cooperatives, in favor of gigantic state farms. This plan for exploiting the rural population he labeled "Trotskyite."[42]

From July 4 to 12, 1928 another plenary session of the party's Central Committee and Central Control Commission discussed agrarian policy and the strategy of the Communist International. At this plenum Leningraders Stetsky and Ugarov (first secretary of the regional labor union council) spoke in opposition to the use of coercion in the countryside. Stetsky argued that state agents ought to pay peasants more for their grain and decried a massacre of villagers in the North Caucasus. Ugarov declared that state procurement agents had confiscated grain not just from kulaks but also from poor and "middle" peasants. Government policy was alienating the mass of the peasantry, Ugarov asserted, and also many workers with close ties to the countryside. I. P. Zhukov, chairman of the Leningrad regional Council on the National Economy, also questioned the Stalin group's tactics in the countryside.[43]

Ugarov and Stetsky made their Right-leaning declarations on the morning of July 7. Two sessions later, on the morning of July 9, Komarov publicly disavowed Stetsky's comments. "Today I read the stenographic report of Stetsky's speech," Komarov said, "and spoke with several comrades, that is our [Leningrad's] members of the Central Committee, and I declare that Comrade Stetsky's evaluation of the situation ought to be understood as his personal opinion, and not the opinion of the Leningrad organization." The "several comrades" Komarov spoke to almost certainly included Kirov. In spite of his earlier Right-leaning declarations on the peasant problem, Komarov chose to stick with the Stalinists at this critical juncture.[44]

On the night the TsK plenum ended, July 12–13, 1928, Stalin hastened to Leningrad, presumably to shore up support there for his position. He stayed at Kirov's apartment. That same night *Leningradskaya pravda* published a Petrovsky lead editorial on the plenum, directly criticizing the theory of extracting "tribute" from the peasants as "Trotskyite." The next day Stalin gave a speech to a joint meeting of the Leningrad party committee and control commission in which he criticized leaders of the Right by name while simultaneously insisting that there was unity within the Politburo. In the question-and-answer period Stalin attacked Petrovsky's article. He insisted that *Leningradskaya pravda* print a revised lead editorial on the plenum results, which it did the next day.[45]

Bukharin was also seeking support for his positions as the July plenum came to a close. Even before the last session, he paid a visit to Kamenev, one of the former leaders of the Left-leaning Zinovievite opposition in 1925–1927. Kamenev took notes on Bukharin's comments that later (January 1929) ended up in the hands of the OGPU. It is not clear how this happened—Kamenev claimed that Trotskyites stole the notes, but it is also possible that he handed them over himself to the OGPU or to the TsKK to curry favor with Stalin and to spite Bukharin. The latter, after all, had led the charge against the Zinoviev-Kamenev opposition in 1926–1927.

Although Bukharin later claimed that Kamenev's notes were not an accurate record of his remarks, they fit well with events recorded elsewhere (for example in the stenographic report of the July 1928 plenum) and they are probably genuine. Bukharin, Kamenev wrote, looked extremely shaken up when he visited. He talked nonstop for a full hour. Evidently there had been a complete break between the Rightists and Stalin. The latter was now moving to take over the newspapers *Pravda* and *Leningradskaya pravda* from Bukharinite editors and to remove Nikolai Uglanov, a Right sympathizer, from the top of the Moscow party organization. Bukharin said that in spite of their earlier factional struggle, he would now be happy to have Zinoviev and Kamenev in the Politburo in place of Stalin. He was feeling out Kamenev for support, and at the same time, he was pessimistic about the Right's chances of victory. Sensing his uncertainty, Kamenev asked Bukharin what "your forces are." Bukharin replied:

> I, Rykov, Tomsky, Uglanov—the *pitertsy* ["Petersburgers," i.e. the Leningraders] are in general with us, but they got scared when talk turned to possibly replacing Stalin, so Komarov disavowed Stetsky's speech, but that night Ugarov came running to me to apologize for Komarov. Andreev is with us. They're removing him from the Urals. Stalin has bought off the Ukrainians by removing Kaganovich from [his post] there. We have great potential strength but (1) the average Central Committee member still doesn't understand the depth of our disagreements; (2) there is great fear of a schism, which is why Stalin's retreat on extraordinary measures has made our attack on him more difficult. We don't want to act as schismatics, because then they'll smash us. But Tomsky in his last speech at the plenum demonstrated clearly that Stalin is the schismatic. Yagoda and Trilisser are with us. There are 150 cases of such small uprisings. Voroshilov and Kalinin betrayed us at the last moment. I think that Stalin has them bound with some kind of special chains. Our task is to gradually clarify the catastrophic role of Stalin and bring the average Central Committee member to support his removal. . . .
>   Sergo (Ordzhonikidze) is no knight in shining armor. He came to me, he cursed Stalin up and down, and at the decisive moment he betrayed me.[46]

Kamenev's notes gained very wide circulation, perhaps because the Trotskyites got hold of them, perhaps because the OGPU deliberately distributed them to discredit the Right, or perhaps for both reasons. Trotskyites published them illegally inside the Soviet Union and they also appeared in the Menshevik organ *Socialist Herald,* then in Berlin. Through Boris Nicolaevsky, the notes fueled speculation much later that Kirov had been a moderate doubtful about Stalin's methods. In an unpublished analysis written sometime after 1950 (probably soon after) Nicolaevsky used the Kamenev document to argue that "the special role of the Leningraders" at the July 1928 plenum indicated that Kirov supported the Right. After all, Kirov led Leningrad, and presumably he set the line for the party organization to follow.[47]

The fundamental problem with Nicolaevsky's argument is the equation of *pitertsy* with Kirov. According to Kamenev's notes, Bukharin mentioned three *pitertsy* by name—Stetsky, Ugarov, and Komarov. Kirov did not come up. Later identification of Kirov with Leningrad, especially in post-assassination literature, obscures the fact that he was not the absolute leader of the city's party/state apparatus in 1928. As already noted, Komarov was almost as significant a figure. A number of other powerful Leningraders, including Boris Pozern, Ivan Zhukov, Georgy Desov, and Aleksei Badaev also played major roles in the city's politics.

It also bears noting that Bukharin was something of a political fantasist. It seems clear that in speaking with Kamenev he exaggerated the extent of support for the Right. In Kamenev's notes he suggests that four persons who turned out to be staunch Stalinists were Right sympathizers. These were Andreev, Voroshilov, Kalinin, and Ordzhonikidze. None of these was ever purged, although Ordzhonikidze in the last days of his life (February 1937) tried to persuade Stalin to limit the scope of repressions among Commissariat of Heavy Industry personnel.[48] At a minimum we can say that Kamenev's notes did not predict who would end up on the outs with Stalin.

The political position in the months between July and October 1928 was fluid. Stalin himself was nervous about where many of his collaborators in the leadership stood, worrying for example that Mikoyan or Kuibyshev might defect to the Right.[49] With regard to Kirov, there is the question of why the Leningrad Region party committee did not fire Petrovsky from *Leningradskaya pravda* until October 13, 1928. While Petrovsky remained at the paper, he managed to get one more Rightist sally published, Bukharin's "Notes of an Economist," which ran on October 1 and 2, 1928. But *Leningradskaya pravda* also published very early open denunciations of the "Right danger" in the party, for example on September 20. Petrovsky no longer had effective control of the paper. Moreover, the *Red Gazette,* run by Kirov's associate from Baku Pyotr Chagin, regularly published articles in the late summer and early fall about peasants hoarding grain, state procurement agents overpaying peasants for grain, and rampant speculation by kulaks and private traders. These were all standard tropes of the anti-Rightist line. Once the dispute between the Stalin and the Right came out into the open in mid-October 1928, *Red Gazette* launched savage attacks on the Rightist leaders. When Bukharin, Tomsky, and Rykov demanded in early November that the Central Committee take a number of measures to halt the anti-Right campaign in the press, they included a call for the firing of Chagin. The Stalinist faction ignored this.[50]

Exchanges of letters between Yemelian Yaroslavsky, Sergo Ordzhonikidze, and Kliment Voroshilov in this period give some idea of Kirov's probable mood. In correspondence running from July 19 through November 16, 1928 all three of these men expressed clear support for the Central Committee line (that is, the Stalin line), but also hopes that Rightist leaders could be reconciled with Stalin and a bitter struggle avoided. They clearly did not relish the prospect of another intra-party fight. Immediately before the November 1928 Central Committee plenum, for example, Ordzhonikidze wrote to Aleksei Rykov in a conciliatory tone asking him to help "make it up" between Stalin and Bukharin. "My conversations with you, and others [Stalin], convince me that there are no essential disagreements between us, and that is the most important thing," Ordzhonikidze assured Rykov.[51]

Similar hope for conciliation and dislike of the prospect of an open battle with the Right, rather than doubts about Stalin's line, probably explain Kirov's mood in a brief letter to his wife written immediately after Stalin's July 1928 visit to Leningrad. "Dear Marusya," he wrote, "I received your letter and telegraphed an answer. Things are not working out very well. But it is useless to talk about it. Stalin was here with me for two or three days. I took him to Volkhov [the hydroelectric power plant]. The day before yesterday he left."[52] What to make of Kirov's statement that "Things are not working out very well"? Not necessarily that he sympathized with the Rightists, but that he was unhappy at the prospect of having to purge them from the Leningrad organization. Petrovsky had criticized Stalin's policies only days earlier and Stetsky had put himself forward as a major spokesman for the Right. Kirov was going to have to deal with both of them. Things were not working out well, indeed.

Yet another reason for Kirov's dealing gently with Leningrad officials who may have leaned Right has to do with the complex and rapidly changing political climate. Peasant policy was not the only issue at stake in 1928–1929. The Stalin group made a decision by the spring of 1928 for breakneck industrialization, with an overwhelming focus of investment in heavy industries like steelmaking, coal mining, and arms production. Part of rapid industrialization was "rationalization" of production and increased pressure for "labor discipline." In other words, workers would have to accept longer hours and lower real wages so that more profits could be reinvested in production. With this goal in mind, a "Face to Production" campaign aimed at crushing what remained of labor union independence was initiated. Kirov provided early support for "Face to Production." Conveniently for Stalin, this campaign resulted in the removal of his Rightist rival

Tomsky from the chairmanship of the central All-Union Council on Labor Unions. In the last days of 1928 Kirov was on board for the final assault on Tomsky's position in the labor union apparatus.[53]

At the same time, the party leadership opened an assault on "bourgeois specialists"—nonparty engineers, managers, scientists, and the like—with the Shakhty trial of mining engineers on trumped-up charges of sabotaging coal production in Ukraine's Don River Basin. The Shakhty trial opened in March 1928, and set off a wave of "specialist baiting" by party officials and ordinary factory workers. The attack on specialists was a centrally sanctioned policy, designed probably to intimidate the targets, scapegoat them for production problems, and vent workers' frustration with stagnant wages and increasingly onerous labor conditions. But it also had the potential to disrupt the day-to-day operations of factories in industrial centers like Leningrad.[54]

Nor was this all. Connected with the Shakhty trial, the Central Committee declared a nationwide campaign of self-criticism in April 1928. Self-criticism in the Soviet context referred not to individual confessions of error, but to the process of identifying and correcting problems with the party/state apparatus. Bolshevik leaders understood that in the absence of "bourgeois" institutions such as the free market or pluralistic politics, they needed other checks on the incompetence and arbitrary powers of local officials.[55] Thus, self-criticism often meant the denunciation by subordinates of upper-level administrators' malfeasance or incompetence. During a self-criticism campaign, Soviet newspapers were supposed to solicit, check, and publicize such denunciations in order to "correct deficiencies" and make the apparatus more efficient. Journalists cultivated grassroots networks of "worker correspondents" and "village correspondents" who could supply the denunciations. Besides the newspapers, there were other reporting channels critics could turn to, such as the OGPU or the party control organs. Starting a self-criticism campaign, however, was something like attempting a controlled burn to clear a field of brush and trees. It was difficult to prevent self-criticism from engulfing institutions or people that were not the original target of the campaign, and to distinguish between baseless and valid denunciations.[56]

For a big industrial city like Leningrad, the self-criticism campaign posed serious challenges. A key issue debated throughout 1928–1929 was whether the campaign was to be targeted primarily at corrupt and/or incompetent bosses or at lower-level workers who needed to be pressured to work harder. In the factories workers and managers tried to use the campaign against one another. Within the city's party organization cliques criticized their rivals in order to gain access to desirable jobs or repay past defeats in local power struggles. The campaign was a problem for Kirov and other provincial party secretaries, because it threatened to turn their organizations upside down. Indeed, with encouragement from the Central Committee's Agitprop Department, newspapers and prosecutors did catalyze major purges of a number of provincial party organizations, including Smolensk, Sochi, Vladimir, Baku, and Astrakhan.

Although Kirov promoted the self-criticism campaign as part of the Central Committee's current "line," he frequently added cautions about going too far, particularly in the factories (Stalin often did the same). At the very outset of the campaign, at the same March 13, 1928 meeting of the regional party committee cited above, Kirov discussed the Shakhty trial and its implications for Leningrad. He advised his audience to read the reporting on the trial carefully, because the GPU had exposed "real counterrevolution" at Shakhty. In Leningrad too, he suggested, counterrevolutionary specialists were sabotaging production. He cited an incident in which Leningrad factories were unable to make use of expensive new equipment purchased from Yugoslavia, calling it "a matter of wrecking" rather than of innocent mistakes. After this preamble, however, Kirov went on to warn against excesses in attacks on specialists and factory management. The basic criterion for judging self-criticism, he noted, was whether it aided or hampered "practical factory work." It was a bad thing, he said, when a factory director never talked to workers, but it was just as bad when a factory's Communist Party secretary tried to run the enterprise himself (for example by encouraging denunciations of management). Kirov thus positioned himself on the side of ordered criticism controlled from above, and against manifestations of worker discontent. He wanted order and production efficiency in his city. This resembled the position on self-criticism taken by Kirov's friend Ordzhonikidze and his colleagues on the Central Control Commission. As for Stalin, he took varying positions on criticism of management in 1928–1929, sometimes emphasizing that it needed to be done with care, and sometimes stressing that worker criticism that was "even five percent true" deserved a hearing. His ambiguous position on the issue was almost certainly deliberate. Stalin did not want disorder per se, but he did want to encourage attacks on his Rightist political rivals.[57]

The menacing background to the self-criticism campaign in Leningrad in 1928 was a series of strikes at city factories early in the year. Workers objected to wage cuts and increased working hours, both imposed by the authorities as part of the industrialization drive. Although the party and the labor unions opposed the work stoppages, a number of Communists at the affected factories joined the strikers, endorsing their demands and signing their petitions. On June 13, 1928 the writer Ivan Zhiga, visiting Leningrad, discussed the strikes in his diary. Zhiga described the mood in the city as "nervous." Workers complained of bread shortages, salary cuts, and increased production quotas. They referred to the "bloating of our whole [government] apparatus," and asked "Why do we have such a life?"[58]

On May 19 the Rightist Petrovsky published an article in *Leningradskaya pravda* excoriating the Communists who had encouraged or participated in the strikes, "behind the backs of the party collectives and the union organs." The job of Communists in the factories, Petrovsky wrote, was to explain to the "backward" workers the necessity of the party's wage-cutting policy, not to encourage their insubordination. Worker complaints should be discussed in private with party cell leaders and union officials, so that they could be resolved quietly.[59]

One of the centers of the strikes was the Khalturina textile factory. In May Khalturina Communists sympathetic to the strikers voted to replace the secretary of the factory's party cell for mishandling worker discontent. Soon afterwards the Central Ward party committee sent a representative to meet with the cell members. He pressured them into reversing their decision by a vote of 500–10. This incident became a citywide scandal after an official by the name of Tagunov published an article in *Leningradskaya pravda* protesting the intimidation of the Khalturina party cell members (May 30). Two days later A. Amenitsky, the senior party secretary of the Central Ward party committee, rebutted Tagunov in a piece entitled "Is It Worthwhile To Stick Your Nose into the Ward Committee Bureau's Business?" Amenitsky argued that a few dissenters had been allowed to speak at the second meeting, which fulfilled the requirements of self-criticism. Beyond that, there was no point in lower-ranking Communists questioning the decisions of party committee bureaus.[60]

A June 15–16, 1928 plenum of the regional party committee debated the self-criticism campaign in general and the Khalturina incident in particular. A number of speakers charged Kirov and other senior Leningrad officials with failure to take self-criticism seriously

One, Filip Ivanov, complained that *Leningradskaya pravda* was publishing exposés only on small enterprises. Ivanov also criticized the Central Ward party committee for "giving it to the [Khalturina] activists in the face." Another speaker, Amatuni, directly attacked Kirov for talking about self-criticism in general terms without naming specific people or institutions. Amatuni wanted to know why demands by Communists from Volodarsky Ward for new elections to the ward party committee had been ignored. Kirov answered that there was not "such a majority" against the present party committee as to justify new elections.[61]

On the day of the plenum, , June 16, I. P. Zhukov, the proto-Rightist head of the regional Council on the National Economy, took a stand against the advocates of more self-criticism of senior authorities. In Zhukov's view the entire campaign was directed unfairly against factory management. Self-criticism was disrupting production. Zhukov even criticized Stalin's "five percent" formula.[62]

The debates about self-criticism in the Leningrad organization in the spring and early summer of 1928 reveal Kirov struggling to reconcile the TsK-sanctioned campaign with maintenance of labor discipline and his own control over the city's party machine. In particular he was concerned with ensuring that dissatisfied factory workers (the supposed "dictators" of the Soviet state!) did not use self-criticism as an opening to challenge management. He was, in short, a typical party boss. Important Right-leaning officials in Leningrad, including Petrovsky and Zhukov, helped him to keep a lid on discontent "from below." On the peasant question they were a thorn in his side, but on the self-criticism issue they were his allies, at least for the time being. Aleksandr Stetsky, the Rightist agitprop official who drew criticism both for "suppressing" self-criticism and for promoting it, also played a key role in this balancing act.[63] The "Rightists" support for Kirov in the self-criticism campaign helps to explain why he did not move decisively against them in 1928.

The publication of Bukharin's "Notes of an Economist" in *Pravda* on September 20, 1928 was a turning point in the struggle between Stalin and the Right. The article took an anti-Stalin position without actually naming Stalin. It contended that excessively high state demands for grain from peasants were leading to hunger, truncating industrial growth rates, and causing shortages of consumer goods. As Bukharin had feared, Stalin used the article to launch a decisive offensive against him and his supporters as "factionalists" undermining the construction of socialism. On October 8 the Politburo passed a resolution censuring *Pravda* for publishing the piece without first consulting with the Central Committee. Following the resolution, activists began attacking Bukharin by name at local party meetings. A joint plenum of the Moscow party committee and control commission removed a number of officials who supported Moscow party secretary Nikolai Uglanov, a key Rightist leader. Thus the Moscow organization was lost to the Right.[64]

As already noted, Petrovsky published "Notes of Economist" in *Leningradskaya pravda* on October 1–2, 1928. At this point Kirov and the regional party committee fired him. This was formally accomplished by a plenum of the party committee on October 13. Addressing the plenum that day, Kirov said:

> It is impossible to ignore any longer the situation that has developed between the regional party committee and the leadership of *Leningradskaya pravda*. Under the circumstances it will be difficult to bear those "differences of opinion" (*raznoboi*), to put it mildly, that at times have occurred between the regional party committee and its print organ. I have to say that we on the side of the bureau and secretariat of the regional party committee did everything we could to resolve painlessly our "relationship," so to speak, with *Leningradskaya pravda*. But as it turned out our measures did not achieve what was necessary for truly . . . fruitful work in the organization. So the bureau of the regional party committee has decided to remove Comrade Petrovsky from the duties of chief editor of *Leningradskaya pravda* (voice from the seats: That's right!).[65]

Pyotr Petrovsky's son reported in the late 1980s that Kirov did not fire his father until he received an angry telephone call from Stalin and a snippy telegram from Molotov. It is quite likely that the telegram existed and still exists in TsK archives, but the Stalin telephone call is another matter. How would L. P. Petrovsky, who makes a number of important factual mistakes in his article, have been privy to Stalin's precise words to Kirov on the secret Kremlin line?[66] It is also important to note that Kirov fired Petrovsky from *Leningradskaya pravda* at approximately the same time that Leftist radical journalists, with a wink and a nod from Stalin, took over effective control of *Pravda* from Nikolai Bukharin. Bukharin was not formally fired from *Pravda* until April 1929. Thus, Kirov was not particularly late in firing "his" Bukharinist from *Leningradskaya pravda*.[67]

By the November 1928 plenum of the TsK, the defeat of the Right was becoming obvious to most informed party members. Stalin's successful attack on the Moscow regional party leadership was decisive. At the plenum the Leningraders demonstrated their fealty to the Central Committee line. B. P. Pozern did most of the talking for the Leningrad delegation and his line was definitely anti-Right. When Rightist leader Aleksei Rykov accused the Leningrad organization of continuing to shelter Zinovievites ("Lefts"), Pozern replied that whatever Leningrad's faults were, the Leningraders had not "organized a campaign against the Central Committee" as the Moscow regional leadership had done. In his final statement, Pozern endorsed "that . . . monolithic unity of which Comrade Stalin spoke," and called for a continued struggle against the "Right Deviation." A. I. Stetsky, who had abandoned his Bukharinist positions, spoke of the need to fight the "Right Deviation" at every level of the party. In conclusion Stetsky assured his audience that "the Leningrad organization in the last years has given many demonstrations of its Bolshevik toughness and firmness. It will continue to show the same toughness in the future."[68]

The stroke that felled the Right for good was Ordzhonikidze's revelation to the party leadership in late January 1929 of Bukharin's July 1928 meeting with Kamenev. An emergency joint session of the Politburo and the Presidium of the Central Control Commission on January 30 discussed the meeting. As rapporteur Ordzhonikidze accused Bukharin and his allies of organizing a secret faction in the party. Stalin followed up with an "accusatory and extremely rude" speech against Bukharin. At this plenum Ordzhonikidze nominated Kirov to the commission that was to prepare a resolution censuring Bukharin. Kirov would also serve on the three-man commission that drafted the anti-Rightist resolution for the April 1929 plenum of the TsK and TsKK.[69]

On February 9, 1929 Bukharin, Rykov, and Tomsky responded to the attacks with a written declaration to another joint session of the Politburo and the TsKK Presidium. In it they labeled the Kamenev notes a forgery, criticized the Stalinist policy of taking "tribute" from the peasantry, referred to Lenin's negative evaluation of Stalin's personality in his 1923 "testament" (the Bolshevik leader's deathbed assessment of Stalin and other Soviet leaders), and accused the TsK majority of an unprincipled campaign of "working over" the Right.[70] The Stalinists reacted by mobilizing the entire party against the three Rightist leaders. In preparation for the forthcoming joint TsK/TsKK plenum, party organizations all over the USSR passed resolutions condemning the Rightist leaders. Leningrad joined in. In early April a joint session of the Leningrad party committee bureau and control commission presidium resolved that "[we] have no doubt that the joint plenum of the TsK and TsKK will decisively censure the line and behavior of Comrades Bukharin, Rykov, and Tomsky and put an end to their attempts to shake the party at a time of difficulties and [we] declare that the Leningrad organization will defend with all decisiveness the line taken by the party. . . ."[71]

At the April 1929 joint plenum F. Ya. Ugarov, the only vocal Rightist left in the Leningrad leadership, complained bitterly of Leningrad party authorities' actions against him and against the Rightist leaders. Ugarov stated that attacks on Rykov, Bukharin, and Tomsky had begun at lower levels of the Leningrad organization immediately after the July 1928 TsK plenum. "I said at a plenum of the regional party committee," he continued, "and in a private conversation with the secretary of the Leningrad party organization Comrade Kirov, the following: the discrediting of the three comrades going on . . . will lead to their firing. In answer to this, they passed more than one special resolution calling me various pleasant names." Ugarov apparently felt that Kirov had let him down by failing to support the Right. "I don't know if Comrade Kirov will remember this [conversation] or not," he said.[72]

Kirov's behavior between the spring of 1928 and the spring of 1929 was circumspect. He did not speak even once at any of the TsK plenums from April 1928 through April 1929. This circumspection did not conceal policy differences with Stalin, although the self-criticism campaign undoubtedly made Kirov's life more difficult, as it did the lives of provincial party officials all over the USSR. Rather, Kirov was waiting to see in what direction Stalin would take the party, trying to keep the Leningrad organization on the Central Committee line, and choosing the proper moment to move against the open Rightists in the city. He seems to have allowed Rightists like Ugarov to read what they wished into his public silences. The result was that Ugarov felt betrayed, as Butiagin and Narimanov had before him.

Both Trotsky and Zinoviev believed Kirov to be firmly in Stalin's camp throughout this period. Thus Trotsky in the opposition platform prepared just before the Fifteenth Party Congress in November 1927 placed Kirov in the party faction of "apparat-centrists." In this group he placed Stalin, Molotov, Kaganovich, Mikoyan, Uglanov (who turned out to be a Rightist in 1928), and Kirov. Bukharin, Trotsky wrote, vacillated between the "apparat-centrists" and the Right. Similarly in December 1928 Zinoviev listed Stalin's "staff" as Molotov,

Voroshilov, Mikoyan, Ordzhonikidze, Rudzutak, Kuibyshev, Kalinin, Bauman, and Kirov.[73]

In considering Kirov's political position during the struggle with the Rightists it is also important to remember that the Stalinists did not stake out a clear position in favor of immediate mass collectivization of the peasantry until November 1929.[74] As Bukharin lamented to Kamenev, Stalin in the spring and summer of 1928 "retreated" on the use of "extraordinary measures," supporting the inclusion of language criticizing them in Politburo and TsK resolutions. He also continued to insist that the NEP was not being revoked, and that the regime's policy was still one of collaboration with the middle peasant. Kirov's continued support in 1928 to early 1929 for the *smychka* with the middle peasant was entirely consistent with Stalin's policy proclamations, particularly given the Leningrad leader's regular calls for a "renewed attack on the kulak."[75]

Kirov's Purge

On the first day of September 1929, at the very end of the summer break for many top party officials, animosities within the Leningrad organization exploded into an open conflagration. That day *Pravda* published an exposé of malfeasance by Leningrad cooperative managers who had sold state goods to private merchants below market price in exchange for large personal "loans." According to the piece, Leningrad newspapermen and party authorities had suppressed complaints from rank-and-file party members about the incident. *Pravda* accused *Leningradskaya pravda* and the regional party control commission of "suppressing self-criticism." In other words, they had ignored denunciations of official corruption "from below." The *Pravda* coverage mentioned by name one member of the regional party control commission, Rekstin, and the head of the Central Ward Party Committee, Korol.[76]

Over the next two weeks *Pravda*, followed by the Leningrad newspapers and the central Komsomol organ, *Komsomolskaya pravda*, published numerous articles on corruption, harassment of worker correspondents, and sabotage at Leningrad's State Properties Department (*Otdel kommunalnogo khoziaistva*), the regional cooperative apparatus, the shipbuilding trust, and the regional control commission. The ultimate result of *Pravda's* attack was the removal of those Leningrad party veterans who had enough status to challenge Kirov's leadership, first and foremost Komarov, but also G. A. Desov (chairman of the regional control commission), Rekstin (Desov's deputy), Ivan Kondratev (Komarov's deputy at the Leningrad soviet), Korol, and Aleksei Badaev (head of the Leningrad Region's cooperative apparatus). The favorable results of the press campaign for Kirov prompt the question of whether he had a part in initiating it. Several authors have discussed the fall 1929 upheaval in Leningrad, but have failed to answer this question definitively.[77]

There was a lengthy prehistory in Leningrad which must be considered in evaluating *Pravda's* campaign. As early as June 1928 Kirov had criticized Desov in a published speech for stalling on investigations of "bureaucratism." Checking into bureaucratic obstructionism was a basic function of the control commissions and their associated state organ, the Workers' and Peasants' Inspectorate (RKI). Moreover, one integral part of the self-criticism campaign was an intensified assault on such "bureaucratism." Kirov implied that Desov was not active in the campaign.[78]

In late 1928, soon after the press began the open campaign against the "Right Deviation," Kirov had "complications" with N. K. Antipov, a senior official and Leningrad veteran transferred back into the city in the spring of 1926 to serve as a secretary on the province party committee. The TsK kicked him upstairs to Moscow, appointing him Commissar of Posts and Telegraphs. Antipov, however, was well connected with the Leningrad Old Bolshevik network, including Komarov and Desov. According to a statement given by the Komarovite official K. Yunosov in 1937, soon after Antipov left for Moscow Leningrad officials began visiting him there to discuss ways of compromising Kirov. A secret battle for control of the city was underway. Echoes of this battle reached leading Rightist circles in Moscow. By the middle of 1929 members of Bukharin's "school" were discussing in private Kirov's record of writing for a Kadet newspaper (*Terek*). If Kirov were a Rightist sympathizer at this point, one would wonder why the Rights themselves viewed him as a Stalinist and were talking about ways to discredit him.[79]

In every major party/state organization the self-criticism campaign led to the accumulation of accusatory materials from worker correspondents and others. This was the case too in Leningrad. Such materials piled up even in ordinary times—the question was who would utilize them, when, and how. Well before *Pravda's* September 1 bomb, Pyotr Chagin's *Red Gazette* was running exposés of disorders at lower-level institutions in Leningrad. Coverage connected with the purge of state institutions initiated by the Stalin group in the summer of 1929, in part to root out Rightist officials. Throughout July 1929 and August 1929 *Red Gazette* denounced "bureaucratism" at the State Properties Department of the Leningrad soviet, kulak infiltration of local cooperatives, nepotism at the Regional Finance Department, theft of state and cooperative property, and production problems at Red Shipwright, the shipbuilding trust at the city's port.[80] All of these disorders were at government, not party, institutions, and they might be considered to reflect poorly on Komarov as the senior state official in Leningrad. It is also important to remember that *Red Gazette*'s editor Chagin was a Kirov associate from Baku. Although Kirov was sometimes exasperated with him (and Kirov would throw Chagin to the Central Committee's dogs in the fall of 1929), it is likely that the Leningrad party chief approved of *Red Gazette*'s muckraking. He undoubtedly could have put a stop to it had he wished to do so.

Another important piece of the background to *Pravda*'s September 1 sally was the resurgence of Left-leaning forces. By the summer of 1928 Stalin's veiled hostility to the Right had convinced Zinoviev, Kamenev, and other former Left oppositionists in the know that they stood a good chance of returning to the political fray. Former Leningrad adherents of the United Opposition, some encouraged by Zinoviev himself, began applying for readmission to the party.[81] The Central Control Commission allowed them to return, provided their confessions of error were sufficiently abject. The Central Committee majority's open declaration of war on the Right also prompted some Left-leaning journalists and Komsomol officials (Shatskin, Sten, Lominadze) to undertake fierce attacks on Rightist leaders, the labor union apparatuses, and bureaucratic institutions such as the Union of Militant Atheists. There was undoubtedly an element of payback in some of these forays for the defeat of the Left Trotskyite and Zinovievite oppositionists in 1926–1927.

The Central Committee Department of Agitation and Propaganda encouraged these assaults. Stalin, on the other hand, repeatedly condemned "sensationalistic" exposés in private letters and public statements. Yet it is very likely that he deliberately encouraged such attacks with his own anti-Rightist rhetoric as well as with behind-the-scenes prompting through the Department of Agitation and Propaganda. Then he could sanctimoniously disavow the attackers and discipline them. Mikhail Tomsky suspected that this was Stalin's game when

Komsomolskaya pravda editors attacked him in the fall of 1928. Standing by and egging on both sides of a fight was part of Stalin's modus operandi throughout his political career.[82]

In July 1929 attacks on supposedly Right-leaning officials peaked throughout the USSR. These assaults had a number of complementary functions, among them signaling the end of NEP cooperation between party officials and private traders. In Baku the TsK removed Levon Mirzoian from the leadership of the Azerbaijani Communist Party following a campaign of anti-Right criticism led by A. A. Artak and Olga Shatunovskaya, a young Communist activist and Baku native. In Astrakhan press denunciations of sweetheart deals between Communist officials and local businessmen were followed by well-publicized show trials.

Kirov was at work in the regional party committee offices in Leningrad that July. On the twelfth he wrote to Ordzhonikidze that he was "stuck at the committee offices alone." Many of the employees were already on vacation, and others were outside the city helping with the ongoing purge of state institutions. Kirov reported that a number of senior TsK and TsKK officers were in the region helping with this purge.

> The First Five Year Plan doesn't just look good on paper, but demands serious effort. The tempos [of production growth] we have approved will obviously be surpassed. One example is tractors. According to the Five Year Plan, Putilov factory is to turn out 1,500 tractors [annually] by the end of the Plan period. This year the factory should give 3,000, and if things work out this way, for next year 10,000, and the year after that, 15,000!
>
> It has to be said that your boys [representatives of the TsKK and its government counterpart, the Workers' and Peasants' Inspectorate] are giving us a good push on this business. It is true that they often go pretty far, but that's not a bad thing. They even managed to get our shipbuilding trust moving. They sat on them for a good long time, and finally things got going![83]

Kirov also wrote enthusiastically about the harvest. He closed with an obligatory injunction to his friend to rest well on his Black Sea vacation. "Soso [a familiar nickname for Stalin] is coming soon" (to join Ordzhonikidze on vacation). And again of Stalin—"By the way, he has done a great job with the economy, he is putting pressure everywhere and with great success."[84]

Kirov and Ordzhonikidze were well aware by this time that their mail might be read by the OGPU.[85] To a certain extent, then, this letter was meant not just for Ordzhonikidze, but for other eyes as well. While it does not necessarily show us Kirov's real thoughts, it does show the attitudes he wished to present to other members of Stalin's political circle. He expresses open admiration for Stalin's ability to "pressure" people into obeying orders, and he endorses huge increases in plan numbers for Putilov tractor production—pushing production tempos to superhuman limits was the standard Stalinist position throughout the First Five Year Plan. Kirov approves of the TsKK/RKI investigations aimed at squeezing more production out of existing industry, although he does show some veiled frustration with their disruptive effects ("they often go pretty far"). He also reveals that he is in touch with Stalin, otherwise he would not know the latter's summer plans.

On July 29, 1929, Ordzhonikidze sent Kirov a letter from Sochi which confirms that both men were working closely with Stalin that summer.

> Hello, dear Seryozha!
> Well, they scratched up our pals good [referring to Lev Mirzoian and other fired leaders of the Baku party], and they [the "pals"] all thought Moscow was going to defend them. Some defense for you! That was a real mess there [Baku]. Gikalo [Mirzoian's replacement] is hardly up to dealing with it. Thursday I arrived with Soso and Klim [Voroshilov]. Tomorrow I'm going to Nalchik. Our countryman [Stalin] is in a fine mood. He keeps telling us about how you and he put the squeeze on "poor" Mikhailov [head of the Leningrad Machine Trust], he's pleased as the devil that Mikhailov agreed to 10,000 tractors. It's obvious we're going to emerge from the agricultural crisis in great shape. The present expansion of sown lands is the final confirmation of our political line. No opposition has ever collapsed as completely or pathetically as our Rightist crackpots. To hell with it, no mercy for them. . . .
> Things are good with us, Kirych! We're really starting to move forward. As long as we refuse to let ourselves be dragged back into the old stale routine, we'll go far in the next year. . . .
> Keep well! With a warm embrace.
> Your Sergo.[86]

Ordzhonikidze's letter refers to the continuous pressure that Kirov and Stalin were exerting on the Red Putilov factory to accept a higher tractor production quota for plan year 1929–1930. VSNKh, together with Kirov, had been pressing Red Putilov director Grachev and M. S.

Mikhailov, head of the Machine Building Trust, to accept higher plan targets since the summer of 1928. Grachev, his technical director Sablin, and factory employees right down to the shop floor resisted repeated increases in the targets on the grounds that they were simply impossible to achieve. Nonetheless VSNKh, Stalin, and Kirov raised annual plan targets for 1929–1930 from 2,500 to 3,000, then to 10,000 and finally to 12,000. The targets were not based on careful evaluation of available resources, but were aimed at squeezing the maximum work out of the labor force. Ordzhonikidze and Kirov evidently found this process of terrorizing their subordinates amusing ("'poor' Mikhailov"). The result, however, was not amusing. The year 1930 saw a major breakdown of tractor production at Putilov, as well as delivery of thousands of unusably defective tractors throughout the USSR. Sablin was arrested and Grachev fired, both scapegoated for the incompetence of their superiors. At a June 1930 conference of the Leningrad Region party organization, Kirov applauded the arrest of Sablin and other factory "specialists" accused of "wrecking."[87]

In general Ordzhonikidze's letter has the tone of a self-satisfied bully. He refers contemptuously to the demotion of Mirzoian, supposedly a friend of his and Kirov's. His crowing about the great successes of Stalin's new agricultural policy—mass coercion of the peasantry— is entirely misplaced. Neither Stalin, Ordzhonikidze, nor Kirov knew much about agriculture, yet they and their colleagues in the party leadership were about to dictate a sweeping and disastrous settlement of Russia's longstanding peasant "problem." The results of that experiment in the early 1930s would be the decimation of livestock herds, a sharp drop in grain production, and mass starvation.

In the summer of 1929, however, the leadership was concerned not with starvation, but with using vigorous self-criticism to force local officials to raise production and follow orders. In the middle of August the Central Committee Department of Agitation and Propaganda sent A. P. Mariinsky, an *instruktor* (a midlevel administrative post), to Leningrad to check on work at *Red Gazette*. Mariinsky met with newspaper staff, A. I. Stetsky, and officials from the Leningrad prosecutor's office. According to Mariinsky, all of these people complained of "suppression of self-criticism" by the Leningrad Control Commission under Desov and the Workers' and Peasants' Inspectorate. Desov demanded that journalists clear all materials for publication with him, and often rejected their articles. In October 1929 Chagin and other *Red Gazette* editors confirmed their meetings with Mariinsky in August, claiming that he had insisted that *Red Gazette* present a report in Moscow to the TsK Agitprop Department.[88]

Mariinsky returned to Moscow on August 23. Sergei Ingulov, head of the Newspaper Sector of the Agitprop Department, and several *Pravda* editors debriefed him on his visit to Leningrad and compared the specific stories on "suppression of self-criticism" that he brought back with him to material already sent to them from Leningrad. They asked him to write a report on the Leningrad press for *Pravda*. Following a further consultation with Mariinsky on the evening of August 31, the central party organ began running the "Leningrad materials."[89]

On Sept. 3, 1929 Chagin and his deputy Rappoport delivered a report on *Red Gazette's* work to officials of the TsK Agitprop Department in Moscow, including Ingulov and Mariinsky. All participants later agreed that Ingulov and Agitprop Department chief Krinitsky told Chagin that "the Central Committee" considered the Leningrad party "leadership" (*rukovodstvo*) "healthy," but that there were other specific targets in the city's party/state apparatus. A comment was dropped that "the Komarov group had grown rotten," but after the fact everyone present would deny responsibility for this. At any rate, it appears from Mariinsky's and Chagin's later accounts that there was an understanding at the meeting that the press campaign would not target Kirov or his deputy Mikhail Chudov, but rather the regional control commission, its director Desov, and possibly "the Komarov group." The stenographic report of the session shows that the Agitprop officials scolded Chagin for not developing self-criticism enough, giving him the impression that they expected much more aggressive coverage from *Red Gazette*. They also accused him of going soft on the Right Deviation.[90]

Pravda's September 1 attack on corruption in Leningrad was too precisely timed to be an accident. It came at the very end of the summer vacation, on the eve of a previously announced joint session of the regional control commission with local control commissions.[91] The joint session was precisely the type of forum where lower-ranking officials could attack the regional control commission leaders (with the proper encouragement from the central press). Ward party committees were also holding plenary sessions in late August, standard preparation for a regional party committee meeting (Kirov would call one for September 7). Mikhail Rosliakov, the finance official, believed that Kirov knew an attack from *Pravda* was coming, although he may have been surprised by "the sharpness" of the attack. Kirov would have known that Chagin, Stetsky, and city prosecutors were telling the TsK Agitprop Department emissary about obstruction of self-criticism by Desov and his control commission. The certainty with which TsK Agitprop officials Ingulov and Mariinsky acted suggests that one way or another Stalin or one of his senior associates let them know that he would look favorably upon an attack on quasi-Rightist officials making trouble for Kirov in Leningrad. Finally, Leonid Kovalyov, *Pravda* editor and Stalin's unofficial agent at the paper, also encouraged the attack.[92] Overall the evidence points toward a coordinated effort by Stalin and Kirov, acting through proxies, to solidify Kirov's position in Leningrad by removing troublesome senior officials from the city. It is unclear whether the plan was for the attack to go as far up as Komarov, but certainly it was aimed at Desov and other lower-ranking officials.

As the regional control commission met on September 2 Kirov called together the bureau of the regional party committee to deal with the *Pravda* materials. The bureau called for "development of self-criticism" throughout the Leningrad organization, and set up three commissions to investigate the charges in *Pravda*. As the commission went to work, ward party committees convened to promote self-criticism. The "Central Committee line" suddenly seemed clear to everyone—denunciation of corrupt Rightist officials throughout the apparatus. At this point the press campaign, probably propelled in part by Agitprop officials' meeting with Chagin on September 3, went into full attack mode. Desov, Rekstin, and other senior officials were denounced by name. On September 5 *Leningradskaya pravda* published an attack on the regional soviet's executive committee, headed by Komarov ("Under the Banner of Bureaucratic Complacency"). On the seventh the editorial board engaged in an open polemic with Komarov and other executive committee officials.[93]

Red Gazette's coverage was even more aggressive, apparently driven by Chagin and a former Zinovievite official who now headed the paper's "Chronicle" department, Nikolai Gordon. The paper widened the assault to include the leadership of the Central and Volodarsky wards (Kirov and Rightist officials had headed off insurrections against these leaders by strike sympathizers in summer 1928—see above) and a number of officials who worked closely with Kirov, such as Rosliakov and G. N. Pylaev, secretary of the Vyborg Ward party organization. The attacks on Desov became more strident, including the September 8 headline "The United Front of . . . Desov and the Landlords: Turning a Blind Eye on the Class War." On that same day the paper called for a purge of "particular representatives of the regional executive committee who have lost their proletarian instincts"—a transparent reference to Komarov.[94]

Also on September 8 *Red Gazette* attacked the leadership of Vyborg Ward, although without mentioning the ward's senior party secretary Pyotr Struppe by name.[95] The campaign had apparently gone about as far as Kirov, or Stalin, wanted it to. From September 7 to 9 Kirov chaired a plenary session of the regional party committee. Desov, Rekstin and others were removed from the regional control commission. A. M. Amenitsky, the Central Ward party secretary involved in suppressing the Khalturina factory activists, and Korol, also a member of the Central Ward party bureau, were removed and replaced by P. A. Irklis, a onetime Zinovievite. Top officials of the Department of State Properties were also fired. According to a June 1930 report, twenty-six "leading workers" were removed from their posts in the aftermath of the September self-criticism campaign. Apart from these personnel changes, Kirov reassured his audience that "the opinion of the party's Central Committee is that we are capable of dealing with these matters ourselves, but work must go on at yet faster tempos." By 1929 the phrase "Central Committee" was a common euphemism for Stalin in such situations. Kirov was claiming to have it straight from the general secretary that his own position in Leningrad was safe. He proceeded to scold "some organs" for taking the campaign of denunciation too far. The excesses of the campaign, he suggested, were due to Trotskyite influence.[96]

Kirov and Stalin both took action now to smother the press campaign. On September 9 Stalin wrote to Molotov from Sochi complaining about *Pravda*'s "shrieking racket about the Leningrad organization." On the thirteenth he blamed the *Pravda* editorial board, including senior member Yemelian Yaroslavsky, and demanded that the "Central Committee once again take control over *Pravda*." He endorsed the "Kirov-Komarov" leadership in Leningrad.[97] Meanwhile, Kirov on September 11 demanded an explanation from Chagin for *Red Gazette*'s overblown attacks. Chagin responded by blaming everything on the TsK Agitprop Department (Mariinsky would in turn blame Chagin). Kirov also called and wrote to Molotov. We know this because the latter then wrote Ordzhonikidze a note, quoting Kirov as condemning the attacks on Komarov as "disgraceful." Kirov blamed Chagin and

Mariinsky both. The Central Commitee soon fired Chagin from *Red Gazette*.[98]

Kirov's letter and telephone call to Molotov indicate either that he genuinely wanted to limit the attack to Desov, leaving Komarov out, or that he needed to make such a pretense. In this context it is interesting that he did not go directly to his friend Ordzhonikidze on the TsKK, but relied on Molotov to pass his opinion along. Molotov was not a native Petersburger, but he was a longtime veteran of the Leningrad Bolshevik organization, with many ties there, including to N. K. Antipov. Kirov may have wished to signal to Molotov that he was not behind the attack on Komarov. The latter was a powerful figure, and Kirov could not attack him openly. Even if he had helped initiate the campaign against Komarov, Kirov may have wished to establish his disapproval of it before Molotov.

With hindsight it seems that Kirov, Chagin, Stetsky, Stalin, the TsK Agitprop Department officials, and *Pravda* editors agreed on an early September offensive against Desov, the Leningrad control commission, and certain city bureaucracies. The documentary evidence indicates that the press campaign then went too far for Kirov's or Stalin's comfort. Both Kirov and Stalin recorded in writing their support for Komarov's position in Leningrad in the second week of September (see above). However, it is possible that one or both men actually expected the campaign to go "too far." Stalin, for instance, used the "excesses" of *Pravda*'s attack on Leningrad institutions to transfer Agitprop Department chief Krinitsky and his deputy Ingulov out of the TsK apparatus. Yet in his correspondence with Molotov he was already discussing Krinitsky's transfer on August 23, 1929, nine days before the press campaign began.[99] Stalin seems to have anticipated that the Agitprop Department executives would run into trouble.

The promotion of A. I. Stetsky, the former Bukharin "schoolboy" who renounced his Rightist views after the publication of "Notes of an Economist," also suggests that Stalin approved beforehand of the self-criticism episode in Leningrad. In the fall of 1929 TsK authorities transferred Stetsky from the Leningrad Agitprop Department to their own central Agitprop Department, where he replaced Krinitsky. Stetsky played a key part in encouraging *Pravda*'s campaign against disorders in Leningrad. The promotion may well have been his reward for doing the dirty work against his old allies.

Veteran Leningraders attacked in the press campaign certainly blamed Kirov. Desov, with probable encouragement from Antipov in Moscow and from Komarov, visited the Leningrad public library and read back issues of *Terek*. Based on selected articles Desov concluded (falsely) that Kirov had been a Kadet before 1917. He denounced him as such to the Central Committee and the Central Control Commission, also complaining that Kirov was neglecting the battle against Trotskyites and Zinovievites, and that he employed many ex–White officers, factory owners, and other "former people" in the Leningrad state apparatus. Ordzhonikidze at the TsKK handled Desov's denunciation (which was also signed by K. Yunosov). He defended his friend, arguing that "even Stalin" had made mistakes before the October Revolution, such as supporting the Provisional Government in March 1917. Desov promptly denounced Ordzhonikidze to the TsK for casting aspersions on Stalin's political correctness before the October Revolution.[100]

The Kirov-Desov dispute went right up to the level of the Politburo, which heard Ordzhonikidze's report on the affair on December 7, 1929. The Politburo then scheduled a joint session with the Presidium of the TsKK for December 10. To make certain that senior members of the Leningrad organization accepted its decision as definitive, the Politburo ordered all members of the Leningrad party secretariat, all TsK members and candidates from Leningrad, and all ward committee secretaries to attend. According to Mikhail Rosliakov, who was not present but heard about the proceedings from senior city official Ivan Kodatsky and Kirov's deputy Mikhail Chudov, Kirov was calm and silent throughout the meeting. In his concluding comments, Stalin stated that Kirov had made mistakes in some of his articles, but that under the prerevolutionary party rules "he had a right" to work at a "liberal newspaper." The Politburo and TsKK confirmed the demotion of Desov and others. Most importantly, they ordered Komarov transferred out of Leningrad. He was first given the chairmanship of a central construction trust, and later (1931) received the post of Commissar of State Properties (*komissar kommunalnogo khoziaistva*) of the Russian Republic.[101]

The fall 1929 fight for leadership of the Leningrad organization epitomizes the methods of political struggle that developed inside the party. Given the leaders' demand that the party present a public face of monolithic unity, conflicts had to be conducted covertly. Thanks to the taboo (actually stated as a formal rule by the Orgburo in 1923) against press organs criticizing officials higher in the party/state hierarchy than themselves, the battles had to be fought first by lower-ranking proxies. Finally, the party/state's solicitation of denunciations to keep the apparatus honest offered a ready-made weapon for use by the antagonists. Kirov proved himself nearly as able as Stalin in political infighting under these rules of the game.[102]

Oleg Khlevniuk concludes that "Kirov emerged from this encounter victorious, thanks largely to the support of Stalin." One reason that Stalin supported Kirov probably was Komarov's wavering at the July 1928 plenum of the Central Committee. Stalin knew from Kamenev's transcript of his talk with Bukharin during that plenum that Komarov and other influential Leningrad Communists had nearly supported the Right. He needed to get all of them out of the city. At the same time, the affair also provided Stalin with compromising information on Kirov and Ordzhonikidze (Kirov's work at *Terek,* Ordzhonikidze's reference to Stalin's 1917 "mistake"). It was Stalin's practice, and the practice of many other Bolshevik leaders, to collect such "materials" on rivals and subordinates.

Probably after Kirov's death, Desov praised him for treating him fairly after the dénouement of their struggle. (Desov was first sent to Germany for medical treatment and then appointed director of a typewriter factory in Leningrad.) Rosliakov claims that he bore no grudge against Kirov.[103] But denunciations to the secret police in the early 1930s tell a different story. The Komarovites expelled from the Leningrad leadership were very, very bitter. According to informers from the Komarovite circle, Desov, Komarov, Rekstin, Badaev, Amenitsky, Ivan Kondratev (Komarov's former deputy at the Leningrad soviet), Korol, and other former Leningraders often met in Moscow in the early 1930s to commiserate and speculate about the possibility that they might return to their home city. Informers quoted Rekstin as referring to Kirov as "a scoundrel," "a creep," "an upstart, sent from Moscow to humiliate the best Petersburg Bolsheviks (Badaev, Komarov, Desov . . .)," and "Stalin's thrall," an incompetent who only held onto his post thanks to the dictator's support. Rekstin himself confessed in early 1935 to uttering such phrases. Informers also reported Desov, Komarov, and others abusing Kirov in private and speculating about their own possible restoration to the Leningrad leadership.[104]

As Kirov's control over the Leningrad organization strengthened, he became a more active fighter against the "Right Deviation." At the Central Committee plenum of November 10–17, 1929, where Bukharin, Rykov, and Tomsky issued a declaration submitting to the TsK majority, Kirov spoke extensively. He took one of the hardest lines against "the Three" at the plenum, arguing that their statement of submission was insincere. "If one reads carefully what is written in the declaration, it turns out . . . that the comrades from the opposition have in their pockets more effective recipes for the construction of socialism, than those of the party . . . " he commented sarcastically.[105]

Probably echoing the frustration of many younger party members with the theoretical squabbles of the émigré generation, Kirov proclaimed that the Rightists just didn't want to finish the job of socialist construction. The plenum had wasted three valuable days discussing the "Right Deviation" when there were many other "urgent questions" to be discussed.[106]

After his grilling by the Politburo and the TsKK Presidium over the Desov affair on December 10, 1929 Kirov returned to Leningrad to prepare for a plenum of the regional party committee. This met on December 17. Chudov explained the verdict in Kirov's favor to the assembled delegates. Then Kirov himself spoke, in honor of Stalin's upcoming fiftieth birthday. He delivered what Amy Knight dramatically calls "Kirov's Secret Speech," a frank assessment of Stalin as a Soviet leader. In this speech, Knight argues, Kirov expressed indirectly serious doubts about Stalin's leadership. In particular, Knight believes that Kirov's comments on Lenin's testament were "sheer heresy." Here is Knight's translation of Kirov's words.[107]

> And, finally, I don't think that it would be wrong for me to bring up what everyone is speculating about, specifically Lenin's testament, in which he characterized individual leading comrades. Ilich [Lenin], for example, talks about Stalin, discussing what arises from all his activity. The one negative trait that Lenin saw in Stalin was that he is rude. True, he added that the rudeness was of such quality that in certain circumstances it could lead to something. This of course is a minus. But aside from the minus, even Lenin, who could see through people (he knew his assistants especially well) didn't observe anything.[108]

In the testament, written in early 1923, Lenin assessed the strengths and weaknesses of the major party leaders, suggesting that Stalin be replaced as general secretary of the Central Committee because he was "too rude," intolerant, and capricious. The document was an open secret among higher-ranking Communists. It was read to all delegates to the Thirteenth Party Congress in May 1924 and published in full in late 1927 in the *Bulletin* of the Fifteenth Party Congress. The *Bulletin,* labeled "for party members only," had a print run of ten thousand. The Rightist leaders brought up the testament again early in 1929. At the April 1929 TsK/TsKK plenum delegates debated the document's implications at length.

Kirov commented on the testament before a closed meeting of the Leningrad regional party committee. All of these men and women would have known about it. His aim was clear—to counter Rightist insistence that Stalin needed to be replaced. After the quotation above, Kirov went on to say opposition leaders always attacked Stalin personally, "and this is not because he has certain character traits, that he is not always easy to get along with and so on. That is rubbish. The blow goes in his direction because he is the main guard and a fierce guard at Lenin's post."[109]

In keeping with his general practice, Kirov was actually following the Stalin group's line very carefully. Stalin had defended himself in similar terms before the Fifteenth Party Congress in November 1927: "I am rude, comrades, towards those who rudely and treacherously destroy and dismember the party." But Kirov's speech followed even more closely comments made by the Stalinists Yemelian Yaroslavsky and N. E. Bauman at the April 1929 plenum of the Central Committee where the testament was debated. Yaroslavsky said of "the attacks on Comrade Stalin," that "it is very characteristic since the death of Lenin, that all groupings in our party, when they begin to distance themselves from the party line, always beat on Comrade Stalin. Why? Because Stalin is the worst offender? No, because he is the true conduit for the party line. . . . Vladimir Ilich's testament is known to the whole party, we've discussed it multiple times. . . ."[110]

Mentioning Lenin's testament in 1929 before a closed meeting of senior party officials was not "sheer heresy." What Kirov said to the December 1929 session of the Leningrad Region party committee was the Stalinist line on the testament at the time. He was defending Stalin against the many doubters in the Leningrad organization, including both ex-Zinovievites and Komarovites. It was only later that discussion of the testament became taboo among top-ranking Communists. Then this particular quote of Kirov's became a scandal requiring concealment.

CHAPTER 3

Kirov in Leningrad, 1930–1934

In the winter of 1929–1930 Stalin and his lieutenants initiated a mass campaign to force Soviet peasants to join collective farms. They did not issue direct orders to use compulsion. Rather, they insisted that party officials in particular regions achieve "complete collectivization" immediately, and issued quotas for the deportation of kulaks and their "lackeys" (*podkulachniki*). The OGPU, Komsomols, Communists, factory workers, and even some Red Army units were mobilized to accomplish the task. They used persuasion, threats of force, and violence. Hundreds of thousands of peasants—supposed kulaks or "kulak lackeys"—were deported from their homes in the first months of the assault. Many perished of neglect in harsh winter conditions. The villagers resisted with pitchforks, riots, and sometimes firearms. The Soviet countryside experienced something like a second Civil War.[1]

Kirov expressed vigorous support for collectivization. In early January 1930 he vowed before a meeting of factory foremen in Volodarsky Ward that "we are going to completely destroy the class enemy." He labeled as kulak sympathizers those who doubted the wisdom of the collectivization campaign: "When we put the squeeze on the kulak, he shrieks. He shrieks so loud that you can hear him even in the city—in the factory and in the plant. His shrieks are sometimes echoed in . . . certain layers of the working class and even in our party."[2]

On March 2, 1930 Stalin published in *Pravda* an article entitled "Dizzy with Success," in which he blamed local cadres for pressing collectivization too far, particularly in "backward" areas such as Central Asia. Coercion was not acceptable in the collectivization drive—

107

peasants had to join voluntarily. "Dizzy with Success" was in all probability a deliberate attempt to scapegoat local officials for the violence and disruption of collectivization, and a signal to ratchet down the levels of state violence in the countryside. Peasants reacted with a mass exodus from the collective farms (many of which existed only on paper anyway). Rural Communists were confused and discouraged by Stalin's intervention, which many viewed as a retreat.[3]

Kirov responded to "Dizzy with Success" in precisely the manner prescribed by Stalin. At a mid-March plenum of the regional party committee, he admonished his listeners that the party line in the countryside had not changed. The collectivization drive had not been "rushed," but "perfectly timed." In response to doubts raised by G. N. Pylaev, Kirov affirmed official propaganda that droves of middle and poor peasants were joining the collective farms of their own free will. The party's task now was to "consolidate the conquered positions" and forswear "distortions of the party line." The distortions Kirov identified—coercing poor and middle peasants, collectivizing their chickens, and using dekulakization as a pretext for theft—had already been labeled as such by Stalin and other spokespeople for the center.[4]

Two months later, Kirov addressed another plenum in similar terms. He now had a new Stalin article, "Answer to the Collective Farm Comrades," published in *Pravda* on April 3, as guidance. His presentation to the regional committee plenum followed Stalin's theses closely. The widespread use of "administrative methods" by "hotheads" in the collectivization campaign had nearly destroyed the alliance between the middle peasants and "the working class" (that is to say, the Communist regime). Stalin's two articles in *Pravda*, however, had cooled the "hotheads" and saved the situation. Kirov also used a variation on one of Stalin's themes, the need to approach collectivization differently in different regions of the USSR. Methods that were appropriate for wheat-growing regions such as Ukraine, he said, could not be "mechanically transferred" to regions (like Leningrad) where wheat culture was not dominant.[5]

Whatever his public stance, did Kirov entertain private doubts about Stalin's choice to wage war on the peasantry? Scholars who believe that he did use a document from this period, six pages of handwritten notes by Kirov, to make their argument. Labeled in the archive with the heading "Sergei Mironovich Kirov's notes on struggle with the Opposition," the holograph consists of three sheets covered on both sides with short notes scribbled by Kirov in various directions. Kirilina excerpts just five fragments (nonconsecutive) from the document:

> On factionalism
> There was none . . .
> Perhaps the Opposition is correct . . .
> A secret struggle inside the party
> I should fight against Tomsky and the other way
>   around (*naoborot*) . . . [6]

Kirilina identifies this document "preliminarily" as notes taken by Kirov about speeches by Bukharin and Rykov at one of the TsK plenums of 1929. She suggests that it shows "Kirov's doubts about the correctness of the line taken by the party with relation to the 'Rightists.'" Knight, who takes the excerpts directly from Kirilina, dates the notes specifically to the April 1929 plenum and also uses them to argue that Kirov had covert Rightist sympathies.[7]

Examination of microfilm of the original document and published transcripts of central party meetings from the period reveals that the notes in fact were taken by Kirov at the Sixteenth Party Congress which met from June 26 to July 1, 1930, and that they have nothing to do with any sympathy on his part for the Right. Indeed, they are part of Kirov's preparations for a blistering attack on the Rightist leaders he delivered at that conference. The notes follow closely consecutive speeches of repentance given by former Rightist leaders Tomsky and Rykov at the Sixteenth Party Congress on the evening of June 29, 1930. It appears that Kirov scribbled fragmentary phrases and paraphrases of the speeches as he listened, an exercise he often engaged in. On the morning of June 30, immediately following the appearances of Tomsky and Rykov, Kirov rebutted them, insisting that their confessions of error were inadequate. Several themes and phrases in the notes appear in Kirov's June 30 philippic.[8]

Three out of four of the statements supposedly indicating Kirov's doubts about the TsK attack on the Rightists are in fact verbatim transcriptions or summaries of Tomsky's and Rykov's words, taken out of context. "Factionalism . . . there was none" corresponds to Tomsky's "my close friends and I did not set ourselves the goal or have the intention of creating a faction." "A secret struggle inside the party" fits Rykov's "I have to say that from a political point of view—[the idea of] a secret struggle inside our party—is stupidity and nonsense." "I should fight against Tomsky and the other way around" summarizes Rykov's response to a hostile comment: "You mean I should fight against Tomsky and Tomsky should fight against me?"

The single statement that does not appear in the published record of the Tomsky and Rykov speeches is "Perhaps the Opposition is correct." The phrase appears in Kirov's notes at the point corresponding to a brief disquisition by Rykov on the Trotskyites. Party leaders tended to refer to the Left Communist dissidents as "the Opposition" and the Right party dissidents as "the Right Deviation." Thus the "Opposition" in Kirov's notes likely refers to the Left followers of Trotsky and Zinoviev. One of the tasks Rykov undertook, as part of his repentance, was to demonstrate that Stalin's course for forced collectivization was not a radical extension of the Trotsky-Zinoviev Opposition's program for squeezing the kulaks (read: peasants) harder. The Stalinists had to show how their actions differed from the Left program that the party had rejected in 1926–1927. Rykov could demonstrate his loyalty by doing this, especially given that he and other Rightists had previously attacked Stalin precisely for taking such a Left line against the peasantry. Because the published versions of party speeches differed somewhat from the actual words spoken, it seems likely that in his speech, Rykov used the rhetorical question, "Perhaps the [Left] Opposition is correct?" to introduce his refutation—"No, the [Left] Opposition is wrong." It is also possible that Rykov never actually said "Perhaps the Opposition is correct," but that Kirov, who was quite skillful at parsing arguments, noted this down as the implied rhetorical question that Rykov was answering.

Kirov was no Right-leaning moderate at the time he took these notes. On June 30 he delivered to the congress a sarcastic rejection of Tomsky's and Rykov's speeches of submission, mocking their "biblical pathos," accusing them of "opposing resolutely every measure the party undertaken in the countryside," and decrying their "vicious attacks" on Stalin. As a reward for his loyalty, he was promoted to full member of the Politburo (Figures 3, 4).[9]

A Soft Line on Collectivization in Leningrad?

If moderation cannot be found in Kirov's public statements or private notes, perhaps it is to be found in his actions as leader of Leningrad. In the early 1930s Leningrad Region had a lower rate of collectivized peasant households than the Soviet Union as a whole. This fact has led commentators beginning with Semyon Sinelnikov (1964) to the conclusion that Kirov treated the region's peasants relatively gently during the collectivization campaign. However, an examination of the differences between specific regions of the USSR reveals that this inference is not justified. On the one hand, the Leningrad rates were low enough to make Stalin impatient. On the other, Leningrad authorities collectivized at a rate comparable with rates in similar regions in European Russia—those that were relatively infertile and contained major urban concentrations. In TsK planning for collectivization, the Leningrad Region fit in the lowest-priority category—it imported food and wheat was not the dominant crop. The highest-priority regions were wheat-exporting areas like the North Caucasus, followed by wheat-growing regions that had a small net excess of food imports over exports.[10]

Official figures for the percentage of collectivized households from September 1931 through July 1932 show that Leningrad's numbers were comparable to those from other food-importing Russian regions with relatively high urban populations. Kirov was not the most ruthless collectivizer, but Leningrad kept pace with similar areas. In this regard, it should be noted that the party secretary of Nizhegorod Region, where the percentage of collectivized households was very close to Leningrad's, was the hard-bitten Stalinist Andrei Zhdanov.

Dekulakization was a major weapon in the collectivization drive, particularly in 1930–1931. According to OGPU figures, between 380,000 and 390,000 peasant families were deported from their home villages in those years, most of them to be used as forced labor. In fer-

TABLE 1. Percentage of Collectivized Households in Selected Regions, 1931–1932

	September 1931	*June 1932*
Leningrad	39.5	38.0
Nizhegorod	39.8	41.8
Ivanov	40.4	43.8
Moscow	47.0	48.0
USSR	59.9	61.5

Source: I. E. Zelenin, "Kolkhoznoe stroitel'stvo v SSSR v 1931–1932 gg.," *Istoriia SSSR,* no. 6 (1960): 19–38.

tile wheat-cropping regions, proportionally far more families were deported than in less fertile areas such as Leningrad. However, the Leningrad authorities kept pace with their colleagues in other less fertile areas, as Table 2 illustrates. It can be seen that the deportation campaign was more intensive in Leningrad than in either Nizhegorod or Ivanovo regions. It is also worth noting that 5,344 of the families deported in the Leningrad Region were moved elsewhere within the region itself. This was because of the high demand for forced labor north of the city. European consuls in Leningrad in the early 1930s monitored Soviet use of forced labor in the region's lumber camps, apatite mines, ports, and other enterprises.[11]

An October 1934 report prepared by Pyotr Irklis, a close associate of Kirov's and former secretary of rural Luga District, sheds light on the reasons for Leningrad's slow rate of collectivization compared to the breadbasket zones. Irklis first noted the varying levels of collectivization within Leningrad Region, with fourteen districts over 80 percent and six under 50 percent. He identified two reasons for low rates of collectivization. In some districts, most notably Pskov, individual farmsteads dominated. These were more difficult to collectivize than villages (presumably because the population was dispersed and the individual farmers less vulnerable to peer pressure). In other areas, typically close to major towns or railroad lines, there were many small enterprises (for example fishing cooperatives, artisanal shops, and lumber camps) that employed peasants. These provided extra income for the inhabitants and made them less vulnerable to financial and procurement pressure from the authorities. State agents, Irklis wrote, tended to press collective farms harder than individual homesteaders

TABLE 2.   Number of Families Dekulakized Divided by Total Rural Population in Select Regions, 1930–1931

	Families Deported	*Rural Population*	*Ratio*
Moscow	10,813	2.7 million	0.4
Leningrad	8,604	2.3 million	0.37
Nizhegorod	9,169	2.7 million	0.34
Ivanovo	3,655	1.5 million	0.24

Sources: For families deported, V. N. Zemskov, "Spetsposelentsy: Po dokumentatsii NKVD-MVD SSSR," *Sotsiologicheskie issledovaniia,* no. 1 (1990): 3–17. For rural population, Frank Lorimer, *Population of the Soviet Union: History and Prospects* (Geneva: League of Nations, 1946). Population figures from Lorimer are based on 1926 census.

for taxes, compulsory labor, and agricultural procurement, because the collective farms delivered a bigger payoff for smaller effort (contact with one collective farm chairman versus contact with dozens of individual household heads). Thus, individual homesteaders found it easy to evade their obligations to the state. In general, the population in fertile wheat-growing regions was concentrated in larger villages than in less fertile northern regions, and thus more vulnerable to the forced collectivization campaign.[12]

Leningrad's slow pace of collectivization appears to have bothered Stalin from time to time. In early 1932 he sent Kirov two telegrams on the subject, separated by one week. In the first he demanded that Leningrad achieve full collectivization by the end of 1932, and in the second, by the end of 1933. Kirilina postulates that Kirov spoke with his boss by telephone between the two telegrams, and persuaded him to accept a later date for 100 percent collectivization. In the event, Leningrad achieved neither goal.[13]

In 1934 Kirov, prompted again by Stalin, ordered a renewed effort to expand the collective farms. On February 27, immediately following the Seventeenth Party Congress, he told the regional party committee that the proportion of collectivized households in Leningrad Region was too low. The chief danger in rural policy was no longer "excesses," but complacency. Leningrad cadres had forgotten the task of collectivization, they were not behaving like Bolsheviks. Forcing the peasants to join the collective farm, Kirov scolded them, entailed "protest and opposition from forces hostile to us." Because the job was difficult, too many rural officials had been avoiding it. Now, however, it was time to return to the attack.[14]

The assault made substantial progress, as the percentage of peasant households collectivized increased from 54.2 to 65.7 between January and October 1934. By January 1, 1935 the number was up to 74.3 percent. The basic method as outlined in Irklis's October 1934 report was to make life difficult for individual farmers by raising their taxes and compulsory labor requirements, forbidding local enterprises from hiring them, and enforcing the harshest legal penalties for "speculation" and tax evasion. At the July 1934 plenum of the regional party committee, Kirov warned that rural officials needed to stop worrying about whether the peasants had enough food to eat and focus instead on forcing them to cough up the taxes and mandatory deliveries they owed the state. Discussing the problem of collective farmers hiding livestock from state procurement agents, Kirov first declared that propagandists could convince them to reveal the animals if they properly explained the reasons for taxes. However, he immediately suggested a more realistic way of determining the size of livestock herds—recruiting informers from among those who had already joined the collective farmers.[15]

It is possible that a detailed study of collectivization in the Leningrad Region would find a "soft" approach fundamentally different from policies in comparable areas of the USSR. However, the evidence in *Leningradskaya pravda*, Kirov's papers, and central archives does not show any significant divergence in policy statements between Kirov and Stalin. Nor was the percentage of peasant households collectivized or dekulakized in the Leningrad countryside outside the normal range for similar regions. Stalin pressed Kirov to accelerate collectivization in 1932 and 1934, but the latter responded with alacrity, in 1934 at least. Kirov did not shirk the assault on the peasantry.

Building Socialism

In the early 1930s Kirov's primary tasks were ensuring that Leningrad industries carried out the central economic plan and expediting the delivery of food and fuel to the populace. Soviet historians generally presented Kirov's years in the city as a chronicle of successes on the "industrial front," hard-won but based on enthusiastic cooperation between the Communist leaders, the workforce, managers, and central planning agencies. There is some truth to this oversimplified picture. The Red Putilov factory raised its production of tractors by several times, the Izhorsky factory set up the USSR's first blooming mill for producing large steel ingots, and other factories pioneered the production of high-pressure marine turbines, synthetic rubber, carburetors, X-ray machines, and other high-technology products. Based on the work of talented Soviet engineers, Leningrad industry's accomplishments were impressive, especially in the areas of machine building and electrical equipment. The Soviet Union seemed to be approaching the goal of independence from the major capitalist powers in the production of advanced technology. At the same time there were many problems, delays, and failures. The collapse of tractor production at Putilov in 1930 (see above, pp. 97–98) is just one example.[16]

Provision of fuel for household and industrial use was a continual headache for Kirov. Given the extreme centralization of the economy and the absence of legal market mechanisms, the responsibility for en-

suring the fuel supply devolved on the Leningrad leader and his immediate subordinates. Correspondence between Stalin and Lazar Kaganovich from 1931 shows "the Leningraders" arguing for the hiring of
foreign ships to transport Baku oil by sea (presumably from a Black
Sea port) to their city. Shipping the oil north along the Volga River,
they claimed, would take too long. Although Ordzhonikidze and
VSNKh chief Valerian Kuibyshev supported them, "the Leningraders"
lost the argument in the Politburo.[17]

Another perennial difficulty was food. The Leningrad Region was
not self-sufficient in vegetables or grain, in part because of its far
northern location, in part because so much of the arable land was
given over to cash-cropping of flax. Food supplies had to be shipped
long distances from Ukraine and the North Caucasus. Kirov monitored closely the transport of vegetables and other agricultural products to Leningrad. Nonetheless, shortages were endemic. To "explain"
these, the regional control commission and the press ran propaganda
campaigns scapegoating officials in the cooperative and state distribution networks. These generally culminated in firings and even arrests.[18]

During the First and Second Five Year Plans competition for central
investment and resources between different industrial regions of the
Soviet Union was savage. The Leningraders, whose region manufactured approximately 15 percent of the Soviet Union's industrial product by value, constantly lobbied VSNKh and other organs for investment. In 1927, for instance, Kirov requested the Council of Labor and
Defense to fund tractor production at Red Putilov. In 1928 he lobbied
VSNKh for money to investigate methods of mass-producing synthetic
rubber. In 1930 he initiated another petition to VSNKh, ostensibly
from workers at the Metallist factory, asking for a contract to construct hydro-turbines for the gigantic Dnepr hydroelectric dam project. Yet these efforts never seemed to yield enough—Kirov and his
subordinates regularly complained that their city was not getting a fair
share of the center's investment funds.[19]

The constant jostling for funds, resources, and food supplies was a
source of tension inside the party leadership. Oleg Khlevniuk reports
several conflicts involving Kirov and Leningrad. On January 5, 1934,
for example, the Politburo dealt with a dispute between Leningrad authorities and the Commissariat of Agriculture over the city's consump-
tion of five thousand tons of grain above plan. Rosliakov describes
how Kirov competed with Moscow authorities, including Kagano-

vich, chief of the city's party organization, for construction materials and financing to build new infrastructure. One important tactic in these battles was exaggerating the size of the city's population. A caricature of Kirov drawn by V. I. Mezhlauk in 1931 shows Kirov inflating a balloon with larger and larger Leningrad population figures on it. Entitled "Elastic Leningrad," the caption is "Blow, Kirov, Blow!"[20]

Khlevniuk concludes that the conflicts recorded in the archives between Leningrad officials and the authorities in Moscow were typical of the Soviet apparatus in the first half of the 1930s. In the struggle for funds and supplies from the center provincial leaders resorted to all sorts of stratagems. They petitioned, they issued demands, and they turned a blind eye when their subordinates used illegal means to secure resources. "Kirov and his subordinates," Khlevniuk writes, "behaved themselves in exactly the same way as all of the other local bosses."[21]

In spite of the authorities' wheeling and dealing, living conditions in Leningrad (and most Soviet cities) worsened between 1927 and 1932. The main reasons were the regime's concentration of resources in heavy industry and the collectivization of the peasants. The drive to increase worker productivity combined with the lack of investment in light industries producing consumer goods meant that real wages fell throughout this period. Shoes and clothes were in short supply, and many urban residents simply did not get enough to eat. Adding to the difficulties was the arrival in the city of hundreds of thousands of peasants, fleeing forced collectivization and seeking jobs in the expanding industrial workforce. Between 1926 and 1932 the population of Leningrad nearly doubled. The modest housing construction program could not keep pace, and most residents had to live in crowded communal apartments.[22]

Declining living standards and a sense of powerlessness led to strikes by Leningrad workers, a serious embarrassment for Communist authorities. In addition to the early 1928 strike at Khalturina factory discussed in Chapter 2, there were strikes in the late twenties and early thirties at brick factories, lumber mills, the city port, No. 5 Hydroelectric Plant, and the Nogin factory. A substantial number of Soviet factory workers saw state repression, tightening industrial discipline, and declining wages as a betrayal of the October Revolution. Some protested. The phenomenon was not confined to Leningrad. In April 1932 textile mills in the Ivanovo Region were rocked by a massive, well-coordinated walkout, followed by days of public demonstrations.[23]

Kirov regularly received angry letters about living conditions from workers and party members. These came both anonymous and signed. On November 15, 1932, a Communist wrote to Kirov, suggesting that he "try to buy boots, a coat, a suit, linen of any kind, manufactures, furniture, a stove. No, you won't find any of these." An anonymous Jewish worker from the Elektroapparat factory complained about the "volunteer Saturdays" he was forced to work. Of the party leadership he wrote, "You have eaten yourselves round with meat. All of the workers say this with one voice, and say that our entire population of 140 million is ruled by terror. Look at yourself in the mirror. You have three automobiles, you eat better than the tsars ever did, and even when there's no war on, or epidemics, or random disasters, you demolish the economy, you keep us, unhappy ones, hungry. You're a sad son of a bitch and your place is on the gallows."[24]

Repression

In the early 1930s the secret police grew rapidly and expanded its functions. The Gulag, a network of forced labor camps that became an important part of the Soviet economy, was founded in 1930. Police card files on "alien elements," which now included party members suspected of disloyalty to Stalin, grew longer. Between 1928 and 1933 the number of persons arrested annually by the secret police multiplied almost fivefold. Stalin personally supervised several nationally publicized show trials and investigations of political crimes, targeted at ex-Mensheviks, economic planners, foreign engineers, cooperative officials, and agronomists. The regular police also ratcheted up levels of coercion. Using the mandatory internal passport system introduced in 1932 they purged the cities of "socially harmful elements" including vagrants, the drunk and disorderly, petty criminals, and "former people" (such as priests, ex–Tsarist police officers, nobles, and businessmen).[25]

Kirov played an active role in the expansion of state repression. In October 1929 he cooperated with a government commission that discovered a purported case of "wrecking" among historians at the Academy of Science in Leningrad that ended with the execution of five persons and the exile of over seventy.[26] Kirov's secret police chief in the early 1930s, Filip Medved, was one of the officers who supervised the operation to lure the émigré Russian physicist Pyotr Kapitsa to the USSR and detain him there.[27]

The case of the Academy historians and Kapitsa are correctives to the "Kirov, friend of the intelligentsia" trope endorsed by post-Stalin Soviet historians and by Kirilina.[28] As party leader in Leningrad, the center of intellectual and scientific life in Imperial Russia and home of the Academy of Sciences until 1934, Kirov had to deal with prominent scientists, engineers, and writers whose services were valuable to the Soviet state. Like Stalin, he ably made use of coercion, threats, persuasion, flattery, and the dispensation of privileges to manage the intelligentsia. The central goal was always to use these men and women for the state's larger purpose of "building socialism."

Both Knight and Kirilina have called attention to Kirov's relationship with Nikolai Bukharin in the early 1930s. Following Bukharin's political defeat, the TsK appointed him chief of the "scientific-technical" section of VSNKh, effectively in charge of "technical propaganda."[29] He served the Stalinists as a go-between to high-ranking scientific and technical specialists, as well as a propagandist for Soviet technological achievements. In this capacity Bukharin made regular trips to Leningrad on business with the Academy of Sciences, and developed a working relationship with Kirov. He sent many work-related requests to the latter and gave him and Maria Lvovna books, copies of his own articles, and other presents. Kirilina claims that he often stayed overnight at Kirov's apartment on his visits to Leningrad. In his letters Bukharin took a familiar tone with Kirov, using *ty*, the familiar form of "you," and signing as "Your Nikolai," or "Your Bukharin." Unsurprisingly, there was no discussion of Stalin or party politics. It is quite likely that Bukharin sought to ingratiate himself with Kirov, Stalin's man in Leningrad. Kirov was cordial in return, in spite of his continuing violent denunciations of Bukharin in public. Stalin too had moments of private geniality with Bukharin in the early thirties.[30]

In addition to collectivization and dekulakization, Kirov also participated in the organization of other police "mass operations" and summary tribunals during the early 1930s. He signed top secret orders for the arrest of two thousand Leningrad residents from among "criminal declassed elements" in April 1932. The arrestees were to be sent to work at the Svir forced labor camp, which provided Leningrad with firewood as well as lumber for building. Kirov also followed closely and probably signed off on the expulsion of about 100,000 Leningraders from the city during the campaign against "socially harmful elements" that took place in 1933 simultaneous with the issuance of internal passports. Kirov's secret police chief Medved was on the commission that planned the campaign. Probably in connection with the passportization campaign, police sweeps netted three thousand children living on the Leningrad streets between April and October 1933. Many were sent to overcrowded children's homes. If Leningrad practice followed all-union norms, older adolescents would have been sent to do forced labor at lumber camps and construction sites. During 1933 Kirov also served with Medved and chairman of the Leningrad soviet I. F. Kodatsky on a troika (a three-person board with summary jurisdiction) charged with issuing death sentences for cases of "insurrection and counterrevolution" in Leningrad Region.[31]

The Soviet state used many of those detained in the mass operations as forced labor. Kirov and his subordinates were involved in this form of repression too. The White Sea–Baltic Canal was constructed between 1931 and 1933 in Leningrad Region, largely with the use of forced labor. Kirov was not among those directly responsible for the canal project, but he conducted inspection tours of the construction area in the summers of 1932 and 1933. At the peak of activity in 1932–1933, the White Sea Canal project used over 100,000 OGPU camp prisoners. Oleg Khlevniuk has called the canal, which was the OGPU's first big construction project, "a defining moment for the future of the camps." At the Seventeenth Party Congress in January 1934 Kirov praised the police officials in charge of the canal construction: "To build such a canal, in such a period of time, is truly heroic work, and one must give their due to the chekists [secret police officers] who directed this work, who literally worked miracles."[32]

Kirov played his part in the organization of state coercion and violence under Stalin. The few cases where he argued for limits to repression, such as his apparent attempt to persuade Stalin to accept a slower pace of collectivization for Leningrad in early 1932, were pragmatically motivated and fit within the normal range of action for the head of a provincial party organization. Outside Stalinist circles he was generally perceived as one of the despot's thuggish henchmen. Reader Bullard, British consul in Leningrad from July 1931 to July 1934, called him "a brutal-looking demagogue who is the Stalin of Leningrad" (Figure 5). The Riutin Platform, composed by a group of Right-leaning party dissidents headed by Martemian Riutin in early 1932, labeled Kirov an "opportunist," who had adapted himself to "the Stalinist regime" in spite of his record "as a former Kadet, and editor of a Kadet newspaper in Vladikavkaz." The Leningrad leader was one of the "pillars of the Stalinist regime. . . . Such people can adapt themselves to any regime, to any political system." Referencing

Desov's denunciation of Kirov to the party leadership in late 1929, the platform stated: "Everyone knows how the attempt of the Leningraders to denounce Kirov . . . ended. They got smashed in the face and were forced to shut up. Stalin . . . resolutely defends his own sons-of-bitches."[33]

Conflict in the OGPU

When Kirov first came to Leningrad in 1926, the chief of the region's OGPU was Stanislav Messing, an Old Bolshevik and veteran chekist who helped to undermine Zinoviev's hold on the city's party organization during the factional struggle. In December 1929 Messing was removed from his Leningrad post, and replaced by Filip Medved, another veteran chekist, with previous experience working in the region. Messing's removal coincided with Stalin's and Kirov's take-down of the Komarovites, and it may be that Messing was associated with that group. It is also known that Kirov, immediately prior to Messing's firing, had intervened to halt a falsified OGPU case against I. P. Zhukov, head of the Leningrad Council on the National Economy. This incident too might have had a bearing on Messing's removal.[34]

In 1931 Medved was peripherally involved in a dramatic clash inside the OGPU leadership. In the summer of that year, a number of higher-ranking officers in the OGPU began openly criticizing the conduct of the operation "Spring" (*Vesna*), prepared against military specialists in Ukraine and central Russia. The critics, who included Ya. K. Olsky, head of the Special Department of the OGPU; Messing, now head of the Foreign Department; and OGPU Collegium member Ye. G. Yevdokimov, claimed that most of the cases in "Spring" were falsified. Their immediate target was the two lead officers on the "Spring" investigation, Israil Leplevsky and Lev Balitsky. But behind Leplevsky and Balitsky stood the titular director of the OGPU, Viacheslav Menzhinsky, and his deputy, de facto director Genrikh Yagoda.

Stalin intervened decisively on the side of Yagoda. On July 25, 1931, at his behest, the Politburo ordered both Olsky and Messing transferred out of the OGPU to other posts, and promoted Balitsky to the position of deputy chairman of the secret police. Balitsky's promotion opened up the position of OGPU chief in Ukraine. The Politburo ordered Stanislav Redens to replace Balitsky, transferred Medved from Leningrad to Redens's former job in Belarus, and replaced Medved with the erring Yevdokimov.[35]

According to the 1960s testimony of D. B. Sorokin, Medved's brother-in-law, Kirov intervened immediately to keep Medved in Leningrad. Whether due to Kirov's intervention or not, the Politburo rescinded Medved's transfer on August 5, 1931. Yevdokimov was dispatched to Central Asia rather than Leningrad. In the aftermath of this incident Yagoda dispatched a circular letter to "all chekists" warning them to check denunciations carefully and to avoid using "the methods of our enemies," such as beating, torturing, and verbally abusing prisoners. Stalin, however, delivered a more powerful message with an August 10 Politburo circular charging Messing, Olsky, and Yevdokimov with undermining the OGPU's "iron discipline." The letter indicated that further "gossip about 'internal weaknesses' of the OGPU organs and their 'incorrect line'" would not be tolerated. "Inflated" cases, as the Soviets called them, were the unspoken order of the day.[36]

This incident probably had more to do with personal rivalries than with principled objections to the OGPU's methods of "inflating" cases. Yevdokimov was one of the managers of the fabricated cases against the Shakhty engineers, and Olsky took a prominent part in dekulakization and the 1930 fabrication of charges of espionage against a number of Soviet microbiologists.[37] The affair certainly does not show that Medved was a supporter of the "soft line" on investigations. In the original scheme, he was to be replaced in Leningrad by Yevdokimov, identified by Stalin on August 10 as a soft-liner. If Medved's problem from Yagoda's or Stalin's point of view was that he would not inflate cases, then why would they replace him with another "soft-liner," who presumably would have the same hesitancy?

In April 1932 Medved received a new deputy, Ivan Zaporozhets. After spending most of the 1920s abroad, working for the OGPU in Poland, Czechoslovakia, Austria, and Germany, Zaporozhets had been transferred to the OGPU section of the Leningrad Military District in November 1931. Five months later, he was appointed Medved's deputy. Many memoirists claim that Yagoda distrusted Medved, and that Zaporozhets was to be the OGPU leader's eyes and ears in Leningrad. Rosliakov reports that many in the city leadership were surprised by the self-assurance with which Zaporozhets conducted himself, answering questions given to Medved, for example, at meetings of the regional committee's bureau.[38]

Leningrad was a hotbed of OGPU activity against foreign nationals and their Soviet contacts in the 1920s and 1930s. It was a major international port and Russia's longtime window on the West. There were ten European consulates in the city in the early 1930s as well as thousands of foreign engineers, sailors, doctors, businessmen, and so on. *Leningradskaya pravda* regularly ran stories of espionage cases against foreign consuls. As the diary of British consul Reader Bullard makes clear, Soviet interpreters and servants employed by foreigners often worked for the OGPU. The secret police also sent provocateurs asking for help escaping from the USSR to a number of the consuls. Zaporozhets was a specialist in foreign espionage, and as Medved's deputy he was responsible for the regional OGPU's Special Department, which handled such "counterespionage" in the early 1930s.

Over the course of his tenure in Leningrad, Medved developed a reputation for slackness. Rosliakov describes him as growing lazy, fond of parties, and indiscrete. At a celebration of the fifteenth anniversary of the founding of the Cheka, Rosliakov witnessed him embracing and kissing jazz singer and band leader Leonid Utyosov. The implication, that they had a homosexual relationship, was not acceptable in Soviet society. In general, Rosliakov writes, Medved "grew heavier, not just physically, but morally, his will to work flagged." According to both Rosliakov and Bullard, Medved's wife Raisa Kopylovskaya had a reputation for flirting and promiscuity. Bullard reported in his diary a rumor that Medved imprisoned the manager of Leningrad's Torgsin store after the latter flirted with his wife. Rosliakov's memoirs and a November 24, 1934 suicide note from an aide to B. N. Chudin, office manager for the Leningrad soviet, hint that Kopylovskaya and Chudin were involved together in corrupt financial deals, some kind of a ménage à trois, and/or procuring adolescent boys for sex. The suicide, age 20, wrote in his note that he refused any longer "to be a prostitute in ripped pants."[39]

Such stories obviously undermined Medved's authority. Tales that his wife had cuckolded him and that he was a homosexual meant, in the context of a highly patriarchal Soviet society, that Medved was weak, soft, and incompetent. By early 1934 rumors were widespread that the secret police chief was not long for the Leningrad job. When Bullard heard Soviet officials retailing the story of Kopylovskaya's flirtation with the Torgsin manager, he concluded that Medved might soon lose his position. Rosliakov reports in his memoirs that Kirov told him in early 1934 that the "Central Committee" wanted Medved out of Leningrad, but that he (Kirov) would resist any transfer. The young journalist V. K. Zavalishin reported years later that some time before Kirov's murder he heard that Medved was slated for transfer from Leningrad to the Far East.[40] Clearly, central authorities viewed Medved as a problem by early 1934.

Kirov's Personal Life

Although he had to travel often, Kirov was well settled in Leningrad by 1930. He was the undisputed head of the region's party organization. As party secretary he indulged his appetite for the good life. He took in plays, ballets, and concerts regularly, continuing a lifelong love for the performing arts. In 1923 he had taken up hunting, the preferred sport of the Bolshevik elite, and he eventually arranged a private lodge and motorboat for his own use outside Leningrad. Kirov's regular hunting companion was his guard and manservant, OGPU Commissar (Officer) Lev Fomich Bukovsky. Medved, other select senior Leningrad officials, Ordzhonikidze, and VSNKh chief Valerian Kuibyshev accompanied him on expeditions at various points. Kirov was in the habit of sending Stalin game he had shot.[41]

Maria Lvovna did not thrive in Leningrad. In the spring of 1929 Kirov had her installed as head of a residential facility for "curing" prostitutes, a job for which her only preparation was some volunteer work with street children in Baku. According to a medic who worked at the facility, Maria Lvovna's idea of therapy was reading to the former prostitutes about the lives of exemplary Bolsheviks and taking them to political meetings. A series of scandals broke out at the "prophylactory," as it was called. In one of these, two student volunteers recruited by Maria Lvovna to help with therapy began pimping the "patients" at a nearby bar. Eventually, in the summer of 1930, Ordzhonikidze visited Leningrad and convinced Maria Lvovna to leave the position.[42]

From the late 1920s onward Maria Lvovna's health deteriorated. She apparently suffered a series of small strokes that left her nearly paralyzed by 1933. As a result she spent most of her time at a rest home in Tolmachevo, in the Leningrad suburbs. Kirov kept in touch with her by letter. When he was traveling he received updates on her well-being from his deputy, Chudov. In September 1934 her condition was sufficiently poor that Chudov arranged for her younger sister, Rakhil Markus, a doctor, to come from the North Caucasus and tend to her physical and mental health. According to Kirilina, Maria Lvovna's illness intensified her querulousness and aristocratic attitude, parodied by Zorich in his 1926 "Two Dogs" feuilleton.[43]

Kirov sought out other female companionship. According to Alla Kirilina, there is documentary confirmation in secret police files of one mistress, a widow with two children who lived in Zagube, on the eastern shore of Lake Ladoga. Not coincidentally, this was one of Kirov's favorite spots for hunting expeditions. In 2004 Kirilina also claimed to have seen a list compiled by the NKVD soon after Kirov's assassination, of women with whom he might have had "an intimate connection." The list, which was quite long, had the names of a number of Leningrad ballerinas on it. Kirilina notes, however, that the NKVD was collecting rumors, and that there is no other evidence that any of these women were Kirov's lovers. The list Kirilina refers to is probably the same one that Soviet KGB veteran Pavel Sudoplatov's wife Emma Kaganova helped to compose after the assassination. In his *Special Tasks,* a work riddled with factual errors, Sudoplatov claims to have solved the Kirov murder based on information Emma gave him about the "Don Juan" list. Sudoplatov's tale is too confused to merit consideration (see Conclusion). It is entirely plausible, however, that Kirov had mistresses among the Leningrad ballerinas.[44]

Keeping his mistresses more or less under cover was just one part of a much larger effort—maintaining his image as an upright, totally dedicated "proletarian" leader. Except as an apprentice in Kazan, Kirov had never done factory work, and he had effectively remade himself as an intellectual in the years before the 1917 revolution. The few remaining photographs from his Vladikavkaz days show a well-groomed young man in a blazer, wearing dress shoes, sometimes in an informal "flat cap." As late as 1921, a number of photographs show Kirov in blazer and tie. As Leningrad leader, however he generally affected a quasi-military outfit including button-down shirt with high collar, greatcoat, and boots (his style resembled Stalin's of the same period). Although he was quite far-sighted by the 1920s and kept four pairs of glasses in his Leningrad apartment, Kirov never wore them in public because they were a marker of intelligentsia status.[45]

Although the posthumous rhetoric about Kirov's leadership qualities is vastly overblown, it does seem that he built effective working relationships with his subordinates in Leningrad, especially after the removal of the Komarovites. Judging by their correspondence in 1934, he and his deputy Mikhail Chudov trusted one another as competent colleagues. Kirov called Chudov "Mikhail" and used the informal *ty* with him. He was also on a *ty* basis with Pyotr Irklis, the Luga party leader promoted to the Leningrad apparatus after Zinoviev's fall. He was close to OGPU chief Medved and saw Medved's family regularly. Medved's son Misha was a particular favorite with Kirov.[46]

Kirov and his subordinates needed one another. The top Communist leaders in Moscow exerted constant pressure on provincial party organizations through the party control commissions, the secret police, the press, and even lower-level party cells. Officials and activists in all of these institutions provided information to central authorities about malfeasance or incompetence in the provincial party leadership. Thus provincial party secretaries like Kirov often sought loyal subordinates who could keep their mouths shut, troubleshoot, and cover up problems. From the center's point of view this behavior was known as "familyness" (*semeistvennost'*) and was a real problem.[47] It prevented Stalin from having good information about the goings-on outside Moscow. By the middle of 1933 Kirov had been in charge of the Leningrad organization for over seven years—an unusually long tenure for the secretary of a provincial party organization. He had had plenty of time to find and promote his "family," even given that he came from Baku almost alone. It is quite likely that Stalin believed that it was time for him to move on.

Kirov's Promotion and the "Moderate Line," 1933–1934

From July 18 to 25, 1933, Stalin, Voroshilov, and Avel Yenukidze visited Kirov and the four of them took a cruise on the Baltic–White Sea Canal, which was under construction with slave labor. The foursome stopped in the northern city of Murmansk and traveled through the Kola Peninsula as well. Upon their return to Leningrad, they made an official inspection of the city's port. A number of photographs have been published of Stalin, Kirov, and Voroshilov in informal poses on the deck of a small steamer during this trip. Yenukidze, shot in 1936, is not shown.[48]

Stalin's 1933 visit prompted a reorganization of security measures for Kirov (see below, pp. 403–409). Stalin, it seems, felt that Kirov was not cautious enough about his own safety, and he ordered the OGPU, and perhaps Medved directly, to strengthen Kirov's guard. Operations Department chief Gubin increased the number of personal bodyguards from three to fifteen, switched Kirov's Smolny office (Figure 6) to a less accessible location, and began preparations to move Kirov from his apartment to a separate house. Kirov's security was now roughly comparable to Stalin's. Given the frequent spy scares in Leningrad, the city's location in a border zone, and the Soviet authorities' growing fear of war following Hitler's seizure of power in Germany, Stalin's concern probably struck those around Kirov as normal. Indeed, in April 1933 central authorities ordered the Leningrad OGPU to strengthen their border guards in anticipation of "terrorists" crossing over from Finland.[49]

Kirov received occasional death threats and warnings of assassination plots that could also have motivated the strengthening of his guard. One such warning, of a German plot (almost certainly imaginary), came in from a Leningrad student on July 2, 1933, just weeks before Kirov's excursion with Stalin.[50]

Based on events in 1934, it nonetheless appears that Stalin could have had motives beyond Kirov's personal safety in ordering an improvement in his guard. It may well be that the dictator was already considering promoting his Leningrad satrap to a position in Moscow. If so, strengthening Kirov's guard would have been a way of raising his profile and tightening Stalin's control over him. Secondly, Stalin may have had the impression of a general laxity in Leningrad, based on stories about Medved, and the continuing employment of prominent former Zinovievites in middle levels of the city's apparatus. Finally, as the original epicenter of the Bolshevik Revolution, Leningrad's industrial neighborhoods and party cells continued to display signs of political instability and restlessness that must have made Stalin nervous. All of these would have been good reasons in Stalin's mind to reinforce Kirov's guard.

In late November 1933, Kirov experienced a nervous crisis, with some physical symptoms. At an examination around November 21, he complained to his physician Dr. G. F. Lang of heart palpitations, listlessness, irritability, and severe insomnia. He had no motivation for work. Lang prescribed a rest. Nervous crises of this sort were not unusual for top party leaders, who worked under immense psychological pressure, and the usual cure was a vacation at a sanatorium. Kirov had many reasons to be anxious. There were the continual struggles to keep Leningrad supplied and meet plan targets. It may also be that Stalin was talking about the possibility of Kirov moving to Moscow by the fall of 1933, and we know that Kirov was not pleased at the prospect.[51]

Kirov spent about one month resting in Tolmachevo with Maria Lvovna, skating and ice-fishing. Returning to work at Smolny in late

December, he was immediately precipitated into preparations for the Seventeenth Party Congress, scheduled to open on January 26, 1934.

The Soviet press dubbed the Seventeenth Party Congress "the Congress of Victors." The central conceit was that collectivization and the First Five Year Plan had succeeded, thus laying the bases for a truly "socialist" society. Speakers hinted at the high human cost of collectivization, speaking of some regrettable "excesses" in the countryside and party policies founded on "repression . . . as the deciding method of 'management'. . . ." There was relief, then, that the "victory" was won. Kirov summed up the officially cultivated mood at the congress, when he said that "the fundamental difficulties are already behind us."[52]

Several former oppositionists spoke at the congress, delivering more or less abject confessions of error and sycophantic paeans to Stalin. The partial rehabilitation of oppositionists had in fact begun before the congress, with the readmission to the party in December 1933 of Zinoviev, Kamenev, and the Trotskyite Ye. A. Preobrazhensky. Over the spring and summer of 1934 the rehabilitation of ex-oppositionists would continue, with the return to the party of former Rightist leader N. A. Uglanov, the release of ex-Trotskyite Kh. G. Rakovsky from exile, and the commutation of a labor camp sentence for Pyotr Petrovsky, the former editor of *Leningradskaya pravda*. All of this was clearly sanctioned by Stalin, who signed off on or even initiated the rehabilitations.[53]

Speakers at the congress harped almost constantly on Stalin's genius. Kirov's role, obviously scripted beforehand in consultation with top TsK officials, was to underscore and add an exclamation point to this theme. In the "discussion" of Stalin's comprehensive report to the congress, Kirov spoke last (Figure 7). He delivered a speech entitled "Comrade Stalin's Report Sets the Program for All of Our Work," which was, as Kirilina notes, "a hymn to Stalin." Mixing his metaphors freely, Kirov praised Stalin as "the best helmsman of our great socialist structure." At the speech's conclusion, he proposed that the congress refrain from passing detailed resolutions, as earlier party congresses had done, but simply "accept for implementation as party law all of the propositions and conclusions in Comrade Stalin's report." There followed the standard round of "prolonged, stormy applause," the same applause that Stalin had received. Stalin then took the podium and announced that in view of the congress's unanimity, he was forgoing his own final comments on the discussion. The scene was undoubtedly planned in advance. The dictator often enjoyed playing the part of the modest but competent servant of the party.[54]

Three circumstances at the congress bear mentioning in light of stories that appeared years later about events there. In one incident highly embarrassing for Leningrad, P. F. Kudelli, an elderly party veteran and member of the Leningrad delegation, made anti-Stalin comments in private during the congress. One delegate remembered Kudelli saying that she "recognized only one genius, V. I. Lenin"; another remembered her saying, "Stalin, Stalin . . . and where is the party?" Two of her interlocutors, including fellow Leningrader Dora Lazurkina, denounced her as a Zinovievite. The delegation leaders then ordered her to leave the congress and confiscated her credentials. In the aftermath Kudelli wrote a letter to Kirov apologizing for her "extremely unfortunate words" and denying that they were as inflammatory as her denouncers claimed.[55]

A second circumstance worth noting is that rumors circulated among congress delegates following the formal voting for Central Committee representatives that there had been a few votes against Stalin. Archival records of the election show three votes of 1,059 total were cast against Stalin's candidacy to the Central Committee. In the early 1960s Karl Ratnek, who had been a delegate to the congress from the Belorussian Republic, reported other delegates saying with surprise that there had been five or six votes against Stalin's candidacy. "This did not seem completely normal," Ratnek wrote. (In fact previous party congresses had seen a number of votes cast against Stalin.) Delegate Yana Straumit remembered hearing of two to four votes against Stalin. Nikita Khrushchev in the 1960s also remembered being taken aback when he heard of "six" votes against Stalin. Given the public adulation for Stalin at the congress, people were shocked that anyone had voted against his candidacy. The rumors even reached the Menshevik organ in emigration, the *Socialist Herald*. On February 25, 1934 the journal published a letter, supposedly from an anonymous correspondent in Moscow, describing the "consternation" when the vote counters discovered that "the largest quantity of votes was received not by Stalin, but by Kalinin, and Stalin ended up only in third place." The *Socialist Herald's* information matches precisely the archival records of the voting at the congress.[56]

A third circumstance important for understanding later folklore about the Seventeenth Party Congress was that rumors apparently circulated among the delegates that Kirov was about to be appointed to a high-profile position at the Central Committee in Moscow. In November 1960 former delegate Nikolai Ostakhov recalled delegates commenting that "Kirov's overdue for a transfer from Leningrad to the Central Committee." Vasily Yegorov recalled that many delegates praised Kirov's speech, commenting, "His place is at the Central Committee."[57] There is some confirmation from December 1934 of these much later accounts. Following the Kirov murder, on December 11, Appolon Chikovani, an aide to Avel Yenukidze at the Central Executive Committee (VTsIK), wrote to Nikolai Yezhov that at the Seventeenth Party Congress the Komarov clique had discussed a rumor that Kirov was bound for Moscow.[58] The ultimate source for the story could have been Stalin himself, who aimed to make such a move, suspected that Kirov would resist, and wanted to pressure him by generating a wave of "popular opinion."

The atmosphere of calm confidence at the Seventeenth Party Congress, deliberately fostered, was part of a larger "moderate" course correction by the party leadership. Signs of this correction appeared as far back as January 1933, when Stalin announced to a TsK plenum that rates of industrial growth would be pruned back in the Second Five Year Plan. For a year following Stalin's announcement officials at the state planning agency Gosplan worked up various versions of the new plan, all assuming decreased levels of overall investment in industry, lower production targets, and greater attention to "Group B" light industries that manufactured consumer goods. In January 1934 the Seventeenth Party Congress rubberstamped the new program. The hope was that it would take some downward pressure off wages and raise production of consumer goods, relieving the dire poverty of most urban dwellers.[59]

In addition to the plan revisions, Stalin and his advisers also took some measures in 1933–1934 to ease up on police repression. One of the most important reasons for this was simply that detention facilities were overcrowded. On May 8–10, 1933, the TsK executive apparatus and Sovnarkom issued orders ending the mass deportation of peasants, prohibiting arrests by anyone other than those legally empowered to do so (the OGPU, prosecutors' offices, the regular police), and ordering the release of 400,000 prisoners with relatively short terms. The directive emphasized that the class struggle in the countryside required "new methods of work"—targeted arrests of individual counterrevolutionaries, propaganda work, and other nonpolice tactics (such as tax penalties and incentives) that would encourage peasants to enter the collective farms. Mass deportations were out. This was the program that Kirov and Irklis were following in the summer and fall of 1934 as they worked to raise the proportion of collectivized households in Leningrad Region.[60]

The year 1934 saw a drop in the number of criminal convictions in the Russian Republic, and a sharp drop (by over two-thirds) in the number of convictions in cases investigated by the secret police (OGPU-NKVD). The Soviet leaders merged the OGPU with the Commissariat of Internal Affairs (NKVD) in July 1934, and substantially reduced (on paper at least) the secret police's power to try cases and detain people without charges. Prosecutors were now to ensure that arrested persons were charged and regular (not secret police) courts were to try them. Stalin approved of this reorganization, and of other measures to regularize police and juridical procedures (see below, pp. 253–256, for a more detailed discussion of these changes).[61]

Khlevniuk makes two very important points about the regime's "moderate" turn in 1933–1934. First, the main motivation for the course change was ending the chaos brought on by forced collectivization and forced-draft industrialization. In 1932–1933 over five million Soviet peasants starved to death, workers struck, and labor turnover reached astronomical proportions as factory operatives "flitted" from site to site seeking better working conditions. Quite possibly Stalin and those around him feared the collapse of their authority in these years. Second, there is no evidence of a "moderate" faction within the party leadership that pressed for the course change, or of a "hard-line" faction that resisted it. Correspondence between senior Stalinists indicates general acceptance of the new party line. There were no important changes in the organization or personnel of the TsK executive apparatus that might explain the "moderate" course as the program of one faction or another.[62]

Immediately following the conclusion of the Seventeenth Party Congress the Politburo met to set the agenda for the TsK plenum set to open that same evening, February 10. Following the usual practice, the Politburo decided on the candidates for the TsK Secretariat and Orgburo, who would be elected later by the plenum. According to Leningrad finance official Mikhail Rosliakov, who heard the story separately from Kirov, Kodatsky, and E. K. Pramnek, Stalin proposed that Kirov leave Leningrad for Moscow, and join the TsK Secretariat. Kirov objected, asking for two more years in Leningrad to complete the Second Five Year Plan. Molotov, speaking more than forty years later, recalled Kirov telling him at the meeting, "What are you talking about?! I'll be no good here. In Leningrad I can do as well as you, but what can I do here?" According to Rosliakov, Ordzhonikidze and Kuibyshev supported Kirov's desire to remain in Leningrad, and Stalin stalked out of the meeting in anger. Kirov followed him out, and they talked. A compromise was reached. The TsK would elect Kirov to the Secretariat, but he would continue to live in Leningrad for the time in being and head the party organization there. To carry out some of the duties Stalin had hoped to assign to Kirov, A. A. Zhdanov would be promoted to Moscow from his post as head of the party organization in Gorky (Nizhny Novgorod/Nizhegorod).[63]

Stalin probably had multiple motives for wanting to shift Kirov to Moscow, as he usually had for his personnel appointments. As already mentioned, he may have concluded that Kirov had developed too close a circle of "family" in Leningrad and needed to be uprooted (Figure 8). Part of this was probably his sense (exaggerated no doubt) that Medved and perhaps Kirov were complacent about security problems in the Union's second city. Khlevniuk notes that Stalin needed a replacement on the TsK Secretariat for P. P. Postyshev, recently transferred to Ukraine. He may have also wanted to counterbalance the strong influence of Lazar Kaganovich, TsK secretary and de facto second-in-command of the party, in the TsK executive apparatus.[64]

As Khlevniuk points out, the conflict between Kirov and Stalin over the transfer from Leningrad had plenty of precedents. "It should be remembered," he writes, "that the transfers of senior leaders to new posts in the late 1920s and early 1930s was quite often accompanied by conflicts and scandals." Kirov himself had resisted the transfer to Leningrad in late 1925. Ordzhonikidze resisted promotion from the Caucasus to the Central Control Commission in the summer of 1926. Stalin had to threaten him with demotion to get him to take the job. In 1931, when Valerian Kuibyshev threatened to resign from his post as head of Gosplan, the central government economic planning agency, Stalin and Lazar Kaganovich went to a great deal of trouble to conciliate him, and ended up giving him six weeks vacation to keep him at his post.[65]

The coincidence of the turn to "moderation" with Kirov's prominent role at the Seventeenth Party Congress and Stalin's move to promote him has led some observers to conclude that Kirov was one of the authors of the new course. Khlevniuk, who has studied the deliberations of the Politburo and other leading TsK organs (Orgburo, Secre-

tariat) as closely as anyone, has found no evidence of this. He writes
that Kirov in the early 1930s "behaved not as a full member of the
Politburo, but more as the influential leader of one of the great party
organizations of the country. Kirov's initiatives were limited to the
needs of Leningrad. . . . He was at Politburo sessions in Moscow very
rarely. . . . In general, based on documents available to date, one cannot even paint a picture of Kirov as taking any part in the development
and implementation of . . . 'high policy,' much less of him as a 'reformer' or leader of an anti-Stalin wing of the party."[66]

Although Kirov remained officially in Leningrad, he visited Moscow more frequently following his appointment to the TsK Secretariat.
In 1934 he spent sixty-three hours in Stalin's Kremlin office, compared
to twenty-three in 1931, twenty-eight in 1932, and ten in 1933. Moreover, Stalin pressed him hard to get involved in central business, calling
him frequently on the direct Kremlin line. The willful dictator still
wanted Kirov in Moscow, and this was one way of importuning him.
Rosliakov reports that this irritated Kirov, who sometimes grimaced
when Stalin called. In 1966 N. F. Sveshnikov remembered Stalin calling Smolny while Kirov was visiting his wife in Tolmachevo. Stalin expressed impatience that Kirov was not available. Mikhail Chudov
jumped into an automobile and went straight to the suburb to let
Kirov know his boss had called.[67]

Whatever tension existed between Stalin and Kirov was due to the
conflict over Kirov's appointment to Moscow, not to policy differences. Claims for Kirov's "moderation" in this period are based on
misreadings of statements and actions that actually fit remarkably well
with the agenda of Stalin and his closest advisers. For example one
supposed index of Kirov's moderation in 1934 was his repeated references to the need for observance of "revolutionary legality" or "proletarian legality" in the countryside and elsewhere. Yet as we have seen,
the TsK and Sovnarkom had issued instructions in May 1933 putting
an end to mass deportations in the countryside. The explicit campaign
for "revolutionary legality" reached back at least as far as the July 1,
1933 Politburo order (issued undoubtedly with Stalin's approval) establishing the USSR Prosecutor's office, which referred to the goal of
"reinforcing the socialist legal order." The campaign was promoted in
Pravda after the Seventeenth Party Congress under headlines such as
that of a May 8, 1934 lead editorial, "Immutable Soviet Laws—The
Basis of Socialist Jurisprudence."[68]

The Italian scholar Francisco Benvenuti and the émigré journalist

Zavalishin have suggested that Kirov took the lead in opposing repression against the peasantry with rhetorical assaults on the Machine Tractor Stations' Political Departments in the late summer and fall of 1934. The Machine Tractor Stations were tractor depots that provided services to collective farms. The Political Departments attached to them were established in January 1933 to strengthen the party's (and OGPU's) authority in the countryside, and to squeeze kulaks and other "harmful elements." They were so-called "plenipotentiary" organs and bypassed the authority of local party committees in rural areas. Benvenuti argues that two Kirov speeches in the fall of 1934 calling for the "reorganization" of the MTS and the Political Departments show that the Leningrad leader spearheaded a move to abolish the departments.[69]

In fact, however, senior party leaders had been discussing abolishing the Political Departments for almost a year at the time Kirov spoke. Lazar Kaganovich, in a set of "Theses" presented in preparation for the Seventeenth Party Congress in early 1934, broached the possibility of subordinating the Political Departments to county party committees. At the congress there was open discussion of the issue, with prominent party leaders such as Pavel Postyshev, Robert Eikhe, I. M. Vareikis, and Boris Sheboldaev expressing dissatisfaction with the Political Departments. The congress adopted resolutions that anticipated their liquidation. In the spring, summer, and fall of 1934 *Pravda* regularly ran articles critical of the Political Departments' efforts to raise agricultural production. On September 3, Kaganovich told a conference of party officials that Political Department personnel would soon be theirs to dispose of. Liquidation was in the offing, and came at the November 1934 TsK plenum. It can be seen that there was absolutely nothing path-breaking about Kirov's criticisms of the Political Departments.[70]

Commentators have also suggested that in early 1934 Kirov stuck his neck out to advocate rapprochement with the Western democracies, citing two speeches in which he emphasized the threat to peace posed by Japan and Nazi Germany. Yet Kirov's comments were squarely in line with Stalin's foreign policy at the time. By the first months of 1934 Hitler was in power, the Rapallo Treaty between the USSR and Germany was effectively dead, Germany and Japan had left the League of Nations, and the Politburo had approved talks for a military alliance with France and a collective security policy that implied cooperation with select capitalist powers. The Soviet Union tentatively began to seek membership in the League. There were certainly revolutionary fundamentalists, including perhaps Kaganovich and Molotov, who opposed alliance with any capitalists at all. Stalin let them have their say, but he also let the advocates of collective security, most prominently Commissar of Foreign Affairs Maksim Litvinov, have theirs. He deliberately let both lines coexist, as the USSR sought its footing in a new and threatening international situation.[71]

From late 1933 through the summer of 1934 the Leningrad authorities supported the placement of a number of former Zinovievites in the state apparatus. This might be read as a sign of unusual tolerance on Kirov's part but for two reasons. First, even before 1933 Stalin, Kirov, and other leaders of the "Central Committee majority" had a relatively complex policy towards former Left oppositionists, controlling them with big sticks and small carrots. On the one hand they kept former Trotsky and Zinoviev supporters under close surveillance and bullied them publicly. On the other they used them to fill middle-level positions in the Soviet apparatus, provided they behaved well. Second, Stalin sent a clear signal at the Seventeenth Party Congress that rehabilitation of repenting Communist dissidents was acceptable.

The official stance of the period 1929–1934 was that former oppositionists who repented fully could be readmitted into the party and participate in "socialist construction." Kirov followed this policy, above all for pragmatic reasons. Given the shortage of competent officials, he was ready to employ ex-oppositionists of proven talents. Just as his friend Ordzhonikidze employed the former Left oppositionist Georgy Piatakov as his deputy at the Commissariat of Heavy Industry, Kirov made use of Mikhail Rosliakov, Pyotr Irklis, and other Leningraders who had supported Zinoviev in 1925. There is also evidence that he used former members of the Left-leaning United Opposition as a counterweight to Right-leaning Komarovites. Former Zinovievites certainly expected that Kirov would employ them after Komarov's and Desov's disgrace in the first two weeks of September 1929. As early as September 11 Kirov received a letter from one former Zinovievite by the name of Devingtal, congratulating him on cleaning up Komarov's "nest of nepotism and cliquishness" and asking for work. During the period 1929–1931 Kirov placed a number of former Zinovievites in middle-level posts in the cooperative and soviet apparatuses. Among these were several who would be charged with his murder.[72]

Most of the former oppositionists who continued to work in official posts were under secret police surveillance from 1928 onward, largely by means of informers. Kirov, through Medved, received regular intelligence reports on their behavior. The Leningrad OGPU placed reports on ex-Zinovievites in at least two files dubbed "Svoiak" ("Brother-in-Law"), which was an all-union operation, and "Politikan" ("Politico/Boss"). Some Komarovites, including Rekstin, were also under OGPU surveillance by the early 1930s.[73]

As with the intelligentsia, Kirov sought to control and make use of repentant former oppositionists. The case of Vladimir Rumiantsev, leader of the Leningrad Komsomol in 1925, is typical of the combination of the bullying and petting he employed. A vocal Zinoviev supporter, Rumiantsev joined the United Opposition and did not recant his views until the late summer of 1928, as the campaign against the Right began. He was readmitted to the party in October. Rumiantsev was able to return to work in Leningrad by 1930, but remained under OGPU surveillance. Following Kirov's fierce attack on former oppositionists at the June 1930 regional party committee conference, Leningrad authorities ordered Rumiantsev out of the city, assigning him work at the Magnitogorsk construction site east of the Urals. He was allowed back to Leningrad some months later. After his return the Vyborg Ward office of the OGPU interviewed him at least once (early 1932) about possible continuing links with the opposition. In the fall of 1933 Filip Medved ordered Rumiantsev's arrest, as part of an all-union campaign to "liquidate" Trotskyite and Zinovievite groups. Medved also planned to pick up a number of other former Trotsky and Zinoviev supporters, including Vladimir Levin, who would be tried with Rumiantsev for Kirov's murder in December 1934. Kirov blocked the arrests of Rumiantsev and Levin (the other arrests went ahead), saying that he wished to talk personally to Rumiantsev. Apparently as a result of this conversation, Rumiantsev wrote a letter of repentance directly to Stalin. Soon after these steps, in April 1934, he was appointed secretary of the Vyborg Ward soviet, certainly with Kirov's approval.[74]

Rumiantsev was not the only ex-oppositionist promoted during the thaw in attitudes towards ex-oppositionists that culminated at the Seventeenth Party Congress. Vyborg Ward party secretary Pyotr Smorodin (together with Nikolai Bukharin) sponsored a request by the physicist and secret police collaborator D. L. Talmud that OGPU chief Filip Medved assign the former Leningrad Komsomol official Ivan Kotolynov, an ex-Zinovievite, to work in his lab. Also in the winter of 1933–1934 some former Zinoviev supporters were allowed to join the Fellowship of Komsomol Militants (*Boevoe zemliachestvo*), an organization of Komsomol veterans who had served in the Civil War. Attached to the Komsomol section of the Leningrad Institute of Party History, the Fellowship published articles and a book on the history of the Komsomol in the Russian Civil War. The book, *The Petrograd Komsomol in the Civil War,* had at least one identifiable former Zinovievite, Georgy Popov, on the editorial board. It presented Stalin in politically correct fashion as the leader of the defense of Petrograd in the spring of 1919. However, it seems that the editors offended by their inclusion of a document referring to M. M. Lashevich, a supporter of the United Opposition in 1926–1927, and by their omission of even a pro forma denunciation of the Zinovievite opposition.[75]

In 1950 the former Leningrad journalist Zavalishin, citing several acquaintances, including onetime *Red Gazette* editor Chagin, laid out a story-line in which Kirov began rehabilitating select ex-oppositionists with skills useful to the state in late 1933. According to Zavalishin, Kirov met with Kotolynov, which led to hopes of rehabilitation among wider circles of former oppositionists. However, other sources show that by July 1934 tolerance for the ex-Zinovievites in Leningrad was already running out. A number were kicked out of the editorial "brigade" connected to the Fellowship of Komsomol Militants. At a stormy meeting at party headquarters in Smolny, Vladimir Rumiantsev was forced to defend himself against charges of links to Zinovievites on the brigade. *The Petrograd Komsomol in the Civil War* disappeared from circulation.[76]

The dichotomies of "repression" versus "legality" or "hard line" versus "soft line" often used in analysis of the year 1934 are not adequate. This was a very complex period. Stalin was considering a major turn in foreign policy, at the same time as he sought to stabilize Soviet society following the chaos of collectivization and the First Five Year Plan. The growing threat of war with Germany and/or Japan was another motivation to seek social stability. At the same time the dictator was growing increasingly impatient with the Old Bolshevik elite of the party. In letters to Kaganovich dating from 1931–1934 he referred to senior party officials individually and collectively in terms of contempt. They were incompetent and loud-mouthed "bureaucratic grandees," "idiots," "appanage princes." Senior journalists, he thought, had a "Bolshevik-philistine striving to generate noise and empty blather."[77]

Different problems required different approaches. Targeted repression combined with "legality" could help to build social stability and prepare for war. Courting the French or British might require a certain show of "moderation" in domestic affairs. On the other hand, corrupt or incompetent officials needed to be threatened or outright repressed. Analysis of policy during this period is further complicated by the fact that Stalin was often deliberately vague about his own policy preferences, to keep his options open and his subordinates guessing.

The Fall of 1934: Sochi and Kazakhstan

One important part of the campaign to stabilize society in 1934 was the aggressive revival of "patriotism" and the first steps to construct a national history that would rehabilitate elements of Russia's Tsarist past and glorify individual heroes. David Brandenberger traces the origins of this campaign to 1931, but describes a significant acceleration in March 1934 at Stalin's initiative. At two Politburo sessions that month Stalin demanded that Soviet historians throw over the dry "sociological" Marxist history they had been writing and produce textbooks for Soviet schoolchildren that described heroic individuals and their actions in history. In particular he sanctioned the presentation of the Soviet Union as a successor state to the Russian Empire. The Russian Empire's "gathering of the peoples" could be presented as a net positive for those peoples, and the Soviet "gathering of the peoples" as homologous.[78]

Revisions in the presentation of Russian history were part of a larger effort to construct a middlebrow Soviet culture that would promote order, loyalty to the state, and family stability. The asceticism, iconoclasm, and lawlessness of the revolutionary period would be replaced. Stalin was seeking cadres for this project, and he evidently settled on Kirov and Andrei Zhdanov, both of whom were relatively well-read and culturally literate, to take part. As early as June 1, 1933, the Politburo placed Kirov on a commission charged with reviewing the musical repertoire of the Russian Republic's Musical Trust as well as technical aspects of record and radio production. One year later, in July 1934, he was assigned to the commission on preparations to commemorate the hundredth anniversary of the death of poet Alexander Pushkin. Although Kirov did not live to see it, the 1937 commemoration campaign birthed a quasi-sacred Pushkin cult that became central to Soviet culture.[79]

In the summer of 1934 Stalin invited Kirov and Zhdanov for a working vacation at the Black Sea resort of Sochi, where they would write instructions for a new generation of history textbooks. Kirov arrived somewhere between August 1 and 3, 1934, and the three men immediately set to work. On August 13 they sent to Politburo members their comments on a précis for the new textbooks prepared by professional historians. The notes were, as David Brandenberger argues, a "transitional stage" between the Marxist internationalism of the 1920s and "the emerging russocentric étatism of the late 1930s." They did not express a simple-minded Russian nationalism, but rather a synthesis of Marxist world history with a more sympathetic view of the Russian state and people than had prevailed in the 1920s. Rather than abusing "Russia" for its imperialism and colonialism, Stalin, Kirov, and Zhdanov targeted "Tsarism," and "the Russian bourgeoisie and landlords." They also emphasized that the Western "bourgeois" powers shared with Tsarism the guilt for imperialism and World War I. Consciously or not, the stage was being set for the exaltation of "the great Russian people."[80]

Kirov was well suited for the task of synthesizing Marxist theory with a patriotic history of the Russian state. As Kirilina shows, he was well-read in literature, history, and philosophy, owning a library of twenty thousand books many of which were heavily marked up. Moreover, as far back as the *Terek* days, Kirov had understood socialism as a means of modernizing, democratizing, and strengthening the Russian state. His view of the Soviet project's relation to Russian history as a whole was consonant with Stalin's own evolving vision. Although some scholars have suggested that Kirov did not take an active part in composing the Sochi notes, Kirilina argues otherwise. The content of the notes prepared in Sochi closely resembles parts of a presentation Kirov gave in July 1934 to the city party committee of Leningrad, entitled "Facts about Our Schools."[81]

On August 14, 1934 the Politburo in Moscow rubberstamped the notes authored by Stalin, Kirov, and Zhdanov. Zhdanov left Sochi soon after. Kirov departed on August 23 or 24, while Stalin remained.[82]

Kirov's private communications from Sochi to his wife, as well as to his subordinate in Leningrad, A. I. Ugarov, show that he had no fun on this "vacation." To Ugarov he wrote on August 16, "By the caprice of fate I've ended up in Sochi, and I'm unhappy about it—the heat here is not 'tropical,' it's hellish." On the same day he wrote his wife that "I am devilishly sick of this place, I'm planning on leaving on the twentieth. The weather here is awful. We had intense heat, then six days and nights of intense rain." And, in another letter to Maria Lvovna, undated, "The heat here is unbearable. You can't walk, can't play for example *gorodki* [a Russian lawn game somewhat resembling bowling], things are completely impossible." Kirov complained to Maria Lvovna that he was bored, could not sleep, and had a bad sunburn.[83]

The fact that Kirov did not enjoy Sochi does not suggest that he was on the outs with Stalin. He does not mention the dictator at all in letters to his wife, a safe enough course of action. First and foremost, he hated the heat. Probably too, being on "vacation" with a capricious, domineering, and manipulative boss was not pleasant. Many loyal Stalinists did not enjoy spending time with "the Chief." Andrei Zhdanov, according to his son Yury, was tense throughout his stay in Sochi that summer. Nikita Khrushchev described several times in his memoirs just how miserable spending time with Stalin could be. "During the war, when I visited Moscow," he recounted, "I suffered. Almost every evening I would get a call from Stalin. 'Come over, we'll have dinner together.' The dinners were horrible; we would return home only toward morning before breakfast. . . ." Stalin threw tomatoes at those who fell asleep.[84]

Whatever his innermost feelings, Kirov was by 1934 a regular and seemingly welcome guest of Stalin. Their personal relationship went back at least a decade. Stalin, Kirov, and Ordzhonikidze had vacationed together at the North Caucasus mineral spa of Kislovodsk in the summer of 1925. Stalin stayed at Kirov's apartment when he visited Leningrad in July 1928. In September 1931 Kirov visited Stalin on the Black Sea. Stalin reported to his wife, Nadezhda Alliluyeva, that "I've been having a good time with Kirov," playing *gorodki* and swimming in the Black Sea. When Stalin, Kirov, Voroshilov, and Yenukidze made their trip up the Baltic–White Sea Canal in July 1933, Kirov was at pains to make sure that every detail of "the Chief's" visit went well. He personally drove the route Stalin took from Moscow beforehand, and he importuned his secretary Sveshnikov to make sure that Stalin had at hand all of important Soviet newspapers.[85]

Relations among members of Stalin's inner circle became considerably more complex following the suicide of his wife, Nadezhda Allilueva, on November 9, 1932. There is some evidence that Stalin leaned on Kirov psychologically following his wife's death, although it may well be tainted by the posthumous Kirov cult. Kirilina asserts that Stalin called Kirov to invite him to Allilueva's funeral and Kirov attended. According to the 1935 memoirs of Ordzhonikidze's wife Zinaida and the 1940 recollections of Maria Lvovna's sister S. L.

Markus, after Allilueva killed herself, Kirov generally stayed at Stalin's apartment when he visited Moscow (previously he had stayed at Ordzhonikidze's). However that may be, Allilueva's death must have made personal relations with Stalin more awkward for his close associates. It was widely known in the upper ranks of party officialdom that Allilueva died a suicide, and it was suspected that Stalin's abuse contributed to her distress.[86]

On the surface at least Stalin and Kirov had a very warm relationship right up to the latter's death. There is remarkable testimony for this in diary entries from November 1934 by Maria Svanidze, the sister-in-law of Stalin's first wife, Yekaterina, who died of typhus in 1907. On November 4, Maria described an informal gathering in Moscow the previous day, during which Stalin called Kirov to invite him to visit "at least for a day." He joked about the forthcoming end of rationing and told Kirov he had to come in order to make sure that prices were not set too high for goods in Leningrad. Kirov apparently demurred, and Stalin handed the phone to Kaganovich, who continued trying to persuade him to come to Moscow. "Stalin loves Kirov," she commented, "and obviously wanted to see him after Sochi, take a Russian steam bath, and clown around. . . ."[87]

Ultimately Kirov did respond to Stalin's summons. On the evening of November 13 Kirov, Stalin, and Stalin's son Vasily visited Stalin's summer house at Zubalovo together, where Maria Svanidze saw them. They had tea together, played billiards, watched a puppet show put on by Stalin's daughter Svetlana and other children, then left in a fast motorcade to have dinner at a different dacha. That night the Zubalovo household ate smelt and whitefish Kirov had sent, perhaps the catch from one of his fishing expeditions. Twelve days later, Svanidze noted that Svetlana, then age nine, was closer to Kirov than to other party leaders. "With Kirov she has a great friendship (because I. [Stalin] is especially close and good with him)."[88]

Svanidze's diary confirms memoir evidence that Stalin and Kirov got along well. Thirty years later Svetlana Allilueva remembered Kirov fondly, writing that, "my father liked him and was attached to him." In 1992 Stalin's guard A. T. Rybin claimed that Stalin and Kirov were very close, and that Kirov was the only person with whom Stalin would take a steam bath naked. N. S. Vlasik, the head of Stalin's bodyguard, wrote in the 1960s that Stalin loved Kirov and the latter's visits were "real holidays" for the dictator. Yury Zhdanov (Andrei's son) who was in Sochi with his father, Stalin, and Kirov in August 1934, remembered that the three got on well, in spite of the tension his father felt.[89]

At one level, the question of Kirov's and Stalin's personal friendship is irrelevant. Many people who knew Stalin have commented that he was a great actor, expert at concealing his real feelings and thoughts. He was undoubtedly capable of greeting someone warmly while plotting against them. Also, surface civility among top leaders and their families in the Stalinist elite often concealed bitter political rivalries. In December 1934, for example, Maria Svanidze's husband Aleksandr would denounce Avel Yenukidze to the NKVD for supposedly plotting a coup against the Soviet leadership.[90] Svanidze and Yenukidze saw Stalin regularly together in cordial home circumstances. Taking all of this into account, however, it is still true that Stalin usually gave signals when one person or another was out of favor, and he generally did not remain as close to subordinates in disgrace as he remained with Kirov to the end.

More evidence that Kirov remained part of the Stalinist inner circle in late 1934 is his assignment to visit Kazakhstan in September 1934 to monitor the grain harvest. Soon after Kirov left Sochi that August, Stalin became impatient with the pace of grain procurements, which had fallen behind 1933 numbers. In an angry letter to Kaganovich, he accused his subordinates of complacency and ordered them to "organize a squeeze" on officials and peasants. He emphasized the need for "tax-cash pressure" to his lieutenant, just as Kirov and Irklis were doing in Leningrad at the same time. However, he did go one step further than Kirov, when he wrote that he was "not against a few coercive measures undertaken 'on your own hook.'" On Stalin's instructions, Kaganovich moved quickly to mobilize members of the Politburo and TsK Secretariat to travel to key regions to put the "squeeze" on local authorities. In the first days of September Molotov was dispatched to Western Siberia, Kaganovich to Ukraine, Voroshilov to Belarus and the Western Region, Mikoyan to the Kursk and Voronezh area, Chubar to the Middle Volga, Zhdanov to Stalingrad, and Kirov to Kazakhstan (two lesser-known officials, Kleiner and Chernov, were also sent to the provinces). Such expeditions had been standard procedure for the harvest season since the late 1920s. Stalin seems to have tailored the assignments to his subordinates' personalities. Molotov and Kaganovich, well-known as the most merciless of the Stalinist cohort, were sent to the two most important and troublesome regions, Western Siberia and Ukraine. Voroshilov, not a particularly effective leader, went to the less fertile areas of western Russia and Belarus. It was almost certainly Stalin who assigned Kirov to Kazakhstan, where the latter's protégé Levon Mirzoian was in charge. The Politburo had assigned Mirzoian there in January 1933, after the state drive to force nomadic herders to join collective farms led to mass starvation and a flood of refugees into neighboring republics. Because the territory was still recovering, Stalin himself sanctioned a relatively "soft" line in Kazakhstan in 1934, blocking the central confiscation of some of the grain reserves that had been sent there in response to the famine.[91]

Matthew Payne believes that one purpose of Kirov's visit to the Kazakh territory was "establishing Mirzoian as a good Stalinist." The latter was in an awkward position in early 1934. Following Central Committee orders, he had been castigating Russian cadres in Kazakhstan for their "great power chauvinism" (Russian nationalism) since his appointment to the republic leadership. In late 1933, however, the party line on nationalism for the entire USSR shifted. Local "bourgeois nationalism" was now supposed to be a greater danger than Russian nationalism. Mirzoian scrambled to toe the new line and establish that he was not a supporter of Kazakh "bourgeois nationalists." Kirov's presence also signaled Stalin's visible support for maintaining some central food aid to the republic and continuing relatively moderate state grain procurement targets.[92]

Kirov left Leningrad on September 3 and Moscow on the fourth, traveling to Central Asia by train. In Kazakhstan he dismissed some local officials he judged as incompetent, issued party censures to others, and expelled several from the party. He threatened MTS chiefs with firing if they failed to meet procurement targets, precisely the kind of pressure that tended to motivate abuse of peasants by lower-ranking apparatchiks. In certain ways, however, Kirov's behavior and rhetoric were relatively temperate. While a lower-ranking TsK plenipotentiary in Kazakhstan attributed low procurements to "sabotage . . . organized by kulak elements," Kirov did not use such inflammatory terms. He also requested from Commissar of Internal Affairs Yagoda the firing of several NKVD officers he believed guilty of neglecting or abusing peasants deported to the region. Finally, he secured from the USSR Prosecutor's Office the firing of the head prosecutor for the East Kazakhstan Region, whom he charged with "breaches of revolutionary socialist legality."[93]

Were Kirov's actions against NKVD commissars and prosecutors in Kazakhstan exceptional for the time? The answer is no. Once more he seems to have been in remarkably close concurrence with Stalin's line of the moment. That fall Stalin took several actions aimed at clipping the wings of the NKVD and restricting extralegal methods of investigation. In September he created a Politburo commission to investigate accusations that a 1933 case against "agronomist-wreckers" supposedly spying for Japan had been partially fabricated by the OGPU using "incorrect methods of investigation." In October and November the commission uncovered other instances of OGPU torture and entrapment using provocateurs, in Saratov Region and Azerbaijan. Members prepared a draft Politburo resolution on "rooting out illegal methods of investigation," but Kirov's murder scotched the project.[94]

Kirov's removal of the East Kazakhstan prosecutor fit quite specifically with the mood among Stalin's closest collaborators in late summer and early fall 1934. On August 1, Kaganovich wrote to Stalin in Sochi about a meeting of prosecutors he chaired in Moscow. Kaganovich, who generally mirrored Stalin's opinions as closely as possible, criticized the prosecutors in attendance as unqualified and noted that too many people were being tried. In some regions more than half of those convicted were acquitted on appeal. This was presumably the kind of problem Kirov sought to remedy in Kazakhstan.[95]

Yet it is also necessary to say that Stalin's actions with regard to the organs of repression in the fall of 1934 were complex and their motives difficult to discern. The situation is further muddied by the development of a bureaucratic war between the NKVD and the prosecutors' offices following the TsK's division of investigation, arrest, and trial functions between them in the summer of 1934. On the one hand Stalin apparently wished tighter control over the activities of the secret police headed by Yagoda. After Yagoda issued an order creating special courts inside NKVD labor camps on August 9, 1943, Stalin had the Politburo rescind the instructions on October 17. This did not mean, however, that he forswore heavy use of state coercion. In September the Politburo dispatched the newly organized Military Collegium of the Supreme Court to the provinces to try espionage cases and empowered troikas to issue summary death sentences.[96] For Stalin the emphasis on "revolutionary legality" had to do with establishing order and riding herd on the NKVD, not necessarily with any concern for reducing state violence. Part of establishing order was making a clear functional differentiation between the NKVD, responsible for intelligence gathering and investigation, and the prosecutorial and judicial organs, responsible for trying cases.

What Stalin wanted from the secret police section of the NKVD (re-named the GUGB or Main Directorate of State Security in July 1934) was greater professionalism, better intelligence collection, and more aggressive but finely targeted investigations. Secret police work, he believed, was sloppy, ineffective, and crude. Senior NKVD officials in the months following the Seventeenth Party Congress instructed their sub-ordinates frequently to implement the May 8, 1933 TsK resolution calling for the targeting of individual kulaks rather than mass deporta-tions.[97] To replace the blunt instrument of "mass operations" with ar-rests of individual "anti-Soviet elements," the secret police needed bet-ter intelligence. To achieve this, the OGPU/NKVD command wanted officers to recruit and supervise informers more carefully. Paid officers were to find more and better qualified "residents," the unpaid agents who stayed in contact with a much wider network of "informers." They were to supervise the residents more closely. In addition the paid officers were to target identified anti-Soviet groups by recruiting "spe-cial informers" who would organize provocations, for example throw-ing parties with police money at which attendees would be encouraged to express anti-Soviet sentiments. Paid informers were not to receive a flat fee for their service, but "reward" payments for specific informa-tion. Overall the point was to winkle out elusive and wily enemies. The class enemy, according to a March 11, 1935 NKVD circular, had "gone into the deep underground" following multiple defeats. The se-cret police had to go deep as well, to dig the enemy out.[98]

From the summer of 1934 if not earlier, Stalin apparently felt that many NKVD officers were not carrying out the new instructions. In some areas indiscriminate arrests continued, in others senior comman-ders had simply interpreted the new course as an excuse to slack off. The first secretary had in mind specific provincial police chiefs whom he aimed to fire, and one of them was Medved.

We know this from an October 1934 memorandum from Yagoda to Stalin found in the Russian presidential archive. According to this doc-ument, in the early fall of 1934, at the conclusion of the summer holi-days, Stalin ordered Yagoda to send investigative commissions to check the Leningrad and West Siberian NKVD directorates. The commis-sion's findings are not available, and second-hand commentary on them is contradictory. In all probability, given the politically loaded context (Yagoda and Stalin wanted Medved out of Leningrad, Kirov may have wanted him to stay), the commission members hedged their bets. On the one hand, they found that Medved and his officers were not devoting enough energy to working up cases against Trotskyites, ex-Mensheviks, and former Socialist Revolutionaries. There were "serious shortcomings in agent-operational and investigative work." On the other hand, the report recognized the Leningrad department's work as "satisfactory" overall.[99]

In his comments to Stalin, however, Yagoda took a clearer stand.

> The actual situation found as a result of the investigations in both Novosibirsk [capital of the West Siberian Region] and Leningrad, has convinced me that neither Alekseev [Nikolai Nikolaevich, head of the West Siberian NKVD] nor Medved is in any way capable of supervising work under the new conditions and guaranteeing that sharp turn in methods of work that is now necessary in the protection of state security.
>
> The reorganization of the agent apparatus and investigative work, in accordance with TsK directives . . . and my orders, has not been carried out in either region. . . .
>
> Alekseev criminally slept through the sabotage of the grain procurements in the region and not only failed to carry on the struggle with kulak saboteurs, but did not even signal it, because he did not see what was going on.
>
> Unable to organize the work of the Directorate of State Security along new lines, Alekseev has in fact disgracefully neglected the struggle with the counterrevolution that is underway in the West Siberian Region.
>
> The situation in Medved's jurisdiction is approximately the same as in Novosibirsk.
>
> Various serious lines of work, especially having to do with the countryside and agent-operational protection of the border from Finns and other refugees and spies, as well as with the organization of the struggle with diversions [in other words sabotage] in the factories, are in a completely unsatisfactory state.[100]

Yagoda proposed to fire Alekseev and Medved, and publicize the move in an NKVD circular to make examples of them. Medved he wished to replace with Leonid Zakovsky, a veteran of dekulakization and head of the Belorussian NKVD, where he had conducted an aggressive operation against a supposed Polish espionage organization in 1933. Stalin admired Zakovsky for his scorched-earth approach to policing. Yagoda recommended transferring Medved to a central job in Moscow, to see "if he is still fit for work in the NKVD or if he is completely burned out" (*uzhe sovsem vyrabotalsia*).[101]

Stalin also showed signs of impatience in the summer and fall of

1934 with recently rehabilitated oppositionists, and this too may have helped to motivate Yagoda's memorandum. On July 14 he chastised Bukharin, now editor of the official state newspaper *Izvestia,* for a May article implying that the Soviet Union had developed heavy industry at the expense of light industry.[102] In August he had Zinoviev fired from his new job on the editorial board of the lead theoretical journal *Bolshevik.*[103] It seems plausible that NKVD instructions issued in August for the arrest of fourteen ex-Zinovievites in Leningrad, including Vladimir Rumiantsev and Ivan Kotolynov, were linked with Stalin's anger at Zinoviev. Kirov signed off on these instructions, but then, according to Medved, canceled the operation.[104] According to the 1956 testimony of Fyodor Fomin, second deputy to Medved, the August arrest list actually included 107 Trotskyites and Zinovievites in Leningrad. Fomin claimed that Kirov told Medved that he did not have the authority to sanction the arrests himself, but had to check with Stalin. Aside from abstract support for "revolutionary legality" (there was no good evidence against the former Zinovievites), there is at least one concrete reason Kirov may have rescinded the arrest orders. In September 1934 the Politburo commission set up by Stalin to investigate violations of "legal methods of investigation" began its work. Given Kirov's handling of Rumiantsev's case in 1933 it is probable that he intended to check with Stalin on the disposition of the ex-Zinovievites when he visited Moscow for the November TsK plenum. Fomin's recollection does not suggest a Kirov who was resisting the arrest of former oppositionists on principle, but a Kirov very concerned to do precisely what Stalin wanted.[105]

It is impossible to be sure whether Kirov still supported Medved in the fall of 1934. Rosliakov claims that early in the year Kirov told him that he wanted Medved to remain in Leningrad. It is entirely possible, however, that the situation had changed by September or October. Kirov had always known how to choose the winning side, and there was clearly nothing to be gained by backing Medved against Yagoda and Stalin. N. F. Sveshnikov in 1960 and 1966 reported tension between the Leningrad leader and his police chief in 1934. In addition the journalist Zavalishin reported hearing in the summer of 1934 that Kirov was unhappy with a trial of local agronomists charged with "wrecking" that Medved had organized. If Kirov was turning on Medved it would not have been the first time he betrayed a colleague or subordinate. Whatever the case, it is entirely possible that he resolved the Medved problem as well as the disposition of the former Zinovievites in private conversation with Stalin when he visited Moscow in November.[106]

The situation in the fall of 1934 was absolutely typical for Stalinist politics. No one was sure of the dictator's precise line on the NKVD, the status of ex-oppositionists, or repression in the countryside. This left a certain latitude for local workers to try to define the line themselves. Stalin often deliberately cultivated such ambiguity. He also played off one subordinate against another, and he may have been playing off Yagoda against Kirov in the fall of 1934. In this difficult situation, however, Kirov had two advantages. First, Stalin apparently kept him relatively well-informed about his policy preferences, as witnessed by the precision with which Kirov's own moves tracked Stalin's initiatives in many areas. Second, Kirov had a well-honed aptitude for following the Central Committee line exactly.

From November 25 through 28, 1934 Kirov attended a plenary session of the Central Committee in Moscow. The plenum focused on the forthcoming end of rationing. Stalin, Kaganovich, and Molotov were the major speakers. The stenographic report shows that Kirov did not play a particularly prominent role, contrary to later rumors. It was in fact Stalin who dominated the plenum, explaining the great importance of market prices and money for the Soviet economy, and justifying his initiative to abolish the rationing of basic food products.[107]

Upon his return from Moscow, Kirov received, but never opened, a plaintive letter from his sisters, Anna and Yelizaveta, whom he had not seen or written to in almost thirty years. Yelizaveta had sent him a letter in December 1932, which Kirov had never replied to. The 1934 letter, dated November 18, reveals a great deal about the sisters' resentment of their powerful brother, the vast gulf between governing and governed in early Soviet society, and the hard conditions in the Russian countryside. Amy Knight refers to it as "an implicit reproach about the discrepancy between (Kirov's) lofty words and . . . grim reality."[108]

The purpose of the letter seems to have been to convince Kirov to pay for Anna, Yelizaveta, and their families to visit Leningrad in the summer of 1935. The sisters gave basic family news. Both were schoolteachers in Kirov's hometown of Urzhum, and Yelizaveta had a son and daughter. They were already "old ladies," they complained, isolated, living on low pay and inadequate rations. Yelizaveta's son had never seen a train, and the first car had visited Urzhum only in 1933. The letter painted a harrowing picture of rural oppression and poverty. The peasants were overtaxed, sometimes even assigned grain quotas

for nonexistent land. If anyone complained about this at a village soviet meeting, "they shut him up." When a bad harvest compounded
their difficulties, many peasants fled the region for Odessa and western
Siberia. There were not enough left behind to do the spring sowing in
1935. In spite of all the hardships, "no one dares to speak up."

Yelizaveta, who had composed the letter, was put out that Kirov had
ignored her 1932 note. In classically passive-aggressive fashion, she
noted that all of her neighbors "were surprised that we do not correspond with you." Then she let loose a damning condemnation of
Kirov, not very subtly concealed as an assurance that she understood
the reasons for her brother's aloofness.

> I wrote, and you did not answer, not because you are prideful and con-
> ceited—no. I know that you have a lot of work, and second as a non–
> party member I could unconsciously compromise you, but believe me
> that although I am non-party, just as Aniuta [Anna] is, we bear our la-
> bor honorably and we are trusted and respected by the local party or-
> gans.[109]

CHAPTER 4

The Scene of the Crime

E arly in the morning of Thursday, November 29, 1934 Kirov arrived back in Leningrad on the Red Arrow sleeper train from
Moscow. The Central Committee plenum that approved the end
of rationing was over. According to Rosliakov, Kirov traveled in a
train car with the Leningrad party delegation rather than using the separate coupé reserved for him. Rosliakov describes the atmosphere as
relaxed, as Kirov reviewed events at the plenum with his colleagues.
"It was very late before the conversations and laughter in the train car
quieted down," he concludes.[1]

Kirov's immediate task was to mobilize the Leningrad party organization to implement the Central Committee resolutions on the end of
rationing. The Soviet rulers had introduced rationing of bread and
other staple foods in 1928–1929, as a temporary means of controlling
scarce food supplies during the collectivization drive. By 1934 collectivization was largely accomplished, the First Five Year Plan was complete, and easier times were supposedly ahead. The Stalinist leadership
extolled the end of bread rationing as the beginning of an era of plenty
for the population, and Stalin himself declared the long-term importance of money and trade for Soviet socialism. Yet the move to end
bread rationing was politically ticklish, for it promised to arouse fear
and doubt among poorer factory workers, a group the Bolsheviks still
considered key for their dictatorship. Many less-skilled, lower-paid
workers feared that they would not be able to afford bread at the new
prices. Such fears were quite strong in Leningrad, which had received
somewhat more grain under the rationing system than most other ar-

eas of the Soviet Union. Kirov and his lieutenants in Leningrad faced a difficult job selling the populace on the end of rationing.[2]

Upon their return home, the Leningrad leaders followed the regular procedure for mobilizing the party after an important Central Committee decision. A meeting of Leningrad party activists open to all Communists (all Communists, that is, who could obtain tickets from responsible officials) was scheduled for 6:00 P.M. on December 1 at the Uritsky Palace. Then on December 2 there would be a joint plenary session of the Leningrad regional and city committees of the party.[3]

By noon on November 29 Kirov was at work on his speeches for both meetings at Smolny. That afternoon he chaired a joint meeting of the secretariats of the city and regional party committees that set the agenda for the December 2 plenum. Mikhail Chudov was charged with chairing a committee that would meet on December 1 at 3:00 P.M. to draft formal resolutions for the December 2 plenum. On November 30 Kirov visited construction sites in the city and put in more time on his speeches.[4]

On December 1, Kirov spent the day in his apartment preparing his presentation to the 6:00 P.M. meeting of party activists. Multiple memoirs of party officials and employees at Smolny attest to this. Rosliakov and Kirov's secretary, N. F. Sveshnikov, later remembered several phone calls from Kirov during the day requesting research materials for his speech. The courier M. F. Fyodorova delivered batches of documents to Kirov at least twice and reported that he answered the door himself because neither his wife nor the maid were at home. Some who talked on the telephone with Kirov had the impression that he was not coming to Smolny to work that day, but would go straight to the activists' meeting at 6:00 P.M. Sveshnikov, however, asserted later that it was Kirov's habit to stop at Smolny in the afternoon before major speeches, and he was expected.[5]

The committee to draft resolutions for next day's plenum convened in Chudov's office, next door to Kirov's, at 3:00 P.M. About twenty people, including Chudov, I. F. Kodatsky, P. I. Struppe, Mikhail Rosliakov, and other leaders of the Leningrad party, were present.[6]

At around 4 P.M. Kirov left his apartment for Smolny. That night two bodyguards on duty on the street outside Kirov's apartment building, Pyotr Pavlovich Laziukov and Karl Mikhailovich Pauzer, testified that they'd "received" him at 4:05 P.M. and walked behind him ("ten steps behind") along Krasnykh Zor Street to the Troitsky Bridge. An observation car followed them and a third guard walked ahead of the group. At the bridge Kirov boarded his own automobile and the guards got into the observation car. Both vehicles proceeded to Smolny. At the main entrance they were met by a group of guards assigned to cover Kirov's entrances and exits at party headquarters. According to Pauzer, Officer Mikhail Borisov, whose job was to guard Kirov inside Smolny, was there and followed Kirov up the main stairway.[7]

· 1 ·

Telegram to NKVD Commissar G. G. Yagoda from F. D. Medved, chief of the Leningrad Region NKVD, December 1, 1934, 6:20 P.M. RGANI, f. 6, op. 13, d. 71, l. 14.

On December 1 at 4:30 P.M. in the Smolny building on the third floor, twenty steps from the office of Comrade Kirov, Comrade Kirov was shot in the head by an unknown assailant who approached him, and who according to his documents is Nikolaev, Leonid Vasilievich, member of the Communist Party from 1924, born 1904.

Comrade Kirov is in his office.

With him are the professors of surgery Dobrotvorsky, Feert, Dzhanelidze, and other doctors.

Preliminary evidence is that Comrade Kirov went on foot from his apartment /Krasnykh Zor St./ to the Troitsky Bridge. Near the Troitsky Bridge he got into his car in the company of his guards, and drove to Smolny. His guard accompanied him to the third floor. On the third floor Kirov was accompanied to the point of the incident by Operations Agent Borisov. After wounding Comrade Kirov Nikolaev attempted to shoot himself, but failed. Nikolaev has been recognized by several employees of Smolny [. . .] as a former employee at Smolny.

The wife of the assassin Nikolaev is Graule [*sic*] Milda, a member of the Communist Party from 1919, she has worked at the Regional Committee of the All-Union Communist Party.

Nikolaev has been arrested and sent to the NKVD Directorate of the Leningrad Military District.

An order for the arrest of Graule has been issued. An investigation is underway at Smolny.

18:20, 12/1/34.

Medved.

Witness statements to police during the evening of December 1 confirm the general outlines of Medved's account. There are, however, two clear inaccuracies in the telegram. First, Medved misspells the last name of Nikolaev's wife, which in fact was "Draule." Second, he implies that the guard Borisov, assigned to protect Kirov inside Smolny, was with the party leader when Nikolaev fired. However, Borisov himself and other witnesses testified on the evening of December 1 that he was walking well behind Kirov at the moment of the assassination. Understandably, Medved did not want to divulge this evidence of possible NKVD negligence.

· 2 ·

Interrogation of Mikhail Borisov, evening of December 1, 1934. RGANI, f. 6, op. 13, d. 71, l. 14.

At approximately 4:30 Comrade Kirov exited his car alone and entered the regional committee building [Smolny]. In the vestibule I was walking behind him at a distance of about fifteen steps. I stayed at this distance up to the second floor. When I stepped onto the first flight of stairs, Comrade Kirov was already on the landing between the first and second floors, and that's how I followed him to the third floor entrance. Once I reached the corridor [on the third floor] I followed him at a distance of twenty steps. Not quite two steps from the turn to the left corridor [on which Kirov's office was located] I heard a shot. As I was pulling my revolver from its holster and cocking it, I heard a second shot. Running down the left corridor I saw two [persons] lying on the floor by the doors to Comrade Chudov's reception room. They lay three-quarters of a meter apart. Next to them lay a Nagan [a common Russian pistol make]. In that same corridor I saw that there was the electrician Platoch. Right away regional committee employees came running out of their offices. I don't remember their names.
Operations Commissar Borisov
Interrogator: Molochnikov

Interrogator Molochnikov later testified that Borisov was extremely upset and unable at first to give direct answers to simple questions. Given Borisov's distraction and his probable desire to cover up his failure to protect Kirov, he may have omitted a lot from his account. Two Smolny employees later claimed to have met Kirov while he was on his way to his third-floor office, and conversed briefly with him, facts Borisov did not report. Borisov also did not mention seeing Nikolaev following Kirov in the main corridor, as the guard should have done if he had had his charge in sight at all on the third floor. Therefore it seems that Borisov was even further behind Kirov than he claimed. He could not have stepped onto the third floor until Kirov and Nikolaev had both taken the turn into the small side corridor. In the 1960s Rosliakov and N. F. Sveshnikov both remembered Borisov appearing at the crime scene only after a sizeable crowd had gathered.[8]

After talking to Borisov, Molochnikov interviewed electrician Seliverst Alekseevich Platoch, whom Borisov saw in the corridor where Kirov was shot. Platoch had been at an electrical box in the main corridor checking circuit-breakers after the lights in some offices went out (investigators later found that electricians in the basement had been testing the breakers, switching the lights on and off). He then met storage clerk Grigory Vasiliev, who asked him for help carrying typewriters from the Secret Department downstairs and over to the Uritsky Palace for the 6:00 P.M. meeting of the activists.[9]

· 3 ·

"Interrogation of Platoch, Seliverst Alekseevich, electrician, [. . .] born 1905, member of the All-Union Communist Party," evening of December 1, 1934. RGANI, f. 6, op. 13, d. 44, l. 22.

Kotulov, an employee of the Mutual Aid Society of the regional committee, dropped in on me in room 451 and asked me to fix the lights in specific rooms and the corridor. When I went to the circuit-breaker box I found that one breaker (*faza*) was not on—then it turned on by itself. Obviously someone below in the basement was turning the lights on and off. When the lights were turned on in all the rooms, I set off for the typing pool [in the Secret Department] to get the typewriters. The supplies clerk Grigory Grigorevich Vasiliev also came with me for the typewriters. Going along the [main] corridor to the left corridor, we saw that Comrade Kirov was catching up with us from behind. Vasiliev asked me to close the glass door in the left corridor leading to the No. 4 cafeteria [at the far end of the left corridor].[10] I ran about eight to ten steps ahead of Kirov, and suddenly heard a shot behind me, when I turned a second shot rang out. I saw that Comrade Kirov was lying on the floor, and a second [person] was slowly sliding to the floor, leaning on the wall. This person had a Nagan in his hands, which I took out of his hands, when I took the Nagan from the hands of the person who shot Kirov he seemed to be unconscious.

Platoch

Interrogator: Molochnikov

One day later Platoch testified to a slightly different version of events. Rather than removing the Nagan from Nikolaev's hand, he picked it off the floor next to Nikolaev and threw it aside. Then, he asserted, he hit Nikolaev two times in the face. On December 9, Platoch's interrogator Molochnikov stated that Platoch had in fact told him about hitting Nikolaev in his first [December 1] interrogation but that he [Molochnikov] had not written that down. Molochnikov also noted that "on the first night Nikolaev did indeed complain that someone hit him." Evidence taken on December 1 from G. A. Yalozo, an official with the Leningrad Housing Authority, confirms that Platoch had already told a number of people that evening that he'd hit Nikolaev.[11]

Other statements by witnesses on the evening of December 1 gave the same general picture—two shots heard, two bodies and a revolver on the floor outside Chudov's office, Kirov face down, Nikolaev on his back or sliding down the wall towards the floor.

· 4 ·

"Protocol of interrogation of Mikhail Lioninok, born 1896, *instruktor* at the Leningrad City Party Committee, by Leningrad Chief of Police Zhupakhin," December 1, 1934. TsA FSB RF, a.u.d. N-Sh44, t. 24, l. 81.

At the moment of the shot I was in the reception room of the Secret Department of the regional committee. The first shot rang out, I threw down my papers, opened the door leading to the corridor, and saw a person with a Nagan in his hands who was screaming, waving the revolver over his head. I pushed the door almost closed. He shot again and fell. After that the Secret Department employees and I left the reception room and entered the corridor. In the corridor, on the floor, opposite the door to Comrade Chudov's office, lay Comrade Kirov face down, and in back of him, one meter behind, lay the person who had shot him, on his back, with his arms spread out wide.

In the corridor a lot of people had already gathered, including Comrades Chudov, Kodatsky, Pozern [all secretaries of the Leningrad regional party committee] and others.

Medical help was immediately called. The shooter began to stir, to raise himself off the ground. I detained him and began to search him, bringing him into a separate room /no. 493, Information Department/. At the same time other comrades carried the wounded Kirov into his office. . . .

Lioninok

Interrogator: Zhupakhin.

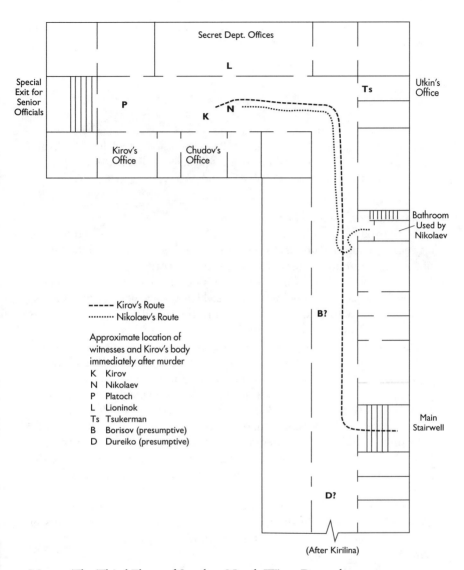

Map 3. The Third Floor of Smolny, North Wing, December 1, 1934.
Based on Alla Kirilina, *Neizvestnyi Kirov* (Moscow: OLMA-PRESS, 2001).

Another witness interrogated on December 1 was Leningrad Circus director Mikhail Tsukerman.

· 5 ·

"Interrogation of Mikhail Tsukerman, born 1886, director of the Leningrad State Circus, member of the Communist Party from 1918 [. . .], by Babushkin, officer of the Secret Political Department (Leningrad NKVD)," evening of December 1, 1934. TsA FSB RF, a.u.d. N-Sh44, t. 24, ll. 84–85.

Statement of essential facts.

At approximately 4:30 P.M. on December 1 I was on my way to see the city party committee *instruktory* Utkin and Voites. As I entered the offices of the city committee, I heard two shots, one after the other. Turning I saw Comrade Borisov from Comrade Kirov's guard. Borisov at the moment was cocking his Browning [probably used here as a generic term for a pistol]. Together with Utkin [. . .] I ran into the corridor leading to the offices of Comrades Kirov and Chudov.

The light in the corridor was dim. Right away I saw a person who appeared to be unconscious lying face up in a fur-lined jacket. Just a little bit ahead of him lay a person turned face down, in the left hand there was a portfolio. Beside him were Comrades Chudov, Kodatsky and the head of the city Health Department Bogen, who was taking his pulse. I immediately recognized the person lying on the floor as Comrade Kirov.

Comrade Utkin and I turned around right away and stood at the exit from the passage [onto the main corridor], so as not to let anyone into the corridor. We stood there until officers of the [Smolny] guard arrived.

After that I and a group of comrades spoke with city committee *instruktor* Nikitina. The latter stated that a few minutes earlier she saw Comrade Kirov walking along the corridor and greeted him, and a person she later recognized as the arrested man [Nikolaev] was walking in front of him. [. . .]

M. Tsukerman.
Interrogator: Babushkin.

Why was Nikolaev in front of Kirov at the point Nikitina claimed to have seen him? In a December 3 statement Nikolaev said that he had been in the third-floor bathroom at Smolny around 4:30, and had run into Kirov (whom he had been stalking for about a month) by chance.

· 6 ·

Excerpt from interrogation of Leonid Nikolaev, December 3, 1934. TsA FSB RF,
a.u.d. N-Sh44, t. 12, ll. 15–16.

———————

Exiting the bathroom I turned left. After taking two or three steps I observed Sergei Mironovich Kirov approaching me along the right wall of
the corridor, perhaps 15–20 steps away. Seeing Sergei Mironovich Kirov,
I first stopped and turned my back on him, so that after he passed me, I
was looking at his back. Letting Kirov get 10–15 steps ahead, I noticed
that there was no one for a great distance around us. Then I followed behind Kirov, gradually overtaking him. When he turned the corner to the
left in the direction of his office, whose location I knew well, fully half of
the [left] corridor was empty—I ran up maybe five steps, pulled the Nagan
out of my pocket, aimed at Kirov's head, and shot him once in the back of
the head, Kirov fell instantly face down.

Nikitina presumably saw Nikolaev in front of Kirov just after the assassin exited the bathroom. In a later memoir another witness, Smolny
courier M. F. Fyodorova, wrote that she saw Nikolaev standing by the
wall, "bending over strangely," probably just before Kirov passed
him.[12]

In archives open to this author, there are interrogation records for
seven witnesses to the murder scene from the evening of December 1,
1934. In addition to Borisov, Platoch, Tsukerman, and Lioninok,
whose testimony is presented above, these are the storage clerk Grigory Vasiliev (mentioned in Platoch's interview); the guard Nikolai
Maksimovich Dureiko, charged that day with policing the Smolny
corridors; and Grigory Aleksandrovich Yalozo, an official with the
Leningrad Soviet Housing Authority.[13] All of these records confirm
one another on several important facts. There were two shots, separated by no more than a few seconds; Nikolaev and Kirov ended up lying on the ground in the small corridor outside Chudov's office, with a
crowd of employees and officials gathering around them; Kirov lay
head toward the "special entrance," and Nikolaev in the opposite direction, with his arms splayed out. Alla Kirilina writes that she has
seen accounts of the scene by participants in the planning meeting in
Chudov's office that also confirm this picture.[14]

It appears that Lioninok, followed by Platoch and Yalozo, were the
first to see Kirov and Nikolaev after the initial fatal shot. Lioninok, as
we have seen, testified to opening a door onto the corridor and seeing

Nikolaev standing, waving his revolver, and screaming incoherently. One week later Lioninok expanded on his testimony, explaining that he actually saw the flash of Nikolaev's second shot, and then shut the door. Afraid of the pistol, he kept the door shut for one and one-half to two minutes, until he heard voices in the hall. At this point he decided the coast was clear and emerged. There was already a sizeable group around the bodies, including members of the regional committee who had been in Chudov's office. Yalozo and Platoch both saw Nikolaev sliding down the wall after the second shot. This must have been moments after Lioninok saw him standing and waving the pistol.[15]

Other witnesses all appear to have arrived on the scene later, including Borisov. All reported Nikolaev lying on the ground, and a group of people gathered around the two prone bodies. Dureiko, for example, asserted that he was at the far end of the main corridor (that is at the main stairwell or beyond) and far from the murder scene when he heard the shots. By the time he arrived, there were many people already there.

In memoirs first put to paper about twenty-five years after the murder, Mikhail Rosliakov, a high-ranking finance official in Leningrad, also confirmed the overall picture. Rosliakov was in the meeting in Chudov's office at about 4:30 when all present heard two shots. A. Ivanchenko, an official sitting closest to the office door, "leapt" out into the corridor and just as quickly leapt back. Then Rosliakov entered the corridor and saw Kirov face down, completely still, with a portfolio or folder of documents under his left arm, and his head within four to six inches of Chudov's cabinet door. Behind Kirov was a man on his back, with his arms splayed and a revolver in his right hand, with his feet about one meter from Kirov's feet. The corridor quickly filled with people from the various offices, including Chudov and other secretaries of the Leningrad party committee. Some tried to kick Nikolaev, but Rosliakov claims that he and A. Ugarov stopped them.[16]

How trustworthy are the early witness statements reproduced in this chapter? How were they prepared and what was their purpose? These accounts were generally labeled "protocol" or "statement" (*pokazanie*) and they were not verbatim transcripts of everything witnesses said. They were summary statements prepared by the interrogating officer, containing what he considered the most salient facts, which the witness and officer both signed. Sometimes they were in the form of a single statement by the witness, sometimes they were presented in a question-and-answer format.

What was the purpose of the interrogation statements of December 1, 1934? A. M. Molochnikov, chief of the Economic Section of the Leningrad Region State Security Directorate, did many of the earliest interrogations and described them in a deposition on December 9, 1934. The deposition was taken as part of the central NKVD inquiry into the possibility that negligence in the Leningrad NKVD had contributed to Kirov's death.

· 7 ·

"Statement by A. M. Molochnikov, chief of the Economic Security Section of the Leningrad NKVD, December 9, 1934." RGANI, f. 6, op. 13, d. 71, ll.15–17.

On December 1 of this year [I was] in the office of Comrade Medved around 4:30 P.M. when the telephone rang. Comrade Medved, putting down the phone, ordered a car to be called as Kirov needed him [Medved's office was in NKVD headquarters at 4 Liteiny Street, approximately three and a half kilometers from Smolny]. In three to five seconds the telephone rang again. Comrade Medved after the first words threw down the receiver, yelling "Kirov's been shot," jumped up from his place, and ran out together with Comrade Fomin who obviously had also received a phone call. [. . .]

In about twenty minutes I got an order to send thirty officers to Smolny, which I carried out immediately. I rode to Smolny with the officers.

At Smolny I found that the murderer was alive and had been sent to the NKVD [headquarters].

At Smolny I [also] discovered that a number of documents had been found on the murderer, including a party card. About forty minutes after my arrival Comrade Medved ordered me and Comrade Gubin to interrogate Commissar Borisov and clarify the circumstances of the attack.

I requested one of the commissars to [. . .] bring Comrade Borisov to me.

They brought me a man in civilian clothes, about fifty years old.

At the beginning of the interrogation [Gubin did not take part] Borisov was so upset that I could not get any kind of straight answer out of him, where he had met Kirov, how he accompanied him, and where he, Borisov, had been at the moment of the killing. I ended up having to draw a map of Smolny, explain to him where the left and right sides were.

At last I managed to figure out from his words that he met Comrade Kirov in the vestibule and was twenty steps from him. When Kirov began climbing the stairs, he remained the same distance from him. [. . .]

To my questions about why he stayed so far from Kirov he gave no answer.

We finally clarified that two to three steps from the turn to the left corridor, Borisov heard two shots, one after the other. He got out his revolver, put in a cartridge, and sprinted into the corridor. Turning into the corridor he supposedly saw two [persons] on the floor, one to two meters apart [. . .] and some people standing around them already. By his own account he did nothing further.

Borisov could not remember a single detail, if we can believe his testimony. Who were these people who surrounded Comrade Kirov as he lay on the floor? For example, to the question of whether Comrade Chudov was among them, he could not answer for a long time.

At the time of Borisov's interrogation it was found that his revolver was under his jacket in its holster and was unloaded.

I sharply rebuked Borisov about this during the interrogation and he became very upset. In connection with this I addressed Comrade Gubin with the words, "we must take care with the old man, he's armed." Two to three minutes later I was told that he had been disarmed.

In view of the fact that Borisov's interrogation did not give a picture of the moment of the attack, I began seeking people who could give me more details about that. I don't remember who pointed out to me Platych [Platoch, the electrician] and, I think, Vasiliev [the supply room clerk with Platoch], whom I then interrogated. [. . .]

I also interrogated one operations officer [Dureiko] who was guarding the [main] corridor, who asserted, if I remember correctly, that he saw Borisov walking far behind Kirov.

My interrogations were obviously not complete. This was because:

(1) My purpose in these interrogations was to get the first witness accounts, and I supposed that I would have the possibility of following up in more detail later. But I was not assigned to interrogate these persons later.

(2) There was no way that I could know that this interrogation was Borisov's last.

Molochnikov.

P.S. To your question of who wrote the first report to Moscow [probably Document 1 above], I confirm that this report was composed one hour after the murder in Ugarov's office. Comrades Medved and Gorin were at the desk. Medved dictated and Gorin wrote, at least that's how it was at first, and I was not present for the entire time.

Molochnikov

The purpose of the December 1 interrogations, then, was to establish what actually happened at the murder scene while witnesses' memories were fresh. Many later interrogations had an entirely different purpose—to build a legal case, or what passed for a legal case in Stalinist courts, against the accused. For this reason the early interviews, particularly those from the night of the murder, are the most valuable evidence for what actually happened in Smolny on December 1. It is also unlikely that the archival copies we have are forgeries. The December 1 accounts confirm one another on the central facts. In addition they are confirmed by the post-Stalin memoirs of Mikhail Rosliakov, who was on the crime scene within seconds of the killing, and who himself believed that Stalin was behind Kirov's killing. If the December 1 documents were Stalin-era forgeries, then we would expect them to fit Stalin's version of the crime—that Zinovievite oppositionists conspired to murder Kirov. By the middle of 1937 this version postulated a massive conspiracy to kill Kirov inside the Leningrad NKVD and party apparatuses. But the December 1 testimony we have provides no evidence of any conspiracy.

Myths, Inconsistencies, and Loose Ends

Descriptions of the Kirov crime scene in literature written before the perestroika era turn out to be mistaken in many details, as Kirilina has demonstrated.[17] To cite one example, the Smolny corridors were not "suspiciously empty" at the time of the murder. To cite another, Nikolaev did not need any special pass to get into Smolny. Former Smolny employees, officers of the Smolny guard, and Nikolaev himself all testified that access to the building's third floor was by party card (Nikolaev had one), and the first and second floors were open to the public.[18]

Many analysts of the assassination, from Stalin's policemen to Western Kremlinologists, have found it suspicious that Borisov lagged so far behind his charge. In context, however, his late arrival on the scene does not look so strange. Borisov had been Kirov's bodyguard since the latter's arrival in Leningrad in 1926, and at first he was attached to Kirov as he moved about town. Later, due to advancing age (he was fifty-three in 1934) and physical decrepitude he was assigned to guard the party secretary inside the Smolny building. Kirov's secretary, N. A. Sveshnikov, in 1966 remembered Borisov as "immobile," sitting in Kirov's waiting room and complaining that he wanted to retire, but that the higher-ups wouldn't sanction it. According to Sveshnikov, Borisov and Kirov very rarely spoke, and the bodyguard stayed quite far from his charge. Kirilina claims that Kirov blocked

Medved at one point from firing Borisov out of personal affection for the old man.[19]

Perhaps Kirov liked Borisov because of his very unobtrusiveness. There are many indications that the first secretary chafed at having bodyguards. On November 30, 1960, for example, P. G. Kulnev, a member of Kirov's guard until November 1934, testified that officers had specific instructions to keep a distance of at least twenty to twenty-five steps from Kirov because he so disliked being escorted. Other officers of Kirov's guard described such instructions in testimony after the killing.[20] There seems also to have been pre-assassination evidence that Kirov was making trouble for his guards. A. A. Gubin, head of the Leningrad NKVD Operations Department that controlled Kirov's guards, defended himself with reference to pre-assassination documents in a statement five weeks after the murder.

· 8 ·

Statement by A. A. Gubin, chief of the Leningrad NKVD Operations Department, January 7, 1934. RGANI, f. 6, op. 13, d. 80, ll. 137–139. (All emphasis added.)

———————

To Comrade Mironov, Chief of the Economic Department of the Directorate of State Security of the NKVD:

I request that the following be attached to my case file, as supplement to my previous testimony.

At the telegraphed request of [central] Operations Department Chief Pauker made on December 1, 1933, a report was presented with the approval of Comrade Medved at the [Leningrad] Operations Department on the organization and conditions of Comrade Kirov's guard. The report stated that Comrade Kirov's lack of cooperation with the guard was an obstacle to maintaining an effective guard */a copy of the report is in the archives of the Operations Department/*. One and a half months ago, on November 16 to be exact, in a personal report to Comrade Pauker, I noted that Comrade Kirov still was not permitting a[n effective] guard.

In light of the above, Borisov's lagging behind Kirov does not seem so suspicious. It is quite likely that he was simply following instructions in keeping his distance from the party secretary. On December 7, 1934 Maly, an officer in the Leningrad Operations Department, testified that he'd seen Borisov crying on the third floor of Smolny on the evening of the murder, and that the latter had told him he'd stayed twenty to thirty meters behind Kirov because "Comrade Kirov did not like it when anyone shadowed him closely."[21]

It is important to remember that the NKVD in 1934 was more of a Rube Goldberg machine than a Swiss watch. The Operations Department, for example, was haphazardly organized—there were no written instructions at all for Kirov's bodyguard.[22] Gubin, Leningrad Operations Department chief, testified on January 13, 1935 that other departments generally did not forward information on suspected terrorists to his department—one indicator of a more general lack of coordination.[23] Much of the Operations Department, and of the NKVD in general, was staffed by persons with little education and no professional training. Borisov's qualifications for his job, for example, were that he was from a working-class family and had once been a nightwatchman.[24]

More recent works on the Kirov murder have used inconsistencies and loose ends in the sources to argue that a second gunman may have been at the murder scene and the Nagan might have been planted on Nikolaev.[25] There are for example contradictions about the disarming and searching of Nikolaev in the reliable sources that might suggest some kind of hanky-panky with the pistol. Platoch, Yalozo, and Rosliakov all claimed to have handled Nikolaev's pistol at one point or another. Lioninok and Operations Department officer Dureiko both claimed to have searched the assassin before removing him from the corridor.[26] But these contradictions are explicable without postulating any extra gunman. A December 4 statement to interrogators by A. D. Mikhalchenko, deputy commander of the Smolny building guards, a separate command from Kirov's security detail, confirms that Platoch, Yalozo, Dureiko, and others all played parts in searching and guarding Nikolaev. Mikhalchenko was the senior officer on duty at the time in Smolny (thus some documents mistakenly identify him as the Smolny commander). He was interrogated on December 4 by I. Chertok, head of the central NKVD Economic Security Directorate as part of the investigation into possible negligence by the Leningrad NKVD. In addition to the question of who detained, disarmed, and searched Nikolaev, Mikhalchenko's evidence sheds light on other murky moments in the chain of events, such as the extinguishing of lights in several offices before the murder, the disposition of building guards afterwards, and the tripping of Smolny's general alarm.

· 9 ·

Interrogation of A. D. Mikhalchenko, deputy commander of Smolny guards,
by I. Chertok, chief of the USSR NKVD Economic Security Directorate,
December 4, 1934. TsA FSB RF, a.u.d. N-Sh44, t. 24, ll. 99–104.

Mikhalchenko, Aleksandr Dmitrievich [...] born 1899, native of
Borovichi, Leningrad Region, parents ... poor peasants, Ukrainian. [...]
Residence: Leningrad, commander of Smolny, married. [...] Education:
elementary. Member of the Communist Party from 1930, convicted of no
crimes. Did not serve with Whites.

Question: Under what circumstances did you become aware of the murder of Comrade Kirov?

Answer: On the first of December at 4:30 P.M. the duty officer at
Smolny, Comrade Bravy, ran into my office and announced that shots had
been fired on the third floor. I immediately sprinted out of my office,
which is located on the first floor, to the third floor. As I ran up to the
guard post at the entrance to the third floor I saw that the doors, which
were usually open, were shut. Officer Ivanov of the Smolny command,
stationed at that post, told me that he heard shots from the direction of
Comrade Kirov's office [and] he shut the door and was not letting anyone
in or out. Arriving at a run at the scene of the crime I saw two persons lying on the floor with a group of twelve to fifteen people standing around
them.

Question: Who did you recognize among the persons at the scene of the
crime when you arrived?

Answer: At the moment I ran up I remember clearly that there was already a group of twelve to fifteen. [...] I remember that among them
were

1. Platoch—regional committee electrician.
2. Yaloz[o]—aide to the director of the Leningrad Soviet Administrative Department.
3. Tsukerman—director of the State Circus.
4. Dutsman—secretary to comrade Ugarov.
5. Sveshnikov—secretary to Comrade Kirov.

I can't remember the others. The explanation for that is that at the moment I arrived at the murder scene, there was constant movement in the
group of people already there. Some were arriving, others running off
somewhere.

Now I remember that among them was also Borisov, standing by Comrade Kirov, and the officer of the [Smolny] command Durenko [Dureiko].

Question: Tell in detail what happened next.

Answer: From the conversations of those at the crime scene I gathered that doctors had already been called. I myself hurried to a telephone and called 22-80 /on-duty officer of the State Security Directorate Operations Department [at NKVD headquarters]/. Then I ordered the closing of all exits and reinforcement of the guard. [. . .]

Question: You say that you heard from eyewitnesses of the crime that Comrade Kirov's murderer also tried to shoot himself. Who were these eyewitnesses?

Answer: Of those who said that he [*sic*] was an eyewitness of the crime, I remember now only the city committee *instruktor* Olonen [a marginal note on the document identifies this "Olonen" as Lioninok], or something like that name. That comrade was soon interrogated at Smolny.

[. . .]

Question: How long did it take you to run from the first floor to the third, that is, from the moment when you heard of the shots to your arrival at the scene of the crime?

Answer: That took no more than one and a half to two minutes, I was at a dead run.

Question: Did you clarify later how the officer of your command Bravy, who notified you of the shots, found out about the murder?

Answer: I did not clarify exactly. As far as I remember, Bravy told me that he heard about it by telephone. It is possible that Bravy heard about the shots in some other manner.

Question: Where was Bravy at the moment of the murder?

Answer: Bravy was in the office next door to mine [it seems that Bravy was seated in an outside office giving onto the corridor, while Mikhalchenko, his superior, had an inner office]

Question: Could Bravy, located in the office next to you [the outer office], have heard the shots on the third floor?

Answer: No, he could not, that is demonstrated also by the fact that when I had run as far as the second floor and asked the officer of the Smolny command on duty there whether he had heard anything, he answered in the negative.

Question: How was it learned that the murderer was alive?

Answer: After I notified the NKVD by telephone of what had happened and ran back [to the crime scene], one of those present—I don't remember who—said that the murderer was moving and he had to be taken away. Then it was decided /at whose order I don't remember/ to carry the murderer to some other room. Platoch, Yaloz[o], and I and somebody else took the murderer by the hands and feet and carried him to the room next to Comrade Ugarov's reception room. Having laid the murderer on the floor and seeing no blood on him, we decided to tie him up. This was done by Platoch, who tied the murderer up with electrical cord. I left Officer Dureiko by the murderer as a guard. [. . .]

Question: Was Comrade Kirov accompanied by anyone at the time that he was walking through Smolny on the way to his office?

Answer: At the entrance to Smolny Comrade Kirov met my aide Comrade Pogudalov and Borisov. Comrade Pogudalov went as far as the second floor, and Borisov, as was usual, followed behind Comrade Kirov all the way to his office.

Question: You say that you saw Borisov at the very moment that you arrived on the scene of the murder. Tell us in detail what you remember about what Borisov did while he was in the group surrounding the murder scene.

Answer: I remember that Borisov was at the scene of the murder and was very upset and distracted. As far as I remember Borisov took no part in calling the doctors, notifying the NKVD directorate of what had happened, or in the detention of the murderer.

Question: Do you know anything about the fact that shortly before the murder of Comrade Kirov in Smolny, the lights went out on the third floor, among other places?

Answer: I heard nothing about that before the murder of Comrade Kirov. After the murder of Comrade Kirov, Smolny electrician Platoch told me that just before the murder [. . .] the lights went out in the rooms next door to Comrade Kirov's office.

On that same day [of the murder] there was an investigation of this issue. It was found that at around four P.M. on the first of December electricians were in fact turning on and off some of the breakers, which caused the lights to go out for a time as long as one minute. [. . .]

Interrogated by: I. Chertok.

Could a putative "second gunman" have escaped easily from the Smolny Building, as Amy Knight has claimed?[27] Mikhalchenko's testimony, together with that of his subordinate, Arkhip Ivanovich Bravy, indicates that word of the murder spread rapidly and Smolny was "sealed" moments after the crime. Bravy testified on or soon after December 4 that he set off the building's general alarm immediately upon receiving a telephone call from Ivanchenko, the Leningrad soviet official at Chudov's meeting on the third floor (also mentioned by Rosliakov, see above). Ivanchenko did not say that Kirov had been shot, but told Bravy to call an ambulance and trip the alarm. The alarm rang throughout the building and signaled guards to close the exits. Thus, egress from Smolny appears to have been blocked within a minute or two of the shots, not ten or fifteen minutes after, or even later, as has been claimed.[28]

Knight, Kirilina, and Bastrykin and Gromtseva have all raised questions about "the man in a GPU uniform" referred to by Nikolaev in one of his early interrogations. Could this unidentified secret police officer have been part of a larger conspiracy to murder Kirov and set up Nikolaev to take the fall? In the testimony in question, dated December 3, Nikolaev described his actions in the seconds after he shot Kirov.

· 10 ·

Excerpt from testimony of Leonid Nikolaev, December 3, 1934. TsA FSB RF, a.u.d. N-Sh44, t. 12, ll. 15–16.

I turned around, to prevent any attack on me from behind, I cocked my pistol, and I fired, intending to hit myself in the temple. At the moment I was cocking the pistol a man in a GPU uniform jumped out of an office opposite me and I hastened to shoot myself. I felt a blow on my head and collapsed. When I awoke and gradually came to I thought I was about to die. Someone rushed up to me, began to examine me, and took me off to some room.

I have read this through and it is an accurate transcription of my words.
December 3, 1934
L. Nikolaev.
Interrogated by: Deputy Chief of the Special Department of the State Security Directorate Sosnovsky.

Sensationalism aside, the "man in the GPU uniform" was almost certainly Platoch. The electrician was wearing a dark blue work uniform (*siniaia spetsovka*), and the uniform for NKVD security officers at the time was also dark blue. Nikolaev, in a state of exalted hysteria, could well have failed to differentiate between the two. Platoch, as discussed above, testified on December 2 (and probably also on December 1) to hitting Nikolaev. It was most likely his blow that Nikolaev described.[29]

The NKVD attempted to track other unidentified people in the third-floor corridors of Smolny at the time of the murder. But the possibility of a second gunman is mitigated by the strong evidence that Nikolaev fired both shots heard in Smolny on December 1. Lioninok testified to seeing Nikolaev waving his pistol and firing the second shot. Nikolaev himself claimed throughout the investigation that he shot Kirov and then fired again with intent to commit suicide. We know from Nikolaev's notes and diary (see Chapters 5 and 6) that he was considering suicide. The murder weapon and ammunition recovered from the crime scene also point to Nikolaev as the murderer. The Nagan pistol found there belonged to Nikolaev—he procured it in 1918 and registered it twice with the police. All seven bullets that fit in the Nagan's magazine were accounted for. One was extracted from Kirov's head and a second (presumably the second shot heard by witnesses) was found on the corridor floor on the right side (facing away from the main hallway). The mark of a bullet ricochet was found on a cornice where the wall met the ceiling. According to a telegram from Medved to Moscow early in the morning of December 2, two expended cartridges were found at the scene of the crime together with the pistol. Five bullets remained in the revolver's magazine, two had been fired. According to a 1966 ballistics analysis done at the order of the Pelshe Central Committee investigative commission the bullet recovered from Kirov's head was fired from Nikolaev's Nagan.[30]

To summarize, it is not likely that there was a second gunman at the crime scene, or that there was a conspiracy inside Smolny on December 1 to let Nikolaev get at Kirov. Throughout the investigation and trial process Nikolaev claimed that he shot Kirov himself, and there are no substantial reasons to doubt his claim. A second point is that there are good explanations for Borisov's distance from the crime scene that do not involve sabotage or criminal negligence. Indeed, Borisov was most likely under orders to keep his distance from Kirov. Based on the documents discussed here, Smolny on the evening of December 1 1934 looks less like the theater for a meticulously prepared assassination plot than like a workplace overtaken by unexpected tragedy.

Within seconds of the shots on the third floor of Smolny, Rosliakov, city Health Department chief Bogen, and others were around Kirov and determined that he had no pulse and was not breathing (Bogen and Rosliakov were both doctors). Office workers called NKVD headquarters and the Smolny medical clinic. Perhaps five minutes after the murder Dr. Maria Galperina and a nurse arrived from the Smolny clinic, just as Rosliakov and others were carrying Kirov's body into his office and laying it on the large table there. In her 1954 memoirs Galperina wrote that Kirov was clearly dead when she first saw him, but she began artificial respiration nonetheless. Around fifteen minutes after the murder Filip Medved arrived from NKVD headquarters, accompanied by the chief of the NKVD medical section S. A. Mamushin. In the meantime Bogen had called for medical help from leading doctors in the city, among them the professors of surgery Vasily Dobrotvorsky and Yulian Dzhanelidze. They began arriving just before 5:00 P.M. Dzhanelidze was one of the last, reaching Kirov's office at 5:40 P.M.[31]

· 11 ·

Certificate of death of S. M. Kirov, December 1, 1934, 7:55 P.M. RGANI, f. 6, op. 13, d. 137, ll. 1–6.

Comrade Kirov was wounded at 4:37 P.M. outside Comrade Chudov's reception room. He was found lying face down, with his legs stretched out and his hands lying by his sides, while blood was coming out of his nose and mouth in clots. Some blood was on the floor. Two to three steps away from him another person, unknown, lay stretched out on the floor.

Upon initial examination by Bogin [Bogen], Rosliakov, and Fridman the presentation was—absence of pulse and respiration. Seven to eight minutes later Comrade Kirov was carried into his office. Dr. Galperina appeared during the transfer of the body and constituted cyanosis of the face, absence of pulse and respiration, pupils dilated and unreactive to light. Hot water bottles were applied to the lower part of the legs and artificial respiration begun. Examination revealed a wound in the back of the head. At the front of the forehead on the left there was a large hematoma [congealed blood under the skin]. A pressure bandage was applied [to the hematoma] and two cubic centimeters of camphor injected three times together with two cc of caffeine twice.

Artificial respiration was continued.

Dr. Cherniak arrived at 4:55 P.M.

Dr. Cherniak found Comrade Kirov on the table, with complete absence of pulse and respiration, cyanosis of the face, blue extremities, dilated pupils unreactive to light. Camphor and caffeine were injected, artificial respiration continued. At 5:10 P.M. Drs. Vainberg, Feiertag, and Tatskin arrived, followed immediately by Professor Dobrotvorsky at 5:15 P.M. [. . .]

At 5:40 P.M. [. . .] the patient was declared dead.

In the back of Comrade Kirov's forage cap, on the left side, was found an entry hole from the bullet. In the skull five fingers behind the left ear in the region of the cerebellum there is an entry wound with slight bruising. An entry hole in the surface of the rear of the skull can be palpated with the fingers.

Above the left brow there is a swelling from subcutaneous bleeding.

Conclusion: Death occurred instantaneously from damage to centers of the nervous system vital to life.

December 1, 1934

7:55 P.M.

Bogen [head of the city Health Department]

Prof. Dobrotvorsky

Prof. Dzhanelidze

Prof. Gesse

Citizen Fridman

Dr. Galperina

Dr. I. Cherniak

Dr. Feiertag [elsewhere spelled "Feert, "Feiertag," "Feiertat," etc.]

Dr. Tsatskikh [second-in-command, city Health Department].

Dr. S. Mamushin.

A commission including Dobrotvorsky and Mamushin performed the autopsy on Kirov's body early in the morning of December 2 at the Sverdlov Hospital. The commission found that the blunt-nosed Nagan bullet had entered Kirov's cerebellum (the part of the brain lowest and furthest back) behind his left ear, passed through the cerebellum and part of the left-side temporal lobe, and bounced backward off the front of the skull, just barely above the left eye. Kirov had fallen face forward with the left side of his forehead hitting the ground first. The bullet ricochet and the impact with the floor had cracked Kirov's skull and caused the massive bruising and subcutaneous bleeding above his brow. The path of the bullet was slightly upward, consistent with an attack at close range from behind by a person shorter than Kirov (as Nikolaev was). After the autopsy Kirov was dressed again in his usual clothes—a military service jacket, trousers, and "Russian boots"—and embalmed.[32]

Medved's second deputy, F. T. Fomin, came upon a scene of pandemonium when he reached Smolny from NKVD headquarters. This was a few minutes after five o'clock. In a letter to the Central Committee twenty-two years later, Fomin described a crowd of Smolny employees gathered in the side corridor where Kirov died, shouting, "Give us the killer, we'll rip him to pieces!" Nikolaev, alternately catatonic and hysterical, was guarded by several NKVD officers in a side room. Fomin and the other officers covered the assassin with an overcoat, carried him downstairs, and transported him to NKVD head-quarters in an ambulance. At headquarters, 4 Liteiny Street, Fomin brought Nikolaev to his office or Medved's and examined the documents that had been found in his pockets and briefcase. According to Fomin's memory in 1956 these were a pass to a cafeteria inside Smolny and a party card. One of these, probably the cafeteria pass, identified him as an employee of the Workers' and Peasants' Inspectorate in Smolny (a job Nikolaev had in fact been fired from in August 1933). Examining the papers in Nikolaev's briefcase, Fomin found a pocket notebook with addresses, including those of family members, whose arrest he ordered immediately. Based on a reference in the first interrogation of Nikolaev on the night of December 1–2 (Chapter 7, Document 36) it appears that the NKVD also found on Nikolaev's person a fragmentary "Plan" for an attack on "K" (Chapter 6, Document 32). It is not out of the question, however, that officers could have found the "Plan" found at Nikolaev's apartment or his mother's.[33]

The Leningrad NKVD determined very quickly who Nikolaev was, as several witnesses on the scene knew him by sight and he was carrying identification. Within hours of the murder, officers raided his apartment and his mother's, arresting most of his immediate relations. According to the 1960 testimony of one of the NKVD men involved, B. A. Yermolaev, Nikolaev's two children and his elderly mother-in-law were at his apartment. The police found Nikolaev's "political testament," a letter to Stalin, and other documents there. At his mother's apartment, the haul seems to have been larger, including multiple letters to family members, more copies of his "political testament," and at least eight different notebooks with his writings.[34]

Back at Leningrad NKVD headquarters Officer Olberto (Alberto?) Kulesh remembered Nikolaev lying on a couch and muttering deliriously soon after his arrival. L. V. Kogan, a section chief in the Operations Department, tried to transcribe what he was saying. Fomin soon had Nikolaev taken to the headquarters clinic to be "brought to consciousness."[35]

An admission report from the clinic, written at 6:40 P.M., described Nikolaev as refusing to answer questions and "groaning and screaming from time to time."[36] The document below describes a more full examination carried out minutes later.

· 12 ·

Report on medical examination of Leonid Nikolaev at Leningrad NKVD clinic,
7 P.M., December 1, 1934. FSB RF, a.u.d. N-Sh44, t. 24, ll. 332–333.

On December 1 of 1934 at the order of the head of the Medical Section
of the NKVD Directorate, we, the undersigned, carried out a medical examination of Citizen Nikolaev, L. V. on the premises of Clinic No. 1 [Med-
ical Section, NKVD], with the following results.

The subject is over thirty years of age, height below average, dysplastic
[abnormal body type], bow-legged, body clean, no abrasions or bruises.
The subject was carried in on a stretcher at 7:00 P.M. in a state of hysteria,
with very limited awareness of his surroundings and some motor disturbance. Under the influence of vibration of a tuning fork and pressure on
the eyeballs, together with verbal reprimands, the subject changed position, began to breathe more calmly, and spoke disjointed phrases, mentioning several names. At this point we noticed an outflow of mucus from
the right nostril, minor burning of the left nostril [the result of dosing with
smelling salts], and significant drooling. By 9:00 P.M. he had come to himself somewhat, which made it possible to bathe and shower him and
change his clothes. During this time he carried on sensible conversation,
answered questions immediately, but not always to the point. Examination found a pulse of ninety, rhythmic, effective action, reflexes normal,
[. . .] pupils of correct form, average diameter, prompt reaction to light,
sensitivity to pain intact. [The subject's] constant theatrical behavior was
noted.

On the basis of the above we conclude that Citizen Nikolaev L. V. was
in a temporary reactive hysterical state with limited awareness of his surroundings, but later grasped his situation. [. . .] There were two phases of
the reactive state—mild muscle spasms and emotive poses of a theatrical
character. There was undoubtedly [an element of] exaggeration, and following that even simulation, that is, an understanding of his situation and
intention to confuse those around him for his own purposes. Future repetition of hysterical attacks is possible.

Consulting doctor and department chief [. . .] Second Leningrad Psychiatric Hospital Gust. Vlad. Reits.

N. Ia. Gandeltan

L. S. Ryvlin

M. E. Gontarev.

In testimony to Central Committee investigative commissions in the
late 1950s and early 1960s Fomin and former NKVD officer Isakov,
who were both present at early interrogations, described Nikolaev as

erratic and hysterical. Kirilina quotes Fomin that "for a long time after coming to consciousness the murderer screamed, babbled, and only towards the morning began to speak and shout 'my shot rang round the world.'" In 1961 Isakov testified that Nikolaev "was not a thinking person, but a bag of bones and flesh, without reason. . . . For a long time Nikolaev simply refused to answer questions. In my opinion there was not a thing in his head . . . he just cried. . . . Nikolaev behaved like a person in a state of intense depression. . . . He fell into hysterics literally every five minutes, and then there'd be some kind of torpor and he'd sit silently, staring at a point in the air."[37]

Based on Fomin's testimony, it seems that NKVD officers were unable to conduct a real interrogation of Nikolaev until around midnight of December 1–2 or even later. They talked to Nikolaev's wife, Milda Draule, considerably earlier. Medved included the complete protocol of her initial statement to the NKVD in a 10:30 P.M. telegram to Yagoda describing the progress of the investigation.

· 13 ·

Telegram to Yagoda from Medved, December 1, 1934, 10:30 P.M. TsA FSB RF, a.u.d. N-Sh44, t. 24, ll. 1–2.

Based on documents recovered, Nikolaev, Leonid Mikhailovich [*sic*] has been a member of the Communist Party since 1924, date of birth 1904, social status: worker.

Nikolaev passed the last party purge as a member of the Smolny work collective. From the protocol of the purge commission it is clear that Nikolaev was born in Leningrad, his parents were workers /father is dead/ his mother is a tram depot cleaning lady, Nikolaev finished elementary school in 1916, then apprenticed with a watch repairman. In 1919–1920 he was the secretary of a village soviet, at the end of 1920 he served as an orderly at the 978th Military Hospital. In 1922–1923 he was an office manager (*upravdelami*) in the Vyborg Ward VLKSM [Communist Youth League or Komsomol]. At the factory Red Dawn (*Krasnaia zaria*) he was a metal worker until 1925 and then went to Komsomol work. From 1927–1929 he worked at Mechanical Factory Number 7. From 1929–1930 at the Karl Marx Factory. From 1931–1932 at the Regional Committee of the Komsomol. In 1931 Nikolaev worked as an assessor (*referent*) in the regional Communist Party apparatus. In addition, in 1932–1934 Nikolaev worked as head of the Financial Section of the Regional Council of the "Down with Illiteracy!" Society (*obschestvo "Doloi negramotnosti!"*). At the time of the purge Nikolaev was a price inspector of the Regional Control Commission of the Workers' and Peasants' Inspectorate. He passed the purge.

In April of 1934 Nikolaev was ordered by the Institute of Party History, where he then worked, to undertake [party] work in transport. [This was a compulsory party mobilization, probably to do propaganda work].

The party collective excluded Nikolaev from the party on the grounds of his refusal to follow this order, although the ward committee later restored him to membership and censured him.

Nikolaev's family consists of: wife born in 1901, member of the party from 1919, an inspector of the Personnel Section of the Commissariat of Heavy Industry [Leningrad] Office.

His mother lives in Leningrad, she is a cleaning lady at the Kalinin tram depot.

His sister Ye. V. Rogacheva is a member of the Communist Party since 1918, a representative of the Workers' Committee for Horticulture.

His sister Pantekhin [*sic*—should be Pantiukhina], Anna Vasilievna, nonparty, is married to an engineer, a candidate member of the Communist Party in Sverdlovsk.

His brother Pyotr served in the Red Army, nonparty, and as a factory labor rate setter. At present he is a deserter [from the Red Army].

[Nikolaev's] wife's sister, Draule, O. P., is secretary of the party committee of the Vyborg House of Culture, a member of the Communist Party from 1925. Relatives in Leningrad have been arrested.

Searches of Nikolaev and his apartment have uncovered a large number of documents.

I transmit the first statement of Nikolaev's wife.

My last name is Draule, Milda Petrovna, date of birth 1901, inspector of the Personnel Section of the Office of the Commissariat of Heavy Industry, member of the Communist Party from 1919, my party card is in my briefcase.

My husband is Nikolaev, Leonid Vasilievich, member of the Communist Party since 1924. I have been married to him since 1925. We met in Luga. There I worked in the district committee of the Communist Party. There he was chief of the General Administrative Department (*Obshchii otdel*) of the county Komsomol.

At present he is not working. In April of 1934 he became an employee of the branch of the Institute of Party History located at Moika 59 in the building of the Managers' Club. At about the same time he was mobilized by the local cell of the Communist Party for work in transport. He refused to go on the grounds that he was sick /he really does sometimes have brief cardiac episodes/. Besides that, he explained his refusal on family grounds. I have two children, /one seven and one three years old/ and my mother is elderly. The local party cell excluded him from the party for his refusal to mobilize for transport work. The ward committee of Smolny Ward restored him to the party /that was in May/ and gave him a strict censure. He appealed this decision to the Party [Control] Commission in Smolny. At Smolny they confirmed the ward committee resolution. Then he appealed to the Central Committee. As far as he has told me, there has been no answer yet.

After his exclusion from the party he has not worked anywhere and has lived on my salary. From that time he hasn't gone out at all. He sits at home and studies.

I don't know any of his close comrades. He used to have a weapon but after the 1926 re-registration it seems to me they took it away from him. He has no weapon at present. He has no weapon at home.

From the moment of his exclusion from the party he fell into a depressed state, he was waiting all the time for a resolution of his case by the Central Committee and did not want to work anywhere. He did turn to the ward committee but they gave him no work there. He couldn't work in production [that is, manual labor] for health reasons, he has neurasthenia and cardiac episodes.

I haven't noticed anything particularly different about him in recent days. He has been the same as always.

I left the house at eight in the morning today. He was still sleeping. Last night he went to bed at about midnight. Before that he played with the children.

My words noted here correctly—Draule.

We have found on Nikolaev a Nagan with five bullets and two expended cartridge cases.

Chief of the NKVD Directorate F. Medved

Medved's December 1 telegrams shed light on the timing of Draule's first interrogation, which has become an important issue in recent literature. Rumors that Nikolaev shot Kirov because the latter was having an affair with Draule began circulating soon after the murder and continue to this day. In a 2000 article historian Yury Zhukov claimed that Draule's first interrogation began at 4:45 P.M. at NKVD headquarters, less than fifteen minutes after the murder. This suggests to Zhukov that Draule was near the scene of the crime at the time of the murder and that she and Kirov were romantically involved. The logic of the claim seems doubtful (if Kirov and Draule had been actually having sex, wouldn't they have been doing it at Kirov's apartment, where multiple witnesses place him throughout the day of December 1?). Moreover, Medved's December 1 telegrams to Yagoda appear to place Draule's first interrogation between 6:20 P.M. and 10:30 P.M. In his 6:20 P.M. telegram to Moscow Medved noted that an order had been issued for Draule's arrest, not that she had been arrested and interrogated. At 10:30 P.M. he forwarded Yagoda the text of her first statement. These telegrams would seem to contradict Zhukov's reconstruction of events.[38]

A complete reading of the protocol of Draule's first statement available in the Yezhov files at the Russian State Archive of Social and Political History suggests a straightforward explanation for this contradiction. Zhukov fixes the time of Draule's interrogation using the time given at the beginning of the protocol—16:45 on the 24-hour clock, or 4:45 P.M. But at the end of the same document the time is given as 19:10 (7:10 P.M.). Given how short Draule's statement is, it seems unlikely that the interrogation went on for two hours and twenty-five minutes. Most likely the 16:45 at the top of Draule's interrogation is a copying error for 18:45 (6:45 P.M.). The numerals "6" and "8" look very similar in most Russian typewriter fonts. The sequence of events then would be:

6:20 P.M. Medved tells Moscow an order has been issued for Draule's arrest. Soon after this Draule is brought in.[39]

6:45 P.M. Draule's first interrogation begins.

7:10 P.M. Draule's interrogation concludes. Twenty-five minutes would have been plenty of time for the NKVD to get the brief statement recorded by the protocol.[40]

In her deposition Draule gave the first hint of a motive for Nikolaev's crime—the latter had lost his job and nearly lost his party membership for a violation of party discipline. Nikolaev's trouble at work was absolutely typical for Communists of his time. He had been "mobilized" by his workplace party organization soon after taking his new job at the Institute of Party History. This meant that the party cell bureau, that is the cell leadership, often consisting at this time of three persons, had ordered Nikolaev to leave his job temporarily to work on some urgent task. The phrase "transport work" indicates that Nikolaev would have been doing party propaganda work among railway workers at a depot, marshaling yard, or construction site. Party members were formally under military discipline—Nikolaev had no choice but to obey. He would have to leave his home and family to travel to a relatively remote area where he would organize political discussion meetings, group readings of party newspapers, classes in "political literacy" (basic Marxist theory, revolutionary history, current tasks of the party), and the like. Most Soviet subjects resented being asked to take part in such activities, and they were not particularly popular even among ambitious party members who had to participate in order to advance their careers. Dragooning tired employees after work into attending political meetings was not easy or fun. Communist party members often tried to avoid such "mobilizations," especially to remote areas. Because these assignments were so undesirable, cell bureaus tended to mobilize members they wanted to get rid of for whatever reason—personal animosity, political rivalries, plain incompetence.

December 1 interrogations of Nikolaev's other relatives and party officials who knew him supplemented the picture painted by Milda Draule of a sickly and resentful man. According to these informants, Nikolaev felt wronged by the party bureaucracy and had hinted in letters to party authorities that he might take drastic steps. He and his wife had actively sought a ticket for him to get into the party activists' meeting scheduled for the evening of December 1.[41]

Just after midnight Medved sent another telegram to Commissar of Internal Affairs Yagoda in Moscow. A search of Nikolaev's apartment had turned up many pages of his writing. It seemed that Nikolaev had been stalking Kirov for at least a month. The documents seemed to suggest that Nikolaev was a disillusioned Communist, and they hinted at possible connections with foreigners.

· 14 ·

Telegram from Medved to Yagoda, December 2, 1934, 12:40 A.M. TsA FSB RF, a.u.d. N-Sh44, t. 24, ll. 3–4.

Additional report: Among the documents found at Nikolaev's apartment there are a "testament" and a number of notes by Nikolaev. Among the notes are such items as: "I wrote my political testament one month ago. It is being fully confirmed, there is no way out now." "I called Sveshnikov, Kirov is not receiving visitors" /November 2/. "If on October 15 or November 5 I couldn't do it . . . now I'm ready." "I am moving towards my own execution, [for me that is] a triviality. Of course that's easy enough to say [now]" (*idu pod rasstrel, pustiaki—tolko skazat' legko*)"

/November 9/. "Today, as on November 5, he [I?] was late. It didn't work out. They've really got him well covered at the train station with the Red Arrow" /November 14/. "From words I have decided to move to deeds, and truly a grand and solemn deed." /November 14/. "I am aware just how serious the matter is, that if I strike with one blow, I'll get ten, one hundred, and more blows in return. The blow must be planned without a single error." "It's hard to break a path through twenty bodyguards. You've got to seize the initiative. And even then success will be unexpected. . . ." "In what way have I remained true to the party and my fatherland? In that I have not broken with the party and taken the route of counterrevolution. They offered me big sums of money for my documents, but I did not make the deal. . . ." "I could have translated my last letters-testaments into three languages, but I refused." "Today Ch[udov] left in a new auto and went to the OGPU. Then they got in my way and I cleared off. . . ." " . . . a thousand generations will pass, but the idea of Communism will not be made flesh. . . ." "I will attack with the same strength with which I defended the new world . . . "

In a notebook taken from Nikolaev, among many other addresses there is the note "Germ. tel. 169-82 Herzen St. 43" /this is the actual address of the German consulate/ and: "Latv. 5-50-63." This is the telephone number of the Latvian consulate.

Chief of the State Security Directorate NKVD—Medved.

Yagoda probably did not see this telegram on the night of December 1–2, 1934. At 12:40 A.M. he was already on a special express train to Leningrad. Together with him were Stalin; Central Committee secretaries Molotov, Voroshilov, Yezhov, and Zhdanov; Komsomol chief A. V. Kosaryov; and a host of high-ranking NKVD officers. Medved was not going to be in charge of the investigation much longer.

CHAPTER 5

Leonid Nikolaev

NKVD officers who interviewed Nikolaev in the hours and days after the murder remembered him decades later with contempt as "a degenerate," drooling, with "short, crooked legs" and "small . . . shifty eyes." F. T. Fomin, who interrogated him on December 1–2, described him as "a half-insane person, at the interrogation he'd say three words and that was it."[1]

His relatives arrested by the Leningrad NKVD were hardly more flattering, describing him as a strange loner, obsessed with his own "sickly condition," and convinced of his "ideological superiority" as a Communist.

· 15 ·

Excerpt from interrogation of Leonid Nikolaev's sister, Yekaterina Vasilevna Rogacheva, December 4, 1934. TsA FSB RF, a.u.d. N-Sh44, t. 3, ll. 69–70.

Question: Has [Nikolaev] visited you often in recent months?

Answer: Yes, in recent months Leonid has dropped in on us a lot, at least once every five days, but he visited our mother more often.

Question: When he visited you, what did you talk about with him?

Answer: Leonid is generally very quiet, recently he has been thoughtful and gloomy. He's been angry that he hasn't been able to get a pass to a sanatorium, he talked of his sickly condition, he said that he couldn't work until he bettered his health, he appealed to all different organizations for a pass to a sanatorium, but was refused everywhere.

I did not have political discussions with him.

179

[...]

Question: Who do you know among your brother's friends and acquaintances?

Answer: Leonid has never had friends and I'm even having a hard time naming any acquaintances.

Nikolaev's brother-in-law (husband of his wife Milda's younger sister Olga), Roman Kulisher, saw Nikolaev as a strange and resentful loner.

· 16 ·

Excerpt from testimony of Nikolaev's brother-in-law Roman Kulisher, December 2, 1934. TsA FSB RF, a.u.d. N-Sh44, t. 24, ll. 227–228.

Kulisher, Roman Markovich, born 1902, native of Kiev, [...] chief of the Planning Department of Leningrad Stamp Trust, married—1. wife O. P. Draule [...] son Marat, age four, incomplete secondary education, member of the Communist Party since 1922.

I've known Nikolaev since 1928. We met periodically, recently more often. I can tell you that Nikolaev has not worked for some time. Around July I offered to set Nikolaev up at a gramophone record factory, at some kind of easy civic/political (*obshchestvennyi*) work /Nikolaev did not want to work in production, claiming that he was sick/. In spite of his lack of employment, Nikolaev limited himself to making a phone call to the record factory and later told me that he did not get through. Several times /in response to my questions about why he wasn't working/ he emphasized that he could get work at any time he wanted, he even showed me his ward committee [work] pass, but he could not work because he had to get better. Recently I've noticed Nikolaev's been kind of cracking up. Once, when we were talking Nikolaev said in an upset way, bitterly, that when he was needed, they squeezed everything out of him, and now they won't let him recuperate and heal. In connection with his mobilization for transport, Nikolaev one time said something like, "I've already gone on many [mobilizations], let someone else go."

In September of this year Nikolaev turned to me with a request that I loan him money for a trip to Moscow in order to get a pass to a sanatorium. I gave him thirty rubles through my wife. But he did not go to Moscow. He said something to the effect that he was getting 500 rubles for his rest cure, but the problem was getting a pass, which he could not do in Leningrad, but which he could get in Moscow.

He said this to me several times.

Nikolaev seemed to me to be a loyal member of the party, but with some strange points. In conversation he always thought it necessary to emphasize his party-mindedness and ideological superiority with excessively popular speech, and elements of posing. By nature he is a secretive person. [. . .] Nikolaev was closest to his brother Pyotr, who serves in the Red Army, and with the brother of his wife Pyotr Petrovich Draule. [. . .] Towards these two people Nikolaev showed uncharacteristic warmth and care. In general, as far as I know, Nikolaev lived a solitary life, practically nobody ever visited him.

Kulisher.

Interrogator: Lulov.

Nikolaev was born on or about May 10, 1904 (Old Style) in St. Petersburg, to Maria Tikhonovna Nikolaeva, who was then about thirty-four years old. The boy suffered from rickets, a common childhood disease among the urban poor in the early twentieth century. Nikolaev seems to have suffered from typical symptoms. He developed short, bowed legs and did not walk until very late—by his own account somewhere between age three and five, according to his wife, at age seven, according to his mother at eleven. A December 1926 medical report from the Red Arsenal Factory, Nikolaev's employer at the time, described him as having "simian arms, short legs, long torso." His growth was probably stunted—his adult height was 153 centimeters (just over five feet one inch), compared to an average height for St. Petersburg workers of 165 centimeters.[2] As an adult he suffered from "rheumatism" and "cardiac episodes" that may also have been related to childhood malnutrition.

Nikolaev's father Vasily was a carpenter. The 1926 medical report used the word *stoliar*—"joiner, cabinetmaker"—to describe him. Nikolaev reported to the medical examiner in 1926 that his father was an "alcoholic" who suffered from "syphilis, tuberculosis, psychological and nervous diseases." He died in 1908 of cholera. Nikolaev's mother, according to Kirilina, was illiterate, and "took whatever work she could to dress, shoe, and feed her children." Fragments of a December 4, 1934 interrogation by the NKVD reveal her as an inveterate gossip obsessed with figuring out which of her relatives and friends were "rich." From about 1918 until 1934 she worked as a night cleaner of city trams at the depots. This is how Maria Tikhonovna described her son's early life to interrogators on the night of December 1, 1934.[3]

· 17 ·

Testimony of Leonid Nikolaev's mother, Maria Tikhonovna Nikolaeva, night of
December 1–2, 1934. RGANI, f. 6, op. 13, d. 1, ll. 58–59.

———————

Leonid was sick by the time he was one year old, he had the "English
sickness" [rickets]—he had a swollen head, a swollen belly, all of his joints
were dislocated, his bones were dislocated, he was hospitalized for two
years in a cast, after that he got sick again and couldn't walk until he was
eleven. Around age twelve he had a seizure—he shook violently, like in a
fever, and he was unconscious. That was the only such attack he had in his
life. As a grown-up he was always sick and he's sick with rheumatism now.
Leonid's father drank like a fish, we lived in a damp basement.

Nikolaev briefly described his early childhood in an "autobiography" he composed in May 1934.

· 18 ·

Excerpt from Nikolaev's autobiography "[My Struggle] for a New Life"
(*Za novuiu zhizn*), fifty-six handwritten pages with 33-page "Supplement,"
spring 1934. RGANI, f. 6, op. 13, d. 24, ll. 24–32 (excerpted in KGB report
of April 1956).

———————

On May 31 [New Style] 1934 I will be exactly 30 years old, for this reason I am presenting a short biography of my life and work—about the entire path I have taken through life.
    . . . Piter [St. Petersburg], the Vyborg Side, is the place of my birth, and
where I live to this day. When I was three or four years old I was still a little one, like my second son Lyonia now. I remember little of this period,
and indeed, there is little enough to tell. Just a few scenes come to mind. I
remember, for example, how I crawled (due to illness I didn't walk until
somewhere between ages three and five) in front of my father, who often
came home in a party mood.

Nikolaev's origins were close to the bottom of St. Petersburg society.
His physical disability probably also made it hard for him to grow up
in Russian working-class masculine society or abide by its mores. As
an adult Nikolaev did not smoke or drink, which suggests social isolation given the habits of the time. As we have seen, relatives and former
co-workers described him as friendless.

However hard life in the imperial capital was, there were people who sought to ameliorate the sufferings of the poor. As a boy Leonid received free medical care for rickets, including many months in hospitals. He finished a six-year primary school in 1916, after which he was put out to work as an apprentice to a watchmaker.[4] When crowds of common people and soldiers took over the streets in St. Petersburg in February 1917, demanding bread and attacking police, Nikolaev was just about to turn thirteen. He later claimed that in 1917 he fought "on the barricades" for the revolution. Whatever the literal truth about the barricades, the revolution's promises of a "new life," peace, freedom, and an epoch of plenty for the "laboring masses" gripped the deprived boy's imagination. In his own mind Nikolaev remained loyal to that vision almost to the end.

It was in 1918 that Nikolaev claimed to have gotten the pistol he later used to murder Kirov—a 1917 model Nagan. In December 1934 Nikolaev told interrogators that a Red Guard (a member of a worker militia that generally supported the Bolsheviks) who lived in his family's apartment gave him the revolver. When asked why a soldier would give a gun to a fourteen-year-old boy, Nikolaev replied that he had fought on the barricades with the Red Guards in 1917 and they saw him as an adult.[5]

Nikolaev did not serve in the Red Army during the Civil War, probably because of his physical problems, and perhaps because of his youth. However, the revolutionary authorities dispatched him at age fourteen to the Samara Region, along the Volga River, where he served as secretary of a village soviet, according to Kirilina from January 1919 into 1920. This was one of the more remarkable aspects of the "world turned upside down" of the Bolshevik social revolution—teenagers, mostly male, from the "lower classes" were suddenly put in charge of local government. It is unfortunate that we do not know more about this episode. The boy Leonid was serving as nominal head of the village assembly in a region torn by fighting between Reds, Whites, local peasant militias, and "bandits." During this period seizure of peasant grain supplies by the Bolsheviks (and their White opponents) led to mass famine and even cannibalism.[6] Peasant "bandits" retaliated by torturing, dismembering, and burning alive Communists they captured. Red Army units in turn used machine guns to massacre crowds of peasants armed with scythes and pitchforks.[7] Nikolaev must have witnessed at least the aftermath of such violence. We can only guess how it affected him. Did he accept that the war against the peasantry was necessary to build the "new life"?

After his tenure at the village soviet, Nikolaev returned to Petrograd and served briefly as a medical orderly with the 978th Military Hospital of the Red Army. He was hired as a clerk in the Vyborg Ward Section of the city soviet's Department of Communal Property on May 28, 1921. Kirilina points out that this was a time of very high unemployment in Petrograd—the Civil War had just ended, industrial enterprises had mostly shut down, and masses of demobilized Red Army soldiers were seeking work. Nikolaev, she suggests, may have found a job through Ivan Sisiaev, an older worker at the Putilov arms and metal factory. Sisiaev lived "almost next door" to Nikolaev, worked in the Department of Communal Property, and later served as Nikolaev's chief recommender for entrance to the Communist Party.[8]

In August 1922 Nikolaev's job was eliminated, but he soon got a more responsible position, as office manager (*upravdelami*) for the Vyborg Ward committee of the Komsomol (Nikolaev was already a member of the Communist youth organization). At the ward committee he worked with local Komsomol leaders whom he later implicated in the Kirov murder—Ivan Kotolynov, Andrei Tolmazov, Lev Khanik, Vasily Zvezdov, and Nikolai Shatsky. Kirilina states, without citation, that Nikolaev knew Kotolynov and others from childhood as the "Vyborg courtyard boys."[9]

There is indirect evidence that Nikolaev's colleagues were not happy with his work in this position. In June 1923 Leonid signed a formal request to be released from his job and transferred "to production"— hands-on factory work. Although this may have been an attempt to establish credentials as a proletarian which could aid in his advancement in the party, it is more likely that Nikolaev was acquiescing in a demotion. Party organizations often sent erring or incompetent members to work "in production" as a punishment and a reeducation in proletarian consciousness. The fact that Nikolaev applied in August 1923 for transfer into an army artillery school supports this hypothesis. If possible he wanted to study rather than work on the shop floor. The Komsomol ward committee, however, refused to sponsor him, and Ivan Kotolynov, committee secretary, signed the rejection. Kirilina suggests that Nikolaev may have born Kotolynov a grudge after this incident.[10]

In October 1923 Nikolaev began work as an apprentice metalworker at the Red Dawn factory. Here he became a Communist during the "Lenin Levy," the mass enrollment of workers that Soviet leaders initiated after Lenin's death to keep the party close to its class roots. On March 4, 1924 the Vyborg Ward committee of the Communist Party accepted Nikolaev as a candidate member, and on April 24 as a full member. The drive to raise the proportion of "proletarians" in the party may explain the speed with which Nikolaev moved from candidate to full member.[11]

Around this time Pavel Sutula, the husband of Nikolaev's sister (probably Yekaterina) taught Nikolaev how to handle his revolver. The two went out beyond the city limits for target practice. In January 1924, however, Sutula deliberately shot himself with the Nagan. It is not clear from available evidence whether he killed himself or not, but the suicide attempt resulted in a criminal investigation and confiscation of the pistol. Early in the fall Nikolaev applied to ward authorities for return of the pistol and got it back. At this point (September 2, 1924) he had to register the pistol and get a permit to carry it. He let the permit expire, however, after one year.[12]

In this period the first evidence appears of Nikolaev as a chronic complainer and "squabbler" (*sklochnik,* in the party terminology of the time). To put this in more positive terms, Nikolaev always stood up for his rights, or what he believed to be his rights. After he did not receive a full set of Lenin's works he had subscribed to, Leonid demanded his money back from the party committee. Kirilina also alludes to complaints to party authorities about conflicts between Nikolaev and co-workers.[13]

Probably at the behest of the Red Dawn party organization, Nikolaev was soon given a nominal promotion that got him out of the factory. In fact the "promotion," to office manager of the rural Luga County Komsomol organization, was not a desirable move. From the big city, the original heart of the Russian Revolution, party authorities dispatched Nikolaev to the rural fastnesses, where Communist organization in the 1920s was weak, peasants were hostile, and living conditions poor. But Nikolaev followed orders. The Luga County Komsomol committee appointed him administrative manager on January 28, 1925.[14]

Kirilina writes, "here too Nikolaev experienced difficulties almost immediately." In March he requested release from the "civic work" obligations all Communists were expected to undertake, in this case leading Komsomol study circles. The Luga Komsomol committee granted the request, but Kirilina believes that Nikolaev's refusal to do "civic work" was behind the committee's refusal to give his appointment as administrative manager final confirmation on May 21, 1925. Then, on December 8, the committee fired him, referring him back to the Leningrad Province Komsomol committee for further orders.[15]

In Luga Nikolaev met and married Milda Petrovna Draule, born in August 1901, and a Communist since 1919. In official documents (the obligatory party autobiographies, for instance) Draule presented herself as the daughter of a landless farm laborer (*batrak*) who immigrated to the Leningrad area from Latvia. In a 1933 political autobiography, Draule wrote that she began to work for landowners herself at age nine, herding pigs and cattle. As she grew older she shifted to garden and field work. During winters she attended elementary school, and in 1916 she completed the equivalent of middle school.[16] Milda's younger sister Olga claimed in a 1926 political autobiography that the Draules had been early supporters of the Bolsheviks in Luga and that White forces under General Yudenich imprisoned and nearly executed Milda in 1919.[17]

Draule's origins and personality are in fact hard to pin down. According to Tatyana Sukharnikova, who has recently seen the secret police files on the Kirov murder, her father was in fact a well-off estate manager for a large landowner in Luga Province. He was able to send her to a *gimnaziia* (elite liberal arts high school) in St. Petersburg, from which she graduated in 1917. Milda joined the Komsomol and played a part in denouncing her father's employer to the Bolsheviks. It is entirely plausible that Draule concealed her class origins as part of constructing her Communist identity. She may have fudged the truth— perhaps her father really once had been a landless laborer, who had risen to the post of estate manager. And probably she had done farm work for the estate owner, even if her father was relatively well-off. However, it is also possible that Sukharnikova's summary biography of Draule draws on NKVD materials falsified after the Kirov murder to make Draule appear to be a "class enemy."[18]

There is at any rate no reason to doubt that Milda was an early and dedicated supporter of the Communists. In 1919 she was hired to work in the executive committee of a township soviet. From there she moved on to a job for the Petrograd Provincial Committee on Foodstuffs, allocating grain delivery quotas and later grain taxes for various regions of the province. In 1921, probably at the age of nineteen, she returned to the township soviet executive committee as secretary, a managerial position. In July 1922 the Luga County Communist Party committee appointed her chief of the Department of Personnel Assignments (*uchraspred*), where she worked until she left Luga with Nikolaev in early 1926.[19]

A photograph of Draule in her teens or early twenties shows a pretty, round-faced young woman in a military forage cap, with short hair, slightly pursed lips, and a serious look. Although one source claims that she had a cleft lip, the photograph indicates that it could not have been more than a minor blemish. In *The Unknown Kirov,* Alla Kirilina provides a sketch of Draule based on interviews with and memoirs of former Leningrad neighbors and co-workers. According to neighbors, Nikolaev and Draule kept to themselves. Kirilina quotes interviewees who described Draule as "nice-looking," "modest," and "guileless." Ex-officials in Smolny who had worked with Draule portrayed her as "serious, independent, devoting a lot of attention to her children." At work Draule must have been hard-put to win respect. Despite party rhetoric about equal rights, Bolshevik men tended to see women as ignorant, undisciplined, and interested only in the profoundly "petty bourgeois" topics of romance and babies.[20]

Vasily Ivanovich Zvezdov, one of the former Zinovievites arrested and shot on fabricated charges after Kirov's killing, described Nikolaev's time in Luga, as well as his relationship with Draule, in a December 12, 1934 interrogation. Zvezdov and Nikolaev were transferred from the Vyborg Komsomol organization to Luga together in early 1925, and shared a room in the Luga House of Soviets. Zvezdov told interrogators that Nikolaev was quiet, that he held himself apart from Komsomol colleagues, and that he reacted in a "morbid" fashion to happenings at work. In Zvezdov's opinion, Nikolaev suffered from an "inflated opinion of himself" (*bol'shoe samomnenie*) and also "bore his personal troubles alone." Zvezdov saw Draule as similar to Nikolaev in her "eccentricities" and her "reserve." He also opined that Nikolaev was "under her influence." It is worth noting that Draule was three years older than Nikolaev. Judging by his writings in 1934, Nikolaev was very dependent on his wife.[21]

What could Draule, evidently a competent and attractive young woman, and veteran of the rural revolution, have seen in Nikolaev, the aloof, difficult, and sickly boy from Leningrad? Whatever his physical disabilities, Nikolaev was handsome in a baby-faced way, with a full, dark head of hair. For Milda he may have represented an opportunity to move to the big city, the center of power, excitement, and opportunity. Leningrad Komsomol boys must have seemed good catches to rural Luga girls—Zvezdov also married during his year in the district.

Nikolaev, who was truly in need of care, probably aroused maternal feelings in Draule, as Zvezdov implied when he described her "influence" over him. In the second interrogation following her arrest, on the night of December 1, 1934, Draule described her husband in terms that were not entirely negative—"a keen person, impressionable, sensitive . . . nervous, passionate." He was also "willful" and "stubborn." He read a great deal and always strove to improve himself. He was sensitive, intelligent, he did not drink, and he apparently enjoyed staying home with the family. Based on his 1926 medical report, it appears that Milda was probably his first sexual partner.[22]

In spite of his spotty work record, it appears that Nikolaev was capable of competent office work. Kirilina has read the transcript of a presentation he gave in Luga on September 13, 1925 to the secretaries of county Komsomol organizations about the technical details of party record-keeping. She reports that it is "very logical, the language of the lecturer is literate, and he presents the various tasks—the proper form for writing protocols, the way to bind documents, the organization of an archive—in a professionally knowledgeable fashion."[23]

Nikolaev's time in Luga overlapped with the beginning of the battle between the Zinovievites in Leningrad and the Central Committee organization led by Stalin. In the 1934 interrogation cited above Zvezdov admitted that every one of the Luga Komsomol leaders supported Zinoviev through most of 1925. Nikolaev, he stated, was present at meetings where they discussed their support for "the opposition." Zvezdov speculated that his roommate "felt solidarity" with the Zinovievites, but denied that he ever spoke either for or against them. He behaved himself in "indeterminate fashion." This really does suggest that Nikolaev was never a vocal supporter of the Zinovievites, for Zvezdov would have been under pressure from interrogators to connect him to them.[24]

By March 1926 Zvezdov was one of only two Zinoviev supporters left in the top ranks of the Luga Komsomol. The others had all gone over to the Central Committee. They fired Zvezdov, and sent him back to the Northwestern Territory Party Committee for further assignment.[25]

Luga connections remained important for Nikolaev and Draule even after they moved to Leningrad. For example, the Old Bolshevik Pyotr Andreevich Irklis, a veteran of the Luga party organization, apparently provided work recommendations for Draule in the city. Irklis and Draule had worked together in Luga, where Irklis headed both the soviet's executive committee and the district party committee, during the Civil War and after. At about the same time Draule moved to Leningrad, Irklis was promoted and also moved there, but remained under surveillance as a former Zinoviev supporter. In a December 3, 1934 interrogation Draule said that she had considered turning to Irklis for help with the family crisis provoked by Nikolaev's 1934 firing and depression.[26]

Upon return to Leningrad Nikolaev got a job at the Red Arsenal factory, where he was registered first as a metalworker, then as a lathe operator (*strogal'shchik*). But in fact he did not serve as a blue-collar worker. Instead he moved from one low-level office position to another, clerking and managing the "Red Corner," a workplace reading center devoted to propagandizing employees. Milda had trouble finding a steady job, temping for the Vyborg Ward committee of the party and doing "production work" at a textile factory. Nikolaev lived with Draule in his mother's apartment at Lesnoi Prospect 13/8, together with his grandmother, his younger sister Anna, his older sister Yekaterina Rogacheva, Yekaterina's husband, and another relative, Aleksandr Vasiliev, a fifty-two-year old handyman who lived in the kitchen. The couple had one room 17.4 meters square (about 160 square feet) to themselves. This was close to average living space per person in Leningrad at the time, which was 8.5 square meters.[27]

In 1927 Milda and Leonid had their first child, a boy they named "Karl Marx," or "Marx" for short (it was common for Communists in the 1920s to name their children after their political heroes—there was a fair number of "Vladlens," for Vladimir Lenin). Milda reported that she had to quit her job in 1928 "due to my child's sickly condition." In 1929 she returned to work, first as a ledger clerk and then as office manager at the Red Woman Worker factory.[28]

In the meantime, Nikolaev was having trouble at work again. He was fired from his position at Red Arsenal probably in the early fall of 1929, around the time of the purge that followed the September 1929 *Pravda* attack on the Leningrad party organization. On October 16 a workshop party committee at Red Arsenal reviewed Nikolaev's party membership, and discussed his firing. Nikolaev complained that he had been fired due to his active participation in "self-criticism" (*samokritika*), the officially sanctioned process in which co-workers gave one another supposedly constructive criticism (see above, pp. 86–103). In other words, he had been finding fault with his fellow workers as part of the official campaign to streamline production processes and root out oppositionists from the party. But there was perhaps more to his firing than self-criticism. At the purge meeting a fellow worker asserted that "In my opinion, it is untrue that Nikolaev was fired due to his participation in *self-criticism*. Nikolaev sat in the storeroom and got the rank six salary, as a metal-worker. Then he began whining that this is not a real job, why are you paying me so little, and asked for a transfer 'to the bench.' So he began to earn two hundred rubles a month. Then he left for the foreman's office. And he sat in Foreman Kartashev's office, and he kept his mouth shut there, but when they cut him, he started to tell everyone that he had been fired for *self-criticism*."[29] At least as far as this co-worker was concerned, Nikolaev was a complainer and a slacker who did not deserve his relatively high salary.

Evidently Nikolaev had passed judgment on his fellow workers in a factory or workshop newspaper, because while the party committee did not expel him, it did censure him for "using the press to start a row." He did not get his job back. However, with the First Five Year Plan and the industrialization drive beginning, jobs were easy to come by. He was soon hired at the Karl Marx factory, officially as a blue-collar worker. Again, however, his real job was to run the "Red Corner."[30]

Leonid did not last long at Karl Marx either, no more than four months or so. Sometime in early 1930 the party cell there "mobilized" him for rural work in support of the forced collectivization of the peasants. He was dispatched to a very remote location, Uiarsk District in east-central Siberia, near the city of Krasnoiarsk and the Mongolian border. The evidence for this is from one of Milda Draule's interrogations on the night of Kirov's murder. During his mobilization Nikolaev apparently remained officially on the list of employees at Karl Marx. He probably left for Siberia in late April or early May.[31]

It is safe to assume that with this "mobilization," Nikolaev's party comrades were once more getting rid of him. And this time the assigned task was especially unpleasant. Collectivization in the Krasnoiarsk area was as brutal as anywhere in the USSR. Tens of thousands of "kulaks" (which often meant simply those who balked at joining the collective farm) were shipped to the far north of Siberia in the middle of the winter of 1929–1930 and dumped in the taiga, often with no shelter and meager supplies. Officials and poorer villagers stole the property of the "dekulakized" and sometimes raped their wives or daughters. Communist activists, troops, and police forced many peasants to sign up for the collective farm at gunpoint. Oral threats were enough to "persuade" others. Peasants responded by rioting, massacring their livestock, killing hundreds of officials and activists in isolated acts of "terrorism," and in at least one district, organizing open rebellion. Due in part to weather, and in part to government confiscation even of peasants' seed grain, much of rural Siberia faced starvation in 1930–1931.[32]

It is quite possible that Nikolaev was one of the "25,000er" worker "volunteers" mobilized with much fanfare in 1929–1930 to administer the new collective farms. A sizeable contingent of "25,000ers" from Leningrad served in central Siberia. Things did not go well for them. According to contemporary reports cited by James Hughes, local authorities often failed to supply the "25,000ers" with winter clothes, arrange shelter for them, instruct them in their tasks, or even pay them. The city Communists generally lacked knowledge of agriculture and were socially isolated. Not surprisingly, many behaved badly, embezzling collective farm funds and abusing the locals.[33]

Nikolaev seems to have anticipated the possibility of violence. Probably in preparation for his assignment in Siberia, he renewed his pistol permit on April 21, 1930. The permit shows stamps for two purchases of ammunition during the year 1930 (a total of twenty-eight bullets), at the Leningrad sporting goods store Dinamo. The store was officially part of the NKVD (Commissariat of Internal Affairs), which has given rise to claims that Nikolaev "got his ammunition from the NKVD." In fact NKVD stores were the only legal channel for purchasing ammunition in the Soviet Union at the time, and the secret police (the OGPU) were not part of the NKVD. It was also commonplace at this time for party members to carry sidearms.[34]

While Nikolaev endured his de facto exile to Siberia, his wife received rapid promotions, probably due to the same quiet competence that she had displayed in the Luga soviet apparatus, and to her connection with Pyotr Irklis, who now headed a department of the Leningrad Region Party Committee. In September 1930 she was appointed to a clerkship at the committee, in the Department of Statistics and Party Membership, the same department in function, if not in name, that she had worked for in Luga. She soon earned promotion to assistant to the chief of the Sector of Cadres for Light Industry.[35] Draule's employment records suggest the difficulties she experienced working, doing her obligatory "civic service" for the party, and caring for her sons all at the same time. Between 1931 and 1934 she took a number of days off to nurse sick children, and she requested and received permission at least twice to skip party meetings and study circles for reasons of childcare. Draule's 1934 interrogation records indicate that she often brought work home to complete in the evenings.[36]

According to Draule in one of her December 1 interrogations, Nikolaev returned to Leningrad early in 1931 after "about one year" in Siberia. Soon after his return, Milda became pregnant with their second son, who was born on November 21, 1931 and named Leonid. Possibly through Milda's intervention with Irklis or other senior contacts, Nikolaev secured a position inside the regional committee apparatus at Smolny in April 1931. He was to serve as an *instruktor-referent* with the committee's Section of Light Artisanal Industry. The words *instruktor* and *referent* translate roughly as "administrator" and "assessor," and they were all-purpose job labels used for many party committee employees who monitored the work of local enterprises and party organizations.[37]

Probably late in 1931 housing authorities assigned Milda and Leonid a three-room apartment of their own, on Batenin Street, which enabled them to move out of Nikolaev's mother's apartment.[38] This was an unusual privilege. In all likelihood it was Milda who arranged it. The infant Leonid was on his way or already arrived, and enlargement of one's family was formal grounds to apply for a new apartment. Moreover Draule's new job at the regional party committee gave her access to special privileges and connections.

Once again Leonid did not last long in his job. In September he was transferred to a position as head of the Financial Department of the regional soviet's literacy program (the "Down with Illiteracy!" Society). Nominally this was a promotion, but given his troubled work history it is likely that Nikolaev was being kicked upstairs. According to the authors of a recent archive-based article, the job at "Down with Illiteracy!" was the thirteenth position listed on Nikolaev's official work record.[39]

In August 1932, after a one-year tenure with the literacy program, Nikolaev moved back to Leningrad party headquarters at Smolny, now as a price inspector for the Workers' and Peasants' Inspectorate (RKI), the watchdog organization charged with monitoring all kinds of government operations and economic enterprises. There remains in the archives a note from the chief of the city or regional RKI, N. S. Osherov, instructing the personnel department to hire Nikolaev. It is unclear who recommended Nikolaev to Osherov. Kirilina suggests his old patron Ivan Sisiaev, who supported him for admission to the party in 1924, and who had worked at the RKI. She also believes that there was a more "weighty" recommendation, because the hiring apparently circumvented usual procedures. This could have come from Irklis.[40]

Nikolaev's Writings

Seven months after Nikolaev began his job at the RKI he started to keep a family journal, apparently as a record for his sons. He hoped Milda would contribute to it too. Leningrad NKVD officers seized this journal together with Nikolaev's "testament" and other "notes" (*zapisi*) when they raided Nikolaev's apartment on the evening of December 1, 1934, immediately after Kirov's murder. The NKVD confiscated various other writings by Nikolaev in a raid on the apartment where his mother and sister Yekaterina lived, probably also on December 1. In the spring of 1956 the KGB provided a Central Committee investigative commission with a transcription of large sections of the journal, along with other writings by Nikolaev. All of the documents reproduced below were part of the 1956 KGB document release. There is good evidence that these documents are genuine, as will be discussed later in this chapter and in the Conclusion.[41]

Nikolaev's family journal covers a period from March 1933 through late November 1934, albeit with some long hiatuses. It provides a more intimate, if still partial, view of Nikolaev's personality and his family's life. It is also a good framework for presenting the entire story of his activities in the two years prior to the assassination. Below the reader will find journal entries interspersed with other documents, outside information, and commentary. The documents are arranged in chronological order.

Nikolaev regularly made grammar errors in Russian, some of which I have tried to represent in English. An autodidact, he often attempted to duplicate "high" style, bringing in clichéd metaphors, the grandiose verbiage of revolutionary proclamations, and words whose meaning he did not actually understand. Occasionally his writing made no sense, but did leave an emotional impression. I have tried to render these nuances into English as faithfully as possible. The KGB transcription available to me also contains numerous ellipses. It is not clear when these duplicate Nikolaev's own gaps, when they represent illegible sections that the transcriber omitted, or when they represent legible sections left out. I have included all ellipses below. In places I have been able to fill in missing words in the 1956 KGB document release by comparing the text to quotes from Nikolaev's writings in other sources, including December 1934 telegrams between Leningrad and Moscow, official reports from the 1950s and 1960s, and recent publications.[42]

· 19 ·

Excerpts from Nikolaev's family diary, "Our Life and Work," 1933–1934.
TsA FSB RF, a.u.d. N-Sh44, t. 12, ll. 401–410.

Diary
Our Life and Work
Year: 1933
1934
To all of you [probably Nikolaev's wife and children]:
Milda, take a look inside and write more!
MARCH 1933
13 March: We got new passports in connection with the introduction of personal passports throughout the USSR.

A big deal—such an event must be taken note of.

On the other hand, they're holding up things for my mother—because she hasn't handed her apartment over to the ZhAKT [a housing cooperative that leased apartments], not only that, they demanded from Matryosha /her sister/ two witnesses, because her husband had died and there were no documents on his class background (*sotsialnoe polozheniia*). Oh, poor *maiter* [apparently an attempt to transliterate in Russian German *mutter* or Latvian *mate*].

On the fourteenth I went to Luga on business and was there until the twenty-third, that's my old hangout, practically my hometown (*rodina*).

Milda and I visited the place where she was born—we even stayed overnight with acquaintances in an old house on a former estate /a unique experience/.

On the thirtieth we got the last of our things from Kalishchi Station—the final break with all of our connections and any hope of vacationing there in the summer (again), as we have for the last three to four years, when your parents (*stariki*) lived and worked there /between the two of them they've now lived around 140 years/.

Now they've opened a Police and Detective's Vacation Home (*dom otdykha*) there.[43]

Now our children have nowhere to run around freely except on Batenin Street.

APRIL

April 1—Happy April Fools Day!—how we used to celebrate today! Now we're much more cultured, and such superstitions aren't for us.

April 2—A while ago I managed to get hold of tickets to the Vyborg House of Culture /Lomansky [Street]/ for the Circuit Session of the People's Court hearing the case of the murder of three children, whose mother was the former secretary of the church council of Spasso Bochatskaya Church /Tikhvin Street—opposite the ward soviet/, now demolished—as leftovers of "the old regime (*starogo mira*)."

I went together with my brother Pyotr. The place was packed. They didn't finish the trial, they extended it to April 4. The priest–common-law husband (*sozhitel'*), recanted his earlier confessions, they took him into custody (he's already 50 years old).

April 3—today we had to turn down a good bundle of products at the ZRK [cooperative store] because Milda didn't have enough money for it.

Marx—"Karl Marx" to be precise—fell sick lay in bed from the morning on. He had a temperature of about forty degrees.

The boy is recovering from his smallpox shots. Today I also got a notice to go for a mandatory smallpox vaccination.

Papa Leonid.

April 4—Got home early from a work trip. . . . Today I'm tired. I feel like going to bed early and besides . . . I can't think of anything [to write]!

Marx turns out really to be sick, the doctor came. He has a temperature of 39.8 degrees. At night we gave him an enema, a mustard-poultice, a compress, and took other measures.

It's already eleven P.M. but no one's gone to sleep yet.

. . . The devil knows how the fleas bother us constantly, there are such a lot of them, they crawl out of the chinks of the floor in our new home [this refers to the apartment on Batenin Street, which they'd moved into about one and a half years earlier].

Mama came by—we put together a package for her sister Niura in Sverdlovsk. But for some reason no one's had a letter from her in a long time.

Today again I spent a lot of time putting together a bed for my Leonid.

There's no time to work on the radio or the bicycle.

Brought home coupon no. 1107 for joining the Red Star cooperative at 60 Bolshoi Street.

I scold Mommy again for not writing here.

L. Nikolaev.

April 5—morning—in the second third of March it seemed like it was like spring was already beginning, the starlings arrived in the woodlot, but today for the second day snow is falling and the temperature is one or two degrees above zero—it's cold and cloudy.

. . . Marksik feels better this morning, thanks to Mama's energetic measures.

L. Nikolaev

I'm rushing to work at the Obl. KK RKI [Regional Control Commission/ Workers' and Peasants' Inspectorate].

Yesterday I finished the bed for L[eonid]. He was scared at first. When I put him into the bed he sat for a long time frightened of something. Then pretty soon, as soon as everybody left the room, he began to act more bravely. Now it's already 11 P.M. and he just won't settle down, he loves it so much in his new bed.

Marx is getting better—his temperature has fallen.

I checked the second printing of the Industrialization Bonds for the Crowning Year of the First Five Year Plan—the numbers don't match.

Milda still hasn't written a single letter even though the diary is in a prominent place!

I want to undertake energetic study of Lenin's works.

Papa.

[Milda's entry] It's already 2:30 in the morning of April 6. I'm sorry that I'm not writing at all, but I don't have the strength now, I'm tired and my hands are frozen from rinsing and squeezing out the laundry in cold water. Everyone's been asleep for a long time. Today the baby [Leonid] only cried in his sleep a few times.

We had to put him back in his old bed, he was just so restless, I was afraid he'd crawl out, because the big bed is not completely finished, it'll have to be done tomorrow. L[eonid] is one year four months old now, he has twelve teeth in his little mouth, but he doesn't know how to use them yet, he's not biting into bread or crackers for real.

He walks from one object to another—more like crossing between them—with unsteady steps. Today he didn't get to play on the accordion because M[arx] is sick. I've got a headache I'm going to bed.

Mama.

Evening of April 6, . . . I spent the whole day at home, the weather was sunny. Pyotr [possibly Leonid's half-brother or Milda's brother] and his daughter came, and Lusya and Valya dropped in.

I have to get to work.

Leonid.

There is almost a nine-month gap in the transcription of Nikolaev's diary at this point. Dramatic events occurred in this period. Nikolaev lost his most recent job and the authorities transferred Milda Draule out of the regional party committee apparatus to the Leningrad offices of the Commissariat of Heavy Industry. These events occurred almost simultaneously and were probably connected. Nikolaev went on summer leave in August 1933 and was formally released from his job on October 1 with the official reason given as "due to his departure for study." On August 23 Draule was transferred from Smolny to the Commissariat of Heavy Industry offices, where she would head the Accounts Group. Nikolaev in his October 1934 "political testament" addressed to the Politburo, and Milda Draule in a December 3, 1934 interrogation, both indicated that Nikolaev was fired due to a conflict with his boss at the RKI, Fuks. Nikolaev also wrote that he was fired the day after he spoke up at a workplace party meeting [presumably criticizing his boss], and that Milda too was "fired" as a result of his speech.

In the second half of 1933 the party leadership mandated a general purge, aimed at ridding the party of passive members, "careerists" and "bureaucrats," criminals, "underminers," and kulak sympathizers.[44] In October and November 1933 Nikolaev and Draule both passed through the purge process. The records shed light on their August work transfers, and on Nikolaev's problems with co-workers.

The regional control commission evaluated Nikolaev's party membership on October 23. At the meeting his former chief at the RKI, Fuks, stated that "The quality of [Nikolaev's] work was not always well thought-out. And one other negative point—he thinks everything can be achieved in one giant leap, he doesn't want to improve himself, although he's capable of it." Kuchnev, evidently another co-worker, said that "Nikolaev must be warned that he should work to improve himself. Otherwise . . . he may end up making a mass of mistakes."[45]

In contrast, Draule's former boss at Smolny, Larin, was complimentary at her November purge commission hearing. Her work was "quite good," and she carried out her party "civic duties" conscientiously. She was "very disciplined, modest, worthy to be a member of the party." Larin supplied a suitably innocuous excuse for her removal from the job, mentioning "staff cuts." Draule's move to the Commissariat of Heavy Industry was evidently not due to any shortcomings in her work.[46]

Nikolaev's response to his latest firing was to apply for study, as his October 1 dismissal letter indicated. Taking time off from work for further education was a standard option for Communists in disfavor during this period, and Nikolaev, judging from his diary and Draule's

interrogation transcripts, had high educational and literary aspirations. He applied to the Leningrad branch of the Institute of Red Professors, a Communist Party school of graduate studies that was supposed to train a new generation of "Red" administrators, publicists,
and scholars with proper proletarian class credentials. Unfortunately
he failed the entrance exam, an episode which he mentioned resent-
fully in his "notes" (and which he also lied about repeatedly). The
party authorities then passed him along to another assignment perhaps intended to fit his intellectual aspirations. On October 14, 1933
the Cultural and Propaganda Department of the Regional Party Committee instructed the director of the Institute of the History of the
Communist Party, Otto Lidak, to hire Nikolaev.[47]

· 19 ·

(continued)

Nikolaev's family diary. TsA FSB RF, a.u.d. N-Sh44, t. 12, ll. 401–410.

———————

Dec. 25, 1933—On Dec. 18 in the morning we went to the park with
our sleds. The boys were very happy. The baby yelled when he had to sit in
the sled to go home, he liked making snow mounds so much. In the
evening M[ilda] and I went out on our skates, we skated two hours and
decided to go out to skate every evening no matter what as soon as I get
back from work. Today we are honorably fulfilling our pledge. It was on
Dec. 22 that our son began to move around on skates on his own. He's
very very happy, he wants to make M[ama] proud. . . .

[apparently written by Milda from this point to Feb. 18, 1934] At first I
let him move about on one skate, then changed the foot it was on. The second evening it was necessary to rationalize things—we put wooden blocks
under the heels /and attached to them five-kopek pieces wrapped in paper,
so they wouldn't slip/.

Now the skates sit firmly. He loves to skate on his own, he just glows
with happiness. He moves with confidence. And the little one laughs—[il-
legible]—ooo! Then he runs to dig in the snow with a spoon.

On December 23 both got diphtheria shots; their arms hurt. Leonid
even has an elevated temperature, so yesterday and today we didn't take
him outside.

Today it was −16 degrees, and yesterday it was o degrees.

Tomorrow we have party cell elections, I'll be getting home late, but
maybe I'll be able to skate with M[arx] before bed.

It's already three in the morning I'm going to bed. Somehow I just don't feel like working.

Good night. Mama.

On Dec. 19 I sent the laundry out, but I doubt it will be returned on time. And P. only remembered to write home on the twenty-first. M[ama?].

There's been a mouse in the cupboard /the top one attached to the wall/ for two days, I don't know how to get him out of there.

M.

Draule's life, a constant round of work, party meetings, laundry, and childcare, was about to get even more difficult. Early in 1934 her brother, Pyotr Petrovich Draule, an employee of the Leningrad police, was charged with embezzling department funds, convicted, and sentenced to three years forced labor. And in February Leonid Nikolaev's half-brother, Pyotr Nikolaev, who had recently been drafted, deserted his Red Army unit and returned to Leningrad. In a much later interrogation Pyotr claimed that he wanted to see his new wife and that army service felt like "jail." Nikolaev's older sister Yekaterina, perhaps informed by Milda, turned him in to the military police the day after he showed up at Nikolaev's apartment.[48]

· 19 ·
(continued)

Nikolaev's family diary (entry from late April 1934). TsA FSB RF, a.u.d.
N-Sh44, t. 12, ll. 401–410.

Marx—He'll be seven soon, his height is 120 cm. Weight—hard to say he hasn't been weighed for a long time health—poor, he just went through the flu. Frequent hiccups—we're working on it, he takes medicine.

He speaks well in two languages [presumably Russian and Latvian]. He reads by syllables words of one to five letters. He counts successfully up to 100. He can make out numbers up to one billion.

He taught little Lyonya [the toddler Leonid] to say the names of a number of letters—especially the soft sign.

He's outside rarely. Today we were out for thirty or forty minutes. Cold. We don't have a nanny and grandma's sick. We are both of us at work all day. He goes to sleep at nine or ten in the evening. He sleeps on his own in the big bed, his sleep is good. He doesn't wet his bed.

M[ama] always puts him to bed, he calls me every night to go to sleep with him for company. In the morning he gets up at nine or ten. He gets dressed on his own. He's pale, often hungry, he doesn't get much good food.

But we do buy milk all the time almost daily we've got it only for . . . for them three liters /three rubles a liter/.

He's shy and fearful. Lyonya sometimes upsets him.

At times he doesn't like me. I have to try to imbue him with proper love for his father.

On April 23 KIROV was in the courtyard escorted by five persons, inspecting the construction site. We were out walking—Marx, Lyonya, and I.

Leonid.

Nikolaev composed this entry two to three weeks after he lost his job at the Institute of History. This time, however, the situation was more serious, for the Communist cell at the Institute expelled him from the party on March 31, before firing him the next day.[49] His transgression was refusal to obey yet another party "mobilization," this time for work in a railroad Political Department in the distant town of Taganrog, a seaport on the Sea of Azov in southern Russia. Nikolaev told acquaintances later that his previous "mobilizations" to the countryside had ruined his health. Milda Draule referred to "cardiac attacks" of some kind in her December 1, 1934 interrogation, and Nikolaev's mother, as we have seen, said he suffered from rheumatism. Nikolaev also based his refusal on "family" grounds—presumably he did not want to leave his wife and two young sons for another long, lonely stretch of political propaganda work. The records of the Institute of History party meetings (there were at least three) that considered Nikolaev's expulsion reveal that part of his "craziness" was his willingness to discuss in public abuses of power by party organization officials. Nikolaev said openly that the supposedly "honorable" assignment to political work on the railroads was a rotten tomato the administrators were handing off to the lowest-ranking members of the collective. He also abused his bosses. At an April 7, 1934 Institute party meeting that discussed his refusal to go to Taganrog, Nikolaev said of the director, Lidak, that "he imagines that he is some kind of a Grand Khalif, some kind of grandee, a Biblical miracle . . . [but in fact] the Institute [would] work fine without [him]."[50] Nikolaev used the informal *ty* to Lidak, insulting when addressed to a workplace superior. The next day the Institute party cell met again, and members were not happy with Nikolaev. In a typical self-criticism ritual, they cast him out of the party collective.

· 20 ·

Excerpt from the protocol of a general session of the party organization of the
Leningrad Institute of Party History, April 8, 1934. RGANI, f. 6, op. 13,
d. 25, ll. 39–43.

———————

Agenda: [. . .] (2) Nikolaev's refusal to accept assignment to transport.

Comrade Avvakumov informed the meeting of Nikolaev's refusal to accept mobilization to transport and read Nikolaev's statement.

Comrade Nikolaev: I worked in the regional control commission of the
RKI, from whence I was sent to the Institute of Red Professors. Due to my
weak health and for other reasons [note that Nikolaev evades discussing
his failure on the entrance exams] I was unable to begin study and was
passed on to work at the Institute of Party History, where I hoped to grow
politically. It seemed that I fulfilled my work as *instruktor* in the Section of
[local] Commissions on the History of the Party in satisfactory fashion. I
received no warnings. On April 1 I was supposed to go on a regular trip to
the districts outside Leningrad. When I arrived at work on March 31,
Comrade Burt called me in for a conversation. Section Chief Comrade Bystrova for some reason was not invited. Comrade Burt asked me what
party work I had done, and then I was handed a card, ordered to go to the
ward party committee for assignment to transport [railroad Political De-
partment], and dismissed. I didn't want to take the card. Then Burt ordered an emergency meeting of the party committee. [. . .] At the party
committee meeting I did not bring up my illness, I wasn't crazy and I did
not refuse the assignment to transport. The question here was of life or
death: who would have to go—Avvakumov and Burt, or me. You can't
construct a story of Nikolaev's "antiparty behavior" just on impressions,
as the opposition does. After the party committee meeting I want to the
ward committee—Comrade Zolina already knew about this business, as
they'd called her on the telephone from the Institute of History, but she
nonetheless asked me to fill out a card. At the ward committee I saw an *instruktor* and one of the secretaries, they suggested that I submit a formal
complaint. I thought that this [complaint] was going to be handled by correspondence, but it was handled by the party committee, which called me
in. At the party committee Lurye proposed not to examine the matter, but
to confirm the earlier decision to exclude me [from the party]. This was
the proposal of Lurye, who was himself [once] let go, because there is a
blot on his record. At the party committee I said that no one had helped
me at work. To my request for leave Comrade Lidak answered that I had
been fired from the Institute. They say that someone from the city committee called the ward committee in order to keep Avvakumov, who
greatly feared the mobilization, in Leningrad. And do they know at the

city committee who Avvakumov really is, he was thrown out of the Institute of Red Professors [but] now holds a responsible post at the Institute and writes about party history. If they're going to check on me, then they'll have to check on Lurye and Avvakumov too. I know that the regional committee would not have mobilized me anyway due to my illness. I never refused to accept the mobilization. I've been treated too harshly. I ask for indulgence.

Questions:

Comrade Kirillov: Why did you (*ty*) say, "I'm not going to go, I've got a job."

Comrade Nikolaev: I never said that.

Comrade Senchenko: You state that Comrade Avvakumov gave an untrue account of events.

Nikolaev: I put it this way: it is possible that due to the reorganization at the Institute they want to get rid of me, so I'll find work myself.

Shidlovsky: Who gave you cause to say that they wanted to get rid of you?

Nikolaev: It seemed like that to me. Not only that, but they wouldn't place my articles in the wall newspaper [workplace newsletter].

Avvakumov: You (*ty*), Nikolaev, said at the party committee that for several months they undermined [you], they wanted to fire you, and you had heard about this from Comrade Korol.

Korol: How could I have said anything to Nikolaev, when I knew nothing about this?

Maiofes: Is Nikolaev's psychological condition normal?

Beloborodov: Do you consider the mobilization to transport an honor?

Nikolaev: Yes.

Sulima: Do you deny the sequence of events, and did you act appropriately when you refused to take the card, and then went to the ward committee without it? Did Avvakumov lay out correctly the sequence of events?

Nikolaev: Avvakumov simply dumped a bucket of garbage over my head. Yes, I really did refuse to take the card.

Krom: What basis do you have for supposing that Avvakumov and Burt sent you in place of themselves?

Nikolaev: People were fighting each other not to go, and to send someone instead of themselves, I turned out to be the victim. If it is a question of life or death, whether to send the director or Nikolaev, then you select Nikolaev and send him off.

Fyodorov: Who chose the candidates?

Avvakumov: The ward committee picked out two [party] cards: mine and Averianov's, and as mine was returned, the party committee selected Nikolaev as the only appropriate candidate, as all the others had been sent to the ward committee and returned for one reason or another.

Discussion:

Comrade Bystrova: Comrade Nikolaev, I had the best opinion of you as an employee, but I am very surprised by you now. You should know the duties of a party member. A member of the party must obey any mobilization, even if he doesn't like it, even if they don't send him on such an honored mission as transport, even on any minor work in the middle of nowhere. You ought to confess your mistake honestly before the party, which you have sinned against in a terrible way.

Comrade Kornatovsky: Confirms all that Avvakumov said.

Even before the session of the party committee and at the session, Nikolaev constantly was saying, "forget it, I'm not going to go, I've got a job." He asserted this categorically several times and so the party committee was called for an extraordinary session. Nikolaev's behavior at the party committee meeting and before the party committee meeting was antiparty, just as it is today. He stupidly and boorishly reduces everything to personal grievances. Nikolaev's actual face is the face of a petty bourgeois self-seeker (*meshchanin-obyvatel'*), a selfish pig, who has broken with the party. The party committee's decision to exclude him must be confirmed.

Comrade Korol: I heard Nikolaev shouting hysterically "that they're firing Bystrova and they want to get rid of me." Nikolaev cites me, supposedly he heard from me that they wanted to fire him, but I have no idea how I would know that. The party committee acted entirely correctly when it put the question of expelling Nikolaev from the party.

Comrade Shidlovsky: When Nikolaev left the party committee meeting he was upset and he yelled that they wanted to get rid of him. That they should have given him his card earlier and he could have found himself work on his own. When they gave the floor to Nikolaev at the second party committee meeting I thought he was going to recognize his mistake, but he didn't do it. I believe the party committee's decision to be correct.

Comrade Berezina: Events at the party committee were precisely as Avvakumov described them. At this meeting they treated Nikolaev very gently, Comrades Lidak, Avvakumov, Burt tried to persuade him to rethink his actions, to think about what it meant for him to refuse to accept the mobilization. Nikolaev behaved in a manner unworthy of a party member. He behaved like an embittered petty self-seeker (*obyvatel'*), at two meetings he acted like a two-faced reprobate (*dvurushnik*); at the second meeting he announced that he wanted to go to the ward committee, but they wouldn't let him. He's got everything wrong in his statement, that's not the way it was. At the party committee he was always whining that he needed work that was easier and higher-paying. I propose confirming the decision of the party committee.

Comrade Beloborodov: We veterans are familiar with such cases. Today Nikolaev refused to go to work in transport on such honorable conditions, so can we count on him to go to the front in the event of war, or will he refuse again? It's shameful that such an incident happened at the Institute of Party History. The party committee acted correctly when it excluded Nikolaev from the party. I suggest that we make a political matter out of this case and publish an article in the press.

Comrade Smirnov: Nikolaev has acted unscrupulously, not only as a party member, but as a person, by denying everything and reducing it all to personal grievances. Nikolaev has nerve to say that they wouldn't let him go to the ward committee. Nikolaev is the epitome of a petty self-seeker who somehow got past the purge, obviously hiding deep his degeneration. Nikolaev got scared of going to the ward committee for discussions, although the question of his assignment had not yet been finally decided. Nikolaev himself should admit that he is not worthy to be in the party, he is not necessary for the party. At the meeting it was made entirely clear that Nikolaev refused to accept the party mobilization and the party committee acted completely correctly when it expelled him from the party.

Comrade Orekhov: Nikolaev's psychological condition needs to be checked on, and if he is healthy, then a political trial must be organized in order to present an example of the kind of member the party does not need.

Comrade Lidak: This is the first such extremely sad incident at our Institute, and it is a blot on the whole Institute. It's humiliating even to admit that such an incident could happen at our Institute of Party History, but it is impossible to keep silent.

I know Nikolaev only through his work, and I had the best opinion of him, but I knew little of him as a party member, and I did not know that he was such a petty self-seeker. I never thought of sending Nikolaev off for good, and I had just assigned him to a work trip to Cherepovets, there was no talk about firing him at all. Nikolaev has the style of a petty self-seeker, he attributes everything to personal grievances and he tries to cover up his own mistakes with the mistakes of others, but this troublemaker's act didn't go over in our collective. The collective turned out to be strong and united and there were no cracks through which his slander could penetrate.

When I was called to the emergency meeting of the party committee I did not believe that Nikolaev was really refusing to go to the ward committee to discuss [the issue]. We tried to get him to understand that his continuing membership in the party was at stake, but he announced, "forget it, don't make a mountain out of a molehill, they don't exclude people from the party for such nonsense, and I'm ready to take some other work." It was clear that he could not remain in the party, the party committee resolved to expel him, of which fact he was immediately notified. After the meeting he went to the ward committee to talk about transport [the mobilization] and not his expulsion. After that it was clear to me that Nikolaev could not remain at the Institute. This is the first time I've met with such an embittered, selfish, petty malcontent inside the party. His declaration upset me, because he told a story that was the opposite of what actually happened. For lack of sincerity and deceiving the party, he needed to be expelled, at the second meeting of the party committee he declared that he had made no mistakes and he proposed that the committee consider the incident closed. Nikolaev has turned a major mobilization for transport into a farce and he's doing the same for the disciplinary process. This sad case will nevertheless be of use to the party, for it helps it to clean its ranks and strengthen itself.

Nikolaev: You wanted me to shut up, submit, and disappear.

Comrade Fyodorov: The fact that there is in our organization such a member, leaves a spot on the whole Institute. The decision of the party committee to expel Nikolaev is absolutely correct, and this is an excellent lesson for others. The only mistake made is that the party committee did not know Nikolaev, who worked mostly in the field, well enough and recommended him for work in transport.

Nikolaev should admit that his behavior was incorrect and petition the ward committee to send him on the transport assignment.

Comrade Burt: talks of those members of the party who take a responsible attitude when the party mobilizes them. He and Comrade Averianov together with about 300 comrades mobilized for transport are now in training, preparing for their new work. They are doing their best to carry out the priority task assigned to them by the party as well as possible.

Comrade Burt's words are interrupted by applause.

Nikolaev: I made a mistake. The comrades' accusations are fair. In 1925–1926 I fought hard for the party's general line. I do not deserve such a harsh punishment. My health is shattered. The party committee did not approach me in a comradely fashion, [but] very harshly [otherwise] I might have thought again and gone to the ward committee. Decide the question as you wish.

Resolved: To confirm the decision of the party committee to expel Comrade Nikolaev from the party for his refusal to obey the party mobilization and for his behavior at party meetings and sessions which demonstrated that he is an embittered petty self-seeker alien to the Leninist party.

Decided unanimously.

[. . .]

Chairman—Avvakumov

Secretary—Yampolskaya

On December 1, 1934, the NKVD detained Otto Lidak, and questioned him about Nikolaev's personality and his firing.

· 21 ·

Protocol of interrogation of Otto Lidak, director of the Institute of History of the
Communist Party, Leningrad, evening of December 1, 1934. TsA FSB RF, a.u.d.
N-Sh44, t. 24, ll. 191–194.

Question: When was Nikolaev assigned to you at the Institute and what
do you know about him?

Answer: Nikolaev was sent to me by the regional party executive committee in December 1933. I appointed him as *instruktor* assigned to the
organization of district departments of party history in Leningrad Region
with a salary of 250 rubles. He coped poorly with work, as he did not have
sufficient preparation. In the entire period of his service at the Institute he
left the city to visit the counties only three times. I personally did not insist
on more trips, because I feared that he would make errors and I was keeping an eye on him.

Question: Under what circumstances did you fire Nikolaev from the Institute?

Answer: [. . .] This is how it happened. In April of this year the Smolny
Ward committee of the Communist Party required that our organization
select several candidates for dispatch to transport. Comrade Burt, secretary of the collective, picked out Nikolaev among others, but he categorically refused not only to work in transport, but even to go to the ward
committee to discuss the question. He gave as the basic reason for his refusal his unwillingness to work in transport, but then began explaining it
as due to his family situation [note that Lidak ignores Nikolaev's claims
that he was sick]. The party cell and its bureau viewed this behavior as antiparty and resolved to expel Nikolaev from the party.

[. . .]

Question: Did Nikolaev approach you for anything after his firing from
the Institute?

Answer: Yes, he did. In May he dropped in on me at the Institute, asking
that I hire him back, but I refused, first because he was a party member
with a strict censure, second, as a bad employee. He approached me again
in September of this year with a demand that he be paid for the entire period of his unemployment, that is from April of this year. I answered that
there is nowhere any rule that someone who has been fired should receive
a salary for the period of time in which he does not work, and that the government would not give me money to do that. Nikolaev announced that
he was going to make a[n official] complaint against me. After that I never
saw him.

Question: With which employees of the Institute did Nikolaev have the
closest relations?

Answer: I don't believe he had any friends at the Institute. No one supported him when we reviewed his case at the party cell, at any rate. [...]

Question: What is your opinion of Nikolaev?

Answer: I told everyone, including Shirokov /regional committee *instruktor*/ and Pokhvalin /regional committee *instruktor*/ that I did not consider Nikolaev a member of the party, because he is an unworthy and undisciplined person. When Pokhvalin told me that Nikolaev had written a complaint to Comrade Stalin and asked me what kind of a party member he was, I characterized him as an antiparty person. [...] Based on my observation, Nikolaev is a morbid individual, an unstable and nervous person [...]

On April 29, 1934 and/or May 5 three officials of the Smolny Ward party committee heard Nikolaev's appeal of his expulsion. Avvakumov and Yampolskaya represented the Institute of History party organization. Nikolaev admitted "his mistakes" and the ward committee restored him to party membership, with a "strict warning" for "indiscipline and a petty, self-seeking attitude . . . towards the party mobilization." The Institute of History, however, did not rehire him.[51] Nikolaev remained angry and frustrated with the verdict. He and his family were now living on Milda's salary and associated rations alone.

CHAPTER 6

Nikolaev Agonistes

The brush with expulsion from the party, the "strict warning," and the loss of his job shocked Nikolaev into a state of depression. Milda Draule in her first interrogation on December 1, 1934 reported that "from the moment of his exclusion from the party [Leonid] fell into a depressed mood, he was just waiting a decision from the Central Committee on his 'strict censure' all the time and did not want to work anywhere."[1] Nikolaev became obsessed with the resolution of his case to the exclusion of all else. A diary entry from mid-May shows his distraction.

· 19 ·
(continued)

Nikolaev's family diary. TsA FSB RF, a.u.d. N-Sh44, t.12, ll. 401–410.

FOR RECOLLECTION (*dlia pamiati*)
On April 29 I lost my fountain pen, then recently I left my cap in the tram, today I lost the most important thing—all of our bread ration cards—five shares.
May 13 Leonid.

At the same time as he blamed party officials, Nikolaev experienced intense feelings of self-reproach about his firing and party warning. He also had an increased sense of dependence on, and guilt towards, his wife. Obsessive waiting, self-reproach, a sense of helplessness—there is little doubt that a psychiatrist today would diagnose Nikolaev as suffering from depression. Thoughts of death and suicide also seem to have haunted him.

· 19 ·
(continued)

Nikolaev's family diary. TsA FSB RF, a.u.d. N-Sh44, t. 12, ll. 401–410.

———————

DEAR MINTSA [an affectionate diminutive for Milda]!
You are uncomplaining and wise, you bear everything, I did not expect [anything] like—this.
Soon it will be one and a half months that I've been sitting at home, five persons are living on your salary, and I have no work. But that's not my only misfortune, I am morally completely dead—excluded from the party and fired from work, worry about you and many [other] thoughts torment me. I've never been so ashamed before you!
How much I've changed my thinking in that time!
No one even wants to understand that outside the party neither work nor life is of any value to me.
Milda, you are my only true companion.
You are wise in all things. I have also become wiser in much and I think that soon, soon all of this will be over.
May 13, 1934. Your Leonid.

Nikolaev's reactions to his party warning and firing may seem overly histrionic, but they were common among young Communists of the time. An editor at the newspaper *Factory Siren* (*Gudok*) who was expelled from the party in the fall of 1930 wrote in his appeal that the expulsion was "political death, and I cannot live outside the party . . . it follows that I cannot continue to exist physically either. . . ." Pyotr Chagin, working in a job he considered beneath him, wrote to Kirov in 1934 that he was "buried alive" in his enforced idleness, a phrase Nikolaev also used in one of his letters. For many young men from the laboring classes like Nikolaev, the Communist Party had become a substitute for absent or dead fathers and the sole source of hope in a severely disrupted society. Bolshevik leaders actively suppressed alternative organizations, setting the party up as the only font of authority and social cohesion. More concretely, employment in the party apparatus meant access to special rations, superior housing, vacation homes, and other perquisites.

For Nikolaev and other expellees feelings of abandonment and mean-
inglessness were compounded by the loss of material benefits.[2]

As summer approached Nikolaev struggled to keep active, reading,
writing and rewriting his "autobiography," which he told Milda was
for his children's education, and gardening. He also sent articles and
letters to local *mnogotirazhki,* the newsletters printed in many Soviet
workplaces and residential complexes. Nikolaev exemplified the Soviet "graphomaniac," the compulsive writer, often an autodidact, who
cherished visions of literary grandeur and who sought to improve him
or herself through "culture." As a writer Nikolaev seems to have imagined himself in several roles—the literary genius, à la Leo Tolstoy or
Maxim Gorky, the bold denouncer of high-level malfeasance, and the
Communist propagandist leading the masses.[3]

In early May Nikolaev sent a typical contribution to his apartment
complex's *mnogotirazhka.*

· 22 ·

May 8, 1934 letter from Nikolaev to his apartment complex's newsletter.
RGANI, f. 6, op. 13, d. 1, ll. 24–32 (excerpted from April 1956 KGB report).

To commemorate the conclusion of the First of May celebrations, as a
holiday of labor, I propose setting up in our courtyard /on a wooden base/
a bust of Karl Marx, as the founder of the precepts of Communism, and
warrior for the liberation of the laboring people, which will beautify our
courtyard and be the best kind of agitation on the front of socialist construction and the development of the consciousness of the broad masses in
the task of improving conditions of housing and everyday life and care for
communal residential facilities. I propose to undertake these measures by
a collection of donations from building residents /for which it will be necessary to appoint a commission and compose a budget estimate/. As a proposal [*sic*] I am contributing two rubles.

Nikolaev also wrote many other proposals to local authorities between April and August, including suggestions to remove the city's
monument to Peter the Great (the famous Bronze Horseman), demolish a chapel, and rename a barber shop. The first two ideas marked
him as a true Communist believer. Nikolaev wished to cleanse the city
of the remnants of the twin pillars of Tsarist authority—the autocracy
and the Orthodox Church.[4]

On May 5, 1934 the Smolny Ward party troika heard Nikolaev's appeal of his expulsion from the party.

· 23 ·

Excerpt from the protocol of the third session of the party troika of the Smolny Ward committee of the Communist Party from April 29 through May 5, 1934. RGANI, f. 6, op. 13, d. 60, ll. 80–81.

Chairman: Tsinit

Members: Meshchersky and Georgiev

Item 12.—On the imposition of a party censure on Nikolaev, L. V. by the party committee of the Institute of Party History.

Nikolaev, Leonid Vasilievich, b. 1904, member of the Communist Party from May 1924, party card number 0156283, elementary school education, worker origin, social status—worker, profession—mechanic, worked in production 10 years. Member of the Komsomol from 1919 to 1929. Present occupation—unemployed. Red Army service—exempt due to illness. No [previous] party censures.

Facts of the case: Excluded from the party on April 8, 1934 by the party committee for refusal to visit the ward committee Selection Commission (*otborochnaia komissiia*) for the TsK mobilization, and for his petty self-seeking reaction to the order to present himself for the mobilization /divisive accusations against a number of senior party workers/ and so on.

Comrade Nikolaev is present. A representative of the party committee is present.

Comrade Nikolaev: "I did not immediately go to the ward committee in response to the order because I had previously been rejected [meaning unclear], later I went to Zolina [at the ward committee], and filled out a form [a petition for exemption from the mobilization?]."

Representative of the party committee Comrade Abakumov [Avvakumov], Yampolskaya state that Nikolaev is not unemployed, that he refuses to go to transport work, and that he can find himself work if he needs it. He went to the ward committee [only] after the present decision of the party committee to expel him. He views his dispatch to the ward committee for transport work as a punishment /the question was not of mobilization, but of selection for the mobilization. Nikolaev behaves in an undisciplined fashion, he threatens the party committee, declaring, "I will admit my mistakes when the party committee admits its own."/

In view of [Nikolaev's] recognition of his mistakes, restore his party membership. For the indiscipline and the petty self-seeking attitude to-

wards the mobilization demonstrated by Nikolaev—issue him a strict
censure to be recorded in his personal party file.

Chairman: Tsinit

Members: Meshchersky and Georgiev

On December 1, 1934 troika member V. E. Meshchersky told police
that, "at the troika meeting Nikolaev left us the impression that he was
a morbid (*boleznennyi)* person and an undisciplined Communist. We
decided that he did not deserve expulsion from the party, but issued
him a strict censure all the same. We did not insist upon a check-up of
his [mental] health."[5]

· 19 ·
(continued)

Nikolaev's family diary (the confused chronological order of entries is in the
document released to the TsK in 1956). TsA FSB RF, a.u.d. N-Sh44, t. 12,
ll. 401–410.

Today Mama visited, yesterday they were at the cemetery.

She told me to come tomorrow for bread she promise [*sic*] to give it to
us from her ration.

I accompanied her home at eleven in the evening, she reminisced about
how she played with me when I was a child, the hospital, the rest home,
and so on.

May 1934. Leonid.

Today I read V[illegible]sky's article—re: the newspaper—good.

I forgot to write about M. Gorky's article on the great initiative for Socialist Realism [a new designation at the time] it was right to the point.

May 20

Today I fixed a third pair of boots. Yesterday I finished the garden, I
planted 45 kilograms of potatoes. Mama and Marx helped.

The weather got cold, my kids are not outside much. Grandma's sick,
Marat and Marta [the children of Olga Draule and Roman Kulisher] are
staying with us, I am unemployed and have no ration card. Tomorrow
we've got to pay eighty rubles for the apartment. Of three rooms half of
the apartment we [they?] wallpapered then gave it up, there's no time
[. . .].

On the day of my birthday—May 31 [according to other sources Niko-laev's birthday was May 23 [New Style]]. I finished the first and second parts of my autobiographical story, in June I'll present the last ten years of our road together, it is a much more serious topic.

Soon I'm leaving for the country for a vacation.

I visited my old office, at the party committee no one is interested in how and for what I'm living . . .

I made my petition, but after that there's no place to turn, not because that's the last level of appeal, but that's the way the times are, a fierce struggle.

I feel like I want to write a few lines about the crux of the situation, what's to happen next. To C[omrade] S[talin]. . . . the First Tsar [of War and] Ind[ustry] . . . in Rus. But, you know, there's no hope, it won't reach h[im]. . . . .

May 5 Leonid.

Nikolaev's diary entry for May 5 appears to be a reaction to the Smolny Ward troika's decision to restore him to the party but censure him. The reference to Stalin as "First Tsar of War and Industry" is the first comment in Nikolaev's available writings with a possible anti-regime shading. Privately Nikolaev had probably entertained doubts about the Stalin regime for some time before the spring of 1934. In his tours of duty in the countryside he had seen brutal struggles between the regime and the peasants. In Leningrad he was undoubtedly aware of the wildcat strikes that rocked major city factories that summer and fall. As a member of the Leningrad party organization he had heard all kinds of attacks on the ruling clique voiced openly in the 1925–1926 battle between Zinoviev and Stalin. If we can believe Draule's evidence in a December 11, 1934 interrogation, Nikolaev had assimilated many criticisms of the regime. According to her, he returned from a trip to the countryside in the winter of 1932–1933 or 1933–1934 criticizing the party for confiscating grain from the peasants with practically no recompense. Draule also attributed to Nikolaev negative comments about regime exploitation of workers, suppression of self-criticism, and excessive military spending.[6]

· 19 ·

(continued)

Nikolaev's family diary. Ts FSB RF, a.u.d. N-Sh44, t. 12, ll. 401–410.

The money's running out, we're taking loans. Today my entire lunch was two glasses of kefir (*prostokvasha*). I went to the garden, took part of a loaf of bread. I dug potatoes . . . I'm physically exhausted—from three until ten in the evening I was there, but it did improve my mood.
    Leonid, July 11, 1934.

NEW DACHA
    It's a beautiful spot, what can you say, near the seaside—Sestroretsk.
    From the seashore it's too far to the other side of the railroad station, beyond the lake by Zabolotnaia.
    It doesn't matter, but the hut is just a nightmare, it's ancient, right next to a cowshed and outhouse.
    The windows are tiny, the chinks are huge. Even so, they're charging an unbearable rent, 150 rubles for the season and the season is one and a half months.
    Our kids have been at the dacha since the thirteenth and they've tanned a bit. The weather's now at its hottest, the rain as a rule falls at night in the majority of cases.
    I've spent two days with them, yesterday Mama left. Olya [Olga Draule] is there. Little Marat [Olga's son] was there.
    July 18, 1934 Leonid.

In the months after his firing Nikolaev often reports that he and the children are hungry, and complains about trouble paying his apartment rent. The loss of his income and the associated rations had a catastrophic impact on the family finances. In 1934 real wages in the Soviet Union were still at the nadir plumbed during the First Five Year Plan and forced collectivization. When Nikolaev and Draule were both working, they had earned almost 500 rubles per month. On this income they supported five people—themselves, their children, and Milda's elderly and sick mother, who had lived with them since the summer of 1933. After Nikolaev lost his job the family lived on Milda's 230 rubles per month. Rent on the family apartment was high—Nikolaev reported it at different points as 65 and 80 rubles. In this period the average Soviet urban family was spending at least 30 rubles per month per person on food. Feeding five people would have cost an absolute minimum of 150 rubles—just about all of the Niko-laev/Draule income after rent payment.[7]

After Kirov's murder, investigators who wished to show that Niko-laev had received money from the Latvian and/or German consulates in Leningrad succeeded in getting testimony from bitter members of his extended family that the Nikolaev/Draules lived well throughout 1934.[8] The NVKD also used the Nikolaev/Draule dacha rental in Ses-troretsk, a popular summer destination for the Leningrad party elite, to make the same case. However, the decision to rent the dacha is un-derstandable without assuming clandestine sources of income. First, the family diary indicates that Leonid and Milda both placed a high value on getting their children outdoors in the countryside. Through 1933 they spent part of most summers in Luga. When Milda's parents moved into their city apartment, there was no place to stay in Luga, so the Nikolaev/Draules rented a place in Sestroretsk. Second, Nikolaev indicated in his diary that he and Milda were borrowing money, prob-ably from relatives. Third, the Nikolaev/Draules probably had some savings that they could have used for the dacha rental.

During the summer months Nikolaev continued to appeal his case. On May 17 the Smolny Ward committee confirmed the troika sentence of May 5. On June 5 a hearings board of the regional party control commission heard his appeal, in which he demanded the annulment of his warning, and restoration of his job at the Institute of Party History. The board rejected both demands. On July 2 the party collegium of the regional control commission ratified the board decision. Nikolaev then requested a second hearing before the board, which again rejected his petition on August 3. In the meantime Nikolaev wrote an appeal to the central Party Control Committee (KPK) in Moscow, dated July 25, 1934. During this period he also sent a letter directly to Kirov request-ing restoration of his job and annulment of his warning.[9]

Nikolaev wrote this letter probably in July or early August. He stressed themes that appeared again and again in his petitions to the authorities over the next few months. Among these were his past work for the RKI and the regional party organization, his participation in the struggle against the "New Opposition" (Zinoviev, Kamenev, and Trotsky), and his loyalty to the party. He complained that he had been without work or rations for nearly four months "but no one pays any attention to this." His situation, he wrote, was hopeless. On August 25 he addressed a similar letter to Stalin, claiming that he had been fired for legitimate self-criticism, describing his straitened material circumstances, and requesting work and a pass to a state sanatorium to restore his health with a rest cure. Nikolaev complained that the party was ignoring him in spite of his "eighteen years of service in the labor force," his "responsible work" in fighting the opposition, and his mother's "unrelenting . . . work in production," for over thirty years.[10]

· 24 ·

Excerpt from Nikolaev letter to Stalin, August 25, 1934. RGANI, f. 6, op. 13, d. 1, ll. 10–53 (April 1956 USSR prosecutor's report on Kirov murder).

I have been sitting without work for five months. All of this has had a deep effect on me, that I am left completely helpless and sick . . . I am asking for some attention. I continue in the hope that I will receive help—an offer of medical treatment. I am asking that I be given work—otherwise outside the party, outside active participation in the party and the new life—I have no life, no work, no path.

It was common in the 1920s and 1930s for senior party officials who suffered nervous breakdowns due to overwork or "working over" in the self-criticism mill to go on extended vacations at state sanatoria, or even abroad. Nikolaev's request for a vacation in a rest home may have been of this sort. It probably grew out of deep despair and was not motivated by purely physical problems. He complained to acquaintances and in his diary that years of overwork had "shattered his nerves."[11] Moreover, some "farewell" letters that he wrote to family members in August, but may not have delivered, suggest that he was considering suicide, or possibly the assassination of party officials.

· 25 ·

Nikolaev's letters to family members, August 1934. RGANI, f. 6, op. 13, d. 1, ll. 60–62.

MY LAST FAREWELL

1. TO MY DEAREST MOTHER

Dear mother, with all of my joy in life I would never have thought to part with you this way, but the cruel struggle for life has swallowed me completely . . .

Of course you will not understand everything that is going on with me. I haven't even complained to you about this, but the fact is I've been sitting for five months without work and without a piece of bread.

But I am strong [enough] to carry the task I have begun to its conclusion. I know well what a mother's love means, but I have to tell you the truth, that soon you will experience great grief and shame . . .

You have worked all of your life, fulfilling your work duties, without seeing a single ray of hope, and I too have entered upon a hard and rocky road. . . .

. . . I thank you for the life that you gave me. Do not be dejected and do not be timid!

Farewell, Mama.

I kiss your wrinkled little forehead and hands, I wish you well forever.

1. For Katya, Niura, Petya [nicknames for Nikolaev's three siblings] and my other relatives and friends I wish all satisfaction and all possible success in life.

YOUR LYONYA.

2. Dear MINTSA.

It is very hard for me to explain myself before you. For your life together with me and for the children you deserve great consideration (*vnimanie*).

. . . but it is not yet given to you to know all that is going on with me.

As you know well the recent events at the Institute of History of the Communist Party shook me deeply.

As on a lifelong friend I depend on your steadfastness and support.

You know, my love, that I have always been patient and undemanding, it was not in vain that we grew together in one idea, in our life as friends, in work, and in our care for the children.

. . . Whatever may happen to me, let the party not judge you.

And am I guilty of anything before her [the party], that I should be cruelly punished . . .

I prostrate myself before your steadfast modesty and pure heart.

I thank you for [our] life and for the children, your care and love will nourish our Marx and Leonid.

My intentions have not changed.

These do not [does he mean "will not"?] trouble you in any way . . .

Forgive me. It is not my fault that you sometimes experienced great deprivation.

A heartfelt kiss to you and the children.

I remain your LEONID

To my dear children—MARX and LEONID.

You, my children, are at the moment of your blossoming, like little azure flowers /one of you is seven, the other is three years old/.

Devoting myself all the time to you, I have never spared my time or energy. I feel for you as for a drop of my own blood. I am not going to press upon you any deep moral lessons, it is too early for that, but do not sin only in this, do not forget your father and your mother. For you I leave my own story and all of my documents.

For you dear Mintsa I hope that you will be able to raise them and educate them.

Let Mama, Grandma, Olya, and the others help you [addressing the children here], I may soon fall asleep for eternity.

Value and do not forget my irreproachable love for you. Live and grow for our happiness, but the strength of love lies so deep in me that I would even be ready to take you with me.

Your father, L. Nikolaev

Leningrad, August 1934.

That August Leonid's sister Anna Pantiukhina and her husband moved to Kuznetsk (it is unclear whether they went to the coal-mining region in southwestern Siberia or the town in Penza Region). In late December and early January 1934 Anna testified to the NKVD about Leonid's reaction to her departure. At her mother's apartment, Leonid gave Anna a copy of his "autobiography," which she "glanced at," noticing sections on their parents and Leonid's time in Siberia. Leonid accompanied the Pantiukhins to the railroad station, where he cried and said that they might never see one another again.[12]

In spite of Nikolaev's histrionics and his desperate appeals to authority, the daily grind of financial and family worries went on. In September his brother Pyotr deserted a second time from his army unit and again showed up at Nikolaev's apartment. Milda hurried over to tell Nikolaev's older sister Yekaterina, who once more turned Pyotr in.[13]

Nikolaev was hard-up for money, especially because he had begun to consider a trip to Moscow to present his case personally at the Central Committee. In September he asked his brother-in-law Roman Kulisher to loan him money for the Moscow trip. Kulisher refused. He also asked his sister Yekaterina for fifty rubles. At about the same time he approached his former boss at the Institute of History, Lidak, and asked him for "back pay" for the entire period of time since his firing at the end of March. Lidak laughed. Nikolaev also tried to sell some state bonds he held (perhaps the "industrialization bonds" party members were more or less obliged to purchase). Apparently he had to get official permission to make the sale. It is doubtful he could have found a buyer except at a very steep discount.[14]

· 19 ·
(continued)

Nikolaev's family diary. TsA FSB RF, a.u.d. N-Sh44, t. 12, ll. 401–410.

———————————

September 30 Grandma is sick temp. 37 degrees, we called a doctor, he stuck in his thermometer, held it two or three minutes, and hurried off. The thermometer showed 36.5.

After him used my therm.—it showed 37.5. M. didn't give the [illegible], I said—I don't know what's going on.

Leonid.

. . . Just got back from my mother's.

I was over there two or three hours.

Sister K and mother all try to calm me.

You'd think it would be possible to find the strength to be calm /but I couldn't/.

Milda puts up with me because she understands my "weak" side—as a good family man. . . .

I took mother to work, it was sad, bitter until tears welled up.

But they forget that I am still strong and want to fight. . . . .

They must not think that I am putting my personal interests above everything. . . . for me the important task is . . . . . and struggle in the name of the general good. . . .

October 17, 1934—12 A.M. Leonid.

Nikolaev felt sad, enraged, and isolated. His family was by now exasperated with his obsession and his failure to find a job. They accused him of selfishness ("they must not think that I am putting my personal interests above everything") while he insisted that his actions served a higher cause ("struggle in the name of the general good"). Family members expressed their bitterness against Nikolaev in early interrogations on December 1 and 2. According to them, he had never really sought work, but indulged his obsession with getting a sanatorium pass and righting the injustice done against him at the Institute of Party History. Milda too was frustrated with Nikolaev. On Dec. 3 she told

interrogator Genrikh Liushkov that she had remonstrated with Nikolaev about his "unhealthy" attitude and refusal to find work. She believed at the time that his behavior was strange and could lead to "an
abnormal life," perhaps alcoholism, but not a "serious political crime."
In what one imagines was a spectacular understatement, she admitted
that her relations with Nikolaev in the months before the murder had
been "somewhat tense."[15]

Having failed to achieve the results he wanted with letters to Kirov
and Stalin, in early October Nikolaev once again tried to contact the
highest authorities.

· 26 ·

Nikolaev letter to the Politburo, October 9, 1934. RGANI, f. 6, op. 13,
d. 1, ll. 65–74.

Air mail. Moscow. Ilinka Street. Central Committee of the All-Union
Communist Party (Bolsheviks)—Politburo
A Last Hope . . .
The strength of my anxiety and endurance force me to turn to you.
In short, my situation is one that I would not wish on anyone.
I have been sitting without work and without rations for seven months
now, they are about to throw my family /four persons/ and I out onto the
street [from our apartment], but no one offers any help.
My conclusion is this—the story of the affair that happened at the
Leningrad Institute of Party History has changed my thinking about a
great many things!
It starts to seem strange to me that as result of my eighteen years of labor work I am beginning to think of my right to life.
A revelation—perhaps that it seems to me that I was climbing a hierarchical ladder, subordinating myself to my service duties and submission
[sic]. Every time that I wished to help facilitate work through [construc-
tive] criticism . . . I was stupidly rejected.
The primary reason for this was my passion, my self-sacrifice . . .
You see, I am not a thief or an enemy . . . and I do not understand why I
am no longer trusted, why there is no access for me to life, to work, to education.
In the eyes of friends and acquaintances, in the eyes of my elderly
mother, who has worked unceasingly for four decades, I am still a martyr
and an exile . . .

I wrote a declaration appeal to the Party Control Commission of the Central Committee, two months have passed, but there are no results at all.

I wrote a letter to KIROV, but it did not reach him. I wrote to STALIN at the Central Committee—the same thing happened.

In the worst case, they are sent back to that individual who innocently tried to punish and defame me [*sic*—Nikolaev obviously meant to apply an adjective, "innocent," to himself].

Besides all of that, I have an entire correspondence of dozens of pages about granting me work and treatment at a sanitary rest home /from the Commissariat of Health, the Regional Labor Union Soviet, from I. Alekseev [*sic*—should be P. Alekseev] personally, the Ward Health Department, and etc., etc./. But they are all no use.

I request that I be granted immediately treatment at a sanitary rest home /as I exhausted myself at work/ and work, but if that is not possible, then I must give up faith and hope in deliverance . . .

October 9, 1934.

This communication reveals in passing that Nikolaev's family was in danger of being thrown out of their apartment, at least ostensibly due to failure to pay the rent. It is also possible that housing authorities considered him persona non grata (a "strict censure" from the party, a brother who deserted from the Red Army, a brother-in-law incarcerated for embezzling state funds), and were enforcing payment deadlines that might otherwise have been flexible. The threat of losing the family's housing must have added to Nikolaev's desperation.

Compared with Nikolaev's earlier writings, this missive shows deterioration in grammar and word usage (misplacement and misuse of the adverb "innocently," the redundancy of "declaration appeal," the inappropriate "endurance" in the first line). The man writing it was living in a chaos of anger and despair. The letter contains a kind of threat—that the writer, once a faithful believer in the Soviet system, may change his whole worldview if the injustices done him are not righted. If no help comes, he will "give up . . . hope." The entire composition bespeaks Nikolaev's tremendous exaggeration of his own importance. Perhaps to satisfy his craving to be heard, Nikolaev imagines himself in personal conversation with party leaders, who he expects, like parents, to understand and respond to his plight. He assumes, in effect, that they will care whether Leonid Nikolaev has lost his faith in Communism or not.

Soviet authorities had in fact fostered the view of the Communist Party as a universal therapist or parent able to provide for every one of its members' psychic needs. The party provided not only a purpose in life and a complete worldview, it also provided concrete benefits such as rest cures, ration cards, office jobs, and decent apartments. Nikolaev responded to this by sublimating the deep longings he had accumulated in the course of a lifetime of humiliation and deprivation (for revenge, for praise, for succor) into an extravagant dependence on the party. But if Nikolaev's "therapist" rejected him, his thralldom could easily turn into rage.

The October 9 letter raises the question of the authorities' handling of Nikolaev's various petitions. It refers to letters "sent back" to the very authorities who had supposedly abused him. According to the 1967 Pelshe commission report, both Nikolaev's August 25 letter to Stalin and his October 9 letter to the Politburo were returned by Central Committee apparatchiks "to the Leningrad city party organization with a request to notify the TsK and the petitioner of the results of investigation." The *instruktor* Pokhvalin, a functionary in the city party organization offices, checked on the Stalin letter. In December 1, 1934 interrogations both Otto Lidak, the director of the Institute of Party History, and another regional party committee official, Shirokov, recalled Pokhvalin talking to them during his inquiry. The Pelshe report states that the city committee forwarded the second (October 9) letter to the Vyborg Ward committee (Nikolaev resided in Vyborg, although his workplace was in Smolny Ward). Vyborg officials summoned Nikolaev to a meeting to discuss the letter, but he did not show up. In a telephone conversation with them he "expressed surprise that his complaint addressed to the Central Committee had ended up at the ward committee." KPK officials interviewing Nikolai Sveshnikov in 1966 mentioned that Vyborg Ward party officials sent the October 9 letter with comments back to the "Special Sector" of the Leningrad regional party committee, addressed to Sveshnikov. The Vyborg Ward committee communication was dated November 28, 1934. In all likelihood no one looked at it before the murder.[16]

Despite their veiled threats and tone of desperation, Nikolaev's letters would not have grabbed the attention of the functionaries who read the party's mail. Party leaders received thousands of letters a year and dozens of them had a tone of desperation, even mental disturbance. In 1934, for example, Kirov received letters from a cashiered army officer who wanted his commission back, from poverty-stricken widows, from authors who wanted him to review their manuscripts, from an unemployed music teacher who needed a job, and from a young woman in search of an apartment who wrote, "the last resort left to me in my life is my hope for help from you." On June 7, 1934 a man wrote to Kirov from the distant city of Orel, asking him to find him and his family an apartment in Leningrad, and addressing Kirov as "My dearest uncle" (*diadenka*). This correspondent concluded with "Love, Vova Finagin." Party leaders received too many such odd missives to check on every one carefully.[17]

Soon after composing the October 9 letter, Nikolaev turned again to Smolny officials in search of an office job (as we have seen he rejected returning "to the bench," where he had little experience anyway, on "health" grounds). He met with the *instruktor* Pokhvalin, probably to discuss his letter to Stalin. He also attempted to speak with Kirov personally, even approaching him in the street on October 15. He was detained by Kirov's NKVD bodyguards, and soon released (this episode will be discussed in more detail in Chapters 10 and 15). Nikolaev's motivation for renewed efforts to resolve his case may have been a sense of obligation to his family.

· 19 ·

(continued)

Nikolaev's family diary. TsA FSB RF, a.u.d. N-Sh44, t. 12, ll. 401–410.

Yesterday I looked at grandma [Milda's mother] and the children with horror. . . .
Hunger has taken a good grip on them, especially on Marx.
The reason is my unemployment.
Today I went to the regional committee. . . . in search of and in hopes of getting work, but the answer everywhere was the same—no work for *you!*
What's left to do?
Leonid.

I visited Pokhvalin tomorrow I'm going to see K[irov]. . . .
He [Pokhvalin] discussed my behavior—it boils down to—it's better to keep your mouth shut and whitewash everything. . . .
Leonid.

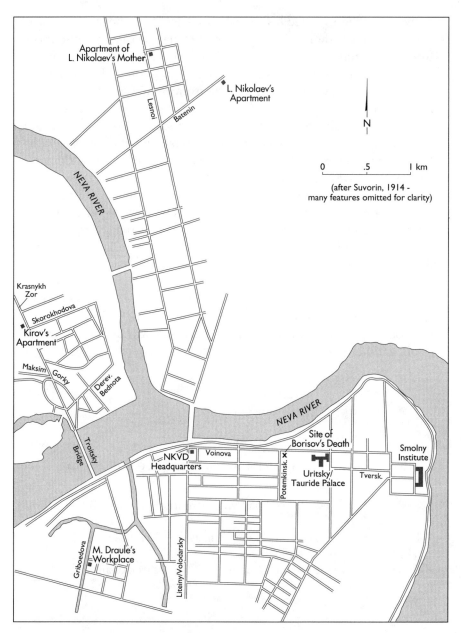

Map 4. Central Leningrad and Vyborg, 1934. Based on Suvorin, 1914, in
S. V. Kalesnik et al., eds., *Peterburg-Leningrad: Istoriko-geograficheskii
atlas* (Leningrad: Geografo-ekonomicheskii nauchno-issledovatel'skii
institut, 1957).

As of mid-October, Nikolaev was also keeping at least one other "diary," which was apparently not out for the family to see. He jotted down entries about his activities, often with dates, plans, and so on, in unsystematic form. These notes provide a bit more detail on his visits to Smolny in the middle of October, including his interview with Pokhvalin and his attempts to see Kirov. It appears that he spent much of October 19 in Smolny, seeking an interview with Kirov, applying for some kind of "extension" at the Institute of Party History (perhaps connected to another request for the "back pay" he believed he was owed since his firing), and either seeing or trying to see Pokhvalin about getting work. Eventually, either on October 19 or soon after, he met the *instruktor*, who was unhelpful. On December 1 Draule remembered Nikolaev talking about the Pokhvalin interview, and how the *instruktor* had "an already-formed attitude" towards him.[18]

Nikolaev was also waiting for the arrival of a circuit tribunal of the Central Control Commission, which he hoped would hear his case. The tribunal did review his grievances on October 25, with Nikolaev present, and confirmed his "strict warning for lack of discipline." According to Nikolaev, his day in court was "a comedy and not a hearing." He considered a trip to Moscow—his diary reads "Oct. 27–Nov. 10—trip to the Central Committee"—to make a personal appeal, even trying to borrow money from his acquaintance Yuskin for the trip. Yuskin refused the money, and Nikolaev did not go.[19]

· 27 ·

Nikolaev's personal diary. TsA FSB RF, a.u.d. N-Sh44, t. 12, ll. 401–410.

On October 19, 1934
11 A.M. to MANKOV to lodge a protest. Waiting for a representative of the Central Committee. Was there on October 21.

12 P.M. to KIROV. To give an explanation.—Didn't work out.

1 P.M. to Institute—to apply for an extension [or postponement]. Telephoned.

2–4 P.M. to POHKVALIN—Nothing.—Telephoned.

On October 25, 1934
At hearing of the Party Control Commission. (A comedy and not a hearing).

Oct. 27–Nov. 10 . . . trip to the Central Committee.

. . . you are counting on the passivity/placidity (*blagodushie*) of the masses but among them you will discover people of courage.

I've written to everyone, there's no one left, I wrote to K[irov], Stal [in], the Politburo, the Commission on Party Control—but no one pays attention, the only one left to write to is the Heavenly Tsar Himself.

A thousand generations will pass, but the idea of Communism will not be made flesh.

I will attack with the same strength with which I defended the new world.

I read WELLS's conversation with STALIN—it is astounding (*porazitel'-noe vpechatlenie sozdaetsia*).

. . . . For themselves, complete personal security (*neprikosnovennost'*), for us the most unbearable measure of punishment.

For themselves, for their wives and children—garages with automobiles—for us stale bread and a cold room . . .

Numberless family ties and [the] children prevent [me] from giving myself up to oblivion.

If you don't want the father and mother to bring them up, then take them yourselves . . .

. . . I wish to die with the same joy with which I was born.

I want to fight with the same strength with which I grew up in the fight for existence.

LEV. . . . ["the Lion"]

These notes from the last days of October show Nikolaev moving through his last attempts to achieve redress towards a decision to take violent action, and a final rejection of the Soviet dream of building Communism. His reaction to H. G. Wells's interview with Stalin (published in the party's theoretical journal *Bolshevik* in September) is somewhat enigmatic, but in context appears to be negative. It is quite likely that Nikolaev was sickened by Stalin's claim that Soviet socialism served the interests of the working class, even the "individual interests" of workers. He could see that this was not so in Leningrad, and he immediately laid out his own view of the party elite's exploitation of the workers—"for themselves . . . garages with automobiles, for us, stale bread and a cold room." This "us versus them" view of the Communist authorities was quite common among Leningrad's non-Communist workers, and the automobile, to which only privileged officials had access, was a common symbol of that social division.[20]

The closing words of the interview probably also rankled with Nikolaev. Wells wondered whether Soviet writers were allowed the wide freedom of expression advocated by PEN, the international writers' organization that he headed. Stalin replied that "We call that self-criticism, and it is widely used in the USSR." For Nikolaev, of course, self-criticism had turned into a cruel joke. One can imagine his anger when he read Stalin equating it with freedom of speech.

A central pillar of Nikolaev's identity, his identification of the Soviet regime with the worker revolution and the "new world" of Communism, was crumbling. He felt desolated, concluding that Communism would never be achieved ("a thousand generations . . . "). Returning to his understanding of the 1917 revolution that had initiated him into manhood, he imagined himself as the lone "lion" (he had not used the nickname "Lev" for himself in previous writings) who would revenge the masses against their new overlords in a purifying moment of violence.

On October 26 Nikolaev penned yet another farewell note to his wife, this time in a reproachful tone. In retrospect, the note, which apparently appeared in one of his journals, indicates he had decided on attempting an assassination.

· 28 ·

Nikolaev note to his wife, Milda Draule, October 26, 1934. TsA FSB RF, a.u.d. N-Sh44, t. 12, ll. 401–410.

October 26, 1934
M[ilda] you could have prevented much, but you did not wish to.
I never imagined our life would turn out this way.
Whatever happens to me, hand over all materials to the Central Committee of the Communist Party.
A decent amount of time has passed, seven months, first with respectful requests, then from indirect to direct warnings [the letters written on October 15], but no one helped. The moment of action has come!
It's hard to say who will truly understand /whose hand aimed the weapon/.
Lev ["the Lion"] is drowning in blood . . .

Much has been made of two phrases in this particular note. Nikolaev's reproach to Milda has been interpreted to refer to a supposed affair between Draule and Kirov. This is possible, although the phrasing is quite soft if that is so. Alla Kirilina offers a more convincing explanation, that Nikolaev believed that Milda could have used her connections (for example with Irklis) to get him yet another "supervisory" office job, but had chosen not to. He was accusing her of not supporting him during his personal crisis.[21]

Pursuant to a different version of the murder, other writers have argued that the phrase, "It's hard to say who will truly understand whose hand aimed the weapon," indicates that NKVD officers or other conspirators put Nikolaev up to it. In this interpretation, Nikolaev's phrase hints that the NKVD had actually instigated the killing. A more probable interpretation of this phrase, which accords with comments he made to interrogators on the night of December 1–2, is that Nikolaev felt that his "persecutors" bore responsibility for the assassination, because they had forced him to take extreme measures.[22]

Other documents dating from October witness Nikolaev's rejection of the existing Soviet regime, and his determination to act against it. In 1956 investigating authorities dated the following note to October 14, although it may well be from later that same month or even from November (evidence from other documents—see Document 26 and commentary above) indicates that Nikolaev made his final decision to assassinate Kirov after October 15).

· 29 ·

Nikolaev note to his wife and "class brothers," probably late October 1934. RGANI, f. 6, op. 13, d. 24, ll. 24–32.

To my dear wife and my class brothers. I am dying for my political convictions, on the basis of historical reality, without even a drop of fear, nor an iota of consolation (*uspokoenie*) . . . Remember and spread the word . . . I was ambitious for the real, living world. Devoted to the new idea, concerned, and of the fulfillment of my duties [*sic*]. Given that there is no freedom of agitation [i.e. political speech], of the press, of free choice in life and I must die. The Central Committee /Politburo/ is not in a hurry to help, because there they are sleeping the sleep of the great lords (*bogatyrskim snom*) . . . Your Beloved Nikolaev.

Also in October Nikolaev composed a long document explaining himself to party authorities and his countrymen. This he and later investigators seem to have referred to as his "testament" or "political testament." Based on other notes he took, it appears that he expected the authorities to find it after the assassination, and he hoped it would be circulated widely. He copied this document several times and left copies in a number of different places.[23]

· 30 ·

Manuscript of L. V. Nikolaev, "My Explanation before the Party and the Fatherland," addressed to the Politburo of the TsK of the Soviet Communist Party, October 9, 1934 or later. RGANI, f. 6, op. 13, d. 24, ll. 24–32 and d. 1, 65–74.

Moscow, Kremlin, Ilinka Street
To the Central Committee of the All-Union Communist Party
My Explanation before the Party and the Fatherland.

My sufferings shocks [*sic*] have gone too deep.

I do not have strength or time to write everything in detail.

In the contents of this letter I will limit myself to what deserves attention.

. . . living and struggling further without support or backing over [*sic*] a live human being—it seems senseless.

A correct development of consciousness and the presence in me of a worker psychology made of me a warrior for the new life—ready always to sacrifice myself.

"Insurmountable" difficulties have stood before me more than once, but at that time they corresponded to that atmosphere /they were within the corresponding limits/ in which I could live—I gathered new strength.

Now for three months I have felt that I am buried alive /!/, I am morally dead, around me they have created an unbreakable chain of slander through which I cannot break again without accepting the one thing / death/ .

For a person who has not a little experience of the real world on his life's road /in thirty-one years/—his [experience of the] present must be real.

Living in one's proletarian fatherland, is it truly possible to imagine a situation without a way out?

It turns out that the answer is "yes," it happens all the time!

For six months I have not received any offer of help for this living human being.

. . . . . While it was possible for me to live and work, I believed in something, there was in me a great and powerful zeal to rally the masses behind me for victory, to carry out the slogans set by the party.

But the immediate future will show what lies in store for me next.

I am not going to judge all, all of the weak points of our life. . . . and as a son of the proletariat I will remain always true to my party and my fatherland.

Over these six months I have thought very hard and only thanks to correct judgment have I held onto a healthy feeling of life.

However, the eighteen years of my working life are [now] far behind. It seemed to me that the revolution facilitated the development of my thoughts and ideas, that the revolution itself raised me to this height.

From active participation on the barricades of the proletarian revolution of 1917 I plunged into work directly in the soviet organs /1918–1922/ . . . working in a factory I felt myself a completely free and equal proprietor (*khoziain*) . . .

I participated most actively in the socialist construction of our country / the factories Karl Marx, Red Arsenal, Red Dawn/ and fought for the general line straight and true of the party.

I worked ceaselessly—day and night for the benefit of the party and it seemed to me that the party valued my merits /I worked in the regional party committee, the regional control commission, the Institute and RKI/ and experience.

Now in the recent years of my life I have risen to the most greatest [*sic*] achievement—the development of my mental powers and abilities. But my deeds and strivings remain like an unfinished building . . .

And, strange as it is, I am forced to speak of the right to life.

It turns out that I was climbing a hierarchical ladder—carrying out my work and subordinating myself to the duties of my job . . .

They excluded me from the party /the Institute party committee/, but then reinstated me.

The reinstatement was not a mistake, perhaps because I do not deserve the highest measure of punishment from my own party.

But those who needed to be punished for their petty tyranny—they remained unpunished and totally self-satisfied.

I am amazed by my own physical strength, profound endurance, and by the confluence of a whole series of circumstances.

. . . Our thoughts and deeds were all devoted to serving one class idea—the new life. My elderly mother has worked constantly for 38 years, and that always at night. My sister has been a party member since 1917. My wife has been a party member since 1919.

I am proud that I was birthed by the proletariat, but they, those people at the Institute, consign the working class to oblivion, they forget what it is capable of!

The confluence of all the circumstances that developed out of the Institute case pushes me towards a grave conclusion.

Moreover the way out in itself is entirely free, no one is interested in how, why, or by means of what I live. So I shift from one sphere of influence to another. . . .

I draw the conclusion that outside the party there is neither life, nor work, nor a path for me.

Perhaps I will swerve from the path, but at the moment I do not find any sin in that.

But the fact that I have sat for six months without work /and without rations/ has great significance.

I have called for help more than once, but no one pays attention everyone stamps the same stamp on my "case" . . .

* * *

I declare openly that by character I am a confirmed protester against all that is alien and unfair in such a great enterprise as our country.

For this I have been persecuted over the course of many years.

They sought revenge against me for everything—for my truthfulness, for my passion, for my abilities.

Here I indicate the reality of which KIROV spoke not long ago /his prophetic words/.

He said that "restless drifters can be sometimes found in our party practice" /July 11 of this year/.

If we turn to the history of the distant past, it is necessary to point out the great role played by Communists who played a not unimportant role in the matter of my education.

1. F. . . . and R. were the first to humiliate me. This was in 1921. For this F. was asked /by the Vyborg Ward Communal Housing Department/ to serve as a judge. Is this not bias?

2. When it was no longer convenient for M. to keep me on, he began by attacking my salary—paying me four kopeks a week and then he was able to squeeze me and fire me from the factory. And here the judicial organs / various commissions and the prosecutor's office/ were helpless against his underground tenure [in the party] and his decoration (*orden*).

3. OGNMI—60 . . . and there was no way /where they tried to fire me in 1924/ I referred [them] to the *Oblavrshkoll.*

4. But the very worst incident of suppression of self-criticism is my second-to-last place of employment . . . where I was promoted from the factory Karl Marx.

In the course of my work as an assessor I was an irreplaceable employee. Proof of this is the following:

From the moment of my arrival at work there were [*sic*] a revival of enthusiasm among the group of assessors—MESHCHERIAKOV, GORIACHEV, VLADIMIROV—SHULMAN told them more than once that [my work] was the way to present the essential information on a case.

POZERN put me in his resolutions, as my informational reports interested him.

I talked with CHUDOV on the same topic on the telephone etc. . . . .

When I made trips to Luga on my days off I was detained there for three to four days /due to bad weather and the great distance/. This happened more than once, but it was never punished . . .

But, it was enough for me to speak at one of the presentations at the party collective, and literally on the next day I was fired /thrown out/ at the order of O [sherov?] . . . without furlough, without compensation, and without work.

My wife suffered too as a result, she was soon fired as well.

The moment was difficult, but I was young and was in "the power of the new thinking, of the new world shining in the distance" . . .

1. Working at the Leningrad Regional [. . .] RKI I also happened upon a disgusting story, which cannot be passed over without a trace.

My former boss F[uks]. . . . the son of an artisan, brought up twenty to thirty persons on the harshest charges because his father had been fired from the *artel* [an artisanal or construction cooperative] . . . L. . . . .

Heaps of people sat with tears in their eyes by the door to his office.

This was reported to the proper authorities, but he is still prospering there under the sponsorship of the Soc . . .

1. And now, about the Institute of History.

Due to my personal development and active participation in one and another branch of socially useful work or government service, I grew and was promoted higher and higher.

In this I saw confirmation of my most powerful abilities.

I won great authority [i.e. respect] at the Institute with my businesslike attitude and my conscientiousness.

They kept me as deputy chief, they praised me at meetings, there was a comradely attitude towards me.

My illness and the moment of my removal from studies /Institute of Red Professors/ I handled very easily. But when I began like a surgeon to expose long-infected wounds, a misfortune happened to me . . .

I expected vindication for this and I began to speak more and more about the abnormal sides of [this] public institution.

But to take revenge against me there were people /B., A[vvakumov]., and L[urye]./ who exacted a cruel retribution /one is an émigré and the other a White officer/ my findings are not taken into account because they have the upper hand /one fool made fifty fools/. I'm not going to expand on this here, I've handed in four statements and made as many oral explanations.

This story of this case has caused me to rethink a great many things.

People give them enthusiastic ovations, but they stick the label of "self-seeker" (*obyvatel'*) on me, a working man. But I remain convinced that if they are not given a scare for a month or two, then they will not ever feel [the wrath of] Soviet Power—all of the Right Deviationists /LURYE, TSU-KERMAN, AVVAKUMOV/.

. . . They took vengeance on me and I suffered—in the same way as that nurse of socialist ideas J. Rousseau.

In spite of the fact that he was a noble person, they all considered him a bad apple and he was subjected to mockery and persecution all of his life.

Voltaire, on the other hand, was a [real] bad apple, but many read him and loved him.

The reason for this could be the following: Rousseau wanted to renew the old world, he acted with the sword destroyed and undermined the grandees [with] the sad truth and so on.

But VOLTAIRE hated baseness /and Rousseau base people/ and spoke in general.

He took the world and. . . . the way it was in reality. He flattered and seduced people of weak character to his side.

That is my sad truth. I thought that I would find a solution and resolved to see the matter through to the end. But my hopes proved vain. The regional party collegium confirmed the decision . . . of the lower-level organizations.

Then I decided that outsiders would see things more clearly and I sent a petition to the Central Committee of the Communist International, but there are still no results /two months/ as if they are asleep there.

Apparently I am supposed to live on the Holy Spirit alone, but I am not alone, I have a family and we are about to be chased out of our apartment onto the street.

Thus, taking the line of greatest resistance I wish to say over the head of bureaucratic departments and the great distances . . . to the entire party, the entire working class.

To speak of the just motives for my act, as I take the last road of my life!

x x x x x x

For me life opened up but then it all began to seem to me to boil down to a simple truth.

Everywhere we see how much is for show, a great hullabaloo is made over the tiniest thing, but often deeds do not match words.

Culture is growing—but between the weak and the strong, between the big and the small /!/ there is a struggle for life going on that is not without mercenary motives.

For us for the working person there is not free access to life, to work, to education.

My mother is a poor and ignorant person, after the revolution she had to continue to work eighteen more years at her hopeless job.

We moved to a new apartment but they charge so much for it that there is no deliverance /they say, for a whole fifty years/.

Here, there and everywhere, just as in past times there hangs the threat of fines.

Money circulates at a turtle's pace.

Hundreds of thousands of automobiles go millions of kilometers every year, all for nothing.

They predict war as they predict the weather . . . perhaps it is so war is inevitable, but it will be destructive and redemptive. The people will not suffer as much as they did in our Revolution 17—30–50 million people— with all the consequences /look at the USSR statistics in the almanac of the Central Directorate of the People's Economy/.

Our life is short enough without that /its ancient foundations have been shaken/.

With each passing year harsh new laws are introduced on the application of the highest measure of punishment—the firing squad.

Every factory worker and office employee survives on the government budget, but this indicates only the state's lack of planning, and the decline of productive forces!

Socialist Realism aims to whitewash real self-criticism.

People are many, but there are few differences between them.

A person's frantic activity creates a fantasy and a soothing effect.

The secret of life and wisdom is held to be loyalty, but loyalty is patriotism, nothing more.

. . . the story of my past outweighs the present.

An illiterate mother found help for her children /free medical care at a hospital and a rest home /. But now that I have knocked at all doors, it turns out that no one is able to help me /bureaucracy has overwhelmed the People's Commissariat of Health, the Ward Health Department, the Regional Labor Union Soviet, and so on and so on./

. . . Oh, if I were to reveal the secret of my sufferings over the last days and months.

I leave an autobiographical story /100 pages/ in which a deep moral can be discerned . . .

I matured long ago, it's not for those people from the Institute to judge my lack of literacy /wasn't it they in the company of MESHCHERSKY who wrote that resolution?/.

Perhaps I wouldn't have done so poorly on the exams for the Institute of Red Professors if they hadn't treated me so pedantically (*akademichno*) /as with L. Tolstoy/.

But this lesson was not wasted on me.

I have read and stored up a great deal in my memory.

I have studied all of the most important works of Lenin, Stalin, Marx's *Capital*.

I know the history of the party and the revolutionary movement, its strategies and. . . .

I saw that mastery of philosophy leads to freedom (*prostor*) in the sense of developing efficient work and a deep understanding of the real world!!!!

As a soldier of the revolution no death frightens me. I am ready for anything now, and no one has the power to stop me.

I am making preparations like A. Zheliabov. . . .

In such actions the single most important thing is—the strength of one's will to sacrifice oneself.

. . . If it was once far to the Tsar, then now it is the Great who are high up.

I visited the secretary of the ward committee the [work] collective with my written testimony, but he did not wish to speak with me.

I sent my testimony letter to K[iro]-v, but it did not reach him.

I sent a letter to STALIN the same thing happened.

Here I am speaking even more courageously, as A. Radishchev did—150–170 years ago, in the epoch of Catherine II's reign.

He was one of the brave people of that time, who dared to protest against the existing social order, against autocracy, against Catherine the Great.

He had neither comrades nor any organization. It was terrifying to speak of the sufferings, to expose the injustice!

But his power was just in this, that he could not remain silent and indifferent when he saw disorders.

Catherine held her power dear and rewarded her favorites according to her caprices, she liked it when they called her Great, Wise, and etc.

And now for some there are honors and fame, and for others sobs over a grave . . .

. . . Yes, there still must be found many more brave people who are ready to sacrifice themselves in the name of a historical mission.

And I am ready to do so—for the sake of/all of/ humanity, leaving my mother, my wife to [the care of] merciful people—my mother, my wife, and my young children.

Greetings to the Tsar of Industry and War—Stalin.

Farewell.

L. Nikolaev

October 1934

Nikolaev had been reading. On December 3, 1934 Milda Draule told interrogators that in the past one to one and a half months he'd been returning home later than usual, at ten or eleven P.M. He told her that he had been reading at the Vyborg Ward House of Culture library, or visiting his mother, who lived near the House of Culture. Draule noted that he showed great interest in history and spent a lot of time at their apartment writing his "autobiography" and other essays. It was most likely at the library that Nikolaev researched the lives of Rousseau and Voltaire; the Russian aristocrat Radishchev, exiled to Siberia by Catherine the Great for his criticism of serfdom; and the People's Will revolutionary assassin Zheliabov, who killed Tsar Alexander II in 1883. Soviet historians gave qualified praise to all of these figures as progressive in the context of their respective epochs, for all had been critics of the nobility, absolute monarchy, and "feudalism." The glorification of rebellious critics and assassins from the past, however, posed a peculiar problem for the Stalinist regime, whose leaders were now bent on stabilizing Soviet society after the earthquakes of revolution and forced collectivization. Nikolaev had seized on the heroes of the Soviet regime's revolutionary pantheon as models for his attack on that same regime.[24]

Also notable is Nikolaev's wholesale rejection of the Soviet regime. Like Tsarist officials, Soviet authorities oppressed their subjects with fines and executions. The lives of the working class, epitomized by his mother, had not improved. Stalin was just another Tsar. The Bolsheviks had failed to eliminate "mercenary" self-interest and "the struggle between weak and strong" continued. The regime conjured up false war threats to justify gigantic expenditures on the military. Socialist Realist literature was window-dressing. Even the state's domination of the economy was a problem. The huge numbers of people employed by the state Nikolaev linked not with full employment and the supposed efficiency of a rational government-run economy, but with chaos and inefficiency ("decline of productive forces"). Nikolaev did not express any coherent understanding of alternative systems—certainly he did not see capitalism and bourgeois democracy as the solution. Instead he harked back to the "barricades" experience of 1917, when, he believed, an energized and heroic working class overthrew their oppressors in the name of a vaguely understood "socialism" which would provide material plenty, a "new life," and freedom for the multitude.

Nikolaev's testament also reflected his transition to full-blown megalomania. He described himself as fearless, immeasurably tough and patient, a warrior for the world proletariat. At his former jobs he had been always a leader, "irreplaceable." Much of this rhetoric reflected the putative traits of the Bolshevik hero—"tempered" like steel, unflinching, overcoming impossible obstacles. But rather than seeing the Bolshevik hero as an ideal to strive towards, Nikolaev simply identified with him. He was the superman.

The flip side of Nikolaev's megalomania was a sense of overwhelming persecution. Like Rousseau, he had been mocked and spit on from every side. No one appreciated his extraordinary abilities. In particular the Communist Party had ignored and ultimately betrayed him. Nikolaev expressed his disillusion with the party in heavy sarcasm. The bosses who had abused him were "Communists who played a not unimportant role in the matter of my education." Stalin was the "Tsar of War and Industry."

The saddest part of Nikolaev's break with reality was his belief that his wife, his mother, and his two sons would be cared for by "merciful people" after his terrorist attack. Somehow he believed that they would be spared the authorities' wrath because of his family's impeccable proletarian credentials. Interrogators would use this bizarre faith effectively to manipulate him in December 1934. In reality, of course, the consequences of his action were fatal for his wife and mother, and disastrous for his children.

In his testament, Nikolaev clearly gave the purpose of the assassination he was planning—to communicate over the heads of the bureaucracy directly with ordinary workers and Communists about the injustices he personally and the working class as a whole were suffering. He placed a high value on his writings, which he hoped that the authorities would find and publicize after the assassination.

On October 30 Nikolaev's nihilistic despair perhaps lightened a bit, and he made one more effort to achieve his goals through regular channels. He composed the following letter to Kirov.

· 31 ·

Nikolaev letter to Kirov, October 30, 1934. Reconstructed by comparison of partial copies in TsA FSB RF, a.u.d. N-Sh44, t. 12, ll. 401–410, and RGANI, f. 6, op. 13, d. 1, ll. 10–53 (April 20, 1956 KGB/prosecutor's report to Molotov commission).

———————————

Comrade K[irov] . . . . my difficult situation has forced me to turn to you . . .

I have sat without work for seven months persecuted for self-criticism.

A party member since 1934. I entered the party after active participation in the struggles at the barricades of 1917 and active work in the Komsomol.

A Petersburg worker, [I] work[ed] at the Karl Marx, Red Dawn, and other factories, the regional control commission of the Workers' and Peasants' Inspectorate, and the Institute of Party History, from which I was fired.

There they ordered me to transfer to transport, but I refused because of my illness.

They knew that I was sick, but before that there were rumors that they wanted to fire me due to [my?] discovery of a number of problems.

There they have recently changed the whole leadership, but a former [Tsarist] officer [Avvakumov] and Right Deviat[ionists] [Lurye, Avvakumov] are still writing history. They would not have supported Soviet Power, without being terrorized for two or three months.

Investigation of this matter has already gone on eight months.

They've slandered me and I have had a hard time finding support anywhere. . . .

No one offers guidance to me and no one will hire me. Even after a letter to STALIN no one has offered help, no one /including Pokhvalin/ has given me work even though I have a family of five.

I request that you look into the Institute case and help me, because no one wants to understand how hard this moment is for me. I have already been taken under suspicion once [this probably refers to Nikolaev's October 15, 1934 detention by the NKVD]. If no one responds, I am ready to take action, because my patience will break, as I do not have the strength for a struggle until the grave. I am not an enemy, I am an active warrior for the party's general line and all of its tasks.

October 30, 1934.

On November 1 or soon after Nikolaev sat down and tried to outline concrete plans for assassinating Kirov.[25] The handwriting on the original first page of his "Plan" is evidently very hard to read—I have available two printed Russian transcriptions of the plan, and they differ at a number of places. In the translation below I have tried to give a sense of where it is clear what Nikolaev meant, and where it is doubtful. The first page of the "Plan" consists of a list of "external and internal circumstances" on the left and a double-columned catalog of possible variants on the assassination attempt.[26]

On the night of December 1-2, 1934 NKVD interrogators claimed that they had found the "Plan" on Nikolaev at the time of the murder, although they may in fact have picked it up at his apartment or his mother's.[27]

· 32 ·

Nikolaev's "Plan" for assassinating Kirov, early November 1934. RGANI, f. 6, op. 13, d. 1, ll. 88–89.

PLAN [left side of first page]
Consideration of External and Intern[al] Circum[stances]
1. Suffic[ient] energy
2. Abs[ence] of susp[icion]
3. Choice of place for action
4. Urgent reasons
5. 2 pr[imary] condit[ions]
6. Until [alternative: up to] . . . . bravery, stealth /conceal[ment]/

LEFT
. . . [?] tasks hide behind . . . . package
RIGHT
Essential /be[?] cunning
Strength

PLAN [right side of first page]

Place of action
In case of interference:
1. From X. to X. it's 200 steps at a run
/in case of
suspic[ious] challenge/
Enter ahead of time K [irov?]
Series of questions:
detain[ed]—call/
[alternative—say]
1. It is building [number] 28
2. Inquire K, P, N, [alternative—KPK

Evening

1. Confirm [or With Shv.]

2. At the en[trance?] /if

3. Inter[nal] suffer[ings/]
and strength of will
/final decision/

3. Akh . . . from Kronv[erskaia Street]
4. Why
5.
Upon exit of K[irov?]—walk to meet.
Preparatn. 1. to at[tack?] or
2. from behind
Give 1, 2, 3 . . . /given successful
preparation m. o.

II. 2–4 seconds follow[ing*]* from behind   Same
K[irov?]
III. 1. at [corner of?] Sk[orokhodova Street]

                                                  Daytime

2. "   " M[axim] G[orky St.]
3. "   " D[erevenskaia] B[ednota Street]
In case of suit[able] circum[stances] after
the first sh[ot] make escape to M. . . . .
(a) break glass and [?]
(b) open door
IV. At Sm[olny]   Same
Immediately upon meeting /master
[own] spirit and decis[iveness?]

Much of this part of the plan is not decipherable with certainty. However it is fairly clear that Nikolaev planned to attack Kirov either at Smolny or outside his apartment building (number 28, Krasnykh Zor Street) at one of the intersections of Krasnykh Zor Street with east-west running streets (Skorokhodova, Maxim Gorky, or Derevenskaya Bednota streets). He considered alternative actions and cover stories if he was stopped and questioned, and he believed that under certain circumstances he might escape after shooting Kirov. He planned for the possibility of assaulting Kirov from in front or from behind. He was also worried that he might falter at the decisive moment and miss his chance. This is consistent with his other writings that indicate he was vacillating between continued pursuit of redress through legal party channels and violent action.

On the back of the "Plan's" first page and on the second page Nikolaev jotted down more factors that would affect the success of the assassination attempt as well as his justifications for the act. These lists are apparently more legible—the two Russian transcriptions are consistent with one another and the meanings are relatively unambiguous.

· 32 ·
(continued)

Nikolaev's "Plan." RGANI, f. 6, op. 13, d. 1, ll. 88–89.

PRESENCE AND EVALUATION OF CIRCUMSTANCES

I. *Purely external*

    1. In the near future.

    2. In case of the confl[uence] of favorable circumstances to take the risk.

    3. Tracks [in damp earth].

    4. Interference—bodyguards or passersby.

    5. In case of failure and capture.

    6. Choice of place and time.

II. *Internal*

    1. Struggle with mood.

    2. Absence of hope.

    3. Toughness—question of decis[iveness].

    4. The [only] way out—a trap.

    5. The latest events—a spur [to action].

    6. Speed and pressure.

    7. Account of missed oppor[tunities]

    8. Almost alone.

    9. Urgent reasons.

Facts and Convictions

My difficult road /autobiog[raphical] notes/

Latest events /testament, letter to the Central Committee

Absence of future hopes—8 months of unemploym[ent]

Hope nourishes youth . . .

Zero attention to petit[tions].

The moment and repentance.

Historical deeds.

Us and Them [note the contraposition of the general population to the Communist elite]

All the rest I have in my mind.

Clarity Thoughts [sic]

1. Deep analysis of all that has occurred.

2. The only way out.

3. The work, humanity, its deeds.

4. The internal and external cover /internat[ional] events/

5. Illusions. . . .

Along with this plan, Nikolaev drew in his notebook sketches show-ing the routes used by Kirov and his security escorts between Kirov's apartment and Smolny. He noted down the license plate numbers of automobiles and motorcycles involved in these movements.[28]

Even as he wrote his "Plan" and drew his maps, Nikolaev continued to call Smolny offices and project visits to check on the progress of his case through bureaucratic channels.

· 27 ·
(continued)

Nikolaev's personal diary. TsA FSB RF, a.u.d. N-Sh44, t. 12, ll. 401–410.

[Entry from November 1—dated based on November 2 entry]
Today I called Ushakova, I wanted to find out the results of the circuit tribunal [of the central Party Control Committee]—she says I won't get an answer for at least one and a half.

I already knew that all that I'm doing and the measures I've taken are pointless.

Tomorrow I am going to call SVESH[nikov]. Then I will go to K[irov]. For two days I haven't been able to get through.

I wrote my Political Testament one month ago [referring apparently to the "Explanation before the Party and Fatherland" translated above] It [the testament] is being fully confirmed, there's no way out now. How deeply I thought everything out, with what shining clarity.

Don't come to my apartment without Central Committee sanction, when you come don't frighten my wife and children.

I called SVESHNIKOV. KIROV is not receiving visitors. . . . Nov. 2.

My secret letters are at home—in the apartment—under the writing table. Nov. 2.

Good thoughts predominate over bad, but . . . Nov. 3.

If I could decide my [own] fate, I would not wish to bid farewell to life ten to twenty years early.

In spite of everything I've thought up and all the measures I've taken, there is no way back. Nov. 6.

If on Oct. 15 and Nov. 5 I couldn't do it. . . . now I am ready, I am moving towards my own execution, [for me that is] a triviality. Of course that's easy enough to say [now] (*idu pod rasstrel, pustiaki—tol'ko skazat legko*)"

Nov. 9.

Today, as on November 5, he [I?] was late. It didn't work out. They've really got him well-covered /so few . . . [?]/at the station with the R[ed] Ar[row] /Nov. 14/

SECRET
Letters for the party and relatives I left at home under the writing table. On the table is my autobiographical story.

Don't come to me at the apartment without Central Committee sanction, when you come, don't frighten the children and my wife.

From words I have decided to move to deeds, and truly a grand and solemn deed.

November 14.

I . . . to M., a serious situation, I know that if I just wave my hand, they'll give it to me in the head.

Didn't they take me in to the "House of Tears" on Oct. 15 just for an attempt to meet?

And now, for a blow . . . I am aware just how serious the matter is, that if I strike with one blow, I'll get ten, one hundred, and more blows in return. The blow must be planned without a single error.[29]

Nov. 14.

Nikolaev explains where his "secret letters" can be found, showing his desire to be heard. His scribblings also indicate that by the second week of November, he was actively seeking out Kirov to try and shoot him. The notes above refer to three different attempts to meet Kirov. One is the October 15 attempt, which probably occurred before Nikolaev actively sought to shoot Kirov, and which resulted in his detention. Nikolaev mentions two other tries, on November 5 and on November 14. The diary entries suggest that on November 14 Nikolaev tried to find Kirov at a railroad station. On December 2, 1934, he explained this note to interrogators, stating that he went to Moscow Station, the arrival point for trains from the capital, in the morning in hopes of catching Kirov disembarking from the Red Arrow express. On that day, Kirov did arrive from Moscow and Nikolaev seems to have caught a glimpse of him but been unable to get close. Nikolaev told the investigators that he did not know Kirov's schedule, but had simply shown up at the station in hopes that Kirov might be coming in that day. He also claimed to have gone to the station twice before November 14 in hopes of catching Kirov getting off the Red Arrow. Nikolaev also explained the reference to a November 5 encounter with Kirov in the same interrogation. Not far from the Leningrad party chief's apartment, he had seen his car go by, but decided not to shoot.[30]

· 27 ·
(continued)

Nikolaev's personal diary. TsA FSB RF, a.u.d. N-Sh44, t. 12, ll. 401–410.

———————————

[Entry from November 19]
From Suvorov Square they were relieved /it's cold to stand there/ there are two less.

Today from ten to two I waited, he didn't come out. . . . .

One meets with St [ruppe]. /516/ more often. He grew a beard. . . . . who needs it.

Podnialov br. in . . . so down with suppress self-criticism.

In his time secretary of the Vyb. Ward committee got it good from him. For self-criticism R[oman?]. Ku[lisher?] . . . /Rebrth.—my six/.

Today I got a letter from the ward committee, there's not much hope. This morning they put our names on the Black Board of Disgrace for not paying our apartment rent.

. . . if they had put corpses up there, they would have pronounced greater and more sinister words. . . .

All the [my?] accumulated experience and knowledge is just stewing in its own juices—it is completely burned up. . . .

I've swallowed a lot for the sake of my hopes . . .

But it all turned out to be in vain anyway. On the other hand I accumulated a lot of material, if it were revealed it would make a big [legal] case.

As the calloused hand beats on the anvil, strong and accurate, so I remain tough—unwavering in the fulfillment of the plans I have made . . .

This is a historical fact. No, I will not resign myself to what I struggled against all my life [with the past, of the past]

The remaining days are numbered, the last hour is near . . .

Nov. 19.

As this entry shows, the Nikolaev/Draules were in danger of being thrown out of their apartment—the "Black Board of Shame" was a public list of persons late with their rent. On November 21, Nikolaev made a last entry in his "Family Diary." Money was short and housing authorities or residents were pounding on the Nikolaevs' door demanding that they pay the rent.

· 19 ·
(continued)

Nikolaev's family diary. Ts FSB RF, a.u.d. N-Sh44, t. 12, ll. 401–410.

Closer and closer. . . . .

I'm leaving [life] twenty, thirty years before I ought to.

All that is left to you my dear children, all that was given to me by the revolution and my labor. . . . no one and nothing will dare to take that away from you!!!

Your Leonid.[31]

Money's going only for the apartment, kerosene, and soap. It's impossible to buy anything else Not even for milk no for the children [sic].

They harass [me/us] every day (*odolevaiut kazhdyi den'*), they pound on the door in the most shameless and extraordinary way, yesterday they went on pounding so long that I involuntarily told [them] to go to Simbirsk to the county soviet [this apparently refers to Nikolaev's assignment as village soviet secretary in Simbirsk in 1919–1920] and bang their fists on the desk there in front of the right person. . . . .

Today I brought back from the garden a half-bag of potatoes. On everyone's faces—smiles, joy. They're so hungry, they'd be happy if you brought them a bag of sh*t.

Of 115 rubles M. brought in [apparently two weeks of Milda's salary] we paid sixty-five rubles for the apartment, on the rest we all [illegible] of us live, and we have to stretch it out for two weeks no less.

November 21, 1934

Your Leonid.

Also on November 21 Nikolaev wrote another farewell letter to his wife.

· 33 ·

Nikolaev letter to Milda Draule, November 21, 1934. RGANI, f. 6, op. 13, d. 1, l. 85.

On the occasion of Lyonya's third birthday

Dear Milda:

Fate has tied us together forever. It was neither [your] maidenly beauty [that] drew me to you nor [as] a wife [sic]—are you my bonded slave? But as the best friend of [my] life . . . as intimate and loyal friends we shall remain.

It's not often that I have been mistaken.

In you I found the truest friend.

How great is your patience and determination, especially your brave conduct in the recent period showed this.

Dear Milda, in the future do not change, remain unwavering. Didn't you and I devote all of our strength. . . .

My days are numbered, no one is coming to our aid.

Forgive me for everything . . .

I will be writing much more to you before my death (my Testament).

Your L. NIKOLAEV.

Nikolaev made private notes as well on November 21. These include a mysterious reference to an offer of money for his writings, seemingly from counterrevolutionary sources. This would prove to be an important starting point for the murder investigation. The notes also show that Nikolaev was observing the comings and goings at Smolny, where he saw Leningrad second-in-command Mikhail Chudov take a car to NKVD headquarters.

· 27 ·

(continued)

Nikolaev's personal diary. TsA FSB RF, a.u.d. N-Sh44, t. 12, ll. 401–410.

I could write so much now, but I keep silent.

. . . we don't have to dress ourselves in armor in order to crush and kill people, and then demonstrate in the squares . . .

It's hard to break a path through twenty bodyguards. You've got to seize the initiative. And even then success will be unexpected.

. . . As I move decisively toward my goal, I am forced to acknowledge many things.

Today Ch[udov] left in a new auto and went to the OGPU. Then they got in my way and I cleared off.

It's not often that I have been mistaken.

I was able to get through and create a school—of the decisiveness and toughness to die for truth for an idea. . . .

Nov. 21, 1934

In what way have I remained true to the party and my fatherland? In that I have not broken with the party and taken the route of counterrevolution. They offered me big sums of money for my documents, but I did not make the deal. . . . I could have translated my last letters-testaments into three languages, but I refused.

Nov. 21.

On November 22 Nikolaev wrote that he had decided to give up on the possibility of shooting from hiding and then escaping. He would expose himself openly to capture and execution in order to complete the assassination. Once again he expressed feelings of hopelessness and isolation, and indirectly, his fierce longing to be heard ("no one pays any attention . . . ").

· 27 ·
(continued)

Nikolaev's personal diary. TsA FSB RF, a.u.d. N-Sh44, t. 12, ll. 401–410.

. . . he who does not know me will think that I am angry, but I was never so.

. . . I have nothing to hide from the party, I gave warning in my letters/declarations more than once—but no one wants to understand that.

I am not sick of life, I fought for life from my first years, but now not only am I powerless and helpless to help people, but I myself am engaged in a battle not for life, but for death.

She [death] is cl[ose?]. . . . . no one pays any attention, everyone is waiting for empty assurances.[32]

I have let many good chances get away, but now I'm not going to shoot from hiding, let them kill me, but let them know how they're tearing and smashing the working class its true sons.

I am not the only one who is suffering and I am ready to fight to my last breath, but I no longer have hope for salvation.

Nov. 22, 1934.

Probably on November 25 Leonid's half-brother, Pyotr, appeared at the Nikolaev/Draule apartment once again. He had deserted his Red Army unit on November 14. Military police visited the apartment of Nikolai's mother and his sister Yekaterina on November 15 or 16 and told them Pyotr was once again on the run. Leonid and Pyotr may have considered going underground together and/or taking a trip to Moscow. That is what Pyotr testified on December 8 at any rate. On the evening of November 26 Leonid went by Yekaterina's workplace

at the Green Space Trust (*Trest zelenogo stroitel'stva*—the parks department), called her out onto the street, and showed her Pyotr, who
was standing on a nearby corner. The three siblings had a brief conversation, and Yekaterina urged Pyotr to return to his unit. He refused.
Leonid again made efforts to help his little brother out. On November
27, he took Pyotr to the doctor, paying two rubles for the visit, in an effort to get some kind of certificate that he was sick, presumably to get
him out of military service. He told Pyotr he should return to the army,
but the latter refused. It is clear from evidence in Pyotr's case that he
shared his older brother's anti-Soviet feelings.[33]

Pyotr now embarked on a five-day spree of threats and violence that
weirdly paralleled his brother Leonid's descent to murder. After leaving Leonid's apartment on November 27, he stole a pistol and other
items from a friend's apartment. He spent the evening of November
27–28 "in the woods." He then turned up at the apartment of his new
wife and her family, threatening them with the stolen gun if they
turned him into the police. He may have spent the two nights of November 28–30 there. The night of November 30–December 1 he stayed
at the home of one of his mother's elderly lady friends, Yevdokiya
Shpatz. The next day, December 1, he fenced some of the things he'd
stolen at the Aleksandrovskaya market. Like Leonid, he wrote in these
last days short notes, as if for a journal, and letters to his relatives. In a
letter apparently addressed to his wife and his father-in-law on November 29, he asked that they not think him a "hooligan who made a
baby and ran off." The fault was not his, he wrote, but that of "para-
sitic Soviet Power, which forces people to starve and live according to
the laws of the prehistoric era, that is, in handcuffs." He wrote multiple suicide notes to various family members. He also wrote a short
missive to "My family," perhaps intended for Yekaterina, Milda, and/
or Leonid, who all had had a part in turning him in to the military police previously. In this note, which he signed, "Your enemy," Pyotr expressed his "thanks" to his family for "thrusting sticks into my wheel
at every turn." "Now you've got what you wanted," he concluded. "I
will perish." When NKVD officers captured Pyotr following Kirov's
murder, he resisted arrest, emptying the magazine of his pistol at
them.[34]

In the meantime, Leonid Nikolaev read in the newspapers that the
Central Committee plenum would be ending on November 28. In anticipation of Kirov's return from Moscow on the Red Arrow, he went
to Moscow Station on the morning of November 29, but missed his

chance again. He spent at least part of the day maintaining his watch on Kirov's apartment. He also left a note for Milda's sister Olga at her place of work, asking her if she could get him a ticket to Kirov's meeting with regional activists on December 1. That evening Nikolaev dropped in at his sister's and mother's apartment. His mother was asleep, and he stayed for no more than fifteen minutes, conversing briefly with Yekaterina and her friend, Anna Gushchina. He left the apartment with Gushchina. By his own account, Nikolaev spent the day of November 30 at home, then went out to see a movie in the evening.[35]

According to Milda Draule, Nikolaev stayed up until midnight on November 30. Milda herself visited her sister Olga with one of her sons at about 10:00 P.M. that night, asking if she could get hold of a ticket for the activists' meeting (obviously for Leonid's use). Olga later claimed to have said she could not. The next morning Milda left the apartment for work at eight, while Nikolaev was still asleep.[36]

Once Leonid awoke on December 1 he called his wife twice at work (probably from a public telephone, as the evidence is that he had no telephone at home), pressing her to find him a ticket to the activists' meeting. Concluding that she could not get one, he headed to the Smolny Ward party committee offices on "Twenty-fifth of October" Prospect in search of a ticket. One official, Gurianov, turned him down; a second, Orlov, promised a pass if Nikolaev returned at the end of the work day. "To make sure," as he put it, Nikolaev went into the regional party headquarters at the Smolny building to ask acquaintances there if they could get him a ticket.[37]

Two days later, on December 3, Nikolaev recounted the succeeding events to interrogators.

· 34 ·

Protocol of interrogation of Leonid Nikolaev, December 3, 1934. TsA FSB RF, a.u.d. N-Sh44, t. 12, ll. 15–16.

Question: How did you get into Smolny on December 1?
Answer: I got in on my party card.
Question: When did you arrive at Smolny?
Answer: Approximately 1:30 P.M., and I was there until 2:30 P.M., then I left and returned back at 4:30 P.M.

Question: How did you spend that first hour in Smolny?

Answer: At first I went to see Comrade Denisova, regional committee *instruktor*, who works next to another employee, Platonovskaya. I have known Denisova personally since 1923. I asked her to give me a pass to the activists' meeting, but she refused me, because she had no tickets, as she explained to me. Then, still on the third floor, I met the city committee employee /Newspaper Section/ Shitik-Shneierson, I asked her also for a ticket and got the answer that she herself had none. On the same corridor I met senior *instruktor* of the city committee Larin, and I asked him for a pass to the activists' meeting, but again was refused. Next I met Smirnov, chief of the Cadres Sector of the regional committee, by his office I asked for a ticket and got the answer that he, Smirnov, had no connection with the distribution of tickets. Smirnov sent me to Room 450 to get a ticket, but I did not go there, as I knew that I had no personal acquaintances in that office. Then I headed to see Petroshevich, secretary of the agricultural group, I dropped in to see him at the office on the left side of the main corridor and chatted with him for about five minutes, first on general themes without any significance, and then I again requested a pass. Petroshevich told me that at that moment he had eight tickets and if any remained, he would give me one. For this purpose Petroshevich asked me to come back in the evening. After that I went downstairs, left Smolny, and took a stroll along Tverskaya and Ochakovskaya Streets, came out on Sovetskaya and returned to Smolny. Going up to the third floor I went into the bathroom, relieved myself, and exiting the bathroom I turned left. After taking two or three steps I observed Sergei Mironovich Kirov approaching me along the right wall of the corridor, perhaps 15–20 steps away. Seeing Sergei Mironovich Kirov, I first stopped and turned my back on him, so that after he passed me, I was looking at his back. Letting Kirov get 10–15 steps ahead, I noticed that there was no one for a great distance around us. Then I followed behind Kirov, gradually overtaking him. . . .

CHAPTER 7

Stalin Responds

Kirov's deputy Mikhail Chudov called Stalin's secretariat from Leningrad with news of Kirov's assassination sometime soon after 5:00 P.M.[1] Stalin was meeting in his Kremlin office with his close collaborators Molotov, Kaganovich, Voroshilov, and Zhdanov at the time. About forty years later Molotov told interviewer and admirer Feliks Chuev that when Stalin got the news over the telephone he exclaimed "Idiots!" ("Shliapy!"), presumably referring to the Leningrad NKVD. It is also quite possible that the word used was actually an obscenity.[2]

NKVD chief Genrikh Yagoda arrived at the office soon after the news, at 5:50 P.M. according to Stalin's visitor log. Karl Pauker, head of the NKVD Operations Department, arrived at 6:15 together with his deputy Gulko and Kremlin commandant Peterson. Pauker, Gulko, and Peterson all supervised guards for the leadership, and Stalin probably issued orders to them for increased security measures. He also instructed Pauker to arrange for a special overnight train to Leningrad for himself and a large delegation of the Soviet leadership. Pauker, Peterson, and Gulko left after just ten minutes. At about this time, Medved's first telegram from Leningrad came in. Members of the Politburo trickled in to the office—Kalinin, Mikoyan, and Ordzhonikidze at 6:20, Andreev at 6:25, and Chubar at 6:30. Avel Yenukidze, head of the Central Executive Committee, arrived at 6:45. The meeting of party leaders lasted until 8:10, when everyone except Stalin and Yagoda left. At that point a group of senior editors and propagandists (Mekhlis, editor of *Pravda*; Bukharin, editor of *Izvestia*; and Stetsky, head of the TsK Department of Agitation and Propaganda), came in

251

and met with Stalin and Yagoda for ten minutes, presumably to discuss the public announcement of the assassination. At 8:20 these men departed, leaving Yagoda alone with Stalin until 8:30. Later that night Stalin and an entourage of senior party officials, NKVD commissars, and guards boarded the overnight train to Leningrad.[3]

The Law of December 1 and the Execution of Hostages

Probably on the night of December 1–2, 1934 Stalin drafted the infamous "Law of December 1," instructing the police and courts to try cases of terrorism without delay, reject appeals, and carry out death sentences immediately upon conviction. Stalin's fellow Politburo members approved it by canvass (an administrator contacted each member for his vote) by December 3. *Pravda* published it on December 4, giving its issue date as December 1.[4]

· 35 ·

Politburo approval of the "Law of December 1" ordering bypassing of regular judicial procedures in cases of terrorism. APRF, f. 3, op. 62, d. 95, l. 1.

Extract from Protocol No. 17 of Politburo Session
Politburo members approved by canvass (*opros*), December 3, 1934.
89. Regarding Trial Procedures for Cases of Planning or Carrying out Terrorist Acts.
The following proposal for a resolution of the Presidium of the Central Executive Committee is approved.
1. Investigatory authorities are directed to handle cases of those accused of planning or carrying out terrorist actions in expedited fashion.
2. Judicial organs are directed not to postpone the carrying out of death sentences in consideration of appeals for clemency by criminals of said category, as the Presidium of the Central Executive Committee does not deem it possible to review such appeals.
3. The organs of the NKVD of the USSR are directed immediately upon sentencing of criminals of this category to carry out death sentences.

It has frequently been argued that the speed with which Stalin issued this decree suggests that he had planned Kirov's killing and prepared the text beforehand.[5] But this is not really the case, as indicated especially by new archival evidence. The decree is very short and worded vaguely. It would not have taken Stalin more than a few minutes to dash it off, especially given that he was working with a document drafted in response to an earlier assassination, that of the Soviet ambassador to Poland P. L. Voikov by a White émigré in Warsaw on June 7, 1927. According to J. Arch Getty and Russian scholars with access to Stalin's archive, the "Law of December 1" was based on a proposal to deal with political terrorism made after Voikov's murder.[6] Then— Deputy Commissar of Justice N. V. Krylenko suggested to the Politburo the establishment of special police tribunals to deal expeditiously with "cases of banditry, counterrevolution, espionage, and other major cases." Krylenko proposed that suspects tried by these "extraordinary tribunals" would have no right to defend themselves in court, no right to counsel, and no right to appeal. Sentences were to be carried out "as soon as possible."[7]

Regime reaction to the killing of Kirov followed the Voikov script in other ways. In both cases Soviet authorities immediately executed prisoners from alien groups they regarded as "hostages." The day after Voikov's murder, Stalin issued orders that the OGPU "declare all well-known monarchists we have in jail . . . hostages," and execute "five or ten" of them immediately. Within three days of the murder, *Pravda* had published news of the execution of twenty White Guard prisoners on charges of terrorism, illegal entry to the Soviet Union, and attempted organization of counterrevolutionary groups. Soon after Kirov's murder, on December 4, *Pravda* announced that the Military Tribunal of the USSR Supreme Court would try the cases of a number of supposed White Guard terrorists. On December 6, 1934, the Soviet wire service TASS reported the trial of seventy persons on charges of "preparing terrorist actions against Soviet authorities." The court sentenced sixty-six to death.[8]

The "Law of December 1" and Kirov's murder also need to be placed in the context of changes in the structure of judicial and police organs during the summer and fall of 1934. The major organs concerned were the security police (OGPU), state prosecutors' offices, courts at all levels, the Commissariat of Justice, and the USSR Supreme Court. On paper the powers of the security police were downgraded. The OGPU was merged with the Commissariat of Internal Affairs (NKVD), and was given a new name, the Main Directorate of State Security (GUGB). The OGPU Collegium which had heard cases of major state crimes such as counterrevolution, espionage, and treason was dissolved and its functions passed to military tribunals, most importantly the Military Tribunal of the USSR Supreme Court. In general the powers of the security police to try cases themselves were curtailed. Prosecutors were instructed to resume the practice of reviewing cases presented to them by police organs to see if they were well grounded and ready for trial. This practice, common in the 1920s, had fell into disuse during the years of collectivization, when prosecutors often rubberstamped the charges brought by police. In an effort to improve the work of prosecutors and judges, the Politburo raised salaries for some legal officials and mandated on-the-job professional training. The major loser in this reform was the Commissariat of Justice, which was divested of all control over prisons and labor camps, and lost most of its supervisory powers to the USSR Prosecutor's Office and the Supreme Court.[9]

The debates within the Soviet leadership about these changes were complex. Personal antagonisms and bureaucratic rivalries played as important a role as policy considerations. Scholarly interpretations vary. Robert Tucker argues that the reduction in security police powers was a feint by Stalin to cover up preparations for the Great Terror, which he was already planning to unleash. These preparations included giving military tribunals jurisdiction over serious crimes against the state and creating the Special Board of the GUGB, which had the power to issue labor camp sentences up to five years in less important cases. Peter Solomon makes a case that the reforms were aimed at stabilizing the Soviet legal system in the wake of the chaos of collectivization, bringing it under tighter central control, and establishing a consistent set of procedures for investigation and trial. Solomon sees the reforms as part of Stalin's efforts from the mid-1930s to build a powerful centralized state and settle Soviet society after the disruptions of social revolution, civil war, and collectivization.[10]

In Solomon's account the Kirov murder was a surprise that temporarily confounded Stalin's new emphasis on "legality." Once again the regime resorted to "extraordinary measures" in an emergency.[11] My own interpretation of the 1934 reforms and the regime's response to Kirov's assassination follows Solomon's closely, except that I doubt that Stalin, Kaganovich, and their associates ever had any intention of renouncing "extrajudicial measures" in the event of an emergency. On the one hand, Stalin wanted to establish an effective rule-bound legal machine that would serve state purposes. Besides being a tool of social control, such a machine could also win the respect of the Western powers whose support the Soviets now sought against Hitler. At the same time, Stalin and his lieutenants sought to intensify security police surveillance over society, and they reserved the option of utilizing extrajudicial terror when necessary against the regime's real or imagined enemies. Intensified surveillance and resort to summary police "justice" were not inconsistent with "legality" in the Stalinist view. The laws were for subjects and lower-level officials to obey. Surveillance was to ensure that no one was breaking the law or fomenting opposition to the regime. Extrajudicial terror was for the leaders to employ when necessary to protect the state or its officials.

In this interpretation, the Soviet regime's response to Kirov's assassination was consistent with Stalin's understanding of the reforms of 1934, just as it paralleled earlier Bolshevik responses to attacks on their officials. In a genuine emergency—Kirov was the first senior party leader to take a bullet since Lenin in 1918—party leaders still claimed the right of resort to state terror. Nor does the summer 1934 transfer of jurisdiction over high crimes against the state from the OGPU Collegium to the Supreme Court's Military Tribunal imply a conspiracy by Stalin. The transfer grew out of the downgrading of the security police's power to try cases, which in turn was connected to "rationalization" of the legal apparatus and, as Solomon and others have suggested, to a propaganda offensive inside and outside the USSR. There is no reason to believe that the OGPU Collegium would have been less receptive than the Military Tribunal to the hundreds of bogus cases investigators fabricated after Kirov's assassination.

The legal changes of 1934 did include a shift in the definition of antiregime crimes with major implications for the treatment of Stalin's former political opponents inside the party. In 1934 propagandists, officials, and Stalin himself began talking less of crimes against the revolution and more of crimes against the state. "Counterrevolution" became "treason." This relabeling fit with the regime's new stress on glorification of the state. On June 9, 1934 the Politburo approved a law "On the Betrayal of the Motherland" (*rodina*) which provided the death penalty for "actions of citizens of the USSR damaging the military power of the Soviet Union, its sovereignty, or the integrity of its territory." Offenses covered included spying, flight across the borders, and communicating state secrets. Family members of traitors were also subject to harsh punishments, even if they were not involved in the crimes concerned.[12]

It is certainly possible that Stalin foresaw using this statute against his former political opponents in the party, many of whom had recently been allowed to return to public life. As ex-oppositionists became more active, the security police had stepped up surveillance of them, presumably to ensure that they behaved in loyal fashion. Should any of the former "Rightists," "Zinovievites," etc., step out of line, Stalin could now accuse them of outright treason. The Soviet leader was suspicious and held grudges. It is plausible that he expected the former oppositionists to undermine him, and he planned for that eventuality.

The Leningrad NKVD Questions Nikolaev

In the middle of the night of December 1–2, perhaps just before midnight, NKVD officers began questioning Leonid Nikolaev. Fyodor Fomin reported in 1956 that officers brought Nikolaev back from the clinic at about 10 P.M. and laid him on a sofa in a room next door to his office. Two guards were put on him to prevent a suicide attempt. He had been banging his head against the wall. According to Fomin, Nikolaev was incoherent during much of this time—"he shouted and babbled and only towards morning began to speak, and yell, 'my shot has been heard around the world!'"[13]

Medved and Fomin led the first formal interrogation.

· 36 ·

Protocol of interrogation of Leonid Nikolaev, December 1, 1934. RGANI, f. 6, op. 13, d. 1, ll. 92–99.

Question: Today, December 1, in the corridor at Smolny you shot Central Committee secretary Comrade Kirov with a revolver. Tell us who else participated in the organization of this attack with you.

Answer: I state categorically that there were no other participants in the attack I made on Comrade Kirov. I prepared the whole thing by myself, and I told no one of my plans.

Question: Since when have you been preparing this attack?

Answer: The idea of killing Comrade Kirov actually occurred to me at the beginning of November of 1934, from that time I have been preparing for this attack.

Question: What reasons motivated you to carry out this attack?

Answer: One reason—my estrangement from the party, from which I was alienated by the events at the Leningrad Institute of Party History, second my unemployment and the absence of material and most importantly moral aid from party organizations.

My whole situation developed from the moment of my exclusion from the party /eight months ago/, which tainted me in the eyes of party organizations.

I wrote to various party instances /the Smolny Ward Committee, the party committee of the Institute of Party History, the Regional Party Committee, and the Central Committee of the Communist Party, the Leningrad Commission on Party Control, and also the Central Control Commission/, of my difficult material and moral situation many times, but I got no real help from any of these.

Question: What specifically did you write in all of these communications?

Answer: I wrote everywhere that I had been trapped in a situation without exit and that I had reached the critical moment that pushed me to commit a political assassination.

Question: What was the main goal of the attack you made today on Comrade Kirov?

Answer: The attempt on Kirov's life had the main goal of making a political signal before the party that over the last eight to ten years of my life's road and work there has accumulated a backlog of unfair attitudes on the part of specific government persons towards a living human being. For a time I bore all of this as long as I was involved in directly useful civic work, but when I ended up discredited and alienated from the party, then I decided to signal all of this before the party.

I have fulfilled this historic mission of mine. I must show the whole party the extreme to which they forced Nikolaev for repressing self-criticism [*sic*—Nikolaev obviously means "with their repression of self-criticism"].

Question: A plan written in your hand for an assassination attempt was found on you during the personal search, tell us with whom you worked up this plan.

Answer: Who could have helped make such a plan? Nobody helped me in making it. I composed it myself personally under the influence of the events around me at the Institute of Party History. In addition I composed it under the influence of the unfair attitude towards me when I worked at the regional committee and the regional control commission.

I affirm categorically that I worked up this plan personally, nobody helped me with it and nobody knew about it.

Question: Your brother Pyotr knew of this plan.

Answer: If he knew of this, he would have handed me over [to the police] instantly.

Question: In your appointment book there is the address and telephone number of the German consulate in Leningrad, written in your hand. Who gave you this address and telephone number?

Answer: The address and telephone number of the German consulate in Leningrad I copied from the 1933 telephone book.

Question: With what purpose?

Answer: I made that notation on purpose in order to show the party afterwards that I allegedly [*sic*] suffered much and in order to take the easiest route to exposure and signaling [of the wrongs done me]. I was obsessed with the idea of drawing down on myself suspicion of contacts with foreigners, and so that due to that [*sic*] I'd be arrested and then I would have the chance to expose all the outrages I knew about.

Question: With what foreigners did you have ties and discuss the attack you were planning?

Answer: I never had any ties or talked with any foreigners. It would have been bad indeed if I'd given my plan to foreigners, comrades. I worked out the whole plan personally myself and I carried it out right to the end by myself.

Question: Tell us more clearly what purpose you were pursuing when you made your attack on Kirov?

Answer: I saw and still see that attack as a political act. With this murder I wanted to get the party to pay attention to a living human being and to the heartless bureaucratic attitude towards him.

I request that you note down that I am not an enemy of the working class and that if my recent hard experiences at the Institute had not occurred, I would have borne all of the difficulties I have suffered and would not have gone so far as attempting the assassination.

Question: How can we make sense of your statement that you "are not an enemy of the working class" when by your actions you have joined the camp of the enemies of the working class?

Answer: Yes, I have to admit that I really did act morally as an enemy of the working class by making my attempt on Comrade Kirov's life, but I did so under the influence of psychological distress and the deep impression made on me by events at the Institute, which placed me in an impossible situation.

Transcribed correctly from my words and read back to me in its entirety.

NOTE: While confirming that the above is correctly transcribed, the interrogated prisoner Nikolaev, Leonid Vasilevich categorically refused to sign the present protocol of his testimony, and attempted to rip it up.
[. . .]

Interrogated by:

Chief of the Leningrad Regional Directorate of the NKVD Medved.

Deputy Chief of the Leningrad Regional Directorate of the NKVD Fomin.

Chief of the Economic Affairs Department of the Regional Directorate of the NKVD Molochnikov.

Deputy Chief of the Special Political Department of the Leningrad Military District Yanishevsky.

Deputy Chief of the Special Political Department of the Regional Directorate of the NKVD Stromin.

In this protocol, Nikolaev alternates between a grandiose presentation, in which he continues to play the lone hero who has accomplished a world-historical deed, and a more detached persona. The grandiose hero uses fragments of party-speak—"political signals," "suppression of self-criticism,"—to explain to the police the motives for his attack. The second, deflated Nikolaev begins to get psychological distance from the murder, to see it as the interrogating officers must see it, and to analyze his own internal state. Yes, he admits, the murder must look like an attack on the working class. Yes, he acted in extreme "psychological distress." Yes, he was "obsessed" (*nosilsia s mysl'iu*) with getting attention. The two personas are linked first by Nikolaev's pride in the act—he did it himself, without aid, he emphasizes again and again—and his insistence that even if he was disturbed when he planned and carried out the attack, that was all the fault of the Institute and the government officials who had abused him. The protocol confirms the picture of Nikolaev's motives that emerges from his diaries, notes, and letters to authority.

For their part the Leningrad NKVD officers seem to be concerned above all with connecting Nikolaev to a foreign conspiratorial organization. The NKVD leadership was worried about penetration of the Leningrad area by White Guard terrorists and spies with support from Finland, the Baltic states, Poland, and Germany. The summers of 1933 and 1934 had seen major operations aimed at capturing such agents in Leningrad Region, so the Leningrad NKVD was probably disposed already to look for foreign connections. They may also have been prompted by Yagoda, the head of the NKVD. In 1956 Fomin reported that while he was in his office with Nikolaev just before sending the latter to the clinic, he received two calls from Yagoda asking whether Nikolaev was wearing any foreign clothes (he was not).[14] Comparison of the times in Fomin's account and Stalin's visitor log indicate Yagoda must have been calling from Stalin's office.

260

Early on December 2 Fomin, Yanishevsky, and Isakov, deputy chief of the Baltic Fleet's NKVD Special Department, interrogated Nikolaev again. Medved was absent, perhaps getting some sleep.

· 37 ·

Protocol of interrogation of Leonid Nikolaev, December 2, 1934. TsA FSB RF, a.u.d. N-Sh44, t. 12, ll. 12–14.

Question: In your notes you write that you were offered a lot of money for the documents you composed. Tell us who offered you the money and what documents you meant.

Answer: I can tell you openly and honestly that that part of my notes is exaggerated.

Question: How are we to understand your phrase "exaggerated"?

Answer: You have to understand that this didn't happen and I simply made it up when I was writing.

Question: Why did you make it up?

Answer: I made it up because I wanted to make the charges against me heavier afterwards, when I was interrogated after accomplishing the murder. To be more specific, I wanted with that note to leave evidence behind, because I did not imagine that having completed the killing, I would fail to end my life by suicide. In addition to that, I was preparing myself morally for the killing and suicide with that note.

Question: Your testimony regarding the note stating that you were offered money for your documents does not correspond to the truth, it is illogical and confused, tell us truthfully, who offered you money for your documents.

Answer: I will say it again, all of that was just my personal fantasy. Nobody offered me any money, I didn't think of handing over any documents to anyone. You can check this yourself and confirm that not one of my personal documents disappeared and I had all of them.

Question: What do you mean when you talk about handing over documents?

Answer: I mean that these documents were my personal letter to my mother and nothing more, and that I wasn't even thinking of any documents when I made my notes.

Question: On November 14 you went to Moscow Station with the intention of meeting Comrade Kirov, who was arriving that morning on the Red Arrow from Moscow to Leningrad, tell us, how did you know that Comrade Kirov was arriving on that day in particular?

Answer: I didn't know the exact day of Comrade Kirov's arrival in Leningrad. I only supposed that after the October Holidays [the anniversary of the October Revolution was on November 7], he ought to be coming back to Leningrad. In connection with that [supposition] I appeared at the station twice before November 14, but without result.

I want to add that on October 15 I met Comrade Kirov (completely by chance) near Uritsky Square, I let him go by, but then turned to follow him and met him again by the Troitsky Bridge. From the bridge I followed him all the way to his home on Kamennoostrovsky [this was the former name of Krasnykh Zor Street] Prospect. Because Comrade Kirov was walking with Comrade Chudov I could not make up my mind to approach him for discussion. I want to emphasize that at the time I had not thought of assassination. After Comrade Kirov and Chudov disappeared inside the entrance, I was detained by a policeman, taken to the police station on the Petrograd Side, from there I was sent to the on-duty NKVD officer just by the entrance to the lower floor. After a check of my party and personal documents I was let go without a search.

This protocol is transcribed correctly from my words, it has been read to me, and I have read it through in its entirety myself.

NOTE: After personally being acquainted with the protocol of the interrogation and recognizing that everything in it was transcribed correctly, the prisoner Nikolaev, Leonid Vasilievich refused to sign the present protocol. Present were:

Deputy Chief of the Regional NKVD, Leningrad Region—Fomin.

Deputy Chief of the Leningrad Military District Special Department—Yanishevsky.

Deputy Chief of the Fleet Special Department—Isakov.

As in the first interrogation protocol, the investigators pressed Nikolaev about possible collaborators in the crime. Most likely they had foreigners in mind. And indeed, the phrase in Nikolaev's writings about receiving an offer of money for his documents is mysterious. Nikolaev's explanation here—that he made up the buyers for his documents to grab the police's attention and to work himself up for the murder—parallels the one he gave in his earlier interrogation for the address of the German consulate in his date book. As with the other explanation, it seems consistent with his psychology, but perhaps too convoluted. Moreover, Nikolaev lied about his documents, claiming that the only one which existed was his letter to his mother.

This interrogation also marks the moment Nikolaev revealed to interrogators his brush with the NKVD on October 15, which was to become a key incident in the development of later narratives of the mur-

der. Note the place of the detention—outside Kirov's apartment—and
the fact that he claims to have been released without a search. In the
protocol he does not state that he was carrying his revolver with him,
or any of his more inflammatory writings (his "testament," for example), or his assassination plan (he probably had not composed this as
of October 15). In March 1956 Fomin recalled this interrogation, but
in somewhat confused fashion. He placed the date of Nikolaev's detention two weeks before the murder, one month after it actually happened, although he correctly remembered Nikolaev's testimony as to
the place of the detention, outside Kirov's apartment. Fomin added
that Nikolaev had told him that when he was detained "I had everything with me that you just took from me." This would imply that
Nikolaev had the revolver with him on October 15. However, Fomin
cannot be relied on for this point. There are demonstrable problems
with his 1956 testimony, starting with contamination from the 1937–
1938 NKVD narrative of the murder (for example, Fomin placed Zaporozhets in Leningrad on October 15). Even if Fomin transmitted
Nikolaev's words on December 1–2 correctly, it is quite possible that
the latter was lying.[15]

Stalin Arrives

On the morning of December 2, Stalin and his entourage arrived in
Leningrad. Fomin and a recent account in the journal *Rodina* give the
time as 10:00 or 10:30 A.M. By the reckoning of NKVD officer Genrikh Liushkov, who was in Stalin's group, the arrival was earlier, at
around 8:00 A.M. Medved accompanied Stalin, Molotov, Voroshilov,
Zhdanov, and Yagoda to Smolny, perhaps stopping at the Sverdlov
hospital morgue to view Kirov's corpse, and possibly visiting his
widow, Maria Lvovna. The group set up shop in Kirov's old office. The
atmosphere was very tense. Stalin had brought his own security guard
with him, consisting of over two hundred men, and it seems he feared
more violence. One regional party committee employee, A. Tammi, remembered more than twenty years later how Stalin entered Smolny
with his entourage: "This was in the main corridor. I see a group of
people walking. I look—in the middle is Stalin. Genrikh Yagoda was
walking ahead of Stalin with a Nagan in his raised hand and ordering,
'Everyone, face to the wall! Stand at attention!'"[16]

In the meantime Yagoda's senior deputy, Yakov Agranov, a director
of show trials and fabricated legal cases going back to 1922, ordered

Fomin to take him to NKVD headquarters and hand over all the Kirov case materials. Agranov told Fomin that he was taking over the inquiry into Kirov's killing. Fomin handed the case materials over by 11:00 A.M. Agranov took over Medved's office and had an immediate conference with Pauker, Fomin, Leningrad police chief Zhupakhin, commander of the Leningrad garrison Bekker, and all of the department heads of the Leningrad NKVD. He put Pauker in charge of guarding the leaders from Moscow, made Fomin Pauker's chief of staff, and put the city's Red Army garrison, NKVD troops, and police at Pauker's disposal.[17]

One of the Moscow delegation's first steps was to order Borisov, Kirov's bodyguard, sent to Smolny for questioning by Stalin and his aides. Two days later, on December 4, N. A. Zavilovich, Operations Secretary of the Leningrad NKVD, wrote the following report to Agranov on what transpired next.

· 38 ·

Testimony of Leningrad NKVD Operations Secretary N. A. Zavilovich on the death of Kirov's bodyguard Mikhail Borisov, December 4, 1934. RGANI, f. 6, op. 13, d. 92, ll. 169–172.

———————

Comrade Medved called to the office of the chief administration (*nachal'stvo*) of the Leningrad regional NKVD, where I was on duty, on the Smolny telephone exchange. He ordered me to have Operations Commissar Borisov sent over to Smolny immediately, to the office of Comrade Fillipova /Comrade Chudov's secretary/. I called Comrade Yanishevsky, supposing that Borisov was [being held] at the Special Department. He told me that Borisov was not at the Special Department.

Then I called Comrade Khviiuzov /Chief of the Third Section/ at the Operations Department, and, discovering that Borisov was in the Operations Department, told Comrade Khviiuzov to send Borisov under the escort of two officers without delay to Smolny.

After a short time, in approximately 25–30 minutes, Comrade Khviiuzov called me and stated that the automobile in which they were transporting Borisov, crashed on Voinov St. without reaching Uritsky Square, and that Borisov was wounded and had been taken to our clinic.

December 4, 1934 N. Zavilovich

Borisov died of wounds to his head soon after the apparent accident. His death naturally aroused the suspicions of Stalin and the central

NKVD officers. Was the Leningrad NKVD grossly incompetent, or had they murdered Borisov to conceal evidence? In later years Nikita Khrushchev and others would use Borisov's death to suggest that Stalin was involved in Kirov's murder and that Borisov knew too much. On the face of it, however, if Borisov was murdered it would seem most likely that the Leningrad NKVD organized the crime to conceal evidence from Stalin. This was what central NKVD officers suspected in December 1934. Combined with the fact that Nikolaev had been detained and released in October, Borisov's death ensured that central authorities would undertake a robust investigation of the Leningrad NKVD.

In line with the developing attack on the Leningrad NKVD central officials may have prompted Zavilovich to distort his testimony to make Medved look worse. Genrikh Liushkov, a senior NKVD officer who was on the scene on the morning of December 2, wrote in 1939 that it was Agranov, not Medved, who issued the order to the Leningrad Operations Department to send Borisov to Smolny. The difference between Liushkov's and Zavilovich's accounts might be due to faulty memory or faulty inferences on Liushkov's part. It is also possible, however, that Yagoda or his subordinates prompted Zavilovich to attribute the Borisov order to Medved rather than Agranov, so as to place responsibility for Borisov's death squarely on the Leningrad NKVD.

Back at Smolny, Stalin had Nikolaev brought in for questioning. Rumors about the encounter proliferated during and after the Great Terror of 1937–1938, especially in Soviet forced labor camps, where prisoners swapped alternatives to the official narrative of the murder. The different versions that have been published in English include a story that Nikolaev pointed to NKVD officers in the room and shouted "They forced me to do it!" or some variant of the same, after which he was severely beaten. Other versions are that he said he committed the murder "on behalf of the party," and that he told Stalin, "But you yourself said to me . . . "[18] All of these accounts are at least third-hand. We will examine their provenance in later chapters.

What did the people who were actually in Smolny on the morning of December 2 say about Stalin's cross-examination of Nikolaev? A. I. Katsafa, an NKVD officer who guarded Nikolaev in his cell from December 2, was not present at the interrogation, but Nikolaev was handed over to him in Smolny directly afterwards. He reported that Molotov, Voroshilov, Nikolai Yezhov, Komsomol leader Kosaryov, and Yagoda were present at the meeting. In November 1960, Katsafa testified that when Pauker's deputy Gulko passed Nikolaev over to his custody, he said that "this creep (*podlets*) Nikolaev was rude to Stalin, he refused to answer his questions, he acted like a hooligan." Gulko also told Katsafa that Nikolaev had answered questions from Voroshilov, saying that he'd shot Kirov because the party wouldn't give him work or a pass to rest home in spite of the fact that he and his family were "also human beings." This account was second-hand when it was put to paper. Katsafa wrote it for investigators from the KPK who aimed to demonstrate that Stalin had been involved in the murder. Thus, any bias introduced by Katsafa's questioners would have been towards a version of the meeting more damning for Stalin.[19]

Another guard in Nikolaev's cell, Guzovsky, reported in 1956 that immediately after his meeting with Stalin, Nikolaev said, "Stalin promised me my life, what nonsense, who's going to believe a dictator? He promised me my life if I would tell him who my co-conspirators were. I have no co-conspirators."[20]

Mikhail Rosliakov, the head of the regional and city finance departments introduced in previous chapters, was on the second floor of Smolny in the office of Ivan Fyodorovich Kodatsky, chair of the regional soviet executive committee, from about noon on December 2. Chudov, Kirov's senior deputy, was upstairs in or just outside of Kirov's office where Stalin was. Kodatsky, who was in and out of Kirov's office, had marshaled a group of senior party officials in his room in case Stalin wished to question any of them. Rosliakov wrote about thirty years later that he and the others in the room got some word from "comrades" about what was going on upstairs. He summarized what they heard.

> They brought Nikolaev to the interrogation in a semiconscious state [among other things, he was severely sleep-deprived]. He did not recognize Stalin immediately, they showed him his portrait, and only then did he realize who he was speaking to. He didn't say anything clear, he cried, he repeated the words, "What have I done? What have I done?" He didn't deny the fact of the attack, but he presented the events in only the foggiest terms. And then they took him [back] to the clinic. Nikolaev's wife Milda Draule was called in. She was very upset, stunned, she stated that she had known nothing and suspected nothing.[21]

This account correlates roughly with what Katsafa heard from Gulko—that Nikolaev did not answer Stalin's questions clearly. Let us now consider the single extant firsthand account of the meeting—by Viacheslav Molotov. There exist in fact two different reports by Molotov. The first is in the form of summary notes taken at a December 31, 1955 discussion of the Stalin-Nikolaev encounter by the party Presidium. The notes summarize Molotov's account of the meeting this way: "it was with the senior chekist [Medved or Yagoda?]. The three of them [us?] talked with Nikolaev. Stalin talked with Nikolaev in our presence. There were no blows."[22]

In the early to mid-1970s Molotov told a more detailed story to his biographer and admirer Feliks Chuev:

> Molotov: That night [December 1] we went to Leningrad—Stalin, Voroshilov, and I. We talked to Nikolaev, Kirov's murderer.
>
> He really looked pathetic, he had been excluded from the party. He said that he killed as a conscious act, for ideological reasons. A Zinovievite. I don't think any woman was involved. Stalin interrogated Nikolaev in Smolny.
>
> Chuev: What kind of a person was Nikolaev?
>
> Molotov: An ordinary person. An office worker. Short. Skinny . . . I think that he was bitter about something, excluded from the party, an angry man. And the Zinovievites used him. Possibly he wasn't a real Zinovievite and not a real Trotskyite.
>
> Chuev: Nikolaev was not the only one convicted, but a whole list of people. . . .
>
> Molotov: The thing is, that they were not convicted for the attack itself, but because they participated in the Zinovievite organization. But as far as I remember there was no actual document [showing] that [the attack] was ordered by the Zinovievite group.[23]

Molotov was a mass murderer, one of the two or three men closest to Stalin in the 1930s. In his interviews with Chuev he lies from time to time, denying, for example, that Stalin sanctioned torture of prisoners, and claiming ignorance of the Soviet massacre of Polish prisoners of war in Katyn Forest. But overall the interviews accord well with archival evidence (it should be noted, however, that Molotov himself had reviewed some of the archival evidence in 1956 and it could have influenced his memories or even served as the basis for fabrication). Molotov had a remarkable memory for the details of meetings and official party resolutions. His stance throughout his conversations with Chuev is unrepentant—there were certain "excesses" under Stalin, but in general the "repression" was justified, because the Soviet Union was under mortal threat from internal and external enemies. His refrain is "it was all necessary." Because Molotov remained proud of what he had done, his memoirs are in some ways more factually accurate than those of many Stalinists-turned-reformers, such as Mikoyan, who felt shame about their past actions, and who were tempted to soften or falsify them.

Molotov's memories of Stalin's encounter with Nikolaev do correlate well with what we know about the assassin, his appearance and motivations, and with Rosliakov's and Katsafa's second-hand descriptions of the interrogation. Moreover, his description of Nikolaev's actual relationship with the Zinovievites is quite precise. "Perhaps," he admits, Nikolaev was not a "real" Zinovievite or Trotskyite. And the people executed with him were not directly involved in the murder. The implication is that because Nikolaev shared some sentiments with the Communist opposition to Stalin, he was "objectively" an oppositionist, and other oppositionists were "morally guilty" of the murder. This is a logic that interrogators and prosecutors used again and again in the investigation and trial of the so-called "Leningrad" and "Moscow Centers" in December 1934–January 1935.

After Nikolaev met Stalin, NKVD guards, including Katsafa, escorted him back to the jail at NKVD headquarters. The streets in the center of Leningrad were crowded with pedestrians, and Katsafa reported in 1960 that Nikolaev began to shout out the car window at them "Remember me, I am the assassin, let the people know who killed Kirov!" This is consistent with Nikolaev's frequently expressed desire that the whole party and working class know of his deed. When one of the guards tried to cover his mouth, Nikolaev bit him. Soon after arrival at the NKVD headquarters, according to Katsafa, Yagoda and L. G. Mironov, head of the central NKVD's Economic Security Department, sat down with Nikolaev to get his biographical information. The Leningrad NKVD had done this already, but the central authorities were starting the case from scratch again. Mironov and Nikolaev promptly got into a loaded argument about Nikolaev's "social origins." Nikolaev said that his father was a "carpenter," but Mironov wrote down that he was a carpenter "who hired wage-laborers." Mironov was trying to show that Nikolaev came from the petty bourgeoisie rather than the working class, because his father had hired help. Nikolaev objected strongly, denying his father had ever had hired anyone. Again he refused to sign the official protocol of the questioning. A loud quarrel ensued, with Yagoda joining in. Yagoda then ordered Nikolaev taken back to his jail cell, and, according to Katsafa, told him, "We will force you to talk, I'll make a bloody mess of you."[24]

That afternoon Stalin and his aides reviewed Leningrad NKVD files on suspected oppositionists and counterrevolutionary conspiracies. It appears that Pyotr Struppe's secretary Ivan Ilin and possibly another Leningrad official, Dora Lazurkina, informed them of an NKVD "secret collaborator" (*sekretnyi sotrudnik*), M. N. Volkova, who in August had reported the existence of an anti-Soviet conspiracy of former kulaks. The Leningrad NKVD had committed Volkova to a psychiatric hospital on October 28, 1934 with a diagnosis of "congenital schizophrenia/systematic delusions of persecution." On December 2 Stalin or one of his lieutenants ordered her released and brought to Smolny for questioning.[25]

Volkova was born sometime between 1905 and 1909 in Vologda Province to a well-off forestry officer. According to Kirilina, she was married in the 1920s and had a child. In mid-decade her family's house burned down. Volkova left the area, evidently without her husband, and moved to Leningrad around 1930. There she worked as a passport clerk and as a nanny in Ilin's family. She picked up other odd jobs as well, such as maid, cleaning lady, and waitress. Volkova became a secret informer to the NKVD, possibly as early as 1931. In this latter position she found her true vocation.[26]

Georgy Alekseevich Petrov, an officer of the Special Department of the Leningrad NKVD, handled Volkova's denunciations in the fall of 1934. After Stalin's delegation questioned him and Volkova, central NKVD officers arrested him on charges of negligence for ignoring Volkova's claims about a "counterrevolutionary" organization. Special Department deputy chief Yanishevsky and his aide Baltsevich were also arrested in connection with the Volkova case on December 2, as was Secret Political Department officer A. A. Mosevich and Ivan Zaporozhets' deputy Belousenko.[27]

Convicted in January 1935 on charges of negligence, Petrov repeatedly sought rehabilitation, submitting statements on the Volkova case in 1939, 1948, 1951, 1956, 1960, and 1964. According to Petrov's depositions from the post-Stalin era Volkova claimed to have detected in Leningrad a counterrevolutionary organization called the "Green Lamp" numbering seven hundred persons.[28] At her first meeting with Petrov she described the "Green Lamp" in vague terms as aiming at overturning Soviet Power and assassinating Communist leaders. In later interviews, Volkova claimed to have found "a bucket full of human meat" at the apartment of a Putilov factory worker, and to have uncovered a printing press for counterfeiting money at a friend's apartment. After missing several appointments with Petrov, she turned up again with a tale of having been kidnapped, taken to the country home of a former Tsarist general, and forced to clean storage rooms. In the rooms she found "stacks of corpses" and boxes of artillery shells. When Petrov asked her for more details, she showed him an old shell casing of the sort "often used on writing tables as a decorative pencil container."[29]

That fall, probably in October, Petrov attended a meeting on "the bloated informer network," where top Leningrad NKVD officials, including Medved, claimed there were too many agents giving false information. Petrov's secret informers were singled out, and Volkova in particular. Petrov claimed in 1956 that Medved called Volkova "a socially dangerous element, as she libels people and misinforms government organs with her letters." Petrov, Medved said, "was wasting his time." He ordered NKVD clinic chief Mamushin to arrange a psychiatric evaluation for her. On October 28 she was committed to a psychiatric hospital.

On December 2 (or possibly December 3) Petrov was called to Kirov's old office in Smolny. Stalin was there, together with Molotov, Voroshilov, Zhdanov, Yagoda, and others. Petrov was unpleasantly surprised to see Volkova as well. Stalin told Petrov that he'd listened to her story and thought "that there might be some truth to it." Yagoda berated Petrov—"You are the son of a kulak and you've lost your class vigilance!"[30] As was his wont when making dramatic decisions before an audience, Stalin walked about the room, smoking, in silence. Finally, he said, "The whole party, the working class, and above all the Leningrad NKVD are guilty in Kirov's assassination." Soon after Petrov left the room he was arrested. Then Nikolai Yezhov asked Petrov if he was willing to testify against the Leningrad NKVD leadership.[31]

Stalin gave Volkova his stamp of approval. She received her formal release papers from the psychiatric hospital on December 3 and was transferred to a clinic of the Sverdlov Hospital, where she received special treatment until her release on February 23, 1935. The authorities then set her up with a large apartment, rations, money, and passes to health resorts. In the meantime Volkova did what was expected of her. By December 15, two weeks after the murder, she had produced denunciations resulting in the arrest of sixty-three persons belonging to six supposed counterrevolutionary groups—the "Leningrad State Philharmonic Terrorist Group," the "Monarchist Group," the "Bogomolov Terrorist Group," the "Livanov Terrorist Group," the "Counterrevolutionary Group of Escaped Kulaks," and the "Counterrevolutionary Kulak Group of Kabachinov et al." In early 1935 she denounced her ex-boyfriend, a Leningrad policeman, as a spy for Poland, Germany, Italy, and Estonia. Her motives were apparently twofold—to get revenge on him for attacking her with a knife, and to force him to come back to her.[32]

For the next twenty years Volkova was well rewarded for producing denunciations. From 1948 to 1955, for example, she sent ninety of them to the "organs." The Leningrad MVD/KGB generated eleven volumes of material investigating these. Volkova denounced her daughter and many neighbors and acquaintances, all for capital crimes. She also loved tall tales, and over time she became convinced that she had warned the NKVD of the Kirov murder beforehand. Already in 1935 she began writing letters to the NKVD stating that she had known Nikolaev before Kirov's assassination, a claim for which there is no credible evidence at all, and which contradicts Petrov's account and evidence from 1934 interrogations of Leningrad NKVD officers. At an interview with KGB officers on June 8, 1956, Volkova admitted that she in fact did not know Nikolaev or the other accused in the "Leningrad Center" trial. Her description of Nikolaev did not match other descriptions or his photograph. Immediately after the June 8 interview Volkova wrote a letter denouncing her interrogators' supposed involvement in a "terrorist plot."[33]

Volkova's youngest daughter described her mother to a Leningrad journalist in the 1980s as "difficult . . . arrogant, suspicious . . . vengeful," and power-hungry. She died in the early 1960s in a Soviet psychiatric hospital.[34]

On the same day Stalin first interviewed Volkova, December 2, Officer N. I. Makarov of the Leningrad NKVD Special Political Department delivered a report to him on the case file "Svoiak" ("Brother-in-law") which held informer accounts of the activities of former Zinoviev and Trotsky supporters. Agranov then ordered Makarov to prepare a list of the Zinovievites in the file, including Ivan Kotolynov and Vladimir Rumiantsev. According to Makarov's testimony in 1956 and 1961, there was no file on Nikolaev in "Svoiak," or indeed in any of the Leningrad NKVD files. None of the informers questioned in the days after the murder mentioned Nikolaev.[35]

When did Stalin decide to target the Zinovievites for Kirov's murder? According to Officer Makarov, Agranov, Nikolai Yezhov, and Genrikh Liushkov told interrogators at a December 3 meeting to press the prisoners hard for evidence implicating the Zinovievite opposition in the killing. If this is so, then Stalin must have spoken to them in the same vein on December 2 or 3. Based in part on this evidence, Aleksandr Yakovlev suggested in 1990 that "Stalin arrived in Leningrad with prepared, well-thought-out ideas, and immediately these began to be implemented. Stalin said from the beginning that Zinovievites had done the deed." I would argue that Stalin was probably thinking about targeting the Zinovievites very early, but that this does not necessarily indicate he had planned the Kirov murder himself. After all, when Stalin moved to shut down the September 1929 turmoil inside the Leningrad party organization, one of his first steps was to insinuate that Zinovievites might have been responsible. In Stalin's mind trouble in Leningrad was Zinovievite trouble.[36]

Stalin, Yagoda, and Nikolai Yezhov, a leading TsK official who was playing a prominent role in the investigation, were also building a substantial case against senior officers of the Leningrad NKVD. Apart from the fact that Kirov's sizeable bodyguard had failed to protect him, there were Nikolaev's detention and release on October 15, Borisov's death, and the quashing of Volkova's denunciations. All three NKVD departments involved in active work in the field (Special, Special Political, Operations) were implicated. On December 3, 1934, Yagoda issued a formal indictment of eight leading NKVD officers, at least four of whom were already in custody.

· 39 ·

Firing of leading officers of the Leningrad NKVD, December 3, 1934.
RGANI, f. 6, op. 13, d. 79, l. 1.

_____

Order No. 319. Re: removal from work and indictment of a number of employees of the NKVD directorate of Leningrad Region.

No. 319. December 3, 1934. City of Leningrad.

The following employees of the NKVD Directorate of Leningrad Region are relieved of their duties and indicted for a negligent attitude towards their obligations to defend state security in Leningrad.

Chief of the NKVD Directorate Medved F. D.

Deputy Chief of the NKVD Directorate Fomin F. T.

Chief of the NKVD Directorate Special Political Department Lundin-Gorin A. S.

Deputy Chief of the NKVD Directorate Special Department Yanishevsky D. Yu.

Aide to the Chief of the NKVD Directorate Special Political Department Mosevich A. A.

Aide to the Chief of the NKVD Directorate Special Department and Chief of the Third Section of the Special Department Lobov P. M.

Aide to the Chief of the Second Section of the Special Department Baltsevich M. K.

Plenipotentiary Officer of the Second Section of the Special Department Petrov G. A.

I hereby assign my deputy Comrade Agranov Ya. S. to the post of acting Chief of the Leningrad Region Directorate of the NKVD.

People's Commissar of Internal Affairs of the USSR—G. Yagoda.

On the day this order was issued, December 3, Stalin had a face-to-face meeting with Medved and his deputy Fomin, in which he discussed their firing. Writing in March 1956, Fomin described how Stalin received both officers at the house in the Kamenny Ostrov neighborhood where the leaders of the Moscow delegation were staying. Molotov was standing to Stalin's right, Voroshilov to his left. Yagoda was standing several steps behind them and Agranov stood by the wall and took notes. Stalin immediately taxed Medved with the release of Nikolaev on October 15 and with Borisov's death. Voroshilov told Fomin, whom he had worked with in the Civil War, that "I knew you . . . as a fighting fellow, now look what's happened to you." Then Stalin told Medved, "Your surveillance files (*uchet*) are lousy, they took a shot at you, and you've only got thirteen people in your card files on suspicion of terrorism, and you don't even have anyone to shoot . . . you've lost your Bolshevik chekist vigor."[37]

Stalin told Medved and Fomin that "Kirov's murder is the doing of some organization, but it's hard to say at the moment what organization." He was less candid than he had been with Yezhov and Agranov, to whom he had probably already issued instructions to build a case against the ex-Zinovievites. According to Fomin, he said that "we have to feed Nikolaev up, buy a nice chicken and some other groceries, feed him, so he'll get stronger, and then he will tell us who ran him, and if he doesn't talk, we'll strew him all over the room, and he'll tell us everything. . . ."[38]

On December 3 *Pravda* published an NKVD bulletin for the first time publicly identifying Kirov's assassin. Curiously, the bulletin described Nikolaev as a former employee of the Leningrad RKI, rather than of the Institute of Party History, where he had last worked.

· 40 ·

Bulletin of the People's Commissariat of Internal Affairs of the USSR on the Kirov assassination, December 3, 1934. *Pravda*, December 3, 1934.

Preliminary investigation has established that the family name of the killer of Comrade Kirov is Nikolaev (Leonid Vasilievich), born 1904, former employee of the Leningrad RKI.

Investigation is continuing.

Probably in connection with the bulletin, NKVD authorities issued an order over Medved's name to several Leningrad officials. The order was dated December 3, 1934, 4:50 P.M. The use of Medved's name was probably a formality, as he had already been effectively removed from leadership of the Leningrad NKVD.[39]

· 41 ·

NKVD order to Leningrad officials, December 3, 1934, 4:50 P.M. RGANI, f. 6, op. 13, d. 69, l. 136.

To: Comrades Osherov, Nazarenko, Struppe, Sveshnikov.

This is to notify you that at the order of the NKVD of the USSR no information of any kind at all about the murderer—Nikolaev, Leonid Vasilievich—is to be given to anyone, no matter what the circumstances. This includes government institutions and reporters, especially reporters from foreign newspapers.

In the event that any persons should request information, immediately notify Comrade Gorin of the NKVD Directorate of Leningrad Region, tel. 23–87 Smolny . . .

Take measures with regard to any of your employees who may have any information about Nikolaev.

Chief of the Leningrad Regional Directorate of the USSR NKVD.
Medved.
December 3, 1934.
City of Leningrad.
4:50 P.M.

This order in all likelihood stemmed from the desire of the NKVD authorities to keep all options open as they sought to find or fabricate the right "enemy" identity for Nikolaev. It was unclear yet who he would turn out to be—son of the exploiting classes, White Guard terrorist, foreign spy, Zinovievite terrorist, or even all of the above. Information about Nikolaev that got out without the NKVD's permission could complicate the task of publicizing the "correct" identity once it was determined. In addition, Nikolaev's real identity, a working-class Communist who had turned against the regime, was potentially devastating for official versions of reality. It needed to be kept quiet.

That night (December 3–4) Stalin and most of his retinue departed Leningrad on an overnight train to Moscow that also carried Kirov's body. Yagoda and Yezhov went with them, leaving Agranov in charge of the investigation in Leningrad. Based on the evidence of Makarov and Genrikh Liushkov, it seems that Stalin had already set the inquiry on course towards implicating former Zinoviev supporters in Kirov's murder. He had fired Medved and his most important deputies, fulfilling a goal he and Yagoda had set for themselves in the fall. Much work, however, remained ahead.

Comparison of Stalin's actions on December 1–3, 1934 with his reactions to other "extraordinary incidents" (*chrezvychainye proisshestviia*—ChP) in the late 1920s and early 1930s reveals many parallels. The similarities to his response to the murder of Ambassador Voikov in June 1927 were discussed at the beginning of this chapter. There are also startling parallels to his reactions following an August 1934 mutiny attempt at a Moscow barracks.

On the morning of August 5, 1934 A. S. Nakhaev, chief of staff of a reserve artillery division organized by Osoaviakhim (the Society for the Support of the Armed Forces and Aviation-Chemical Defense, which had its own reserve military formations), led two hundred of the division's infantrymen, recently called up for training, onto the barracks grounds of the Second Moscow Proletarian Infantry Division, located at Sukharyovskaya Square in downtown Moscow. Ordering the volunteers into formation, he delivered a speech denouncing the Bolsheviks for betraying the October Revolution. The factories did not belong to the workers, nor the land to the peasants, he declared. A tiny clique of Jewish Communists was running the country. Nakhaev called for the soldiers to turn their weapons against the Soviet government, and finished his speech with shouts of "Down with the old authorities! All hail the new revolution! All hail the new government!" Most of the soldiers did not follow Nakhaev's orders, but he persuaded a few to try to seize the Second Infantry Division's guard post. Guards and other soldiers, probably from the conscript Second Infantry Division, subdued the mutineers.[40]

On the day of the mutiny Stalin's right-hand man Lazar Kaganovich wrote to him in Sochi, where he was vacationing on the Black Sea. The Politburo had put Agranov in direct charge of the investigation (just as in Leningrad four months later). Agranov reported that Nakhaev seemed to be "normal, but had some kind of nervous breakdown," and that his statements under interrogation were "obscure" (*tugo*). Voroshilov, Commissar of Defense, was calling Nakhaev "a psychotic."[41] As in the Kirov murder, lower-level authorities concluded early that they were dealing with a psychologically disturbed perpetrator. Like Nikolaev four months later, Nakhaev apparently was prepared to commit suicide—he had a bottle of poison with him. Also like Nikolaev, he seems to have been motivated by poverty as well as politics. At the time of the mutiny he was living with his wife in a "corner" four meters square in a village outside Moscow.[42]

Stalin responded with cold rage, dismissing the possibility that psychological problems played a role in the crime. In an August 8 letter to Kaganovich, he voiced the same assumptions that guided his response to Kirov's murder—the perpetrator must belong to a counterrevolutionary conspiracy, the organization where he worked must have lacked vigilance, and the chekists were being too "soft." He also suspected a foreign connection, an angle the NKVD also worked hard in the Kirov murder.

> The Nakhaev case is a son-of-a-bitch. He is obviously (*obviously!*) not alone. We have to nail him to the wall, force him to talk—tell the whole truth, and then punish him as harshly as possible. He is probably an agent of the Poles and Germans (or the Japanese). The chekists are a joke when they discuss his "political views" with him (they call this an *interrogation!*). A hired dog doesn't have political views—if he

did he would not be an agent of outside forces. He called armed personnel to action against the government—he must be destroyed. Obviously all is not well at Osoaviakhim.[43]

On August 12, following another bulletin on the Nakhaev case, Stalin instructed Kaganovich to "squeeze [Nakhaev] harder." On August 26 Agranov reported success in a telegram to Stalin in Sochi. Nakhaev had "confessed" that the former Tsarist general Leonid Nikolaevich Bykov, with whom he had worked at a physical education school, had ordered him to foment a mutiny. Nakhaev also claimed that a former Tsarist officer who had served with Bykov in the same Imperial Army regiment was now chief of staff of the Estonian armed forces. The NKVD arrested Bykov. On August 28 Kaganovich, obviously aiming to impress Stalin with his own "vigilance," wrote to Stalin that, "one assumes that [the foreign connection] is not just Estonia." Almost two months later (November 15) Yagoda notified Stalin that interrogators had managed to link Bykov to the Estonian diplomatic mission in Moscow. On December 5 the Politburo passed Nakhaev's case on to the Military Tribunal of the Supreme Court (the same body which would try Nikolaev). He was shot in short order.[44]

As in the Kirov case, one of Stalin's main concerns following the Nakhaev case was with the laxness of guards who let the Nakhaev incident go so far. Immediately after the mutiny Stalin ordered a full-scale investigation of the effectiveness of sentries guarding Moscow garrison units. The results were disappointing. Investigatory personnel without documents easily got into military schools and barracks. In response the Politburo issued an order for tighter security.[45]

The Nakhaev case is also important for what it reveals about Stalin's shifting political inclinations and plans for the future. When the case unfolded in August Stalin insisted that Nakhaev was linked to a counterrevolutionary group with foreign connections. White Guard and foreign capitalist espionage/terrorism inside the USSR were old chekist storylines, with a certain thin thread of truth to them. Moreover, regime leaders' fear of foreign intervention seems to have escalated following Japan's seizure of Manchuria and Hitler's rise to power. In 1934 the security organs reported to Stalin dozens of supposed cases of foreign espionage on Soviet territory.[46]

What Stalin did not suggest after Nakhaev's mutiny, and what no one else suggested to him, was that ex-oppositionists from within the Communist Party were involved. But just four months later, he suggested to Yezhov and Agranov that Zinovievites were behind Kirov's murder. Moreover he apparently did so within forty-eight hours of the crime. Clearly he was ready to blame the ex-oppositionists for whatever trouble might come up. What had changed between August and December?

At the same time that he corresponded with Kaganovich about the Nakhaev case Stalin was very angry with Grigory Zinoviev about a conflict involving the flagship party theoretical journal *Bolshevik*. Zinoviev, who had been expelled from the party twice, in 1927 and 1932, was readmitted and given a post on the editorial board of *Bolshevik* in late 1933. In the early summer of 1934 he was one of the editors who proposed to publish an 1888 letter of Friedrich Engels that Stalin did not like because it denigrated the Russian state. The *Bolshevik* editors did not publish the offending letter, but they ran an article discussing it and summarizing its contents. On August 5 Stalin wrote an enraged letter to Kaganovich demanding that Zinoviev be fired. On August 16 the Politburo complied.[47]

It is clear that Stalin in the early 1930s was bent on monitoring ex-oppositionists closely and crushing any hint of recalcitrance on their part. The summer 1934 incident with Zinoviev must have heightened his vigilance toward the ex-Zinovievite opposition. It is not particularly surprising that he blamed them in December for the assassination in Leningrad.

The Nakhaev mutiny and numerous other incidents show that Stalin's reaction to the Kirov murder was typical for him personally and for the Bolshevik regime as a whole. The insistence that a counter-revolutionary conspiracy must be behind the assassination, the immediate resort to extrajudicial procedures, the execution of hostages, the search for a foreign connection, and the anger at the NKVD's supposed incompetence were all practically reflexive. Stalin's reactions to the killing can be integrated into a narrative in which he ordered the Kirov murder, but they do not really strengthen any argument for such a story line. They are equally or more consistent with response to an unexpected act of terrorism. The same holds for Stalin's early decision to inject the Zinovievites into the case. A quick decision on Stalin's part to blame them for Kirov's murder is entirely plausible.

Stalin did not just follow earlier patterns in his handling of the Kirov murder. He was also learning. His "suggestion" to NKVD officers that they follow up on Volkova's accusations appears to be his first use of low-ranking women angry at abuse by male authorities to generate mass denunciations. The Leningrad NKVD had exploited Volkova as a secret informer, then forcibly committed her to a psychiatric hospital. Her policeman boyfriend had attacked her with a knife. Now with Stalin's help, she would get back at everyone. In the coming years, Stalin made use of other women in similar fashion. In April 1937 he received a letter from Moshkova, an economist in Kursk, claiming that a "Trotskyite" friend had told her all about a gigantic oppositionist plot in the early 1930s to murder Kirov. Moshkova's description of the plot was clearly inspired by Stalin's own speech to the February-March TsK plenum of 1937. Using phrasing very similar to his recommendation in the Volkova case, Stalin told Yezhov, now chief of the NKVD, that although there was much that was "confused" in Moshkova's denunciation, "there might be some truth in it."[48]

Nikita Khrushchev recalled two other "hysterical" female denouncers endorsed by Stalin, the history graduate student Nikolaenko in Kiev and a Komsomol official in Moscow, Mishakova. According to Khrushchev, Nikolaenko, who had been expelled from the Ukrainian Institute of History party organization in 1936, played a key role in the Great Terror cases against Pavel Postyshev, Stanislav Kosior, Chubar, and other officials in Ukraine. Mishakova played a similar role in the downfall of Komsomol "chieftain" Aleksandr Kosaryov during the Terror. In the prosecution of the so-called Doctors' Plot just before his death, Stalin again used a woman pushed around by her male superiors, the doctor Lidiya Timashuk, although Timashuk was probably not psychologically ill in the clinical sense, as Volkova and Nikolaenko seem to have been.[49]

Stalin's cynical use of exploited, desperate, and sometimes psychologically ill women was a particularly vicious instance of a basic practice of Soviet governance—mobilizing the inchoate resentment of "the masses" against officials deemed obstructionist or otherwise inconvenient by the leadership. The practice was especially ugly because Soviet policies themselves—the granting of arbitrary privileges to party members, collectivization, the constant search for "enemies"—exacerbated such resentment. Frighteningly, however, the oppressive policies, the mass rage, and the scapegoating constituted a coherent, functioning system.

Figure 1. Group of leading Leningrad officials in 1926. From left to right: I. F. Kodatsky, P. A. Alekseev, N. K. Antipov, S. M. Kirov, N. F. Sveshnikov, I. I. Kondratev, Sobolev. Bearded man standing is unidentified. RGAKFD.

Figure 2. Dedication of Lenin statue before the main entrance to the Smolny Institute, 1927. The banner reads "Vyborg Ward." RGAKFD.

Figure 3. Politburo members sit among the Leningrad delegation to the Sixteenth Party Congress, July 1930. Stalin is visible, wearing a white outfit, in the third row at center. Kirov, his face partly concealed, sits behind Stalin and to his right. Directly in front of Stalin is Lazar Kaganovich, to Kaganovich's left, Viacheslav Molotov. Valerian Kuibyshev sits behind Molotov, and Sergo Ordzhonikidze, in white, is behind Kuibyshev and to his left. RGAKFD.

Figure 4. Stalin and Kirov on Sverdlov (Teatralnaya) Square, Moscow, between sessions of the Sixteenth Party Congress, 1930. RGAKFD.

Figure 5. On the Kremlin grounds, 1932. From left to right: Kirov, Kaganovich, Ordzhonikidze, Stalin, Mikoyan. RGAKFD.

Figure 6. Kirov's office and desk in the Smolny Institute. RGAKFD.

Figure 7. Kirov speaks at the Seventeenth Party Congress, 1934 (behind him, from left to right, Voroshilov, Kuibyshev, Postychev). RGAKFD.

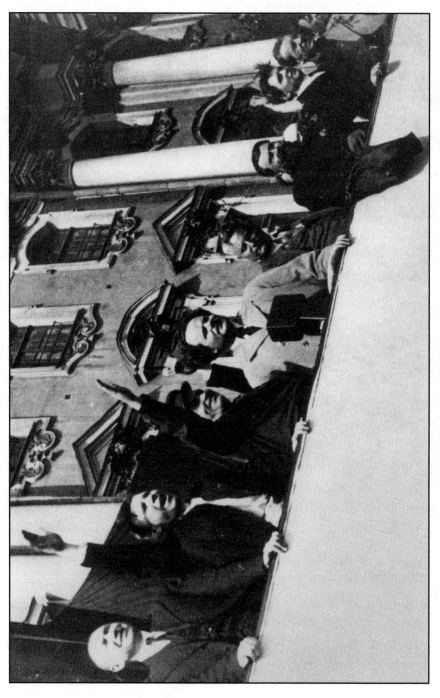

Figure 8. Leading Leningrad officials on the podium at May First celebration, Uritsky (Tauride) Square, Leningrad, 1934. From left to right, beginning with Kirov: S. M. Kirov, Mikhail Chudov, I. F. Kodatsky, P. I. Struppe, P. A. Irklis (others unidentified). RGAKFD.

CHAPTER 8

Fingering the Zinovievites

J ust after noon on December 4 most of the Politburo gathered in
Stalin's office for a three-hour meeting. A number of security and
legal officials were also present for at least part of the time, including Yagoda, Pauker, Redens (chief of the Moscow Region
NKVD), Avel Yenukidze (who among other things had charge of
Kremlin security), USSR chief prosecutor Ivan Akulov, his deputy Andrei Vyshinsky (who had already made a name for himself as a show
trial prosecutor), and Commissar of Justice Krylenko. The assassination, the security organs' response, and future criminal proceedings
were presumably the main topics on the agenda. The meeting adjourned at 3:25 P.M.—some of those present were to stand in the first
honor guard by Kirov's body, which had been displayed for public
viewing in Moscow from 1:30 P.M. that afternoon. In the evening a
group of Politburo members and provincial party secretaries convened
again at Stalin's office at 10:40 P.M. Nikolai Yezhov, a prominent TsK
official who had risen rapidly due to his hard work and mastery of Soviet bureaucratic technique, was present.[1]

That same day, December 4, Agranov sent Stalin a large number of
interrogation protocols and other documents in the Kirov murder
case. Right down to the executions of Nikolaev and other supposed
members of the "Leningrad Center" on December 29, Agranov kept
his boss posted daily on developments in the investigation. Stalin received more than 260 interrogation protocols related to the Kirov
murder case. Agranov also forwarded all of his reports, and probably
at least some of the interrogation protocols, to Yagoda. Yezhov also re-

ceived the reports, although his name does not appear as an addressee on the copies still extant.[2]

· 42 ·

Agranov telegram to Stalin, December 4, 1934. APRF, f. 3, op. 24, d. 198, l. 1.

To: Secretary of the Central Committee of the All-Union Communist Party Stalin.

I am sending to you the following documents in the case of Nikolaev, Leonid Vasilevich:

1. Interrogation protocol for Nikolaev, Leonid from 12/3/1934.

2. Two interrogation protocols for Nikolaev, Pyotr from 12/3/1934.

3. Two interrogation protocols for Platych (Platoch), S. A., from 12/1 and 12/2/1934.

4. Two interrogation protocols for Vasiliev, G. G. from 12/1 and 12/3/1934.

5. Interrogation protocol for Borisov from 12/1/1934.

6. Four interrogation protocols for Draule, Milda from 12/1 and 12/3/1934.

7. Six letters of Nikolaev, Pyotr and notes from his diary.

Deputy Chief of the NKVD USSR Agranov

December 4, 1934.

The first thing to note about the list of protocols is that most of the more important interrogations after the night of December 1–2 were conducted by central rather than Leningrad NKVD personnel. A second important point is that all of the documents sent to Stalin on December 4 are still extant in party archives. I have read every document on this list. They deal with the whereabouts and activities of both Nikolaev brothers in the days before the murder, the sequence of events at the crime scene in Smolny, "anti-Soviet" comments in Nikolaev's diaries, Milda Draule's failure to denounce Nikolaev's planning for the assassination, and Draule's possible foreign contacts, including her relatives in Latvia and German engineers working at the Commissariat of Heavy Industry. There is no mention of the Zinovievites or other specific Communist opposition groups. Overall these documents indicate that central interrogators on December 2 and 3 were still working on basic questions about the crime—how it was done and who the possible accessories might be. They were particularly interested in possible foreign connections to the assassination, which was in line with the direction of many NKVD investigations in 1933–1934.[3]

Later comments by Nikolai Yezhov and Genrikh Liushkov confirm that the initial direction of the central NKVD investigation was towards foreign involvement. On February 5, 1939 Yezhov, in a letter of self-justification to Stalin (he was in prison awaiting trial) wrote, "I carried out your order—to seek the enemy among the Zinovievites, at the time when the chekists were trying to turn the case into one of foreign espionage, and limit it to that." Genrikh Liushkov confirms that the initial thrust of the investigation was towards a connection with foreign consulates in Leningrad. Based on Yezhov's comments on March 3, 1937 to the February/March 1937 plenum of the TsK, Yagoda may have offered some resistance to turning the case against the Zinovievites. Yezhov said, "Comrade Stalin, as I remember it, called in me and Kosaryov and said, 'Look for the killer among the Zinovievites.' I should note that the chekists did not believe in that. . . . Comrade Stalin had to intervene. Comrade Stalin called Yagoda and said, 'Look, we're going to smash their faces.'"[4]

As we saw in the previous chapter, Stalin and his aides were already examining the police files of ex-oppositionists in Leningrad on December 2. Stalin's directive to "Look for the killer among the Zinovievites" probably came on December 2 or 3. At any rate, interrogation protocols show a sharp turn in the investigation on December 4. On that day Agranov began pressing Nikolaev for the first time about his connections with the Zinovievites (there is no mention of the latter in any of the interrogation protocols from December 3).

· 43 ·

Agranov interrogation of Leonid Nikolaev, December 4, 1934. TsA FSB RF, a.u.d. N-Sh44, t. 12, ll. 95–96.

Question: What influence did your connections to former oppositionists-Trotskyites have on your decision to kill Comrade Kirov?

Answer: My ties with the Trotskyites Shatsky, Vanya Kotolynov, Nikolai Bardin, and others influenced my decision to kill Comrade Kirov. However, I knew these people not as members of any group, but as individuals. I met these people over a period of a number of years, and some of them quite recently. I have not met Bardin recently.

Question: Did these individuals take part in your crime?

Answer: No, they did not. Around August of this year, one afternoon as I was keeping under observation the building where Kirov and Chudov live—on Krasnykh Zor Street—I met Shatsky. He complained to me of his alienation from the party, of his dissatisfaction. He said that in his place someone else would be ready for anything. At the moment of our conversation secretary of the regional party committee Chudov went by in auto no. 713. Chudov was going with his guards to his dacha in Sestroretsk. Comrade Chudov's car halted by the tram stop and then went on. That auto caught our attention—we glanced at one another.

I saw Kotolynov at the Polytechnic Institute in Leningrad [also known as the Leningrad Industrial Institute] just before the October holidays [on November 4], but did not converse with him. Just before that I met Sokolov, a member of the Communist Party, in Smolny. From Smolny we took the tram home to the Vyborg Side. Sokolov has tight connections to the former oppositionists. He is a student of the Naval Academy. As a result of our conversation we decided to establish closer relations. At Smolny we wanted to get tickets to the gala [to celebrate the anniversary of the October Revolution] at the Mariinsky Theater on November 6. I wanted to make an attempt on Kirov on the fifth or sixth of November, but then I postponed my plans, in connection with the October holidays. When I talked with Sokolov we were feeling each other out. Sokolov lives on Nizhegorodskaya Street. He graduated from the Industrial Technical School.

L. Nikolaev.

Interrogated by: Deputy Chief of the NKVD Agranov and Chief of the Economic Security Department of GUGB NKVD USSR Mironov.

Who were the men named by Nikolaev? Shatsky was born in 1899 in the Tula Region; his father was a railroad worker. Unlike most Leningrad workers, he had a diploma, from the Leningrad Mechanical Institute. In 1934 Shatsky was married, with two children. He joined the Communist Youth League in 1917 and served in the Red Guards and Red Army during the Civil War. He held a number of elected Komsomol positions, including at the Vyborg Ward committee, where he became acquainted with Nikolaev. In 1923 he joined the party, but was excluded in 1927 for distributing "Trotskyite literature." Unlike many of his contemporaries from the (Trotsky-Zinoviev) "United Opposition" in Leningrad, he did not appeal his expulsion or write public letters of repentance. Leaving Leningrad he worked for some time as an engineer at the new tractor factory in Cheliabinsk in the Urals. He returned late in 1933 or early in 1934, only to lose two factory jobs in rapid succession due to his oppositionist record.[5]

Ivan Kotolynov had been a major figure in the Leningrad Komso-mol prior to 1926. He was a Vyborg native, born in 1905 in a working-class family. According to one record he was admitted to the party in 1921, at the age of sixteen. In the early to mid-1920s he was a secretary on the Vyborg Ward and Leningrad committees of the Komsomol and a member of the All-Union Komsomol Central Committee. He was ex-cluded from the party in late 1927 for supporting the "United Opposi-tion," and restored in 1929 after a public statement to the Central Control Commission recanting his "mistakes." At the time of Kirov's murder he was in his final year of studies at the Leningrad Industrial Institute. His wife was also a student there, and they had a one-year-old son.[6]

Georgy Sokolov, born in 1904, was a student at the Naval Academy in late 1934 and a former Komsomol activist who knew Nikolaev from his Vyborg days. He had no record of opposition activity. Niko-laev knew Sokolov relatively well and had talked with him more than once in 1934. Nikolai Bardin was an oppositionist, labeled a Trot-skyite by the regime, who had been exiled to Kazakhstan in 1932.[7]

On December 5 Agranov's men arrested Kotolynov and Shatsky; on the sixth they detained Sokolov. Getting their hands on Bardin would take longer because he had to be sent back to Leningrad from Kaza-khstan for questioning.[8]

Agranov had good reason to question Nikolaev about Kotolynov and Shatsky. In the NKVD library there were informer reports on both men in a file labeled "Politikan" ("Politico"), which covered the activ-ities of former Zinoviev supporters in Leningrad.[9] And Nikolaev men-tioned both men in his writings (probably in his "autobiography," composed beginning in late May 1934). At the time he wrote the ex-cerpt below Nikolaev clearly still identified with Stalin's "general line" and viewed the former oppositionist Kotolynov as a traitor to the party.

> I remember how I. Kotolynov and I visited managerial offices (*khozi-aistvennye organizatsii*) collecting funds for Komsomol work. In the ward committee there was a strong team—Kotolynov, Antonov, and Shatsky on the periphery. In 1924–1926 Kotolynov joined the new op-position and at one of the Komsomol congresses traitorously declared that we are not St[alinists] but L[eninists], now he gnaws the granite of science.[10]

Government investigators in 1956 and 1990 used the fact that both Nikolaev and his interrogators at first labeled Kotolynov and the other oppositionists Trotskyites to argue that as of December 4 Stalin had not decided to target the Zinovievites. This argument requires clarification. The boundary between Zinovievites and Trotskyites was not clear, either in reality or in the minds of the regime's security officers. Followers of Trotsky and Zinoviev had fought together in the "United Opposition" against Stalin in 1926–1927, and there was not a clear distinction between Zinovievite and Trotskyite ideas. Informer reports on suspected Trotskyites and Zinovievites were intermingled in the same case files at the Leningrad NKVD.

Investigators were certainly under pressure from Stalin to produce interrogations that would implicate oppositionists of some stripe, and Agranov was frustrated. When he sent the protocol of the December 4 interrogation above to Stalin, he noted that "Nikolaev is behaving extremely stubbornly."[11] Despite all he could do, the assassin would not name Kotolynov, Shatsky, or any others as accessories to the crime.

One measure of Agranov's desperation is a schoolboy lie he concocted probably on December 4, perhaps even before the interrogation cited above. The lie can be reconstructed by backtracking from a communication he sent to Stalin on December 4. The text read in part, "via an agent report, based on Nikolaev's own words, it has been established that his best friends were the Trotskyites Kotolynov, Ivan Ivanovich and Shatsky, Nikolai Nikolaevich." Agranov stated that he had ordered the arrest of both men.[12]

An April 1956 KGB report based on interviews with two of the officers who guarded Nikolaev in his cell, Katsafa and Radin, clarifies the origin of Agranov's communication to Stalin. The "agent" mentioned by Agranov was Nikolaev's prison guard Katsafa.

· 44 ·

April 1956 KGB report on 1956 testimony of Nikolaev's guards. RGANI, f. 6, op. 13, d. 24, l. 29.

Katsafa claimed that several days after his arrest Nikolaev gave revealing testimony of his participation in the Zinovievite organization. Katsafa at the time supposedly heard Nikolaev pronounce in his sleep the phrase, "If they arrest Kotolynov, there's no need to worry, he is a strong man, but if they arrest Shatsky, he's a punk (*meliuzga*), he'll give everything away." Katsafa then supposedly wrote this phrase down in his notebook and immediately reported it to Agranov and Mironov, after which he received an order to prepare a detailed official report.

Katsafa's claim is dubious, as Radin, whom we [also] questioned, who was together with Katsafa in the cell with Nikolaev, does not confirm it, but says that Nikolaev [...] often spoke deliriously in his sleep, mentioned some last names, but never pronounced complete phrases.

For this reason it is to be supposed that Katsafa, who was the person [the guard] closest to the leaders of the USSR NKVD /a relative of Leplevsky [I. M. Leplevsky, a prominent security official in Ukraine and Belarus in 1933–1935]/ could have received from them the task of persuading Nikolaev to confess to being a participant in the Zinovievite opposition, and [*sic*] they also gave him [Katsafa] the names of Kotolynov and Shatsky.

On December 5 Agranov had much more to report. He and his officers interrogated Nikolaev five times that day. The latter still refused to incriminate Kotolynov, Shatsky, or Bardin directly in the crime but he declared that he believed them capable of terrorism.[13]

· 45 ·

Agranov telegram to Stalin and Yagoda, December 5, 1934. RGANI, f. 6, op. 13, d. 71, ll. 23–26.

———————

I am reporting on the further course of the investigation in the case of L. Nikolaev.

1. According to the testimony of Nikolaev, Leonid, the Trotskyites Shatsky, Bardin, and Kotolynov were of a terrorist disposition.

Nikolaev deposed:

"Bardin, Nikolai is undoubtedly disposed to terrorism; he had the same sentiments as I did, I even think that Bardin had even stronger sentiments than I."

Further, in answer to the question whether Kotolynov was involved in the preparation of a terrorist act against Kirov, Nikolaev deposed:

"I did not recruit Kotolynov, because I wanted by my convictions to be the sole executor of the terrorist act against Kirov. In the second place, Kotolynov, I believed, would not agree to murdering Kirov, but would demand attacking [someone] higher, that is carrying out a terrorist act against Comrade Stalin, which I would not have agreed to."

Nikolaev also stated that by chance he became acquainted with an employee of the Leningrad mint, whom he wished to recruit to maintain surveillance of Comrade Kirov. Nikolaev did not give the family name of this woman, describing only her features.

Protocols of Nikolaev's interrogations will be sent to you today.

2. A Browning revolver was found in the search of the detainee Kotolynov, which he possessed without a license.

3. The suspect Pyotr Nikolaev declared that he considers himself a confirmed enemy of Soviet Power. He testified that he maintained connections with the German colonist Beldiug, who resides in the Leningrad suburb Grazhdanka, where there live German colonists.

4. Upon interrogation, Maksimov, the father of Pyotr Nikolaev's wife, deposed that both Pyotr and his brother Leonid Nikolaev have acquaintances among the German colonists in the Leningrad suburbs. Maksimov also testified to the kulak and anti-Soviet sentiments of Pyotr Nikolaev.

5. According to the deposition of Olga Draule, the sister of Leonid Nikolaev's wife, [Leonid Nikolaev] was acquainted with Kuznetsov, the former secretary of the Komsomol organization in the city of Luga—a Trotskyite, exiled to Siberia.

6. Seliverstov, an electrician at the Leningrad Philharmonic arrested on the evidence of Volkova, deposed that Odakhovsky, the foreman (*brigadier*) for elevator maintenance at the Philharmonic, who worked for the Polish concession "Jan Serkowski," asked him more than once in the past about attendance at the Philharmonic by members of the government, among them Kirov. After he heard about the murder of Kirov and the arrest of the murderer, Odakhovsky said, "Well, there's still courageous people around, it takes a lot of bravery to do something like that," and expressed regret at the arrest of the assassin.

According to NKVD data the concession "Jan Serkowski" was a front for the Second Department of the Polish General Staff, and was liquidated in 1930.

In Odakhovsky's work group (*brigada*) the former [Tsarist] staff captain Ivanov works as a mechanic. We have arrested him today.

Odakhovsky was hired at the Philharmonic on the recommendation of the mechanic Dukhnitsky, with whom he worked at the concession "Jan Serkowski." Dukhnitsky, as previously reported, has been arrested.

7. We have arrested Kornev, a consulting engineer at the administrative department (*khoziaistvennyi otdel*) of the Directorate of the Leningrad Region NKVD, mentioned in Volkova's testimony as the person who promised to help the former [Tsarist] Colonel Kamensky in his illegal border crossing.

8. Kamensky's female relatives Sofia and Kleopatra have been located by us. Kamensky has not yet been found. Korsunsky will be arrested today.

9. The commission of forensic experts /names of the commission mem-

bers are given in the report of December 4 of this year/ determined in its conclusion about Borisov's death that "the death of Borisov was accidental, resulting from an automobile crash." A copy of the accident report and conclusion will be sent to you today.

Interrogations in the Borisov case are proceeding at an accelerated pace. I will give you a supplementary report on the course of that investigation.

Deputy Chief of the USSR NKVD Agranov.

December 5, 1934

City of Leningrad.

Agranov was keeping a number of balls in the air. His men were questioning the guards, the dispatchers, and the driver in Borisov's death. They were making arrests based on Volkova's denunciations of counterrevolutionary plots at the Philharmonic and in the Leningrad NKVD's administrative department. They were also working to use Nikolaev's relatives against him. Leonid's volatile half-brother Pyotr, the deserter, was the most promising prospect in this direction. In letters seized by the NKVD Pyotr blamed "parasitical Soviet Power" for his troubles, and on December 3 he had already testified that Leonid had known of his desertion but had not turned him in. On that day Pyotr also told interrogators how he quit the Komsomol in 1930 because he hated the "voluntary" political activities—attending lectures, reading for study circles, and so on. His father-in-law, whom Pyotr had threatened with his stolen pistol, was happy to provide testimony about the Nikolaev brothers' "kulak" and "anti-Soviet" moods. There would be no problem presenting Pyotr as a counterrevolutionary.[14]

Leonid Nikolaev's own testimony, of course, was the center of attention. Agranov personally conducted most of his interrogations throughout December. On December 5 he and his deputy Dmitriev questioned the assassin at least three times. By encouraging him to monologue about the "moods" of his old Komsomol acquaintances, Agranov and Dmitriev seem to have nudged Nikolaev towards incriminating them directly in Kirov's murder. For example, they had him describe again his meeting with Shatsky in August. In Nikolaev's quite plausible account Shatsky expressed anger at Stalin's Seventeenth Party Congress speech calling for the firing of former oppositionists, connecting this with his own two recent firings. He told Nikolaev that he was under NKVD surveillance (literally *na uchete*, registered with them or on their watch list). Agranov and Dmitriev also prompted Nikolaev about the supposed terrorist moods of Kotolynov and Bardin until he said that "If I'd had trouble killing Kirov myself, I'd have recruited Bardin, Shatsky, and Kotolynov, and they'd have agreed to do it." Of Bardin specifically, Nikolaev noted that he had had a weapon in the past, the OGPU had arrested him twice, and he had supposedly invited Nikolaev to his apartment for a "serious talk" in 1932, presumably to recruit him for the opposition.[15]

On December 6 Agranov, Dmitriev, and L. G. Mironov, head of the NKVD's Economic Security Department, interrogated Nikolaev at least seven separate times. Eventually Nikolaev "confessed" that he had recruited Shatsky to watch Kirov's apartment for him, and strongly implied that Kotolynov had masterminded a conspiracy to murder Kirov. Moreover, he said that Kotolynov was planning to go to Moscow to assassinate Stalin. Nikolaev also implicated Vladimir Rumiantsev, the former Zinovievite who had returned to a prominent position on the Vyborg Ward executive committee, and Ignat Grigorevich Yuskin, a longtime acquaintance. Following up on Nikolaev's evidence, the NKVD arrested Yuskin and Rumiantsev on December 6.[16]

How were these and later confessions extracted from Nikolaev? Like police interrogators all over the world, NKVD officers alternated soft treatment with coercion, threats, promises, and bargaining. For much of his imprisonment, Nikolaev was treated as a privileged prisoner, albeit with no privacy. On December 24, 1960 Dr. Boris Danovich, employed by the NKVD in 1934, gave eyewitness testimony on Nikolaev's treatment in police custody. Danovich confirmed that when Nikolaev arrived at the NKVD clinic between 6:00 and 7:00 P.M. on December 1, he was "extremely disturbed." One to two days later, the NKVD assigned Danovich to be one of three doctors on call for Nikolaev. He had a room next to the prisoner's cell. From Danovich's account it appears that the investigators usually questioned Nikolaev late at night and into the next morning. Danovich was only called once to his cell. He noticed a pack of expensive cigarettes, with fruit and other hard-to-get food on a table next to Nikolaev's cot. The guards asked Danovich to give Nikolaev an enema, as he had not had a bowel movement for several days. They told him that a specially assigned cook prepared whatever meals Nikolaev requested. Danovich described Nikolaev as "gloomy," silent, and smoking constantly.[17]

According to his guards, interrogators promised Nikolaev his life in exchange for giving the testimony they desired. An Officer Gusev, who guarded Nikolaev during his trial on December 28–29, testified in

1956 that "For some reason Nikolaev was convinced . . . that he was going to get 3–4 years of exile in Siberia. . . ." In addition Nikolaev was almost certainly promised that his family would not be harmed if he cooperated in the investigation. He was very anxious that harm not come to Milda or the children. Kirilina quotes him as telling his interrogators, "my wife knew nothing," and asking for "mercy for her." According to a 1956 KGB report on the Kirov case, investigators lied to Nikolaev, claiming that Milda had not been arrested. They even organized for him a supposedly "illegal" secret correspondence with her. Probably they got Milda's cooperation in writing letters to Leonid by promising lighter sentences for her and perhaps her husband.[18]

Given Nikolaev's readiness before the assassination to believe that the government would not harm his family after he killed Kirov, and the hope he expressed in his writings that top-level government officials would somehow come to his rescue, it is easy to believe that the NKVD could fool him with such bogus guarantees. But they did not succeed in keeping him calm all the time. After incriminating his acquaintances and former workmates on December 6, Nikolaev seems to have had a fit of extreme remorse. On December 7 and 8 he twice attempted suicide, once by trying to jump out of a fourth-story window during an interrogation. Guards restrained him. He declared a hunger strike, and resisted leaving his cell. To get him to interrogations the guards had to put him in a straitjacket and carry him down the hall while he struggled and shouted, "It is I, Nikolaev, they're torturing me, remember me!"[19]

On December 7, Agranov sent the following telegram to Moscow.

· 46 ·

Agranov telegram to Stalin and Yagoda, December 7, 1934. APRF, f. 3, op. 24, d. 197, ll. 84–86.

I am reporting on the further course of the investigation in the case of L. Nikolaev.

(1) Today, the seventh of December 1934, Pyotr Nikolaev gave testimony that he participated in the murder of Comrade Kirov, but refused to answer questions about the circumstances of his participation, or any other questions connected with the murder of Comrade Kirov.

(2) When presented with eighteen photographs of various persons, in-

cluding one of the Latvian consul, Nikolaev immediately picked out the photograph of the Latvian consul [. . .]

(3) Rumiantsev, named in Nikolaev's deposition from December 6, has been arrested.

(4) Bardin, named in Nikolaev's testimony, is in exile in the South Kazakhstan Region. Orders have been issued for his arrest and dispatch to Leningrad.

(5) Sokolov, arrested on December 6, in his first interrogation testified that: (a) among the former oppositionists with whom he worked in Vyborg Ward, he knows [family names are listed before given names here] Khanik, Lev, Nikanorov, Vasily, Tolmazov, Andrei, Antonov, Nikolai, Vinogradov, Vasily, Rumiantsev, Vladimir, Zvezdov, Vasily, and Nikolaev, Leonid; (b) although these persons officially declared their withdrawal from the opposition, they still represent a particular [social] circle, which opposes itself to the party; (c) ideologically and organizationally Nikolaev was connected with this circle, and (d) the antiparty mood of this circle influenced Nikolaev, L., and to a great degree determined the development of his counterrevolutionary intentions.

In the same deposition Sokolov says that on the eve of the October holidays he met L. Nikolaev at Smolny and they had a lively conversation in which they felt each other out. This corresponds to Nikolaev's testimony about this meeting.

We are tracking down and questioning Khanik, Nikanoforov, Tolmazov, Antonov, Vinogradov, and Zvezdov without delay.

[. . .]

Agranov also announced the arrest of three members of the "counterrevolutionary group" denounced by Volkova beginning in August. One of them, Livanov, had confessed to "counterrevolution" and implicated a number of coworkers at Skorokhod factory, all of whom had been arrested. Finally, he notified Stalin of further developments in the investigation of Leningrad NKVD negligence in Nikolaev's detention and release on October 15.

In the Nikolaev case, Agranov had made progress with Pyotr Nikolaev's "confession" of his participation in the plot to murder Kirov. Agranov was pursuing two versions of the crime, which he probably hoped in the end to link up. There was the putative "counterrevolutionary group" consisting of former oppositionists from the Vyborg Ward Komsomol and other acquaintances of Nikolaev, and there was the matter of Nikolaev's possible connections with foreign consulates, in particular the Latvian one.

In the case of the "counterrevolutionary group" that would eventually become the so-called "Leningrad Center," Sokolov had so far proved the one really productive arrest (other than Leonid Nikolaev himself). Although he did not confess to involvement in a murder plot, he named a large number of former oppositionists who supposedly constituted a group still opposed to the party, and he placed Nikolaev inside the group. This was progress towards "proving" the kind of conspiracy that Agranov had to create for Stalin.

Shatsky and Kotolynov, on the other hand, did not give the interrogators what they were looking for. On December 6 Genrikh Liushkov asked Shatsky about his contacts with former oppositionists from the Vyborg Ward. In response Shatsky named six men, four of whom would end up indicted as members of the "Leningrad Center" (the four were Tolmazov, Zvezdov, Antonov, and Rumiantsev). Of the four, Shatsky had seen only one, Tolmazov, in 1934. He denied knowing Leonid Nikolaev. The next day, upon being shown a photo of Nikolaev, Shatsky admitted that he did know him.[20]

· 47 ·

Protocol of interrogation of Nikolai Shatsky by officers Liushkov and Dmitriev, December 7, 1934. TsA FSB RF, a.u.d. N-Sh44, t. 12, ll. 45–46.

Shatsky, Nikolai Nikolaevich, born 1899, Tula Province. Father [. . .] deceased, was railroad worker, mother [. . .] deceased. [. . .] Place of residence: Leningrad. Engineer [. . .] at the Electrotechnical Institute. Married, wife Elena Ignateva, age 35, daughter Lidiya, age 12, son Oleg, age 5. [. . .] Nonparty. Member of Komsomol 1917–1923, of party 1923–1927, excluded in 1927 for membership in the Trotskyite-Zinovievite Opposition, as demonstrated by distribution of Trotskyite literature. [. . .]

Testimony on the central facts of the case.

Question: Where did you first meet Nikolaev, the person you recognized in the photograph presented to you?

Answer: I know Nikolaev [. . .] from 1923. He was a secretary in the Vyborg Ward committee of the Komsomol—a technical secretary. At that time I was secretary of the Komsomol organization at the Red Vyborg factory and had dealings with Nikolaev on Komsomol business.

Question: Did you meet Nikolaev during 1934?

Answer: Yes, I did, once in about February or March 1934, and again in the summer, in July or August.

FIRST MEETING—I was in the building where the Institute for the History of the Komsomol Movement was located, the so-called Istmol [a branch of the Institute of Party History]. I visited the bureau of the Fellowship of Komsomol Militants, which was in the same building.

I met Nikolaev by chance, he had a job at Istmol. He asked me why I was visiting the Institute, where I was working, what I was doing. After my answers he showed me where the bureau was and we parted.

SECOND MEETING—this took place on the corner of Krasnykh Zor Street and Tolstoy Square, not far from Kirov's apartment.

Question: What did you talk about with Nikolaev during this second meeting?

Answer: I told him that it was tough to be outside the party, I complained that I was alienated from the party, that I had twice been fired from Soviet work as a former oppositionist, I said [. . .] that "Soviet Power no longer trusts me."

Question: During the time of your conversation with Nikolaev did you see an automobile in which the secretary of the regional party committee [. . .] Chudov was riding?

Answer: Yes, the auto passed the tram stop where we were talking. Nikolaev nodded in the direction of Chudov and asked, "Do you know him?" I looked over at Chudov. [At the trial of the Leningrad Center on December 28–29 Shatsky recounted the conversation as follows: Nikolaev: "You know, Chudov just went past." Shatsky: "Ruler of men's fates."]

Question: Exactly when were you fired from work as a former oppositionist?

Answer: In the spring of 1934 I was fired from work at the Ilich works, where I started as a mechanics' assistant. In June 1934 I was removed from work as a shop engineer at the Progress factory. [. . .]

Interrogated by: Deputy Chief of the Special Political Department of the USSR NKVD Liushkov, and aide to the Chief of the Economic Security Department [. . .] Dmitriev.

Shatsky had met Nikolaev twice during 1934, and Chudov's car had passed them once. That was all Shatsky had to say on December 7. Kotolynov's connection to Nikolaev was even more tenuous. In his first testimony, on December 6, Kotolynov admitted to maintaining social ties with several former Trotskyites, including the exiled Maria Natanson (wife of Nikolai Gordon, who had been prominent in Leningrad under Zinoviev), but denied these had any political content. Taxed with possessing notebooks and letters with anti-Stalin content, Kotolynov confessed "I am guilty of this," but stated that the notebooks dated from the 1926–1927 factional struggle, and the letters were written by his brother. He also admitted possessing a revolver without a license.[21]

On December 7 interrogators asked Kotolynov whether he knew Leonid Nikolaev.

· 48 ·

Protocol of interrogation of Ivan Kotolynov, December 7, 1934. TsA FSB RF, a.u.d. N-Sh44, t. 12, l. 40.

Question: Do you know Nikolaev, Leonid, a former Komsomol employee in the Vyborg Ward?

Answer: I remember that during the period of my Komsomol work in Leningrad in 1921–1924 I encountered a Nikolaev through work, but I don't remember his name and patronymic. Nikolaev is short, with big protruding lips, and brown hair. I had the impression that Nikolaev was a gloomy and rude person. In conversation he made poisonous comments and inappropriate jokes. I remember well that Nikolaev did not have a senior post, but I don't remember what his job was.

Question: Have you met with Nikolaev [recently], when and where?

Answer: I met him in passing in the summer of 1932 or 1933, I don't remember exactly, on the premises of the Army Medical Academy /Cafeteria no. 1 of the Vyborg Ward committee/.

I. Kotolynov.

Also on December 7 Genrikh Liushkov and a second officer questioned Ignaty Yuskin, who by Kirilina's account had known the Nikolaev family since childhood. Kirilina reports, evidently based on personal files from the Leningrad party archive, that Yuskin, who was six years older than Leonid Nikolaev, helped care for him during the period in his childhood when he was crippled. He carried him downstairs from the Nikolaevs' apartment to sit on a bench in the courtyard and watch the other children play.[22] Yuskin, however, told the NKVD that he and Nikolaev had first met face-to-face in 1930. The NKVD appears to have arrested Yuskin based on the December 4 testimony of Nikolaev's older sister Yekaterina, who told interrogators that Leonid had visited or called Yuskin several times in November. Yekaterina had definitely known Yuskin's wife Anna since childhood, although judging from their interrogations there was bad blood between them. Yuskin did not have any oppositionist record and the NKVD was unable to connect him to Kotolynov and the other former Zinovievites.

· 49 ·

Protocol of interrogation of Ignaty Yuskin by officers Liushkov and Fyodorov,
December 7, 1934. TsA FSB RF, a.u.d. N-Sh44, t. 12, ll. 41–42.

Yuskin, Ignaty Grigorevich—b. 1898, son of a peasant, village of Tr.
Pargolova, Leningrad Region, Russian, citizen of the Russian Soviet Socialist Federal Republic, resident of Leningrad, Lesnoi Prospect, Bldg. 13/
8, Apt. 52. Student of the Leningrad Industrial Academy /second year/
[. . .] wife Anna Yakovlevna, Leningrad, Lesnoi 13/8. Mother had two
dachas in Pargolova, now she has one. Member of the Communist Party
from 1925. Member of the party committee of the Russian Diesel factory
for five years, secretary of workshop cell, now a member of the party committee of the Industrial Academy and editor of the [wall] newspaper.

Question: Are you acquainted with Nikolaev, Leonid Vasilevich?

Answer: Yes I am. I have known Nikolaev through his sister Rogacheva,
Ye. V. since 1926. My wife and Nikolaev's sister are old acquaintances
from childhood.

From 1926 I lived in the same building with Nikolaev /Lesnoi Prospect,
Building 13, Entrance 8/. Until 1930 I knew of Nikolaev's existence only
through my wife, not having met him personally yet.

In 1930 I put in a telephone at my apartment, in connection with which
Nikolaev dropped in several times with a request to use the telephone.
From that time we began to greet each other upon meeting. From 1931–
1932 I lived in Moscow. When I returned to Leningrad Nikolaev had already left our building for a new apartment.

I have only met with Nikolaev about nine times in total.

Question: What do you know about the anti-Soviet moods of your acquaintance Rogacheva, Yekaterina Vasilevna?

Answer: I don't know anything about the anti-Soviet moods of Rogacheva, Yekaterina. [. . .] I do know about her immorality in everyday
life [in the officially puritan world of early Soviet Communism, this might
refer to sleeping around, drinking parties, etc.].

Question: When did you last meet with Nikolaev, L. V.?

Answer: This year I saw Nikolaev just three times. The first time I met
Nikolaev on the street at the beginning of this year. The second time the
meeting happened at my apartment on October twenty-something—he
came to use the telephone. The third and last time I saw Nikolaev was on
the twenty-sixth of October when he dropped in on me again at my apartment.

Question: Tell us the content of your conversations with Nikolaev at
your last two meetings.

Answer: At the first meeting Nikolaev told me that he had been assigned to work in the countryside, but wanted to take a rest cure before doing that and he was applying for place at a sanatorium. Nikolaev was at my place for five minutes and left.

At the second meeting Nikolaev told me that he had received approval for a pass to a sanatorium he would have to pay for. He said that if he was not able to get a free pass, then he intended to get one through the regional union [Council of Labor Unions?] with the help of Comrade Kodatsky, and if he did not succeed there, then he was planning to go to Moscow and apply for a pass there. My understanding was that in Moscow Nikolaev intended to petition the Central Committee of the Communist Party.

After telling me of his intention to go to Moscow, Nikolaev said that he had no money for the trip and asked me to lend him some for the trip. I said that after I received my stipend I could give him fifteen rubles and no more.

Question: The investigation possesses evidence that at his meeting with you Nikolaev expressed his anti-Soviet feelings.

Answer: Nikolaev, L. V. never expressed his anti-Soviet feelings when he met with me.

Question: The investigation also has evidence that in conversation with you Nikolaev mentioned to you the necessity of killing Comrade Kirov.

Answer: He did not say anything to me about the necessity of killing Comrade Kirov.

I have read this testimony and it is correctly transcribed from my words. I wish to make the following corrections.

1. I heard of Nikolaev's existence not from my wife, but from his sister Yekaterina Rogacheva.

2. I cannot say anything about Rogacheva's immoral behavior in everyday life, but there are several minor unethical things she has done to me. Yuskin.

Liushkov's evidence that Nikolaev had made anti-Soviet comments to Yuskin came from Nikolaev himself on December 6. Nikolaev claimed that he had told Yuskin that he couldn't get a meeting with Kirov, and added, "It's like he somehow knows that I'm trying to kill him." Yuskin supposedly answered, "Why Kirov? Why not Stalin?"[23]

At this point, without good evidence yet of an oppositionist conspiracy to murder Kirov, Agranov returned to Moscow to consult with Stalin. He took the overnight train on December 7–8. Komsomol leader Kosaryov, who played a major role in supervising the investigation, probably traveled with him. The following afternoon (December 8) Agranov and Kosaryov met with Stalin, Kaganovich, Molotov, Ordzhonikidze, Zhdanov, Voroshilov, Yagoda, and Yezhov from 3:25 to

6:20. Stalin relieved Agranov of the post of acting director of the Leningrad Region NKVD, so that he could concentrate on running the investigation of the Nikolaev case. In Agranov's place he would appoint Leonid M. Zakovsky, of whose harsh methods and wholesale roundups of Polish "spies" in Belarus he approved, and whom Yagoda had proposed to replace Medved earlier in the fall. That night Agranov returned to Leningrad, with Yezhov along as Stalin's personal emissary and overseer of the investigation. It appears that this was the point at which Yezhov, who had probably not been in Leningrad since the night of December 3–4, took over direct supervision of the inquiry there. It was also the point at which the investigation turned decisively towards incriminating the Zinovievites.[24]

Early on the morning of December 9, just hours after the meeting in Stalin's office, the NKVD arrested seven former members of the Leningrad party leadership under Zinoviev—Ivan Bakaev, Pyotr Zalutsky, Grigory Yevdokimov, Artyom Gertik, Grigory Fyodorov, Aleksei Perimov, and Sergei Gessen. The Fifteenth Party Congress had excluded all of these men from the party in late 1927 as oppositionists, and all were readmitted in 1928. All but one were arrested in Moscow (Gessen was detained in Smolensk). Stalin was closing in on Zinoviev himself, and his former ally Lev Kamenev.[25]

But Zinoviev and Kamenev were not the only targets. Even as they fabricated charges against the Leningrad Zinovievites, NKVD investigators were constructing a case that would link Stalin's great rival in exile, Trotsky, to foreign spies. They began with Nikolaev's supposed contact with the Latvian consul in Leningrad, Georgs Bissenieks.

The Latvian Consul

As we have seen, Nikolaev wrote down the addresses of the Latvian and German consulates in his date book, and his notes referred to a supposed offer of money for his writings, which he said he could have translated into three languages. NKVD interrogators immediately focused on these, seeking a link to foreign agents, just as they had in the Nakhaev case four months earlier. On the night of December 1–2 Leningrad NKVD officers questioned Nikolaev about the meaning of the addresses and the offer of money. Nikolaev's early explanations, that he had only fantasized about selling his papers, and that he had put the addresses in his date book to attract attention, are certainly possible given his histrionic imagination and his evident desire for fame. But they must have rung false to interrogators, and they do seem strange, especially given that Nikolaev lied about the extent of his writings on the morning of December 2. Officers of the central NKVD did not forget the addresses in Nikolaev's date book. On December 5 they got him to confess to visiting the Latvian consulate in Leningrad.

· 50 ·

Protocol of interrogation of Leonid Nikolaev by Agranov and Dmitriev, December 5, 1934. RGANI, f. 6, op. 13, d. 14, ll. 19–20.

Question: In your date book the telephone number of the Latvian consulate is written down. Explain how this came to be there.

Answer: I decided to link up with the Latvian consulate with the goal of carrying on counterrevolutionary work. This was several days before the execution of a gas attack drill in the city. I found the telephone number and address of the consulate at the information bureau. I headed directly to the consulate, located on Herzen Street. The consul received me in his office, which is on the third floor of the building. The consul, I could see, lived right there himself. I concluded this because some rooms of the consulate had the obvious appearance of residential quarters.

At the time of my conversation with the consul his secretary, who spoke good Russian, was present.

Question: What kind of conversation did you have with the consul?

Answer: Out of caution I did not want to tell the consul the real goal of my visit right away. I began by saying that I had relatives in Riga, from whom I was to receive an inheritance. The consul wanted to know what kind of inheritance this was—fixed assets or money. I answered that it was money. I told the consul that I was corresponding with my relatives in Riga, that my mother lived in Siberia; I gave him the impression that I was Latvian, I spoke in broken Russian; and by the way, just in case I brought with me the Latvian passport of Grandfather [the prerevolutionary passport of Milda's father, which showed that he had originally resided in Latvia, then part of the Russian Empire]. I was counting on getting some monetary help from the consul at our first meeting.

At this point I broke off the conversation with the consul, because the secretary, whom I feared, was present in the office. I decided to go to the consulate another time to continue the conversation.

Question: What specifically did you want to talk about with the consul at your next meeting?

Answer: I wanted to present myself as a Red Professor [i.e. a member of the Institute of Red Professors], to say that I had valuable [journalistic] material to be sent abroad, and to request money from the consul.

Question: Did the second meeting with the consul take place?

Answer: No it did not. This is what happened. One day soon after I called the consul on the telephone and asked him to receive me; he answered, "I can't right now, come tomorrow," and he gave me the visiting hours. When I arrived at the building where the consulate was, there was a car parked in front with license plates that had a red line through the registration number, 10168. This meant, I believed, that the auto belonged to the military. The suspicion occurred to me that my arrest was planned; I went upstairs to the consul's quarters, but decided not to go in. I did not go to the consulate again, I decided to hook up with the German consulate.

Question: What kind of materials specifically did you want to give to the consul?

Answer: I wanted to give the consul materials and an article of a critical, anti-Soviet character on the situation inside the country.

Question: Describe for us the consul's distinguishing features.

Answer: The consul is tall, completely gray-haired, with his hair combed back.

Transcribed from my words correctly and read through by me. L. Nikolaev.

Interrogated by:
Agranov, Dmitriev.

The idea that Nikolaev visited the Latvian consul in roughly the manner described here is not far-fetched. Based on secret Latvian diplomatic correspondence examined by the Soviets after their takeover of the Baltic nation, it appears that many Soviet subjects of Latvian origin visited the Latvian embassy in Moscow as well as the Leningrad consulate to complain about life in the USSR, seek visas to Latvia, contact relatives, and even collect inheritances, as Nikolaev claimed he wished to do.[26] Foreign consuls believed, correctly, that some of their visitors were Soviet police provocateurs. After attending a dinner party on February 11, 1934, Reader Bullard, the British consul in Leningrad, wrote in his diary about comments the English wife of the Latvian consul had made to him. "She is very nervous because the OGPU are paying the Latvian Consulate too much attention. Bissineks [*sic*] says that two Russians had come (not together) asking whether they might escape into Latvia. He said that if the applicant could run faster than a bullet he might succeed. Why? Because both the Soviet *and* the Latvian frontier guards would fire at him."[27]

Nor was Nikolaev's presumptive plan to sell his writings to the consul quite as absurd as it might seem. During periods in the 1920s and probably the early 1930s the Latvian embassy in Moscow was an important information channel between underground members of the Menshevik party in the USSR and the Menshevik delegation in exile. The Latvian Social Democratic Party, one of the two largest political parties in the republic, was Menshevik-oriented, and often held ministerial posts in the government. The Latvian embassy in Moscow distributed hundreds of copies of the Menshevik organ-in-exile, the *Socialist Herald,* to Soviet subjects, and presumably some of the reports from inside the USSR published in that journal came out via the same route. It is reasonable to assume that the Leningrad consulate served similar functions, especially given that Bissenieks, who was appointed to his post in 1933, was a Social Democrat with a record of underground activism in the years before 1917. Moreover, in the early 1930s the *Socialist Herald* carried occasional reports from Leningrad.[28]

Nikolaev was desperate for money in the fall of 1934—we know that he asked his acquaintance Yuskin, his brother-in-law Roman Kulisher, his sister Yekaterina, and his mother for loans. He also imagined himself as a literary figure, and he could easily have told himself a dramatic story about how he would be paid for his secret reports from the USSR in the émigré press. His decision to present himself as a Red Professor on his second visit (which according to this interrogation never happened) is consistent with his psychology and history as well. It was to the Institute of Red Professors that Nikolaev had applied but failed the entrance exam. But as he projected his next visit to the Latvian consul, he could fancy that he was a Red Professor himself, and a revolutionary intriguer to boot. He does not seem to have considered that a Red Professor would hardly have spoken "broken Russian," nor that if he were truly Latvian, the Latvian consul might have expected him to speak in Latvian, not "broken Russian."

Certain elements of Nikolaev's December 5 interrogation seem to confirm that he really visited the consul. According to Latvian ambassador to Moscow Bilmanis, Nikolaev accurately described the location and interior of the Latvian consulate. His description of Bissenieks was accurate too as far as it went. On December 6, as Agranov notified Stalin, Nikolaev picked out Bissenieks' photograph from among eighteen presented to him. The NKVD could easily have arranged for Nikolaev to pick the "right" photo, but there is at least confirmation that there was a real gallery prepared, in 1960–1961 testimony from the officer who put it together.[29]

There is some evidence beyond Nikolaev's own testimony that he visited the consul, although none of it is conclusive. On December 13, Milda Draule testified that she remembered him looking for her dead father's old imperial passport (which would suffice to identify the holder as Latvian), although she did not know that he had actually visited the Latvian consulate. She also recalled Nikolaev saying in October, "it would be good to go abroad."[30] It is quite possible that this was simply testimony demanded by the NKVD to incriminate Nikolaev. However, Genrikh Liushkov, who was Draule's main interrogator, believed her testimony. He concluded that Nikolaev did visit the Latvian consulate once, seeking a visa with an eye to fleeing abroad with his family (see Conclusion, Document 127). If the visit took place in early November, Nikolaev would still have been seriously considering escape from the murder scene rather than suicide.

On December 6 interrogators pushed Nikolaev to expand his testimony about links with foreign consuls.

· 51 ·

Excerpts from protocols of Nikolaev's December 6, 1934 interrogations.
RGANI, f. 6, op. 13, d. 14, ll. 21–22.

———————

/From the protocol of Nikolaev's third interrogation on December 6./
Question: When did you turn to the German consulate?
Answer: This was several days after my visit to the Latvian consulate. In the telephone book I found the telephone number of the German consulate and called there. I managed to speak to the consul himself only after a number of calls.
Question: What kind of conversation did you have with the consul?
Answer: I recommended myself to the consul as a Ukrainian writer, giving a made-up name, I asked the consul to hook me up with foreign journalists, I said that as a result of my travels through the Soviet Union I had various journalistic materials, I mentioned that I wanted to sell this material to foreign journalists to use in the foreign press.

To all this the consul answered with a suggestion that I contact the German mission in Moscow. This attempt to contact the German consul thus ended unsuccessfully.
/From the protocol of Nikolaev's fourth interrogation on December 6./
Question: When did you turn to the English consulate to establish ties?
Answer: Along with my attempt to establish ties with the German con-

sulate, I also tried to contact the English consul. I began to observe the arrival and departure of the consul from the consulate building. I also considered turning to one of the employees of the consulate outside the building with a request to connect me with the consul. But nothing came of this plan because I was unable to meet with any employee of the consulate.

By the way, at one point I studied the English language with a dictionary with the aim of facilitating making contact with the English consul.

Nikolaev's testimony above is plausible, but cannot be confirmed from any documents available to me. He did need money, and judging from his diaries considered selling what he felt were his valuable literary materials. The Russian historian Yuri Zhukov claims to have seen transcripts of testimony that Nikolev visited the German consulate several times in the summer and fall of 1934 and immediately afterwards headed to the Torgsin hard currency store and made purchases in marks. It is very hard to see, however, why the German consul would have given Nikolaev money. In all likelihood this is testimony extracted from Nikolaev after December 19 or so, at which point he was signing the most fantastic depositions. Or it may be a report by some other malleable witness made on NKVD orders and intended to prove Nikolaev's (and hence the oppositionists') connections to foreigners.[31]

In any event, the foreign connection that the NKVD chose to pursue was the Latvian. Nikolaev did have a real connection with Latvia, through his wife. But this was just one factor in the choice to focus on that country. As observers from Trotsky to Latvian diplomats noted, if the Soviet authorities wished to construct a story linking the Kirov murder with foreign espionage, it would have been dangerous to accuse Germany or any other major power of inciting it. This could have led to serious international complications. It was safer to implicate a small country like Latvia.

There were also more specific reasons why the Soviets might have been interested in pressuring Latvia. From April 1934 through May 1935 the Soviet government conducted difficult negotiations with the French government regarding a mutual defense pact, aimed at containing Nazi Germany. This was a period of rapid and confusing reorientation in Soviet foreign policy, as the leadership sought an effective response to the Nazis and to the Japanese advances in China. Ultimately Stalin chose, with stops and starts and efforts to keep other channels open, to tone down Bolshevik rhetoric about world revolution and to conciliate France and moderate social democratic political parties in the West. The Soviet entry into the League of Nations in 1934 was one key indicator of this change.[32]

The Baltics were a key strategic zone for the Soviets. In 1917–1919 German troops and later White armies supported by British naval forces had approached Petrograd through the Baltic region and nearly captured the former imperial capital. Soviet diplomats hoped they could convince the French to promise to help defend the Baltics, presumably against German aggression. And Latvia was arguably the most important Baltic state for the Soviets. From 1926 until 1934 it was the only one of the Baltic republics to maintain relatively cordial relations with the USSR, including a mutually beneficial trade pact. The powerful Latvian Social Democratic Party was not unfriendly towards the Soviets. However, in May 1934 Karls Ulmanis, the leader of the conservative Agrarian Union, took power in a coup and ended representative democracy. Ulmanis's foreign policy was resolutely neutralist, but the right-wing coup sparked Soviet fears that Latvia might seek an accommodation with Hitler.[33]

Soviet authorities may have sought inside information on Latvian policies, and/or pressure points to use to persuade Latvia to join a mutual defense pact with the USSR and France. They may have sought to intimidate the Latvian government into keeping away from Nazi Germany. They could also have been concerned to shut down or send disinformation along the Mensheviks' communication channels in and out of the USSR. In general the Soviets viewed all of the Leningrad consulates as a particularly troublesome nest of foreign espionage activity. In 1934–1935 NKVD agents had an informant inside the Latvian consulate (the cleaning lady). They tailed the consul whenever he went out, and they frequently sent provocateurs to visit him and offer to spy for Latvia.[34]

Bissenieks, then, was a desirable target for NKVD recruitment. His political profile also suggested that he might be willing to aid the Soviets. As a Social Democrat he was isolated from and unsympathetic to the new Ulmanis government in Latvia. In fact, the Leningrad NKVD Special Department, with the approval of the central NKVD authorities, apparently had a plan to recruit him prepared *before* Kirov's murder. They were going to use Jan Lentsmanis, an old contact of Bissenieks from the pre-1917 Social Democratic movement in Latvia. Lentsmanis worked in the Comintern (Communist International) apparatus and had done intelligence work in Leningrad before, inciting Latvian sailors visiting the city to strike.[35]

On December 5, as Leningrad boiled with rumors in the wake of Kirov's murder, NKVD authorities executed their plan to contact Bissenieks. It is not clear whether they still aimed to recruit the consul or whether they wanted to scare him out of Leningrad and make him appear guilty of connection with the assassination. That day Lentsmanis called Bissenieks from the Astoria, the most exclusive hotel in the city, used his old party alias, and invited him for a get-together. Bissenieks agreed. That night the two men drank and talked so late that Bissenieks ultimately slept over at the hotel. Lentsmanis had along an NKVD minder, an Officer Fortunatov of the Leningrad Special Department, who did not know the purpose of the meeting, and whose job was to make sure that Lentsmanis actually met Bissenieks. He was also to monitor the conversation, although he did not know Latvian (more evidence that the NKVD was hardly a well-oiled machine).

According to a December 8 NKVD report, Bissenieks and Lentsmanis discussed the Kirov murder, with Bissenieks expressing perplexity about who might have organized it. The Latvian Social Democrats and Mensheviks, he said, did not believe that terrorist methods would be effective in changing the situation inside the USSR. Thus, they would not have organized the assassination. According to Bissenieks' account to Latvian authorities almost four weeks later, when the NKVD minder left for a minute to use the bathroom, Lentsmanis urged him to leave the USSR. It is impossible to know for sure whether this was part of the NKVD script, or whether Lentsmanis was trying to protect his old revolutionary comrade from arrest. At the conclusion of the evening, Bissenieks and Lentsmanis agreed to meet again, but soon afterwards Sosnovsky, the central NKVD officer serving as acting head of the Leningrad NKVD Special Department, ordered no further contacts with Bissenieks. Efforts to connect him to Kirov's assassination, however, continued.[36]

The "Leningrad Center"

Nikolai Yezhov returned to Leningrad with Agranov on the morning of December 9 to supervise the Kirov inquiry. His notebooks show that on December 9–10 he questioned witnesses about Leningrad NKVD negligence in guarding Kirov and about the accident that Borisov died in. However, he also worked with Agranov on interrogations in the Nikolaev case, assigning interrogators to particular witnesses and analyzing testimony.[37]

Stalin had by December 9 chosen a framework for the conspiracy case he was building against ex-oppositionists in Leningrad and Moscow. The ultimate targets were Zinoviev and Kamenev. According to separate reports by Olga Shatunovskaya and Party Control Committee officials, there exists a note in Stalin's archive listing members of two supposed conspiratorial groups—a "Leningrad Center" and a "Moscow Center." Control Committee officials stated in 1989 that the note is in Yagoda's handwriting, with corrections by Stalin. (Olga Shatunovskaya claimed in 1988 that the handwriting was Stalin's, and others have apparently identified it as Yezhov's.). If the Control Committee officials are correct, Stalin moved Zinoviev and Kamenev from the "Leningrad Center," where Yagoda had placed them, to the "Moscow Center." Shatunovskaya, whose testimony is sometimes unreliable, claimed in the late 1980s that there was a date on the note, December 6.[38] It is significant that the first mention of prominent former Zinovievite Vladimir Rumiantsev in interrogations was also on December 6. Whatever the date of the note, by about December 10 Yezhov was outlining connections between the two "centers" in his notebook.[39] It seems likely that the "Leningrad Center—Moscow Center" framework, with Zinoviev and Kamenev at the head of the whole organization, was decided upon at the December 8 meeting in Stalin's office attended by Yagoda, Agranov, and Yezhov, if not a day or two before.

On December 9 Vladimir Rumiantsev, arrested on December 6, provided interrogators with the first "evidence" of what might be interpreted as conspiratorial activity by Zinoviev and Kamenev. Rumiantsev, who appears in case documents first in Nikolaev's, Sokolov's, and Shatsky's depositions of December 6, had been an important figure in the Vyborg Komsomol Zinovievite opposition. He had been debriefed by OGPU officers at least once (1932) and probably multiple times. Ultimately he had been allowed to take a leading position on the Vyborg Ward executive committee, in all likelihood with the nod from Kirov himself. The Leningrad NKVD had also issued and then withdrawn two orders for his arrest.

· 52 ·

Protocol of interrogation of Vladimir Vasilevich Rumiantsev by officers Liushkov and Petrovsky, December 9, 1934. TsA FSB RF, a.u.d. N-Sh44, t. 12, ll. 77–78.

Question: Who did you meet among the former participants in the counterrevolutionary Trotsky-Zinovievite Opposition during your stay at the resort in Kislovodsk [a vacation town with mineral springs in the North Caucasus] in 1934?

Answer: In late September or early October, while I was vacationing in Kislovodsk, I met the former Zinovievite Rotskan by chance in Piatachka, and then soon after Mushtakov, Andrei Andreevich [Mushtakov had been a member of the Leningrad Province party committee under Zinoviev and a Leningrad delegate to the Fourteenth Party Congress in December 1925] arrived from Leningrad at the Leningrad soviet's sanatorium with his wife. I did not know that Mushtakov was coming.

Question: What kind of conversations did you have during your meetings at Kislovodsk with Mushtakov and Rotskan?

Answer: I met very frequently with Mushtakov as we were living in the same sanatorium, Mushtakov frequently drank too much and as a result got involved in particular misunderstandings. Mushtakov and I had conversations about things we read in the newspapers. Our conversations had a proper party character and I did not notice any unhealthy attitudes with regard to the party on Mushtakov's part. During my meeting with Rotskan the latter told me that Zinoviev and Kamenev were in Kislovodsk at the Turgenev dacha and suggested that I drop in on them, Rotskan took my address and promised to visit me, and he gave me his sanatorium address as well, I think that it was the "Tenth Anniversary of October" sanatorium.

Question: Did your meeting with Zinoviev and Kamenev take place?

Answer: The meeting did not take place, as I did not go to see them at the dacha.

Question: In your opinion, what might have motivated Rotskan's invitation to you to go to the dacha to see Zinoviev and Kamenev? Do you consider this proposal a coincidence?

Answer: I imagine that this invitation was not a coincidence and possibly was motivated by the desire of Zinoviev and Kamenev to feel out the mood of the Leningraders.

Question: Did you meet with Rotskan after that conversation?

Answer: No, I did not meet him again in Kislovodsk or in Leningrad.

This protocol is transcribed from my words correctly and has been read through by me.

V. Rumiantsev.

On the evening of December 9, Agranov reported to Stalin on Rumiantsev's testimony and a number of other arrests and interrogations. Six former oppositionists named by Sokolov had been arrested, four of whom—Antonov, Zvezdov, Tolmazov, and Khanik—would stand trial twenty days later with Nikolaev and the rest of the "Leningrad Center." Pyotr Nikolaev testified that on November 25 Leonid suggested that they both go underground, using a diploma from the Leningrad Economics Institute in the name of Koshvilo as fake identification for Pyotr. According to Pyotr, Leonid said that they would head to Moscow. Milda Draule "confessed that she shared the anti-Soviet views of her husband . . . " The cases based on Volkova's denunciations continued to progress, with a new arrest, as well as testimony from Nikolai Binkerov, a member of the supposed counterrevolutionary group at the Leningrad Philharmonic, that he was acquainted with several employees of the German consulate.[40]

With the arrests of Antonov, Tolmazov, and Zvezdov, Agranov's men began to accumulate substantial evidence about continuing social ties between former Zinoviev supporters. These were treated as threads in an extended web of political conspiracy. Stalin and the central NKVD officers were extraordinarily suspicious of *dvurushnichestvo* ("two-facedness") among the former Zinovievites. In particular they were concerned about a directive Zinoviev supposedly issued his followers in 1928 to recant their views and rejoin the party. Stalin and Agranov chose to view this directive as a sign that Zinoviev sought to undermine the party from within.

The December 10 deposition of Nikolai Antonov demonstrates these concerns of the interrogators. Antonov, born in 1903 to a working-class family in Leningrad, had joined the Communist Youth League in 1917, and the party in 1922. Because of his very poor eyesight, he did not serve in the Red Army during the Civil War. He was acquainted with Leonid Nikolaev from the Vyborg Ward committee of the Komsomol before 1926, and possibly also from his work at the Red Arsenal factory. Because of his support for Zinoviev during the 1925–1926 struggle for the Leningrad party organization, Central Committee authorities dispatched him to a post in the Vologda Region with a "strict warning." In early 1928 he was allowed back to the second capital after a petition recanting his oppositionist views. After he had done a stint as a worker at the Russian Diesel factory, the party sent Antonov to the Leningrad Industrial Institute to study.[41]

· 53 ·

Protocol of interrogation of Nikolai Semyonovich Antonov by Chief of the First Section of the NKVD Special Political Department B. Petrovsky, December 10, 1934. TsA FSB RF, a.u.d. N-Sh44, t. 12, l. 87.

Question: Are you aware of the existence [. . .] of a directive letter of Zinoviev, instructing the Zinovievites about the desirability of returning to the party, and if so, from whom [did you hear about it]?

Answer: After the Fifteenth Party Congress I arrived in Leningrad from Vologda in 1928, and dropped in at the apartment of Volodya Rumiantsev. Muravyov, Mikhail, who had also belonged to the Zinovievite opposition, was with me. At that time Rumiantsev had not yet left the opposition. Rumiantsev was [. . .] dissatisfied with the position taken by Zinoviev, who advocated return to the party under particular conditions. At that time Rumiantsev showed me a letter from Zinoviev, written in red pencil on a small piece of white paper, in which Zinoviev instructed Rumiantsev to return to the party.

Transcribed correctly from my words,
N. Antonov.

In an effort to link the Leningrad *komsomoltsy* with Zinoviev in a counterrevolutionary conspiracy, the inquiry was zeroing in on the moment in 1928 when many Zinoviev supporters recanted their views and applied for readmission to the party. Among the Leningrad oppositionists there were fierce debates, monitored by the GPU through informers, about whether or not to submit and apply for readmission to the party. Opponents of reconciliation became known as "nonreturners." Among the prominent "nonreturners" were Rumiantsev and Kotolynov, although both later rejoined the party. Grigory Zinoviev himself petitioned for readmission in the spring of 1928 and encouraged Rumiantsev and others to do so as well.[42]

In 1928 Zinoviev's actions could be seen as supportive of the party and the Central Committee—unlike Trotsky who remained defiant, he persuaded his fellow oppositionists to "disarm." Now, in December 1934, police and prosecutors would portray the oppositionists' return to the party in 1928 as "two-facedness," part of a plot to undermine Communism from within.

Three more former oppositionists from the "Politikan" files were arrested by the NKVD on December 10. These were Vladimir Levin, Lev Sositsky, and Nikolai Miasnikov. All three had fought in the Civil

War, and Levin and Sositsky had served in the Red Army until 1926. None of these men had ever met Nikolaev. Their guilt rather consisted in their support during the 1920s for Trotsky and for the Zinovievite Red Army commander, Lashevich. Each had been excluded from the party in 1927 and later reinstated. Kirilina notes that when Levin could not find a job in 1927 due to his oppositional activity, Kirov assigned him to party work in Luga (this was after Nikolaev left that town). At the time of their arrest Levin, Sositsky, and Miasnikov held supervisory positions in the Leningrad government (respectively, head of the city residential housing cooperative, director of the Leningrad soviet's auto repair workshops, and deputy chief of a department in the Leningrad soviet administration).[43]

In the course of the investigation and trial of the "Leningrad Center," Miasnikov, Levin, and Sositsky confessed to membership in a secret counterrevolutionary organization of Zinovievites, but not to foreknowledge of or participation in Kirov's murder.[44]

It appears to have been Vasily Zvezdov who provided Agranov with breakthrough "evidence" about the existence of a well-organized "Leningrad Center" conspiring against the party leadership. Like Antonov and Kotolynov, Zvezdov was a student at the Leningrad Industrial Institute when he was arrested. Like Antonov, he had been sent out of the Leningrad Region (to Pskov) in 1926 after participating in the Zinovievite opposition. Zvezdov knew Nikolaev from the Vyborg Komsomol days and from their period as roommates in Luga (see Chapter Five above, pp. 187–188). Like Shatsky, he admitted meeting Nikolaev in the spring of 1934 and discussing how to join the Fellowship of Komsomol Militants, but at first he resisted identifying him as a Zinovievite. On December 10 Zvezdov confessed to meeting former oppositionists Antonov, Nodel, Kotolynov, and others in 1933–1934. When questioned as to why he had met these men, he answered, "personal friendship based in part on shared political views." He denied knowledge of any "underground antiparty group of former Zinovievites."[45]

Two days later Zvezdov was more cooperative. Although he did not discuss Nikolaev he did "confirm" the existence of an underground Zinovievite organization dedicated to fighting the party leadership.

· 54 ·

Protocol of interrogation of Vasily Zvezdov by Deputy Chief of the Special
Political Department Stromin, December 11, 1934. TsA FSB RF,
a.u.d. N-Sh44, t. 12, l. 98.

Question: What do you know about the existing counterrevolutionary
organization of former Zinovievites?

Answer: I am aware that in the course of 1933–1934 the former leaders
of the Zinovievite opposition, Bakaev, Kharitonov, Gertik, and Zinoviev
himself, renewed their efforts to revive their organization.

The former leaders of the Zinovievite opposition who were in Moscow
and were [also] tightly connected with Leningrad hoped to drag our old
Komsomol group of former Zinovievites into a battle with the party and
the party leadership. Antonov, Nikolai, with whom I study at the Institute,
told me about this.

Question: Where did Antonov hear about this, when he told you about
it?

Answer: Antonov heard about this from Kotolynov. Our conversation
took place at the Industrial Institute in October 1934.

Question: What else did Antonov say about Kotolynov?

Answer: He passed along to me Kotolynov's instruction that it would
not be a good idea for us to become close to Nodel, Mikhail, who according to Kotolynov's information was connected with the OGPU organs.

Question: What did Antonov say to you about political instructions received from Moscow?

Answer: He said that now the old ties were being activated and a new
attack on the party leadership was being prepared.

This protocol written down from my words correctly.

Zvezdov.

The next day Stromin had Zvezdov listing the members of a "Moscow Center" and a "Leningrad Center" consisting of five separate
conspiratorial "groups." As we have seen, Stalin, Yagoda, and/or Yezhov were the real creators of both "centers." Zvezdov was following
their script.

310 *Fingering the Zinovievites*

· 55 ·

Protocol of interrogation of Vasily Zvezdov, December 12, 1934. TsA FSB RF, a.u.d. N-Sh44, t. 12, ll. 112–116.

Question: In your depositions of December 11 [. . .] you assert the existence in Moscow of a counterrevolutionary organization, founded on the base of the old Trotsky-Zinoviev bloc. Specify the organizational structure of this organization, its ties with other cities, including Leningrad, and what you know about its practical activities.

Answer: In elaboration of my earlier testimony with regard to the existence and activities of the Moscow Center of our organization I declare the following:

The Moscow Center was [. . .] formed in the course of 1933. The former leaders of the Trotsky-Zinoviev bloc—Zinoviev, Yevdokimov, Bakaev, Gertik, Sharov, Kharitonov, and Gorshenin—joined it.

With regard to the question of the ties of the Moscow Center with other cities, I know only of the existence of ties with our Leningrad organization, which acted exclusively according to directives received from Moscow. [. . .]

Question: What was the structure of your Leningrad organization?

Answer: At the head of the organization stands the so-called "Local Center /Leningrad/." This center, in its turn is connected with the representatives of individual wards of the city of Leningrad, that is: Petrograd, Volodarsky, Vasileostrovsky, and others, and also with the leaders of groups that are [. . .] the smaller associations of members of our organization. This particular form of organizational structure was chosen due to considerations of facilitating connections between members of the organization and, most importantly, the necessity of observing secrecy (*konspiratsiia*).

Question: Lay out for us the membership of the Center and the other branches of the Leningrad organization.

Answer: The membership is as follows:

1. The Leningrad Center.
   a. Rumiantsev, Vladimir—leader of the organization.
   b. Kotolynov, Ivan.
   c. Tsarkov, Nikolai.
   d. Severov, Pyotr.
   e. Tseitlin, Yakov.
   f. Surov, Pavel.
   g. Tolmazov, Andrei.
   h. Nikolaev, Leonid [emphasis added].
2. The Group Attached to the Leningrad Fellowship of Komsomol Militants.

a. Popov, Yegor/"Gosha"—leader of the group.
b. Khanik, Lev.
c. Zhestianikov.
d. Vasileva, Raisa.
e. Burmistrov, Pavel.
f. Driazgov, Grigory.
g. Seredokhin, Aleksandr.
3. The Group at the Industrial Institute.
   a. Kotolynov, Ivan—leader of the group.
   b. Nadel [*sic*], Mikhail.
   c. Antonov, Nikolai.
   d. Zvezdov.
   e. Loginov, Pyotr.
   f. Panfilov.
4. The Group at the Student Section of the [Council of] Labor Unions.
   a. Sokolov, Georgy—leader of the group.
   b. Panfilov.
   c. Apanasevich [Afanasevich?], Konstantin.
5. The Group at the Vyborg Apartments.
   a. Antonov, Nikolai.
   b. Faddeev [Fadeev?], Fyodor.
   c. Vinogradov, Vasily.
   d. Khanik, Lev.
   e. Tsarkov, Nikolai—leader of the group.

[. . .]

Question: In your evidence from December 11 you speak of the special tactics used by your organization in order to protect your people inside the party and the Komsomol, that is the cadres of the former participants of the Trotsky-Zinoviev bloc. Tell us specifically what these special tactics are.

Answer: The essence of the instructions which exist about this matter is under no circumstances to tell anyone [at the control commissions of party organizations] about participants in the opposition who for one reason or another have not yet been uncovered. In the event that someone is summoned to a party organization control commission or other organization to testify about opposition figures, it was proposed not to give honest evidence, but [. . .] not to name new names or connections. In the last resort, it was recommended to speak only of those persons who had already received party censures.

Question: From whom exactly did these instructions that you speak of come?

Answer: They came from the Moscow Center of the organization. I found out about this from one of the members of the Leningrad Center—Tsarkov, who passed them on to me [. . .] as directives.

Question: What principles guided your organization in the recruitment of like-minded people?

Answer: With regard to this, there existed rules that were very precise. We had orders from the Center that it was necessary first to restore and activate to the maximum old ties with the former Trotsky-Zinoviev bloc and check up on each carefully to see who was capable of being useful for the organization's activities. In addition we made a direct connection with the Trotskyites, whom we also recruited into the organization /Bardin, Nikolai and Korshunov, Nikolai [probably actually Efim]/. In general our organization, in pursuit of the goal of changing the party's course and the present party leadership, considered it possible and imperative to unite and take charge of all active forces hostile to the party, not just from among the members of former antiparty groups, but [from among] nonparty [persons]. /For example Bogoslovsky, a student of the Industrial Institute, son of a professor, nonparty./

Question: What do you know about the preparation of the terroristic act against Comrade Kirov, why was this act undertaken by a member of your organization—Nikolaev, Leonid, on whose orders was he acting?

Answer: I did not know of the fact of the preparation for this terrorist act, nor do I know if in this case Nikolaev acted at the behest of our entire organization, or if he acted on his own initiative.

However, I should state directly that Nikolaev's act is a logical consequence of all of our political views and principles. All of us were resolute opponents of the policies and measures carried out by the present leaders of the Communist Party, considering them to be at root responsible for the difficulties that the working class and the peasants are experiencing right now.

All of our hopes for possible change in personnel at the very summit of the Politburo have been dashed; we were in reality supporters of removing from the leadership Comrade Stalin and Comrades Molotov, Kaganovich, and Kirov, whom we believed to be [. . .] the main culprits in the defeat of Zinoviev's policy.

In this light, obviously, Nikolaev's act appears completely natural, opening as it did the way to the achievement of the goals we set ourselves.

This protocol is transcribed correctly from my words, and has been read through by me. Zvezdov.

Interrogator: Stromin.

Zvezdov gave the interrogators almost everything that they needed. He placed Nikolaev inside a tightly organized "counterrevolutionary group" that aimed to replace Stalin. The group was made up of former Trotskyites and Zinovievites. It had strict rules of secrecy, so that the following Alice in Wonderland reasoning could be applied—the lack of evidence of a conspiratorial organization could serve to demonstrate just how top secret, insidious, and widespread the organization really was. Zvezdov and the interrogators also cooked up an early example (perhaps the first) of the sort of partial confession that prominent former party leaders such as Zinoviev, Kamenev, Bukharin, and Rykov would soon be repeating at public show trials: I did not participate in a conspiracy to assassinate Kirov (or Stalin or some other leader), but I helped to foster the anti-leadership attitudes that inspired the assassin. Therefore I bear moral responsibility for the crime.

Why did Zvezdov and other purported members of the "Leningrad Center" confess? Some of the same techniques applied to Nikolaev probably worked on them, including promises of clemency for themselves and their families. Then there was physical abuse. Beatings and other direct physical torture were not officially permitted by the NKVD leadership at this time, but they undoubtedly occurred. Interrogators certainly used other forms of torture such as sleep deprivation, continuous interrogations, exposure to extreme temperatures, and forcing prisoners to stand for hours on end. But it is not just the problem of confession that needs to be solved, but the logic of the widespread *partial* confessions. Arthur Koestler's 1940 novel *Darkness at Noon* attempts a solution. In the novel the interrogator Ivanov convinces his former Civil War comrade Rubashov to admit at a public trial to participating in a counterrevolutionary organization, but not to plotting the assassination of the leader, "No. 1." Thus, Ivanov persuades Rubashov, he will serve the revolution through a public spectacle of repentance and submission, while also saving his own life so that he can once again, after several years of incarceration, join the march of human progress (which is to say party work).[46] There are other possible motives for the partial confessions. Prisoners might try to stretch out the period of the inquiry by cooperating but holding back a full confession, in hopes that some political turn or other happenstance might save them. Or they might have believed that the political police were helping them to cleanse their psyches of impure, "class-alien" attitudes of the past, as Stepan Podlubny, the diarist analyzed by Jochen Hellbeck, believed when he became an NKVD informer.[47] At their trial several of the members of the "Leningrad Center" described their relationship with their interrogators as this kind of therapy.

Darkness at Noon and Ivan Kotolynov's testimony also suggest the probable relationship to reality of the elaborate organization of "centers" and "groups" Zvezdov described. As with Rubashov in *Darkness at Noon,* many of the arrested former oppositionists had met and exchanged anti-Stalin comments and analysis with one another. From the point of view of Rubashov's first interrogator Ivanov, this kind of talk was already indistinguishable from participating in a counterrevolutionary organization. If you weren't already acting on your talk, you could be expected to do so soon. The same held for the real interrogators and prisoners in the case of the "Leningrad Center." At the trial of the "Leningrad Center," Kotolynov testified that he had belonged to a "counterrevolutionary Zinovievite organization," but that all the members did was stay in contact with one another. They had no specific agenda or division of responsibilities. Kotolynov denied hearing of any "Leningrad Center" or "Moscow Center" before the interrogators introduced the terms. But the original admission was enough to convict him.[48]

Andrei Ilich Tolmazov provided testimony similar to Zvezdov's on the same day, December 12. Tolmazov, a Red Army veteran from the Civil War days, born in 1899, had been one of the most prominent leaders of the Leningrad Komsomol under Zinoviev. Prior to 1926 he served as head secretary of the Vyborg Ward organization, as one of the secretaries of the Leningrad Province Komsomol, and as a Zinovievite delegate to the Fourteenth Party Congress in December 1925, where Stalin and the Central Committee crushed the Leningrad oppositionists. Posted out of Leningrad, he issued a statement of "repentance" for his "mistakes" after the Fifteenth Party Congress in late 1927. Eventually he was able to return to the city to a senior post in the cooperative apparatus. In April 1934 Kirov sanctioned his appointment as Deputy Director of Workers' Provisioning at the Red Putilov factory.[49]

· 56 ·

Protocol of interrogation of Andrei Ilich Tolmazov by Chief of the Fourth Section of NKVD Special Political Department L. Kogan, December 12, 1934. TsA FSB RF, a.u.d. N-Sh44, t. 12, ll. 127–129.

Question: Tell us about the organizational forms of the organization you belonged to.

Answer: The counterrevolutionary organization to which I belonged has its center in Moscow, consisting for the most part of former chiefs of the Trotsky-Zinoviev bloc. According to Rumiantsev and Kotolynov, Zinoviev, Yevdokimov, Bakaev, and Gertik belong to the center. [. . .] Personally I have not met with members of the center.

The Leningrad group for the most part consists of Rumiantsev, Kotolynov, Antonov, Zvezdov, Fadeev, and myself, Tolmazov.

The contacts and mutual support that existed among us occurred in such fashion that we could meet very rarely. [. . .] Communication with Moscow was maintained by Kotolynov and Rumiantsev. This year Yevdokimov visited from Moscow. He saw Rumiantsev and they chatted. Rumiantsev himself told me this. He asked me if I had seen Yevdokimov and when I answered in the negative, he said that he had talked with him. The conversation between Rumiantsev and me took place in the Vyborg Ward soviet, as afar as I can remember. I do not know the content of the conversation between Rumiantsev and Yevdokimov. Rumiantsev himself showed me a personal letter he received from Zinoviev. This letter evidently was not sent by post. I do not remember exactly the contents of the letter, I only remember that the topic was the situation inside the organization. [. . .] Rumiantsev also visited Moscow, but I don't know whom he met there. I already testified about Kotolynov's trip to Moscow and his meetings there with Faivilovich and Tarasov [both had been important officials in Leningrad under Zinoviev]. I also tried to meet with Faivilovich during one of my trips to Moscow, in early 1934. I dropped in at his place, but he wasn't home.

One of our illegal forms of work was the Fellowship of Komsomol Militants, created as part of the Leningrad department of Istmol. The fact that the core of the Leningrad Komsomol cadres belonged to the Trotsky-Zinoviev bloc and until very recently belonged to the organization was used by us to create a counterrevolutionary organization by the name of the Fellowship of Komsomol Militants, headed by [. . .] Lev Khanik, a member of [our counterrevolutionary] organization. Rumiantsev, Antonov, Fadeev, Seredokhin, and I, Tolmazov, belonged to the Fellowship.

I forgot to tell you that in 1930, I think [. . .] Seredokhin and I were in Moscow and visited Kuklin [another prominent Leningrad official under Zinoviev]. We drank tea and talked about general questions. When I asked Kuklin if he was meeting with Zinoviev, he answered in the positive. On the same visit to Moscow we met with Safarov, who cursed Zinoviev as a "dirty rag" in the sharpest tone, holding nothing back from us.

Question: With which members of the organization was Leonid Nikolaev directly connected?

Answer: I did not know Leonid Nikolaev personally. I left Vyborg Ward Komsomol work in 1923. Nikolaev did not work under me at the ward committee. Zvezdov, Antonov, and Kotolynov worked together with him. I don't know where and how they met. During the period of the oppositional struggle Nikolaev attached himself to the Trotsky-Zinoviev bloc.

Question: What can you tell us with regard to the organization of the terrorist act against Comrade Kirov by Nikolaev, a member of your organization?

Answer: Our organization, in whose heart Nikolaev grew up and upon whose ideological nourishment he battened, bears the entire political and moral responsibility for the murder of Comrade Kirov. [. . .] Tolmazov.

Ivan Kotolynov provided parallel but less specific testimony to Genrikh Liushkov on the same day as Tolmazov's confession (December 12). Kotolynov confessed that after the defeat of the opposition in 1927 the Zinovievites continued to maintain "an autonomous organization," and that their rejoining the party in 1928 was a "deliberate maneuver." He admitted that the ex-Zinovievites bore "political and moral responsibility for the murder of Kirov" because they had "nourished Nikolaev in an atmosphere of hostility to the Communist Party leadership."[50]

After obtaining depositions from Tolmazov, Zvezdov, and Antonov confirming the existence of the Moscow and Leningrad "Centers," Agranov and his deputies persuaded Nikolaev to sign a protocol naming Shatsky, Kotolynov, Yuskin, Antonov, and Zvezdov as his co-conspirators in the plot to assassinate Kirov. Nikolaev underwent several interrogations that day, December 13.

· 57 ·

Protocol of interrogation of Leonid Nikolaev, December 13, 1934. TsA FSB RF, a.u.d. N-Sh44, t. 12, ll. 131–135.

Question: Do you admit that you were part of a counterrevolutionary group of former oppositionists which existed in Leningrad, consisting of Kotolynov, Shatsky, Yuskin, and others?

Answer: Yes I affirm that I was part of a group of former oppositionists consisting of Kotolynov, Shatsky, Yuskin, and others, which carried out counterrevolutionary work.

Question: What political views did the participants in the group hold?

Answer: The participants in the group took their stand on the platform of the Trotsky-Zinoviev bloc. They considered it essential to replace the existing party leadership by any means necessary.

Question: Who sanctioned the murder of Comrade Kirov?

Answer: The murder of Comrade Kirov was sanctioned by [. . .] Kotolynov and Shatsky in the name of the entire group.

Question: What kind of instructions did you get from Kotolynov [and] Shatsky about how to behave yourself during the investigation?

Answer: I was supposed to present the murder of Kirov as an individual act, so as to hide the participation of the Zinovievite group in it.

[. . .] L. Nikolaev

Interrogated by: Agranov, Mironov, Dmitriev.

The final line of this interrogation confirms that the early protocols of Nikolaev's interrogations are correct—he did testify on December 1–2 that he had killed Kirov on his own. It also implies that his diary and letters existed at the time of the murder. Both the early interrogations and the writings posed a problem for Agranov's project, because they indicated that Nikolaev was a lone gunman. The interrogators' solution was typically heavy-handed—they got Nikolaev to "confess" that all of the early evidence was part of a plot to hide the existence of a major counterrevolutionary organization. If the early evidence never existed, then the interrogators would not have needed to add this clunky device to the storyline.

Nikolaev's testimony is particularly implausible given the Russian tradition of revolutionary terrorism. Political terrorists such as Andrei Zheliabov, Vera Figner, and Maria Spiridonova had striven for maximum public exposure so as to propagate their views. They were proud of their acts and seemed to welcome punishment. Nikolaev showed the same attitude in his diary and early interrogations. Now, however, he suddenly changed his testimony to suggest a reluctance to expose the alleged conspiracy.

· 58 ·

Protocol of interrogation of Leonid Nikolaev, December 13, 1934. TsA FSB RF, a.u.d. N-Sh44, t.12, ll. 131–135.

———————

Question: Who among the former Zinovievite oppositionists were part of the counterrevolutionary organization to which you belonged?

Answer: Following up on my earlier depositions, I affirm that the following former oppositionists belonged to the organization: Kotolynov; Rumiantsev; Shatsky; Zvezdov; Antonov; Sokolov; Yuskin; Khanik, Lev; Tolmazov; Aleksandrov; Popov, G.; Tsarkov and a number of other persons. In the organization were two terrorist groups. One group was headed by Kotolynov, it included: me—Nikolaev, Vasily Zvezdov, Nikolai Antonov, Georgy Sokolov, Yuskin. The other group was headed by Nikolai Shatsky, Rumiantsev, Georgy Popov, and N. Tsarkov belonged to it.

Question: What work did each of the terrorist organizations do?

Answer: Kotolynov's group prepared the terrorist act against Kirov, and its execution was assigned personally to me. I carried out my task on December 1, 1934.

I heard from Shatsky that his group got the same task, moreover this work was carried out [. . .] independent of our preparations for a terrorist act. I heard from Kotolynov that his group prepared a terrorist act against Stalin, using those ties that they had in Moscow. As is stated in my interrogation protocol of December 6, 1934, Shatsky and [. . .] his group also carried out preparations for a terrorist act against Stalin.

Thus each of the groups had particular terrorist tasks, which they carried out independent of one another, although the actual goals corresponded. This can be seen from how preparations for the Kirov murder went, which I undertook mainly around Smolny, and Shatsky for the most part around Kirov's apartment. [. . .]

L. Nikolaev.

Interrogated by: Agranov, Mironov, Dmitriev.

Also on December 13 Lev Khanik, arrested five days previously, gave testimony implicating in the murder conspiracy members of the Fellowship of Komsomol Militants, in which he had played a prominent role. Khanik, born in 1902, came from a worker family in western Ukraine. He was an early volunteer for the Red Army, enlisting in March 1918, at age fifteen or sixteen, and serving to the end of the Civil War. His mother was also a Bolshevik in the revolutionary years. He had served as an official in the Vyborg Ward Komsomol apparatus with Nikolaev and trained as an apprentice metalworker. Although he apparently sympathized with the Zinovievite opposition, records do not indicate he was ever expelled from the party. He had received at least three party warnings for drunkenness, indiscipline, and conflicts at work. In 1934 he worked as a party *instruktor* in the island town of Kronstadt (site of the eponymous naval base) near Leningrad. He had a wife, son, and daughter.[51]

· 59 ·

Protocol of interrogation of L. O. Khanik, December 13, 1934. TsA FSB RF,
a.u.d. N-Sh44, t. 12, ll. 160–163.

Question: The investigation disposes of evidence that you belong to a
counterrevolutionary organization of former Zinovievites, what can you
tell us about this?

Answer: I confess that I am guilty of being a member of a Leningrad
counterrevolutionary organization, founded on the basis of the Trotsky-
Zinoviev bloc. Our organization was formed definitively in 1933 at the instance of Moscow [. . .] where an all-union center was being organized at
the initiative of Zinoviev.

Rumiantsev, Vladimir and Levin, Vladimir, who revived the old oppositional ties, calling upon them [*sic*] to take part in the further struggle
against the present [. . .] party leadership, played the organizational and
leading roles in the creation of this organization in Leningrad. Nearly all
of the former participants in the Vyborg Zinovievite group, the so-called
"youth," were members of this organization in the early phases of its existence.

Question: Who specifically belonged to the Moscow and Leningrad
Centers of your organization?

Answer: In the Moscow Center there were Zinoviev, Kamenev, Yevdokimov, Bakaev, Kuklin, Gertik, and Sharov, and in the Leningrad Center there were Rumiantsev, Vladimir; Levin, Vladimir; Mandelshtam,
Sergei; Kotolynov, Ivan; Miasnikov, Nikolai; and Sositsky, Lev . Also I believe (*predpolagaiu*) Bograchev /a deputy/ member of the Leningrad soviet presidium. All of this I heard from Rumiantsev.

Question: What role did you play personally?

Answer: I was the leader of a separate group of the organization, existing under the aegis of the Leningrad Region Istmol in the Fellowship of
Komsomol Militants of former Komsomol participants in the Civil War.

Question: Who belonged to your organization, and what tasks did you
set yourself?

Popov, Yegor/Georgy; Vasileva, Raisa; Tolmazov, Andrei; Zhestianikov, Isolit; Sorokin, Vsevolod; Lukin, Vasily; Aleksandrov, Aleksandr;
Borovichkov, Ivan; Burmistrov, Pavel; and Fadeev, Fyodor. I set myself the
task of using the Fellowship as a legal opportunity for the collection and
consolidation around our organization of those forces which might be directed against present party policies. Aside from the careful recruitment of
new supporters, our group published a series of literary works on the history of the youth movement, which had the aim of smoothing over the

antiparty and counterrevolutionary essence of the Zinovievite opposition in the Komsomol and party. In addition, we could not have put out our literature had we not controlled particular posts in publishing organizations /Vasileva, Raisa; Burmistrov; Driazgov, Lukin, Sorokin/.

Question: What do you know about the structure of your organization as a whole?

Answer: For reasons of secrecy, only members of the [Moscow and Leningrad] center[s] had information on the structure of our organization. However, based on what Rumiantsev told me, I know that our organization had a number of branches in places where youth concentrated. For example, there were branches at the Industrial Institute, the Student Section of the [Council of] Labor Unions, and Istmol. Each branch was connected to the Leningrad Center through one member; I personally was connected with Rumiantsev according to this principle.

Question: How did you formulate the organization's ideological-political principles?

Answer: The ideological-political principles of the organization flowed from the platform of the Trotsky-Zinoviev bloc directed towards [. . .] the replacement of the party leadership with the leaders of our organization Zinoviev, Kamenev, and others. [. . .]

Question: The investigation disposes of evidence that the leaders of your organization cultivated among the members a feeling of resentment and hatred towards the chiefs of the Communist Party. What can you tell us about this?

Answer: This proposition corresponds to reality. The leaders of our organization constantly affirmed that all our problems were the responsibility of the present leadership of the party, Comrades Stalin, Molotov, Kaganovich, and Kirov. In connection with this, the leaders of our organization inculcated in us, especially in the so-called youth, the belief that difficulties would continue in the country /achievements were discounted/ until such time as real leaders headed the party. It was these counterrevolutionary principles and convictions that made possible the terrorist act committed against Comrade Kirov by Leonid Nikolaev, a member of our organization.

Question: What do you know about the preparation of this terrorist act?

Answer: I know nothing personally, as Leonid Nikolaev was not connected with me, but with Kotolynov.

Question: How do you know that Nikolaev was connected specifically with Kotolynov?

Answer: I heard it from Rumiantsev, Vladimir. Nikolaev was linked to Kotolynov for many years, beginning in 1922, when they worked together in the Vyborg Ward committee of the Komsomol.

I have read this protocol, which accurately transcribes my words.
Khanik.
Interrogator: Stromin.

Khanik was listed in the pre-assassination NKVD Special Political Department file "Politikan," along with all of the other men executed with Nikolaev besides Yuskin and Shatsky. The interrogators were particularly interested in using him to discredit recent works published by the Komsomol's "History of Youth" publishing program. In all likelihood this was connected with the accelerating campaign to rewrite Soviet history. The thrust of the campaign was to exaggerate Stalin's role in making the Bolshevik Revolution, and to disparage or even erase the deeds of his intraparty opponents.[52]

Agranov continued to work Nikolaev over. On December 15 and 16 the two of them put together a story of the conspiracy's development that relied on falsifying the conversations that occurred at Nikolaev's actual meetings with Shatsky and Sokolov, and on making up meetings with Kotolynov. In this version of events, Shatsky told Nikolaev of the existence of the Zinovievites' counterrevolutionary organization when the two ran into each other near Kirov's apartment in August 1934. Nikolaev then had a series of (almost certainly imaginary) meetings with Kotolynov, in which the latter gave him instructions for Kirov's murder. One important remaining hole in the case was that Nikolaev could not or would not provide convincing evidence that he'd actually belonged to the Zinovievite organization anytime during the 1920s. On December 14 interrogators tried to get such evidence, but all Nikolaev came up with was a story that he had once spoken against the expulsion of an oppositionist from the party organization of the Red Arsenal factory.[53]

Agranov and his men also wanted to further discredit Nikolaev's notebooks and other materials that showed him to be a lone gunman. The assassin's December 13 dismissal of this evidence as a deliberate subterfuge to protect his Zinovievite collaborators was apparently not enough, presumably because word had leaked out in Leningrad about the documents. On December 16 the interrogators got an entire statement from Nikolaev on his diaries and letters.

· 60 ·

Protocol of interrogation of Leonid Nikolaev, December 16, 1934. TsA FSB RF, a.u.d. N-Sh44, t. 12, ll. 218–219.

Question: Explain why it is that, in the notes found at your apartment [. . .] there are no indications that you had collaborators and acted in the name of the counterrevolutionary organization of Zinovievites.

Answer: It is true that there are no indications in the documents that the terrorist act was prepared by the counterrevolutionary organization and that I had collaborators. Obviously I couldn't put such things in my notes, as this would have been incriminating evidence against the Zinovievite organization. Moreover, I wanted to give vent in those notes to the terrorist feelings which developed in me on the basis of my sharp disagreements with party policy.

I had direct orders from Kotolynov not to let drop in the notes any kind of pointer to my collaborators. All the same, it is possible if you read the notes carefully to discover a few allusions to the fact that I was not acting alone. For example, in the document [. . .] dated November 1 and headed "Plan," under the rubric "Internal," point number eight, there is at one point the phrase "almost alone." These words gave away the fact that I did not act alone.

In the letter "My Explanation before the Party and the Fatherland" I compared myself to Andrei Zheliabov, saying, "I am carrying out preparations like Andrei Zheliabov." Since Zheliabov did not act alone, there is an allusion in these words to the fact that I too did not act on my own. [. . .]

Nikolaev, L.
Interrogated by: Agranov, Mironov, Dmitriev.

Agranov's case in Leningrad was well-nigh complete by December 16. In the meantime, Yagoda in Moscow had reeled in the big fish— Zinoviev and Kamenev.

CHAPTER 9

The Trials of the Moscow and Leningrad "Centers"

The roundup of Zinoviev supporters in Moscow began on the morning of December 9, with the arrests of Ivan Bakaev, Pyotr Zalutsky, Grigory Yevdokimov, Artyom Gertik, Grigory Fyodorov, Aleksei Perimov, and Sergei Gessen. The first five are all identifiable as prominent officials in Leningrad under Zinoviev in 1925.[1] Four days later, in the small hours of December 13, Yagoda arrested eight more former Zinovievites in Moscow—Ivan Gorshenin, Boris Bravo, Aleksandr Gertsberg, Leonid Faivilovich, Anna Bakaeva (probably the wife of Ivan Bakaev), Ivan Naumov, Aleksei Bakaushin, and Sergei Mandelshtam. Of these, Faivilovich and Ivan Naumov had been senior officials under Zinoviev in Leningrad. Gorshenin, Bravo, Gertsberg, and Faivilovich would be tried as members of the "Moscow Center."[2]

Sergei Mandelshtam was the only Moscow arrestee to be tried with the "Leningrad Center." He was an industrial planner who resided in Leningrad but was in Moscow on business on December 13. A member of the party since 1917, he was born in 1896, making him the oldest defendant at the "Leningrad Center" trial. He had solid proletarian roots at the Putilov factory, where he worked before and after 1917. He also served four years in the Red forces during the Civil War. In 1928 the provincial control commission expelled him as a Zinoviev supporter and exiled him temporarily to a job at the northern port of Arkhangelsk. He was readmitted to the party in 1928 or 1929.[3]

All of the Moscow arrestees were transferred in short order to Leningrad. There Agranov's men quickly racked up evidence against Zinoviev. On December 11 Artyom Gertik revealed that a secret, "illegal" meeting of ex-Zinovievites (including Yevdokimov, Gertik himself, and Kuklin, another prominent member of the Leningrad party committee under Zinoviev) took place at Ivan Bakaev's Moscow apartment in 1932. As we have already seen, on the twelfth and thirteenth Zvezdov, Tolmazov, and Khanik named Zinoviev as the head of a secret counterrevolutionary organization. Also on the thirteenth Genrikh Liushkov took a damning "confession" from Rumiantsev, who detailed supposed connections between the Moscow and Leningrad "Centers." Levin, Miasnikov, and Kuklin traveled back and forth between the cities, according to Rumiantsev. In a fall 1934 visit to Leningrad, he claimed, Kuklin had brought word that Zinoviev and Kamenev were "strong . . . inclined to fight the present party leadership."[4]

On December 14 Ivan Kotolynov testified that the former Zinovievites maintained ties, talked politics, and hoped that Stalin might be replaced. This was enough for the NKVD to claim they constituted a "counterrevolutionary group." Kotolynov evidently did not contest the label.

· 61 ·

Protocol of interrogation of Ivan Ivanovich Kotolynov, December 14, 1934.
TsA FSB RF, a.u.d. N-Sh44, t. 12, ll. 108–109.

Question: Do you confess that you returned to the party [in 1928] with a concealed (*dvurushnicheskaia*) aim in accordance with Zinoviev's directive which you read and discussed at the apartment of Vladimir Rumiantsev in July of 1928?

Answer: Yes, I confess it.

Question: What do you know about the present counterrevolutionary Zinovievite organization and its activities?

Answer: I know that in Leningrad the establishment of systematic ties between former participants in the Trotsky-Zinoviev bloc led in effect to the creation of a counterrevolutionary organization. I was connected to Vladimir Rumiantsev, with whom I met periodically to exchange information. I know that links were maintained to Moscow. I personally saw I. Tarasov and Faivilovich at their apartments in Moscow in December 1933. At first we exchanged our thoughts about those among us who made it through the purge [of 1933] and how they did it, and then the conversation turned to the party leadership. In the course of the discussion all of us made the most hostile counterrevolutionary attacks against Comrade Stalin. Following that, I don't remember how the transition went, we had a talk about the question of who might replace Comrade Stalin. It was mentioned that although Kaganovich was not a bad organizer, he did not have the trust of the party and could not be allowed to become party leader.

In connection with this conversation about the replacement of Stalin, Faivilovich named Zinoviev, arguing that he—Zinoviev—could become leader of the party. Besides this, the question of the possibility of promoting Bakaev, Yevdokimov, Gertik, and Kharitonov to leading work in the party was touched upon.

Upon my return from Moscow, in December or at the beginning of 1934, I dropped in at V. Rumiantsev's apartment [and] told him that I had seen Tarasov and Faivilovich, and informed him of the content of my conversation with them. Tolmazov was present at my conversation with Rumiantsev.

Question: Who do you know among the persons connected with Rumiantsev, V., in the counterrevolutionary organization?

Answer: I know the following persons who are regularly in touch with Rumiantsev on business of the counterrevolutionary organization: Tolmazov, Andrei Ilich; Mandelshtam, Sergei; Antonov, Nikolai. It seems to me that Fadeev, Fyodor also visits him.

Kotolynov.

Interrogators: Liushkov [. . .] Chief of the Sixth Section of the NKVD Special Political Department Korkin.

By the evening of December 13 Yagoda and Agranov were ready to make a public case that the murderer Nikolaev belonged to a counterrevolutionary group of ex-Zinovievites who had inspired, if not organized, the assassination. They also had depositions that Zinoviev headed the group. Moving with remarkable speed, the TsK executives called plenary sessions of the regional party committees in Moscow and Leningrad for December 15–16. Each meeting was presided over by one of Stalin's closest associates—Kaganovich in Moscow, and Andrei Zhdanov, already designated as Kirov's successor, in Leningrad. On the first day of the plenums Kaganovich and Zhdanov announced to their respective audiences that Zinoviev and his supporters were behind the killing. The next day Agranov told the Leningrad plenum that onetime Zinoviev supporters from the Leningrad Komsomol had plotted the murder, and that their "ideological inspiration" came from Zinoviev, Kamenev, and other senior members of the Zinovievite faction. According to Mikhail Rosliakov, who was present, Agranov named Kotolynov, Rumiantsev, and Shatsky as plotters.[5]

Rosliakov reports that "the atmosphere at the plenum was tenser than tense, in the hall there was a graveyard silence, not a whisper, not a rustle, the only thing to be heard was the voices of the comrades giving their speeches." P. I. Smorodin and P. I. Struppe, both of whom had headed the Vyborg Ward party organization in the past, gave "speeches of repentance," presumably because so many of the supposed assassins worked or had worked in the Vyborg party or Komsomol apparatus.[6]

Early in the evening of December 16, Yagoda, who was in charge of operations on the Moscow end of the inquiry, sprang the trap on Zinoviev, Kamenev, and G. I. Safarov, a senior Leningrad official under Zinoviev and former editor of *Leningradskaia pravda*. The police confiscated old opposition documents (the latest from 1928) from all three. These included Zinoviev's 1920s correspondence with Trotsky. Yagoda dispatched Zinoviev and Kamenev to Leningrad that same evening, and Safarov the following day.[7]

As the police searched his apartment on December 16, Zinoviev scribbled a frantic note, which Yagoda handed on to Stalin.

· 62 ·

Zinoviev note to Stalin, December 16, 1934. APRF, f. 3, op. 24, d. 199, l. 45.

To Comrade I. V. Stalin.

At this moment [December 16, 7:30 in the evening], Comrade Molchanov and a group of chekists have presented themselves at my apartment and are conducting a search.

I can say to you honestly, Comrade Stalin, that from the moment that I returned from Kustanaya with the Central Committee's leave, I have not taken one step, nor said even one word, nor written a single line, I have not had even one single thought, which I might want to hide from the party, from the Central Committee, from you personally. I thought only of one thing: how to win the trust of the Central Committee and you personally, how to reach the point that you would include me in [the party's] work.

I have and could have nothing more than old archives /all that I have accumulated in more than thirty years, including the years of the opposition/.

I am guilty of nothing, nothing, nothing before the party, before the Central Committee, and before you personally. I swear to you by everything that a Bolshevik can hold sacred, I swear to you by Lenin's memory.

I cannot imagine what could have sparked suspicion against me. I beg you, believe this honest truth. I am shaken to the depths of my soul.

G. Zinoviev.

Safarov penned a similar note to Stalin while the police searched his apartment. Perhaps because of Safarov's lower status in the party, it was a great deal more obsequious than Zinoviev's.

· 63 ·

G. I. Safarov note to Stalin, December 16, 1934. APRF, f. 3, op. 24, d. 199, l. 46.

Deeply Respected Joseph Vissarionovich, Great Leader of the Party and Country,

I would prefer not to live rather than live to see the day of such a fatal, terrible misunderstanding. I honorably and frankly broke with counter-revolutionary Trotskyism, I did everything I could to help in the struggle against it. Those comrades who saw my work can attest that this work was entirely suffused with the desire to do everything to expiate my crime before the party. *There is no life for me outside the party and I beg you to investigate and clear up this fatal misunderstanding* [emphasis in the original]. I will prove that I am worthy of your trust as a foot soldier in the great army of the great Lenin and the great Stalin in the most remote corner of the country, at the most grueling tasks.

Comrade Stalin! You must believe that there is not a grain of falsehood here and help me!

G. Safarov.

The time had come for the press to reveal the "true" perpetrators of the crime. On December 17 *Pravda* and *Leningradskaia pravda* ran the same lead editorial, "Without Mercy We Must Root out the Remnants of Our Smashed Enemies!"[8] The editorial stated that "Zinovievites" were responsible for Kirov's assassination. The next morning *Leningradskaia pravda's* lead editorial presented the new official interpretation of the crime: "Comrade Kirov was murdered by an evildoer sent by the despicable scum of the former Zinovievite antiparty group. It is hard to find more abominable criminals, it is hard to imagine a more monstrous crime against the working class, against the proletarian revolution. *The leftover Zinovievite slime has degenerated into White Guard Fascists.*" To expand upon these boldface words, the paper ran a page two article entitled "From Opposition to Terror." This piece by V. Bystriansky argued that because oppositionists lacked any popular support, they had no choice but to hide themselves inside the party, pretending to be loyal Communists, and to undertake individual acts of terrorism. Thus, he wrote, "they become direct agents of the class enemy, they resort to the ultimate White Guard bandit, Fascist method of struggle—terror." Bystriansky's essay foreshadowed the fundamental logic of the Moscow show trials of 1936–1938. When Nikolai Yezhov began writing his (never-published) book "From Factionalism to Open Counterrevolution" for Stalin in the early spring of 1935, his thesis closely resembled Bystriansky's. In the manuscript Yezhov linked the Rightists, the Zinovievites, and the Trotsky faction, and he charged the latter two groups with plotting Kirov's murder. The logic of the show trials, that past opposition to the Central Committee's "general line" led inexorably to counterrevolutionary terrorism, was already developed less than three weeks after the Kirov murder.[9]

On December 20 the Party Control Commission excluded Zinoviev, Kamenev, Safarov and twenty-two others from the party "as counterrevolutionaries."[10]

Once Agranov and his subordinates had Zinoviev in custody, they pressed him relentlessly to confess to three main charges—that he had encouraged his supporters to return to the party in 1928 with the "two-faced" goal of saving Zinovievite cadres for a later struggle against the party leadership, that he had criticized collectivization and other party economic policies in 1932, and that he had continued ties with the "terrorists" of the "Leningrad Center" up to the time of Kirov's murder. One of Zinoviev's depositions from December 22 shows the interrogator (Liushkov) pushing these accusations. In it Zinoviev also gives a very credible description of the real moods and motivations of those whom the investigators accused of counterrevolution.

· 64 ·

Protocol of interrogation of Grigory Yevseyevich Zinoviev, December 22, 1934.
APRF, f. 3, op. 24, d. 200, ll. 163–173.

Question: The investigation once again demands [. . .] that you tell us all that you know about the organization of former participants in the so-called Zinoviev opposition in Leningrad, about the Moscow center of this organization, and about your role in all of this.

Answer: In 1927–1928 in Leningrad there was an underground organization of Zinovievites, existing parallel to the party organization, with its own ward [committees], connections, and so on. But after that the elements of the organization melted away and after 1929 there was no organization at all. What remained in Leningrad of the former Zinovievite organization [. . .] could [only] have viewed those in Moscow—me, Kamenev, Yevdokimov, Bakaev, and others, as an obvious "moral" center. But in reality there was no Moscow center. [. . .]

After the Fifteenth Party Congress [late 1927] I had hopes, in connection with the appearance of the Rights, of a future regrouping in the party, of an open discussion. It seemed to me, by the way, that the "nonreturners" among the youth /Rumiantsev, Kotolynov, and others/ returned to the party and turned from the road they had taken [. . .] for the same reason. It is possible that when I was in Leningrad in 1929, there was a conversation with the persons named in the interrogation /Rumiantsev, Mandelshtam, Levin, and others/ and if there was a conversation, that it followed the sense of the note found on Shvalbe.

There were arguments made from my side to Kamenev and others: "Reenter the party, preserve your forces, they'll be useful for the struggle with the Rightists."

In 1929 Kamenev's and my hopes that we would be "called upon" to participate in the party leadership strengthened, in connection with the party's struggle with the Rightists. This was, obviously, a tangled mass of feelings. On the one hand, we had been sitting around [. . .] without work or with work that did not satisfy us, on the other the pace of collectivization and the growth of industry alone created favorable conditions for a blow against the Rightists. My political line in general corresponded with that of the party during this time. But I was not willing at this time to follow the orders of the Central Committee simply as a "rank-and-filer," instead I wished to negotiate with the Central Committee as a "Power" in my own right; the hope of [. . .] participating in the leadership had not yet disappeared. [. . .]

More than once I met with leading figures of the party and the Soviet government, before my exile to Kaluga [. . .] and after my return from Kustanaya.[11] The comrades knew of the underground methods of struggle with which I had been connected in the past, but no one asked me—tell us, who are these people, how did they work, name the names! It was as if there were a silent accord that if I submitted politically, everything would work out. [. . .]

I do not consider myself without sin. But the issue is not just my individual character, but how difficult and nearly impossible any kind of painless transition was from my previous role in the party to the situation that developed for me later. Embittered by the memory of the role that I played in the past, I tried in spite of everything to be in the thick of politics, and I did not understand that after my struggle against the party, after my colossal political mistakes, it was possible for me to return to the party only as a rank-and-file member.

I was not the only one in that situation. To a greater or lesser degree, it applied to the whole group of former Leningrad leaders/"elders" who fought by my side in the opposition. A whole group of such people formed. In part it formed based on personal ties, and, more importantly, on a shared situation and dissatisfaction with this situation. The [. . .] peak of such feelings among us after the Fifteenth Party Congress was the appearance of the Rightists. [. . .]

I did not understand that the exposure of Bukharin, Rykov, Tomsky. and the others as opportunists did not mean that it was possible for me to receive a political amnesty, much less a promotion. I did not understand that the Central Committee and not I had the right to decide the question of how, when, and by what methods to smash the Rightists. [. . .] More than once I made a vow of loyalty to the party, and in general from 1929 I did agree with the general line, but up until 1932 I continued to have the psychology of a person who feels himself somehow, at least in part, correct. [. . .]

The moods I have described remained with me until 1932. Naturally, in such a mood I cursed the party leadership and Comrade Stalin personally. But from the time I returned from Kustanaya I have had no such unhealthy feelings. I did not meet with anyone, I did not have any antiparty conversations, I know of no organization nor do I know about any center.

Question: To the protocol of your interrogation from December 19 you added a note that a number of persons, including Rumiantsev, Kotolynov, Mandelshtam, and others about whom the investigation questioned you, broke with the group of former Leningrad oppositionists and formed a special group of "nonreturners" or "Lefts" after the Fourteenth [*sic*—Fifteenth] Party Congress.

Answer: These are the persons whom the investigation informs me are members of the Leningrad center of the organization to which I supposedly belonged. I consider that one of the arguments against this might be to point out that these people broke with me and with my supporters. At the moment of the break they were much closer to the Trotskyite group with which we also broke, than to the group that I belonged to then.

Question: According to the depositions of Rumiantsev, Kotolynov, and Mandelshtam, which you cite in your note appended to the protocol of December 19, the later struggle with the party and the Soviet government which the said persons carried on erased their hostile disagreements with you. Your letter of June 13, 1928, addressed to Rumiantsev, confirms [. . .] that the disagreements were liquidated, and [your] ties with this group, the so-called "nonreturners," were restored. What can you tell us about this?

Answer: I no longer saw any of them. My letter, addressed to Rumiantsev, confirms just the opposite, the [continued] existence of disagreements /otherwise, why would I try to persuade him [to rejoin the party]/ and as I know absolutely nothing about what happened to him after this, what kind of struggle he undertook, I have nothing to tell you about this. [. . .]

I can say that I knew several of them personally. [. . .] I considered Rumiantsev at the time to be a valuable person, a young working man who took a wrong turn. I tried to convince him [to rejoin]. I had no meetings with him after that, and as to what kind of person he was after that, I wasn't interested.

Question: You were interested in Rumiantsev not for himself, but because he was connected to the group of [Komsomol] youth. As is evident from Rumiantsev's depositions, your letter to him was aimed at keeping him, and the group of youth connected with him, under your influence. When Rumiantsev returned to the party eventually, he did not do so alone. He carried on negotiations with the Central Control Commission together with Tarasov and Kotolynov, who headed the group of former Zinovievite opposition youth. They turned directly to Kamenev, who by the way edited their petition to the Central Control Commission, which had, as they have confessed, a two-faced character. In this connection, your letter to Rumiantsev had an obviously two-faced character. Do you confirm this?

Answer: Anything is possible. It is possible that they were prevaricating (*oni i dvurushnichali*), but I called on Rumiantsev to return to the party without any concealed thoughts. I tried to persuade many people to return to the party.

Question: Did you ever say anything to Gorshenin about the organization of Zinovievites that existed in Leningrad?

Answer: In 1928 I might have said something, but if you are talking about later events, then no. At the end of 1928—that's possible.

Question: It has been established by the December 19 deposition of Gorshenin, that at the end of 1928 you told him about the existence in Leningrad of a conspiratorial organization of former members of the so-called Zinovievite opposition, at the head of which stood Levin, Vladimir and Rumiantsev, Vladimir. You characterized this organization to Gorshenin as "in a fighting mood." Do you confirm this?

Answer: No I cannot confirm it. [. . .]

Question: On the basis of all the materials that the investigation disposes of, the materials of your interrogation, your organizational ties with Levin, Rumiantsev, and others are completely obvious. The investigation has determined that an organization of former participants in the so-called Zinovievite opposition [. . .] formed in Leningrad not just with your knowledge, but at your order.

The investigation insists that you give an honest answer about your real role in the creation of this organization. [. . .]

Answer: I told you today in detail that I led no organization [. . .] nor did I participate in one, that in late 1928—early 1929 I truly had hopes of a return to a leadership position in the party, and that on these grounds there were naturally conversations. My moods and attitudes about this are most clearly shown in the notes that were confiscated from Shvalbe and which are in your hands. There was hope for a new discussion, we even supposed that the comrades and I could return to Leningrad to battle against the Rightists. Moods such as these could have existed, but that was far from the creation of any kind of an organization. [. . .]

Question: [. . .] The deposition of Bakaev from December 21 establishes that in the summer of 1932 you personally discussed with him the utility of composing a collective letter to the TsK of the Communist Party about the supposed difficulties in the country and the necessity of party members demanding information about same from the Central Committee.

Answer: That did not happen and could not have happened.

Question: Do you assert that there was no conversation with Bakaev?

Answer: There was no such proposition from my side, nor could there have been. [. . .]

Question: Did you see Bravo in 1932, where, and what was the character of your conversation with him?

Answer: I saw him in Ilinsky. I remember above all his conversation about his impressions from the countryside /he had gone there on the grain mobilization/. It was a typical conversation of that year, difficulties, and so on.

Question: Did Bravo give you intelligence about the countryside?

Answer: Why do you put it that way—"intelligence"? He told me his impressions of what he saw. I don't remember exactly where he went.

Question: It has been established by the testimony of Bravo from December 19 that in August 1932 he was at your dacha in Ilinsky with Yevdokimov, where he found you with Kamenev, Kuklin, and one other person, identity unknown. As a result of your conversation with Bravo, who worked on the procurements committee of the Council on Labor and Defense, you gave a negative evaluation of the situation in the country, you concluded, in part, that a general deterioration of the food situation in the country could be expected. Do you confirm this?

Answer: I cannot confirm it. What kind of specialist am I in food procurement problems? Obviously, the difficulties in 1932 were serious.

Question: What kind of conclusions did you draw from that?

Answer: In 1932? What kind of general conclusions could I draw? In all probability I viewed things in the same way everyone did: the matter would depend on future harvests, above all, and on the success of collectivization. [. . .]

Question: The depositions of Gorshenin establish that at the end of 1933 [at the time of] the Fascist coup in Germany and Hitler's coming to power, you personally explained to him the incorrect line of the Comintern and the Central Committee of the Communist Party, which facilitated Hitler's coming to power.

Answer: I cannot confirm that in any way. I have written plenty on the Fascist coup and Hitler's coming to power; I was considered to some degree a specialist in this question and I have laid out what I truly thought about this issue. [. . .]

Question: The depositions of Safarov from December 20 establish that in the summer of 1932 at a meeting at your dacha in Ilinsky, you told him that the country was experiencing a feeling of alarm in the face of difficulties, that elements of dissatisfaction were growing in the country, you gave a slanderous evaluation of the party's handling of the situation in the country, and so on.

What do you have to say about this?

Answer: Everything depends on the way things are formulated. Of course there was talk of the difficulties of 1932, but not in the context that the policies as a whole were mistaken—that wasn't how it was. That particular news from particular regions elicited alarm—that is possible, but to say that the leadership's policy was mistaken—that didn't happen. I wouldn't want to claim, of course, that I was in general without sin in 1932. I did have some unhealthy moods, vacillations, connected with the difficulties which the country was then living through.

G. Zinoviev.

Interrogators: Agranov. Liushkov.

Zinoviev's deposition reveals several typical techniques of interrogators and prosecutors in the years of the Great Terror. As we have seen in the protocols of other interrogations, the police construed social connections as prima facie evidence of conspiracy. They took past political actions out of context to construct retrospective accusations of political crimes (Zinoviev's encouragement of his supporters to rejoin the party in 1928 was "two-faced"). They also used incriminating testimony from associates to pressure the accused to confess. It is likely that interrogators represented to Zinoviev's former associates that he himself was to blame for their plight, suggesting that there might be clemency for those who recognized their errors and denounced their leader. At the trial of the "Leningrad Center" on December 28–29 Anto-

nov, Zvezdov, Tolmazov, Miasnikov, Khanik, Sositsky, and Rumiantsev, that is seven out of fourteen persons in the dock, blamed Zinoviev
for leading them astray.[12] Interrogators presumably encouraged arrestees to accuse their former chief of ultimate responsibility for the
murder. There is good evidence that Safarov, who had called Zinoviev
"a dirty rag" in 1930, was informing on the latter as part of proving
his loyalty to the party. Thus Liushkov and Agranov were able to use
evidence from Kotolynov, Rumiantsev, Mandelshtam, Safarov, Bakaev,
Bravo, and Gorshenin against Zinoviev on December 22.

Wrapping up the Case of the "Leningrad Center"

In preparation for the trial of the "Leningrad Center" officials of the
USSR prosecutorial apparatus arrived in Leningrad on the morning of
December 18 or 19. In accordance with formal procedures for "prosecutorial oversight" of criminal investigations, Ivan Akulov, Chief
Prosecutor of the USSR, Andrei Vyshinsky, Deputy Prosecutor, and
Sheinin, an investigator for the Office for High Priority Cases, questioned each of the accused in the "Leningrad Center" case. Most, if not
all, of the interviews were held on December 19. According to a 1956
report from the USSR prosecutor's office, the protocols of these interviews were often just one or two sentences long. The officials asked the
accused simply to confirm their previous testimony, making no effort
to resolve contradictions or delve into the specifics of the case. In violation of Russian Federation law at least some of the accused were not
provided access to the evidence in the case. Several of the interview
protocols were not signed.[13]

In April 1956 Sheinin described the interviews:

· 65 ·

Testimony of Sheinin, investigator for the Office for High Priority Cases, April
1956. Excerpted from late April 1956 USSR prosecutor's report to Molotov
commission on the Kirov murder in RGANI, f. 6, op.13, d. 1, ll. 153–194.

Upon arrival in Leningrad Akulov and Vyshinsky began to question the
accused in very summary fashion, and I took down the testimony. These
interrogations had a purely formal character and lasted twenty to thirty
minutes, and members of the Central Committee commission on the [Ki-

rov] case were present in the persons of Yezhov and Kosaryov. The interrogations boiled down to asking the accused whether he confirmed his testimony given to the organs of the NKVD, and whether he admitted his own guilt. The processing of the case for delivery [to the judicial organs] was done in a great hurry, because of the Law of December 1.

Between December 18 and 20 the NKVD organized a number of face-to-face confrontations (*ochnye stavki*) between suspects, a standard Soviet police procedure. Presumably this was done in the hopes of squeezing out more confessions or tying up loose ends. The records of these confrontations provide important information about the relations between Nikolaev and four of the arrestees who had contact with him in the months before the murder, namely Shatsky, Kotolynov, Yuskin, and Sokolov.

· 66 ·

Protocol of confrontation between Ivan Ivanovich Kotolynov and Leonid Vasilevich Nikolaev, December 18, 1934. TsA FSB RF, a.u.d. N-Sh44, t. 12, ll. 260–261.

The accused Kotolynov, I. I. and Nikolaev, L. V., summoned to a confrontation, after mutual confirmation that they are personally acquainted with one another, deposed:

Question to Kotolynov: Do you confirm that you were a member of a counterrevolutionary Zinoviev-Trotskyite organization?

Answer: Yes, I confirm that I was. [. . .]

Question to Nikolaev: Did you belong to a counterrevolutionary Zinoviev-Trotskyite organization and who recruited you?

Answer: Yes I belonged to a counterrevolutionary Zinoviev-Trotskyite organization; I was recruited into the organization by Kotolynov; this was in September 1934 at the building of the Polytechnical Institute where Kotolynov studied.

Question to Kotolynov: Do you confirm that you recruited Nikolaev into the Zinoviev-Trotskyite organization?

Answer: No, I deny it.

Question to Nikolaev: Did Kotolynov propose in the name of the Zinoviev-Trotskyite organization that you kill Comrade Kirov, did you accept the proposal, and under what circumstances did this take place?

Answer: Yes, a proposal to kill Kirov was made to me by Kotolynov in the name of the Zinoviev-Trotskyite counterrevolutionary organization; I accepted this proposal in September 1934; the proposal was made at the Polytechnic Institute where I went to meet Kotolynov.

Question to Kotolynov: Do you confirm Nikolaev's testimony that he killed Kirov at your orders?

Answer: No, I deny it. [. . .]

Nikolaev, L. V. Kotolynov, I. I.

Confrontation supervised by: Mironov Liushkov Dmitriev.

At his trial Kotolynov continued to maintain the stance he took in this confrontation, accepting that his contacts with former opposition-ists amounted to a "counterrevolutionary organization," but denying any involvement in Kirov's murder.

The following day Mironov, Dmitriev, and Fyodorov presided over a confrontation between Yuskin and Nikolaev. The NKVD had already extracted from Yuskin an admission that he did say to Nikolaev, "Why Kirov? Why not go for Stalin?" but only in jest (December 10). Based on all of Yuskin's available interrogations the reality seems to be that Nikolaev made some reference to the assassination of Kirov, but Yuskin did not take him seriously and replied flippantly. Yuskin had also "con-fessed" on December 15 and 18 that he knew from their meetings that Nikolaev planned to attack Kirov. It is likely that Yuskin's interrogators omitted from the protocols Yuskin's attempts to explain that his com-ments about killing Stalin were meant sarcastically.[14]

· 67 ·

Protocol of confrontation between Ignaty Yuskin and Leonid Nikolaev, December 19, 1934. TsA FSB RF, a.u.d. N-Sh44, t. 12, ll. 280–281.

———————

Question to Yuskin: What did you hear from Nikolaev about the ques-tion of preparations for the murder of Comrade Kirov?

Answer: In October 1934 Nikolaev, who was at my home, confided to me that he was preparing the assassination of Comrade Kirov.

Question to Nikolaev: Do you confirm that you really did tell Yuskin about preparations for the murder of Kirov?

Answer: Yes, I confirm [it]. [. . .]

Question to Nikolaev: Did Yuskin participate in the preparation of the murder of Comrade Kirov?

Answer: Yes, he participated; his participation consisted in his telling me where it would be best to make the attack on Kirov. He advised me at what point on Kirov's [habitual] routes it made sense to attack.

Question to Yuskin: Do you confirm that you were a participant in the preparations for the murder of Comrade Kirov?

Answer: No, I deny it.

Question to Nikolaev: Did you know that Yuskin was a participant in the counterrevolutionary Zinoviev-Trotskyite organization, and did you tell him that you yourself belonged to that organization?

Answer: Yes, I knew, Yuskin himself told me; I told him in turn that I also belonged to that organization.

Question to Yuskin: Do you confirm Nikolaev's testimony that you told him of your membership in the Zinoviev-Trotskyite counterrevolutionary organization, and that he told you of his participation in that organization?

Answer: No, I deny it.

Question to Yuskin: Did you suggest to Nikolaev that he organize a terrorist attack on Comrade Stalin and did you agree to be a participant in preparation of that act?

Answer: Yes, in conversation with Nikolaev I told him that kill Kirov [*sic*] it was necessary to kill Stalin.

Question to Nikolaev: Do you confirm Yuskin's testimony?

Answer: Yes I confirm it. I want to add that in this conversation Yuskin also talked with me about a trip to Moscow to make preparations for a terrorist attack on Stalin.

Nikolaev, L. Yuskin, I.

Confrontation supervised by: Mironov Dmitricv Fyodorov

In his interview with Akulov and Vyshinsky, which took place on the same day as the confrontation with Nikolaev, Yuskin changed some of this testimony, perhaps hoping for a more sympathetic hearing from the prosecutors. He admitted knowing of Nikolaev's terrorist intentions, and admitted that failing to denounce him made him an accessory to Kirov's murder. However, he denied any participation in planning for the assassination.[15]

The NKVD also organized a confrontation between Nikolaev and Shatsky.

· 68 ·

Protocol of confrontation between N. N. Shatsky and Leonid Nikolaev, December 20, 1934. TsA FSB RF, a.u.d. N-Sh44, t. 12. ll. 288–291.

Question to Shatsky: Did you meet with Nikolaev [. . .] in February–March 1934? If so, where did this meeting take place?

Answer: Yes, I met with Leonid Nikolaev in February–March on the premises of Istmol, on the Moika [Canal]. [. . .]

Question to Nikolaev: What kind of conversation did you have with Shatsky at this meeting?

Answer: I told Shatsky that we had to reestablish ties with the old cadres of the Zinoviev opposition, that we had to organize; Shatsky agreed with this; Shatsky showed hostility to the leadership of the party. At that same time Shatsky expressed a desire to go to work in Vyborg Ward, where the old opposition cadres were concentrated.

Shatsky came to Istmol with the intent of linking up with oppositionist-employees of Istmol, Popov and others.

Question to Shatsky: Do you confirm that you really did talk about this with Nikolaev.

Answer: No, I do not confirm it.

Question to Shatsky: Did you have another meeting with Nikolaev, if so, when specifically and at what location?

Answer: Yes there was a meeting, around July or August not far from the building where Kirov lived, on Krasnykh Zor Street. [. . .]

Question to Nikolaev: Tell us the content of your conversation with Shatsky at this meeting.

Answer: At the time of this August meeting Shatsky said to me that he was a member of the counterrevolutionary Zinovievite organization, that he had established ties with the organization, with Rumiantsev, Kotolynov, Sokolov, and others, that the organization was preparing [. . .] a terrorist act against Kirov and that in connection with this Shatsky was carrying out surveillance of Kirov.

Question to Shatsky: Do you confirm this testimony of Nikolaev's?

Answer: No, I deny it.

Question to Shatsky: Did you see the regional party committee secretary Chudov who rode past you during the said conversation with Nikolaev?

Answer: Yes. [. . .]

Question to Nikolaev: What kind of conversation did you have with Shatsky, in connection with the encounter with Comrade Chudov?

Answer: In connection with the encounter with Chudov, Shatsky said that Chudov was not a suitable target for a terrorist act.

Question to Shatsky: Do you confirm this testimony of Nikolaev's?

Answer: No, I do not.

Question to Shatsky: During the August conversation with Nikolaev, did you talk with him of the fact that you had been removed from work more than once for oppositional activity?

Answer: Yes, I told Nikolaev that I was fired from work, and suggested that this was due to my previous oppositional activity.

Question to Nikolaev: What can you say about this?

Answer: Shatsky told me that he had been removed from work as an oppositionist in the past and that he was under OGPU surveillance (*na uchete*).

Question to Nikolaev: Did Shatsky tell you at the said meeting that he was preparing a terrorist act against Comrade Stalin?

Answer: Yes, Shatsky said this to me.

Question to Shatsky: Do you confirm this testimony of Nikolaev's?

Answer: No, I do not confirm it.

Question to Nikolaev: Did Shatsky propose that you link up with Kotolynov to carry out counterrevolutionary work?

Answer: Yes, Shatsky proposed this to me.

Question to Shatsky: Do you confirm this testimony of Nikolaev's?

Answer: No I do not confirm it.

Question to Nikolaev: On the anniversary of the October Revolution in 1934 did you meet Shatsky near Comrade Kirov's apartment?

Answer: Yes, I met Shatsky near Comrade Kirov's apartment on Krasnykh Zor Street on the anniversary of October in 1934, but I did not approach him because I understood that he was keeping Comrade Kirov under surveillance for the accomplishment of a terrorist act; for this reason I shifted my surveillance of Kirov to Smolny, agreeing upon this with Kotolynov. As is known I committed the murder of Kirov in Smolny.

Question to Shatsky: Do you confirm Nikolaev's testimony.

Answer: Yes, on the day of the 1934 anniversary of October I was in fact on Krasnykh Zor Street, [but] I deny that I was at that place with the aim of keeping Kirov under surveillance, for the accomplishment of a terrorist act.

Question to Nikolaev: Did Shatsky talk with you about the necessity of making connections abroad, what proposal did you make to Shatsky, and later Kotolynov, about this question, and how was it received?

Answer: Yes, Shatsky told me that he wanted to make connections abroad through Moscow, using Rumiantsev's ties with the Comintern; I proposed to Shatsky that we try to make connections abroad through consulates in the city of Leningrad: Shatsky accepted my suggestion.

Question to Shatsky: Do you confirm this testimony of Nikolaev?

Answer: No, I do not confirm it.

Question from Shatsky to Nikolaev: Does Nikolaev remember who sat next to our table in the same room when the conversation of Shatsky with Nikolaev took place at their meeting in February–March 1934?

Nikolaev's Answer: There were just the two of us at the table.

Shatsky L. Nikolaev.

Confrontation supervised by: Mironov Liushkov Dmitriev Fyodorov.

Shatsky admitted to two conversations with Nikolaev, and to complaining about the party's treatment of him. But he insisted right up to his execution that he was not involved in any counterrevolutionary organization, much less a plot to assassinate Kirov. He was the only one of the accused to reject completely the interrogators' logic that opposition to Stalin equaled counterrevolution, which in turn implied terrorist activity.

Liushkov and his fellows pressed for revelation of a foreign connection in this confrontation. Nikolaev obliged them, discussing possible connections through the Comintern apparatus and the consulates in Leningrad. "Rumiantsev's ties to the Comintern," mentioned by Nikolaev, almost certainly refers to Georgy Safarov, mentioned above, who was deputy chief of the Eastern Secretariat of the Comintern at the time of his arrest. After Safarov's arrest the Comintern executive committee's party organization set out to "cleanse" itself, expelling Ludwig Magyar, a Hungarian Communist close to Safarov and Zinoviev, on December 29, 1934. A number of other executive committee employees were expelled from the party and arrested in the succeeding months.[16]

Nikolaev also took credit in this confrontation for proposing that the counterrevolutionaries make contact with the outside world through the Leningrad consulates. The NKVD had not stopped work on the case of the Latvian consul. On December 10–11, interrogators elicited testimony from Nikolaev's sister Yekaterina and from Olga Draule that Leonid never had money problems and had turned down work offered to him after he lost his position at the Institute of History.[17] The purpose of such testimony was probably to demonstrate that Nikolaev was receiving money from illicit outside sources, such as a foreign consulate. The fact that Leonid and Milda had a decent apartment, and that they had vacationed in a dacha (albeit a very humble one) in Sestroretsk in the summer of 1934, made the testimony more plausible. Recent commentators have used Yekaterina's and Olga's evidence to argue that Nikolaev really was receiving money from some suspicious outside source. In fact, however, it is likely that their depositions were exaggerated, and that Nikolaev's family was indeed out of money in the fall of 1934, as his diary indicates (see Chapter 6).

On December 14 interrogators returned to Nikolaev's testimony of December 5 and 6 about his supposed attempts to visit foreign consulates. They persuaded Nikolaev to embellish his previous depositions with the claim that Kotolynov, Shatsky, and the "counterrevolutionary organization" had supported his efforts to contact the consuls. Nikolaev also stressed on December 14 that the Zinovievites had hoped to trade "materials presenting the internal situation of the country in an anti-Soviet spirit" for the consuls' aid in making contacts abroad. In all likelihood the NKVD hoped to link him to the Menshevik or Trotskyite clandestine information networks inside the USSR.[18]

Six days later, on December 20, Nikolaev signed an interrogation protocol giving a much more elaborate story about his relations with the Latvian consul. This protocol contains the tell-tale sign of an interrogation supervised by Nikolai Yezhov, a sudden statement by the accused that he has been lying and will now tell the whole truth. During Yezhov's tenure as NKVD chief (1936–1938), this theatrical device became a commonplace in interrogation protocols.

· 69 ·

Excerpt of protocol of interrogation of Leonid Nikolaev, December 20, 1934. RGANI, f. 6, op. 13, d. 14, ll. 27–28.

Question: What more evidence can you provide us about your links with consuls in the city of Leningrad?

Answer: I have decided to tell the whole truth about my links with consuls in the city of Leningrad.

My relations with the Latvian consul went much further than I have testified previously to the investigation.

I had several meetings with the consul, at which I told him that I belonged to an underground anti-Soviet organization, I explained just what our organization was, who some of the participants were, our connections with the Communist Party.

The consul showed great interest in my explanation, he showered me with questions to clarify what kind of persons belonged to the organization, [. . .] what the organization had in common with the former Leningrad opposition.

I asked the consul to connect our group with Trotsky, I noted that it was in the consul's power to give us the kind of help that we would be very grateful for.

I stated that we were always prepared to help the consul with accurate information of what was going on inside the Soviet Union, here I had in mind the conversation I had with Shatsky and Kotolynov about the necessity of interesting the consul in materials of an anti-Soviet character about the internal situation of the USSR, of which I wrote in my deposition of December 14 1934.

Further, I asked the consul to provide me with material aid, stating we would return him the money we received from him as soon as our financial situation changed.

At the next meeting in the consul's building—the third or fourth meeting—the consul told me that he was ready to satisfy my request and handed me 5,000 rubles.

He also said that he was able to make contact with Trotsky if I had any kind of letter from the group for Trotsky.

I told Kotolynov of my conversation with the consul, giving him 4,500 rubles of the money I received, and keeping 500 for myself.

The handover of the letter to the consul was put off, as Kotolynov held it up, for reasons unknown to me. [. . .]

L. Nikolaev.

Interrogated by: Mironov Dmitriev.

The interrogators had finally forged (in both senses of the verb) a link between the ex-Zinovievites in the USSR and Trotsky abroad.

Sometime on December 20–21 Agranov returned to Moscow to meet Stalin, perhaps on the same train with Vyshinsky and Akulov. At 7:30 P.M. on the twenty-first he entered Stalin's office for what was almost certainly a planning meeting for the trial of the "Leningrad Center." Also present were Vyshinsky and Akulov from the USSR prosecutor's office, Yagoda, and V. V. Ulrikh, the chairman of the Military Collegium of the USSR Supreme Court who would preside over the trial the following week. Kaganovich, Molotov, Ordzhonikidze, Voroshilov, and Andreev, among Stalin's closest associates at the time, attended the meeting as well.[19]

One apparent result of this meeting was an NKVD bulletin, the first to lay out in public the case against the former Zinovievites. Stalin edited this announcement before it was released to the press on December 22. It stated that Nikolaev was "a member of an underground anti-Soviet terrorist group, formed from among the participants in the former Zinovievite opposition in Leningrad." The bulletin claimed that Kotolynov had conveyed to Nikolaev orders from the terrorist group to execute Kirov. The goal of the killing was to "disorganize the leadership of the Soviet government" and "achieve a change in external policies in the spirit of the so-called Trotsky-Zinoviev platform." This accusation suggests that one of Stalin's major concerns was opposition among the Bolshevik Old Guard, especially the "Lefts," to the new policy of reconciliation with France and moderate socialist parties in Europe. Zinoviev and Trotsky were both associated with such opposition, at least in Stalin's mind. A second motive the bulletin gave for the murder was revenge against Kirov for dethroning Zinoviev from his post in Leningrad.[20]

On December 21 Mironov, deputy chief of the Economic Security Department of the NKVD and one of the senior interrogators on the Kirov case, issued an instruction on further interrogations to Genrikh Liushkov in Leningrad. It may be that this order originated from the evening meeting in Stalin's office. Be that as it may, it shows that NKVD officials were concerned with demonstrating at trial that Niko-laev had belonged to the Zinoviev opposition in the 1920s, that he was not of worker background, and that he had belonged to the "counter-revolutionary Zinovievite-Trotsky organization" in 1934. They also wished to solidify the "evidence" that Rumiantsev and Tolmazov, the most prominent former members of the Zinoviev opposition among the accused, really did belong to the presumptive 1934 counterrevolu-tionary organization.

· 70 ·

Note from Lev Grigorevich Mironov, chief of the Economic Security Department of the NKVD, to Officer Genrikh Liushkov, December 21, 1934. RGANI, f. 6, op. 13, d. 34, l. 94.

Comrade Liushkov!

I request that no later than tomorrow, the twenty-second at 8:00 P.M., you question all of the arrestees held by the Special Political Department about the following issues:

1. Do they know whether Nikolaev belonged to the opposition during the years it was active? What facts are there confirming this?

2. Do they know whether Nikolaev was a member of the counterrevo-lutionary Zinoviev-Trotskyite organization? Sokolov testifies to this; Anto-nov, Zvezdov, and others should be questioned first about this issue.

3. What do the arrestees know about Nikolaev's biography and his worker origins? It is extremely important to obtain proofs of Nikolaev's real social origins.

I request that you carry out interrogations re these points very thor-oughly, taking into account the absolutely vital significance of these is-sues.

Mironov.

21 December 1934

[Handwritten note:] It is very important that Antonov confirm this connection and membership in the counterrevolutionary organization, as he is linked to Rumiantsev, and Tolmazov is linked to the latter [Rumiantsev].

It seems likely that Nikolaev as a point of pride was still insisting on his worker origins, as the NKVD had to turn to other witnesses to rebut his claim. The great importance of the issue indicates just how threatening the fact of a worker's attack on the regime was for Bolshevik identity as the party of the proletariat. That a worker should reject the Soviet government as antiworker, as Nikolaev had done in his notes, and then attack one of the leaders, was a disaster for Soviet propaganda. A number of commentators in the weeks following the murder would point to the fact that a worker and a Communist had turned on Soviet Power to argue that the regime was both illegitimate and unstable (see Chapter 12). But Nikolaev's attack was probably not just a public relations problem for Stalin and other Soviet leaders. It may well have provoked rage precisely because it was a secret rebuke to regime leaders' own sense of themselves.

Agranov returned to Leningrad immediately after the December 21 meeting with Stalin. Yezhov may have returned with him for a two-day stay. On December 23 the NKVD notified the accused in the "Leningrad Center" case that the pretrial investigation was complete. On December 25 the USSR prosecutors' office completed the indictments in the case, and Yezhov notified Stalin as follows.[21]

· 71 ·

Yezhov note to Stalin re meeting to finalize indictments of Leonid Nikolaev et al., and Stalin's reply, December 25, 1934. RGANI, f. 6, op. 13, d. 34, l. 36.

Note to Secretary of the Central Committee I. V. Stalin.
The indictments in the case of Nikolaev are ready, they have been delivered to the secretariat of the Central Committee.
[Please] set a time to discuss them.
[signed] Yezhov, Akulov
[Stalin's handwriting] Notify other members of the Politburo.
I propose we meet tomorrow or tonight. Best would be today at 9:00 P.M.
I. Stalin.

That evening at 9:15 the members of the Politburo convened in Stalin's office together with Akulov and Vyshinsky from the prosecutor's office, Ulrikh, Yezhov, Yagoda, and Commissar of Foreign Affairs Maksim Litvinov. This was clearly the meeting Yezhov and Akulov had requested to discuss the indictments. Litvinov was probably present because the indictments charged that a foreign consul was linked to the murder, and this accusation would have consequences in the international arena. The presence of Ulrikh, chairman of the Supreme Court's Military Collegium, indicates that the meeting probably also considered procedures for the trial, which began just three days later.[22]

The draft indictments read in part as follows.

· 72 ·

Draft indictments in "Leningrad Center" case, completed December 24–25, 1934. TsA FSB RF, a.u.d. N-Sh44, t. 1, ll. 1–16.

INDICTMENTS

In the case of Nikolaev, L. V., Kotolynov, I. I., Miasnikov, N. P., Shatsky, N. N., Mandelshtam, C. O., Sokolov, G. V., Zvezdov, V. I., Yuskin, I. G., Rumiantsev, V. V., Antonov, N. S., Khanik, L. O., Tolmazov, A. I., Levin, V. S., and Sositsky, L. I., accused of crimes falling under Articles 58-8 and 58-11 of the Criminal Code of the Russian Soviet Federated Socialist Republic.

On the first of December 1934 at 4:30 P.M. in the city of Leningrad, in Smolny, Comrade Sergei Mironovich Kirov, member of the Presidium of the Central Executive Committee of the USSR, member of the Politburo of the Central Committee of the Communist Party, and Secretary of the Central and Leningrad Committees of the Communist Party, was killed by a revolver shot.

The murderer, Nikolaev, Leonid Vasilevich, age thirty, office worker, excluded in March 1934 from the ranks of the Communist Party for breach of party discipline, but later restored to the rights of a party member in view of his formal statement of repentance, was detained at the scene of the crime.

The inquiry into this case has determined that Nikolaev, L. V. is a member of a counterrevolutionary terrorist underground group, formed from among the participants in the former Zinovievite anti-Soviet group in the city of Leningrad, and that the murder of Kirov was carried out by Nikolaev, L. V., at the order of the underground terrorist Leningrad Center.

FORMATION OF THE UNDERGROUND COUNTERREVOLUTIONARY
TERRORIST GROUP IN LENINGRAD

The inquiry has determined that, in spite of the capitulation of the former Zinovievite anti-Soviet group, the underground work of the most active participants of this bloc did not cease and continued up until the most recent period.

This work became especially active in 1933–1934, when an underground terrorist anti-Soviet group headed by the so-called Leningrad Center was formed from among the former participants in the Zinovievite group.

With regard to the establishment and organizational formation of this group the accused Zvezdov testified that:

" . . . the organizational formation of our group occurred gradually, and the role of primary organizers was played by Rumiantsev, Vladimir and Kotolynov, Ivan. . . ."

The accused Sokolov, G. V. in his depositions of December 7, 9, and 12 likewise confirmed these assertions, emphasizing that:

" . . . beginning in October 1934, the persons belonging to this group began to activate their connections, to establish among themselves closer ties. . . . the group united on the basis of the old Zinovievite platform. . . ."

The accused Khanik, L. O. gave an even more complete picture of the organization of this counterrevolutionary underground terrorist group in his depositions, which stated that he:

". . . . was truly a member of this group, organized [. . .] on the basis of the former Trotsky-Zinovievite bloc. . . ."

As established by the inquiry, at the head of this group stood the underground terrorist Leningrad Center, at the head of which stood Kotolynov, Shatsky, Rumiantsev, Mandelshtam, Miasnikov, Levin, Sositsky, and Nikolaev—all former members of the Zinovievite opposition.

[The indictment here quotes testimony of Rumiantsev, Miasnikov, Khanik, and Mandelshtam about the formation of the "center" in Leningrad—Rumiantsev, however, did not use the specific term "Leningrad Center."]

The murderer of Comrade Kirov, L. V. Nikolaev, belonged to this same underground anti-Soviet terrorist group, the Leningrad Center.

The accused Zvezdov testified as follows about the participation of the accused Nikolaev in this group.

" . . . He /Nikolaev, Leonid/ was connected with us for an extended period of time, beginning in 1924. He worked at one time under the direct supervision of Kotolynov, when the latter was secretary of the Vyborg Ward committee of the Komsomol. Nikolaev was indoctrinated (*vospitan*) by us; he was nourished on the ideological juices of our group and undoubtedly took in all of the experience of our factional struggle against the party and the party leadership.

"It should also be noted that Nikolaev belonged to that category of reserved people who are, however, ready for decisive actions. . . ."

Among the former Zinovievites, Sokolov, Antonov, Kotolynov, Khanik, Yuskin, and Shatsky likewise testified to the participation of Nikolaev in the underground anti-Soviet group.

Nikolaev, L. V. himself, in his testimony of December 13, attested that he belonged to the group of former oppositionists consisting of Kotolynov, Shatsky, Yuskin and others, which carried out counterrevolutionary work. [. . .]

GOALS AND METHODS OF THE COUNTERREVOLUTIONARY UNDERGROUND TERRORIST GROUP

The pretrial inquiry has established that the core task of the underground anti-Soviet terrorist group was the striving to disorganize the leadership of the Soviet government by means of terrorist acts directed against the most important leaders of Soviet Power, and to achieve by those means change in current policies along the lines of the so-called Zinoviev-Trotskyite platform.

Having lost all hope for the support of the masses, and being themselves a closed and politically isolated anti-Soviet group, the participants took the road of direct terror.

The accused Khanik, one of the active members of this group, describing its "political-ideological" formation, recognized that it flowed from:

"the platform of the Trotsky-Zinovievite bloc [calling for] the subversion of the authority of the present party leadership and replacement of that leadership with the leaders of our organization—Zinoviev, Kamenev, and others. . . ."

The accused Khanik also testified that:

" . . . The leaders of our organization constantly affirmed that all our problems were the responsibility of the present leadership of the party, Comrades Stalin, Molotov, Kaganovich, and Kirov. In connection with this, the leaders of our organization inculcated in us, especially in the so-called youth, the belief that difficulties would continue in the country / achievements were discounted/ until such time as real leaders headed the party. It was these counterrevolutionary principles and convictions, that made possible the terrorist act committed against Comrade Kirov by Leonid Nikolaev, a member of our organization. . . ."

The accused Rumiantsev, himself "the strongest advocate of terrorist methods of action" according to the testimony of the accused Tolmazov, characterizes the mood reigning in this group in analogous fashion.

The accused Rumiantsev confessed that:

"In such a hardened atmosphere of sharp hatred of the leadership of the Communist Party attitudes of a terrorist type could not fail to grow. . . ."

" . . . the direct result of such attitudes," the accused Tolmazov testified, "was Nikolaev, Leonid's shot at Kirov . . . "

The accused Nikolaev, L. V. gave exhaustive testimony with regard to the terrorist methods of struggle mastered by this underground anti-Soviet organization.

" . . . we could not expect any change in the party leadership by means of intraparty democracy. We concluded that that route was closed off. Thus there remained to us one road—the road of terrorist acts.

When I shot at Kirov, I judged thus: our shot would be a signal for attacks against the Communist Party and Soviet Power inside the country. . . ."

Without confidence in the development of such attacks "inside the country," however, the said group placed its bets on help "from outside"—on armed intervention and help from several foreign states.

The hope for intervention, as the sole means of overturning Soviet Power, was characteristic of the views of Nikolaev himself, who did not hide this from the persons closest to him.

Thus, Nikolaev, Pyotr, the brother of Nikolaev, Leonid, questioned as a witness in the present case, testified:

" . . . Leonid told me also that it was possible to overturn Soviet Power only by way of an attack by foreign capitalist states, and that if he were abroad, he would do everything to aid any capitalist state that attacked the Soviet Union in order to overturn Soviet Power."

[The indictment then cites the testimony of Leonid's brother-in-law Kulisher, to the same effect.]

The inquiry has established that accused Nikolaev, by agreement with the accused Kotolynov, a member of the Leningrad Center, visited several times the Latvian consul in Leningrad G. I. Bissenieks, with whom he conducted negotiations about possible forms of aid to this group [the "Leningrad Center"] and to whom Nikolaev gave information about several questions of interest to the consul [there follows an extensive excerpt from Nikolaev's December 20 testimony about his supposed meetings with Bissenieks, including the claim that the consul had promised to put him in touch with Trotsky.]

Thus, the goals and methods of struggle of this counterrevolutionary terrorist group in Leningrad correspond fully to the goals and methods of those open enemies of the people, the émigré White Guard landlord capitalist organizations the Russian Military Union (*Rossiiskii obshchevoinskii soiuz*) and the Brotherhood of Russian Truth (*Bratstvo Russkoi pravdy*)—the Denikinists—which openly advocate terror and systematically infiltrate their agents into Soviet territory with the aim of organizing and carrying out terrorist acts against the representatives of Soviet Power, and which effected the murders of Comrade Vorovsky, V. V. and Comrade Voikov, P. L.

PREPARATIONS FOR THE MURDER OF COMRADE KIROV

In the process of the inquiry it has been established that there were two terrorist centers active in Leningrad in this period. One of them was headed by member of the Leningrad Center Kotolynov, and included Nikolaev, Zvezdov, Antonov, Sokolov, and Yuskin.

The other group, according to the words of Nikolaev himself, acted under the leadership of Shatsky, N. N.

[. . .]

The accused Kotolynov, who knew Nikolaev intimately since 1922 in connection with their work in the Vyborg Ward, and who became especially close to Nikolaev in recent years in the fall of 1934, directly put the question of assassinating Comrade Kirov at one of their meetings.

This is how the accused Nikolaev himself describes the meeting:

" . . . This was in the middle of September after the meeting with Shatsky in August 1934. Kotolynov talked with me about the work of the counterrevolutionary group of Zinovievites. He referred to my August meeting with Shatsky and proposed that we begin work. . . . From this conversation Kotolynov could have concluded that I was prepared to carry out the most extreme actions, including the execution of terrorist acts. At the following meeting, which took place that same September in the building of the Institute, Kotolynov talked of terror. Kotolynov asked me if I was prepared to carry out a terrorist act against Kirov. I answered that I was ready to take upon myself the direct execution of the act. . . . "

[. . .]

Nikolaev himself has admitted that the accused Kotolynov took a direct part in working out a plan for the attempt on Comrade Kirov's life.

This plan, dated November 1 of this year, found on Nikolaev's person at the time of his detention, and attached to the case file as an item of material evidence, was worked out down to the smallest details, even providing for difficulties and obstacles that might be met with in the course of its fulfillment.

Speaking of the role of his collaborators in the preparation of the murder of Comrade Kirov, the accused Nikolaev deposed that:

" . . . Kotolynov, having worked out directly with me the technique for accomplishing the act, approved these techniques, [and] specially checked how accurately I could shoot; he was my direct supervisor in the accomplishment of the act. Sokolov clarified how appropriate this or that location on Kirov's usual travel routes was, thus making my own work easier.

[. . .] Yuskin was informed of the preparation of the attack on Kirov; he worked out with me the variant of an attack in Smolny.

"Zvezdov and Antonov knew of preparations for the attack. They were connected directly to Kotolynov, from whom I know that they were used to collect information about Smolny."

[. . .]

The accused Nikolaev over a period of several months /August–November 1934/ "wore out," as he put it, the Nagan revolver earmarked for the murder of Comrade Kirov, systematically practicing his aim. At the same time the accused Nikolaev L. made preparations for going underground in connection with which he prepared forms with the stamps of various government institutions. Here it is worth noting that with the aim of hiding clues to the crime and his collaborators, and also with the aim of masking the true motives for the murder of Comrade Kirov, the accused Nikolaev L. V. prepared a number of documents /a diary, petitions to various institutions, and so on/ in which he tried to represent his crime as an act of personal despair and dissatisfaction due to his supposedly difficult material situation, and as an act of protest against "a backlog of unfair attitudes on the part of specific government persons towards a living human being."

The accused Nikolaev L. himself admitted the falsehood and artificiality of such a version of events, explaining that he created this version with the previous agreement of members of the terrorist group, who decided to present murder of Comrade Kirov as an individual act, and in this fashion to hide the real motives of this crime.

[. . .]

This matter finds its confirmation in the fact, as the inquiry proved in exhaustive fashion, that the accused Nikolaev, L. decisively and systematically rejected all offers to set him up with a job, referring to the poor state of his health and the necessity of furthering his education, and to various other circumstances supposedly standing in the way of his taking a new position.

By means of the depositions of various persons questioned as witnesses in this case, including the mother of the accused Nikolaev, M. T. Nikolaeva, and his wife, Draule, Milda, the inquiry has established that the accused Nikolaev did not experience material deprivations during this period of time, just as his family did not experience deprivation. The facts that Nikolaev had a well-furnished three-room apartment and furthermore rented a dacha from a private owner at the Sestroretsk resort indicate the absence of any kind of material difficulties on the part of the accused Nikolaev L. One can also judge Nikolaev's material situation and means based on his own testimony, cited above, that he received a substantial sum of money from the Latvian consul G. I. Bissenieks.

[. . .]

INDICTMENTS

Analyzing the evidence above, the inquiry considers it established that:

1. In the period 1933–1934 in Leningrad an underground terrorist group setting itself the goals of disorganizing the leadership of the Soviet government by means of terrorist acts directed against the leaders of Soviet Power, and of changing by this means present policies in line with the so-called Zinoviev-Trotskyite platform, was organized [. . .] from among the former participants in the Zinovievite anti-Soviet group.

2. Members of this underground counterrevolutionary terrorist group included the following persons accused in the present case: Nikolaev, L. V., Kotolynov, I. I., Miasnikov, N. P., Shatsky, N. N., Mandelshtam, S. O., Sokolov, G. V., Zvezdov, V. I., Yuskin, I. G., Rumiantsev, V. V., Antonov, N. S., Khanik, A. O. [*sic*—L. O.], Tolmazov, A. K., Levin, V. S., and Sositsky, L. I.

3. That this underground counterrevolutionary group was led by an illegal terrorist Leningrad Center consisting of the accused Kotolynov, I. I., Shatsky, N. N., Rumiantsev, V. V., Mandelshtam, S. O., Miasnikov, N. P., Levin, V. S., Sositsky, L. I., and Nikolaev, L.;

4. That the counterrevolutionary terrorist Leningrad Center, based on its criminal goals given above, and also inspired by motives of revenge against Comrade S. M. Kirov [. . .] who smashed the Leningrad group of former Zinovievites ideologically and politically, worked out the plan for and organized the murder of Comrade S. M. Kirov, which was carried out on December 1 of this year by Nikolaev, L. V.

The persons accused in the present case testified in summary as follows with regard to the charges against them:

1. Nikolaev, L.—confessed himself guilty in full and gave the evidence presented above;

2. Kotolynov—confessed that he was guilty of belonging to an underground counterrevolutionary group, formed from among former participants in the Zinovievite anti-Soviet group, and of being one of the group's leaders. While denying his direct participation in the murder of Comrade S. M. Kirov, the accused Kotolynov recognized that as an active member and leader of this group he bore responsibility for this crime;

3. Shatsky—did not confess guilt, but is implicated by the depositions of Nikolaev, Kotolynov, Rumiantsev, Mandelshtam, and others;

4. Sokolov—confessed that he was guilty of belonging to an underground counterrevolutionary group, but denied his direct participation in Nikolaev's preparations for the murder of Comrade Kirov;

5. Zvezdov—confessed himself guilty in full;

6. Yuskin—while denying his membership in the group described above, confessed that he knew [beforehand] of the premeditated murder of Comrade Kirov;

7. Antonov—confessed himself guilty in full;

8. Rumiantsev—confessed only to being guilty of belonging to an underground group of former Zinovievites;

9. Mandelshstam—confessed himself guilty of belonging to said group, and of being a member of the Leningrad Center, but denied knowledge of this group's terrorist methods of action;

10. Tolmazov—confessed himself guilty of belonging to the group described above;

11. Levin—confessed himself guilty of being one of the leaders of the Leningrad underground group of former Zinovievites;

12. Khanik and

13. Miasnikov—confessed themselves guilty only of belonging to an underground group of former Zinovievites;

14. Sositsky—confessed himself guilty of belonging to the Leningrad Center and of knowledge of the terrorist moods of members of the underground anti-Soviet group of former Zinovievites.

On the basis of the above it is charged that Nikolaev and the others [there follows a list of all fourteen men with summary biographical data], as members of an underground counterrevolutionary terrorist group in the city of Leningrad, organized and planned the murder of Comrade S. M. Kirov, which was carried out on December 1, 1934, that is that they committed crimes falling under Articles 58–8 and 58–11 of the Criminal Code of the Russian Soviet Federated Socialist Republic.

Based on the above, and in accordance with the decrees of the Central Executive Committee of the USSR dated July 10 and December 1, 1934, all of the persons listed above are to be tried by the Military Collegium of the Supreme Court of the USSR.

These indictments were prepared in the city of Leningrad, December 25, 1934.

Assistant Prosecutor of the USSR A. Vyshinsky

Investigator for High Priority Cases [. . .] L. Sheinin

Attested—Chief Prosecutor of the USSR I. Akulov.

One of the important reasons that Stalin and the prosecutors opted for a secret hearing, as opposed to a public show trial, is that the case for Zinovievite involvement in terrorist activity was so weak. Many of the ex-oppositionists had confessed to anti-Stalin conversations and continued meetings with their former comrades, and some had even agreed to the NKVD's formula that such contacts were tantamount to the formation of Moscow and Leningrad "Centers." The majority, perhaps convinced by interrogators that Nikolaev really was a former Zinovievite, had admitted that "anti-Soviet moods" among the ex-oppositionists could have helped inspire the attack. But apart from Nikolaev's own confessions, there was scant evidence that any of the former oppositionists were involved in planning the murder or any other "terrorist acts." Late in the course of the investigation (December 17 and after), Antonov, Zvezdov, and Sokolov all claimed that they had heard in general that the organization of ex-Zinovievites was planning terrorist action against the Soviet leadership (Antonov and Zvezdov said that Kotolynov had told them). This was as far as any of the ex-Zinovievites the NKVD placed in the "Leningrad Center" went in confessing terrorist activities. The indictments' assertions that Antonov and Zvezdov had "confessed themselves guilty in full" were deceptive.[23]

Nor was the case for Zinovievite connections with the Latvian consul any stronger. It depended almost entirely on Nikolaev's evidence. Nikolaev's brother Pyotr and brother-in-law Roman Kulisher eventually signed depositions claiming that Leonid hoped for a foreign capitalist attack on the USSR, and Milda remembered him looking for her father's passport. But none of the family members claimed direct knowledge of any visit by Nikolaev to the Latvian consul. Nor did the members of the putative "Leningrad Center," aside from Nikolaev, testify about efforts to contact the Latvian consul or Trotsky.[24]

The indictments identified every one of the accused as "student," "white-collar employee" (*sluzhashchii*), or, in Shatsky's case, "engineer." They thus obscured the fact that every one of the defendants came from solid Leningrad working-class backgrounds (in unpublished documents of the investigation most were identified as "workers"). All were genuine veterans of the proletarian revolutionary movement of 1917. But as Sheila Fitzpatrick has pointed out, Soviet use of class labels in the 1920s and 1930s was flexible and imprecise. Although authorities, co-workers, and neighbors often assigned "class" designations based on the occupations of a person's parents, they might also use that person's own present occupation or occupation in 1917 as the criterion. The prosecutors chose in the case of the "Leningrad Center" to use present occupations to determine the "class" of the accused, so as to conceal their proletarian origins.[25]

The indictments divided the accused into two groups—eight members of the "Leningrad Center," who had supposedly taken a leading role in organizing counterrevolutionary activity, and six members of a supposedly larger counterrevolutionary organization who followed orders from "the Center." The "Leningrad Center" included Kotolynov, Shatsky, Rumiantsev, Mandelshtam, Miasnikov, Levin, Sositsky, and Nikolaev. The remaining, lower-ranking, members of the supposed organization were Yuskin, Sokolov, Antonov, Zvezdov, Tolmazov, and Khanik. These latter were the suspects who had cooperated most with the investigators. Antonov, Sokolov, Zvezdov, Tolmazov, and Khanik gave the names of many-ex-Zinovievites who were still in contact with on another, they provided detailed testimony on the supposed structure of the "counterrevolutionary organization," and they had all at one point or another attested to "terrorist moods" among the former oppositionists. Yuskin testified that he knew Nikolaev was planning to attack Kirov beforehand, although he gave no evidence at all about any of the actual ex-Zinovievites.

The division of the accused into two groups suggests that the trial planners may have considered giving less harsh sentences to the "followers," for example, ten years of hard labor as opposed to death. In nationally publicized Soviet show trials from 1928 to 1938 it was common to have at least one or two defendants who got off "easy." The division also hints at the possibility that investigators promised lighter sentences to the "followers" in exchange for testimony incriminating the "leaders."

Soviet newspapers published the indictments on December 27, 1934. *Pravda* and *Leningradskaia pravda* followed the wording of the December 25 indictments slavishly. The single difference between the unpublished and published versions was that the newspapers did not reveal which foreign consul in Leningrad was accused of aiding Nikolaev. Presumably the Soviet government ordered this omission to avoid the international complications that might arise if the Latvians demanded public release of the very thin evidence against their consul.

As the trial neared several of the accused took what actions they could to head off a death sentence. On December 21 Lev Khanik wrote a petition to the Leningrad NKVD Special Political Department, begging for his life so that he could serve the party.[26] At his meetings with prosecutors Vyshinsky, Akulov, and Sheinin on December 19, Mandelshtam recanted an earlier confession that he belonged to a counterrevolutionary Zinovievite organization. Presumably he hoped that the prosecutors would give him a fairer hearing than the NKVD.[27] Ivan Kotolynov wrote an appeal to the USSR prosecutor on December 27, after viewing the indictments. Kotolynov now suspected that the investigators had lied when they told him that Nikolaev had belonged to the Zinovievite opposition. With these lies they had tricked him into his partial confessions of responsibility for the murder.

· 73 ·

Excerpt from Ivan Kotolynov's statement to the USSR prosecutor's office, December 27, 1934. RGANI, f. 6, op. 13, d. 24, ll. 24–32 (late April 1956 KGB report to Molotov commission).

Now and throughout the investigation I have insisted that I was entirely ignorant of Nikolaev's political attitudes and political views. Nor did I know whether he had belonged to the Zinovievite opposition or not, much less whether he has recently belonged to the group of former Zinovievite oppositionists.

But, trusting in the assurances of the investigation that Nikolaev belonged to the Zinovievite opposition and that as an employee of Istmol and the bureau of the Fellowship of Komsomol Militants, where he constantly moved among former oppositionists and was under their strong influence, I stated that the political responsibility for Nikolaev's action lay with the illegal group of the former Zinovievite opposition, within which there was cultivated a mood of resentful hostility towards the party leadership and which, objectively speaking, could have given birth to terrorist attitudes among hotheads. . . .

. . . As for Nikolaev's testimony about me, this is all lies, slander, or the delirium of an insane person.

Vladimir Rumiantsev, one of the prime targets of the NKVD, was particularly active in trying to defend himself. He wrote a letter to Stalin on December 19, and one to chief USSR prosecutor Akulov on December 27. The first appeal (to Stalin) read in part as follows.

· 74 ·

Vladimir Rumiantsev letter to Stalin, December 19, 1934. RGANI, f. 6, op. 13, d. 1, ll. 112–113.

Yesterday I was notified of the decision of the Committee on Party Control to exclude me from the ranks of the Communist Party as a counterrevolutionary. I recognize this decision as completely correct, as I did not prove myself worthy of the party's trust after I rejoined following my struggle against it. I did not entirely break my criminal ties with the Zinovievite counterrevolutionary organization. I knew their attitudes (*nastroeniia*) and I did not denounce them to the party. Thus I was directly connected to these undefeated remnants of the class enemy, who took the road of fascism and fascist terror. But I did not preach or share terrorist views. I did not sink to such filthy and monstrous treachery against the working class and against my party, which nurtured me and in which I passed the whole of my conscious political life from age sixteen onward. One would have to be a fanatic enemy with a bestial hate for Soviet Power [to sink to that level]. I never became such an enemy. In 1929 I broke all of my old ties with the leaders of the center /Zinoviev, Kamenev, Bakaev, Yevdokimov, Gertik, Zalutsky, Naumov, Fyodorov/, they called on me, they sought me, but I deliberately chose not to respond to their overtures. In Leningrad I broke off my connections with the majority of the members of the counterrevolutionary organization, but not with all of them. My crimes are great and I do not minimize them. I bear full political and moral responsibility for the evil crime committed by Nikolaev, whom I did not know personally, but who according to the investigators was a member of the Zinovievite counterrevolutionary organization. I ask you, Comrade Stalin, to help me break free of the counterrevolutionary swamp into which Zinoviev dragged me. I took the first step out of that swamp when I returned to the party. I have worked with especially great diligence at the Vyborg Ward—sponsored House of Culture, at the Magnitogorsk construction site [in the Urals where the Soviets were building a city and a giant steel manufacturing complex from scratch], and for three and a half years at the Vyborg soviet. Comrades Smorodin and Baranov can tell you about it. I shall curse for the rest of my life that horrible day when I took the road of struggle against the party, the worst day of my life. I ask you to grant me the possibility of expiating my shameful, base counterrevolutionary crimes as a Soviet citizen at any of the most difficult posts.

December 19, 1934, former member of the Communist Party from 1920 V. Rumiantsev.

On December 27, after NKVD officers showed him the charges in the case, Rumiantsev petitioned the prosecutor to call specific witnesses in his defense.

· 75 ·

Petition of Vladimir Rumiantsev to USSR Prosecutor Akulov, December 27, 1934. RGANI, f. 6, op. 13, d. 1, ll. 114–116.

To the Prosecutor of the USSR Comrade Akulov
From former member of the Communist Party [. . .] Rumiantsev, V. V.
Declaration
    1. I have been notified by Comrade Mironov that I am charged under Article 58-8 and 58-11 of the Criminal Code with being one of the leaders

of a counterrevolutionary organization in Leningrad that undertook terrorist action. This is a direct and fatal error. It is true that up until 1929 I was one of the "nonreturners," [but] I broke with them in connection with Kamenev's talks with Bukharin during the party purge of 1929. I request that you check this through the comrade chairman of the control commission Comrade Nulinov [. . .] and Yulina, former secretary of the party collegium. [. . .].

2. I was not a member of the Fellowship of Komsomol Militants and I did not visit their premises even once. I knew of the unhealthy attitude and the grouping together of former oppositionist cadres under Khanik from Comrade Panov, now chairman of that Fellowship, who knows my point of view [supporting] his [Khanik's] firing and immediate handover to the GPU. This [view] was stated [by me] in the presence of many comrades at Smolny as early as July or August.

3. Upon my return to the party I did not open Zinoviev's letter, and I showed it to the secretary of the ward committee Comrade Kairova, the prosecutor Kozlov, GPU officer Galin, chairman of the Soviet Baranov (and many others). [. . .]

4. I ask that you summon me to give the names of those who can attest to my behavior in 1929.

5. It is true that I had three to four meetings with Zinovievites in the last five years, which I revealed in good faith to the investigation. On the basis of these meeting I came to the firm conclusion that the Zinovievites as an organization do exist. I did not share their views, I did not propagate those views, I did not receive or carry out orders from them. This I say frankly and honestly. I have worked in the [Vyborg] soviet since 1931, thousands of people know me, many Communists with whom I became friendly [. . .] know me. [. . .] I ask that you summon Comrade Yeremeev, of the Administrative Department of the Vyborg soviet, deputy chairman of the Regional Court Khodyrev. [. . .] On the question of the job Antonov was given, I ask that you question Nikolaev, Ivan, former chief of the Cadres Department of the soviet [. . .] who selected him for the ward committee [job] himself. [. . .] in connection with [his vacillations during the period of the opposition struggle] I did not recommend hiring him.

6. At the interrogations I testified that I did not know Nikolaev, no one questioned me about terror, I did not preach terror, and I am neither insane nor an enemy of Soviet Power, which nurtured me and educated me.

7. Antonov came to me from Fadeev, I request that you question him [Fadeev] about the list of old Komsomol members made at the order of ward committee Komsomol secretary Vrublyovsky, whom I also request that you summon. This was done [. . .] because the old list of members for the Fellowship of Komsomol Militants had been lost by Panov, now chairman of the Fellowship.

8. I gave 150 rubles to Tsarkov as [he was] a former secretary of the former ward committee of the Komsomol and a [veteran] Red Guardsman who had discussed [finding] work with the comrade deputy secretary of the ward committee and Dolotov. This was done as a regular practice and with the approval of the chairman of the soviet Baranov.

V. Rumiantsev

27 December

Like most of the other accused in the case, Rumiantsev sought a way out of "the fatal mistake" by confessing to limited relations with the former opposition, but denying charges of terrorism. Probably he hoped that the authorities would treat his case like those of other oppositionists arrested by the security police or disciplined by the party control organs in the early 1930s, such as Mikhail Riutin, N. B. Eismont, or A. V. Tolmachev. The latter three were sentenced to various prison terms for their "counterrevolutionary activity" (advocating removal of Stalin from leadership of the party). Other party officials suspected of anti-Stalin attitudes got off with expulsion from the party or lesser disciplinary measures following ritual confessions of error. J. Arch Getty has argued that rituals of confession before leading party organs functioned to sustain the unity of the Communist elite.[28] Rumiantsev and others among the accused in the trial of the "Leningrad Center" probably hoped that if they could rebut the charges of actual terrorism, and make the ritual confessions of "mistakes" and "incorrect attitudes," they would be allowed to live. Carrying out the ritual would fulfill their duty to the party. Stalin, however, was determined to smear former party oppositionists with charges of terrorism. On December 26, at a final pretrial meeting in Moscow, Stalin ordered Ulrikh to finish the trial in two days and execute all of the defendants. When Ulrikh left for Leningrad, he already had multiple copies of the sentences in hand for signature by the other two members of the Military Collegium.[29] Neither confessions nor denials were going to save any of the accused.

The Trial

The trial of Nikolaev and his supposed co-conspirators was held in camera in Leningrad beginning at 2:20 P.M. on December 28, 1934. It ran all night, concluding at 5:45 on the morning of December 29. The presiding judges of the Military Collegium were Ulrikh, Matulevich, and Goriachev. Vyshinsky led the prosecution. Yakov Agranov telephoned regular bulletins on the trial's progress to Yagoda in Moscow, and it seems likely that Stalin and Yezhov also read these. Besides the texts of these bulletins, evidence on the trial consists of archival transcripts of the proceedings and interviews conducted by Soviet authorities in 1956 with Matulevich, Goriachev, and a number of others present in the courtroom.

In accordance with the provisions of the "Law of December 1," the accused had no defense lawyers and no right of appeal. But in camera the conduct of the trial violated even that law. According to a 1956 report by the USSR prosecutor's office, no one notified the accused of their rights to question one another, call witnesses, add new evidence to their case files, challenge the court's jurisdiction, or speak in their own defense. The indictments were not read in court. The defendants were brought into the courtroom for questioning individually or in small groups, so that they could not hear or question one another's testimony. This was particularly important to protect Nikolaev's "evidence," for the assassin routinely contradicted himself and embellished previous testimony with new and fantastic details. Other defendants he implicated in the killing could have made use of such inconsistencies in their own defense.[30]

At least one of the defendants attempted to assert his right to question witnesses (in this case the other accused prisoners). At the opening of the court session, Mandelshtam asked about "procedures for questioning." Ulrikh replied, "What questions? There are no questions. The court establishes procedures, and it will implement those procedures. The Chairman of the Court regulates the procedures, not the accused."[31]

The precautions taken to ensure a definitive outcome to the trial proved wise. In 1956 interviews, judges Matulevich and Goriachev, court secretary Batner, and Ulrikh's common-law wife, who attended the trial, all asserted that Nikolaev, upon first facing the Collegium, recanted his previous testimony and declared that he had acted alone. Then, under intense questioning by Ulrikh, he reversed himself again, and confirmed his depositions about a plot by the "Leningrad Center" to murder Kirov.[32]

Neither Agranov's first bulletin to Yagoda nor the trial transcript record this embarrassing moment. Agranov's earliest communication was clearly intended to reassure Yagoda that all was going smoothly. "All of the accused [. . .] are behaving calmly," it read. Nikolaev confirmed to the court that he had linked up with the Latvian consul, and that Shatsky and Kotolynov had helped him to plan the attack on Kirov. He also claimed that Antonov knew of his visits to the Latvian consul. Finally, according to Agranov, he "revealed" the existence of a trunk full of his notes which the NKVD, unbeknownst to him, had already found in a storage space at his mother's apartment.[33]

In reality, Nikolaev's testimony did not go as smoothly as Agranov told Yagoda. The witness was erratic. He went into a long digression about the "military vehicle" that had scared him away from the Latvian consulate, an artifact of his December 5 and 6 interrogations. Whereas Nikolaev had stated on December 5 that he saw the car on his second visit to the consul, now he claimed that he had seen it on his fourth visit. Ulrikh cut him off with "What's the point of this 'military vehicle' here?" Nikolaev, however, rambled on, claiming that he had thought that the car might belong to the "Military Tribunal" itself—a weird insertion of Ulrikh's own court into testimony regarding a period months before the trial. "What's the point of the Military Tribunal here?" Ulrikh snapped.[34]

There were other problems with Nikolaev's testimony about the Latvian consul, a subject on which the NKVD had apparently failed to tutor him enough. When Ulrikh asked Nikolaev whom he wanted to contact through the consul, Nikolaev replied, "Unfortunately, I cannot explain that." Ulrikh prompted "Were you thinking of particular newspapers?" Then he asked, "You must know about conditions in Riga [. . .] you must be oriented about what parties there are there, what newspapers, and so on?" Nikolaev could only reply "I didn't discuss this with the consul." Ulrikh now salvaged the situation with "The consul was supposed to decide [where to send your materials]?" "Yes, yes," Nikolaev interjected.[35]

In his first round of testimony, Nikolaev also repeated his disclaimer about his writings and earliest depositions. These, he said, concealed the fact that he'd worked with a conspiratorial group.[36]

After a ten-minute break, officers brought Antonov, Zvezdov, Yuskin, and Sokolov into the courtroom. These were all men from the "lower-ranking" group, and they had been among the most helpful of the suspects to their interrogating officers. The strategy of the trial organizers, directed at the select audience of police and party elites, was evidently to present the most cooperative witnesses first, so as to undermine later defendants who might assert their innocence. Agranov's report to Yagoda, transmitted at 7:30 P.M. on December 28, noted that Antonov pled guilty, confirming all of his depositions, that Zvezdov did the same, and that Yuskin confessed that he knew of Nikolaev's plans to murder Kirov, but did not take them seriously. Sokolov testified to being a member of a counterrevolutionary organization, and to knowing about preparations for an unspecified terrorist act.[37]

Agranov was once again glossing over or ignoring inconvenient testimony. Antonov had in fact denied specific knowledge of preparations for any terrorist attack, and declared that "Terrorist acts are against my principles." Under questioning by Ulrikh he confessed that he still bore responsibility for the murder because he had done nothing to stop it. Antonov also said that he had only met Nikolaev once since 1923, and that was in 1932. This of course would put into serious question whether the two could have worked together on any plot at all in 1934. Zvezdov denied knowledge of any terrorist plot against the Soviet leaders, declaring that he had hoped that they could be removed from their posts through political action. He claimed not to have met Nikolaev since the spring of 1934.[38]

Careful reading of Yuskin's testimony in one archival transcript reveals that although he pled guilty to all charges, he admitted no wrongdoing under examination. He denied ever belonging to any antiparty group. He asserted that "I had no idea of Nikolaev's political identity (*litso*)." Yuskin also described the conversation that led to his comment to Nikolaev, "Why Kirov? Why not go for Stalin?" According to Yuskin, after Nikolaev said that he was planning to go to Moscow to appeal for a sanatorium pass, he (Yuskin) suggested turning to Kirov in Leningrad for help. Nikolaev stated, "Kirov won't receive me. I've been trying to meet him for an entire month. It's as if he suspects I'm going to kill him." Yuskin testified that he had not taken Nikolaev's comment seriously, considering it "idle chatter" (*obyvatel'skaia briakhnia*). He replied with a joke, "Why Kirov? Why not go for Stalin?" In spite of aggressive questioning from Ulrikh, Yuskin insisted that he had had no idea Nikolaev was planning a murder. The prosecutors then brought out Nikolaev, who claimed that Yuskin had "approved" of his terror plan.[39]

Sokolov, who had been the first witness to link Nikolaev to a "counterrevolutionary" group of former Zinovievites in Leningrad (December 6), was the most cooperative of this group of defendants. He followed the NKVD script closely, incriminating Zvezdov, Antonov, Kotolynov, and Nikolaev in a terrorist conspiracy, but without giving specifics. Following his testimony, the court adjourned for one hour.[40]

The trial resumed with Kotolynov's testimony. According to Agranov's communiqués to Yagoda, Kotolynov confessed to belonging to a counterrevolutionary organization that had "cultivated terrorist moods" and so bore responsibility for the murder. Agranov omitted many details of Kotolynov's cross-examination that were troublesome for the prosecution. In fact Kotolynov stated that he was guilty only of one charge—belonging to a Zinovievite counterrevolutionary organization. This organization, he said, had no "clear goals," nor was there any division of duties among its members. He had never heard of any kind of "Leningrad Center." He did state that the leaders of the Leningrad Zinovievites were Rumiantsev, Levin, Mandelshtam, and Tolmazov. He himself was the senior member among the "youth." Kotolynov allowed that the Zinovievites could have unwittingly inspired "some hotheads" to terrorism, but denied that they planned terror or "cultivated terrorist moods."[41]

Nikolaev, present for Kotolynov's testimony, interrupted to claim that the two of them had had "anti-Stalin conversations" in September–October 1934, but Kotolynov insisted that he had not met Nikolaev in 1934 and had in fact "lost him from view" after 1924. Kotolynov noted that there were numerous contradictions in Nikolaev's testimony and declared, "I can smash these depositions into dust." After a brief exchange with Antonov, whom he admitted meeting in late October (he rejected Antonov's claim they had talked about terrorism), Kotolynov returned to the subject of Nikolaev. He announced that he was withdrawing his admission of moral and political responsibility for the murder. He had signed a deposition to that effect because he had "trusted the investigators when they said that Nikolaev was a Zinovievite," but he no longer believed this. In all likelihood Kotolynov had concluded that Nikolaev was an NKVD provocateur.[42]

Shatsky rejected all charges, even after Nikolaev testified against him. He confirmed only two encounters with Nikolaev in 1934 (not three, as the latter claimed), and he also admitted visiting Rumiantsev's apartment once. In the course of Shatsky's cross-examination, Kotolynov interjected that they had not met since 1924. Shatsky thought that their last encounter was in 1926.[43]

Tolmazov was more cooperative, pleading guilty to the charge of belonging to a counterrevolutionary organization led by Rumiantsev and Kotolynov. Rumiantsev, he asserted, had "terrorist moods." However, Tolmazov also indicated that he had met supposed members of the counterrevolutionary organization very few times. He had met Nikolaev just once and knew "nothing" of him. He had seen Kotolynov just once in 1934, at a meeting at Rumiantsev's apartment where there was discussion of possible changes in the party leadership. Antonov was a relative, but Tolmazov hadn't seen him in four to five months. He had only a nodding acquaintance with Vladimir Levin. It is hard to see how a conspiracy could have been arranged on the basis of so few meetings.[44]

Nikolai Miasnikov, the former Red Army officer working in the Leningrad soviet at the time of his arrest, pled guilty to belonging to the counterrevolutionary organization of Zinovievites. He described trips back and forth to Moscow as a courier for Zinoviev, Kamenev, Bakaev, and Gertik. Although Miasnikov confessed to the usual formula of "moral and political responsibility" for Kirov's assassination, he also denied any concrete knowledge of the plot.[45]

Lev Khanik, the former official of the Fellowship of Komsomol Militants, pled guilty to belonging to an underground Zinovievite organization from 1930 through July 1933, when he was assigned to work as a propagandist on the island of Kronstadt. At this point, he claimed, he had broken ties with the organization. According to Khanik, Rumiantsev had told him about "the center," which included Levin, Miasnikov, and Sositsky. Rumiantsev told Khanik that he hoped for another oppositional struggle like that of 1926–1928, or for other opportunities to replace the Stalinist leadership, such as a peasant rebellion or foreign invasion. The Zinovievites, Khanik claimed, also considered an alliance with "Rightists."[46]

Khanik's evidence was problematic for the prosecution in two ways. First, he denied meeting Nikolaev after 1923, even when Nikolaev testified that they had run into one another several times in Smolny in 1931–1933. Second, he claimed to have left the Zinovievite organization in the middle of 1933, which the indictments pinpointed as the time when the oppositionists increased their activity. According to Khanik, then, he had lost contact with the Zinovievites even before they supposedly began plotting terror.[47]

Just before midnight Vladimir Levin, another former Red Army officer, pled guilty to being a leader of the Zinovievite organization in Leningrad. According to Levin, after Zinoviev returned from internal exile, joined the editorial board of *Bolshevik,* and spoke at the Seventeenth Party Congress, Zinovievite hopes of "penetrating" the party revived. Levin affirmed that the Zinovievites hoped to replace Stalin and "spread provocative, counterrevolutionary, slanderous rumors against the party leadership," but he never mentioned terrorism. He also denied any acquaintance with Nikolaev.[48]

Lev Sositsky, director of the Leningrad soviet's auto repair workshop, began with a guilty plea, but like Yuskin, he then rebutted most of the charges. He hadn't met Levin, one of his supposed co-conspirators, at all in 1934, and he knew nothing about Nikolaev or his relationship to the Zinovievites. Although Sositsky confessed that he and his fellow oppositionists had "considered violent methods" against the party leadership, he refused to specify what these methods were. Anti-Stalin conversations among the Zinovievites, he admitted, "led to the evil act of Kirov's killing." But when Ulrikh interrupted to insist that "your group incited, your center supervised, Nikolaev shot, it's completely logical," Sositsky replied, "I didn't incite anyone and I never heard of anyone doing so." He went on to tell the court that he "would never have committed a terrorist act [. . .] if I heard of such a thing, I'd have denounced it immediately." In frustration Ulrikh cut him off—"That's enough already, sit down." Agranov's account of Sositsky's testimony omitted these exchanges.[49]

Next up was Rumiantsev, one of the NKVD's main targets. It was now well past midnight, and everyone in the courtroom must have been exhausted. Rumiantsev pled guilty only to being a "nonreturning" oppositionist in 1928. After he finally rejoined the party, he had maintained infrequent social contacts with Vladimir Levin, Lev Sositsky, and Moscow resident Kuklin, another former Leningrad administrator under Zinoviev. However, he had "nothing in common" politically with any of the Zinovievites after 1929. Ulrikh hounded Rumiantsev to admit that "his organization [. . .] cultivated hate in the spirit of terrorist moods," which Rumiantsev denied. Then, the pressure apparently too much, he exploded "I take full responsibility!"[50]

After Rumiantsev spoke, Miasnikov and Tolmazov denounced him as a member of the "Leningrad Center." Levin denied that any "Leningrad Center" existed, but stated that "I maintained ties with Miasnikov, and he with Rumiantsev." It seems possible that the NKVD used Levin's, Miasnikov's, and Tolmazov's preexisting suspicions of Rumiantsev to motivate their denunciations. Rumiantsev had been a "nonreturner" in 1928, while they had not. Moreover, he had since taken a relatively senior post in the Leningrad city government. In early 1932 Rumiantsev was in contact with a GPU "resident," an officer who collected information from informers, and in 1933 he had avoided arrest and negotiated a promotion directly with Kirov. Levin, Miasnikov, and Tolmazov may have believed him to be an informer, and not without justification.[51]

The final defendant cross-examined by the court was Mandelshtam, arrested in Moscow on December 13. He admitted to being a member of the "Leningrad Center" and confessed that his "counterrevolutionary, antiparty activity" as a Zinoviev supporter could have fostered "terroristic, counterrevolutionary fascist moods" in those around him. However he "categorically" denied participation in or planning of terrorist activities. He reaffirmed that he had never met Nikolaev before, and he refused to incriminate anyone as leader of the "Center." Until the interrogators told him, he had not known that Kotolynov was a "Center" member.[52]

Following Mandelshtam's testimony, Ulrikh called a brief recess before the accused made their final statements.

When the judges returned, the defendants spoke in the same order as they had given evidence. First was Nikolaev, who pled for mercy based on the claim that the Zinovievites had brainwashed him and on his cooperation with the interrogators. Agranov's summary of Nikolaev's last words to the court, sent to Yagoda the following afternoon, corresponds with the trial transcript.

· 76 ·

Yakov Agranov's summary of Nikolaev's last words to the court, December 29, 1934. TsA FSB RF, a.u.d. N-Sh44, t. 34, ll. 25–32.

Nikolaev stated that in the 28 days that had passed since the crime he committed, he had done everything possible to reveal to the investigators the whole truth about the counterrevolutionary organization, which had fought against the party and Soviet Power and sanctioned the terrorist act that he had carried out against Comrade Kirov. He asserted further that all of his counterrevolutionary activity was the consequence of the influence of the "chiefs" of the Zinovievite opposition, including Kotolynov. [. . .] They had a great influence on him, they fed him on all kinds of oppositional materials, and they slandered the party leadership. He resorted to terror because the former Zinovievite opposition once more decided to try its strength in a new struggle against the party: they decided to use all of the difficulties the country had experienced due to its growth, to create material on the basis of which they could mobilize forces inside the party to battle for the return of Zinoviev and Kamenev to the party leadership.

Nikolaev once again confirmed that he had a direct order from Kotolynov to resort to a terrorist act against Comrade Kirov, as the organization aimed at the violent removal of Stalin, Kirov, and other party leaders from power. At the end of his speech Nikolaev declared that he had told the court the whole truth, and requested mercy.

The 1956 testimony of NKVD Officer Gusev, who guarded Niko-laev, sheds light on the latter's state of mind during the trial, and the nature of the police efforts to secure his cooperation.

· 77 ·

Testimony of Nikolaev's guard Gusev on Nikolaev's behavior during his trial, given to KGB in April 1956. RGANI, f. 6, op. 13, d. 2, ll. 78–107 (August 1956 KGB report to Molotov commission).

On December 28, 1934 I was sent with other servicemen of the regi-ment to guard the accused from the Nikolaev-Kotolynov group, and I was assigned to guard Nikolaev during the trial.

There was a separate room assigned to him next to the courtroom.

Besides me, there were two other NKVD officers, unknown to me, in the room; one of them was about forty years old, heavy-set [. . .] the other about 28–30 years old. Both of them were constantly conversing with the accused Nikolaev, I was forbidden to talk. My comrade from the regiment /I can't remember his name/ and I took the guard in turn every two hours.

From time to time Nikolaev was called into the courtroom, and twice he returned in tears, once in a semihysterical state, repeating as if to himself, "What have I done! What have I done! Now they'll call me a rat (*podlets*)! It's all over!" and so on.

For some reason he was convinced the whole time that he was going to get three to four years exile in Siberia. [. . .]

[. . .] the two officers present, especially the older one, constantly con-firmed him in this opinion, calmed him, imbued him with hope in a soft punishment.

Every ten to fifteen minutes [. . .] one other military serviceman un-known to me without insignia of rank came into the room; he was dealing with Nikolaev's state [of mind], he gave instructions to the other two /usu-ally in whispers or behind the door/ and also supported Nikolaev's hopes.

Antonov pled guilty to "awful crimes." Like Nikolaev he begged for clemency because the Zinovievites had led him astray. Zvezdov took a similar line, describing how the oppositionists had (presumably in the 1920s) molded his "yet unformed political psyche," making of him "a blind tool." Probably seeking favor with the judges, he tore into Ko-tolynov for his "insolent" denial that he had issued orders for terror attacks. He requested a chance to expiate his guilt.[53]

Yuskin's final words closely resembled his testimony under cross-examination. He admitted only to expressing antiparty opinions and failure to recognize Nikolaev's terrorist intent at their meetings in October. His phrase, "Why Kirov, why not go for Stalin?" he had meant ironically. At the same time, Yuskin gave thanks to the party in the following terms: "I should have just given thanks to the party for all it has given me, but my self-satisfaction, my lack of vigilance, my tongue that won't stay in its place—these created a petty self-seeking attitude (*oby-vatel'shchina*) that led to anti-Sovietism." Yuskin asked the court to spare his life.[54]

Sokolov echoed the earlier pleas, confessing guilt, expressing thanks to the party for his higher education, and requesting mercy.[55]

Kotolynov's final speech was the most carefully thought out, and next to Shatsky's, the most courageous of all the defendants' statements. He confessed that his membership in the Zinovievite opposition in the 1920s was a crime against the party, and that it could have inspired terrorists like Nikolaev. In this sense he bore responsibility for Kirov's murder. Kotolynov did not request mercy, and he made it clear that he understood that he would probably be shot. In this situation, he asserted, his final duty to the party was to tell the whole truth, and this was that "I did not participate in this murder. [...] I did not know, I did not participate, I did not organize, and I did not meet Nikolaev." He proceeded to attack Nikolaev's evidence on a number of points. Nikolaev claimed, for example, that Kotolynov had recruited him into the terrorist organization at a meeting in September 1934. But Milda Draule had testified that Nikolaev had been preparing a terrorist attack since March 1934. Moreover, Nikolaev had met Shatsky in August 1934, before he saw Kotolynov. Therefore, Kotolynov argued, it appeared that Nikolaev had been plotting an attack long before September.[56]

Kotolynov denied meeting Nikolaev in mid-September 1934 or Shatsky in August. He denied receiving 4,500 rubles from the Latvian consul via Nikolaev, and described his own poor living conditions. Using evidence that the NKVD itself had gathered to link Nikolaev with the Latvian consul, Kotolynov argued that the assassin was in fact very well-off, and asked that the court look into the sources of his money. He declared that he had never seen Yuskin or Sokolov before. Although he did know both Antonov and Zvezdov, he had never discussed murdering Kirov with them.[57]

Kotolynov followed other defendants in emphasizing that the opposition had corrupted his originally pure loyalty to the party. He insisted, however, that he had been loyal in 1933–1934: "I had no disagreements with the general line of the party. I frequently criticized Zinoviev and Kamenev."[58]

Kotolynov was trying to shift the terms of indictment to those of the late 1920s—factionalism, undermining party unity, and so on. At the same time as he rejected all charges of terrorism, he declared himself ready to accept execution to advance the party's unity. In words worthy of Koestler's *Darkness at Noon,* he declared:

> I request no mercy, I demand with great joy . . . the harshest punishment. Why? Because I will die not as a counterrevolutionary, but as a revolutionary who, gathering all his courage, repented, and completely disarmed himself, ideologically and politically.
> . . . Now the counterrevolutionary Zinovievite scum must be utterly annihilated. Whatever punishment the party and the proletarian government appoint for me, I will die with the slogan, "All hail the Leninist Party and the Leninist leadership of the magnificent chief Comrade Stalin, down with Zinoviev!" on my lips.[59]

It seems that Kotolynov may have maintained some small hope of clemency. In a passage that did not appear in some official transcripts of the trial, he thanked his interrogator Dmitriev for "frank discussion" and for showing him "his future possibilities."[60] Kotolynov's interrogators had evidently persuaded him that honesty and full recognition that his past oppositional record was criminal still might win mercy from the court.

Shatsky flatly rejected every charge.[61]

The remaining seven defendants, Tolmazov, Miasnikov, Levin, Sositsky, Khanik, and Rumiantsev all made similar pleas, denouncing Zinoviev and Kamenev for leading them astray, and confessing in abstract terms to criminal support of counterrevolutionary views. Mandelshtam demanded that the court "shoot us down to the last man"; all of the others pled for mercy. Khanik rambled on so long about Zinoviev and Kamenev "hoodwinking" party youth that Ulrikh cut him off with "What does that have to do with anything now?" Rumiantsev thanked Agranov, Mironov, and Liushkov "who helped me break free of the counterrevolutionary swamp." Sositsky and Khanik expressed gratitude to their interrogators in similar terms.[62]

But even in these last pathetic petitions there were hints that the indictments and supporting evidence were false. Tolmazov and Miasnikov disavowed knowledge of any terrorist plot, as did Rumiantsev.

The latter said, "believe me, if I knew that Kotolynov was organizing the murder, I myself would have put a bullet in him, and turned him over to the OGPU. [. . .]" Rumiantsev further averred that he did not know Nikolaev, Yuskin, or Sokolov. Mandelshtam confirmed Rumiantsev's testimony "as to the facts," suggesting that he too had not belonged to any terrorist group. "I am not a counterrevolutionary," he stated, "but I have slid into an abyss." The implications of the word "abyss" were not clear. Did Mandelshtam mean that his Zinovievite views had led him into the abyss? If so, was that the fault of Zinoviev, or of the Stalinists who persecuted dissenters? In a passage that was not reproduced in some transcripts, Mandelshtam discussed his December 19 confession, retracted later the same day, that he belonged to a counterrevolutionary terrorist group. "On December 19," he stated, "I was in such a condition that I would have signed anything." The implication would seem to be that he had been tortured.[63]

It was 2:30 A.M. on December 29 when the court adjourned, to ratify sentences that had been decided days before. It is possible to imagine the judges and prosecutors getting in a nap over the next three hours. Perhaps some of the accused did so too—Shatsky was certainly resigned to his fate, and maybe too Kotolynov, who had declared to the court, "for ten days I have been in such a tense state that death is not that frightening to me."

In his final plea Mandelshtam had requested permission to write a letter to the party leaders. Part of this letter was found in his case file in 1956. It began:

· 78 ·

Fragment of Mandelshtam's letter to Stalin, December 29, 1934. RGANI, f. 6, op. 13, d. 24, ll. 51–68.

———————————

Dear Yosif Vissarionovich:
When this letter reaches you, I will no longer be among the living. For this reason, please understand that I am writing honestly, with all of my heart's blood, so to speak. [. . .]

Mandelshtam swore to Stalin that he had not been an oppositionist since 1929. Unfortunately the final section of the letter was not in his case file when it was examined in 1956.

· 79 ·

"Special Bulletin No. 6 from Deputy Commissar of the NKVD Agranov to
Commissar of the NKVD Yagoda on the course of the trial of Nikolaev,
L. V. and others." TsA FSB RF, a.u.d. N-Sh44, t. 34, ll. 25–32.

[. . .] at 5:45 A.M. on December 29 the court announced sentences in
the case, in which all of the fourteen accused [. . .] were sentenced to be
shot. Nearly all of the accused greeted the sentences in subdued fashion.
Nikolaev exclaimed "How cruel!" and dropped his head onto the divider
in front of the defendants' bench. Mandelshtam said quietly, "All hail Soviet Power, all hail the Communist Party," and exited the courtroom with
the other accused.

[. . .] Agranov.

Dec. 29, 1934.

Apart from Agranov's bulletin, there exist transcripts of 1956 interviews with NKVD guards that describe the prisoners' reactions to the
sentences, as well as their executions. It should be noted that these descriptions may be embellished, and that one of the witnesses, Katsafa,
gave clearly unreliable evidence on another aspect of the case.[64]

Gusev, the guard whose testimony about the NKVD efforts to manipulate Nikolaev is excerpted above, told interviewers that "when the sentence was announced, Nikolaev was led back (into the holding room)
with hands tied behind his back, and he was repeating as if to himself,
"Can it really be? It can't! It can't!"[65] Katsafa said that Nikolaev shouted
"They lied to me!" when the sentence was read.[66] Sheinin from the prosecutor's office claimed in 1956 to have heard from Vyshinsky that Nikolaev before his death protested, "But I exposed those bastards!"[67]

Katsafa also claimed to have witnessed Kotolynov's final words on
the execution ground. On April 3, 1956 he deposed as follows.

· 80 ·

Testimony of Kirov's guard Katsafa on execution of the convicted in the trial of
the "Leningrad Center," April 3, 1956. RGANI, f. 6, op. 13, d. 24, ll. 51–68.

First Nikolaev, Shatsky, Rumiantsev and the others were shot. Kotolynov was last. When he alone was left alive, Agranov and Vyshinsky took
him aside. They said to him, "They're going to shoot you now, so tell us

the truth, who organized the murder of S. M. Kirov?" To this Kotolynov answered, "This whole trial is garbage. People have been shot. Now I'm going to be shot. But none of us, with the exception of Nikolaev, are guilty of anything. That's the absolute truth."

If this conversation actually took place, Agranov and Vyshinsky were most likely hoping that Kotolynov, in a last desperate hope of saving himself, would "confess" to the charges. The attempts to manipulate the prisoners' most primal fears and hopes did not stop until they were dead. Kotolynov, however, did not take the bait.

At 7:20 on the morning of December 29 Agranov sent the following telegram to Yagoda in Moscow.

· 81 ·

Agranov telegram to Yagoda on execution of the convicted in the trial of the "Leningrad Center," December 29, 1934. TsA FSB RF, a.u.d. N-Sh44, t. 34, l. 83.

Report.

Today, the twenty-ninth of December, 1934 at 5:45 A.M. the Circuit Session of the Military Collegium of the Supreme Court of the USSR sentenced to death for the murder of Comrade Kirov: Nikolaev, Leonid, Zvezdov, Antonov, Yuskin, Sokolov, Kotolynov, Shatsky, Miasnikov, Tolmazov, Levin, Khanik, Sositsky, Rumiantsev, and Mandelshtam. At 6:45 the sentences were carried out.

Deputy Chief of the NKVD of the USSR Agranov.

In Leningrad it was still dark out.

What was the reality behind the "Leningrad Center"? Based on interrogation and court records, it appears that a group of former Komsomol leaders who had been prominent under Zinoviev maintained contact in the early 1930s with Zinoviev's closest associates (also former Leningrad officials) in Moscow. Tolmazov went to Moscow in early 1934 and tried unsuccessfully to see some of the ex-Zinovievite leaders there. In 1933–1934 Miasnikov, Kotolynov, and Levin paid visits to former Zinovievite officials in Moscow, among them Gessen, Gertik, Kuklin, Bakaev, and Faivilovich. Rumiantsev was part of this group, although his role was ambiguous. He himself paid a visit to Kuklin in Moscow at one point, and he was apparently present at two get-togethers in Leningrad in 1933–1934 where news from Moscow was discussed. The group of Leningrad Zinovievites was not tightly knit. At their occasional meetings they discussed politics, criticized Stalin, and hoped for a day when they might return to more prominent positions in the party.

Rumiantsev's place in this group is somewhat mysterious. Kirov and other authorities may have viewed him as a competent worker and as some kind of intermediary between the old Zinovievite cadres and the Stalinist leadership. Rumiantsev had met an OGPU resident at least twice (in 1929 and 1932) and he apparently had a good relationship with Pyotr Ivanovich Smorodin, first secretary of the Vyborg Ward committee since 1929. Smorodin was in turn close to Kirov, and Rumiantsev himself in all probability knew Kirov personally. In 1933, when the Leningrad NKVD planned his arrest, Rumiantsev had escaped the net and won a promotion after sending declarations denouncing the opposition to Stalin, the party control organs, and Chudov. Most likely he had met Kirov at this time to discuss his future. It is reasonable to wonder if Rumiantsev provided information on the former Zinovievites' activity to Leningrad leaders and to the police. At the same time he was perhaps expected to "save" some of the ex-oppositionist "youth" for the party. It is clear that he had a patron-client relationship with some of the lower-ranking former oppositionists— in 1932–1934 he helped place Tolmazov's sister and Antonov in jobs, he helped Tolmazov replace a lost identification card, and he provided Kotolynov with passes to the Vyborg Ward committee cafeteria.[68]

Lev Khanik claimed to have been close to the Moscow-connected group prior to his reassignment to Kronstadt in July 1933. He served as chief of the Fellowship of Komsomol Militants but was evidently dismissed under political pressure after he recruited former oppositionists to write for Istmol publications (the Fellowship, the reader will remember was attached to the Komsomol history section of the Institute of History). This was probably when he was transferred to propaganda work at Kronstadt. Rumiantsev claimed to have denounced Khanik for his Istmol work at a meeting in Smolny in "July or August" of either 1933 or 1934. In November 1933 Khanik received a party censure for "ignoring the party organization and the orders of the director." This was probably related to the end of his tenure at the Fellowship.[69]

Although the sequence of events is not entirely clear, it seems that Khanik was fired from Istmol, and that Rumiantsev denounced him and demanded that the security police investigate him. This would certainly have provided an incentive for Khanik to incriminate Rumiantsev at the trial of the "Leningrad Center."

The fact that Khanik was fired from Istmol in the summer of 1933 was covered up in a number of documents from the trial and investigation. The NKVD wished to present the Fellowship of Komsomol Militants as a center of oppositional activity under Khanik. But of those accused in the "Leningrad Center" trial, only Antonov and Tolmazov had belonged to the Fellowship at the same time as Khanik. Zvezdov and Shatsky had both talked to Nikolaev about joining the Fellowship in early 1934, by which time Khanik was already in Kronstadt.

The episode around the Fellowship of Komsomol Militants provides a tantalizing glimpse of the internal politics of the Leningrad organization, which become quite opaque after the 1929 defeat of the Komarovites by Kirov. The book put out by the Fellowship, *The Petrograd Komsomol in the Civil War* (see above, p. 136) included many references to Smorodin, who had been an important Komsomol leader in Petrograd during the Civil War. The attack on the Fellowship may have been a proxy attack on Smorodin, going after the ex-Zinovievites he had taken under his wing.

It is not clear from available sources where the attack on the Fellowship came from. One possible hypothesis is that supporters of the Komarovite faction were behind it. In 1929 Kirov had used some ex-Zinovievites, such as Pyotr Irklis, against the proto-Rightist Komarovites. It is probable too that Smorodin had been a Zinovievite sympathizer in 1925, and Kirov also used him against the Komarovites in 1929. In 1933 at least one Komarovite under OGPU surveillance, Korol, had been allowed to return to Leningrad. A Korol, who may have been the same man, appears as a Smolny Ward party committee official in the transcript of Nikolaev's April 1934 hearing at the Institute of Party History that resulted in his firing. Nikolaev in his writings referred to the Institute of History bosses (Lidak, Lurye, Avvakumov) who fired him as "Rightists." It may be that Komarov sympathizers at the Institute were behind the 1933–1934 attack on the Fellowship of Komsomol Militants, which was recruiting former Zinovievites. If this is so, then this clash might have been important background to Nikolaev's party mobilization for transport work and subsequent firing. Although Nikolaev was apparently never an open Zinoviev supporter, he may have been perceived as Left-leaning.[70]

However, the hypothesis of Komarovite involvement in the attack on the Fellowship of Komsomol Militants or in Nikolaev's firing from the Institute of History is speculative. In addition, available OGPU surveillance files from the early 1930s show that there was some intermingling of former Zinovievites and Komarovites, both of whom expressed private resentment of Stalin and Kirov and doubts about collectivization. It is hard to tell if the two groups really existed any more as discrete cliques by 1933.

Antonov and Zvezdov were also peripheral to the group of former oppositionists in touch with Zinoviev's circle in Moscow. Antonov was Tolmazov's cousin and had lived with him and another former Zinovievite, Fyodor Fadeev, in the same apartment in the late 1920s. He and Tolmazov socialized from time to time. He also knew Kotolynov—both were students at the Leningrad Industrial Academy. However, he had not seen Rumiantsev since 1928, and he had no other links to the Moscow-connected group. Zvezdov was another Industrial Academy student, acquainted with both Kotolynov and Antonov.

Nikolai Shatsky had worked together with Kotolynov and other defendants in the Komsomol in the 1920s, but his connections with them were mostly broken. Unlike them he had not rejoined the party, which made him a Trotskyite in the official typology of oppositionists. Moreover, he had only recently returned from work in Stalingrad. Among those tried with the "Leningrad Center," he had seen only Nikolaev and Tolmazov in the year before the murder. He also had contact with two ex-Zinovievite members of the Fellowship of Komsomol Militants, Georgy Popov and Fyodor Fadeev, who had been detained in the Kirov case. In a face-to-face confrontation during the investigation Popov charged Shatsky with "terrorist moods."[71]

Yuskin had no discernible connections with any of the accused other than Nikolaev. The NKVD targeted him because Nikolaev named him as a recent social contact, and perhaps because his wife went on record about his anti-Soviet statements. Her testimony could be used to pressure him.[72]

Georgy Vasilevich Sokolov, the thirty-year-old naval cadet, was the most enigmatic of the defendants. A longtime Komsomol member, he joined the party in 1931. Sokolov was a physical education instructor in the Vyborg Ward Komsomol apparatus in the early 1920s, when Nikolaev met him. After that job, he worked at the Red Vyborg factory. The factory's party organization recommended him for study at the Electrical Welding Institute. Sokolov must have been an exemplary student and party member, because in October 1933 the Central Committee and the Leningrad city committee of the party selected him to matriculate as a cadet at the central Soviet naval academy in Leningrad.

Although he was listed in the OGPU's "Politikan" file in the early thirties, Sokolov had no record of party censures for oppositional activity. Of all of the arrestees in the "Leningrad Center" case, Sokolov was the most cooperative. Upon his arrest on December 6, he immediately signed a protocol that previewed the entire NKVD case against the "Leningrad Center." Sokolov was the first witness to link Nikolaev unequivocally to the Moscow-connected group of former Zinovievites, and he was the first to utter the formula that dominated the confessions at the trial, namely that expression of oppositional views was tantamount to inciting terror. Sokolov was also the only person listed in the "Politikan" file to meet Nikolaev after February 1934.[73]

It is interesting, then, that not one of the accused in the trial of the "Leningrad Center" besides Nikolaev mentioned meeting Sokolov at all. A number of them probably knew him from work together in the Vyborg Komsomol organization in the early 1920s, but no one testified to seeing him (again, besides Nikolaev), and most did not even mention his name in their testimony. Sokolov claimed to have met Antonov once in 1933 and once more in the fall of 1934, but Antonov did not confirm either of these meetings in the documentation I have seen.

How did Nikolaev fit into the social networks described above? His direct contacts with the Moscow-connected group in 1933–1934 were nil, with the possible exception of an exchange of greetings with Kotolynov. Rumiantsev, Levin, Mandelshtam, Miasnikov, and Sositsky had never met Nikolaev at all, and Tolmazov had no memory of him from the Vyborg Ward days. Kotolynov testified that he had last met Nikolaev in 1932 or 1933, and that only in passing. Khanik had not seen Nikolaev in many years and professed not to remember him. The assassin did, however, have some connection to Antonov and Zvezdov, on the periphery of the Moscow-connected group. Antonov he had last seen in 1932. Zvezdov he encountered once in early 1934 at the Istmol offices, when Nikolaev was still employed by the Institute of Party History.

Apart from Zvezdov, the defendants Nikolaev had seen in 1934 were Yuskin, Shatsky, and Sokolov. With the possible exception of Sokolov, none of these men had regular social connections with the former Zinovievites tried on December 28–29. Yuskin was a student

and party committee member at the Industrial Institute, where Kotolynov, Zvezdov, and Antonov were enrolled, but the Institute was huge
and there is no evidence of social connections between him and them.
Shatsky's only recent connection with the former Zinovievites seems to
have been a brief visit to Tolmazov's apartment in July 1934 to talk
about the prospects for reentering the party and finding a job. Sokolov
claimed to have met Antonov in late 1933 on the premises of the regional students' union, and to have watched a soccer game with him in
the fall of 1934. However, Antonov did not mention these meetings in
any of the documents I have had access to.

Nikolaev and Sokolov both testified that they had met at Smolny
just before the October anniversary holiday in 1934, and had had a
conversation that was a "mutual-feeling-out." Late in the investigation Sokolov stated that he knew Nikolaev was preparing a terrorist
action, but had not aided him. His evidence at trial was contradictory.
Sokolov first claimed that he did not know Nikolaev was "preparing a
terrorist act" when he met him before the October holiday, but then,
under pressure from Ulrikh, confessed that he knew Nikolaev had
"terrorist intentions."[74]

It is not possible to analyze the relations among the veteran Zinovievites without taking into consideration the constant presence of
police informers, possibly even provocateurs. Rumiantsev, as already
noted, had been in contact with GPU residents as well as party control
organs in 1929–1933. Georgy Popov at the Fellowship of Komsomol
Militants, who was questioned in the Nikolaev case, had been interviewed at least once previously by the security police. Kotolynov told
Antonov in the fall of 1934 that he believed fellow Industrial Institute
student Mikhail Nodel to be a police informer. Nodel too was detained
in the case. Remaining GPU-OGPU records from Leningrad confirm
that as early as 1928 the police had sources well-placed inside the Zinovievite opposition in the city. One might even describe the "organs"
and the oppositionists as participating in a delicate dance of accommodation, punishment, police "therapy" for erring party members,
and the exchange of information for privileges and promotions. The
Kirov murder stopped the music.[75]

If one asks about possible informants or provocateurs among Nikolaev's contacts in the months before the murder, one possible candidate
is Sokolov. He admitted to "feeling out" Nikolaev's political mood in
their conversation before the October holidays, a discussion Nikolaev
confirmed early in the investigation. His exemplary party record, com-

bined with his past history of contact with oppositionists, would have made him an ideal candidate for "secret collaborator" (*sekretnyi sotrudnik*) from the security police's point of view. Moreover, his cooperation with the inquiry was extraordinary, perhaps until he realized that he himself was likely to be eliminated. Against this hypothesis is the fact that he only met Nikolaev once in 1934 and he had had practically no social contact with other ex-Zinovievites in recent years.

Shatsky seems an unlikely candidate for police informer because of his refusal to cooperate during the investigation and trial. Yuskin also seems unlikely because there is not evidence that he knew any of the ex-Zinovievites. Antonov had apparently not seen Nikolaev since 1932.

Whether or not Nikolaev was in contact with NKVD collaborators, or was one himself, it is evident that tight police surveillance of the former oppositionists created a volatile situation in 1934. And events at the Seventeenth Party Congress only exacerbated the situation. The appearance of Zinoviev and other former oppositionists at the congress, combined with Zinoviev's appointment to the editorial board of *Bolshevik,* gave ex-Zinovievites hope for public advancement and greater tolerance. Based on the evidence of the defendants at Nikolaev's trial, it seems that many began to talk of renewing "former ties" and taking a more active role in political life. At the same time, Stalin warned at the congress that persons who broke party directives needed to be weeded out of the party/state apparatus. Vigilance against internal enemies, including the old oppositionists, was still the order of the day. According to Leonid Raikhman, former officer of the Leningrad Secret Political Department, orders had come down from Stalin to monitor the conversations of party officials for anti-Stalin or antiparty comments. In a 1989 article Raikhman noted that "we had our informers everywhere, including inside the party organs. The order to 'give a good working-over' to party members in search of careless conversations came from Molchanov (head of the USSR NKVD Secret Political Department), who cited Stalin's personal instructions: "We knew exactly who was having anti-Soviet conversations and where they did so, where people made negative comments about Stalin."[76] Multiple orders had been issued and rescinded for the arrest of prominent ex-Zinovievites including Rumiantsev, Kotolynov, and Levin in 1933–1934.

Seventeen days after the conclusion of the "Leningrad Center" trial, on January 15–16, 1935, the Military Collegium heard the case of the

"Moscow Center," which consisted to a large extent of residents of the capital who had direct or indirect associations with Zinoviev. Most of those charged were veterans of the Leningrad party organization from Zinoviev's tenure there. Many of them had been mentioned in depositions by the defendants in the "Leningrad Center" trial, including Tarasov and Faivilovich, Yevdokimov, Kuklin, Tsarkov, and of course Zinoviev and Kamenev themselves. The defendants by and large followed the formula used by most of the accused in the "Leningrad Center." That is, they confessed to moral and political responsibility for the terror attack against Kirov due to their cultivation of "bitterness and open hatred for the leaders of the Party and Soviet power." They did not, however, admit to direct participation in Kirov's murder, and Zinoviev apparently continued to deny that any organized "center" existed. On February 3, 1935 Agranov admitted to a meeting of senior NKVD officers that "We were not able to prove that the 'Moscow Center' knew about the preparations for a terrorist attack on Comrade Kirov."[77]

The official Soviet wire service TASS released the following report on the proceedings.

· 82 ·

TASS report on "Trial of the Moscow Center," January 16, 1935. RGANI, f. 3, op. 16, d. 25, ll. 85–86.

———————

Trial of the "Moscow Center," an Underground Counterrevolutionary Group of Zinovievites.

January 15–16, 1935.

The Military Collegium of the Supreme Court of the USSR, after hearing the case of the "Moscow Center," an underground counterrevolutionary group of Zinovievites, handed down the following sentences:

1. Zinoviev, Grigory Yevseevich, as the main organizer and most active leader of the underground counterrevolutionary "Moscow Center," sentenced to ten years of prison,

2. Gertik, Artyom Moiseevich,

3. Kuklin, Aleksandr Sergeevich,

4. Sakhov, Boris Naumovich—as the most active participants in the counterrevolutionary underground group of Zinovievites—sentenced to ten years of prison,

5. Sharov, Iakov Vasilevich,

6. Yevdokimov, Grigory Eremeevich,

7. Bakaev, Ivan Petrovich,

8. Gorshenin, Ivan Stepanovich,

9. Tsarkov, Nikolai Alekseevich—for active participation in the said underground counterrevolutionary group—sentenced to eight years of prison,

10. Fyodorov, Grigory Fyodorovich,

11. Gertsberg, Aleksandr Vladimirovich,

12. Gessen, Sergei Mikhailovich,

13. Tarasov, Ivan Ivanovich,

14. Perimov, Aleksei Viktorovich,

15. Anishev, Anatolii Isaevich,

16. Faivilovich, Leonid Iakovlevich—for participation in the said group—sentenced to six years of prison,

17. Kamenev, Lev Borisovich,

18. Bashkirov, Aleksandr Fabianovich,

19. Bravo, Boris Lvovich—as the least active participants in the said group—to five years of prison.

The indictments and sentences state that the "Moscow Center" for a number of years supervised the counterrevolutionary activity of various underground groups of Zinovievites, including the Leningrad group of Nikolaev-Kotolynov that murdered S. M. Kirov. [The Moscow Center] was the ideological and political leader of the Leningrad group of Zinovievites, knew of the terrorist moods of that group, and took all measures to incite them; it attempted at various times to organize a counterrevolutionary bloc with various anti-Soviet groups, with the aim of opening a struggle against Soviet power.

Simultaneous with the trial of the "Moscow Center," the Special Board of the NVKD, invested by the summer 1934 reorganization of the security organs with the right to issue administrative sentences of up to five years hard labor, reviewed charges against the "Leningrad Counterrevolutionary Zinovievite Group of Safarov, Zalutsky, and Others." Seventy-seven persons were indicted in this group, including former prominent Leningrad officials Zalutsky, Safarov, and I. K. Naumov, as well as Zinoviev's ex-wife Sara Ravvich. The NKVD also threw into the group Leonid Nikolaev's mother Maria Tikhonovna, his older sister Yekaterina, his half-brother Pyotr's wife Anna Maksimova-Nikolaeva, his cousin Georgy Vasilev, his younger sister Anna Pantiukhina, and Anna's husband Vladimir Pantiukhin. Seventy-six of the seventy-seven indicted received various terms of hard labor or exile. Most died in the camps or were executed in 1937–1939 when state terror intensified.[78]

On January 18, 1935 the Central Committee issued a letter on the Kirov murder, authored by Stalin, to all party organizations. Headed "Lessons learned from the events connected with the villainous murder of Comrade Kirov," the circular asserted that Zinovievites in the "Leningrad Center" had committed the assassination. The "Moscow Center" of the Zinovievites had general supervision of the "Leningrad Center," encouraged its terrorist sentiments, but "apparently" did not know of specific preparations against Kirov. The Zinovievites, "having lost the trust of the working class," had now gone deep underground, plotting individual acts of terrorism and consorting with the Latvian consul in Leningrad, supposedly a German agent. With their new strategy, the Zinovievites (supposedly allied with the Trotskyites) were "something entirely new for which there is no precedent in the history of our party." Unlike previous Communist oppositions, Stalin claimed, the Zinovievites had decided to present themselves as completely loyal Communists. Yet in fact they were "in essence, a White Guard organization in disguise." Parts of this declaration by Stalin had earlier precedents—the assertion that party oppositionists operated in secret, and that they were aiding the class enemy. Other parts, however, were new. Prior to the Kirov murder, the Stalinists had claimed that oppositionists objectively served the interests of the class enemy, although they might not themselves understand this. Now Stalin was claiming that the Zinovievites and Trotskyites had consciously conspired with the class enemy. Moreover, his letter's accusation that the oppositionists were masquerading as loyal Communists made it impossible for suspects to defend themselves. Avowals and even acts of loyalty would be interpreted as part of their "double-dealing."[79]

Stalin also attacked the Leningrad party organization and NKVD savagely for "complacency [. . .] and negligence unbecoming Bolsheviks in matters of security." Repeating one of his favorite themes, he warned that such complacency was due to the mistaken belief that the more defeats the class enemy suffered, the more "tame and harmless" he became. In fact, Stalin claimed to believe, the class struggle sharpened as the defeated class enemy grew more desperate. Party members needed to reject all complacency, and "exterminate and extirpate" double-dealing former dissidents.[80]

Stalin's letter also contributed to the rapid proliferations of myths and half-truths about the murder. As part of his tirade against the Leningrad NKVD's slackness, he wrote as follows.

· 83 ·

Excerpt of Central Committee circular on the Kirov murder, January 18, 1935,
authored by Stalin. RGANI, f. 6, op. 13, d. 13, l. 18.

How can we [...] explain the fact that the murderer of Comrade
Kirov, the monster Leonid Nikolaev, detained three weeks before the accomplishment of the crime next to Comrade Kirov's car when he rushed at
Comrade Kirov as the latter approached the vehicle, was not even searched
because he showed the chekists his party card? Is it that difficult for a
chekist to understand that a party card can be forged, or stolen from its
owner, that the party card in and of itself, without any check of its gen-
uineness, and especially without any check of its holder's identity, cannot
serve as a sufficient guarantee when one is dealing with a person more
than suspect, behaving himself in worse than suspect fashion as Comrade
Kirov approached his waiting automobile. Where has vigilance disappeared to? [...]

Stalin's story of Nikolaev's attempt to approach Kirov does not
match any event recorded in the 1934–1935 layer of documents. It is
possible that some NKVD commissar whose testimony lies in the secret police archives passed along the tale. It is more likely that Stalin
was conflating several events. There was Nikolaev's well-attested detention on October 15, when the NKVD did indeed check his party
card. Then, on November 5, he watched Kirov's car drive past. This
was approximately twenty-six days, or about four weeks, before the
murder. Finally, on November 14, seventeen days before the murder,
he had tried to approach Kirov at Moscow Station, but there were too
many bodyguards. There is no evidence that NKVD officers touched
Nikolaev at all in the last encounter, much less examined his passport.
Stalin may not have had a detailed memory of all testimony in the case
(he was most interested in testimony implicating the Zinovievites), and
he could have taken the passport check from the October detention,
the car from November 5, and the "three weeks before the murder"
from either the November 5 or the November 14 encounters. Whatever the case, Stalin's account of Nikolaev's detention spawned a mass
of stories in the following decades about Nikolaev jumping on the running board of Kirov's car, etc., for which there is no other documentary
evidence from 1934–1935.

In the aftermath of the trial of the "Leningrad Center," Soviet authorities used Nikolaev's testimony against the consul Bissenieks to apply pressure to Latvia. Just hours after the conclusion of the trial, Soviet Deputy Commissar of Foreign Affairs Boris Spiridonovich Stomoniakov summoned Latvian ambassador Bilmanis for an interview. He informed him that the investigation had found connections between Bissenieks and the assassin. Because the USSR desired good relations with Latvia, Stomoniakov said, his government would not make this fact public, but he demanded that Bissenieks leave the Soviet Union immediately. The workers of Leningrad, he explained in a transparent threat, were very angry about Kirov's murder and if word that the Latvian consul was involved got out, there could be "explosions of indignation at the consulate, demonstrations, and so on." After Stomoniakov and Bilmanis discussed the fact that Bissenieks was "a Social Democrat and a Menshevik," Bilmanis tacitly conceded that the consul had been collecting information and passing it on to socialists abroad. "I deplore [. . .] such activities," he stated.[81]

Publication of the indictments in the Kirov murder case prompted worried discussions among the ten consuls resident in Leningrad about which of them might be implicated. When Bilmanis ordered Bissenieks to exit the USSR by midnight on December 31, word spread among them rapidly. At a meeting of the consuls on the thirty-first the British consul Gilliat-Smith (Bullard's replacement) and the German consul Sommer wanted to accompany Bissenieks to the train station as a gesture of solidarity, but none of the others supported them.[82]

The Commissariat of Foreign Affairs had an agent in Leningrad, Vainshtein, whose job was to maintain contact with the city's consuls and gather intelligence on them. In the first days of January Vainshtein reported to Stomoniakov about conversations he had with the Swedish consul Assarson and the Dane Schraeder. According to Vainshtein, Assarson told him the following story. Bissenieks had confidentially told Gilliat-Smith, his close friend, that he had in fact met Nikolaev and lent him a small sum of money, "but that he could never have dreamed that in giving him funds he was [. . .] providing aid and comfort to a terrorist group." Gilliat-Smith mentioned this to the Finnish consul Westerlund, who in turn had told Assarson. Vainshtein then asked Schraeder to check on this story directly with Gilliat-Smith. Gilliat-Smith denied he'd said anything of the sort, claiming Westerlund must have been drunk and imagined he'd heard it. Westerlund himself then backtracked, telling Schraeder that he "must have misunderstood."[83]

Taken by itself, this tale, fourth-hand when Vainshtein put it to paper, would deserve little consideration. But when matched with Nikolaev's detailed knowledge of the Latvian consulate and other evidence discussed in the previous chapter, it does strengthen the possibility that the assassin really had visited the Latvian consul. Furthermore, in confidential interviews with Latvian officials Bissenieks never categorically denied meeting Nikolaev (see below).

Latvian ambassador Bilmanis, upon receiving Stomoniakov's order for Bissenieks to leave the USSR, sent one of his deputies in Moscow, Filholds, to take over the Leningrad consulate. When Filholds reached Leningrad he interviewed Bissenieks about the Kirov charges (this must have been on December 30 or 31, before Bissenieks left the USSR), and sent a report back to Bilmanis. Bissenieks described to Filholds his meeting with Soviet agent Lentsmanis at the Astoria on December 5, an encounter Filholds concluded was "fatal." The NKVD, Filholds believed, was seeking scapegoats for the Kirov killing and Bissenieks had fallen into their trap. With regard to Nikolaev, Bissenieks stated that "I don't know Nikolaev, and as you don't have a photograph of him, I cannot tell you whether he was at the consulate or not." He also denied knowing Draule. At the same time he said that visitors to the consulate did not always give their names, so that he couldn't be sure whether either the assassin or his wife had visited.[84]

Bissenieks had intended to travel from Leningrad to Tallin, in Estonia, but when he arrived at the train station at around 6 P.M. on New Year's Eve, there was no train there. So he and his wife rode to Helsinki, in Finland, instead. There he rousted the Latvian ambassador out of bed at 8 A.M. on New Year's Day with a phone call. He was out of money. Later in the day the ambassador met Bissenieks at the embassy and they discussed recent events. On January 4 he sent a report to V. Munters, the general secretary of the Ministry of Foreign Affairs, and the de facto minister, in Latvia. After a summary of Bissenieks' misadventures, the ambassador gave an account of rumors about the murder that the consul had picked up in Leningrad. "He has some reason to believe," the ambassador wrote, "that Nikolaev's fatal step can be explained at least in part by romantic motives." In an excellent demonstration of just how inaccurate rumors about the murder could be, Bissenieks had explained to the ambassador that "Kirov's wife Draule" was Latvian, and Nikolaev was having an affair with her.[85]

Back in Moscow, Bilmanis and Stomoniakov met again on January 3. Bilmanis presented the Soviet representative with Filholds' report on his interview with Bissenieks, which Stomoniakov dismissed as "not worthy of attention." Stomoniakov in turn showed Bilmanis excerpts from Nikolaev's testimony against Bissenieks.[86]

Following the second meeting with Stomoniakov, Bilmanis sent his analysis of the situation to Karls Ulmanis, President of Latvia and titular Minister of Foreign Affairs. He was very unhappy with Bissenieks, emphasizing that he had a loose tongue and poor judgment. For one thing, he had made a stupid error by visiting Lentsmanis at the Astoria on December 5. A second problem was related to Nikolaev's testimony that the Latvian consul had given him five thousand rubles. Bilmanis wrote that on December 2, the day after the Kirov murder, Bissenieks had called him from Leningrad and asked for that sum so that he could pay the rent for the consulate's premises. Bilmanis sent him two thousand. In Bilmanis' view, the NKVD must have been eavesdropping on the telephone line (the Soviet police had recently begun bugging telephones, using new technology imported from Germany). They had heard the reference to five thousand rubles and used it. "Why talk about money on the telephone, especially in Russia?" wrote Bilmanis.[87]

The NKVD was indeed well-informed about goings-on at the Latvian consulate, and officers used their information to link Nikolaev more closely to Bissenieks. At the trial of the "Leningrad Center," Nikolaev had testified that he had not signed a receipt for the five thousand rubles, but that the "accountant" at the consulate had "formulated" the expenditure "as if it were for renovations." There had in fact been renovations to the consulate apartment throughout much of 1934, and these had cost between four and five thousand rubles. Knowing about this (the cleaning lady at the consulate was an NKVD informer) the NKVD aimed to use Nikolaev's testimony to assert that receipts for the renovations were in fact receipts for money paid to Nikolaev.[88]

Bilmanis believed it quite possible that Bissenieks had really met Nikolaev: "My conclusion [. . .] is that whatever happened, happened, who can know for sure. [. . .] Some 'Red Professor' [at one point Nikolaev testified he'd told the consul he was a "Red Professor"] comes in and complains about his tough life and informs—there are lots of those types. But the whole misfortune is that one out of the hundred who constantly [come in to] grouse turns out to be Kirov's killer. [. . .] We get all kinds during our visiting hours. With all kinds of troubles and requests."[89]

On January 7, Bissenieks, now returned to Riga, met with Munters for a debriefing. Munters questioned the former consul closely about the details of Nikolaev's testimony, which Bilmanis had forwarded to Riga. Although the Latvians (and Soviet investigators in the 1960s) would use Bissenieks' testimony to argue that he had never met Nikolaev, in reality the former consul's answers were curiously indeterminate. Nikolaev's first pretext for supposedly visiting the Latvian consul had been to inquire about a Latvian inheritance. Bissenieks told Munters that such questions were "relatively frequent." Visitors had shown him imperial passports, of the sort Nikolaev's father-in-law had possessed, but in connection with citizenship claims, not inheritance issues. Bissenieks did not remember anyone claiming to be a Red Professor, as Nikolaev reputedly had done, but he did remember a number of "persons engaged in scholarship" (*nauchnye rabotniki*). He did not recall anyone offering him information on the internal situation in the USSR, but his hearing was poor and he might not have understood them if they had done so.[90]

Bissenieks provided Munters with an account of major consulate expenditures in 1934, including the renovations and thirteen hundred rubles for rent. He had also purchased a fur coat for his wife, paying five to six thousand rubles out of his own pocket. There had been no expenditures of precisely five thousand rubles. The secretary at the Latvian consulate, Elvira Apinis, confirmed Bissenieks' account to Filholds, the new consul in Leningrad.[91]

The Latvians concluded the charges against Bissenieks were bogus (as they certainly were, even if Nikolaev had been at the consulate once). They were doubly outraged because the Soviet authorities were doing everything that they could to spread the word that Bissenieks was implicated in the Kirov murder, short of actually publishing his name. At a New Year's Day reception in Moscow the Italian ambassador, evidently intervening for the Latvians, warned Stomoniakov that knowledge of Bissenieks' expulsion was spreading too far. The Italian understood that the Press Department of the Commissariat of Foreign Affairs had informed some foreign reporters of the incident.[92] Then, on the morning of January 4, Soviet newspapers ran a TASS report (also released abroad), that the accused consul had been expelled from the USSR, and that the ambassador of the same country had been shown the materials incriminating him. The following day *Pravda* and *Izvestia* both published stories asserting that the anonymous consul had participated in the plot to kill Kirov and helped the "terrorists" to prepare a plan for escape abroad. The story said that a "small government" was aiding in preparations for an attack on the USSR by a "large government." In the opinion of Latvian diplomatic officials, the "small government" was obviously supposed to be Latvia, the "large government" Germany.[93]

The Latvians initially sought to use Soviet breaches of protocol to pressure the Commissariat of Foreign Affairs to enter negotiations for a closer relationship. They also wanted information about Soviet negotiations with France over an "Eastern Pact" against Hitler that might involve a joint guarantee of Latvian independence. On January 7, 1935 Bilmanis visited Stomoniakov to complain about the Soviet press pieces of January 4 and 5 implicating Bissenieks in the Kirov murder and Latvia in Nazi plans to attack the USSR. After Stomoniakov disingenuously claimed that the Commissariat of Foreign Affairs could not control what Soviet journalists chose to publish, Bilmanis requested that Stalin and Molotov receive Munters, for a state visit. Munters, he explained, wished to discuss possible cooperation in the League of Nations, the "Eastern Pact," a possible trade pact, and intensified cultural exchanges. Stomoniakov's reply was evasive.[94]

From this point tensions escalated. On January 15 Munters sent a circular to all Latvian embassies asserting Bissenieks' innocence and detailing the Soviets' breach of their promise to keep the case quiet. One week later Julijs Feldmanis, Latvia's representative at the League of Nations, visited Soviet Commissar of Foreign Affairs Maksim Litvinov in Geneva to complain about Soviet smears of Latvia and Bissenieks. This was followed by a diplomatic note to Stomoniakov demanding the "moral satisfaction" of allowing Bissenieks to return briefly to Leningrad. The Soviets rejected the demand, and Molotov publicly repeated the charge that the guilty consul's "small government" was aiding a "large government" with designs on Soviet territory.[95]

In the spring of 1935 the hullabaloo around the consul's expulsion died down. Neither side had given ground. As for Bissenieks, he never served again in the Latvian diplomatic corps. When the Soviet Union occupied Latvia in 1940, the NKVD soon arrested him. He was charged in the Kirov murder, found guilty, and executed on July 27, 1941, as German troops stormed through the Baltics toward Leningrad. Throughout the investigation and at trial Bissenieks denied the charges against him.[96]

The entire episode sheds light on Soviet reasons for targeting the

Latvian consul in particular (we can assume that the NKVD aimed to find some foreign "sponsor" for the "terrorists"). First there was the fact that Nikolaev had a previous connection to the consul, even if it was only the consulate address in his date book. The second reason the Soviets chose Bissenieks was Latvia's weakness in the international arena. Accusing Germany directly of aiding and abetting Kirov's assassination (Nikolaev had written down the German consul's address as well as the Latvian consul's) would have led to serious complications for Soviet foreign policy. A third probable reason the NKVD was interested in Bissenieks was that they suspected he was passing information about conditions in the USSR to Menshevik and other socialist correspondents abroad.

As the Latvians pressed their defense of Bissenieks in the early months of 1935, the NKVD turned to Nikolaev's immediate relatives for new "evidence" to incriminate the consul. On January 10, 1935 Milda Draule signed testimony asserting that Nikolaev had visited Bissenieks to discuss "the question of detaching various national regions from the USSR." In mid-January, to answer Latvian questions about the timing of Nikolaev's putative visit to the consul, interrogators pressured Milda's sister Olga Draule to testify that she knew of an October visit. On March 8, 1935 they persuaded Milda to affirm that she knew of an October visit and of the consul's supposed five-thousand-ruble "loan" to Nikolaev.[97]

After this deposition, Milda Draule was no longer useful to the NKVD. When she gave her testimony on March 8 she was already appointed for execution.

· 84 ·

Telegram of Ulrikh, head of the Military Tribunal, to Stalin, March 11, 1934.
RGANI, f. 6, op. 13, d. 33, ll. 49–50.

To: Secretary of the Central Committee Comrade I. V. Stalin.

On March 9 of this year the circuit session of the Military Collegium of the Supreme Court of the USSR under my chairmanship reviewed in closed session in the city of Leningrad the case of Leonid Nikolaev's accomplices Milda Draule, Olga Draule, and Roman Kulisher.

To the question of what goal she was pursuing when she sought a ticket to the meeting of the party activists on December 1, [. . .] where Comrade

Kirov was to deliver his report, Milda Draule answered that she "wanted to help Leonid Nikolaev." With what? "That should have been obvious from the circumstances." In this fashion we have determined that the accused intended to aid Nikolaev in the accomplishment of a terrorist act.

All three were sentenced to the supreme measure of punishment—shooting.

On the night of March 10 the sentence was carried out.

I request instructions: should an announcement be distributed to the press?

V. Ulrikh

March 11, 1935.

CHAPTER 10

Investigating the Leningrad NKVD

On December 3, 1934, Genrikh Yagoda issued an order for the firing and arrest of eight officers of the Leningrad regional NKVD: Medved, his second deputy Fomin, chief of the Special Political Department Gorin-Lundin, deputy chief of the Special Department Yanishevsky, head of the Third Section of the Special Department P. M. Lobov, Special Political Department Officer Mosevich, and Special Department officers Baltsevich and G. A. Petrov. Yanishevsky, Lobov, Mosevich, Baltsevich, and Petrov were all involved in suppressing Volkova's denunciations before the murder. Medved, Fomin, and Gorin-Lundin were the most senior NKVD officers in Leningrad on the day of the assassination. In late January the Military Collegium tried all of these men for negligence. Four more colleagues joined them in the dock. These were Aleksandr Gubin, head of the Leningrad NKVD Operations Department, his subordinate and head of Kirov's guard Mikhail Kotomin, Medved's first deputy Ivan Zaporozhets (who also headed the Special Department), and Zaporozhets' senior aide Aleksandr Belousenko. Gubin and Kotomin were charged in connection with failure to protect Kirov. Zaporozhets and Belousenko were tried on the same charge, but also in connection with the Special Department's suppression of Volkova's denunciations.[1]

Zaporozhets was not arrested until five to six days after the murder, when he returned to Leningrad after several months' leave of absence. Multiple witnesses in different time periods testified to the fact that Zaporozhets had injured his leg in August, by several accounts while taking part in an equestrian dressage event at Leningrad's Dinamo Stadium. He was on leave throughout the fall on the Black Sea, in Moscow, and possibly also in the countryside outside Leningrad. On November 13 he left Leningrad for the Black Sea resort of Sochi, and did not return until after Kirov's murder. According to 1963 testimony by S. A. Annushkov, Operations Secretary for the Leningrad NKVD Special Department in 1934, there were no Zaporozhets signatures at all on Leningrad NKVD documents from September through December 1934. Fomin had charge of the Special Department during this period. In 1990 Zaporozhets' widow confirmed that he did no NKVD work that fall.[2]

Nikolaev's Detention and Kirov's Guard

In one of his confiscated journals Nikolaev mentioned being taken to "the House of Tears," a reference to NKVD offices, on October 15, 1934. He reported the same detention in the small hours of December 2 to NKVD interrogators (see Chapter 7, Document 37). At this point he described following Kirov and Chudov on foot west from Uritsky Square to the Troitsky Bridge, across the bridge, and northwest along Kamennoostrovsky Prospect (officially Krasny Zor Street) to Kirov's apartment. After Kirov and Chudov entered their apartment building, he said, guards detained him and took him back across the bridge to NKVD headquarters on Liteiny (Soviet name Volodarsky) Street. There "the on-duty officer" checked his documents and released him without a search. Nikolaev averred that "at the time I had not thought of assassination."

Leaders of the Central Committee commission must have heard soon after their arrival that the Leningrad NKVD had detained and released Nikolaev in October. There was documentary confirmation of the event in the daily log of the Fourth Section of the Operations Department (Kirov's bodyguard) for October 15, 1934.

· 85 ·

Leningrad NKVD Operations Department daily log report on Nikolaev's detention, October 15, 1934. RGANI, f. 6, op. 13, d. 34, l. 86.

In the course of guarding Comrades Kirov and Chudov on their way from Smolny to Krasnykh Zor Street an officer of the Fourth Section detained an unknown citizen who attempted to approach Comrade Kirov. The citizen was taken to the regional NKVD, where it was determined that he was the party member Nikolaev, unemployed, former *instruktor* of the Institute of History of the Communist Party. Nikolaev wanted to ask Kirov for permission to visit him to discuss the question of finding work. Nikolaev was freed after his identity was ascertained.

Nikolaev's description of events and the log book account were generally consistent, except possibly with regard to the point of detention. Nikolaev placed his arrest close to Kirov's apartment on Krasnykh Zor Street/Kamennoostrovsky Prospect, but the log book seemed to imply that it occurred before Kirov and Chudov turned onto Krasnykh Zor Street. (The log book fits with the testimony of guard Karl Pauzer on December 5, 1934—see below.) I In light of other corroborating details, at any rate, it seems clear that Nikolaev and the log book refer to the same detention. Both accounts refer to the same date, to Kirov and Chudov walking together, and to a relatively perfunctory verification of Nikolaev's identity at NKVD headquarters. Finally, Nikolaev's December 2 statement that he had not yet decided to murder Kirov squares with the log's note of his explanation about wanting to speak to Kirov about work.

It is possible to explain the difference in detention sites between the two accounts in one of two ways. Nikolaev was a highly unreliable narrator, liable to overdramatize events and embellish stories on the spur of the moment. This is clear from the verbatim transcript of his testimony at his trial. It may have fit his fancy to claim he'd followed Kirov and Chudov all the way to their apartment building, when in fact the NKVD detained him before he had even crossed the Troitsky Bridge. A second possibility is that the guards did not take Nikolaev into custody until he reached Kirov's apartment building, but that they placed the detention earlier on the walking route in order to emphasize their own vigilance.

Genrikh Liushkov questioned Milda Draule on December 3 about Nikolaev's apprehension. According to the interrogation record, he did not provide her with the detention date. It is significant, then, that Milda remembered that sometime "before the October holidays" (i.e. before the November 7 New Style anniversary of the revolution), Nikolaev had come home "at midnight." Draule's account is consistent with a detention date in mid-October. When Milda asked Leonid why he was so late, he answered that the police had arrested him and sent him to the NKVD headquarters. Nikolaev told his wife that the police had made a mistake, and expressed a suspicion that he was under surveillance—"it could be that they're following me."[3]

On December 5–6 central NKVD officers questioned several of the Operations Department officers involved in Nikolaev's October 15 detention.

· 86 ·

Protocol of interrogation of Karl Pauzer, member of Kirov's security detail. RGANI, f. 6, op. 13, d. 13, ll. 72–75.

——————————

Protocol of interrogation of Pauzer, Karl Mikhailovich, born 1891, city of Libava, father was worker, Latvian, citizen of the USSR, lives in Leningrad suburbs, Lakhta Station [. . .] served in NKVD organs from 1919 as operations commissar of the [. . .] NKVD of Leningrad Region, nonparty, served in the Red Army 1918–1919, did not serve in White forces, no court or police record.

Question: What do your duties in the Operations Department of the regional NKVD consist of?

Answer: My duties consist of guarding members of the government. From the beginning of 1932 I have been assigned to Comrade Kirov's street guard (*naruzhnaia okhrana*).

Question: Were there instances in which you detained suspicious persons following Comrade Kirov while accompanying Comrade Kirov?

Answer: Yes, there were such instances.

Question: Tell us about these instances in more detail.

Answer: I remember particularly well the last case, when I detained a suspicious person following Comrade Kirov from Smolny to Voinov Street, where I detained said citizen.

Question: What elicited your suspicion and caused you to detain this citizen?

Answer: It happened somewhere in the middle of October of this year around five or six P.M., I remember well that evening was coming on, Comrade Kirov left Smolny alone and headed on foot along Tverskaya Street towards Voinov Street. I noticed an unknown citizen who was shadowing (*nabliudal*) Comrade Kirov. *It shocked me especially that the unidentified citizen was not only shadowing Comrade Kirov, but looking around, as if checking to see if anyone besides himself was following Comrade Kirov* [emphasis in archival copy].

Now I remember something, please take a correction. Comrade Kirov was not walking alone, but together with Comrade Chudov.

Question: Did you alone notice the suspicious behavior of the unknown citizen or did any of the other officers of the Operations Department remark it as well?

Answer: It was also noticed by officers Piotrovsky, Borisov, and someone else from among the accompanying officers, I can't remember who now.

Question: On what basis do you say that the suspicious behavior of the unknown citizen attracted the attention of the other officers?

Answer: I know that Piotrovsky and Borisov also observed the unknown citizen because, after I noticed him, I called the attention of Piotrovsky and Borisov to the unknown person with a nod and a glance. I recall well that Piotrovsky and Borisov noted my nod and glance and took the said [. . .] person under observation.

Question: You earlier testified that you detained this citizen. Tell us how long this citizen observed Comrade Kirov, what distance he maintained, and when, how, and by whom he was detained.

Answer: The unknown person followed Comrades Kirov and Chudov for 35 to 40 minutes [. . .] from Smolny along Tverskaya, [then] along Voinov Street to Volodarsky [also known as Liteiny] Prospect. He was walking behind Comrades Kirov and Chudov at a distance of 15–20 steps. This was when he was walking behind [them] on the same side [of the street]. There were times when the unknown subject crossed to the other side of the street. Then he would stay level with Comrades Chudov and Kirov.

The unknown subject was detained at my initiative on the corner of Voinov Street and Volodarsky Prospect. I organized his detention in the following manner: as we approached the NKVD building, I told Piotrovsky to keep a close eye on the unknown person until I returned with an operations commissar and we detained [him]. After this I ran to the [Operations] Department and asked senior commissar [. . .] Comrade Griunvald to send a commissar to detain the unknown person. Running back outside again, I caught up to the unknown person at the corner of Voinov Street and Volodarsky Prospect, where I detained him. Petrovsky did not help me with the detention of the unknown subject because when he ran out onto the street behind me he did not notice me and went on past.

Question: To whom did you hand over the unknown subject?

Answer: I handed over the unknown subject to Senior Operations Commissar Comrade Griunvald.

Question: Did Comrade Griunvald request a detailed explanation of the reasons for the detention? [. . .]

Answer: Yes, he did. I explained to Comrade Griunvald the reasons for the detention, telling him how the unknown subject behaved when he was following Comrades Kirov and Chudov.

Question: Did anyone at that time or afterwards demand of you a written report on the reasons for the detention?

Answer: No, they did not.

Question: What happened next with the detainee?

Answer: I don't know, as I immediately returned to my post.

Question: Did any ranking officers of the section or the department call you in later and ask you about the circumstances of the detention? [. . .]

Answer: No, they did not.

Question: Do you know the last name of the person you detained?

Answer: No, I do not know his last name.

Question: What did the unknown subject look like?

Answer: The features of the unknown subject were: below average height, dark hair, shaven face, [. . .] frail body, around thirty years old.

Question: How was the unknown subject dressed?

Answer: He was dressed in a dark pea jacket, pants worn over his boots, a cap on his head.

Question: Did the unknown subject have anything on his person?

Answer: The unknown subject had a briefcase with him.

Question: Are you certain that the unknown subject had a briefcase?

Answer: Yes, I am certain of it.

Question: What color was the briefcase?

Answer: Black.

Question: Do you recognize the person in this photograph as the subject you detained?

Answer: Yes, I do.

Question: Did you ask Comrade Griunvald or anyone else later about the fate of the person you detained?

Answer: No, I did not.

Question: You observed the suspicious behavior of the unknown person who was following Comrades Kirov and Chudov for an extended period of time. Said person was detained at your initiative. As soon as you handed the arrested man over, you left, as you had to hurry back to your duty post. But it remains puzzling why you showed no further interest in the fate of the person you had detained, especially given that you could have given the investigation more detailed information about the suspicious behavior of this person.

Answer: No one asked me further about this and for that reason I said nothing.

Question: Do you not find that such lack of interest in the operations that you yourself carried out is criminal and unacceptable in a chekist?

Answer: Yes, I fully agree with that formulation.

Question: Weren't you instructed by your supervisors that you had to make a written report after every incident during your time on duty?

Answer: No I was not.

Pauzer

Interrogated by Deputy Chief of the Special Department of the USSR

NKVD Sosnovsky and Chief of the Third Section of the Economic Security Department of the USSR NKVD Chertok.

Griunvald, to whose custody Pauzer had transferred Nikolaev, was questioned on December 6. He confirmed that the incident occurred in mid-October. Pauzer had come into his office, announcing that he had apprehended a suspicious person who had followed Kirov from Uritsky Square to the corner of Voinov St. and Volodarsky Prospect. The detainee was sitting outside Griunvald's office in the corridor. Griunvald ordered Officer Tereshchenko, who was sitting in the same room and heard Pauzer's report, to check Nikolaev's identity, then left immediately on other urgent business. He did not ask Pauzer whether he had already searched Nikolaev. In an apparent attempt to evade responsibility for failing to search Nikolaev himself, Griunvald stated that in such cases the plainclothes guards were expected to search detainees. He also testified that practice in the department was only to give "oral reports," rather than written ones, on routine detentions. In a second interrogation, around the same date, Griunvald indicated that Kirov's guards stopped "suspicious persons" in their charge's vicinity two to four times per month. No formal record was kept of every detention. Detained persons were taken to the nearest police, NKVD, or military police post. They were then transferred to the Operations Department offices in the NKVD Directorate building. Kirov's guards, he said, were supposed to search the detainee's person, but not on the street. They were to wait until they reached the police or military post. If these were in fact the instructions, they were problematic. For guards there was a conflict between orders to "isolate" detainees at a police post and search them, and the imperative to stay at their duty post with Kirov.[4]

A 1960 or 1961 report by the Party Control Committee states that in 1934 Officer Tereshchenko was not questioned. On the one hand, it is possible that Tereshchenko did do a body search of Nikolaev, but that central NKVD officers decided not to put him on record saying so. In this way they could claim in court that Nikolaev had never been searched, and strengthen the charges of negligence against Leningrad NKVD officers. On the other hand, Nikolaev testified on the night of December 1–2 that the NKVD had not searched him during the October 15 detention (see Chapter 7, Document 36). Presumably he was referring to a body search. So it may be that Tereshchenko simply assumed that Pauzer or Griunvald had already searched Nikolaev's person. It is clear at any rate that either Tereshchenko or Kotomin opened up Nikolaev's briefcase and examined the contents (see Kotomin's testimony below).

Questioned in 1939, as the Terror wound down, Tereshchenko wisely stonewalled investigators, denying he'd ever met Nikolaev before the night of the trial of the Leningrad Center on December 28–29, 1934, when he had guard duty in the courtroom.[5]

Tereshchenko took Nikolaev (or just his documents) to the chief of Kirov's guard, Mikhail Kotomin.

· 87 ·

Testimony of Mikhail Kotomin, head of Kirov's NKVD security detail, December 5, 1934. RGANI, f. 6, op. 13, d. 13, ll. 7–45 (1961 Klimov report to KPK on multiple detentions of Nikolaev).

———————

I do not remember precisely on what date in November one of the operations commissars, I can't remember which, brought into my office a person detained by the guard who turned out to be, according to his own word and documents, Nikolaev.

. . . I personally checked all of the documents he had on him, his party card, his old Smolny employment identification card, the card identifying him as an *instruktor* at the Institute of the History of the Party. He also had with him a briefcase, torn, with books and various old papers and newspapers in it. . . .

Question: Did the detainee Nikolaev have a weapon?

Answer: I don't remember whether he had a weapon, it seems to me that he had among his documents a license to carry a weapon [Nikolaev did indeed have such a document, albeit expired—see above, p. 191].

Question: Did you run any checks on the detainee Nikolaev?

Answer: I ordered one of my subordinates, I don't remember who, to check with the Address Bureau by telephone to see whether the detainee really lived at the address he had given us. This subordinate reported that the Address Bureau confirmed his address. After that I left the detainee in the office with one of my subordinates, I can't remember which, and I myself took all of the detainee's documents to the office of Operations Department Chief Comrade Gubin. I reported to him all the circumstances of Nikolaev's detention and our inquiry.

Comrade Gubin heard me out, examined the documents and ordered the detainee freed, which I did. . . .

Question: How did Nikolaev explain the fact that he tried to approach Comrade Kirov on the street?

Answer: To my question about that Nikolaev answered that he wanted to speak to Comrade Kirov as a party member with a personal question about work. At this point Nikolaev said: I didn't think that Comrade Kirov had a guard on the street, otherwise I wouldn't have tried to approach him on the street.

Question: Tell us, did you give your opinion about the best way to proceed with Nikolaev to your supervisor Comrade Gubin?

Answer: I reported only the factual side of the question of his detention, his documents, and the correctness of his address. I asked, "What should we do with him?" and did not give my opinion about his arrest or release. Comrade Gubin ordered the release of the detainee Nikolaev. In general I concurred with his decision. . . .

Question: Was a personal search of Nikolaev carried out after he was taken into custody?

Answer: I cannot answer this question, I believed that he had been searched, as there is a rule that each detained person is to be searched by the person who apprehended him before he is brought to me.

Question: Why was there no protocol drawn up about the search of Nikolaev, or his questioning?

Answer: I believed that to be superfluous given that his identity was obvious to me.

In another section of this interrogation that the author does not have permission to publish, Kotomin also stated that the guard had detained four or five persons a month in October–November 1934. Standard procedure was for these persons to be taken to Kotomin in the Operations Department Fourth Section. The latter would check their identification and report on the results to Gubin. Gubin would decide on their disposition. The Operations Department had ultimately released all persons taken into custody this way in October and November.[6]

In response to a question about Nikolaev's behavior in detention, Kotomin said that he had acted "calmly, normally . . . more calmly than many detainees."[7]

Another potentially significant point appears in sections of Kotomin's December 5 testimony not published here. Interrogators asked the chief of Kirov's guard whether anyone had checked for Nikolaev's name in the Directorate's "card catalogue" or inquired about Nikolaev with other NKVD departments. Kotomin said that he believed no one had. The question might (but does not necessarily) imply the possibility that there *was* a record on Nikolaev in the catalogue or at one of the departments, which the Operations Department failed to find.[8]

The December 6, 1934 evidence of Senior Operations Commissar Griunvald also contains a hint that some other department of the Leningrad NKVD might have had information on Nikolaev. Griunvald's interrogator Sosnovsky wanted to know if the Operations Department had ever received orders to keep an eye out for particular persons. In general, Griunvald answered, no, but there had been orders before the October holidays to watch out for "some Latvian."[9] The reference to "some Latvian," together with the attempt to recruit Bissenieks in December 1934, and the summer mass operations in search of espionage agents, indicates that the Leningrad NKVD was on the alert in the summer and fall of 1934 for spies and terrorists from Finland and the Baltics.

On December 6 central interrogators examined Gubin, chief of the Operations Department.

· 88 ·

Interrogation of Gubin, head of the Leningrad NKVD Operations Department (responsible for Kirov's guard detail), December 6, 1934. RGANI, f. 6, op. 13, d. 13, ll. 7–45 (1961 Klimov report to KPK on multiple detentions of Nikolaev).

I ordered the release of the detainee Nikolaev based on the following considerations:

(1) Nikolaev's identity was fully established.

(2) Nikolaev was a party member.

(3) Nikolaev, who worked in Smolny, knew S. M. Kirov.

(4) I considered Nikolaev's attempt to approach Comrade Kirov with a request for a job assignment natural and not suspicious, as there had been such cases before and afterwards.

. . . Chief of the Fourth Section of the Operations Department Kotomin reported to me on the detention of Nikolaev and the identity check. He also brought me all documents found on Nikolaev, I looked through these documents carefully /I remember well that one of his employment identification cards was dark red/. I also remember that I felt some doubt due to the fact that there were no stamps for payment of party dues on Nikolaev's party card for the last few months. Comrade Kotomin explained to me that this was in order, because Nikolaev was unemployed. . . .

Question: Did you yourself see Nikolaev?

Answer: No, I did not see him. . . . I heard about all of the circumstances of Nikolaev's detention and the reasons for that detention, that is [. . .] his suspicious behavior, from Comrade Kotomin alone. . . .

Question: What did you know about the results of any personal search of Nikolaev after his detention and at the time his identity was checked in the Operations Department?

Answer: I did not ask Kotomin about the results of the personal search of Nikolaev, as I already supposed /I was certain/ that a search had been done. I also supposed this was so first on the basis of existing regulations on the actions with regard to detainees, and second, on the basis of the entire content of Comrade Kotomin's report and his answers to my questions. Thus, to my question about what had been found in Nikolaev's briefcase Comrade Kotomin answered, "it's full of newspapers, obviously, since he's unemployed he has nothing to do and he is reading a lot. . . ."

Question: Did the group of Kirov's plainclothes guards have orders to carry out at least a superficial search of persons detained upon approaching Comrade Kirov and of those acting in a suspicious manner?

Answer: There are no particular general instructions or orders about this issue. However, in the course of our work it was said to officers that those detained on the street ought to be taken away from the place of detention, to the nearest police station or the Operations Department, where a search was to be immediately carried out. Searches were not done on the street.

I recognize and I admit that the check-up on Nikolaev was inadequate. The most important omission was that I did not ask about whether there had been a personal search of Nikolaev, or the results of that search, and that under these circumstances I decided to release Nikolaev based exclusively on my personal impressions of him, which derived only from Comrade Kotomin's report.

One day later (December 7) Agranov mentioned Nikolaev's October detention in one of his regular reports to Stalin and Yagoda.

· 89 ·

Excerpt from Agranov telegram to Stalin, December 7, 1934. TsA FSB RF, a.u.d. N-Sh44, t. 12, l. 87.

In the case of the release of L. Nikolaev after his detention on October 15, it has been determined that the chief of the Operations Department of the Leningrad regional NKVD Directorate, Gubin, and the head of the Fourth Section of said department, Kotomin, did not take the most elementary measures to check Nikolaev's identity, nor did they carry out a

search of Nikolaev's briefcase, where there was a revolver and counterrevolutionary materials. Gubin and Kotomin were arrested [. . .] on December 6.

Agranov.
December 7, 1934.
Leningrad.

Agranov's bulletin was deceptive. Kotomin claimed to have searched
Nikolaev's briefcase, and Gubin backed him up. Kotomin also claimed
that he had checked Nikolaev's identity with some care, and the Operations Department log description of Nikolaev confirms his story at
least in part. The real issue in the interrogations was whether anyone
had searched Nikolaev's person.

Agranov also stated in his bulletin that Nikolaev had his pistol and
"counterrevolutionary materials" in his briefcase when detained. This
too was deceptive. Based on the evidence accumulated prior to December 8, it seems quite likely that Nikolaev did not have his weapon
or such "materials." Kotomin, as already noted, asserted that he had
gone through Nikolaev's briefcase and found only identification documents, books, and old newspapers. Nikolaev himself claimed on December 2 that at the time he was detained he was not considering
shooting Kirov, and his writings from this period indicate that this is
quite plausible. Clearly Agranov was exaggerating the culpability of
Kirov's guard in the Nikolaev detention, part of the overall attack on
the Leningrad NKVD that followed the assassination and which Yagoda's September/October 1934 memorandum [see above, p. 145] foreshadowed. One way or another it was obvious that Stalin wanted punishment for the "idiots" in Leningrad who had allowed the murder to
happen. Agranov had to deliver evidence to justify this.

On December 8, just one day after Agranov's bulletin cited above,
Nikolaev signed testimony that backed up the bulletin's hitherto unsubstantiated claims. One might speculate that Agranov, who left for
Moscow on the night of December 7–8, had ordered his subordinates
to get such "evidence" from the assassin. Nikolaev gave this testimony
during or immediately after the period when he refused to cooperate
with investigators, attempted suicide, and resisted leaving his cell (December 7–8). It can be viewed either as the result of his readiness to incriminate officers of the same organization that was tormenting him or
of the investigators once again "breaking" him to their will.

· 90 ·

Excerpt from Leonid Nikolaev's testimony of December 8, 1934. RGANI, f. 6, op. 13, d. 13, ll. 7–45 (1961 Klimov report to KPK on multiple detentions of Nikolaev).

On October 15 there was supposed to be a meeting of the city party organization. I went to Smolny one hour before the meeting [. . .] because I was not able to get a ticket to the meeting beforehand and hoped to get one just before the meeting. I don't remember from whom I heard that Kirov and Chudov were not going to be at the meeting—Ugarov was running it—and that they had just left for home on foot towards Krasnykh Zor Street. I decided that I had to use the excellent opportunity that presented itself and I went after them. I followed Kirov and Chudov all the way to number 28 [Krasnykh Zor Street/Kamennoostrovsky Prospect] without shooting; I refrained from an attack because I thought that I'd have to shoot at both and this did not enter into my plans. At that moment I was arrested by Kirov's guard, who thought that my behavior was suspicious. I was taken by car to the building of the NKVD Directorate of Leningrad Region to the on-duty officer. . . .

Question: At the moment of your arrest did you have with you your Nagan and your notes of an anti-Soviet character?

Answer: Yes, the Nagan and the notes of an anti-Soviet character were on me. Everything was in the briefcase I was carrying with me.

Question: Were you searched at the moment of your detention or when you were brought into the NKVD Directorate?

Answer: No. Inside the NKVD Directorate building the on-duty officer asked if I had a weapon and whether I had been searched. I answered in the negative to both questions and nonetheless was released without being searched.

Nikolaev's account of his visit to Smolny to get a ticket to the city party meeting and his decision to follow Kirov and Chudov may well correspond to reality. However, his claim that he was carrying a weapon with the intention of murdering Kirov on October 15 is questionable. For one thing, it looks very much like an add-on from his interrogators who wished to implicate the Leningrad NKVD in negligence. For another, Nikolaev's explanation that he chose not to attack because shooting both Kirov and Chudov "did not enter into my plans" does not make much sense. It is more likely that Nikolaev followed Kirov and Chudov with the intention of talking to Kirov about a job assignment and the injustice done him at the Institute of Party

History. Moreover, if we accept Kotomin's and Gubin's testimony, the Leningrad NKVD did search his briefcase. They would have found the pistol and the anti-Soviet literature had they been there.

The change in the story of Nikolaev's detention, made by Agranov before any evidence corroborated it and then extracted from Nikolaev in contradiction to his earlier description of events, had fateful consequences. In the central show trials of 1936–1938 prosecutors backed up their assertions of a gigantic conspiracy to kill Kirov with the tale that the Leningrad NKVD officers had found a revolver and counter-revolutionary documents on Nikolaev on October 15, but released him anyway. Stalin used the claim of a gigantic conspiracy to incriminate his real and imagined political rivals; Khrushchev and de-Stalinizers later used it to implicate Stalin.

Agranov and Yezhov returned from Moscow on December 9. Among other things, Yezhov apparently had a mandate from Stalin to work up a case for the incompetence of Kirov's guard. This included not just the question of Nikolaev's release on October 15, but also that of the guards' failure to stop the assassin on December 1. Jottings in Yezhov's notebook dated December 9 indicate that he questioned Medved and Fomin, guard officer Dureiko, Operations Department chief Gubin, Smolny deputy commandant Mikhailchenko, his deputy Bravy, the electrician Platoch, the circus director Tsukerman, and Molochnikov, the chief of the Leningrad NKVD Economic Security Department, who had conducted many of the first interrogations in the case on the evening of December 1. In his notes Yezhov focused on events at the scene of the crime. One of his aims, for example, was to demonstrate that Medved had lied in his first telegraphic report on the assassination, when he claimed that Borisov had been with Kirov at the moment he was killed.[10]

Yezhov also distrusted the testimony of the third-floor guard Dureiko, whom he labeled "an unreliable person." He scribbled, "Dureiko in reality left," presumably suggesting that Dureiko was nowhere near Kirov when the killing occurred. "Dureiko is obviously lying about Borisov" indicated that Yezhov did not believe his testimony placing Borisov just a few steps behind Kirov at the moment Nikolaev fired. When Yezhov questioned Dureiko about his duties, the latter indicated that his superiors had given him no instructions or training for the job.[11]

Yezhov noted of Molochnikov that he might not have interrogated Borisov until four to five hours after the crime. In Fomin's testimony

Yezhov noted that forty minutes after Kirov's killing (when Fomin arrived on the scene), the third-floor corridors in Smolny had not been cleared and there were about seventy persons milling about. Fomin had no idea whether Borisov had been near Kirov at the time of the murder. With regard to Gubin, the head of the Operations Department, Yezhov wrote, "Put on trial for negligence. An idiot . . . an old chekist who has lost his connection to the party."[12]

There is no documentary evidence on the charges of negligence Yezhov proposed against Gubin until January 7, 1935. On that day Gubin addressed a statement to L. G. Mironov, the head of the central NKVD Economic Security Department who seems to have been handed charge of the Leningrad NKVD case in late December. Gubin defended himself stubbornly. His letter also contains important evidence on the history of Kirov's guard in 1933–1934.

· 91 ·

Self-defense of Gubin, head of Leningrad NKVD Operations Department, to
L. G. Mironov, January 7, 1935. RGANI, f. 6, op. 13, d. 80, ll. 137–139.

To the Chief of the Economic Security Department of the NKVD Comrade Mironov:

As a supplement to my earlier depositions, I request that you attach the following to my case file.

At the telegraphed request of [central] Operations Department chief Comrade Pauker, on December 1, 1933 a report was presented, with the knowledge of Comrade Medved, to the Operations Department of the former OGPU on the procedures and circumstances associated with guarding Comrade Kirov, and on the measures necessary to guard him. In the report it was stated that resistance (*nesoglasie*) to the guard from Comrade Kirov himself was an obstacle to maintaining a real guard over him /a copy of the report is in Operations Department files/.

One and a half months ago, on November 16 to be precise, in a personal report to Comrade Pauker, I advised him that Comrade Kirov still refused to permit any [effective] guard.

As the most recent example of this situation I brought up the following episode: during the first half of October 1934 (before October 15) Comrade Medved informed me that Comrade Kirov, during his latest walk around the city, noted a Ford auto following him, concluded that this was an NKVD vehicle, and directly ordered Comrade Medved to stop this practice of trailing him. I also reported to Comrade Pauker that in connection with these circumstances I lived in fear that the slightest public exposure (*rasshifrovka*) of the guard or its discovery by Comrade Kirov would lead to a final and categorical prohibition on any guard.

To this Comrade Pauker responded with an order that things must not be allowed to go so far, and that it was essential to write to the Central Committee [that is, to Stalin]. Upon my return from Moscow on November 22 I reported to Comrade Medved on my presentation to Comrade Pauker and his orders.

With all of the above I wish to show that I always strove to improve and did improve Comrade Kirov's guard.

With regard to the question of my participation in the guard, I declare that on all security assignments where Comrades Kirov or Chudov were expected to be present, I was always present. I personally checked on the guard, checked the posts. At the site I checked the guards' knowledge of their duties, and when necessary, instructed them. I also generally had an officer reporting to me whose duty was to monitor the work of the guards. Upon the arrival of Comrade Kirov or Chudov I myself stuck close by them. I was always at the railroad station when Comrade Kirov departed or arrived, in order to guard him. In order to guard him I was also at every meeting where Comrade Kirov was expected to be present, and at the plenary sessions of the regional party committee in Smolny.

In order to check and monitor the work of the guards there was a procedure set up such that any movements of Comrade Kirov were immediately reported to me by the guards on the scene. The officers accompanying Comrade Kirov by car also communicated to me the routes of his travels through the city.

In addition I checked up directly on the permanent guard posts, I made the last check between November 10 and 20, 1934. I recall that at that time I discovered the absence of the police post set up at the demand of the Operations Department by the building where Comrade Kirov lived. I reported this to Chief of Police Comrade Zhupakhin, with whom I made arrangements for cooperation in guard duties in the future.

The most recent training in vigilance for operations commissars guarding Comrade Kirov was conducted by me on November 14, 1934.

During my last interrogation in Comrade Agranov's office, I was asked some questions that I did not have time to answer. (1) Under what circumstances was Officer Borisov appointed to the guard and (2) Did I report Nikolaev's detention to anyone.

I declare:

(1) When I took over the Operations Department [. . .] the secretary of the [. . .] department Maksimov told me that in 1930, soon after Comrade Kirov's arrival from Tiflis [*sic*], the former section chief of the Oper-

ations Department Comrade Yakubenko returned from a meeting looking very disturbed, and gave an order to immediately remove Officer Bravy from the guard, replacing him with Borisov, as [the latter was] a better fit for the job. This was done immediately.

(2) On October 16 I reported in writing to Comrade Medved and his deputy Comrade Fomin on the October 15 detention of Nikolaev for attempting to approach Comrades Kirov and Chudov on the street. On the log, which Comrade Fomin had, there is a note in his hand (the log is in Operations Department files).

I also declare that in the report of the Operations Department duty officer for October 15, 1934, in which there were supposed to be included all incidents that occurred during the day, the fact of Nikolaev's detention was not noted. On October 16 I wrote a note on the original report ordering the inclusion of the detention, which was done by hand by the chief of the Fourth Department Kotomin. The most serious or urgent intelligence from the Operations duty officer's report and information coming from the other subdepartments of the Operations Department were included in the daily Operations Department digest which was produced to the regional NKVD leadership. This was done on October 16 [as usual].

/The duty officer's report for October 15 and the digest from October 16 are in the Operations Department files/

The fact that in order to ascertain who Nikolaev was I personally and carefully checked the detainee Nikolaev's documents presented to me by Comrade Kotomin, including his party card/which showed that he had been a Communist Party member since 1924 or 1926/, that I checked with Kotomin that Nikolaev was from among the workers/the name of the factory and his specialization I do not remember/, that the photographs on two of the identification cards /from the regional Control Commission and the Institute of History of the Party/ were identical with the detainee, that the address given by Nikolaev corresponded to that registered at the Address Bureau, and the [fact of] the other measures taken to clarify Nikolaev's identity, and also, the fact that I insisted that the case of Nikolaev's detention that was omitted from the duty officer's report be included, and that I forwarded [the report on Nikolaev's detention] to the leadership of the regional NKVD, all demonstrate that I was not negligent in my duties, that I recognized the significance of this matter, hid nothing, and did not shirk.

January 7, 1935
Gubin

Gubin enlarged on the history of Kirov's guard in an interrogation on January 13, 1935. He had been appointed to head the Leningrad NKVD Operations Department in June 1933, at which point there

were only three officers in the guard—Borisov whose duty post was
Smolny, the doorkeeper at his apartment, and Bukovsky, the personal
assistant who guarded Kirov on trips outside the city (police and
OGPU troops, however, assisted with the guard in public places).[13]
Just days after taking over the Operations Department Gubin received
a "strict censure for carelessness" in the organization of Kirov's guard.
This was in July 1933. Kirov had driven from Leningrad to Moscow
with only Bukovsky along to protect him. Gubin claimed that Medved
had ordered him not to send any other guards along.[14]

Evidence given by Kirov's secretary N. F. Sveshnikov and Operations Department officers nearly thirty years after the murder fills gaps
in Gubin's account of events in the summer of 1933. As Gubin noted
in his January 1935 testimony, he was appointed chief of the Operations Department in summer 1933, probably in June. According to
former Operations Department officer Ivan Ivanovich Baskakov, Medved fired the previous Operations Department chief, Eduard Fyodorovich Lampe, after a knife-wielding assailant attacked I. Brodsky, a
painter friendly with Kirov, inside Smolny. N. F. Sveshnikov in 1966
remembered the same incident, placing it on the building's first floor,
and recalled that Kirov called Medved afterwards to demand "some
kind of order in Smolny."[15]

Sveshnikov reported to Party Control Committee investigators in
1966 that Kirov's July 1933 drive to Moscow was connected to Stalin's
visit to the Leningrad Region later that month. Apparently Stalin was
considering going to Leningrad by car rather than rail. To ensure that
road conditions were acceptable, Kirov drove to Moscow and back.
According to Sveshnikov, he then returned to Moscow by auto, picked
up Stalin and Voroshilov, and drove back to Leningrad. From July 18
to 25 Stalin, Kirov, Yenukidze, and Voroshilov toured Leningrad, the
newly completed White Sea Canal, and the port of Murmansk. At the
end of "the Chief's" visit, Kirov was exhausted.[16]

Officer Baskakov provided further details on Kirov's security arrangements and Stalin's 1933 visit to Leningrad. Baskakov served
from 1933 until October 1934 as deputy chief of the Leningrad Operations Department "for general operational questions" and was involved in the organization of Kirov's security detail. He testified to
Party Control Committee officials in January 1961 that Medved told
him Stalin had not stayed in Kirov's apartment during his 1933 visit
because he did not like being in a "large building of rented apartments."
Instead "the Chief" stayed in a separate house (*osobniak*) where secu-

rity was tighter. Based on Stalin's doubts about the safety of Kirov's housing, Medved ordered Operations Department officers Bukovsky (Kirov's personal assistant) and Tereshchenko (involved in handling Nikolaev's October 15 detention—see above) to scout out possible separate houses that Kirov could be moved to. Baskakov stated that Bukovsky and Tereshchenko found four possibilities, but the move was not made "for reasons unknown to me." Rosliakov reports that construction on a new house for Kirov was begun on Krestovsky Island (perhaps after the rejection of the possibilities suggested by Bukovsky and Tereshchenko?). In any event it is clear that security officials initiated a project in 1933–1934 to move Kirov into a separate house.[17]

These accounts show that Stalin was unhappy with the security arrangements for Kirov when he visited Leningrad in the summer of 1933, and they strongly imply that he ordered them strengthened. It was most likely Stalin himself who suggested to NKVD officials that they censure Gubin for allowing Kirov to drive to Moscow and back almost unaccompanied. It was probably Stalin too who told Yagoda or Medved that Kirov ought to be moved to a separate house. Clearly Stalin could have had more than one aim when he sought to strengthen Kirov's guard. He probably wanted to protect Kirov—within six months he promoted him to a more prominent role in the Politburo and sought to transfer him to Moscow. He may also have sought tighter control over the Leningrad leader and his surroundings.

In his interrogation of January 13, 1935 Gubin described the measures he took to improve Kirov's guard following Stalin's visit. He fired the doorkeeper at Kirov's apartment because he was a drunk and replaced him with two sober Operations Department officers and two "elevator operators." Sometime in the winter of 1933–1934 Gubin began sending two guard officers with a car and driver to Kirov's building at 9 or 9:30 A.M. to accompany Kirov when he traveled about the city. Three Operations Department officers were stationed by the main entrance at Smolny to cover Kirov's arrivals and departures. Gubin also placed a roving guard officer on the third floor of the party headquarters (this was Dureiko's post on the day of the murder). He told interrogators that he had not issued written instructions to guards, but provided frequent oral ones. Gubin stated that he reported directly to Medved on questions of the guard. In Medved's absence he dealt with Zaporozhets or Fomin. During this period the number of men formally assigned to Kirov's NKVD guard increased from three to fifteen.[18]

Gubin's testimony reveals that the central NKVD Operations Department monitored Kirov's guard in the year and a half between Stalin's visit and the assassination. Gubin reminded his interrogators that he had traveled to Moscow to report on the guard in September 1933, May 1934, and November 1934. During the May 1934 trip "Moscow" (presumably the central Operations Department) approved the Operations Department staff who were part of the Smolny *komendatura*. Moreover, Gubin reported, Pauker and Gulko regularly instructed him by telephone on the organization of the guard.[19]

In 1960–1961 Officer Baskakov and former Smolny deputy commandant A. D. Mikhalchenko each testified about a project both had worked on to improve Kirov's security following the knife attack and Stalin's visit in the summer of 1933. Access to the (previously open) regional and city party committee premises on the third floor was restricted to holders of party cards or special passes from first-floor offices. Kirov's office was moved away from the main stairway on the third-floor central corridor to larger rooms on the small corridor. The special side entrance for the exclusive use of high-ranking officials was set up, although Kirov used it rarely, if at all. There were plans to require special passes to see Kirov, but these were not implemented before the murder.[20]

A picture emerges from the interrogations of Operations Department commissars in 1934–1935, supplemented with testimony from the early 1960s, of Leningrad NKVD officers under pressure from the center to strengthen Kirov's guard. Kirov, however, as testified to by many witnesses, did not like being hemmed in by his security. He resisted the assignment of a car to follow him on his walks through the city, he insisted that guards on foot keep their distance, he refused to use the special side entrance at Smolny established for him, and he seems to have delayed his move to a separate house. In his November 16, 1934 report to Moscow NKVD officials on Kirov's security detail, Gubin noted that "As in the past Kirov does not accept a guard . . . during his most recent drive through the city he noticed the [guard's] automobile shadowing him . . . [and] ordered Medved to put an end to the shadowing." Medved was caught between a rock and a hard place. Sveshnikov in 1966 recalled tense conversations between him and Kirov about the security detail. Rosliakov, also in the 1960s, claimed that Kirov was not eager to leave his apartment for a separate house. Gubin's 1934–1935 evidence shows that even Karl Pauker, head of the central Operations Department, was at a loss to deal with the resistance of Kirov, who was after all a Politburo member, and apparently in favor with Stalin. When Kirov threatened to forbid the automobile escort, Pauker could only tell Gubin that he had to write to "the Central Committee," that is to Stalin.[21]

With regard to Nikolaev's detention or detentions by the NKVD, it is very likely that October 15 was the only date that he was taken into custody. The October 15 detention is the only encounter with Nikolaev that figures in the 1934–1935 evidence taken from officers involved with Kirov's guard. It is possible that there were other occasions when Nikolaev tried to approach Kirov, under the pretext of presenting a petition to him, but was blocked by guards. This may have happened at Moscow Station, for example, on November 14. Years later a number of guards claimed to have participated in multiple detentions of Nikolaev, but as we shall see this evidence was severely contaminated by the denunciatory bacchanalia of the Great Terror. It is also likely that NKVD officers who read Nikolaev's "diaries" passed on his stories about being detained on October 15, seeing Kirov drive past a bus stop on Krasnykh Zor Street on November 5, and his attempt to get at Kirov at the railway station on November 14. Through telling and retelling, a chain of interlocutors could have blown up these incidents into much more dramatic tales—of Nikolaev jumping onto the running board of Kirov's car, for example.

Another source of rumors about multiple detentions of Nikolaev appears in the 1960–1961 evidence of Officer Baskakov. On November 22, 1960 Baskakov told Party Control Committee officials that he remembered a suspicious detention that took place "maybe in the spring of 1934." He was on duty in place of Operations Department chief Gubin, when a call came in from the police guard post outside Kirov's apartment building. The policeman on duty had detained "an unknown person who was trying to approach Kirov as he exited his car." The "unknown person" turned out to have a loaded Nagan pistol in his briefcase. Operations Department officers brought the arrested man to Baskakov, who wrote up a protocol of his detention and search. Baskakov stated that the arrestee was a student of the Forestry Academy, who was also carrying release documents from a psychiatric hospital. Medved turned the case over to one Officer Migbert, head of the Counterrevolutionary Organizations Subdepartment of the Leningrad OGPU/NKVD. Later Migbert told Baskakov that in spite of a "long struggle" he had not been able to connect the arrested forestry student to any group. He appeared to have acted alone.[22]

Just over one year after Baskakov's initial testimony, in February 1962, Control Committee investigators uncovered documentation in the Leningrad KGB archive on the arrest of the "forestry student." He turned out to be Fyodor Romanovich Nikolenko, and he was arrested on March 24, 1932, not in the spring of 1934, at the bus/tram stop near Kirov's apartment building. As Baskakov had recalled, the arresting officer, Safronov, was on duty at the guard post by Kirov's building. The officer had observed Nikolenko standing at the tram stop just after midnight for about one hour. He did not take any of the trams or buses that stopped. When he tried to enter the apartment building, Safronov arrested him and brought him to the nearest police station. Nikolenko had a loaded Nagan in his briefcase and more ammunition in his pocket. Under interrogation he stated that he had been waiting for his sister at the stop. He also claimed that for about two weeks he had been considering suicide due to his family's poverty (seven persons in an apartment of twenty-six square meters) and his impending break-up with his common-law wife. Hence the loaded pistol. Witnesses accused Nikolenko of anti-Soviet talk and assaulting his wife. The OGPU Collegium convicted him of plotting to murder Kirov and sentenced him to five years hard labor. In 1940 the NKVD executed him.[23]

It seems very likely that some later rumors in the Leningrad NKVD about multiple detentions of Leonid Nikolaev were in fact based partly on Nikolenko's arrest. The similarity in family names and the "Nagan in the briefcase" element of the story could well have caused former officers of the guard to connect Nikolenko and Nikolaev. So too could the fact that Nikolaev in December 1934 claimed that he'd been detained outside Kirov's apartment, as Nikolenko had been in reality two and a half years earlier.

In considering stories about multiple detentions and other rumors about Nikolaev, it is also important to remember Alla Kirilina's point that the family name Nikolaev was ubiquitous in Leningrad. There were other Nikolaevs working in the Leningrad regional party committee apparatus. Probably around 0.5 percent of the population bore the name. In fact, Alla Kirilina has found that there was another Communist Leonid Vasilevich Nikolaev in Leningrad at the time, a Communist factory worker also born in 1904. The second Leonid Nikolaev died in May 1934. There are complete sets of party records for both, for example, from the 1929 party purge. Their biographies were different, and they had different party card numbers. The existence of so many Nikolaevs, and of one other Leonid Vasilevich Nikolaev, could easily have sparked rumors in later years from people who mistakenly believed that they had met Kirov's assassin.[24]

Nikolaev's Acquaintances in the NKVD and Smolny

Central NKVD officers did not limit their search for conspiracies and incompetence to Nikolaev's October 15 detention. On December 8 they questioned the assassin about his sources of information inside Smolny on Kirov's movements. Nikolaev testified that Vladimirov, a *referent* (assessor) for the city party committee with connections inside Kirov's secretariat, had told him about Kirov's habits, when he had lunch, and so on. It was Vladimirov, Nikolaev said, who informed him that Kirov's office was being moved.[25]

Nikolaev also claimed he'd received useful information from regional party committee employee Petrashevich, city committee employee Karmanov, and a female clerk in the mailroom whose name he didn't know. Petrashevich, besides engaging to get him a ticket to the December 1 activists' meeting, had given him information on the dates and times of plenary sessions of the city and regional party committees. He'd also told him when Kirov would be speaking. Karmanov discussed personnel changes in the Smolny offices with Nikolaev. The unidentified clerk had let him know when Kirov was returning from at least one of his sojourns outside the city. On December 8 Nikolaev did not accuse these people of consciously abetting his crime. He implied that they had simply been making conversation with him.[26]

On December 9 Agranov, Mironov, and Dmitriev asked Nikolaev about his acquaintances and contacts in the NKVD. Nikolaev named three, Yaroslants, Ponomarenko, and Pankratev. Yaroslants he had known in 1924–1925 (before Yaroslants joined the NKVD) when both did Komsomol work in Leningrad and Luga. After that time they had had only "chance encounters." In August of 1934, Nikolaev told interrogators, he had gone to NKVD headquarters in Leningrad and called Yaroslants, who headed a section of the Leningrad NKVD Economic Security Department, from downstairs. Nikolaev wanted to know how to put in a formal request that his brother-in-law Pyotr Draule, recently sentenced for embezzling police funds, serve his term not in a Far Eastern labor camp, but near Leningrad. Yaroslants directed Nikolaev to the Directorate of Corrective Labor Institutions of Leningrad Region. Nikolaev then got off the phone. This was the only recent contact he'd had with Yaroslants, he said. When interrogators asked why Nikolaev hadn't made a formal request through the courts, he replied, plausibly enough, that he had no personal contacts in the judiciary.

Nikolaev knew Ponomarenko, now an officer in the Special Department of the Baltic Fleet NKVD, from 1931 to 1932. They had worked together in the "Down with Illiteracy!" association at Smolny. Nikolaev had visited Ponomarenko once in his apartment, but said that he had not seen him since 1932.

At the beginning of the December 9 interrogation, Nikolaev mentioned Pankratev, an employee of the Communications Department, as one of his NKVD acquaintances. However, later in the same session he denied direct acquaintance. He had heard of Pankratev from the latter's mother, who lived in the same apartment building with him.[27]

On December 13 interrogators returned to questions about Nikolaev's contacts inside Smolny and the NKVD.

· 92 ·

Protocol of interrogation of Nikolaev, December 13, 1934. RGANI, f. 6, op. 13, d. 1, l. 98.

Question: Did you have collaborators in the terrorist attack on Comrade Kirov among Smolny employees?

Answer: I had no collaborators. I used a number of employees of Smolny to ascertain Kirov's movements. I have already given evidence on this. I did not even need direct collaborators from among the Smolny office workers, because I found out what I needed to accomplish the terrorist attack by means of conversations with workers I knew, and besides, Kotolynov gave me quite a bit of help in determining Kirov's movements.

Question: Without collaborators among the employees in Smolny there is no way that you could have had such precise information about Comrade Kirov's movements. The investigation orders you to name which of the Smolny office workers was a direct collaborator in the murder.

Answer: Once again I repeat that I had no collaborators in Smolny. I had no need of them.

Question: Did you have collaborators among the employees of the regional NKVD directorate?

Answer: [. . .] I have already testified that I had no collaborators.

Question: Did any of the other participants in the counterrevolutionary organization have connections with employees of the NKVD directorate, and were they utilized for the accomplishment of the terrorist action?

Answer: I know nothing about that, personally I had no such connections, if you don't count my acquaintances Yaroslants and Ponomarenko, who I have already testified about. They had no relation to the terrorist act.

Question: Were you acquainted with Officer Borisov of the regional NKVD directorate, who guarded Comrade Kirov?

Answer: No, I don't know him.

Question: From whom did you hear about the existence of the special entrance to Smolny, which Comrades Kirov, Chudov, and Kodatsky used regularly?

Answer: [. . .] I found about the existence of that entrance by observing Comrade Kirov's entrances and exits at Smolny.

Transcribed from my words correctly.

I have read through this protocol.

L. Nikolaev

Interrogators: Agranov, Mironov, Dmitriev.

Obviously this interrogation does not prove Nikolaev had no contact with NKVD agents, open or clandestine, before Kirov's murder. But it does raise serious doubts about central NKVD involvement in any plot to kill Kirov using Nikolaev. The central NKVD went to great lengths to investigate any possible Leningrad NKVD enmeshment with Nikolaev. If the chief officers of the central NKVD had been "running" Nikolaev, with or without his knowledge, would they have initiated such a serious investigation, which could uncover awkward facts that might become more widely known inside and outside the police apparatus? It does not seem likely.

Borisov's Death

At around 11 A.M. on the morning of December 2, Medved or Agranov had ordered the NKVD to send Kirov's guard Borisov to Smolny for questioning by Stalin (see above, p. 263). Officer Noya Zavilovich at NKVD headquarters called the Special Department, but officers there were not holding Borisov. Then he called Khviiuzov, head of the Third Section of the Operations Department. On December 4 Khviiuzov testified to receiving the call and dispatching Borisov from NKVD headquarters in a one-and-a-half-ton Ford pickup truck with a driver, Kuzin, and two escorting officers, Maly and Vinogradov. Borisov, however, never reached Smolny. On Voinova Street the truck reportedly had an accident and Borisov died of head injuries within minutes. Central NKVD officials, Yezhov, and presumably Stalin too, immediately suspected foul play. Borisov was supposed to be guarding Kirov at the time of the murder. Could Leningrad NKVD officers, fearing that Borisov would provide evidence of their negligence in guarding Kirov, have murdered him? The day of the accident the central NKVD arrested and interrogated Kuzin, Maly, Vinogradov, and N. S. Maksimov, an Operations Department officer who helped escort Borisov to the truck before he left NKVD headquarters. An expert commission was organized to make an accident report, and eyewitnesses to the accident—there were at least four, including two police officers on duty near the accident scene and one regional party committee *instruktor*—were questioned.[28]

· 93 ·

Protocol of interrogation of Nikolai Ivanovich Vinogradov, officer of the Operations Department of Leningrad Region NKVD. Interrogator: Mironov. December 2, 1934. TsA FSB RF, a.u.d. N-Sh44, t. 24, ll. 255–256.

Vinogradov, Nikolai Ivanovich, b. 1906, native of Ivanovo Industrial Region, [. . .] Russian, of poor peasant origins, [. . .] married, wife Anna Mikhailovna (dependent), holds no property, secondary school education, candidate member of Communist Party from 1931, no court record, subject to military service, has not served.

Today, Dec. 2, I received an order from my boss, Officer Maly of the Operations Department, to accompany him in the execution of said order [bringing Borisov from Leningrad NKVD headquarters to party headquarters at Smolny]. Maly ordered me to find Borisov and bring him with me. Comrade Maly and I located Borisov in the office of Chief of the Operations Department Fourth Section Kotomin, where he was asleep. We woke him and at Maly's order he came with us. The three of us [. . .] accompanied by a driver, whose name I do not know, left NKVD headquarters and got into a one-and-a half-ton truck. This is how we disposed ourselves in the truck: Officer Maly sat with the driver in the cabin, while Borisov and I sat in the back on a bench attached to the driver's cabin. I sat on the left side /oriented in the direction of the truck's motion/ and Borisov sat on the right, both of us with our backs to the truck cabin. Comrade Maly ordered the driver to take us to Smolny. Leaving NKVD headquarters, the driver developed a speed of 50–60 km/hour. In a little while the auto began to zigzag, then tilted strongly to the left and at that very moment turned suddenly to the right with a sharp jolt and hit the wall of a building with great force [. . .] with the side on which [. . .] Borisov was sitting. The truck hit at high speed and after the powerful impact with the wall turned to the left, away from it.

Borisov hit his head hard on the wall of the building and I was thrown to the right, but I managed to grab the bench and oppose the force of impact with the wall. Maly managed to jump out of the truck after it hit the wall, while the driver remained at the wheel the entire time. Comrade Maly stopped a light automobile that was passing and we transported Borisov to the Medical Department [of the NKVD] for first aid. Borisov's head and coat were covered with blood, as blood was flowing out of his nose and mouth from the blow. I did not receive any injuries. We brought Borisov to the Medical Department and handed him over to medical personnel, after which I returned to work at the NKVD offices.

Vinogradov.

Officer Dmitry Maly rode in the passenger seat of the truck cab, with the driver Kuzin.

· 94 ·

Protocol of interrogation of Dmitry Zinovevich Maly. Interrogator: Liushkov. December 2, 1934. TsA FSB RF, a.u.d. N-Sh44, t. 24, ll. 253–254.

Dmitry Zinovevich Maly, b. 1901, Sevastopol, Russian, father from middle peasants, an artisan/cooper [. . .]. Operations Officer of the Operations Department of the Leningrad Region NKVD. Married [. . .]. Finished seven-year primary school. Member of the Communist Party from 1928. Served in NKVD organs from 1922. No court record. No service with Whites.

Q: What orders did you receive today, December 2, before you left for Smolny, and who gave them to you?

A: Around 11 A.M. this morning, December 2, I received an order from the Chief of the Third Section of the Operations Department Comrade P. Khviiuzov, to go immediately to Smolny with Officer Borisov, Comrade Kirov's guard, and report to Comrade Chudov's office. To accompany Borisov, Khviiuzov suggested I bring with me another officer. At my own initiative I took Officer of the Third Section of the Operations Department Vinogradov, whom I ordered to go to the Red Corner—that's where the on-duty drivers usually waited—and get a driver.

As Vinogradov said that there were no light autos available, Comrade Khviiuzov ordered me to take a one-and-a-half-ton truck. I then woke Borisov, who was asleep in the office of Fourth Section Chief Kotomin, and we all—that is, Vinogradov, Borisov, the driver /whose name I do not know/, and I—went to the truck, which was parked by the NKVD head-quarters building on Voinova Street.

First I put Borisov with Vinogradov in the back of the truck, and then I myself got into the cabin next to the driver.

Question: Describe the circumstances of the auto accident.

Answer: We traveled away from the NKVD building on Voinov Street, headed toward Smolny with a speed of no more than 25 km/hour. The road was completely dry, there was not much traffic. Gradually the truck sped up, but it seems to me that we did not go faster than 40 km/hour. I did not rush the driver, although he knew of the urgency of our trip. After we crossed the intersection with Potemkin St. the truck turned suddenly to the left, the driver began to turn to the right [to counteract the left turn], but the truck did not respond well to the steering. Before we hit the wall the driver managed to shout to me "the steering!" Then the truck banged hard with its right side into the wall of a building on the right side of the street [. . .] not far from Uritsky Square. After the impact the truck turned away to the left, zigzagging, and /after I had jumped out of the smashed cabin/ stopped about fifteen meters from the place where it hit the wall, possibly because it was braked. Given that the truck continued to move after the impact I presume that despite losing control of the steering, the driver did not apply full pressure to the brakes. After the accident I imme-diately ran to the truck and saw Borisov unconscious and with a broken head, supported by Vinogradov. Vinogradov and I took Borisov to the Medical Department of the NKVD in a light auto that was passing.

Maly

Maly's statement that Vinogradov had reported there were no cars available in the NKVD auto pool bears noting. Investigators later would come back again and again to the question of why Operations Department officers put Borisov in the back of an open-bed truck, a dangerous place to travel, when they dispatched him to Smolny. How plausible was Maly and Vinogradov's claim (Khviiuzov made the same assertion) about the lack of cars? Quite plausible. A large central gov-ernment commission with two hundred guards had arrived in Lenin-grad that morning, and the city's NKVD was also engaged in arresting dozens of potential suspects in the murder. Demand on the motor pool was high, and it makes sense that all the cars were in use. In 1988 for-mer Special Department officer Leonid Raikhman told Alla Kirilina,

"Many today greatly oversimplify the situation in Leningrad on December 2. You see, a whole cavalcade of top authorities had arrived in the city. All of the light automobiles, and not only those of the regional NKVD offices, were in use. Stalin wanted to interrogate Borisov . . . they took Borisov to Smolny as fast as possible in a truck. . . ."[29]

The NKVD also interrogated the truck driver immediately following the accident.

· 95 ·

Protocol of interrogation of Vasily Mikhailovich Kuzin. Interrogator: B. Agas. December 2, 1934. TsA FSB RF, a.u.d. N-Sh44, t. 24, ll. 259–262.

———————

Vasily Mikhailovich Kuzin, born 1908, Russian, Western Region [. . .] driver of Transport Department of Leningrad regional NKVD. Employed as driver from 1930, first with Red Army in Central Asia in 10th Cavalry Regiment of Armored/Mechanized Division, then from the beginning of 1933 at NKVD. Prior to 1930 was chimney sweep in Leningrad. Resident of Leningrad from 1925. Parents—middle peasants. Elementary education, finished driving school in Leningrad in 1929. Candidate member of Communist Party from 1932, Komsomol member from 1928. No criminal record, never under criminal investigation.

My assignment is a one-and-a-half-ton Ford truck No. 2-12-15. At approximately 11 A.M. on Dec. 2, 1934 I was ordered to take three comrades to Smolny. I do not know their names, I am only acquainted with one, who was in uniform. The two others were in civilian clothes. One of them was elderly [Borisov], he sat on the right side of the truck, the other one /in civilian clothes/, on the bench behind the driver's cabin, and the third (in uniform) sat next to me in the cabin. The truck that I received from Chopovsky, my colleague on the other shift, was in order and drove normally. In spite of the fact that the comrade sitting next to me ordered me to get them to Smolny post haste, I drove at a speed under 30 km/hour. On Voinova St. the truck suddenly turned sharply to the right, the wheel instantly turned to the side and I lost control of the steering for a short time. The truck rode up onto the sidewalk and grazed a drainpipe on a building. The comrade sitting on the side of the truck hit the drainpipe. After hitting the drainpipe I turned the wheel hard to the left and directed the truck back into the roadway. The accident occurred because the right front tire went flat. The road was dry. When the truck approached the wall, the comrade sitting by me in uniform wanted to jump out of the truck, but I did not let him—I grabbed his greatcoat. He got out of the truck when it stopped.

Transcribed correctly from my words and read by me.

Kuzin.

These three protocols corroborate one another on most details. The few divergences can be explained by the deponents' efforts to present their own actions in the best light. Thus, Vinogradov claimed that Borisov, who was under his charge in the back of the truck, sat on a bench attached to the cabin of the truck, while Kuzin said that he sat in a much more hazardous position, on the side wall of the cargo bed. Vinogradov did not want to admit allowing Borisov to take a dangerous position. Similarly, Maly and Vinogradov claimed that Kuzin drove at forty kilometers per hour or faster, while Kuzin gave his top speed as only thirty kilometers per hour. The driver, obviously, did not want to confess to speeding. Kuzin blamed Maly for urging him to go faster; Maly explicitly denied doing so.

Kuzin's account also differed from Maly's and Vinogradov's with regard to the impact with the wall and the way in which Borisov was wounded. Kuzin's claim that the truck hit a drainpipe, so that Borisov's head smashed into the pipe, not the building, was probably made to minimize the seriousness of the accident. However, Kuzin, who was driving, was in no position to see what happened to Borisov during the accident. Vinogradov's account is more trustworthy on these counts because, sitting in the back of the truck, he saw what happened to Borisov, and he could not be held responsible for bad driving.

Police Officer I. V. Krutikov was on duty and saw the accident from a distance of thirty or forty meters. Hours later he testified that

Today, December 2, at around ten in the morning on Voinova St. . . . there was a truck driving, a one-and-a-half-tonner. A man in uniform sat next to the driver and on the left and right sides [of the cargo bed] there sat two citizens in civilian dress. The truck was going at a normal speed. The traffic officer let the truck through Chernyshevsky Square and then about ten meters after it had passed through the square, the truck turned to the left (towards the tram line) and then after another ten meters or so, it turned to the right, . . . rode up onto the sidewalk, traveling at an angle [to the direction of traffic]. Just when the truck was about to hit the wall of the building, it straightened out parallel to the wall . . . and passed along the wall for about five meters, leaving scrapes on the wall. At this moment the man sitting on the right side hit his right temple on the wall. The man sitting on the left side was unharmed. When the truck stopped the driver and the man in uniform got out.[30]

Interrogated by Yezhov on December 10, Krutikov indicated that he had not seen precisely what happened to Borisov, only that he "fell." Party committee *instruktor* Voitas, near the scene by chance, reported that he had not seen the accident but its immediate aftermath. He had recognized the wounded man as Borisov.[31]

The expert commission, which consisted of a tire production engineer from the Red Triangle factory, two engineers and an auto pool manager from the Commissariat of Heavy Industry, and two accident investigators from the traffic police, went to work within a couple of hours of Borisov's death. Commission members discovered that the driver Kuzin had concealed a key fact in his initial testimony—that a spring in the truck's forward suspension system, consisting of multiple steel strips or "leaves" stacked one upon another, was loose. Confronted with this evidence, Kuzin admitted that the forward suspension had been loose when he left the NKVD garage before the accident, but again tried to minimize his own responsibility for taking an unsafe vehicle on the road. He asserted that the condition of the suspension had worsened during the drive (a leaf had fallen off one of the springs) but that regardless the cause of the accident was a flat tire.

· 96 ·

Second interrogation of Kuzin (by expert commission), December 3, 1934.
TsA FSB RF, a.u.d. N-Sh44, t. 24, ll. 259–262.

Question: How do you receive your vehicle in the morning?
Answer: Today my colleague on the previous shift told me that one leaf in the forward springs had broken and he had tightened the center clamp [that held the spring together and in place]. In my opinion one more leaf in the springs fell off during the trip. [. . .]
Q: Your route?
A: From the stop at Tekhnichesky Alley I turned left and followed Voinova St., stopping about fifty meters from the point of the accident and the policeman on duty. At the intersection with Potemkin St. there was a green light, I slowed down before the light. When I crossed the tram line [at the intersection] my speed was 10–15 km/hour, before that it was 20–25 km/hour.

Q: Did you hit anything when you were going through the final intersection?

A: I did not notice anything.

Q: How did the accident happen?

A: The truck turned suddenly to the right, I began to turn to the left, but the response was slow. I lost control of the steering when I tried to restrain my neighbor who tried to jump out.

Q: At the time of departure was the air pressure in the inner tube checked; at the moment of the truck's turn were there signs of lowered pressure?

A: [The air pressure] was checked, I noticed no sign of lowered air pressure.

Q: Did the truck hit the wall?

A: No, it only hit the drainpipe. At the moment of impact the door was open.

Q: Did you try to stop the truck at the moment of the sharp turn to the right?

A: I tried to brake before I ran up on the sidewalk, but mostly I tried to turn the truck to the left.

Q: Why didn't you stop the truck at the moment of the accident?

A: I did not stop the truck until I was ordered to do so, as I intended to stop once I was off the sidewalk. After the impact, I put the truck in third gear and got off in that gear.

Q: When you crossed the tram rails you first turned to the left and then to the right. Was it immediately after the turn to the right that the car turned further in that direction?

A: Yes, immediately.

Q: What do you consider to have been the cause of the accident?

A: A flat tire [literally, "The release of air pressure from the inner tube"].

[Signatures of expert commission members][32]

Kuzin's testimony about several details was doubtful. For example, his claim that the passenger side door was open at the moment of the accident (supposedly because Maly was preparing to jump out of the truck) seems to be an attempt to explain the damage to the door. He needed some explanation for this because he also asserted that the truck had never actually collided with the wall. Yet the notion that Maly would try to jump out of a truck moving at ten kilometers per hour at least and likely much faster, as it turned out of control toward a nearby masonry wall, is bizarre. Another example of Kuzin's unreliability was his claim that he was driving only ten to fifteen kilometers per hour when he lost control of the truck. Based on the evidence of every other witness, it is likely that the truck was going at least forty kilometers per hour at that moment.

By the evening of December 2 the expert commission had prepared a preliminary accident report that refuted Kuzin's version of the events. The driver lost control of the truck not because of any sudden flat tire, but due to the preexisting problems with the front suspension. Moreover, the truck *had* struck the wall—there were "traces of lime/chalk from the wall masonry on the right door handle."

· 97 ·

Report of expert commission on the truck accident that killed Borisov, December 2, 1934, evening. TsA FSB RF, a.u.d. N-Sh44, t. 24, ll. 242–244.

Today (December 2, 1934) truck no. 24215 had an accident on Voinova Street, opposite number 50. It has been determined that the truck was traveling along Voinova Street from Volodarsky Prospect; 35 meters past the intersection with Potemkin Street the truck turned toward the sidewalk, at an angle of 35 degrees, traveled three meters to the sidewalk, hit the curb with its wheel, then traveled 9 1/2 meters and hit the ledge of a blocked-up window opening with its right-side door and the corner of the truck body. After this, the truck rode along the sidewalk another 6 1/2 meters, passed back onto the main roadway, and continued straight on. Then, 56 meters from the point where it first left the road, the truck stopped.

Inspection of the accident site revealed:

1. Tracks [skid marks?] of the tires begin before the truck passed onto the sidewalk, at a distance of perhaps 3 meters from said sidewalk, after which the marks continue for the whole distance the truck traveled on the sidewalk, and continue after it left the sidewalk for 2 1/2 meters.

2. Tracks of the right front wheel prior to running up on the sidewalk do not show obvious signs of lowered tire pressure. From the point that the wheel passed over the curb, the tracks are clearly widened, demonstrating a complete lack of air in the inner tube.

3. The width of the traveling lane was 5 1/2 meters from right edge of the [tram] rails to the curb. The roadway is paved with asphalt and has a slight incline towards the sidewalk. Roadway was dry.

4. A tongue-shaped break was found in the inner tube of the right front wheel, precisely corresponding to a break in the cloth of the tire casing,

while the rubber tread has no cuts at the point of the break. This leads to the conclusion that there occurred a sharp impact with the edge of the sidewalk curb. Placement of the inner tube under water revealed no other breaks/flaws in the rubber.

5. Condition of the automobile: the glass of the right door of the cab is broken, there are deep dents for approximately 1/5 of the length of the steel trim [. . .] attached to the main frame, there are traces of lime/chalk from the wall masonry on the right door handle, the right forward wheel well is bent, the right front fender is slightly bent, the truck body is displaced backward by 10–12 millimeters.

6. After replacing the damaged tire, the brakes and steering mechanism were checked. During the test only a left turn was produced /left from the driver's point of view/, and the auto was brought to a stop from a speed of 46 km/hour /according to said automobile's speedometer/ in about 20 meters. A strong pull to the left was noted in the steering. After the automobile was stopped, a displacement of the forward axle to the left, visible to the eye, was discovered. In driving the automobile involved in the accident back to the garage, taking a right turn from Voinova Street to Narimanov Street, and then traveling down Roshal Prospect to the intersection at Decembrists Square, the auto ran up onto the sidewalk twice when the steering wheel was turned in normal fashion.

Examination of the auto in the garage revealed the following. There was noticeable vertical play in the center clamp of a forward spring— however, this did not exceed ten millimeters. On each bolt of the clamp there was one nut, each bolt had a cotter pin about ten millimeters from the nut. The nut on the right forward bolt could be unscrewed by hand. There were seven leaves in the spring (the base leaf and six more of the set), and each leaf had the normal thickness for a 14-leaf spring. The leaves were displaced to the right with relation to the axis of the central bolt. . . . The central bolt was missing and only its head remained. Examination of the latter revealed traces of the break. [. . .]

Examination of the main components of the steering mechanism and the forward axle showed both to be in full working order.

7. According to the report of Comrade Malkevich, based on the words of Krutikov, the policeman on duty, after the truck passed through the regulated intersection of Voinova and Potemkin Streets, it broke the traffic rules by developing a speed of 40 km/hour as opposed to the 35 km/hour speed limit. No signs of sharp braking were noted in the tracks [of the accident].

On the basis of the above the commission concludes:

1. There is no basis for believing that the accident was caused by the damage to the inner tube and tire that were discovered.

2. The presence of nuts screwed down the full length of the thread on

the bolts of a spring center clamp, in the absence of [some of] the leaves of the spring, could be the direct cause of inadequate affixing of the spring, as a result of which the entire forward axle/front end could be subject to sideways displacement. Such a sideways displacement could serve as the direct reason for the automobile's turn to the right, which occurred in this case. This is confirmed by the fact that neither the central bolt, nor any broken leaves were found at the accident site [i.e. they probably were missing before the accident].

I. V. Komarnitsky, Technical Director of Tire Production at the Red Triangle factory, B. L. Grinberg, Engineer-Inspector of the Leningrad Region Office of the Commissariat of Heavy Industry, V. N. Ivanov, Senior Chemical Engineer of the Commissariat of Heavy Industry, Oskar Ivanovich Aigro, Director of the Office of the Commissariat of Heavy Industry Garage, Malkevich, Senior Inspector of the First Section of ORUD [*Otdel regulirovaniia ulichnogo dvizheniia*—the traffic police], and Oskotsky, Accident Investigator of the First Department of ORUD.

R. W. Rivers, auto accident reconstructor and author of *Evidence in Traffic Crash Investigation and Reconstruction* (2006), as well as a number of other books in the field, reviewed the above accident report and the witness depositions. Rivers concludes that although "important details of the site and vehicle are not included in the statements," the available evidence gives a plausible picture of the accident and its causes. If the truck's left wheels crossed the tram rails in the center of Voinova Street, this could well have "caused the vehicle to weave in its path of travel (a very well known occurrence when traveling over such rails)." When Kuzin attempted to turn the truck back into the main travel lane, it swerved towards the sidewalk. The slant of the road surface towards the sidewalk would also have "pulled the vehicle in that direction."[33]

Rivers calculates that the damage to the truck points to "an impact speed of 60 kilometers per hour rather than 40." This fits with Vinogradov's report that the truck accelerated to fifty or sixty kilometers per hour before the driver lost control. Kuzin was probably traveling much faster than either he or Maly admitted.[34]

Whether Borisov was sitting up on the side of the truck or on the bench attached to the back of the cabin, collision with the wall would have "cause[d] him to be . . . projected toward the wall at an expected angle of approximately 35 degrees, the angle at which the vehicle left the roadway." His head would have traveled about 0.6 meters before hitting the wall. If the truck were moving at a speed of forty to sixty kilometers per hour the result would be "severe head injury." Rebounding off the wall, Borisov would have ended up in the bed of the truck. This is where the autopsy summary translated below places him, and where Maly's testimony implies that he was after the collision.[35]

The results of the post-accident testing of the truck are largely meaningless, Rivers writes, except for the fact that the brakes were functioning. However, "there is sufficient evidence from the inspection to suggest the probability of poor vehicle maintenance relating to the front suspension system, such that steering by an operator would probably be adversely affected." The steering system too most likely had "many worn parts and improper front wheel alignment, resulting in shimmy, wobble and difficulty in steering control, particularly if the vehicle was driven over a rough roadway."[36]

Rivers agrees with the expert commission's conclusion that the flat tire did not cause the accident, but resulted from impact with the curb after Kuzin lost control. Overall he concludes as follows.

1. The findings of the expert commission were essentially correct.

2. In all probability the vehicle first began to go out of control when it drove over the tram rails. That is approximately where it first veered to the left. Kuzin then attempted to correct the direction of travel by steering to the right, traveling to and striking the curb. That is where the tire went flat. The flat tire did not contribute to the initial loss of vehicle control. [. . .].

3. An unevenness or roughness of the roadway (probably the tram rails), the poor mechanical condition of the steering, and excessive speed were the major contributing factors in this accident.[37]

Borisov died within minutes of the accident, in all likelihood before Vinogradov and Maly got him back to the clinic at NKVD headquarters. His corpse was not buried until December 19, apparently due to the ongoing investigation of his death.[38] In later years Soviet and Western commentators would contest hotly whether he was murdered or not. Apart from the accident reports already discussed, two important pieces of evidence survive. The first is a summary of autopsy findings on Borisov, dated December 4, 1934. The second is a series of photographs taken of Borisov's skull when his remains were exhumed on the orders of the Party Control Committee in December 1960.

The autopsy summary below was probably written in connection with the issuance of Borisov's death certificate. Labeled "Conclusion," it was signed on December 4 by five Leningrad doctors, including the head of the NKVD headquarters clinic Mamushin. According to a KGB report from August 1956, the blue ribbon medical commission that prepared this report examined Borisov's body and visited the accident site as well.[39]

> The death of Borisov, M. V. was the result of depression of the activity of the brain centers associated with breathing and circulation. This resulted from bleeding in the cavity of the fourth ventricle of the brain due to fractures of the roof and the base of the skull. Death was not instantaneous, but occurred over the course of several minutes (probably not more than ten). Injury to the soft tissues of the skull was caused by impact of the skull with a hard, flat object (such as a masonry wall). The direction of the impact was from behind towards the front and from the right towards the left. Such a blow could have been received as the automobile turned sharply to the left away from the wall. One may suppose that at the moment of impact the deceased was located on the right side of the automobile with his right shoulder forward and after impact could have ended up thrown onto the truck bed. Abrasions on the hip, the left subscapular area and the abrasions to the skin of the head to the left of the hemorrhaging could have occurred as the deceased fell onto the truck bed and played no role in accelerating death.
>
> Given the age of the deceased (52 years old) and the changes in his internal organs discovered in the autopsy, his state of health must be recognized as satisfactory. Considering the autopsy data, the absence of signs of external violence, and the circumstances of the case, it can be concluded that Borisov's death was the result of an accident in connection with the automobile crash.[40]

Dr. James A. J. Ferris, professor emeritus of forensic pathology at the University of British Columbia, and Jennifer Prutsman-Pfeiffer, forensic anthropologist and pathologist's assistant at the University of Rochester's Strong Medical Center, independently reviewed all of the evidence on Borisov's death available for this book, including the 1934 autopsy report, the 1960 photographs of Borisov's skull, witness depositions, and R. W. Rivers' accident report. Both experts reached similar conclusions. Prutsman-Pfeiffer notes that the cracks in the skull indicate a very strong impact with a large flat object rather than being the result of a blow with a weapon. Had someone hit Borisov with a hammer, bat, or similar object, it would have probably left a bruised impression on the skin, which the pathologists doing the autopsy could have noted.[41] Ferris, who has performed over 9,500 autopsies, including 900 on homicide victims, concludes that Borisov died as the result of the traffic accident, not as the result of an attack with a blunt instrument. He writes in part:

> In over forty years of forensic pathology practice I have examined many reports from a variety of countries and jurisdictions of post-mortem examinations and exhumations and I think that the translated report of the original examination is clear and concise and shows a high degree of professionalism by the original forensic medical examiners. Their description of the skull fractures appears accurate and I agree with their general conclusion that the main impact was to the right occipital area of the skull. I also agree with the conclusion that death was probably not instantaneous. The evidence of bleeding into the fourth ventricle indicates severe injury to the brain-stem and death would have been rapid and likely taken not more than ten minutes. Such hemorrhage into the area of the fourth ventricle is consistent with the skull fractures around the foramen magnum and is strong evidence to support the severe deceleration forces to which Borisov's skull was subjected.
>
> The photographs of the skull show an area of comminuted fractures in the right occiput with a fissured fracture radiating forwards along the line of the right temporo-parietal suture line. More significant however is the pattern of fractures radiating across the floor of the skull.
>
> There is a wide fissured fracture extending forwards to the foramen magnum and then extending in the midline through the pituitary fossa into the cribriform plate between the orbits in the area of the roof of the nose. . . .
>
> A third fissured fracture extends into the right middle fossa passing through the structures of the right inner ear. This would almost certainly have resulted in blood emanating from the right ear.
>
> The amount of force required to produce this pattern of comminuted fracturing with clear evidence of a single impact area associated with at least three distinct radiating fissured fractures across the skull is entirely *inconsistent* with an assault with a heavy weapon. It would be virtually impossible to generate sufficient impact force with a weapon, even a heavy metal rod, and produce this pattern of skull fractures. In order for such a theory to have any possibility, the head of Mikhail Borisov would need to have been on a hard surface at the time of such an impact. If this had been the case, there would have been clear evidence of reciprocal fractures caused by the side of the skull opposite the weapon impact area impacting the ground. No such reciprocal fractures were present.[42]

The analyses by Ferris and Prutsman-Pfeiffer validate the findings not only of the 1934 autopsy report on Borisov's corpse but also of the December 1960 Soviet medical commission which examined his exhumed skull. According to this commission, the injuries to the skull matched up well with the autopsy findings and witnesses' testimony about the accident in 1934. In 1967 and again in 1989 Soviet medical experts reached this same conclusion, using photographs of the exhumed skull.[43]

It is clear that in spite of witness accounts, autopsy results, and the December 2 accident report, central authorities, in particular Yezhov, pressed hard in the following weeks for evidence that Leningrad NKVD officers had murdered Borisov. The central NKVD kept Kuzin, Maly, and Vinogradov in custody for two months after Borisov's death. It was presumably also central authorities who delayed the burial of Borisov's body until December 19. Investigators questioned numerous witnesses, including Medved, NKVD garage personnel, and a second policeman on duty at the scene of the accident, and others. Between December 10 and 14 Yezhov, Kosaryov, and Agranov again questioned Kuzin, Maly, Vinogradov, Khviiuzov, and Krutikov, seeking evidence of foul play in Borisov's death. All five stuck by their previous descriptions of the incident. On December 12 investigators reexamined the accident scene and found a scrap of Borisov's overcoat, which had been torn in back during the accident, stuck on a metal clamp securing a drainpipe to the wall that Kuzin had hit.[44]

In the absence of evidence of murder, Yezhov and Stalin eventually accepted an official finding that Borisov died in an auto accident, albeit one attributable to Leningrad NKVD incompetence.

The Volkova Case

Of the eight NKVD officers arrested on December 3, five were charged with suppression of Volkova's denunciations in fall 1934. These were Georgy Petrov, Special Department head Yanishevsky, his deputy Baltsevich, Special Political Department officer Andrei Andreevich Mosevich, and Zaporozhets' aide Belousenko. Central NKVD officials repeatedly demanded that these men confess to negligence or even counterrevolutionary intent in their handling of Volkova. All five eventually admitted to the former, but not the latter.[45]

The protocols of these interrogations are the earliest evidence in the

Volkova case available to date, and they contain information that does not appear in later documents, in particular in Petrov's multiple petitions for rehabilitation. In conjunction with other evidence they suggest that Volkova may have been more than an isolated psychiatric case Stalin chose to use on December 2.

On December 3, D. M. Dmitriev, deputy chief of the central NKVD Economic Security Department, interrogated Petrov twice about his handling of Volkova's denunciations. Volkova, Petrov stated, had shown up at a military post in the city with a letter for an officer there. The NKVD liaison officer attached to the post, Driapkin (alternative spelling Drapkin, forwarded the letter to Petrov at the Special Department, with a request that the latter inform deputy chief Baltsevich about it. According to Petrov, Volkova's letter stated that a counterrevolutionary group was meeting at the apartment of one Livanov (alternative spelling Levanov). In the 1950s and 1960s Volkova and Petrov would both label this group the "Green Lamp" or the "Green Army." Volkova named five members of the group—Livanov, Masliakov, Kabachnikov, Zvezder (referred to as Zvezdr by Volkova in 1956 and Zvezdris by Agranov in December 1934), and Korshunov. "Most" (four?) of these she probably was acquainted with because they came from her home region in the province of Vologda. Kabachnikov and Zvezder, Volkova said, had taken part in the 1918 rebellion against the Soviet government in the Yaroslavl region, which bordered on Vologda.[46]

Under Baltsevich's supervision, Petrov began to work with Volkova. They first met in early October, and Petrov questioned her at least two more times before her commitment to the psychiatric hospital on October 28. From the outset, he said on December 3, he was suspicious of her. She claimed to have a letter she was supposed to deliver from Masliakov to Korshunov, which had counterrevolutionary content (information about the arrest of a supposed fellow conspirator). But she could only produce a "copy" of the letter for Petrov, because she'd "lost" the original. Volkova also showed Petrov an old artillery shell casing she claimed to have gotten from a certain Karlinsky she worked for as a maid.[47] This was evidently supposed to be evidence of an illegal weapons cache. The shell casing, however, was of a old type often used as a souvenir pencil holder on desks. When Petrov questioned her about Karlinsky, Volkova admitted that the latter had no ties with the "counterrevolutionary group" she had denounced.

Petrov and Baltsevich ordered Operations Department agents to recruit Korshunov and other supposed members of the "Green Lamp" as NKVD informants. They also put a tail on Volkova and set up surveillance of Korshunov's and Livanov's apartments. The results were disappointing. The agent at Korshunov's apartment said neither Volkova nor any of the other "conspirators" ever visited there. Livanov lived in a communal apartment and no meetings happened there. Nor would a communal apartment crowded with outsiders have been an appropriate place for counterrevolutionary meetings. The supervisor of the building Volkova lived in told Petrov that Volkova was a "gossip" who bragged about being a secret police agent (as in Tsarist times, building supervisors were regular informants for the police).[48]

Petrov also tried having Volkova deliver her letter to Korshunov, the original addressee. Considering her unreliable, he had her call Korshunov while he listened in on another line. When Volkova identified herself to Korshunov, the latter asked in confusion "What Volkova?" She then said quickly that she was going to visit him and hung up before he could reply, "obviously not wishing to continue the conversation." Acting chief of the Special Department Yanishevsky then ordered Livanov, Korshunov, and other "counterrevolutionaries" brought in for interrogation. After face-to-face confrontations (*ochnye stavki*) with Korshunov and the others Volkova confessed that she had falsely accused them (Volkova later claimed that the Leningrad Special Department officers had extracted the confession with threats). The Special Department officers concluded that the whole "conspiracy" was made up. On October 28 Zaporozhets' aide Belousenko forcibly committed Volkova to a psychiatric clinic.[49]

According to Baltsevich (interrogation of December 9, 1934), Petrov reported "all the details" on the Volkova case to senior officers of the Leningrad NKVD several times—twice to Fomin and once to Medved. In 1956 Petrov described Medved's reaction to the Volkova materials at one of the directorate's regular "operational meetings." The entire leadership of the Leningrad NKVD was present at the meeting, which discussed the handling of informer networks. According to Petrov, officers at the meeting criticized him for collecting "counterfeit cases" (*legendarnye dela*) from informers, especially Volkova, an "element dangerous to society." Medved instructed Dr. Mamushin of the NKVD Medical Department to arrange a psychiatric examination for Volkova. On the basis of the examination, the NKVD committed Volkova to the psychiatric hospital.[50]

Thus, the whole Leningrad NKVD was potentially complicit in ignoring the existence of a counterrevolutionary organization under their noses. This is precisely what Dmitriev and other interrogating officers from the central NKVD were trying to demonstrate. Again and again they pressed Petrov and Baltsevich to admit negligence. They even suggested that the Leningrad Special Department deliberately aimed to discredit Volkova and wished to cover up the existence of the "Green Lamp." The interrogators got Petrov to accuse Baltsevich of actually forbidding him from putting a tail on Korshunov, and then used this to pressure Baltsevich. At a confrontation on December 21, Petrov reminded Baltsevich how of the latter had said that they had "to put an end to this hoax (*lipa*)."[51]

Petrov's and Baltsevich's interrogations in December 1934 reveal two suggestive facts. First, when Petrov was dealing with Volkova in the fall of 1934 he did not know that she was already an NKVD secret collaborator. In 1960 he claimed that he even checked with the Statistics and Records Section of the Leningrad NKVD and did not find her registered there. He apparently did not find out that Volkova was a police informer until December 2 or 3. Probably central NKVD officers told him. Second, the "counterrevolutionary group" denounced by Volkova had a curious composition. Four of them were apparently people Volkova knew because they came from her home region. In Russian terms, they were her *zemliaki*. One, however, was very different. The Korshunov she named probably was Yefim Korshunov, a former secretary of the Central Ward soviet executive committee and onetime Zinovievite who was a student at the Industrial Academy in the fall of 1934. After Kirov's murder Korshunov was arrested and sentenced to four to five years of exile as a member of the "Leningrad Counterrevolutionary Zinovievite Group of Safarov, Zalutsky, and Others" (see above, p. 379). He crops up in interrogations of Boris Lvovich Bravo, a former supporter of the Trotsky-Zinoviev Opposition living in Moscow, and N. P. Miasnikov, one of the former Zinovievites from Leningrad shot with Nikolaev on December 29. On December 17, 1934 Chertok, Dmitriev's deputy from the central NKVD Economic Security Department, interrogated Korshunov about a 1928 letter sent to him by Zinoviev's close associate Ivan Bakaev.[52]

In October 1934 Petrov found that Korshunov had no connection with Volkova or her *zemliaki*—he had simply been lumped together with Livanov and the others in a single imagined conspiracy. Yet in spite of the fact that she did not even know Korshunov, Volkova had somehow selected the ex-oppositionist, connected with leading figures among the former Zinoviev supporters, for denunciation. The strangeness of this "coincidence" is heightened by the fact that Volkova did not make just one denunciation of her "counterrevolutionary organization." In the late summer and fall of 1934 she strewed Leningrad offices with her accusations. According to an Agranov memorandum to Stalin from January 1935, Volkova wrote separate denunciations on August 17, September 7, 10, and 12, and October 13 and 18. Based on statements of Leningrad policemen Gromov and Kazansky written in the immediate aftermath of Khrushchev's February 1956 Secret Speech, and on a petition written by Georgy Petrov in 1956, it seems that Volkova contacted the regular Leningrad police Criminal Investigation Department as well as the NKVD. In addition to the NKVD Special Department, she also independently contacted the NKVD Special Political Department, where Officer Andrei Andreevich Mosevich was assigned her case.[53]

Volkova also told her onetime employer Ilin (Volkova had been or still was a nanny for Ilin's child in the fall of 1934), aide to regional party committee secretary P. I. Struppe, about her "counterrevolutionary group." In October–November 1934 Ilin tried to bring her accusations to the attention of party officials in Smolny. He may have been the first person to notify Stalin of the Volkova case after Kirov's murder. We know this because in August 1937, charged in an unconnected case with helping a "village merchant" obtain an internal passport, Ilin wrote to Kirov's successor in Leningrad, Andrei Zhdanov, that "I am the same person from whom you, together with comrades Stalin, Molotov, and Voroshilov, heard a report on December 2, 1934 . . . my statement about how I tried for over two months to expose the existing terrorist organization denounced by Volkova that was planning an attack on the leaders of the party, among them on Kirov."[54]

Like Nikolaev's firing from the Institute of Party History and the 1933–1934 attacks on the Fellowship of Komsomol Militants, the Volkova case can be interpreted in terms of conflict between Left (Zinovievite) and Right (Komarovite) cliques in Leningrad. In the spring of 1926 Struppe apparently identified with Komarovite resentment of the newcomer Kirov. In September 1929 he came under attack from Left journalists in Leningrad as a Rightist. It is possible that there are echoes of Left-Right conflict in the efforts of Struppe's aide Ilin to bring Volkova's evidence against putative Zinovievites to the attention of the NKVD and party leadership.[55]

It is doubtful that Volkova specifically mentioned a forthcoming attack on Kirov in her denunciations before December 1934. Agranov's January 1935 memorandum to Stalin summarizing Volkova's pre-assassination denunciations does not discuss any warning of a possible attack on Kirov, nor do Agranov's reports to the dictator in December 1934 or the 1934 depositions of Petrov, Baltsevich, or Yanishevsky. The earliest mention of such a warning in connection with Volkova is in the sentencing document from the January 23, 1935 trial of senior Leningrad NKVD officers. The sentence states that "In the fall of 1934, aide to chief of the Special Political Department Mosevich, having received from citizeness Volkova information about the presence in Leningrad of a number of counterrevolutionary terrorist groups, *in part of a planned terrorist attack against Comrade Kirov,* did not attribute proper significance to this material, and filed it without action."[56] However, this claim could be an exaggeration aimed at further implicating Leningrad NKVD officers in criminal negligence. Ilin's assertion in 1937 that Volkova had denounced a coming attack on Kirov could well be due to hindsight and exposure to the charges in the 1935 trial of Leningrad NKVD officers and the August 1936 show trial of Kamenev and Zinoviev.

Volkova's denunciation of Korshunov, whom she did not know, her service as a "secret collaborator," and her very persistence in pressing her denunciations on Leningrad authorities in fall 1934 all indicate that she was something more than a lone crazy lady. Who was using Volkova as a "secret collaborator," and who suggested that she include the ex-Zinovievite Korshunov in the "Green Lamp"? Without access to the closed archives of the Russian state security police (and quite possibly even with such access) it is impossible to answer these questions definitely. Available documents do, however, suggest a possible answer.

Volkova herself in statements in 1956 and 1960 claimed that she was a secret informant for the Smolny Ward office of the NKVD at least as far back as the summer of 1934. In evaluating this claim, it is important to remember that both Volkova's statements are full of demonstrably false and even fantastic elements. In 1956, for example, Volkova claimed that before the Kirov murder she met Zinoviev, Kamenev, and Yevdokimov in the Leningrad suburb of Ligovo, where they were unloading munitions from a German submarine. In 1960 she claimed that she'd met Milda Draule in 1956, twenty-one years after the latter was executed. She also described meeting Leonid Nikolaev months before the murder, getting drunk together, and visiting the

German consulate. There Nikolaev got fifteen thousand rubles and took Volkova to the Astoria, the premier luxury hotel in Leningrad. In fact documentation on the case shows that Volkova did not begin claiming that she'd met Nikolaev until 1935. In a 1956 interview with the KGB she admitted that in 1935 Nikolai Yezhov had shown her Nikolaev's photograph and "convinced" her that she knew him.[57]

But there are also elements of Volkova's 1956 and 1960 statements that fit with the December 1934 testimony of Petrov, Baltsevich, et al. In 1956 she described carrying a letter from "Zvezdr" to Korshunov, which parallels Petrov's 1934 testimony about her "letter" from Masliakov to Korshunov (see below for more on the letter from Zvezder). She also remembered interviews with Driapkin, Petrov, Baltsevich, and Yanishevsky. In 1960 she remembered, with some inaccurate details, her face-to-face confrontation with Korshunov, as well as the phone call she made to him on Petrov's instructions.[58]

Stripped of their more fantastic elements, such as trips to the Astoria with Leonid Nikolaev and lemonades at the Amerikanka restaurant with Kotolynov and Shatsky, Volkova's 1956 and 1960 accounts of events in the months before Kirov's assassination are worth consideration. On July 24, 1934, she claimed, she stumbled onto the meeting of the "counterrevolutionary group" of Livanov and the others at the communal apartment where her Vologda girlfriend Morozova lived. On July 25 she went to the Smolny Ward office of the NKVD (a different address from NKVD headquarters for the city) to tell her handler about the group. She named her handler as Officer Sokolov, head of the Smolny Ward NKVD office, and in 1956 she stated that he was a recent replacement for her previous NKVD contact Malinin (Malinin is identifiable from a 1961 interview with the Party Control Committee as an officer in the Leningrad NKVD). Sokolov showed great interest in the supposed conspiratorial group. He told her to visit Livanov's apartment more often and report to him on conversations among the "conspirators." Then the latter supposedly asked her to carry letters. Petrov in his December 1934 evidence testified that Volkova told him of just one copy of a letter from Masliakov to Korshunov. Volkova in 1956 claimed that Nikolaev gave her two letters to take to members of the "Green Lamp" in the Leningrad suburbs, Zvezder and Masliakov. She delivered these and carried back to the city letters from Zvezder to Miasnikov (later of the "Leningrad Center") and Korshunov. All of these letters she showed to Sokolov at the Smolny Ward NKVD, and he copied each of them.[59]

Volkova's account of the letters she carried is certainly confused. Among other things she mentions Nikolaev and Miasnikov, neither of whom appears in the 1934–1935 testimony of Leningrad NKVD officers about her case. However, when juxtaposed with Petrov's testimony about her claim to have a copy of one letter, from Masliakov to Korshunov, Volkova's description of Sokolov copying letters is suggestive. Korshunov, according to Petrov in December 1934, had no connection with Volkova or the "counterrevolutionaries" at Livanov's apartment. Yet Volkova claimed to have a letter for him. If Volkova in fact had a contact officer in the Smolny Ward NKVD office, Sokolov or someone else, it seems that he sought to entangle the ex-Zinovievite Korshunov with the Livanov group. He may have done so by fabricating or soliciting provocative letters to Korshunov.

Evidence on Zvezder from 1934 also suggests strongly that Volkova was part of an NKVD-run "provocation" aimed at incriminating former Zinovievites in Leningrad. After hearing about the "Green Lamp," Agranov immediately ordered the arrest of the members named by Volkova, that is Livanov/Levanov, Zvezder/Zvezdr/Zvezdris, Masliakov, and Kabachnikov. Korshunov had been arrested on the night of December 1–2. Reports from Agranov to Stalin dated December 6 and 9 indicate that the NKVD tracked down Zvezder through Masliakov, finding him in the village of Konduia, Tosno District, Leningrad Region, where he headed a village school. After his arrest, Agranov wrote Stalin, Zvezder declared that he was a secret informer for the police.[60] Volkova in 1956 described taking a letter to "Zvezdr" at Vyritsa Station, which is located in Gatchina District, next to Tosno. She also described taking letters from "Zvezdr" to N. P. Miasnikov (to repeat, one of the ex-Zinovievites tried with Nikolaev) and Korshunov.[61] Thus, she was carrying letters from an NKVD informer to fairly prominent former Zinovievites in Leningrad. This certainly sounds like a classic NKVD "provocation" aimed at creating "evidence" of counterrevolutionary activity on the part of Miasnikov and Korshunov.

According to Volkova, Sokolov aggressively sought to draw the attention of senior officers in the Leningrad NKVD to her information on the "Green Lamp." In September and October 1934 he took her to see Special Department acting chief Yanishevsky, Special Political Department chief Gorin-Lundin, and Zaporozhets' aide Belousenko. After the Special Department put a tail on her (Petrov's and Baltsevich's depositions from 1934 confirm that officers were assigned to tail

Volkova), Sokolov intervened, but was unable to persuade senior officers to suspend the surveillance.[62]

If we accept that Volkova actually had a handler (we will call him Sokolov, as she did in 1956 and 1960) at the Smolny Ward office who encouraged her to collect information on Livanov's supposed counterrevolutionary group and to pass provocative letters from the group on to Korshunov, then a startling picture comes into focus. Sokolov was running his own "secret collaborators" from the Smolny Ward NKVD office without the knowledge of senior officers in the Leningrad NKVD (remember that Petrov did not know Volkova was an informer). He was also seeking or fabricating evidence that ex-Zinovievites in Leningrad were engaged in counterrevolutionary activities. Senior officers in the city security apparatus, confronted with Sokolov's obviously bogus evidence, quashed it. A number of ex-Zinovievites held middle-level administrative positions in the city government and they were probably protected by higher-ranking party secretaries in the Vyborg, Smolny, and other wards. The Leningrad NKVD did not want to let a denunciatory "St. Bartholomew's Day" happen inside the city's party organization. Too many vested interests were at stake.

Yagoda and Stalin, we know from Yagoda's early October memorandum on the Leningrad and Western Siberia NKVD organizations, wanted to shake up the Leningrad NKVD and move Medved. The central NKVD had ordered a series of arrests of former Trotskyites and Zinovievites in Leningrad in 1933–1934, some of which Kirov apparently blocked. Moreover, central security authorities and Stalin himself were demanding a "reconstruction" of work with the networks of informers and secret collaborators. This meant, as we have seen, insisting that the NKVD's collaborators actively solicit counterrevolutionary statements and activities, rather than passively monitor conversations. Lower-ranking NKVD officers, such as Volkova's Sokolov, may have been instructed directly from the center (that is by Yagoda or his subordinates) to find evidence incriminating ex-Zinovievites and present it directly to their nominal supervisors in Leningrad. If Medved or his subordinates rejected the evidence, they could be accused of incompetence, negligence, or worse. Or it may be that the Sokolovs were responding to nonspecific signals from the center about "improving work with the agent network" and incriminating former oppositionists.

Aside from Sokolov, Struppe's secretary Ilin and the Criminal Investigation Department of the regular Leningrad police pressed Volkova's

denunciations on the regional NKVD. Ilin, as we have seen, claimed in
1937 to have urged Leningrad authorities in the fall of 1934 to take
Volkova seriously. The Criminal Investigation Department was using
Volkova as a secret informer under the apt codename of "Snake" well
before Kirov's murder. According to the 1956 testimony of Leningrad
policemen Gromov and Kazansky, cited above, Criminal Investigation
officers sent one of Volkova's written denunciations to city NKVD
headquarters. They were notified soon after that Volkova was psychologically ill and had been committed to a mental hospital. One has to
wonder whether Ilin and/or the police were knowingly involved in gin-
ning up a false case against former oppositionists in Leningrad.[63]

It should be repeated here that there is no evidence of any direct link
between the Volkova case and Nikolaev. Agranov's January 1935 memo
summarizing the content of Volkova's pre-murder denunciations shows
this. Also, in 1960 a number of Leningrad NKVD officers denied that
Volkova ever mentioned Nikolaev in her pre-murder interrogations.
Among them was Anton Bozhichko, who questioned Volkova on the
orders of Andrei Mosevich.[64] But the Volkova case, particularly Petrov's December 1934 testimony, does suggest that before the Kirov
murder someone was trying to fabricate evidence of counterrevolutionary activity against ex-Zinovievites inside the Leningrad party/state
apparatus. That somebody may have been Yagoda, acting on Stalin's
instructions. If so, a second important goal of the operation was to discredit the Leningrad NKVD leadership, Filip Medved in particular.

Trial of the Leningrad NKVD

Interrogations in the case of the Leningrad NKVD officers continued
right up to the eve of the trial, January 22. Based on the post-Stalin testimony of Rosliakov, Fomin, and D. Sorokin, Medved's brother-in-
law, it seems that five of the senior officers (certainly including Medved, Fomin, and Zaporozhets), were not actually arrested until early
January. Rosliakov saw Medved at Moscow Station in Leningrad just
after midnight on December 3–4, as a special train departed with Kirov's remains. He describes the former chief of the Leningrad NKVD
as "under house arrest" at that time. Fomin testified in 1956 that he
and the other "arrested" officers were sent from Leningrad to Moscow
on December 10. On January 12 (in Sorokin's account "early January") the senior officers who were still nominally free were confined at

NKVD headquarters on the Lubianka in quite comfortable conditions (Sorokin). They were subjected to renewed interrogations in preparation for their trial. Fomin claimed that Yagoda, his deputy G. E. Prokofev, Mironov, and Berdichevsky tutored the accused intensively, urging them to take the whole responsibility for failing to prevent Kirov's murder on themselves, and to avoid any mention of the central NKVD. Yagoda aimed to script the entire trial beforehand. Sorokin, citing the words of Medved, confirms that Yagoda supervised the preparation of prisoners for the upcoming trial.[65]

Stalin probably discussed final plans for the trial with Yagoda, Akulov, Vyshinsky, and Ulrikh, who as chair of the Military Collegium of the Supreme Court would again be presiding, early on the evening of January 17, 1935. On this date all five men, plus Kaganovich, Molotov, Kalinin, and Kuibyshev, met in Stalin's office from 4:30 to 8:30 P.M. Two days later G. E. Prokofev forwarded to Yagoda a draft of proposed sentences in the Leningrad NKVD trial, noting that Vyshinsky had not yet approved it. The final sentencing document, translated below, closely followed the draft, with the exception of the sections dealing with Kuzin, Khviiuzov, Maly, and Vinogradov, the driver and officers involved in Borisov's death. Although the draft author noted that all four were "accused of . . . a negligent attitude towards the fulfillment of an operational order," resulting in the truck accident, he also recommended that they be freed. Yagoda and Stalin ultimately approved this recommendation. None of the four stood trial. They were released by the end of the month, following a brief meeting with Agranov, who explained that the central NKVD had determined that Borisov had died in an auto accident.[66]

Sometime between January 19 and 22 Yagoda forwarded the proposed sentences to Stalin, after getting Vyshinsky to sign off on them. Stalin approved them.[67]

The trial took place on January 23. In the documents available for this book, there is no complete transcript of the proceedings, only excerpts and summaries of testimony. One of the issues Ulrikh focused on was Nikolaev's October 15 detention and release. Medved asserted that there were standing orders "as a general rule" to search all detainees. Kotomin explained again the sequence of events on October 15 from his point of view. In contrast to earlier interrogations he now claimed that someone had told him Nikolaev had been already been searched.

· 98 ·

Testimony of Mikhail Kotomin at the trial of Leningrad NKVD officers,
January 23, 1934. RGANI, f. 6, op. 13, d. 13, ll. 7–45 (1960–1961
Klimov report on the detention[s] of Nikolaev).

————————

At the time Nikolaev was detained I was in a meeting with the section
chief [Gubin], there I was told by one of the officers (*sotrudniki*), that a
citizen following behind Comrade Kirov's guard had been detained and
turned over to an operations commissar. When I returned to my office I
saw on my desk a briefcase and documents in the name of the detainee, citizen Nikolaev. At that point someone, I can't remember who, told me that
they had searched him. I looked through the contents of the briefcase,
there were three newspapers and two books inside, I didn't find anything
else. I don't know who did the personal search of Nikolaev, nor do I know
what Nikolaev had in his pockets. Besides the briefcase Nikolaev had
identification from his work and a party card stating that he had been a
party member since 1924.

[Ulrikh]: Did Nikolaev have a weapon?

[Kotomin]: I don't know, I did not search him.

[Ulrikh]: Did Nikolaev have a license for a weapon?

[Kotomin]: I don't know, I have the impression he did, I don't remember.

[Ulrikh]: Why did you report to Gubin that Nikolaev had nothing suspicious on him?

[Kotomin]: Given that I had his briefcase, I believed that he had already
been searched.

[Ulrikh]: When you reported to Gubin, did you tell him you had
searched Nikolaev?

[Kotomin]: No.

[Ulrikh]: Did Gubin ask you about this?

[Kotomin]: No.

[Ulrikh]: Who interrogated Nikolaev?

[Kotomin]: I don't know . . .

[Ulrikh]: Who stopped you from carrying out a search of Nikolaev?

[Kotomin]: No one, I believed he had already been searched. . . .

[Ulrikh]: /Reads [Kotomin's] evidence from December 5, 1934 about
the question of whether any search of Nikolaev was done after his detention [. . .]/

[Kotomin]: That is incorrect. The instructions are that upon detention
there has to be a search.

Member of the Court Matulevich: What were the standing instructions
for detention and release [of detainees]?

[Kotomin]: Upon the detention of any suspicious person, there was supposed to be a mandatory search, and only I could authorize release. Besides this, I was supposed to receive all confiscated documents, I would examine them, and then draw the appropriate conclusions.

[. . .]

Member of the Court Matulevich: Who reported to you on Nikolaev's detention?

[Kotomin]: The operations commissar [presumably Tereshchenko].

Member of the Court Matulevich: If you yourself did not search Nikolaev and did not interrogate him, then how could you determine that he was not a suspicious person?

[Kotomin]: That was my mistake.

Kotomin's evidence in court differed somewhat from his statements on December 5, 1934. In his earlier interrogation, the chief of Kirov's guard indicated that he'd directly questioned Nikolaev; now he said that he had not. The "operations commissar" (almost certainly Tereshchenko) had by implication handled both the search and the interrogation of Nikolaev.[68] Yet in court Kotomin seemed to cover for Tereshchenko, claiming that he did not remember his name. Kotomin may have agreed as part of the trial scripting to take responsibility himself for negligence in checking up on Nikolaev on October 15, or he may have genuinely been covering for Tereshchenko. Whatever the case, the fact that central NKVD officers did not put Tereshchenko on record about his handling of Nikolaev suggests that the latter's testimony was not convenient for them. Possibly he had searched Nikolaev, but found nothing.

Under questioning by Ulrikh Gubin tried to minimize his own responsibility for the supposed negligence in Nikolaev's detention. He stated that Kotomin had told him that he'd personally spoken with Nikolaev, and he insisted that the detaining officer had the responsibility for searching suspicious persons.[69]

There was no evidence available for this book on the statements of senior Leningrad NKVD officers at the trial, but there are summaries that combine their pretrial depositions and statements in court. Medved confessed to "elements of self-satisfaction, as a result of which . . . operations work was in a neglected state." He admitted that there were no written instructions for Kirov's guard, and that he personally had not checked up on the guard posts (Gubin and Griunvald both testified to checking guard posts and training guards). Finally he accepted responsibility for inability "to achieve the arrest in Leningrad of a number of counterrevolutionaries from among the Trotsky-Zinoviev activists (*aktiv*), including Rumiantsev, Levin, and others. . . ."[70]

Zaporozhets asserted that Medved, not he, had supervised Kirov's guard. He admitted that during the 1933 all-union campaign to arrest Trotskyite "counterrevolutionary elements" he should have insisted to Medved on the arrest of Rumiantsev and Levin. But at the same time he noted that he had found no grounds for the arrest of Rumiantsev, Levin, or other "Trotsky-Zinovievite elements" in any of the reports on their activities he heard between late 1933 and August 1934. Zaporozhets' 1935 testimony is important confirmation that the arrest of prominent ex-Zinovievites in Leningrad was on the NKVD agenda in 1933–1934 and was a contested issue.[71]

Like Zaporozhets, Fomin denied responsibility for Kirov's guard, assigning it to Medved.[72]

Gorin-Lundin, head of the Secret Political Department which was charged with the surveillance of ex-oppositionists, confessed that he was guilty of failure to uncover the counterrevolutionary activities of the "Zinovievite group" in Leningrad. He testified that Rumiantsev, Levin, and Kotolynov were all under surveillance as Zinovievites. But like Zaporozhets he insisted that before the murder his department had not found incriminating evidence against them.[73]

According to Petrov's early 1960s testimony, only he, Lobov, and Fomin refused to plead guilty to the charges against them.[74]

The final sentences in the case read as follows:

· 99 ·

Sentences at the trial of Leningrad NKVD officers, January 23, 1935.
RGANI, f. 6, op. 13. d. 79, ll. 99–104.

———————

Military Collegium of the Supreme Soviet of the USSR
Consisting of:
Chairman—V. Ulrikh
Members: I. O. Matulevich and I. T. Goliakova
Secretary: Shaposhnikova
On January 23, 1935, without the participation of prosecution or defense, in the city of Moscow heard in closed session the case against the accused:
1. Medved, Filip Demianovich, former Chief of the NKVD Directorate

[. . .] of Leningrad Region, b. 1890, member of the Communist Party from 1907, served in the former VChK-OGPU, and later the NKVD from 1918;

2. Zaporozhets, Ivan Vasilevich, former First Deputy Chief of the NKVD Directorate [. . .] of Leningrad Region, b. 1895, member of the Communist Party from 1919, served in the former VChK-OGPU, and later the NKVD from 1921;

3. Fomin, Fyodor Timofeevich, former Second Deputy Chief of the NKVD Directorate [. . .] of Leningrad Region, b. 1894, member of the Communist Party from 1917, served in the former VChK-OGPU, and later the NKVD from 1919;

4. Gorin-Lundin, Aron Solomonovich, former Chief of the Secret Political Department of the NKVD Directorate [. . .] of Leningrad Region, b. 1900, member of the Communist Party from 1926, served in the former VChK-OGPU, and later the NKVD from 1919;

5. Gubin, Aleksandr Antonovich, former Chief of the Operations Department of the NKVD Directorate [. . .] of Leningrad Region, b. 1893, member of the Communist Party from 1918, served in the former VChK-OGPU, and later the NKVD from 1919;

6. Kotomin, Mikhail Ivanovich, former Chief of the Fourth Section of the Operations Department of the NKVD Directorate [. . .] of Leningrad Region, b. 1891, member of the Communist Party from 1918, served in the former VChK-OGPU, and later the NKVD from 1921;

7. Yanishevsky, Dionis Yulianovich, former Deputy Chief of the Special Department of the NKVD Directorate [. . .] of Leningrad Region, b. 1898, member of the Communist Party from 1918, served in the former VChK-OGPU, and later the NKVD from 1922:

8. Petrov, Georgy Alekseevich, former plenipotentiary officer of the Special Department of the NKVD Directorate [. . .] of Leningrad Region, b. 1904, member of the Communist Party from 1929, served in the former VChK-OGPU, and later the NKVD from 1932;

9. Baltsevich, Mechislav Konstantinovich, former aide to the Chief of the Third Section of the Special Department of the NKVD Directorate [. . .] of Leningrad Region, b. 1900, nonparty, served in the former VChK-OGPU, and later the NKVD from 1918 /with breaks/ has a brother, officer in the Polish Army, in Poland;

10. Mosevich, Andrei Andreevich, former aide to the Chief of the Secret Political Department of the NKVD Directorate [. . .] of Leningrad Region, b. 1903, member of the Communist Party from 1927, served in the former VChK-OGPU, and later the NKVD from 1927;

11. Belousenko, Aleksandr Makarovich, former Operations Secretary to the Deputy Chief of the NKVD Directorate [. . .] of Leningrad Region [Zaporozhets], b. 1903, member of the Communist Party from

1926, served in the former VChK-OGPU, and later the NKVD from 1920;

12. Lobov, Prokopy Maksimovich, former aide to the Chief of the Special Department of the NKVD Directorate [. . .] of Leningrad Region, b. 1898, member of the Communist Party from 1918, served in the former VChK-OGPU, and later the NKVD from 1922–

All twelve charged with crimes under Article 193—17, Paragraph (a) of the Criminal Code of the Russian Federated Soviet Socialist Republic.

The Military Collegium of the Supreme Court of the USSR [. . .] determined the following:

The leaders of the NKVD Directorate of Leningrad Region, Chief of the Directorate Medved, his deputies Zaporozhets and Fomin, Chief of the Secret Political Department Gorin-Lundin, and Deputy Chief of the Operations Department Yanishevsky did not show the necessary energy and persistence in carrying out the orders of the OGPU and NKVD for reconstruction of operational/agent and investigative work [. . .] their monitoring of the agent network was totally insufficient, they did not give proper attention to the investigation of agents' information and they did not provide the necessary training for their subordinates. As a result of the criminally negligent attitude towards their service obligations taken by Medved, Zaporozhets, and Gorin-Lundin, Zinovievite counterrevolutionary elements residing in Leningrad were able to activate their counterrevolutionary work and undertake preparations for a terrorist attack, in spite of the fact that some were under Secret Political Department surveillance (*na uchete*).

Besides this, Medved, Zaporozhets, and Fomin had a criminally negligent attitude towards the organization of Comrade S. M. Kirov's guard: they did not take the necessary measures to strengthen the Operations Department with sufficiently qualified personnel, they did not prepare written instructions for the persons guarding Comrade Kirov, and they did not assign an [. . .] experienced commissar for constant guard over Kirov.

Besides this, the work of the Operations Department was not connected with other departments of the Directorate, there was no mutual exchange of information between these departments about the working up of terrorist cases, as a result of which the Operations Department could not adjust handling of the guard.

Chief of the Operations Department Gubin and Chief of the Fourth Section of the same department Kotomin, who had direct responsibility for guarding members of the government [. . .] not only failed to take adequate measures to improve the guard, but took a criminally negligent attitude towards their service duties. They illegally released from custody, without a personal search and without checking into the circumstances of detention, the terrorist Leonid Nikolaev, detained on October 15, 1934, a member of the Leningrad counterrevolutionary terrorist center, who was obviously following Comrade Kirov on the streets of Leningrad. It was later determined that at the moment of his detention Nikolaev was carrying on his person a Nagan-system revolver.

In the fall of 1934 Mosevich, aide to the Chief of the Secret Political Department, after receiving from citizeness Volkova information on the presence in Leningrad of a number of terrorist groups, in part on a terrorist attack in preparation against Comrade Kirov, did not attribute proper significance to this material, and held this material up without processing. At this same time analogous material from Volkova came into the Special Department of the Leningrad [. . .] NKVD. Baltsevich, aide to the Chief of the Second Section of the Special Department, assigned to check on the denunciations (*zaiavleniia*) by Special Department Deputy Chief Yanishevsky, decided immediately, without any basis at all, that Volkova's denunciations were false. He ordered Officer Petrov of the Special Department to take the working up of Volkova's material in the direction of proving the falsehood of her denunciations, rather than exposing the persons denounced by Volkova. At Baltsevich's order, Volkova was put under surveillance, which prevented her from further working up [her case]. Then Petrov, on Baltsevich's instructions, arrested Volkova with the intention of getting from her a confession that her denunciations were false.[75] In the upshot Volkova, at Baltsevich's order and with the approval of Yanishevsky, was sent without any justification to a psychiatric hospital.

During the time that Volkova's case was being processed, the latter complained of the criminally irresponsible attitude towards her denunciations to Belousenko, Operations Secretary to the Deputy Chief of the NKVD Directorate. Instead of taking measures towards a real inquiry into Volkova's complaints, the latter confined himself to hearing explanations by Baltsevich and Petrov that investigation of Volkova's claims showed that they were supposedly false, and that Volkova herself was supposedly psychologically abnormal.

The same Baltsevich, after receiving the case files on the Mikheevs, who confessed to agreeing with the Latvian consul to collect espionage information for Latvian military intelligence on conditions in Leningrad military industries, illegally suspended the investigation and freed the Mikheevs from confinement.

Lobov, aide to the Chief of the Special Department, took a criminally negligent attitude towards his service duties, failed to supervise members of the department, failed to check their work, failed to reorganize work with the agent network, and utterly neglected working up a case on the counterrevolutionary Zinovievite group.

Thus, it has been established that all of the accused in this case are guilty of demonstrating criminal negligence of the basic demands of state security, failing to take essential measures to guard Comrade Kirov, who was killed on December 1, 1934 by Leonid Nikolaev, a member of the Leningrad counterrevolutionary terrorist center.

The crimes of the accused are classified under Paragraph "a," Article 193–17 of the Criminal Code of the Russian Federated Soviet Socialist Republic.

Sentences:

1. Baltsevich, Mechislav Konstantinovich, for a criminally negligent attitude to his service obligations in the protection of state security and for a number of illegal actions in the investigation of specific cases is sentenced to incarceration in a concentration camp for a period of ten years.

2. Medved, Filip Demianovich, and

3. Zaporozhets, Ivan Vasilevich, for a criminally negligent attitude to their service obligations in the protection of state security are sentenced to incarceration in a concentration camp for a period of three years each.

4. Gubin, Aleksandr Antonovich,

5. Kotomin, Mikhail Ivanovich, and

6. Petrov, Georgy Alekseevich, for a criminally negligent attitude to their service obligations in the protection of state security are sentenced to incarceration in a concentration camp for a period of three years each.

7. Fomin, Fyodor Timofeevich,

8. Gorin-Lundin, Aron Solomonovich,

9. Yanishevsky, Dionis Yulianovich,

10. Mosevich, Andrei Andreevich,

11. Belousenko, Aleksandr Makarovich, and

12. Lobov, Prokopy Maksimovich, for a negligent attitude to their service obligations in the protection of state security are sentenced to incarceration in a concentration camp for a period of two years each.

With the apparent exception of Baltsevich, all of these men would serve their sentences not as prisoners, but as officers in the administration of the Gulag forced labor complex at Kolyma in far northeastern Siberia. Beginning in the summer of 1935 many would be joined by their families.[76]

The sentencing document follows closely the lines of questioning central interrogators took with indicted Leningrad NKVD officers in December 1934–January 1935. The Leningrad NKVD leadership is taxed with failure to intensify work with the informer network, by which is meant among other things building cases on more dubious denunciations. The authors note poor communication between departments, in particular implying that the Operations Department was not receiving information on potential terrorists from other departments.

This was an issue interrogators had raised in sessions with Kotomin and Griunvald. The sentencing document repeats the charges of neglecting Kirov's guard, omitting to search Nikolaev, suppressing Volkova's evidence, and failing to arrest members of the supposed Zinovievite underground in Leningrad.

The sentences distort the facts to exaggerate the failures of the Leningrad security police. The document claims that Nikolaev was carrying his revolver when detained on October 15, when this was probably not so. It also presents the check on Nikolaev's identity as more perfunctory than the testimony of Operations Department officers actually indicated. And finally, the document states that Volkova had evidence of an attack in preparation against Kirov, a claim for which there is no earlier evidence.

The indictments listed in the document introduce one important new piece of evidence, namely the reference to a case against "the Mikheevs" of cooperating with the Latvian consul to spy on Leningrad military industry. Although there is no other mention of the Mikheevs in the sources available to me, the reference is nonetheless important. It indicates that Bissenieks was probably a target of the NKVD, or perhaps just the central NKVD, before the murder. The Mikheevs may have been part of a provocatory operation aimed at incriminating or recruiting him. Baltsevich could have released them with the aim of continuing or initiating such an operation, or he may have believed their evidence hopelessly unreliable.

Much of the variation in sentencing is hard to explain, but the cases of Baltsevich and Fomin stand out. Baltsevich's heavy sentence may have been due in part to the fact that he was a non-Communist with relatives in "bourgeois" Poland. But it was in all likelihood due mostly to the fact that central authorities held him more than anyone else responsible for squelching Volkova's denunciations. Medved and Zaporozhets as the senior responsible officers received the next-longest labor camp terms. In this context Fomin's relatively light sentence is worth noting. Formally speaking, he was responsible only for the border guard units of the Leningrad NKVD, and this could have been the justification for his short term of forced labor. But as we have seen, Special Department Operations Secretary S. A. Annushkov claimed in 1963 that Fomin was actually in charge of the Special Department during Zaporozhets' medical leave.

It is often alleged that the punishments meted out to the Leningrad NKVD officers in January 1935 were unusually light, and that this suggests they were in fact complicit with Stalin in a murder plot against Kirov. However, comparison of the officers' treatment in 1935 with that of other security officials penalized for mistakes (as opposed to corruption or spying) in the early 1930s indicates that this is not so. In late June or the first days of July 1932 Japanese authorities in Manchuria arrested a Korean "subversive" who confessed that he was an OGPU operative sent to blow up bridges in the Japanese-occupied territory. Stalin, who wanted no trouble with Japan at this point, was angered by this "criminal violation of the Central Committee directive on the unacceptibility of subversive operations . . . in Manchuria." He demanded "draconian measures against the criminals at the OGPU. . . ." In the end the Politburo censured the OGPU agent who had recruited the Korean and transferred him to a new job. After the mutiny of civil defense commander Nakhaev on August 5, 1934, the Politburo punished a number of civil defense officers Stalin held responsible, but apparently not with arrests or executions (see above, pp. 274–277). From Sochi Stalin ordered TsK leaders to give Moscow Military District commander A. I. Kork a "tongue-lashing."[77]

On January 26, 1935 the NKVD released a secret circular to all of its local branches chastising the Leningrad NKVD for complacency and incompetence and insisting on an implacable struggle with the class enemy, iron discipline, and constant vigilance. Attached to the circular were selected transcripts of testimony by Medved and other Leningrad officers tried for negligence. Under the circumstances the circular's admonition that the struggle be carried out "on the basis of the strictest revolutionary legality" must be viewed as a fig leaf. Within a month the new head of the Leningrad NKVD, Leonid Zakovsky, would undertake the arrest of every single person on the Directorate's watch lists.[78]

Only a partial copy of the January 26 NKVD circular was available for this book. In addition there were two partial copies of drafts of the circular, both worthy of attention. Yagoda was the author of both drafts. In the first, the Commissar of Internal Affairs defends himself against charges of negligence in a very angry, personal tone. He insists that before the murder he ordered Medved and Zaporozhets to improve Kirov's guard and to "reorganize" work with the informer network. He implies that the Leningrad NKVD should have arrested the supposed conspiratorial center of ex-Zinovievites long before the murder, and derides Operations Department officers for their incompetence in guarding Kirov and transporting Borisov. Following the sentencing document, he overstates the Operations Department's culpability in Kirov's death by stating as fact the claim that Nikolaev was carrying his gun when detained on October 15. Without comment he also includes a verbatim transcription of Stalin's story, included in the January 18 TsK circular, of Nikolaev's attempt to approach Kirov beside his car three weeks before the murder. If this made it into the final circular, it would undoubtedly have contributed to rumors that Nikolaev was arrested twice before the murder, rather than once.

· 100 ·

Draft NKVD circular authored by Yagoda around January 20, 1935. RGANI, f. 6, op. 13, d. 92, ll. 173–177. (All emphasis in the original.)

The investigation in the case of the villainous murder of Comrade Kirov, carried out by Leonid Nikolaev, member of the "Leningrad Terrorist Center," has established that the murder was possible due only to the complete deterioration and collapse of the NKVD apparatus in Leningrad, which turned from an organ of battle against the counterrevolution into an abominable desolation (*merzost zapusteniia*).

The burden of responsibility for the murder of a most prominent member of the government and the shame which has shrouded the organs of the NKVD [. . .] is only worsened by the fact that the assassination could without a doubt have been prevented, if those officers of the Leningrad NKVD Directorate responsible for the guard of Comrade Kirov had worked to take even the most elementary measures to protect and guard Comrade Kirov.

First and foremost, I must state that more than once I personally warned the chief of the NKVD Directorate in the Leningrad Region Medved about the presence of terrorist elements in Leningrad, about the absence of any signs at all of serious operational work in the apparatus subordinate to him, and about the fact that the most important, the most urgent task of the Directorate was the battle with counterrevolutionary terrorists and the implementation of concrete measures for the prevention of terrorist attacks.

I personally warned Medved and his deputy Zaporozhets that they would answer with their heads for the personal security of Comrade Kirov. Nevertheless, the leading officers of the Leningrad Directorate of the NKVD, including Comrades Medved, Zaporozhets, Fomin, Yanishevsky, Gorin, Gubin, Kotomin, and others, flagrantly ignored the energetic operational orders of the NKVD.

The Release of L. Nikolaev on October 15, 1934

The fact is that the murderer of Comrade Kirov, Leonid Nikolaev, was in the hands of the Leningrad NKVD apparatus *just one and a half months* before his attack, but *he was released from custody* thanks exclusively to a complete lack of discipline and shocking irresponsibility.

On October 15 of last year Nikolaev, L. was detained by officers of Kirov's guard, in view of his suspicious behavior *as he followed Comrade Kirov.* Delivered to the Chief of the Fourth Section of the Operations Department Kotomin, responsible for Kirov's guard, Nikolaev was not subjected to a personal search nor was his name checked against the list (*uchet*) of suspicious persons. And this was while Nikolaev at that very moment had in his briefcase a loaded Nagan and notes, wherein his concrete plans for a terrorist act against Comrade Kirov were laid out.

After his second arrest [i.e. after Kirov's murder] Nikolaev deposed that if the officers of the NKVD had bothered to take a look in the briefcase at the time of his first arrest, his evil plans would have been thwarted, and he himself would have "had time to cool his heels behind the walls of a solitary confinement cell." The chief of the Operations Department Gubin, to whom Kotomin reported Nikolaev's detention, agreed with Kotomin's proposal to free Nikolaev from arrest without asking for the reasons for freeing him.

It is not inappropriate to note that Nikolaev was freed only on the basis of his own statement that he was a member of the Communist Party and intended to speak to Comrade Kirov on the street about a personal question. [. . .]

[There follows a long direct citation from Stalin's January 18, 1935 Central Committee circular on the murder (Chapter 9, Document 83), referring to the alleged incident in which guards seized Nikolaev as he approached Kirov's car, but released him upon presentation of his party card.]

Organization of Kirov's Guard

Comrade Kirov's guard was organized in particularly chaotic fashion. The leaders of the Leningrad Directorate of the NKVD did not have the ability, the persistence, or the necessary boldness to carry out the clear and direct orders [. . .] of the center for the [. . .] organization of Comrade Kirov's guard.

Above all, the senior Leningrad officers of the NKVD *looked on indifferently while Comrade Kirov regularly took walks and rode his automobile around the city without any guard at all. They took no decisive measures to maintain any guard.*

Inside the Smolny building itself, Borisov, *a specially assigned commissar of the Operations Department,* was responsible for Kirov's guard. It must be said that this so-called "bodyguard" was 53 years old [. . .] [and] before beginning work in the NKVD organs in 1924 was a night watchman and had never worked in production.

Could this elderly night watchman guarantee the personal safety of Comrade Kirov against armed terrorists?

As it turned out, at the moment that Nikolaev committed his terrorist act Commissar Borisov was not on the scene. [. . .] It is clear from the investigation evidence that Borisov in the best case was somewhere in the corridors of Smolny, a good several hundred meters from the place of Kirov's murder, and obviously could not have stopped the hand of the assassin. He was one of the last to turn up at the scene of the crime, well after the murder was committed.

Unfortunately, the investigation was deprived of the possibility of questioning Borisov personally about his behavior at the moment of the killing because Borisov, summoned on December 2, 1934 from the NKVD Directorate to Smolny to give testimony to members of the government, perished as the result of an automobile accident.

It must be said that the death of Comrade Borisov shows the inability of leading officers of the Leningrad Regional Directorate of the NKVD to carry out what one would suppose were the simplest operational instructions. First and foremost, the leaders of the [. . .] Directorate, and especially Comrade Medved, did not think to arrest immediately Borisov, who had disregarded his duties.

When Comrade Khviiuzov (chief of the First Section of the Operations Department) [. . .] was ordered to send Borisov to Smolny, he could find no better means to carry out this order than dispatching Borisov on a truck that happened to turn up, which had an accident due to the negligence of the driver, who failed to notice that the steering mechanism of the vehicle was not in order.

Here you have a brief summary of the way in which Comrade Kirov's guard was organized in Leningrad, if one can even call such unheard-of lack of discipline "organization of a guard."

As everyone now knows, there long existed in Leningrad a terrorist center of the counterrevolutionary Zinovievite organization in the persons of Rumiantsev, Levin, Kotolynov and others, on whose orders Nikolaev carried out the villainous murder of Comrade Kirov. [. . .]

An inspection of the work of the Leningrad Region Directorate of the NKVD by an NKVD brigade in October 1934 found total operational inactivity.

In spite of the very concrete instructions of the brigade, no real measures for the decisive reorganization (*perestroika*) of work were taken by the leadership of the [. . .] Regional Directorate. [. . .]

From the above the following conclusions are entirely obvious.

1. For an extended period of time the leadership and part of the apparatus of the Leningrad [. . .] NKVD have demonstrated criminal inactivity.

2. Among the employees of the NKVD Directorate a mood was cultivated of frivolous indifference, lordly laziness, and condescension towards direct, practical operational work, which was handed over to the whims of unscreened, unknown person who often had dubious pasts and suspicious foreign connections /for example Baltsevich/.

3. As a consequence of [. . .] demoralization, the absence of vigilance, and the contamination of the NKVD apparatus in Leningrad [with "alien" elements], signals from the agent network and direct orders from the NKVD USSR for a decisive struggle with terrorist elements were given no attention at all.

4. The most important task of the Regional Directorate of the Leningrad NKVD—*guaranteeing the protection of Comrade Kirov with all available forces—was not the center of attention even for the Operations Department, much less the entire apparatus.* [. . .]

The other available draft of the January 26 NKVD letter resembles the one excerpted above, except for the inclusion of specific comments on the Volkova case.

> The villainous murder of Comrade Kirov could have been prevented if it were not for the criminal self-satisfaction and operational inactivity of the Leningrad apparatus, if the senior . . . operational officers had paid even the slightest attention to the alarming signals from the agent network about the preparation of terrorist acts against Comrade Kirov.
>
> In a whole series of reports to the Leningrad Directorate of the NKVD beginning in August 1934 Volkova warned of the existence in Leningrad of a counterrevolutionary, terrorist organization, consisting of kulaks, the members of which discussed . . . the organization of an attack on Comrade Kirov at their get-togethers . . . [79]

The claim that Volkova uncovered a plot against Kirov specifically in the summer of 1934 parallels statements in the charges against the Leningrad NKVD officers. In all probability Yagoda made the assertion to deepen the apparent responsibility of Medved and his subordinates for Kirov's death.

The evidence on the central investigation of the Leningrad NKVD in 1934–1935 is indispensable for understanding the Kirov murder, Stalin's reaction, and the overall context for both. To begin with the most obvious conclusions, the investigation documents, supplemented by interviews with witnesses from the Khrushchev era, show that Kirov's guard Borisov almost certainly perished in a truck accident, and that before Kirov's murder the Leningrad NKVD only took Nikolaev into custody once. It was Operations Department chief Gubin who ordered his release, not Yagoda acting through Zaporozhets. Moreover, Nikolaev may well not have been carrying a weapon when he was detained. These conclusions undermine a later narrative of the murder suggested in slightly different variations by Khrushchev, Medvedev, Antonov-Ovseenko, Rybakov, Tucker, and Conquest, among others.

The evidence also reveals tensions between central authorities and the Leningrad NKVD leadership that predated the Kirov murder. The central NKVD, apparently prompted by Stalin's expressed desire to protect Kirov more effectively, monitored arrangements for the Leningrad leader's guard beginning in the summer of 1933. Stalin and Yagoda shared a sense that the Leningrad NKVD was lax. A second point of conflict was the ongoing surveillance of ex-Zinovievites who held middle-level positions in the Leningrad party/state apparatus. Two separate orders were issued for the arrest of Rumiantsev and Levin in 1933–1934, evidently under pressure from Yagoda or his subordinates. Medved claimed that Kirov countermanded these orders. As discussed in Chapter 3, he may have done so based on the general course towards limited rehabilitation of ex-oppositionists set by the TsK in 1933–1934. At any rate, Leningrad NKVD officers after Kirov's murder unanimously stated that they had no evidence of oppositional activity by the former Zinovievites in 1933–1934.

Documents from the investigation hint that Volkova's denunciations in the summer and fall of 1934 could have been part of some kind of coordinated effort to fabricate evidence of counterrevolutionary activity against ex-Zinovievites in Leningrad. This operation may have been run out of the Smolny Ward NKVD office, with or without the direct sanction of central NKVD authorities. Certainly the ongoing efforts of central authorities to arrest Rumiantsev and Levin suggest that the central NKVD could have been involved. Regular Leningrad police investigators and/or party officials (Ilin) might also have been involved in preparing a provocation against the ex-Zinovievites.

Stalin, Yagoda, and their deputies swept into Leningrad on December 2 determined to smash the leadership of the city NKVD. Given earlier efforts to remove Medved from his post and the tension between the city and central NKVD apparatuses, Kirov's murder made this inevitable. Throughout their investigation central interrogators sought to maximize the culpability of Leningrad NKVD officers. This fact is important to keep in mind when assessing the probability, for example, that Leningrad NKVD officers murdered Borisov or that Zaporozhets masterminded Nikolaev's release from custody on October 15. Interrogation protocols as well as memoirs from the 1950s and early 1960s indicate that Yezhov and Agranov (and behind them, Stalin) were bent on finding every piece of evidence that might demonstrate local security forces' incompetence or even implicate them in Kirov's murder. If there was good evidence that the Leningrad NKVD murdered Borisov, or that Zaporozhets ordered Nikolaev's release, central NKVD investigators would have probably have discovered and used it in the winter of 1934–1935. The same logic applies to possible connections between Leonid Nikolaev and Volkova's denunciations—if they existed, the central NKVD would have been glad to find them.

CHAPTER 11

The Kirov Murder and the Great Terror

S oviet subjects understood immediately that the Kirov murder would provoke large-scale state retaliation. Apprehension was particularly widespread among Communist Party members and the intelligentsia. Yevgeniya Ginzburg, a Communist activist and teacher, describes fear and confusion in the Kazan party organization in the days following the killing. The fact that Nikolaev was a Communist was seen as particularly ominous. Leningrad journalist Zavalishin in 1950 reported widespread anxiety among Communists in the city, especially those with histories of belonging to other parties during the revolutionary era. In post–World War II accounts of the Kirov murder, some memoirists began attaching the general anxiety to a supposed inchoate sense that Stalin was behind the murder. In 1934, however, what people seem to have experienced was a more free-floating dread.[1]

Fear is easily transformed into rage, and fear of the oppressor into identification with him. The result in December 1934 was an ecstasy of denunciation. In the weeks following the murder, Leningrad authorities had party organizations meeting nearly every day to discuss events. Following the December 17 announcement in *Pravda* that Zinovievites were responsible for the assassination, party meetings all over the city passed resolutions demanding "merciless punishment of the terrorists." Reports from the Leningrad party's Information Department stated that "everyone" was demanding harsh reprisals against the Zinovievites. Communists stumbled over one another in the rush to denounce compatriots who had expressed any sympathy for dissidents. Former oppositionists were terrified. According to one Information Department memorandum, ex-oppositionists appealing for clemency at a Lenin Factory party meeting "were very nervous and spoke even with tears in their eyes."[2]

In the wake of the Kirov murder, the Leningrad government, no doubt terrified of Stalin's wrath, moved to "cleanse" the city of suspected Zinovievites. In the prevailing mood of terror and rage, no doubt there were many ready to provide compromising information on co-workers and neighbors. Nikolai Yezhov, soon to be TsK secretary and now Stalin's de facto overseer of NKVD work, supervised the purge, although formally a commission of Leningraders was responsible. Yezhov reported to Stalin that the city's government and party institutions were "infested with doubtful elements, former Tsarist officers, persons with ties abroad, children of persons deprived of civil rights (*lishentsy*), kulaks, Trotskyites, Zinovievites, and so on." Yezhov and new Leningrad party chief Andrei Zhdanov supervised the checking of 223 employees of the city and regional party committees, firing 80, including 31 of 111 "supervisory personnel." At the regional executive committee, the Leningrad soviet apparatus, and the regional control commission, 119 people were fired of 292 checked.[3] Thousands were also exiled from Leningrad. According to a 1960 summary of materials in the Leningrad regional party archive, this purge resulted in the expulsion of 2,331 persons from the city in January–February 1935 and the firing of over 200 employees from the government apparatus.

· 101 ·

Summary report on materials in the archives of the Leningrad regional committee of the Communist Party on the expulsion from the party and exile of Communists from Leningrad following the Kirov murder, prepared by *instruktor* of the Leningrad regional party committee Poleshchuk, November 22, 1960.
RGANI, f. 6, op. 13, d. 16, ll. 19–21.

———————

A commission composed of Nizovtsev, M. Bogdanov, Tsarev, Smirnov, Tsyganov, Tsesarsky, with the participation of first secretaries of appropriate ward committees, reviewed the cases of 1,610 former Zinovievites from January 1 to February 3, 1935. Of this number 654 persons were expelled from the party and exiled from Leningrad, 421 persons were posted to work in other areas, 265 were exiled from the Leningrad, and 270 were allowed to remain in Leningrad.

On February 13, 1935 Leningrad ward committees excluded 626 persons from the party. Between January 27 and February 17 365 persons were ordered to work outside Leningrad [by the ward committees].

On February 17, 1935 the party collegium of Leningrad Region reviewed 487 appeals. Of all appeals, expulsion from the party was confirmed in 425 cases, and restoration [to the party] in 5. [The original decisions] were changed to restoration in 54 cases, and to expulsion in 3.

In addition, a commission to vet employees of the city and regional party committees, the regional and city executive committees, the regional and city committees of the Komsomol, composed of Nizovtsev, M. Bogdanov, Voitas, S. Smirnov, Tsyganov, [. . .] worked from December 25, 1934 through January 27, 1935.

[The commission] [. . .] decided to dismiss from work 28 employees out of 78 vetted from the Regional Executive Committee, 82 out of 171 vetted at the Leningrad soviet, nine out of 35 at the Soviet Control Commission, 7 out of 17 at the Leningrad Planning Department, 19 out of 39 at the Regional Planning Department, and 22 out of 56 at the city and regional committees of the Komsomol. A total of 245 persons were dismissed out of 628 vetted. . . .

Among those fired and expelled from the party was S. M. Petrashevich (sometimes spelled Petroshevich), the secretary of the regional party committee Agriculture Department who had offered to help get Nikolaev a ticket to the activists' meeting on December 1, and had apparently told him the Kirov was to speak at the meeting. Two other Smolny employees who had spoken to Nikolaev, Vladimirov and Karmanov, were also excluded from the party. Several of the people transferred to jobs outside the city were senior officials, including Georgy Pylaev, a Leningrad veteran who headed the city's office of the Commissariat of Heavy Industry in 1934; N. F. Sveshnikov, Kirov's office manager and regional party committee member; Serganin, head of Leningrad's cooperative network; and T. S. Nazarenko, secretary of the city soviet's executive committee. At least one of those transferred, Mikhail Rosliakov, had briefly stood with Zinoviev in late 1925.[4] The Soviet and party apparatuses were not the only organizations affected. Beginning on December 10, 1934 Nikolai Yezhov supervised a purge of the regional NKVD office, which resulted in the dismissal or transfer of 298 employees of 2,747 checked. He also ran the "cleansing" of the regular police, firing or transferring 590 of 3,050 employees.[5]

In addition to exiles and transfers, there were thousands of arrests. In February and March 1935 the Leningrad NKVD carried out a massive operation to arrest every single city resident on their watch lists. This project was separate from the purges of the party and state apparatuses described above. It was spearheaded by the new director of the regional NKVD, Leonid Zakovsky. Zakovsky, who had a reputation for ruthlessness, proposed the operation to Yagoda in a February 16 memorandum that warned of "the serious infestation of enterprises, institutions of higher learning, and government institutions of the city of Leningrad with the remnants of defeated bourgeoisie, major officials of the former [Tsarist] government apparatus (including the police), the relatives of executed terrorists, diversionists, spies, and even well-known representatives of the former Tsarist aristocracy, the commanding staff, and their relatives." He noted that there were 11,095 persons on the watch lists, including 941 relatives of executed counterrevolutionaries, 2,360 former tsarist aristocrats, 5,044 former landlords and wealthy merchants, 620 former Tsarist police officers, and 585 "middle- and high-ranking" clerics not serving in active churches. Zakovsky characterized these people as "unoccupied . . . with any useful activity," and busy with "active counterrevolutionary activity." Many had ties abroad.[6]

Yagoda wrote to Stalin, who approved the plan on February 26, proposing that the operation be spread out over a two- to three-month period in order to avoid too much negative coverage in the international press. The cases of the arrestees were to be tried by the NKVD's Special Board (created in the July 1934 "reforms"), which had the right to sentence the accused to up to five years of labor camp. Two days later the arrests began, and they continued until March 27 (apparently Stalin wanted faster results than the two to three months proposed by Yagoda). On March 31 Zakovsky reported that 11,702 people had been arrested (something like one in every two hundred residents of the city). They were charged with crimes including distribution of counterrevolutionary literature, planning terrorist attacks, espionage, and connections with White émigrés abroad. Most of those arrested were sent to forced labor camps. Although over 6,000 of the detainees appealed their sentences to the NKVD or the prosecutor's office, no more than a few hundred were allowed to remain in Leningrad.[7]

Zakovsky and the central NKVD authorities made a thorough canvass for counterrevolutionary plots. Based on the denunciations of Maria Volkova alone, the NKVD arrested sixty-three persons in the two weeks following Kirov's assassination, supposedly belonging to six counterrevolutionary groups. The reality behind the charges against these "counterrevolutionaries" seems mostly to have been offhand sarcastic comments about Stalin, other Soviet leaders, or Soviet Power in general. Based on a January 1935 Zakovsky memorandum referring to the "liquidation" of counterrevolutionary groups and/or persons, it seems that the NKVD may have executed several hundred people in Leningrad following Kirov's murder.[8]

A large proportion of those arrested as counterrevolutionaries were university students. Some sense of the anguish, hopelessness, and isolation experienced by these student prisoners can be gleaned from the unpublished memoir of V. I. Rudolf-Yurasova, solicited by Boris Nicolaevsky in the early 1950s. Rudolf-Yurasova passed through the Shpaliorka jail in Leningrad in 1937, where she read messages scratched into the surface of the cafeteria's aluminum cups by students arrested following the Kirov murder. One girl wrote, "Yulia Reznikova, student of the Tekhnolozhka [short for the Technological Institute]. Jailed in the Kirov case. 58 [the article of the Soviet criminal code most often used in cases of terror and "counterrevolution"]. Age 19. Tell my mama —13 Solianaia Alley. We may never see each other again." On a second cup was scraped: "Kira Baranova. Forestry Academy. Arrested 10/11/35. Not guilty. I can't take any more."[9]

Repressions continued in the region from 1936 to 1939. A check of party documents running from the summer of 1935 into early spring 1936 (see below), uncovered 2,708 "direct, open enemies of the party and Soviet Power" in the Leningrad Region and the Karelian Autonomous Republic. In April Chudov requested permission from the Central Committee to expel all of these people from the area. Ultimately there were about 90,000 arrests in the Leningrad Region during the Great Terror.[10]

As Stalin's January 18 Central Committee circular makes clear, the dictator was determined to use the Kirov assassination to root out from the party and destroy former Trotskyite and Zinovievite oppositionists. Yet from the first days of the murder investigation, he and Nikolai Yezhov cast an even wider net for Communist malcontents. Yezhov's partially legible notes for a presentation to Stalin, probably delivered between December 8 and 21, 1934, indicate that he proposed putting "Rightists" on trial for the murder, in addition to the Trotskyites and Zinovievites. He apparently intended to ask Stalin whether the Komarovites, Kirov's onetime opponents in the Leningrad organization, should be tried or given party censures.[11] It is not known what Stalin told Yezhov at this meeting. However, by early January the latter was working with a secret police file labeled "Zanoza" ("Thorn in the Flesh," or, more loosely, "Pain in the Ass") that contained denunciations of and intelligence on a number of former Komarovites. On January 2, the NKVD called in Rekstin, one of the members of the Leningrad party control commission fired by Kirov in 1929, to make a written statement. Rekstin confessed to "clinging to my humiliation" after 1929, spreading rumors about Kirov (his work at *Terek*), and having "antiparty" conversations with Georgy Desov and other Komarovites as recently as 1934. The NKVD arrested Rekstin on January 8 for "cliquishness" (*gruppovshchina*) and antiparty conversations. In the course of interrogations running into February, Rekstin confessed to various anti-Kirov utterances, in which he also implicated Komarov. At around the same time as Rekstin, the NKVD also arrested Anna Korol, apparently the wife of a Komarovite member of the Leningrad control commission fired in 1929. Korol and Rekstin's testimony, as well as informer reports from 1933–1934, implicated former Leningrad officials Desov, Badaev, Amenitsky, Messing, and others in nasty comments and general hostility towards Kirov and in some cases Stalin as well. The secret police materials also appeared to show that the Komarovites had complex connections with ex-Zinovievite veterans of Leningrad (Faivilovich, P. A. Zalutsky), and the Bukharin "schoolboys" (Tseitlin). The boundaries between Left and Right were not clear-cut. After February 1935 there are no further data on the disposition of Rekstin's and Korol's cases, but they almost certainly perished in 1937–1938. The materials in their files were rich with leads that the NKVD no doubt made good use of during the Great Terror.[12]

Further incriminating material for NKVD use was provided by the efforts of one clique or another to settle old scores or wring advantage out of Kirov's killing. Two of what were probably many denunciations based on Leningrad's internal party politics remain in Nikolai Yezhov's archive today. On December 11, an aide to Avel Yenukidze at the Central Executive Committee, Appolon Chikovani, wrote a denunciation based on conversations with a Leningrad soviet department head, Rappoport, who had chaired the regional control commission immediately after Desov's dismissal (see above, pp. 98–104). Chikovani's letter was somewhat coy, but he suggested that people working with Kirov before his death had clandestine ties with Komarov and former Zinovievites. Chikovani specifically accused N. F. Sveshnikov, Kirov's office manager, of "playing on two fronts," that is of connections with the Komarovites. A second letter, dated December 25, came in to Stalin personally from N. Tagunov, a disgraced former Leningrad official who had tangled with Amenitsky and lost when Komarov's clique was still powerful in the city. Tagunov's narrative was somewhat disconnected, but in essence he accused Komarov's people of setting up the ex-Zinovievite Vladimir Rumiantsev (executed in the "Leningrad Center" case) with various jobs in Vyborg Ward in the early 1930s. According to Tagunov, N. Osipov, who had headed the regional party committee's personnel department for a while in the early 1930s, was Komarov's "right-hand man." Osipov now worked for Kaganovich in the Central Committee.[13]

Obviously there were plenty of materials to support a purge in Leningrad. But the effort to clean out "anti-Soviet elements" from the state apparatus reached beyond that city to the entire USSR. After Kirov's assassination, Stalin ordered checks into the background of state employees throughout the country. Given that an "insider" had assassinated the Leningrad party secretary, the NKVD conducted a particularly thorough check for "enemies" among Kremlin personnel. This investigation, which quickly became linked with the purge of the Central Executive Committee apparatus, resulted in the so-called "Kremlin Case" of 1935.[14]

The "Kremlin Case," involving a supposed plot to murder Stalin, led to the removal of Stalin's old comrade Avel Yenukidze from the secretariat of the Central Executive Committee, where he had charge of the Kremlin command (*komendatura*) responsible for the security of the Soviet leadership. The commander of the Kremlin guard, R. A. Peterson, was also fired. Presumably at Stalin's order, Yagoda, Molchanov, and Pauker reorganized the Kremlin guard, which was removed from the control of the Central Executive Committee and placed under the NKVD. A regiment of special NKVD troops replaced the Red Army soldiers previously charged with the guard. As can be seen from these moves, the case was at least in part connected with an effort to strengthen Stalin's security in the wake of Kirov's killing.[15]

Investigation of the case began with supposed "anti-Soviet rumors" spread by three young Kremlin cleaning ladies and denounced to the Kremlin command in early November 1934, several weeks before Kirov's murder. The cleaning ladies had reportedly griped about Stalin and other Soviet leaders living in luxury, while the population nearly starved. They had also gossiped about Stalin (he wasn't Russian, but "Armenian") and his wives (both, they said, had died "unnatural deaths"—true in Allilueva's case). A memorandum on these conversations reached Kremlin commander Peterson and Yenukidze, both of whom chose to ignore the whole incident, presumably as insignificant gossip. After the Kirov murder, however, the denunciation of the cleaning ladies appeared in a new light. On January 20, 1935 Pauker and Molchanov interrogated all three of them.[16]

Yagoda and his subordinates quickly declared the three "a counter-revolutionary group." Based on their interrogations, the NKVD arrested more Kremlin employees, including other janitors, a telephone operator, a postal clerk, and a couple of librarians. Under questioning these prisoners denounced one another for a variety of subversive conversations, namely gossip that Allilueva had died "an unnatural death," rumors that Nikolaev had killed Kirov "on romantic grounds" (because Kirov was sleeping with his wife), discussions of Lenin's testament, and complaints that Stalin had made life harder for the general population.[17] By pressuring lower-ranking employees, investigators were ultimately able to charge a librarian who was the former wife of Lev Kamenev's brother and leading officers of the Kremlin command with plotting to assassinate Stalin. It was then easy to manufacture charges of negligence against Peterson, who was transferred to Ukraine, and Yenukidze, who was demoted, transferred out of Moscow, and expelled from the party at a TsK plenum in June 1935. Lev Kamenev was convicted of foreknowledge of the assassination plot and ten years were added to his five-year prison term from the "Moscow Center" case. A total of 112 people were arrested in the "Kremlin Case" and nearly all were sentenced to punishments ranging from internal exile to execution.[18]

The entire course of the "Kremlin Case" paralleled closely the purges in Leningrad following Kirov's murder. In both cases the people in charge of security measures—Medved in Leningrad and Yenukidze and Peterson in Moscow—were chastised as lax and dismissed or transferred. In both cases the NKVD identified putative terrorist plots by ex-oppositionists who had supposedly sold out to White Guard "class enemies." The NKVD targeted Trotsky, Zinoviev, and Kamenev as ultimate culprits in both investigations. In Leningrad and Moscow alike Nikolai Yezhov, now Stalin's point man on policing and internal security issues, supervised an extensive purge of the party/state headquarters. After Kirov's assassination, Moscow NKVD chief Redens purged the city of "anti-Soviet elements," just as Zakovsky did Leningrad.[19]

The parallels laid out above strongly suggest that Stalin genuinely feared an attempt on his life by an "insider" like Nikolaev. Hence the changes in the Kremlin guard and the purge of the Kremlin staff.

Whether or not he believed literally that Zinoviev and Kamenev had plotted Kirov's murder, the evidence indicates that he viewed ex-oppositionists as a real threat to him. Kirov's murder he undoubtedly saw as a chance to crush them before they could do him harm. Stalin's real fear of losing his life and his power were central to the "Kremlin Case." If this is so, then it also implies that Stalin did not engineer Kirov's murder. The assassination surprised and frightened him. Members of his immediate circle fed this fear for their own purposes. According to Yuri Zhukov, the Kremlin investigation began after Stalin's brother-in-law Aleksandr Svanidze denounced Yenukidze and Peterson in early January 1935 for supposedly plotting a coup d'état against Stalin.[20]

There is other evidence that Stalin's fear of assassination increased following the Kirov murder. About one year before the murder, in August–September 1933, he was involved in two accidents, both of them potentially fatal. In the first, his automobile nearly collided head-on with a truck on a dark road outside Sochi. In the second a border detachment fired on his motorboat by accident near Gagra on the Black Sea. Stalin ordered measures taken to investigate each incident and prevent anything similar in the future, but he did not treat either as a potential assassination plot. After Kirov's murder, according to several eyewitnesses testifying in the perestroika and post-Soviet eras, Stalin had his security beefed up. He continually prompted the NKVD to find murder plots against him and other Soviet leaders.[21]

In limited and subtle ways Yagoda resisted Stalin's demands to find gigantic counterrevolutionary conspiracies among former oppositionists. It was Nikolai Yezhov, the TsK secretary charged with oversight of the NKVD, who really pressed the conspiracy narratives, often much farther than Stalin would go in public. At the June 1935 plenum of the TsK, Yezhov directly accused Zinoviev, Kamenev, and Trotsky of plotting to kill both Kirov and Stalin. The Rightists, Yezhov asserted, were also implicated in the conspiracy, because they had negotiated for an alliance with the Zinovievites in the early 1930s. Yet Zinoviev and Kamenev were not tried on charges of plotting to kill Kirov and Stalin until August 1936, nor did arrests of Rightists begin until the late spring of 1937.[22]

J. Arch Getty argues for two possible explanations of the delay. It may be, he writes, that "quiet opposition in the Central Committee" to executing Zinoviev and Kamenev gave Stalin pause. But more likely Stalin chose to leave the two ex-oppositionist leaders hanging by a thread, either because he himself had not decided on the final disposition of their cases, or because he wanted Yezhov and Yagoda to force from them a direct confession to murdering Kirov.[23] The last explanation rings true. First, because Stalin generally preferred to undermine his enemies covertly and gradually, out of his innate caution and possibly out of sadism as well. Second, because direct confessions had assumed a place of central importance in high-profile Soviet trials and Bolshevik political culture. To the untutored mind a direct confession "from the horse's mouth" was the most irrefutable proof of guilt. Confessions seemed to prove the state's case against counterrevolutionaries, and they were the simplest means of doing so. Moreover, confessions, even if doubted, proved the overweening power of the party/state apparatus, which could force people to corroborate whatever version of reality the leaders chose to endorse. For these reasons, Stalin frequently appended confessions of convicted "counterrevolutionaries" to TsK circulars. And probably for these reasons he sought full confessions before trying Zinoviev and Kamenev, and later Rykov, Bukharin, and Yagoda.

According to recent accounts by Getty and Oleg Khlevniuk, Kirov's assassination did not spark an immediate, radical break in Soviet leadership policies. The number of police and NKVD arrests recorded dropped slightly between 1934 and 1935, and the number of executions fell from 2,056 to 1,229. Levels of overall repression remained constant, more or less, but the organs of state security focused their efforts much more tightly on former party oppositionists and cases of "anti-Soviet agitation." Khlevniuk argues that in 1935 as in 1934 Stalin aimed to stabilize Soviet society with a combination of targeted terror and "conciliation." When possible, he wanted the NKVD to replace indiscriminate "mass operations" with the surgical removal of "anti-Soviet elements" from society. Among the measures taken to conciliate society were Stalin's endorsement of sizeable private plots for collective farmers, and the release of thousands of prisoners arrested on charges of petty theft of state property.[24]

The changes in Stalin's attitude from 1934 to 1935 had to do with his determination to deal with former oppositionists, at least those on the Left, for good; his growing fear of war; and his increasing frustration with provincial party secretaries and the Old Bolshevik elite in general. The fear of war with Nazi Germany, Poland, or Japan was manifest in a TsK-authorized campaign to screen political émigrés for foreign spies, begun in March 1935. Yezhov was instrumental in the organization of this effort. Stalin's perennial frustration with the provincial party secretaries was exacerbated by the party document check conducted in the second half of 1935 (which had been planned before Kirov's murder). He and Yezhov, who supervised the check, hoped to winkle former oppositionists out of the upper ranks of provincial party organizations. In the event, however, the party secretaries tended to "deflect the purge downward to the rank and file" (Getty) in an effort to protect their "families." In late September 1935 Yezhov complained that provincial party leaders were not cooperating with the NKVD in the document check.[25]

The case of Avel Yenukidze epitomizes Stalin's anger at senior Old Bolsheviks. Before the Kirov assassination, Yenukidze was already in difficulties with Stalin over a 1934 reprint of his memoirs which presented Stalin accurately as a minor player in the Caucasian revolutionary movement at the turn of the century. This contradicted the falsified, grandiose history of Stalin's early revolutionary activities already being worked up by Lavrenty Beria, first secretary of the Transcaucasus Region party committee. On January 16, 1935 Yenukidze published a *Pravda* article admitting "mistakes," but not going far enough for Stalin.[26]

In June 1935 a plenum of the TsK stripped Yenukidze of his membership and expelled him from the party. The latter vote was split, suggesting a certain amount of resistance from TsK members to the persecution of Yenukidze. For Stalin, the whole affair was part of an ever-growing resentment (and perhaps fear) of the Old Bolsheviks, many of whom were gossiping about him in private. He heard about much of this gossip, from the informers the NKVD had now placed throughout the Bolshevik leadership, and possibly through the use of new eavesdropping equipment. On September 7, 1935 Stalin wrote to Kaganovich, Yezhov, and Molotov about intelligence that Ordzhonikidze and Transcaucasus party veteran Mikhail Orakhelashvili had both visited Yenukidze, who was "playing the victim" and complaining about his lot. One day later, in a letter to Kaganovich, the dictator noted that "it was strange" that Ordzhonikidze and Orakhelashvili still spent time with Yenukidze, "a person alien to us." He also quoted Lenin's reference to the Old Bolshevik émigrés as a bunch of "old farts."[27]

Reopening the Kirov Case

In December 1935 or January 1936 Stalin decided to reopen the investigation into the Kirov murder. The immediate trigger cannot be determined for certain, but Getty proposes that it could have been the arrest of Valentin Olberg, a supposed Trotskyite who may have been an NKVD double agent. During this period the NKVD and the USSR Prosecutor's Office reported to Stalin the discovery of a "Trotskyite" terrorist group in Moscow, a "Zinovievite" terrorist group in Leningrad, and several "White Guard" groups, all seeking to assassinate Soviet leaders. Whatever the specific trigger, if any, for reopening the Kirov investigation, Stalin's decision was obviously part of his ongoing drive to crush former party oppositionists. In February 1936 Stalin ordered the NKVD to provide Yezhov with copies of all documents about Trotskyites. The TsK secretary would supervise Yagoda's inquiry into Trotskyite involvement in the Kirov murder.[28]

In the succeeding months, Yezhov and Yagoda moved to "liquidate the Trotskyist underground," arresting hundreds of former Trotsky supporters. They also interrogated Zinoviev and Kamenev about Kirov's assassination, and eventually squeezed from them full confessions of guilt. Torture may have played a role in the confessions—Yezhov ordered the NKVD to take off "the kid gloves." Interrogators' promises to spare the prisoners' lives in exchange for the "service" to the party of show trial testimony probably also motivated Zinoviev and Kamenev. Zinoviev wrote an entire book manuscript, "A Deserved Sentence," which he sent to Yezhov two weeks before his trial. There would seem little reason for him to have done this other than hope of saving his own life.[29]

The first of the infamous Moscow show trials began on August 19, 1936. Stalin oversaw Yezhov, Yagoda, and Vyshinsky, now Chief Prosecutor of the USSR, in scripting the drama of the "Trotskyite-Zinovievite Terrorist Center." Zinoviev, Kamenev, and the other fourteen defendants were charged with conspiracy to murder Stalin, Kirov, Voroshilov, Kaganovich, Ordzhonikidze, Zhdanov, Kossior, Postyshev, and other high officials. Most of those charged confirmed the government's scenario. Supposedly six of them, plus Kamenev's former aide Grigory Sokolnikov, met at Kamenev's Moscow apartment in the summer of 1934 and "decided to expedite the assassination of S. M. Kirov." The former Leningrad officials Ivan Bakaev and Grigory Yevdokimov played key roles in the organization of the subsequent plot. Bakaev testified that he'd traveled to Leningrad in the fall of 1934 where he had met with members of the "Leningrad Center" (Mandelshtam, Sositsky, Rumiantsev, Miasnikov, and Nikolaev). At this meeting he recruited Nikolaev for the murder.[30]

Lev Kamenev had the responsibility of making the big connections. He testified that he'd linked up with the Left group of Shatskin and Lominadze, with the former Workers' Opposition, and with the "Rights" Tomsky, Rykov, and Bukharin. Thus he implicated all of these groups in Kirov's killing, and limned the outline of an even larger conspiracy than the "Trotskyite-Zinovievite Center." At the end of the trial, Vyshinsky declared that he was beginning an inquiry into the possibility that the Rightists Tomsky, Bukharin, and Rykov and the ex-Trotskyites Karl Radek and G. L. Piatakov were involved in the assassination conspiracy.[31]

The court sentenced all sixteen defendants to death, as decided beforehand, and they were shot immediately. In cases connected to the August show trial, the state ultimately executed 160 people, including veterans of the old Zinovievite leadership in Leningrad such as Artyom Gertik and Leonid Faivilovich.[32]

The show trial of Zinoviev and Kamenev made it clear that Stalin's agenda was total destruction of the former Left opposition. Experienced officials could also discern that ex-Rightist leaders were in very deep trouble. Things began to move rapidly as the summer holidays concluded. On the day following the end of the trial, Mikhail Tomsky committed suicide, impelled by Vyshinsky's threat of an investigation of the Rights. Tomsky's wife, possibly seeking revenge against her husband's NKVD tormentor, told Yezhov that Tomsky before his death had said that Yagoda had worked for the Right in 1928–1929. Yezhov passed the accusation along to Stalin, and it hit home. Yezhov had been insinuating for months that he wanted Yagoda's job, and Stalin was now ready to give it to him. He sent a telegram from Sochi on September 25, also signed by Zhdanov, stating, "We deem it absolutely necessary and urgent to have Comrade Yezhov appointed People's Commissar of Internal Affairs. Yagoda has definitely proved himself incapable of unmasking the Trotskyist-Zinovievist bloc. The OGPU [NKVD] is four years behind in this matter." Yagoda was appointed People's Commissar of Communications, replacing the ex-Rightist Rykov, recently dismissed.[33]

From the late summer of 1936 onward, Stalin and Yezhov developed an offensive against an ever-broadening range of targets. On September 12 the NKVD arrested the ex-Trotskyite Piatakov, Ordzhonikidze's deputy at the Commissariat of Heavy Industry, based in part on the fact that his ex-wife still had in her possession Trotskyite documents from the 1920s. The entire TsK, including Ordzhonikidze, approved Piatakov's expulsion from the Communist Party. In addition, a number of specialists and administrators in Ordzhonikidze's commissariat were charged with sabotage, and some were arrested. Ordzhonikidze made an effort to defend some of these men, which culminated in a private conflict with Stalin on the eve of the February 1937 TsK plenum, and Ordzhonikidze's death, probably by suicide.[34]

The second major show trial of the Terror opened on January 23, 1937. Stalin and Yezhov supervised. The state constructed a giant conspiratorial edifice on the basis of private grumbling about Stalin and a few grotesque confessions of terrified defendants. The proliferation of murderous plots was bewildering. The prosecutors charged the prominent ex-Trotskyites Piatakov and Karl Radek, along with Kamenev's former aide Sokolnikov and fourteen other prisoners, with engineering train wrecks, arson, working for Japanese intelligence, and conspiracy to murder Kirov, Stalin, Kaganovich, and Yezhov. Piatakov testified that he had helped recruit a "Trotskyite Reserve Center" in Leningrad that would back up the Zinovievites' plot to kill Kirov. Sokolnikov claimed to know of yet another, more recently organized terrorist group in Leningrad, headed by the ex-Zinovievite Zaks-Gladev (briefly editor of *Leningradskaia pravda* in December 1925). This group's goal was to assassinate Kirov's successor Zhdanov. Bukharin was incorporated into the fabrication by Piatakov, who charged him with joining a "Right Reserve Center" to back up the various Left groups.[35]

Of the seventeen accused, the court sentenced thirteen to death. Radek and Sokolnikov were among the four sentenced to prison terms. Sokolnikov may have survived for the moment because he provided key "evidence" for the trial.[36]

Until January 1937 Stalin had targeted mainly former oppositionists. Senior party officials who had never been in open opposition could still imagine themselves safe from persecution. But now, as Getty has suggested, the center's pressure on provincial party organizations to root out ex-Trotskyites, which had increased throughout 1936, began to threaten the provincial party secretaries themselves. In January 1937 the TsK transferred Boris Sheboldaev, head of the Azov–Black Sea Territory party organization, and reprimanded Pavel Postyshev, second secretary of the Ukrainian Republic. Both men were charged with "blindness" to the Trotskyites supposedly infesting the party, lack of vigilance, and "familyness." Party meetings in Ukraine and the Azov–Black Sea Territory followed the TsK cues and attacked their leaders.[37]

In late February and early March 1937 the Central Committee assembled in Moscow to hear the latest word from their leaders on the alleged counterrevolutionary conspiracy that now overshadowed all of party life. Stalin told the audience that the "Zinoviev-Trotskyite Bloc" had schemed with a multitude of foreign intelligence services and White émigrés to overthrow Soviet Power. Yezhov accused Bukharin and Rykov of foreknowledge of the Kirov assassination and of intriguing to kill other Soviet leaders. He proposed their trial and execution. Although the ex-Rightist leaders denied the charges, the NKVD arrested both men at the plenum. Ominously, Stalin warned that many senior party officials had been complacent about the oppositionist and foreign threats.[38]

The February/March plenum saw Yezhov and Yakov Agranov give Yagoda, who was present, a severe working over. Leonid Zakovsky, still chief of the Leningrad NKVD, joined in. The essence of the charges was that Yagoda, and his deputy Molchanov (already arrested), had ignored the supposed Trotskyite-Zinovievite danger before Kirov's assassination and resisted a full-scale purge of Trotskyites and Rightists afterwards. A full-scale attack on Yagoda and the NKVD was in the offing. About two weeks after the conclusion of the plenum senior NKVD officers met in Moscow to discuss the resolutions passed. Yezhov told attendees that the NKVD was honeycombed with traitors, including Yagoda himself. Just days later the Politburo ordered the arrest of the former People's Commissar. Many of Yagoda's former subordinates were also detained around this time. By June all but one of the NKVD operational department heads who had served under Yagoda were in custody.[39]

The Terror and the Distortion of Evidence in the Kirov Case

The course of the murderous campaign that Stalin and Yezhov now unfolded can be summarized briefly, if at the high cost of reducing immense human suffering to a few statistics. In May 1937 the NKVD imprisoned the first prominent party officials who had no oppositional record. By July the trickle of arrests became a flood that swept away most of the Central Committee and nearly every one of the eighty provincial party secretaries. The majority of these officials were executed. The party elite was decimated in 1937–1938. Of the 1,966 delegates to the Seventeenth Party Congress (1934), 1,108 were eventually arrested, and many of these were shot. Simultaneously the senior officer corps of the Red Army was purged of supposed traitors, beginning with the secret trial in early June of Marshal Tukhachevsky and other generals on charges of plotting a coup d'état. Tukhachevsky and his fellows were tortured and shot. In 1937–1938 the NKVD arrested almost 10,000 Red Army officers.[40]

In July 1937 Stalin ordered "mass operations" against "former kulaks, criminals, and other anti-Soviet elements." These operations were indiscriminate sweeps aimed at "cleaning up" society and bore some resemblance to Nazi "social hygiene" campaigns against supposed undesirables. The Stalinist leadership drove the mass operations onward by issuing mandatory quotas for arrests and executions to provincial NKVD organizations. Another component of the Terror was the arrest or deportation from border regions of hundreds of thousands of members of ethnic minority groups considered a security risk. Poles and Koreans are the best-known examples.[41]

Official records indicate that the NKVD arrested over 1.5 million people in 1937–1938. Of these 681,692 were executed, and hundreds of thousands more died of abuse in the camps. There were undoubtedly other victims uncounted by the state.[42]

There is of course a sizeable literature on the causes of the Terror, much of which resembles the proverbial blind men grasping at the elephant. Tucker and Conquest portray Stalin as a kind of demonic chess master, plotting mass repression of his "enemies" years in advance, while Getty focuses on conflicts between provincial party elites and the center, as well as on Bolshevik rituals of accusation and confession. Moshe Lewin sees the Terror as an entirely unrealistic attempt by Stalin to solve the problem of an inefficient, corrupt, and ever-growing bureaucracy, which in turn had its roots in backward peasant Russia. Gabor Rittersporn argues that Soviet leaders elaborated conspiracy theories to explain systemic problems with Communist administration that they would not admit. The conspiratorial mindset that developed among party cadres also fueled the Terror. Recently Paul Hagenloh has illuminated the role of changes in policing practice in paving the way for the "mass operations."[43]

There is some truth to most of the explanations listed above. There are also problems with them. It seems to me, for example, that Getty is mistaken to take seriously the repeated charade in which Stalin played the forbearing father, holding out for softer penalties for malefactors, while his subordinates clamored for blood. Stalin himself was a master of evading responsibility for decisions, and this was one of his tactics.

But his underlings knew his real inclination towards harsh punishments, and they "worked towards" him, just as Hitler's henchmen "worked towards the Fuhrer." The system of "signals," in which central authorities used indirect hints, show trials, news items, and apparently obscure theoretical articles to convey desired policies to the party at large, facilitated Stalin's avoidance of responsibility.[44]

At the same time, the hypothesis that Stalin was plotting the annihilation of the Old Bolshevik elite as early as 1934, which Conquest and Tucker sometimes appear to endorse, has no backing in reliable evidence. Stalin was not omniscient or omnipotent, despite the claims made by the manufacturers of his leader cult. He could not see or determine the future three years in advance. Indeed, one of his greatest strengths as a politician, at least up to the Great Terror, was his ability to respond flexibly to circumstance, a trait that would seem to preclude the kind of long-range, mechanical, chess-move type plotting that has been attributed to him. He was a murderous opportunist. We know from Stalin's letters that already in 1934 he intensely disliked a number of Old Bolsheviks who had never been open oppositionists, and that he was impatient and irritated with what he viewed as the rank incompetence and dishonesty of much of the provincial party leadership. But Stalin was frequently impatient or angry even with his closest collaborators, including Molotov, Kaganovich, and Ordzhonikidze.

It is also important to note that Stalin alone did not make the Terror. The mass killing would not have been possible without an entire complex of social and structural factors. Getty is right to foreground the explosive center-periphery tensions developed by Bolshevik political practice. And Soviet society, wracked by class resentments, tormented by decades of violence and deprivation, and encouraged by the Bolshevik leaders to engage in mass denunciation, was ready to react explosively to Stalin's prodding. In my view discussion of these realities does not discount the Bolsheviks' responsibility for the Terror, it deepens it. It was the Bolsheviks who established a one-party dictatorship without effective limitations on the leaders' power. It was the Bolsheviks who chose to use mass denunciation to root out "alien" social groups and monitor the state apparatus. It was the Bolsheviks who subjected Soviet society to the trauma of collectivization, who resorted repeatedly to secret police terror in time of crisis, who pressed down ordinary people's living standards and then scapegoated the intelligentsia, local bosses, kulaks, and an amorphous "class enemy" for the resulting poverty.

The contingent history of the 1930s also facilitated the Terror. The real threats of Nazi Germany to the west and Japan to the east made the mass repressions seem to some a necessary destruction of potential "fifth columnists."

But to return to the Terror's immediate cause—Stalin ordered it. He was a vengeful and power-hungry man, and possibly a sadist in the clinical sense. But we can be more specific than that in reconstructing his motivations and mental state. I would emphasize two points. First, as Sheila Fitzpatrick has suggested, the Terror brought a definitive conclusion to the Russian Revolution.[45] Apart from the holocaust of the Nazi invasion, imposed from without, the course of Soviet society after 1938 was by and large towards stabilization, and ultimately ossification. Stalin knew that he was ending the revolution, although he would have called it consolidating the revolution. This is clear from the deliberation with which he embarked on the various measures to stabilize society that Nicholas Timasheff summarized controversially as "the Great Retreat." Like "the Great Retreat," the Terror helped to end the revolution, by destroying the fractious, critically inclined first generation of revolutionaries. No doubt, too, Stalin hoped that the "mass operations" would stabilize society. At the same time, his resort to mass operations was a gesture of frustrated rage, of throwing up his hands at what he believed to be the failure of the NKVD to target "anti-Soviet elements" more precisely.

The second point requires looking at Stalin's conditions of daily work. He was a desk worker above all, with few recreations beyond movie screenings and meals with "friends"—his political collaborators. He stayed in his office, and he read and commented on paperwork. By 1934 he was participating in fewer formal political meetings. In these isolated circumstances, he was exposed to a relentless barrage of reports on kulak sabotage, counterrevolutionary plots among Komsomol youth, intelligentsia resentment of the regime, and foreign espionage. As James Harris has suggested, this could only have heightened his native suspiciousness and paranoia.[46] Always inclined to believe the worst, he demanded that the secret police and other subordinates focus obsessively on potential threats, and they obliged. In a disastrous feedback cycle, the constant reports of threats only intensified Stalin's suspiciousness and his demands for more evidence of counterrevolution and espionage. This is not to reduce Stalin's responsibility for the atrocities he committed. It is to suggest how he might have brought himself to the kind of break with reality that led him to suspect mass subversion among party officials who supported him.

This is where Kirov's assassination comes into the story. Stalin's daughter Svetlana Allilueva and personal acquaintances of the dictator have testified that his wife's suicide and Kirov's murder were both watersheds in his life. Allilueva, who witnessed her father in mourning as a nine-year-old child, concluded in the late 1960s that after Kirov's death Stalin trusted no one. In her 1934 diary Maria Svanidze recorded Stalin telling his brother-in-law, Pavel Allilueva, "I'm utterly an orphan now" just days after the murder.[47] Discounting any notion of Stalin ever trusting anyone, and making allowances for both witnesses' considerable melodramatic flair, it still seems plausible that Kirov's assassination, assuming Stalin did not order it himself, greatly increased his sense of isolation and looming threat. In Stalin's world, at least, it was also logical to suspect the Zinovievite oppositionists, many of whom still lived and worked in Leningrad. Kirov had, after all, driven them from the city's leadership and persecuted them. Some of Nikolaev's comments in his letters and diaries smacked of Zinovievite rhetoric—the attacks on the Institute of History bosses as "Rightists" and the greetings to Stalin, "Tsar of War and Industry." Once Stalin decided that the oppositionists were in some sense responsible, the details of individual guilt or innocence did not bother him. It was the NKVD's job to put together whatever evidence was necessary.

In the course of the Terror, Stalin masterminded the distortion of evidence in the Kirov murder. The most persistent distortions came about in the course of Yezhov's fabrication of cases against Yagoda, which began with the former NKVD chief's arrest in the last days of March 1937. Yezhov took Yagoda's negligence in the Kirov case and his supposed sympathy for the Right as starting points. On April 28, 1937 he sent to Stalin a transcript of Yagoda's testimony from two days earlier. A number of Yagoda's subordinates, including Karl Pauker, had already accused him of plotting to kill government leaders, but Yagoda continued to deny these charges. He did confess to Rightist sympathies and to forming a "reserve Right Center" inside the OGPU/NKVD.[48]

Meeting resistance from Yagoda, Yezhov set about using the Leningrad NKVD officers exiled to Kolyma against him, using torture and promises to spare prisoners' lives. There were also objective factors favoring Yezhov's work. The Leningrad officers all had plenty of reason to resent Yagoda, who had set out to break their organization, and who had let them take the fall for the Kirov murder. Even Zaporozhets, Yagoda's client, could not have been happy that his patron had left him flapping in the breeze. Yezhov's starting point appears to have been the Leningrad NKVD Operations Department, and Kirov's guard.

As was standard NKVD practice, Yezhov started at the bottom of the hierarchy and worked his way up, forcing subordinates to incriminate their bosses. On May 10, 1937 N. S. Maksimov, former secretary of the Third Section of the Operations Department gave his interrogators the following statement.

· 102 ·

Testimony of N. S. Maksimov, former secretary of the Leningrad NKVD
Operations Department Third Section, May 10, 1937. RGANI, f. 6, op. 13,
d. 13, ll. 7–45 (Klimov report on detention[s] of Nikolaev, 1960 or 1961).

I know for a fact that Kirov's murderer, the terrorist Nikolaev, was twice detained by Kirov's guard and taken to the Operations Department, and that Gubin and Kotomin talked to him and freed him.

In order to hide this fact from the government commission, Officer Gusev of the Operations Department late on the night of December 1–2, at the orders of Khviiuzov, destroyed all files on persons detained by Kirov's guard at various times.

One detention became two, in the effort to exaggerate Gubin's and Kotomin's negligence. To explain why 1934 evidence showed only one detention, the interrogators and Maksimov cooked up the story of the document burning, which was inherently implausible. First, if there was a mass holocaust of documents on the night of December 1–2, 1934, how did the records of Nikolaev's October 15 detention survive? Second, when Stalin and the government commission arrived in Leningrad on the morning of December 2, 1934 the fear in Leningrad was so thick that some NKVD employee would have denounced any document destruction. Such a move was simply too risky for Leningrad NKVD officers to take. Plenty of documents damaging to the Leningrad NKVD were in fact found by the Stalin commission, covering Nikolaev's October 15 detention, the Volkova case, and surveillance of the ex-Zinovievites.[49]

Maksimov's testimony suffered from what one might call evidentiary "overkill." He knew everything that NKVD interrogators in 1937 needed him to know, not just about multiple detentions of Nikolaev, but about Borisov's death. In June 1937, for example, he claimed that Zaporozhets and Gubin had murdered Borisov to prevent him from giving information to Stalin's government commission.[50]

Next up the ladder was Gubin, who was arrested in the Far East on April 30, 1937. Presumably interrogators used Maksimov's testimony against him. Gubin may well have resisted confessing, because his first recorded deposition useful for the prosecution was dated June 5. From that point on, however, he proved very cooperative. He confessed to membership in a "counterrevolutionary group" consisting of his fellow officers Màly, Vinogradov, Maksimov, and Khiiuzov, which killed Borisov to cover traces of the Kirov murder. He charged Yagoda and Zaporozhets with "bringing the Operations Department to collapse, and effectively annulling [Kirov's] guard."[51] He also provided "evidence" implicating Zaporozhets and Yagoda in Nikolaev's October 1934 release and Kirov's assassination. In doing so he shifted responsibility for freeing Nikolaev off his own shoulders.

· 103 ·

Testimony of Gubin, former head of the Leningrad NKVD Operations
Department, June 1937. RGANI, f. 6, op. 13, d. 13, ll. 7–45
(Klimov 1960/1961 report on detention[s] of Nikolaev).

In October Nikolaev was detained next to Kirov's car. In his briefcase he had a diary with various notes and a plan, and also a Nagan revolver. All of this spoke directly and clearly of the fact that Nikolaev was a terrorist and approached Kirov's car with the intention of killing Kirov.

Immediately after the guards detained Nikolaev, I reported this by telephone to Zaporozhets, Zaporozhets was sick and was at his apartment; I explained to him in detail about the discovery of the objects enumerated above on Nikolaev, and of my suspicions that Nikolaev was a terrorist. Zaporozhets told me to wait for him to call me back. Twenty minutes later I called him again, and he answered that he'd talked to Yagoda, who had ordered him released immediately. I carried out Zaporozhets' orders and freed Nikolaev, knowing well that we were choosing to free a terrorist, who had come to Smolny to shoot Kirov.

Question: And after freeing Nikolaev, did you discuss this issue with Zaporozhets?

Answer: Yes, I did, and during that conversation Zaporozhets said to me directly, "Your idiots nearly screwed up everything with the detention of Nikolaev, and if that happened our heads would have flown off, including yours, Gubin."

Question: And did you have any other conversation with Zaporozhets with regard to the detention of the terrorist Nikolaev?

Answer: Yes, there was an even more detailed discussion, when Za-porozhets came back from his vacation. In the fall of 1934 he called me in to his apartment and said, "Make sure that we don't have a repetition of the business with Nikolaev, and with others, be absolutely sure that Niko-laev is not stopped again, you can screw up everything. Check and see that everything about Nikolaev's detention is well-concealed from prying eyes." Zaporozhets with special emphasis said, "Do not get in Nikolaev's way, he could fall into the hands of our people again on Kirov's usual walking routes. Take measures to be sure they don't detain him, and that if they detain him, they immediately let him go without taking him to the NKVD headquarters. Keep in mind, you must not interfere. . . ."

There are a number of tip-offs that Gubin's testimony here was made up almost out of whole cloth. For one thing he conflates Nikolaev's Oc-tober 15 detention, when Kirov was on foot, with Stalin's false account of Nikolaev's approaching Kirov's car. For a second, he makes the false statement that Nikolaev had his diary and notes in his briefcase when he was stopped in October, and the probably false statement that he had a revolver as well. For a third, he indicates that Zaporozhets came back to work in Leningrad in the fall of 1934, when in fact the latter was *hors de combat* from August until December 7, 1934. Fourth, there is the tell-tale overkill in the interrogation. Gubin's questioners obvi-ously wanted to make sure that he fully incriminated Zaporozhets and Yagoda. Hence the two discussions about the detention and Zaporo-zhets' repetitive warnings—"you must not interfere. . . ."

This scenario became the core story-line of the March 1938 show trial of Yagoda, Bukharin, and Rykov.

In the meantime, Yezhov moved another step up the Leningrad NKVD chain of command, to Zaporozhets, reportedly arrested in April 1937 in the Far East.[52] In all likelihood he brought Gubin's testimony to bear and demanded that Zaporozhets denounce Yagoda. On June 16 Zaporozhets obliged.

· 104 ·

Testimony of Ivan Zaporozhets, former deputy chief of the Leningrad NKVD, June 16, 1937. RGANI, f. 6, op. 13, d. 13, ll. 7–45 (Klimov 1960/1961 report on detention[s] of Nikolaev).

As far as I remember there were no materials about any preparations for a murder attempt on Comrade Kirov in any department of the Leningrad

NKVD; nor were there any arrests in that line other than the Operations Department's chance detention beside Kirov's car of Leonid Nikolaev, who later killed Kirov. . . .

Carrying out my orders to report to me all incidents connected with Kirov's guard, Gubin called me at home on October 15, as far as I remember /I was sick at the time/ and announced that one Nikolaev, Leonid had been detained by Smolny next to Kirov's automobile. In his briefcase there had been found a loaded revolver and some kind of plan with notes. Gubin asked me for my orders, stating that Nikolaev was undoubtedly a terrorist, who had come to Smolny to kill Kirov. I immediately called Yagoda on the special direct line and reported Nikolaev's detention to him and that a weapon was found on him. Yagoda examined me thoroughly and in detail about the detainee, forcing me to repeat everything, and then attacked me sharply for this chance detention. He ordered me to release Nikolaev immediately, saying that "You have detained exactly the person whom you should not have detained under any circumstances, this is that very valuable person, of whom I spoke about in Moscow." For me it was completely clear that this Nikolaev, Leonid was [to be] the agent of a terrorist action against Kirov.

I remember Yagoda added on the telephone, "Your idiots don't even know who they're taking into custody anymore," and then he repeated, "This is that same person I was talking about." Yagoda once again ordered me to free Nikolaev immediately and hide all traces of his chance detention. At the end of the conversation Yagoda said to me that "It would be a good thing for you to find some pretext to leave work for a while." I ordered Gubin to release Nikolaev . . . the assassin of Kirov, Leonid Nikolaev, was freed by me on Yagoda's orders.

Zaporozhets begins with a statement that was probably true—the Operations Department had detained Nikolaev once on October 15. He then moves on to the fabrications, repeating Gubin's conflation of the October 15 detention and Stalin's version "by the car." There follows the story of Gubin's report, and Zaporozhets' phone call to Yagoda, obviously intended to pass as much as possible of the responsibility for releasing Nikolaev to the People's Commissar. The identical phrasing of parts of this deposition to Gubin's strongly suggests that interrogators were dictating to Zaporozhets, or even that they gave him a prepared statement to sign.

The NKVD executed both Zaporozhets and Gubin on August 14, 1937.[53]

Interrogators got testimony on Nikolaev's detention(s) from a number of other Leningrad NKVD officers. Khviiuzov, head of the Third

Section of the Operations Department, claimed one detention of Nikolaev, in October, next to Kirov's car, with the revolver and the incriminating documents. On August 18, 1937 V. Ya. Tyshkevich, a special assignments officer, claimed to have detained Nikolaev twice as he tried
to follow Kirov from Smolny. Tyshkevich's evidence was a denunciation of Senior Operations Commissar Griunvald, with whom he seems
to have had a personal conflict. Tyshkevich had previously denounced
Griunvald and Kotomin in February 1935, claiming that they had released Nikolaev after he stopped him. Investigators at that time had
shown Tyshkevich photographs of different "terrorists," asking him
to identify Nikolaev, and concluded that he could not recognize the
man he'd supposedly detained. It cannot be ruled out that Tyshkevich
stopped Nikolaev, but it is more likely that he lied and/or recalled
other persons he'd detained. By the summer of 1937 the "folk wisdom" in the NKVD was that Nikolaev had been detained multiple
times and Kirov's guard had been grossly negligent. This fueled more
and more accounts of detentions such as Tyshkevich's.[54]

Griunvald was arrested, perhaps on Tyshkevich's testimony, and
died in prison, supposedly a suicide.[55]

In September 1937 Filip Medved was arrested at the Magadan/
Kolyma Gulag complex, transported to Moscow, and held at the
Lefortovo Prison. In all likelihood Yezhov could not fabricate any convincing plot in which Medved and Yagoda had worked together, because the bad blood between them was so well known in the NKVD.
Therefore, he opted for implicating Yagoda in a plot involving Zaporozhets. Medved's case was a sideshow. The NKVD charged him
with joining yet another plot to murder Kirov, this one supposedly run
by former Commissar of Defense Yosif Unshlikht and "the Polish Military Organization." Medved resisted confessing at first, but eventually broke. He was shot without a hearing on November 27, 1937.[56]

In addition to multiplying Nikolaev's detentions, Yezhov fabricated
a tale that Kirov's guard Borisov had been murdered. Central NKVD
officers, Stalin, and Yezhov had all had strong suspicions in December
1934 that there was foul play in Borisov's death. Now Yezhov, working through Zakovsky in Leningrad, pressed for evidence showing that
Yagoda or his agents had killed the guard. In early June Zakovsky arrested Kuzin, who had driven the truck in which Borisov died, and escorting officers Maly and Vinogradov.

At first all three prisoners stood by their 1934–1935 accounts of the
accident, in spite of beatings with rubber truncheons and long periods

on the "conveyor" of continuous interrogation. The driver Kuzin was the first to break, after several days of questioning. Changing his testimony, he claimed that Officer Maly, riding next to him in the passenger seat, had grabbed the steering wheel and directed the truck against the wall. He now sought to escape with his own life at the expense of the other two prisoners. Over the next three decades Kuzin's descriptions of the accident would vary greatly one from another, but in all of them he was innocent, and Maly and Vinogradov guilty.[57]

In April 1956 Kuzin described his 1937 interrogations.

<h2 style="text-align:center">· 105 ·</h2>

Testimony of Kuzin, driver of the truck in which Borisov died, April 1956. RGANI, f. 6, op. 13, d. 2, ll. 78–107 (August 31, 1956 KGB report to Molotov commission).

I was arrested by officers of the regional NKVD on June 6, 1937. After I arrived at the sixth floor of the regional NKVD, about eight officers surrounded me and one of them announced that I was arrested as a participant in a counterrevolutionary organization and an enemy of the people. I answered that I had never been a participant in any counterrevolutionary organization. Then he came up to me and hit me hard in the chest.

I asked him: "Why are you hitting me? I am a Soviet citizen." Then one of the officers around me with stars [on his uniform] said, "Interrogate him as a Trotskyite." And they interrogated me for 23 days in a row. At the interrogations they did not let me sit down. They stood me in a corner and they questioned me without a break. When one interrogator got tired, another replaced him, and I continued to stand. They constantly demanded that I confess that I was a member of a counterrevolutionary terrorist group, but I could not admit that because I had never belonged to such an organization. Among the investigators who interrogated me was Yakushev.

It seems to me that it was on the tenth day after my arrest, while I was standing in the corner, that I fell and blood began to flow out of my mouth. I became very ill, and I told the investigator Smirnov: "If you want my life, take it." And after that I began to sign all of the interrogation protocols that Yakushev gave me. I didn't even read the protocols.

Maly and Vinogradov held out longer than Kuzin, as did N. S. Maksimov (see above), who had dispatched Borisov to Smolny and who was also charged in the case. Referring to the NKVD practice of continuously interrogating detainees for days, Officer Leonid Raikhman of the Leningrad NKVD told Alla Kirilina in the late 1980s that "the investigator Reznikov . . . told me 'I kept Maly on the conveyor for 15 days.' After 15 days on the conveyor, you're ready to say anything. . . ."[58]

Eventually Maly, Vinogradov, and Maksimov "confessed" to murdering Borisov. At their September 2, 1937 hearing before the Military Collegium of the USSR Supreme Court, all three men recanted their confessions. After a twenty-minute session, the court ordered them shot.[59]

The Case of the "Anti-Soviet Bloc of Rights and Trotskyites," March 1938

From March 2 to 13, 1938, USSR Prosecutor Vyshinsky tried Bukharin, Rykov, Yagoda, and seventeen other defendants before the Military Collegium of the Supreme Court on charges of treason. The scenario was even more grandiose than that of the earlier show trials. The prosecution charged that a huge conspiratorial network of Rightists, Trotskyites, and Zinovievites had plotted since 1932 to murder Soviet leaders and public figures. In addition to Kirov, the conspiracy had also supposedly assassinated Maxim Gorky, his son Maksim Peshkov, OGPU chief Menzhinsky, and Politburo chief Valerian Kuibyshev.[60] The conspirators had worked together with the Polish, German, and Japanese secret services to plan the invasion and partition of the Soviet Union. Remarkably, the prosecution claimed that the antiparty conspiracy went back to 1909. Details of internal party debates before the revolution were rehashed. Several of the defendants were charged with working for the Tsarist secret police before 1917.[61]

The prosecution used the version of the Kirov murder worked up by Yezhov and his interrogators over the previous year. As laid out in the published testimony of Yagoda's former aide Bulanov and Vyshinsky's closing statement, the story went like this. The Right-Trotskyite Bloc "entrusted" Yagoda with Kirov's murder. Yagoda ordered Zaporozhets to get the job done. Two months before the murder the Leningrad NKVD accidentally detained the assassin Nikolaev, and found he was carrying a revolver and a map of Kirov's walking routes to and from Smolny. Zaporozhets consulted with Yagoda, who ordered Nikolaev released. After the killing, Yagoda ordered Zaporozhets to kill

Borisov, who had "had a hand" in Kirov's assassination and might rat the plotters out.[62]

Although all of the defendants eventually pled guilty to charges of treason, Bukharin, Rykov, and Yagoda contested concrete details of the imagined conspiracy. In his final words to the court, Bukharin confessed himself guilty of "treason to the Socialist Fatherland" in general terms, but proceeded to deny connections with foreign espionage or involvement in Kirov's murder. Rykov too denied "any direct part" in the murders of Kirov, Kuibyshev, Menzhinsky, Gorky, or Peshkov.[63] Yagoda, who at earlier points in his testimony admitted to some "complicity" in Kirov's murder, had this to say at the trial's conclusion:

· 106 ·

Excerpt from Genrikh Yagoda's closing statement, March 1938 Moscow show trial. RGANI, f. 6, op. 13, d. 2, ll. 78–107 (August 31, 1956 KGB report to Molotov commission).

Not only is it false to say that I was an organizer, but even to say that I was an accomplice in the murder of Kirov. I am guilty of a very serious dereliction of duty [that is, he did not prevent Kirov's murder], that is true. I will answer for that in full measure, but I was not an accomplice. "An accomplice"—you know as well as I do, comrade prosecutor, what that means. None of the materials of this trial or the preliminary investigation demonstrate that I was an accomplice in this villainous murder.[64]

The only witness to testify to Yagoda's ordering Kirov's murder was his former aide, Bulanov. As early as May 1937, Bulanov had signed statements charging that Yagoda used Nikolaev to kill Kirov. He claimed that Yagoda had told him the whole story, one-on-one. Now that he was on the stand, however, Bulanov had a very hard time keeping his story straight. For example, although the official transcript of the trial shows Bulanov narrating a clear account of Yagoda ordering Zaporozhets to have Borisov killed, the actual, uncorrected stenogram of his testimony is quite different:

I am afraid to tell it to you exactly—the story was very dark, but it has remained in my memory that Commissar Borisov, who was the only participant in the murder, who was supposed to give to the members of the government, who themselves had gone there and carried out an investigation, he was supposed to give what evidence he could give, that Yagoda was there too, and so this Commissar Borisov could not appear at the interrogation and was killed in an automobile accident. When he told me that he had been informed of the murder, I understood then the unusual concern for Yagoda, which he showed when Medved, Zaporozhets, and the other officers were ordered to be arrested and handed over to the court.[65]

The state's main witness to Yezhov's version of the Kirov murder was almost totally incoherent. Nevertheless, the court sentenced all but three of the defendants to death.

Fate of the Leningrad Leadership

The Great Terror devastated the Communist leadership of Leningrad. Although this has often been put down to Stalin's special hatred for the city, or for Kirov's "family," it may have been simply a function of the general annihilation of the party elite. After all, of 139 members and candidates elected to the Central Committee at the Seventeenth Party Congress, 98 were arrested and shot. Every single TsK member and candidate arrested was executed.[66]

The way in which the chronology of arrests and executions tracked the historical chronology of opposition inside the party is uncanny. Stalin was systematic in his destruction of his real and imagined political opponents. The Zinovievites, one of the earlier opposition groups, were largely annihilated by the fall of 1936. Stalin then moved on to officials who had once been open Rightists in 1928–1929. D. P. Rozit, for example, a vocal Rightist at the 1928–1929 TsK plenums, was arrested on January 3, 1937, and sentenced to death on July 1 of the same year.[67] After the Rightists came the suspected Rightists, in the truly sweeping purge that began in late June. On June 29, 1937 the TsK expelled the current and former Leningrad officials N. K. Antipov, I. P. Zhukov, S. S. Lobov, N. P. Komarov, Mikhail Chudov, Ivan Kodatsky, and Pyotr Struppe. Evidence from the 1928 TsK plenums suggests that Komarov and Zhukov, at least, had sympathies with the Right. In addition, Antipov and Komarov had once been Kirov's antagonists in Leningrad. No doubt the denunciations of Komarovites that came in to Stalin and Yezhov immediately after Kirov's death were used in Komarov's case. All of these men were arrested within weeks.[68]

The NKVD set about fabricating a "Reserve Right Center" using the Leningraders' testimony. Antipov, who had once been involved in the 1929 effort to discredit Kirov, seems to have been the center of this case. Arrested on July 21, 1937, he was severely tortured. An NKVD officer involved in his interrogations testified in the mid-1950s that "Using illegal methods of investigation, Antipov was brought to such a state that he was ready to give any testimony at all." He confessed to having been a Tsarist secret agent since 1914, and to organizing the "Right Reserve Center" that supposedly included Komarov, S. S. Lobov, I. P. Zhukov, Kodatsky, Struppe, and Chudov. Antipov claimed that Rykov had put him up to all of this.[69]

Zakovsky was in charge of fabricating the "Right Reserve Center," which he and Yezhov considered putting on stage for a show trial. The testimony of a lower-ranking Leningrad official, A. I. Rozenblium, given in the mid-1950s, shows the methods Zakovsky was using. According to Rozenblium, after his 1937 arrest, he was taken to Zakovsky's office. The Leningrad NKVD chief told him that there was no point to resisting, because the only exit from his situation was jail. If Rozenblium gave the required false testimony about the existence of a "wrecking, diversionist, terrorist, espionage center" in Leningrad, he could escape torture and death. Zakovsky showed him various versions of the "Center," and told him that a big show trial involving four to five chiefs of the so-called "Center" was in preparation. He named Chudov, A. I. Ugarov, Smorodin, Pozern, and others as possible accused. The case, he said, had to be "solid," and Rozenblium's long record of party service would help with that. "You need not do anything, or think up anything," Zakovsky assured Rozenblium. "We will provide you with the material to memorize. Your fate will depend on how you do. You can save your own head, and we'll feed and clothe you until you die."[70]

There was also some talk in the NKVD of using Antipov at the big March 1938 Moscow show trial. Although his name came up there, neither this plan nor Zakovsky's big show trial came off, perhaps because interrogators concluded that their prisoners could not be trusted to cooperate in the courtroom. The defendants were doomed to summary secret hearings before the Military Collegium, and execution. N. P. Komarov, who according to his interrogators simply signed whatever was put before him, was sentenced to death on November 27, 1937. Chudov, who confessed at his trial to belonging to "a Leningrad antiparty group of Rightists," was shot on October 30, and Kodatsky at about the same time. As with a number of the other Lenin-

graders, Chudov's case included charges of plotting to murder Zhdanov. Kirov's friend and Milda Draule's patron Pyotr Irklis was sentenced to death on September 9. Most of the other men arrested in
mid-summer were probably executed in the fall of 1937.[71]

In early 1938 the first signs appeared that Stalin might let the Terror
abate. The Central Committee expelled Pavel Postyshev, now party
secretary in the city of Kuibyshev (Samara), for sanctioning indiscriminate mass repressions. Certain state organs issued instructions warning against mass detentions. That April Yezhov opened a new round of
arrests among senior NKVD officers, many of whom were now accused of fabricating cases and excess arrests. By August Yezhov had a
new deputy at the NKVD, Lavrenty Beria, who would soon replace
him. The main reason for slowing the Terror down was that it was seriously undermining the stability of the state apparatus. Perhaps, too,
Stalin had killed most of those he believed dangerous.[72]

The changing political situation led to a new round of repressions in
Leningrad. The search for scapegoats was on. On April 14, 1938 the
Politburo fired Leonid Zakovsky, chief of the Leningrad NKVD, in
part for fabricating "inflated" cases. Zakovsky did not have long to
live. Boris Pozern, a leading Old Bolshevik with a record of continuous
service in the city since 1917, was arrested on July 9, 1938. As prosecutor of Leningrad Region in 1937 Pozern had been heavily involved
in carrying out the Terror. The NKVD apparently also imprisoned A. I.
Ugarov, who had been one of Kirov's key deputies in the city, at about
the same time as Pozern.[73]

Zakovsky's fall and the wind-down of the Terror coincided with a
last round of arrests in the Leningrad NKVD. Early in the spring of
1938 Officer N. E. Tereshchenko, who had been involved in the chain
of custody in Nikolaev's October 15 detention, was arrested along with
several other Operations Department officers, apparently including
V. Ia. Tyshkevich, Karl Ivanov, and Karl Pauzer. Early in their interrogations Tereshchenko and several other officers confessed to membership in the supposed "Right-Trotskyite Bloc" that had plotted Kirov's
murder. Interrogators seem to have pressed officers for stories of multiple detentions of Nikolaev that would implicate Tereshchenko, Kotomin, and former Smolny deputy commandant Mikhalchenko. Perhaps
they sought evidence that could silence Mikhalchenko and Kotomin,
both of whom knew well that the 1938 show trial version of the Kirov
murder was false. There may have been higher-level targets in the
Leningrad NKVD directorate, either Zakovsky's men or leftovers from

the Medved years. Or it is possible that this was simply a reflex of the security apparatus, a last spasm before the end of the Terror.

Special assignments officer Tyshkevich, who had already reported two detentions in his denunciation of Griunvald from August 1937, repeated his story with more detail during the 1938 investigation. He claimed to have stopped Nikolaev once in August as the latter tried to follow Kirov and Chudov from Smolny, and again "ten to fifteen days later," in the entrance to Kirov's apartment building. No car was mentioned. When questioned as to how he knew that the man he'd detained was Nikolaev, Tyshkevich stated that he'd seen Nikolaev from a distance after the murder as Medved led him into Smolny. Yet there is no evidence that Medved personally escorted Nikolaev anywhere after the murder. Needless to say Tyshkevich's identification of Nikolaev was very dubious, even if he was remembering two real detentions.[74]

Karl Ivanov on May 26, 1938 testified to two detentions, roughly similar to those Tyshkevich described (interrogators may have been prompting him from Tyshkevich's evidence, given three days earlier). He claimed to have been on duty at the Operations Department both times Nikolaev was brought in, but he identified the arresting officer in the second detention as Pauzer, not Tyshkevich. He claimed that Kotomin and Griunvald had threatened to fire Tyshkevich and Pauzer, because they had detained "a person they were not to detain" (note the echo of the 1937 testimony of Gubin, Zaporozhets, and others). Ivanov, in an obvious effort to deepen the guilt of Kotomin, claimed that he and other junior Operations Department officers had repeatedly warned the latter that Kirov's guard under the present orders was "useless."[75]

On February 23, 1939, the case of the Leningrad NKVD Operations Department was passed on to Officer Grigory Matveevich Krutov, possibly because his predecessor had been purged. In early 1961, at a time when Party Control Committee officials were trying desperately to prove multiple detentions of Nikolaev, Krutov testified that when he first interrogated the former Operations Department officers, they all recanted their previous evidence (including that about multiple detentions of Nikolaev), which had been extracted by torture. Although Krutov did not discuss this in his 1961 evidence, documents from 1939 make it clear that he then set about proving the prisoners guilty of negligence in guarding Kirov, perhaps using torture himself.[76]

In the two months that Krutov ran the investigation, Nikolaev's detentions pullulated like maggots. Karl Ivanov on March 7, 1939 testified to knowledge of *four* detentions of Nikolaev, rather than the two he had previously described. According to Ivanov, "Kotomin didn't want to liquidate terrorists, he shared their mood." "Witness" V. S. Noskov claimed that Officer Ya. S. Yesinov, belonging to the Operations Department's uniformed security service (not Kirov's guard), had told him that he had detained Nikolaev "several times on the routes that Kirov drove." According to Noskov, Yesinov told him that each time "he took [Nikolaev] to the Operations Department, but at the Operations Department, as a rule, Nikolaev was immediately freed by . . . Tereshchenko . . . Kotomin, and . . . Gubin." Yesinov under interrogation denied ever detaining Nikolaev, but allowed as how "at my orders very many suspicious persons were stopped on the street that Comrade Kirov used."[77]

On March 15 Officer I. S. Komovich asserted that he had detained "a suspicious person" in Kirov's entrance way, and passed that person on to Leningrad police chief Zhupakhin. Komovich admitted that he "didn't know who the suspicious person was."[78]

Karl Pauzer, who had stopped Nikolaev in the one well-attested detention, on October 15, 1934, now claimed that he had detained Nikolaev twice, once in October, and once "by Smolny" in the summer of 1934. Krutov apparently was targeting Mikhalchenko. Under Krutov's interrogation, both Pauzer and Ivanov (who were relatives) testified that Mikhalchenko had released Nikolaev after one of the reported summer detentions. However, Mikhalchenko, who had wisely resigned his commission and kept a low profile after his sister was denounced as a White espionage agent in July 1937, was never arrested or questioned in the case.[79]

Officer Tereshchenko's defense was to deny meeting Nikolaev at all until the trial of the "Leningrad Center," where he had been a guard. In the face of his stubborn resistance, Krutov even brought in his wife, and Kotomin's, for questioning. Both confirmed the story of Nikolaev's single detention as uncovered by the 1934–1935 investigation. Other than that, they provided no incriminating evidence against either Tereshchenko or Kotomin.[80]

On April 25, 1939 Krutov handed his case over to prosecutors. By this time, however, the official line on repressions had changed— Yezhov was under arrest, Beria in charge of the NKVD, and Stalin's minions were now talking about the possibility that "wrong decisions had been made" in individual prosecutions. Krutov heard later that his case against Tereshchenko and the others had been thrown out on a technicality. Some of the defendants had been arrested one month before official warrants were issued by the prosecutor. Everyone involved in this round of investigation was off the hook. The "evidence" of multiple detentions of Nikolaev, however, remained in secret police archives.[81]

Many of the NKVD officers who would provide testimony in 1960–1961 suggesting a plot by Stalin to murder Kirov were deeply compromised by the Terror. Several went further than giving false testimony under duress. Officers P. P. Petrovsky of the Leningrad Operations Department and P. M. Lobov, aide to Zaporozhets in the Special Department, took more active roles in the repression. Probably in connection with Yezhov's early 1935 purge of the Leningrad NKVD, Petrovsky was transferred to clerical duty at a concentration camp in Central Asia. There he was in charge of the "card catalogue," probably the register of camp prisoners. Soon after the March 1938 show trial in which Yagoda was sentenced to death, Petrovsky wrote a denunciation to Yezhov. It is unclear whether he decided to write on his own, or whether his letter was prompted. Either way, it was in essence an offer to Yezhov of his services as a false witness. His goal, one assumes, was to get out of the concentration camp.[82]

Petrovsky who was a low-ranking guard in the Leningrad NKVD, noted early in his letter that "now, after the uncovering of the Right-Trotskyite Bloc I see all that was going on in Leningrad after the Kirov murder." He referred to "the despicable and traitorous work of the traitor Yagoda," which he had not noticed before the March show trial. "Now I see how they killed Borisov," he wrote, and launched into a very confused and factually inaccurate account of the death of Kirov's bodyguard. According to Petrovsky, when Borisov was put in the truck for transport to Smolny, escorting officer "Vladimirov" (*sic*) ordered the driver to go fast as possible. The other escorting officer, Maly, Petrovsky characterized as "a real con-man, and so on and so forth." According to Petrovsky (who was nowhere near the scene of the accident), the truck driver had killed Borisov by slamming on the brakes so that the latter flew out of the back of the truck.[83]

There was more. Petrovsky asserted falsely that Smolny deputy commandant Mikhalchenko had had charge of Kirov's guard, along with Griunvald (another falsehood). They had ordered the guard officers to keep their distance from Kirov, thus exposing him to attack. Petrovsky also claimed that he'd heard Mikhalchenko instructing his boss Nikitin, Smolny commandant, on how to testify in the Borisov case. He closed his letter by assuring Yezhov again that "now after the trial of the Right-Trotskyite Bloc I understand everything."[84]

Petrovsky's letter elicited a response. On June 4, 1938 Officer Viatkin of the Leningrad NKVD wrote to the camp authorities asking them to interrogate Petrovsky about "the criminal activities of Kotomin, Griunvald, Tereshchenko, and others in the work of Kirov's guard, how they aided the murder." Viatkin also wanted information on the relations of the above officers with Operations Department chief Gubin, Nikolaev's detention "in August 1934" (*sic*), and anything else Petrovsky might know about the case. Viatkin's missive reveals a great deal about NKVD investigative methods at this point. In essence he was asking Petrovsky to show him just how good a witness he could be—how far he would go in corroborating any story interrogators fed him. Documents available for this book reveal nothing about the further disposition of Petrovsky's case, except that he survived the Terror and gave testimony on the Kirov murder to the Party Control Committee on December 1, 1960 (see below, pp. 609–610).[85]

P. M. Lobov sank even further than Petrovsky. In January 1935 the Military Collegium sentenced him to two years of forced labor in the case of the Leningrad NKVD officers charged with negligence following Kirov's murder. Like the others convicted, he did his time as an officer at the Magadan/Kolyma Gulag complex. We do not know how his case developed next, but in all likelihood he provided testimony against Zaporozhets in 1937, and was himself incriminated by one or more of his fellow officers. Presumably to expiate his guilt, he murdered G. Sokolnikov, Kamenev's associate and political ally, in jail in 1939 on the orders of the new NKVD commissar Beria. He then received a light sentence of three years exile to Kazakhstan. In 1948 he was again sentenced, this time to five years exile in Kolyma. Beginning in 1956 Lobov provided copious and conflicting evidence on the Kirov murder.[86]

Like the state security officers of most countries, the NKVD men were not necessarily of the highest moral caliber. Petrovsky, Lobov, and other NKVD veterans who provided evidence in the Kirov case, including the defectors Aleksandr Orlov and Pavel Sudoplatov, were opportunists and practiced, perhaps pathological, liars. Lobov, Orlov, and Sudoplatov were also murderers. Yet party investigators and Western scholars often accepted the testimony of one or another of these men with breathless credulity, as we shall see in coming chapters.

CHAPTER 12

Rumors, Speculation, and the Martyr Cult

N ews of Kirov's murder spread rapidly throughout the USSR. Soviet radio made an announcement at 11:30 P.M. on December 1, which reached thousands of receivers at factories on night shift (home receivers were still a rarity in 1934). Leningrad party leaders met at Smolny beginning at 6 P.M., little more than one hour after Kirov's death, to write an official announcement, order Kirov's office sealed, and begin preparations for memorial ceremonies. They immediately ordered party organizations to meet during the night shift at city factories. Ward party secretaries ran these meetings during the small hours of December 2, just as Moscow party organizers had done on the night of Lenin's death eleven years before. Members of the Leningrad Region Party Committee, including Pyotr Smorodin, spoke at several of the gatherings. On the tram the next morning one Leningrad woman heard Communists complaining that they'd been rolled out of bed in the middle of the night to participate. Several ward newspapers also managed to get special editions out in the middle of the night. The morning editions of the major national newspapers carried word of the killing throughout the USSR.[1]

Stalin himself edited the Politburo's announcement of Kirov's death which appeared in *Pravda* on December 2. Words he inserted are underlined below. Some are additions, and some are replacements of earlier text.

· 107 ·

Politburo bulletin on the death of S. M. Kirov, December 1–2, 1934.
APRF, f. 3, op. 62, d. 95, ll. 14–150b.

A great misfortune has befallen our party. On December 1 Comrade Kirov died at the hands of an <u>evildoer</u>-assassin, <u>sent by class enemies.</u> Not only for us, his close friends and comrades, but for all who knew him from his revolutionary work, who knew him as a warrior, a comrade and a friend, Kirov's <u>death</u> is an irredeemable <u>loss.</u> At the hands of the enemy perished a man who gave all of his brilliant life to the cause of the working class, the cause of Communism, the cause of mankind's liberation.

Comrade Kirov was an <u>exemplar</u> (*obrazets*) of the Bolshevik who knows no fear and surrenders to no obstacles in the struggle to achieve the magnificent goal the party has set itself. Directness, iron fortitude, and the inspirational qualities of a revolutionary tribune were combined in him with that personal cordiality and gentleness in relations with friends and comrades, with that radiant warmth and modesty that characterize the true Leninist.

Comrade Kirov worked in many parts of the USSR during the years of the underground and after the October Revolution—<u>in Tomsk and Astrakhan, in Vladikavkaz and Baku</u>—and everywhere he held high the banner of the party and won over to the cause of the party millions of working people with his inexhaustible, energetic, and always fruitful revolutionary work.

For the last <u>nine</u> years Comrade Kirov led our party organization in the city of Leningrad and Leningrad Region. In such a short and sad letter it is impossible to express the value of his activity among the laborers of Leningrad. [. . .]

<u>You</u> [Stalin here inserted *ty*, as opposed to the more formal *vy*] were dear to all of us, Comrade Kirov, as a true friend, a favorite comrade, a dependable companion-in-arms. To the last days of our lives and our struggle we will remember you, dear friend, and feel the burning pain of our loss. You were always with us in the years of our hard struggles for the triumph of socialism in our country, you were with us always in the years of wavering and trouble inside our party, you lived through all the difficulties of the last years with us, and we lost you at the very moment when our country had achieved great victories. In all of this struggle, in all of our achievements, there is much of your doing, much of your energy, strength, and ardent love for the cause of Communism.

Farewell, our dear friend and comrade, Sergei!

[Signatures of members of the Politburo and the All-Union Central Executive Committee follow.]

Stalin accentuated the malevolence of the criminal by inserting the noun "evildoer." His addition of the phrase "sent by class enemies" was important but unsurprising. Any rank-and-file party agitator, and most Soviet subjects, would have known without Stalin's guidance the politically correct response to Kirov's assassination—the class enemy did it. Resolutions published in *Leningradskaya pravda* the morning after the murder stated that Kirov had been killed by "the hand of a despicable hired killer . . . a bullet of the class enemy," "the despicable hand of the class enemy's hireling," and "the hand of a foul agent of the enemies of the proletarian revolution." In fact almost no one, including probably Stalin, knew anything about the murderer at this point.[2]

The bulletin set the tone for the Kirov martyr cult that would endure for the next sixty years, presenting the Leningrad party leader as a typical Bolshevik "positive hero"—tough yet "warm," untiring, "iron," devoted to the cause, yet "modest," and possessed of unflagging devotion. There was no hint of a private life. These were the qualities of the hero of the new official literary genre of Socialist Realism, inaugurated just four months earlier at the first Congress of Soviet Writers.[3] Propaganda officials and writers consciously designed such heroes as models for ordinary Communists to emulate. Stalin inserted the word "exemplar" to hold up the idealized Kirov as a paragon of the true "Leninist" personality.

By listing the names of the cities where Kirov had worked Stalin emphasized his long revolutionary pedigree, which his opponents inside the Leningrad organization had questioned in 1929. Replacing *vy* with *ty*, the dictator tried to give the reader a sense of personal intimacy with Kirov. A standard exercise in modern mass politics, this was an attempt to provide millions of rank-and-file Communists with a substitute for personal contact with the great Bolshevik heroes they had never met.[4]

Funeral planning began on the night of December 1–2, and must have been the object of some push and pull. The Leningrad party leadership formed one committee to begin funeral planning on the evening of December 1. In Moscow, in the meantime, the Politburo appointed a similar committee that included Yenukidze, Mikhail Chudov, and P. Alekseev from Leningrad, Yan Gamarnik from the Red Army, and N. A. Bulganin. The following morning at 10:00 A.M. a joint commission including officials just arrived from Moscow (Zhdanov, Khrushchev, Yagoda) and a number of senior Leningrad party figures met at Smolny.

The formation of two different committees by the central and Leningrad leaderships suggests some tension over funeral arrangements. During questioning in 1966 Sveshnikov reported hearing from Ivan Kodatsky, who was on the commission that met in Smolny on the morning of December 2, that the latter had asked Stalin if they could bury Kirov in Leningrad. Stalin answered "as you couldn't protect him here, we'll bury him in Moscow." It seems quite likely that Kodatsky's story reflected some contestation between Leningrad and central representatives on the morning of December 2 over the site of the burial.[5]

By the afternoon of December 2 it appears that the question of the funeral location was settled, as were planning arrangements. The Leningrad commission that met on the morning of December 2 apparently handled preparations in Leningrad, where Kirov's body was to lie in state in the Uritsky (formerly Tauride) Palace on December 2–3 before transport to Moscow on the night of December 3–4. Another commission met in Moscow on December 2 to make arrangements for Kirov's lying in state and burial there. It was headed by Yenukidze, who had also headed the commission planning Lenin's funeral in January 1924.[6]

Preparations for the lying in state and funeral were meticulous and followed precedents from Lenin's funeral. In both Leningrad and Moscow honor guards of high party officials, including Leningraders, would stand post by Kirov's coffin. Stalin did a turn in the honor guard in both cities. The train bearing Kirov's body would be accompanied upon arrival in Moscow by a squadron of Red Army aircraft, and orchestras were to play at the lying in state and the cremation. Kirov's body was to lie in the Hall of Columns at the House of Soviets in Moscow from the afternoon of December 4 to the evening of December 5. That night it would be cremated. On December 6 his ashes would be interred by the Kremlin wall, where many other Bolshevik martyrs, including the assassinated diplomats Vorovsky and Voikov, were buried. Although Red Army units and "mobilized" workers would make up most of the audience for the funeral in Red Square, entrance to the lying in state was open in Leningrad and Moscow. Planners wanted to ensure that a maximum number of Soviet subjects saw Kirov and mourned him.[7]

The Kirov funeral and the memorial ceremonies that preceded it had multiple purposes. The participation of much of the leadership in the honor guards was an exemplary demonstration of the party unity that obsessed the Bolshevik elite. The Soviet press published dozens of photographs of the honor guard during the mourning period. The worker delegations represented the regime's supposed popular support. By providing open access to Kirov's lying in state, the memorial planners aimed to involve as much of the populace as possible in the emotional drama of his death, and hence prompt a closer identification with Soviet Power. This was essentially the same purpose that motivated the mummification of Lenin in 1924, according to Benno Ennker.[8]

The Kirov Memorial Campaign

The memorialization of Kirov involved far more than the disposal of the body and the associated rituals. There was also a cycle of public meetings and press coverage that began the day after the assassination and went on for a month. On the morning of December 2 party agitators received daily newspapers and other propaganda materials at local party offices, with the most important sections of text underlined. At lunch or at the conclusion of the day shift they held party meetings on the assassination. At some factories there were also meetings of the entire staff. On the night of December 1–2 and the day of December 2 these meetings produced resolutions promising retribution against the assassin(s), generally labeled "the class enemy," and lauding Kirov as "one of the best sons of our beloved Mother—the All-Union Communist Party . . . " One resolution referred to "the shining, miraculous image of our beloved Sergei Mironovich," evoking representations of the saints in medieval Russian icons. A *Leningradskaya pravda* report described an elderly worker standing silently at the podium during a memorial meeting, overwhelmed by grief, with tears trickling down his face.[9]

The party and workplace meetings associated with Kirov's death went on for about one month, in Leningrad and throughout the Soviet Union. Party activists were well practiced in the organization of such events, and many would have remembered the propaganda campaign that accompanied Lenin's death. Indeed, the propaganda campaign that followed Kirov's murder resembled in a number of ways the mass mourning of Lenin organized by the Bolshevik leadership in 1924, as Benno Ennker points out. Both campaigns involved the same system of organizing popular and party response to the leaders' deaths. Party activists led public meetings, orchestrating the passage of resolutions expressing the sentiments prescribed by the Soviet leadership. Dissenters and doubters were reluctant to speak up due to social pressure and the presence of secret police and party informers. Newspapers published selected resolutions of the meetings, thus generating the appearance that state policies and rhetoric had broad popular backing. There was also a sense in which the party succeeded in fooling itself. Many of the comments made at meetings by individuals eager to demonstrate their political loyalty found their way into secret reports on popular mood prepared by the party Information Department. Party officials reading these reports naively would have had the impression of overwhelming support for their initiatives, when the reality might well have been indifference or even hostility.[10]

As in the Lenin memorials, official mourning for Kirov included a variety of events besides mass meetings. Documentary film of the dead leader was released. A campaign to sell bonds to factory workers opened. There were even efforts directed at children. A child's picture published in 1989, entitled "Kirov is dead," shows a woman at a kitchen table with her face in her hands and appears to have been a school assignment. *Leningradskaya pravda* on December 3 ran a story about schoolchildren vowing "We will be like Kirov!" There was also a rash of commemorative renaming of places and institutions. On December 5 the Central Executive Committee renamed the town of Viatka, capital of the region where Kirov was born, Kirov. The Red Putilov factory became the Kirov factory and the Leningrad ballet became the Kirov Ballet. The Azerbaijani town of Ganje, where the Red Army troops had crushed the forces of the independent Azeri republic, became Kirovbad.[11]

In the weeks following the murder *Leningradskaya pravda* published a number of memoirs of Kirov written by co-workers and subordinates at Smolny. These pieces filled out the foundation for a Kirov martyr cult laid by the government's initial announcement of the assassination. In them the hortatory tone of the standard newspaper obituary was heightened by the grandiose rhetoric of Bolshevik martyrdom and the Stalinist leader cult. A joint statement on Kirov's death, published by *Leningradskaya pravda* on December 2 and signed by a number of senior city officials, including Chudov, Ugarov, Irklis, Struppe, and Pozern, established the pattern for memories published in coming days.

· 108 ·

"To the Shining Memory of Our Leader, Friend, and Comrade."
Leningradskaya pravda, December 2, 1934, 1.

Comrade Sergei Mironovich Kirov, the most true son and gifted figure of our Bolshevik Party, is dead at the vile hands of an enemy of the working class.

Comrade Kirov gave all of his storied life to the working class. In the Tsarist underground, in the October Days, at the fronts of the Civil War, in his work in Baku, Vladikavkaz, and Astrakhan Comrade Kirov was an unbendable warrior for the cause of the party, the cause of Lenin-Stalin.

The entire party and all of the laboring masses of our country feel the news of the death of Comrade Kirov with the deepest grief.

We, who worked under the direct leadership of Comrade Kirov, suffer the loss of our dear Mironych with special pain.

The life and work of Leningrad Bolsheviks, of all the men and women workers of the city of Lenin, are unbreakably bonded with the name of Comrade Kirov. Our victories and conquests in the last nine years, our storied road of struggle for the general line of our party and her Central Committee, are tied up with name of Comrade Kirov.

Mironych is no longer among our fighting ranks, Kirov is no more, he who was the living incarnation of Bolshevik party-mindedness (*partiinost'*), for whom there was nothing more holy in life than selfless devotion to the cause of the freedom of the laborers, for whom there was nothing higher than the title "member of the Communist Party," is no more.

An ardent and fearless proletarian revolutionary, he approached the daily needs of the laboring masses with great love and care. All of the laborers of our great city knew him and warmly loved him, seeing in him their close and dear chief and comrade.

Comrade Kirov inspired all of our work for the construction of a happy new socialist life. Our industry, our agriculture, our cultural construction, the industrial development of the North, the working and mastery of the mineral wealth of the Leningrad Region—for all of this we are in great measure indebted to the leadership of Comrade Kirov.

There is not a single corner of our [socialist] construction, where the man and woman worker, the collective farmer, the engineer, the teacher, the scholar did not feel the careful and loving attention to business of Comrade Kirov, his friendly help and advice, directed at all of our work.

Comrade Kirov did not know doubt and never feared difficulties in the resolution of the great tasks set by the party. He was a true Leninist, a true and unwavering student of Comrade Stalin.

He united in himself the iron determination and the Bolshevik passion of the revolutionary with a rare simplicity and sincerity.

He was a true chief of the working masses, an ardent tribune of the people. [. . .]

We have suffered an irreparable loss. But the ranks of Leningrad Bolsheviks, of men and women workers, are unwavering. We will follow the shining example of Comrade Kirov. [. . .]

Close the ranks tightly around our Bolshevik Party and her Central Committee, around our chief and teacher Comrade Stalin!

Pyotr Chagin, former editor of *Red Gazette*, who would twenty-five years later become an important proponent of the theory that Stalin ordered Kirov's killing, published a similar eulogy/memoir in *Leningradskaya pravda* on December 3. The article, titled "Chief, Comrade, Human Being," praised Kirov in lush superlatives: "The strongest and strictest discipline, the brilliant qualities of a chief and tribune were combined in Kirov with unusual modesty, with warm concern for his class and party comrades, with a tender care for people. . . ." Chagin referred to Kirov as "one of the most faithful companions-in-arms of the great Stalin." He also mentioned specifically one of the incidents that would later become an important part of the "Kirov as anti-Stalin" myth—"the stormy, enthusiastic reception which . . . accompanied Sergei Mironovich's speech to the Seventeenth Party Congress. . . ." Decades later commentators would claim that Stalin must have felt threatened by this applause, even though the dictator received just as enthusiastic a reception, and Kirov's speech was a paean to him.[12]

Even Kirov's enemies joined in the praise of the fallen hero, motivated by their instinct for self-preservation and their desire for political advancement. Ivan Butiagin, who had clashed with Kirov during the Civil War campaign to retake the North Caucasus and had denounced him to the Central Committee as a waverer and Menshevik in 1921, produced a glowing memoir for a collection published in 1935. Georgy Desov, who had denounced Kirov to the TsK after his ouster from the Leningrad leadership in 1929, praised Kirov for treating him kindly after the conflict.[13]

Not only did the early publications of the memorial campaign turn Kirov into a plaster saint, they also exaggerated his stature in the party leadership. Perusal of *Pravda* and even Leningrad's hometown *Leningradskaya pravda* from 1934 suggests that Kirov's public profile before his death was substantially lower than that of Kaganovich, Molotov, or Ordzhonikidze. Coverage of the Leningrad leader was comparable to that of Pavel Postyshev and other second-level party officials. The overstatement of Kirov's power and prestige during the memorial campaign contributed to later assertions that he was a serious rival to Stalin.

Subversive Responses to the Memorial Campaign

Despite the tremendous effort put forth by agents of the party/state to direct popular response to Kirov's assassination, secret NKVD and party intelligence reports studied by Lesley Rimmel and Sarah Davies reveal that many people did not accept the official version of murder by the "class enemy." Nor did everyone accept the grandiose claims that the press made for Kirov's Communist virtue and service to the proletariat. Although these reports give us no data on the frequency of dissident comments about the murder, they do indicate that a substantial number of people in Leningrad doubted the official story and interpreted events in ways hostile to the Soviet regime. In spite of recent claims in the scholarly literature for the overwhelming power of Bolshevik propaganda to shape the consciousness of the population, these reports indicate that many individuals could see that official "reality" was patently unreal. This does not mean that a majority of the population was longing for liberal democracy and capitalism. Almost certainly they were not. But it does mean that many retained the ability to see that official rhetoric contradicted reality. The intelligence reports also indicate that Soviet society in the 1930s was riven by tensions and resentments, many of them created or exacerbated by the Bolsheviks themselves.[14]

Since scholars gained extensive access to former Soviet archives in the early 1990s, there has been controversy about the value of the intelligence reports (svodki) on popular mood. They are a very tempting source because they seem to provide hard data on a question that has been very hard to answer—how did ordinary people feel about the regime? However there are serious difficulties with using the *svodki* as sources on "popular opinion." One problem is suggested by Terry Martin, who argues that the secret police reports on popular mood derived from evidence gathered against specific people on police watch lists. In short, selection was overwhelmingly for negative comments, and some of the negative comments may even have been exaggerated or made up. In the case of the Leningrad reports cited below, there is some corrective for this problem, because many of them were compiled by the Party Information Department, often in connection with the memorial meetings described earlier in this chapter. Most of the comments collected by the Party Information Department came from the notebooks and reports of grassroots party agitators, and from other sources such as the anonymous notes that audience members were allowed to hand in to speakers at some Soviet meetings. Although there was without doubt some overlap between the party agitators as a group and the NKVD's network of informers, the Information Department's reports did not derive only from materials gathered to incriminate "anti-Soviet elements" under surveillance.[15]

A second consideration in evaluating the intelligence reports on popular mood is the immense pressure to parrot official rhetoric exerted by party leaders, activists, and the secret police. This pressure was particular intense in major cities like Leningrad, where the party and police presence was strong as compared to the countryside. We must assume, then, that people who voiced negative, indifferent, or subversive opinions about the Kirov memorial campaign represented a larger body of the population that had similar thoughts but chose silence.

Like the assassination of any public figure, Kirov's killing was a sensation, and at first much of the Leningrad population wanted to know more about it. In early December several ward party secretaries reported that sales of newspapers were up. Agitators noted relatively high attendance (70–90 percent) at mass meetings held for factory employees.[16] Most people's interest, however, did not stem from "politically correct" motivations. Like "bourgeois" viewers tuning into a television special on Princess Di's fatal car accident, Leningraders wanted to hear the story of a sensational death.

According to Lesley Rimmel, "negative" comments reported to the party Information Department in the first two weeks following the murder frequently expressed doubts about the state's accusations and Kirov's "heroic status." A number of commenters said that the state had overreacted in one way or another. One stated that the "White Guard" prisoners executed immediately after the assassination were not guilty, but had simply been killed as hostages to the state. Several of the commenters said that too many people were executed in retaliation for the killing. A staff member at the Academy of Sciences said, "Now they're going to start shooting right and left, and even innocents will fall." Doctors in a private conversation criticized the Law of December 1 as illegal, and noted that "Kirov wasn't such an important figure, despite the way he's being portrayed in the press. . . . This incident is being used to raise the spirit of class struggle . . . and to revive class hatred and vigilance."[17]

Other people were skeptical of the government's claim that the "class enemy" was responsible for the killing. At a party history study circle in the Svetlana factory a student asked "How do we know that Kirov was killed by order of class enemies?" Many suggested, accurately, that an insider, a Communist and/or a worker, rather than a "class enemy," had committed the murder. A physics teacher told his interlocutor that "maybe [Nikolaev] was an honest party member who became disenchanted with [the party's] policies. It can happen that we waver, for example under the influence of the hunger in Ukraine and the Urals." Sometimes the authors of such comments gave them an anti-Communist spin that turned the official narrative on its head—it wasn't the "class enemy" but the Communist enemy who had murdered Kirov. A construction worker suspected that "the Communists themselves have sold Kirov for gold. I heard that the murderer is a Communist, but foreigners gave him 30,000 gold rubles, so he killed Kirov for money. All of the Communists are selling themselves for money." A peasant at a village meeting explained to his audience that the assassin was a Communist, and that Communists were always committing evil acts—"they rob us—the state procurements are excessive."[18]

In contrast to the official propaganda, there were a number of negative comments about Kirov himself. Some noted character flaws—he was a careerist, he "lorded it over others and stuffed his own pockets," he was "a tsar" and "crude." Other negative commentary focused on the hunger experienced by the general population, often contrasting it ironically with Kirov's chunky body (by the early 1930s the Leningrad leader was quite overweight, as a few private photographs reveal). One worker said of the killing, "That's the way to go—that's just what [Kirov] deserved, because the people are exhausted and kicking the bucket from hunger. . . . this means . . . 800 extra grams of bread [a day] for the population." A worker at the Red Dawn factory commented, "Kirov was so plump lying in his coffin," while a woman worker said, "What did Kirov ever do for the workers besides develop a paunch?" A young peasant woman was recorded as saying: "They've killed Kirov and that's fine; he's brought us all to hunger and exhaustion. We will remember him for that. If I knew where he was buried, I'd shit on his grave." Among the peasants, Rimmel contends, anti-Soviet commentary was more direct and less ironic than in the city. Another peasant said simply, "A dog's death for a dog."[19]

The intelligence reports record some people taking the ultimate subversive stance, viewing the assassin Nikolaev as a hero. One commenter, who feared that the end of bread rationing would mean less food for the common people, said that Nikolaev had been sent on his mission by the workers and peasants, "in connection with the repeal of bread rationing." At the Red Putilov factory one worker praised Nikolaev for his courage in attacking Kirov out in the open, "directly . . . within the walls of Smolny." A few Leningraders identified Nikolaev with the revolutionary terrorist heroes of the past: "It's clear that not all the Zheliabovs have disappeared in Russia, the struggle for freedom goes on." Rimmel also notes a number of comments generally approving of the murder: "Way to go!," "Thank God!," and "That's the way to send him off!" Once the press unveiled the charges of Zinovievite involvement, a number of workers expressed sympathy for the oppositionists. A foreman at the Stalin Metallurgical Factory told his subordinates, "if the Zinovievite group were in power we'd live a lot better."[20]

There was also widespread resistance to the propaganda campaign around Kirov's death that did not involve direct anti-Soviet, anti-Kirov, or anti-Stalin commentary. Much of this came from attendees at the mass meetings who asked difficult questions, challenged party agitators, or made snide comments. Some audience members asked why the authorities had not expelled Nikolaev during the 1933 purge of the party, or why the party had tolerated the ex-Zinovievites in its ranks for so long. Following the widespread agitation for execution of Zinoviev and Kamenev in early January 1935, meeting leaders had to explain to restive audiences why they had not been sentenced to death. Some compared the death sentences in the "Leningrad Center" trial with the prison sentences for the "Moscow Center," and concluded that there were softer standards for the elite: "They shoot the little people, but as for Zinoviev, Kamenev, and so on, they don't shoot them—it's not fair." At some meetings the audience asked the orator uncomfortable questions, such as "What is the platform of the Zinoviev Opposition?"[21]

Not surprisingly, people resented demands made by party agitators during the memorial campaign. When an activist asked workers to donate to a fund for Kirov's funeral, someone said, "We've been completely skinned alive—what more do you want?" At one power plant not a single Communist contributed to a fund for building a "Kirov Squadron" for the air force. Many people simply resented the endless compulsory meetings. A frustrated worker at the Kronstadt naval shipyard told Communist activists, "What are you grieving for? So [Kirov's] been killed—Fuck him. . . ." Even party cadres did not always hide their boredom. At the Red Instrument machining plant, activists played dominoes during a memorial meeting on December 4 or 5.[22]

To their credit a number of Communist officials and activists in Leningrad resisted the central authorities' drive to blame former oppositionists for the murder. Presumably they recognized the likelihood that this would lead to a bloody massacre. The authors of Information Department reports in late December 1934 fretted about several cases of meeting leaders' apparent reluctance to attack the ex-oppositionists. Speaking at the Electrical Apparatus factory around December 18 or 19, Boris Pozern mentioned nothing about the connection of the opposition to the murder. The report on Pozern mentioned six other factory meetings where there was no mention of the Zinovievites' alleged responsibility for the crime. At two other factories speakers mentioned the oppositionists only in passing.[23]

Rimmel argues that the most characteristic reaction to Kirov's death in Leningrad was "jokes, disrespect, and boredom." Although it is not possible to support her claim statistically, it makes intuitive sense. The memorial campaign was a major imposition on people's daily schedules, and there is scant contemporary evidence that Kirov was widely "loved" among the city's general population. Typical comments recorded in party Information Department reports were "What does this have to do with me?" "Who cares?" "There'll be others to take his place." Most common of all was "Enough already" (*Nu i ladno*). At the Volod factory a worker told party members, "So you've passed your resolution [on the "Moscow Center"], but nothing will come of it. And anyway, this is your own party affair . . . you deal with it yourselves." Such comments reflect the gap between Communists and non–party members, the most important social divide in the early Soviet Union. Non-Communists knew very well that Bolsheviks viewed them as the preterite, left-over masses who required leadership from the party avant-garde. They also knew about and resented the privileges of party officialdom, petty as these might seem to present-day inhabitants of far richer capitalist societies.[24]

Rumors, Speculation, Conspiracy Theories

The near silence of the official media on the concrete facts of the Kirov murder in early December left an information vacuum that was filled with a cloud of rumor and supposition. As Adam Ulam pointed out almost forty years later, Soviet political culture determined that the murder could only be interpreted as the result of a conspiracy. For at least a decade Bolshevik authorities had promoted the idea that there were no accidents in the USSR, no incompetence, no random crimes, no freak catastrophes. Industrial accidents, production below plan, theft, murder, and rape were "not coincidental." They all had political meanings; they were all perpetrated by saboteurs, class enemies, and foreign intelligence services. Accordingly, the assassination of a high official could not but be the outcome of a political conspiracy.[25]

In Leningrad speculation and rumors about Kirov's killing embraced just about every conceivable scenario. There were stories that Medved had provided the assassin with a pass to Smolny, that Medved himself had pulled the trigger, and that Chudov had ordered a hit on Kirov. Some Leningraders talked of a conflict between A. I. Ugarov and Kirov. Other tales implicated German, Finnish, Polish, or Turkish secret agents. There was speculation about a larger plot that included attempts on the lives of Maxim Gorky, Kaganovich, and German Communist leader Ernst Thälmann. Another rumor circulating was that Kirov had killed himself. Russian nationalist and anti-Semitic interpretations of the killing also surfaced. "They shot the only Russian" in the Bolshevik leadership, went one such comment. A twenty-year-old worker at the Red Seamstress factory said, "It was a Jew who killed Kirov."[26] The French Communist A. Rudolph, working at Leningrad's *Red Gazette,* recalled in 1950 that every new arrival at the editorial offices on the morning of December 2 had a different story about the murder—the assassin was a personal enemy of Kirov's, he had been excluded from the party, he was a terrorist financed by foreign powers.[27]

One of the rumors in the days after Kirov's assassination was that Stalin had ordered the killing. An employee of a village cooperative store, hardly likely to be privy to any inside information, said, "Kirov was a genius, and enjoyed great authority which grew with every day, among the workers as well as the peasants. Stalin was afraid that Kirov was competing for his position, and so he sent the murderer. . . ." Davies points out that rumors of personal quarrels among party leaders were very common even before Kirov's death. In the absence of any sound information about what was going on in the upper echelons of power, Leningraders speculated. Davies quotes two such tales: "Once upon a time Stalin and Voroshilov knifed each other while they were drunk." "When Krupskaya was drunk she shot Stalin, who was also drunk, because he does not allow her to speak up for the workers' children." In the context of widespread rumors and conspiracy theories about relations among Soviet leaders, the appearance of a story indicting Stalin for Kirov's murder does not have particular significance. This rumor, however, did not die, but later grew in strength among ex-Communists imprisoned in forced labor camps.[28]

Davies and Rimmel agree that one of the more common rumors was that a romantic rival or jilted husband had killed Kirov. Tales of romantic conflict and sexual disorder among party leaders were quite common in popular discourse, Davies suggests. Most of the tales about Kirov's murder were vague, referring only to a "jealous man." None of those uncovered by Rimmel referred to Milda Draule by name. A publishing house deputy director, Boris Latynin, speculated that the murder was "a case of some tart" (*po bab'emu delu*). The "driller Romanov" at Plant Number Eight in Moskva Ward said that Kirov had "three wives" and was pursuing the assassin's wife when he was shot. At least one person retailing the "romantic version" of Kirov's murder, however, sounded better informed. A senior librarian at the Academy of Sciences, K. K. Mozheiko, reportedly said that "Kirov was known to the entire city as a skirt chaser, he'd had affairs with all of the female staff of the regional party committee, including Nikolaev's wife. In addition, at the alleged suggestion of Kirov, Nikolaev was expelled from the party during the party purge, then reinstated. And so, because of all this, Nikolaev, from feelings of personal revenge, killed Kirov. . . ."[29]

Suggestions by Roy Medvedev, Robert Conquest, and Anton Antonov-Ovseenko that the security police created the "jealous husband" rumor to counter the "Stalin did it" version of the murder are not plausible. As Rimmel points out, Medvedev argues that the NKVD created the rumor long after the murder, when in fact it was circulating in Leningrad within days. Nor would the NKVD have put the rumor into circulation earlier. For one thing, the "Stalin did it" story was not dominant in December 1934. For another, discussion of party leaders' sexual liaisons was so taboo that Alla Kirilina, trained as a historian in the Soviet era, did not admit that Kirov had affairs until 2004. The party leaders and the NKVD believed that rumors of sexual escapades undermined their authority. As Rimmel shows, party agitators in Leningrad struggled to stamp out all kinds of rumors in the wake of the Kirov murder, including the "jealous husband" story.[30]

Like the version implicating Stalin, the "jealous husband" tale had staying power. Indeed, it reached high-ranking party officials in Moscow within days, if not hours. This could have been via Academy of Sciences connections, but there were plenty of other routes for it to spread. At any rate, the story was a commonplace among Kremlin staff by late December, judging from testimony given in the "Kremlin Case" (see above, pp. 459–461). Lidia Shatunovskaya (no relation to Olga), claimed in her 1982 memoir, *Life in the Kremlin,* that "everyone" in the party elite who inhabited the famous "House on the Embankment" believed that Nikolaev was a jealous husband. Shatunovskaya's version of the story was particularly lurid, with Nikolaev "barging in" on a "tryst" between Kirov and Draule.[31] Avel Yenukidze believed this narrative of the murder and evidently spread it widely. A September 1936 report to the NKVD by an informer close to Yenukidze describes in some detail his version of the assassination, which resembles the December 1934 rumor retailed by Academy of Sciences librarian Mozheiko.

· 109 ·

NKVD officer's report on Avel Yenukidze's comments on the Kirov murder, September 1936. RGANI (archivists in 2007 were not able to locate a citation for this document. The author has a 1996 photocopy in his possession).

———————

Previously, in 1935, I reported on how A. S. Yenukidze reacted to the murder of S. M. Kirov in his intimate circle. From the point of view of the facts, uncovered during the trial of the Trotsky-Zinoviev bloc [August 1936], some aspects of A. S. Yenukidze's comments at that time have taken on new interest.

In December 1934, when the entire country was waiting for the publication of the results of the investigation into the case of Kirov's murder, member of the government A. S. Yenukidze disseminated among his acquaintances living in Building No. 1 of the Central Executive Committee, in part to the Vetoshkin family, a counterrevolutionary version of the reasons for Nikolaev's crime.

To the official announcement that S. M. Kirov died "at the hands of the class enemy," A. S. Yenukidze opposed *his own* version, stating that there was supposedly no political side to Nikolaev's crime at all, that Nikolaev killed S. M. Kirov out of personal motives, allegedly as a result of a "blood insult" he had received from Kirov. A. S. Yenukidze claimed that supposedly S. M. Kirov was "courting" Nikolaev's wife, who worked in the apparatus of the Leningrad regional committee of the party and in connection with this situation Nikolaev was ordered to go to work in the countryside. Nikolaev refused this move, for which he was excluded from the party. According to A. S. Yenukidze, this served as the grounds for Nikolaev's "personal revenge."

Evidence that A. S. Yenukidze disseminated this counterrevolutionary version, which one of his acquaintances, Vera Mikhailovna Vetoshkina, almost immediately told with exactly the same details [*sic*]. On the day after Yenukidze developed this version in the circle of his friends, V. M. Vetoshkina talked about it in her apartment in Building No. 1 of the Central Executive Committee in the presence of several persons. The husband of V. Vetoshkina, E. Z. Kiselgof /a party member presently working for the Northern Sea Route Trust/ and L. A. Okhitovich /presently working for the All-Union Central Council of Labor Unions/, and others [*sic*].

[...]

Yenukidze's "strange" behavior in connection with the fact of S. M. Kirov's murder cannot in any way be put down to mere liberalism and philistine gossip. There are uncontestable facts indirectly indicating that A. S. Yenukidze's "apolitical" attitude in relation to Nikolaev's crime has deeper roots, as can be seen from the example below.

On the day of S. M. Kirov's funeral in Moscow, in December 1935 [*sic*], A. S. Yenukidze opened the meeting on Red Square with an introductory speech. In this speech [...] Yenukidze, in contrast to all of the other orators without exception, did not say a single word about the fact that Kirov fell at the hands of the class enemy. The entire content of this speech witnesses the fact that even on the day of the funeral, when a great deal was already clear, A. S. Yenukidze did not in any way recant his version [of the murder].

Given that A. S. Yenukidze himself belongs to the circle of people who are very well-informed, his stubbornness cannot be explained away as idle chatter. The facts indicate that here we see in all probability his [expression of] a particular political position.

The author of this report unwittingly reveals a great deal about the nature of the "truth" in Bolshevik rhetoric by the middle 1930s. The officer treats the centrally controlled show trial of August 1936 as establishing a "true" revolutionary narrative, while dismissing Yenukidze's alternative narrative as "counterrevolutionary." Evidence for the competing narratives is irrelevant—the sole criterion for truth is now the declarations of the central authorities or the story-lines presented in the mass spectacles organized by them. Moreover, believers in the Stalinist "truth" care far less about whether it corresponds to the real world than whether they can demonstrate their power by forcing others to reiterate its tenets. For Stalin and his loyalists the ability to get the entire populace to repeat their "true" narrative of events both indexed and reproduced their power. Any challenge to their narrative was thus a challenge to their power. Needless to say, this attitude towards "truth" was and is not unique to Stalinists.[32]

The informer also points to the importance of Yenukidze's speech at Kirov's funeral. Yenukidze's failure to pin the responsibility for the assassination on "class enemies" indicates his "apolitical" and hence "counterrevolutionary" attitude. Yenukidze's 1934 correspondence with his friend Lev Karakhan, former Deputy Commissar of Foreign Affairs, confirms that this omission was significant not just in the minds of diehard Stalinists. Karakhan and presumably Yenukidze himself saw it as a gesture rejecting bloodthirsty calls for revenge. Karakhan's letters to Yenukidze in December 1934 are worth describing because they illuminate not just the meaning of the funeral speech, but also the reaction of one member of the party elite to Kirov and his assassination.

In the last months of 1934 Karakhan, recently demoted, was serving in Ankara as ambassador to Turkey. On December 2 he wrote to Yenukidze that he had heard the news of Kirov's killing on Soviet radio the previous night. Of Kirov, Karakhan wrote, "he had many qualities, which everyone will be writing all about. But there was one . . . for which I felt the greatest respect and simply loved him for—this was his great simplicity and modesty. It was as if he tried not to be noticed." Karakhan's description resembles Mikoyan's, quoted by Khrushchev in his memoirs: "At meetings [Kirov] did not once speak about any question at all. He kept his mouth shut, and that was it. I don't even know what that meant."[33]

Ten days later Karakhan wrote again to Yenukidze. He praised his friend's speech at Kirov's funeral, which he had heard on the radio, and expressed his intense dislike for calls for revenge. "Dear Avel, how agitated I was to hear your voice from Red Square. . . . I should tell you that your few words touched me more than any others, they were said simply and humanly, without clichés. . . . In spite of Manuilsky's [a

Comintern official] stupid shriek about how we don't know how to cry, but only how to revenge ourselves . . . I could not tear myself away from the radio until the end." The clear implication of these words is that Karakhan disapproved of the calls for vengeance, and that he appreciated Yenukidze's refusal to include any in his speech. It seems reasonable to conclude that Yenukidze, who was quite close to Karakhan, felt the same way, and made a deliberate choice to omit any reference to "class enemies."[34]

In their efforts to explain Stalin's destruction of the Old Bolshevik elite during the Great Terror, scholars have referred to Kirov's supposed blocking of the execution of oppositionist Mikhail Riutin in 1932 and an effort to replace Stalin with Kirov at the Seventeenth Party Congress in 1934. Both of these incidents are probably mythical (see below, pp. 530–536, 616–618). Rather than such dramatic incidents of outright opposition, we need to look at a more quiet resistance to Stalin's escalating power, manifest in myriad smaller incidents of obstructionism and refusal to parrot certain formulas of the new Stalinist "truth." In his unwillingness to participate fully in the falsification of Stalin's early biography and his rejection of the "class enemy" and "oppositionist" explanations of the Kirov murder, Yenukidze exemplifies this resistance. The tension was heightened by NKVD reports on the opinions Old Bolsheviks expressed in private, not always flattering to Stalin. It is the accumulation of such incidents against the background of Stalin's personal vengefulness and paranoia that explain the dictator's ultimate decision to annihilate most of the Bolshevik Old Guard.

The NKVD was interested not only in the reactions of Soviet subjects to the Kirov murder, but also in those of foreigners inside and outside the USSR. In addition to reading the foreign press, NKVD operatives intercepted letters sent out of the country by foreigners living in the Soviet Union—for example, one dated December 31, 1934 and mailed to a Berlin address. The author was in contact with diplomats in Leningrad and with Communist officials and his letter was in German. He may have been a German diplomat, but more likely was a journalist and/or unofficial agent for the German Socialist Party, now in hiding from Hitler. The letter reads like an intelligence report.

· 110 ·

Letter on the Kirov murder, originally in German, translated into Russian by
Soviet security services, mailed to a Berlin address, December 31, 1934.
RGANI, f. 6, op. 13, d. 104, ll. 182–189.

The Kirov murder caused great upset in the upper party leadership, the
more so because it was impossible at first to foresee the meaning and the
importance of this attack. Evidence of this is that fact that the three most
senior figures of the government, namely Stalin, Molotov, and Voroshilov,
left for Leningrad that same evening, obviously in order to clarify the situation at the scene and decide what measures had to be taken.

From the start the opinion has circulated among the public here that the
murder of Kirov was committed for personal revenge by a deceived activist or spouse.

As is now obvious [. . .] the government from the very beginning decided not to permit such a version but to use the attack for its political
goals. Thus, directly after the assassination, it was officially published that
Kirov died "at the traitorous hands of an enemy of the working class." But
then, the next day the murderer was found in the person of the former civil
servant named Nikolaev. [. . .] Everything possible was done by [. . .] official circles to dispel the opinion of the public that the murder was committed for personal motives, and to represent the attack as a deliberate
maneuver by the enemies of the Soviet Union.

[. . .]

In the process of [the case's] further development, the striving of the Soviet government to represent the attack as the deed of the hand of a secret
anti-Soviet organization became ever clearer. Following multiple bulletins
about the underground machinations carried out by the remnants of opposition elements from the Zinovievite camp, who were accused also of
involvement with counterrevolutionary circles abroad, there came the announcement on December 22 [. . .] that the investigation [. . .] had determined that the assassination was committed at the orders of a terrorist
organization, the so-called "Leningrad Center." [. . .]

The difference [between the "Leningrad Center" case and earlier show
trials] is that in the trials of 1925, 1928, 1932, and 1933 the accused were
persons outside the party, such as professors, engineers, technologists, and
foreigners, whereas here for the first time all of the accused belong to the
ruling party. [. . .] They confess themselves guilty of fighting against the
present party leadership with all means possible. [. . .]

Speaking of the indictments, one must note the passage in which it is
stated that Nikolaev falsified his own diary and also his petitions to various Soviet organs, in order to represent his action as "an act of individual

despair and protest against unfair treatment of a human being by particular government persons."

This passage could provide fruitful soil for the rumors in circulation about personal motives for the attack. [. . .]

The present merciless suppression of all open statements of one's opinion [. . .] could lead to the conclusion that there is total unity in the Communist Party of the USSR, [. . .] but in reality not only do the masses of the peasant population and a not insignificant portion of the workers feel themselves deceived in the hopes brought about by the revolution, but even party circles do not fully approve of the developments that the "general line" has taken in recent years. Although it is not permitted to criticize openly the measures taken by the party leadership [. . .] in closed circles and at private gatherings party members more frequently and firmly say that the present "general line" has [. . .] little in common with the teachings of Marx and Lenin and is a foul betrayal of the real principles of Communism. [. . .]

The complete power and satisfying lives of some, alongside the helplessness and terrible need of others, has led to the formation inside the party of a stratum of those who have always been able to adapt themselves to the "general line" in a timely fashion and get hold of good posts and other perquisites, [. . .] at the same time as others feel themselves deceived in part in material, in part in ideological hopes, and for that reason have an oppositional mood. [. . .] This tendency strengthened following the end of the rationing card system for bread, a measure that will probably lead to a worsening of the material condition of the broad masses who are receiving low wages. It cannot be hidden from the party leaders that their decision to end the rationing card system for bread, which is supposed to be a brilliant demonstration of the success of their economic policies, is cursed in some party circles as treason against the Communist idea and the betrayal of the interests of the proletariat. [. . .]

To take on such tendencies in open battle would obviously be unpleasant for the party leadership. [. . .] For this reason they seek other means with which to prove that the opposition is wrong, to force it to shut up, and to destroy it. And at such a moment an accident comes along to help them. The assassination of Kirov is a magnificent weapon. What could be easier than to connect the murder with the inconvenient oppositionists in [the party's] ranks? [. . .]

Any means are acceptable to achieve this goal, and so they make up farfetched accusations against old oppositionists who have long ago made peace. [. . .]

The letter writer believed that the end of bread rationing was a key to the mood of the general populace as well as of some party circles, a hypothesis that finds support in NKVD and party Information Department reports. "The public," by which the writer probably meant educated professionals, believed that the murder was a matter of personal revenge, though not necessarily on romantic grounds. The letter writer's linking of Nikolaev's act with the growing gap between successful opportunists and failed purists in the party is quite shrewd and fits with the evidence from Nikolaev's diaries. Also astute is his suggestion that Stalin and his henchmen targeted Zinoviev, Kamenev, and the Leningrad oppositionists in part to intimidate wider circles of the party who were dubious about the "general line." The writer's contention that there was widespread doubt about Stalin's policies in the party fits with the picture advanced in this chapter of a gradual build-up of tension between some of the Old Bolsheviks and Stalin. Stalin would have been well aware of such doubt without any direct challenge from Kirov.

Another group whose reactions to the assassination interested the NKVD was the oppositionists themselves. On March 21, 1935 Molchanov, chief of the Special Political Department, sent Yagoda a copy of an analysis of the murder and its consequences written by David Borisovich Rubinshtein, a Trotskyite. Rubinshtein was a lawyer who had once taught at Moscow State University. A dedicated and tough revolutionary, he continued to resist the regime even while in prison. Arrested in 1931, he was exiled to Siberia, where he "undertook active underground work," according to Molchanov. He was arrested a second time and imprisoned in a special prison for political dissidents, the Upper Urals "political isolator." At the time he wrote the document below, in early January 1935, Rubinshtein was organizing a hunger strike among his fellow prisoners.

It seems unlikely that Rubinshtein had read Trotsky's commentary on the murder, written in exile (Chapter Thirteen, Document 113), but his analysis follows it closely. Rubinshtein was certainly familiar with Trotsky's general attempt to explain the Stalinist regime, however. Because Marxism downplayed the significance of individual "great men" in determining the course of history, Trotsky argued that Stalin represented a social force, a bureaucratic caste that had hijacked the Russian Revolution and now ruled the USSR. Rubinshtein tried to fit his analysis into this scheme.

· 111 ·

Analysis of the Kirov murder by David Borisovich Rubinshtein, an imprisoned Trotskyite, early January 1935. RGANI, f. 6, op. 13, d. 33, ll. 51–86.

The entire staging of the case of Kirov's murder, the indictments and the sentences of the military tribunal, and the execution of the fourteen [members of the "Leningrad Center"] leaves no doubt that this is only the prologue to a renewed and this time bloody attack on the opposition. To prepare the way to lead us to the guillotine, the government of the USSR is thinking up a bloody plot against the opposition. [. . .]

The bureaucracy is thirsty for our heads and for Trotsky's head above all. [. . .] to pay him back with death for the organization of the October Revolution, for the smashing of the White armies and the [Allied] Intervention in Russia, and to get rid of the most gifted, talented, and great chief of the Bolsheviks and international Communism. Even if the shot in Smolny was not organized deliberately, it is still being deliberately used to facilitate the murder of L. D. Trotsky and the punishment of his followers in the USSR.

[. . .]

Time has shown, however, that the roots which the October Revolution sunk in the working class cannot be so easily ripped up [. . .] that even the virtuoso opportunism and flexibility of the Stalinist bureaucracy cannot cope with the situation, that [. . .] the forces of the revolution are sinking deeper and deeper into the underground, digging [. . .] the grave of the (seemingly) triumphant reaction. [. . .] The workers and the popular masses of the USSR, deprived of rights, tormented by the burdensome exploitation of labor, poor and half-starving, atomized and spit on by the bureaucracy, resist the crushing attack of the Stalinist regime, [albeit] in unorganized and formless fashion. [. . .]

The years 1933 and 1934 did not bring any improvement in the country. All of the demagogic measures of the bureaucracy failed one after another, [while] the working class and the popular masses remained silent. On the surface everything appears smooth, but deep behind the official facade so much powder and explosive material has accumulated, that it could suddenly burst and destroy not only the brick facade, but the entire many-storied building of the ruling house of Stalin and his myrmidons. Helpless and strengthless [. . .] the bureaucracy could have decided to undertake against the revolution the sharpest provocation—"burning the Reichstag" at Smolny, so as to give the signal for a new pogrom against the opposition. Then the punishment of the Trotskyites and revolutionaries in preparation in the USSR would be justified and legalized in the eyes of the laborers and workers of the USSR and the whole world.

Besides the false official story of the circumstances and aims of the Kirov murder, the following versions can be proposed:

1. Nikolaev shot at Kirov on direct orders from the NKVD, whose agent he had long been.

2. Agents of the NKVD supervised Nikolaev. Unconscious of this, he was convinced [. . .] that he alone was carrying out this act of revenge for himself and others and became a traitor and NKVD agent after completion of the murder [i.e. when he began to make false confessions incriminating ex-oppositionists].

3. Inside the official Communist Party there formed some kind of very small group of terrorists, connected with no one, at whose order Nikolaev carried out the killing. He gave no evidence and the NKVD fabricated all of his depositions.

4. Nikolaev carried out an act of purely individual terror, run by no one else. [. . .]

5. A combination and cross-cutting of several of the versions above. Whatever version may be correct, it is incontestable that the bureaucracy has decided to use the murder in Smolny to set up a sweeping and bloody pogrom against the Bolshevik-Leninists and to prepare public opinion for silent acceptance of the execution of oppositionists. [. . .]

We, the Russian Trotskyites, are a branch of the international revolutionary Communist movement, the inheritors and bearers of all the best revolutionary traditions of Bolshevism in Russia. We censure and reject individual terror, considering it detrimental to the revolutionary struggle. [. . .]

At present every shot of INDIVIDUAL TERROR IS AN ACT OF PROVOCATION, whatever the subjective intentions of the terrorist. [Each shot] serves as a signal for mass arrests of and reprisals against oppositionists, for the gloating of the reactionary bureaucratic clique which rejoices at the deaths of tens and hundreds of Communists.

Where is the gain when Sergei Kirov is replaced by Andrei Zhdanov? [. . .]

Why does [the bureaucracy] thirst for our heads now, why is it preparing the murder of Trotsky? Because the Trotskyite opposition is the only revolutionary force in the USSR which is [. . .] dangerous to the ruling bureaucracy, because "Trotskyism" has been transformed from a term of abuse by our enemies into the banner of revolutionary Communism [. . .] because the word "Trotsky" is no longer just the name of a gifted chief, but has become a symbol and a password of revolution, because "All Hail Trotsky!" means "Down with Stalin!," because in the gathering catastrophe, and in the case of war the eyes of the proletariat, not only in the USSR but in all countries will seek out Trotsky and listen to his voice, because in the end Trotsky is a living rebuke and constant threat to Stalin.

[. . .]

Among the ruling circles of the bureaucracy there were and remain major disagreements about the "disposition" of the Kirov murder case. Many of them felt that no one would believe all of the inventions in the indictments, but the group that decided to undertake this provocation, no matter what happened [. . .] won out.

[. . .]

Let us begin with Nikolaev's evidence. All of the depositions he gave prior to December 13 are hidden, excerpts have been given only of his testimony on December 13 and 20. What did he say before that? Why is this hidden? Only once does the indictment refer to Nikolaev's diary, in which he wrote that he committed the murder of Kirov "as an act of personal despair and protest against the unjust treatment of a living human being by particular government personages." It is clear that in those depositions concealed by the indictment, Nikolaev did not say what the NKVD demanded. That is why the Central Executive Committee had to issue a special resolution prolonging the investigation to December 20. [. . .]

Why should we believe Nikolaev's deposition of December 13 [if he even gave it himself] and not his earlier testimony or the entries in his diary? Indeed, every one of the accused mentioned by Nikolaev, including the most important [. . .] figures Kotolynov and Shatsky did not just refuse to confirm his testimony, but categorically rejected Nikolaev's assertions. Even in the indictment it is stated that Kotolynov confessed only belonging to a group of former Zinovievites and nothing more. [. . .]

What happened in reality? Who killed Kirov and why? Which of the five variants we have proposed is correct? If Nikolaev shot at the orders of the NKVD, then it is possible that one part of the ruling bureaucracy did not have the means to [. . .] suppress certain disagreements among the bureaucrats and decided to get rid of a bureaucrat who was inconvenient to it by means of a bullet. [. . .] It is possible that the task given was the arrangement of an [. . .] "attack" on the chief and his nearest collaborators, that the shot was supposed to distract the attention of the masses from the struggle and not to be fatal. But the perpetrator carried out the task seriously and "conscientiously," whether by accident or design. If this was the case, then the leadership of the Leningrad department of the NKVD was removed not for negligence and passivity, as was announced in the press, but for excessively aggressive action, for exceeding its authority, and for "overfulfilling the plan." Whatever the actual goals of the shot at Kirov were, it is entirely plausible that the physical perpetrator of the murder may not have been a direct agent of the NKVD. Having received the orders to get rid of Kirov, the NKVD could have specially sought out Nikolaev, knowing his individual terrorist moods, and guided him, supposedly in the name of some group of terrorists.

It must be supposed that among the fourteen executed persons there were 3–4 agents of the NKVD. The fact that they were also shot makes perfect sense. [. . .]

According to the daily assurances of the entire press, the speeches of orators great and small, the resolutions of all congresses and conferences, the country is blossoming, the working class lives satisfied and well taken care of, the collective farmers are becoming well-off, in the Communist Party there is total unity. [. . .] And then suddenly the government announces that in the most monolithic Communist Party organization in the industrial heart of the country, in the much-praised Leningrad organization, in Smolny, a plot and an organization of terrorists has been uncovered, consisting not of [. . .] anonymous rogues, but of persons rooted in the Leningrad proletariat, of youth who were brought up and educated after October, who set themselves the task of overthrowing the "wise" leadership and carrying out the platform of the opposition. Thus the bureaucracy has recognized that the superficial appearance of monolithic unity is no more than an illusion. [. . .]

Everyone and everything is now frightening for the bureaucrats. Each one suspects the others, and the "Wise Chief," having lost his footing, is terrified of finding himself suddenly alone on the Kremlin Square. [. . .] The bureaucracy aims to terrorize the revolutionaries inside the country with reprisals, and show its foreign allies, the French and other governments [. . .] that it is sufficiently strong to deal with the threatening situation and that the imperialist allies can count on it. [. . .] The coming years will bring a cataclysmic earthquake for the present regime. If we turn out to be unprepared and unable to head the new proletarian revolution of the Russian working class, if we are unable to link up with the proletarian masses, become their avant-garde and their party [. . .] if we do not take the road of class activity of the masses, then a sad lot and a pathetic end await us.

> We tighten the stays and haul up the sails,
> With comradely whispers we chase away the easy dreams
> And boldly we set sail and sing our song loudly

That will be a funeral song for the bureaucracy and a victory song for the revolution!
Hold fast, Comrades!

Thus the Trotskyite Rubinshtein, starving himself to death in prison. Yet one can see that this declaration could have frightened Stalin. Rubinshtein claimed that an extensive Trotskyite underground existed, that it was growing stronger, and that it had "sunk roots" in the proletarian population. His manifesto was, in effect, a direct threat against

Stalin. Moreover, the dictator had access to intelligence on strikes, and he knew that large numbers of Soviet workers were unhappy with their lot. He and Rubinshtein had both participated in the overthrow of the Tsarist autocracy, and they understood the state as a fragile structure, easily overthrown by mass unrest. They may not have appreciated (Rubinshtein certainly did not) just how powerful a modern state apparatus was under ordinary conditions. The Russian autocracy collapsed only after two and a half years of shattering military defeats and the loss of support from just about every group in imperial society.

The Trotskyites openly challenged Stalin's status as a revolutionary and "the best student of Lenin." They struck directly at the heart of his political identity, and perhaps his personal identity too. They turned all the terms of the Stalin cult and Stalinist ideology upside down. Trotsky, not Stalin, was the chief of the world revolution; Stalin was a reactionary of the darkest hue. It was not Trotsky who collaborated with foreign imperialist powers, as suggested by the indictment in the Kirov murder, but Stalin, who was making a military alliance with France. The Stalinist bureaucracy was congruent with the old imperial bureaucracy. Rubinshtein's manifesto does not in any way justify Stalin's decision to wipe out suspected oppositionists, but it helps to explain it. Such direct challenges must have aroused his rage and fear.

Because of his commitment to orthodox Marxism, Rubinshtein downplayed Stalin's personal leadership role, but his suggestion that the "bureaucracy" might stand behind Kirov's murder obviously implicated the dictator. Here too the Trotskyites turned Stalinist rhetoric upside down in the most simple-minded fashion—it wasn't Trotsky who ordered Kirov's murder, but it might well have been Stalin. Rubinshtein had no evidence for the proposal, which he himself presented as speculation.

The Trotskyites' direct experience of secret police persecution led them to believe that Kirov's murder, could have been the result of an NKVD conspiracy. Stalin or some other leader of "the bureaucracy" might have ordered the assassination, or perhaps the NKVD had prepared a provocation, an assassination plot that was not to be completed, but unmasked. The fabricated conspiracy would then serve as the pretext for reprisals against oppositionists and ex-oppositionists. The plan had gone awry and the assassin had completed the job. Trotsky himself, writing in France, suggested the same scenario in late December.

As the last lines of Rubinshtein's manifesto show, the Russian Revolution had come full circle. The Communist government was now threatened by the romantic vision of revolution that had inspired its own founders in the years before 1917. Underground conspiracy, idealism, and the solidarity of warriors in the proletarian cause were threats to the state. To save the revolution, Stalin had to end it.

Concentration Camp and Terror Rumors

During and after the Great Terror Stalin's victims in the labor camps, in particular former Communist officials, swapped and elaborated tales of the Kirov murder that countered the official narrative. James Scott has suggested that exploited subordinate groups from American slaves to Southeast Asian peasants develop "hidden transcripts" that defy and negate the dominant culture. These "hidden transcripts" can take the form of rumors, gossip, "world-turned-upside-down" imagery, anonymous threats to power, and folk tales such as the African-American "B'rer Rabbit" stories.[35] In the case of the Communists imprisoned by Stalin, the hidden transcripts reversed official narratives with remarkable, almost mechanical precision. Accused during the Terror of collaboration with the Tsarist secret police, Communists in the camps charged Stalin with the same crime. Accused of espionage for capitalist powers, they charged their arch-enemy with collaboration with German intelligence to frame Marshal Tukhachevsky. Denounced for betraying the heritage of Lenin, they identified Stalin as the real traitor to the cause. Accused of conspiring to kill Kirov, they charged Stalin with killing him.

It was true that Stalin was a murderous tyrant. Many of the tales told about him in the camps had more than a grain of truth to them. The camp rumors are worthy of study as a "hidden transcript" of resistance to Stalinist oppression (at the same time that many of the Communists in the camps, such as Filip Medved or Olga Shatunovskaya, had participated in that oppression). And the survivors' narratives of their own experiences in the camps and their meditations on the Gulag nightmare deserve attention as historical and moral documents. But the third-, fourth-, or more-hand rumors that circulated in the camps are not accurate historical sources for events in Stalin's inner circle.[36]

One of the earliest sources of rumors was the Leningrad NKVD officers exiled to Kolyma in 1935. Multiple documents indicate that these men felt a strong sense of grievance over their scapegoating for Kirov's death. They blamed Yagoda, his man in Leningrad Zaporozhets, and perhaps, in the most private conversations, Stalin. On December 19, 1956 Medved's former deputy Fyodor Fomin wrote to another Leningrad NKVD survivor, Georgy Petrov, that "I believe that not one Leningrad chekist is guilty" in the Kirov case. Fomin, who may have testified against Zaporozhets and Yagoda in 1937–1938, blamed the two for the assault on the Leningrad NKVD leadership in the aftermath of the Kirov murder.[37] At his January 1935 trial, according to Georgy Petrov, Filip Medved faulted Zaporozhets for "tying his hands" with respect to Kirov's guard.[38] Medved's anger at being faulted in the Kirov case may lie at the base of tales reported in the late 1950s and 1960s by Leonid Kirchakov and D. B. Sorokin. In 1956 Kirchakov reported to party authorities a story he had heard from his onetime boss, Yan Olsky. Olsky was one of the senior officers transferred out of the secret police in 1931 following a row with Yagoda. He was also apparently a friend of Medved's. Kirchakov worked for Olsky at a food processing trust in the years immediately before the Terror. He claimed that in late 1936 or early 1937 Olsky told him that "Medved's suffering was completely unjust, that Medved was the closest and most sincere friend of Comrade Kirov, and that Medved was not guilty in the murder of Comrade Kirov."

Thus far, Kirchakov's story is entirely plausible. It seems quite likely that Medved would have told friends in letters or in person what Olsky passed on to Kirchakov. The next part of Kirchakov's tale, however, is more dubious. He recounts a version of Stalin's interview with Nikolaev, supposedly passed from Medved to Olsky, in which Nikolaev, when asked why he killed Kirov, answered that "the chekists told him to do it," and then pointed to a group of central NKVD officers in the room. Kirchakov specified that Medved and Zaporozhets were both on the other side of the room from the central chekists. There are a number of problems with the story, including the fact that Zaporozhets was not in Leningrad on December 2 when Stalin interviewed Nikolaev (see above, p. 389). The story's exculpation of Medved is also suspiciously clear—Nikolaev points away from him but toward the central NKVD officials. It is possible that Kirchakov experienced confusion as to the source of one or both parts of his story ("source amnesia"—see above, p. 10) and that the tale of Nikolaev's interview did not come ultimately from Medved.[39]

Tales retold by D. B. Sorokin, Medved's brother-in-law and an employee of Molotov's secretariat in Sovnarkom in the 1930s, appear also to have their origin in the Leningrad NKVD chief's resentment of his treatment following the Kirov murder. Sorokin reported to central party authorities in 1962 that while at liberty in Moscow awaiting his trial, Medved visited him. Sorokin, who had fairly accurate inside knowledge of personnel appointments at the top levels of the Leningrad NKVD, claimed that Medved had told him about a meeting with Stalin, in which Stalin scolded him for failing to protect Kirov, and asked where he wanted to serve his punishment. On a wall map, Medved indicated Kolyma. When Sorokin asked "Isn't Stalin interested in the details of the murder of S. M. Kirov?" Medved supposedly said, "Stalin does not need my services in the matter. He knows the history and the prehistory of the murder of S. M. Kirov perfectly well, and he knows too the executors of that villainous murder, Yagoda and Zaporozhets." He added, "if you manage to survive, [you'll see] that everything about it will come to light. Time will claim its due."[40]

It is entirely possible that Medved spoke to Sorokin (who adopted his daughter after his execution) in Moscow in December 1934 or January 1935, and expressed anger at Stalin, Yagoda, and Zaporozhets. Given Stalin's fabrication of the case against the oppositionists, Medved may also have made a sarcastic comment to the effect that "Stalin already knows everything about the murder that he needs to know—he doesn't need my help." Beyond that there are real problems with Sorokin's testimony. First, his narrative follows the story-line prepared by the NKVD in 1937 and presented at the March 1938 show trial, a story-line which is almost certainly inaccurate. It is probable that Sorokin consciously or unconsciously adopted that story-line. He may even have testified to it during the Great Terror, as payback against Yagoda for taking down Medved. Second, Sorokin's story implies that Medved was barely questioned at all in the Kirov murder, whereas the documents indicate that Yezhov, Stalin's right-hand man on the investigation, debriefed him extensively. Third, Medved's alleged references to "if you survive" and "Time will claim its due," smack far too strongly of hindsight. It is extremely unlikely that Medved in the winter of 1934–1935 foresaw the annihilation of much of the party elite. Testimony in 1939 of a Leningrad police officer who saw Medved during this period indicates that he suspected foul play of some sort in Borisov's death, but that he did not have theories about any conspiracy in Kirov's killing.[41]

Another source of rumors was Leningrad Communist leaders and their families repressed by Stalin during the Great Terror. Stalin killed most of the officials and imprisoned many of their wives and children. They had good reason to speculate about the reasons for Kirov's killing and to wonder if it had not been a deliberate provocation, perhaps organized by Stalin. People went over the events of December 1 and 2 in their minds repeatedly, exchanged stories that they had heard, and built up a body of often self-contradictory oral legend. For example, Roy Medvedev reported in the late 1960s a story from M. Smorodina, daughter of Pyotr Smorodin, that when Medved attempted to get into Smolny right after the murder, "unknown chekists from the Moscow NKVD" stopped him. Not only was this story at least third-hand, and possibly fourth- or fifth-hand when Medvedev heard it, but there is no other evidence of any such incident.[42]

A number of people passing on supposedly "inside" stories on the Kirov assassination gave Mikhail Chudov as the ultimate source, although none seem to have spoken to him directly. For instance, Anna Larina, Bukharin's wife, claimed to have spoken to Chudov's wife in early 1938. Chudov's wife told her that "Zinoviev didn't need to get Kirov. This came down from the very top, on orders from the Chief. [. . .] After Kirov was shot, many Leningraders understood this. Chudov did too." At first glance this account appears to be inside information on the murder, coming from Kirov's deputy. Read more closely, it is simply an empty statement of "common knowledge." In other words, many people were speculating that orders for the murder came down from "the Chief." Another version of Stalin's interview with Nikolaev, including the "Nikolaev-accused-the-chekists-and-was-beaten" narrative, was also sourced to Chudov, reaching Medvedev via Chudov's friend "V. Sh." This tale seems to have circulated widely among the Leningraders, and those telling it in the early 1960s cited at least four different "original" sources. In no case was the story first-hand when put to paper, and it appears to have been third- or more-hand in most versions. It is very likely that there was substantial source displacement in people's memories as well as outright falsification of the chain of transmission by a few to make the narrative seem more plausible (see Chapter Fifteen and the Conclusion for more discussion of such stories and whether any of them constituted good evidence).[43]

Rumors and speculation about Stalin's involvement in Kirov's killing spread far beyond Leningrad leadership circles. V. I. Rudolph-Yurasova, who spent time in a concentration camp with a number of wives of former people's commissars, wrote about her experience in

1950. The commissars' wives "all said that the assassination was a 'provocation'" used by Stalin to get rid of the opposition. Given the ways in which the term "provocation" was used in Russian at the time, this could have implied that Stalin organized the murder, or that he simply used it for his own political purposes. Either way, these women, imprisoned by Stalin, had developed an alternate narrative of the Terror, in which the dictator himself was to blame.[44]

Further Development of the Official Martyr Cult

The Stalinists built up the Kirov martyr cult to fantastic heights in the years following the Leningrad leader's murder. Like Red Army Day, the anniversary of the October Revolution, and the commemoration of Lenin's death, the anniversary of the Kirov assassination became the occasion for party meetings, the publication of memoirs, and other rituals. In late November 1935 Central Committee authorities set the pattern for the future when they instructed provincial Communist officials how to commemorate the anniversary of the murder. Stalin personally edited the circular before its dispatch (words cut by Stalin are underlined below).

· 112 ·

TsK circular to provincial party organizations on commemorating Kirov's death,
November 26, 1935. APRF, f. 3, op. 62, d. 96, ll. 62–63.

———————

To all territorial and regional party committees, and the central committees of the national republic Communist parties.

On December 1 it will be one year from the day of death of S. M. Kirov, killed in villainous fashion by the despicable scum of the Zinoviev-Kamenevite opposition.

The Central Committee of the Communist Party orders you on that day to illuminate in the press, party meetings, schools, study circles, and agitational conversations the heroic life of Comrade Kirov, devoted completely to the party /the building up of the party in the underground, the heroic struggle versus the enemies of the USSR during the Civil War, the struggle for the rebuilding of industry in Baku, the struggle for the Leninist-Stalinist line in the party against the thrice-accursed, foul Zinovievite-Trotskyite opposition and the Right opportunists, the struggle for the socialist reconstruction of Leningrad, etc./. It is essential that you present Comrade

Kirov as one of the greatest leaders of our party, <u>the closest comrade-in-arms of Comrade Stalin,</u> tribune of the party, the favorite of all laboring people in the USSR.

It is simultaneously necessary to show that the Zinoviev-Kamenevite group, smashed by the party, <u>took the road of two-faced conspiracy and</u> became the most evil enemy of the party and Soviet power, that in its beastly hatred of the party and its leadership this counterrevolutionary group joined up with the White Guards and fascists, carrying out their orders and accepting their <u>methods</u> influence.

The Central Committee of the Communist Party orders you at meetings and in articles devoted to the anniversary of Comrade Kirov's death, to explain the necessity of further increasing the vigilance of every party member and all party organizations and all mobilized members of the party towards better study of the history of the Communist Party, the history of the party's struggle against all of the antiparty groups, for the triumph of the Leninist-Stalinist cause.

November 26, 1935.

Stalin sought to use the commemoration to whip up more hatred against the Zinovievite opposition, a plan which did not bode well for Zinoviev and Kamenev personally. He enjoined party members to study with care the new, revised version of party history, which emphasized the defeat of the various groups that had challenged him. Stalin also showed a bit of his false modesty, crossing out the reference to Kirov as his "closest companion." Stalin frequently referred to himself as "the Central Committee" and his subordinates also sometimes used this phrase. Behind the false modesty that eschewed personal references lay the extraordinary grandiosity of identifying himself as the Central Committee, and in effect as the entire party.

Stalin also ordered provincial party committees to show Kirov as "one of the greatest leaders of our party." This exaggeration was now plausible due to Kirov's martyrdom and its connection to the supposedly titanic struggle against the oppositionists. Acceptance of Kirov's new status was mandatory for party members, as the TsK circular made clear.

The development of the official Kirov cult was conditioned by the publication of memoirs, selected documents, novels, and eventually scholarly studies. The Central Committee press published the first collection of memoirs and documents, *Biographical Material—S. M. Kirov,* just weeks after the murder. In the introduction the editors of this short book praised Kirov as "a well-tempered and staunch warrior" with a "shining intelligence, calm decisiveness, and self-sacrificing devotion." He was a "passionate revolutionary, an irreconcilable foe of the slightest deviation from Bolshevism," and of course, "the closest comrade-in-arms, student, and friend of the great Stalin." The collected memoirs falsified Kirov's biography by omission and exaggeration. Kirov was credited with organizing the 1905 demonstration against Bloody Sunday in Tomsk and with leading the defense of Astrakhan during the Civil War. Of his tenure in Azerbaijan, the editors wrote that Kirov "was a favorite of the Baku proletariat."[45]

The editors of *Biographical Material* commissioned memoirs from a number of people from Kirov's distant past, including his Tomsk companion Mikhail Popov, now facilities construction director for the Communist Academy; G. Shpilev, another SD acquaintance from Tomsk; and his boyhood friend Aleksandr Samartsev. These men added their contribution to the growing pile of Kirov elegies written by Leningrad Communists and published in *Leningradskaya pravda* and the history journal *Red Chronicle (Krasnaia letopis').*

The first anniversary of Kirov's death saw the publication in *Leningradskaya pravda* and *Red Chronicle* of more Leningrad memoirs, as well as the release of the memoir collection *Comrade Kirov. Comrade Kirov* embellished the information published in *Biographical Materials.* Now Kirov was a leader of student rebellion in Kazan, an active opponent of the Mensheviks in Tomsk in 1905–1906, "a major party figure" in Vladikavkaz, and an eyewitness to the storming of the Winter Palace during the October Revolution. A story surfaced that Trotsky as Red Army commander wanted to abandon Astrakhan during the Civil War, but Kirov resisted. There appears to be a grain of truth to this tale, but Kirilina has demonstrated that Lenin never overruled Trotsky with a telegram ordering the Red Army to "Defend Astrakhan to the last!" *Comrade Kirov* skipped over the issue of Kirov's father's abusiveness and alcoholism, and devoted a long section to the smashing of the opposition in Leningrad in 1926.[46]

By 1937 Kirov had become relentlessly "cheerful" and tougher. That year, as the Terror got underway, Boris Pozern edited a biography titled *Sergei Mironovich Kirov, 1886–1934.* Pozern added a class warfare component to his account of Kirov's childhood, blaming the exploitation of labor for his father's difficulties and describing how the young Sergei had fist fights with "merchants' sons." The boy Kostrikov was portrayed as a leader of the orphanage students, "strong, sharp, and full of the joy of life." Pozern emphasized Kirov's poverty and ascetic life in Kazan. Kirov/Kostrikov was now the leader of the

SD student group that disrupted the liberal banquet in Tomsk in January 1905, and of course, a relentless fighter against Mensheviks and Socialist Revolutionaries, who "feared his sharp tongue like fire." During 1905–1906 he fought in armed skirmishes with government troops (a claim Kirov himself never made). In the Tomsk jail he plotted to escape. He was single-handedly responsible for the defense of Astrakhan and the reorganization of the Eleventh Army. Trotsky's order to abandon Astrakhan during the Civil War was now not a strategic mistake, but treason, thwarted by Kirov. Unlike earlier biographical works, *Sergei Mironovich Kirov* referred not just to his battles against Trotskyites, Zinovievites, and Mensheviks, but also against the Rights. This fit with the arrests of Bukharin and Rykov and preparations for the March 1938 show trial.[47]

In 1939 the State Publishing House put out a revised and expanded version of *Sergei Mironovich Kirov.* Pozern, who had been arrested, was no longer editor. Kirov was now even more "staunch" and unbending, and there were few references to his "tenderness for people" or his love of children. He even fought the Mensheviks inside the Tomsk jail. Kirov's eyes were "penetrating," seeing through the subterfuges of Fascists, White Guards, and party traitors. His energy was "inexhaustible." The enemy he fought was if possible even further dehumanized. Trotsky was now "the Judas Trotsky," and the party oppositionists were "the detestable enemies of the Soviet people, the Trotskyite-Bukharinite monsters." The final paragraph of the book was a call to "remember all of this and be vigilant."[48]

During the Great Terror Soviet studios released Fridrikh Ermler's two-part film, *A Great Citizen,* a fictionalized drama based on Kirov's battle with the opposition and his assassination. Part One came out in 1937, Part Two in 1939. *A Great Citizen* showed the "Kirov" character, Shakhov, first defeating the Zinoviev and Kamenev characters, Borovsky and Kartashov, in an open battle resembling the TsK's takeover of Leningrad in 1926. The second part followed the evil duo as they wove a conspiracy to kill Shakhov, aided by Shakhov's deputy Zemtsov, a stand-in for the recently arrested Chudov. According to Yevgeny Dobrenko, on the surface *A Great Citizen* was a relatively simple Manichaean story. It projected onto the screen sections of the Stalinist *Short Course* in party history, in preparation while the movie was filming. The oppositionists were power-hungry, neurotic, unprincipled, and evil. They achieved their goals through subterfuge and conspiracy, since they had no hope of popular support. As for Shakhov/

Kirov, Dobrenko quotes the Soviet director Grigory Roshal's contemporary description of the character: "A Stalinist, full of friendly clarity and love for people, passionate in his loving heart, carrying within him the sunny joys of our era, Shakhov is splendidly handsome with the beauty of the new communist image. His clash with the gang of scoundrels that had lost its senses and was forging a new chain of treachery in the new, bright Stalinist world—this great clash came to a victorious conclusion in spite of the death of Shakhov." At the same time that Shakhov was full of "love for people," he was a Stalinist strongman, who "defeats [the oppositionists] with direct blows—simple blows which paralyze the seeming complexity of the enemies' thoughts."[49]

Dobrenko argues that *A Great Citizen* contained an unspoken but clear threat to Soviet audiences in the late 1930s. The oppositionists in the movie have no political goals or platform, they are just congenitally evil, and the "good" Bolsheviks like Shakhov find them out not in the course of rational debate, but by their "scent." If there were no objective criteria defining who the enemies were, then anyone, including audience members, might turn out to be one. The only psychological escape route from fear of this threat was to love the Shakhov/Kirov character, as well as the other heroes of late 1930s party/historical movies, such as the Bolshevik official "Maksim," and Lenin himself. Dobrenko writes, "In the name of self-preservation the viewer had to love these amazing people. They were specially created objects for the sublimation of fear." If Dobrenko is right, then the Terror itself must have led some Soviet audience members, and perhaps party members in particular, to cathect the mythical Kirov very powerfully.[50]

By the last years of the Stalin era, Kirov was a paternalistic Soviet Godfather who crushed enemies and cared for his "family," the common people. The novel *The Dangerous Year (Groznyi god)*, published in 1955 but written in 1946–1951, before Stalin's death, was the story of Kirov's defense of Astrakhan during the Civil War. Although the novel was grossly inaccurate, the author, Georgy Khlopov, presented it as historical truth. He showed Kirov and his right-hand man, the chekist Atarbekov, crushing the traitors Aleksandr Shliapnikov (historically a leader of the Workers' Opposition) and of course Trotsky. In *The Dangerous Year* Kirov is a threatening figure, who walks with heavy footfalls and sees through his interlocutors with "penetrating eyes." At the same time he shows care for his simple subordinates, for example by leaving part of his dinner for the cleaning lady to eat (!).

The Dangerous Year also incorporates Cold War and anti-Semitic motifs typical of late Stalinism. Behind the British plotting to seize control of the Caspian Sea stand American imperialists. The most important White spy inside the Soviet camp is a nurse with the unmistakably Jewish name Kaufman and the headquarters of the White rebellion in Astrakhan is the home of the merchant Rozenblium.[51]

Beginning in the late 1950s Khrushchevite authorities and their sympathizers in party publishing wrought an emphatic change in Kirov's image. In keeping with the new emphasis on "general humanitarian values" and on the real problems and strivings of individuals in Soviet society, they turned Kirov into a personable character with feelings and a difficult personal history, as well as a humane Communist who opposed the excesses of the Stalin years. In 1962 the "Kirov" publishing house put out *It All Happened in Urzhum*, presented as memoirs of Kirov's sisters about their brother's boyhood. Yelizaveta and Anna, who were both in their seventies, probably received substantial help in producing the book. They described Kirov's childhood in frank terms, including his father's alcoholism and abusiveness, previously a taboo subject. Sergei they portrayed as a dutiful boy loved by his teachers and caretakers.[52]

The Kirov of *It All Happened in Urzhum* is a kind of model revolutionary Boy Scout, "direct, frank, and honorable." Indeed, the book was probably published with a youth audience in mind. It was still important to present Sergei Kostrikov as an active revolutionary, and Yelizaveta and Anna (or their editors) drew on previous exaggerations of his early subversive activities and his standing among fellow socialists. Some sense of the distortions involved in producing *It All Happened in Urzhum* can be gained by comparing Yelizaveta and Anna's 1962 descriptions of their brother with their 1934 letter to Kirov in Leningrad. In 1962 they refer to Kirov's "astounding personal charm," to his "respect for labor," and his "humanitarianism." But judging from their last letter to Sergei (see above, p. 149), in 1934 they resented him for cutting contact with them, and saw him as the "prideful and conceited" representative of an exploitative and distant party elite.[53]

In 1964, as one faction of party officials strove to present Kirov openly as a genuine alternative to Stalin, Semyon Sinelnikov published *Kirov* in the Komsomol publishing house's "Lives of Remarkable People" series. An awkward cross between an inspirational biography aimed at an adolescent audience and a scholarly history, Sinelnikov's work stressed Kirov's ability to settle personal conflicts and win over political opponents to the Bolshevik side. In his effort to portray the Bolshevik movement as a unified band of brothers (betrayed by Stalin, although the author did not go so far as to say that openly), Sinelnikov smoothed over every political battle in Kirov's life, other than the fights with the Whites and the Trotskyite-Zinovievite oppositionists. In Sinelnikov's recounting, Kirov's conflict with the Piatigorsk Bolshevik Andzhievsky over the formation of the Socialist Bloc in the North Caucasus in spring 1918 was a misunderstanding. His defeat and exile of Nariman Narimanov, the Azeri Communist leader, was a close working friendship. And the expulsion of the Komarovites from Leningrad never happened. Nor did the "cleansing" of Leningrad or the brutal pacification of the Azerbaijani countryside.[54]

In Sinelnikov's biography Kirov became a model Khrushchevite party secretary. In Baku he worried about getting more consumer goods to the population, an echo of the Khrushchevite shift of investment from heavy to light industry. He was also a promoter of international cooperation, supervising the Azerbaijani oil company's special concession to sell oil directly abroad, and arranging a treaty with Iran for cooperation in the eradication of agricultural pests. His method of work was democratic persuasion, not "naked administrationism." In Leningrad he constantly struggled to improve food supply for the workers, and he "cared about people." Last but not least, he rejected the "excesses" of Stalinist collectivization, and followed a more gradual path.[55]

To depict Kirov as human, humane, and tolerant, Sinelnikov made extensive use of eulogies written by Leningrad Communist leaders and other Soviet notables in 1934–1937. The cited authors included S. S. Lobov (Kirov knew how to save "honest Communists" from the opposition's snares), Boris Pozern ("he found ardent words to inspire the weary"), Komsomol leader Aleksandr Kosaryov (Kirov loved youth "with a Bolshevik love"), and museum director Aleksandr Fersman ("With Kirov all was calm and bright"). Lobov, Pozern, and Kosaryov had been dead for twenty-five years, all shot in the Terror.[56]

In 1969, as the last embers of the Khrushchevite "Thaw" died, the publishing house Lenizdat put out a small print run of *Our Mironych*, a collection of memories of Kirov written by co-workers and others who had met him. The book was a late product of the "Thaw," following the Khrushchevite line of emphasizing Kirov's human warmth and collegiality. The titles of some of the essays convey the overall tone—"Friend of the Workers," "His Charm and Inspiring Conviction," "Always among the People," "With the Help of Mironych," "Kirov and Children," and "Care for People." Like Sinelnikov, the editors of *Our Mironych* relied heavily on eulogies of Kirov written in the middle 1930s. Many of the articles were in fact reprinted from *Leningradskaya pravda, Red Chronicle,* and other periodicals where they had appeared in 1934–1935.[57]

Kirov had immense utility as a cult figure for Stalinist and for Khrushchevite propagandists, for several reasons. First, as David Brandenberger has described in the case of the rehabilitation of Tsarist generals and Russian feudal princes in the second half of the 1930s, Kirov was a useable hero. According to Brandenberger, the Great Terror disrupted Bolshevik propagandists' search for concrete historical heroes they could use to inculcate patriotism in the Soviet population. Many of the Communist candidates were executed, their memories befouled by charges of treason. One solution was to turn increasingly to long-dead heroes of the Russian imperial state, such as Peter the Great. The other was to use Communists who had died before the Terror, including Lenin himself, Mikhail Frunze, Yakov Sverdlov, and a few others.[58] As a Communist leader who had died in good odor before the Terror, Kirov was a suitable figure for the campaign to foster Soviet patriotism. The real Kirov's remarkable ability to cleave closely to the party line, as well as his caution and reserve, meant that most of his documents and speeches could be used with relatively little editing. The eulogies written by friends, co-workers and acquaintances provided plentiful source material to portray him as a tolerant and humane leader. According to Stalinist mythology, a demonic conspiracy of traitors to Communism had martyred Kirov. Many Soviet Communists had internalized and cathected this story. All the de-Stalinizers had to do was place Stalin at the head of the devilish antiparty conspiracy, and they would have a powerful tool of political propaganda, perfect for dethroning the dead tyrant in the minds of Communists throughout the Soviet Union.[59]

CHAPTER 13

The Kirov Murder in the West, 1934–1956

Soon after Kirov's murder readers of the Soviet press from abroad understood that the NKVD was seeking to implicate former party oppositionists and "class enemies" in the crime. Russian socialists in exile anticipated large-scale repressions. On January 10, 1935 the *Socialist Herald* (*Sotsialisticheskii vestnik*), organ of the Menshevik Central Committee in Paris, ran the headline "New Wave of Terror in the USSR" over a resolution denouncing Stalin's accusations against Zinovievites and "Zinovievite-Trotskyites." The resolution noted that party opposition groups inside the USSR did not advocate terror and it blamed the killing on a lone assassin unbalanced by the atmosphere of fear created by Stalin.[1] Stalin's exiled rival Leon Trotsky also anticipated a full-scale attack on oppositionists within the USSR. In late December 1934, writing in his journal, *Bulletin of the Opposition*, Trotsky concluded based on official Soviet press coverage that Nikolaev might have had the support of a group of low-ranking Communists. That Communists would undertake a terrorist act against a Soviet leader, Trotsky argued, was the fault of "the bureaucracy," which was destroying the legacy of October. He predicted that Stalin was now going to fabricate a "judicial 'amalgam'" that implicated Zinoviev and Kamenev in the murder. Trotsky believed that this was probably the prelude to a large-scale crackdown on oppositionists.[2]

One month later, after following the trials of the Leningrad and Moscow "Centers" in the Soviet press, Trotsky had developed quite a different view of the crime. He suggested that the local NKVD, under Stalin's orders, might have been trying to use Nikolaev to stage an attempted attack on Kirov that could be used as a pretext for repressions. The plan, Trotsky speculated, had gone awry and Nikolaev had succeeded in killing Kirov.

· 113 ·

L. D. Trotsky, "Step by Step, Everything Falls into Place (A Letter to Our American Friends" (*Vse stanovitsia postepenno na svoe mesto [pis'mo amerikanskim druz'iam]*)," *Biulleten' oppozitsii,* no. 42 (1935).

On January 23 the Military Tribunal sentenced twelve officers of the Leningrad GPU [NKVD], headed by their chief Medved to harsh punishments: imprisonment for two to ten years! The sentencing document charges them with nothing more nor less than the fact that "they were informed of the planned attack on Kirov, but showed . . . criminal carelessness /!/, . . . failing to take the necessary measures to guard him." Recognition of the fact of GPU collaboration in the crime is covered over with the sad phrase about "carelessness." Can we suppose for even one minute that such a pillar of the GPU as Medved could in reality show "carelessness" with regard to the preparation of an assassination attempt on Kirov? No, we are not dealing with "carelessness" here. Excess zeal, a game of chance with Kirov's head—this explanation fits more closely the gist of the matter.

When preparations for the terrorist attack had already begun, with the knowledge of the GPU, the task of Medved and his fellow officers did not consist of arresting the plotters—that would be too simple. An appropriate consul had to be found, he had to be hooked up with Nikolaev, Nikolaev had to trust him, and so on. At the same time a connection had to be established between the Zinovievite-Kamenev group and the Leningrad terrorists. This was not simple work. It demanded time. But Nikolaev did not wait. The difference in work tempos between Medved and Nikolaev led to the bloody conclusion.

The sentence of the tribunal directly states that Medved, Zaporozhets, and the others "did not take measures to uncover and halt in time" the activities of the terrorist group. It is impossible to express things more clearly. They could have prevented the murder, but they did not do so. Why? Out of carelessness, answers the tribunal. Who believes that? Medved and the others could not take preventative measures because they had not yet completed the task with which they were entrusted. [. . .]

Medved "knew," the tribunal tells us. We have no doubt of it. Through whom did he know? Through his own agents, participating in the preparation of the attack and at the same time observing Nikolaev. What happened to those agents? Not a word was said about them at Medved's trial. That is not surprising! Their case was decided at the same time as Nikolaev's; there were undoubtedly agents of the GPU among the fourteen executed conspirators. [. . .]

It is completely obvious, however, that Medved could not carry out this game of chance on his own account. The participation of the foreign consul could not be his secret alone. In a matter of such great importance Medved could not but report daily on the telephone to Yagoda, and Yagoda to Stalin. The matter was one involving the heads of people of worldwide fame, after all. Moreover, even the "happiest" outcome of the amalgam involving the consul threatened diplomatic complications. Without the direct sanction of Stalin—most likely without his personal initiative—neither Yagoda nor Medved could ever have decided on such a risky enterprise.

No one, we hope, will gainsay us now. But Medved himself admitted that the tribunal's charges were "true." Of course! What else could he do? The accused chose the lesser of two evils. They could not in reality declare that they participated in a criminal provocation with the aim of producing an amalgam on the direct orders of Yagoda. Such a declaration would have cost them their heads. [. . .]

But what about the consul? That is one question to which we hear no answer. The consul of Latvia gave 5,000 rubles for the organization of Kirov's murder. The court has confirmed this fact. What more? By the time of the trial the consul ended up in Finland, not in the hated USSR and not in his native Latvia, but in "neutral" Finland. What a fortunate consul, to have friends who gave him a warning! It is clear, at any rate, that the consul did not finance Kirov's murder on his initiative and at his own risk. Such plots are too much for a small-time functionary. If the consul was not a GPU agent, as Stalin's lackeys assure us, then he could have acted only on the orders of some foreign government, Latvian or German /as the Soviet press has hinted/. Why not reveal the criminal band? [. . .] In fact Stalin has shown no interest in the terrorist-diplomat and his inspirers. [. . .]

There is another side to this riddle. Why is the consul himself silent? He is now outside the USSR and could, it would seem, uncover the whole truth. [. . .]

Documents of the 1934–1935 investigation of the Kirov murder provide answers to a number of Trotsky's questions. They indicate that the charges of "carelessness" against the Leningrad NKVD were based on the single detention of Nikolaev and the ignoring of Volkova's denunciations. Stalin, Yagoda, and Yezhov were determined to punish the Leningrad NKVD leadership for allowing the assassination to happen. Moreover, Yagoda's and Stalin's hostility to Medved pre-dated the murder. As for the consul, he never did give Nikolaev 5,000 rubles. There was no mystery about his departure from the USSR—the Soviets expelled him. He ended up in Finland because of the extremely short warning he was given. Once in Latvia he denied any involvement in the murder, and the Latvian government backed him up.

Trotsky seems to have been fooled by the Soviet authorities' fabrica-tion of an amalgam after the murder—the inclusion of the Latvian consul in the putative conspiracy, the linking of Nikolaev to the ex-Zinovievites in Leningrad. He mistakenly concluded that the Lenin-grad NKVD, under central direction, had fabricated these connections before the murder.

Trotsky's January 1935 theory of the murder is nonetheless worth attention for two reasons. First, we cannot dismiss the possibility that local NKVD officers had contact with Nikolaev before the murder and may even have been trying to use him as a provocateur against ex-Zi-novievites. Second, Trotsky's suggestion that Stalin was involved in the killing, albeit unwittingly, influenced many later writers on the subject.

The August 1936 trial and execution of Zinoviev and Kamenev prompted further discussion of the possibility that Kirov's murder had been plotted at the highest levels of the Soviet leadership. The trial script hinted that the Rightists might be connected to the supposed Trotskyite-Zinovievite cabal. Kamenev and Zinoviev both testified that they had hoped that Rightists might join their conspiracy against the Stalinist leadership. It appeared, then, that Stalin was going to bring the former leaders of the "Right Deviation" under renewed at-tack. Prosecutor Vyshinsky's declaration at the trial's conclusion that he would investigate possible Rightist links with the alleged assassina-tion plots strengthened that impression.[3]

Based on the August show trial and other events, such as the May 1935 disbanding of the Society of Old Bolsheviks, Menshevik and Trotskyite exiles came to the conclusion that Stalin was preparing a full-scale assault against the entire cadre of Old Bolsheviks who had led the Communist Party through the October Revolution and the Civil War. The October 1936 edition of Trotsky's *Bulletin of the Op-position*, which was entirely devoted to analysis of the August trial, ar-gued that "the heritage of the October Revolution is being liquidated." The editors noted Stalin's diplomatic efforts to build alliances with the hated bourgeois powers, police repression of workers, the Soviet state's return to Tsarist educational methods, and other arguably "counterrevolutionary" policy changes. They predicted that in order to solidify his reactionary dictatorship Stalin would have to undertake more "bloody reprisals against Bolshevism," and they foresaw that he would eventually murder not just Left oppositionists, but the former Rightist leaders Bukharin and Rykov.[4]

Mensheviks in Paris drew similar conclusions. Writers in the *Socialist Herald* had for years discussed the Old Bolsheviks' loss of power under Stalin's dictatorship. Now they began to suspect worse lay ahead for the veterans of October. On January 17, 1937, Pyotr Garvi wrote that Stalin was preparing to attack not just Kamenev and Zinoviev, but the former Rightists and a host of other "old students and co-workers of Lenin, old undergrounders, makers of October, chiefs of the Comintern. . . ."[5] The same issue of *Socialist Herald* carried a piece entitled "How the Moscow Trial was Prepared: The Letter of an Old Bolshevik," which predicted the "crucifixion" of prerevolutionary veterans of the party. In a dramatic announcement, the editors declared this "Letter" to be a direct message from an Old Bolshevik (by implication still inside the USSR) containing "fascinating news of the mood and the struggle of tendencies among Soviet higher-ups." This qualified it as a sensation, for by 1936 the personal relationships and decision-making processes of Soviet leaders were almost entirely opaque to outside observers.[6]

The "Letter" appears to be the first published source to identify Kirov as a moderate counterweight to Stalin. It claimed, for example, that Kirov had successfully opposed Stalin's desire to execute Mikhail Riutin, a former Rightist party official who in 1932 helped to author a clandestine "platform" criticizing the dictator. The "Letter" represented the Soviet leadership in 1933–1934 as split into two camps, one favoring reconciliation with former Communist oppositionists, abolition of terroristic repression, and a Western-oriented foreign policy, and the other opposed to all of these changes. According to the "Letter," Kirov and Maxim Gorky headed the first camp, Central Committee secretaries Kaganovich and Yezhov headed the other. The two groups were engaged in "*a fight for influence over Stalin,* a struggle for his soul, so to speak" (emphasis in the original). The "Letter" strongly implied that Kaganovich and Yezhov had engineered Kirov's death to ensure their own victory in this conflict. Yakov Agranov, the chief investigator in the Kirov case, had convinced Stalin, most likely at the behest of Kaganovich and Yezhov, that former Zinovievites were behind the assassination. Stalin had ultimately drawn the conclusion that the majority of the Old Bolsheviks opposed him. The "Letter" foresaw that Stalin would destroy them in retaliation.[7]

· 114 ·

"Letter of an Old Bolshevik," *Socialist Herald*, December 1936–January 1937, reprinted from Boris Nicolaevsky, *Power and the Soviet Elite*, 1965 (all emphasis in the original).

[After Hitler came to power] there gradually ensued the change in foreign policy that soon led to Russia's entry into the League of Nations, and to the creation of the "Popular Front" in France. Naturally this change did not take place without a great deal of discussion. [. . .] This was all the more difficult because it was clear that a new orientation in the direction of the democratic parties of Western Europe would inevitably lead to considerable changes in the *internal policy* of the Soviet Union. It was at this time that Kirov began to gain great influence.

Kirov played an important part in the Politburo. He was a hundred-percent supporter of the general line, and distinguished himself during its operation by great energy and inflexibility. This caused Stalin to value him highly. But there was always a certain independence in Kirov's attitude that annoyed Stalin. The story is told that Stalin had prevented Kirov from attending the meetings of the Politburo in Moscow for several months under the pretext that his presence in Leningrad was indispensable. However, Stalin could never make up his mind to take strong measures against Kirov. It would have been folly to add to the already large number of dissidents an important Party leader such as Kirov. [. . .] In the winter of 1933–1934 Kirov had so strengthened his position that he could afford to follow his own line. He aimed not only at a "Western orientation" in foreign policy, but also at the conclusions that would follow logically from this new orientation as far as domestic policy was concerned.

The task, therefore, was not only of creating a mighty army in preparation for the impending military conflict [. . .] but also, politically speaking, of creating the proper psychological frame of mind on the home front. There were two alternatives: to pursue the former policy of crushing all dissenters, with the administrative pressure ruthlessly tightened and the terror intensified, or to try "reconciliation with the people," to gain their voluntary cooperation in the political preparation of the country for the coming war. The most convinced and most prominent advocates of the *second alternative* were Kirov and Gorky. [. . .]

Kirov stood for the idea of *abolition of the terror,* both in general and

inside the Party. We do not desire to exaggerate the importance of his proposals. It must not be forgotten that when the first Five Year Plan was being put into effect, Kirov was one of the heads of the Party, that he was
among those who inspired and carried through the notoriously ruthless
measures against the peasants and the wiping out of the kulaks. The Kem
and Murmansk coasts, with their prison camps, etc., were under his jurisdiction. Furthermore, he was in charge of the construction of the Baltic–
White Sea Canal. This is enough to make it clear that Kirov could not be
accused of undue tenderness in the manner in which he disposed of human
lives. But this very fact added to his strength in the official circles in which
he had to defend his point of view. [. . .] Kirov's line of thought ran as follows: The period of destruction, which was necessary to extirpate the
small proprietor element in the villages, was now at an end; the economic
position of the collectives was consolidated. [. . .] as the economic situation continued to improve, the broad masses of the population would become more and more reconciled to the government; the number of "internal foes" would diminish. [. . .] In one of his speeches, Kirov is said to
have stated that there were now "no more irreconcilable foes of any importance." The old groups and parties had melted away during the fighting period of the first Five Year Plan and they were now no longer a factor
of consequence. [. . .]

Kirov's viewpoint /put forward even more emphatically by Gorky/
gained considerable influence among *those at the head of the party*. The
period of struggle for the Five Year Plan had been no easy one for them.
The horrors which accompanied the transformation in the villages, and of
which you have only a faint idea, beggar description. [. . .]

Hence, early in the summer of 1933, when it became certain that the
harvest would be good, Kamenev, Zinoviev, and a number of other former
members of the Opposition were once again readmitted as members of the
Party. They were even permitted to choose their spheres of work, and
some of them actually received invitations to the party congress (February
1934).

At that congress, Kirov appeared in triumph. Previously his election in
Leningrad had been celebrated as was no other. At ward conferences in
various parts of the city, all of which he toured on the same day, he had
been received with wild cheers. "Long live our Mironych," the delegates
shouted; it had been an exceedingly impressive demonstration and it
showed that the entire Leningrad proletariat was behind Kirov. At the
party congress, too, Kirov received an extraordinarily enthusiastic reception. He was cheered, the entire assembly rising to its feet on hearing his
report. During the recess there was discussion as to who had the more tu-
multuous reception, Kirov or Stalin. This very comparison shows how
strong Kirov's influence had become.

Not only was Kirov reelected to the Politburo, but he was also chosen a secretary of the Central Committee, making it necessary for him to move to Moscow within a short time to take over direction of a whole group of departments which had heretofore been under Postyshev and Kaganovich. This was to ensure putting into effect the new line that Kirov had inspired. His removal to Moscow was delayed, however. The official reason given was that his presence in Leningrad was indispensable. [. . .] In spite of this, he took part in the work of the Politburo, and his influence there continued to grow.

[. . .] The news of the new course soon spread through Party circles. Under its influence, a number of prominent members of the Opposition abandoned their implacability, including men like Rakovsky, Sosnovsky, etc. This, too, was regarded as a great success for the policy of reconciliation. Those who "repented" were immediately given permission to live in Moscow and to take up responsible work. Rakovsky was even welcomed by Kaganovich personally. Sosnovsky was able to resume his journalistic work, if not on *Pravda*, at least in *Izvestia;* and further examples could be given. Kirov's success reached its zenith at the plenary session of the Central Committee in November, 1934. This session discussed a number of concrete measures which were to be taken in accordance with the new course. Kirov presented the report on the question and was the hero of the hour. His transfer to Moscow was again discussed and it was definitely decided that it would occur very shortly. All those sections of the Party secretariat having to do with "ideology" were to be under his direction. He was to return to Leningrad for only a short time to transfer his duties to his successor. All the more shocking, therefore, was the news by telephonogram telling of his assassination. [. . .]

The "Letter" appeared to offer an inside view of the Soviet leadership in 1933–1934, which made it a very tempting source to use before the opening of Soviet archives. However, Getty has argued, it was not what it seemed to be. In 1959 the *Socialist Herald* revealed that the author of "Letter of an Old Bolshevik" was in fact Boris Nicolaevsky, a Menshevik émigré who had left the Soviet Union in 1922, brother-in-law of Aleksei Rykov, and a regular contributor to the journal. Nicolaevsky asserted that he had based the "Letter" on a series of informal conversations he had with Nikolai Bukharin in March and April of 1936 while the latter was in Amsterdam and Paris negotiating for the Soviet purchase of the German Social Democratic Party's (SPD) archive of manuscripts, which included a number by Karl Marx himself. Nicolaevsky, who had served as a volunteer administrator for the Russian section of the archive, represented the German socialists, while Bukharin and two other representatives, V. V. Adoratsky, head of Moscow's Marx-Engels-Lenin Institute, and A. Ya. Arosev, chief of the All-Union Society for Foreign Cultural Exchange, represented the Soviet side. The negotiations failed, as the Social Democrats, in exile and desperate for funds, asked more money than the Soviets were willing to pay.[8]

Nicolaevsky's claim that the "Letter" was based on discussions with Bukharin was problematic, among other reasons, because the article included commentary on events that occurred months after Bukharin left Paris, most importantly the August 1936 show trial. In 1964–1965 Nicolaevsky gave a more detailed description of the way he composed the "Letter" in *Power and the Soviet Elite,* an anthology of English translations of his writings. In an interview published as part of this book, Nicolaevsky said that in addition to Bukharin's conversations, he had relied on other sources for the "Letter," including Charles Rappoport, a Franco-Russian Communist who had been the Paris correspondent for *Izvestia* in the early 1930s. The bulk of his information on the situation inside the Soviet Union after April 1936, Nicolaevsky stated, came from Rappoport. Manuscript materials for *Power and the Soviet Elite* in Nicolaevsky's archive strengthen the impression that the "Letter" was actually based on a variety of sources, and not simply on Nicolaevsky's talks with Bukharin. In a list of recommended footnotes to the book, Nicolaevsky included a statement that his description of the Seventeenth Party Congress "as a moment when Stalin's influence weakened" was "based on the account of N. I. Bukharin, *reinforced by analysis of documents*" (emphasis added). But the editors or Nicolaevsky himself cut the italicized phrase from the footnote in the published text. This substantially altered its meaning, leaving the impression that Nicolaevsky relied on Bukharin's comments alone when writing about the congress.[9]

In his 1964 interview Nicolaevsky actually backed off from any claim that Bukharin had provided him with specific information about high-level Soviet politics. At one point he asserted that Bukharin "did not speak directly about the situation in the USSR," and at another that "Bukharin hardly mentioned Stalin's name . . . he was very restrained in his remarks to me."[10] Yet Stalin is an important presence in the "Letter," from his demand for the execution of Riutin to his supposed stonewalling of Kirov's planned move to Moscow. Nicolaevsky was apparently trying to explain such contradictions when he stated in his 1964 interview that "from certain remarks, from [Bukharin's] silences, or his questions, I could get some idea of his attitudes on various matters, even though he did not define them."[11] If this is how Nicolaevsky was "reading" Bukharin in the spring of 1936, it is difficult to imagine how he got his description of the alleged debate over Riutin's execution from the Soviet visitor. The same caveat applies to a number of other incidents covered by the "Letter," such as the secret meeting where Kamenev reportedly declared his "love" toward Stalin and the two reconciled.[12]

As the above suggests, Nicolaevsky made substantial use of his imagination when composing the "Letter." In 1964 he admitted that he had no notes on his conversations with Bukharin when he wrote it. Moreover, he made it quite clear that in writing the "Letter," he used his memories of his talks with Bukharin to convey above all a "mood," "the shade of some sort of doom" among Old Bolsheviks as a group. He wanted to transmit "the general atmosphere of [Bukharin's] stories, as they reflected the mood at the time of a specific cohort of 'Old Bolsheviks'. . . ."[13]

Overall Nicolaevsky's comments in 1964 convey the impression of a man who wanted to be honest about how he composed the "Letter" but wished at the same time to preserve the text's status as a genuine message from inside the Soviet leadership. On the one hand he admitted using multiple sources and disavowed responsibility for *Socialist Herald*'s original misrepresentation of the "Letter" as a direct missive from inside the Soviet leadership (he blamed Fyodor Dan, chief editor of *Socialist Herald,* with whom he had had a bitter political break in 1940).[14] On the other hand he spent most of the interview reminiscing about his meetings with Bukharin and how they affected his text. The tension between these conflicting desires probably accounts for the intense anxiety Nicolaevsky expressed in correspondence with editors about the precise wording of the final, published version of his interview.[15]

Archival evidence contradicts many of the factual claims made by Nicolaevsky in the "Letter" and in his 1964 interview. For example, Khlevniuk examined the paper trail on the October 1932 sentencing of Mikhail Riutin, and found no evidence of Stalin advocating the death penalty or Kirov opposing him (and indeed, it was more typical of Stalin to play the role of merciful Tsar, opposing executions while his subordinates, who understood the game perfectly well, demanded death for enemies of the revolution). After discussion of the Riutin case by plenary sessions of the Central Committee and the TsKK, Stalin and five other Politburo members confirmed a ten-year prison sentence for

Riutin. Kirov's signature was not on the sentencing document, most likely because he spent the bulk of his time in Leningrad and missed most Politburo sessions. The "Letter," which is the sole independent source to describe Kirov's alleged intervention on behalf of Riutin, indicates that discussion of the latter's sentence occurred at a meeting of the Politburo, but there is no record of any such Politburo session. And, as Khlevniuk points out, if there were some super-secret conspiratorial meeting of the Politburo, how would Bukharin or any other informant available to Nicolaevsky know about it? Bukharin did attend some Politburo sessions open to Central Committee members in 1932, but he did not attend the tighter, closed meetings. He was in political disgrace and was not close to the inner leadership circle.[16]

Central Committee archives also contradict the "Letter's" claim that Kirov was a major player in the Politburo and a leader of reform in the period 1930–1934. Based on Politburo records, Khlevniuk writes that "Kirov's initiatives were limited to the needs of Leningrad (petitions for new investments and resources, attempts to prevent the transfer of Leningrad officials, requests to open new stores, etc.). Kirov was at sessions of the Politburo in Moscow very rarely." Nor was Kirov the chief rapporteur on reform issues at the November 1934 Central Committee plenum, as the "Letter" claims. Stalin, Molotov, and Kaganovich presented the major reports to that plenum and were the most active in discussions. Khlevniuk concludes that Kirov did not participate in making high policy, was not a reformer, hewed closely to the party's "general line" as defined by Stalin, and behaved as the party chief of the Leningrad Region rather than as a leader of national stature.[17]

The "Letter" contains a garbled version of Kirov's impending transfer to Moscow in 1934. Its story is that Kirov was slated to take on a major role in planning further reforms, but that Stalin stonewalled the move. The memoirs of Leningrad finance official Mikhail Rosliakov, confirmed at points by Central Committee records, controvert this version. A Moscow assignment for Kirov, it is true, was in the works. As we have seen, however, it was Stalin himself who demanded the transfer. No doubt confused rumors of this situation reached Nicolaevsky in Paris and prompted his upside-down version of events.

Anna Larina, Nikolai Bukharin's wife in 1936, issued a sweeping challenge to the authenticity of the "Letter" in her 1989 memoirs, *Nezabyvaemoe* ("This I Cannot Forget"). Larina, who was in Paris with Bukharin for the last three weeks of his three-month visit to Western Europe (February–April 1936), argued that the "Letter" was almost entirely false and indeed that its publication was a deliberate Menshevik provocation aimed at getting Bukharin into further trouble with Stalin. She claimed that Bukharin scrupulously avoided negative comments about conditions inside the USSR in the meetings she witnessed. Bukharin was well aware that Stalin could use any indiscretion against him.[18]

There are nonetheless problems with Larina's critique of Nicolaevsky. She was only with Bukharin for the last three weeks of his trip, and much of the negotiation over the Marx archives took place earlier. It cannot be excluded that Bukharin did share with Nicolaevsky some of his views of Stalin and/or Soviet politics, perhaps before Larina's arrival in Paris. *Socialist Herald* editor Fyodor Dan's wife Lidia reported in her memoirs that Bukharin spoke in confidence to her husband about his hatred of Stalin. American newspaper correspondent William Reswick and French writer André Malraux also reported decades later that Bukharin had shared with them his distress about the political situation in the USSR. If these accounts are accurate, then it seems possible that Bukharin might have confided something to Nicolaevsky. Of course Nicolaevsky in his 1964 interview denied that Bukharin confided anything of importance to him about Stalin or the internal Soviet political situation. One plausible hypothesis is that Bukharin made certain fairly innocuous observations to Nicolaevsky, perhaps for example about Kirov's work to promote science and letters in Leningrad, which Bukharin knew well, or about Kirov's big ovation at the Seventeenth Party Congress. Nicolaevsky misunderstood and/or inflated these observations, and combined them with his imagination and other sources to produce the "Letter."[19]

The language of the "Letter of An Old Bolshevik" indicates just how uncertain many of its propositions are. Although the missive is purportedly a direct communication from a well-informed Old Bolshevik, most of it reads like a journalistic analysis of events. Only nine sentences contain a first-person pronoun. Moreover, the "Letter's" putative narrator indicates that many of his specific facts come from third persons. The sentence introducing the "Letter's" account of the Riutin affair, for example, begins, "They say" (*peredaiut*), indicating that the narrator was not witness to the debate. A substantial portion of the "Letter" is dominated by passive constructions that obscure who is relating particular parts of the narrative and which political actors took what actions. We read that Kirov "was not only reelected to the Politburo, but was chosen a secretary of the Central Committee. Ahead was his transfer to Moscow. . . ." Here it is a mystery who ordered Kirov's transfer to Moscow.

The narration also subtly qualifies key assertions as uncertain. When the "Letter" discusses Kirov's moderate "line of thought," for instance, it begins with a series of statements that could just as well have come from Stalin's mouth in 1933–1934 about the success of collectivization and the passage to an easier era following the struggle to destroy the kulaks. But it concludes with a supposed quote from Kirov that could never have come from Stalin—that there were now "no more irreconcilable foes of any importance." However, this final citation is introduced by the phrase "In one of his speeches, Kirov *is said to* have stated" (emphasis added). So the "Old Bolshevik" narrator did not hear this speech himself, and he is not telling us who reported it to him. What on first glance appears to be a direct quote from Kirov is on more careful reading revealed to be a vague rumor, at least third-hand from the reader's point of view.

Many of the problems related to the composition of the "Letter" disappear if one assumes that it was in fact a complex cut-and-paste job masquerading as a unified account of events by a single narrator. One likely source was pre-1937 reports from *Socialist Herald*'s "regular" correspondents in the USSR. Most issues of the Menshevik journal in the early to mid-1930s contained a section titled "From Russia," with reports from anonymous writers in the Soviet Union. Nicolaevsky edited this section in the 1920s, according to André Liebich, and it seems likely he continued to do so in the 1930s.[20] In its impersonal narrative voice, its frequent resort to reporting what "they say," and its speculations about relations between top Soviet leaders, "the Letter" strongly resembles letters by Moscow correspondents "A," "N," "T," and "X" published in *Socialist Herald*. Indeed, some of the "Letter's" content seems to be directly traceable to these reports. The story that Kirov was slated in 1934 for a transfer to Moscow to take over from Kaganovich as Stalin's closest adviser appeared in a report by "T" just after Kirov's murder, and the "Letter's" discussion of Yenukidze's fall seems much indebted to reports by "N" and "P" in the summer of 1935.[21]

From about 1930 onwards *Socialist Herald*'s reports "From Russia" deal in information and rumors widely available in the middle ranks of party officialdom. As far as can be determined the journal had no reliable high-placed informants during this period. Nicolaevsky's brother-in-law Rykov, the onetime Rightist leader and former chair of Sovnarkom was in political disgrace, serving in the relatively junior ministerial post of Commissar of Communications. Other suspected informants including A. Troianovsky, David Riazanov (Nicolaevsky's brother), and V. G. Groman, were very far from the centers of power by the early thirties. At least one informant, the engineer "Nikolai Petrovich," turned out to be a Soviet agent feeding the *Herald* disinformation.[22]

There are various possible explanations for the stylistic and narrative parallels between the "Letter" and the correspondence published in "From Russia." All would seem to weaken claims that Bukharin was the preeminent source for the "Letter." One explanation is that Nicolaevsky was making extensive use of excerpts from the anonymous correspondence. A second is that he was deliberately imitating the style of one or more of the anonymous correspondents when he wrote the "Letter." A third is that he himself heavily edited or even authored some of the anonymous correspondence as well as the "Letter" itself.

A great deal of the "Letter's" content was available in the Soviet press and it is fair to conclude that Nicolaevsky made extensive use of this source. For example, the its description of local Leningrad party meetings greeting Kirov with "wild cheers" of "Long live our Mironych!" in early 1934 could have and probably did come straight out of *Leningradskaya pravda* (the appellation "Our Mironych" was a staple of Kirov's personality cult both before and after his murder). Such coverage was part of the multiple personality cults established at the time around regional party leaders.[23] The author of the "Letter" then proceeds to draw exactly the conclusion party propagandists intended readers to—that "the entire Leningrad proletariat was behind Kirov." Ironically, later Western commentators often accepted the "Letter's" claims for Kirov's popularity, which probably derived directly from Soviet propaganda.

The "Letter of an Old Bolshevik," then, was based on multiple sources, probably including print media, Nicolaevsky's own imagination, Charles Rappoport, Bukharin, the anonymous letters sent from the USSR to *Socialist Herald,* and other contacts Nicolaevsky had in the European socialist world. Nicolaevsky obscured the sourcing, both to maintain the fiction of the "Letter's" authorship, and to conceal that a substantial portion of the article was his own speculation.

In André Liebich's book on the Mensheviks after 1921, Nicolaevsky emerges as a sympathetic figure, a survivor, and an assiduous researcher, but also as a conspiracy theorist and wheeler-dealer. Liebich notes that Nicolaevsky could be very cagey about his sources and that he was prone to flights of fancy about "Stalin's secret sickness" and other speculative topics. Dan, who had been Nicolaevsky's editor at *Socialist Herald* in the 1930s, later wondered, "Who are these correspondents of Nicolaevsky from whom nothing can be hidden?" and criticized his analyses for their resemblance to detective stories. Boris Souvarine, a French socialist of Russian origin, respected Nicolaevsky's scholarship but thought he had an "obsession" with the "Letter."[24]

Documents in Nicolaevsky's archive suggest that Souvarine was right. In the early 1950s Nicolaevsky was pestering his contacts from the new post–World War II wave of Soviet emigration to provide sensational information on the Kirov case. On April 15, 1951, for instance, he wrote to former Leningrad journalist V. K. Zavalishin asking him to speed up completion of his memoir about the Kirov murder. He believed that he could get Zavalishin a hundred dollars for the piece in the American "literary-journalistic world," but that "if the memoirs are interesting and to the point (*obstoiatelnye*), this sum could easily be increased."[25] Apparently in response to Nicolaevsky's prompts, Zavalishin wrote in some irritation that he could not speculate on the connections between the assassin Nikolaev and the men convicted with him in the "Leningrad Center" trial. "I have never asked myself this question. . . . How could I imagine that I would end up abroad and would meet people who took an interest in what I'm now writing?" Zavalishin's manuscript was never published.[26]

It is time to move beyond reflexive defenses of Nicolaevsky's honor and recognize that author of the "Letter of An Old Bolshevik" had a broad streak of the trickster, the con-man, and even the double agent in him.[27] Recently declassified documents from Nikolai Yezhov's archive on the Soviets' 1935–1936 negotiations for the sale of the SPD's Marx archive do not show Nicolaevsky in a flattering light.

Prior to Bukharin's spring 1936 visit to Paris there was at least a half-year of preliminary discussion of the sale between Nicolaevsky, the Social Democrats, the French socialist author and Soviet sympathizer Romain Rolland, and the French government. The archive had originally been part of the Social Democratic Party's central library in Berlin. When Hitler took power in 1933, Nicolaevsky worked with French socialists to arrange the French government's purchase of parts of the library and their transport to Paris. The Marx archive and other documents were smuggled out of Berlin together with the library volumes. In Paris, the French authorities refused to store the smuggled archival materials, which they had not purchased. Nicolaevsky began to seek a home for them. He also sought a permanent post for himself as curator of the archive.[28]

In August 1935 Soviet agents contacted Nicolaevsky to discuss purchase of the Marx archive.[29] During September A. Arosev and a second Soviet representative, Tikhomirov, engaged in talks about the archive at the apartment of Romain Rolland. Although the archive legally still belonged to the SPD, Rolland and Nicolaevsky each behaved at times as if it belonged to them personally. Rolland wanted a commission on the deal of between 15 and 20 percent (Nicolaevsky initially proposed a sale price of five million francs, or more than $2.5 million in 2006 dollars). During these initial negotiations, the Soviets paid for Nicolaevsky's purchase of documents for his own library and for his trip to Prague to talk with representatives of the Social Democratic Party. Nicolaevsky also provided the Soviets with intelligence about a secret split threatening the unity of the Social Democrats. According to the Soviet representatives' report to Yezhov, Nicolaevsky represented himself as allied with the left-leaning "opposition" inside the party. This faction, Nicolaevsky suggested, was willing to sell the Marx archive out from under the noses of the SPD Central Committee. The Soviets apparently tempted Nicolaevsky with an offer of a job at the Marx-Engels Institute in the USSR.[30]

The SPD leaders in Prague, whom Nicolaevsky visited late that September, were reluctant to make a deal. In response to the SPD Central Committee's position, Nicolaevsky began to plot the theft of the archive. In a scenario he discussed with the Soviets, he would transfer the documents to Rolland's apartment, from whence they could be spirited away to the USSR. The Soviets would presumably have paid both Nicolaevsky and Rolland for their services. In a September 25, 1935 report to Yezhov and Adoratsky, Arosev wrote that "Nicolaevsky is in this question entirely on our side," and that as soon as the archival materials were at Rolland's apartment "he will give them to us legally or illegally." "For this," Arosev concluded, "we need to negotiate with him and make a deal." To his credit, Nicolaevsky also apparently brought up the release or better treatment of Soviet political prisoners as part of the "deal."[31]

Nicolaevsky and Rolland did not go through with their scheme, although it is unclear why. By December 1935 the SPD Central Committee had voted against any sale to the Soviets, but one SPD leader, Friedrich Adler, was still proposing to "internationalize" the archive under the aegis of the Labor and Socialist International and sell it to the Soviets for 25 million rubles. When the Soviets threatened to break off negotiations, Nicolaevsky became frantic. Based on a letter sent by Tikhomirov to Arosev, and forwarded to Stalin, it appears that he and Rolland once again offered to sell the archive on their own hook for a lower price. Arosev told them that since he expected the purchase money to end up in the hands of the Soviets' enemies, the Mensheviks, he did not want to buy. Nicolaevsky then began calling Arosev several times a day, requesting a meeting. He swore that the purchase funds would not go to *Socialist Herald,* but to the establishment of an "Institute for the Study of Marx" outside Paris, headed by the Left Social Democrat Hilferding, with himself (Nicolaevsky) as "scholar-in-residence" (*uchenyi sekretar'*).[32]

In the end the negotiations for the sale of the Marx archive foundered, probably due more to the beginning of the Terror than to differences over price.[33] Nicolaevsky was forced to move to New York by the Nazi victory over France, and his archive eventually followed him. Following World War II, he remade himself as an American cold warrior, participating for example in the Congress for Cultural Freedom, an organization of European intellectuals partially funded by the CIA. He remained a moderate democratic socialist to the end, a fact that the editors of *Power and the Soviet Elite,* concealed, presumably to make his work more palatable to conservative American audiences.[34]

It is clear that the "Letter" is not a credible source on the Soviet leadership in general or Kirov in particular. It is true that outside sources confirm certain of the "Letter's" assertions, such as the claim that Kirov's assassin Nikolaev was inspired by the example of Russian People's Will terrorist Zheliabov. However, many of these facts were openly reported by the Soviet press. Other claims are belied by evidence from Central Committee archives, Leningrad archives, and memoirs like Rosliakov's. The "Letter of an Old Bolshevik" requires a subtitle, perhaps "An Improvisation Inspired by Meetings with Nikolai Bukharin," or simply "A Speculation on Soviet Politics."

The direct suggestion that Stalin himself might have ordered Kirov's murder first appeared in print in 1939, in the aftermath of the final great Moscow show trial which resulted in the execution of Bukharin,

Rykov, and Yagoda, as well as many other defendants. The two authors who introduced the idea, Greek journalist G. N. Grammatikopoulos and Soviet NKVD defector Walter Krivitsky, were both concerned to rebut the official Soviet narrative of the crime put forth at the March 1938 trial. According to the Stalinist version Kirov had been killed by a conspiratorial "Right-Trotskyite Bloc" determined to overthrow the Soviet state and restore capitalism. Prosecutors claimed that Avel Yenukidze, as head of the Kremlin guard, had ordered the second-in-command of the Leningrad NKVD Zaporozhets to arrange Kirov's execution. Former Rightist leaders Bukharin and Rykov, former NKVD commissar Yagoda, and many others were also supposed to have been in on the plot.[35]

In the first two issues of the *Socialist Herald* from 1939 Grammatikopoulos, who had witnessed two of the three major Moscow trials, rebutted the Stalinist script. Grammatikopoulos focused on the problem of confession by the accused, but he also speculated that Kirov's murder might have been "a direct provocation" rather than a plot by Stalin's enemies. In other words, Stalin or his close associates might have been the true perpetrators. He also asserted that "Kirov in the last years of his life had gradually moved to de facto opposition to Stalin and had become the center of developing democratic and reformist tendencies inside the Central Committee." This last he may have picked up from Nicolaevsky's "Letter," but there is no way to be certain.[36]

Soviet secret police defector Walter Krivitsky made a more explicit suggestion that Stalin had killed Kirov in June 1939 in the *Saturday Evening Post*. Krivitsky, who had served as an officer in Soviet military intelligence and an underground NKVD agent in Holland, reiterated the claim that Kirov had been a moderate and implied strongly that Stalin could have been involved in his murder. ("Besides Stalin, there are probably no more than three or four people alive who could solve the Kirov mystery.") He also claimed that Stalin had learned much from Nazi dictator Adolf Hitler's 1934 purge of the SA. The Stalin-Hitler comparison and the notion that the two dictators were influencing each other was also a commonplace observation in the *Socialist Herald* during this period.[37]

Krivitsky's piece, "Why Did They Confess?" appears to be an amalgam of sections of Nicolaevsky's "Letter," the official transcript of the Bukharin show trial, and word of mouth from other NKVD officers. It repeats the "Kirov as moderate" story from the "Letter" using very similar language and presentation. There can be little doubt that this section of "Why Did They Confess?" is based on the "Letter." To cite just two similarities between the documents, both refer to Lenin's warning against applying the death penalty to party members and to the Jacobin precedent for the Stalinist Terror.[38]

Krivitsky's article also referred directly to the transcript of the March 1938 show trial of Bukharin et al. According to this transcript, the Nikolaev had been detained by Leningrad NKVD officers once before the crime (he was supposedly trailing Kirov) and relieved of a pistol and a diary, both of which were returned to him at the order of Leningrad NKVD second-in-command Zaporozhets. This story was part of the larger narrative inculpating Yagoda in Kirov's murder. Krivitsky used the incident of Nikolaev's detention to heighten the aura of mystery he was building around the case. He ignored the absurdity of presenting testimony from one of Stalin's kangaroo courts as established fact.[39]

In his *Saturday Evening Post* piece Krivitsky did not indicate any source for his speculation that Stalin might have engineered Kirov's death. It may have come from rumors inside the Soviet NKVD, or from conversations in Menshevik circles in Paris, or it may have been his own idea. He did quote Abram Slutsky, director of the NKVD's foreign espionage department, to the effect that "this case is so shady . . . that it is best not to pry into it."[40] But Slutsky's quote is hardly evidence of Stalin's complicity in the killing itself. It could just as easily be referring to the dictator's fabrication of a case against the Zinovievites during the subsequent investigation.[41]

We cannot know where Krivitsky got the idea that Stalin might have organized the murder—but we can estimate why he published it in the *Saturday Evening Post*. The *Post* pieces repeated much of the content from a series of articles Krivitsky wrote for the *Socialist Herald* immediately after his defection, which ran in the first months of 1938. However, the *Socialist Herald* series did not even imply the possibility that Stalin had ordered Kirov's murder, indicating instead that Krivitsky and his NKVD colleagues suspected Leningrad NKVD chief Filip Medved of organizing the crime. Nor did Krivitsky's essays in the *Socialist Herald* mention the Riutin case or Kirov's alleged "moderation." In other words, between early 1938 and June 1939 Krivitsky added to his account of the Kirov murder interpolations closely paralleling Nicolaevsky's "Letter." He also added speculation that Stalin might have ordered Kirov's execution.[42]

Between March 1938 and June 1939 Krivitsky had moved from France to the United States and found a literary collaborator and agent, Isaac Don Levine. Levine was an author and freelance journalist who had done much work for the Hearst newspaper chain. A pre-revolutionary immigrant from Kiev, Levine began his journalistic career during World War I, writing analyses of the Imperial Russian war effort and later the Russian Revolution. During the Civil War and NEP years he traveled in Russia. Levine was an avid reader of the Soviet and émigré Russian presses. His remarkable, if somewhat purple, 1931 biography of Stalin shows deep knowledge of the Soviet Union. By the time he published this biography Levine was an intense, committed anti-Communist with a special interest in exposing Stalin and the terrorist methods of his secret police. This was both his life mission and his bread and butter. As a sometime writer for the Hearst papers Levine would have understood well the value of a sensation in selling a story to the mass circulation American press.[43]

In his autobiography Levine writes that he had been following Krivitsky's case long before the defector arrived in the United States. Krivitsky, Levine claims, had run out of money and "was seeking major outlets and a wide reading public for the publication of his rich experiences in the Soviet underworld." The two men conferred together for a week, after which Levine pitched a series of articles by Krivitsky to one of his contacts at the *Saturday Evening Post*. Once Krivitsky had a contract, Levine served as his ghostwriter. It is likely that Levine encouraged Krivitsky to include in his articles at least a hint that Stalin had ordered Kirov's murder, as a means of making them more attractive to editors.[44]

According to a story put to paper by Lidia Dan, based on conversations with Menshevik émigré David Shub, Krivitsky was very unhappy when he saw the final proofs for the *Saturday Evening Post* article. He called Shub, who had originally referred him to Levine, and told him that Levine had inserted words and stories of his own into the original text. Krivitsky was also upset that the *Saturday Evening Post* referred to him as a general, which was inaccurate. At the moment he spoke to Shub, Krivitsky was ready to rip up the contract with the *Post*. "I cannot put my signature under such a text," he reportedly said.[45] Levine would later betray secrets Krivitsky told him in confidence to British intelligence.[46]

Levine, whose 1931 biography presents Stalin as a cold-blooded dictator with a virtuous private life, became in later years a collector of tales about Stalin's personal depravity, most of them now discredited.

In a 1956 book, *Stalin's Great Secret,* Levine publicized a document, later proved a forgery, which supposedly showed the young Stalin acting as an informer for the Tsarist police. In the same book Levine asserted that Stalin had poisoned Lenin and shot his own wife, Nadezhda Allilueva (most scholars now consider that Allilueva was a suicide). For Levine the direct execution, starvation, and torture of millions were perhaps not dramatic or monstrous enough. Personal murderousness and dissoluteness made Stalin's evil more real for the reader.[47]

With Krivitsky's *Saturday Evening Post* series the Kirov murder intersected with American domestic politics, and specifically with accusations that Soviet spies had penetrated the Roosevelt administration. At the time he met with Krivitsky, Levine was also negotiating with former Communist Whittaker Chambers, trying to convince him to reveal the names of administration officials he had worked with when he was a courier for Soviet intelligence officers in the United States. Years later Levine's anti-Communist journal *Plain Talk* would break the story of Chambers' accusations of espionage against State Department officials, among them Alger Hiss.[48] (The accusations against several of the officials Chambers accused have since been substantiated, and Hiss, too, in all probability passed classified information to the Soviets.)[49] Kirov's assassination, in other words, was now in play in a highly charged field of American politics. It became part of a sensationalization of the Communist threat that went beyond Levine's dubious "inside" stories to John F. Kennedy's 1960 presidential campaign claim that the United States was behind in the deployment of nuclear-capable missiles.

To illustrate the ambiguities of Levine's role in the anti-Communist struggle, it is worth looking at the contents of his magazine, *Plain Talk.* In the late 1940s Levine ran articles supporting a preemptive attack on the Soviet Union, a letter from *Gone with the Wind* author Margaret Mitchell denouncing the "Communist Negro" slant of the "Negro press and public," and cartoons lampooning "Professor Pinko." One contributor opined that "If a liberal gets himself tagged a 'Communist,' the chances are he deserves it." The Stalinist logic of the last quotation was impeccable, although Levine presumably did not understand the irony. Much of *Plain Talk* partook of what Whittaker Chambers himself referred to as the "crackpotism" of sections of the American Right.[50]

In 1945 Alexander Barmine, a Soviet diplomat who defected from his post in Greece during the Terror, published *One Who Survived.* In it he repeated the "Letter of an Old Bolshevik's" account of Kirov's "moderation" as well as the Yagoda-Zaporozhets-Nikolaev version of the conspiracy bruited at the 1938 Moscow show trial. As J. Arch Getty has pointed out, an earlier (1939) version of Barmine's memoirs did not argue for Stalin's involvement in the murder. Nor did it allude to Kirov's moderation or any other elements of the "Letter's" story. Barmine's case resembles Krivitsky's in that he was not at the scene of the murder in Leningrad, and seems to have inserted elements from the "Letter" and the show trial transcripts in the later version of his memoirs. He could have borrowed these elements directly, or indirectly through Krivitsky's *Saturday Evening Post* series.[51]

The case of Alexander Orlov, an NKVD defector, also resembles that of Krivitsky. Orlov defected while on duty in Spain during the Spanish Civil War and he brought with him to the United States about sixty thousand dollars in cash (probably stolen from NKVD coffers). When his savings began to run out in 1952 Orlov went to work on a memoir which came to be titled *The Secret History of Stalin's Crimes*, and which opened with a description of Stalin's supposed plot to kill Kirov. Like Krivitsky, Orlov needed to sell his work quickly. According to a 1993 biography based in part on KGB archives Orlov spent much time researching Soviet history at the White Memorial Library in Cleveland before writing his book. The section of *The Secret History* dealing with the Kirov assassination includes the Yagoda-Zaporozhets-Nikolaev conspiracy story from the 1938 show trial and an account of Kirov's "moderation." Orlov was in London at the time of the assassination and did not return to the Soviet Union until October 1935, ten months afterwards. In his book Orlov did not hide the fact that what he heard about the killing in 1935 from police colleagues was third- or fourth-hand. It is safe to assume that his account of Kirov's murder derived in part from his library reading and in part from what Getty has called "corridor gossip . . . among some of his NKVD friends."[52]

Orlov's account of Stalin's plot to murder Kirov is wildly inaccurate. He claims that Kirov had a major conflict with Ordzhonikidze (in reality his closest friend in the Soviet leadership) in 1934. He describes with fair accuracy Yagoda's 1931 attempt to replace Medved in Leningrad with Yevdokimov, but misdates the incident to 1934. He asserts that Nikolaev was stopped at the entrance to Smolny once before the assassination, and guards found a pistol and diary in his briefcase. Orlov also exaggerates the security measures at Smolny, claiming that

Nikolaev would not have been able to enter without inside help from Zaporozhets. There are numerous other factual errors.[53]

There are other reasons for skepticism about Orlov's account. His recent biographers, John Costello and Oleg Tsarev, show that the defector had contact with a Soviet KGB officer as late as 1971. Orlov concealed much of his own biography from CIA and FBI interviewers, including his role in organizing the execution of Trotskyites during the Spanish Civil War. At a time when Soviet archives were closed, the Soviet press muzzled, and the Soviet leadership closeted it was perhaps reasonable to use Orlov as a source on Bolshevik high politics. But it is no longer.

The early years of the Cold War saw the publication of numerous sensationalist exposés of Stalin's crimes, including Levine's *Stalin's Great Secret* and Orlov's *Secret History*. These works promiscuously mixed fact, surmise, and rumors. Elizabeth Lermolo's memoir *Face of a Victim* (1955), which also implicated Stalin directly in Kirov's murder, was the most extreme example of the genre.

Lermolo claimed to be the daughter of a Russian landholding family who was imprisoned on charges of conspiring to kill Kirov. Like Orlov and earlier memoirists she centered her work around Kirov's assassination. Lermolo's book reads like a soap opera and is full of factual errors and bizarre stories. The text presents itself as a compendium of events witnessed and stories heard by the author while in prison. To cite just a very few of the factual errors, Lermolo claims that Nikolaev led the 1926 purge of the Leningrad party apparatus with Kirov and Chudov; that Aleksandr Slepkov, a member of Nikolai Bukharin's "school" of young party intellectuals, was invited by Sergei Kirov to work in Leningrad in 1929; that the pistol with which Nikolaev shot Kirov was stolen from the head of the Society of Former Political Prisoners; and that NKVD deputy-in-chief Zaporozhets was executed on Stalin's orders immediately after Nikolaev's interrogation in early December 1934.[54] Zaporozhets shows up in Lermolo's tales with obsessive regularity—now taking Nikolaev personally under his wing, now checking entrance passes into Smolny on December 1, and then murdering Borisov in his car on December 2.[55]

Then there are Lermolo's more tabloidish stories, as when she states that Aleksandr Slepkov had a love child with a forty-nine-year-old veteran Bolshevik named Zinaida Gaiderovo. The baby died during birth and Slepkov, preoccupied with building socialism, kept the corpse in a shoebox on his desk until it began to stink. Lermolo also claims that she witnessed a fistfight between Zinoviev and one of his denouncers in a Cheliabinsk prison; that she was in the same transport car with Zinoviev and Kamenev and overheard them joking about the charges against them; that Anna Pantiukhina, Nikolaev's sister, was the illegitimate daughter of a Finnish baron; that his other sister Katya was a nymphomaniac; and that Stalin beat, choked, and shot his wife Nadezhda to death after a quarrel about an affair the dictator was having with Lazar Kaganovich's daughter Roza. Lermolo also gives the improbable figure of 500,000 arrests in Leningrad following the Kirov assassination (approximately one-fifth of the city's population).[56]

Another remarkable feature of Lermolo's book is the number of personal encounters she supposedly had in prison with leaders and former leaders of the Communist Party, and with eyewitnesses to crimes. Not only did she meet Zinoviev and Kamenev, but also former leader of the Workers' Opposition Aleksandr Shliapnikov, Yezhov, Yagoda, Stalin's secretary Poskrebyshev, and of course, Stalin, who supposedly interrogated her on the night of December 2–3, 1934. In addition she spoke to eyewitnesses to Lenin's poisoning, Nadezhda Allilueva's murder, and Kirov's killing. Another jail acquaintance had a niece who attempted to assassinate Stalin. She also met Avel Yenukidze, who personally explained to her how Stalin planned Kirov's murder, utilizing Yagoda, Zaporozhets, and Nikolaev to get the job done.[57]

"Elizabeth Lermolo" was a pseudonym, and historians who used her evidence during the Cold War did not speculate about her identity.[58] After the collapse of the Soviet Union, however, Amy Knight (1999) and Bastrykin and Gromtseva (2001) identified her as Elizaveta Fyodorovna Yermolaeva (sometimes spelled Yermolova), one of the accused in the "Leningrad Counterrevolutionary Zinovievite Group of Safarov, Zalutsky, and Others," the seventy-seven supposed accessories to the Kirov assassination tried by the NKVD Special Board in January 1935. Knight's identification was tentative, but Bastrykin and Gromtseva went so far as to call her "Princess Ermolova," without providing an accurate citation for their claim.[59]

Internal evidence in *Face of a Victim* suggests that the author had inside knowledge of the Leningrad and central NKVD unavailable in any open sources. She describes being interrogated by an officer by the name of Malinin, which matches the name of a Leningrad NKVD officer referred to by Volkova and in other official documents.[60] She also mentions meeting an Officer "Katsapha," who would appear to be the Katsafa who guarded Nikolaev early in the investigation.[61] Lermolo's descriptions of NKVD interrogation techniques (being forced to stand in one place for hours at a time, for example) and obsessions (officers frequently sought to implicate her or her acquaintances in spreading rumors about Nadezhda Allilueva's death) sometimes ring true.

Lermolo also seems to know a few accurate details about Nikolaev and his family which were not available in open Soviet sources and which suggest that she either met them personally or heard rumors about them in or around Leningrad. She refers to Nikolaev as crippled, although she does not get the nature of his physical problem right—she calls him club-footed. She writes that he had unnaturally long arms, which fits the description in his 1926 medical exam report. She is aware that Nikolaev's mother worked in a "tram barn." She knows that Nikolaev sought a pass to a sanatorium and was refused. Generally her information on Nikolaev's living situation in Leningrad—he and Milda had two children and Milda's mother in their apartment—is accurate. At the same time, much of what she reports about the family is nonsense—Draule never worked as a stenographer for Kirov, for example, and Nikolaev did not work under Chudov in Pskov for six years either.[62]

Lermolo claims to have met Nikolaev before the murder, and to have been imprisoned with his two sisters, Yekaterina Rogacheva and Anna Pantiukhina, his mother, and Milda Draule.[63] Rogacheva, Pantiukhina, and Nikolaev's mother Maria Tikhonovna were all sentenced as part of the "Leningrad Counterrevolutionary Zinovievite Group." Lermolo also asserts that she met three other people sentenced as part of the same group, Zinaida Gaiderova, Ye. K. Korshunov (whom Volkova attempted to incriminate—see above, p. 434), and Anna Yuskina (wife of the Yuskin executed with Nikolaev) while incarcerated. These assertions would seem to strengthen her identification as E. F. Yermolaeva, who was also sentenced with the "Leningrad Counterrevolutionary Zinovievite Group."[64]

If Lermolo was Yermolaeva/Yermolova (and I want to stress that this is a big "if"), then it appears that she was telling some whoppers in *Face of a Victim*. Yermolaeva comes up in available documents from the "Leningrad Center" case four times—in pretrial interrogations of Nikolaev and Yuskin, and in trial testimony by the same men. On December 14, 1934, one day after Nikolaev began to cooperate fully with the NKVD, Agranov or one of his aides asked him "Who helped you to prepare an assassination attempt on Stalin?" Nikolaev answered that "Yermolaeva" had, and identified her as a Communist Party member and third-year student at the Leningrad Industrial Academy. He then proceeded to weave a tale about how, after getting orders from Kotolynov and Shatsky to prepare the assassination of Stalin, he began to look for qualified accomplices. Yuskin gave him Yermolaeva's name. Nikolaev then had a telephone conversation with her in which he ascertained that she had "an antiparty mood." Apparently during the same phone call Nikolaev asked her for "material support." By Nikolaev's own account, Yermolaeva replied by asking how he had gotten her telephone number. He told her Yuskin had given it to him, and the call ended there.[65]

On December 18 the NKVD interrogated Yuskin about Yermolaeva. During this interrogation he admitted that he knew of Nikolaev's plot to kill Kirov (at trial he would recant, insisting that he thought Nikolaev was joking—see above, p. 361). He claimed to have known Yermolaeva for two years, and he labeled her "alien to the party." She was always spreading "anti-Soviet anecdotes and rumors," he said, and they were all "secret." Yuskin believed that she had "big connections" with senior officials in Smolny. Judging by the phone conversation he overheard when Nikolaev called Yermolaeva from his (Yuskin's) apartment, the two were "close." Yuskin disavowed any knowledge of whether Yermolaeva knew about the assassination plot beforehand.[66]

Nikolaev's and Yuskin's account of the former's phone conversation with Yermolaeva conflicted sharply. Nikolaev claimed Yuskin had advised him to call Yermolaeva whom he didn't know and who was unresponsive. Yuskin claimed that it sounded as if Nikolaev and Yermolaeva knew each other well.

A different picture of events emerged at the trial. Nikolaev, testifying against Yuskin, stated that the latter had "approved" of his terrorist plot, and suggested that he link up with Yermolaeva, a student at the Industrial Academy. Yuskin, Nikolaev stated, had told him that she had "big connections in Moscow," knew a lot about Kirov, and could help him out. Yuskin had then contacted Yermolaeva for him. This account, like Nikolaev's December 14 interrogation record, was obviously distorted and meant to inculpate Yuskin.[67]

Ulrikh, chairman of the Military Tribunal, turned to Yuskin, who was on the witness stand, and asked, "What do you say to this?" Judging from the trial transcript, Yuskin was surprised by Nikolaev's story. "I'm having difficulty answering . . . ," he began. He then told a somewhat disjointed, but basically coherent story. When Nikolaev first began visiting Yuskin's apartment to use the telephone, they had casual conversations. Yuskin inquired after Milda's health, and so on. But in one of these conversations, Yuskin said, Nikolaev had told him "gossip" about Yermolaeva. Nikolaev had come in to use the phone, and asked Yuskin, "Do you have a Yermolaeva?" referring to the Industrial Academy party organization of which Yuskin was a committee member. Yuskin answered, "Yes," there was a Yermolaeva in the Industrial Academy party group. Nikolaev then claimed that he'd known her since 1922. (Elizabeth Lermolo, in *Face of a Victim,* writes that she was arrested because her phone number was in the pocket address book Nikolaev was carrying on December 1.) "How did she act at the purge?" Nikolaev asked. Yuskin replied that she was "sick" and acted strangely. Nikolaev came back with, "That's not strange. She's from the priesthood [presumably her father was a priest] and practices palm-reading." Yuskin, who as a member of the committee apparently felt responsible for checking on charges that "anti-Soviet elements" had snuck into the party, asked Nikolaev for a written statement, which he refused to give. Yuskin apparently later sought to meet Nikolaev and try again to persuade him to write a formal denunciation of Yermolaeva.[68]

Disallowing Nikolaev's hopelessly unreliable testimony, the following picture of events seems to emerge. Yuskin, as a member of the party committee at the Industrial Academy, had known Yermolaeva for about two years. By his account she was a Communist, but liked gossip and sometimes made "anti-Soviet" comments. One day in October (see above, p. 294) Nikolaev showed up to use the telephone and brought up Yermolaeva, said he'd known her for twelve years, and characterized her as "class-alien" (origins in the priesthood). He and Yuskin both agreed that she was a strange character. Yuskin asked Nikolaev for a written statement so that he could pursue an investigation of Yermolaeva through formal party channels. Nikolaev never wrote the statement. It appears, however (based on Yuskin's December 18 interrogation), that Yuskin later prevailed upon Nikolaev to call Yermolaeva on his telephone, perhaps hoping to entrap her, or arrange a meeting with her. Yuskin concluded from the part of the conversation he overheard that Nikolaev and Yermolaeva knew each other fairly well.

The simplest interpretation of what went on is that Nikolaev swapped some nasty gossip with Yuskin about an old acquaintance, and Yuskin, fulfilling his party duty of vigilance, pressed Nikolaev to follow up. But Yermolaeva needs a closer look. If one is looking for a provocateur (NKVD or otherwise) who could have influenced Nikolaev, she is the strongest candidate of anyone who appears in archival records. According to Yuskin, Nikolaev had long conversations with her and claimed to know her well. She engaged in "anti-Soviet" conversations, enjoyed gossip, and bragged (as many informers, including Volkova, did) about her "connections." Her "alien class background" made her vulnerable to NKVD pressure, and hence, to NKVD recruitment. The NKVD was careful to keep her out of any public documents on Nikolaev's trial.

If one assumes further (and again, this may well be a false assumption), that Lermolo and Yermolaeva were the same person, then the possibility that this person was an NKVD informer or provocateur increases. Lermolo knew the name of Officer Malinin, who was Volkova's contact officer at the Smolny Ward office of the NKVD until the summer of 1934. She knew something of Nikolaev's family. Her fantastic stories and gossip recall Volkova's fantasies, and suggest that she could be easily manipulated to generate imaginative denunciations.

Tantalizingly, Lermolo in her memoir describes meeting Yuskin's wife ("Madame Yuskina") in jail soon after the arrest. Yuskina told her how Nikolaev used to come to their apartment to use the telephone.[69] Published Soviet sources indicate that Yuskina was sentenced together with Yermolaeva as a member of the "Leningrad Counterrevolutionary Zinovievite Group."[70]

If Elizabeth Lermolo was Elizaveta Fyodorovna Yermolaeva, then she misrepresented drastically both herself and the facts of her acquaintance with Nikolaev. Elizabeth Lermolo in *Face of a Victim* was a young non-party woman in exile in the town of Pudozh, in Karelia not far from Petrozavodsk, because her former husband had once been an officer in the Tsarist army. She claimed to have met Nikolaev there in the summer of 1934, while he was visiting his aunt who lived in the same cooperative apartment with her (there is no record of Nikolaev visiting Pudozh, although the possibility cannot be excluded).[71] Elizaveta Fyodorovna Yermolaeva was a Communist student at the Leningrad Industrial Academy, who had apparently been acquainted with Nikolaev for some years. Unlike Lermolo, who claimed to have been entirely "apolitical" in 1934, Yermolaeva had a reputation (perhaps undeserved) for "anti-Soviet" comments and being well-connected with party officials.

My conclusion is that the author of *Face of a Victim* was probably Yermolaeva, or some other person arrested by the NKVD in Leningrad in the first days after Kirov's murder. If she was Yermolaeva, she chose to conceal her onetime membership in the party to appear in the best light before Western audiences (including government debriefers). Whoever he or she was, the author gained some reliable information on Nikolaev and his family through repeated interrogations and/or access to written records of their testimony. Lermolo claimed that in the course of multiple interrogations in December 1934–January 1935 she learned many details of the supposed cases against Nikolaev and many others.[72] This might account for some of the accurate, unpublished details on the assassin and his family. If Lermolo was Yermolaeva, then she apparently did know Nikolaev, and she may have spent time in confinement with female members of Nikolaev's family as well as Yuskin's wife. It is also possible that she was an NKVD informer or provocateur in touch with Nikolaev before the murder.

Another possibility that cannot be excluded is that Lermolo was in 1934 a Leningrad NKVD employee or the wife of an officer or party official who had access to written records of the case or who heard extensive discussion of it. Whatever the case, the author of *Face of Victim* was a wild confabulator, conscious or unconscious. The book is wholly unreliable as a historical source.

By the mid-1950s, educated opinion in the West was that Stalin had been a mass murderer running a system that relied heavily on state terror. In this sense the history was clear (there was more debate about Lenin's legacy). But with regard to the more detailed political history of Stalin and Kirov confusion was compounding confusion. Bereft of reliable sources inside the USSR, commentators relied upon speculations and rumors in the writings of Krivitsky, Orlov, Barmine, Nicolaevsky, and Lermolo, who were often simply citing one another (frequently enough without acknowledgment). De-Stalinizers in the Soviet Union, for their own reasons, were about to add to the confusion.

CHAPTER 14

The Politics of Rehabilitation and the Kirov Murder, 1953–1957

Joseph Stalin's death on March 5, 1953 began a succession struggle among his collaborators in the party leadership. Continuing practices established by Stalin himself, Lavrenty Beria, Nikita Khrushchev, Georgy Malenkov, and their respective allies scrambled to gather compromising information on one another and pose as reformers. Discrediting one another was not difficult, as all of the rivals were directly implicated in the mass violence wrought by the Stalinist regime. Khrushchev, the victor in the succession battles, proved the master of mobilizing archival documents and party memory against his competitors, but Beria, the first loser, employed the same tactics. It was Beria who, just days after the dictator's death, began the process of reexamining Stalin-era legal cases and rehabilitating many of those convicted. Simultaneously, he accumulated in his safe materials incriminating other party leaders. After the other Central Committee Presidium members managed to arrest Beria on June 26, 1953, they portrayed him as the mastermind of state terror and a foreign spy. In the next four years Khrushchev, who emerged on top in the months following Beria's arrest, took on the mantle of white knight, defeating his rivals Malenkov, Molotov, and Kaganovich in part by using the KGB to expose their participation in Stalin's terror. Thus, ironically, the succession conflict between Stalin's henchmen led step by step toward exposure of the atrocities they and their dead leader had committed.

There were also motives beyond the seizure of power involved in the drama of de-Stalinization. Khrushchev and many of his allies genuinely did want to end mass terror and improve life for ordinary Soviet subjects. Self-interest strengthened moral qualms about mass repression. Party leaders and lower-level apparatchiks had an obvious interest in changing the Stalin-era rules of political struggle, in which the penalty for defeat was often arrest or death. Stalin had operated a de facto hostage system, imprisoning or exiling close relatives and political associates of his lieutenants on the usual trumped-up charges of espionage. Among these were Molotov's wife, Anastas Mikoyan's sons, Khrushchev's daughter-in-law, and Beria's political protégés from Mingrelia, accused of "bourgeois nationalism." In the first two months following Stalin's death, Beria freed all of these hostages with the approval of the other members of the Central Committee Presidium.[1]

The process of rehabilitation of "repressed" (arrested, exiled, or executed) persons, begun by Beria and expanded by Khrushchev and his allies, was a complex struggle in which political power and the creation of some kind of coherent party history of the Stalin years were tightly bound together. It was confined almost entirely to party and professional elites, with the *narod,* the common people, excluded. Participants in the struggle had sundry motivations. Communist survivors of prisons and labor camps sought to drive a stake through the heart of Stalinism by revealing the dead dictator's crimes. Molotov, Malenkov, and Kaganovich, who because of their higher-level posts in the 1930s and longer history with Stalin arguably were more culpable than Khrushchev for the Great Terror of 1937–1938, sought to evade responsibility. Khrushchev aimed to secure his own position as party leader by exposing them. Other players, mainly associated with Khrushchev, worked to create a useable, heroic party history that would nonetheless acknowledge Stalinist terror. This history would legitimate the rule of a reformed Communist Party. Yet others, such as Dmitry Shepilov in June 1957 and Mikhail Suslov in June 1956, wished to put the brakes on public reevaluation of the Stalin years because they believed such discussion undermined the foundations of Communist rule. At the same time they did not advocate a return to full-blown Stalinist repression.

Feuds, friendships, and factional resentments going all the way back to the days of the revolution shaped the battle over de-Stalinization. Anastas Mikoyan quietly encouraged surviving comrades from the Bolshevik Revolution in Baku to research and publicize the Great Terror. Veterans of the Leningrad party leadership who survived Stalin's purge of the city organization in the notorious "Leningrad Affair" of 1949–1950 proved eager to attack Malenkov for his role in organizing those repressions. Ivan Serov, who ran the KGB for Khrushchev from

1954 to 1958, had worked together with his boss in the Ukraine in 1939–1941. There are many more examples.

Thus, the usual distinctions between reformers and Stalinists, or "liberals" and "conservatives," which still tend to dominate discussion of the Khrushchev years, do not capture the complexity of the political battles around the rehabilitation of Stalin's victims. The history of the Khrushchev-era commissions that reexamined Sergei Kirov's assassination, and ultimately tried to create a new narrative of Soviet history, must be understood in this context—of desperate struggles for power and an equally desperate desire to escape from the Stalinist nightmare and return to the revolutionary dreams of 1917.

Between 1956 and 1967 the Presidium/Politburo of the party Central Committee created five different commissions to study the show trials of 1936–1938 and the annihilation of party cadres in the same period. The first commission, headed by former *Pravda* editor and TsK secretary for ideology Pyotr Pospelov, was appointed on December 31, 1955: the second, created in April 1956, was chaired by Stalin's former deputy Molotov; the third, established sometime in 1960, was chaired by second-level party veteran N. M. Shvernik; the fourth, established in May 1961, was also chaired by Shvernik. A fifth commission, established in 1963, worked for four years under the de facto leadership of Khrushchev ally Zinovy Serdiuk and later of G. Klimov, chief controller of the KPK. None of these commissions was devoted exclusively to probing the Kirov murder. Rather, they were charged with investigating what we now call the Great Terror as a whole. As Alla Kirilina and J. Arch Getty have observed, these investigations were politically motivated. Their findings depended greatly on the balance of forces in the Central Committee leadership. The argument presented in this chapter derives from Kirilina's, with additional data and conclusions.[2]

The practical work of the commissions was mostly done by the staff of the Party Control Committee (KPK), the disciplinary and investigative organ of the Central Committee. N. M. Shvernik, chairman of the KPK from 1956 through 1966, chaired the 1960 and 1961 commissions. The KPK Chief Controller (*otvetstvennyi kontroler*), Olga Shatunovskaya from 1955 to 1956 and G. Klimov from 1956 to 1967, played an important role in directing commission work and authoring reports to the Presidium of the Central Committee. KPK staff conducted interviews and did archival research. It was usually the KPK which requested information from the chief prosecutor's office of the

Soviet Union and the KGB. The role of the special investigative commissions seems to have been to bring some senior party leaders in to review the KPK conclusions and provide guidelines for future work.

A three-year submerged history preceded Khrushchev's not very secret "Secret Speech" at the Twentieth Party Congress (February 1956) that began open de-Stalinization. It was a history of conversations, speeches, amnesties, and personnel appointments about which rank-and-file party members, not to mention ordinary Soviet subjects, knew next to nothing. It was a history of business conducted inside the closed circles of the party elite, often in private one-on-one conversations. During these years Mikoyan and Khrushchev quietly sponsored labor camp returnees and scholars who laid the groundwork for de-Stalinization and the investigation of the Terror.

As already noted, the review and dismissal of high-profile espionage/murder cases, such as the "Doctors' Plot," began within days of Stalin's death. Direct criticism of the dictator was another matter. The Soviet press would not undertake this until years after Stalin's death. However, party leaders were feeling each other out on the subject as early as July 1953. With the possible exception of Beria (there is one report of him referring to Stalin as "a son-of-a-bitch" and a "tyrant" in private between March and June 1953), they did so with great circumspection. The attitudes of Stalin's former lieutenants toward their dead master were conflicted, and conditioned by powerful taboos. They might best be compared to the psychology of hostages or of children severely traumatized by their parents. Khrushchev and his fellows hated the tyrant who had abused them, but they also identified with him (they were all his collaborators), and they feared the consequences of denouncing him. Most of all they felt a supernatural awe of him. On the day of Stalin's death the Presidium discussed a proposal to build a huge "pantheon" in Moscow to the memory of "the Chief." According to Dmitry Shepilov, Khrushchev spoke in favor.[3]

But three months later, at the July 1953 Central Committee plenum, Khrushchev pointed out that the dictator was not infallible, saying "we all respect Comrade Stalin but the years tell, and recently Comrade Stalin did not read documents, didn't receive visitors, had weak health. . . ." Mikoyan observed that worship of Stalin had gone too far, using the phrase "cult of personality" that later became the Soviet shorthand for denunciation of Stalin-era crimes and incompetence. Conveniently, he blamed Beria for inflating the cult of personality and cited Stalin's own complaints about it. It is important to note that this was a closed discussion of the top several hundred party members in the country, and in 1953 all present would have understood the need not to disseminate Khrushchev's and Mikoyan's comments. These words were strictly for those at the top.[4]

Khrushchev emerged as the most powerful man inside the "collective leadership" of the party earlier than Western observers recognized—according to William Taubman, in the spring of 1954. Key to his consolidation of power was his appointment as first secretary of the Central Committee (September 1953), Stalin's old party position. In the early expansion of his political network, Khrushchev secured two appointments with great consequences for de-Stalinization and rehabilitation of the repressed—R. A. Rudenko as chief prosecutor of the USSR (at the July 1953 TsK Plenum), and Ivan A. Serov as head of the KGB (March 1954).[5]

On June 29, 1953, three days after Beria's arrest, the Presidium appointed Rudenko as chief prosecutor, ordering him to investigate the deposed security chief. Rudenko was a Khrushchev client. As first secretary of the Ukrainian Republic Central Committee, Khrushchev promoted Rudenko in 1942 from a position as chief prosecutor of Lugansk Region to assistant prosecutor of the republic. Rudenko served in the post from 1942–1944 and then as Chief Prosecutor of Ukraine from 1944–1953. In addition, he gained international fame as the chief Soviet prosecutor at the Nuremberg Nazi war crimes trial in 1945–1946. In his memoirs, Khrushchev implies that Rudenko was in debt to him—during the Terror of the late 1930s arrested "enemies of the people" gave evidence against Rudenko, and in 1942 Khrushchev prevented his promotion to a higher-profile position in Moscow where that evidence might have been used against him. Instead Khrushchev promoted Rudenko to assistant prosecutor in his own bailiwick, "with the provision that there were denunciations against him, and it was necessary to keep an eye on him . . . "[6]

Ivan A. Serov also had longtime ties to Khrushchev. Serov began his career as an artillery officer but transferred into the NKVD in February 1939. At the time newly appointed commissar Beria was purging the NKVD of officers associated with Yezhov (the second NKVD purge in two years), and promoting masses of new recruits from the party and the Red Army. Serov was one of these. In September 1939 he became NKVD chief for the Ukrainian Republic, where he worked closely with Khrushchev and General Georgy Zhukov. During this period Serov ran the "cleansing" of the occupied city of Lvov of "bourgeois and nationalist elements" (in other words mass deportations) and participated in the execution of nearly 15,000 Polish prisoners of war in the Katyn forest in 1940. Soon after Serov's transfer from the Ukrainian post in February 1941, Germany and its allies invaded the USSR. During the war, Serov, as one of the deputy chiefs of the NKVD, specialized in mass arrests and mass deportations from areas recaptured by the Red Army. He took part in deportations of the Kalmyks, Chechens, Ingush, and Volga Germans, and in purges of suspected collaborators and "bourgeois nationalists" in Ukraine, Poland, and Lithuania. He also served as the NKVD chief for the First Belorussian Front commanded by Zhukov. In the course of the Red Army advance through Ukraine and Belorussia, he maintained a close working relationship with Khrushchev.[7]

Serov had served at the center of Stalin's state security apparatus, and he was deeply compromised. Not only had he taken part in mass repressions, but one of his mistresses, whom he recruited as an intelligence agent, had defected to Romania before World War II. He was also implicated in lucrative illegal business dealings while stationed in occupied Lvov (1939–1941) and in Germany at the end of World War II. Multiple observers have concluded that Serov was Khrushchev's creature during the post-Stalin years precisely because his shady past made him vulnerable to pressure. Khrushchev's rivals feared Serov both because of his dependence on Khrushchev and his Stalinist history. In his memoirs Dmitry Shepilov, expelled from the leadership after participating in the 1957 attempt to replace Khrushchev, described Serov as "a deeply amoral . . . person," but "close to Khrushchev and ready to carry out any illegal order of his and to satisfy his personal caprices with slavish devotion." Until his removal from the chairmanship of the KGB in 1958, Serov accompanied Khrushchev on his foreign tours as chief of his bodyguard. Shepilov remembers him personally serving Khrushchev soup in China.[8]

In his memoirs Khrushchev is defensive about Serov, repeating several times that in his view Serov was "an honorable person." At the same time, he shows clear awareness that Serov was tainted by his participation in state terrorism. "If there was something on him," the former Soviet leader writes, "as there was something on all chekists, then he was a victim of the overall policies made by Stalin."[9]

As is evident from Khrushchev's patronage of Rudenko and Serov, de-Stalinization was conducted using Stalinist methods (with the very important difference that after Beria the losers were not arrested or executed). This is paradoxical, but not surprising. Lazar Kaganovich and Stalin himself were Khrushchev's mentors. Khrushchev's political style after 1953 resembled Stalin's in a number of ways.[10] These included his reliance on trusted cronies, his readiness to undermine and then abandon those same cronies, his use of highly compromised persons in key positions, his pretend modesty covering a ravenous hunger for adulation, and his propensity for keeping those around him guessing by maintaining at least two different "lines" on a given issue. On the other hand, Khrushchev was more flamboyant than Stalin, more impulsive, and much less bloodthirsty.

In the spring of 1954, Khrushchev and Mikoyan were both taking the first steps toward de-Stalinization. In the case of Khrushchev, at least, these steps also eroded the position of his rivals, in particular Georgy Malenkov. On May 3, 1954, the Presidium passed a resolution that in effect annulled the convictions of the accused in the "Leningrad Case" of 1950, in which Leningrad party leader and war hero A. Kuznetsov and a number of subordinates were executed or imprisoned on trumped-up charges of treason. The resolution blamed the unjust persecution of Kuznetsov and others on Beria and his old lieutenant V. S. Abakumov. In the background, however, was Malenkov, who played an important role in organizing the Kuznetsov trial (three years later Frol Kozlov, Khrushchev's party chief in Leningrad, would say that "the blood of Leningraders is on Malenkov's hands"). Two days after the passage of the Presidium resolution, Khrushchev and Rudenko traveled to Leningrad, where they spoke to a meeting of leading party activists. In his presentation Rudenko denounced Beria and Abakumov using the rhetoric of Stalinist show trials, claiming that they aimed at "the seizure of power, the overthrow of the Soviet state, and the restoration of capitalism." Khrushchev asserted that Stalin, although he was "a big man, a brilliant Marxist," had had too much power, and his "cult of personality" had been "inflated."[11]

Mikoyan and Khrushchev also sponsored the return of high-ranking Communists accused of "counterrevolutionary crimes" from exile, labor camps, and prison. On May 4, 1954, the same day as the rehabilitation of the leading figures in the "Leningrad Case," the TsK Presidium established a commission including Rudenko and Serov to review these other cases.[12] Several of the men and women released from state custody in the following months became key advocates of full-scale de-Stalinization. Those with personal ties to Mikoyan and Khrushchev in particular became important players.

A. I. Snegov was one early rehabilitee who immediately took on an important political role. Khrushchev had worked with Snegov, a Communist veteran of the Bolshevik Revolution and Civil War, in the Ukrainian Republic in the late 1920s. Snegov was also an old and close friend of Rudenko. According to accounts originating with Khrushchev and his relatives, Khrushchev released Snegov from the camps so that the latter could testify against Beria at his secret trial. (Snegov had at one point been a department head in the Transcaucasus party committee and had incriminating information on Beria.) It appears from party documentation that immediately after testifying (presumably in December 1953), Snegov was sent out of Moscow again, but to exile in the Komi Autonomous Republic, not to a labor camp. Two months later, in February 1954, he was again "summoned to Moscow." On March 6, 1954 Rudenko's office annulled his criminal conviction, and on March 13 the Party Control Committee reinstated him as a Communist Party member. Khrushchev soon appointed him as head of the corrective labor camp department of the Ministry of Internal Affairs (MVD), charged with reforming the camp system.[13]

Snegov's case is instructive first because it shows Khrushchev using personal connections with Communist camp survivors to take down his political enemies and accomplish his goals. It also shows how the battle for de-Stalinization became mythologized and memories distorted. In his 1990 memoirs Khrushchev's son Sergei relates what he says Snegov told him about his own rehabilitation in the early 1960s. In this account Rudenko returned Snegov to the labor camps for two years after Beria's trial. Then on the eve of the Twentieth Party Congress, Khrushchev recalled Snegov's name and asked where he was. Khrushchev's assistants rescued Snegov from prison—"he was brought to Moscow straight from prison, hungry and unshaven. There he exchanged his prison outfit for a suit and was given a guest pass to the Kremlin." This is a good story, but does not stand up upon comparison with party documentation. Snegov was exiled to Komi for two months, not sent back to a concentration camp for two years after Beria's trial. He did not make a last-minute return to Moscow on the eve of the Twentieth Party Congress. When William Taubman asked Sergei Khrushchev to explain these discrepancies, the latter replied that Snegov "could hardly have forgotten the date of his own liberation; the version he recounted to me must have seemed more dramatic to him. In any event, I didn't want to alter his account to correct the inaccuracy."[14]

De-Stalinization was a just struggle against heavy odds. It is not surprising that in later years those who fought to expose Stalinist mass murder would mythologize the conflict to some extent. And historians, memoirists, and journalists who respected the legacy of the de-Stalinizers would be reluctant to question any part of the history, including the mythologized elements. Sergei Khrushchev's brief comment reveals this dynamic. Out of respect for Snegov, Khrushchev says, he transmitted the more dramatic, but factually inaccurate, version of his release.

A second early returnee from the camps, and one crucial to the investigation of the Kirov murder, was Olga Shatunovskaya. Born in 1901, Shatunovskaya was the child of a Jewish lawyer in Baku. She attended the same *gimnazium* (elite liberal arts high school) as the children of Stepan Shaumian, the leader of the Baku Bolsheviks. In 1917 Shatunovskaya threw herself into the Bolshevik revolutionary movement in Baku. In addition to her activities as a street activist, she served as Shaumian's secretary and head of the Baku Council of People's Commissars Press Department in the months after the October Revolution. When Turkish forces helped Mensheviks and Azerbaijani nationalists (the Musavat) overthrow Soviet rule in Baku in September 1918, Shatunovskaya was captured and by her own account nearly executed. (The new regime did execute Stepan Shaumian and twenty-five other leaders of the Baku Soviet, turning the "twenty-six commissars" into Bolshevik martyrs.) Released, she joined the Bolshevik underground movement in the Caucasus, working closely with Anastas Mikoyan, among others.[15]

In the following years Shatunovskaya started a family with her second husband, Yury Kutin, and established herself as an important party official. She served in Baku, Briansk, Siberia, and Moscow. She was acting chief of the Moscow Party Committee's Department of Leading Party Organs when the NKVD arrested her in November 1937 on charges of Trotskyite activity. During her imprisonment Shatunovskaya sent several letters to Mikoyan disputing the case against her and seeking his help. Mikoyan did not reply or take any action until 1945, when he forwarded one of her appeals to Beria and secured her release (though according to Shatunovskaya, Mikoyan was still afraid to meet her when she returned to Moscow). In August 1948 the NKVD returned to her case, exiling her to Krasnoiarsk Region. Through her childhood friend Lev Shaumian, son of the Baku Commissar Stepan, she again appealed to Mikoyan, and Mikoyan supposedly appealed to Stalin for clemency. Stalin refused.[16]

When Mir Bagirov, author of one of the denunciations that led to Shatunovskaya's arrest and longtime chief of the Azerbaijani Communist Party, was himself arrested in March 1954 on suspicion of collaborating with Beria, Shatunovskaya petitioned Khrushchev for release from exile. Notified of her rehabilitation in May, Shatunovskaya made her way to Moscow, where, she writes, Khrushchev invited her for a private meeting. Khrushchev's assistants soon provided her with an apartment in the capital, a car, and a position as Chief Controller of the KPK. Khrushchev told her he wanted to accelerate rehabilitation.[17]

In the coming years Shatunovskaya became the most dedicated proponent inside the party apparatus of the theory that Stalin had organized Kirov's killing. Hence it is important to give a fuller description of her character and the reliability of her assertions. Shatunovskaya was courageous, histrionic, and combative. Late in life she described herself in childhood as a "hooligan," and she never seems to have stopped being one. She served in the Red Army in the revolutionary years, in addition to her very risky underground work in Baku. In the course of these struggles she adopted as her own the party's practices of vehement political denunciation. In the 1920s she was a very active supporter of the evolving Central Committee "general line" defined by Stalin and his allies. She fought with enthusiasm against "Trotskyites" in Baku, participating in debates and meetings of party cells all over the city. In 1928–1929 she joined the struggle against the "Right Deviation," leading a campaign to oust Azerbaijani Communist Party secretary Mirzoian (Kirov's client), whom she charged with being soft on the Rightists. After Mirzoian had her fired from her position on one of the ward party committees in Baku, Shatunovskaya denounced him to the Central Committee. Stalin used the hubbub to remove Mirzoian from Baku, but in a private letter to Molotov he also expressed contempt for Shatunovskaya and her allies as noisy do-nothings. He ordered Shatunovskaya's transfer into an intensive course of study at the Communist Academy in Moscow, a common enough move at the time for elite party members who had gotten into trouble with their local organizations.[18]

According to her daughter, Jana Kutin, Shatunovskaya either loved or hated people. "She loved to death and she scorned to death," Kutin writes. When she felt someone had slighted her, or had made an immoral choice, she was capable of rejecting them utterly. This character trait comes across in Shatunovskaya's memoirs of the rehabilitation period. In her account, the protagonists are either "Leninists" (good) or "Stalinists" (evil). In at least two cases she summarily dismisses loyal supporters of Khrushchev as enemies of reform.[19] Her readiness to dismiss those with whom she had work conflicts as crypto-Stalinists puts in doubt a number of Shatunovskaya's claims about obstruction of the rehabilitation process, in particular about the supposed destruction of documents.

In her memoirs, dictated from the early 1970s through the late 1980s, Shatunovskaya tells and retells stories from Communist Party history. But the details sometimes conflict with party documents and others' memoirs. She claims, for example, that during the Great Terror Mikoyan signed no execution or arrest lists, but Mikoyan in his memoirs admits signing at least one, in Armenia.[20] She describes a supposed episode in 1920, when Beria, arrested by the Menshevik government of independent Georgia, escaped to Baku. Kirov, who was at the time the Soviet ambassador to Georgia, telegraphed Baku to arrest Beria as soon as he arrived, because he was under suspicion of having served as a Musavat spy against the Bolsheviks. Shatunovskaya's tale seems to be a topsy-turvy reworking of two different events, one well attested to, the other more obscure. Beria was an agent of Bolshevik intelligence and was arrested twice by Georgian authorities. After the first arrest, he was freed and went underground working for Kirov in the Soviet embassy under an assumed name. When Beria was arrested again, Kirov petitioned the Georgian government for his release. The second event that may have influenced Shatunovskaya's story is more uncertain. Based on the 1953 testimony of former chekist N. F. Safronov, it is possible that Azerbaijani Communist authorities briefly arrested Beria in Baku in 1920. But there is no evidence Kirov had anything to do with this. The well-documented narrative of Beria's arrest in Georgia shows Kirov doing his job as Soviet ambassador, petitioning for Beria's release and aiding Bolshevik espionage in Georgia. But the story as Shatunovskaya tells it fits better with the requirements of her narrative—Kirov, the good Leninist, denounces the evil Beria.[21]

Shatunovskaya's account of Stalin's relations with his brother-in-law Aleksandr Svanidze, probably based on rumors, also has a "good" Bolshevik, in this case Svanidze himself, opposing the evil Stalin. According to Shatunovskaya, Svanidze protested the arrest of Avel Yenukidze to Stalin. But from his wife's diary and other documents Svanidze emerges as a relentless flatterer of Stalin, desperate to improve his position. In fact, Yuri Zhukov, who has had privileged access to KGB/FSB archives, writes that Svanidze initiated the case against Yenukidze by writing a denunciation of him (quite possibly at Stalin's suggestion) to the NKVD.[22]

Another example of Shatunovskaya's inaccurate reporting is her exaggerated claims for the total number of arrests and executions during the Stalin era. She states that 22 million people died during collectivization. During the Great Terror, she asserts, the government arrested nearly 20 million persons and shot 7 million. No reputable scholar today believes that the numbers were this high. Demography alone shows that they are impossible.[23]

There are several explanations for Shatunovskaya's imprecisions. First, she seems to have been a gossip with a gift for dramatic storytelling (she loved reminiscing about her old romances, including one with Anastas Mikoyan). Second, when she dictated the memoirs, Shatunovskaya had to recall from memory KPK documents she had not seen for ten years or more. It is not surprising that she did not remember all of them exactly. Third, Shatunovskaya was not a historian, but a political activist engaged in a crusade for justice. It appears that she collected any stories she heard that reflected poorly on Stalin, no matter what the source.

On the other hand, Shatunovskaya got a lot right in her memoirs. Her accounts of Sergo Ordzhonikidze's final conflict with Stalin, of Bukharin's letters to Stalin from jail, and of the late 1930s show trials all square with currently available documents. And she was undoubtedly right that Stalin was a brutal dictator. Although her memoirs and interviews late in life are unreliable on details, one has to sympathize with a woman whom anti-Semitic Stalinists referred to in the 1990s as "the provocateur Shatunovskaya" and "the liar Shatunovskaya."[24]

Shatunovskaya's long history with Anastas Mikoyan and his circle is a central part of the story of the investigation into Kirov's assassination. As already noted, she worked closely with Mikoyan in the Baku underground and claimed in old age that he had been her suitor. She also had attended *gimnazium* with Lev Shaumian, whom Mikoyan in effect adopted after the execution of his father, the Baku commissar. In 1954–1955 these three Baku Commune veterans laid the groundwork for Khrushchev's complete overturn of the official history of Stalin's rule at the Twentieth Party Congress. Shatunovskaya and Shaumian also became vigorous promoters of the theory that Stalin had killed Kirov. Another Baku veteran who played an important role in promoting the story that Stalin had ordered Kirov's assassination was Pyotr

Chagin, who had edited the flagship newspaper of the Baku party organization, the *Baku Worker,* under Kirov, and who had later transferred to Leningrad to run *Red Gazette.*[25]

All of these veterans shared a deep resentment of Lavrenty Beria and his client, Mir Bagirov, first secretary of the Azerbaijani party organization from 1933 to 1953. During the Great Terror Beria, with Bagirov's assistance and Stalin's approval, wiped out many of the old Caucasian cadres who had served with Ordzhonikidze and Kirov in the early days of Bolshevik rule. There were clashes between Beria and Ordzhonikidze clients, such as Mamia Orakhelashvili, as early as 1931–1932. In response Stalin pressed a number of Ordzhonikidze's clients out of leadership positions in the Georgian, Azerbaijani, and Transcaucasian apparatuses, based on his perception that they were incompetent. Lavrenty Beria, who of course worked to foster Stalin's sense that Ordzhonikidze's clients were bunglers, was promoted from head of the Transcaucasian Republic GPU to first secretary of the Georgian and Transcaucasian Communist parties. The Politburo removed Mamia Orakhelashvili from his post as first secretary of the Transcaucasian party in October 1932, and replaced him with Beria. In 1934–1935, as part of the campaign to present a new (falsified) history that exaggerated Stalin's role in the prerevolutionary Bolshevik movement, Beria's clients attacked Orakhelashvili and other Old Bolsheviks from the Caucasus who supposedly denigrated Stalin's importance. In 1937–1938 Orakhelashvili, Yenukidze, and other Caucasian Old Bolsheviks attacked by Beria were executed.[26]

Two decades later, Baku veterans such as Shatunovskaya and Mikoyan, as well as Ordzhonikidze's widow Zinaida, came to suspect Beria in Ordzhonikidze's death in early 1937, and even in Kirov's death in December 1934. The fact is, however, that in 1934 the methods of struggle between cliques within the party, while plenty dirty, certainly did not involve secret assassinations. Beria did not have a national political network at that time, nor would he have dared to engineer an assassination without Stalin's go-ahead. The Baku veterans who claimed that Beria had a hand in Kirov's death seem to have anachronistically projected the methods of 1937–1938 back to 1934. As for Ordzhonikidze's death in February 1937 Oleg Khlevniuk has argued persuasively that this was a suicide and that Beria had nothing directly to do with it.[27]

The Baku veterans played a key role in de-Stalinization efforts in the 1950s. According to Mikoyan's memoirs, Lev Shaumian (who, as we have seen, was effectively a member of Mikoyan's family and the intermediary for Shatunovskaya's appeals for clemency to Mikoyan) was instrumental in the early rehabilitation efforts of 1954–1955. Shaumian himself had never been repressed. But, while working in the party apparatus as an editor of newspapers and also of the *Great Soviet Encyclopedia,* he did maintain contact with some in the camps. Following Stalin's death, many imprisoned Communists used Shaumian as an intermediary to petition Mikoyan for review of their cases. Mikoyan says that it was Shaumian who "brought to me" Shatunovskaya and Snegov, and that he (Mikoyan) in turn brought them to Khrushchev's notice. Shatunovskaya and Snegov, Mikoyan writes, "opened my eyes to a great deal, telling me of their arrests, the tortures used during the interrogation process, and the fate of dozens of our acquaintances. . . ."[28]

Approximately half a year before the Twentieth Party Congress of February 1956, Mikoyan claims that he asked Shaumian to do some quiet research into the fate of delegates to the Seventeenth Party Congress of 1934. Specifically, he wanted a list of the Central Committee members and candidate members elected at that congress who were arrested or executed during the Terror. When Shaumian gave him the list about a month later, Mikoyan claims that he was "shocked." He went to Khrushchev and persuaded the latter that they were going to have to tackle the issue of Stalinist repressions at the Twentieth Party Congress. It is worth noting that whatever general desire Mikoyan and Khrushchev felt to review Stalinist history and rehabilitate the dictator's victims, there was also a very concrete motivation for bringing the issue up at the forthcoming congress. At the July 1955 plenary meeting of the Central Committee, Khrushchev and Molotov clashed openly. Mikoyan's conversations with Shaumian would have come after that plenum, and one of the purposes of Shaumian's research was probably to gather material compromising Molotov.[29]

Around the time that Mikoyan asked Shaumian to research the fate of the 1934 Central Committee, or soon after, he also requested that Shatunovskaya send him an official letter recounting a story she had told him relating to the Kirov assassination. The letter was forthcoming. In it Shatunovskaya described conversations she had with one Dr. Kirchakov and a nurse, Dusia Trunina, while hospitalized at the Kolyma labor camp in 1943–1944. Kirchakov, she wrote, had heard directly from Filip Medved an eyewitness account of Stalin's interrogation of Leonid Nikolaev the day after Kirov was killed. Medved was in exile at the time (1937), working at Kolyma in the NKVD, and expected to be rearrested soon. He supposedly told Kirchakov that when Stalin asked Nikolaev "Why did you kill Kirov?" Nikolaev accused officers of the Leningrad NKVD who were in the room at the time of providing him with the murder weapon and "persecuting" him until he agreed to assassinate Kirov. When Nikolaev said this, "they beat [him] on the head with their Nagans, he collapsed, and they carried him out. . . ."[30]

Before proceeding, it is necessary to make two notes about Shatunovskaya's story. First, it was third-hand by her own account—Medved had supposedly told Kirchakov, who told her. Second, the story places Zaporozhets in the interrogation room with Stalin, Medved, Nikolaev, Yagoda, and a number of other Leningrad NKVD officers. But as we have seen, several sources indicate that Zaporozhets was not in Leningrad at the time. On multiple counts the story conflicts with the account of Mikhail Rosliakov (see above, p. 265), who was waiting at the time of interrogation in a room one floor below.[31]

Mikoyan forwarded Shatunovskaya's letter to Khrushchev with a note on the envelope—"To Comrade N. S. Khrushchev—for his eyes only." Khrushchev evidently put the letter on the agenda of the Presidium of December 31, 1955. The only record of the meeting is a "working summary" of the discussion, which indicates that Bulganin read the letter out loud. While he was reading Voroshilov interrupted with a shout of "Lies!" Molotov, according to the summary, noted that he was present when Stalin interviewed Nikolaev and "no one was hit." Mikoyan asserted that "Stalin was extremely upset. The chekists had a hand in the whole thing." Khrushchev agreed that "if you look at the business, it doesn't smell right," and proposed interviewing the doctor (Kirchakov), the driver of the car in which Borisov died, and "Kuprianov" (identity not established). Molotov, perhaps afraid of what charges might surface in oral interrogations, expressed skepticism that interviews would provide useful information, and suggested "checking the documents." Kaganovich seems to have taken the claim that NKVD officers were involved, and to have tried to defuse it by interpreting in the spirit of the 1934–1935 investigation into the Leningrad NKVD—the chekists' negligence had allowed the assassination to happen. The Presidium resolved to look at the files of the 1930s cases against Yagoda, Yezhov, and Medved.[32]

Khrushchev, with the help of Mikoyan and his associates, was clearly preparing for a serious discussion of Stalinist repressions (at least those against Communists after 1934) at the forthcoming party congress. Molotov, Kaganovich, Malenkov, Voroshilov, and other party leaders outside Khrushchev's inner circle had to be nervous. But Khrushchev, who controlled the KGB (Serov), and the USSR prosecutor's office (Rudenko), and had key allies in the army (Zhukov) and the KPK (Shatunovskaya and others) had the upper hand. He was able to force a very uncomfortable discussion of the Stalinist years on his rivals on his own terms. At the same time, his power was not unlimited. He proceeded cautiously, using Mikoyan's people, whom he could always cast loose, to do the research, and forbearing to charge Molotov and the others directly with collaboration in the Terror.

Khrushchev's colleagues had much to fear, but they too had to proceed very carefully. They acceded to the proposal for an informal inquiry into the Kirov murder. At other Presidium meetings in the months before the Twentieth Party Congress Molotov, Kaganovich, Voroshilov, Bulganin, and Malenkov all voiced their support for revealing to the party congress some of Stalin's unjustified persecutions of Communists. At the same time they called for doing so "with a cool head," and for reaffirming Stalin's great accomplishments in building socialism. In reply a chorus of junior Presidium members who supported Khrushchev (Aristov, Saburov, Suslov, Pervukhin, and others) insisted that the Presidium had to tell the congress "everything" (Suslov), that Stalin had no good points (Pervukhin), and that Stalinist repressions were not "faults" but "crimes" (Saburov). By early February 1956 everyone knew what the party line was—even Kaganovich was saying "we can't deceive history . . . Khrushchev's proposal for a report is correct."[33]

In the meantime, the Presidium appointed a commission consisting of junior Presidium members Pyotr Pospelov, Komarov, Aristov, and Nikolai Shvernik to investigate issues related to rehabilitation. On February 9 this commission reported to the Presidium on "reasons for the mass repressions against members and candidates of the Central Committee elected at the Seventeenth Party Congress." Almost certainly the commission relied in part on the evidence on the same topic gathered earlier by Lev Shaumian. Using documents that were top secret at the time, the commission reported that 1.5 million persons were arrested and 681,692 executed in 1937–1938. The report stated that of 139 members and candidates elected to the Central Committee by the Seventeenth Party Congress, 98 were arrested and shot—numbers Khrushchev used in his "Secret Speech" weeks later. It described the methods by which cases were fabricated against high-ranking party members in 1937 and after. It also identified as key to the Terror's development Kirov's murder and the subsequent Law of December 1. There was no discussion of the possibility that Stalin had deliberately organized the assassination himself.[34]

The Twentieth Party Congress and After: Serov and Rudenko Investigate

On February 25, 1956, at the conclusion of the Twentieth Party Congress, Khrushchev gave his "Secret Speech," denouncing Stalin's "cult of personality," his arrests and executions of party members after 1934, and his failure to prepare for the Nazi attack on the Soviet Union in June 1941. Khrushchev also acknowledged Stalin's supposed accomplishments (such as the industrialization of the USSR). He did not suggest that there were systemic problems other than "the cult of personality," nor did he question the forced collectivization of agriculture, or the expulsion of oppositionists from the party.

Following up on the February 9 Pospelov report and Mikoyan's earlier question to Lev Shaumian, Khrushchev addressed the question of the mass annihilation of Central Committee members after the Seventeenth Party Congress. He attributed the extermination to Stalin's unchecked power, but did not offer more specifics. Immediately following this part of the speech, he noted that "mass repressions and gross violations of socialist legality" began after Kirov's murder. With regard to the assassination itself, he said:

> One has to note that the circumstances connected with the murder of Comrade Kirov are to this day befogged with much that is incomprehensible and mysterious, and demand careful investigation. There is reason to believe that someone among those charged with guarding Comrade Kirov aided the murderer Nikolaev. One and a half months before the murder of Kirov Nikolaev was arrested for suspicious behavior, but was released and not even searched. The fact that the chekist attached to Kirov ended up dead in an auto "accident" on December 2, 1934 while being driven to interrogation is extremely suspicious. After the murder of Kirov the leading officers of the Leningrad NKVD were removed from their posts and given very light punishments, but in 1937 were shot. It is conceivable that they were shot in order to clean up the traces of the organizers of Kirov's murder.[35]

Khrushchev's speech reveals him to be a "master of dosing" almost as great as Stalin himself. He did not directly state that Stalin or other party leaders were involved in preparing Kirov's murder. But by placing his suggestion that there had been a conspiracy to kill the Leningrad party leader immediately after his discussion of the destruction of the TsK membership after 1934 and his note that the orgy of killing followed Kirov's death, he signaled his readiness to accept a specific narrative of the Terror. This would be one in which Stalin himself and/ or his closest assistants at the time (Molotov, Kaganovich) had plotted the killing to justify the subsequent extermination of party cadres. This narrative would make sense of the Terror, and it would also bring Khrushchev's major rivals for power—Molotov, Kaganovich, and Malenkov—crashing down. It would exonerate "true" Bolshevism of responsibility for the Terror, laying it all at the feet of Stalin and his closest lieutenants in 1934–1938. It would also exonerate junior members of the Bolshevik leadership who supported Khrushchev in 1956–they "had no idea" about the mass repressions in the 1930s, they just followed orders.

Many party officials, ambitious or afraid, or both, responded with alacrity to Khrushchev's signal. This response followed the Stalinist pattern, in which subordinates rushed to carry out wishes the leader expressed only in hints and insinuations. Pyotr Pospelov was one such subordinate.

As part of his work on the commission on Stalinist repressions created on December 31, 1955, Pospelov prepared a report on Kirov's murder, which he presented to the Presidium on April 23, 1956. This report is important for the light it sheds both on the rumors about the assassination reported by Shatunovskaya in her 1955 letter and on the construction of an alternative history of the murder. Pospelov and his colleagues looked into Shatunovskaya's letter, summoning the doctor and nurse she cited to Moscow for interviews. Doctor Kirchakov indicated he had not heard the story he told Shatunovskaya about Nikolaev's interview with Stalin directly from former Leningrad NVKD chief Medved, but from an ex-NKVD officer, Olsky (see above, p. 515). Olsky had told Kirchakov that his friend Medved had insisted that he had been punished unjustly for Kirov's murder—that he was Kirov's "closest and truest friend." Olsky also repeated, ostensibly from Medved's mouth, the story about Nikolaev's supposed dramatic interview with Stalin, in which he denounced central NKVD officers for putting him up to the assassination. The nurse Trunina testified that Kirchakov had told her the same story he told Shatu-novskaya.[36]

In short, the story that Nikolaev denounced the Leningrad NKVD officers in his interview with Stalin was not third-hand, but fourth-hand (Medved to Olsky to Kirchakov to Shatunovskaya) when Sha-tunovskaya put it to paper. Moreover, in Kirchakov's retelling, the Nikolaev episode was merely a postscript to an otherwise believable account of Medved denying his guilt in Kirov's murder. Understand-ably, Pospelov concluded that Kirchakov's tale could not be relied upon.

Can we believe Pospelov's account of his interviews with Kirchakov and Trunina? Perhaps, as a longtime Stalinist, he was simply trying to discredit evidence that might link "the Chief" to the murder. The an-swer is that he was not. In the remainder of his report, Pospelov con-structed a case that Stalin had ordered Kirov's murder. He began by dismissing Leningrad NKVD third-in-command Fomin's testimony (probably given on March 26, 1956) that Borisov's death really was an accident ("obviously false evidence"). He also dismissed the 1934–1935 investigative materials as tainted by the efforts to build a case against Kamenev and Zinoviev, and as going too easy on the Lenin-grad NKVD. Pospelov then proceeded to state his preference for mate-rials from 1937–1938 investigations of Yagoda, Yenukidze, Zapo-rozhets, and the Leningrad NKVD officers accused of murdering Borisov. In other words, in order to implicate Stalin, he chose to rely on "evidence" that was extracted under torture in the process of fabricat-ing a case against arrested NKVD chief Yagoda. Pospelov's version of the crime duplicated the March 1938 show trial version, except that Stalin replaced the "Right-Trotskyite Center" as the source of the or-der to kill Kirov.[37]

A very likely interpretation of Pospelov's report is this. The author, an old Stalinist (like Khrushchev, Shatunovskaya, Mikoyan, and nearly everyone else at the top of party in the 1950s), was producing what he knew "the Chief" (once Stalin, now Khrushchev) wanted. Re-garding Shatunovskaya's fourth-hand tale as too far-fetched even for his purposes, he cherry-picked the 1937–1938 confessions, which at least were on paper and usually signed by their supposed authors, to produce a coherent story of how Stalin had Kirov killed. He generated the narrative that Khrushchev demanded. Now it was up to Khru-shchev how, when, and in what forum to use that story-line.

Khrushchev's "Secret Speech" on de-Stalinization set off a furor that in many ways resembled a traditional Bolshevik "self-criticism" campaign. At upper levels of the party potential targets of the campaign (Molotov, Malenkov, Kaganovich) publicly applauded but behind the scenes strove to protect themselves by obstructionism and delaying tactics. Inside the TsK executive apparatus officials like Pospelov worked to produce texts that Khrushchev might need in pursuit of the campaign. Professional elites and lower-ranking party members victimized and/or disgusted by Stalin's tyranny spoke out against the dead dictator. A few even dared to discuss before public meetings the responsibility of the entire party leadership for the reign of fear. At some workplaces employees tore down or defaced portraits of Stalin. Meanwhile Stalin's defenders took to the streets. In Georgia the republic leaders imposed martial law after pro-Stalin riots on the anniversary of the dictator's death. Soviet security forces killed twenty people in the suppression of the disorders.[38]

An integral part of any "self-criticism" campaign was letters of denunciation "from below." After party meetings in Leningrad devoted to the "Secret Speech," former police and NKVD officers began sending letters to the province party committee concerning the Kirov murder. V. M. Yakushev, the NKVD officer who had conducted the second (1937) investigation of Borisov's death, wrote one that captured the attention of Frol Kozlov, Leningrad party chief and Khrushchev ally. In late March or early April, Kozlov wrote to Khrushchev that "From Yakushev's statement it is clear that Borisov's murder was accomplished according to a plan worked out beforehand."[39]

Yakushev based his report on the 1937 testimony of Kuzin, the driver of the truck Borisov died in, and Vinogradov, one of the officers accompanying Borisov. His account followed the 1937–1938 show trial scenario prepared to incriminate Yagoda. According to Yakushev, Zaporozhets feared that Borisov would reveal the alleged Yagoda-run plot against Kirov. Zaporozhets ordered Khviiuzov (second-in-command of the Leningrad NKVD Operations Department) to have Borisov killed. A plan was hatched to do away with him under the guise of a car accident. When Borisov was on the way to Smolny for interrogation by Stalin, Maly, one of the accompanying officers, grabbed the steering wheel from Kuzin and ran the truck off the street against a wall. Simultaneously, Vinogradov, the officer in the back of the truck with Borisov, smashed the latter's head with a steel bludgeon, killing him (for more details of this version of events see Chapters 11 and 15).[40]

Yakushev was a perpetrator, a torturer, and a collaborator in Stalin's fabrication of false cases against Yagoda and dozens of others. His 1956 letter seems to have been a preemptive strike—by providing his version of events to party leaders, he not only insured himself against prosecution, he also curried favor with them. And Kozlov, Khrushchev's associate, was buying what Yakushev had to sell. In his letter to Khrushchev, Kozlov also accepted uncritically statements from former members of the Criminal Investigation Department of the Leningrad police that they had uncovered plots against Kirov's life in 1933–1934. These officers claimed that the NKVD had dismissed their findings out of hand. Two of the officers' statements derived from the evidence of Maria Volkova, the compulsive denouncer. Based on these highly dubious claims, Kozlov concluded "These facts demonstrate, obviously, that several different plans for killing Kirov were worked out in the organs of the MVD [NKVD]."[41]

While Pospelov, Aristov, Kozlov, and other TsK members worked to create a narrative that would implicate Stalin (and probably also Molotov or Kaganovich) in Kirov's assassination, the KGB and the USSR prosecutor's office had begun interviewing surviving witnesses about the case, and someone inside the TsK or KPK apparatus was soliciting letters from people who might have first-hand knowledge of the circumstances of the crime. On March 26, 1956 Fyodor Fomin, who had resided in Leningrad since his release from the camps, sent a formal statement to the Secretariat of the TsK. As early as April 3, 1956 the KGB began interviewing the NKVD officers who had guarded Nikolaev during his imprisonment and trial, as well as a number of former senior officers in the Leningrad NKVD. Also sometime in April the Prosecutor's Office interviewed two members of the military tribunal that sentenced Nikolaev and the other thirteen defendants to death.[42]

On April 13, 1956 the Presidium created a commission to investigate "materials of the open trials of the cases of Bukharin, Rykov, Zinoviev, Tukhachevsky, and others." This commission would look into the Kirov case as well, but it is important to note that its mandate was much broader—in effect, to explain that part of the Terror directed against the upper levels of the Communist Party. At first glance, the composition of the commission was strange. Of nine members, three, Molotov, Kaganovich, and Voroshilov, had been involved at the highest level in orchestrating the Terror, and thus were themselves potential targets of investigation. They were, however, outnumbered by the six members of the commission from the junior ranks of the TsK leadership, all of whom supported Khrushchev during this period—Suslov, Furtseva, Shvernik, Aristov, Pospelov, and Rudenko. Shvernik, a Khrushchev supporter during the "Thaw," had just been appointed chairman of the Party Control Committee on which Shatunovskaya served.[43]

Putting Molotov, Kaganovich, and Voroshilov on the commission may have been a sop to them and to others nervous about where the party's investigation of the Terror might lead. It may also have been an exercise in harassment and disciplinary power by Khrushchev. At the commission sessions Molotov and the others would be subject to insinuations, badgering, and generally uncomfortable discussions. Finally, Khrushchev may have considered that getting the signatures of the veteran Stalinists would be the final validation of commission findings. Given the party tradition of unanimous approval of such reports, he may have hoped that all three could ultimately be forced into signing whatever report the commission issued, and, perhaps, incriminating themselves.[44]

On April 16 the commission met for the first time. All members were present except for Rudenko, the head of the prosecutor's office, who was represented by one of his deputies, Baranov. Also present was Khrushchev's KGB chief Serov. The commission (hereafter the Molotov commission, after its chairman) began its work with a consideration of the Kirov assassination. This was in accordance with Khrushchev's identification at the Twentieth Party Congress of the murder as the starting point of the Terror. The commission resolved as follows.

· 115 ·

Protocol number one. Session of the Central Committee commission for review of materials from the trials, April 16, 1956. RGANI, f. 6, op. 13, d. 43, l. 1.

———————

Present: Comrade Molotov /chairman/. Members of the commission comrades Voroshilov, Kaganovich, Suslov, Shvernik, Furtseva, Aristov, Pospelov, Serov, Baranov.

I. On the schedule of the TsK commission for reviewing materials on the trials.

　1. Begin the review of trial materials with the case of the murder of Comrade Kirov.

　2. Order Comrades Serov and Baranov:

　　a. to forward to the members of the commission within three days a report on documents and agent materials /primary sources/ held by the KGB and the Prosecutor's Office on the assassination of S. M. Kirov and the stenographic record of the trial of Nikolaev, Kotolynov, and others in this case.

   b. to prepare the basic documents in the case of S. M. Kirov's murder and send them to the members of the commission within one week. Review them at the next session of the commission.

II. On the next session of the commission. Schedule for Monday, April 23 at 3 P.M.

   Commission Chairman: V. Molotov

In response to the commission's request, Serov and Baranov forwarded on April 20 a "Report on Investigative Materials in the Case of the Villainous Murder of S. M. Kirov." Attached to the report were copies of selected materials from the case (including excerpts from Nikolaev's diary) and a note that commission members could examine all documents related to the murder at the KGB headquarters. Many of the primary sources on Kirov's assassination cited earlier in this book were part of this document release.[45]

The next commission meeting came off as scheduled, on April 23.

· 116 ·

Protocol number two. Session of the Central Committee commission for review of materials from the trials, April 23, 1956. RGANI, f. 6, op. 13, d. 43, l. 2

Present: Comrade Molotov /Chairman/.

Commission members: Comrades Voroshilov, Kaganovich, Suslov, Shvernik, Furtseva, Aristov, Pospelov.

Comrades Serov, Baranov.

At the session there was an exchange of opinion regarding the materials on the case of the murder of S. M. Kirov presented by the KGB [. . .] and the USSR Prosecutor's Office on April 20.

   1. The commission considers that the murder of S. M. Kirov by Nikolaev had a political character, that Nikolaev had a hostile attitude towards the party and its leadership. Based on his psychological condition, Nikolaev could and should bear responsibility for the crime he committed.

   2. Instruct the KGB /Comrade Serov/ to present to the commission by April 28:

      a. Detailed data on Nikolaev's political characteristics, his political ties and relationships, on his political moods in the last years before the assassination of S. M. Kirov, etc.

   b. Materials on the antiparty work and terrorist moods of the Trotsky-Zinoviev group in the period 1932–1934 /prior to the murder of
S. M. Kirov/ in Moscow and Leningrad.

   c. Material on the political behavior, connections, and political
moods of the group including Kotolynov, Shatsky, et al. before their
trial for the murder of S. M. Kirov.

   d. A report as to how satisfactorily the NKVD guard of Comrade
Kirov was organized in 1934.

   3. Instruct Comrade Shvernik /KPK/ to prepare by April 28 for the
commission as complete information as possible on Nikolaev's political
identity (*litso*) during his time in the party, the reasons for his exclusion
from the party, his restoration to the party, etc.

   4. Order the USSR Prosecutor /Comrade Baranov/ to study and present
to the commission materials on the validity and legality of the preliminary
investigation, inquest, and trial in the case of the murder of S. M. Kirov.

   5. Schedule the next session of the Central Committee commission for
May 3, 1956.

   Commission Chairman: V. Molotov

The Russian State Archive of Contemporary History holds three reports to the Molotov commission from late April 1956, as well as one
apparent draft report. An initial joint report to the commission from
Serov and Baranov was delivered on April 20. Based on internal evidence (reports of interview dates with witnesses, etc.) the other three
were prepared and handed over several days later, after the commission's request for more information on April 23. Comparison of these
reports' contents with the April 23 commission minutes reveals two
radically different agendas at work. On the one hand, the April 23
commission meeting resolved, probably at the prompting of Molotov,
Kaganovich, and/or Voroshilov, that Nikolaev's murder was a "political" act, and dismissed the issue of Nikolaev's psychological state.
Commission members asked Baranov, the KGB, and the KPK (Shvernik) to answer a series of questions related to the official 1934–1935
version of the crime. These questions boiled down to: Was Nikolaev a
Zinovievite? What were his ties to Zinovievite groups? What activities
in Leningrad were the Zinovievites up to? These questions are attributable to the desire of Molotov and his allies to defend at least the
1934–1935 version of the crime as presented at the trials of the
Moscow and Leningrad "Centers." Nikolaev was a Zinovievite terrorist, and hence his trial, the trials of Kamenev and Zinoviev, and
probably also the later show trials of 1937–1938, were justified.

   On the other hand, item 4 of the April 23 minutes looks more like something pushed for by the reformers, probably Aristov for one, and points toward questioning the official 1934–1935 official version of events. And the reports produced in late April by the KGB (Serov) and the prosecutor's office (Rudenko/Baranov) took precisely this direction. Using investigation records from 1934–1935 and the April interviews with witnesses from the NKVD, the prosecutor's office, and the military tribunal, all of these reports explicitly denied the argument that the murder was political or that Nikolaev had connections with actual Zinovievite oppositionists. The trial of Nikolaev and the "Leningrad Center," according to these memoranda, was a fabrication created by the NKVD leadership in collaboration with Stalin. Nikolaev was a lone "pyschopathic" killer.

· 117 ·

KGB report on the Kirov investigation to Molotov commission, late April 1956.
RGANI, f. 6, op. 13, d. 24, ll. 24–32.

We have examined materials of the investigation into the villainous murder of S. M. Kirov and interrogated the following persons: former officers of the NKVD Katsafa, A. I., Radin, L. D., Makarov, N. I., Lobov, P. M., Tsomaev, Yu. Kh., and also [. . .] Gusev, K. S., who guarded Nikolaev during the trial, and Yanovsky, A. V., who conversed with Tsomaev in 1935.

On the basis of these materials we conclude that the murderer of S. M. Kirov—Nikolaev L. V., was undoubtedly a psychologically ill person.

Nikolaev's father was an alcoholic, Nikolaev himself suffered from an aggravated case of rickets in childhood, he [only] began to walk at age 11, at age 12 he had some sort of attack, [and] he was regularly sick as an adult.

The notes, diaries, letters, and declarations taken from Nikolaev at the time of his arrest demonstrate his psychological defectiveness (*nepolnotsennosti*). [There follow excerpts from several of Nikolaev's documents reproduced in earlier chapters, including his autobiography, his diaries, his "political testament," and his May 8 letter to his apartment building wall newspaper.]

[. . .]

Nikolaev L. V. was arrested on December 1, 1934 at 4:30 P.M. at the scene of his assassination of Comrade Kirov, S. M.

As can be seen from a report of a medical examination of Nikolaev dated December 1, 1934 at 6:30 P.M., Nikolaev was in a state of "general nervous excitement," he did not answer questions, he groaned and screamed.

From the medical examination report composed on December 1, 1934 in Leningrad regional NKVD clinic number 1, it can be seen that Nikolaev was brought to the clinic "on a stretcher at 7:00 P.M. in a state of hysteria, with very limited awareness of his surroundings. . . . By 9:00 P.M. he had come to himself. . . . During this time he carried on sensible conversation, answered questions immediately, but not always to the point."

Former NKVD officers Katsafa, A. I. and Radin, L. D., who were stationed in one cell with Nikolaev throughout the entire investigation, say that he behaved himself strangely: at times singing songs, at times shouting, "Why don't they shoot me, I killed Kirov." At points he refused to go to his interrogations and had to be carried on a stretcher.

Prior to the moment of his arrest the NKVD organs had no materials on any participation by Nikolaev in the opposition. Nor are there any party documents to this effect.

In the first days after his arrest Nikolaev asserted in interrogations that he killed S. M. Kirov for personal reasons and did not say anything about any kind of anti-Soviet organization.

Colonel N. I. Makarov, of the reserves, who was working on the Zinovievites in Leningrad in 1934, claims that there were no materials regarding Nikolaev's belonging to the opposition in the regional NKVD [files], and that he personally first heard the name [Nikolaev] only in connection with the murder of S. M. Kirov.

Also deserving of attention is Makarov's evidence that on December 2, 1934 the files on Kotolynov, Rumiantsev, Shatsky, and others /Nikolaev was not in these files/ were taken from him and presented to I. V. Stalin. Two days later, that is on December 4, the names of Kotolynov, Shatsky, and others first appeared in Nikolaev's interrogations. From the investigative materials it is clear that Nikolaev was acquainted with Kotolynov and others in the period 1921–1924 from his work in the Vyborg Komsomol organization, and after that he had two to three chance meetings with them, in the course of which no political conversations occurred. Kotolynov confirmed this, stating that "I did not know Nikolaev as a member of a counterrevolutionary Zinovievite organization."

However, in our review of the investigative materials we came upon a plan of work, composed by one of the leaders of the USSR NKVD who came [to Leningrad] to carry out the investigation of Nikolaev's case. In this plan the first issue noted is:

"1. Direction of investigation into the counterrevolutionary Zinovievite organization:

"a. the Moscow Center,

"b. the Leningrad organization."

It can be inferred that leading officers met with Stalin about this plan, for on the typewritten plan several questions were noted in pencil.

Our proposal is backed up by the fact that on December 6 Nikolaev. named Kotolynov, Shatsky, and the others as his collaborators, and on December 13 he turned them into the leaders of a terrorist Zinovievite organization. [The report then explains Katsafa's supposedly overhearing Nikolaev saying Kotolynov and Shatsky's names in his sleep, and postulates that this was a fabrication. See Chapter Eight, Document 44.]

[. . .]

It is clear from the materials of the review and the investigative files that the investigation pursued the goal of connecting the murder of S. M. Kirov by Nikolaev with persons formerly belonging to the Zinovievite opposition, and of portraying them as participants in a terrorist group [led by] Zinoviev that planned and carried out the terrorist act against S. M. Kirov.

However, this version, "confirmed" in the depositions of Nikolaev and several other of the accused in this case, is obviously illogical:

First, because Nikolaev himself gave contradictory evidence. Until December 4 he said that he was a lone gunman and did not even mention the names of Kotolynov and the others at all. On December 4 he testified that he was acquainted with the Trotskyites Kotolynov, Shatsky, and others. On December 6 he named them as co-conspirators, because they "shared" his terrorist intentions. On December 13 he now deposed that he killed S. M. Kirov at the orders of Kotolynov and Shatsky.

Second, in the case [files] there is no objective evidence of the presence of any ties at all between Nikolaev and Kotolynov and the others. Kotolynov testified during the inquiry and in court that he met with Nikolaev only in 1924.

Third, Nikolaev cannot be believed because, as is clear from the testimony of Katsafa and Gusev, he was promised his life if he would confirm in court his testimony that he killed Kirov at the orders of the Zinovievite organization.

[. . .]

Analysis of all materials on hand indicates the following conclusions.

1. The murder of Comrade Kirov was carried out by a psychopathic personality, Nikolaev, L. V., who had no connections with the Trotsky-Zinovievite opposition.

2. The investigative organs used the fact of personal meetings between Nikolaev and Kotolynov, Shatsky, and other former participants in the Zinovievite opposition many years before the terrorist act to connect them artificially to the Nikolaev case. [. . .]

A second memorandum added substantially to the picture of a lone gunman and a fabricated criminal case against the Zinovievites. This was the initial April 20 joint report by the KGB and prosecutor, requested by the Molotov commission on April 16. It used citations from interrogations and the stenographic report of the trial of the "Leningrad Center" to argue that no such "Center" had ever existed. The authors demonstrated that the trial had violated standard Soviet rules for criminal trials. They also analyzed the changing testimony of the witnesses in the death of the guard Borisov, contending that the 1937–1938 confessions implicating NKVD officers in murdering him were bogus.

· 118 ·

"Report on Materials in the Case of the Villainous Murder of S. M. Kirov." Joint KGB/USSR prosecutor's report to the Molotov commission, April 20, 1956. RGANI, f. 6, op. 13, d. 1, ll. 10–53.

I. On the Circumstances of the Crime.

On December 1, 1934 at 4:30 P.M. in the city of Leningrad, in the Smolny Building, twenty steps from his office, Sergei Mironovich Kirov was killed by a shot in the back of his head from a revolver.

The murder of S. M. Kirov was committed by Nikolaev, Leonid Vasilievich, who was detained at the scene of the crime.

[The remainder of Part I of the report presents excerpts from the testimony of Smolny witnesses Borisov, Platoch, and Lioninok, see Chapter 4, Documents 2, 3, and 4.]

II. Nikolaev, Leonid Vasilievich, born 1904, was a member of the Communist Party from 1924.

At the moment of Nikolaev's arrest, the NKVD organs had no materials on his participation in the opposition. Nor were there any party documents to this effect.

On March 31, 1934 Nikolaev was expelled from the party for refusing to work in transport. In connection with this he was fired from the Leningrad regional party committee's Institute of Party History. On April 29, 1934 the Smolny Ward committee of the party rescinded the decision on Nikolaev's expulsion from the party, limiting itself [. . .] to the issuance of a strict censure to be noted in his personal file. This decision was confirmed by the party collegiums of the Leningrad Region and the KPK.

After his expulsion from the party and firing from the Institute of Party History, Nikolaev petitioned the Leningrad Region party committee and the Central Committee for a review of the decision in his case, but without success.

As a result of his long period /eight months/ of unemployment, Nikolaev and his family were having trouble making ends meet.

[The report then presents excerpts from Nikolaev's August 25, 1934 letter to Stalin, his October 9, 1934 letter to the Politburo, his "political testament," and his October 30, 1934 letter to Kirov (Chapter 6, Documents 24, 26, 30, and 31). It also excerpts his diaries and depositions from his relatives (see Chapter 5, Documents 15, 16, and 17 for some of his relatives' evidence), as well as the NKVD doctors' December 1 examinations of Nikolaev (Chapter 4, Document 12) and the evidence of his guards Katsafa and Radin (Chapter 8, Document 44).]

III. Preliminary Investigation of the Case.

Interrogated on the day of the murder, Nikolaev testified:
"I state categorically that there were no other participants in the attack I made on Comrade Kirov. I prepared the whole thing by myself, and I told no one of my plans."

He further testified that his hard material situation and moral state, which were the results of his firing from work and expulsion from the party, pushed him to murder S. M. Kirov.

[The report then cites Nikolaev's testimony of December 1 (Chapter 7, Document 36) and discusses his first mention of Kotolynov and Shatsky on December 4.]

In an interrogation on December 5 Nikolaev gave obviously self-contradictory testimony about Kotolynov. First he declared that upon meeting Kotolynov he did not start a conversation with him because he was sure that the latter would urge him to carry out immediately the murder of S. M. Kirov, which he planned on completing only after the October holidays. And on this same page, Nikolaev answered, to the question why he did not recruit Kotolynov for the commission of a terrorist act against S. M. Kirov, that "Kotolynov, I believed, would not agree to the murder of Kirov, but would demand a higher-level target, that is, the commission of a terrorist act against Stalin, to which I would not have agreed."

On the one hand, Kotolynov appears as an advocate of the immediate murder of Kirov, but on the other he considers it best not to touch S. M. Kirov, but to prepare an attack on I. V. Stalin.

Although Nikolaev testified on December 4 and 5 that he saw Kotolynov before the October holidays, but did not speak with him, by December 6 he was already saying that he had a conversation with Kotolynov, during which he told Kotolynov of his plans to kill S. M. Kirov, and the latter supposedly approved of this, and declared that he himself would plan a terrorist attack on Stalin.

Nikolaev's testimony about Shatsky was just as self-contradictory. On December 4 he deposed that when he met Shatsky on Krasnykh Zor Street Shatsky complained about his lack of connection to the party. After Chudov's automobile went by the two silently glanced one at the other. On December 5 he now testified that Shatsky stated his terrorist intentions and with hostility spoke of Stalin's declaration on the necessity of removing oppositionists from their jobs. On December 6 it is written in Nikolaev's depositions that Shatsky told him that he had recruited V. Rumiantsev to prepare a terrorist attack on Stalin. Also on December 6, but in another deposition, Nikolaev . . . testified that Shatsky was preparing simultaneously terrorist attacks on Stalin and on Kirov. [. . .]

[The memorandum then covers the testimony of Nikolaev's guards Katsafa and Radin (Chapter 8, Document 44), and the lack of evidence against the accused in the "Leningrad Center" case. The authors continue with a discussion of Nikolaev's testimony on December 14 that Shatsky, Sokolov, and Kotolynov recruited him to the Zinovievite terrorist organization in 1934.]

The tale of the supposed recruitment of Nikolaev by Shatsky, Sokolov, and Kotolynov or anybody else is clearly a fabrication.

All of the "recruiters" named by Nikolaev categorically denied recruiting him. From the depositions of Nikolaev himself and the others accused it is evident that in the course of 1934 he had three chance meetings on the street with each of these persons. Prior to that he had not met them for about ten years. The case looks then like this: persons who were never particularly close to one another, who had not met for ten years, meet on the street and one of them recruits the second into a counterrevolutionary organization. Then he immediately orders him to kill a member of the Politburo, a secretary of the party's TsK.

Nikolaev's depositions cannot be accepted as trustworthy for the following reasons.

1. Nikolaev, as is evident from the materials of the case, was a psychologically ill person.

2. His testimony is self-contradictory and often simply implausible.

3. The review has determined that Nikolaev was promised his life if he gave the testimony demanded of him in court.

4. During the investigation Nikolaev was deceived. The illusion was created that his wife had not been arrested, and a supposed illegal correspondence was organized between him and his wife. [. . .]

[The report then covers the pre-1928 oppositional activity of the accused in the "Leningrad Center" and notes that there was no plausible evidence that any of them engaged in such activity later, in spite of the confessions forced from them. The description of Mandelshtam's testimony during the investigation is typical:]

Mandelshtam testified at his interrogations that there existed in Leningrad a counterrevolutionary Zinovievite organization, of which Nikolaev was a member. Mandelshtam did not say from what sources he knew of Nikolaev's membership in this organization.

At his meeting with Vyshinsky, Mandelshtam declared that "I admit the fact of the existence of an organization only in the sense that the participants in the former opposition represented in themselves a particular social circle that retained a certain element of factionalism, but had no particular unity of views or action."

[. . .]

IV. Trial of the Case

The trial of the case of Nikolaev, Kotolynov, and the others took place with gross violations of procedural norms.

After receiving copies of the charges a number of the accused petitioned to call additional witnesses before the court and attach documents [to their case files], but the court did not review these petitions.

At the outset of the trial the accused were not explained their rights in court and they were not asked whether they had any petitions to present before the trial began. The indictments were not read in court and the accused were not asked whether they pled guilty to the charges or not. [. . .]

Despite the fact that Nikolaev was the main defendant in the case, he was the one who denounced all the others for participating in the murder of S. M. Kirov; the presiding judge Ulrikh established an illegal trial procedure by removing from the courtroom all of the accused except for Nikolaev, questioning the latter in the absence of the other accused.

After the conclusion of Nikolaev's cross-examination, the other accused were brought into the courtroom one by one. None of them knew how those cross-examined earlier had conducted themselves. They were thus deprived of the possibility of cross-examination or explanations with regard to the testimony of their fellow accused.

The cross-examinations of the accused were constructed such that they could not go beyond the framework of their earlier depositions given during the preliminary investigation.

[. . .]

Sositsky [. . .] refused at the trial to confirm his testimony from the preliminary investigation that he had terrorist attitudes. He tried to give an explanation in this regard. The following conversation took place between Ulrikh and Sositsky.

"Chairman: No explanations are necessary.

"Sositsky: No . . .

"Chairman: I am not asking you about that. You gave a deposition / reads/. . . . Do you confirm this testimony?

"Sositsky: No, I did not go so far as terror. In the preliminary investigation I testified to the effect that . . .

"Chairman: I am reading your deposition, which you signed: "and thus our organization, in accordance with an inevitable logic, resorted to terror /reads/ . . .

"Your group instigated, your center provided guidance. Nikolaev shot —totally logical."

[. . .]

Former member of the Military Tribunal A. D. Goriachev, interrogated by us, testified that at the beginning of the trial Nikolaev announced that he had carried out the murder of S. M. Kirov for his own reasons independent of any ties with the Zinovievites, and he took this back only after Ulrikh began to tax him with his earlier statements.

The majority of the accused denied Nikolaev's claims. [. . .]

The accused Zvezdov testified to the court that he knew absolutely nothing about the preparation of the assassination of S. M. Kirov, that such a thought had never even entered his head. [. . .]

Nor did the accused [. . .] Shatsky confess himself guilty of belonging to any counterrevolutionary organization or participating in the murder of Kirov.

The accused Rumiantsev denied categorically his participation in the terrorist group and stated that he did not even know Nikolaev. [. . .]

Mandelshtam stated to the court, "I categorically deny any participation in terrorist activities, their preparation, or their discussion—because I was not an advocate of individual terror."

[. . .]

V. Behavior of the Accused after Announcement of the Sentence.

Certain information uncovered about the behavior of the accused following the announcement of their death sentences is significant for the evaluation of the evidence accepted by the court in the case of Nikolaev, Kotolynov, and the others.

As noted in the December 29, 1934 report of the deputy commissar of the NKVD /Agranov/, after the announcement of the sentence Nikolaev banged his head on the barrier and exclaimed, "How cruel!" Katsafa . . . who was present at the trial, stated [in 1956] that Nikolaev screamed "They lied to me!" This testimony is indirectly strengthened by the explanations of Gusev K. S. [Nikolaev's other guard] and Sheinin L. P. [investigator for the prosecutor's Office for High Priority Cases]. Gusev states that Nikolaev upon return from the courtroom exclaimed, "Can it really be? It can't! It can't!" Sheinin, citing the words of Vyshinsky says that Nikolaev before his execution said, "But I exposed those bastards."

[. . .]

VI. Circumstances of the Death of M. V. Borisov

[. . .] Khviiuzov, Kuzin, Maly, and Vinogradov categorically asserted [during the 1934–1935 investigation] that Borisov's death was the chance result of an automobile accident and that they never got from anyone an order to murder Borisov.

In June 1937 Khviiuzov, Vinogradov, and Maly were arrested and in the preliminary investigation confessed their guilt in the premeditated murder of Borisov. They asserted that at their interrogations in December 1934 they gave false evidence as to the reasons for Borisov's death. [. . .]

At the trial of his case Vinogradov recanted his confessions, declaring, "I gave them falsely, hoping thus to save my life."

[. . .]

In June 1937 the driver Kuzin was arrested and with regard to the death of Borisov testified:

" . . . The accident occurred not because the truck was not in working order, as I stated in 1934, but was caused by Maly, who grabbed the steering wheel while we were driving at high speed, turned the truck to the left, which caused it to crash and kill Kirov."

At an interrogation on June 29, 1937 Kuzin, affirming that Borisov had been killed by Maly and Vinogradov, in support of this assertion offered the following claims.[46]

"1. The speed of the automobile by the wall at the moment of the accident was negligible, it could not under any circumstances have caused a fatal blow to those sitting in the automobile by the building wall no matter what their position in the back of the automobile at the moment of the accident.

"2. Maly, who was sitting next to me, instantly jumped out the moment the auto stopped and went to the back where Borisov and Vinogradov were.

"3. Immediately following the accident, while I was still in the passenger cabin of the car, I heard from the back a muffled blow, after which Vinogradov, who had been sitting there, threw himself out of the back of the automobile and only Maly remained there after that.

"4. When I jumped into the back of the auto, Borisov was already half-dead and I saw that blood was pouring out of the right side of Borisov's head while in fact the blow from the car accident could only have wounded him on the left side of the head." [. . .]

Interrogated on April 19, 1956 Kuzin fundamentally changed his testimony of 1937, confirming only that the auto accident happened because Maly, riding in the cab with him, grabbed the wheel.

Now Kuzin claims that Maly did not get into the back of the truck after the accident, but stood by the radiator, that he heard no muffled blows from the back of the truck, that he saw no foreign objects in the back of the truck, nor did he see Borisov bang his head on the wall.

Explaining the contradictions in his testimony from 1934, 1937, and 1956, Kuzin stated that he always had said the same thing, but the investigators had not noted down his words precisely. [. . .]

At a face-to-face confrontation with his former interrogator Yakushev on April 20, 1956, Kuzin asserted that soon after his arrest in 1937 he was subjected to beatings, and then had to stand in a corner for about twenty days, until he collapsed. All this time he was interrogated on the "conveyor" by four to five investigators who demanded that he confess to belonging to a Trotskyite-Zinovievite organization.

As is evident from the materials of our review, the 1937 investigation of Borisov's death was carried out in very tendentious fashion. [. . .] materials of the investigation into this matter in 1937 were falsified.

The thrust of this report, then, was that the accused former oppositionists in the "Leningrad Center" trial had almost certainly not conspired with Nikolaev, and that the 1937 version of Borisov's death (murdered by Leningrad NKVD officers) was extracted under torture and probably false. The report also discredited Yakushev, author of the March–April letter claiming that the Leningrad NKVD had killed Borisov. Kuzin himself, who had incriminated Maly and Vinogradov, and was responsible in part for their executions, temporized in 1956, protecting himself and pursuing his own agenda. He denounced Yakushev for torturing him, while at the same denying that any of his earlier testimony was false. Thus, he could not be held responsible for the executions of Vinogradov and Maly in 1937.[47]

The report contained an interesting coda, covering the trial of Leningrad NKVD officials for negligence in the Kirov case in January 1935. This section, excerpted below, could be used to suggest a conspiracy to assassinate Kirov, not among Zinovievite oppositionists, but within the Leningrad NKVD. Such a conspiracy could, of course, fit within a larger story of Stalin planning Kirov's murder (following the outlines of the 1938 show trial narrative, but with Stalin replacing the "Right-Trotskyite Center"). The April 1956 report did not make any such suggestions, but the potential of the evidence was probably important.

· 118 ·

(continued)

Joint KGB/USSR prosecutor's report on the Kirov murder, April 20, 1956. RGANI, f. 6, op. 13, d. 1, ll. 10–53. (All emphases added.)

After the murder of S. M. Kirov the former head of the Leningrad Region NKVD F. D. Medved, his deputies I. V. Zaporozhets and F. T. Fomin, the chief of the Operations Department A. A. Gubin, the chief of the Secret Political Department A. S. Gorin-Lundin, the section chief M. I. Kotomin of the Operations Department, and other officers of the Leningrad Province NKVD, twelve persons in all, were arrested and charged with criminal negligence of their professional duties. [. . .]

Medved, Zaporozhets, and Fomin were charged with failure to maintain a satisfactory guard for S. M. Kirov and failure to take measures to uncover and halt in timely fashion the activities of the counterrevolutionary terrorist Zinovievite group in Leningrad. [. . .]

During the investigation [. . .] Medved testified that there were no written instructions for the persons guarding S. M. Kirov, and there was no general plan for the guard. He did not undertake any checks of the guard posts.

Medved confessed himself guilty in that he "was not able to arrest in Leningrad a number of counterrevolutionaries among the Trotsky-Zinovievite activists, among them Rumiantsev, Levin, and others, and I did not put this question before the former OGPU or NKVD." [. . .]

During the investigation Zaporozhets, *who was interrogated only once,* on January 14, 1935, testified that direct control over Kirov's guard was in the hands of Medved, and he dealt with issues related to the guard only when Medved was absent. [. . .]

Gubin and Kotomin were accused of "illegally freeing L. V. Nikolaev, *who was bearing a revolver and counterrevolutionary writings at the time, without checking his identity or searching him,*" and of not taking necessary measures to guard S. M. Kirov. [. . .]

The checking of Nikolaev's identity, as Gubin testified further, was inadequate, and his release was made only on the basis of personal impressions of him [that Gubin gathered] from Kotomin's [oral] report. [. . .]

In addition Gubin testified that neither Medved nor Zaporozhets gave him special instructions for the guard of S. M. Kirov, and they heard reports from him [Gubin] on the guard only on a case-by-case basis.

Medved, Zaporozhets, and Fomin were not interrogated about the incident of Nikolaev's detention. [. . .]

Lobov, interrogated in April 1956, testified that after the trial he, Medved, Zaporozhets, and others were transferred to Kolyma to serve out their terms of imprisonment. Although they rode in a prison train car, in fact their freedom during the trip was not limited in any way.

According to Lobov, upon arrival in Magadan [near Kolyma] they were immediately appointed to supervisory positions in the Dalstroi system. [. . .]

While at Kolyma, Zaporozhets told Lobov that before he was sent to Kolyma *Yagoda had called him in and announced that supposedly Stalin had issued an order not to punish harshly the NKVD officers guilty of failure to maintain an adequate guard for Kirov, and after a short period of time, to restore them to their work and to the party.*

The italicized passages in the excerpt above all hint that there might have been some kind of conspiracy within the Leningrad NKVD, possibly abetted by central authorities, to let Nikolaev get at Kirov. The last section, taken from the 1956 testimony of P. M. Lobov, deserves special attention. Lobov, who had been Zaporozhets' deputy in Leningrad and who had murdered Sokolnikov on Beria's orders in 1939, was clearly hinting that Stalin had gone easy on the Leningrad NKVD for a reason—perhaps their negligence had not been unwelcome. Serov and Rudenko probably also included this testimony in their report for a reason. It opened a possible line of inquiry that would point from the Leningrad NKVD to the center—to Stalin, or perhaps one of his closest lieutenants, like Molotov.

While Lobov's testimony is dramatic, it may have been tainted by 1937 testimony against his superior Zaporozhets, and against Yagoda. Lobov may have testified at that time that Yagoda had ordered soft treatment of the Leningrad NKVD, because they had helped in the supposed anti-Stalinist plot to kill Kirov. By "tainted," I mean that he may have chosen to confirm his 1937 testimony in 1956, regardless of its truth or falsity. Whatever the case, in the years after 1956 Lobov would repeatedly enlarge upon his testimony until Zaporozhets at Kolyma was telling him the whole story of a putative Stalin-Yagoda-Zaporozhets plot to kill Kirov—again, almost precisely the story-line of the 1938 show trial of Yagoda and the leaders of the "Right-Trotskyite Bloc."

The memorandum in some ways contradicted itself. It did not point towards a single version of Kirov's assassination (in contrast, for example, to Kozlov's letter to Khrushchev in March). Its account of Borisov's death as an accident undermined the hints of Leningrad NKVD involvement in Kirov's death. This could be due to two reasons, not mutually exclusive. First, the memorandum's authors seem to have made an effort to grapple with the actual evidence at hand, which was in some ways contradictory. Second (see below), they wished at once to undermine any claim that Nikolaev was part of a real Zinovievite conspiracy, and to leave open the possibility that the Leningrad NKVD, and perhaps Stalin or his underlings, were involved the murder.

A third report from April 1956 came from the USSR prosecutor's office in response to the April 23 query from the Molotov commission for "materials on the validity and legality of the preliminary investigation, inquest, and trial in the case of the murder of S. M. Kirov." This memorandum repeated the contents of the two already analyzed, albeit with some different data. The authors contended forcefully that Nikolaev was a lone gunman, psychologically disturbed, who had no conspiratorial connections to any of the other accused in the trial of the "Leningrad Center." They argued that the trial was an obvious fabrication that was "in direct violation of the law" of December 1, 1934 on expedited trials for accused terrorists. The document gave a definitive "no" in answer to the Molotov commission's implied queries as to whether Nikolaev was a Zinovievite and whether there was a Zinovievite terrorist group involved in the Kirov murder. In other words, it took what was almost certainly a strongly anti-Molotov position. Unlike the April 20 memorandum, it did not discuss Borisov's death or the issue of Leningrad NKVD negligence in organizing Kirov's guard.[48]

Central to this book is the question of what, if anything, the KGB might have concealed when it released documents from the Kirov investigation to the party Central Committee. Was Serov, for example, concealing key evidence against Stalin or key evidence against Leningrad NKVD officers when he released investigation materials to the Molotov commission on April 20, 1956? Given the facts covered in this chapter so far, this seems unlikely. Serov was Khrushchev's man throughout this period. There was no reason for him not to be. Khrushchev controlled the situation in the spring of 1956. He had key men in other positions by this time, most importantly Rudenko as USSR prosecutor and Shvernik as head of the KPK. And he had made it clear both in the "Secret Speech" and in Presidium meetings that he was interested in "solving" the Kirov murder, and that the solution might implicate Stalin or his closest lieutenants at the time. Khrushchev had looked favorably, for example, upon Shatunovskaya's letter reporting rumors that Leningrad NKVD officers had "run" Nikolaev, and that Stalin had turned a blind eye.

To understand the positions that Serov and the USSR prosecutor's office took in their memoranda, it is necessary to see precisely what was at stake in the deliberations of the Molotov commission. The commission was charged with investigating the show trials of the later 1930s and determining whether the charges were valid. The Kirov murder and the trials of the "Leningrad Center" and "Moscow Center" that immediately followed were just the starting point of the inquiry, but everything that followed depended on these events. If the official charges in the first two trials—that former Zinoviev supporters had conspired to murder Kirov—were entirely bogus, then the indictments in all of the succeeding show trials collapsed. The later indictments were built on the earlier ones, albeit in a confused and illogical way. But if there was some truth to the charge that Zinovievites conspired to kill Kirov, then that preserved the possibility of arguing that the later charges were also valid, at least in part. Therefore Serov and Rudenko (or their subordinates who authored the memoranda) chose to make a clear-cut argument that Nikolaev had had no relationship at all with the ex-Zinoviev supporters convicted in the trial of the "Leningrad Center."

It appears that Serov or his boss had thought through this strategy, to deny any connection at all between Nikolaev and the Zinovievites, even before the "Secret Speech." On January 27, 1956 the KGB destroyed central records on the case file "Svoiak," the all-union surveillance operation against the Zinovievites. It seems likely that "Svoiak" contained more evidence than Serov wanted Molotov to see, either of counterrevolutionary talk among former Zinovievites and/or of Nikolaev's connections with the accused in the "Leningrad Center." Serov concealed other evidence of connections between Nikolaev and the ex-Zinovievites Kotolynov, Antonov, and Shatsky. The excerpts from Nikolaev's diaries that he released to the Molotov commission in April 1956 contained no references to these men. But we know from later releases of data that Nikolaev did mention all three in his diaries. Serov presumably feared that Molotov would construe such connections as evidence of criminal conspiracy.[49]

At the time the Molotov commission was debating these issues, Rudenko, Serov, and KPK officials were already taking actions based on the assumption that the charges in the show trials were false. In his memoirs Khrushchev reports a conversation with Rudenko some time before the creation of the Pospelov commission (that is, before December 31, 1955), in which the prosecutor told him that the charges against Bukharin, Rykov, Krestinsky, and others in the 1930s show trials were baseless.[50] Moreover, in early 1956 the ongoing rehabilitations of Central Committee members who perished in 1936–1938 were creeping in the direction of the accused in the open show trials. On April 25, A. I. Stetsky, executed in late 1938 for supposed conspiratorial ties with the "Right-Trotskyite Bloc," and a former close associate of Bukharin, was rehabilitated by the USSR prosecutor's office. On May 5, 1956, the same office rehabilitated former Leningrad official N. K. Antipov (one of the veteran Leningraders hostile to Kirov), who at one point had been slated for public trial together with Bukharin and Rykov.[51]

Nevertheless, Molotov, famous for his stubbornness, continued to defend the show trials. On May 9, 1956 the Molotov commission met for the third time and discussed the reports on the Kirov case submitted by the KGB and the USSR prosecutor's office. Apparently the commission members could reach no consensus on an interpretation of the assassination and trial of the "Leningrad Center." Therefore, they resolved to lay aside consideration of the case for the moment and move on to investigate later proceedings. The commission would return to the Kirov affair at a later date.[52]

In the meantime reaction to the "Secret Speech" inside and outside the USSR led to doubts among some Central Committee leaders about further public revelations of Stalinist repression. In the USSR the pro-Stalin riots in Georgia and numerous reports of party members questioning the entire Soviet system at meetings caused uneasiness. In late June thousands of strikers in the Polish city of Poznan demanded "Bread and Freedom," while in Hungary participants in a youth forum established by the party leadership turned on the Communist leader, Matyas Rakosi. In June the Italian Communist leader Palmiro Togliatti suggested that the Soviet Union might have undergone "a bureaucratic degeneration." In response the Central Committee Presidium tasked Pospelov with drafting a resolution on the "Secret Speech." The draft, with minor changes, was approved by the Presidium on June 30, 1956 under the title "On Overcoming the Cult of Personality and its Consequences."[53]

Soviet reformers of the time and many Western historians came to view the June 30, 1956 Presidium resolution as a fundamental setback to, or even a reversal of de-Stalinization. But the impact of the resolution and its regressive content have been exaggerated. It is hard to see what other reaction the party leadership could have had to condemnations of the entire Soviet system as corrupt and degenerate—in effect unsalvageable. The leaders, including Khrushchev, naturally assumed that the system of one-party rule and state ownership of the economy was sound—indeed, that it represented the future of humanity. In response to the disorders and to criticisms of the Soviet system as a whole, then, they reaffirmed that Stalin had made great mistakes and committed many crimes, but that he was a genuine fighter for socialism. Flaws in his personality, noted by Lenin, together with the pressures of fighting capitalist enemies without and their collaborators within, had been too much for Stalin, and the sad result was the cult of personality. The "cult of personality," the resolution stated, was "in contradiction to the nature of Soviet society (*stroi*)." It was an alien growth that needed to be removed. At the same time, the Soviet people "were justified in their pride that our Motherland was the first to build the road to socialism."[54]

The June 30 resolution did put a damper on denunciation of Stalin in the upper levels of the Soviet Communist Party. And it followed Molotov's formula of noting Stalin's accomplishments as well as his "shortcomings." But the resolution did not signal the end of de-Stalinization. Work continued on the rehabilitation of party members repressed in the Terror, on restoring the rights of deported peoples and former POWs, and on compensating camp survivors for confiscated property.[55]

The changing atmosphere seems to have made the old Stalinists on the commission, led by Molotov, bolder. Between May 10 and July 30 the Molotov commission met seven times. Protocols of the meetings provide scanty information on proceedings, but combined with other evidence suggest an escalating struggle between the old Stalinists and the younger Khrushchev backers. The commission examined documents of the major trials of 1935–1938 provided by Serov and Rudenko. On May 30, members were unprepared to deliver a scheduled written report to the Presidium on its findings, and resolved instead to present an oral summary. On June 1, the Presidium agreed to postpone the report. Questions put by the commission to Serov on July 25 suggest that Molotov was pushing hard his view that the defendants in the trials were guilty of at least some of the charges. Commission members wanted information on meetings of various accused with Trotskyites abroad, on Bukharin's possible connections with the old Socialist Revolutionary Party, and on Nikolaev's connections with foreign consuls in Leningrad. On July 30 the commission resolved to return to discussion of the Kirov murder, requesting "detailed conclusions" on the matter from Rudenko and Serov before breaking for the summer holidays.[56]

Khrushchev's point man on the commission, Aristov, continued to work with Serov on the Kirov murder. On July 18, 1956 Serov sent a memorandum to Aristov headed "On the Results of Investigation of M. N. Volkova's Letter on the Murder of S. M. Kirov." Volkova, familiar from earlier chapters as the denouncer Stalin pulled out of a mental hospital on December 2, 1934 and used to purge Leningrad of supposed terrorist plotters, had written a denunciation to the Central

Committee in May 1956. She claimed that she had known Nikolaev personally, that he had been a member of a counterrevolutionary organization dedicated to assassinating Kirov, Molotov, and Voroshilov, and that some participants in the conspiracy were still alive and well in Leningrad. Serov attached a report from KGB colonels Dobrokhotov and Kallistov that detailed Volkova's history of compulsive denunciation and destroyed her credibility.[57]

Given that Serov's letter was addressed to Aristov, it seems that the latter had probably asked for a KGB evaluation of Volkova's denunciation. The denunciation itself could have been used by Molotov or his antagonists on the Molotov commission. It suggested a wide-ranging conspiracy to murder Kirov, true, but one directed against the Stalinist leadership as a whole (which would fit the 1938 show trial version of events). The KGB debunked the denunciation completely, perhaps to ensure that Molotov could make no use of it. A later commission, on which Shatunovskaya played a decisive role, would return to Volkova's evidence in an effort to find evidence implicating Stalin in the murder.

Late in the summer, Serov (or his assistants) produced yet another report on the Kirov murder, in response to the Molotov commission's July 30 demand for "detailed conclusions." This memorandum squarely opposed the efforts of Molotov and his allies to suggest that there had been a real Zinovievite conspiracy to kill Kirov. The authors marshaled a great deal of evidence from the 1934–1935 investigations to argue that Nikolaev was a lone gunman and Borisov had died in an auto accident. They also went over testimony about the Kirov murder from the later show trials, demonstrating that the defendants, including Yagoda, were almost certainly innocent of any conspiracy.

· 119 ·

August 31, 1956 KGB (Serov) report in response to Molotov commission queries of July 30, 1956. RGANI, f. 6, op. 13, d. 2, ll. 78–107.

To Comrade Shvernik, N. M.

I am sending to you this report re: the questions raised in the protocol of the Central Committee commission of July 30, 1956.

I. Serov.

August 31, 1956

[Parts I and II of the report cover the crime scene and Nikolaev's personality. They follow the same lines and reproduce much of the same testimony as the April 1956 reports to the Molotov commission and the documents translated in Chapter 4.]

III. Evolution of Interpretation of the Evidence in the Murder of S. M. Kirov between 1934 and 1938.

In the beginning the investigators in the murder of S. M. Kirov interpreted the circumstances as follows—Nikolaev, a person with anti-Soviet inclinations, was a lone terrorist, acting without collaborators.

From the available documents it is clear that later, without any basis, the investigation changed tracks in the direction of collecting "proofs" that supposedly confirmed the existence of criminal connections between Nikolaev and the group of former participants in the Zinovievite opposition. In this way the case against Kotolynov, Rumiantsev, and others appeared. Moreover it is worth noting that even on the eve of trial the investigators had no evidence of any interest on Nikolaev's part in any of the former oppositionists, much less of [closer] connections between him and Kotolynov, Rumiantsev, or others among the accused.

Before the case went to trial, Zinoviev, Kamenev [. . .] and a series of other former participants in the opposition were arrested without any evidence of participation in the assassination of S. M. Kirov. This case was then carried through under the banner of the "moral responsibility" of the former leaders of the opposition for the murder of S. M. Kirov, insofar as the assassin /for no reason whatsoever/ was labeled as one of the Zinovievites. On this charge, that of moral responsibility, the accused confessed themselves guilty.

However, later, when Nikolaev, Kotolynov, Rumiantsev, and the others were no longer among the living, and hence, there were no persons who could confirm or deny any new versions of the murder of S. M. Kirov, an entirely new interpretation of the role of Zinoviev, Kamenev, and the others was accepted.

Based only the statements of the accused, and in spite of the fact that these clearly contradicted their earlier explanations and materials made at previous trials, it was presented as proven that the Trotsky-Zinovievite Center directly managed the organization of S. M. Kirov's murder, and its representative Bakaev personally met with and instructed the killer Nikolaev.

Even later, after Zinoviev, Kamenev, Yevdokimov, Bakaev, and others had been shot, yet another new version appeared, to wit, that the murder of S. M. Kirov was carried out at the order of a Right-Trotskyite Bloc. Moreover, this version was accepted as proven based only on the statements of Yagoda, which he himself [. . .] retracted in his last words to the court. [This version] was accepted as proven in spite of the fact that it was debunked by Bukharin and Rykov, and by all the materials of the earlier trials.

Thus it turned out that, given the absence of documentary evidence, the fewer persons remained alive whose evidence the court should have considered in its decision (and this includes the investigators who took part in the inquiries for the previous trials), the larger the circle of persons grew who turned out to be guilty in participating in the murder of Kirov. [. . .]

[Part IV debunks the December 1934 case against the "Leningrad Center" in similar terms to the April 1956 reports. Some of the evidence presented in Chapters 8 and 9 is reproduced.]

V. The Participation of Zinoviev, Kamenev, and Others in the Murder of S. M. Kirov at the trials of 1935–1936

In the sentences in the case of the "United Trotskyite-Zinovievite Center" [August 1936] all of the accused were convicted in the assassination of S. M. Kirov.

During the investigation and during the trial Zinoviev, Kamenev, Yevdokimov, and Bakaev testified that S. M. Kirov was killed in accord with the decisions of the "Trotskyite-Zinovievite Center." If one accepts the formal approach to this testimony, as the court did, it is possible to accept as proven the guilt of the accused, and the sentence was in this sense justified. However, comparison of the various statements with one another, with consideration of the other materials at the disposal of the court and the investigation, and the data collected during the review of 1956, gives reason to affirm that the accusations against Zinoviev, Kamenev, and other persons on trial in the case of the "United Trotskyite-Zinovievite Center" on charges of murdering S. M. Kirov were falsified. None of them were complicit in the murder.

The statements of Zinoviev, Kamenev, Yevdokimov, and Bakaev, unsupported by any other evidence, are diametrically opposed to the statements they gave to the court in January 1935. Previously they all asserted that the murder of S. M. Kirov was as unexpected to them as for all Soviet persons. These statements [of August 1936] are also refuted by all the investigative materials on the case of Nikolaev, Kotolynov, Rumiantsev, et al., as none of the accused in this case gave any evidence of the participation of Bakaev, Zinoviev, Kamenev, and others in the murder of S. M. Kirov.

It also should be noted that the statements of Zinoviev, Kamenev, et al. in 1936 do not stand up when compared directly to one another, and in a number of instances include obviously untrue assertions. For example, Bakaev said that the decision to kill Kirov was taken in 1934, while Yevdokimov said it was 1932. Some [of the accused] testified that Bakaev was charged with managing the organization of the terrorist act against S. M. Kirov, but he said that he had just a onetime assignment—to check up on preparations. Bakaev [. . .] testified that Yevdokimov recommended Nikolaev to carry out the terrorist act, as he had known him for many years. Yevdokimov himself did not testify to this, although he did state in court that he recognized the photograph of Nikolaev as a person he'd known in 1925–1926. At this time Yevdokimov was secretary of the Leningrad Province committee of the party, and Nikolaev—the manager of the Luga County committee of the Komsomol. For this reason Nikolaev could hardly have been acquainted with Yevdokimov. [. . .]

VI. Participation of the Rightists in the Murder of S. M. Kirov

On March 13, 1938 the Military Collegium of the Supreme Court of the USSR found Bukharin, Rykov, Yagoda, and other accused, tried in the case of the so-called "Right-Trotskyite Bloc," guilty in carrying out the villainous murder of S. M. Kirov. [. . .]

Rykov and Bukharin, who supposedly made the decision to carry out this terrorist act, during the investigation and in court categorically denied not just participating in, but even knowing anything about this affair. [. . .]

In his final words to the court Yagoda declared:

"Not only is it false to say that I was an organizer, but even to say that I was an accomplice in the murder of Kirov. I am guilty of a very serious dereliction of duty, that is true. I will answer for that in full measure, but I was not an accomplice. 'An accomplice'—you know as well as I do, comrade prosecutor, what that means. None of the materials of this trial or the preliminary investigation show that I was an accomplice in this villainous murder."

In this declaration Yagoda in essence recanted his earlier testimony with regard to the participation of the Rightists in the murder of Kirov. [. . .]

It has been determined by the inquiry of 1956 that during the investigation process measures of physical pressure were used against Yagoda, and that before the trial Yezhov promised him his life, if he said in court what was demanded of him. [. . .]

IX. Conclusions [. . .]

1. Nikolaev, the murderer of S. M. Kirov, was a person with anti-Soviet inclinations.

2. In the period of the struggle of the party against the oppositions, Trotsky, Zinoviev, Kamenev, and their supporters strove to sow distrust in the leadership of the party and the country. Their slanderous assertions about degeneration of the party, about the necessity of changing the composition of the party leadership, their attempts to take the intraparty struggle "to the streets" [. . .] facilitated the growth of terrorist moods among politically immature, unstable persons. [. . .] However, neither in [. . .] the investigation nor [. . .] in the recent review was any evidence found of the existence of any connection of Trotsky, Zinoviev, et al., with the concrete facts of S. M. Kirov's assassination. The version of the direct participation of Zinovievites, Trotskyites, and [. . .] "Rights" in the mur-

der of S. M. Kirov is completely made up, and their false testimony [. . .] was obtained as a result of use of measures forbidden by law. [. . .]

3. The death of Borisov was the result of an accident.

4. The officers of the Leningrad Province NKVD, accused of the murder of Borisov, were executed without reason based on falsified materials.

In this report Serov omitted any evidence that might point to a conspiracy by Stalin, Yagoda, and/or local NKVD officials to kill Kirov. Yet behind the scenes investigators continued to collect such evidence, even the most unreliable. On July 20, P. M. Lobov, Zaporozhets' former deputy, enlarged on his April testimony. Not only had Zaporozhets told him about Stalin's order to Yagoda to take it easy on the Leningrad NKVD, Lobov said, he had also told him that the Leningrad NKVD had detained Nikolaev more than once, and that Yagoda, through Zaporozhets, had ordered Nikolaev's release. Here again, Lobov's testimony followed the story-line of the March 1938 show trial on the purported conspiracy to murder Kirov.[58]

The Molotov commission did not meet again until November 19, 1956, perhaps because the discussions had reached an impasse, perhaps because the Soviet leaders were occupied with summer holidays, the Suez war in Egypt, and revolution in Hungary. But when it did meet, members moved quickly to produce a report to the Presidium. After discussion of the memorandum on the Kirov murder from Serov (excerpted above) and Rudenko, the commission charged Rudenko with preparing a draft report to the Presidium. On December 4 the commission approved Rudenko's draft, recommending minor changes.[59]

The commission's conclusions were an incoherent and contradictory mess, but an overall victory for Molotov. The memorandum emphasized that because there were real enemies inside and outside the Soviet Union in the 1920s and 1930s the repressions of the period were justified. Although there was no conclusive evidence of "criminal ties" between Nikolaev and any Zinovievites, the latter bore responsibility for encouraging terrorism by struggling against the party majority. In particular oppositionist rhetoric in Leningrad fed Nikolaev's hatred of Kirov. In the absence of any evidence of an oppositionist conspiracy to murder Kirov, the verdicts of the show trials of 1935–1938 were nonetheless justified because the accused in those trials had undermined the construction of socialism. Yet at the same time the authors concluded that Stalin's unlimited power had allowed him to undertake a full-scale attack on the party itself in the wake of Kirov's murder, aided by "careerists and provocateurs" in the NKVD.[60]

Khrushchev evidently was unhappy with the report. It seems likely that he wanted a complete rejection of the show trial verdicts and some sort of indictment of Stalin. On December 14, 1956 the Presidium resolved to "take note of" the Molotov commission's report and order it back to work. The Presidium also put Serov on the commission (previously he had attended sessions only as a rapporteur, not as a member). Presumably this was because Khrushchev wanted to strengthen his influence on the deliberations.[61]

In the following months relations rapidly deteriorated between Khrushchev and a number of other party leaders. Molotov, Kaganovich, Voroshilov, and Malenkov must all have feared the personal consequences of further public de-Stalinization. But others, including Bulganin and USSR Foreign Minister Shepilov, also came to view Khrushchev as out of control and dangerously power-hungry. De-Stalinization was not the only issue for this group. While Shepilov for one has written that he feared further public denunciations of Stalinist repression would undermine the stability of the Soviet regime, none of these men wished to return to the extreme state terror of the Stalin era. Rather, they were afraid of Khrushchev's accumulation of power, they were afraid of his control of the KGB through Serov, and they were appalled at some of his policy initiatives, most notably his January 1957 proposal to decentralize the management of industry. There was also a general perception that Khrushchev was a rash big-mouth.[62]

Although Khrushchev has been portrayed as unaware of the widespread dissatisfaction with his power, there is some evidence that he was deliberately pushing affairs towards a confrontation. Pyotr Demichev, a Khrushchev assistant in 1957, and Shepilov both believed Khrushchev knew that an attempt to remove him was in the works. Shepilov asserted that Serov, who was eavesdropping on the other party leaders, must have told him. Putting these claims together with Khrushchev's aggressive behavior towards Molotov, Malenkov, and Kaganovich in the spring of 1957, it appears quite plausible that the Soviet leader was pressing towards a final showdown with his rivals.[63]

The scanty records of the Molotov commission suggest that Khrushchev used it to apply heavy pressure to the Molotov group. On April 8, 1957 the commission met for the first time after a four-month hiatus, with Serov now on board as a full participant. Members chose to define a narrow issue for investigation, namely the death of Kirov's guard Borisov. Serov and Rudenko were assigned to prepare a draft report to the Central Committee. On April 13 the commission discussed the draft, but apparently Aristov, Khrushchev ally and aggressive de-Stalinizer, was unhappy with it. The commission agreed to postpone presentation of a report to the Central Committee for ten days, while Aristov gathered new materials on Borisov's death. Unfortunately, we do not know what materials, if any, Aristov provided.[64]

On April 23, 1957, after some discussion, commission members assigned Rudenko, Serov, and Pospelov to prepare by the end of the day another draft memorandum on Borisov. Apparently they were under pressure to present their report quickly to the Presidium. The final report was, like the December memorandum on the 1930s show trials, an awkward, inconclusive document. It was clear why there were "doubts" about Borisov's death—he was the only one seriously hurt in the truck accident, and his failure to maintain a close guard on Kirov led to the latter's death. But the 1937 testimony of the driver and guards who accompanied Borisov on December 2 was extracted under torture, and was therefore untrustworthy. Hence, there was no hard evidence of foul play. The commission stated that since events had occurred so long ago, there was no possibility of finally determining the truth, and therefore the inquiry should be closed.[65]

Khrushchev remained determined to force a repudiation of the show trials and the Terror on Molotov. On the afternoon of April 25 the Presidium met to discuss the rehabilitation of Tukhachevsky, Yakir, and Uborevich, the three leading generals executed for treason in 1937, and of victims of other Terror cases. Khrushchev threw down the gauntlet to Molotov and company. During discussion of the rehabilitation of E. E. Rubinchik, a former factory director convicted for sabotaging the design of an amphibious tank, Khrushchev stated sarcastically that "my friend Georgy Malenkov played an unseemly role in this affair." When the Presidium considered the Tukhachevsky rehabilitation, Khrushchev challenged, "let the old members of the Politburo tell us how they decided the question of bringing Yakir to trial, how this first step was prepared." Marshal Zhukov seconded Khrushchev with "we've got to get to the bottom of this." According to Brezhnev's account two months later, at the June 1957 TsK plenum, Khrushchev asked, "What are we going to do with those guilty of these executions? Will we return to this issue, or will we just continue to keep out mouths shut about them. . . ."[66]

During May Rudenko and Serov continued to press rehabilitation in a direction that the old Politburo cohort could not have liked. On May 18, 1957 the two recommended the rehabilitation of Akmal Ikramov, tried and convicted together with Bukharin in the March 1938 trial of the "Right-Trotskyite Bloc." Ikramov was the first rehabilitee from among those convicted in the open show trials of the Terror. In their memorandum, Serov and Rudenko debunked the evidence presented against Ikramov, including his own "confessions." The rehabilitations moved one step closer to the leaders of the Right themselves, Bukharin and Rykov, and to a complete rejection of the show trials.[67]

On June 18, 1957 tensions between Khrushchev and the Molotov group erupted. With the support of seven of eleven full members of the Presidium, the old Stalin guard attempted to fire Khrushchev from the post of first secretary of the Central Committee. For four days Presidium members locked in intense debate, with the majority of full members savaging Khrushchev for arrogance, incompetence, and construction of his own cult of personality. A number of Khrushchev's rivals complained that Serov was spying on them, and there was apparently a proposal to remove Serov as KGB chief. Kaganovich argued that Khrushchev's supposed sympathies with the Trotskyites were motivating his efforts to review the great show trials of the Terror.

The Khrushchev faction fought back. Zhukov and Shvernik denounced Molotov's, Kaganovich's, and Malenkov's prominent roles in the Terror, with Zhukov apparently reading aloud from archival documents. Khrushchev rallied candidate members of the Presidium and a number of TsK secretaries to his side. Behind the scenes Serov and Zhukov flew dozens of Central Committee members to Moscow on military transport aircraft. With the military, the KGB, and the majority of the party elite below Presidium level on his side, Khrushchev forced his opponents to agree to a full session of the Central Committee, which began on June 22.[68]

Khrushchev was in undisputed control of the TsK plenum that followed, which was devoted to denunciation of the "antiparty group" of Molotov, Malenkov, and Kaganovich. These three, together with Shepilov, were expelled from their leadership posts and from the Central Committee. Pervukhin, Saburov, and Bulganin "confessed" their errors early in the plenum and got off for the time being with demotions. Khrushchev let Voroshilov off the hook, more a gesture of contempt than anything else.[69]

The June 1957 TsK plenum was above all about the history of the Stalin era. With Khrushchev victorious, dozens of Central Committee members jostled to denounce Molotov, Malenkov, and Kaganovich for participating in the annihilation of party higher-ups under Stalin.

Furtseva referred to their "monstrous crimes"; Brezhnev denounced their "fanatical approach to cadres"; Kozlov criticized Malenkov's leading role in the execution of Leningrad leader Kuznetsov in 1949; and first secretary of the Uzbek Communist Party Mukhitdinov said that in trying to remove Khrushchev the three leaders of the "antiparty group" were mainly concerned with hiding their role "in the mass extermination of leading cadres." Speakers cited documents from the KGB archives on the scale of repressions, with Khrushchev himself giving the figures of 1.5 million arrested and 681,692 shot in 1937–1938 that had previously only been revealed at Presidium meetings. Serov had a major part in the denunciation of Kaganovich, describing his leadership of mass purges in Ukraine. Rudenko described working with Serov on the rehabilitation of thousands of repressed party members. He also attacked Malenkov and Kaganovich for obstructing the investigations into the Stalin era, and Molotov for justifying the murder of party cadres.[70]

Aristov in particular shed light on the history of the Molotov commission, albeit from the point of view of the Khrushchevites. According to him, "we sat on that commission endlessly. The debates were extremely harsh." Voroshilov "just got outraged," while Kaganovich and Molotov said the trials during the Terror were "correct," "in the interests of the party," and "the right thing to do." Serov and Rudenko provided documents, Aristov said, that ultimately forced Molotov and Kaganovich to recognize "maybe half" of the crimes committed. Kaganovich confessed "there were excesses," while Molotov stated, "there were good political reasons for all of that." Because of Serov's and Rudenko's services in providing documents on the crimes of the Stalinist leadership, Aristov said, the "antiparty group" had aimed to fire Serov after Khrushchev's removal. Molotov, Malenkov, and Kaganovich, he claimed, had wanted to "break through" into the archives of the KGB and the TsK commissions on repressions, in order to destroy documents that incriminated them.[71]

The real bomb-thrower was V. N. Malin, head of the Central Committee General Administration Department (*Obshchii otdel*) and onetime Leningrad official, who had witnessed Kuznetsov's trial in 1949. Malin asserted that the mass executions of the later 1930s were not just Stalin's doing. "No, Kaganovich and Molotov—they're guilty. I'll go further—Kirov's ghost hangs over Molotov. Let him answer why Medved was destroyed, why Yenukidze was destroyed. . . . The case of Kirov's assassination is a case that has not yet been deeply examined.

Based on the documentary materials we have, I'm prepared to say that."[72]

In his concluding speech to the plenum, Khrushchev disavowed Malin's assertions, but somewhat in the manner of a Mafia boss ruing the excessive enthusiasm of his enforcers. "I respect [Malin], but he has his character, yesterday you saw that character." Yet Khrushchev was in effect using Malin to issue an implied threat about possible accusations that could be deployed against the "antiparty group." Indeed, later in the same speech, Khrushchev returned to the Kirov murder, and while he did not mention Molotov's name, he did indicate that further investigation was necessary.

> I still can't make sense of all the circumstances of Kirov's murder. There is much that remains unexplained. It's not clear why, after Kirov's death, it was necessary to kill Borisov when Stalin arrived in Leningrad and Borisov—Kirov's guard—was being driven to an interrogation. They killed Borisov and said that he died as the result of an auto crash. The driver who survived said that the chekist grabbed the wheel from him, and directed the truck against a building, and he heard noise in the back, and when he got out, the guard Borisov was dead. And now we've determined that the two chekists in the (back of the) truck, killed Borisov with picks (*lomikami*—possibly "crowbars"). Who needed this? It's clear that this was necessary to cover the traces. Even today I do not believe that Zinoviev had anything to do with this. We had a battle of ideas with Trotsky, Bukharin, and Zinoviev, and we smashed them. But after Kirov's murder hundreds of thousands of heads were laid on the execution block. Why was this necessary? Even today this is a mystery, and it would be a good thing to look into. But does Molotov get it? No. He trembles before this, he fears even hints about this question; Kaganovich is in the same situation.[73]

No one was "covering" for Stalin at this moment—the Khrushchevites revealed many of his most heinous crimes, as well as the collaboration of Molotov, Kaganovich, Malenkov, Beria, and others in mass murder. These revelations were not for the general population, but strictly for members of the party elite, to discredit for good the "antiparty group." If the KGB or other instances had documents that might connect Stalin or any of the "anti-party group" to Kirov's assassination, directly or indirectly, Khrushchev supporters at this plenum would have revealed them.

Khrushchev's words to the plenum on the Kirov murder are telling.

In order to suggest the involvement of Stalin and the Molotov group in the assassination, Khrushchev resorted to the 1937–1938 show trial version of events, and to testimony extracted under torture (that of the truck driver in Borisov's death). In doing so he omitted any reference to the 1934–1935 investigation results, with which Serov had acquainted him and the Molotov commission. Instead he presented as simple truth a version of Borisov's death that was unsubstantiated and dubious— that two NKVD officers had murdered Borisov with picks in the back of the truck transporting him to his meeting with Stalin. This was the best "evidence" he could deploy for the involvement of the Stalin group in Kirov's assassination.

CHAPTER 15

Shatunovskaya's Investigation and After

Following the June 1957 plenum and the defeat of the "antiparty group," the prosecutorial apparatus under Rudenko and the KGB under Serov continued to exonerate high-ranking victims of the Terror. On November 20, 1957 Serov and Rudenko reported to the TsK on the rehabilitation of three of the defendants in the March 1938 Moscow show trial, Levin, Kazakov, and Pletnev (all doctors charged with murdering their patients). This report also cited the recent admission of "expert witnesses" at the trial that their testimony had been worthless. Serov and Rudenko thus crept closer to a truly radical step, the rehabilitation of Bukharin and Rykov, the leaders of the "Right Deviation." Meanwhile the KPK was dotting the "i's" of the accusations flung around at the June 1957 plenum, preparing a thorough report on Malenkov's participation in the Terror. Yet the process of preparing a new official story-line for the Stalin years seems to have stalled. There was no publication of the revelations delivered in secret at the 1957 plenum, and no further investigation of the Kirov murder.[1]

Then, in the fall of 1960, soon after the return of party leaders from their traditional summer holidays, the KPK suddenly renewed the investigation of the Kirov murder. The earliest document of this investigation that I was able to see in the KPK archives is a September 9, 1960 letter from Pyotr Chagin, the former editor of *Red Gazette* in Leningrad, addressed to the Central Committee. Chagin wrote that the Central Committee had solicited his letter, based on the contents of earlier correspondence. He claimed that in the late 1920s and early 1930s Kirov had expressed some doubts about Stalin's accumulation of power. Chagin also repeated a story that a number of regional and territorial party committee chairmen had approached Kirov at the Seventeenth Party Congress to suggest that he ought to replace Stalin as general secretary of the TsK. Kirov reportedly told Stalin, who responded, "Thank you, you've saved the party."[2]

KPK documentation indicates an acceleration of the investigation in early November 1960, under the direction of Olga Shatunovskaya. Within three months (January 28, 1961), the KPK delivered to Khrushchev a report stating that Stalin had organized the Kirov murder using Yagoda, Zaporozhets, and Leningrad NKVD officers, that Borisov's death was murder, that Nikolaev was detained multiple times before the murder, and so on. The memorandum reported that Stalin had ordered Kirov's assassination because of the supposed initiative by provincial party secretaries to make the latter general secretary. It also asserted that the results of voting for the TsK at the Seventeenth Party Congress had been falsified and that in fact Stalin had received hundreds of "No" votes.[3]

The January 1961 report was an attempt to create an entirely new narrative of the Terror that would provide Khrushchevite reformers with a useable reforming hero, Kirov, who had supposedly stood against Stalin's tyranny. The narrative was composed by and based mostly on the evidence of Old Bolsheviks who had supported Stalin through 1937 but nonetheless been arrested during the Terror (Shatunovskaya, who led this phase of the investigation, exemplifies the type). These men and women sought to portray Stalin as the lone devil who had derailed the Communist project. This would absolve them of responsibility for the mass murder, demonstrate that their cohort had attempted to resist the dictator, and rehabilitate a supposedly pristine Leninism as the basis for the Soviet future. Unfortunately the evidence gathered for the new story-line was flimsy, and at times downright deceptive. To understand the evidence presented below, and this book's argument, it is vital to grasp that the Shatunovskaya commission made an all-out effort to gather any evidence at all implicating Stalin in the murder. Shatunovskaya and her subordinates showed no interest in protecting the dictator's reputation. Moreover, according to Shatunovskaya herself, "all of the archives were open" to them.[4]

The January 1961 report soon disappeared into the KPK archive, in part because of its poor quality, in part for political reasons. In May 1961 the Presidium of the TsK ordered the creation of another commission, with the addition of new members, to deal again with the Kirov assassination and subsequent trials. On September 26, 1961 this commission issued a short report describing in detail Stalin's use of the Kirov assassination to fabricate cases against ex-oppositionists and deviationists. This report did not even mention the question of Stalin's involvement in the Kirov murder. Thus, the narrative of the Terror prepared by the earlier commission was rejected. But evidence collected by the Shatunovskaya commission eventually made its way, in more or less distorted form, into works by Roy Medvedev, Anton Antonov-Ovseenko, Robert Tucker, and other scholars. In the late perestroika era (1989–1991) the Soviet press gave it wide coverage.[5]

Why did the KPK take up the Kirov assassination and the Terror when it did? There were most likely several overlapping motivations. The January 1961 report was titled "Memorandum of the Control Committee of the Central Committee of the Communist Party on V. M. Molotov's Participation in the Organization of Mass Repressions in 1935–1938." It laid the groundwork for attacks on Molotov and Kaganovich at the Twenty-Second Party Congress in October 1961 and their expulsion from the party in 1962. Molotov, effectively in exile as ambassador to Mongolia and later Soviet representative to the International Atomic Energy Agency in Vienna, had provoked Khrushchev with frequent missives to the Central Committee attacking the general secretary's policies. Molotov was particularly critical of Khrushchev's management of relations with China, and at points seemed to take Mao's side against Khrushchev.[6]

The topic of Sino-Soviet relations was particularly sensitive in 1960. At the June 1960 congress of the Romanian Workers' Party in Bucharest, and again in November at a Moscow meeting, Khrushchev clashed with Chinese and Albanian representatives. Moreover, the Soviet Union was in the early stages of its courtship with Castro's Cuba, and the Chinese represented an alternative, and arguably more radical, center of revolutionary charisma. Although such considerations in retrospect might seem secondary, Ken Jowitt has argued persuasively that the USSR's status as "sacred center" of the Leninist world was integral to the Soviet leaders' Communist identity. They reacted very strongly to any challenge to that status.[7]

Under these pressures, Khrushchev and his fellows apparently decided upon a bold offensive. Two of the reasons for the muted public criticism of Stalin in the USSR after 1956 were the leaders' deference to the Chinese sense that the denunciations had gone too far, and fear of seeding further instability like the 1956 Polish and Hungarian anti-Stalinist disorders. Now, however, someone high in the leadership sanctioned the articulation of a reformist, "humanitarian" version of socialism that they would contrast openly with Stalinist Albania (the transcript of the Twenty-Second Party Congress in October 1961 is replete with denunciations of Enver Hoxha's "cult of personality") and by implication with Mao's China. Presumably this would place the USSR once again at the head of world socialism.[8]

As part of the offensive, the KPK went to work to prepare a new history of the Stalinist era. Also connected with the offensive was a grandiose program for the construction of Communism by 1980 presented to the Twenty-Second Party Congress in October 1961.[9]

One more factor to consider in the timing of the KPK investigation is the ascendancy of former Leningrad party chief Frol Kozlov in the summer of 1960. The May 1960 plenary session of the Central Committee demoted a number of Khrushchev's old supporters in the Presidium and TsK Secretariat (Kirichenko, Beliaev, Aristov, Furtseva, and Ignatov), and promoted Kozlov to the Secretariat. On June 2 the Presidium charged Kozlov with preparing the agenda for and chairing TsK Secretariat meetings. As already noted, Kozlov had recruited (dubious) testimony suggesting Stalin's involvement in Kirov's murder in 1956, and sent it on to Khrushchev. He seems to have taken it ill that Serov and Rudenko dismissed "his" materials. The KPK's new investigation of the assassination made extensive use of Kozlov's documents.[10]

Rewriting the History of Stalinism

Judging from the handwritten depositions collected by the KPK, Shatunovskaya and her subordinates A. I. Kuznetsov and G. Klimov used investigative methods that were bound to distort their informants' accounts. Before a witness gave evidence, a KPK functionary (often Klimov) had a "conversation" with him or her, recalling the witness's duty to the party (nearly all interviewees were Communists), asking leading questions, and possibly laying out other deponents' descriptions of events. This process left traces in the formal depositions. P. P. Petrovsky, the Leningrad NKVD guard who denounced his bosses to Yezhov in 1938 (see above, p. 485) wrote to Klimov and Shatunovskaya on December 23, 1960 that "After your summons and my conversation with you, I remembered everything that happened in December 1934 from beginning to end." In answer to a question about how he knew that Nikolaev had a weapon and "notes" in his briefcase when detained, Petrovsky wove a tale about how he now "recalled" that during Nikolaev's interrogations in December 1934 he had delivered documents to the interrogating officers and overheard them talking about the incident. In his 1938 "evidence" Petrovsky never mentioned Nikolaev's pistol, much less visiting his interrogation room. The formula "our conversation resurrected X in my memory" appears also in the testimony of Simon Viksin (see below). It appears that KPK functionaries prompted witnesses with an account of an alleged event (for example, the supposed move by provincial party secretaries to make Kirov general secretary) and asked if they "remembered" it.[11]

The formula about suddenly recalling major political events at the prompting of party authorities or official documents is quite transparent. In his memoirs, penned in the late 1960s and early 1970s, Anastas Mikoyan uses it several times. In his account of the Seventeenth Party Congress, he writes that when he saw Pospelov's February 9, 1956 report on the repressions, "I involuntarily remembered two facts known to me in the past." What Mikoyan "remembered" was that many votes were cast against Stalin at the congress, and that there was a move afterwards to replace Stalin with Kirov. These were not trivial events. It is remarkable that Mikoyan "forgot" them and then "remembered" them in the years after the January 1961 report implicating Stalin in Kirov's murder. (Mikoyan's memoirs are the first evidence we have of any such "memories." He did not bring up them up in Presidium discussions in 1956 or afterwards.)[12]

Shatunovskaya and her collaborators also showed or read back to a number of witnesses (especially NKVD witnesses) their testimony from the years of the Terror, and asked them if they confirmed it. Many did so, and some simply wrote, "I confirm my testimony of dates X and Y." Karl Ivanov, an officer who sometimes guarded Kirov in the early 1930s, used this formula to confirm his evidence of May 26, 1938 and March 7, 1939 about Nikolaev's multiple detentions. Ivanov actually gave conflicting testimony about the detentions during the Terror, first claiming two and later four (see above, p. 483). Yet in his January 1961 deposition he did not resolve this contradiction. Obviously Shatunovskaya's practice of asking witnesses to confirm their testimony from the Terror years led to the perpetuation of falsehoods extracted under torture.[13]

How Many Votes Were Cast against Stalin at the Seventeenth Party Congress?

Let us examine the findings of the January 1961 report in chronological order, beginning with the Seventeenth Party Congress in February 1934. Part of the widely accepted narrative of the Great Terror presented by Medvedev, Conquest, Tucker, and others is the claim that at this congress somewhere between 270 and 300 delegates voted against Stalin's membership in the Central Committee.[14] According to this narrative, Lazar Kaganovich ordered most of the offending ballots destroyed and the results of the vote falsified. Supposedly the revelation of widespread opposition to his rule inside the Central Committee enraged Stalin and led to his annihilation of much of the membership during the Terror. This version of events was first put together in Shatunovskaya's 1960–1961 investigation. As far as I can determine there are no references to large numbers of votes cast against Stalin prior to November 1961. Earlier stories relate that there were some votes against Stalin (true, based on the existing archival record of the Seventeenth Congress), that Stalin did not get the most votes (true), or that Kirov got more votes than Stalin (false).[15]

According to KPK records, on November 10, 1960 Olga Shatunovskaya and her assistants opened up the sealed materials of the Seventeenth Party Congress's Electoral Commission. They found that although there were 1,225 certified voting delegates to the congress (that is, those "with mandates") there were only 1,059 ballots in the sealed records, leaving a shortage of 166 ballots. Comparison with earlier party congresses, however, shows that 134 voting delegates did not return ballots at the Sixteenth (1930) and 43 at the Fifteenth (1927). In 1934 the number of unreturned ballots may have been unusually high due to a flu epidemic among the delegates.[16]

The claim of massive falsification of balloting originated with V. M. Verkhovykh, a delegate from the Moscow organization who was a member of the 1934 congress's Electoral Commission. (Claims that only three of sixty-four commission members survived the Terror are false. In 1960 the KPK tracked down nine living members.) Like so many other congress delegates, Verkhovykh was later repressed, but survived the camps. On November 23, 1960, two weeks after the examination of the Electoral Commission records, Verkhovykh presented to the KPK a handwritten deposition. In it he claimed that in the actual balloting Stalin, Molotov, and Kaganovich had received more

"No" votes than any other TsK members, "each over 100." "It seems to me Stalin had 123 or 125 against, Kaganovich, 126 or 125, Molotov 121." In addition, Verkhovykh testified that there were some anti-Stalin notes on ballots and on separate pieces of paper placed in the voting urns.[17]

In 1990 Shatunovskaya stated that Verkhovykh had testified to 289 ballots cast against Stalin at the Seventeenth Party Congress, and suggested that some documents in the case had been destroyed and replacements forged.[18] I have seen the original Verkhovykh deposition which indeed refers to 123 or 125 votes. Although I am not an expert on detecting forged documents, I can testify that the deposition is handwritten in faded purple ink on yellowed paper that resembles that used in other handwritten commission documents. It is signed in Verkhovykh's name.

Verkhovykh's deposition and an undated "supplement" to it (in the same handwriting with the same signature) display a problematic evidentiary overkill. Not only did Verkhovykh testify to the votes against Stalin and the notes against him, he also claimed to have heard from Ukrainian party chief S. V. Kosior at the congress of a proposal to replace Stalin with Kirov as general secretary of the TsK. Moreover, he asserted that he'd met Medved at Kolyma, and that the latter had complained to him of central NKVD interference in his work at the Leningrad NKVD. This last is particularly confusing and questionable. Verkhovykh wrote as if Medved had spoken to him in Kolyma before his dismissal from Leningrad and conviction on charges of negligence. But Medved was not stationed in Kolyma until after his January 1935 conviction. Furthermore it is very likely that Verkhovykh himself was not arrested until mid-1937, that is, months after Medved had been removed from Kolyma and sent back to Moscow for interrogation in the Yagoda case.[19]

Other members of the Electoral Commission gave testimony to the KPK in 1960–1961 and later about the voting at the Seventeenth Party Congress. Support for Verkhovykh's deposition came from Simon Ottovich Viksin, a Latvian Old Bolshevik who was around seventy-five years old in 1961. Viksin wrote on January 14, 1961 that Stalin had received more "No" votes than any other TsK member, but he could not remember how many, or even how many there were in his own urn (each commission member was assigned to count votes from one of the thirteen urns in which ballots were deposited by delegates).[20] (Note that the claim that Stalin received more "No" votes than Mikhail

Tomsky or even Yakov Yakovlev is preposterous.) Viksin's letter was formulaic, referring to Kirov as "the favorite of the party, despicably murdered from hiding . . . " at a time when his authority in the party was "especially high." He also referred to baseless rumors of a top-secret TsK plenum held in October 1937 where TsK member Khataevich demanded that Stalin resign as general secretary.[21]

One other member of the 1934 Electoral Commission testified to the KPK in 1960–1961. This was N. V. Andreosian, a former schoolmate of Mikoyan's in Tbilisi. Andreosian remembered that members of the Electoral Commission were shocked that there were some votes against Stalin (according to the commission records opened by the KPK, there were in fact three votes against Stalin). He did not remember how many such votes there were but "no more than three." He also recalled commission members' consternation that there were three ballots with anti-Stalin notes on them. The January 28, 1961 KPK report to Khrushchev misrepresented Andreosian's deposition, stating falsely that the three votes against Stalin he mentioned referred to votes from his urn only. The report's authors then argued that because they had not found any votes against Stalin in the ballots from Andreosian's urn, these must have been destroyed. Yet Andreosian had not written specifically of three votes against Stalin in his own urn. He was almost certainly referring to three votes against Stalin among all ballots. Several surviving delegates to the congress (not members of the Electoral Commission) also remembered hearing with surprise of a few votes (three to six) cast against Stalin.[22]

In the documents available to me, there is no record of any evidence taken in 1960 from the other six members of the 1934 Electoral Commission who survived.

It is probable that there were three anti-Stalin notes placed in the balloting urns at the Seventeenth Party Congress, as Andreosian testified. That would correspond to the three votes against Stalin in the official election tally. It is also conceivable that some ballots against Stalin were destroyed to put a better face on the results of the voting. But given the evidence presented above, it is very unlikely that three hundred or even one hundred delegates voted against Stalin's membership in the TsK. First, delegates were well aware that there would probably be efforts to track down those who crossed out Stalin's name.[23] Second, there was no tradition of congress delegates using their ballots to protest the preferences of the TsK executive apparatus. Voting totals for the TsK tracked closely the standing of the candidates with the top party leadership. The voting results recorded in the archives for the Seventeenth Party Congress did the same.[24] Third, there exist only two reports of large numbers of votes against Stalin at the congress, and these are explicable as "sharpening" (see above, p. 10) of factual rumors that there had been a few votes cast against Stalin. In addition to the unreliability and implausibility of Viksin's and Verkhovykh's depositions, there is the sheer and excessive convenience of this claim for the party itself in 1960–1961. It fit well within a new narrative of the Stalin era, in which Stalin, Kaganovich, and Molotov were the evil geniuses who set out to destroy the pristine heritage of Leninism (note the key role Kaganovich reputedly played in falsifying the voting results). Honorable members of the party, the story went, had stood up to defend true Leninism, but had been cut down. The new story-line restored the party's honor and limited responsibility for the Terror to a small group of degenerates in the leadership.

Was There a Move to Replace Stalin with Kirov?

Also central to the KPK's January 28, 1961 report was the claim that a number of delegates to the Seventeenth Party Congress wished to abolish the office of general secretary and return the party to "collective leadership" (not coincidentally a key slogan of the Khrushchev era). The report also cited Verkhovykh's testimony that Stanislav Kosior had told him that some senior officials had discussed with Kirov the possibility that he could replace Stalin as general secretary. The authors did not indicate clearly which version of events they preferred. Roy Medvedev passed on these reports in summary form in *Let History Judge,* and thus they entered the Western literature on Soviet history. However, the original KPK evidence was hearsay, and appears to be based on exaggerations of historically known circumstances at the congress.[25]

In files 23 and 78 of the KPK archive on the Kirov assassination are collected twenty-three depositions of surviving delegates to the Seventeenth Party Congress taken during Shatunovskaya's investigation. Two of these depositions, those of Verkhovykh and Z. N. Nemtsova, report hearing second- or third-hand stories of proposals to replace Stalin with Kirov as general secretary. We have seen the problems with Verkhovykh's testimony already. Nemtsova reported hearing rumors from fellow members of the Leningrad delegation that other delegations had asked Leningrad to propose Kirov as "general secretary."

This could easily be a distortion of rumors circulating at the congress about Kirov's projected promotion to secretary of the TsK, a move that was truly in the works. Moreover, as Alla Kirilina has pointed out, party congresses did not choose the general secretary—TsK plenums did. Thus, there was absolutely no precedent for the Leningrad delegation to propose Kirov to the congress as general secretary. And, given the correlation of forces in the party at the time, such a move would have been absurd.[26]

Two other depositions (those of Kisis and Rosliakov) mentioned hearing stories at the congress of a proposal to abolish the office of general secretary and return to "collective leadership." Kisis asserted that his friend Eikhe had told him that Kosior was considering such a move. Rosliakov told investigators in 1960–1961 that he had heard the story from Kodatsky, a top official in Leningrad at the time of Kirov's murder. However Rosliakov abandoned the whole tale when he wrote his memoir in the mid- to late 1960s. Instead he provided a realistic explanation for stories that delegates at the Seventeenth Party Congress had talked about replacing Stalin with Kirov. Senior party officials and activists, Rosliakov wrote, often evaluated the qualities of this or that party leader in casual conversation. "But indeed, speaking frankly, in conversations about replacements, no one ever proposed the immediate or violent replacement of Stalin: generally the talk was that the party had matured, grown stronger, that there were even people capable of replacing Stalin if the necessity arose."[27]

Eighteen of twenty-three depositions from Seventeenth Party Congress delegates did not mention or explicitly rejected the claim that there had talk of replacing Stalin with Kirov or of abolishing the office of general secretary. Three more delegates deposed later (1965–1967) also denied hearing any such conversations or rumors.[28]

How might rumors about proposals to replace Stalin with Kirov have developed? They could well be exaggeration and sharpening of conversations related to the possibility of Kirov's transfer to Moscow and promotion to TsK secretary. Indeed, it is likely that Stalin encouraged such discussion among provincial party secretaries in order to increase the pressure on Kirov to make the move. Eight of the twenty-three depositions taken in 1960–1961 explicitly mentioned that Kirov's authority at the congress was high and/or that his concluding speech was well received. Nikolai Ostakhov mentioned hearing talk that Stalin was looking older, and it was time for Kirov to go to Moscow to help him out. (Stalin himself used similar lines more than once in his career, speculating that the time for his retirement might be approaching.) Vasily Yegorov reported delegates saying, "Kirov's place is in the Central Committee"—that is, in its executive apparatus.[29]

Five of twenty-three deponents indicated that they had not considered the possibility that Kirov was a rival to Stalin until long after the Seventeenth Party Congress. Khrushchev's de-Stalinization drive was one catalyst for rethinking events at the congress. Karl Ratnek wrote that Kirov's speech made a big impression, "but it was only a good deal later that I heard rumors that Stalin 'envied' Kirov, and supposedly saw in him a rival." Matilda Cherniak said, apparently in response to strong prompting to "remember" evidence that Stalin had it in for Kirov, "I have to say in all frankness that right up to the moment I learned about Comrade Khrushchev's report to the Twentieth Party Congress it never occurred to me that the Kirov murder was Stalin's doing." It seems very likely that Khrushchev's authoritative speech caused some party members to reconstruct their memories of the Seventeenth Party Congress that had met over twenty years earlier.[30]

Three other witnesses interviewed by the Shatunovskaya commission provide a separate example of the influence of Khrushchev's "Secret Speech" on accounts of the Seventeenth Party Congress. These men reported hearing a story not in 1934, but in the months after Khrushchev's 1956 speech, of a move to replace Stalin with Kirov as general secretary. These were Pyotr Chagin, writing in September 1960, I. I. Mitiaev, writing in December, and A. Andreev. All three referred to A. T. Sevastianov, a former Kirov associate in Baku and Leningrad, as the source. Sevastianov, each said, had told them the tale in late 1956 from his deathbed. It is doubtful that Andreev actually heard the story from Sevastianov, because he admitted also hearing the story in 1959 from Mitiaev. According to Chagin and Mitiaev, Sevastianov told them that Kirov had told him how Boris Sheboldaev and other provincial party secretaries approached him with a proposal to become general secretary. Kirov said he'd refused, and told Stalin about the incident. Stalin reportedly said, "Thank you, you have saved the party."[31]

Even aside from the fact that this story was at least third-hand by the time Chagin and Mitiaev put it to paper in 1960, there are other problems with it. For instance, why didn't Chagin, who had written letters to the Central Committee after the "Secret Speech," immediately write to some party authority about Sevastianov's tale, rather than waiting four years? There is also the later history of the Sevastianov story. In 1990 Shatunovskaya described a note that Sevastianov's wife supposedly found among his effects after the Twenty-Second Party Congress in 1961. In this note, dated June 1956, Sevastianov himself laid out the story of the proposal to replace Stalin with Kirov. The note came to light at an expedient time, five years after Sevastianov's death, at a moment when Shatunovskaya was locked in a battle with other KPK officials to defend the findings of her 1960 investigation. In 1989–1990 KPK archivists could not locate the note, and Shatunovskaya claimed that someone inside the apparatus must have destroyed it. Yet other documents Shatunovskaya said were "burned" by the KPK have in fact been found. Given all of these circumstances, the 1956 Sevastianov note probably did not exist, and the Sevastianov rumor about a proposal to replace Stalin with Kirov seems very questionable.[32]

In 1990, Shatunovskaya asserted that Sofia L. Markus, the sister of Kirov's wife, also reported in 1960 hearing the Sevastianov story from Kirov's own mouth. In the January 1961 report prepared by the Shatunovskaya commission, there is no trace of such a story, although the authors cite Markus for a vague tale of an unspecified conflict between Stalin and Kirov. Kirilina has, moreover, demolished Markus' credibility. In 1959, she notes, Markus wrote a glowing memoir about the friendly relations between Stalin and Kirov which contradicts her later account (or accounts) of conflict between them. In addition, Kirov disliked his sister-in-law, who rarely visited (she did not live in Leningrad until after Kirov's death) and sometimes used go-betweens to ask favors of him. It is improbable that he would have told her about such an explosive incident. It is also relevant that Markus was an active denouncer of co-workers to the NKVD during the Terror.[33]

The stories about hundreds of votes against Stalin at the Seventeenth Party Congress and a move by some party officials (Eikhe, Sheboldaev, Kosior, and Ordzhonikidze have been mentioned frequently) to replace Stalin with Kirov are quite fantastic when compared with the actual situation in the party in early 1934 as revealed by documents of the time. Kirov was a Leningrad leader above all, known for his "modesty" and reluctance to undertake big policy initiatives on his own. Rumors about Kirov as a rival to Stalin seem to have their origin in badly distorted oral accounts of Stalin's efforts to promote Kirov out of Leningrad to Moscow, and gossip at the Seventeenth Party Congress about the three votes cast against Stalin. Such stories became part of the folklore of Old Bolsheviks sent to the labor camps or otherwise beaten down by Stalin. As discussed in Chapter 11, this folklore simply stood on its head the Stalinist narrative of the Terror. Stalin postulated a grand conspiracy among veteran Bolsheviks to destroy Communism; the repressed Old Bolsheviks postulated a grand conspiracy by Stalin to destroy Communism.[34]

The "Hunt" for Kirov

According to the Shatunovskaya investigation report, after the Seventeenth Party Congress, Stalin began a "perfidious game" with Kirov. The latter knew that "they were hunting him without a break." The story of Stalin's assassins hunting Kirov is based on assertions of multiple detentions of Nikolaev, and on evidence of Pyotr Chagin and Sofia Markus about what Kirov's wife Maria Lvovna supposedly told them. In September 1960 Chagin wrote that after Kirov's murder he visited Maria Lvovna who told him how "they were 'hunting' [for Kirov] outside the entrance to their apartment building."[35] There are a number of reasons that Maria Lvovna would have mentioned a "hunt" for Kirov that do not involve assassins dispatched by Stalin. As Kirilina has pointed out, it was common for petitioners to attempt to approach Kirov on the street or at the entrances to his apartment building and Smolny. These were Leningraders seeking favors or redress from some injustice. It would not be surprising if Kirov and his family considered them a nuisance, and if Maria Lvovna later connected some of them with the assassination. Second, Kirov received occasional anonymous death threats. Third, Maria Lvovna may have been influenced by stories of Nikolaev's multiple detentions.

In 1960 Sofia Markus gave similar testimony about her sister's take on the murder. However, she claimed to have heard these stories in the summer of 1934 from Kirov and from Maria Lvovna. Her assertions were also more elaborate than Chagin's. Several of them made their way directly into the Shatunovskaya commission report. Markus claimed that Kirov had told her about the proposal to make him general secretary and commented "Now my head is on the block." As Kirilina has pointed out, the reference to the "execution block" was anachronistic —Stalin had not begun imprisoning, much less executing major party figures in 1934. Markus also referred to mysterious burglars in Kirov's apartment in 1934, and quoted her sister to the effect that "they were hunting him without break." Yet Markus did not live in Leningrad in 1934 and whatever she heard from Maria Lvovna she almost certainly heard after the assassination. Kirilina, who worked with Markus at the Kirov Museum in Leningrad, claims that by the early 1950s she suffered from age-related memory problems and often could not recall people's names.[36]

There was, of course, other evidence of the "hunt" for Kirov—the supposed multiple detentions of Nikolaev. The January 28, 1961 KPK report indicated that Nikolaev had been detained "a number of times" while in possession of his revolver and his plan for murdering Kirov. "Each time" senior NKVD officials had ordered his release and threatened to punish the apprehending officers. To back their claims up, KPK investigators relied on testimony from the 1937–1939 interrogations of Leningrad NKVD operatives that Nikolaev had been detained and released two or more times before Kirov's murder. Khrushchev would make this version of events public at the Twenty-Second Party Congress.

KPK reports, the written depositions of surviving NKVD officers, and the transcripts of the 1937–1939 interrogations all demonstrate just how flimsy the claim for multiple detentions was (see Chapter 11 for details on the NKVD's development of the "multiple detentions" story in 1937–1939). Even apart from internal inconsistencies and contradictions with the 1934 evidence, the embellishment of evidence to absurd lengths to make a more "solid" case is a tip-off that the material was unreliable. A 1960 report signed by KPK Chief Controller G. Klimov, "Clarification of the Question of L. V. Nikolaev's Detention Prior to His Carrying Out the Murder of S. M. Kirov," apparently was the basis for the January 28 KPK report's assertion of multiple detentions. It begins with an analysis of Nikolaev's diary and testimony.

· 120 ·

Excerpts from G. Klimov report to KPK on detention(s) of Nikolaev, winter of 1960–1961. RGANI, f. 6, op. 13, d. 13, ll. 7–45.

———————

[. . .]

In the course of the preliminary investigation Nikolaev testified that he made the decision to kill Kirov in July, began to prepare "more energetically" in August 1934, and attempted to carry out his intention by meeting Kirov near his home, at Moscow Station when he returned from Moscow, and near Smolny.

With regard to his detention on October 15, 1934, which is mentioned in his notebook, Nikolaev gave contradictory depositions. For example at an interrogation on December 2 he testified [. . .]:

" . . . on October 15 I met Comrade Kirov (completely by chance) near Uritsky Square, I let him by, but then turned to follow him and met him again by the Troitsky Bridge. From the bridge I followed him all the way to his home on Kamennoostrovsky Prospect [Krasnykh Zor Street]. Because Comrade Kirov was walking with Comrade Chudov I could not make up my mind to approach him for discussion. I want to emphasize that at the time I had not thought of assassination. After Comrade Kirov and Chudov disappeared inside the entrance, I was detained by a policeman, taken to the police station on the Petrograd Side, from there I was sent to the on-duty NKVD officer just by the entrance to the lower floor. After a check of my party and personal documents I was let go without a search."

At an interrogation on December 8, Nikolaev gave somewhat different testimony:

" . . . On October 15 there was supposed to be a city party meeting. I went to Smolny one hour before the beginning of the meeting. I did so because I had not been able to get a ticket to the meeting earlier and I was counting on getting one just before the meeting itself. I don't remember who told me that Kirov and Chudov would not be at the meeting— Ugarov was to conduct it—and that they had just left for their homes on Krasnykh Zor Street. I thought that I had to use this excellent opportunity presented to me for an attack and I went after them on foot. I followed Kirov and Chudov right up to Building No. 28, without shooting. I refrained from shooting because I figured that I'd have to shoot at both and that did not come into my plans. At that moment I was arrested by Kirov's guard, to whom my behavior seemed suspicious. They took me by car to the building of the NKVD Directorate [. . .] to the duty officer."

"Question: At the moment of your arrest did you have on your person the Nagan and your notes of an anti-Soviet character?"

"Answer: Yes, I had the Nagan and the notes of an anti-Soviet character on me. They were all in the briefcase that I was carrying."

"Question: Were you searched when you were detained or when you were brought into the NKVD Directorate?"

"No [. . .]"

As can be seen from these depositions, at first Nikolaev claimed that on October 15 he met Kirov "completely by chance" "near Uritsky Palace," and he emphasized that at that time he had "not even thought about carrying out a murder." Later he declared that on that day, upon arrival at Smolny for the city party meeting at Smolny and the discovery that Kirov would not be at that meeting and was going home on foot, he decided "to use the favorable opportunity for an attack" and followed him. In these depositions Nikolaev speaks of completely different circumstances when he followed Kirov on October 15. But the inquiry did not attempt to clear up these contradictions in Nikolaev's evidence [. . .]

[There follow extensive citations of 1934–1935 testimony from Operations Department Officers Pauzer, Gubin, and Kotomin, and a summary of Officer Griunvald's depositions. See Chapter Ten, Documents 86–88, for excerpts from this testimony.]

From the above-detailed testimony of Pauzer it can be seen that Nikolaev was detained by him personally in the middle of October 1934 at the corner of Voinova Street and Volodarsky Prospect /opposite the NKVD building/ and taken to Griunvald. Griunvald confirmed the testimony of Pauzer as to the place of detention. Thus, compared with Nikolaev's depositions, this testimony speaks of completely different circumstances of Nikolaev's detention. Nikolaev gave his evidence on December 2 and 8, while Pauzer and Griunvald testified on December 5 and 6, that is, at the same time [as Nikolaev]. In essence these depositions witness different detentions of Nikolaev in October 1934. In Kotomin's testimony there is mentioned [another] detention of Nikolaev, in November. However, the investigation did not attempt in any way to explain these contradictions in the evidence.

[. . .]

In the secret Central Committee circular, "Lessons of the Events Connected with the Villainous Murder of Comrade Kirov," dated January 18, 1935 [authored by Stalin—see Chapter 9, Document 83] completely different circumstances and a different time are given for the detention of Nikolaev [there follows an excerpt from the circular].

[. . .]

From this excerpt it is clear that the topic is a detention of Nikolaev "three weeks before the murder of Kirov" and not "October 15" and not "in the middle of October" as appears in the materials of the investigation. Kotomin also wrote of the detention of Nikolaev in November. The TsK circular speaks of a detention [. . .] in which Nikolaev threw himself at Kirov as the latter approached the automobile waiting for him, that is under other circumstances than those that obtained during the two [other] detentions of Nikolaev uncovered by the inquiry. Investigation has established that in both the detention of Nikolaev by Kirov's building and that by the NKVD building, no automobile waiting for Kirov was involved. Thus, the "Secret Letter" refers to some other, third detention of Nikolaev. [. . .]

Out of minor contradictions between Nikolaev's and Pauzer's 1934 testimony and Stalin's probably inaccurate circular, Klimov conjured three detentions. Using this approach on evidence collected during the

Terror, he was able to generate even more. He made extensive use of 1937–1938 depositions from Gubin, Zaporozhets, other Leningrad NKVD officers, Yagoda, and Yagoda's former deputy Bulanov, extracted under torture and used to incriminate Yagoda at the March 1938 trial. Most of these follow the basic story-line of the trial (Yagoda ordered Zaporozhets to order Gubin to free Nikolaev), but contradict one another in details (for example, was Zaporozhets in Moscow, or at his apartment in Leningrad when Nikolaev was detained?). Klimov also used testimony from officers arrested during the 1938–1939 investigation of the Leningrad NKVD that followed Zakovsky's ouster (see above, p. 482). Officer Tyshkevich, who gave evidence against colleagues in both 1937 and 1938, claimed to have detained Nikolaev two times personally, while at the same time admitting that he didn't "recognize [. . .] Nikolaev until after the accomplishment of his terrorist act." Tyshkevich lied to the commission, claiming that no one had interrogated him about Nikolaev's detentions after Kirov's murder.[37]

Other officers questioned in 1960–1961 (Pauzer, Kruglov, Ivanov) explicitly confirmed their testimony from the Terror years. Pauzer even provided an explanation for his 1934 evidence pointing to a single detention of Nikolaev—he had mentioned the second detention, but the investigating officers refused to write it down. Given the eagerness of central investigators to find dirt on the Leningrad NKVD in the days after Kirov's murder, this is hardly plausible. Yet Klimov uncritically used these officers' 1937–1939 testimony, which they chose to confirm in 1960–1961 probably to protect themselves from charges of perjury and responsibility for the deaths of those they had denounced.[38]

Another witness deployed by Klimov was P. M. Lobov, who had murdered Grigory Sokolnikov in 1939 for Beria. Lobov's post-Stalin testimony showed extensive embellishment and grew more florid over time. Thus, in 1956 he testified that at the Kolyma labor camp Zaporozhets had told him that Nikolaev had been taken into custody once and that Yagoda had ordered him freed (see Chapter 14, Document 118 [continued]). In 1960 Lobov went much farther, stating that he had personally interrogated Nikolaev, who intimated that he had high-level connections. He also claimed that at Kolyma Zaporozhets had told him that Stalin himself had ordered Nikolaev's release. This was precisely the smoking gun that Shatunovskaya and the other investigators needed to accuse Stalin of Kirov's murder. Lobov delivered this evidence, which he had not mentioned in 1956, very conveniently for the KPK in October 1960.[39]

Based on the sloppy multiplication of Nikolaev's detentions, the authors of the Shatunovskaya commission report concluded that the NKVD had stopped the assassin and found a weapon (and assassination plan) on him multiple times. Moscow had ordered Nikolaev freed "each time" and threatened the detaining officers with punishment. Lobov's 1960 evidence was used to pin responsibility for releasing Nikolaev on Zaporozhets.[40]

The "Kozlov Materials" and Borisov's Death

To make the case that the guard Borisov had been murdered the 1960–1961 investigation relied chiefly on witnesses recruited by Frol Kozlov in Leningrad in March 1956.[41] Above all these were the driver of the truck in which Borisov died, Kuzin, and the interrogator Yakushev who had helped prepare the 1937 case against the former chief officers of the Leningrad NKVD. As already described (Chapter Ten), investigators in 1934 concluded after a thorough inquiry that Borisov had died in an accident caused by the absence of a central bolt and loose pieces of a leaf-spring in the truck's suspension system. Forensic pathologists (Ferris and Pfeiffer-Prutsman) and accident reconstruction specialist Robert Rivers, who reviewed the 1934 evidence as well as photographs of Borisov's skull exhumed in 1960, concluded that Kirov's guard almost certainly died in an auto accident. Genrikh Liushkov, one of the lead three or four officers on the case, who was present in Leningrad when the accident occurred, confirmed the 1934 investigation results after he defected to Japan in 1938.

But in the early 1960s Kuzin and Yakushev both continued to repeat the 1937 version of events that Yakushev had extracted from Kuzin and NKVD escorts Maly and Vinogradov under torture, to wit, that Maly and Vinogradov had murdered Borisov. In Kuzin's case this was most likely because he bore partial responsibility for the executions of the two escorts—his testimony had incriminated them. Yakushev, a perpetrator and torturer, was presumably trying to evade punishment for his actions.[42]

Kuzin's written testimony, dated January 18, 1961, differed substantially from his earlier post-Stalin evidence, given in 1956, and also from his accounts of 1934 and 1937. For example, in an obvious attempt to make Yakushev a more credible witness, Kuzin now claimed that Yakushev had not beaten and tortured him, but had rescued him from an earlier, more sadistic interrogator. He stated that the transcript of his 1956 face-to-face confrontation with Yakushev, in which he accused his former interrogator of torturing him, had been falsified.[43]

The January 28, 1961 report of the KPK relied heavily on the testimony of a second NKVD driver, Yanelis, who had contacted Kozlov in March 1956. I was unable to determine whether Yanelis was interrogated during the preparation of the 1937–1938 cases against Yagoda and the Leningrad NKVD. But whether tainted by 1937–1938 testimony or not, Yanelis' 1960–1961 deposition is not credible. In his eagerness to please his audience, Yanelis went too far, trying to provide them with every detail they needed. He claimed to have witnessed (from inside a different vehicle) Borisov refusing to sit in the open back of an NKVD truck, and Maly dragging the "limp" Borisov onto the truck bed, and forcing him to perch perilously on one of the side panels. Yanelis testified that he had opened the door of his car and yelled at Maly, "It's not allowed to sit passengers on the side panels." Maly swore at him. After the truck departed, Yanelis, for no apparent reason, hung around the buffet at the seventh floor of NKVD headquarters, and then went downstairs just in time to witness Maly and Vinogradov carrying Borisov, with a "horribly mutilated head," back into the building. It is also worth noting that Yanelis, in his earlier letter to Kozlov (1956), testified only that he heard Borisov express to Maly fear of sitting on the truck side panel. Yanelis' warning to Maly and his witnessing Borisov's being carried back into NKVD headquarters were details added in 1960–1961.[44]

A February 10, 1961 report on Borisov's death by the KPK, based on the same material as the January 28 memorandum on the Kirov murder, presented as fact a number of propositions which were demonstrably false based on 1934 testimony. It claimed, for instance, that Borisov had personally detained Nikolaev multiple times on the street, when according to the 1934 testimony Borisov was involved only in the one detention of Nikolaev. The report asserted that a third NKVD driver, Chopovsky, had testified that the truck in which Borisov died had been in complete working order, when in fact Chopovsky had admitted in December 1934 that he knew before the accident that parts of the truck's suspension system were missing.[45] Without explanation, the report cited Chopovsky's account of Borisov's "murder," in spite of the facts that Chopovsky was not an eyewitness to the accident, and that his testimony contradicted on important points every one of the known accounts by eyewitnesses. P. P. Petrovsky, the NKVD guard who had contacted Yezhov in 1938 and proven willing to provide whatever testimony the authorities needed, was cited for his assertion that Borisov had been severely beaten before his arrest.[46]

The KPK report on Borisov's death also utilized the testimony of Dr. S. A. Mamushin, in 1934 chief of the NKVD Medical Department in Leningrad. Like the drivers, Mamushin came to the attention of the KPK commission through Frol Kozlov. On November 11, 1960 Mamushin had deposed that the conclusion of the 1934 medical commission on Borisov's death, on which he had served, was "obviously mistaken."[47] Mamushin had given evidence about Borisov's death in writing a number of times. He had signed the 1934 medical commission's report on Borisov's death, which asserted that all the data were consistent with an accident. Alla Kirilina states that at his rehabilitation hearing (she gives no date or details of Mamushin's repression), Mamushin confirmed the conclusions of the 1934 commission. But in his March 1956 letter to Kozlov, Mamushin had stated that even in 1934 he had doubts about the reason for Borisov's death, "as a result of the absence . . . of any kind of precise evidence on the causes of death." In the written depositions he gave to the KPK in November 1960, Mamushin described a recent (1960) Leningrad meeting with KPK officials and two drivers in the case (Kuzin and probably Yanelis). At this meeting, Mamushin wrote, Kuzin had convinced him that Borisov had been killed by a blow on the head with a paving stone. Still later, on October 15, 1964, Mamushin changed course again, confirming the findings of the 1934 medical commission and explaining his 1960 testimony as the result of "the influence of the times, and my conversation with the drivers."[48]

In the various narratives of Borisov's "murder," there was no agreement over the means by which the guard was killed. In 1960 Mamushin specified the murder weapon as "a paving stone," claiming that Kuzin had told him this. In 1956 Yakushev had testified that the NKVD escorts murdered Borisov with a pick or crowbar (*lomik*). Yet according to forensic pathologist Ferris the fractures to Borisov's skull are incompatible with an attack by a person wielding a blunt instrument. In 1960 Yanelis suggested that the NKVD escorts had deliberately placed Borisov in a very dangerous position sitting on the truck side panel, so that he would suffer injury in the "accident." P. P. Petrovsky told investigators in 1938 that one of the escorting guards (Maly) stamped on the truck's brakes and in the resulting sudden stop Borisov was catapulted over the top of the cab to his death.[49]

Yet in spite of the implausibility and contradictions of the 1960 testimony, both KPK reports (the general one dated January 28, 1961 and the one on Borisov's death from February 10) influenced Khrushchev's description of Borisov's death at the Twenty-Second Party Congress in October 1961. Khrushchev presented as fact the evidence of Kuzin that the NKVD escorts had killed the guard. Khrushchev's assertion and the original KPK documents in turn determined Roy Medvedev's account of Borisov's death, that NKVD officers killed him with crowbars in the back of a "closed truck" (in fact Borisov rode in an open flat-bed truck). Robert Conquest (1989) relied on Medvedev, while Tucker (1990) used Khrushchev's account at the Twenty-Second Party Congress. Anton Antonov-Ovseenko also apparently relied on Medvedev's or Khrushchev's account of Borisov's death, although he provided no citation.[50]

Conclusions of the Shatunovskaya Commission Report

The authors of the January 1961 KPK report to Khrushchev—probably Klimov and Shatunovskaya—proposed a new official version of the Kirov murder. Stalin, they claimed, had ordered it, and NKVD officers carried it out using Nikolaev. In consequence, the Communist Party should recognize publicly that the show trials of the Terror were falsified and the mass repressions unjustified. Molotov, the authors wrote, should be excluded from the party for "monstrous crimes," for plotting against the party's "general line" during the "antiparty conspiracy" of 1957, and for obstructing the work of the 1956–1957 commission on the Kirov assassination and show trials. This last charge explained much of the report's content, which was aimed at proving the findings of the earlier commission absolutely false.[51]

The report also recommended excluding Malenkov, Kaganovich, and Bulganin from the party for crimes similar to Molotov's. In addition, the authors wanted an investigation of former KGB chief Serov, demoted in 1958 to head of Soviet military intelligence, and of USSR prosecutor Rudenko (who remained chief prosecutor until 1981) for their supposed role in thwarting the 1956–1957 investigation. Unfortunately, their charge that Serov and Rudenko had cooperated with Molotov to fix the earlier commission's findings was absurd. Records of the Molotov commission indicate clearly that Serov and Rudenko opposed Molotov all along, arguing that the Terror was unjustified. The Shatunovskaya commission, it seems, condemned them for making the case that Kirov's killer was a lone gunman, not a tool of Stalin. But there were personal/political motives at work here. The commission's report stressed that Serov and Rudenko had not trusted the materials provided by Frol Kozlov. It would seem that Kozlov had an animus against both of them.[52]

The KPK's 1961 report to Khrushchev painted Kirov in glowing colors as "a genuine organizer of the masses," "an extraordinarily popular man," and "the favorite of the working masses of Leningrad." It praised his "great authority," "personal charisma (*lichnoe obaianie*)," "truly Leninist style of work," and "selfless service to the revolution." These formulae drew directly on the preexisting Kirov martyr cult. In addition the report quoted Kirov deputy Mikhail Chudov to the effect that his boss was "an educated Marxist," and "a person of great humanitarianism." This last seems an anachronism, as promotion of a "humanist" Leninism was a central theme of party discussion in the later Khrushchev years, but a relatively inconspicuous trope in the early to middle 1930s. The report's authors clearly contrasted Kirov the educated humanitarian Leninist with the anti-Leninist tyrants Stalin, Molotov, and Kaganovich. The humanitarian Communist Kirov, in this version of Stalinist history, prefigured the humanitarian Communist Khrushchev.[53]

Reliability of the Witnesses: Chagin and Sorokin

It is not possible in the space of a single book to debunk all of the rumors about high Soviet politics in general or the Kirov murder in particular that continue to circulate—the top-secret party plenums that left no paper trail, the fifth-hand reported conversations with Stalin, the stories that Nikolaev "was seen" (by whom?) at NKVD headquarters in Moscow before Kirov's assassination, and so on. Such stories flourished in the atmosphere of secrecy, mystery, and conspiracy maintained by Stalin and his successors. They generally contradict one another as well as the archival record and the vast majority appear to be third-hand reports at best.

However, to underscore just how unreliable many of the oral reports collected in the early to middle 1960s are, further examination of two of the more important witnesses, Pyotr Chagin and Dmitry Sorokin, is warranted. Chagin in September 1960 claimed to have been a close personal friend of Kirov, who was frequently at his apartment. In addition to the tales of the Stalin origin of the "Two Dogs" satirical feuilleton directed at Kirov's wife, the 1934 move to replace Stalin, and the "hunt" for Kirov, he related a whole sequence of stories opposing Kirov to Stalin. In 1926, he wrote, he had been at Kirov's apartment with Stalin when the latter went off on a rant about the Russian people's need for a "Tsar." Then he claimed to have been in Kirov's apartment on the evening the latter heard of the death of Stalin's wife, Nadezhda Allilueva (probably the evening of November 10, 1932). In a scene worthy of a screenplay, Kirov was sitting at his desk with a copy of the bulletin of the 1927 Party Congress open at the copy of "Lenin's Testament" criticizing Stalin. "Ilich foresaw everything as in a crystal ball," Chagin supposedly heard him say.[54]

One problem with Chagin's testimony is that it makes too comprehensive a story, suggesting that it was embellished. A second problem is that most of it appeared only in 1960. When Chagin wrote to Khrushchev in March 1956, he described only Stalin's 1926 comments about the Russian people needing a Tsar. He came up with his other stories later.[55]

Yet another problem with Chagin's evidence is that he was not as close to Kirov in the 1920s and early 1930s as he later asserted. In one 1928 note expressing irritation with him, Kirov referred to the editor as "Comrade Chagin," rather than with the more familiar first name that he used with subordinates he was friendly with. In late 1932 or 1933, Chagin wrote to Kirov begging him for work and reminding him that he had served as editor of the newspaper *Star of the East* in Tbilisi, Georgia in 1931–1932. Neither the letter of request nor the reminder should have been necessary had Chagin been as close to Kirov as he later claimed. Again, in November 1934 Chagin wrote to Kirov pleading for a new job assignment and complaining that the latter would not meet him. Again, neither the plea nor the complaint suggest a close relationship between the two.[56]

A final problem is Chagin's history of aggressive denunciation. He himself confessed that Kirov reprimanded him in early 1926 for attacking veteran Leningrad cadres that they both had to work with. In 1929 Chagin was a key player in the attack on the Desov-Komarov group. Kirov then threw him to the TsK dogs as a scapegoat for the excessive "sensationalism" of the assault. In the early 1930s Chagin took the Stalinist side in debates that resulted in the arrest of a number of prominent philosophers, including some orthodox Marxists. The editor had a history of jumping to toe whatever party line the leadership chose to draw.[57]

Dmitry Sorokin's evidence shares some of the difficulties of Chagin's letters. Sorokin served in the Cheka/GPU/OGPU from 1920 until 1926, when he transferred to Molotov's office at the Central Committee. He served there until 1938, when he was demoted (but apparently never arrested). Sorokin wrote two letters to Molotov and two to Khrushchev in the months after the Twentieth Party Congress in 1956, responding to the denunciation of Stalin and the hints of his involvement in the Kirov murder. The TsK did not answer these letters. Following Khrushchev's much broader suggestion at the Twenty-Second Party Congress that Stalin had plotted the Kirov killing, Sorokin wrote to the TsK again. This time his letter came to the attention of Klimov at the KPK, who interviewed him in February 1962. Following this interview Sorokin penned a deposition.[58]

Sorokin married Medved's sister in 1920. He apparently knew Medved well as a former Cheka colleague and brother-in-law. After Medved's arrest, he and his wife adopted Medved's daughter Viola. He was well informed on the conflict between Yagoda and the Messing/Olsky group in 1931, although he misdated it to 1930. He had good information on other aspects of the Leningrad NKVD's work, including Zaporozhets' absence from the city in the months before Kirov's assassination. As already described (above, pp. 515–516) he claimed in 1962 that Medved had strongly implied to him that Stalin and Yagoda had engineered Kirov's death. This story was probably based on Medved's resentment of Yagoda and Zaporozhets, who had in fact worked to remove him from the Leningrad job, and of Stalin, who had scapegoated him for the Kirov murder.[59]

Even more than Chagin, Sorokin developed his evidence into a fully coherent, and probably embellished, story. On the eve of the January 1935 trial of the Leningrad NKVD officers, he claimed to have been at the apartment of V. V. Ulrikh, presiding judge of the Military Tribunal. Ulrikh assured Sorokin that Medved and the others would get off easily. Sorokin also reported that he'd heard rumors about the falsification of voting results at the Seventeenth Party Congress, although his version differed fundamentally from Verkhovykh's (Sorokin claimed that one Makhover, who was not a member of the Electoral Commission at all, had supervised the falsification).[60] In 1962 Sorokin also told a highly degraded version of the auto accident in which Borisov died. In Sorokin's variant, it was Medved who was involved in an auto accident on December 2, which he survived.[61] He was mixing up elements of different stories he had heard, and he probably suffered from source amnesia as well.

In December 1966 Klimov and the KPK questioned Sorokin again, seeking to clarify contradictions in his stories. In response Sorokin generated almost the entire Shatunovskaya commission narrative of the murder, including many incidents that he had not mentioned in 1962 and could not possibly have seen. He described the putative attempt to "fulfill Lenin's Testament" and get rid of Stalin at the Seventeenth Party Congress, the falsification of the voting results, and Stalin's determination to get rid of Kirov "because of his growing authority among the party and the people." He included the story of Zaporozhets ordering the Leningrad NKVD to free Nikolaev after his first detention. At the same time he omitted his 1962 claim that Medved had implicated Stalin in the murder, even noting that relations between Stalin and Medved were "normal."[62]

Sorokin and Chagin's stories suffer from embellishment, factual inaccuracies, and the presentation of rumors as fact. This is not to say that all 1960s testimony about the murder was inaccurate. The Leningrad official Mikhail Rosliakov, for example, was careful to note when he was reporting something he had not witnessed himself. Rosliakov also took pains to give the sources of oral stories he heard. Although he suspected in the 1960s that Stalin was behind Kirov's killing, he introduced a good deal less hearsay into his account of the murder than either Chagin or Sorokin. Much of his evidence fits well with archival records and press reports of the time. Other witnesses, such as Smolny deputy commandant Mikhalchenko, NKVD Officer Baskakov, and Seventeenth Party Congress delegate Karl Ratnek, gave evidence to the Shatunovskaya investigation that checks out well against archival records and other witnesses' accounts. Like Rosliakov, the latter three men were generally careful to specify what they remembered clearly and what they did not. They also differentiated clearly between what they had seen themselves and what they had heard from others.

After the Shatunovskaya Commission

The findings of Shatunovskaya's winter 1960–1961 investigation apparently generated controversy at the highest levels of the party leadership. On May 5, 1961 the Presidium of the TsK set up a commission of Nikolai Shvernik, Zinovy Serdiuk, Shatunovskaya, Rudenko, Aleksandr Shelepin, and N. Mironov to review the political trials of 1934–1938, beginning with the trial of the "Leningrad Center." Shvernik, Serdiuk, Shatunovskaya, Rudenko, and Shelepin were all clearly Khrushchev supporters at this time, although there were obvious differences between Shatunovskaya and Rudenko, for example, about the interpretation of Kirov's murder. At a meeting on June 13, 1961 the commission debated Shatunovskaya's January 28 report. A majority of members agreed, quite reasonably, that "the data provided . . . do not provide the basis for such categorical conclusions and require deeper investigation." Of the six commission members, it seems probable that Shatunovskaya and possibly Shvernik defended the conclusions of the January 28 memorandum (Shvernik's signature was on it), while the other four commission members expressed doubts.[63]

It would not be accurate to view the doubts expressed about the Shatunovskaya report in the spring and summer of 1961 as signs of a recrudescent Stalinism. The new commission continued to work on the assumption that Stalin was the chief instigator of the Terror. Moreover, in April 1961 the Presidium put Shvernik and Frol Kozlov, both early backers of the Stalin-killed-Kirov narrative, in charge of a review of KPK staff aimed at removing those who "expressed disagreement with the decisions of the Twentieth Party Congress about the cult of personality." At least one vocal Stalinist, Boitsov, was retired from the KPK as a result. In 1961 the de-Stalinizers were in the driver's seat.[64]

That September the commission produced a report on the trial of the "Leningrad Center" that climbed down from extravagant claims about a Stalin conspiracy to murder Kirov and focused on his fabrication of a case against the ex-Zinovievites. The report was in fact a summary of the commission's findings about the assassination in general, not just the "Leningrad Center" trial. It was issued with attached materials and detailed reviews of the falsification of evidence in the three major show trials of 1936–1938.[65]

· 121 ·

"On the results of the review of materials in the criminal trial of the case of the murder of S. M. Kirov," September 1961. RGANI, f. 6, op. 13, d. 39, ll. 1–7.

[. . .]

In the course of the inquiry the investigative-judicial file on the charges against Nikolaev, Kotolynov, Shatsky, and others in the Kirov murder was studied. Documents and materials stored in the archives of the Secretariat and Presidium of the Central Committee, the Party Control Committee, the Leningrad regional party committee, and the Leningrad Institute of History of the Communist Party were reviewed. Many materials located in the archives of the NKVD-KGB of the USSR, the USSR Ministry of Foreign Affairs, the Supreme Court of the USSR, and other organizations were reviewed. A number of documents and circumstances with a direct relation to the case of the Kirov murder were subjected to graphological and other expert analysis.

In addition interviews were conducted and depositions received from 120 persons who had in the past some relation to the trial or who knew the accused personally. Among those questioned were former party officials, officers of the NKVD, the court, the prosecutor's office, and relatives and acquaintances of the accused.

[. . .]

After reviewing the materials of the trial we have determined that only Nikolaev was correctly charged and sentenced to execution [. . .] in the murder of S. M. Kirov. As regards the remaining persons found guilty in this case, the charges that they created an underground terrorist Zinovievite group headed by the so-called "Leningrad Center" and [participated] in the murder of S. M. Kirov were fabricated.

Materials of the review of the Kirov murder case are laid out in detail in the attached report [no attached report was available to me—M. L.].

The murderer of S. M. Kirov was the terrorist Nikolaev, L. V., b. 1904, Russian, a member of the Communist Party since 1924. In the past Nikolaev had done Komsomol work, worked for a time as an *instruktor* of the Leningrad regional party committee and the Leningrad Institute of History of the Communist Party. In April 1934 Nikolaev was fired from that Institute and did not work anywhere up to the time of the killing.

Nikolaev developed anti-Soviet convictions and terrorist inclinations [. . .] in the fall of 1934. His lack of psychological and moral balance played a role in the formation of these views and intentions. In addition the situation in which Nikolaev found himself after his expulsion from the party organization of the Institute for refusal to undertake work in transport [. . .] contributed to the development of his terrorist intentions.

Nikolaev, who considered that he had unfairly "ended up discredited and alienated from the party . . . decided to signal all of this before the party." Nikolaev chose to kill Kirov, a well-known party and government figure in the country, to make this political signal.

Nikolaev began to prepare a terrorist action in October–November 1934. With this goal in mind he carried a weapon with him and followed S. M. Kirov, attempted to approach him on the street and in other places. For his suspicious behavior he was detained [. . .] by officers of Kirov's guard and taken to the Operations Department of the Leningrad regional NKVD, but freed without any consequences. Taking advantage of this criminal attitude of the NKVD operatives, Nikolaev accomplished the criminal act he intended on December 1, 1934. [. . .]

The murder of S. M. Kirov was used by Stalin for the physical isolation and annihilation of the leaders of the Zinoviev opposition, as well as their former supporters, in spite of the fact that the Zinoviev opposition had been ideologically and organizationally smashed by the party by 1934. In the first days of December 1934 Stalin began to assert that the terrorist act against Kirov had been accomplished by the Zinovievites, which oriented the investigation on the fabrication of charges against them. [. . .]

Officers Agranov, Mironov, Liushkov, and Dmitriev, as the direct supervisors and organizers of the investigation, carrying out the will of Stalin, took all possible measures to connect Kirov's murder to the activities of the Zinovievite opposition and "prove" Nikolaev's attachment to the Zinovievites and the existence in Leningrad of an underground terrorist center of Zinovievites that supposedly committed the murder.

In pursuit of these goals the officers of the NKVD, using threats and deception, blackmail and promises to spare Nikolaev's life, as well as the organization of privileged conditions of imprisonment for Nikolaev, were able to win Nikolaev around and incline him to give false evidence about the participation of the Zinovievite opposition in the murder of S. M. Kirov and traduce the group of former Zinovievites arrested in the case. [. . .]

The "helpful" testimony of Nikolaev and several others of the accused is not confirmed by the materials of the case and is refuted by the review we have conducted.

First and foremost, it is now established that Nikolaev never belonged to the Zinovievite opposition, the Trotskyites, or any other antiparty groups and did not share their views. During the time of his work in the Komsomol (1922–1923) he was in fact personally acquainted and connected through work with Kotolynov, Shatsky, and several other persons who later became active participants in the Zinovievite opposition. Nikolaev himself denied the existence of any accomplices at all in the crime, although he admitted that he had committed the murder for political reasons.

[. . .]

The accused who were named as members of the terrorist "Leningrad Center" [Kotolynov, Shatsky, Rumiantsev, Mandelshtam, Miasnikov, Levin, Sositsky, and Nikolaev], all [. . .] denied the existence of this center or their participation in same. Not one of the "participants" in the "Leningrad Center" manufactured by the investigators testified that Nikolaev was a member. [. . .] Even the supervisors of the investigation Agranov and Mironov, in spite of all their attempts to represent Nikolaev as an active participant in an underground terrorist organization, did not include Nikolaev in the membership of the "Leningrad Center."

The review has determined that Nikolaev was placed in the membership of the "Leningrad Center" by Stalin himself. On December 21, 1934 the NKVD presented Stalin with a draft announcement for the press of the results of the investigation of the cases of Nikolaev and the others. In this draft Nikolaev did not appear as a member of the "Leningrad Center." In his own hand Stalin, in contradiction to the materials of the case, wrote Nikolaev into the membership of the terrorist "Leningrad Center." In a second edit he added Rumiantsev to the composition of this center, and excluded Antonov and Zvezdov.

The review disconfirms the story of the criminal connections of the Latvian consul in Leningrad Bissenieks with Nikolaev. [. . .]

At the time that the formal charges in the case [. . .] were composed, Stalin had at his disposal 260 protocols of interrogations of the arrested and a significant number of special reports on the course of the investigation. Disposing of these documents, Stalin actively intervened in the investigation of the case, demanding from the investigators the development of materials backing up the baseless story that the Zinovievites participated in the murder of S. M. Kirov. [. . .]

At the conclusion of the investigation Stalin gave Ulrikh, the chairman of the Military Tribunal of the Supreme Court of the USSR, an order to carry out the trial in two days and shoot all fourteen accused. [. . .] The trial was conducted with the most serious violations of Soviet criminal and procedural law. [. . .]

In January 1935 Stalin personally composed in the name of the Central Committee the text of the secret letter, "Lessons of the Events Connected with the Villainous Murder of Comrade Kirov." which was sent to party and Komsomol organizations. In this letter [. . .] the Zinovievite factional group was declared to be "the most traitorous and the most despicable of all the factional groups in the history of our party [. . .] [the factional group] considered it permissible to resort to terror as a method of struggle against the party and its leadership." Based on this judgment, the "Secret Letter" demanded repressive measures against the Zinovievites and their supporters.

These directives of Stalin sowed suspicion and mistrust among the members of the party and led to further mass repressions not only against former participants in opposition groups, but against the body of party, soviet, and economic officials, and also against the command staff of the army and fleet.

In 1935–1938 the trials of the so-called "Moscow Center," "United Trotskyite-Zinovievite Center" and the "Right-Trotskyite Bloc" were conducted and the persons who stood trial were accused of murdering S. M. Kirov on the basis of the same falsified materials. [. . .]

The memorandum concluded with a recommendation that the sentences in the cases of all defendants in the "Leningrad Center" trial except Nikolaev be annulled. The authors also suggested the rehabilitation of ex-Latvian consul Bissenieks, executed in 1941.[66]

At the Twenty-Second Party Congress that met in late October 1961 Khrushchev, at the height of his power, chose to flirt with the Shatunovskaya report's story-line on the Kirov murder, despite the evident doubts of many of his subordinates. The congress was open season on Molotov, Kaganovich, and Malenkov, the "antiparty group" of 1957. Delegates hastened to condemn them in general terms and bathe Khrushchev in lush praise. When it came to specifics, however, Nikolai Shvernik in his report on KPK work stuck to the well-documented involvement of Molotov, Kaganovich, and Malenkov in the Great Terror. He did not discuss directly either the Kirov murder or the verdicts in the major show trials of 1936–1938. A. N. Shelepin, chief of the NKVD, declared that Stalin, Molotov, and Kaganovich "used the murder of Sergei Mironovich Kirov as an excuse for the organization of retaliation against persons inconvenient for them, against major figures in our government."[67] Khrushchev, however, went further.

> The basis for the mass repressions was laid down following the murder of Comrade Kirov. It is still necessary to make a great effort to understand truly who was guilty in his death. The more deeply we study the materials connected with the death of Kirov, the more questions appear. The fact that Kirov's murderer was twice detained near Smolny with a weapon on his person is suggestive. But both times he was freed on someone's order. And then this person turns up in Smolny with a weapon in the same corridor that Kirov habitually passed through. And somehow it turned out that at the moment of the killing the chief of Kirov's guard was far behind S. M. Kirov, although according to orders he had no right to be at such a distance from his charge.
> Another fact is exceedingly strange. When the chief of Kirov's guard

was transported to an interrogation, and he was to be questioned by Stalin, Molotov, and Voroshilov, then on the road, as the driver of the vehicle has related, those who were supposed to be escorting the chief of the guard to the interrogation deliberately caused an accident. They declared that the chief of the guard died as the result of an accident, although in reality he was killed by the persons escorting him.

In this way the person who guarded Kirov was killed. Then they shot those who killed him. This, obviously, was no coincidence, this was a deliberate crime. Who could have done it? At present there is a careful review underway of the circumstances of this complex case.

It turns out that the driver of the vehicle that transported the chief of Kirov's guard to the interrogation is still alive. He told how, when they were riding to the interrogation, an officer of the NKVD sat next to him. The vehicle was a truck. [. . .] Two other officers of the NKVD were in the back of the vehicle with the chief of Kirov's guard.

The driver said more. When they were driving down the street the person sitting next to him suddenly grabbed the wheel from him and steered the car directly into a building. The driver grabbed the wheel back and corrected the vehicle's course, so that it only hit the building wall with its side. Then they told him that Kirov's guard died during the accident. [. . .]

You can imagine how difficult it was to figure out such questions, when people who were themselves guilty of abuse of power, of mass repressions, were on the Presidium of the Central Committee. They [Molotov, Kaganovich, Malenkov] stubbornly opposed all measures to expose [Stalin's] cult of personality. [. . .]

Of course they did not want to review such matters. You heard Comrade Shelepin's speech. He said much at this congress, but obviously he did not say all that has now been uncovered. Thousands of persons guilty of nothing perished. [. . .]

Of course, those people on the Presidium of the TsK who were responsible for the violations of legality, for the mass repressions, resisted in every way possible the exposure of the arbitrary tyranny during the time of the cult of personality, and then they undertook an antiparty factional struggle against the leadership of the TsK, and above all they concentrated their fire on me, as the first secretary of the TsK, because I, in pursuit of my duties, had put such questions on the agenda.[68]

As the reader can see, Khrushchev presented dubious assertions— two detentions of Nikolaev, Kuzin's story of Borisov's death—as indisputable fact, relying at least in part on Shatunovskaya's report. There were also unquestionable factual errors—Borisov was not "the chief of Kirov's guard," for example, but a low-level officer assigned to a post of very little responsibility.

Khrushchev's main purpose, as revealed in the final three paragraphs quoted, was to charge Molotov, Malenkov, and Kaganovich with obstructing the 1956 investigation into the murder, and thus further discredit them. As the last sentence indicates, this was a very personal feud for him ("they concentrated their fire on me . . . "). Khrushchev's determination to push beyond the attested facts about the Terror probably also had to do with a desire to drive a stake through the heart of Stalinism by implicating the dictator himself in the murder of Kirov. His readiness to go beyond the positions recommended by his more sober advisers (including probably Zinovy Serdiuk and Shelepin) also resembled his grandiose promises that Soviet living standards would match those of the United States by 1970. These too he insisted on proclaiming at the Party Congress, against the advice of his subordinates.[69] Such hubris ultimately contributed to his downfall three years later.

In the remaining years of Khrushchev's reign the narrative of the Terror proposed in the KPK's January 1961 report teetered on the edge of official recognition. The 1962 edition of the *History of the Communist Party of the USSR* declared that "many delegates" at the Seventeenth Party Congress had wanted to "transfer Stalin from the post of general secretary to some other job."[70] On February 7, 1964 Mikoyan's friend, the editor and researcher Lev Shaumian, wrote in *Pravda* of "over 300 votes" cast against Stalin at the Seventeenth Party Congress and again mentioned the supposed initiative to demote him. In the meantime the Kirov cult flourished. *It All Happened in Urzhum,* a memoir of Kirov's childhood attributed to his sisters, came out in 1962. In 1964 S. Sinelnikov published his laudatory *Kirov* in the Komsomol publishing house's series, "Lives of Extraordinary People" (see above, pp. 523–524).[71] The same year the State Publishing House of Political Literature released Stepan Krasnikov's biography, *Sergei Mironovich Kirov: Life and Accomplishments.*[72]

Inside the party leadership, however, there was dissatisfaction with the exaggerations of the Shatunovskaya narrative. In the spring of 1962 Olga Shatunovskaya was removed from the commission working on the Terror trials and then formally retired from the KPK at the end of the year. In a later account that does not lay out a clear chronology of events, Shatunovskaya attributed her firing primarily to the efforts of Mikhail Suslov, the advocate of stability and an end to discussion of Stalin's crimes. Her interpretation certainly makes sense, as does her charge that her aggressive investigations of corruption among high-level officials made her many enemies. But Shatunovskaya also unwittingly made it clear that she had alienated just about every reform-minded party leader as well, in part with an outburst in which she told Khrushchev, "The people around you are no Leninists!" Probably in the spring of 1962, Shvernik delivered a report to the Presidium denigrating her work at the KPK. Shatunovskaya also reports being reprimanded by Khrushchev's secretary Vladimir Lebedev (who stuck with his boss during his overthrow in October 1964), Frol Kozlov, and her old patron Mikoyan. Zinovy Serdiuk, another steadfast Khrushchev supporter, also opposed her continued tenure at the KPK. The fact that loyal Khrushchevites got rid of Shatunovskaya during the warmest period of the "Thaw" suggests strongly that it was her investigations of corruption and the poor quality of her January 1961 report, rather than a desire to conceal Stalin's crimes, that motivated her ouster.[73]

Shatunovskaya was concerned that KPK functionaries or other party officials might destroy the evidence she and her subordinates had gathered on the Kirov murder. In a letter to Khrushchev dated May 22, 1962 she summarized again the version of the murder from the January 1961 memorandum and enumerated what she considered the most important documents in the case. She referred to the evidence of Chagin, Verkhovykh, and A. Andreev on the Seventeenth Party Congress, and to the Sevastianov note that purportedly confirmed their testimony. She listed early 1960s depositions by Dr. Kirchakov and several others (see above, pp. 572–573) that either repeated the story of Nikolaev accusing the NKVD of putting him up to the murder during his interrogation by Stalin, or simply affirmed that the NKVD had organized Kirov's assassination on Stalin's orders. All of these depositions were at least third-hand when they were put to paper nearly three decades after the crime.[74]

Around the time that Shatunovskaya was removed from the KPK, the drive to rehabilitate the most prominent show trials victims stalled. Shelepin's statement to the Twenty-Second Party Congress that Stalin had used Kirov's murder to get "inconvenient" people out of the way, including major party leaders, sent a signal that Bukharin, Rykov, Zinoviev, Kamenev, and the other accused in these proceedings were probably innocent. In the last days of the Twenty-Second Party Congress, Bukharin's widow Anna Larina and Rykov's daughter requested the rehabilitation of the ex-Rightist leaders. But Khrushchev and the Presidium never got round to rehabilitating Bukharin, Rykov, or the Left leaders. The main concern seems to have been that this would throw into question the party's whole course from the 1920s onward, including the establishment of such key Soviet institutions as the collective farms. In addition rehabilitation of the really famous victims would entail tremendous loss of face for the Communist Party. Shatunovskaya reported later that when she asked Khrushchev to publish the materials exonerating Bukharin and the others, he told her that they had to wait fifteen years. In the event, the wait turned out to be about twenty-five years.[75]

The KPK investigation of the Kirov murder continued in 1962–1964, led by Zinovy Serdiuk, the commission's deputy director. Useful evidence was gathered, for example, from A. F. Annushkov, former operations secretary of the Leningrad NKVD Special Department. Annushkov debunked the March 1938 show trial version of events in which Zaporozhets ordered Nikolaev's release before Kirov's murder. Following Annushkov's testimony, beginning in late 1963, the KPK conducted an exhaustive search for surviving employees of the Leningrad NKVD from the first half of the 1930s, focusing on the Special Department and going right down to the level of apprentice clerks. The wives of former Leningrad NKVD Officers Kotomin, Gorin-Lundin, and Mosevich submitted depositions in 1964 at the commission's request. Other than Mosevich's widow's vague memory that her husband and his colleagues had said "there were some kind of materials on Nikolaev, but not in the Special Political Department, but in some other department of the NKVD—the Special Department, it seems to me," these inquiries found no evidence pointing to an NKVD conspiracy to murder Kirov.[76]

Although official discussion of the Kirov murder in 1963–1964 was muted, the ongoing investigation appears to have been impartial. The investigators' work was top-secret, intended only for the eyes of senior party leaders, who would then decide what to do with the findings. Thus, there was no need to doctor conclusions. In addition, Serdiuk and the KPK continued to orient their other work on exposure of secret police abuse of power, the Terror, and rehabilitation of Communist victims. In February 1963 the KPK produced an extremely valuable, comprehensive report on the Terror, signed by Shvernik, Shelepin, Serdiuk, Rudenko, N. Mironov, and new KGB chief Vladimir Semichastny. It was not published until 2003. The commission also "readmitted" to the party second-level figures executed by Stalin for oppositional views, including V. N. Tolmachev and L. A. Shatskin. Serdiuk authored a report on the OGPU's creation in the 1920s of fake counterrevolutionary organizations that sought to entrap politically suspect Soviet subjects and White sympathizers abroad. These organizations also passed false information to foreign intelligence services and White émigré organizations. In short, the KPK continued to follow Khrushchev's injunction at the Twenty-Second Congress to investigate the entire history of the Terror and secret police abuse of power.[77]

After Khrushchev's Fall

In October 1964 a coalition of prominent Presidium members, including former Khrushchev allies and protégés such as Shelepin, Suslov, and Leonid Brezhnev, forced the general secretary to retire. They charged him with behaving rudely, ruling arbitrarily, conducting an impulsive and ineffective foreign policy, risking an apocalyptic war by placing missiles in Cuba, failing to improve Soviet agriculture, constructing his own personality cult, and other missteps. One Presidium member, D. S. Poliansky, criticized Khrushchev for "indecent" attacks on Stalin. Like Suslov, he feared that continuing discussion of the Terror would destabilize the party and discredit it abroad.[78]

On March 16, 1965 officials familiar with the Kirov investigation submitted a brief on the inquiry's progress to the party leadership (most likely addressed to the Presidium). Zinovy Serdiuk, who was still in charge of the investigation, probably authored or at least reviewed this report. The memorandum summarized the evidence in the 1934–1935 investigation, and the history of the post-Stalin investigative commissions. The authors repeated that Stalin and NKVD investigators had falsified evidence on a massive scale in 1934 and again in the show trials of 1936–1938. The fabrication of cases during the Terror had greatly complicated later investigations. Nonetheless, the authors argued, the investigation ought to be continued in hopes of a breakthrough.[79]

· 122 ·

Excerpts from KPK report on progress of the KPK investigation of the Kirov murder, March 1965. RGANI, f. 6, op. 13, d. 40, ll. 36–54.

[. . .]

After the conviction of Nikolaev and the other participants in the so-called "Leningrad Terrorist Zinovievite Center," new circumstances of the Kirov murder were "discovered" over the course of several years, and the circle of persons supposedly responsible for this crime expanded, which confused and complicated to a greater and greater degree the already complex case of the [. . .] assassination. At the same time, the wide publicity in both the open and the limited-access Soviet press [that is, confidential party reports] of the trials of the Zinovievites, Trotskyites, and Rightists, which contained contradictory information about the circumstances of Kirov's murder, disoriented public opinion inside the country and abroad, and created fertile soil for various types of doubts and invented versions of events around [. . .] the assassination of Kirov. [. . .]

As study of the criminal files in the case of the "Leningrad Terrorist Zinovievite Center" and connected cases has shown, many questions of [. . .] extremely great significance for any final conclusions [. . .] about the Kirov murder and the death of Operations Commissar Borisov have not been answered. The investigation of the case and the trial in 1934 were carried out in tendentious fashion, with a lack of objectivity, and in gross violation of the law. All efforts of the investigation were directed towards "proving" the version propounded by Stalin, to wit that the Zinovievites organized the murder of Kirov. The most elementary investigative actions, absolutely necessary for any criminal inquiry, were omitted. There are no protocols in the case files for the description of the crime scene, the search of Nikolaev, enumeration of the objects found at the scene, or analysis by weapons experts. The situation at the time of the crime /the positions of Nikolaev, Borisov, and other witnesses, etc./ was not reconstructed. Nikolaev's first explanations of his reasons for committing the crime and the information on hand about distortions in his psyche were not checked. The investigation had in its hands diaries and other manuscripts supposedly belonging to Nikolaev, in which he laid out his terrorist intentions and his plan for killing Kirov. In spite of the extraordinary value of these documents as evidence in the case they were not analyzed by experts in handwriting, and Nikolaev was only interrogated about a few of them, and even then very superficially. [. . .]

Simultaneous with the inquiry into the cases of Nikolaev and the others in 1934, an investigation into the circumstances of the death of Opera-

tions Commissar Borisov was carried out. However, the original paperwork from this investigation has not been located. [. . .] From the available copies of certain documents, including the protocols of interrogations of the operational officers of the Leningrad Region NKVD who
guarded Borisov——Maly, Vinogradov, the driver Kuzin, and other persons——it is evident that on the morning of December 2, 1934 officers of
the regional NKVD Operations Department received orders to take
Borisov immediately to Smolny to an interrogation by Stalin. On the way
there was an auto accident in which Borisov perished. Immediately after
the accident Maly, Vinogradov, and Kuzin were arrested. Yezhov, who
was at that time a member of Orgburo of the TsK, and Kosaryov, a member of the Orgburo of the TsK and first secretary of the Komsomol Central
Committee, took part in interrogating them. Maly, Vinogradov, and Kuzin were accused of the premeditated murder of Borisov, but they categorically rejected this charge. [. . .] In January 1935 Maly, Vinogradov, and
Kuzin were released and continued to work in the NKVD organs.

In 1937 Maly, Vinogradov, and Kuzin were rearrested and under interrogation changed their previous testimony. Maly and Vinogradov confessed to guilt in the deliberate murder of Borisov. Kuzin denied collaborating in the murder of Borisov, and deposed that the auto accident was
the fault of Maly, who grabbed the wheel from him and directed the automobile against the wall of a building. During the accident Maly and Vinogradov killed Borisov. Despite Vinogradov recanting his confession in
court, he and Maly were sentenced [. . .] to execution by firing squad.
[. . .]

After the Twenty-Second Party Congress (1961), declarations related to
the Kirov murder and the death of his guard began to come in to the Central Committee, the Soviet of Ministers, the KGB, and to local party and
soviet organs. The TsK commission (on investigating the Kirov murder
and Terror) received around 200 such declarations. The declarations
made a myriad of claims about the circumstances of Kirov's murder and
the death of Borisov, the essence of which can be summarized as follows:

—Kirov's murder was organized by Stalin.

—Yagoda, Yenukidze, Yezhov, and Vyshinsky were connected to the organization of the terrorist act.

—Kirov was not killed by Nikolaev but by some other person.

—Nikolaev committed the crime out of jealousy.

—Nikolaev was never shot but was held in some detention center under
a different name.

—Nikolaev was an agent of the NKVD and was used by that organ "in
the dark."

—Nikolaev was detained several times by the NKVD organs with a
weapon in places frequented by Kirov and for some reason freed.

—in Leningrad there existed several terrorist groups which were planning the assassination of Kirov.

—the organs of the NKVD did not react to signals they received about the preparations for a terrorist attack on Kirov.

—the guard Borisov was physically gotten out of way, in order to hide the real organizers of the Kirov murder.

[. . .]

Given the importance of the claims made in these declarations, a general investigation [. . .] was organized.

In the course of this investigation a great quantity of archival investigative documents were checked, as were operational materials and documents stored in central and local party, soviet, and military archives, museums [. . .]

To follow up on declarations of particular interest, visits were made to Ukraine, Belorussia, Kazakhstan, Turkmenistan, Armenia, Georgia, Azerbaijan, Lithuania, Latvia, and Estonia, as well as to Khabarovsk and the Primore, and the Leningrad, Rostov, Voronezh, and Magadan regions, and to other regions, towns, and population centers of the USSR.

Substantial work has been carried to locate persons referred to in the declarations, as well as persons through whom it might be possible to check the claims made by the declaration authors. Several hundred persons have been called in for conversations, and explanations taken from them. [. . .]

The review of the declarations is essentially complete. The majority of the claims made in them have not been confirmed. Investigation continues on a few of the declarations. [. . .]

Work to clarify the true circumstances of Kirov's murder and the death of Operations Commissar Borisov has taken on an especially difficult character. This is because three decades have passed since the time of the events in question. For the most part the former senior officials of the Leningrad city and regional party committees, the regional executive committee and the Leningrad soviet, the leading officers of the Leningrad regional NKVD and the central NKVD apparatus, who could shed light on one question or another, were repressed. Many direct witnesses of these events and persons connected to the investigation of the case are no longer among the living. Some very important materials, for example the files of Kirov's guard detail, the case files on Borisov's death, and others have not been preserved in the archives. [. . .]

Research into questions connected to the Kirov murder and the death of his bodyguard are complicated further by the fact that in the materials on hand [. . .] there are many contradictions, mutually exclusive versions of events, and various interpretations. The variegated stratification [of evidence] from past years and the conjunctures of historical circumstances,

[. . .] and at times delusions held in good faith by particular persons, are not least [among the complications].

Yet in spite of the existence of significant difficulties, it is worthwhile to continue the investigation into the assassination of Kirov and the death of his bodyguard, as the possibilities of the investigation are not yet exhausted. [. . .]

In the process of work to review the Kirov assassination case, the absolute necessity of getting evidence from Molotov, Voroshilov, and Kaganovich has become clear. It would make sense to call these persons to a session of the [investigative] commission or to talk with some of its members, so as to get from them explanations about the most important questions.

Several people /Pantiukhina—Nikolaev's sister, the driver Kuzin, the former commandant of Smolny Mikhalchenko and others/ whose evidence has very great significance for the case, are behaving themselves in extremely guarded fashion, and, judging from certain objective information, deceptively. It might be worthwhile to carry out appropriate operational measures through the KGB with regard to such persons, as exceptional cases.

The authors of the 1965 KPK report recommended further research, including investigations of accounts in the foreign press, another medical investigation into Borisov's death, a search for the originals of 1934 interrogation records known only through copies, and a review of the supposed evidence that Yagoda had connived at killing Kirov. They wanted to carry out ballistics tests on Nikolaev's Nagan, analysis of the handwriting in Nikolaev's diaries and notes, and a technical study of the auto accident in which Borisov died. Ominously, they asked if the KGB should not undertake "appropriate operational measures" on witnesses they believed were not telling the whole truth. In effect, they asked the leadership for permission to torture these people.

As the authors of the 1965 report noted, important documents in the Kirov case had been destroyed, in particular the originals of the Borisov case files and the records of Kirov's guard. It should be noted that the destruction of such documents would be just as consistent with an effort to hide 1934 evidence contradicting the official Stalinist version of the crime as it would be with a cover-up of any Stalin involvement in the assassination. Moreover, copies of documents in the Borisov case survived and the disposal of the records of Kirov's guard may well have been routine (see Chapter 11).

The March 1965 brief on the Kirov investigation indicates that KPK officials were still seeking to uncover the truth about the assassination, and that in private they fully recognized Stalin's guilt in organizing the Terror. They understood the mechanisms by which evidence in the case had been contaminated, including Stalin's fabrication of cases against his former political rivals. At the same time the memorandum shows that the inquiry had uncovered no credible evidence of a conspiracy to murder Kirov.

During 1965–1967 a majority of party leaders gradually came to the conclusion that they wanted no further public discussion of the Terror at all. As early as January 1966 *Pravda* ran an article calling for a "reevaluation" of Stalin. When in March 1966 a group of Soviet writers addressed a collective letter to Brezhnev asking that Stalin not be rehabilitated, Vladimir Semichastny, chairman of the KGB, treated their petition as subversive. In a brief for the Central Committee, Semichastny simultaneously denied that any rehabilitation was in the wind and referred to a new "scientific" approach to the dictator. On November 10, 1966 the Politburo (the party's leading body had taken back its former name) met to discuss "the history of the party and the criticism of the cult of personality of I. V. Stalin." Brezhnev, Suslov, N. V. Podgorny, and other members bitterly decried the harm that Khrushchev had supposedly done to the Soviet government with his denunciations of Stalin and resolved upon the creation of a new canonical historical narrative. Led by their new chairman, Arvids Pelshe, KPK officials began to harass independent-minded historians such as Aleksandr Nekrich, author of a book exposing Stalin's failure to prepare for the Nazi attack on the USSR in June 1941, and Leonid Petrovsky, son of Pyotr Petrovsky, the former editor of *Leningradskaia pravda* persecuted by Stalin. By 1969 the KPK was actively pursuing and punishing camp survivors like Aleksei Snegov who continued to denounce Stalin's crimes in public.[80]

This was the context for a June 5, 1967 KPK report on the Kirov murder forwarded by Arvids Pelshe to the Central Committee. The brief revealed that the commission investigating the Kirov murder had taken some of the steps recommended in the March 1965 report, conducting a ballistics analysis of Nikolaev's pistol and a reconstruction of the auto accident in which Borisov supposedly died. The authors took the position that Nikolaev was a lone gunman, and argued that fabrication of evidence during the Terror had contributed, for example, to later claims that Kirov's guard Borisov had been murdered. They dismissed as hearsay early 1960s stories of hostility between Stalin and Kirov and of hundreds of votes against Stalin at the Seventeenth Party Congress. Their purpose was to close the book on the assassination, as the conclusion makes clear.

· 123 ·

"Summary report on results of the investigation into the circumstances of the
murder of S. M. Kirov" ("Pelshe report"), May 19, 1967. Excerpts.
RGANI, f. 6, op. 13, d. 117, ll. 1–18.

[. . .]
The materials that we have at hand give the following picture of the circumstances of the murder of Kirov.

On December 1, 1934 Sergei Mironovich was at home in the morning, preparing for his report on the results of the November plenum of the TsK to a meeting of the Leningrad party organization *aktiv*, which was to begin at 6 P.M. in the Uritsky Palace. One and a half hours before the opening of the meeting he rode to Smolny, went upstairs to the third floor, and was killed by a shot in the back of his head not far from his office.

Employees of the regional party committee who came running at the sound of shots apprehended Nikolaev, in an unconscious state, at the scene of the crime. Nikolaev had on his person a party card and other documents identifying him. Near him there lay a revolver with five live cartridges and two empty shells. Doctors determined that the detainee was in a "reactive hysterical state." Interrogation of [Nikolaev] began only several hours later.

As Nikolaev testified, he came to the regional party committee to get a ticket to the party activists' meeting from his former co-workers. He got into the building using his party card, and, seeing Kirov on the third floor, he took advantage of the fact that there was no one nearby, and followed him. In the small corridor he shot him in the head from a short distance. He attempted to kill himself with a second shot, but failed.

From the materials of the inquiry it is not clear [. . .] whether Nikolaev knew beforehand of Kirov's arrival at Smolny or whether he met him by chance. According to the testimony of former employees of the Special Sector of the regional committee, Kirov as a rule prepared his lectures at home, but prior to his speeches dropped in at Smolny. Employees of the regional party committee named by Nikolaev confirmed that not long before Kirov's murder he had approached them with requests to provide him a ticket to the party activists' meeting. Nikolaev's relatives also testified that he intended to attend the meeting of the party activists.

At his first interrogations Nikolaev categorically denied that he had any collaborators. Suspicions that someone aided Nikolaev at the moment of

Kirov's killing were not confirmed by the investigation. After the attack all the exits from Smolny were closed and the building cordoned off. A check found no suspicious persons.

Under questioning Operations Commissar Borisov, whose duty was to guard Kirov in Smolny, deposed that he had walked behind Kirov along the main corridor at a distance of approximately twenty steps. He heard the shot before he turned into the small corridor, and while he was "drawing [his] revolver from its holster and cocking it" there was a second shot. Running into the small corridor he saw there "two [persons] lying on the floor by the doors to the reception room." Those persons who were among the first on the scene of the crime testified that they saw Borisov—some at the corner of the main and small corridors as he cocked his pistol, others already at the scene of the murder.

The Nagan system revolver found on the scene of the crime belonged to Nikolaev. It was registered by him in 1924, but after April 1931 the license to bear the weapon was for some reason not renewed. In 1966 experts who examined Nikolaev's revolver and the bullet extracted from Kirov's head concluded that the murder was committed with that same weapon.

In explaining the motive for the crime at the beginning of the investigation, Nikolaev testified that he was pushed to act by his "estrangement from the party" and his "unemployment and the absence of material and most importantly moral aid from party organizations." In his words, "the attempt on Kirov's life had the main goal of making a political signal before the party." In this way he wanted "to get the party to pay attention to a living human being and to the heartless bureaucratic attitude towards him," and he had fulfilled this "historic mission." Nikolaev's initial depositions on the motive for the murder correspond [. . .] to the content of his writings seized in the searches. Later, when the fabrication of the case of the "Leningrad Terrorist Zinovievite Center" began, Nikolaev gave different testimony, declaring that he had committed the crime at the orders of the Zinovievites. [There follows a description of Nikolaev's biography and his writings.]

[. . .]

The organizers and instigators of this evil deed were first presented as the Zinovievites, then the Trotskyites, and then the Rightists, who used for their purpose Yagoda and the deputy chief of the Leningrad regional NKVD Zaporozhets. Beginning in 1956 writers of letters, declarations, and depositions began to express the suspicion, and later the conviction, that the murder of Kirov was organized by the same Yagoda and Zaporozhets, but at the order of Stalin. The interest of Stalin in the physical elimination of Kirov was explained by the growing authority of Kirov, and by policy disagreements between them that led Stalin to have a hostile attitude towards Kirov. [. . .] It was also stated that there were conversations among delegates to the Seventeenth Party Congress, which became known to Stalin, about the promotion of Kirov to his post, and that Kirov was elected to the Central Committee almost unanimously, while Stalin received many "No" votes, but that the true results of the voting were hidden from the delegates.

In the process of investigation no direct evidence of the participation of Stalin in Kirov's murder was found and the materials on hand do not support such a charge.

The question of the relations between Stalin and Kirov is very difficult [. . .] above all due to the complexity and contradictions of Stalin's personality. Persons making claims about unfriendly relations between Stalin and Kirov were not closely acquainted with either, were not present at their meetings, and given their social positions could not have directly observed the interactions of Stalin with Kirov. [. . .] At the same time there is evidence that Kirov spoke warmly of Stalin, that when he visited Moscow he visited him at home and spent his free time with him, and that Stalin in his turn looked favorably on Kirov.

[. . .]

A copy of an NKVD memorandum to Stalin has been preserved, "On the results of the investigation of M. N. Volkova's reports." It lays out her "most characteristic reports" for August–October 1934. In the NKVD memorandum there are no data indicating that Volkova knew the terrorist Nikolaev or denounced his criminal plans. Nor are there such data in the criminal case files on Nikolaev or the officers of the Leningrad regional NKVD.

It should also be noted that in October–November 1934 the state of operational work in Leningrad was reviewed by the USSR NKVD. Serious shortcomings in agent-operational and investigative work were uncovered by the commission, but in its report there is not one mention of any case of signals of terror being ignored.

[The report then covers Borisov's death and the extraction of "confessions" from Borisov's guards by torture in 1937.]

[. . .]

In 1967 a joint commission of experts in auto engineering, traffic accident reconstruction, and forensic medicine, after studying the materials on hand and carrying out necessary analysis and experiments, came to the following conclusion: Borisov was transported in an automobile with serious technical problems, which under the circumstances could have led to the accident in which Borisov smashed into the wall of the building and received a fatal blow to his head.

[. . .]

As a result of the review of the circumstances of the Kirov murder we believe it possible to conclude the following.

S. M. Kirov was killed by Nikolaev. He committed the crime for political reasons. There was no basis for the convictions of the persons charged in the same case as Nikolaev as his accomplices.

Operations Commissar Borisov died accidentally as the result of an automobile crash.

Materials on the participation of Stalin and NKVD officers in the murder of Kirov are not confirmed by objective data.

In connection with the terrorist attack on Kirov, several employees of the Leningrad regional NKVD and relatives of the murderer Nikolaev were convicted baselessly. It would be desirable to review the courts' decisions regarding these persons according to established legal procedures.

Chief Controller of the KPK Klimov.

Prosecutor of the Main Military Prosecutor's Office Baturin.

Deputy Section Director of the KGB Investigative Department Kuzmin.

Senior Investigator for High Priority Cases/KGB Investigative Department Zamaraev.

The KPK's 1967 report on the Kirov murder was not "Stalinist." The authors denied that there was an oppositionist conspiracy to murder Kirov, and they acknowledged that Stalin and the NKVD had fabricated cases against the accused in the trials of 1934–1938. Based on my own examination of KPK files on the murder, their evaluation of the evidence appears to be objective. The reason for this objectivity was simple: in this case the evidence corresponded to the desire of Brezhnev, Suslov, and other Presidium members to put a stop to discussion of Stalin's crimes. Nikolaev killed Kirov, end of story. However, the question of the verdicts in the show trials was left hanging. The Central Committee never released the 1967 report's findings, nor did the Politburo sanction the rehabilitation of the persons wrongly executed in either the "Leningrad Center" trial or the show trials of 1936–1938. A deafening public silence descended, not just about the facts of the Kirov assassination, but also about the mass murders of the late 1930s and Stalin's use of the assassination to justify them.

Nevertheless reform-oriented Communists from Mikoyan's circle kept alive in private conversations and unpublished manuscripts the memory of the Terror, and of Shatunovskaya's investigation. Among them were Shatunovskaya herself, Lev Shaumian, Pyotr Petrovsky's son Leonid, Mikoyan's son Sergo, Khrushchev's son Sergei, Aleksei Snegov, and Bukharin's widow Anna Larina. The dissident historian Aleksandr Nekrich also associated with this group before his expulsion from the USSR. Jana Kutin, Shatunovskaya's daughter, remembers the gatherings where this informal group discussed the history of Stalinism late into the night. The atmosphere was grief-stricken. "When they met around the table . . . and talked of camps, of jails, of exile, of mines and lumber camps, of interrogators, of the basement of the Lubianka, of Beria and Stalin, I wanted to disappear from that room, so thick and black was the cloud of memory. Inside it seemed that there was nothing to breathe, that the cloud was going to crush me with its weight. . . ."[81]

The researcher Roy Medvedev, attached to an educational institute in Moscow, also seems to have had extensive contacts with the group of Leninist dissidents. Medvedev began working on a history of the Stalin era in 1962, at the height of the effort to produce an official revised narrative of the Terror that would expose Stalin. In the summer or fall of 1967 he showed TsK authorities, at their demand, a copy of eight chapters of his thirteen-chapter manuscript, already entitled "Let History Judge." A November report to Mikhail Suslov labeled the work "politically harmful" among other reasons because it did not discuss Stalin's putative accomplishments, showed Leon Trotsky (accurately) as a major figure in the October Revolution, and condemned forced collectivization and "superindustrialization." The report recommended that Moscow city party committee discipline Medvedev. He was expelled from the Communist Party in 1969.[82]

Unable to publish in the USSR, Medvedev brought out *Let History Judge* in English in 1971. He apparently made extensive use of the Shatunovskaya investigation's findings, conveyed to him orally, most likely by Shatunovskaya herself and by Old Bolsheviks interviewed by the KPK in the early 1960s. As a result of the oral transmission, and the imprecise memories of the interviewees, Medvedev's account of the Kirov murder corresponded neither with the 1934–1935 evidence nor with the written depositions submitted to the KPK in the early 1960s. Medvedev referred to the purported attempt of party officials to replace Stalin with Kirov at the Seventeenth Party Congress, drawing on unspecified "reports" that probably originated at the KPK. He also claimed that 270 delegates at the congress voted against Stalin's membership in the Central Committee, more than doubling the number specified in V. M. Verkhovykh's initial deposition. Medvedev cited Pyotr Chagin's description of a "hunt" against Kirov in 1934. He repeated the NKVD's 1937–1938 narrative of the murder, claiming that Nikolaev was detained two times before the murder and relieved of a revolver; that both times Zaporozhets, on Yagoda's order, instructed officers to return Nikolaev's pistol and free him; and that Nikolaev, at his interview with Stalin, had blamed the NKVD for putting him up to the murder. Medvedev relied on a somewhat garbled transmission of the driver Kuzin's testimony about Borisov's murder, claiming that after the truck's accident escorting officers killed Kirov's guard by smashing his head with crowbars. Medvedev also distorted the testimony of Nikolaev's jail guard Katsafa (Chapter 8, Document 44; Chapter 9, Document 80), probably unintentionally, claiming that Nikolaev told Katsafa "how the assassination had been arranged, and how he had been promised his life if he implicated the Leningrad Zinovievites." In the context of the book, the phrase "how the assassination had been arranged" unquestionably implied that Nikolaev had told Katsafa that the NKVD had aided him in committing the crime. But the records of Katsafa's testimony in the KPK archive show him saying nothing of the sort.[83]

Western historians writing on the murder, lacking any access to archival documentation, made use of Medvedev's evidence.[84] Nikita Khrushchev's brief discussions of the assassination at the Twentieth and Twenty-Second Party Congresses seemed to confirm it, and there was nothing implausible about Stalin arranging the assassination of a political rival.

With the publication of *Let History Judge,* internal Soviet evidence on Kirov's killing converged with émigré accounts by Nicolaevsky, Krivitsky, Orlov, and others. This convergence also seemed to confirm the "Stalin did it" version of events. In fact, however, the convergence was illusory for several reasons. Both the Soviet and the émigré streams of evidence/speculation about Kirov's killing drew to a great extent on a common pool of rumor laid down in the middle to late 1930s inside the USSR. Moreover, the two streams had fed one another throughout the 1950s and 1960s. During the Khrushchev years Boris Nicolaevsky was acutely aware of revelations about the Stalinist terror in the Soviet press, and cited them in his articles written from 1956 onward. These revelations included both accurate information on the mass murder and dubious evidence on the Kirov assassination itself. Conversely, Olga Shatunovskaya at the KPK knew and read Nicolaevsky's commentary on Soviet history and it may well have influenced her. One interesting possibility is that Shatunovskaya originally drew the idea of a move at the Seventeenth Party Congress to replace Stalin with Kirov from Nicolaevsky's 1956 *Socialist Herald* articles arguing that Kirov had led a "moderate" Politburo majority, including Ordzhonikidze and Kuibyshev, that secretly opposed Stalin in 1934. The Menshevik organ was still read inside the Soviet leadership, and it was four years later that Shatunovskaya began gathering evidence of pre-assassination tension between Stalin and Kirov.[85]

It took courage to stand against the whole Soviet state apparatus for an open discussion of the history of Stalinism. And the Leninist dissidents were right in their overall appraisal of Stalinism as a terroristic system and of Stalin as a mass murderer. However, their adoption of the dogma that Stalin ordered Kirov's murder was probably mistaken. Why did they insist on this canard when Stalin's overall responsibility for the Terror was so clear? First, Shatunovskaya and her fellow investigators worked in the atmosphere of rumor, secrecy, and conspiracy that Stalin and his allies had so strengthened during their rule. It was difficult to determine what evidence was reliable. Second, they were part of a party political culture (dating back well before 1929) in which history was at the service of the party's tactical decisions and present "line." The 1960 KPK investigators sought "facts" to back up a possible new "line." Third, these dissidents (dissidents, that is, after Khrushchev's fall) remained Leninists, and longed passionately for a useable history of a renewed Communist Party. Thus they embraced Lenin as the touchstone of all that was good in party life, and they sought eagerly for evidence of opposition to Stalin inside the party. If Stalin and a few of his associates were the demons who had subverted Leninism, then once they were purged the Soviet system could perhaps be made truly humanitarian.

Perestroika

Following the accession to power of Mikhail Gorbachev in 1985, reform-minded journalists, authors, and propaganda officials began a new effort to promote a humane, just and law-bound "Leninism." In this context the figure of Kirov, the Leninist man of the people, was attractive. In 1986 Alla Kirilina, then a scholar at the Institute of Party History in Leningrad, published *Kirov and Time,* an illustrated biography, with I. P. Donkov. The book included much valuable historical material. It also reproduced a series of Socialist Realist paintings depicting Kirov interacting with ordinary people. "S. M. Kirov Leads a Workers' Study Circle," for example, depicted the young Kirov in Tomsk instructing workers in a tight room. The work drew on models from the painting of the Enlightenment, representing the illumination of Marxism as a lamp in the middle of a small table. At the head of the table sat Kirov, his face bathed in light, expounding upon a point to an audience of workers leaning towards him in rapt attention. Only the faces were lit; the edges of the room receded into darkness. The thrust of the narrative and the images was to connect Kirov (and thus, the Communist Party) with ordinary people. One of the last illustrations in *Kirov and Time* was a photograph of Mikhail Gorbachev meeting with workers at the Kirov factory in Leningrad. The factory had once been the Putilov and later the Red Putilov works, the heart of the Bolshevik Revolution in October 1917. The photograph identified Gorbachev with the "man of the people" Kirov, the revolution, and the working class.[86]

Gorbachev and his supporters soon undertook a review of the history of Stalinism, with the expressed aim of achieving "an honest understanding of the past" and making "honor" the center of Communist identity. There must also have been a political element to Gorbachev's decision to reopen discussion of the Stalin years. He was now pursuing a more radical "reconstruction" of Soviet society and wanted to mobilize the support of the old Leninist reformers, the common people, and younger Communist innovators. On September 28, 1987 the Politburo set up a commission to study "materials connected with the repressions that took place in the period of the 1930s–1940s and the early 1950s." Among the commission members were the reform-minded Aleksandr Yakovlev, a middle-level official with a long career as a diplomat and party functionary, and P. N. Demichev, the most "liberal" party leader to retain high-level party/state posts throughout the 1970s and 1980s. The commission began work in January 1988, with nervous members debating the risks of rehabilitating such long-denigrated "oppositionist" figures as Bukharin and Rykov.[87]

On September 5, 1988 Olga Shatunovskaya, now in her late eighties, wrote a letter to Aleksandr Yakovlev summarizing the findings of the KPK investigation she had led in 1960–1961, including the conclusion that Stalin had organized Kirov's assassination. The letter mentioned the three hundred votes against Stalin at the Seventeenth Party Congress, the move to replace Stalin with Kirov, three detentions of Nikolaev, and Borisov's supposed murder.[88]

In response to a February 1989 request from the commission reviewing Stalinist repression, officials from the Central Committee archives prepared a response to Shatunovskaya's letter, excerpted below in part. The authors opened their brief with a summary history of the investigative commissions that met in the 1950s and 1960s. However, they omitted any mention of Shatunovskaya's 1960–1961 investigation or the January 28, 1961 report that resulted.

· 124 ·

"On the letter of Comrade Shatunovskaya, O. G. of September 5, 1988." Draft reply, probably by TsK archivists. Excerpts. RGANI, f. 6, op. 13, d. 138, ll. 1–9.

On May 6, 1961 a commission of the Presidium headed by Chairman of the KPK [. . .] Comrade Shvernik was created. Comrade Shatunovskaya was among the members of this commission.

On September 26 1961 the Shvernik commission reported to the TsK on the results of the investigation of materials from the trial in the case of the murder of S. M. Kirov. [. . .] In the commission's memorandum there is no mention of the organization of Kirov's murder by Stalin, [but] [. . .] it is concluded that "the murder of S. M. Kirov was used by Stalin for the physical isolation and annihilation of the leaders of the Zinovievite opposition as well as their former supporters."

The memorandum was signed by Shvernik, Serdiuk, Shelepin, Rudenko, Shatunovskaya, Mironov.

[. . .]

As is clear from documents stored in the archives of the TsK Politburo, nowhere in the materials of the Presidium commissions [. . .] is it concluded that Kirov was killed at Stalin's order.

In 1967 yet another commission was created under the chairmanship of A. Ya. Pelshe, which studied the question of the Kirov murder. The report of this commission is not present in the archive of the Politburo. [. . .]

With regard to other questions raised in Comrade Shatunovskaya's letter, it is possible to state the following.

1. In the materials of the above-mentioned commissions there is no information about any secret meeting of several members of the TsK at the apartment of G. K. Ordzhonikidze during the Seventeenth Party Congress, or about any proposals to make S. M. Kirov general secretary.

2. With regard to the falsification of the results of the secret balloting for the leading organs of the Communist Party at the Seventeenth Party Congress. In the Central Party Archive of the Institute of Marxism and Leninism [. . .] there are stored the protocols of the congress's Electoral Commission and 1,059 ballots from the secret voting. In the protocol of the Electoral Commission it is stated that 1,059 delegates took part in the balloting. [. . .] As there were 1,225 delegates at the congress with a right to vote, the question of why 166 delegates did not take part in the voting

remains unclear. The version that the missing quantity of bulletins was destroyed because Stalin's name was crossed out on them deserves consideration, but is not confirmed by any documents.

3. The assertion of O. G. Shatunovskaya that the murderer of S. M. Kirov L. Nikolaev was detained by guards three times and released three times does not find any confirmation. [. . .]

4. [. . .]

5. The claim recounted by Comrade Shatunovskaya that Nikolaev was beaten during his interrogation by Stalin, and that he was supposedly deceived by promises to spare his life if he should denounce the illegal terrorist center—cannot be checked, as the claims are not first-hand, but only communicated through third persons.

6. Comrade Shatunovskaya's assertion that the KGB of the USSR sent to the investigative commission data on the repressions by year which totaled 19,840,000 arrests of "enemies of the people," of whom seven million were shot [. . .] between January 1, 1935 and June 22, 1941, are not supported. Comrade Shatunovskaya completely ignores her own declaration to the TsK in 1960 that between 1935 and 1940 two million persons were repressed, of whom 688,000 were shot.

The TsK staff members who authored this note sought to stonewall the investigation of Kirov's assassination. They concealed the existence of the Shatunovskaya investigation report and many of the depositions collected in 1960–1961, including materials related to the supposed voting against Stalin and the alleged move to replace him at the Seventeenth Party Congress. The reply to Shatunovskaya reveals that party authorities were now trapped in a fantastic maze of lies that they and their predecessors had constructed. The Shatunovskaya investigation's evidence for Stalin's involvement in Kirov's killing was very weak. Nevertheless, the Central Committee authorities, fearful that their audience would draw the "wrong" conclusions, concealed it. They lied to cover up a false narrative constructed by their predecessors that they feared would now be taken for the truth.

The commission on Stalinist repressions continued its work until June 1990, when the members issued a public report declaring that "Stalin inspired and organized the mass repressions. He personally sanctioned arrests, [and] controlled the course of investigations into the cases of the most well-known party and state personages. . . ."[89] As a result of the commission's work Soviet courts annulled the convictions of nearly all defendants in the great show trials of the Terror, and of all the accused in the "Leningrad Center" trial except Nikolaev. Yakovlev, who chaired the commission from October 1988, writes in his 2003 memoirs that although there were sharp debates among the commission members, "the atmosphere of the time facilitated principled decisions." Commission members, even the somewhat recalcitrant V. A. Kriuchkov, chairman of the KGB, were able to agree on wide-ranging public exposure of the facts of the Terror. One of the few issues that they never reached agreement on, however, was the question of Stalin's involvement in the Kirov murder.[90]

In early 1990 every commission member but Yakovlev agreed to sign a statement that Stalin had used the murder to justify the Terror, but had probably not organized it. Yakovlev responded to the commission's proposed report on the Kirov murder with a memorandum dated March 16, 1990."

· 125 ·

Aleksandr Yakovlev, "To the members of the Politburo commission . . . for the further investigation of materials connected to the repressions that took place in the period of the 1930s, 1940s, and early 1950s," March 23, 1990. RGANI, f. 6, op. 13, d. 135, ll. 1–9.

In the draft report that we discussed at the commission meetings, the facts and documents collected by Central Committee commissions charged in the 1950s and 1960s with clarifying the circumstances of the assassination of S. M. Kirov were subjected to a thorough analysis. The fundamental conclusions that the most recent investigation reached are that the materials at hand indicate that the terrorist act against S. M. Kirov was conceived and carried out by L. V. Nikolaev alone. In 1933–1934 there existed no counterrevolutionary terrorist center in the city of Leningrad and no "Leningrad Center." Nor is there any evidence to support the charges that G. Ya. Bissenieks, consul of bourgeois Latvia in Leningrad, took part in preparing the murder of S. M. Kirov. There is no evidence of the existence of a conspiracy with the aim of killing Kirov's guard M. V. Borisov, who died accidentally as the result of an automobile crash. And finally, the report contains the assertion that there is no evidence in the investigative files on Nikolaev, Kotolynov, and the others, nor in the materials of the reviews of 1956–1967 or 1988–1989, to indicate the participation of I. V. Stalin and the organs of the NKVD in the organization and commission of the murder of S. M. Kirov.

From my personal point of view, these conclusions and their supporting [evidentiary] base cannot be considered beyond dispute. There remain questions to which there are, as yet, no convincing answers.

It seems to me that all of the reviews to date have set themselves the narrow goal of finding data that would directly unmask persons suspected of participating in the accomplishment of the crime. It is necessary to note that this primarily *juridical* approach was in great measure typical of earlier investigations, as can be seen from the materials on hand.

It is well known that there exist several versions of the circumstances of the murder of S. M. Kirov.

First version. The murder was carried out by Nikolaev, a member of a counterrevolutionary organization to which former participants in the Zinovievite opposition belonged. Officers of the central apparatus and the Leningrad Directorate of the NKVD participated directly in the preparations for and organization of the murder.

The *second version* is that Nikolaev was merely a tool in the hands of NKVD officers acting at the order of Stalin.

The *third version* claims that Nikolaev acted alone, and that personal motives had great importance. The organs of the NKVD and Stalin were not party to the murder.

It is in fact this last version that is proposed to us now.

It must be said that all of the investigations of the 1960s and 1980s in the final account considered only these three versions, and effectively relied in their analyses of the circumstances of the murder on the same group of facts and testimony utilized by the organs of the NKVD in the 1930s, and the Shvernik and Pelshe commissions in the 1960s. The only differences were in the evaluations of the facts and the statements of the accused and the witnesses.

The same facts and documents, the contradictory depositions of those years are in the hands of persons participating [today] in the investigation of the circumstances of Kirov's murder. But at times those facts that support a given version are cherry-picked without justification to prove one or another point of view. Simultaneously documents and evidence that contradict the chosen position are thrown out. That at least is the impression that I have.

In effect, no search for new documents has been organized, nor have new circumstances discovered by historians been reviewed. The system of study remains unchanged. New questions that have arisen now, 55 years after the murder, are not discussed. In general the focus is on two questions: (a) Was Nikolaev a lone murderer? (b) Did Stalin participate in the murder of Kirov? In addition Stalin's participation is attributed to a personal dislike of Kirov and a desire to eliminate him as a rival. These are the decisive considerations when conclusions are under discussion.

If there are facts indicating that Kirov and Stalin had comradely relations, then it is concluded that Stalin was not a participant in the murder. If Stalin saw in Kirov a rival then he was the organizer of the killing. Unfortunately, we have not been able to go beyond the range of versions proposed to date /by and large as early as the 1930s/, and this includes possible organizers of the murder.

It must be said that in the course of the investigation of the circumstances of the tragic events of December 1, 1934 almost nothing has been done to look into the relations between Kirov and Stalin. Everything is boiled down to superficial evaluation of a few facts that are not actually adequate to permit judgment of the real character of these relations. We know from the documents that the last letters from the correspondence of Kirov and Stalin as well as Kirov and Ordzhonikidze were taken by M. Orakhelashvili.[91] What were these letters? What were they about? Do they shed any light on events? Nothing is known.

However, we cannot limit ourselves to considering only the relations between Kirov and Stalin. A broad investigation of all political circumstances is necessary. It is known, for example, that in 1933 the Leningrad Directorate of the NKVD presented to the regional party committee for approval a proposal to arrest a list of former participants of the Zinovievite opposition. However, S. M. Kirov did not approve the arrest of all of the persons on this list. The head of the Leningrad NKVD Directorate Medved testified in 1934 with regard to this incident that "Rumiantsev, Levin, and other names I do not remember were on the operational lists for the liquidation of former representatives of the Trotskyite-Zinovievite opposition that I presented to the regional committee of the party for approval in 1933. When I consulted with Comrade Kirov about this list, Comrade Kirov did not sanction the arrest of Rumiantsev and Levin, in part because he intended to talk to Rumiantsev personally."

On December 2, 1934 Stalin heard a report on the files on the former participants in the Zinovievite opposition Kotolynov, Shatsky, Rumiantsev, Miasnikov, Mandelshtam, and others, that is, those persons who were convicted with Nikolaev as organizers of Kirov's murder.

As the investigation has shown, none of Nikolaev's fellow defendants were engaged in illegal counterrevolutionary or underground activity. However, all of them were already grouped together in [the records of] the regional NKVD and thus falsified materials were prepared in order to represent this group as active underground counterrevolutionaries. They were prepared for the trial that followed just a few weeks after the murder of Kirov.

In January 1935 the Military Collegium of the Supreme Court of the USSR sentenced the former leaders of the NKVD's Leningrad Directorate, F. D. Medved, I. V. Zaporozhets, F. T. Fomin, G. A. Petrov, P. M. Lobov, and others to various terms of imprisonment for "carelessness" and "criminal negligence towards their essential duty of protecting government security." The accused were charged with failure to take timely measures to uncover and halt the activities of the terrorist Zinovievite group in Leningrad. The jail sentences were varied. M. K. Baltsevich, whose duties were directly related to cases of terrorism, was sentenced to ten years of confinement in a concentration camp. All of the remaining accused were sentenced to concentration camp terms of two to three years.

Thus, to judge by the documents of this trial, the leadership of the Leningrad NKVD Directorate was accused of negligence in guarding S. M. Kirov and failure to take necessary measures to stop the terrorist activity of the Zinovievite counterrevolutionary group.

However, two years later [*sic*] during the trial of N. I. Bukharin, A. I. Rykov, and others, G. G. Yagoda, former People's Commissar of Internal Affairs, was named as the organizer of S. M. Kirov's murder. Supposedly with the aid of co-conspirators in the central apparatus of the NKVD and leaders of the Leningrad Directorate, among them the deputy chief, I. V. Zaporozhets, he supposedly prepared and executed the murder of S. M. Kirov. In 1937 nearly all leading officers of the Leningrad NKVD were shot. Only one of the deputy chiefs, F. T. Fomin, and two officers—G. A. Petrov and P. M. Lobov—remained among the living.

At the Twentieth Party Congress N. S. Khrushchev proposed a new version of the murder of S. M. Kirov. Ignoring the question of the participation of the "Trotsky-Zinovievite Center" in the execution of the terrorist act, he avowed that the murder of Kirov was organized by Yagoda [. . .] who acted at the personal order of Stalin. Khrushchev's words suggested that he had in his hands complete information on the case.

In the report presented to us any possibility that the organs of the NKVD had a hand in Kirov's murder is completely rejected, and a corresponding evaluation is given of isolated facts connected with the activities of NKVD officers. However [. . .] not all possibilities have been utilized for deeper study of all facts that would allow us to judge whether officers of the NKVD were involved in the murder of S. M. Kirov.

Why did Yagoda take upon himself the guilt of organizing Kirov's murder? At the 1938 trial he publicly stated that officers of the central apparatus and Leningrad Directorate of the NKVD organized and carried out this murder. Why was this false public confession, prepared by the investigation, of crimes that Yagoda and the persons he named had not committed, necessary? Yagoda was falsely placed among the members of the nonexistent "Right-Trotskyite Bloc." Not only was he not connected with a single one of the so-called "participants" in this bloc, he actually had unpleasant and even hostile relations with them. We do not know what was discussed at the closed sessions of the trial, where Yagoda testified. Have there been attempts to clarify what matters Yagoda requested that the court review separately in closed session? Yagoda had one and only one chief—Stalin. Was there any discussion of him at the closed sessions of the court?

How did Yagoda behave in the pre-December days and in the first half of December 1, 1934? Where was he, what did he do, whom did he meet, what was he interested in, was he received by Stalin?

The trials in which the leaders and officers of the Leningrad Directorate of the NKVD were twice judged in the same case have likewise remained without attention. Have the course of investigation, the material evidence, or the charges against the NKVD officers been subjected to investigation? If we accept that the murder was organized by organs of the NKVD, then it is necessary to clarify who might have stood behind Nikolaev. By the Twentieth Party Congress only three persons were still alive from among the 12 officers of the Leningrad Directorate of the NKVD who were convicted for negligence in guarding Kirov—F. T. Fomin, [. . .] P. M. Lobov, [. . .] and G. A. Petrov. [. . .] Only G. A. Petrov has been juridically rehabilitated. Why haven't the documents, letters, memoirs, and testimony of those close to [. . .] officers of the Leningrad Directorate been analyzed?[92]

All activity of the central apparatus of the NKVD and the Leningrad Directorate for the year 1934 requires close study, including the lists of former oppositionists, their program and goals, that were kept. Obviously it is necessary to check in KGB archives whether any reports were received in 1934 from officers posted abroad on the dispatch of two terrorists from the "Russian Military Union" to Leningrad with the aim of carrying out a terrorist act against Kirov. Was there an operation organized by Frinovsky in the summer of 1934 in Leningrad to catch them? What were the results of this operation, what conclusions were reached?[93]

The case of the "Green Lamp" [the counterrevolutionary "kulak" group reported by Volkova in the summer and fall of 1934] played an important part in the investigation of the circumstances of Kirov's murder in December 1934. In the fall of 1934 M. N. Volkova reported to the Leningrad Directorate the existence of this group. G. A. Petrov, plenipotentiary officer of the Leningrad Directorate's Special Department, undertook the inquiry into this report. The investigation failed to confirm the existence of this organization. Volkova herself was subjected to tests by psychiatric specialists at the orders of the leadership of the Directorate. The result was a finding that Volkova was psychologically ill. After this she was confined to an NKVD clinic at the Obukhov Hospital in Leningrad. Several days prior to these events Volkova attempted to see the chairman of the Leningrad executive committee P. I. Struppe at his office, but he was not in. Then Volkova told his secretary that officers of the Leningrad Directorate of the NKVD were preparing the murder of Kirov. She supposedly heard this from drunken officers with whom she was vacationing at the NKVD rest home several days previously. When this was reported to Struppe, he was not able to talk to her, as she was already in the psychiatric hospital by that time.[94]

According to D. A. Lazurkina, on December 2, 1934 she told N. I. Yezhov about all of these facts. On December 3 Volkova was taken from the psychiatric hospital to Smolny, where she conversed with Stalin. Following this conversation, every item of evidence given by this psychiatrically ill person was accepted as absolute fact. The next day, December 4, Nikolaev—Kirov's murderer—changed his earlier testimony. Now he no longer spoke of himself as a lone assassin, but named collaborators in the terrorist act—members of the underground Zinovievite group.

By 1956 there remained alive two witnesses who could characterize the personality of M. N. Volkova and shed light on the circumstances and character of her medical records. These were G. A. Petrov, mentioned above, and the chief of the Medical Department of the regional NKVD Directorate S. M. Mamushin. Unfortunately they were not questioned by the corresponding commissions, documents held by G. A. Petrov have not been attached to the investigation (case files) on the [. . .] Kirov murder. And the entire story of the "Green Lamp" organization still remains beyond the ken of those investigating the events of December 1, 1934.

Evaluation of the behavior of NKVD Officer Borisov, charged with the guard [of Kirov] on that day, has an important place in the investigation of the circumstances of Kirov's death. As is known, at the moment of S. M. Kirov's passage through Smolny Borisov was well behind him and this allowed Nikolaev the chance to shoot at Kirov when they ended up alone together in the corridor at Smolny.

Why did Borisov commit such a gross violation of his instructions? Did he halt somewhere or did someone stop him? What were the circumstances leading to Kirov's ending up alone, without a guard?

Borisov was the most important witness for the investigation of the facts of the death of Kirov. As is well known, however, he perished the next day, when he was being taken to Smolny for interrogation by Stalin. The [present] inquiry avows that this was the result of an automobile accident.

Can we accept this version without question? In my opinion, we cannot.

First. There are various depositions by the driver of the vehicle that Borisov was conveyed in. In one case he claims that there really was an accident, in another he tells how Officer Maly of the Leningrad NKVD Directorate grabbed the steering wheel from him and the auto hit the wall of a building with its side. Unfortunately, the report [prepared by the 1989–1990 Politburo Commission] does not offer reasons for accepting one deposition and completely rejecting the other.

Second, there exists a letter of the former chief of the Medical Department of the Leningrad NKVD Directorate S. A. Mamushin which claims that Borisov's death was a premeditated murder, and not an accident. Mamushin himself was a member of the medical commission [that investigated Borisov's death in 1934] and writes that its conclusion with regard to Borisov's death was reached in spite of the findings of the investigation The autopsy of Borisov's skull showed the presence of many radially diverging fractures of the skill, which were the results of a blow to the head with a heavy object, while in the autopsy report it was written that there was only one fracture of the skull, which indicated impact of the head with a stone wall. S. A. Mamushin's testimony demands close study and should be attached to the case files.[95]

Third. All the documents describing the automobile accident are accepted as reliable, worthy of trust, their conclusions are cited without question as indubitable facts. In fact they require critical study and investigation. Although much time has passed, I believe that specialists could pass judgment on the possibility of such consequences following a truck accident moving at about 30 kilometers per hour with two passengers in the back. Upon hitting the wall of the building none of the persons accompanying Borisov suffered, while he received a fatal wound and died on the spot. There is no report of wounds to the officer accompanying Borisov in the rear of the truck. Not all possible consequences of the accident have been investigated, they are accepted as valid fact. In reality they require investigation and analysis by qualified specialists. It seems to me that this could be done even now, on the basis of documents in the case files.[96]

For a complete clarification of the circumstances of Kirov's death further study is needed of the system of passes to the city and regional party committees prevailing at the time. There is testimony that even employees of the Leningrad soviet offices on the first floor had to get a special pass to get onto the third floor where the regional party committee was located. As is known, not long before the attack on Kirov the number of his guards was increased from three to fifteen persons. In spite of this we have no thorough analysis either of the system of organization of Kirov's guard or of the location of the guards at the moment of the murder. Obviously these questions require further investigation.[97]

The central conclusion reached as a result of the investigation of the circumstances of Kirov's murder by the Prosecutor's Office and the KGB is that the terrorist act was conceived and executed by L. V. Nikolaev alone. But if such is the case, then [it is surprising that] the commission's report pays almost no attention to these most important questions—an explanation of the reasons leading Nikolaev to carry out the terrorist attack, an evaluation of this action, an explanation of the whole series of circumstances that allowed him to carry out the murder. [Rather,] the emphasis is first on demonstrating that Stalin did not know about and did not have any connection to the organization of the attack on Kirov, second that he did not participate in the murder. Third, the lack of connections between Nikolaev's activities and the former oppositionists and the fact that no counterrevolutionary terrorist organization called "the Leningrad Center" ever existed [are emphasized]. Fourth, [the fact is stressed that] the murder of Kirov was used broadly by Stalin to organize mass repressions in the country.

It is stated in the report that Kirov's murder was an act of personal revenge by Nikolaev, and an act of political terror. If it was an act of political terror, then obviously very little attention has been paid to research on the documents taken from Nikolaev by police search, and in particular to his personal diary. A. A. Zhdanov mentioned this diary in a number of his speeches in 1935–1937, stating that in it there were supposedly phrases like "We'll never build Communism," "To kill someone. Maybe Lidak or maybe Gudov, no, Kirov would be better." In the report it is claimed that [documents titled] "Autobiography," "Farewell . . . ," "To My Dear Wife and Class Brothers," "Political Testament /My Answer before the Party and the Fatherland/," and so on, were taken from Nikolaev. These expressed his readiness to sacrifice himself for the sake of justice "in the name of my historical mission," and included references to the preparation of a terrorist act. If this murder was committed due to Nikolaev's political convictions, then, obviously, all of these documents are in need of thorough and deep analysis. Also necessary is detailed analysis of the factors leading to Nikolaev's political position. Nikolaev's acquaintances and co-workers noted his psychological lack of balance, his aggravated self-love, his inability to get along with others, that is, the personal characteristics of a man with a difficult character. But no one speaks of the character of his political statements. He never participated in any opposition group, nor did he join any cliques (*gruppirovki*). When and how did Nikolaev's striving to commit a political crime "in the name of my historical mission" appear? There are no documents reflecting Nikolaev's work on the regional party committee. No analysis of his circle of acquaintances, which is indispensable, has been done.

Nor has sufficient research been done on the Kirov murder as an act of personal revenge by Nikolaev. We do not have the texts of his declarations to various instances, in which he writes of personal despair, dissatisfaction, his difficult material situation, and of his unfair treatment by government personnel. Where are the appeals written by Nikolaev to the Party Control Committee (July–August 1934)? According to the records of the Leningrad party archive (*fond* 24), they were sent to the Party Control Committee in 1936. Were there other declarations by Nikolaev during this period? For example, the [present] report states that he sent a letter to Kirov in July 1934, to Stalin in August, and to the Politburo in October.

There remain many other questions connected with the organization of Kirov's murder. In the Leningrad party archive there is a document indicating that Nikolaev got the cartridges for his pistol at "Dinamo," the sports club of the NKVD.

As is known, in 1934 the passport system at Smolny was tightened, and a special pass was necessary to get on to the third floor, where the regional party committee was housed. Why did Nikolaev still have his pass, even though he had not worked in the regional party committee organization for several months?

Could Nikolaev have determined Kirov's route, the time of his arrival at Smolny, was Kirov summoned by anyone to Smolny or did he himself make the decision to go there, were the officers of the guard informed of Kirov's movements and of his possible arrival at Smolny, who at Smolny knew that Kirov was on his way there, and are there any documents remaining in the KGB archives or at the Leningrad Directorate which might provide answers to these questions? Aren't there too many coincidences in this case?

Behind Nikolaev could have stood officers of the NKVD's central directorate, who acted behind the back of Medved and Zaporozhets both. There are depositions that Nikolaev was seen in the NKVD building at Lubianka Square [headquarters in Moscow]. Can this be checked? Are there any archival documents remaining by which one could judge the probability that Nikolaev was connected with officers of the central NKVD?

The [present] report cites the "good relations, warm and friendly, even intimate (*priiatelskie*) between Stalin and Kirov as evidence excluding the possibility of Stalin's involvement in the organization of Kirov's violent removal from the scene.

The character of relations between the two cannot serve as unconditional proof for the acceptance or rejection of the version of events implicating Stalin in direct participation in or at the very least prior knowledge of the preparation of an attack on Kirov. Stalin's cunning, falsehood, and perfidy are known to everyone. At one time he had good, even friendly relations with Kamenev, with Zinoviev, and especially with Bukharin. But all the same he sent them to their deaths. Didn't he have warm, friendly relations with Ordzhonikidze /in fact Ordzhonikidze probably had the closest, most trusting relations with Stalin of any Politburo member/? And what did this friendship end with? Ordzhonikidze's death, whether by suicide or murder we do not yet know.

By the very way in which they ask the question of Stalin and Kirov's mutual relations they [the report authors] wish to show that Kirov was not Stalin's rival, that he supported him in every way and was even his mouthpiece, praising him in every one of his speeches. And on this basis suspicions of Stalin's personal interest in harming Kirov are supposedly baseless. Asked in this way, the question boils down to personal mutual relations. It is true that if personal motives alone /revenge, personal dislike, the desire to get rid of a rival/ lay at the base of the Kirov murder, then this might be true. But the Kirov murder is attributable above all to political goals.

The attack on Kirov created a serious political basis for repression. The Kirov murder was only the pretext for the political acts that followed. It is connected with the taking of repressive measures. Obviously one cannot exclude the possibility that the [organizers of the] provocation did not foresee its fateful conclusion, but their plan went out of control and a shot was fired that the plan did not anticipate. Perhaps there was the desire only to stage a fake attack, and then it was necessary to demonstrate Kirov's closeness to Stalin, his loyalty, and to exaggerate somewhat his actual place in the party and Politburo. It is worth noting, by the way, that before December 1 Kirov hardly enjoyed the popularity of Molotov, Voroshilov, or Kalinin. We understand his place in the party leadership in connection with the events of December 1, 1934 and the subsequent propaganda campaign around his name, the mass renaming of cities, worker neighborhoods, streets, squares, industrial enterprises, educational institutions, collective farms, and so on, after him. It seems likely that after 1935 there was not a single city in the Soviet Union that did not have a street, or square, or neighborhood named after Kirov. That which was done in memory of a murdered member of the Politburo gradually was transformed in the social consciousness into a sense of his grand role in the party, his leadership.

The beginning of the investigation of the circumstances of Kirov's murder, with the participation of Stalin, demonstrates that the latter came to Leningrad with prepared, well-thought-out ideas which were immediately put into action. Before he even found out the identity of the attacker and the circumstances preceding the killing, Stalin immediately told those around him that this was the "hand of the Zinovievites." In his deposition of January 12, 1937 to the Central Committee, Bukharin wrote " . . . it was on the day after the murder, if I am not mistaken, that I heard that Nikolaev was a Zinovievite. Stalin told me of his name and the Zinovievite connection when he called me in to the Politburo."

At a face-to-face confrontation with Radek presided over by Stalin, Molotov, Voroshilov, and Yezhov on January 13, 1937 at the Central Committee Bukharin reaffirmed his declaration, stating that "on the second day after the murder of Kirov Mekhlis and I were summoned to the Politburo and Comrade Stalin told me that Kirov had been killed by the Zinovievite Nikolaev. Stalin confirmed the content of his conversation with Bukharin, but corrected him, stating that this occurred "probably on the eighth day" after the murder.

Speaking on March 3, 1937 at the February–March 1937 plenum of the TsK, Yezhov declared that "Comrade Stalin, as I recall it now, called in Kosaryov and me and said, 'Look for the murderer among the Zinovievites.' I should note that the chekists did not believe this, and covered themselves . . . using another line . . . the foreign line. . . . At first our relations with the chekists were quite difficult. . . . Comrade Stalin had to intervene. Comrade Stalin called Yagoda: 'Look, we're going to smash them in the face. . . .'"

Thus from the earliest days of the investigation Stalin and Yezhov counted Nikolaev among the Zinovievites and in this manner laid upon them responsibility for the murder of Kirov.

Stalin, naturally, always strove to hide his own role in the supervision of the machinery of mass terror. Many times he presented himself as the champion of fairness, who wanted to put an end to arbitrary rule. He wished to give the appearance that he had nothing in common with the arrests and violence that were going on in the country. Often he succeeded. This gives all the more reason to examine the first act of the tragedy in which he appears as a direct participant, a direct organizer of violence against a large group of persons guilty of nothing. Can we ignore his direct participation in the organization of the investigation, his intervention, the pressure he exerted, his efforts to promote his own point of view? To what end was all of this directed, and what were the consequences? All of this has been left out.

In sum, all of the above forces us to return once more to the investigation of all the circumstances connected with the murder of S. M. Kirov.

March 3, 1990

A. Yakovlev

Many of the questions raised by Yakovlev do have straightforward answers. The most important ones are enumerated below.

The Leningrad NKVD had files on most of those tried in the case of the "Leningrad Center" (there were no files on Nikolaev and Yuskin) because Stalin chose after the murder to target ex-oppositionists who had NKVD surveillance records.

In his "Reflections" Yakovlev asked why Yagoda confessed to organizing the Kirov murder at the March 1938 show trial, and what evidence he gave at the closed sessions of that trial. As we have seen, Yagoda recanted his confession at the trial's end. The closed sessions of the show trial dealt in part with the charges that Yagoda murdered Maxim Gorky's son and with the affair he was having with the latter's wife. The Soviet government did not want the affair discussed before the Soviet public or international observers at the trial. Other closed sessions were dedicated to the detailed charges against various defendants of espionage for foreign governments. The Commissariat of Foreign Affairs did not want the names of specific diplomats or foreign organizations mentioned in open court, for fear of international complications.[98]

In his memorandum, Yakovlev asked "Why did Borisov grossly violate his instructions?" As we have seen, Kirov's guards had no written instructions, and several testified that there were oral orders to keep their distance from their charge, who did not like being surrounded by tight security.

Yakovlev noted accurately that Nikolaev obtained the bullets for his revolver from the shop at the NKVD (at the time OGPU) sport club "Dinamo." However, this hardly indicates that the security police assisted him in the assassination. The OGPU was the only legal ammunition dealer in the USSR at the time, and Nikolaev bought the bullets legally from the organization.[99]

Yakovlev's "Reflections" contain a number of factual errors, which may stem from inadequate knowledge of the archival sources underlying the commission report. Based on the confused testimony of Dora Lazurkina, he claims that Maria Volkova warned Pyotr Struppe's secretary Ilin about an NKVD plot against Kirov before the assassination. In fact, as we have seen, Volkova did not warn of a specific plot against Kirov, much less an NKVD conspiracy against him. Yakovlev also mistakenly asserts that NKVD Officer G. A. Petrov was not questioned by the post-Stalin investigative commissions regarding Maria Volkova's evidence. He takes seriously the highly suspect testimony of the driver Kuzin and Dr. Mamushin in Borisov's death. He suggests inaccurately that there was no careful study of Nikolaev's diary and notes. Finally, Yakovlev mistakenly implies that the investigation of Leningrad NKVD employees had been superficial, whereas documents in the KPK archives indicate quite a thorough inquiry.[100]

Some points made by Yakovlev deserve serious consideration. Central NKVD officials could well have organized a conspiracy against Kirov through junior officers in Leningrad, behind the backs of Medved, Zaporozhets, or Fomin. Nor can the possibility be dismissed that Nikolaev was part of a provocation organized by the NKVD to implicate former Zinovievites in Leningrad in planning an attack on Kirov. The attack was not supposed to take place, but the NKVD lost control of Nikolaev. Trotsky was the first to propose this version of events in print. Yakovlev was also correct to suggest that a thorough study of

NKVD operational documents, particularly in Leningrad, might yield more evidence in the case.[101]

Immediately following Yakovlev's submission of his comments to the commission on Stalinist repressions, officials of the USSR prosecutor's office, the military prosecutor, and the Criminal Investigative Department of the KGB prepared an exhaustive rebuttal, which they signed on June 14, 1990. The report accepted as given that Stalin had planned and directed the Terror, and used the Kirov murder as the justification to execute innocent persons. Its authors did not seek to conceal Stalin's responsibility for mass murder. But, based largely on evidence in KPK files and KGB archives, they argued that he was probably not involved in Kirov's murder. They also provided new information about the case, giving an extensive description of the surveillance files on Kotolynov and the other supposed members of the "Leningrad Center" that remained in KGB archives. My own extensive examination of the KPK files used by the report authors indicates that they cited documents accurately and analyzed them objectively. The authors also included information inconvenient for their own argument.[102] For these reasons I have treated evidence from the June 1990 rebuttal to Yakovlev (cited in the notes as "Reply to Iakovlev") as generally reliable.

In an interview given to the newspaper *Trud* ("Labor") in December 1990, one of the rebuttal's authors, Yu. I. Sedov, a senior official in the USSR prosecutor's office, shed light on the investigators' level of archival access, and their attitudes towards the Stalinist system. Sedov told the interviewer:

> We brought to light several archives [where the authorities] . . . do not like the eyes of outsiders, and which to this day are still closed. . . . These are the agent surveillance documents on persons counted as Zinovievites and other well-known oppositionists. We are talking about, for example, the organization under the code name "Green Lamp," the former NKVD agent Volkova, the operational file "Svoiak," on which Stalin was briefed on December 2, 1934, and the file "Politikan."
>
> The agents of the OGPU worked tirelessly, writing reports to their ever-vigilant chiefs about each meeting, party, or trip to another city of the so-called oppositionists. They wrote even of their intimate relationships. For each concrete person there was a case file where all reports were concentrated. Each agent . . . had his or her own pseudonym and password. Those who were hunted by these bloodhounds

had no idea what kind of microscope they were under. These old OGPU-NKVD denunciations stink, they stink to high heaven.[103]

Elsewhere in the interview Sedov charges Stalin with responsibility for establishing the system of surveillance and denunciation. Suffice it to say that he was not interested in exonerating the dictator or rehabilitating Stalinism.

In the later years of perestroika the veteran Leninist reformers seized with a will the opportunity to denounce Stalinist repression. Larina, Sergo Mikoyan, Leonid Petrovsky, and others published widely. Before her death in 1991 Olga Shatunovskaya gave multiple interviews laying out her version of the work of the 1960–1961 commissions on the Kirov murder. Perhaps the most prominent feature of perestroika culture was the renewed and sharp discussion of the history of Stalinism.[104]

Members of the old reformist circles had long seen Kirov as a moderate, humane alternative to Stalin. Now some reimagined him as a potential Gorbachev of the 1930s, creating an alternative fantasy history in which true Leninism triumphed over Stalinism. In his *Stalinism As I Saw It* (1991) Anastas Mikoyan's son Sergo imagined how the revolution might have developed had Lenin lived fifteen years more, or Bukharin chosen to fight Stalin earlier, or Kirov become general secretary. Soviet Communism would then have developed in a more "social democratic direction," without forced collectivization or the intervention of the security organs in politics. Had Stalin not murdered Kirov, Mikoyan wrote, the Leningrad party chief could have been "the Gorbachev of his time."[105]

But the old reformers' obsession with party history and counterfactual alternatives to Stalinism became increasingly irrelevant as the USSR came apart for reasons that they themselves hardly understood. Economic decline and the restiveness of national minority elites weakened the Soviet regime. And the unrestricted revelation of Stalinist atrocities that Snegov, Shatunovskaya, and many others believed would save Leninism only seemed to undermine it further. By the first years of the new century Sergo Mikoyan's 1991 comparison of Kirov to Gorbachev sounded as quaint as a Derzhavin ode to Catherine the Great.

Conclusion

With the collapse of the Soviet Union, Kirov was once more transformed in accord with the spirit of the times. As censorship collapsed, television channels went to work selling footage of corpses, naked women, and shows like "Road Patrol," in which reporters monitored police radio and drove to accident scenes to videotape grisly footage. Pornography, detective novels, and harlequin romances appeared in the same streetside booths that had once sold *Pravda*. In this atmosphere, Kirov became a nymphomaniac shot by a jealous husband. Tales of Kirov's sexual escapades proliferated. As one Moscow friend said when I mentioned this project to him: "Kirov? Everyone knows what happened to him. He screwed anything walking on two legs!"

One impetus for the renewed dissemination of the "jealous husband" version of the killing was the publication in 1994 of former NKVD officer Pavel Sudoplatov's memoirs *Special Tasks*, which claimed that Nikolaev shot Kirov after the latter had an affair with his wife. Sudoplatov was a onetime protégé of Lavrenty Beria, NKVD chief after Yezhov, who beginning in the late 1930s had helped to organize a number of assassinations—the "special tasks" of the title. Imprisoned during the "Thaw," Sudoplatov was eventually released by Khrushchev's more "patriotic" successors, who understood his actions as services to the state. In *Special Tasks* his brief and formulaic paragraphs of repentance are forced and he reveals a steady contempt for the forces of democratization in Russia. Yet in spite of his extraordinary record of crime and deceit, Western commentators and the Russian reading public accepted his memoirs uncritically when they came out.[1]

Sudoplatov's account is rife with factual errors, on the Kirov murder and other matters. Relying on word-of-mouth accounts from his wife, who worked in the Special Political Department of the central NKVD, and allegedly from former NKVD officer Leonid Raikhman, Sudoplatov claims that Milda Draule was a Jewish "waitress" in one of the Smolny cafeterias when Kirov had an affair with her. Yet Raikhman, who interrogated Draule on the morning of December 2, 1934 told Kirilina in a late 1980s interview that the murder had nothing to do with an affair between Kirov and Draule. Between Sudoplatov's account of Raikhman's stance on the "jealous husband" version and Kirilina's I unhesitatingly trust Kirilina's.[2]

In 2005 researchers and medical experts from the Federal Government Guard Service and the Russian Ministry of Defense, in cooperation with the Kirov Museum in Leningrad, published an article in the journal *Rodina* ("Motherland") hinting very broadly that Nikolaev caught Kirov and Milda Draule in flagrante delicto and shot Kirov right there. A television show was linked with this alleged discovery. The authors built their conclusion on very unsteady grounds, implying, for example, that Draule's documented absences from work and party meetings were related to her alleged affair with Kirov. In fact Draule's declared reasons for taking days off—related to childcare— were entirely plausible. The authors of the *Rodina* article declared that Draule did not need to take time off for childcare because both her elderly parents lived with her and Leonid. However, Nikolaev's diary indicates that Draule's parents did not move to Leningrad until the winter of 1932–1933, and both documents on work/meeting absences cited in the *Rodina* article date from earlier.[3]

The *Rodina* authors claim to derive further evidence for the "jealous husband" version from physical evidence—the clothes Kirov was wearing when he was shot. The Kirov Museum turned these clothes over to a forensics laboratory of the Russian Ministry of Defense. Apparently they had not been washed since the killing. The forensics technicians found dried semen on the inside of Kirov's underwear. They also used the bullet hole in Kirov's forage cap and the break the bullet left on the top edge of his overcoat collar to argue that "at the moment he was wounded Kirov was not in a vertical position."[4]

The *Rodina* article implication that Kirov was shot from behind by Nikolaev while having sex with Draule is worth a laugh for those with a black sense of humor, but no more. The authors' claim to have derived Kirov's position at the moment of the shooting from the hole in the back of his forage cap makes no sense. Because the precise position of the forage cap in Kirov's head at the time of the shooting is not known, no firm deductions about his "horizontal" position can be made. The semen stains are explicable in a number of ways. One is that Kirov, who was in his apartment all day "working," had sex with his "housekeeper," who some witnesses claim was there as well. It was a fairly common practice for senior Bolshevik officials to have partners identified as "housekeepers"—Stalin in his later years did. Masturbation is also a possibility. In fact, the flagrante delicto scenario raises more questions than it answers. If Nikolaev shot Kirov while he was having sex with Draule, was this before or after orgasm? If after, where did the supposedly sizeable sperm stains come from? Where did the shooting take place? In Kirov's office in Smolny? If so, how did Nikolaev get past the secretary and Borisov? Wouldn't Kirov have locked the door? And so on.

Other reports in the Russian press, based on the radical misreadings and exaggerations of the *Rodina* article, are not worth consideration. One 2005 newspaper article entitled "Kirov Died with His Pants Down" (a better title would have been "Kirov Died with Dirty Underwear"), claims that Draule was found at the scene of the crime (supposedly Kirov's Smolny office) naked. This appears to be based on an NKVD document published in the 2005 *Rodina* article listing the items on her person at the time of her arrest. The only clothing inventoried was her overcoat. Yet the parallel document for Milda's sister Olga Draule lists only an overcoat, black shoes, and a hat. Perhaps Kirov was engaged in a ménage à trois with both sisters when Nikolaev shot him.[5]

What Has This Investigation Established?

In my opinion, new archival evidence on the Kirov murder, considered against the background of earlier evidence, establishes firmly that:

1. Stalin used the Kirov murder to fabricate false charges against ex-oppositionists, cultivate an atmosphere of terror in the USSR, and justify the executions and arrests of millions of innocent subjects.

2. Kirov was not a "moderate" political rival to Stalin at any point, although he was probably less inclined towards the use of violence and repression than some other of the dictator's henchmen, such as Kaganovich. It should be noted that such relative "softies" as Mikoyan survived the Stalin era in the party leadership. Kirov could have done the same had he lived.

3. Nikolaev was not detained repeatedly by the NKVD, nor was a pistol found on his person and returned. He was probably only taken to NKVD headquarters once, on October 15, 1934, although guards may have pushed him away from Kirov at some other point, such as when Kirov disembarked from the Red Arrow at Moscow Station on November 14.

4. Borisov was not murdered, but died in a genuine truck accident.

5. The version of the crime in which Yagoda, acting on orders from Yenukidze, or Stalin himself, worked through Zaporozhets to arrange Kirov's killing is a red herring. It was fabricated by NKVD investigators in 1937–1938 to serve Stalin's political goals, namely liquidating the "Rightist" leaders and Yagoda.

The new evidence also strongly indicates (although it does not prove) that there was no proposal from provincial party secretaries or any other party officials to replace Stalin with Kirov at the Seventeenth Party Congress in 1934. It is also quite unlikely that hundreds of delegates to the congress voted against Stalin's membership in the Central Committee.

In light of the above, can a case still be made that Stalin ordered Kirov's assassination?

The Strongest Case for Stalin Ordering Kirov's Killing

There is certainly evidence of some tension between Kirov and Stalin in 1934. It is clear that Stalin wanted to transfer Kirov out of Leningrad, but met resistance and agreed to a compromise solution. He did not give up on his goal, however, involving Kirov a good deal more in central work and high policy making than he ever had before. According to Mikhail Rosliakov Stalin called Kirov more frequently in Leningrad that year and Kirov did not like this. Stalin was also pressing Kirov to complete collectivization in the Leningrad Region, a demand that Kirov responded to promptly.

As discussed already, rumors about a move by party secretaries to replace Stalin with Kirov probably had their origin in Kirov's promotion to TsK secretary and Stalin's efforts to transfer him to Moscow. The tale of hundreds of votes against Stalin at the Seventeenth Party Congress, which really had just one source—Verkhovykh—probably developed from true gossip about the handful of votes cast against the general secretary. However, it is conceivable that there was more fire than this behind the smoke cloud of rumors. NKVD surveillance documents related to the Seventeenth Party Congress are nearly complete, including the "Special Reports" on delegate conversations from January 31, 1934, the day of Kirov's famous speech to the congress. Surveillance reports from January 26 to February 6 show only one comment about Kirov, from a factory director complaining that he was getting too much praise. However, surveillance reports from February 7 to 10 are missing from the file.[6] Perhaps these reports contained anti-Stalin, pro-Kirov comments from some delegates, comments which could have aroused Stalin's suspicions. Perhaps thirty or forty votes, rather than three, were cast against Stalin's candidacy for the TsK.

We do know that Yagoda, and probably Stalin, also wanted Medved transferred out of Leningrad. In September Yagoda sent an investigative commission to Leningrad to find dirt on Medved, but the commission's findings were inconclusive.

Why did Stalin want Kirov and Medved transferred? Although Kirov took pains to check with Stalin on his hiring of ex-oppositionists (for example in the case of Rumiantsev), the dictator may have suspected that he was coddling former Zinovievites. The two arrest orders for former Zinovievites/United Oppositionists in Leningrad in 1933–1934 suggest this interpretation. On the other hand, from mid-1933 Stalin seems to have had a policy of greater toleration for oppositionists, and this could explain Kirov's ability to get the arrest warrants dropped.

A case for Stalin's ordering an operation against Kirov would assume that the above considerations, combined with his unnatural suspiciousness, led the dictator to decide on solving his problems with murder. A turning point for the decision could have been his anger with Zinoviev over the latter's summer 1934 commentary on Engels in *Bolshevik*. This would have led to the August arrest order for some of the ex-Leningrad Zinovievites, followed by Kirov's blocking of the order. If we assume this scenario, it is possible that Stalin acted through Yagoda, but Zaporozhets was almost certainly not involved. At any rate, there were undeniably many channels through which Stalin could have worked. He could have utilized Komarovite connections in Leningrad, perhaps through the former Leningraders employed in Kaganovich's secretariat. Stalin could also have used junior Leningrad NKVD officers stationed, for instance, at the Smolny Ward office of the security organs.

In this scenario someone familiar with Nikolaev or his letters of complaint would have brought the unemployed Leningrad Communist to the attention of the conspirators (most likely not to that of Stalin personally). One way or another, the party officials or NKVD officers involved would have stoked Nikolaev's rage and directed it against Kirov. One way of doing this would have been anonymous letters about an affair between the latter and Milda. Another would have been to get to him using a provocateur, perhaps someone posing as a party oppositionist, who would have encouraged Nikolaev's grudge against the authorities. As discussed in Chapter 9, Georgy Sokolov, the Naval Academy cadet tried with the "Leningrad Center," is one possible candidate for the role of provocateur. Korol, the Smolny Ward official who supposedly warned Nikolaev that Institute of Party History administrators were out to get him, is another. Kirilina does not believe in a Stalin plot, but she does suggest that Nikolaev's brother-in-law, Roman Kulisher, could have fed Nikolaev tales about an affair between Draule and Kirov. Yuskin's evidence from the 1934 investigation and trial indicates that the Industrial Institute student Yermolaeva, possibly the same person as Elizabeth Lermolo, bragged of "connections" in Smolny, knew Nikolaev well, and engaged in provocative "anti-Soviet" conversations. Of all the people known to be in touch with Nikolaev before the murder, Yermolaeva seems to me the best candidate for the role of NKVD informer or provocateur.

It must be said, however, that the search for potential provocateurs is entirely speculative. There are no indications beyond a few mildly suggestive circumstances that Sokolov, Kulisher, Korol, or Yermolaeva were NKVD informers, much less provocateurs. The only evidence of Korol's contact with Nikolaev is two lines in the minutes of one Institute of Party History meeting. According to the 1934 evidence Sokolov only talked to Nikolaev once in the fall of 1934. Kulisher's and Yermolaeva's "anti-Soviet" conversations were probably just "idle chatter," to use Yuskin's phrase. There is no evidence that Yermolaeva had contact with any of the ex-Zinovievites tried with Nikolaev. Nor does Lermolo in *Face of a Victim* seem to know anything about these men (she claims to have met Kotolynov once in jail after Kirov's killing).

There remain a great many problems with the "Stalin did it" version of the Kirov murder. Given that Kirov was not a rival to Stalin, and strove hard to stick precisely to the dictator's party line, it becomes very hard to see why Stalin would have tried to kill him. As Adam Ulam pointed out in 1973, political assassination was for Stalin "a very clumsy and dangerous way to get rid of somebody." Among other problems it set a bad example that other terrorists might follow against Stalin himself. It also led foreign observers to conclude that the Soviet Union was weak and internally unstable.[7]

To press Kirov out of Leningrad, Stalin had other means available to him. He could have used N. P. Komarov and other sympathetic figures to signal their followers in Leningrad that attacks on Kirov's subordinates would be looked on favorably. Indeed, there are a few bits of evidence, such as the 1933–1934 assault on the Fellowship of Komsomol Militants, that this was going on. Attacks on lower-ranking officials would have led ultimately to an all-out assault on Kirov, with Stalin looking on, "regretful" at the revelation that another old friend had failed him. This was the standard modus operandi in party politics, at least prior to the Terror. Secret assassination was for enemies abroad, such as Trotsky or NKVD defectors, who were out of reach of Soviet "justice."

Nikolaev seems like an extraordinarily unlikely choice for assassin. Erratic and unstable, he would have been difficult to "aim" and unlikely to accomplish the deed. With the exception of a botched assassination attempt on Trotsky involving the Mexican painter David Siqueiros, the Soviet security services generally used trained men whose political loyalty was well established. Trotsky's killer Roman Mercador is one example. Pavel Sudoplatov himself, who killed the Ukrainian nationalist leader Yevhen Konovalets in Rotterdam in 1938, is another. The 1948 murder of actor and director Solomon Mikhoels, with which the Kirov murder is sometimes compared, was carried out at Stalin's orders by uniformed officers of the MVD.[8]

In evaluating the "Stalin did it" version of the Kirov murder, it is vital above all to keep in mind the context of political practices in 1934. All of the seemingly suspicious phenomena discussed above— the behind-the-scenes struggles between party cliques, the squabbles over resources between Kirov and Kaganovich, Kirov's resistance to leaving Leningrad, Stalin's irritation and impatience with his subordinates, the uncertainty about the dictator's true "line," the secret police surveillance of ex-oppositionists, the omnipresent informers—were routine for the Soviet Union in 1934. The question for the reader is whether these phenomena, which taken each in isolation were quite ordinary, converged in Leningrad in the summer and fall of 1934 in such an extraordinary way as to indicate an assassination plot by Stalin.

Trotsky's Version

In the weeks after Kirov's murder, Leon Trotsky speculated that Nikolaev was part of an NKVD "provocation" gone awry (see Chapter 13, Document 113). Specifically, he suspected that the security police well before the assassination had sought to implicate former oppositionists in Leningrad in a fabricated plot against Kirov. The fabrication also involved the Latvian consul, so as to tie the alleged conspirators to nefarious forces abroad. The suggestion of such a conspiracy is not as far-fetched as it might seem. In the 1920s the NKVD had set up fake White organizations abroad to control and monitor anti-Soviet émigrés and spread disinformation.[9] In his discussion of the Kirov murder, Trotsky used a less grandiose example of security police provocation, in which an NKVD agent entrapped a young Left sympathizer into distributing clandestine opposition literature.

As discussed in Chapter 10, there is evidence that lower-ranking NKVD officers in Leningrad sought to fabricate evidence in the summer of 1934 against former Zinovievites using the psychologically ill secret informer Maria Volkova. Medved blocked the move. The junior officers' efforts could well have been part of a drive to discredit Medved and remove him from Leningrad, and even to dislodge Kirov from the city. They could have been run directly on Yagoda's orders, or the officers involved could have acted on their own initiative, having a good idea what the center wanted and hoping for a reward. A good question is whether Nikolaev, like Volkova, could have been part of a similar operation, not to kill Kirov, but to stir up a hornets' nest that would drive him and Medved out of the city. Could NKVD officers have used him to gather information on or provoke his acquaintances among the former Zinovievites in the city? Or could someone else, such as Yermolaeva, with her "connections," been provoking Nikolaev as part of a similar effort?

A second possibility to consider is that Nikolaev was an NKVD provocateur sent to the Latvian consulate in Leningrad to draw the consul into some sort of espionage scheme. The consul received many visitors whom he suspected of being NKVD collaborators, and there is some evidence that Nikolaev really did go to the consulate (see above, p. 300). There are also two fragments hinting at the possibility of such a scenario. First, soon after Kirov's murder Leningrad NKVD Operations Department Senior Commissar Griunvald remembered being warned that his guards should watch out for "some Latvian," who one

might speculate was actually Nikolaev. Second, the wife of Special Political Department Officer Mosevich in the early 1960s recalled her husband and his colleague Gorin-Lundin referring to materials on Nikolaev
in the Special Department, which among other things handled espionage
directed against foreign consulates. There is also a single hint in the
December 5, 1934 interrogation of Operations Department officer
Mikhail Kotomin that some other department of the Leningrad NKVD
might have had information on Nikolaev before the murder (see p. 397).
Of course, if Nikolaev was part of an NKVD operation against the Latvian consulate, this does not exclude him also acting as a provocateur/
informer vis-à-vis the ex-Zinovievites. The NKVD goal could have
been to link the former oppositionists to the consul.

If Nikolaev had pre-murder contact with the NKVD, it is more
likely that it was as an informer or provocateur targeting former oppositionists and/or the Latvian consul, than as an assassin put up to
killing Kirov. This would be consistent with junior NKVD officers' attempted use of Volkova to incriminate ex-oppositionists and the
multiple attempts to recruit or entrap the Latvian consul Bissenieks.
Against this is the unanimous testimony of credible Leningrad NKVD
officers who survived the Terror (credible meaning minus P. M. Lobov
and P. P. Petrovsky) that they could not find Nikolaev on any watch list
or agent list after the murder (note, however, that G. Petrov did not
find Volkova in Leningrad NKVD files in October 1934 either).

The provocation-gone-wrong scenario accounts for the facts (and
the more or less probable alleged facts) adduced in favor of a Stalin
murder plot against Kirov, without positing that very implausible scenario. It is thus the more attractive and likely hypothesis. However, all
the scenarios listed above are speculative. Readers may wish to compare them to the detailed evidence offered in earlier chapters and reach
their own conclusions. But before they do so, there remains one last
witness, arguably the most important one in the Kirov murder case, to
be examined.

Genrikh Liushkov

Early on the morning of June 13, 1938, a lone Soviet officer appeared
out of the predawn mist and hailed a detachment of Manchurian police patrolling the border between the USSR and the Japanese puppet
state of Manchukuo. He approached the patrol behaving in a "jovial,"
ingratiating fashion. According to his identification card, which was

signed by Soviet NKVD chief Nikolai Yezhov, he was Genrikh Liush-kov, Commissar Third Class of the NKVD. He was in fact the commander of the NKVD in the entire Soviet Far Eastern department. The police relieved him of two pistols, a quantity of Soviet and Japanese currency, an Order of Lenin medal, a photograph of his wife, and two letters from A. I. Lapin, commander of an air corps in the Soviet Far East. Lapin had committed suicide while under interrogation on charges of treason. His letters, which recanted all of the confessions he had made, were reportedly written in his own blood.[10]

At the Hunchun base of the Japanese occupation army, intelligence officers concluded that Liushkov was a high-ranking NKVD officer. They sent him on to the army headquarters in Seoul, Korea being then a Japanese colony. Upon notification of Liushkov's defection, the Japanese General Staff ordered Korea Army to send Liushkov to Tokyo post-haste, for interrogation by the Russian Section of central military intelligence. Over the next seven years Liushkov lived in Tokyo, more or less under house arrest, and worked for Japanese military intelligence, providing assessments of Soviet military strength and political developments, and writing Russian-language propaganda.[11]

Generals of the Japanese occupation force in Manchuria, the so-called Kwantung Army, angry that they had not received custody of Liushkov, soon released news of his defection to Manchukuo's Chinese-language press. By June 24, 1938 military intelligence in Poland, which monitored closely all things Soviet, had word of the event, and German news agencies reported it on July 1. On July 2 Japanese newspapers picked up the story. Their hand forced by the press, Japanese intelligence officers released a statement by Liushkov on July 3. "I have committed great crimes against the people," Liushkov wrote, "continuing almost up to the present day, by working actively with Stalin to carry out his political deceptions and terrorism." He continued, "I have betrayed Stalin, but I never betrayed my fellow countrymen or my fatherland." On July 13 he appeared at a press conference at Tokyo's Sanno Hotel.[12]

Liushkov was born in Odessa in 1900, son of a Jewish tailor. He joined the revolution in 1917, serving the Odessa soviet and fighting with the Bolshevik underground against the German occupation of Odessa in 1918. During the Civil War he served as a political commissar in a number of Red Army units on the Southern Front and against the Poles. He joined the Cheka in 1920. Although Liushkov's education was limited to elementary school and a few night courses, he advanced rapidly due to his great intelligence. An able linguist, he learned as a young adult to speak German with a native accent, and served as a covert agent in Germany in the 1920s. He earned praise from Stalin himself for his analysis of work at the Junkers aviation plants in that country. As the information he provided to the Japanese demonstrates, Liushkov had a remarkable memory for detail, including names and statistics.[13]

In 1934 Liushkov was deputy chief of the Secret Political Department of the central NKVD, serving under department head G. A. Molchanov. He arrived in Leningrad on the morning of December 2, 1934 with Stalin's delegation, and played a central role in the investigation of the Kirov murder. He is on record as conducting at least twenty-one interrogations of arrestees ranging from Milda Draule to Zinoviev. He observed face-to-face confrontations between Shatsky and Georgy Popov, of the Fellowship of Komsomol Militants, on December 18, between Kotolynov and Nikolaev on December 18, and between Nikolaev and Shatsky on December 20. Immediately after the accident that killed Borisov he questioned escorting Officer Maly. On December 21 he was the recipient of a note from deputy chief of the NKVD Economic Security Department L. Mironov with specific instructions on the interrogation of all suspects. It appears that he may have been temporarily in charge of the investigation while Yezhov and Agranov visited Moscow.[14]

Liushkov was an able interrogator. He single-handedly extracted Milda Draule's various admissions of guilt, making him responsible ultimately for her death. He got key "confessions" as well out of Yuskin, Rumiantsev, and Zinoviev. In short, Liushkov was one of the two or three most important investigators on the Kirov murder case in the winter of 1934–1935. This is what he had to say about the assassination in his press release of July 3, 1938.

· 126 ·

Genrikh Liushkov statement to the international press, *Yomiuri shinbun*, July 3, 1938, translated by NKVD Special Bureau from Japanese into Russian.
RGANI, f. 6, op. 13, d. 102, ll. 54–56.

————————

I fled Soviet Russia in spite of the fact that I held a high-ranking position in the Soviet government because for various reasons I sensed that I was threatened [. . .] by the Red purge. . . .

[. . .] I felt my first vacillations at the time of Kirov's murder by Nikolaev at the end of 1934. This was a fatal incident for the country, just as it was for the party. Not only did I participate directly in the investigation of the Kirov murder case, but I took an active part in the public trials and repressions conducted after the murder under the leadership of Yezhov.

I was involved in the following cases.

1. The case of the so-called Leningrad Terrorist Center in early 1935.

2. The case of the terrorist center that plotted against Stalin in the Kremlin in 1935.

3. The case of the so-called United Trotsky-Zinovievite Center in August 1936.

Before the entire world I can confirm with full responsibility that none of these fake conspiracies ever existed and all of them were fabricated deliberately. There is no question that Nikolaev did not belong to Zinoviev's group. He was an abnormal person, suffering from megalomania. He resolved to perish, so as to become a great hero of history. This is clear from his diary. . . .

Stalin used this convenient opportunity connected with the Kirov case, to get rid of these people through the fabrication of wide-ranging anti-Stalinist plots, espionage activities, and terrorist organizations.

Thus, Stalin used any means necessary to get rid of political opponents and of those who might become such in the future. Stalin's devilish methods led to the fall of even very experienced and strong persons. My tragedy is the result of his actions. This happened not only because of Stalin's hysterical suspiciousness, but due to his unwavering decision to get rid of all the Trotskyites and Rightists, who are his political opponents and could represent a political danger in the future. . . .

In April 1939, Liushkov published in the Japanese popular journal *Kaizo* a lengthy commentary on the Terror, focused on refuting the Soviet government's case in the March 1938 show trial of the "Right-Trotskyite Center." Here, he expanded on his earlier comments on the Kirov assassination.

· 127 ·

Genrikh Liushkov, "An Open Letter to Stalin," *Kaizo*, April 1939,
106–125, excerpted. Co-translator, Mari Lenoe.

I was the lead interrogator during the investigation of Zinoviev and Kamenev in connection with the Kirov murder and several other incidents. During this long process Zinoviev and Kamenev gave testimony on the way the anti-Trotsky struggle had been carried out. The methods used are described more than adequately in Trotsky's writings; there is no need for me to repeat facts that are already public knowledge here. However, the facts [Zinoviev and Kamenev] testified to are an important confirmation that the anti-Trotsky struggle was a case of provocation. At any rate, it is absolutely clear that among Stalin's most important "achievements" were the repression of party members, their arrest, imprisonment, torture, and execution, together with application of pressure to them through the fabrication of legal cases. These were an important part of his arsenal of struggle. They were all tools of political struggle.

The fabrication of cases has reached its peak in the period since the Kirov assassination. Since the murder the falsified cases have taken on terrifying dimensions.

First of all, I can confirm that Kirov's murder was the individual deed of Nikolaev. Nikolaev was a psychologically unbalanced person who suffered from many anxieties and was unhappy with life. He believed that he had the abilities to accomplish anything and he imagined himself as a man of intrigue. In reality he was a constant complainer who could not get along with people. Confronted at every turn by the horrifying inertia of the state apparatus, he nonetheless fought always to maintain the right and battle corruption. Society's indifference aroused in him hatred and an intense desire for revenge. Those around him either ignored this turbulent man or subjected him to attacks and blows. All of Nikolaev's petitions for redress to various agencies ended in failure. The attitude of society itself pushed Nikolaev to the conclusion that the problem was not individual corruption, but the system as a whole.

And so Nikolaev's disenchantment with the party apparatus drove him to make plans for the assassination of one of the party leaders. By means of this act he wished to voice his protest against the bureaucratism and inertia of the party agencies and apparatus, and motivate a correction of the entire situation. Nikolaev had no great mission other than this, as is clear not only from his initial statement, but also from his diary. This obsession grew on him until he lived only for it. He concentrated his attention on the biggest man in Leningrad, Kirov.

Fantasies of political intrigue and personal vainglory influenced [Nikolaev]. He imagined himself in the company of Charlotte Corday, Karyaev, and all the other [revolutionary] terrorists. He investigated history, researched historical terrorists, and made them his model. In short, he came to see himself in the mirror of history as a heroic terrorist.

Nikolaev pursued Kirov in earnest, following him closely. Once at the railroad station he attempted to get a shot at him, but failed because of the large number of Kirov's guards.

Nikolaev's only co-conspirator was Shatsky. At the time of the revolution, Shatsky was an anarchist, but he became a Bolshevik. During the period when the Trotskyite movement was legal, he was a sympathizer and for this he was expelled from the party. From this time he was under surveillance. At last, having lost his job, suffering from hunger, he developed a powerful feeling of rage. Nikolaev was acquainted with Shatsky. They talked, and Nikolaev, learning that Shatsky had the same feelings, recruited him to keep watch on Kirov. Of course Nikolaev concealed [the details of] his plot completely from Shatsky.

On the day of the assassination, Kirov was scheduled to give a report to the Leningrad party *aktiv* on the decisions of the November plenum of the Central Committee of the All-Union Communist Party. Nikolaev decided to kill Kirov at this assembly. To accomplish this, he went to the Leningrad regional party committee offices to get a pass for the meeting. Exiting the toilet inside Smolny, Nikolaev ran into Kirov in the corridor, while the latter was on his way to his office. At this moment the NKVD officer responsible for guarding Kirov, Borisov, was lagging behind, so Kirov was walking alone. This chance coincidence was later used by Stalin as the basis for accusations against the Leningrad NKVD and Yagoda, when they were charged with participating in a plot to kill Kirov. I will explain this below.

In an instant Nikolaev decided to carry out his scheme. He pulled out his Nagan and shot Kirov to death. Probably because of the long period of tension he had experienced, Nikolaev fainted right there and was arrested at the scene of the crime. Because I was involved in the preparation of this case for trial, I was able to follow its development step by step.

I arrived in Leningrad 15–16 hours after the crime by train, together with Stalin, Molotov, Voroshilov, Yagoda, and others. Arriving in Leningrad, Stalin proceeded directly to Smolny to interrogate personally Nikolaev, his wife, and other relatives. This paralleled the way in which Nicholas I personally interrogated the Decembrists, but it gave no results. Stalin was unable to clarify the case. At the beginning Stalin had not yet made the decision to give the case a political direction. This can be concluded also from the official announcement in the newspapers of the execution of former White Guard elements. However, after a certain period of time, he ordered /through Yezhov, to whom he had entrusted the investigation/ that the Zinoviev group be targeted. Stalin used the Kirov assassination as an opportunity to suppress the former oppositional factions. Conveniently, the vast majority of the Leningrad party organization had once supported Zinoviev, so that it was not necessary to look far for connections. Nikolaev himself was well-suited for this. Specifically, when he was a member of the Komsomol, he had sympathies for the Zinovievite faction. So Stalin selected them for sacrifice.

Stalin carried out his plans in the following fashion. Yezhov would periodically go to headquarters [Moscow?] to receive Stalin's instructions. Upon his return he would call a meeting of the investigators on the case and present these as his own proposals and opinions. However, everyone understood these to be orders. This is the way in which the outlines of the "Leningrad Terrorist Center" and the "Coordinating Zinovievite Center" [that is, the "Moscow Center"] were sketched. As far as the structuring of the "connections" and the actual deeds goes, these were developed in the course of the interrogations of the accused, and frequently depended on the skill and speculations of the interrogators.

When Zinoviev and Kamenev were first arrested there was no evidence of their complicity /this was yet another fabrication/. The "evidence" was created in the course of their interrogations, but was limited to moral and political responsibility for Kirov's killing. These charges [. . .] were announced at the Leningrad court session of January 1935. At that point Yezhov /that is to say, Stalin/ was not making particularly unreasonable demands [on the investigators]. However, the ink was not even dry on the verdict when Stalin began to create an even bigger case.

During the investigation/trial of the case in Leningrad, Yezhov tried every possible way of bringing Trotskyites into the case. The connection between Trotsky and the assassination was finally made through the investigation of the Latvian consul in Leningrad. The actual circumstances were that Nikolaev, whose wife was Latvian, had applied to the consul in question for a visa to accompany his family to Latvia. This was utilized for the fabrication. Nikolaev was planning to escape the country after accomplishing his feat. As a result of the investigation it was discovered that said Latvian consul was a member of the Latvian Social Democratic Party. This was used as evidence to authenticate the claim that Trotsky communicated with the terrorists through the consul. This issue resulted in an official investigation by the Latvian ambassador /at the insistence of the Commissariat of Foreign Affairs/ and the consul was made to admit that he had met Nikolaev.

Of course the idea that Trotsky was connected with the assassination was at this time expressed only in the vaguest terms. This is because up until the trial of the Leningrad Center the fabricated case was of limited extent. But later, Stalin's repression of "unreliable elements" took on frightening dimensions, and consequently the fabrications became blatantly obvious. The Kirov assassination came to be handled as one episode in the operations of a giant conspiratorial party headed by Trotsky. At the various trials, different scenes in the conspiracy were presented and refined. Later on the Latvian consul matter was dropped as if no one had ever heard of it, and this was of course no accident. This means of creating a fabricated case involves a high risk that the entire construction of a fake conspiratorial plot will be exposed. If in fact a conspiratorial clique participating in major affairs of state, with control over NKVD operations inside and outside the USSR, had aimed to communicate with Trotsky, would they have chosen such a clumsy method? The stupidity of the consul case was so extreme that it beggars description. Such an approach to the case of Kirov's murder made the fabrication itself obvious to a child.

Although later it was said that Yagoda himself had been running Nikolaev, the facts that Nikolaev had at home a map of Kirov's routes and a Nagan revolver with an expired registration, together with the detailed diary he was keeping, tell more than enough about the oafishness of this version. If Nikolaev had been directed by a group of experienced conspirators, wouldn't they have avoided such infantile methods, given their constant fear of discovery? In order to provide a veneer of authenticity to the fabrication, which went counter to the findings of the entire preliminary investigation in Leningrad, the childishness of Nikolaev's behavior was put down to the plotters' efforts to pretend that [the assassin] acted alone. The same explanation was given for the failure of the conspiratorial group to confess fully their hidden plot.

The Kirov murder became the central pillar of several cases that followed. The Leningrad case went as described above, but at the August 1936 show trial, Zinoviev and Kamenev were the leaders of the conspiratorial organization and Bakaev was presented as the direct organizer [of the killing]. Here I myself can serve as a witness. I was the person who conducted the interrogation of the aforementioned three men, and I can confirm that their confessions were completely false. Yagoda transmitted Stalin's orders to me and these orders were embodied in the text of Zinoviev, Kamenev, and Bakaev's confessions.

At the January 1937 show trial the circumstances of the assassination case [the fabricated version] did not change, with the exception of Radek's testimony that Ramchikovsky recruited him into the Kirov assassination plot. However, at the March 1938 show trial, the Kirov murder case was presented in a new way. The grand finale of the Kirov circus was Bulanov's testimony at this trial. Bulanov testified that Yagoda told him that headquarters guard Borisov had participated in Kirov's murder, and that when the high-level government officials who'd hurried to Leningrad summoned Borisov to Smolny to interrogate him as a witness, Zaporozhets, who feared that Borisov would reveal the conspirators behind Nikolaev, decided to kill him. Furthermore, it was claimed that at Yagoda's orders Zaporozhets had arranged for the truck in which Borisov was riding to have an "accident," in which Borisov died. This was in order to get rid of the most dangerous witness.

The events around Borisov's death occurred during my stay in Leningrad. Borisov had formerly been charged with the duty of guarding Kirov. He was an older man completely unsuited for the duties of a police officer, but Kirov viewed him with special favor. When Medved proposed to replace Borisov, Kirov rejected the idea out of hand. Borisov always followed Kirov and he was always lagging far behind. At the time of Kirov's assassination in the Smolny corridor, he was not at Kirov's side. Borisov was behind Kirov at the end of the corridor around the corner. I was present when Volovich suggested to Agranov on the telephone that Borisov be dispatched immediately to Smolny. This was on the morning of December 2, in Medved's office. During the conversation there were two others present besides myself—Dmitriev—at the time deputy director of the International Economic Affairs Department of the state security organs—and Gorin /former head of the Leningrad NKVD Headquarters Special Department/. Agranov called the Operations Department, where Borisov was being held, and ordered him sent to Smolny immediately. Approximately thirty minutes later Agranov was informed of Borisov's death.

This incident struck me as strange, and we had our doubts about it. Judging whether or not this was a chance accident was difficult. After this Agranov, under Yezhov's direction, launched an inquiry into the incident. As it turned out, at the time Borisov was to be convoyed to Smolny there was not a single NKVD automobile available. The summons for him was extremely urgent, so they put him in an NKVD truck parked by the entrance. This freight truck had a broken steering mechanism. The driver recklessly developed a high speed. After a sharp turn the steering mechanism suddenly went wrong, and the truck hit the wall of a building on the side Borisov was sitting on. At the time Borisov was summoned, Yagoda was at Stalin's side. As I stated before, the catastrophe occurred just thirty minutes later. Could Yagoda have accomplished Borisov's murder in such a short time? Let us consider the assertion that Yagoda could have carried out the murder in just a few minutes /ten minutes elapsed between Agranov issuing the order and Borisov's departure from the NKVD building/. [If one does so] decisive evidence demonstrating the falsehood of the above proposition quickly comes to light. According to Bulanov, Zaporozhets acted to kill Borisov at Yagoda's order. However, one small detail was forgotten in the fabricated plot line—Zaporozhets was not in Leningrad at the time of the murder, before it, or for some time after it. The fabricated story-line was so absurdly haphazard that it did not even take into account whether the persons who had supposedly committed the crime had been at the scene or not. The fact that all of the witnesses were no longer alive was convenient for the fabrication of such blatant falsehoods.

This leads to doubt about the handling of the later terror cases as well. It is a fact that Kuibyshev, Gorky, Menzhinsky, and Gorky's son died. However, if one accepts that they all died at the hands of terrorists, one might as well also agree that Turkish President Kemal died as the result of a conspiracy.[15]

The *Kaizo* article adds two new pieces to the Kirov murder puzzle. First, Liushkov believed that Nikolaev did visit the Latvian consulate, in order to get a visa. Second, he concluded that Shatsky had in fact provided Nikolaev with information on Kirov's movements, although he did not know that Nikolaev intended to kill Kirov. Presumably Shatsky thought that Nikolaev wanted to meet Kirov face to face to petition for redress.

Liushkov's evidence, which has been ignored or downplayed by Western writers on the Kirov killing, is in fact the most important in the case. Unlike Krivitsky and Orlov, who were working abroad at the time of Kirov's killing, Liushkov was at the very center of the first NKVD investigation. He interrogated key witnesses repeatedly and seems to have had full access to written records of the case, including Nikolaev's documents. He also would have been privy to the private conversation and workplace banter of the other interrogators. Moreover, Liushkov gave his evidence outside the Soviet Union, free from the dictates of the party line, and under the protection of the Japanese military police (after World War II Japanese officers who worked with Liushkov testified that he did fear a Soviet assassination attempt).

Unfortunately the Japanese military executed Liushkov in Manchuria in August 1945, and destroyed his records. We are left with publications in the Japanese press by and about him, the transcript of one of his 1938 interrogations passed on by the Japanese to U.S. military intelligence before World War II, a few other miscellaneous documents, and postwar interviews conducted by U.S. historian Alvin Coox with Japanese officers who "handled" Liushkov. These documents reveal that Liushkov gave the Japanese remarkably accurate information on Soviet NKVD operations, politics, and military dispositions. Now that we can compare NKVD defectors' and memoirists' accounts with Soviet archival documents, it is obvious that Liushkov's testimony compares very favorably with Orlov's, Krivitsky's, and Sudoplatov's.[16]

A few examples of Liushkov's accuracy should suffice. At the time of his appointment as chief of the Far Eastern NKVD, which he dated to late July 1937, Liushhkov claimed to have had a meeting with Stalin, Voroshilov, Yezhov, and Molotov in the Kremlin, followed by a one-on-one session in which the dictator ordered him to purge the regional leadership of the party, military, and NKVD. Stalin's office log confirms that precisely such a meeting took place in Stalin's office on July

28, 1937, with Stalin talking to Liushkov alone from 6:00 to 6:15 P.M.[17] In his July 1938 press release ("Escape Notes") and his Sanno Hotel press conference, Liushkov claimed that over two million people had been arrested "in the last few years" in the USSR. This number correlates well with official figures on the Terror published recently, indicating that the secret police arrested 1,466,174 persons in 1934–1937, and another 630,509 in 1938 (note that Liushkov defected in mid-June 1938, so that he could not have known official arrest numbers for any later than May 1938). His assertion of "several hundred thousand executions" also fits with official statistics showing that the NKVD executed 357,477 people in 1934–1937 (the vast majority in 1937), and 328,618 in 1938.[18]

Liushkov's evidence on the Kirov murder is extraordinarily important because it confirms entirely the picture of the crime that emerges from documents of the 1934–1935 investigation (discounting of course the Stalinist accusations against the Zinovievites). Nikolaev was a psychologically unbalanced lone gunman, Borisov died in an accident, Stalin fabricated a case against the former Zinovievites, and so on. Writing outside the Soviet Union from an anti-Stalin perspective just four years after the events, Liushkov, who was closely involved in the original investigation and who was a reliable witness on verifiable facts beyond the Kirov murder, confirms the evidence of the documents released by the KGB to the Central Committee in 1956 and later. His testimony demonstrates that these documents were not forged and that they give an accurate outline of what happened in Leningrad in 1934. It also indicates that the KGB document releases were substantially complete—no important facts were hidden.

Liushkov knew nothing of any conspiracy to murder Kirov. His evidence invalidates the Yagoda-Zaporozhets version of the killing put forward at the March 1938 show trial. If there was a plot by Stalin, it must have involved a tiny handful of people, and probably not Yagoda or other senior NKVD officials. It is also worth mentioning that Liushkov discusses briefly the OGPU investigation of the Riutin Platform, but never mentions anything about Kirov preventing Riutin's execution. In fact he never even hints that Kirov was a "moderate."

One other veteran of the 1934–1935 NKVD investigation of the Kirov murder, Leonid Raikhman, survived the Terror and ultimately testified in a relatively free political environment (the late perestroika Soviet Union). In late 1988 Alla Kirilina interviewed Raikhman, who in 1934 was an officer in the Leningrad NKVD's Special Political Department. His eyewitness account of the investigation confirms the picture of events presented by Liushkov and the 1934–1935 primary source documents presented in this book. Raikhman told Kirilina that on the night of the crime the Leningrad NKVD could find no record of Nikolaev in their various card catalogues and watch lists. Interrogated by Raikhman on the morning of December 2, Milda Draule denied categorically any affair with Kirov.[19]

It is notoriously difficult to prove a negative, and the available evidence does not "prove" that Stalin did not conspire to murder Kirov. However, Liushkov and Raikhman were the only two veterans of the original investigation to testify in more or less neutral political environments, and they both confirm the evidence of the investigation documents released by the KGB in 1956. My conclusion is that Nikolaev very probably acted on his own. He may have had some contact with NKVD agents or informers, but not as a prospective assassin. If there was such contact, it was probably fleeting and coincidental. The hostility to authority that Nikolaev expressed in his 1934 diary entries would seem to militate against his consciously providing information to the police.

Contrary to the denigration of the new archival sources by some senior scholars, new documents on the Kirov murder force us to revise received views of the development of the Great Terror of 1937–1938. The assassination remains a turning point in the chain of events that led to the Terror, but not because Stalin the master plotter ordered it. Rather, he used it. The murder frightened the Soviet leadership and probably Stalin himself. Stalin seized the opportunity presented by this fear to justify a nationwide hunt for counterrevolutionary terrorists, a hunt which he escalated steadily in 1935–1937. Fearful for their own safety, and perhaps still attached to some humanitarian ideals, Old Bolsheviks like Yenukidze grumbled about Stalin and engaged in low-level obstructionism. As NKVD surveillance of senior party members intensified, using new technology such as phone tapping, Stalin heard reports on more and more of this grumbling. The growing danger of war with imperialist Japan or Nazi Germany added to the tension. Ultimately the dictator, vengeful and suspicious to begin with, decided on the mass execution of anyone who could be identified as a potential opponent of his personal despotism. The arrests and executions of millions followed.

It also seems probable that we need to discard some of the more tabloidish elements of older narratives of the Terror. In addition to the story that Stalin ordered Kirov's killing, these would include the list of poisonings attributed to Stalin from 1923 through the Terror years. The claims that Stalin arranged the death by poison of Maxim Gorky, his son, NKVD chief Menzhinsky, and Politburo member Valerian Kuibyshev derive from the March 1938 show trial, when the "Right-Trotskyite Bloc" was charged with these "medical murders." Liushkov believed that all of the deaths were natural and he offered good arguments for his claim in the April 1939 *Kaizo* article. The real facts of the Terror are sensational and sickening enough without such dubious embellishment.

False embellishment in my view trivializes the sufferings of the victims by turning real history and the stories of real people into a screenplay starring a cackling, mad villain. The reality is far worse—Stalinist repression was for those who lived it in camps and prisons a boring, grinding existence, which often enough concluded in an extended, agonizing death by starvation, disease, and exhaustion. The "statesmen" who subjected millions to this treatment did so out of considerations they believed to be "realistic" and "rational." It may well be that Stalin was a kind of moral monster—in the terminology of the modern psychological profession "character disordered," in that of the Abrahamic religions, "evil." But many of his followers were, like Nazi official Adolf Eichmann, or Kirov himself, "terribly and terrifyingly normal." They were not screenplay villains. They committed mass murder on the basis of ideological and realpolitik considerations that they and those around them accepted as rational and necessary. The uncomfortable truth is that under the "right" circumstances ordinary men and women are capable of horrifying acts of evil.[20]

Embellishment and sensationalism also carry with them the danger of forgetting the systemic background to the Terror. The annihilation of so many would have been far more difficult without the extraordinary concentration of political power that developed in the Soviet Union during the 1920s. Official cultivation of denunciation as a basic tool of social control also foreshadowed and facilitated the Terror, as did the constant rhetoric of hatred against "class enemies." The extreme disruption of society brought about by the Bolsheviks' forced collectivization of the peasants and falling standards of living after 1927 contributed too. As the story of Nikolaev himself demonstrates, Soviet society was riven by social conflict and hostility to authority. This was in part the result of Bolshevik leaders' policy choices. Stalin made adept use of the population's resentments during the Terror.

None of this should be understood to diminish Stalin's responsibility for the Terror, or that of his immediate subordinates. Stalin made the key decisions for mass executions, and his subordinates endorsed and implemented them. That they may have subjectively believed such extreme measures were "necessary" when they sanctioned them does not reduce their guilt. Behind their decisions were longstanding attitudes which they had accepted and cultivated in themselves—indifference to human suffering, pride in taking an unyielding stand against "enemies," contempt for written law or formal limitations on their power, and above all the conviction that "you can't make an omelet without breaking eggs." These attitudes had become a part of the everyday culture of the Communist Party.

In February 2005 Marx Draule, an elderly resident of the Russian Federation, submitted a formal request that the General Prosecutor determine whether he was the son of Leonid Nikolaev. Draule's only memories of his life before admission to an orphanage were of living in Leningrad with his mother, father, grandmother, and younger brother, in rooms over the entrance arch of a large apartment building. Following an investigation the prosecutor's office determined that Draule was in fact the older son of Milda and Leonid, admitted to Leningrad Orphanage No. 44 in January 1935. He was formally recognized as a victim of political repression.[21]

With the aid of Tatiana Sukharnikova, director of the Kirov Museum in St. Petersburg, Marx Draule and his cousin, Valeriya Petrovna Draule (probably the daughter of Milda's brother, Pyotr Draule), applied for access to the secret police (NKVD/KGB/FSB) case files on the Kirov murder. Through the Draules, Sukharnikova was able to see the entire fifty-eight-volume set of records. In an interview in late 2007, she summarized some of her findings. Sukharnikova confirmed that the originals of Nikolaev's diaries and notebooks are in his own writing, and that they contain no evidence either of an affair between Milda Draule and Kirov or of contact between Nikolaev and NKVD agents or other provocateurs. She concludes that "Nikolaev's main motive (for the murder) was . . . his firing from work."[22]

In her November 2007 interview, Sukharnikova describes Nikolaev's "diaries and notes" in some detail.

He kept his diaries and notes in notebooks resembling accounting books, on separate sheets of paper, even on ripped-up fragments of such sheets. All of these were in fact found at his apartment or his mother's apartment. Along with them there are some small pocket notebooks, also written in his hand. Overall it appears that Nikolaev took down brief notes so as not to forget thoughts that seemed to him very important, and later fixed these in more detail in his "account books." The pocket notebooks were only for his personal reading, the elaborated versions were for other members of the family. By the way, he kept a simple chronicle of his life, with the intention of telling the children, when they grew up, about himself, his wife, and about events which concerned him the most. For example, there is in the diaries a description of his revolutionary youth. In 1917 he did everything but actually fight on the barricades. At first, Nikolaev wanted his wife, Milda Draule, to write entries together with him. There are few such entries, and they are all about the children.

It is obvious from the text that during the last year of his life Nikolaev suffered from graphomania. The diaries begin with a biography and an extremely detailed genealogy. . . .[23]

Sukharnikova's direct examination of Nikolaev's diaries and the other documents in the secret police files takes us as near as we ever may come to closing the Kirov case. At a minimum, her findings confirm that the KGB's 1956 document release did not hide any key evidence. Taken together with Liushkov's 1939 testimony in the Japanese press and the documents translated in this book, they indicate strongly that Nikolaev acted alone. Based on this evidence, the Kirov murder is not the story of a complex, fiendishly plotted political assassination. It is rather a tale of one government's use of a sensational crime and a pathetic, psychologically ill assassin to terrorize the populace and settle political scores.

APPENDIX

Biographical Sketches

Main Sources Used: J. Arch Getty and Oleg Naumov, *The Road to Terror* (New Haven: Yale University Press, 1999); Alla *Kirilina, Neizvestnyi Kirov* (Moscow: OLMA-PRESS, 2001); V. V. Zhuravleva et al., eds., *Deiateli SSSR i revoliu-tsionnogo dvizheniia Rossii: Entsiklopedicheskii slovar' Granat* (Moscow: "So-vetskaia entsiklopediia," 1989); A. A. Fursenko et al., *Prezidium TsK KPSS, 1954–1964* (Moscow: ROSSPEN, 2004); L. Kosheleva et al., eds., *Pis'ma I. V. Stalina V. M. Molotovu, 1925–1936 g.g.* (Moscow: ROSSPEN, 1995); V. N. Khaustov et al., eds., *Lubianka: Stalin i VChK-GPU-OGPU-NKVD, ianvar' 1922–dekabr' 1936* (Moscow: Mezhdunarodnyi fond "Demokratiia," 2003); A. I. Kokurin et al., eds., *Lubianka: Organy VChK-OGPU-NKVD-NKGB-MGB-MVD-KGB, 1917–1991. Spravochnik* (Moscow: Mezhdunarodnyi fond "Demo-kratiia," 2003); J. Arch Getty and Oleg V. Naumov, *Yezhov: The Rise of Stalin's "Iron Fist"* (New Haven: Yale University Press, 2008); Russian State Archive of Contemporary History (RGANI); Russian State Archive of Social and Political History (RGASPI).

Persons mentioned once or twice in the text may not be included.

Adoratsky, Vladimir Viktorovich (1878–1945). Party member from 1904. During revolution and Civil War worked in Commissariat of Enlighten-ment (education). Taught at Institute of Red Professors and the Sverd-lov Communist Academy. Deputy director of the Central Archives Directorate, 1920–1929. Director of the Marx-Engels-Lenin Institute, 1931–1939. Involved in negotiations with Boris Nicolaevsky and oth-ers for purchase of Marx papers from German Social Democratic Party, 1935–1936.

Agranov, Yakov Saulovich (1893–1938). Born in Gomel Province. Mem-ber of Socialist Revolutionary Party, 1912–1915. Social Democratic Labor Party member (Communist) from 1915. Secretary of Soviet Republic Sovnarkom, 1918–1919. Cheka work from 1919. Headed GPU Special Bureau for the Exile of Anti-Soviet Elements and Intelligentsia, 1922–1923. "Stage manager" of 1922 trial of Socialist Revolutionaries. Deputy director and director of OGPU Special Department, deputy chief of Secret Operations Directorate, 1923–1931. Chief of OGPU Special Political Department, 1931. OGPU plenipotentiary for Moscow Region, 1931–1933. Deputy director of OGPU, 1933–1937. Ran 1934–1935 Kirov murder investigation under orders from Yezhov, Stalin. Arrested July 20, 1937. Sentenced to death on August 1, 1938.

Akulov, Ivan Alekseevich (1888–1937). Party member from 1907. Secretary of Ukrainian party committee, various provincial party committees, 1918–1922. Chairman of Ukrainian Council of Labor Unions, member of All-Union Council of Labor Unions Presidium, 1922–1929. Deputy director of Workers' and Peasants' Inspectorate, 1930–1931. Deputy chairman of OGPU, 1931–1932. Chief prosecutor of the USSR, 1933–1935. Secretary of USSR Central Executive Committee, 1935–1937. Arrested July 23, 1937.

Aleksandrov, I. A. Guard assigned to Smolny entrance on December 1, 1934. One of his duties was to accompany Kirov from his automobile into Smolny. Testified to Pelshe commission in 1966 on the situation around Smolny at the time of the Kirov murder.

Alekseev, Nikolai Nikolaevich (1893–1937). Son of zemstvo (local government organ) agronomist. Member of Socialist Revolutionary Party, 1910–1917. Communist Party member from 1919. Cheka work from 1920. Plenipotentiary officer of Cheka Foreign Department, 1920–1922. Deputy director of GPU Special Operations Directorate's Special Bureau for Administrative Exile of Intelligentsia and Anti-Soviet Elements, 1922–1925. Chief of Western Siberian Territorial OGPU/NKVD, 1925–1935. Repressed.

Alekseev, P. A. (1893–1939). Party member from 1914. Party work in Petrograd after revolution. Chairman of the Leningrad Region Council of Labor Unions, 1929–1934. Candidate member of TsK, 1927–1930, full member 1930–1937. Repressed.

Allilueva, Nadezhda Sergeevna (1901–1932). Stalin's second wife. Member of party from 1918. Worked in secretariat of Sovnarkom, 1919. Student at Moscow's Industrial Academy, 1929–1932. Committed suicide in November 1932.

Amenitsky, Aleksandr Mikhailovich. Party member from 1910. Under Zinoviev was member of Petrograd party committee and head of the province party personnel department (*orgotdel*). Supporter of Zinovievite opposition, transferred out of Leningrad, January 1926. Returned to Leningrad. In 1928–1929 secretary of Central Ward party committee. Monitored by OGPU in case file "Zanoza" in early 1930s for supposed connections with Komarovites.

Andreev, A. Testified to Shatunovskaya commission in 1960–1961 that Kirov told Sevastianov who told him (in 1956) about an attempt at Seventeenth Party Congress to replace Stalin with Kirov. Also admitted that he had heard the same story in 1959 from Mitiaev, who heard it from Sevastianov via Kirov.

Andreev, Leonid (1871–1919) Well-known Russian playwright at the turn of the twentieth century, author of *The Black Maskers, Life of Man,* and other plays. An early favorite of Kirov's.

Andreosian, Napoleon Vasilevich. Mikoyan client on the Electoral Commission at the Seventeenth Party Congress (1934). Arrested on May 17, 1938, charged as member of "Right-Trotskyite Opposition." Freed December 22, 1939. Testified to the Shatunovskaya commission on November 12, 1960 that he and other ballot counters were "outraged" that there were three cases in which Stalin's name was crossed out on TsK ballot.

Andzhievsky, Grigory Grigorevich (1897–1919). Bolshevik Party member from 1917. Chairman of the Piatigorsk Region party committee in the North Caucasus. Left Communist who opposed coalitions with other socialist parties in 1918. Hanged by White forces.

Annushkov, A. F. In 1934 operations secretary of the Leningrad NKVD Special Department. Testified in 1963 on the situation in the Leningrad NKVD in 1934.

Antipov, Nikolai Kirillovich (1894–1938). Skilled metalworker in Petersburg before revolution, party member from 1912. Member of Presidium of All-Union Council of Labor Unions, 1922–1924. Senior party work in Leningrad from mid-1926 to late 1928. Transferred to Moscow due to conflict with Kirov. Commissar of Posts and Telegraphs from 1928. Also worked in Molotov's secretariat. Deputy chairman of Sovnarkom and Council on Labor and Defense, 1935. Apparently had anti-Kirov Komarovite connections in Leningrad. Arrested 1937, executed 1938.

Antonov, Nikolai Semyonovich (1903–1934). Worker origin. Komsomol member from 1917, party member from 1922. Worked with Leonid Nikolaev in the Vyborg Ward Komsomol apparatus, and at the Russian Arsenal factory in the early 1920s. For supporting Zinovievite Opposition, he received a censure from party authorities and was sent from Leningrad to work in Vologda. Allowed to return to Leningrad, 1928. Employed at Russian Diesel factory. In 1934 a student of Leningrad Industrial Institute. Excused from military service due to poor eyesight. Tried and executed with Leonid Nikolaev in the "Leningrad Center" case, December 1934.

Apinis, Elvira Martynona (b. 1899). Graduate of commercial technical school in Riga, 1915. Secretary in Latvian Ministry of Popular Welfare, 1919–1921. Secretary in Latvian embassy in Helsinki, 1932–1933. Secretary in Latvian consulate in Leningrad, 1933–1935.

Aristov, A. B. (1903–1973). Secretary of TsK, 1952–1953, 1955–1960. Deputy chairman of TsK Russian Republic Bureau, 1957–1961. Soviet ambassador to Poland, 1961–1971. Key supporter of de-Stalinization and Khrushchev, 1956–1957.

Aristov, Mina Lvovich (1887–1942). Party member from 1905. Chairman of the Astrakhan Temporary Revolutionary Committee, December 1917. Member of Astrakhan provincial soviet executive committee, Red Army regimental commander, and military commissar of Astrakhan, 1918–1919. Led coup against Cheka units in Astrakhan, July 1919, and arrested Georgii Atarbekov.

Arosev, A. Ya. Chief of the All-Union Society for Foreign Cultural Exchange in 1935–1936. Involved in negotiations with Boris Nicolaevsky and others for purchase of Marx papers from German Social Democratic Party.

Atarbekov, Georgy Aleksandrovich (1892–1925). Party member from 1908. Moscow University student, early party work in Moscow. Chairman of the Astrakhan Cheka, head of the Eleventh Army Special Department, 1919. Later Cheka/OGPU plenipotentiary in Armenia and Azerbaijan.

Badaev, Aleksei Yegorovich (1883–1951). Party member from 1904. Commissar of Supply for Petrograd, 1919. Chairman of Petrograd Consumer Cooperatives Union, 1921–1929. Leningrad Province party committee secretariat, January 1926. Chairman of Tsentrosoiuz (central cooperative organ in Moscow), 1930–1933.

Bagirov, M. A. (1895–1956). First secretary of TsK of Azerbaijani Republic, 1933–1953. Client of Lavrenty Beria and Cheka/OGPU veteran. Involved in repression of older Baku/Caucasian revolutionary cohort, in particular associates of Anastas Mikoyan. Instrumental in arrest of Olga Shatunovskaya in 1937. Executed in 1956.

Bakaev, Ivan Petrovich (1887–1936). Party member from 1906. Chairman of Petrograd Province Cheka, 1919–1920. Chairman of Petrograd party control commission, 1922–1926. Member of TsKK, 1925–1927. Participant in Zinovievite and United oppositions, excluded from party in 1927 and later readmitted. Tried with "Moscow Center" in January 1935. Executed in same case, 1936.

Balitsky, Vsevolod Apollonovich (1892–1937). Father was accountant. Member of party from 1915. On collegium of Ukrainian Cheka from December 1918. Chairman of Ukrainian GPU, 1923–1931. Ukrainian Republic Commissar of Internal Affairs, 1924–1930, 1934–1937. Deputy chief of OGPU, 1931–1934. Repressed.

Baltsevich, Mechislav Konstantinovich (b. 1900). Served in Cheka/OGPU/NKVD from 1918 with breaks in service. One brother was an officer in the Polish army. Not a party member. Aide to the head of the Leningrad NKVD Special Department, Second Section, 1934. At the trial of Leningrad NKVD officers for negligence on January 23, 1935 in Moscow, Baltsevich was sentenced to ten years in a concentration camp.

Baranov, P. B. (b. 1905). Deputy chief prosecutor of the USSR, 1954–1957. Researcher for and participant in the 1956 Molotov investigation of the Kirov murder.

Bardin, Nikolai Alekseevich (1905–1936). Party member from 1921. Participant in United Opposition. Exiled to Aktiubinsk, Kazakhstan in 1932. Mentioned by Leonid Nikolaev in December 4, 1934 interrogation. Arrested and brought back to Leningrad for interrogation. Sentenced in case of the "Leningrad Counterrevolutionary Zinovievite Group of Safarov, Zalutsky, and Others," January 1935. Presumably executed in 1936.

Baskakov, Ivan Ivanovich. Employee of Leningrad Cheka/OGPU/NKVD, 1921–1939. In 1931 transferred from Secret Political Department (political dissidents) to Operations Department (guard duty, arrests, searches, etc.) as chief of Political Guard Service Subdepartment. In charge of guarding Kirov and other public figures in public places in Leningrad. In summer 1933 made Deputy Chief for General Operational Questions. Demoted to clerical post by Medved, October 26, 1934. Testified to Shatunovskaya commission on November 22, 1960 and January 18, 1961, and to later KPK commission on June 20, 1961. Testimony generally accorded with 1934–1935 documents and Mikhalchenko's testimony.

Beliaev, N. I. (1903–1966). First secretary of Altai Region party committee, 1943–1955. Secretary of TsK, 1955–1958. First secretary of Stavropol Territory party organization from 1960. Retired, 1960.

Bilmanis, Alfreds (1887–1948). Latvian ambassador to Moscow. 1934–1935.

Bissenieks (Russian: Biseneks or Bisseneks), Georgs (1885–1941). Joined Latvian revolutionary movement in 1902, probably as member of Social Democratic Labor Party. In emigration in England from 1912. Hired by Ministry of Foreign Affairs of newly independent Latvia in December 1918. Latvian ambassador to England, 1921–1924. Member of Latvian Social Democratic Party, which had close ties with Mensheviks. Appointed Latvian consul in Leningrad on September 14,

1933. Expelled from Soviet Union on December 31, 1934. Arrested on October 3, 1940 (following Soviet takeover of Latvia), charged with terrorist attack on Kirov and spying for England. Sentenced to death and executed on July 27, 1941.

Borisov, Mikhail Vasilievich (1881–1934). Personal guard of Kirov inside Smolny, officer of Leningrad NKVD Operations Department. Non-party member. Former night watchman. Eyewitness to scene in Smolny third-floor corridors soon after Kirov's murder. Died in auto accident (or murdered) on December 2, 1934.

Bosh, Evgeniya Bogdanovna (1879–1925). Party member from 1901. Commissar of Internal Affairs for Soviet Ukraine, 1917–1918. Member of Astrakhan Province party committee and TsK Special Plenipotentiary for Political Work to Red Army's Caspian-Caucasian Front, 1918–1919. Recalled to Moscow, February 1919. Died a suicide.

Bravy, Arkhip Ivanovich (b. 1894). Party member from 1925. Red Army service, 1917–1922. Cheka service from 1922. Officer of Smolny building command (guard). On afternoon of December 1, 1934 was officer on duty at Smolny command office.

Buachidze, Samuil (1882–1918). Party member from 1902 and political émigré of Georgian origin. Schoolteacher of peasant origin. Came to Vladikavkaz in May 1917 and propagandized Lenin's call to eschew cooperation with the Mensheviks. Delegate with Kirov to the Mozdok Congress of the Peoples of the Terek Region, January 1918. Assassinated at political meeting in Vladikavkaz.

Bukharin, Nikolai Ivanovich (1888–1938). Party member from 1906. Exiled from Russian Empire, 1911–1917. Member of Politburo, 1924–1929. Member of Presidium of Comintern Executive Committee, 1919–1929. Leader of "Right Deviation" in 1928–1929. Chief of the Scientific-Technical Section of the All-Union Council on the National Economy, early 1930s. Editor of *Izvestia*, 1934–1937. Tried and executed on charges of treason, March 1938.

Bukovsky, Lev Fomich (b. 1896). Native of Leningrad. Worker origin. Party member from 1916. Red Army service, 1917–1921. NKVD/OGPU service from 1930. Senior operations commissar of Leningrad NKVD Operations Department. Assigned as Kirov's personal bodyguard from November 1931. Accompanied him on trips in and outside of Leningrad, managed his personal affairs, arranged and took part in hunting and fishing trips, etc.

Bulganin, Nikita Aleksandrovich (1895–1975). Party member from 1917. Cheka service, 1918–1922. Chairman of the Moscow city soviet's executive committee, 1931–1937. Member of the State Defense Committee during World War II. Deputy chairman of the USSR Council of Ministers, 1947–1950, Minister of USSR Armed Forces, 1947–1949. Member of TsK Politburo/Presidium, 1948–1958. Chairman of the USSR Council of Ministers, 1955–1958. Chairman of Stavropol Council on the Economy, 1958–1960. Retired, 1960.

Butiagin, Yuri Pavlovich. Party member from 1902, compatriot of Kirov's in Terek Social Democratic movement, 1917–1918. Commander of Eleventh Army for three months in late 1919. Commander of Red Army detachment during Red reconquest of North Caucasus, spring 1920. Later Red Army staff and economic management work.

Bystriansky, Vadim A. (1886–1940). Party member from 1907, former student at St. Petersburg University. Arrested and exiled. Returned to St. Petersburg, 1917. Editor of *Petrogradskaia gazeta*, 1918. Later publishing and journalism work. One of the earliest proponents of the "from opposition to terror" reading of the Kirov murder. Late 1930s, head of the Leningrad Institute of Party History.

Chagin, Pyotr Ivanovich (b. 1898). Party member from 1918. Editor of the newspaper *Baku Worker* and secretary of the Azerbaijani Communist Party, 1922–1925. Editor of Leningrad newspaper *Red Gazette*, 1926–1929. Head of USSR Academy of Sciences publishing house, 1930–1931. Editor of newspaper *Star of the East* in Tbilisi, Georgia, 1931–1932. Later editorial work. Key proponent of and witness for the theory that Stalin masterminded Kirov's murder, 1956–1960.

Chertok. Chief of the Third Section of the Economic Security Department of the USSR NKVD. Interrogator in Kirov case, 1934–1935.

Chubar, Vlas Yakovlevich (1891–1939). Party member from 1907. Member of VSNKh Presidium, 1918–1923. Chairman of Ukrainian Sovnarkom, 1923–1934. Deputy Chairman of Sovnarkom and of Council on Labor and Defense, 1934–1938. Member of Ukrainian Politburo, 1921–1934. Candidate member of USSR Politburo, 1926–1935, full member from 1935. Repressed.

Chudov, Mikhail Semyonovich (1893–1937). Party member from 1913. Worker origin. Chairman of Tver Province soviet executive committee, 1920. Second secretary of Leningrad Region party committee, 1928–1936 (?). Member of TsK from 1925. Repressed.

Chugunov, Pavel Petrovich. Party member from 1905, worker origin. Imperial Army veteran. Member of Astrakhan soviet executive committee, commissar of Astrakhan, commander of Astrakhan garrison, 1919. Attempted to arrest Kirov in October 1919.

Dan, Fyodor (1871–1947). Early member of Russian Social Democratic Labor Party, sided with Mensheviks. Member of Petrograd soviet executive committee after February 1917 revolution. Prominent leader of Mensheviks in exile, first in Paris and later in New York.

Dan, Lidia. Wife of Fyodor Dan.

Danovich, Boris Zinovievich. Doctor in Leningrad NKVD clinic, involved in examination and treatment of Leonid Nikolaev for "hysteria" in hours after latter murdered Kirov. Later assigned to be on call for Nikolaev during his detention in December 1934. Testified on his experiences to KPK's Shatunovskaya commission, December 24, 1960.

Demichev, P. N. (b. 1918). Secretary of Moscow Region party committee, 1956–1958. First secretary in 1959. Secretary of the TsK, 1961–1974. USSR Minister of Culture, 1974–1986. Candidate member of Politburo, 1964–1988. Member of perestroika commission that investigated Kirov's murder.

Desov, Georgy Aleksandrovich. Chairman of Leningrad regional control commission in 1928–1929. Purged from Leningrad organization in 1929 with other Komarovites. Retaliated in fall 1929 with a denunciation of Kirov for working on "bourgeois" newspaper *Terek*. Monitored by OGPU in early 1930s for anti-Kirov, Komarovite connections under case file "Zanoza."

Dmitriev, D. M. Deputy chief of the NKVD GUGB Economic Security Department, 1934. Lead interrogator in the Kirov murder investigation of 1934–1935.

Drapkin (Drabkin, Driapkin), Grigory Ilich (b. 1897). Party member from 1931 In 1934 officer of the Third Section of the Secret Political Department of Leningrad NKVD. Forwarded Volkova's denunciation of the "Green Lamp" group to Georgy Petrov in summer 1934.

Draule, Milda Petrovna (1901–1935). Wife of Leonid Nikolaev. Probably daughter of an estate manager in Luga District. Party member from 1919. Worked in Luga District party apparatus until 1926, then moved to Leningrad. In late 1934 worked as inspector in the Personnel Section of the Leningrad branch, Commissariat of Heavy Industry. Arrested after Kirov's murder. Executed on March 10, 1935.

Draule, Olga Petrovna (d. 1935). Sister of Milda Draule. Married to Roman Kulisher. In 1934 employed at Vyborg Ward House of Culture, where she was a secretary of the party committee. Party member from 1925 (?). Executed in 1935.

Draule, Pyotr Petrovich. Younger brother of Milda Draule, Leonid Nikolaev's wife. Employee of Leningrad police department. Arrested in early 1934 for embezzling department funds, sentenced to three years forced labor.

Dureiko, Nikolai Maksimovich (b. 1906). Ukrainian peasant origin. Red Army service, 1928–1931. Candidate member of Communist Party from 1931. Officer of Smolny command. On third floor roving guard duty on afternoon of December 1, 1934.

Dzerzhinsky, Feliks Edmundovich (1877–1926). Party member from 1895. Head of the Cheka/GPU/OGPU, 1918–1926. Soviet Commissar of Internal Affairs, 1919–1923. Chairman of VSNKh, 1924–1926. Candidate member of Politburo, 1924–1926.

Efendiev, Sultan Medjid (Najmutdin) (1891–1937). Dagestan native, pre-revolutionary experience in Baku oil fields. Member of Azeri socialist party Hummet, then from 1917 a Bolshevik. In 1918 conducted Bolshevik propaganda among the Muslim population of Astrakhan. Plenipotentiary for Caucasian Affairs of Soviet Republic Commissariat of Foreign Affairs, 1919. Commissar of Internal Affairs and party chief in Dagestan. Then work in Baku organization, early 1920s. Possible source of materials for Zorich's 1926 feuilleton satirizing Kirov's wife's lifestyle, "Two Dogs." Supporter of Ordzhonikidze's and Kirov's centralization drive in the Caucasus and Azerbaijan in particular. Rival of Nariman Narimanov, the most prominent Azeri leader and opponent of Kirov and Ordzhonikidze.

Eikhe, R. I. (1890–1940). First secretary of the Siberian and West Siberian territorial committees, 1929–1937. Commissar of Agriculture, 1937–1938. Repressed.

Filholds, J. Latvian diplomat, stationed in Moscow in late 1934. Sent to Leningrad in late December to replace Georgs Bissenieks, who was expelled from the USSR, as Latvian consul.

Fomin, Fyodor Timofeevich (1899–1971). Party member from 1917. Scout in Imperial Army during World War I. Cheka work from 1918 in Ukraine. Chief of Cheka Special Department on Ukrainian and Tsaritsyn fronts during Civil War. Graduated from Soviet Military Academy in 1927. Stationed in Leningrad from 1930 as commander of border guards and NKVD troops. In April 1933 appointed second deputy of Filip Medved in Leningrad OGPU. Sentenced to two years of labor camp for neglect of duty at January 23, 1935 trial of Leningrad NKVD officers. Dispatched to Kolyma where worked in labor camp administration. Arrested in 1939, tortured, sentenced to eight years of hard labor. Sent deposition on Kirov murder to Frol Kozlov (Leningrad), March 26, 1956. Testified to Shatunovskaya commission in 1960–1961. Author of *Zapiski starogo chekista* (1962).

Frunze, Mikhail Vasilievich (1885–1925). Party member from before 1903. Key Red Army commander in the Russian Civil War. Replaced Leon Trotsky as Commissar of Military and Naval Affairs in early 1925. Died during an operation in October 1925.

Furtseva, Ye. A. (1910–1974). From 1942 secretary of Frunze Ward party organization in Moscow. First secretary of the Moscow city party committee, 1954–1957. Secretary of TsK, 1956–1960. Member of Presidium, 1957–1961. Member of TsK, 1956–1974. USSR Minister of Culture, 1960–1974.

Fyodorov. Officer of the central NKVD GUGB Special Political Department. Interrogator in Kirov case, 1934–1935.

Fyodorov, Grigory Fyodorovich (1891–1936). Party member from 1907. Member of Petrograd soviet executive committee, 1917. After October Revolution, Deputy Commissar of Labor. Party work in Nizhny Novgorod, Saratov, chief of Red Army's Thirteenth and Fourteenth Armies political departments during Civil War. Prominent official in Leningrad under Zinoviev until 1926, member of Leningrad Province party committee. Supporter of Zinovievite and United oppositions. Expelled from party in 1927, restored in 1928. Arrested and sentenced to six years of prison in the case of the "Leningrad Counterrevolutionary Zinovievite Group of Safarov, Zalutsky, and Others."

Gatuev, Dzakho. Poet published in *Terek*. Prerevolutionary acquaintance of Kirov's who published 1935 memoir of him.

Gertik, Artyom Moiseevich (1879–1936). Party member from 1902. Senior official in Leningrad under Zinoviev before 1926, member of Leningrad Province party committee. Arrested and sentenced to ten years of prison in the case of the "Leningrad Counterrevolutionary Zinovievite Group of Safarov, Zalutsky, and Others."

Gessen, Sergei Mikhailovich (1898–1936). Party member from 1916. Prominent official in Leningrad under Zinoviev before 1926. Arrested and sentenced to six years in prison in the case of the "Leningrad Counterrevolutionary Zinovievite Group of Safarov, Zalutsky, and Others."

Glebov-Avilov, Nikolai Pavlovich (1887–1942). Party member from 1904. Father was cobbler. Member of Petrograd committee of Russian Social Democratic Party, 1917. Member of first Sovnarkom, October 1917. Party work in Leningrad from 1922. In 1925 head of the city's council of labor unions. Supported Zinovievite opposition. Repressed and probably died in camps.

Glushkova, Anastasia. Sister of Irina Glushkova.

Glushkova, Irina. Chief matron at the Urzhum orphanage where Kirov lived from age seven.

Gordon, Nikolai. Party member from 1903. Leningrad official under Zinoviev—member of Leningrad Province party committee, head of the printers' labor union. Demoted as supporter of Zinovievite opposition. As editor of the *Red Gazette* "Chronicle" department in September 1929 led the newspaper's attacks on Komarovites in Leningrad. Wife, Maria Natanson, exiled from Leningrad in 1932 as "Trotskyite."

Gorin-Lundin, Aron Solomonovich (1900–1939). Born in Minsk, secondary education, party member from 1926. Cheka work from 1921. In Leningrad OGPU from 1925. Chief of Leningrad NKVD Special Political Department, 1934. Sentenced to two years of labor camp at January 23, 1935 trial of Leningrad NKVD officers for negligence. Sent to Kolyma. Arrested August 21, 1938 during business trip to Moscow. Sentenced to death on February 21, 1939.

Gorky, Maxim (1868–1936). In the late nineteenth and early twentieth centuries a journalist, fiction writer, and playwright of revolutionary sympathies. Broke with Bolsheviks following their seizure of power. Left the Soviet Republic in 1922 for exile in Italy. Returned in 1932 following major Soviet publicity campaign and virtually canonized as founder of Soviet literature.

Grammatikopoulos, G. N. Greek journalist present at the March 1938 show trial of Bukharin, Rykov, et al. Introduced the idea that Stalin might have ordered the assassination of Kirov into the Western press with the publication of his account of the show trial in *Socialist Herald* in early 1939.

Griunvald, Gerbert Yanovich (b. 1896). Latvian, worker origin. Red Army service, 1919–1923. Cheka/OGPU/NKVD work from 1921. Assigned to Leningrad NKVD Operations Department in October 1933. In late 1934 headed the plainclothes section (*neglasnaia okhrana*) of Kirov's guard. Ordered Nikolaev released after his detention on October 15, 1934.

Gubin, Aleksandr Antonovich (1893–1937). Party member from 1918, Cheka service from 1919. Leningrad NKVD Operations Department chief from June 1933. Sentenced to three years of labor camp at trial of Leningrad NKVD officers for negligence on January 23, 1935. Provided key testimony implicating Ivan Zaporozhets in murder of Kirov in 1937 before his execution.

Guzovsky. NKVD officer who guarded Nikolaev before his execution on December 29, 1934. Testified on Kirov murder in 1956 to KGB investigators.

Ignatov, N. G. (1901–1966). First secretary of Gorky (Nizhny Novgorod) regional party committee, 1955. Chairman of Russian Republic Soviet Presidium, 1959, 1962–1966. Deputy chairman of USSR Council of Ministers, 1960. Member of Presidium, 1957–1961.

Ilin, Ivan Pavlovich (1893–1937). Party member from 1918. Red Army soldier during Civil War. Commissar on submarine service, 1918–1925. Investigator for Leningrad Region party control commission, 1925–1929. Deputy director of party's Leningrad Region Commission for the Purge of the Soviet Apparatus, 1929–1931. Secretary of Pyotr Struppe during his tenure as chairman of the Leningrad Region executive committee, 1931–1937. Maria Volkova was nanny for his family in the early 1930s. Attempted to bring Volkova's denunciations of terrorist plot in Leningrad to the attention of authorities in the late summer and fall of 1934. Probably informed Stalin on December 2, 1934 of Volkova's denunciations and her confinement in a mental hospital. Arrested and executed, 1937.

Ingulov, Sergei. Head of TsK Department of Agitation and Propaganda Newspaper Section, 1928–1929, former Trotskyite. Later worked in publishing. Repressed 1938.

Irklis, Pyotr Andreevich (1887–1937). Party member from 1905. Chairman of Luga District (Leningrad Province) soviet executive committee in early 1920s. Promoted to Leningrad city party apparatus in late 1925 or early 1926. Zinovievite delegate to Fourteenth Party Congress (1925). Secretary of Leningrad Region party committee in early 1930s. Patron of Milda Draule, who worked in the Luga party apparatus until 1926. Arrested July 23, 1937, sentenced to death, September 9, 1937.

Ivanchenko, A. A. Worked with Kirov in Astrakhan in Civil War. Head of regional trade department of Leningrad regional and city soviets in 1934. One of first witnesses at murder scene after Kirov's death. After Filip Medved was arrested, his family lived with Ivanchenko briefly. Arrested 1937.

Ivanov, Karl Aleksandrovich (b. 1897). Native of Riga, Latvia. Leningrad NKVD Operations Department officer, 1934. Denounced A. D. Mikhalchenko in 1939 for supposedly ordering Nikolaev released after he was detained near Smolny before the murder of Kirov. On March 7, 1939 testified to three detentions of Nikolaev, denounced Kotomin, other Leningrad NKVD officers. Not on rolls of Kirov's guard in December 1934. On January 19, 1961 "confirmed testimony of May 26, 1938 and March 7, 1939" to Shatunovskaya commission.

Kaganovich, Lazar Moiseevich (1893–1991). Party member from 1911. Member of Saratov party committee, 1917. Commissar of All-Russian Collegium for the Organization of the Red Army, 1918. Chairman of Nizhny Novgorod Province party committee, 1918–1919. Member of TsK Turkestan bureau from 1920. TsK department head from 1922. Secretary of TsK, 1924–1925, 1928–1939. General secretary of Ukrainian Republic TsK, 1925–1928. First secretary of Moscow Region party committee, 1930–1935. Candidate member of Politburo, 1926–1930, full member 1930–1957. Close associate of Stalin, especially in late 1920s to mid-1930s. Expelled from party, 1962.

Kamenev, Lev Borisovich (1883–1936). Party member from 1901, in emigration 1908–1917. Chairman of All-Union Executive Committee, 1917. On Southern Front as representative of Council of Defense during Civil War. Member of Politburo, 1919–1925. Later work in publishing and diplomacy. Important leader of Zinovievite and United oppositions, 1925–1927. Expelled from Communist Party, 1927, readmitted 1928. Shot in 1936.

Kapitsa, Pyotr Leonidovich (1894–1984). Prominent Russian physicist who began his professional career in England after fleeing Russia during the Civil War. Detained while on visit to USSR in 1934 and forced to work there at the Institute for Physics Problems, founded for him. Kirov was peripherally involved in managing his detention.

Karakhan, L. M. (1889–1937). Party member from 1917. USSR representative in China, 1923–1926. From 1927 Deputy Commissar of Foreign Affairs for the Soviet Union. In late 1934 USSR ambassador to Turkey.

Karaulov, Mikhail. Duma deputy and Cossack leader dispatched by the Provisional Government in early spring 1917 to serve as Terek regional commissar. Led Cossacks against October Revolution. Native of the Terek region.

Katsafa, A. I. NKVD officer who guarded Nikolaev from December 2, 1934 until his execution on December 29. Relative of Israil Leplevsky. Concocted story of Nikolaev talking in his sleep about Ivan Kotolynov and Nikolai Shatsky. Testified to KGB and KPK investigators of Kirov murder in 1956 and 1960.

Kazarov, S. I. Owner of *Terek*, the newspaper in Vladikavkaz where Kirov was employed, 1909–1917.

Khanik, Lev Osipovich (1902–1934). Native of western Ukraine. Red Army service, 1918 to 1920 or 1921. Party member from 1920. Served in the Vyborg Ward Komsomol apparatus with Lev Nikolaev in the early 1920s. Received at least three party censures for drunkenness, lack of discipline, and conflicts at work. In 1933 he was chief of the Fellowship of Komsomol Militants at the History of Youth section of the Institute of Party History. Received a party reprimand in November 1933, probably in connection with his removal from the fellowship. At the time of his arrest Khanik was an *instruktor* for Industry and Transport in the Kronstadt District party committee. Tried and executed with Leonid Nikolaev in the case of the "Leningrad Center," December 1934.

Khrushchev, Nikita Sergeevich (1894–1971). Worked as a joiner before 1917, labor union activist. Party member from 1918. Red Army service in Civil War. First secretary of Moscow city party committee, second secretary of Moscow regional party committee, 1934–1935. First secretary of the Ukrainian party TsK, 1938–1947. Member of the Chairman of the Ukrainian Sovnarkom, 1944–1949. USSR TsK Politburo/

Presidium member, 1939–1964. Secretary of USSR TsK from 1947. First secretary of the USSR TsK, 1953–1964. Chairman of the USSR Council of Ministers, 1958–1964. Led the Soviet Union during the de-Stalinization efforts of the late 1950s and early 1960s. Removed from leadership, October 1964, and placed under house arrest.

Khrushchev, Sergei Nikitich. Son of Soviet leader Nikita Khrushchev, aerospace engineer. Helped father compose his memoirs.

Khviiuzov. Head of the Leningrad NKVD Operations Department Third Section. Involved in the chain of orders that sent Borisov to Smolny on December 2, 1934 (on which trip Borisov died). Arrested and then cleared in Borisov's death during 1934–1935 investigation. Rearrested June 11, 1937, shot September 20, 1937.

Kirchakov, Leonid Pavlovich (b. 1895). Onetime member of party TsK. Medical doctor. Employed by Commissariat of Food Industry, 1932–1937. Arrested 1937, sentenced to fifteen years of labor camp. Called to Moscow in February 1956 on initiative of Olga Shatunovskaya to give evidence in Kirov case. On February 10, 1956 submitted deposition to Frol Kozlov, head of Leningrad party organization, claiming to have heard in 1936–1937 from Yan Olsky that Filip Medved had insisted on his innocence in neglect case and that Nikolaev at his interrogation with Stalin had implicated central NKVD officers in Kirov murder. Submitted new deposition on Kirov murder to KPK on March 5, 1965.

Kirichenko, A. I. (1908–1975). First secretary of Odessa Region party committee, 1945–1949. Secretary of Ukrainian TsK, 1949–1957. Secretary of USSR TsK, 1957–1960. Member of TsK Presidium, 1955–1960. First secretary of the Rostov Region party committee, 1960. Retired 1962.

Klimov, G. Chief controller of the KPK, 1956–1967. Important participant in the Shatunovskaya investigation of the Kirov murder in 1960–1961 and later inquiries in the 1960s.

Kodatsky, Ivan Fyodorovich (1893–1937). Party member from 1914. Acquainted with Kirov from defense of Astrakhan in Civil War. Deputy chairman, then chairman of Leningrad Region Council on the Economy. Chairman of Leningrad soviet executive committee from 1930. Member of TsK, 1930–1937. Member of Leningrad Region party committee and secretary of same, early 1930s. Repressed.

Kogan, L. Chief of the Fourth Section of NKVD Special Political Department in December 1934. Interrogator in 1934–1935 investigation of the Kirov murder.

Komarov, Nikolai Pavlovich (1886–1937). Party member from 1909. Prerevolutionary member of Petrograd and Vyborg committees of Social Democratic Party, deputy to Petrograd soviet, 1918. Member of

All-Russian Central Executive Committee, 1918. Cheka service. Chairman of Leningrad soviet and Leningrad soviet executive committee, 1926–1929, member of Leningrad Province/Region and city party committees' leadership, 1926–1929. Commissar of Communal Properties, 1931–1937. Member of TsK, 1921–1934. Arrested June 1937, sentenced to death November 27, 1937.

Komarov, P. T. (1898–1983). First secretary of Vologda Region party committee, 1937–1943. First secretary of Saratov Region party committee, 1942–1948. Deputy chairman of KPK, 1952–1959. Retired 1959.

Kondratev, Ivan Ivanovich (b. 1887). Party member from 1905. Secretary of Leningrad Province soviet executive committee, 1926–1929. Purged from Leningrad party apparatus in fall 1929 attack on Komarovites, and transferred to Siberia.

Kononov, Osip. Student killed in Tomsk demonstration against Bloody Sunday, January 18, 1905.

Kopylovskaya, Raisa. Komsomol activist, Minsk, 1920. Married Filip Medved. Acquaintance of Mikhail Rosliakov and Dmitri Sorokin.

Korkin. Chief of the Sixth Section of the NKVD Special Political Department in 1934. Interrogator in 1934–1935 investigation of Kirov murder.

Korol. Latvian. Secretary of Central Ward party committee, head of committee's Organizational Department and member of Leningrad Region party control commission, 1929. Removed from both posts in purge of Komarovites, fall 1929. Returned to Leningrad in 1933. Monitored by OGPU in early 1930s (case file "Zanoza") for supposed anti-Kirov, anti-Stalin Komarovite comments, etc. Possibly the same "Korol" involved in Leonid Nikolaev's firing from the Leningrad Institute of Party History.

Korshunov, Yefim Konstantinovich. Secretary of Leningrad's Central Ward executive committee under Zinoviev, a former Zinovievite/ United oppositionist. In 1934 a student of the Leningrad Industrial Academy. In December 1934 "confessed" social connections with ex-Zinovievites Ivan Bakaev and Vladimir Levin. Arrested and sentenced to labor camp in the case of the "Leningrad Counterrevolutionary Zinovievite Group of Safarov, Zalutsky, and Others," January 1935.

Kosaryov, A. V. (1903–1939). First secretary of the Komsomol TsK, 1929–1939. Lead interrogator, along with Nikolai Yezhov, in the first ten days of the Kirov murder investigation. Repressed.

Kosior, Stanislav Vikentevich (1889–1939). Party member from 1907. Commissar of Finance of Ukrainian Soviet Republic, 1918. Underground work in Ukraine, 1918–1919. Secretary of Ukrainian TsK, 1919–1920. General secretary of Ukrainian TsK, 1928–1938. Politburo member from 1930. Arrested May 3, 1938, sentenced to death February 26, 1939.

Kostrikov, Miron Ivanovich. Father of S. M. Kirov.

Kostrikova, Anna (b. 1883). Older sister of S. M. Kirov.

Kostrikova, Melania Avdeevna. Paternal grandmother of S. M. Kirov.

Kostrikova, Yekaterina Kuzminichna. Mother of S. M. Kirov.

Kostrikova, Yelizaveta (b. 1889). Younger sister of S. M. Kirov.

Kotolynov, Ivan Ivanovich (1905–1934). Worker origin, from Vyborg Ward in Leningrad (father was tailor). Party member from 1921. Early to mid-1920s—member of Vyborg Ward Komsomol committee, Leningrad Region Komsomol committee, USSR Komsomol TsK. Supporter of Zinovievite and United oppositions. Expelled from party in 1927 and readmitted in 1929 after publicly recanting his "mistakes." In 1934 he was in his final year of studies at the Leningrad Industrial Institute. Tried and executed with Leonid Nikolaev in the "Leningrad Center" case, December 1934.

Kotomin, Mikhail Ivanovich (1891–1943). Communist Party member from 1918, Cheka service from 1921. In 1934 officer of Leningrad Region NKVD Operations Department, chief of Kirov's personal guard (Fourth Subdepartment of Operations Department). Worker origin, born in St. Petersburg. "Red Guard" and Red Army service during revolution and Civil War. Promoted to chief of Kirov's guard, September 1933. Detained after Kirov murder and tried with eleven other Leningrad NKVD officers for neglect of duty, January 23, 1935. Sentenced to three years of labor camp in Far East. As of May 1939 was officer in Far Eastern labor camp system. Returned to Leningrad in 1940, worked in Kirov (formerly Putilov) factory in foundry workshop. Applied for readmission to party, February 2, 1941, but rejected by KPK, which confirmed his negligence in guarding Kirov. Evacuated with family to Cheliabinsk during siege of Leningrad. Died December 1943 of natural causes.

Kozlov, Frol R. (1908–1965). First secretary of Leningrad city party committee from 1950. First secretary of Leningrad regional party committee, 1953–1957. Chairman of Soviet of Ministers (Sovmin), 1957–1958. First deputy chairman of Sovmin, 1958–1960. TsK secretary for defense matters, 1960–1964. Member of TsK Presidium, 1957–1964. Gathered materials implicating Stalin in Kirov's assassination in Leningrad in spring 1956. Following the Shatunovskaya commission report of January 1961 rejected these materials.

Kriuchkov, Vladimir Aleksandrovich (1924–2007). Party member from 1944. Diplomatic and TsK work, until joined KGB in 1967. Headed KGB Foreign Operations Department, 1974–1988. Chairman of KGB,

1988–1991. Member of Politburo, 1989–1990. Participated in coup attempt against Mikhail Gorbachev in August 1991. Member of the perestroika era commission that investigated the Kirov murder.

Krivitsky, Walter (1899–1941). Born in Polish part of Russian Empire. Officer of Red Army military intelligence from Civil War years. On undercover foreign assignments in Europe for much of 1920s and 1930s. Defected while operating in the Netherlands, October 1937. Published in the Menshevik *Socialist Herald* in Paris in 1938. Emigrated to the United States in late 1938. Published articles in the *Saturday Evening Post* and the book *In Stalin's Secret Service* (1939). Died in a Washington, D.C., hotel on February 10, 1941, probably a suicide, although it has also been speculated that Soviet agents may have killed him.

Krupskaya, Nadezhda Konstantinovna (1869–1939). Lenin's wife, member of party from 1898. Head of Main Directorate of Political Education (Glavpolitprosvet), 1920. From 1929 deputy director, Commissariat of Enlightenment. Supporter of Zinovievite opposition in 1925.

Krutov, Grigory Matveevich. NKVD officer, constructed case in spring 1939 against various Leningrad NKVD officers for supposed criminal neglect in guarding Kirov and possible complicity in his murder. Evidently using torture, Krutov extracted testimony from Leningrad NKVD officers Karl Ivanov, Karl Pauzer, and others of multiple detentions of Nikolaev under various different circumstances. Assigned to Leningrad NKVD guard officers case on February 23, 1939. Completed case on April 25, 1939. Case eventually thrown out on technical grounds.

Krylenko, Nikolai Vasilevich (1885–1938). Party member from 1904. Member of Petrograd Military Revolutionary Committee, 1917. Member of collegium of Soviet Republic's Commissariat of Justice, 1918. Member of TsKK, 1927–1934. USSR Commissar of Justice, 1931–1936. Author of 1927 proposal for summary trials of "terrorists" that served as a model for Stalin's "Law of December 1" in 1934. Repressed.

Kudelli, Praskovya Frantsevna (1859–1944). Party member from 1903. Active revolutionary before 1917. From 1917 employed at Institute of Party History in Petrograd/Leningrad. Head editor of journal *Red Chronicle* (*Krasnaia letopis'*). Delegate to Seventeenth Party Congress, where she made negative comments about Stalin and was forced to return home early by Kirov.

Kuibyshev, Valerian V. (1888–1935). Party member from 1904. Head of Samara Bolshevik organization, 1917. Member of Revvoensovet of Southern Group of Red Army's Eastern Front, other posts during Civil War. Participant in defense of Astrakhan. Chairman of VSNKh, 1926–1930. Chairman of Gosplan, 1930–1934. Deputy chairman of Sovnarkom and the Council on Labor and Defense, 1930–1935.

Kuklin, Aleksandr Sergeevich (1876–1936). Party member from 1903. Party work in Petrograd after 1917. Member of Leningrad Province party committee, 1925, and participant in Zinovievite opposition. Arrested and tried in "Moscow Center" trial, January 1935. Later shot.

Kulesh, Olberto (Alberto?) Kazimirovich. Party member from 1937. In 1934 worked in Leningrad NKVD Secret Political Department under L. V. Kogan. Assigned to type copy of Nikolaev's address book, evening of December 1, 1934. Testified to Shatunovskaya commission on November 30, 1960.

Kulisher, Roman Markovich (1903–1935). In 1934 husband of Olga Draule (sister of Milda, Leonid Nikolaev's wife). Red Army service in Civil War. Party member from 1923, but expelled three times (1924, 1927, 1929). In 1929 expelled without right of return as "a degenerate element alien to the party" after abandoning a young Komsomol woman pregnant by him. Employed in Leningrad party propaganda apparatus for some time. In 1934 chief of the Planning Department of the Leningrad Stamp Trust. Intelligentsia origin (father was a doctor).

Kulnev, Pyotr Grigorevich. Leningrad NKVD Operations Department officer, 1934. Member of Kirov's guard until November 1934. Testified to one detention of Nikolaev to Shatunovskaya commission, November 30, 1960.

Kuzin, Vasily Mikhailovich (b. 1908). Komsomol member from 1928, candidate member of party from 1932. Professional driver in Red Army units, 1930–1933. In 1934 driver for Leningrad NKVD Communications Department. Drove the truck in which Kirov's guard Mikhail Borisov died on December 2, 1934. Testified in December 1934 that Borisov died in accident. Changed testimony in 1937 under torture, claiming the Borisov was murdered. Testified in 1956 and 1961 that Borisov was murdered, although his evidence differed substantially between these dates.

Kuznetsov, Aleksei Aleksandrovich (1905–1950). Worker origin. Party member from 1925. Komsomol work in Novgorod and Leningrad Provinces/Regions, 1924–1932. From 1932 *instruktor*, later department head in Leningrad Region party apparatus, secretary of ward party committee. Hero of defense of Leningrad in World War II. First secretary of Leningrad Region party committee, 1945–1946. Secretary of TsK and head of the TsK Directorate of Cadres, 1946–1949. Purged by Stalin and Malenkov during "Leningrad Affair" of 1949–1950 and executed.

Lampe, Eduard Fyodorovich (b. 1890, d. 1950/51 in tram accident). Chief of Leningrad NKVD Operations Department until June 1933, replaced by Gubin. Ivan Baskakov reported him as "energetic and loyal" but alcoholic. In early 1924 headed Secret Section of Criminal Investigative Department of Soviet Republic's Commissariat of Internal Affairs.

Lang, Georgy Fyodorovich (1875–1948). Cardiologist, Kirov's personal doctor in 1934.

Larina, Anna Mikhailovna (1914–1996). Wife of Nikolai Bukharin from 1934. Imprisoned in labor camps, 1938. In exile until 1959. Memorized Bukharin's final "Testament" and recited it to KPK officials in early 1960s.

Lashevich, M. M. (1884–1928). Party member from 1901. From 1925 Deputy Commissar for Military and Naval Affairs. Candidate member of TsK in 1925–1926. Excluded from party in 1927 as Trotskyite. Readmitted to party in 1928.

Laziukov, Pyotr Pavlovich. Officer of Kirov's guard at time of murder. Assigned to guard Kirov on trips around Leningrad and its outskirts. OGPU work from September 21, 1931. Worked in Kirov's guard from March 1934.

Lazurkina, Dora Abramovna (1884–1974). Party member from 1902. Headed Department of Preschooling in Commissariat of Enlightenment, 1918–1922. *Instruktor* in Petrograd/Leningrad city party apparatus, member of the regional and city party committees. Arrested 1937, rehabilitated 1955.

Lentsmanis, Yan (Latvian Jan Lencmanis). Member of Latvian Social Democratic Party before 1917. Sided with the Bolsheviks. Employed in the Comintern apparatus in 1934. Because he was an old contact of Latvian consul to Leningrad Georgs Bissenieks, the USSR NKVD used him in attempt to recruit and/or threaten Bissenieks in December 1934.

Leplevsky, Israil M. (1894–1938). Chief of OGPU Special Department (counterespionage, foreign espionage) from late 1931. From February 20, 1933 simultaneously deputy chief of Ukrainian GPU. Repressed.

Lermolo, Elizabeth. Pseudonymous Soviet émigré who published *Face of a Victim* (1956) about her experiences in the Soviet prison system.

Levin, N. Kirov's lawyer at his 1912 trial on charges of setting up an illegal printing press in Tomsk.

Levin, Vladimir Solomonovich (1897–1934). Party member from 1917. Red Army service, 1918–1926. At time of separation from army was chief of the Political Department of the Leningrad Fortified Region. Apparently removed from army for support of Zinovievite and United oppositions. Expelled from party, 1927, and later readmitted. Fired from pharmacy job, June 1927, and eventually reassigned to Luga. Returned to Leningrad in 1928. Mobilized by party in winter 1932–1933 for work on livestock requisitions. In December 1934 was chairman of the residential cooperative of the Leningrad Residential Rental Trust. Tried and executed with Leonid Nikolaev in the case of the "Leningrad Center."

Levine, Isaac Don (1892–1981). Born in Kiev, emigrated to the United States with his family as a child. Journalist for Hearst newspapers, traveled extensively in the USSR in the 1920s. Author of a number of books on Stalin. Publisher of anti-Communist journal *Plain Talk* in the 1940s. Ghost writer for Walter Krivitsky's articles in the *Saturday Evening Post* in 1939.

Lidak, Otto Avgustovich (1891–1937). Party member from 1911. Underground work in Orenburg, Baku during Civil War. *Instruktor* of Commissariat of Internal Affairs in Moscow from 1919. Student in History Department of Institute of Red Professors, 1924–1928. Sent by TsK to work in Leningrad. Director of Vorovsky Communist Institute of Journalism in Leningrad, 1931–1933. From January 1933 to 1935 director of Leningrad Institute of Party History. Fired Leonid Nikolaev, April 1934. Repressed.

Lioninok, Mikhail Dmitrievich (b. 1896). *Instruktor* in the Leningrad city party committee apparatus in late 1934. Eyewitness to moments after Kirov's murder.

Litvinov, Maksim Maksimovich (1876–1951). Party member from 1898. USSR Commissar of Foreign Affairs, 1930–1939.

Liushkov, Genrikh (1900–1945). Born Odessa, son of a Jewish tailor. Underground activist during German occupation of Ukraine. Party member from 1917 or 1918. Political officer in Red Army units, 1919, graduate of Ukrainian Soviet Republic's Political Training School in Kiev, 1919. Cheka work from 1920, including espionage in Germany. From 1933 deputy director of OGPU/NKVD Secret Political Department. Chief of the Azov–Black Sea Territory NKVD, 1936. Commander of NKVD in Far Eastern Territory from summer 1937. Defected to Japan, June 1938. One of lead interrogators in the Kirov murder investigation of 1934–1935 and in preparations for the August 1936 show trial of Zinoviev, Kamenev, et al.

Lobov, Prokopy Maksimovich (b. 1898). Party member from 1918. Chief of the Third Section, Special Department, Leningrad NKVD in 1934, and aide to the Special Department chief (Zaporozhets). Sentenced to two years of labor camp at trial of Leningrad NKVD officers for neglect of duty on January 23, 1935. Sent to Kolyma in Far East. Murdered Grigory Sokolnikov, his cellmate, in 1939 on orders from Lavrenty Beria. From 1956 to 1961 provided often contradictory testimony on Kirov murder tending to implicate Zaporozhets, Yagoda, and ultimately Stalin.

Lobov, Semyon Semyonovich (1888–1937). Party member from 1913.

Factory worker. Member of Petrograd party committee, 1917. Member of VSNKh Presidium, 1924–1930. USSR Deputy Commissar of Supply from 1930. Commissar of Lumber Industry, 1932–1936. Repressed.

Lominadze, V. V. (1897–1935). Party member from 1917. Member of Comintern Executive Committee Presidium, 1925–1929. Demoted from TsK member to candidate member in December 1930 for private criticisms of collectivization. Secretary of Transcaucasian territorial party committee from 1930. Suicide, 1935.

Makarov, N. I. Officer of the Leningrad NKVD Secret Political Department in 1934. Delivered "Svoiak" and other case files on former oppositionists in Leningrad to Stalin on December 2, 1934. Testified in 1956 to KGB investigators and in 1961 to the Shatunovskaya commission that there was no information on Nikolaev in Leningrad NKVD files on ex-oppositionists.

Maksimov, N. S. Secretary of Leningrad NKVD Operations Department in 1934, arrested June 5, 1937. Testified under torture that Ivan Zaporozhets and Operations Department chief Gubin ordered Borisov killed on December 2, 1937.

Malenkov, Georgy Maksimilianovich (1902–1988). Secretary of TsK, 1939–1946, 1948–1953. Chief of TsK Directorate for Cadres, 1939–1946. Chairman of USSR Council of Ministers, 1953–1955. Member of Politburo/Presidium, 1946–1957. Demoted to hydroelectric plant director after failure of Molotov group to remove Khrushchev from power in 1957. Retired in 1961.

Malin, V. N. (1906–1982). Secretary of Belorussian Republic TsK, 1939–1947. Secretary of Leningrad city party committee, 1949–1952. Chief of the General Affairs Department (*obshchii otdel*) of TsK, 1954–1965. Rector of USSR Academy of Social Sciences, 1965–1970.

Malinin, Pavel Ivanovich (1900–?). Worker origin. Red Army service as political education officer (*politruk*), 1922–1924. Party member from 1929. Officer of Leningrad OGPU/NKVD, 1927–1934. While stationed at Smolny Ward office of the NKVD was in contact with Maria Volkova (1934). Also mentioned by Elizabeth Lermolo in *Face of a Victim*. Survived to give evidence to investigative commissions in early 1960s.

Maly, Dmitry Zinovievich (1904–1937). Party member from 1928. Worker. Plenipotentiary officer of Leningrad NKVD Operations Department, 1927–1937. One of the officers who escorted Kirov's bodyguard Mikhail Borisov on the trip to Smolny in which he died, December 2, 1934. Executed 1937.

Mamushin, Sergei Aleksandrovich (1888–1966). Graduated from medical school in Saratov. Party member from 1918. Red Army doctor, 1917–1918. Head of county health department in Saratov, later Piatigorsk. Headed Leningrad NKVD medical section, 1929–1936. Involved in autopsy of Mikhail Borisov, examination of Leonid Nikolaev after the Kirov murder, and commitment of Maria Volkova to a psychiatric hospital in October 1934. Repressed but survived. Provided multiple and conflicting depositions on the question of Borisov's death, 1954–1964.

Mandelshtam, Sergei Osipovich (1896–1934). Native of Riga. Party member from 1917. He was a worker at the Putilov factory before the revolution. Red Army service in Civil War, returned to Putilov upon demobilization. Transferred from Leningrad to work in Arkhangelsk in early 1926 for supporting Zinoviev. Expelled from party, 1928. Readmitted and allowed to return to Leningrad in 1929. At time of arrest Mandelshtam was the director of "organizational planning" for a trust in Leningrad (Gipromez). Tried and executed with Leonid Nikolaev in the case of the "Leningrad Center."

Mariinsky, A. P. *Instruktor* in TsK Department of Agitation and Propaganda, 1929. Involved in investigating Komarovite suppression of criticism (*samokritika*) and instigating *Pravda*'s and *Red Gazette*'s attack on the Komarovites that led to their purging in Leningrad, fall 1929.

Markus, Maria Lvovna (1882–1940). Kirov's wife from 1912.

Markus, Rakhil Lvovna (d. 1959). Sister of Maria Lvovna Markus, Kirov's wife. Doctor.

Markus, Sofia Lvovna. Sister of Kirov's wife Maria Lvovna. Prerevolutionary underground Social Democratic activist. Strong advocate of stories linking Stalin to Kirov's murder late in the Khrushchev era.

Markus, Yakov Lvovich. Brother of Kirov's wife Maria Lvovna Markus, underground Social Democratic activist. Served on the Terek soviet's executive committee in spring 1917 with Kirov. Commissar of Enlightenment in the Terek Republic. Killed by the Whites in 1919.

Martov, Yuly. Prominent in the prerevolutionary Social Democratic Party, leading Menshevik.

Mavromati, Spiridon. Student exiled to Urzhum from St. Petersburg. Leader of secret revolutionary study circle that Kirov joined in 1903.

Mdvani, Polikarp ("Budu") Gurgenovich (1877–1937). Party member from 1903. Member of Eleventh Army Revvoensovet, 1918–1920. Member of Communist Party Caucasian Bureau, 1920–1921. Chairman of Georgian Revolutionary Committee, member of Presidium of Georgian Communist Party TsK, 1921–1923. After 1923 work on foreign concessions. Excluded from party as Trotskyite, 1928. Readmitted, 1931. Commissar of Light Industry, 1931–1936.

Medved, Filip Demianovich (1889–1937). Party member from 1907. Originally a worker. Member of Cheka collegium, chairman of Tula Cheka, chairman of Leningrad Cheka, chief of Soviet Republic's concentration camp system, 1918–1920. Deputy chief of Moscow Cheka, 1921–1923. OGPU plenipotentiary in Western Territory and chief of Cheka in Belarus, 1924–1925. OGPU plenipotentiary in Far Eastern Territory, 1926–1929. Head of Leningrad Region OGPU/NKVD, 1930–1934. Following the Kirov murder arrested and sentenced to labor camp in Far East for neglect of duty. While serving sentence chief of Southern Mining Industry Section of Far Eastern Construction Conglomerate (Dalstroi). Rearrested in Kirov case, September 1937 and executed in November 1937.

Mekhanoshin, Konstantin Aleksandrovich (1889–1942). Party member from 1913. Representative on Petrograd Soviet of Workers' and Peasants' Deputies. Member of the Revvoensovet of the Red Army's Southern Front and later Eleventh Army, 1918–1919. Later work in Gosplan and higher education.

Menzhinsky, Viacheslav Rudolfovich (1874–1934). Child of professor in Petersburg. Completed law education. Party member from 1902. Deputy Commissar of Finance, 1917–1918. Deputy Commissar of Ukrainian Workers' and Peasants' Inspectorate and member of collegium of Ukrainian Cheka, 1919. From 1919, member of RSFSR Cheka Presidium. Chief of Cheka Special Department, 1920–1922. Head of GPU Secret Operational Department, 1922–1924. Chief of OGPU, 1926–1934.

Meshchersky, Vasily Yegorovich (b. 1888). Worker origin. Party member from 1912. Served in Red Guard and Red Army during Civil War. In 1934 *instruktor* on the Smolny Ward party committee. Member of the ward committee party troika that heard on or about May 5, 1934 Nikolaev's appeal of his expulsion from the party and firing. Arrested and charged with "Trotskyite activity" during the Great Terror.

Messing, Stanislav Adamovich (1889–1937). Party member from 1907. Chairman of Sokolniki Ward Committee Cheka in Moscow, 1918. Member of Moscow Cheka collegium, 1918–1919. Chairman of Moscow Cheka, 1921. Chairman of Petrograd Cheka, 1921–1929. Transferred from Leningrad OGPU in late 1929. From 1931 removed from OGPU and sent to foreign trade and diplomatic work.

Miasnikian (Miasnikov), Aleksandr Fyodorovich (1886–1925). Party member from 1906. Veteran of Imperial Army. Commander of Red Army Western Front, 1917–1918. Senior posts in Bolshevik government of Belorussia, 1918–1919. Chairman of Armenian Sovnarkom, 1921. Member of Presidium of Transcaucasus Territorial Committee of the Communist Party, 1922–1925.

Miasnikov, Nikolai Petrovich (1900–1934). Native of Syzran, Volga Region. Party member from 1917. Ten years service in Red Army from revolutionary era forward. Stationed in Siberia. Supporter of United Opposition. Expelled from party in 1927, and readmitted. In December 1934 was deputy chief of the Leningrad soviet's personnel department (*orgotdel*). Tried and executed with Leonid Nikolaev in the trial of the "Leningrad Center," December 1934.

Mikhalchenko-Mikhalsky, Aleksandr Dmitrievich (b. 1899, identified in text as "Mikhalchenko"). Poor peasant origin, Ukrainian nationality. Security police work from 1927, party member from 1930. Assigned to Leningrad NKVD Operations Department, 1934. Deputy commander of NKVD Smolny guard on December 1, 1934. Senior NKVD officer on duty in Smolny at time of Kirov's murder. Gave testimony in Kirov murder case, December 4, 1934. Continued as deputy commandant of Smolny. Resigned on grounds of nervous illness, July 23, 1937. Gave depositions on Kirov murder to KPK investigatory commission (Shatunovskaya commission) on November 25, 1960, January 17, 1961, January 19, 1961. Mikhalchenko's early 1960s testimony accords well with archival documents from 1934 and early 1960s testimony of other Leningrad NKVD officers not "contaminated" by 1937–1939 "Terror" testimony.

Mikoyan, Anastas Ivanovich (1895–1978). Bolshevik leader in Baku during Civil War. Secretary of the North Caucasus territorial party committee, 1924–1926. Commissar of Domestic and International Trade, 1926–1930. Commissar of Supply, 1930–1934. Commissar of Foodstuffs Industry, 1934–1938. Deputy Director of Sovnarkom and associated posts, 1938–1946. Deputy Director of Council of Ministers (formerly Sovnarkom), 1946–1955. Candidate member of Politburo, 1926–1935, full member, 1935–1966.

Mironov, Lev Grigorevich (1895–1938). Father was Tsarist bureaucrat. Graduated from *gimnazium*, spent three years at Kiev University. Chairman of Cheka in Piriatin, Poltava Province, 1918–1919, and also deputy director of Communist Revolutionary Committee there. Political work in Red Army, Deputy Commissar of Justice for the Turkestan Autonomous Republic, 1919–1924. In OGPU/NKVD work from 1924. OGPU plenipotentiary in Central Asia, 1930–1931. Chief of the Economic Security Department of the NKVD in 1934. One of the lead interrogators in the Kirov murder investigation, 1934–1935. Executed in 1938.

Mirzoian, Levon Isaevich (1897–1939). Party member from 1917. Participant in Civil War in Caucasus region. Secretary of Azerbaijani TsK, 1925–1929. First secretary of Kazakh Communist Party, 1933–1937. Close to Kirov from the early 1920s when they worked together in Baku. Repressed.

Mitiaev, Ivan Ignatevich. Party member from 1937. Testified to Shatunov-skaya commission on December 12, 1960 that he heard from Aleksei Sevastianov in July 1956, who heard from Kirov in 1934, that Kirov had told Stalin of a secret move by some TsK members to replace Stalin with him (Kirov) as general secretary of the TsK.

Molchanov, Georgy Andreevich (1897–1937). Party member from 1917. Served in Red Army intelligence on Eastern Front, 1918–1919. Chairman of Grozny Province Cheka, 1919–1921. Chief of Cheka Special Operations Directorate and deputy director of Caucasus Cheka, 1921–1922. Chief of OGPU for Ivanovo-Voznesensk Province/Region, 1925–1931. Head of OGPU/NKVD Special Political Department, 1931–1936. Arrested March 1937, executed October 9, 1937.

Molochnikov, A. L. Chief of the Economic Security Department of the Leningrad NKVD in late 1934. Interrogated various witnesses in the Kirov murder on the evening of December 1, 1934. Later interrogated himself by central NKVD officers and Nikolai Yezhov.

Molotov, Viacheslav Mikhailovich (1890–1986). Party member from 1907. Member of Petrograd "Bolshevik Group," 1915–1917. Member of Petrograd Voenrevkom (Military Revolutionary Council), October, 1917. Chairman of Nizhny Novgorod soviet executive committee, 1919. Secretary of TsK from 1920. Member of TsK, 1921–1957. Member of Politburo/Presidium of TsK, 1926–1956. Close associate of Stalin. Excluded from party 1962.

Mosevich, Andrei Andreevich (1903–1954). Party membership and OGPU service from 1927. Deputy director of Special Political Department of Leningrad NKVD under Gorin-Lundin in 1934. Sentenced to two years labor camp at January 23, 1935 trial of Leningrad NKVD officers and dispatched to Kolyma. Worked at Kolyma camps until 1951.

Moskvin, Ivan Mikhailovich (1890–1937/1938). Party member from 1911. Chief of Petrograd Province party committee personnel department (*orgotdel*), 1921–1923. Promoted to TsK's Northwest Territory Bureau personnel department, 1923. Head of TsK personnel department (*raspredotdel*), 1926–1930. Repressed.

Munters, Vilhelms (1898–1967). Native of Riga. Latvian Deputy Minister (and de facto Minister) of Foreign Affairs in 1934. Head diplomat for Latvia in negotiations on allowing a "Soviet garrison" there, 1939–1940. Arrested 1941, freed 1954. During Soviet era worked in Latvian Academy of Sciences as translator.

Nagli, Vladimir Naumovich. Eyewitness to scene on third floor of Smolny around time of Kirov murder. Deputy director of State Drama Theater in Leningrad. Party member from 1921. Seventh Red Army command staff duty, 1919–1921.

Nakhaev, A. S. (1903–1935). Graduate of Leningrad Artillery School, 1925. Party member 1927–1928, resigned due to sympathy for opposition. Worked in Moscow and Odessa, 1928–1933, after discharge from army. Instructor at the Moscow Institute of Physical Fitness and chief of staff of the Moscow civil defense authority's artillery division. Executed after attempt to incite mutiny at division barracks in August 1934.

Narimanov, Nariman (1871–1925). Party member from 1905. Doctor. Leader of Hummet, a socialist party of Azeris allied with the Bolsheviks, 1917–1918. Participant in defense of Astrakhan, 1919. Deputy Commissar of Nationalities from summer 1919. Chairman of Azerbaijan Revolutionary Committee, chairman of Azerbaijani Council of People's Commissars, member of Soviet TsK Caucasian Bureau, 1920–1923. Then to work in Moscow.

Natanson, Maria. Wife of Nikolai Gordon, former Zinovievite official in Leningrad. Exiled from Leningrad in early 1930s as "Trotskyite." Social contact of Ivan Kotolynov up to 1931.

Naumov, Ivan Kuprianovich (b. 1895). Party member from 1913. Senior official in Leningrad under Zinoviev until 1925–member of Leningrad Province party committee bureau, head of the party committee's Department of Agitation and Propaganda. Supporter of Zinovievite and United oppositions. Sentenced to labor camp in January 1935 in case of the "Leningrad Counterrevolutionary Zinovievite Group of Safarov, Zalutsky, and Others."

Nikitin, Ivan Klementevich. Commander of NKVD Smolny guard in late 1934. Not on duty at time of Kirov's murder. According to A. D. Mikhalchenko involved in decision in 1933 to move Kirov's residence from apartment at 26/28 Krasnykh Zor Street to separate home on Krestovsky Island. Died in Siberia on NKVD service, 1941 or 1942.

Nikolaev, Pyotr Adolfovich (sometimes "Aleksandrovich"—apparently his paternity was uncertain) (1911–1935?). Half-brother of Leonid Nikolaev. Milling machine operator at Russian Diesel factory. Komsomol member in 1930, but soon quit. Repeatedly absent without leave from his Red Army unit in during 1934, and arrested on December 1–2. Ultimately executed in Kirov assassination case.

Nikolaeva, Anna Vasilevna. *See* Pantiukhina, Anna Vasilevna.

Nikolaeva, Maria Tikhonovna (b. 1870). Mother of Leonid Nikolaev. Worked for decades before 1934 as cleaner of trams at city tram park. Also mother of Yekaterina Nikolaeva (later Rogacheva), Anna Nikolaeva (later Pantiukhina), and, by a different father, Pyotr Nikolaev.

Nikolaeva, Yekaterina. *See* Rogacheva, Yekaterina.

Nicolaevsky, Boris (1887–1966). Native of Ufa. Attended *gimnazium* in Samara. Sympathizer of Social Democratic Labor Party from 1903.

First arrest in 1904. Supported the Bolsheviks, 1904–1905, and later the Mensheviks. Active revolutionary with multiple arrests, 1904–1917. Editorial board of Menshevik *Rabochaya gazeta* and member of Petrograd soviet executive committee, 1917. Worked for Mensheviks inside new Soviet Republic, 1918–1921. Imprisoned by Bolsheviks, 1921–1922, then exiled. Active Menshevik, journalist and archivist in Berlin, 1922–1933, Paris, 1933–1940, then in the United States. Author of the "Letter of an Old Bolshevik," published in the Menshevik *Socialist Herald* in 1937, *Power and the Soviet Elite* (1965) and many other works.

Nikolenko, Fyodor Romanovich (1899–1940). Non–party member, native of Kherson in Ukraine. Higher education, radiologist by profession. Detained on night of March 24/25, 1932 for loitering at bus stop outside Kirov's apartment building. Search found that he was carrying a loaded Nagan. Claimed that he was planning to commit suicide due to end of his marriage and suffering from ulcers. Charged with plotting to shoot Kirov, sentenced to five years of concentration camp by OGPU collegium circuit court, June 19, 1932. Executed 1940.

Nikonov. Acquaintance of Kirov's from Urzhum. Accompanied him to Tomsk in 1904.

Olsky, Yan Kalikstovich (1898–1937). Gentry origin. Member of party from 1917. Work in military counterintelligence from 1919 in Special Department on Red Army Western Front. Chairman of Belarus Cheka, 1920–1923. In 1930 chief of OGPU Special Department (foreign espionage/counterintelligence). After opposing fabrication of cases against Red Army officers in "Vesna" (1931), transferred from OGPU work to Commissariat of Food Industry. Repressed.

Orakhelashvili, Mamia Dmitrievich. (1881–1937). Party member from 1903, graduate of Military Medical Academy (1908). Chairman of the Vladikavkaz Bolshevik party committee with Kirov in 1917 and member of the Caucasus territorial party committee, 1917–1920. Chairman/secretary of Georgian Communist Party during 1920s. Secretary of the Transcaucasus Soviet Republic territorial party committee, 1926–1930. Editorial staff of *Pravda,* 1930. Central Committee member, 1927–1934. Deputy Director of the Marx-Engels-Lenin Institute, 1932–1937. Repressed.

Orlov, Alexander (1895–1973). Imperial Army service during World War I and Red Army service in the Civil War. Border guard service and Soviet law school, 1921–1924. Officer of OGPU Foreign Department with undercover missions in Western Europe, United States, 1926–1936. Soviet advisor to Spanish Republican government, August 1936–July 1938. Defected to the United States. Author of *The Secret History of Stalin's Crimes* (1954).

Ordzhonikidze, Grigory Konstantinovich (1886–1937). Social Democratic Party member from 1903. Member of Petrograd Bolshevik party committee in 1917. Chairman of North Caucasus Council of Defense, 1918–1919, member of various Red Army military revolutionary councils, 1919–1920. Prominent leader of Bolshevik reconquest of North Caucasus, 1920. From 1920 member of the Caucasus Bureau of the Communist Party. First secretary of the Transcaucasian territorial and North Caucasus territorial party committees, 1922–1926. Chairman of TsKK, 1926–1930. Chairman of USSR VSNKh, 1930. Commissar of Heavy Industry, 1932–1937. Candidate member of Politburo, 1926–1930, full member, 1930–1937. Committed suicide.

Osherov, N. S. Head of Leningrad Workers' and Peasants' Inspectorate in 1933–1934. Hired Leonid Nikolaev as price inspector in August 1932.

Pankratiev. Employee of Leningrad NKVD Department of Communications and Transport (*otdel sviazei*), whose mother lived in the same building with Leonid Nikolaev. In a December 9, 1934 interrogation, Nikolaev claimed to know of him, but never to have met him.

Pantiukhina, Anna Vasilievna (b. 1907). Younger sister of Leonid Nikolaev. Arrested in Kuznetsk, early December 1934, and sent to Leningrad for interrogation. Interrogated on December 17, 1934 and January 9, 1935. Sentenced to five years of labor camp in January 1935 in case of the "Leningrad Counterrevolutionary Zinovievite Group of Safarov, Zalutsky, and Others." Released from labor camp in 1947 but exiled to Yakutsk in Siberia. As of 1964 resided in Magadan Region.

Pauker, Karl Viktorovich (1893–1937). Born in Austrian Empire. Barber from 1906 to 1914. Served in Austrian Army during World War I, then a POW in Russia. Party member from 1917. Head of Secret Operations Department of Samara Cheka, 1918–1919. Student at Communist Academy, 1919–1920. Cheka/OGPU investigator, 1920–1922. Deputy director, then director of central OGPU/NKVD Operations Department, 1922–1937. Monitored Kirov's bodyguard from fall of 1933, probably on Stalin's orders. Arrested on April 21, 1937. Sentenced to death on August 14, 1937.

Pauzer, Karl Mikhailovich (b. 1892). Leningrad NKVD Operations Department officer in late 1934, not a party member. On December 5, 1934 testified to one detention of Nikolaev on December 5, 1934. On March 13, 1939 testified to two detentions of Nikolaev. Testified that Mikhalchenko freed Nikolaev after one of these. On January 11, 1961 testified to Shatunovskaya commission, again to two detentions. Falsely claimed that he had submitted written reports on "both" detentions.

Pelshe, Arvids (1899–1983). Party member from 1915. Cheka work, 1918, Red Army political commissar, 1919–1929. Graduate student and later professor of history, Moscow, 1929–1940. Secretary of Latvian Republic TsK, 1941–1959, first secretary, 1959–1966. Member of TsK, 1961–1983. Member of Politburo, 1966–1983. Chairman of the KPK from 1966.

Pervukhin, M. G. (1904–1978). Commissar/Minister of Electrical Industry, 1939–1940, 1953–1954. First deputy chairman of Council of Ministers, 1955–1957. Chairman of State Committee on Foreign Trade, 1957–1958. Soviet ambassador to East Germany, 1958–1963. Member of USSR Presidium, 1952–1957.

Peshkov, Maksim. Son of Maxim Gorky, died 1935. Peshkov's wife was reportedly Yagoda's mistress.

Petrov, Georgy Alekseevich (b. 1904). Party member from 1929. OGPU work from 1932. In 1934 an officer of Leningrad NKVD's Special Department. Chief "handler" of compulsive denouncer Maria Volkova in the fall of 1934. Sentenced to three years of labor camp at trial of Leningrad NKVD officers for negligence on January 23, 1935. Freed from Sevvostlag labor camp on June 30, 1938. Transferred to road construction management in Moscow, 1941. Filed multiple petitions for rehabilitation. Provided key evidence on Maria Volkova to KGB and party investigators, 1956–1961.

Petrovsky, Leonid Petrovich. Son of Pyotr Petrovsky. Historian and journalist.

Petrovsky, P. P. Cheka work from 1921. Assigned to Leningrad NKVD Operations Department in 1933. Transferred out of Leningrad to clerical work at NKVD labor camp in Central Asia, February 1935. Testified to Shatunovskaya commission on December 1 and 23, 1960.

Petrovsky, Pyotr Grigorevich. Son of prominent Social Democrat and Bolshevik Grigory Ivanovich Petrovsky, chairman of Ukrainian Central Executive Committee, 1919–1938. Editor of *Leningradskaya pravda,* 1928 (fired in mid-October). Vocal supporter of "Right Deviation."

Petrovsky, V. Chief of the First Section of the Special Political Department, central NKVD GUGB. Interrogator in Kirov case, 1934–1935.

Piatakov, G. L. (1890–1937). Party member from 1910. Deputy chairman of VSNKh in 1923. Trotsky supporter. Chairman of State Bank directorate, 1929–1930. Deputy Commissar of Heavy Industry, 1931–1936. Convicted in January 1937 Moscow show trial and executed.

Piotrovsky, P. A. Leningrad NKVD Operations Department officer and party member, late 1934. Assigned to guard Kirov on trips around Leningrad and its outskirts.

Platoch, Seliverst Alekseevich (b. 1905). Member of Communist Party in late 1934. Electrician at Smolny. Eyewitness to the moments before and after the Kirov murder on the third floor of Smolny. Helped detain Leonid Nikolaev.

Pokhvalin. *Instruktor* in the Leningrad city party committee organization. Handled Nikolaev's appeal of his case to the TsKK and TsK in fall 1934.

Polner, V. F. Prominent citizen of Kirov's hometown of Urzhum, board member on Society of Charity that sponsored Kirov's education.

Ponomarenko. Officer of the Baltic fleet NKVD Special Department. Leonid Nikolaev was acquainted with him from work together in the Leningrad Region "Down with Illiteracy!" Society (*Obshchestvo "Doloi negramotnosti!"*) in 1931–1932. Nikolaev visited his apartment once, in 1932, and had no contact with him after that.

Popov, Georgy. Former Petrograd Zinovievite on editorial board of the Fellowship of Komsomol Militants in 1933–1934. Editor of *The Petrograd Komsomol in the Civil War* (1934).

Popov, Mikhail. Member of Tomsk Social Democratic organization in 1905–1906, friend of Kirov throughout the prerevolutionary years.

Pospelov, Pyotr N. (1898–1979). Party member from 1916. Member of TsKK, 1930–1934, KPK, 1934–1939. Editor of *Pravda,* 1940–1949. Director of Marx-Engels-Lenin Institute, 1949–1952, 1961–1967. Secretary of TsK, 1953–1960.

Postyshev, Pavel Petrovich (1887–1939). Party member from 1904. TsK secretary, 1930–1934. Candidate member of Politburo, 1934–1938. Second secretary of Ukrainian TsK, first secretary of Kiev Region and later Kharkov Region party committee, 1933–1937. Arrested on February 21, 1938, sentenced to death February 26, 1939.

Pozern, Boris Pavlovich (1882–1939). Party member from 1902. Member of Minsk soviet presidium, 1917. Commissar of Northern Front during Civil War. Secretary of TsK Northwest Bureau, 1922–1923. Member of TsKK, 1923–1930. Leningrad regional party committee member, 1929–1938. Rector of Leningrad University.

Pramnek, Ye. K. (1899–1938). Second secretary of Gorky (Nizhny Novgorod) Region party committee, 1930–1934. First secretary, 1934–1937, replacing A. A. Zhdanov, who was transferred to Moscow.

Purishkevich, Vladimir. Prerevolutionary Duma deputy, anti-Semitic monarchist, associated with the "Black Hundreds" gangs of right-wing thugs.

Pylaev, Georgy Nikolaevich (1894–1939). Party member from 1912. Peasant origin. Member of TsKK, 1923–1924. Headed Leningrad branch of Commissariat of Heavy Industry, where Milda Draule was employed, 1934.

Radek, Karl (1885–1939). Party member from 1903. Also member of

Polish and German Social Democratic parties in early 1900s. Member of TsK, 1919–1924. Expelled from party as Trotskyite in 1927, but readmitted. Member of *Izvestia* editorial board, rector of Chinese Workers' University, Moscow, 1925–1927. Murdered in prison on orders of Lavrenty Beria.

Raevsky, Aleksandr Sergeevich. Teacher of Kirov at Urzhum Municipal School, active in the 1905 revolution. Author of a letter of recommendation for Kirov.

Ratnek, Karl Karlovich. Party member from 1910. Belorussian delegate to Seventeenth Party Congress. Testified to KPK, probably in 1961, on question of votes against Stalin at the congress.

Redens, Stanislav Frantsevich (1892–1940). Party member from 1914. OGPU plenipotentiary in Belarus, 1931, Chairman of Ukrainian GPU, 1932–1933. OGPU plenipotentiary in Moscow Region from 1933. Arrested November 1938. Executed.

Rekstin, Ivan Petrovich (b. 1881). Latvian. Party member from 1903. Imprisoned by Tsarist regime, 1907–1917. Member of Leningrad Region party control commission, 1929. Komarovite who came under attack in fall 1929 purge of Leningrad organization. Monitored by OGPU in early 1930s as Stalin/Kirov opponent in case file "Zanoza."

Riutin, Martemian Nikitich (1890–1937). Party member from 1914. Secretary of Irkutsk Province party committee, 1921–1922, secretary of Dagestan Region party committee, 1923. Secretary of Krasnopresnensk Ward party committee in Moscow, 1925–1928. Candidate member of TsK, 1927–1930. Member of Presidium of VSNKh, 1930. Supporter of "Right Deviation" who refused to recant and was expelled from party, 1930. Co-author in early 1934 of secret "Riutin Platform" criticizing Stalin's domination of the Communist Party. Sentenced to prison, executed in 1937.

Rogacheva, Yekaterina Vasilevna (1899–1938). Older sister of Leonid Nikolaev. Party member from 1928. In 1934 employed by Leningrad Green Space Trust. Arrested after murder and sentenced to five years of hard labor in January 1935 in the case of the "Leningrad Counterrevolutionary Zinovievite Group of Safarov, Zalutsky, and Others." Shot in 1938.

Rosliakov, Mikhail Vasilevich (1897–1985). Party member from 1918. *Gimnazium* and medical school graduate, veteran of Imperial Army. From 1925 employed in Leningrad Council on the Economy, Planning Department. Deputy director of Leningrad Region planning apparatus, 1926–1934. Member of Leningrad Region party and city committees. After Kirov's murder dispatched to work in Gorky (formerly Nizhny Novgorod). Arrested in 1937. Rehabilitated in 1956. Author of an important memoir of Kirov's assassination, published posthumously (*Ubiistvo Kirova,* 1991).

Rozit, Dav Petrovich (1895–1937). Party member from 1917. Vocal Rightist at TsK/TsKK plenums in 1929. Arrested and executed, 1937. Rehabilitated 1965.

Rudenko, R. A. (1907–1981). Chief prosecutor of Lugansk Region, Ukraine, promoted to assistant prosecutor of the Ukrainian SSR, 1942. Head prosecutor of Ukrainian SSR, 1944–1953. Head USSR prosecutor during the Nuremburg war crimes trials. Head prosecutor of the USSR, 1953–1981. Khrushchev client early in his career.

Rumiantsev, Vladimir Vasilevich (1902–1934). Party member from 1920. Head of the Leningrad Komsomol under Zinoviev in 1925. Supporter of Zinovievite and United oppositions. Expelled from the party 1927/1928 and readmitted, October 1928, after publicly renouncing his views. Returned to work in Leningrad in 1930, remaining under OGPU surveillance. That same year dispatched to work on construction of new steel manufacturing complex at Magnitogorsk, and returned again to Leningrad. Two orders for arrest apparently issued by OGPU/NKVD in 1933–1934 and blocked by Kirov. Chairman of Vyborg Ward soviet, Leningrad, April–December 1934.

Rykov, Aleksei Ivanovich (1881–1938). Party member from 1898. Deputy chair of Moscow soviet presidium, 1917. Commissar of Internal Affairs in first Soviet government. Chairman of VSNKh, 1918–1921, 1923–1924. Politburo member 1922–1930. Leader of "Right Deviation." Sentenced to death at March 1938 Moscow show trial.

Saburov, M. Z. (1900–1977). First deputy chairman of the Council of Ministers, 1955–1957. Member of the TsK, 1952–1961, member of the Presidium, 1952–1957. Chairman of the State Economic Commission of the USSR, 1955–1957. Director of Syzran Heavy Machine Building Factory, 1958–1962. Retired 1966.

Safarov, Georgy Ivanovich (1891–1942). Party member from 1908. Member of Petersburg Social Democratic Labor Party Committee, 1917. Member of Turkestan Bureau of TsK and head of the Eastern Department of the Comintern from 1921. Editor of *Leningradskaya pravda* and secretary of Smolny Ward party committee in Leningrad, 1922–1925. Supporter of Zinovievite and United oppositions. Expelled from party in 1927 and readmitted in 1928. Repressed and apparently died in the camps.

Saks, Sergei Yevgenevich (1889–1938). Party member from 1917, veteran of Imperial Army. Member of the Revvoensovet of the Red Army Caspian-Caucasus Front and commander of the Red Astrakhan-Caspian naval squadron, 1918–1919.

Samartsev, Alexander. Boyhood friend and neighbor of Kirov.

Semichastny, V. E. (1924–2001). First secretary of Ukrainian Komsomol, 1947–1950. Secretary of USSR Komsomol TsK, 1950–1958. First secretary from 1958. Chairman of the KGB, 1961–1967.

Serdiuk, Zinovy T. (1903–1982). Member of TsK of Ukrainian Republic, 1938–1954. First secretary of Lvov (today Lviv) Region party committee, 1952–1954. First secretary of Moldavian Republic TsK, 1954–1961. From 1961 first deputy chairman of the KPK.

Serebrennikov, Ivan Fyodorovich. Underground revolutionary comrade of Kirov's in Tomsk, married to Nadezhda Serebrennikova. Kirov followed the couple to Vladikavkaz in 1909, and visited them in Moscow in 1912.

Serebrennikova, Nadezhda Germogenevna. Underground revolutionary comrade of Kirov's in Tomsk, 1905–1906. Kirov followed her and her husband to Vladikavkaz in 1909 and later visited them in Moscow (1912). Probably a romantic interest of Kirov's.

Serge, Victor (1890–1947). Russian anarchist/socialist author born in Belgium to political exiles. Communist Party member, 1919–1928. Worked in Comintern and Grigory Zinoviev's secretariat, 1919–1923. Assigned to work in Germany, 1923–1925. Resident in Leningrad, 1925–1933. Persecuted as active supporter of the Left, Zinovievite, and United oppositions. Arrested 1933. Released and expelled from the USSR, 1936.

Serov, Ivan Aleksandrovich (1905–1990). Graduate of Leningrad Military School, 1928. Red Army artillery officer. Student of Frunze Military Academy, 1935–1939. February 1939, chief of USSR NKVD police (regular, not secret). July 1939, head of the GUGB Secret Political Department. Participant in execution of Polish POWs in Katyn Forest, 1940. Candidate member of TsK, 1941. Deputy director of NKVD with various posts, 1941–1954. NKVD plenipotentiary to First Belorussian Front of Red Army, late World War II. Deputy director of USSR regular police, 1947. Chairman of the KGB, 1954–1958. Chief of Red Army military intelligence (GRU), 1958–1962. Excluded from party, 1965.

Sevastianov, Aleksei Timofeevich (1897–1956). Party member from 1917 (1919?). Fought in defense of Astrakhan with Kirov during Civil War. Apparently friendly with Kirov's wife Maria Lvovna Markus and her sister Sofia Lvovna Markus. Arrested October 10, 1939, acquitted December 29, 1939. In late 1960 cited by Ivan Mitiaev to Shatunovskaya commission as source of story that Kirov had been approached at Seventeenth Party Congress by regional party secretaries to replace Stalin.

Shatskin, L. A. (1902–1937). Party member from 1917. Member of TsKK, 1927–1930. Involved in heavy Left attacks on Right Deviationists in the Komsomol organ *Komsomolskaya pravda*, summer 1929, to Stalin's annoyance. Repressed.

Shatsky, Nikolai Nikolaevich (1899–1934). Worker origin. Graduated from Leningrad Mechanical Institute. Komsomol member from 1917, Red Guard and Red Army service during revolution and Civil War. Party member, 1923–1927. Member of Vyborg Ward party committee. Expelled from party in 1927 for distributing Trotskyite literature. Later employed at tractor factory in Cheliabinsk. Returned to Leningrad in the winter of 1933–1934. Unable to hold a job there due to oppositionist record. Tried and executed with Nikolaev in the "Leningrad Center" case, December 1934.

Shatunovskaya, Olga (1901–1990). Member of party from 1916. Party activist during revolutionary era in Baku. Party work in Baku and in Briansk, Siberia. Head of department on Bailovo Bibi-Eibatsk Ward party committee in Baku, 1927–1929. Anti-Right activist in Baku, 1929, played part in pushing Levon Mirzoian out as chief of the Azerbaijani party organization. Transferred from Baku to study at Institute of Marxism-Leninism, October 1929, then party work in Moscow. Acting chief of Moscow Party Committee's Department of Leading Party Organs when arrested, November 1937 on charges of Trotskyism. Released 1945 following petition from Anastas Mikoyan but exiled to Krasnoiarsk, 1948. Rehabilitated 1954. Work in KPK, 1955–1962. Spearheaded investigatory commission into Kirov murder, winter 1960–1961. Member of a second investigatory commission formed in May 1961. Retired, 1962. Published articles and sent petitions to Central Committee arguing that Stalin ordered Kirov's murder, 1988–1990.

Shaumian, Lev Stepanovich (1904–1971). Son of Stepan Shaumian. Unofficially adopted son of Anastas Mikoyan. Journalist. As editor of *Great Soviet Encyclopedia* in 1955 did research on the Great Terror for Mikoyan.

Shaumian, Stepan (1878–1918). Active member of the Russian Social Democratic Labor Party from early 1900s, participant in Baku strikes of 1905–1907. Translated the *Communist Manifesto* into Armenian. Chairman of the Baku soviet in 1917–1918 and leader of the Baku Bolsheviks and the Baku Commune of 1918. Executed by White forces along with the other "Twenty-Six Baku Commissars" in September 1918.

Sheboldaev, B. P. (1895–1937). Secretary of North Caucasus Territory party organization, 1931–1934. Secretary of the Azov–Black Sea Territory party committee, 1934–1937. Repressed.

Sheinin, L. P. Investigator for the USSR Prosecutor's Office for High Priority Cases, 1934. Testified to USSR prosecutorial investigators in 1956. Author.

Shelepin, A. N. (1918–1994). First secretary of the Komsomol TsK, 1952–1958. Chairman of the KGB, 1958–1961. Secretary of the TsK, 1961–1967. Chairman of the Committee on Party-State Control (successor to the TsKK and KPK), 1962–1965. Member of Presidium/Politburo, 1964–1975.

Shepilov, Dmitry T. (1905–1995). Graduate of Moscow University law school, 1926. Work in TsK agricultural management apparatus and teaching duties, 1935–1941. Political commissar during World War II. From 1947 in the TsK Directorate of Agitation and Propaganda, rising to chief of the directorate. Chief editor of *Pravda,* 1952–1956. Secretary of TsK, 1955–1956. USSR Minister of Foreign Affairs, 1956–1957. Demoted to archival work after failure of Molotov group to remove Khrushchev from power in 1957. Retired 1982.

Shliapnikov, Aleksandr Gavrilovich (1885–1937). Party member from 1901. Commissar of Labor in Soviet Republic, October 1917. Chairman of the Red Army Caspian-Caucasian Front's Military Revolutionary Committee, 1918–1919. Member of TsK 1921–1922. Leader of Workers' Opposition, 1920–1922. Repressed.

Shpilev, G. Member of Tomsk Social Democratic organization in 1905–1906, author of a brief memoir of Kirov (1935).

Shvernik, Nikolai Mikhailovich (1888–1970). Party member from 1905. Member of TsKK, 1923–1925. Secretary of Leningrad Province party committee and TsK's Northwest Territory Bureau, 1925–1926. First secretary of All-Union Central Council of Labor Unions, 1930–1944. Member of TsK, 1925–1970. Chairman of KPK, 1956–1966. Key player in TsK defeat of Zinovievite opposition in Leningrad, 1925–1926, and in de-Stalinization.

Sisiaev, Ivan Petrovich (b. 1874). Party member from 1920. Worked in Putilov factory in Petersburg before 1914. Later, following some higher education, did bank work before 1917. Served in Rabkrin and Soviet banking system. Provided official recommendation for Leonid Nikolaev's entrance into party in 1924.

Skrynnnikov, N. P. Prominent leader of the Vladikavkaz Menshevik organization in 1917–1918. Opponent and sometime ally of Kirov in political maneuvering of the time.

Skvortsov-Stepanov, Ivan Ivanovich (1870–1926). Party member from 1896. From 1918 work at *Pravda.* Member of All-Union Executive Committee (VTsIK). Member of TsK, 1925–1926. Editor of *Leningradskaya pravda* briefly in early 1926.

Smirnov, Ivan Nikitich (1881–1936). Party member from 1899. Member of Military Revolutionary Council of Red Army's Eastern Front in Civil War, 1918–1920. Secretary of Petrograd Province party committee, early 1920s. Deputy chairman of VSNKh, 1922–1923. Commissar of Posts and Telegraphs, 1923–1927. Expelled from party and exiled from European Russia, 1927. Readmitted to party following "repentance," 1930. Following discovery of his correspondence with Trotsky's son Lev Sedov in Berlin (1933) arrested and expelled from party. Sentenced to five years prison. Executed August 1936.

Smorodin, Pyotr Ivanovich (1897–1939). Party member from 1917. Worker. Regimental commissar in Red Army, 1918–1922. Secretary of Petrograd Komsomol committee, 1920–1921. Secretary of Komsomol TsK, 1921–1924. Head of Vasilevsky Ward (Leningrad) party committee personnel department (*orgotdel*), then ward committee secretary, 1928–1929. First secretary of Vyborg Ward party committee, 1929–1936. First secretary of Moscow Ward party committee (Leningrad), 1936–1937. First secretary of Stalingrad Region party committee, 1937–1938. Repressed.

Snegov, Aleksei I. Bolshevik veteran of Civil War and revolution. Worked in Baku and Ukraine in 1920s, 1930s, a contact of Mikoyan's Baku group and Khrushchev. Arrested and sentenced to labor camp, 1938. Rehabilitated in 1954 and put in charge of the labor camp system under the Ministry of Internal Affairs. Strong advocate of de-Stalinization throughout the 1960s.

Sokolnikov, Grigory Yakovlevich (1888–1939). Party member from 1905, in emigration, 1909–1917. Menshevik before 1917. Russian Republic Commissar of Finance, 1922–1926. Leading member of Zinovievite and United oppositions. Excluded from party in 1927, readmitted and excluded again in 1936. Diplomatic work in early 1930s. Arrested January 1937. Murdered in jail on orders of Lavrenty Beria, May 1939.

Sokolov, Georgy Vasilevich (1904–1934). Komsomol activist in Vyborg Ward, early 1920s. No official record of oppositional activity. In 1934 was student at Naval Academy in Leningrad. Also worked as a physical education instructor. Tried and executed with Leonid Nikolaev in case of the "Leningrad Center," December 1934.

Sorokin, Dmitri Borisovich (b. 1901). Native of Tula, son of fitter. Factory work from age fourteen. Party member from 1918. Work in Tula Cheka, 1918–1919. Political work with Red Army Southern Front, 1919–1920. Cheka/GPU/OGPU officer to 1926. *Referent* in Molotov's secretariat, 1926–1937. Married to Filip Medved's sister, 1920. Adopted Filip Medved's daughter Viola after Medved executed. After 1937 demoted, went three years without work. From 1956 to 1966 wrote multiple declarations and depositions to TsK, TsK investigatory commissions on the Kirov murder, Stalin's possible role in it, and Medved's reaction to it.

Sositsky, Lev Ilich (1899–1934). Arrested and executed with Leonid Nikolaev in the trial of the "Leningrad Center," December 1934. Native of Leningrad. Party member from 1919. Nine years of Red Army service beginning in Civil War. At time of separation from army was commissar of the Fifty-Eighth Rifle Regiment. Signatory to oppositional "Platform of the Thirteen" and "Platform of the 83." Expelled from party, 1927, later readmitted. Director of Leningrad soviet auto repair workshops at time of arrest.

Sosnovsky. Deputy chief of the GUGB NKVD Special Department (*Osobyi otdel*) in 1934. Interrogator in 1934–1935 investigation of the Kirov murder.

Stasova, Yelena Dmitrievna (1873–1966). Key organizer of Communist Party Central Committee secretariat in 1917. Central Committee secretary, 1917–1920. Largely involved in Comintern work after 1920.

Stetsky, Aleksei (or possibly Aleksandr) Ivanovich (1896–1938). Party member from 1915, student of Petersburg Polytechnical Institute. Underground work in Germany, early 1920s. Graduate of Red Army Military Academy. Editor of *Komsomol'skaia pravda*, 1925. Head of Department of Press, Agitation, and Propaganda for TsK Northwest Bureau and Leningrad Province/Region, 1926–1929. Initial supporter of "Right Deviation," 1928. Head of TsK Agitprop Department, 1930–1938. Repressed.

Straumit, Yana Martynovna. Party member from 1912. Delegate to Thirteenth, Fifteenth, and Sixteenth Party Congresses. Delegate to Seventeenth Party Congress (1934) from East Siberian territorial party committee, Irkutsk city party committee. Testified on January 5, 1961 on question of votes against Stalin at Seventeenth Party Congress.

Stromin. Deputy Chief of the Special Political Department of the Leningrad NKVD, December 1934. Interrogator throughout 1934–1935 investigation of Kirov murder.

Struppe, Pyotr Ivanovich (1889–1938). Party member from 1907. Member of Samara Revvoensovet during Civil War. Secretary of Kirgiz Territory party committee in Orenburg. From 1923 work in Pskov Province party committee. From April 1926 secretary of TsK Northwest Bureau. Secretary of Vyborg Ward party committee in Leningrad, 1927–1930 (?). Secretary of Leningrad Region party committee, 1931–1934/1935. Chairman of Leningrad Region soviet executive committee 1932–1934/1935. Candidate member of TsKK from 1930. From 1936 headed Sverdlovsk state farm apparatus. Repressed.

Sudoplatov, Pavel (1907–1996). Cheka work from 1921, Ukrainian GPU Secret Political Department from 1927. Central OGPU/NKVD from 1933. Assignments under cover abroad, including 1938 assassination of Ukrainian nationalist Yevhen Konovalets in Rotterdam. Chief of NKVD foreign operations from 1939. NKVD/MVD Bureau for Special Tasks (sabotage behind enemy lines in World War II, sabotage abroad), 1941–1953, with interruptions. Claims to have supervised the plot to assassinate Trotsky in 1940. Headed suppression of Ukrainian nationalist guerrillas in early 1950s. Sentenced to fifteen years of prison upon fall of Lavrenty Beria in 1953. Released in 1968. Published autobiography, *Special Tasks*, in 1994.

Sudoplatova (née Kaganova), Emma. (1905?–1988). Wife of Pavel Sudoplatov. Graduate of *gimnazium*. Undercover work for OGPU in Odessa German community. In 1934 she worked in the NKVD Secret Political Department in the section supervising the Bolshoi Theater and the Leningrad Ballet. Following Kirov's assassination Sudoplatova apparently had a part in composing the "Don Juan" list of Kirov's possible lovers at both institutions.

Sundstrem, Liudmila Gustavovna. Sister-in-law of V. F. Polner, Kirov's landlady in Kazan, apparently mother of a daughter by Kirov.

Suslov, Mikhail A. (1902–1982). Poor peasant origin. Komsomol member from 1918, party member from 1921. Graduated from Plekhanov Economics Institute, 1928. From 1931 inspector in the party TsKK. First secretary of Ordzhonikidze (Stavropol) Territory party organization, 1939–1944. Secretary of TsK, 1947–1982. Editor of *Pravda*, 1949–1951. Member of Politburo/Presidium, 1952–1982, with short break in 1953. Khrushchev supporter early in de-Stalinization, but prime mover in his overthrow in 1964.

Svanidze, Maria Anisimovna (1889–1942). Wife of Aleksandr Svanidze, who was the brother of Yekaterina Svanidze (d. 1907), Stalin's first wife. Opera singer in Tbilisi, early 1920s. Executed 1942.

Sverdlov, Yakov (1885–1919). Party member from 1902, Bolshevik. Imprisoned or in internal exile, 1906–1917. Member of Bolshevik TsK, Petrograd, 1917. Head of Soviet Republic's Central Executive Committee, October 1917–March 1919. Died of influenza.

Sveshnikov, Nikolai Fyodorovich (1888–1969). Party member from 1907. Petrograd Cheka from February 1919. Chief of Administration Department (*Obshchii otdel*) of Leningrad provincial/regional party committee, 1920–1934. Student at Industrial Academy in Moscow, 1935–1938. Section head of Military Department of Commissariat of Machine Building, 1938–1939. Officer of Commissariat of Machine Building Inspectorate, 1939–1940. May 1940 to retirement, director of Red Shock Worker factory.

Tereshchenko, Nikolai Yefimovich. Reportedly head of Kirov's uniformed guards. Denied knowing Nikolaev at all in March 1939 interrogations.

Tolmachev, V. N. (1886–1937). Russian Republic Commissar of Internal Affairs, 1928–1930, Head of Sovnarkom's Main Directorate of Road Transport, 1931. Expelled from the party and sentenced to labor camp for private remarks critical of collectivization, 1932.

Tolmazov, Andrei Ilich (1899–1934). Party member from 1919. Red Army service in Civil War. Under Zinoviev in Leningrad he was first secretary of the Vyborg Ward Komsomol organization, and a secretary in the Leningrad Province Komsomol TsK. As a delegate to the Fourteenth Party Congress, December 1925, he supported the Zinovievite Opposition. Posted out of Leningrad in punishment. Allowed to return to city after issuing statement of "repentance." Appointed deputy director of Worker Provisioning at Red Putilov factory by Kirov in April 1934. Tried and executed together with Leonid Nikolaev in the case of the "Leningrad Center," December 1934.

Tomsky, Mikhail Pavlovich (1880–1936). Party member from 1904. Member of Moscow committee of party from 1909. Chairman of All-Union Council of Labor Unions (VTsSPS), 1918–1919, 1922–1929. Member of Politburo, 1922–1930. One of the leaders of the "Right Deviation," 1928–1929. Director of OGIZ (state publishing house), 1932–1936. Suicide.

Trotsky, Leon Davidovich (1879–1940). Participant in Social Democratic movement from 1897. Leaned towards Menshevik faction. Key leader of 1905 revolution in St. Petersburg. In emigration, 1907–1917. Joined Bolsheviks. Key organizer of Red Army during Civil War. Chairman of Soviet Revvoensovet, 1918–1925. Member of Politburo, 1919–1926. Leader of Left and United oppositions, expelled from USSR in 1929. Assassinated in Mexico on Stalin's orders.

Tseitlin, Ye. V. (b. 1898). Party member from 1918. Member of Presidium of Comintern Executive Committee, member of *Pravda* editorial board, 1926–1928. Member of Rightist "Bukharin School." Deputy director of Technical Propaganda (the director was Nikolai Bukharin) for the Commissariat of Heavy Industry, 1931–1933. Repressed.

Tsinit, Avgust Andreevich (1898–1954). In 1934 chairman of party troika of Smolny Ward party committee. On or about May 5, 1934 the troika heard Nikolaev's appeal of his firing from the Institute of History and expulsion from the party. The troika representatives restored Nikolaev to the party but confirmed his firing. In 1937 Tsinit was arrested as "enemy of the people." Sentenced to eight years hard labor on September 1, 1939 for "counterrevolutionary Trotskyite activity." Rearrested on same accusation in October 1949 and exiled to Krasnoiarsk Territory.

Tsukerman, Mikhail Yefimovich (b. 1886, St. Petersburg.) Director of Leningrad State Circus at time of Kirov murder. Before revolution worked as printer. Party member from 1918. One of earliest witnesses on murder scene after shooting.

Turygin, I. Ya. Terek region Bolshevik in 1917. Served on Terek soviet's executive committee with Kirov in spring 1917.

Tyshkevich, Vladimir Yakovlevich. Leningrad Operations Department officer, 1934. Testified to two detentions of Nikolaev in 1937 and early 1960s.

Ugarov, A. I. (1900–1939). Party member from 1918. Completed university. Served in Red Army, 1919–1921. On Moscow's Krasnopresnensk Ward party committee, 1921–1922. Study at Institute of Red Professors, 1922–1925. Trip abroad to United States, Western Europe, 1925–1926. Sent to work in Leningrad by TsK, first as head of the regional party committee's Department of Agitation and Party Work, then head of the Department of Culture and Propaganda. From December 1929 head editor of *Leningradskaya pravda*. Secretary of Leningrad city party committee, 1932–1934, second secretary, 1934–1936. Important aide to Kirov in early 1930s. In early 1930s member of Leningrad Region party committee bureau, and Leningrad soviet executive committee. Candidate member of TsK, 1934–1937, full member, 1937. Repressed.

Ugarov, F. Ya. Head of Leningrad Region labor union council, 1928–1929, supporter of "Right Deviation."

Uglanov, Nikolai Aleksandrovich (1886–1937). Party member from 1907. Secretary of the Petrograd Province party committee, 1921. Secretary of Nizhnyi Novgorod Province party committee, 1922–1924. Secretary of Moscow provincial and city party committees, 1924–1928. Commissar of Labor, 1928–1930. Candidate member of Politburo, 1926–1929. One of the leaders of the "Right Deviation," 1928–1929.

Ulrikh, V. V. In 1934 chairman of the Military Collegium of the USSR Supreme Court. Presided over trials of the Leningrad and Moscow "Centers" in December 1934–January 1935.

Ulmanis, Karlis (1877–1942). Participant in Russian revolution of 1905. In exile in United States, returned to Russian Empire in 1913 upon declaration of an amnesty by Tsar Nicholas II. First prime minister of independent Latvia, 1918–1921. In 1920s and early 1930s headed the conservative Agrarian Union Party. Led coup on May 15, 1934 that established an authoritarian regime. Arrested by the Soviets in July 1941, died of dysentery in 1942 while in prison.

Uritsky, Moisei Solomonovich (1873–1918). Menshevik revolutionary. Joined the Bolsheviks in 1917. Head of Petrograd Cheka, with brief break, in 1918. Assassinated by former military cadet, August 30, 1918.

Utkin, Nikolai Alekseevich (b. 1907?). Native of Leningrad. Party member from 1929. In late 1934 secretary to deputy secretary of Leningrad city party committee Kasparov. On third floor of Smolny at time of Kirov's murder.

Vasilenko, Matvei Ivanovich (1888–1937). Imperial Army staff captain. Red Army from 1919. Commander of Eleventh Army, December 1919–March 1920. Party member from 1932.

Vasiliev, Grigory Grigorevich (b. 1876). Supply clerk in the Leningrad regional party committee apparatus at Smolny, late 1934. Father was apartment doorman/supervisor (*dvornik*). Served in Imperial Army, 1916–1917, and in Red Army in Civil War. In Smolny apparatus as clerk from 1922. Party member from 1924. Eyewitness to situation on third floor of Smolny around time of Kirov murder.

Verkhovykh, Vasily Mefoldovich. Moscow delegate to the Seventeenth Party Congress (1934). Veteran of the congress's Electoral Commission who testified in November 1960 that there were 123 or 125 votes against Stalin in the balloting for the Central Committee.

Viksin, Simon Ottovich (b. 1887). Party member from 1912. Long-time resident of Petersburg/Leningrad. First secretary of Stalingrad city party committee, 1931–1935. Former member of TsKK. Member of Electoral Commission at Seventeenth Party Congress. Testified in January 1961 that Stalin "received more 'No' votes than anyone else" in balloting for the Central Committee at that Congress.

Vinogradov, Nikolai Ivanovich (1906–1937). Peasant origin. Candidate member of party from 1931. Plenipotentiary officer of Leningrad NKVD Operations Department in 1934. One of two officers who escorted Kirov's bodyguard Mikhail Borisov on December 2, 1934 on the trip that ended in Borisov's death. Executed 1937.

Voikov, P. L. Soviet ambassador to Poland, assassinated by White émigré, June 7, 1927.

Volkova, Maria. Daughter of forest warden in Vologda Province, born between 1905 and 1909. Arrived in Leningrad, 1930. Worked as passport clerk, nanny for Ivan Ilin, waitress, and at other odd jobs while serving as a secret informer for the police and NKVD from 1931. After making a number of false denunciations, she was forcibly committed to a psychiatric hospital on the orders of the Leningrad NKVD in October 1934. Removed from hospital on Stalin's orders on December 2 or 3, 1934. Lived on state funds as a "professional" denouncer into the early 1950s. Died in a Leningrad psychiatric hospital in early 1960s.

Volodarsky, V. (1891–1918). Jewish Bund and Menshevik revolutionary in Tsarist Russia. Exile in the United States. Returned to Russia and joined Bolsheviks, 1917. Editor of *Red Gazette* and head of the Petrograd area press, 1918. Assassinated by Socialist Revolutionary, June 20, 1918.

Volovich, Zakhar Ilich (1900–1937). Merchant origin, party member from 1919. Red Army service, 1919–1922. OGPU service from 1924. Espionage assignments in Turkey and Western Europe. One of organizers of abduction of former White general Kutepov from Paris. In 1934 deputy director of central NKVD Operations Department under Karl Pauker. Traveled to Leningrad with Stalin's entourage on December 1–2, 1934 and involved in early investigation of Kirov murder. Repressed.

Voroshilov, Kliment Yefremovich (1881–1969). Party member from 1903, son of railroad guard. Deputy to Petrograd soviet, 1917. Commander of Red Fifth Ukrainian Army, 1918 Commander of Tenth Army in Tsaritsyn area, 1919. Member of USSR Revvoensovet Presidium from 1924. Commissar of Defense, 1925–1940. Politburo member, 1926–1960.

Vyshinsky, Andrei Yanuarevich (1883–1954). Party member from 1920 (prior to that a Menshevik). Rector of Moscow University, 1926–1931. Deputy Chief Prosecutor of USSR, 1933–1935. Chief Prosecutor of USSR, 1935–1939. Deputy chairman of USSR Sovnarkom, 1939–1944.

Yagoda, Genrikh Grigorevich (1891–1938). Son of artisan. Anarchist before 1917. Party member from 1917. Newspaper editor (*Krestianskaya bednota*) 1917–1918. Chief administrator (*upravlaiushchii delami*) for Cheka/OGPU, deputy chief of Cheka Special Department and Secret Operational Directorate, 1920–1922. Head of OGPU Special Department, Special Operational Directorate, 1922–1929, Second deputy chairman of OGPU, 1923–1929. First deputy chairman of OGPU, 1929–1934 (and de facto chairman for much of this time). USSR Minister of Internal Affairs, 1934–1936. Commissar of Communications, 1936–1937. Arrested March 1937. Tried and sentenced to death at March 1938 show trial of the "Right-Trotskyite Center."

Yakovlev, Aleksandr Nikolaevich (1923–2005). Red Army service in World War II, party member from 1944. Chief of TsK's Department of Ideology and Propaganda, 1969–1973. USSR ambassador to Canada, 1973–1983. Director of USSR Academy of Sciences Institute of World Economy, 1983–1985. Member of Politburo, 1987–1991. Important adviser to Mikhail Gorbachev in early phases of perestroika. Member of the perestroika-era committee that investigated the Kirov murder.

Yakushev, V. M. NKVD officer who supervised second (1937) inquiry into Borisov's death. Coerced confessions to murder by Maly, Kuzin, N. S. Maksimov, and Vinogradov. Kuzin, the driver involved in transporting Borisov, testified in 1956 that Yakushev used torture.

Yalozo, Grigory Aleksandrovich. Aide to the director of the Leningrad soviet Administrative Department in 1934. Witness to the scene on Smolny third floor immediately after Kirov shot.

Yanelis. Driver for Leningrad NKVD, 1934. Does not appear in 1934–1935 documents on case.

Yanishevsky, Dionis Yulianovich (b. 1898). Party member from 1918. Cheka/OGPU/NKVD service from 1922. In 1934 was deputy chief of the Leningrad NKVD Special Department under Ivan Zaporozhets. Acting chief in fall of 1934 due to Zaporozhets' incapacitation. Sentenced to two years hard labor at trial of Leningrad NKVD officers for negligence, January 23, 1935. Probably executed during the Terror.

Yaroslants. Head of the Fourth Section of the Leningrad NKVD Economic Security Department in 1934. Acquainted with Leonid Nikolaev from Komsomol work in 1924–1925, when Yaroslants was office manager (*upravdelami*) for Leningrad Region Komsomol committee. Nikolaev spoke to him once by telephone in 1934, asking for advice on how to get Milda Draule's brother Pyotr Draule, imprisoned on charges of embezzlement, transferred to a labor camp in the Leningrad area.

Yaroslavsky, Yemelian (1878–1943). Party member from 1898. Party work in Perm and Siberia, 1920–1922. Secretary of TsKK and later KPK, 1923–1939.

Yenukidze, Avel Safronovich (1884–1936). Party member from 1898. Member of Petrograd Military Revolutionary Council (Voenrevkom) in 1917. Secretary of Presidium of VTsIK, 1918–1922. Secretary of Presidium of USSR TsIK, 1922–1935. Member of TsKK, 1924–1934, member of TsK, 1934–1935. Excluded from party for "moral decrepitude" and laxness in managing Kremlin Guard, July 1935. Repressed.

Yermolaeva, Elizaveta Fyodorovna. Third-year student of the Leningrad Industrial Academy in 1934, party member. Possibly identical with Elizabeth Lermolo, Soviet émigré and author of *Face of a Victim* (1956).

Yevdokimov, Grigory Yeremeevich (1884–1936). Member of party from 1903. Red Army service during revolution and Civil War. Deputy chairman of Petrograd soviet, chairman of Petrograd Council of Labor Unions, 1920–1925. First secretary of Leningrad Region party committee, 1925. Supported the Zinovievite and United oppositions. Expelled from the party, 1927 and readmitted, 1928. Later work in regional party organizations, the cooperative network, and the food processing industry commissariat. Tried in "Moscow Center" case, January 1935. Executed in August 1936.

Yevdokimov, Yefim Georgievich (1891–1940). Party member from 1918. Chief of the Special Department of Moscow Cheka, 1919. May 1921–chief of the Ukrainian Cheka Special Department. OGPU plenipotentiary to North Caucasus Territory, 1924–1926. Member OGPU collegium, head of OGPU Secret Operational Directorate. From 1931 OGPU plenipotentiary in Central Asia. To party work (regional party secretary) in 1934. Arrested November 1938.

Yezhov, Nikolai Ivanovich (1895–1940). Putilov factory worker before revolution. Drafted into Imperial Army, 1916. Party member from 1917. Red Army service in Civil War. Chief of Agitprop Department, Tatar Republic, 1921. First secretary of Mari Province party organization, 1922–1923; first secretary of Semipalatinsk Province party organization, 1923–1924. High posts in Kirghiz Region party committee, Kazakh Territory party organization, 1924–1926. Student at Communist Academy in Moscow, 1926–1927. Official in TsK personnel department (*orgraspred*), 1927–1929. Deputy Commissar of Agriculture, 1929–1930. Head of TsK *raspredotdel* (personnel), 1930–1934. Orgburo member from 1934. Supervised 1934–1935 investigation of Kirov murder for Stalin. Chairman of KPK from 1935. Commissar of Internal Affairs, 1936–1938. Played a major role in implementing the Great Terror for Stalin. Arrested April 10, 1939. Executed 1940.

Yuskin, Ignaty Grigorevich (1898–1934). Peasant origin. Former worker at Russian Diesel factory. In 1934 second-year student of Leningrad Industrial Academy, member of the academy's party committee, and editor of its newspaper. Party member from 1925. Yuskin's wife Anna, and possibly Yuskin himself, knew the Nikolaev family from childhood. Leonid Nikolaev visited Yuskin's apartment from time to time from 1930 to use his telephone. Tried and executed with Leonid Nikolaev in the case of the "Leningrad Center," December 1934.

Zakovsky, Leonid Mikhailovich (1894–1938). Peasant origin, party member from 1913. Scout, Cheka commander, head of Red Army Caspian-Caucasus Front Special Department, head of Moscow Cheka Special Department, 1918–1920. Chairman of Podolsk (Moscow Province) Cheka, 1921–1922. Head of Odessa Province GPU, 1923–1925. Plenipotentiary OGPU representative in Siberian Territory, 1926–1931. OGPU plenipotentiary in Belorussia, 1932–1934. Commissar of Internal Affairs for Belorussian Republic, 1934. Chief of Leningrad Region NKVD, December 1934–January 1938. Arrested April 1938, executed in August 1938.

Zaks-Gladnev, Samuil Markovich (1884–1937). Party member from 1906. Married to Grigory Zinoviev's sister. After 1917 underground work in Germany. Briefly editor of *Leningradskaya pravda* in December 1925. Supporter of Zinovievite and United oppositions. Shot March 1937.

Zalutsky, Pyotr A. (1887–1937). Senior official in Leningrad under Zinoviev before 1926, supported Zinovievite and United oppositions. Chairman of Lower Volga Council on the National Economy, 1928–

1934. Arrested and sentenced in the case of the "Leningrad Counter-revolutionary Zinovievite Group of Safarov, Zalutsky, and Others."

Zaporozhets, Ivan Vasilevich (1898–1937). Peasant origin. Imperial Army veteran of World War I. Prisoner of war in Austria, 1915–1918. Party member from 1919. Cheka officer from 1921. Espionage work abroad, 1921–1924, under diplomatic and foreign trade covers, 1923–1924. Special agent (*osoboupolnomochennyi*) of OGPU Foreign Department, 1924–1929, with assignments abroad. From late 1931, deputy OGPU plenipotentiary, Leningrad Military District. First deputy chairman of Leningrad Region OGPU/UGB, 1931 or early 1932–1934. Arrested for neglect of duty in Kirov case, December 7, 1934 (in fact he was on leave from August 1934 to December 1934 following a horse-riding accident). Sentenced to three years of labor camp in Far East, where he supervised road construction. Arrested again, May 1, 1937. Shot on August 14, 1937.

Zavilovich, Noya A. Operations secretary of Leningrad NKVD, late 1934. Apparently secretary for Leningrad NKVD chief Filip Medved.

Zhdanov, Andrei Aleksandrovich (1896–1948). Party member from 1915. Political work in Red Army, 1918–1920. From 1924 to 1934 first secretary of Nizhnyi Novgorod (later Gorky) party committee. Secretary TsK from 1934. Worked with Stalin and Kirov on draft proposal for reforming Soviet history textbooks, August 1934. First secretary of Leningrad Region and city party committees, 1934–1944. Candidate member of Politburo from 1935, full member from 1939. Chairman of USSR Supreme Soviet, 1946–1947.

Zheliabov, Andrei Ivanovich (1851–1881). Russian revolutionary, Populist. Member of the People's Will terrorist group and organizer of the assassination of Tsar Alexander II. Tried and executed.

Zhukov, Georgy Konstantinovich (1896–1974). Peasant origin. Imperial and Red Army service in World War I and Civil War. Commander of Soviet troops in Battle of Khalkin Gol/Nomonhan against Japanese (1939). Leading Soviet general in World War II (commander of forces in Battle of Moscow, 1941–1942, Stalingrad, 1942–1943, and Operation Bagration, 1944). Minister of Defense of the USSR, 1955–1957. Supported Khrushchev against Molotov group in June 1957. Khrushchev forced his retirement in 1958.

Zhukov, Ivan Pavlovich (1899–1937). Party member from 1909. Chairman of the Leningrad regional Council on the National Economy in 1928–1929. Deputy Commissar of Communications, 1933–1936. Repressed.

Zhupakhin. Chief of the Leningrad police (regular, not NKVD) in late 1934. Interrogated witnesses to Kirov murder on the evening of December 1, 1934.

Zinoviev, Grigory Yevseevich (1883–1936). Party member from 1901, in emigration 1908–1917. Member of Central Committee, 1912–1927. Member of Politburo, 1921–1926. Chairman of the Petrograd/Leningrad soviet and effective leader of that city's party organization, 1917–1926. Major leader in the Zinovievite and United oppositions in 1925–1927. Executed after show trial, August 1936.

Zorich, Aleksandr (1899–1937). Soviet satirist published in *Pravda* and *Izvestia*. One of founders of the journal *Ogonyok* in 1923. Zorich published the 1926 article "Two Dogs," satirizing the self-indulgent lifestyle of Kirov's wife, Maria Lvovna, in *Ogonyok*.

Zvezdov, Vasily Ivanovich (1902–1934). Worker at Elektrosila factory and student of Leningrad Industrial Institute in 1934. Party member from 1923. Served with Nikolaev in Luga, 1925.

Notes

1. Sheila Fitzpatrick, *Education and Social Mobility in the Soviet Union, 1921–1934* (Cambridge: Cambridge University Press, 1979).

2. Roy Medvedev, *Let History Judge: The Origins and Consequences of Stalinism* (New York: Knopf, 1971); Robert Conquest, *The Great Terror: Stalin's Purge of the Thirties* (New York: Macmillan, 1968).

3. See Library of Congress online exhibit, "Revelations from the Russian Archives," webpage on "Repression and Terror: Kirov Murder and Purges" at http://www.loc.gov/exhibits/archives/repk.html. See also Robert Conquest, *Stalin and the Kirov Murder* (Oxford: Oxford University Press, 1989); Robert Tucker, *Stalin in Power: The Revolution from Above, 1928–1941* (New York: Norton, 1990), 238–302; Amy Knight, *Who Killed Kirov? The Kremlin's Greatest Mystery* (New York: Hill and Wang, 1999); Simon Sebag Montefiore, *Stalin: The Court of the Red Tsar* (New York: Knopf, 2004), 126–157. Montefiore quote is from 150.

4. J. Arch Getty, *Origins of the Great Purges: The Soviet Communist Party Reconsidered, 1933–1938* (Cambridge: Cambridge University Press, 1985), 211–220.

5. Alla Kirilina, *Rikoshet* (St. Petersburg: "Znanie," 1993); *L'assassinat de Kirov: Destin d'un Stalinien, 1888–1934* (Paris: Seuil, 1995); *Neizvestnyi Kirov* (Moscow: OLMA-PRESS, 2001); O. V. Khlevniuk, *Stalin i Ordzhonikidze* (Moscow: "Rossiia Molodaia," 1993); *Politbiuro: Mekhanizmy politicheskoi vlasti v 30-e gody* (Moscow: ROSSPEN, 1996).

6. Email communication to author from Mikhail Iurevich Prozumenshchikov, deputy director of RGANI, Sept. 5, 2005.

7. Shatunovskaia made the "three detentions" claim in an interview with the newspaper *Argumenty i fakty* in the summer of 1990. See "Fal'sifikatsiia: Vospominaniia veterana partii," *Argumenty i fakty,* June 2–8, 1990, 6–7.

8. Graham Davies, "Witnessing Events," in Graham Davies, ed., *Memory in Everyday Life* (Amsterdam: North Holland, 1993), 367–401.

9. Elizabeth F. Loftus, "Remembering What Never Happened," in Endel Tulving, ed., *Memory Consciousness and the Brain: The Tallinn Conference* (Philadelphia: Psychology Press, 2000), 106–118.

10. On source amnesia, see Daniel Schacter, "Memory Distortion: History and Current Status," in Daniel Schacter, ed., *Memory Distortion: How Minds, Brains, and Societies Reconstruct the Past* (Cambridge: Harvard University Press, 1995), 1–46.

11. Stephen J. Ceci, "False Beliefs: Some Developmental and Clinical Considerations," in Schacter, *Memory Distortion,* 91–125; Loftus, "Remembering What Never Happened"; Loftus, "The Reality of Illusory Memories," in Schacter, *Memory Distortions,* 47–68.

12. On the effects of partisanship, see Graham Davies, "Witnessing Events," 367–401; and Ceci, "False Beliefs," 91–92. Multiple studies indicate that elderly subjects are particularly prone to source amnesia. See Larry Squire, "Biological Foundations of Accuracy and Inaccuracy in Memory," in Schacter, *Memory Distortion,* 197–225, esp. 218.

13. Alice M. Hoffman and Howard S. Hoffman, *Archives of Memory: A Soldier Recalls World War II* (Lexington: University Press of Kentucky, 1990).

14. Gordon W. Allport and Leo Postman, *The Psychology of Rumor* (New York: Henry Holt, 1947), 61–115.

15. Ibid., 134–138.

16. Ibid., 116–127.

17. Certain publications, such as Anton Antonov-Ovseenko's *In Stalin's Time: Portrait of a Tyranny* (New York: Harper and Row, 1981), are so riddled with error, at least as regards the Kirov murder, as to be unworthy of serious consideration.

18. Email communication to author from Mikhail Iurevich Prozumenshchikov, deputy director of RGANI, Sept. 5, 2005. A note from KGB chief Ivan Serov accompanying the KGB document release of April 20, 1956 stated that all documents on the Nikolaev case were available to TsK investigators at the central KGB archive.

19. See "Bush Issues New Secrecy Executive Order," Society of American Archivists website, http://www.archivists.org/news/secrecyorder.asp.

20. Robert Conquest, *The Great Terror: A Reassessment* (Oxford: Oxford University Press, 1990); Conquest, *Stalin and the Kirov Murder*; Tucker, *Stalin in Power*; Knight, *Who Killed Kirov.*

21. J. Arch Getty and Oleg V. Naumov, *The Road to Terror: Stalin and the Self-Destruction of the Bolsheviks, 1932–1938* (New Haven: Yale University Press, 1999).

22. See Getty, *Origins of the Great Purges,* 216–217; Kirilina, *L'assassinat de Kirov,* 223.

23. L. Michael White, *From Jesus to Christianity* (San Francisco: Harper San Francisco, 2004).

24. "Rushing Off a Cliff," *New York Times,* Sept. 28, 2006; "Challenging the Military Commissions Act," *Jurist: Legal News and Research* (University of Pittsburgh School of Law), Oct. 4, 2006; Seymour M. Hersh, "The Gray Zone: How a Secret Pentagon Program Came to Abu Ghraib," *New Yorker,* May 24, 2004;

"Mr. Gonzalez's Record," *Washington Post,* Nov. 22, 2004, A18; James Risen and Eric Lichtblau, "Bush Lets U.S. Spy on Callers without Courts," *New York Times,* Dec. 16, 2005; Jonathan S. Landay, "Report: Abusive Tactics Used to Seek Iraq–al Qaida Link," McClatchy Newspapers, April 21, 2009, at http://www.mcclatchy dc.com/227/story/66622.html; Lawrence Wilkerson, "The Truth about Richard Bruce Cheney," *The Washington Note,* May 13, 2009, at http://www.thewashington note.com/archives/2009/05/the_truth_about.

25. Glenn Greenwald, "Obama's Pretty Words on Secrecy and Torture Last Night," *Salon Magazine,* April 30, 2009, at http://www.salon.com/opinion/ greenwald/2009/04/30/obama/; "Public Remains Divided over Use of Torture," *Pew Research Center for the People and the Press,* April 23, 2009, at http://people -press.org/report/510/public-remains-divided-over-use-of-torture.

CHAPTER 1. SERGEI KIROV, 1886–1925

1. On the "positive hero" of Socialist Realism, see Katerina Clark, *The Soviet Novel: History as Ritual* (Chicago: University of Chicago Press, 1981), 57–64, 72–77.

2. See Alla Kirilina, *Neizvestnyi Kirov* (Moscow: OLMA-PRESS, 2001), 9–12; and S. Sinel'nikov, *Kirov* (Moscow: Molodaia gvardiia, 1964), 6–8.

3. Sinel'nikov, *Kirov,* 6–8; A. M. Kostrikova and E. M. Kostrikova, *Eto bylo v Urzhume: Vospominaniia o S. M. Kirove* (Kirov: Kirovskoe knizhnoe izdatel'stvo, 1962), 4–5.

4. Kostrikova and Kostrikova, *Vospominaniia,* 17; Sinel'nikov, *Kirov,* 10–11; Kirilina, *Neizvestnyi Kirov,* 12–13.

5. Sinel'nikov, *Kirov,* 11; Kostrikova and Kostrikova, *Vospominaniia,* 10–11, 21–24, 33, 57–58.

6. Quoted in Sinel'nikov, *Kirov,* 24.

7. Kirilina, *Neizvestnyi Kirov,* 13–14; Sinel'nikov, *Kirov,* 37–38; Kostrikova and Kostrikova, *Vospominaniia,* 65–68.

8. Kirilina, *Neizvestnyi Kirov,* 15, writes that Sundstrem closed down her rooming house. Kirov's party autobiography is reproduced in *Entsiklopedicheskii slovar' "Granat": Deiateli SSSR i revoliutsionnogo dvizheniia Rossii* (Moscow: "Sovetskaia entsiklopedia," 1989), s. v. "Kirov, Sergei Mironovich."

9. Kirov's sisters mention in their 1962 memoir that Sundstrem "adopted" a daughter after running the hostel in Kazan, which strengthens the hypothesis that she and Kostrikov really did have a child together. See Kostrikova and Kostrikova, *Vospominaniia,* 65. For the KPK report on the filmmakers' discovery of Kirov's daughter, see Andrei Artizov and Oleg Naumov, eds., *Vlast' i khudozhestvennaia intelligentsiia* (Moscow: Mezhdunarodnyi fond "Demokratiia," 2002), 322–324.

10. *Tovarishch Kirov* (Moscow: Profizdat, 1935), 27–28; Sinel'nikov, *Kirov,* 50; Kostrikova and Kostrikova, *Vospominaniia,* 74.

11. Sinel'nikov, *Kirov,* 59–60. Nicholas Riasanovsky and Mark Steinberg, *A History of Russia* (Oxford: Oxford University Press, 2005), 369–370, 378–381.

12. *Entsiklopedicheskii slovar' "Granat,"* s. v. "Kirov."

13. Kirilina, *Neizvestnyi Kirov,* 33; Adam Ulam, *The Bolsheviks* (New York: Collier Books, 1965), 187–235.

14. Kostrikova and Kostrikova, *Vospominaniia,* 92–93; *S. M. Kirov, 1886–1934* (Moscow: Partizdat, 1934), 19–20; *Entsiklopedicheskii slovar' "Granat,"* s. v. "Kirov"; *Kirov i vremia* (Leningrad: Lenizdat, 1986), 27–28. See also Kirilina, *Neizvestnyi Kirov,* 17.

15. *Entsiklopedicheskii slovar' "Granat,"* s. v. "Kirov"; *Tovarishch Kirov,* 30–31.

16. On the Social Democratic organization in Tomsk, see David Lane, *The Roots of Russian Communism* (University Park: Pennsylvania State University Press, 1968), 193–196, based largely on the 1920s memoirs of N. Baransky, an early participant in the Siberian Social Democratic movement.

17. *Entsiklopedicheskii slovar' "Granat,"* s. v. "Kirov"; *Tovarishch Kirov,* 35.

18. Sinel'nikov, *Kirov,* 86–89.

19. Police report reproduced in *S. M. Kirov, 1886–1934,* 24–25, and *Tovarishch Kirov,* 41.

20. Kirilina, *Neizvestnyi Kirov,* 18; *Entsiklopedicheskii slovar' "Granat,"* s. v. "Kirov."

21. See Lane, *Roots,* 176–206.

22. Sinel'nikov, *Kirov,* 102–106; memoirs of M. Popov in *Tovarishch Kirov,* 44–47.

23. Riasanovsky, *History,* 381–382; John Stephan, *The Russian Far East: A History* (Stanford: Stanford University Press, 1994), 104–105; Kirilina, *Neizvestnyi Kirov,* 19; Sinel'nikov, *Kirov,* 109.

24. Kirilina, *Neizvestnyi Kirov,* 19; *S. M. Kirov 1886–1934,* 25–29; *Ugolovnoe ulozhenie 22 marta 1903 g.* (Riga: Knigoizdatel'stvo "Leta," 1922), 485–486; Sinel'nikov, *Kirov,* 110–112.

25. *Ugolovnoe ulozhenie,* 465, 485–486; *Entsiklopedicheskii slovar' "Granat,"* s. v. "Kirov."

26. *S. M. Kirov, 1886–1934,* 20; Kostrikova and Kostrikova, *Vospominaniia,* 27, 97–99. In a 1934 letter to Kirov, Elizaveta claimed that the last communication from Sergei was in 1911, rather than 1908 (see below, p. 147).

27. *S. M. Kirov, 1886–1934,* 30, Kirilina, *Neizvestnyi Kirov,* 20, Sinel'nikov, *Kirov,* 118–119.

28. *Entsiklopedicheskii slovar' "Granat,"* s. v. "Kirov."

29. For an example of a largely fictional account of Kirov's activities in the Vladikavkaz region, see G. K. Dolunts, *Kirov na severnom kavkaze* (Moscow: Politizdat, 1973), 25, 27, 48–53, 63–65, 78–79, 81–82.

30. Sinel'nikov, *Kirov,* 148.

31. Krasnikov, *Sergei Mironovich Kirov,* 49; Kirilina, *Neizvestnyi Kirov,* 26–28; V. I. Kliukin and S. A. Sheshina, *Sergei Mironovich Kirov* (Kirov: Volgo-Viatskoe knizhnoe izdatel'stvo, 1986), 62.

32. Kirilina, *Neizvestnyi Kirov,* 21, 27; Dolunts, *Kirov na severnom kavkaze,* 14–18.

33. Dolunts, *Kirov na severnom kavkaze,* 14–15.

34. Kirilina, *Neizvestnyi Kirov,* 22–29; Sinel'nikov, *Kirov,* 121, 139–141.

35. Richard Douglas King, *Sergei Kirov and the Struggle for Soviet Power in the Terek Region, 1917–1918* (New York: Garland Publishing, Inc. 1987), 47–49.

36. Sinel'nikov, *Kirov,* 127–137. Sinel'nikov and *S. M. Kirov, 1886–1934,* 30–

37, give different dates for Kostrikov's arrest in 1911. It is not clear whether the latter work gives the date in the Julian (old) or Gregorian (new) calendar.

37. *Tovarishch Kirov,* 77–78; Sinel'nikov, *Kirov,* 136–137.

38. *Tovarishch Kirov,* 77–78.

39. Kirilina, *Neizvestnyi Kirov,* 32–33, 332–333; Sinel'nikov, *Kirov,* 120–121; Kliukin and Sheshina, *Sergei Mironovich Kirov,* 63. Maria Lvovna also had a younger sister, Rakhil (Rachel), who eventually became a doctor.

40. The Kostrikov-Markus correspondence is partially reproduced in Sinel'nikov, *Kirov,* 129–134. There are also excerpts from the letters in Kliukin and Sheshina, *Sergei Mironovich Kirov,* 64–65, and Kirilina, *Neizvestnyi Kirov,* 29–30. Knight, *Who Killed Kirov,* 47–50, also discusses Kirov's letters to Maria Lvovna. On Gorky's heroine Varenka Olesova, see Maksim Gor'kii, "Varen'ka Olesova," in M. Gor'kii, *Sobranie sochinenii,* vol. 2 (Moscow: Gosudarstvennoe izdatel'stvo khudozhestvennoi literatury, 1960), 5–77; and Peter Kropotkin's brief discussion of the piece in Peter Kropotkin, "Maxim Gorky," *The Independent* 57, no. 2924 (Dec. 15, 1904): 1371–1378.

41. On Andreev's career and popularity, see Frederick H. White, *Memoirs and Madness: Leonid Andreev through the Prism of the Literary Portrait* (Montreal: McGill-Queen's University Press, 2006). For English translations of some of his works, see Clarence L. Meader and Fred Newton Scott, trans., *Plays by Leonid Andreyeff: The Black Maskers, The Life of Man, The Sabine Women* (New York: Scribner, 1915), including the introductory essay by V. V. Brusyanin. See also Leonid Andreyeff, *Anathema* (New York: Macmillan, 1910).

42. Kliukin and Sheshina, *Sergei Mironovich Kirov,* 64.

43. For the "dilettante" quote, see Knight, *Who Killed Kirov,* 48–49.

44. Klikushin and Sheshina, *Sergei Mironovich Kirov,* 64.

45. Knight, *Who Killed Kirov,* 41; Kirilina, *Neizvestnyi Kirov,* 30–31; Ivan Zhukov, "Neizvestnyi Kirov" (interview with Alla Kirilina), *Argumenty i fakty,* Dec. 1, 2004; Krasnikov, *Sergei Mirovonich Kirov,* 45.

46. Kirilina, *Neizvestnyi Kirov,* 30–31; Sinel'nikov, *Kirov,* 137; Krasnikov, *Sergei Mironovich Kirov,* 45.

47. Krasnikov, *Sergei Mironovich Kirov,* 45–46.

48. Kirilina, *Neizvestnyi Kirov,* 31; Sinel'nikov, *Kirov,* 138; Krasnikov, *Sergei Mironovich Kirov,* 46. The name "Kornev" was adapted from that of another journalist at *Terek,* who one way or another probably helped Kostrikov get his fake passport. Dmitry Zakharovich Korenev (there is a one-letter difference in the spelling of the last name from the passport) joined *Terek* in the spring of 1911 (Sinel'nikov, *Kirov,* 138).

49. *Tovarishch Kirov,* 74–79.

50. Dolunts, *Kirov na severnom kavkaze,* 18.

51. King, *Sergei Kirov,* 59–70.

52. Ibid., 35, 69–82.

53. Ibid., 73, 87–88.

54. Ibid., 116–151.

55. Ibid., 150–151; Kirilina, *Neizvestnyi Kirov,* 33.

56. King, *Sergei Kirov,* 174–178, 323; Kirilina, *Neizvestnyi Kirov,* 33–35.

57. King, *Sergei Kirov,* 182, 184–188, 189–192.

58. Ibid., 210–240.

59. Ibid., 224–230, 240–251, 254–258, 261–264, 310–325, 338–343, 349–350, 362–372; Kirilina, *Neizvestnyi Kirov,* 36.

60. King, *Sergei Kirov,* 396–397; Knight, *Who Killed Kirov,* 64.

61. This is taking into account that Kirov could not openly write in *Terek* about the overthrow of the autocracy.

62. King, *Sergei Kirov,* 388–389; Kirilina, *Neizvestnyi Kirov,* 44–45.

63. Kirilina, *Neizvestnyi Kirov,* 38–39; Sinel'nikov, *Kirov,* 171–173. Kirilina believes that reports of Kirov meeting Lenin in late May are probably spurious (Sinel'nikov, *Kirov,* and Knight, *Who Killed Kirov,* 71–72 cite such reports).

64. Kirilina, *Neizvestnyi Kirov,* 38–39; Sinel'nikov, *Kirov,* 171–173. Knight, *Who Killed Kirov,* 72–73.

65. Sinel'nikov, *Kirov,* 184–185; V. P. Butt et al., eds., *The Russian Civil War: Documents from the Soviet Archives* (New York: St. Martin's Press, 1996), 46; Kirilina, *Neizvestnyi Kirov,* 44–48.

66. Kirilina, *Neizvestnyi Kirov,* 44–48; N. A. Efimov, "Sergei Mironovich Kirov," *Voprosy istorii,* nos. 11–12 (1995): 49–67.

67. Kirilina, *Neizvestnyi Kirov,* 49–50.

68. Ibid., 48–55; Efimov, "Sergei Mironovich Kirov," 54–56.

69. Efimov, "Sergei Mironovich Kirov," 54–56.

70. Ibid.

71. Kirilina, *Neizvestnyi Kirov,* 55–57; Efimov, "Sergei Mironovich Kirov," 54–55; S. A. Mel'gunov, *Krasnyi terror v Rossii* (New York: Izdatel'stvo BRANDY, 1979), 50–51 (original publication date 1923).

72. Quoted in Kirilina, *Neizvestnyi Kirov,* 62–63.

73. Kirilina, *Neizvestnyi Kirov,* 47–67, esp. 65.

74. Ibid., 50–51, 60–61; Efimov, "Sergei Mironovich Kirov," 56; Sinel'nikov, *Kirov,* 223–226; M. S. Iskenderov, *S. M. Kirov v Azerbaidzhane* (Baku: Azerbaidzhanskoe Gosizdat, 1970), 17–20.

75. Sinel'nikov, *Kirov,* 232–237, Kirilina, *Neizvestnyi Kirov,* 70.

76. Efimov, "Sergei Mironovich Kirov," 53; Kirilina, *Neizvestnyi Kirov,* 41–43.

77. Kirilina, *Neizvestnyi Kirov,* 71–75, Efimov, "Sergei Mironovich Kirov," 56. On the Hummet Party, see Audrey L. Altstadt, *The Azerbaijani Turks: Power and Identity under Russian Rule* (Stanford: Hoover Institution Press, 1992), 47–48.

78. Kirilina, *Neizvestnyi Kirov,* 78.

79. Altstadt, *The Azerbaijani Turks,* 82.

80. Ibid., 96–99, 108–110; Kirilina, *Neizvestnyi Kirov,* 78–79; Sinel'nikov, *Kirov,* 240; Stephen Blank, "Bolshevik Organizational Development in Early Soviet Transcaucasia: Autonomy vs. Centralization, 1918–1924," in Ron Grigor Suny, ed., *Transcaucasia, Nationalism, and Social Change: Essays in the History of Armenia, Azerbaijan, and Georgia* (Ann Arbor: University of Michigan Press, 1983), 307–340.

81. Altstadt, *The Azerbaijani Turks,* 108–112. See also Bruce Grant, "An Average Azeri Village (1930): Remembering Rebellion in the Caucasus Mountains," *Slavic Review* 63, no. 4 (Winter 2004): 705–731. Grant's account suggests that

substantial anti-Soviet violence continued in the Azeri countryside throughout the 1920s.

82. Kirilina, *Neizvestnyi Kirov*, 81–83; Ron Grigor Suny, *The Making of the Georgian Nation* (Bloomington: Indiana University Press, 1994), 205–206; Blank, "Bolshevik Organizational Development," 329.

83. Kirilina, *Neizvestnyi Kirov*, 82–83. Quotations are from Knight, *Who Killed Kirov*, 87.

84. Kirilina, *Neizvestnyi Kirov*, 83–85; Blank, "Bolshevik Organizational Development," 330, notes that Kirov and Stalin "were active in fomenting unrest in Georgia" in the summer of 1920, based on G. K. Zhvaniia, *V. I. Lenin, TsK Partii i bol'sheviki Zakavkaz'ia* (Tbilisi: Meranii, 1969), 239–240.

85. Kirilina, *Neizvestnyi Kirov*, 84–85, Knight, *Who Killed Kirov*, 87–89.

86. Knight, *Who Killed Kirov*, 88–89.

87. On the Chechen rebellion, see Moshe Gammer, *The Lone Wolf and the Bear: Three Centuries of Chechen Defiance of Russian Rule* (Pittsburgh: University of Pittsburgh Press, 2006), 119–140; Marie Benningsen Broxup, "The Last *Ghazawat*: The 1920–1921 Uprising," and Abdurahman Avtorkhanov, "The Chechens and Ingush during the Soviet Period and Its Antecedents," both in Broxup et al., *The North Caucasus Barrier: The Russian Advance Towards the Muslim World* (New York: St. Martin's Press, 1992), 112–194.

88. Knight, *Who Killed Kirov*, 89–91. My own interpretation of events differs from Knight's. She sees Kirov more as a moderating counterweight to Ordzhonikidze and Stalin than as their enabler.

89. Richard G. Hovannisian, "Caucasian Armenia between Imperial and Soviet Rule: The Interlude of National Independence," in Suny, *Transcaucasia, Nationalism, and Social Change*, 261–294; Blank, "Bolshevik Organizational Development," 328–331; Knight, *Who Killed Kirov*, 92. Although Knight calls Kirov's support of the invasion of Armenia "atypical," he had previously lobbied aggressively for the invasion of Azerbaijan, and he subsequently argued for the invasion of Georgia.

90. Blank, "Bolshevik Organizational Development," 330–333; Kirilina, *Neizvestnyi Kirov*, 85.

91. Terry Martin, *The Affirmative Action Empire: Nations and Nationalism in the Soviet Union, 1923–1939* (Ithaca: Cornell University Press, 2001); Blank, "Bolshevik Organizational Development," 317–327; Kirilina, *Neizvestnyi Kirov*, 71–72.

92. Martin, *Affirmative Action Empire*, 21. I have modified the quote by replacing references to the specific soft-line policy of *korenizatsiia* with references to soft-line policies in general.

93. Khlevniuk, *Stalin i Ordzhonikidze*, 9–10.

94. For a short summary of events, see Geoffrey Hosking, *The First Socialist Society: A History of the Soviet Union from Within* (Cambridge: Harvard University Press, 1992), 89–92.

95. Knight, *Who Killed Kirov*, 93–94.

96. Altstadt, *The Azerbaijani Turks*, 114–119; Blank, "Bolshevik Organizational Development," 333–334; Suny, *The Making of the Georgian Nation*, 212–214.

97. Altstadt, *The Azerbaijani Turks,* 114–119; Blank, "Bolshevik Organizational Development," 334; Knight, *Who Killed Kirov,* 96.

98. Altstadt, *The Azerbaijani Turks,* 118–120; Sinel'nikov, *Kirov,* 259–260; M. S. Iskenderov, *S. M. Kirov v Azerbaidzhane* (Baku: Azerbaidzhanskoe Gosizdat, 1970), 82; Knight, *Who Killed Kirov,* 101. Knight suggests that Kirov was reluctant to institute the purge but "he had no choice but to follow through with orders." Unfortunately there is no evidence that Kirov was reluctant about the purge. To the contrary, it was part of Stalin and Ordzhonikidze's centralizing policy which he consistently and enthusiastically supported.

99. Altstadt, *The Azerbaijani Turks,* 122–125; Blank, "Bolshevik Organizational Development," 338–339; Sinel'nikov, *Kirov,* 273–277. Sinel'nikov puts a positive spin on the *korenizatsiia* efforts, while conceding that there was shortage of "native" cadres.

100. Altstadt, *The Azerbaijani Turks,* 123–124, Knight, *Who Killed Kirov,* 101–102.

101. Sinel'nikov, *Kirov,* 261–268, Altstadt, *The Azerbaijani Turks,* 113, n. 41, 269.

102. Iskenderov, *S. M. Kirov,* 62; Sinel'nikov, *Kirov,* 258, 366; Kirilina, *Neizvestnyi Kirov,* 476; Knight, *Who Killed Kirov,* 102. On the labor union debate, see Robert Daniels, *Conscience of the Revolution: Communist Opposition in Soviet Russia* (Cambridge: Harvard University Press, 1960), 121–136.

103. On the Trotsky controversy in the winter of 1923–1924, see Daniels, *Conscience of the Revolution,* 209–235. For Stalin's Dec. 17, 1923 communication to Kirov and the resolution of the meeting of Baku activists, see Valentina Vilkova, *The Struggle for Power: Russia in 1923* (New York: Prometheus Books, 1996), 289–291. See also Sinel'nikov, *Kirov,* 258–259 and Knight, *Who Killed Kirov,* 105–107. Knight argues that Kirov's insistence that Trotsky should remain in the party leadership suggests his "moderation," while in fact he was simply following Stalin's own "moderate" line to the letter. Knight mentions that Kirov's statements to this effect were edited out of his collected speeches following his death, indicating that they were somehow subversive. They were indeed subversive in the post-1934 era, when Trotsky was the Soviet Communist Party's designated enemy number one. They were not subversive in 1924, when they represented the official Central Committee line determined personally by Stalin.

104. A. Zorich, "Dve sobachki," *Ogonek,* no. 43 (Oct. 24, 1926): 7–8, and Chagin letter to Party Control Committee (Shatunovskaia), late 1960 or early 1961, RGANI, f. 6, op. 13, d. 23, l. 37.

105. With regard to Kirov's enjoyment of liquor and good accommodations, Frania Marschak, a Menshevik who attended the Mozdok Congress of Peoples of the Terek in January 1919 remembered in the late 1970s how Kirov and fellow leaders of the Socialist Bloc would drink heavily every night in the luxury railroad car they lived in. See Knight, *Who Killed Kirov,* 68–69. No doubt Kirov's ability to hold his liquor made him a real *muzhik* (literally, "peasant," meaning a "homey," or a "good old boy") in the eyes of his fellows. For Chagin's 1960 evidence, see Chagin to Shatunovskaia, RGANI, f. 6, op. 13, d. 23, l. 37.

106. For the actual political situation, including Narimanov's steady opposition to centralization initiatives sponsored by Ordzhonikidze and Kirov, and Efendiev's

support for the same initiatives, see Altstadt, *The Azerbaijani Turks,* 110–114, 121–124, and Blank, "Bolshevik Organizational Development," 321–322, 334–336. It is clear that Ordzhonikidze could not have "fired" Zorich from *Pravda* or from *Ogonek* because the latter continued to publish regularly in both periodicals throughout late 1926 and all of 1927. See the list of his publications in *Russkie sovetskie pisateli-prozaiki,* vol. 7, part 1 (Moscow: Izdatel'stvo "Kniga," 1971), 280–304. On the "sensationalistic" coverage in 1926 of sex crimes and corruption in party officialdom see Matthew Lenoe, "Stalinist Mass Journalism and the Transformation of Soviet Newspapers, 1926–1929" (Ph.D. diss., University of Chicago, 1997), 749–756, 768, 841–851; and Eric Naiman, *Sex in Public* (Princeton: Princeton University Press, 1999). On Stalin's pressure on Ordzhonikidze to take the TsKK position in late summer 1926, see Khlevniuk, *Stalin i Ordzhonikidze,* 15–18.

107. See excerpts from Miasnikov's diary (written before Kirov's death) in Sinel'nikov, *Kirov,* 254–255, Knight, *Who Killed Kirov,* 97, and Sinel'nikov, *Kirov,* 257–268.

CHAPTER 2. CONQUERING LENINGRAD, 1925–1929

1. Robert V. Daniels, *The Conscience of the Revolution: Communist Opposition in Soviet Russia* (Cambridge: Harvard University Press, 1960); Alla Kirilina, *Neizvestnyi Kirov* (Moscow: OLMA-PRESS, 2001), 92–96. For examples of the Zinovievite side of the polemics, see Petr Andreevich Zalutskii article in *Leningradskaia pravda,* Aug. 13, 1925, 3; or G. I. Safarov, ibid., Sept. 19, 1925, 1.

2. On Zinoviev's fall 1925 position in the "socialism in one country" debate, see Daniels, *Conscience,* 264–267. On Stalin's development of the slogan, see also Robert Tucker, *Stalin as Revolutionary* (New York: Norton, 1973), 377–390.

3. *Leningradskaia pravda,* Nov. 18 and 19, 1925; Daniels, *Conscience,* 255, Kirilina, *Neizvestnyi Kirov,* 96–98.

4. See Komarov speech at the Fourteenth Party Congress in *Leningradskaia pravda,* Dec. 23, 1925, 3. See also Yevdokimov's comments on the same page.

5. Kirilina, *Neizvestnyi Kirov,* 101–103; Tucker, *Stalin as Revolutionary,* 308–312; Daniels, *Conscience,* 268–270. Quotation from Kirilina, *Neizvestnyi Kirov,* 103.

6. For Kirov's comments, see *Leningradskaia pravda,* Dec. 27, 1925, 3.

7. Kirilina, *Neizvestnyi Kirov,* 104.

8. Ibid., 105–109; *Leningradskaia pravda,* Dec. 24–29, 1925. "Kulak deviation" reference is from Dec. 26, 1925, 1. On the provincial party committee blocking the Vyborg Ward meeting, see ibid., Dec. 30, 1925, 1.

9. Kirilina, *Neizvestnyi Kirov,* 107–110. For text of the appeal, see *Leningradskaia pravda,* Dec. 30, 1925, 1.

10. On the "Savage Division" moniker for the TsK delegation, see Chuev's interviews with Molotov in Feliks Chuev, *Molotov: Poluderzhavnyi vlastelin* (Moscow: OLMA-PRESS, 1999), 370.

11. Kirilina, *Neizvestnyi Kirov,* 110; "Vyborg raion–za liniiu XIV s"ezda," *Leningradskaia pravda,* Dec. 30, 1925, 1; Mikhail Rosliakov, *Ubiistvo Kirova: Politicheskie i ugolovnye prestupleniia v 1930-kh godakh* (Leningrad: Lenizdat, 1991), 97–98.

12. See *Leningradskaia pravda,* Jan. 3, 1926, 2, Jan. 5, 1926, 2; and Kirilina, *Neizvestnyi Kirov,* 112. On the Zinovievites' nicknames for Kirov, see Rosliakov, *Ubiistvo,* 99.

13. "Nasha sila—edinstvo," *Leningradskaia pravda,* Jan.19, 1926, 3.

14. I. V. Stalin, *Sochineniia,* vol. 7 (1925) (Moscow: OGIZ, 1947), 231, 282.

15. Kirilina, *Neizvestnyi Kirov,* 111–117; *Leningradskaia pravda,* Jan. 14, 1926, 1.

16. On Kirov's early insistence that the Leningrad appointment be temporary, see Kirilina, *Neizvestnyi Kirov,* 120–121. Kirov letter to Mariia L'vovna excerpted in Amy Knight, *Who Killed Kirov: The Kremlin's Greatest Mystery* (New York: Hill and Wang, 1999), 109–110, and Kirilina, *Neizvestnyi Kirov,* 118. My translation is from the Kirilina text.

17. On Ordzhonikidze's resistance to the TsKK promotion, see O. V. Khlevniuk, *Stalin i Ordzhonikidze* (Moscow: "Rossiia Molodaia," 1993), 15–18.

18. Kirilina, *Neizvestnyi Kirov,* 119.

19. Ibid., 119; *Leningradskaia pravda,* Jan. 21, 1926, 1. Interview with Molotov ibid., Jan. 22, 1926, 1, and Kirilina, *Neizvestnyi Kirov,* 120.

20. *Leningradskaia pravda,* Jan. 1, 1926, 1. The Vyborg Komsomol opposed the TsK in spite of the ward party organization's support.

21. "Plody politicheskogo razvrata," ibid., Jan. 30, 1926, 1; Molotov's speech to Volodarsky Ward party committee ibid., Feb. 10, 1926, 2; "Rezoliutsiia plenuma Leningradskogo gubkoma RLKSM ot 8-II 26 goda," ibid., Feb. 12, 1926, 2.

22. RGASPI, f. 80, op. 26, d. 40, ll. 1–5.

23. *Leningradskaia pravda,* Dec. 10, 1925 and Feb. 13, 1926; Daniels, *Conscience,* 271.

24. Daniels, *Conscience,* 271.

25. See Bukharin and Kirov speeches reported in *Leningradskaia pravda,* Feb. 11 and 12, 1926.

26. Ibid., Feb. 13, 1926, 1.

27. Rosliakov, *Ubiistvo,* 99; Kirilina, *Neizvestnyi Kirov,* 120.

28. Rosliakov, *Ubiistvo,* 100; Party Control Committee interview with N. F. Sveshnikov, Oct. 20, 1966, RGANI, f. 6, op. 13, d. 73, ll. 96–132.

29. Victor Serge remembered Komarov, not Kirov, heading the city leadership on the reviewing stand at a major demonstration in the summer of 1926. See Victor Serge, *Memoirs of a Revolutionary* (New York: Writers and Readers, 1984), 219.

30. Daniels, *Conscience,* 273–321; L. Kosheleva et al., eds., *Pis'ma I. V. Stalina V. M. Molotovu, 1925–1936 gg.* (Moscow: "Rossiia Molodaia," 1995), 48–55.

31. RGASPI, f. 80, op. 27, d. 62, l. 6.

32. RGASPI, f. 80, op. 27, d. 62, l. 6, and Kirov to Mirzoian, March 4, 1926, RGASPI, f. 80, op. 27, d. 62, ll. 1–10b. On the affair of the Baku Opposition and its supposed leader, S. Medvedev, see Daniels, *Conscience,* 279–281, and the Baku Communist Party organ, *Bakinskii rabochii,* July 12, 1926, 1–2.

33. Serge, *Memoirs,* 212–222.

34. Ibid., 192–199. Quote on Lenin from S. Krasnikov, *S. M. Kirov v Leningrade* (Leningrad: Lenizdat, 1966), 31. Kirov quote from Kirilina, *Neizvestnyi Kirov,* 123.

35. Knight, *Who Killed Kirov*, 122-130.

36. V. P. Danilov and O. V. Khlevniuk, "Aprel'skii plenum 1928 g.," in Danilov, Khlevniuk, et al., eds., *Kak lomali NEP*, 5 vols. (Moscow: Mezhdunarodnyi fond "Demokratiia," 2000), vol. 1: *Obedinennyi plenum TsK i TsKK VKP[b] 6–11 aprelia 1928 g.*, 16–18.

37. RGASPI, f. 80, op. 12, d. 2, ll. 1–4.

38. TsGAIPD SPb, f. 24, op. 1, d. 38, l. 100.

39. Danilov and Khlevniuk, "Aprel'skii plenum 1928 g.," 21–27 and stenogram of April 1928 plenum in Danilov et al., *Kak lomali NEP*, 1:36–58, 77, 129–131.

40. See Daniels, *Conscience*, 332, and Leon Trotsky, *The Challenge of the Left Opposition (1928–1929)* (New York: Pathfinder Press, 1981), 122–123. On the Politburo's removal of Slepkov from the editorial board of *Pravda*, see Danilov et al., *Kak lomali NEP*, vol. 4: *Obedinennyi plenum TsK i TsKK VKP(b) 16–23 aprelia 1929 g.*, 700 n. 19. A letter from Bukharin to Stalin of August 1928 confirms that Slepkov got in trouble for a meeting in Leningrad (A. V. Kvashonkin et al., eds., *Sovetskoe rukovodstvo: Perepiska, 1928–1941 g.* [Moscow: ROSSPEN, 1999], 39).

41. Danilov et al., *Kak lomali NEP*, 4:439, 657–658. See also L. P. Petrovskii, "Poslednyi rot front," in A. V. Afanasev, ed., *Oni ne molchali* (Moscow: Politizdat, 1991), 179–198. I found this source through Knight, *Who Killed Kirov.*

42. See "Zernovye fabriki," *Krasnaia gazeta*, June 27, 1928, 2; "Smeloe otkrytic," *Leningradskaia pravda*, June 29, 1928, 2; Petrovskii, "Poslednyi rot front," 182–183; Danilov et al., *Kak lomali NEP*, 4:439, 657–658.

43. Danilov et al., *Kak lomali NEP*, vol. 2: *Plenum TsK VKP(b), 4–12 iiulia, 1928 g.*, 245–248, 258–259, 325–326.

44. Ibid., 301–302.

45. Petrovskii, "Poslednyi rot front," 183–185; Danilov et al., *Kak lomali NEP*, 4:55–58, 703 (n. 61).

46. Danilov et al., *Kak lomali NEP*, 4:558–563.

47. Boris I. Nicolaevsky Collection, Hoover Institution Archives, Series 236, Box 411, File 1. The source is Nicolaevsky's preface to the memoir of former Leningrad journalist V. K. Zavalishin, "Vokrug ubiistva Kirova," which was evidently never published. I learned of the existence of this document from Knight's *Who Killed Kirov.*

48. Khlevniuk, *Stalin i Ordzhonikidze*, 83–129.

49. Danilov, Khlevniuk, and Vatlin, "Noiabrskii plenum TsK VKP(b) 1928 g.," in Danilov et al., *Kak lomali NEP*, vol. 3: *Plenum TsK VKP(b), 16–24 noiabria, 1928 g.*, 5–29.

50. N. Bukharin, "Zametki ekonomista," *Leningradskaia pravda*, Oct. 1, 1928, 2, Oct. 2, 1928, 3–4. Petrovskii, "Poslednyi rot front," 186, gets the publication dates of "Notes of an Economist" wrong. He claims that his father Petr got the article into the paper by a subterfuge, giving it to sympathetic printers just before typesetting. The fact that the piece ran on two consecutive days suggests that this story is incorrect. The Petrovskii article is full of other factual errors, such as misattributing to Petr Petrovskii the speeches of his father Grigory Petrovskii at the July 1928 plenum of the TsK and TsKK.

For September 1928 anti-Rightist coverage in *Leningradskaia pravda,* see "Bor'ba s pravoi opasnost'iu," *Leningradskaia pravda,* Sept. 20, 1928, 1. For anti-Rightist articles in *Red Gazette* see *Krasnaia gazeta,* Aug. 3, 1928, 1 ("Khlebozagotovki"); Aug. 18, 1928, 1 ("Vsesoiuznoe khlebnoe soveshchanie"); Aug. 19, 1928, 1 ("Khlebozagotovitel'nye bezobraziia"); Aug. 30, 1928, 2 ("Chastnik na khleb-nom rynke"). For the text of the Bukharin-Rykov-Tomsky demands, see Danilov et al., *Kak lomali NEP,* 4:436–438. On the timing, see ibid, 3:16–17.

51. Kvashonkin et al., *Sovetskoe rukovodstvo,* 36–58, 58–59.

52. Knight, *Who Killed Kirov,* 126.

53. For early Kirov comments on the "Face to Production" campaign, see his speech to the mid-June 1928 plenum of the regional party committee in *Lenin-gradskaia pravda,* June 19, 1928, 2–3. See Hiroaki Kuromiya, *Stalin's Industrial Revolution: Politics and Workers, 1928–1929* (Cambridge: Cambridge University Press, 1988), esp. 35–39, on the purge of the labor union apparatuses and Tomsky's removal from the chairmanship of VTsSPS. For one example of an attack by Kirov on the labor unions for their inadequate "ties with the masses" see his speech reprinted in *Leningradskaia pravda,* Dec. 13, 1929, 1.

54. Kuromiya, *Stalin's Industrial Revolution,* 28–35.

55. See for example Kirov speech to activists of Petrograd Ward in *Leningrad-skaia pravda,* May 20, 1928, 2 on the need to substitute for "bourgeois" controls on corruption and inefficiency.

56. Matthew Lenoe, "Stalinist Mass Journalism and the Transformation of So-viet Newspapers, 1926–1929" (Ph.D. diss., University of Chicago, 1997), 749–830.

57. See Kirov speech to regional party committee in RGASPI, f. 80, op. 12, d. 2, ll. 1–16. For the positions of Stalin and Ordzhonikidze on self-criticism in 1928–1929, see Lenoe, "Stalinist Mass Journalism," 782–784, 794–803.

58. See discussion of strikes at the April 25, 1928 plenum of the regional party committee in TsGAIPD SPb, f. 24, op. 1, d. 38; and P. Petrovskii, "Borb'a s khvos-tizmom: Samokritika i proletarskaia demokratiia," *Leningradskaia pravda,* May 19, 1928, 2. Zhiga diary entry in RGALI, f. 1844, op. 1, d. 1, ll. 38–41.

59. Petrovskii, "Bor'ba s khvostizmom."

60. See "Kak rukovodit' rabochim nel'zia," *Leningradskaia pravda,* May 30, 1928; and A. Amenitskii, "Stoit li bespokoit'sia za liniiu biuro raikoma?," ibid., June 1, 1928, 3.

61. TsGAIPD SPb, f. 24, op. 1, d. 39, ll. 44, 56–59, 75–76. See also transcripts of plenum in *Leningradskaia pravda,* June 19, 1928, 2–3.

62. TsGAIPD SPb, f. 24, op. 1, d. 40, ll. 49–52.

63. See for example the records of the mid-June 1928 regional party committee plenum. Stetsky was attacked for complacency about the campaign (TsGAIPD SPb, f. 24, op. 1, d. 39, ll. 75–76) and for promoting it too aggressively (ll. 107–108).

64. V. P. Danilov et al., "Noiabrskii plenum TsK VKP(b) 1928 g.," in Danilov et al., *Kak lomali NEP,* 3:5–29.

65. TsGAIPD SPb, f. 24, op. 1, d. 42, l. 171.

66. Petrovskii, "Poslednyi rot front," 186–187, 198 n. 8. See also Knight, *Who Killed Kirov,* 127–128.

67. On the Stalinist takeover of the *Pravda* editorial offices, see Matthew Lenoe, *Closer to the Masses: Stalinist Culture, Social Revolution, and Soviet Newspapers* (Cambridge: Harvard University Press, 2004), 151–161. In September 1928 elections for officers of the *Pravda* editorial office party organization resulted in de facto Stalinist control of the newspaper.

68. Danilov et al., *Kak lomali NEP*, 3:291–296, 477–479, 524–526.

69. Ibid., 4:6–10, 523, 597. Quoted phrase from p. 9.

70. Ibid., 604–619.

71. Ibid., 44.

72. Ibid., 126–127, 364–369, 708 n. 125. After Ugarov, who was head of the Leningrad Council of Labor Unions, opposed Stalin's purge of the central labor union apparatus at the Eighth Congress of Soviet Labor Unions (December 1928), the Leningrad party organization removed him from his position (March 23, 1929). He remained, however, a member of the Leningrad party committee and a delegate to the April plenum.

73. Iu. Felshtinskii, ed., *Kommunisticheskaia oppozitsiia v SSSR, 1923–1927: Iz arkhiva L'va Trotskogo* (Benson, Vt.: Chalidze Publications, 1988), 150–151; Danilov et al., *Kak lomali NEP*, 4:694–698.

74. Stephen Cohen, *Bukharin and the Bolshevik Revolution: A Political Biography, 1888–1938* (Oxford: Oxford University Press, 1980), 310–336.

75. Amy Knight uses Kirov speeches in favor of the *smychka*, technical aid to middle peasants, and so on to argue that he leaned toward supporting the Right in 1928. See Knight, *Who Killed Kirov*, 128–130.

76. RGASPI, f. 17, op. 113, d. 815, ll. 1020b–1050b (TsK Orgburo materials on the incident); Kirilina, *Neizvestnyi Kirov*, 149.

77. See Rosliakov, *Ubiistvo*, 106–110; Knight, *Who Killed Kirov*, 133–137; Khlevniuk, *Stalin i Ordzhonikidze*, 19–20; Lenoe, "Stalinist Mass Journalism," 803–818. Rosliakov, who worked in Leningrad at the time, attended key meetings, and was generally well placed to know what was going on behind the scenes, believes Kirov knew about the attack before it happened.

78. *Leningradskaia pravda*, June 19, 1928, 2–3.

79. Kirilina, *Neizvestnyi Kirov*, 153–154; Rosliakov, *Ubiistvo*, 106–110. Yunosov was not under arrest at the time he wrote the statement. On Moscow Rightist circles' discussion of Kirov's career in "bourgeois" journalism, see testimony of V. I. Vorobyov before the party cell of the Moscow Industrial Academy, Sept. 19, 1929, reproduced in Danilov et al., *Kak lomali NEP*, vol. 5: *Plenum TsK VKP(b), 10–17 noiabria, 1929 g.*, 598–619, esp. 606, 610.

80. See issues of *Krasnaia gazeta* (Leningrad) from July to August 1929.

81. See Kamenev's January 1929 declaration to Ordzhonikidze as head of the TsKK, Zinoviev's July 12/14, 1928 letter to Kamenev, and June 1930 evidence of former Leningrad Zinovievite Filip Shvalbe to the OGPU, published in Danilov et al., *Kak lomali NEP*, 4:564–565, 683–693, 694–698. See also "Zaiavlenie gruppy byvshikh chlenov VKP(b) i VLKSM," in *Smena*, July 8, 1928, 2, in which a number of former Zinovievite oppositionists announced their repentance and desire to return to the party. Among them were two future defendants in Kirov's murder, Vladimir Rumiantsev and Lev Khanik.

82. For an evaluation of the rhetoric of the TsK Agitprop Department and

Stalin during the self-criticism campaign, see Lenoe, *Closer to the Masses,* 182–197. For an example of Stalin rejecting Left attacks in the summer of 1929, see his letter to Molotov, July 29, 1929, in L. Kosheleva et al., eds., *Pis'ma I. V. Stalina V. M. Molotovu, 1925–1936 gg.* (Moscow: "Rossiia Molodaia," 1995), 135–137. Tomsky's account of Stalin's campaign against the Right at the April 1929 plenum of the TsK and TsKK is in Danilov et al., *Kak lomali NEP,* 4:55–67.

83. Kvashonkin et al., *Sovetskoe rukovodstvo,* 84–85.

84. Ibid.

85. Knight, *Who Killed Kirov,* 127.

86. Kirilina, *Neizvestnyi Kirov,* 186–187.

87. Kuromiya, *Stalin's Industrial Revolution,* 175–178; Krasnikov, *S. M. Kirov v Leningrade,* 56–69. For Kirov's commentary on the arrest of Sablin and others, see *Leningradskaia pravda,* June 12, 1930, 2.

88. GARF, f. 374 s. ch., op. 27s, d. 1898, ll. 14–16ob (Mariinskii to Krinitskii on Leningrad visit, probably mid-September 1929); RGASPI, f. 85, op. 27, d. 108, ll. 8–11 (Mariinskii to Ordzhonikidze on whole incident, Sept. 16, 1929), l. 7 (Chagin to Kirov, Sept. 11, 1929).

89. Mariinskii to Ordzhonikidze, Sept. 16, 1929, RGASPI, f. 85, op. 27, d. 108, ll. 8–11.

90. Ibid., and Chagin et al. to Kirov, Sept. 11, 1929, RGASPI, f. 85, op. 27, d. 108, ll. 6–7. Stenographic report of Sept. 3 meeting is in GARF, f. 324 s.ch., op. 27s, d. 1898, ll. 39–75ob (materials on TsKK investigation of incident).

91. Rosliakov, *Ubiistvo,* 106. See also announcement of regional control commission meeting in *Krasnaia gazeta,* Aug. 29, 1929, 1.

92. On Kovalyov's role at *Pravda,* see Lenoe, "Stalinist Mass Journalism," 648–678, 809–817.

93. *Leningradskaia pravda,* Sept. 3, 1929, 1; "Fakty i tsifry," ibid., Sept. 7, 1929, 2.

94. *Krasnaia gazeta,* Sept. 4–8, 1929.

95. "Kak dushili samokritiku v Vyborgskom raione," ibid., Sept. 8, 1929, 2–3.

96. See Bogdanov, "O rabote OblKK VKP(b)," *Leningradskaia pravda,* June 9, 1930, 2; *Krasnaia gazeta,* Sept. 11, 1929, 3 (Kirov quote); *Leningradskaia pravda,* Sept. 10, 1929, 1–2; Krasnikov, *S. M. Kirov v Leningrade,* 49–56. Kirov's "faster tempos" comment suggests that one aspect of the September 1929 Leningrad press campaign was firing or intimidating local managers who were resisting high plan targets for industry.

97. Kosheleva et al., *Pis'ma,* 160–162, 164–165.

98. Chagin to Kirov, Sept. 11, 1929, RGASPI, f. 85, op. 27, d. 108, ll. 6–7; Molotov to Ordzhonikidze, ll. 1–2.

99. Kosheleva, *Pis'ma,* 152–154.

100. Khlevniuk, *Stalin i Ordzhonikidze,* 19–20; Khlevniuk, *Politbiuro: Mekhanizmy politicheskoi vlasti v 30-e gody* (Moscow: ROSSPEN, 1996), 120; Rosliakov, *Ubiistvo,* 108–110; Kirilina, *Neizvestnyi Kirov,* 149–154; Knight, *Who Killed Kirov,* 130–134. Kirilina presents the sequence of events in a confused fashion. She believes that Desov's denunciation preceded the *Pravda* press campaign. This would make the Desov-Komarov group the "aggressor" in the affair. In fact the sequence of events was the reverse.

Knight argues that Stalin provoked the incident in hopes both of getting rid of the Komarov group, and shaking up Kirov a bit. She also finds it probable that Kirov did not know of the upcoming *Pravda* attack. I differ for the reasons explained in the text. Most important here is Rosliakov's sense that Kirov knew roughly what was coming, as well as the testimony of Stetsky, the Leningrad prosecutors, and *Red Gazette* journalists to Mariinsky in August that Desov was "suppressing" self-criticism.

In her argument that Stalin aimed to shake up Kirov, Knight claims that a reference to Astrakhan in *Pravda's* Sept. 1, 1929 coverage was a not very veiled threat to Kirov, because he had once been prominent there. In fact *Pravda* almost certainly referred to the 1929 ongoing anticorruption cases in Astrakhan, which brought down the party leadership. *Pravda* actually emphasized that unlike Astrakhan, the Leningrad party leadership (that is, Kirov) was sound. Thus the reference to Astrakhan had precisely the opposite meaning from that which Knight assigns it.

101. See above, note 100.

102. Lenoe, "Stalinist Mass Journalism," 13–15.

103. Rosliakov, *Ubiistvo*, 109.

104. RGASPI, f. 671, op. 1, d. 129, ll. 61–80; f. 80, op. 17, d. 70, ll. 1–2.

105. Danilov et al., *Kak lomali NEP*, 5:242–245.

106. Ibid.

107. Knight, *Who Killed Kirov*, 137–141.

108. Ibid., 139. The quote is Knight's translation, with minor punctuation changes and an added note.

109. Ibid., 138–139.

110. Danilov et al., *Kak lomali NEP*, 4:40–41. For Bauman's comments see ibid., 105–106.

CHAPTER 3. KIROV IN LENINGRAD, 1930–1934

1. See Andrea Graziosi, *The Great Soviet Peasant War: Bolsheviks and Peasants, 1917–1933* (Cambridge: Ukrainian Research Institute, Harvard University, 1996), 46–70; Moshe Lewin, *Russian Peasants and Soviet Power: A Study of Collectivization* (New York: Norton, 1968), 446–477.

2. *Leningradskaia pravda,* Jan. 11, 1930, 2.

3. I. V. Stalin, *Sochineniia,* vol. 12 (1929–1930) (Moscow: Gosizdat, 1949) 191–199; Graziosi, *The Great Soviet Peasant War,* 55; Robert Tucker, *Stalin in Power: The Revolution from Above, 1928–1941* (New York: W. W. Norton, 1990), 184–186.

4. *Leningradskaia pravda,* March 19, 1930, 2–3.

5. See ibid., May 23, 1930, 3, and Stalin, "Otvet tovarishcham kolkhoznikam," *Sochineniia,* 12:202–228.

6. Alla Kirilina, *Neizvestnyi Kirov* (Moscow: OLMA-PRESS, 2001), 185.

7. Ibid., 185–186; Amy Knight, *Who Killed Kirov? The Kremlin's Greatest Mystery* (New York: Hill and Wang, 1999), 129–130.

8. Kirov notes are in RGASPI, f. 80, op. 12, d. 13, ll. 1–6. All references to Tomsky's and Rykov's June 29, 1930 speeches and Kirov's June 30, 1930 rebuttal are from *Shest'nadtsatyi s"ezd vsesoiuznoi kommunisticheskoi partii (b): Steno-*

graficheskii otchet (Moscow: Gosizdat, 1930), 142–148 (Tomsky), 148–154 (Rykov), 155–160 (Kirov).

9. *Shest'nadtsatyi s"ezd*, 155–160.

10. See S. Sinel'nikov, *Kirov* (Moscow: Molodaia gvardiia, 1964), 310; Tucker, *Stalin in Power*, 240; and Knight, *Who Killed Kirov*, 144–146, on Kirov's supposed soft line on collectivization. On the relative priority of different regions for collectivization, see V. P. Danilov and N. V. Teptsov, "Kollektivizatsiia: Kak eto bylo," *Pravda*, Aug. 26, 1988, 1, 3, and Sept. 16, 1988, 3.

11. Kirilina, *Neizvestnyi Kirov*, 188; Julian Bullard and Margaret Bullard, eds., *Inside Stalin's Russia: The Diaries of Reader Bullard, 1930–1934* (Charlbury, UK: Day Books, 2000), 24–25, 42, 66, 93, 97, 124–125, 150.

12. Irklis report in RGASPI, f. 80, op. 18, d. 135, ll. 1–30. V. P. Danilov, *Rural Russia under the New Regime* (Bloomington: Indiana University Press, 1988), 48–51, discusses the greater ease of collectivizing larger villages located in wheat-growing regions.

13. Kirilina, *Neizvestnyi Kirov*, 187.

14. RGASPI, f. 80, op. 18, d. 8, ll. 1–45.

15. RGASPI, f. 80, op. 18, d. 12, ll. 1–84. Kirov's and Irklis's recommendations for pressuring the individual householders closely followed those issued by Stalin at a June 1934 TsK meeting on finishing the task of collectivization (Danilov and Teptsov, "Kollektivizatsiia: Kak eto bylo," *Pravda*, Sept. 16, 1988, 3). For the Jan. 1, 1935 percentage of peasant households collectivized see Lesley Rimmel, "The Kirov Murder and Soviet Society: Propaganda and Popular Opinion in Leningrad, 1934–1935" (Ph.D. diss., University of Pennsylvania, 1995), 182.

16. Stepan Krasnikov, *S. M. Kirov v Leningrade* (Leningrad: Lenizdat, 1966), 56–91, 96–104; Sinel'nikov, *Kirov*, 295.

17. O. V. Khlevniuk et al., eds., *Stalin i Kaganovich: Perepiska, 1931–1936 g.g.* (Moscow: ROSSPEN, 2001), 45–47, 61.

18. For monitoring of produce deliveries, etc., see Kirov-Chudov correspondence, 1934, RGASPI, f. 80, op. 18, d. 122, ll. 3, 16, 20. For attacks on cooperative and state distribution managers, see *Leningradskaia pravda*, April 8, 1930, 1, 2, 4; "Vrediteli rabochego snabzheniia," ibid., Jan. 12, 1934, 3.

19. On the competition for investment funds, see James R. Harris, *The Great Urals* (Ithaca: Cornell University Press, 1999). For Leningrad's percentage of total Soviet industrial production, see Kirov speech to Leningrad regional party committee meeting in *Leningradskaia pravda*, May 23, 1930, 3. For examples of Kirov lobbying VSNKh for investment, see Krasnikov, *S. M. Kirov v Leningrade*, 57–58, 83–86, 101. For complaints about lack of investment in Leningrad, see I. P. Zhukov to the November 1928 TsK plenum, in V. P. Danilov et al., *Kak lomali NEP*, vol. 3: *Plenum TsK VKP(b), 16–24 noiabria, 1928 g.* (Moscow: Mezhdunarodnyi fond "Demokratiia," 2000), 5–29, 260–261.

20. Oleg Khlevniuk, *Politbiuro: Mekhanizmy politicheskoi vlasti v 1930-e gody* (Moscow: ROSSPEN, 1996), 122–125; Mikhail Rosliakov, *Ubiistvo Kirova: Politicheskie i ugolovnye prestupleniia v 1930-kh godakh* (Leningrad: Lenizdat, 1991), 112–115; Alexander Vatlin and Larisa Malashenko, *Piggy Fox and the Sword of Revolution* (New Haven: Yale University Press, 2006), 46–47.

21. Khlevniuk, *Politbiuro*, 125.

22. N. B. Lebina, *Povsednevnaia zhizn' sovetskogo goroda: Normy i anomalii, 1920/1930 gody* (St. Petersburg: "Letnii sad," 1999), 167, 190–191, 199–202, 204–227; Hiroaki Kuromiya, *Stalin's Industrial Revolution: Politics and Workers, 1928–1929* (Cambridge: Cambridge University Press, 1988), 228–235; Sheila Fitzpatrick, *Everyday Stalinism. Ordinary Life in Extraordinary Times: Soviet Russia in the 1930s* (New York: Oxford University Press, 1999), 40–66.

23. On the Leningrad strikes, see Aleksandr Bastrykin and Ol'ga Gromtseva, *Teni izchezaiut v Smol'nom: Ubiistvo Kirova* (St. Petersburg: Evropeiskii dom, 2001), 28–29. On the Ivanovo strikes and worker resistance to Stalinism in general, see Jeffrey Rossman, *Worker Resistance under Stalin: Class and Revolution on the Shopfloor* (Cambridge: Harvard University Press), 2005.

24. Kirilina, *Neizvestnyi Kirov,* 190–191.

25. J. Arch Getty and Oleg Naumov, *The Road to Terror: Stalin and the Self-Destruction of the Bolsheviks, 1932–1939* (New Haven: Yale University Press, 1999), 588; Paul Hagenloh, "'Socially Harmful Elements' and the Terror," in Sheila Fitzpatrick, ed., *Stalinism: New Directions* (London: Routledge, 2000), 286–308; Kuromiya, *Stalin's Industrial Revolution,* 258; V. N. Khaustov et al., eds., *Lubianka: Stalin i VChK-GPU-OGPU-NKVD, ianvar' 1922–dekabr' 1936* (Moscow: Mezhdunarodnyi fond "Demokratiia," 2003), 256, 258.

26. Knight, *Who Killed Kirov,* 147.

27. Kirilina, *Neizvestnyi Kirov,* 164–174.

28. Sinel'nikov, *Kirov,* 333–348; Kirilina, *Neizvestnyi Kirov,* 156–164, 174–181.

29. See Stalin's Aug. 30, 1931 letter to Kaganovich in Khlevniuk, *Stalin i Kaganovich,* 71–73.

30. Knight, *Who Killed Kirov,* 150–152; Kirilina, *Neizvestnyi Kirov,* 189.

31. Knight, *Who Killed Kirov,* 149–150; Khlevniuk, *Politbiuro,* 77; Kirilina, *Neizvestnyi Kirov,* 133–134; Lebina, *Povsednevnaia zhizn',* 68–69; Khaustov et al., *Lubianka, 1922–1936,* 339–340, 428.

32. See Kirilina, *Neizvestnyi Kirov,* 127–130; Oleg V. Khlevniuk, *The History of the Gulag from Collectivization to the Great Terror* (New Haven: Yale University Press, 2004), 24, 35–36.

33. Bullard, *Diaries,* 194–195; Khlevniuk, *Politbiuro,* 121. On the Riutin Platform, see Getty, *Road to Terror,* 52–58.

34. One informer on the Komarov-Rekstin-Desov group, writing to the Leningrad party control commission in July 1933, identified Messing as part of that group. See RGASPI, f. 80, op. 17, d. 70, ll. 1–2. On the case against I. P. Zhukov, see Kirilina, *Neizvestnyi Kirov,* 363, 396.

35. Sorokin to Khrushchev, March 5, 1962, in RGANI, f. 6, op. 13, d. 67, ll. 7–14; Khaustov et al., *Lubianka, 1922–1936,* 275, 805 n. 87; Mikhail Ilin'skii, *Narkom Yagoda: Dvadtsat' let v maske* (Moscow: "IAUZA/EKSMO," 2005), 172.

36. For Kirov's intervention in the decision to move Medved, see Sorokin's letter to Khrushchev, March 5, 1962, in RGANI, f. 6, op. 13, d. 67, ll. 7–14. He misdates the incident to 1934. Sorokin gave multiple versions of this and other tales between 1956 and 1966, sometimes differing in details. See Knight, *Who Killed Kirov,* 161 for a slightly different version. For the Politburo decision of August 5

and Yagoda and Stalin's circulars, see Khaustov at al., *Lubianka, 1922–1936,* 276–280.

37. A. I. Kokurin and N. V. Petrov, eds., *Lubianka: Organy VChK-OGPU-NKVD-NKGB-MGB-MVD-KGB, 1917–1991. Spravochnik* (Moscow: Mezh-dunarodnyi fond "Demokratiia," 2003), 53.

38. Rosliakov, *Ubiistvo,* 70–71; Kokurin and Petrov, *Lubianka,* 49.

39. Rosliakov, *Ubiistvo,* 68–70; Bullard, *Diaries,* 243. The suicide note reference is in RGASPI, f. 671, op. 1, d. 112, ll. 1–30b.

40. Bullard, *Diaries,* 243; Rosliakov, *Ubiistvo,* 71; V. K. Zavalishin, "Vokrug ubiistva Kirova," Boris I. Nicolaevsky Collection, Hoover Institution Archives, Series 236, Box 411, File 1, 1–55.

41. Sinel'nikov, *Kirov,* 351; Knight, *Who Killed Kirov,* 160.

42. Lebina, *Povsednevnaia zhizn',* 95–96.

43. Ivan Zhukov, "Neizvestnyi Kirov" (interview with Alla Kirilina), *Argumenty i fakty,* Dec. 1, 2004; RGASPI, f. 80, op. 18, d. 122, ll. 9–11; Kirilina, *Neizvestnyi Kirov,* 324.

44. Zhukov, "Neizvestnyi Kirov"; Pavel Sudoplatov, *Special Tasks* (Boston: Little, Brown, 1994), 50–51.

45. For photographs from various periods of Kirov's life, see A. A. Kirilina and I. P. Donkov, *Kirov i vremia* (Leningrad: Lenizdat, 1986). On Kirov's glasses, see Lebina, *Povsednevnaia zhizn',* 216–218.

46. For Kirov's correspondence with Chudov, see RGASPI, f. 80, op. 18, dd. 62, 63, 122. For one of his letters to Irklis, see RGASPI, f. 80, op. 18, d. 121, ll. 174–176. On his relationship with Medved, see Zavalishin, "Vokrug ubiistvo Kirova," and Rosliakov, *Ubiistvo,* 68.

47. On "familyness" and information flow (or lack thereof) in the Stalinist political system, see Graeme Gill, *The Origins of the Stalinist Political System* (Cambridge: Cambridge University Press, 1990), 129–130.

48. A. N. Pazi, ed., *Nash Mironych* (Leningrad: Lenizdat, 1968), 447. Because of his execution on charges of treason in 1937, Soviet secondary sources, all of which date from later, ignore Yenukidze's presence on the trip. In an Aug. 30, 1933 letter to Voroshilov, however, Yenukidze enthused about the good time he had. See A. V. Kvashonkin et al., eds., *Sovetskoe rukovodstvo: Perepiska. 1928–1941 g.* (Moscow: ROSSPEN, 1999), 252–253.

49. RGANI, f. 6, op. 13, d. 73, ll. 96–132 (Sveshnikov interview, 1966); RGANI, f. 6, op. 13, d. 13, ll. 263–274 (Baskakov deposition, 1961); RGANI, f. 6, op. 13, d. 13, ll. 112–114 (Gubin evidence, 1935); "Prikaz OGPU No. 00325 'O distsipline v organakh i voiskakh OGPU,'" in Kokurin and Petrov, *Lubianka,* 541–545. Stalin's bodyguard commander Vlasik mentions nine bodyguards around his vacation dacha in Sochi and two or three to accompany him on walks. This is roughly comparable to Kirov's security in Leningrad after the summer of 1933 (fifteen guards total, two or three accompanying him on walks, etc.).

50. On the assassination plot warning, see Kirilina, *Neizvestnyi Kirov,* 194.

51. On the nervous crisis, see Knight, *Who Killed Kirov,* 167–168; Sinel'nikov, *Kirov,* 357–358; Krasnikov, *S. M. Kirov v Leningrade,* 179–183.

52. Khlevniuk, *Politbiuro,* 100–104.

53. Ibid., 102, 104, 128.

54. Kirilina, *Neizvestnyi Kirov*, 308–309; Knight, *Who Killed Kirov*, 170–172.

55. Kirilina, *Neizvestnyi Kirov*, 319, and 1960s accounts of congress delegates Mariia Karpova, Anastasia Plotnikova, and Anastasia Slin'ko in RGANI, f. 6, op. 13, d. 78, ll. 6–53.

56. N. Mikhailov and V. Naumov, "Skol'ko delegatov XVII s"ezda partii golosovalo protiv Stalina?" *Izvestiia TsK KPSS*, no. 7 (1989): 114–121. I. F. Kodatsky, from Leningrad, and Mikhail Kalinin were the only two TsK members elected unanimously. Stalin received three votes against, and Kirov four. See also *Sotsialisticheskii vestnik*, no. 4, (Feb. 25, 1934): 13; RGANI, f. 6, op. 13, d. 23, ll. 122–124 (Ratnek); RGANI, f. 6, op. 13, d. 23, ll. 114–115 (Straumit); RGASPI, f. 56, op. 2, d. 36, l. 23, f. 58, op. 1, d. 46, l. 2 f. 56, op. 2, d. 36, l. 23 (results of voting for the Fourteenth and Fifteenth Party Congresses; Strobe Talbott, ed., *Khrushchev Remembers* (Boston: Little, Brown, 1970), 48–49.

57. Egorov and Ostakhov memoirs in RGANI, f. 6, op. 13, d. 78, ll. 6–32.

58. RGASPI, f. 671, op. 1, d. 112, ll. 12–14.

59. Khlevniuk, *Politbiuro*, 134–140.

60. Ibid., 100–101; Khaustov et al., *Lubianka, 1922–1936*, 436–440.

61. Khlevniuk, *Politbiuro*, 108–110; Peter Solomon, *Soviet Criminal Justice under Stalin* (Cambridge: Cambridge University Press, 1996), 153–195; Getty, *Road to Terror*, 114–139.

62. Khlevniuk, *Politbiuro*, 118–140.

63. Rosliakov, *Ubiistvo*, 28–29; Feliks Chuev, *Molotov: Poluderzhavnyi vlastelin* (Moscow: OLMA-PRESS, 1999), 375–376; Kirilina, *Neizvestnyi Kirov*, 312.

64. On Stalin's possible desire to reduce Kaganovich's power, see Khlevniuk, *Politbiuro*, 114, 159–162. In 1935–1936, Khlevniuk shows, Stalin did reduce Kaganovich's responsibilities, dividing some of them among A. A. Andreev and Nikolai Yezhov.

65. Khlevniuk, *Politbiuro*, 114; O. V. Khlevniuk, *Stalin i Ordzhonikidze* (Moscow: "Rossiia Molodaia," 1993), 16; R. W. Davies et al., *The Stalin-Kaganovich Correspondence, 1931–36* (New Haven: Yale University Press, 2003), 44–45, 49–55; Oleg V. Khlevniuk, "The First Generation of Stalinist 'Party Generals,'" in E. A. Rees, ed., *Centre-Local Relations in the Stalinist State, 1928–1941* (New York: Palgrave Macmillan, 2002), 37–64.

66. Khlevniuk, *Politbiuro*, 121–122. See also Kirilina, *Neizvestnyi Kirov*, 321–322, and Rosliakov, *Ubiistvo*, 112–115.

67. Khlevniuk, *Politbiuro*, 290; Rosliakov, *Ubiistvo*, 33. Sveshnikov's comments are in RGANI, f. 6, op. 13, d. 73, l. 105.

68. Knight, *Who Killed Kirov*, 177, and Francisco Benvenuti, "Kirov in Soviet Politics, 1933–1934," CREES Discussion Papers, no. 8 (University of Birmingham Centre for Russian and East European Studies, 1977) suggest that Kirov's emphasis on "revolutionary legality" marked him as a maverick. On the broad campaign for "revolutionary"/ "proletarian"/"socialist" legality in 1933–1934, see Getty, *Road to Terror*, 119; "Nezyblemost' sovetskogo zakona–osnova sotsialisticheskogo pravoznaniia," *Pravda*, May 8, 1934, 1; D. Lur'e, "O klassovoi bor'be v derevne," ibid., Oct. 2, 1934, 2.

69. Benvenuti, "Kirov in Soviet Politics," 18.

70. Robert F. Miller, "The *Politotdel:* A Lesson from the Past," *Slavic Review* 25, no. 3 (September 1966): 475–496; "Potonuli v melochakh," *Pravda,* May 24, 1934, 2; "Reshitel'no povysit' tempy khlebosdachi," ibid., Oct. 3, 1934, 1.

71. Jonathan Haslam, *The Soviet Union and the Struggle for Collective Security in Europe, 1933–1939* (New York: St. Martin's Press, 1984), 27–34. There is no basis for claiming as Knight does (*Who Killed Kirov,* 178–179) that "Kirov was taking the lead in this new policy direction" (forming a common front with antifascist forces in the capitalist democracies).

72. Kirilina, *Neizvestnyi Kirov,* 154–155, 284–291.

73. Iu. I. Sedov, N. V. Kulish, and A. Ia. Valetov, "Spravka rabotnikov prokuratury SSSR i sledstvennogo otdela KGB SSSR po povodu zapiski A. N. Iakovleva 'Nekotorye soobrazheniia po itogam izucheniia obstoiatel'stv ubiistva S. M. Kirova,'" in A. Artizov et al., eds., *Reabilitatsiia: Kak eto bylo,* vol. 3: *Seredina 80-kh godov–1991* (Moscow: Mezhdunarodnyi fond "Demokratiia," 2004), 459–508 (hereafter cited as "Reply to Iakovlev"), esp. 469–471. For surveillance of Komarovites, see "Agenturnoe delo 'Zanoza'," in RGASPI, f. 671, op. 1, d. 129, l. 61.

74. "Reply to Iakovlev," 470–471; RGASPI, f. 671, op. 1, d. 121, l. 31; Rumiantsev testimony at trial of "Leningrad Center," Dec. 28–29, 1934, in RGASPI, f. 671, op. 1, d. 128, l. 142; Kirilina, *Neizvestnyi Kirov,* 286, 363.

75. On Talmud's request that Kotolynov be posted to his lab, see "Ubiistvo v Smol'nom," *Rodina,* no. 10 (1995): 62–66. On the *Boevoe zemliachestvo,* see Rumiantsev letter of Dec. 27, 1934 in RGANI, f. 6, op. 13, d. 1, ll. 114–116.

See also *Piterskii Komsomol v grazhdanskoi voine* (Leningrad: Molodaia gvardiia, 1934), passim. Lashevich reference is on p. 124. Lev Khanik "confessed" to interrogator Stromin in a December 13, 1934 interrogation that one of the goals of the supposed Zinovievite conspirators in the Fellowship of Militant Komsomols was to "smooth over the antiparty and counterrevolutionary essence" of the Zinovievite opposition (RGASPI, f. 671, op. 1, d. 114, ll. 202–205). This would suggest that the absence of any denunciation of the oppositionists in the fellowship's publications was a problem, even though the history that they covered was years before the factional battles of 1925–1927.

76. Zavalishin, "Vokrug ubiistvo Kirova," 15–16; V. V. Rumiantsev appeal to USSR prosecutor, Dec. 27, 1934, RGANI, f. 6, op. 13, d. 1, ll. 114–116; Khanik interrogation of Dec.13, 1934, TsA FSB RF, a.u.d. N-Sh44, t. 12, ll. 131–135; Khanik statement to prosecutors, Dec. 19, 1934, in Kirilina, *Neizvestnyi Kirov,* 427.

77. O. V. Khlevniuk et al., eds., *Stalin i Kaganovich: Perepiska, 1931–1936 g.g.* (Moscow: ROSSPEN, 2001), 68, 80, 121–122, 558.

78. David Brandenberger, *National Bolshevism: Stalinist Mass Culture and the Formation of Modern Russian National Identity, 1931–1956* (Cambridge: Harvard University Press, 2002), 27–34.

79. For Kirov's musical and Pushkin assignments, see Andrei Artizov and Oleg Naumov, eds., *Vlast' i khudozhestvennaia intelligentsiia: Dokumenty TsK RKP(b)-VKP(b) o kul'turnoi politike, 1917–1953* (Moscow: Mezhdunarodnyi fond "Demokratiia," 2002), 201–218. On the Pushkin cult, see Stephanie Sandler, "The 1937 Pushkin Jubilee as Epic Trauma," in David Brandenberger and Kevin Platt, eds., *Epic Revisionism: Russian History and Literature as Epic Propaganda*

(Madison: University of Wisconsin Press, 2006), 193–232. On Zhdanov's relative *kul'turnost'* and his role in the 1934 congress of the Union of Soviet Writers and the preparation of new history textbooks, see Kees Boterbloem, *The Life and Times of Andrei Zhdanov, 1896–1948* (Montreal: McGill-Queen's University Press, 2004), 43, 114–116.

80. See Kirilina, *Neizvestnyi Kirov,* 324–328; Brandenberger, *National Bolshevism,* 359–360 n. 6.

81. Kirilina, *Neizvestnyi Kirov,* 324–328.

82. Ibid., 328.

83. Ibid., 141, 324–325; Knight, *Who Killed Kirov,* 180.

84. Boterbloem, *Andrei Zhdanov,* 115; Jerrold L. Schecter and Vyacheslav Luchkov, *Khrushchev Remembers: The Glasnost Tapes* (Boston: Little, Brown, 1990), 66.

85. Kirilina, *Neizvestnyi Kirov,* 306. For quotes, see September 1931 correspondence between Stalin and Allilueva in Iu. G. Murin, ed., *Iosif Stalin v ob'iatiiakh sem'i* (Moscow: "Rodina," 1993), 35–38. On Kirov's management of Stalin's July 1933 trip to Leningrad, see below, pp. 405–406, and Sveshnikov's 1966 testimony in RGANI, f. 6, op. 13, d. 73, l. 104.

86. Kirilina, *Neizvestnyi Kirov,* 307; Rosliakov, *Ubiistvo,* 116.

87. Murin, *Iosif Stalin,* 158–159.

88. Ibid., 160–162.

89. Svetlana Allilueva, *Twenty Letters to a Friend* (New York: Harper and Row, 1967), 138; A. T. Rybin, *Riadom so Stalinym: Zapiski telokhranitelia* (Moscow: Izdatel'stvo "Veteran," 1992); Boterbloem, *Andrei Zhdanov,* 115; Vladimir Loginov, *Teni Stalina: General Vlasik i ego soratniki* (Moscow: "Sovremennik," 2000), 97. Without the confirmation of Svanidze's diary, these memoirs, especially those of Vlasik and Rybin, would be dubious sources.

90. Iurii Zhukov, *Inoi Stalin* (Moscow: "Vagrius," 2003).

91. See Stalin-Kaganovich correspondence of Aug. 25–30, 1934 in Khlevniuk et al., *Stalin i Kaganovich,* 454–468; Kirilina, *Neizvestnyi Kirov,* 329–330; Matthew Payne, "Seeing Like a Soviet State: Settlement of Nomadic Kazakhs, 1928–1934," unpublished ms. (Emory University, 2007); Kvashonkin et al., *Sovetskoe rukovodstvo,* 245–248; personal communication (email) from Payne to the author, July 9, 2007.

92. Email communication from Matthew Payne, July 9, 2007. Among Payne's sources are *Shestoi plenum kazakhskogo kraevogo komiteta VKP(b), 10–16 iiulia 1933 goda* (Alma-Ata: Kazakhstanskoe Kraevoe Izdatel'svo, 1936); *VIII Kazakhstanskaia kraevaia konferentsiia VKP(b) 8–16 ianvaria 1934 g.; Stenograficheskii otchet* (Alma-Ata: Kazakhstanskoe Kraevoe Izdatel'svo, n.d.); and a 1934 report of the territorial control commission. On Stalin's support for sustaining grain reserves in Kazakhstan, see above, note 91.

93. Kirilina, *Neizvestnyi Kirov,* 331–332.

94. Khlevniuk, *Politburo,* 129–133. That October the Politburo also rescinded an August order issued by NKVD chief Yagoda creating special courts in NKVD camps that could sentence inmates to death with no right of appeal. The August order contradicted the terms of the July 1934 reorganization of the secret police and courts.

95. Khlevniuk et al., *Stalin i Kaganovich*, 421.

96. Khlevniuk, *Politbiuro*, 129–130, 134.

97. Khaustov et al., *Lubianka, 1922–1936*, 812 n. 124. Khlevniuk, *Politbiuro*, 153, discusses Stalin's desire for more targeted repression from the security organs.

98. See Kokurin and Petrov, *Lubianka*, 505–522 (Sept. 1930 instructions to Ukrainian GPU organs, giving basic information on relationship of paid officers [*upolnomochennye*] to the *agentura* [i.e. residents] and the "network" [i.e. informers]); 548–552 (March 11, 1935 NKVD circular on "reconstruction of operational work" summarizing multiple previous orders on the new methods). See also Yezhov's notes for December 1934 or January 1935 presentation to Stalin in RGASPI, f. 671, op. 1, d. 271, ll. 565–565ob. See also January 1935 sentences for Leningrad NKVD officers accused of negligence in the Kirov murder (RGANI, f. 6, op. 13, d. 79, ll. 99–104).

99. "Reply to Iakovlev," 472; Khaustov et al., *Lubianka, 1922–1936*, 820 n.154; Pel'she report (RGANI, f. 6, op. 13, d. 117, ll. 1–18).

100. Khaustov et al., *Lubianka, 1922–1936*, 569–571.

101. Ibid., 264–266, 467–468. On Stalin's admiration for Zakovsky's methods, see quotation from his February 1938 letter to Yezhov in A. Artizov et al., eds., *Reabilitatsiia: Kak eto bylo*, vol. 2: *1956–nachalo 80-kh godov* (Moscow: Mezhdunarodnyi fond "Demokratiia," 2003), 579 (February 1963 KPK report on terror).

102. Kvashonkin at al., *Sovetskoe rukovodstvo*, 277–278, 293–295.

103. Khlevniuk et al., *Stalin i Kaganovich*, 419, 427–429, 430–431.

104. "Reply to Iakovlev," 473.

105. Fomin deposition in RGANI, f. 6, op. 13, d. 62, ll. 62–76. Fomin claims that the arrest list was formulated "one month" before Kirov's murder, rather than in August 1934, but he made several such minor factual errors in his post-Stalin testimony.

106. RGANI, f. 6, op.13, d. 73, l. 102 (Sveshnikov interview, 1966); Zavalishin, "Vokrug ubiistva Kirova," 34–35; Rosliakov, *Ubiistvo*, 71.

107. Khlevniuk, *Politbiuro*, 125–127.

108. Knight, *Who Killed Kirov*, 163.

109. RGASPI, f. 80, op. 18, d. 121, ll. 67–70.

CHAPTER 4. THE SCENE OF THE CRIME

1. Mikhail Rosliakov, *Ubiistvo Kirova: Politicheskie i ugolovnye prestupleniia v 1930-kh godakh* (Leningrad: Lenizdat, 1991), 38–39.

2. See Lesley Rimmel, "Another Kind of Fear: The Kirov Murder and the End of Bread Rationing in Leningrad," *Slavic Review* 56 (Autumn 1997): 481–499; and Oleg V. Khlevniuk, *Politbiuro: Mekhanizmy politicheskoi vlasti v 1930-e gody* (Moscow: ROSSPEN, 1996), 125–126.

3. Rosliakov, *Ubiistvo*, 38–39; Alla Kirilina, *Neizvestnyi Kirov* (Moscow: OLMA-PRESS, 2001), 210–211.

4. Kirilina, *Neizvestnyi Kirov*, 210–211; Rosliakov, *Ubiistvo*, 40.

5. Kirilina, *Neizvestnyi Kirov*, 211–214; Rosliakov, *Ubiistvo*, 40; Party Con-

trol Committee interview with Sveshnikov in RGANI, f. 6, op. 13, d. 73, ll. 114–115.

6. Kirilina, *Neizvestnyi Kirov*, 211–214; Rosliakov, *Ubiistvo*, 40.

7. See Dec. 1, 1934 testimony of Laziukov and Pauzer in RGASPI, f. 671, op. 1, d. 113, ll. 9–11.

8. RGANI, f. 6, op. 13, d. 71, ll. 15–17 (Molochnikov testimony); Kirilina, *Neizvestnyi Kirov*, 214–215 ("two employees"); Sveshnikov to KPK, 1966, RGANI, f. 6, op. 13, d. 73, ll. 96–132; Rosliakov, *Ubiistvo*, 41.

9. Smolny commander Mikhalchenko testified on Dec. 4 about the electricians in the basement (TsA FSB RF, a.u.d. N-Sh44, t. 24, ll. 99–104.). See also December 4 testimony of Smolny employee I. I. Kutylov, who first asked Platoch to fix the lights (RGASPI, f. 671, op.1, d. 113, ll.41–42).

10. In testimony on Dec. 1 and 3 Vasiliev explained that the glass doors to the cafeteria also led to the special "secretaries' entrance" to Smolny, for use only of select senior officials. There were a stairwell and an elevator at this entrance. The glass doors were to be kept locked as a security measure, and only persons authorized to use the cafeteria and the special entrance had keys. Vasiliev opened the doors to facilitate carrying typewriters through to the elevator for transport downstairs and over to the Uritsky Palace. See RGANI, f. 671, op. 1, d. 113, ll. 6, 25–30.

11. RGASPI, f. 671, op. 1, d. 113, ll. 18–20 (Platoch testimony, Dec. 2, 1934); RGANI, f. 6, op. 13, d. 71, ll. 15–17 (Molochnikov testimony, Dec. 9, 1934); RGASPI, f. 671, op.1, d. 113, ll. 16–17 (Yalozo testimony). On December 3 Nikolaev stated in written testimony that someone hit him on the head around the time he fired his second shot. See his testimony excerpted in this chapter.

12. Kirilina, *Neizvestnyi Kirov*, 215.

13. Interrogation records for Vasiliev, Dureiko, and Yalozo are in RGASPI, f. 671, op. 1, d. 113, ll. 6, 8, 16–20, 25–38.

14. Kirilina, *Neizvestnyi Kirov*, 218. Testimony available to me (from RGASPI and RGANI) from Dec. 2 through Dec. 8 also confirms the basic picture of the murder. The one exception is a deposition by Nikolai Alekseevich Utkin, assistant to Kasparov, second secretary of the city party committee, on December 8, which differs from that of the other witnesses on important points (RGASPI, f. 671, op. 1, d. 113, ll. 55–58). Utkin claimed that there were forty to sixty seconds between the shots, that he saw Borisov running down the corridor *away* from the murder scene soon after the second shot, and that he (Utkin) was first upon the scene of the killing. I have chosen to disregard most of Utkin's evidence (except that the electrician Platoch was in dark blue work overalls) because it was inconsistent with all of the earlier depositions on multiple points and because it fit too well with central NKVD investigators' efforts to find evidence of negligence by the Leningrad NKVD—in particular his testimony that he saw the guard Borisov actually running away from the scene of the crime.

15. Lioninok's Dec. 8, 1934 testimony is in RGASPI, f. 671, op. 1, d. 113, ll. 48–52.

16. Rosliakov, *Ubiistvo*, 40–41. N. F. Sveshnikov, head of Kirov's secretariat and an important party official, confirmed the same general picture at an interview with the KPK in 1966 (RGANI, f. 6, op. 13, d. 73, ll. 96–132).

17. See Kirilina, *Neizvestnyi Kirov*, 204–209, discussing descriptions in Alexander Orlov, *The Secret History of Stalin's Crimes* (New York: Random House, 1953); Robert Conquest, *The Great Terror* (New York: Macmillan, 1973); and Anton Antonov Ovseenko, *Portret tirana* (New York: Ermitazh, 1980).

18. Iu. I. Sedov, N. V. Kulish, and A. Ia. Valetov, "Spravka rabotnikov prokuratury SSSR i sledstvennogo otdela KGB SSSR po povodu zapiski A. N. Iakovleva 'Nekotorye soobrazheniia po itogam izucheniia obstoiatel'stv ubiistva S. M. Kirova,'" in A. Artizov et al., eds., *Reabilitatsiia: Kak eto bylo*, vol. 3: *Seredina 80-kh godov–1991* (Moscow: Mezhdunarodnyi fond "Demokratiia," 2004), 493 (hereafter cited as "Reply to Iakovlev"); RGANI, f. 6, op. 13, d. 13, ll. 252–262 (Mikhalchenko, 1960).

19. Kirilina, *Neizvestnyi Kirov*, 342; RGANI, f. 6, op. 13, d.73, ll. 110–111 (Sveshnikov).

20. RGANI, f. 6, op. 13, d. 13, ll. 188–195 (Kulnev).

21. "Reply to Iakovlev," 494.

22. On the lack of orders for handling detainees, see Gubin's Dec. 6, 1934 interrogation, reported in "K vyiasneniiu voprosa o zaderzhanii Nikolaeva L. V. do soversheniia im ubiistva S. M. Kirova," RGANI, f. 6, op. 13, d. 13, 7–45. On the absence of written instructions in general see "Reply to Iakovlev," 494.

23. RGANI, f. 6, op. 13, d. 13, ll. 112–114.

24. See Kirilina, *Neizvestnyi Kirov*, 343–344.

25. See Amy Knight, *Who Killed Kirov? The Kremlin's Greatest Mystery* (New York: Hill and Wang, 1999), 190–199; Aleksandr Bastrykin and Olga Gromtseva, *Teni izchezaiut v Smol'nom: Ubiistvo Kirova* (St. Petersburg: Evropeiskii dom, 2001), 347–360. Bastrykin and Gromtseva's book is poorly footnoted and rife with contradictory speculations. Bastrykin argued in a 2000 article in *Moskovskii komsomolets* that Nikolaev was "only a witness" to the crime, not the murderer. As Kirilina points out, this ignores a mass of evidence that Nikolaev was the killer. According to official transcripts, Nikolaev never denied that he had murdered Kirov (Kirilina, *Neizvestnyi Kirov*, 219–222).

26. Rosliakov, *Ubiistvo*, 41; RGASPI, f. 671, op. 1, d. 113, l. 8.

27. Knight, *Who Killed Kirov*, 198–199. Knight cites the 1989 testimony of Dr. A. G. Dembo that when he arrived at Smolny, probably between five and six P.M., there were no guards at the building entrance or Kirov's office (Knight, *Who Killed Kirov*, 198, 308 n. 92). Kirilina points out that there are records of the officers guarding the Kirov office after the murder including a log noting the arrival of various doctors, beginning before 5 P.M. Kirilina demonstrates that Dembo's unpublished memoirs, his 1989 article in the newspaper *Smena*, and his 1989 letter to Mikhail Gorbachev are inconsistent with one another and with documentary evidence from 1934 (Kirilina, *Neizvestnyi Kirov*, 226–228.)

28. Bravy's testimony is in RGASPI, f. 671, op. 1, d. 113, ll. 72–73. Bravy's and Mikhalchenko's testimony about the moments after the shooting differed, as interrogators noted. Bravy was the duty officer that afternoon and next up the chain of command was Mikhalchenko, deputy commander of the Smolny guard. Mikhalchenko, in his testimony excerpted above, claimed that Bravy ran into his office (Bravy sat in a main outer office and Mikhalchenko had an inner room) and said that there had been shots on the third floor. Mikhalchenko then ran upstairs,

saw the murder scene, and called NKVD headquarters, probably from a phone in one of the third-floor offices. Bravy, interrogated by the same central NKVD officer as Mikhalchenko (Chertok) and probably close to the same date, testified that he got telephone calls from Ivanchenko and another Leningrad soviet official, Nazarenko, and activated the general alarm. He did not know where Mikhalchenko was, nor did he know precisely what had happened. Nonetheless, he called the NKVD headquarters Operations Department to notify them something was up. Soon after that Mikhalchenko ran into his office and called NKVD headquarters.

The differences between the two accounts suggest that Mikhalchenko may not have been in his office when notified of the shots. Presumably he chose to conceal this fact in his December 4 interrogation, in order to present himself as at his post when the emergency began. Bravy's account has the advantage of explaining the two calls that came into NKVD headquarters one after the other (see Molochnikov's testimony in this chapter). According to Molochnikov, the first caller simply stated that Medved was needed urgently at Smolny. This could have been Bravy's call, before he knew precisely what had happened. Literally seconds later, Mikhalchenko called, saying that Kirov had been shot. Bravy's interrogation is in RGASPI, f. 671, op. 1, d. 113, ll. 72–73.

The earliest witnesses on the murder scene do corroborate that Mikhalchenko arrived at roughly the time he claimed. Vladimir Nagli, the director of the State Drama Theater, told interrogators on December 8 that he remembered Mikhalchenko helping to carry Nikolaev to a side room after the latter began to stir. Nagli reported that Mikhalchenko stopped him from punching Nikolaev in the face. Mikhalchenko also remembered Nagli at the scene. Nagli's testimony is in RGASPI, f. 671, op. 1, d. 113, l. 53.

In general it is quite likely that NKVD officers in Smolny at the time of the killing were omitting facts and telling minor lies to interrogators in order to avoid charges of negligence.

29. See Bastrykin and Gromtseva, *Teni izchezaiut,* 344–360; Knight, *Who Killed Kirov,* 193–199; and Kirilina, *Neizvestnyi Kirov,* 219. On Platoch's *siniaia spetsovka,* see testimony of N. A. Utkin, an assistant to city party committee secretary Kasparova, who was also at the crime scene early (RGASPI, f. 671, op. 1, d. 113, ll. 55–58). On OGPU/UGB/GUGB/NKVD uniforms, see http://members .tripod.com/~otlichnik/uniformo.html.

30. Rosliakov, *Ubiistvo,* 43–44. On Nikolaev's pistol permits see Kirilina, *Neizvestnyi Kirov,* 354, citing a 1990 interview with A. Ia. Valetov, of the KGB Investigative Department. Knight, *Who Killed Kirov,* 205–206, confirms that copies of Nikolaev's two permits for his pistol are in Nikolaev's file at the Kirov Museum in St. Petersburg. See also N. Petukhov and V. Khomchik reporting on results of the perestroika era investigation in "Delo o 'Leningradskom tsentre,'" *Vestnik verkhovnogo suda SSSR* 5 (1991): 15–18.

The bullet that hit the cornice is reported by Rosliakov, *Ubiistvo,* 43, who implies that it was actually embedded there. NKVD Officer Kulesh, who arrived on the scene with Medved on the evening of December 1, reported in 1960 finding the second bullet on the floor underneath a richochet mark "on the wall" (RGANI, f. 6, op. 13, d. 13, ll. 314–316).

Medved telegram is in RGANI, f. 6, op. 13, d. 71, ll. 22–23. Pelshe commission report is in RGANI, f. 6, op. 13, d. 117, ll. 1–18. See also Kirilina, *Neizvestnyi Kirov,* 220, and Petukhov and Khomchik, "Delo o 'Leningradskom tsentre.'"

31. See Rosliakov, *Ubiistvo,* 41–42; Kirilina, *Neizvestnyi Kirov,* 221–228; Knight, *Who Killed Kirov,* 195–196; Bastrykin and Gromtseva, *Teni izchezaiut,* 9.

32. Kirilina, *Neizvestnyi Kirov,* 223–225, gives the complete text of the autopsy report. The report does not note that the direction of the bullet upward was consistent with an attack by a person shorter than Kirov—that is my observation.

33. Fomin statement of March 26, 1956 in RGANI, f. 6, op. 13, d. 62, ll. 62–76. For the text of the "Plan," see Chapter 6, Document 32. See Chapter 7, Document 36 for the reference to the "Plan" found during the "personal search" of Nikolaev.

Medved's deputy Fomin enlarged upon (or possibly embellished) his March 1956 testimony on Sept. 1, 1956 and later. In his Sept. 1, 1956 deposition, Fomin claimed that on the evening of Dec. 1, 1934 he and Special Department Officer Yanishevsky found in Nikolaev's briefcase a handwritten map of Kirov's habitual walking route from Smolny to his apartment. Fomin elaborated on this testimony to the Shatunovskaya commission on Jan. 18, 1961, when he claimed that the map was not in Nikolaev's handwriting, and that it was "drawn by a person with some connection to drafting work" (Klimov report on detention[s] of Nikolaev in RGANI, f. 6, op. 13, d. 13, ll. 7–45).

Tat'iana Sukharnikova, who has recently examined the originals of Nikolaev's diaries and notebooks (see Conclusion) reports that these contain sketches in Nikolaev's hand of routes used by Kirov and his security escorts between Kirov's apartment and Smolny (Tat'iana Sukharnikova, "My nagnali takoi velichaishii, podobaiushchii strakh revoliutsii," interview by Iuliia Kantor, *Vremia,* Nov. 29, 2007). It may be that Fomin's "map" refers to these sketches, which were in materials found at Nikolaev's apartment and his mother's, not on Nikolaev's person. Although this book relies on Fomin's testimony to help reconstruct events in Leningrad on Dec. 1–2, his evidence contains multiple demonstrable factual inaccuracies, from minor ones such as the misstatement of the name of Kirov's personal assistant Bukovsky to major ones such as his claim that Zaporozhets was present in Leningrad when Nikolaev was detained in October 1934. I suspect that his evidence is heavily contaminated by his testimony against Yagoda (unavailable to me) during the Great Terror.

34. See B. A. Yermolaev testimony of Nov. 20, 1960 in RGANI, f. 6, op. 13, d. 13, ll. 202–203ob. and a KGB memorandum, probably to the 1956 Molotov commission, in RGANI, f. 6, op. 13, d. 71, ll. 4–5. A copy of the official report on the search of Nikolaev's mother's apartment in RGANI, f. 6, op. 13, d. 70, ll. 71–71ob gives the date as Dec. 4, 1934 but this is almost certainly an error.

35. Fomin statement of March 26, 1956 in RGANI, f. 6, op. 13, d. 62, ll. 62–76. Kulesh testimony in RGANI, f. 6, op. 13, d. 13, ll. 314–316.

36. "Reply to Iakovlev," 465.

37. Fomin's and Isakov's signatures are both on December 1 and 2 interrogations of Nikolaev. See RGANI, f. 6, op. 13, d. 1, ll. 91–99, TsA FSB RF, a.u.d. N-Sh44, t. 12, ll. 12–14. See Kirilina, *Neizvestnyi Kirov,* 250–251, Petukhov and Khomchik, "Delo o Leningradskom tsentre." In a 1956 or 1957 report to Khru-

shchev, Petr Pospelov gave a longer excerpt from Fomin's post-Stalin testimony about Nikolaev. See "Zapiska P. N. Pospelova ob ubiistve Kirova," *Svobodnaia mysl'*, no. 8 (1992): 64–71.

38. See Iu. N. Zhukov, "Sledstvie i sudebnye protsessy po delu ob ubiistve Kirova," *Voprosy istorii*, no. 2 (2000): 36.

39. As we have seen from Molochnikov's testimony, Medved sent his 6:20 P.M. telegram from Smolny. Draule was probably first interrogated at NKVD headquarters. In an interview with Kirilina, Leonid Fedorovich Raikhman (pseudonym R. O. Popov), an officer of the Leningrad NKVD Secret Political Department who interrogated Draule on December 2, says that the latter spent the night of December 1–2 at NKVD headquarters, sleeping on chairs in a corridor. So it is most likely that she was arrested and brought straight to the NKVD building rather than Smolny. See Kirilina, *Neizvestnyi Kirov,* 252.

40. RGASPI, f. 671, op. 1, d. 114, ll. 1–2 (copy of the protocol of Draule's first interrogation). My thanks to J. Arch Getty for directing me to this document.

41. See RGANI, f. 6, op. 13, d. 1, ll. 58–59; TsA FSB RF, a.u.d. N-Sh44, t. 24, ll. 191–194, 217–219.

CHAPTER 5. LEONID NIKOLAEV

1. Iu. I. Sedov, N. V. Kulish, and A. Ia. Valetov, "Spravka rabotnikov prokuratury SSSR i sledstvennogo otdela KGB SSSR po povodu zapiski A. N. Iakovleva 'Nekotorye soobrazheniia po itogam izucheniia obstoitel'stv ubiistva S. M. Kirova,'" June 14, 1990, published in A. Artizov et al., eds., *Reabilitatsiia: Kak eto bylo,* vol. 3: *Seredina 80-kh godov–1991* (Moscow: Mezhdunarodnyi fond "Demokratiia," 2004), 464–465 (hereafter "Reply to Iakovlev").

2. TsA FSB RF, a.u.d. N-Sh44, t. 45, paket 7, l. 1.

3. Alla Kirilina, *Rikoshet* (St. Petersburg: "Znanie," 1993), 37. Excerpts from Nikolaev's mother's Dec. 4, 1934 interrogation are in RGANI, f. 6, op. 13, d. 13, ll. 330–331.

4. Medved telegram to Iagoda, 10:30 P.M., Dec. 1, 1934, TsA FSB RF, a.u.d. N-Sh44, t. 24, ll. 2–4; "Reply to Iakovlev," 463.

5. RGASPI, f. 671, op. 1, d. 114, ll. 92–94.

6. Alla Kirilina, *Neizvestnyi Kirov* (Moscow: OLMA-PRESS, 2001), 240–241, 244; Orlando Figes, *Peasant Russia, Civil War: The Volga Countryside in Revolution, 1917–1921* (Oxford: Oxford University Press, 1989), 267–284, 351–353. Nikolaev did not serve in the peacetime Red Army. In 1925 and 1926 medical commissions granted him exemptions from service due to his physical disabilities. In 1927 Nikolaev applied for and received an exemption from service based on his "family situation," presumably meaning the birth of his son.

7. Figes, *Peasant Russia,* 346–351.

8. Kirilina, *Rikoshet,* 38. On Nikolaev's military hospital service see RGANI, f. 6, op. 13, d. 71, ll. 22–23 (Medved telegram to Iagoda, Dec. 2, 1934).

9. Kirilina, *Rikoshet,* 38–39.

10. Ibid.

11. Ibid., 39.

12. Nikolaev interrogation of Dec. 9, 1934, RGASPI, f. 671, op. 1, d. 114, ll.

92–94; RGASPI, f. 671, op. 1, d. 114, ll. 92–94; "Gibel' Kirova: Fakty i versii," *Rodina,* no. 3 (2005): 60.

13. Kirilina, *Rikoshet,* 39.

14. Ibid., 40.

15. Ibid.

16. See Draule's 1933 political autobiography published in "Gibel' Kirova," 57–65.

17. Ibid., 61.

18. Tat'iana Sukharnikova, "My nagnali takoi velichaishii, podobaiushchii strakh revoliutsii," interview by Iuliia Kantor, *Vremia,* Nov. 29, 2007. Online at www.vremya.ru/2007/219/13/19305.html.

19. "Gibel' Kirova," 60–61.

20. Kirilina, *Neizvestnyi Kirov,* 253–254. On male Communists' attitudes towards their female "comrades," see Anne Gorsuch, "'A Woman is not a Man': The Culture of Gender and Generation in Soviet Russia, 1921–1928," *Slavic Review* 55, no. 3 (Fall 1996): 636–660. Photograph of Draule from "Gibel' Kirova," 62. Tat'iana Sukharnikova, director of the Kirov Museum in St. Petersburg, asserted in a 2003 interview that Draule had a cleft lip (Sukharnikova, "Ugolovnogo dela po faktu ubiistva Kirova ne vozbuzhdalos'," interview by Iuliia Kantor, *Izvestiia,* Dec. 1, 2003).

21. RGASPI, f. 671, op. 1, d. 114, ll. 96–99.

22. See RGASPI, f. 671, op. 1, d. 114, ll. 3–5. The 1926 medical reports "beginning of sexual life" for Nikolaev as age twenty. This would mean between April 1924 and March 1925. Photographs of Nikolaev were published by Amy Knight in *Who Killed Kirov? The Kremlin's Greatest Mystery* (New York: Hill and Wang, 1999), 174–175; and in "Gibel' Kirova," 62.

23. Kirilina, *Rikoshet,* 40.

24. RGASPI, f. 671, op. 1, d. 114, ll. 96–99.

25. Ibid.

26. RGASPI, f. 671, op. 1, d. 114, ll. 23–27; Kirilina, *Neizvestnyi Kirov,* 255–256, 496. An NKVD list of members of the Leningrad regional Communist Party committee prepared for Nikolai Yezhov after Kirov's murder lists Irklis as a former member of the Zinovievite Opposition (RGASPI, f. 671, op. 1, d. 116, ll. 67–68).

27. Kirilina, *Rikoshet,* 41, "Gibel' Kirova," 61. On norms for living space and actual average residential space per person in Leningrad see Natalia Lebina, *Povsednevnaia zhizn' sovetskogo goroda: Normy i anomalii, 1920/1930 gody* (St. Petersburg: ITD "Letnii sad," 1999), 191.

28. "Gibel' Kirova," 61.

29. Kirilina, *Rikoshet,* 41.

30. Ibid., 41–42.

31. RGASPI, f. 671, op. 1, d. 114, ll. 3–5; Kirilina, *Neizvestnyi Kirov,* 244. I base my estimate of Nikolaev's probable departure date on his second registration of his Nagan pistol in Leningrad on April 21, 1930, see below, p. 191. Nikolaev's sister Anna Pantiukhina also referred to his time in Siberia in one of her interrogations (there were two, on Dec. 17, 1935 and Jan. 9, 1935). See RGANI, f. 6, op. 13, d. 71, ll. 7–8 (1960s summary of Pantiukhina's testimony).

32. James Hughes, *Stalinism in a Russian Province: A Study of Collectivization and Dekulakization in Siberia* (New York: St. Martin's Press, 1996), 136–198.

33. Hughes, *Stalinism*, 168. On the "25,000ers," see Lynne Viola, *The Best Sons of the Fatherland: Workers in the Vanguard of Collectivization* (Oxford: Oxford University Press, 1987).

34. "Reply to Iakovlev," 466–467.

35. "Gibel' Kirova," 61; Kirilina, *Neizvestnyi Kirov,* 255–256.

36. "Gibel' Kirova," 62; RGASPI, f. 671, op. 1, d. 114, ll. 19–21.

37. "Gibel' Kirova," 62; Kirilina, *Rikoshet*, 42. The Dec. 1, 1934 interrogation of Draule referenced is recorded in RGASPI, f. 671, op. 1, d. 114, ll. 3–5.

38. "Gibel' Kirova," 61.

39. Ibid., 62.

40. Kirilina, *Neizvestnyi Kirov,* 244–245.

41. KGB report from 1967 on cases against Nikolaev's family members, RGANI, f. 6, op. 13, d. 71, ll. 4–5.

42. Tat'iana Bakhmeteva, who went over the Russian originals of Nikolaev's diaries with me, confirms my impression of his style.

43. Tat'iana Sukharnikova indicates that Milda Draule's parents were living in a separate house on the estate that her father had managed before the revolution. They were forced to leave the house in 1933 when it was converted into a vacation hotel for police (Sukharnikova, "My nagnali takoi velichaishii, podobaiushchii strakh").

44. J. Arch Getty, *The Road to Terror* (New Haven: Yale University Press, 1999), 125–129. The purge ultimately expelled 18 percent of all party members. Note that being purged from the party at this point in Soviet history (as opposed to four years later, during the Great Terror) did not necessarily mean arrest.

45. Kirilina, *Neizvestnyi Kirov,* 245.

46. "Gibel Kirova," 62.

47. On the Institute of Red Professors (IKP) see Michael David-Fox, *Revolution of the Mind* (Ithaca: Cornell University Press, 1997), 133–191. On Nikolaev's application to the IKP, see Draule interrogation of Dec. 1, 1934, RGASPI, f. 671, op. 1, d. 114, ll. 3–5. On Nikolaev's hiring at the Institute of Party History, see Kirilina, *Neizvestnyi Kirov,* 245.

48. RGASPI, f. 671, op.1, d. 114, l. 3–5, 30–31.

49. "Reply to Iakovlev," 463.

50. Ibid., 465.

51. RGANI, f. 6, op. 13, d. 60, ll. 80–81.

CHAPTER 6. NIKOLAEV AGONISTES

1. TsA FSB RF, a.u.d. N-Sh44, t. 24, ll. 2–4.

2. Orlando Figes in *Peasant Russia, Civil War: The Volga Countryside in Revolution, 1917–1921* (Oxford: Clarendon Press, 1989), 230, notes that the "typical" young rural Bolshevik had lost his father early. The case of the *Gudok* editor is covered in Matthew Lenoe, "Stalinist Mass Journalism and the Transformation of Soviet Newspapers, 1926–1932" [Ph.D. diss., University of Chicago, 1997], 603–604. For the Chagin petition, Oct. 5, 1934, see RGASPI, f. 80, op. 18, d. 121, ll. 178–179.

3. Milda Draule, under interrogation on Dec. 3, 1934, testified that Nikolaev "wanted to give the style of his autobiography a literary character, and to do so he read Tolstoy, Gorky, and other authors, as he put it, to master their style." See RGANI, f. 6, op. 13, d. 24, ll. 24–32, and RGASPI, f. 671, op. 1, d. 114, ll. 19–21. On "graphomania" see Svetlana Boym, *Commonplaces: Mythologies of Everyday Life in Russia* (Cambridge: Harvard University Press, 1994), 168–214; and Michael Gorham, "Tongue-tied Writers: The *Rabsel'kor* Movement and the Voice of the 'New Intelligentsia' in Early Soviet Russia," *Russian Review* 55, no. 3 (July 1996): 412–429.

4. N. Petukhov and V. Khomchik, "Delo o Leningradskom tsentre," *Vestnik verkhovnogo suda SSSR,* no. 5 (1991): 15–18.

5. RGASPI, f. 6, op. 13, d. 1, ll. 58–59.

6. RGASPI, f. 671, d. 114, ll. 132–133.

7. On real wages and household expenditures in the 1930s USSR, see Alec Nove, *An Economic History of the USSR, 1917–1991* (London: Penguin Books, 1992), 203–210, 250–256; S. Prokopovich, *Narodnoe khoziaistvo SSSR,* t. 2 (New York: Izdatel'stvo imeni Chekhova, 1952), 121–122.

8. See Agranov report to Iagoda, Dec. 11, 1934, RGASPI, f. 671, op. 1, d. 114, l. 104.

9. See Alla Kirilina, *Neizvestnyi Kirov* (Moscow: OLMA-PRESS, 2001), 247; RGASPI, f. 671, op. 1, d. 112, l. 5 (record of Oct. 20–29, 1934 session of Central Committee Party Collegium Circuit Tribunal meeting in Leningrad); and Iu. I. Sedov, N. V. Kulish, and A. Ia. Valetov, "Spravka rabotnikov prokuratury SSSR i sledstvennogo otdela KGB SSSR po povodu zapiski A. N. Iakovleva 'Nekotorye soobrazheniia po itogam izucheniia obstoiatel'stv ubiistva S. M. Kirova,'" in A. Artizov et al., eds., *Reabilitatsiia: Kak eto bylo,* vol. 3: *Seredina 80-kh godov–1991,* (Moscow: Mezhdunarodnyi fond "Demokratiia," 2004), 464 (hereafter cited as "Reply to Iakovlev").

10. RGANI, f. 6, op. 13, d. 117, ll. 1–18 (Pelshe report, 1967); and "Reply to Iakovlev," 466. The full text of Nikolaev's August 25 letter to Stalin was published in 2007 by Tat'iana Sukharnikova in "My nagnali takoi velichaishii, podobaiushchii strakh revoliutsii strakh," interview by Iuliia Kantor, *Vremia,* Nov. 29, 2007. The interview is online at www.vremya.ru/2007/219/13/19305.html.

11. For the complaint in Nikolaev's diary, see "Reply to Iakovlev," 466.

12. From a 1967 summary of Pantiukhina's and her husband's evidence in RGANI, f. 6, op. 13, d. 71, ll. 7–8.

13. See Petr Nikolaev's interrogation of Dec. 3, 1934 in RGASPI, f. 671, op. 1, d. 114, ll. 30–31, and Rogacheva's Dec. 4 interrogation in TsA FSB RF, a.u.d. N-Sh44, t. 3, ll. 69–70. Petr may also have visited Nikolaev's apartment during another AWOL episode, in October 1934.

14. RGANI, f. 6, op. 13, d. 1, ll. 60–62. Nikolaev's request for money from Yekaterina is referenced in a summary of her depositions in RGANI, f. 6, op. 13, d. 71, l. 6.

15. TsA FSB RF, a.u.d. N-Sh44, t. 24, ll. 227–228 (Roman Kulisher, Dec. 1, 1934); TsA FSB RF, a.u.d. N-Sh44, t. 24, ll. 217–219 (Olga Draule, Dec. 1, 1934); RGASPI, f. 671, op. 1, d. 114, l. 127 (Yekaterina Rogacheva, Dec. 11, 1934); RGASPI, f. 671, op. 1, d. 114, ll. 23–27 (Milda Draule, Dec. 3, 1934).

16. RGANI, f. 6, op. 13, d. 117, ll. 1–18 (Pelshe report, 1967), ll. 7–8. See also 1966 interview with Sveshnikov, RGANI, f. 6, op. 13, d. 73, ll.96–132.

17. RGASPI, f. 80, op. 18, d. 121.

18. RGASPI, f. 671, op.1, d. 114, ll. 3–5.

19. On Nikolaev's KPK hearing, see his comments in his diary in TsA FSB RF, a.u.d. N-Sh44, t. 12, ll. 401–410, and the protocol of the hearing in RGASPI, f. 671, op. 1, d. 112, l. 5. Yuskin's testimony is in TsA FSB RF, a.u.d. N-Sh44, t. 12, ll. 41–42. There is no credible evidence that Nikolaev visited Moscow during this period. His own diary places him in Leningrad from Nov. 2–9, 1934.

20. "Beseda tov. Stalina s angliiskim pisatelem G. D. Uellsom, 23 iiulia, 1934 goda," in I. V. Stalin, *Sochineniia,* vol. 1 (1934–1940) (Stanford: Hoover Institution on War, Revolution, and Peace, 1967–continues official Soviet series, in which this volume would be 14), 11–36; Sarah Davies, *Popular Opinion in Stalin's Russia: Terror, Propaganda, and Dissent, 1934–1941* (Cambridge: Cambridge University Press, 1997), 124–144.

21. Kirilina, *Neizvestnyi Kirov,* 253.

22. My thanks to Tat'iana Bakhmeteva for suggesting the last interpretation in this paragraph.

23. RGANI, f. 6, op. 13, d. 117, ll. 1–18 (Pelshe report).

24. Draule testimony in RGASPI, f. 671, op.1, d. 114, ll. 23–27.

25. On December 16 Nikolaev told interrogators he wrote his "Plan" on November 1, but in the "Plan" itself he says that he has been without work for "eight months." This would suggest that the plan dates from late November, but it is also possible that Nikolaev did not calculate the months since his firing precisely when he composed the "Plan."

26. Translation of Nikolaev's "Plan" based on transcription in RGANI, f. 6, op. 13, d. 1, ll. 88–89, and partial transcription in Petukhov and Khomchik, "Delo." Street names and references to "K" (Kirov) are from Petukhov and Khomchik.

27. Also relevant to the question of whether the NKVD found Nikolaev's assassination plan on his person is the testimony of Leningrad NKVD Operations Officer B. A. Yermolaev to the KPK on Nov. 20, 1960, RGANI, f. 6, op. 6, d. 13, ll. 202–203ob. Yermolaev claims that Stromin (Leningrad NKVD) told him on the telephone on the evening of Dec. 1, 1934 that a "Plan" and a "diary/notebook" had been found on Nikolaev.

28. On Nikolaev's sketches see Tat'iana Sukharnikova, "My nagnali takoi velichaishii, podobaiushchii strakh revoliutsii strakh." The license plate numbers are reproduced in several of the copies of Nikolaev's writings released by the KGB to the TsK in April 1956.

29. At this point I have used Medved's telegram of Dec. 2, 1934, 12:40 A.M. (Chapter 4, Document 14) to reconstruct text which is incomplete in the transcription of Nikolaev's diary in the April 1956 KGB document release.

30. See TsA FSB RF, a.u.d. N-Sh44, t. 12, ll. 12–14 for interrogation. It seems that Nikolaev truly did not have knowledge of Kirov's schedule. On November 5, when he apparently tried to catch Kirov returning from Moscow, the latter was in fact in Leningrad. See A. Pazi, ed., *Nash Mironych: Sbornik* (Leningrad: Lenizdat, 1969), 450.

31. The date of this entry is unclear, but the following entry is from November 21.

32. The Russian that I have translated as "She [death] is close . . . " reads "Ona bl. . . ." An alternate possible translation is "She [death? life?] is a bitch/whore (*bliad'*) . . . " This would be something like the English colloquial "life's a bitch" or "death's a bitch." The entire previous paragraph is about life and death, which more or less excludes the possibility that "She's a whore" might refer to Milda and a putative affair with Kirov.

33. Evidence from Yekaterina Rogacheva interrogation, Dec. 12, 1934, RGASPI, f. 671, op. 1, d. 114, ll. 173–174, and Petr Nikolaev's interrogations, Dec. 3, 1934, RGASPI, f. 671, op. 1, d. 114, ll. 32–36, and as reported in Agranov telegram to Stalin and Iagoda, Dec. 9, 1934, RGASPI, f. 671, op. 1, d. 114, ll. 68–70.

34. Petr Nikolaev interrogation, Dec.3, 1934, and attached documents, RGASPI, f. 671, op. 1, d. 114, ll. 32–43. On Petr Nikolaev's capture, see March 26, 1956 statement of Fomin to Central Committee, RGANI, f. 6, op. 13, d. 62, ll. 62–76.

35. For Nikolaev's activities on Nov. 29–30, see his interrogation of Dec. 9, 1934, RGASPI, f. 671, op. 1, d. 114, ll. 79–81. On his note to Olga Draule, see Olga Draule testimony of Dec. 1, 1934, TsA FSB RF, a.u.d. N-Sh44, t. 24, ll. 217–219. For his visit to his mother's apartment, see Dec. 4 testimony of Yekaterina Rogacheva, TsA FSB RF, a.u.d. N-Sh44, t. 3, ll. 69–70, and summary of Mariia Tikhonovna's testimony in RGANI, f. 6, op. 13, d. 71, ll. 5–6.

36. Medved telegram to Iagoda, Dec. 1, 1934, 10: 30 P.M., TsA FSB RF, a.u.d. N-Sh44, t. 24, ll. 2–4, and Olga Draule testimony of Dec. 1, 1934, TsA FSB RF, a.u.d. N-Sh44, t. 24, ll. 217–219.

37. Nikolaev interrogation of Dec. 9, 1934, RGASPI, f. 671, op. 1, d. 114, ll. 79–81.

CHAPTER 7. STALIN RESPONDS

1. Iu. I. Sedov, N. V. Kulish, and A. Ia. Valetov, "Spravka rabotnikov prokuratury SSSR i sledstvennogo otdela KGB SSSR po povodu zapiski A. N. Iakovleva 'Nekotorye soobrazheniia po itogam izucheniia obstoitel'stv ubiistva S. M. Kirova,'" June 14, 1990, published in A. Artizov et al., eds., *Reabilitatsiia: Kak eto bylo*, vol. 3: *Seredina 80-kh godov–1991* (Moscow: Mezhdunarodnyi fond "Demokratiia," 2004), 491 (hereafter "Reply to Iakovlev").

2. Feliks Chuev, *Molotov: Poluderzhavnyi vlastelin* (Moscow: OLMA-PRESS, 1999), 376.

3. A. V. Korotkov et al., eds., "Posetiteli Kremlevskogo kabineta I. V. Stalina," *Istoricheskii arkhiv*, no. 3 (1995): 119–177.

4. See Robert Tucker, *Stalin in Power: The Revolution from Above, 1928–1941* (New York: Norton, 1992), 297; and Robert Conquest, *The Great Terror: A Reassessment* (New York: Oxford University Press, 1990), 41, 497 n. 10.

5. See, for example, Tucker, *Stalin in Power*, 296–297.

6. J. Arch Getty and O. V. Naumov, *The Road to Terror: Stalin and the Self-destruction of the Bolsheviks, 1932–1939* (New Haven: Yale University Press,

1999), 145; V. N. Khaustov et al., eds., *Lubianka: Stalin i VChK-GPU-OGPU-NKVD, ianvar' 1922–dekabr' 1936* (Moscow: Mezhdunarodnyi fond "Demokratiia," 2003), 795 n. 55, 796 n. 60. My thanks to Terry Martin for first bringing to Krylenko's 1927 proposal to my attention.

7. Khaustov et al., *Lubianka, 1922–1936*, 137.

8. See Ibid., 133, 795; *Leningradskaia pravda*, Dec. 6, 1934, 2; and Robert Conquest, *Stalin and the Kirov Murder* (Oxford: Oxford University Press, 1989), 44–47.

9. See Peter Solomon, *Soviet Criminal Justice under Stalin* (Cambridge: Cambridge University Press, 1996), 162–167; Tucker, *Stalin in Power*, 272–276; Krylenko to Kaganovich, Aug. 3, 1934, in Khaustov et al., *Lubianka, 1922–1936*, 547–548.

10. Tucker, *Stalin in Power*, 272–276; Solomon, *Soviet Criminal Justice*, 153–155.

11. Solomon, *Soviet Criminal Justice*, 166.

12. Khaustov et al., *Lubianka, 1922–1936*, 531–532.

13. RGANI, f. 6, op. 13, d. 62, ll. 62–76.

14. RGANI, f. 6, op. 13, d. 62, ll. 62–76.

15. RGANI, f. 6, op. 13, d. 62, ll. 62–76.

16. See Fomin statement of March 26, 1956 in RGANI, f. 6, op. 13, d. 62, ll. 62–76, and Alla Kirilina, *Neizvestnyi Kirov* (Moscow: OLMA-PRESS, 2001), 232. On the time of Stalin delegation's arrival in Leningrad see also "Gibel' Kirova," *Rodina*, no. 3 (2005): 57–65. See also Genrikh Liushkov's description of events in the Conclusion, below, pp. 683–686.

17. RGANI, f. 6, op. 13, d. 62, ll. 62–76.

18. See Tucker, *Stalin in Power*, 294; and Conquest, *Stalin and the Kirov Murder*, 41.

19. RGANI, f. 6, op. 13, d. 21, ll. 86–93.

20. For Guzovsky's testimony, see "Reply to Iakovlev," 460.

21. Mikhail Rosliakov, *Ubiistvo Kirova: Politicheskie i ugolovnye prestupleniia v 1930-kh godakh* (Leningrad: Lenizdat, 1991), 46.

22. A. Artizov et al., eds., *Reabilitatsiia: Kak eto bylo*, vol. 1: *Mart 1953–fevral' 1956* (Moscow: Mezhdunarodnyi fond "Demokratiia," 2000), 296.

23. Feliks Chuev, *Sto sorok besed s Molotovym* (Moscow: "Terra," 1991), 310–311.

24. RGANI, f. 6, op. 13, d. 21, ll. 86–93.

25. RGANI, f. 6, op. 13, d. 28, l. 233; Kirilina, *Rikoshet*, 56; "Reply to Iakovlev," 474. See below, pp. 431–436, for more on Ilin.

26. Kirilina, *Neizvestnyi Kirov*, 269; "Zapiska Serova A. B. Aristovu," July 18, 1956, in Artizov et al., *Reabilitatsiia*, 1:163–167.

27. "Reply to Iakovlev," 474.

28. Ibid., 477–478; Kirilina, *Neizvestnyi Kirov*, 269–270. According to both sources, there is no evidence in Leningrad party archives or KGB archives of Volkova denouncing a specific plot against Kirov prior to Dec. 1, 1934. Petrov's multiple statements confirm this.

29. See Petrov statement of Dec. 2, 1960 in RGANI, f. 6, op. 13, d. 28, ll. 196–205; "Reply to Iakovlev," 475; Kirilina, *Neizvestnyi Kirov*, 269–271.

30. On Dec. 19, 1956 Fomin wrote to Petrov that "I remember how Yagoda called you a son of a kulak in front of Stalin." See RGANI, f. 6, op. 13, d. 28, ll. 228–231.

31. Petrov testimony of Dec. 2, 1960 in RGANI, f. 6, op. 13, d. 28, ll. 196–205.

32. "Reply to Iakovlev," 476–480; Volkova's interview with Shatunovskaya and A. I. Kuznetsov, Nov. 24, 1960, in RGANI, f. 6, op. 13, d. 28, ll. 7–75.

33. "Reply to Iakovlev," 480; "Zapiska Serova A. B. Aristovu," July 18, 1956, in Artizov et al., *Reabilitatsiia*, 1:163–167.

34. Kirilina, *Neizvestnyi Kirov*, 269–271; Alla Kirilina, *Rikoshet* (St. Petersburg: "Znanie," 1993), 54–55.

35. Makarov's 1961 testimony to the KPK is summarized in "Reply to Iakovlev," 471, 473. His 1956 testimony is summarized in a KGB report from that year in RGANI, f. 6, op. 13, d. 24, ll. 51–68. See l. 52.

36. Kirilina, *Rikoshet*, 59–60; "Reply to Iakovlev," 473, 482.

37. Fomin 1956 testimony in RGANI, f. 6, op. 13, d. 62, ll. 62–76.

38. RGANI, f. 6, op. 13, d. 62, ll. 62–76.

39. Kirilina, *Neizvestnyi Kirov*, 264–265.

40. For summaries of the Nakhaev mutiny, see O. V. Khlevniuk et al., *Stalin i Kaganovich: Perepiska, 1931–1936* (Moscow: ROSSPEN, 2001), 411–412; and Khaustov et al., *Lubianka, 1922–1936*, 818–819 n. 147.

41. Khlevniuk, *Stalin i Kaganovich*, 419–421.

42. Ibid., 411.

43. Khaustov et al., *Lubianka, 1922–1936*, 550.

44. Khlevniuk, *Stalin i Kaganovich*, 432, 459, 411–412. Agranov telegram to Stalin in Khaustov et al., *Lubianka, 1922–1936*, 565.

45. Khaustov et al., *Lubianka, 1922–1936*, 818 n. 147.

46. See documents for the year 1934 ibid.

47. Khlevniuk, *Stalin i Kaganovich*, 419, 428; R. W. Davies at al., The *Stalin-Kaganovich Correspondence, 1931–36* (New Haven: Yale University Press, 2003), 252 n. 2, 375–380.

48. V. N. Khaustov et al., eds., *Lubianka: Stalin i glavnoe upravlenie gosbezopasnosti NKVD, 1937–1938* (Moscow: Mezhdunarodnyi fond "Demokratiia," 2004), 127–130.

49. N. Kovaleva et al., *Molotov, Malenkov, Kaganovich, 1957: Stenogramma iiul'skogo plenuma TsK KPSS i dr. dokumenty* (Moscow: Mezhdunarodnyi fond "Demokratiia," 1998), 247–248, 751; Jonathan Brent and Vladimir P. Naumov, *Stalin's Last Crime: The Plot against the Jewish Doctors, 1948–1953* (New York: HarperCollins, 2003), 14–16, 24–28, 46–47, 157–166, 292–293.

CHAPTER 8. FINGERING THE ZINOVIEVITES

1. A. V. Korotkov et al., eds., "Posetiteli kremlevskogo kabineta I. V. Stalina," *Istoricheskii arkhiv*, no. 3 (1995): 119–177; Alla Kirilina, *Rikoshet* (St. Petersburg: "Znanie," 1993), 34–35. On Yezhov, see J. Arch Getty and Oleg V. Naumov, *Yezhov: The Rise of Stalin's "Iron Fist"* (New Haven: Yale University Press, 2008). In December 1934 Yezhov was a member of the TsK Orgburo, head of the

Party Control Committee, and chief of the TsK personnel assignment department (Raspredotdel).

2. Findings of Shvernik commission, 1961, RGANI, f. 6, op. 13, d. 39, ll. 1–7; Getty and Naumov, *Yezhov,* 138. For an example of a copy of an Agranov report in Yezhov's archive, see RGASPI, f. 6, op 13, d. 114, ll. 8–10. The fact that Yezhov does not appear on the reports as a recipient suggests that Agranov and perhaps others were finessing the awkward fact that Yezhov and not Yagoda was Stalin's "go-to" man for the Kirov investigation.

3. Nikolaev's Dec. 3 interrogation covers his day on Dec. 1 and is reproduced in part in Chapters 4 and 6. Other interrogations are available in Nikolai Yezhov's archive, RGASPI, f. 671, op. 1, dd. 113, 114.

4. For the comments of Yezhov and Liushkov, see Iu. I. Sedov, N. V. Kulish, and A. Ia. Valetov, "Spravka rabotnikov prokuratury SSSR i sledstvennogo otdela KGB SSSR po povodu zapiski A. N. Iakovleva 'Nekotorye soobrazheniia po itogam izucheniia obstoitel'stv ubiistva S. M. Kirova,'" June 14, 1990, published in A. Artizov et al., eds., *Reabilitatsiia: Kak eto bylo,* vol. 3: *Seredina 80-kh godov–1991* (Moscow: Mezhdunarodnyi fond "Demokratiia," 2004), 482–483 (hereafter cited as "Reply to Iakovlev"); and Liushkov's *Kaizo* article from April 1939, Conclusion, Document 127.

5. Shatsky interrogation of Dec. 7, 1934 in TsA FSB RF, a.u.d. N-Sh44, t. 12, ll. 45–46; Rumiantsev interrogation of Dec. 13, 1934 in RGASPI, f. 671, op. 1, d. 114, ll. 197–198; Alla Kirilina, *Neizvestnyi Kirov* (Moscow: OLMA-PRESS, 2001), 285.

6. Kotolynov interrogation of Dec. 6, 1934 in TsA FSB RF, a.u.d. N-Sh44, t. 12, ll. 34–36 and Kirilina, *Neizvestnyi Kirov,* 284–285.

7. Kirilina, *Neizvestnyi Kirov,* 286, 482.

8. For arrest dates, see "Protest Prokuratury SSSR po delu L. V. Nikolaeva, I. I. Kotolynova, N. N. Shatskogo, i drugie obviniaemykh v ubiistve t. Kirova," RGANI, f. 6, op. 13, d. 136, ll. 28–40. The possibility should be noted that many of the people discussed in this chapter were detained by the police earlier than their official arrest dates. The NKVD apparently conducted mass arrests of suspected oppositionists on the night of Dec. 1–2 as a "prophylactic" measure.

9. "Reply to Iakovlev," 469.

10. Ibid., 462.

11. Kirilina, *Neizvestnyi Kirov,* 277.

12. RGASPI, f. 671, op. 1, d. 114, ll. 8–10. For dates of arrest of Kotolynov and Shatsky see "Plenum Verkhovnogo suda SSSR: Protest po delu L. V. Nikolaeva . . . ," Nov. 12, 1990, in RGANI, f. 6, op. 13, d. 136, ll. 28–40.

13. Prosecutor's report to Molotov commission, late April 1956, RGANI, f. 6, op. 13, d. 1, ll. 153–194.

14. RGASPI, f. 671, op. 1, d. 114, ll. 30–46.

15. RGASPI, f. 671, op. 1, d. 114, ll. 15–17.

16. See RGANI, f. 6, op. 13, d. 1, ll. 153–194 for the number of Nikolaev's interrogations on Dec. 6. It is possible that the number represents one long "conveyor" session with alternating interrogators that produced seven separate protocols. For protocols of some of the Dec. 6 interrogations see RGASPI, f. 671, op. 1,

d. 114, ll. 58–59, 61–64. For arrest dates of Yuskin, Rumiantsev, and Sokolov, see "Plenum Verkhovnogo suda SSSR: Protest po delu L. V. Nikolaeva . . . ," Nov. 12, 1990, in RGANI, f. 6, op. 13, d. 136, ll. 28–40.

17. RGANI, f. 6, op. 13, d. 31, ll. 307–309.

18. For Gusev's testimony, see RGANI, f. 6, op. 13, d. 2, ll. 78–107 (August 1956 report to KPK Chairman Nikolai Shvernik). Kirilina, *Neizvestnyi Kirov,* 251, provides the evidence that Nikolai hoped to save his family. Unfortunately she does not provide a cite for her quotes. They may come from interviews with former officers in the Leningrad NKVD, e.g. Raikhman, or from her sources inside the former Leningrad NKVD/KGB archive who have seen interrogation protocols not yet open to researchers. See KGB report in RGANI, f. 6, op. 13, d. 24, ll. 51–68 for Nikolaev's "secret correspondence" with his wife.

19. See Kirilina, *Neizvestnyi Kirov,* 277; "Reply to Iakovlev," 461.

20. TsA FSB RF, a.u.d. N-Sh44, t. 12, ll. 37–38.

21. TsA FSB RF, a.u.d. N-Sh44, t. 12, ll. 34–36.

22. Kirilina, *Neizvestnyi Kirov,* 286.

23. "Reply to Iakovlev," 467.

24. For Stalin's office log see Korotkov et al., "Posetiteli kremlevskogo kabineta I. V. Stalina." Yezhov attended meetings in the office on December 4, 5, and 8. It is possible that he was in Leningrad on December 6–7.

On Agranov's replacement as head of the Leningrad NKVD, see APRF, f. 3, op.24, d. 197, l. 88; Getty and Naumov, *Yezhov,* 126–138, 189. Getty and Naumov argue that notes by Yezhov on the investigation date from Dec. 3, 1934, but misread some very messy writing. In fact the passage in question reads "Plan (of investigation) through 3/I/35 (i.e. Jan. 3, 1935)" and other internal evidence shows that it was composed on Dec. 9, 1934 or soon after. Hence my conclusion that Yezhov was put in overall charge of the inquiry at the December 8 meeting.

25. APRF, f. 3, op. 24, d. 197, ll. 117–118.

26. See letter of Bissenieks' replacement in Leningrad, Juris Filholds, to Latvian foreign minister Wilhelm Munters, Jan. 9, 1935, RGANI, f. 6, op. 13, d. 14, ll. 164–165, and letter of Latvian ambassador to Moscow Alfreds Bilmanis to Prime Minister Karlis Ulmanis, Jan. 4, 1935, in RGANI, f. 6, op. 13, d. 14, ll. 96–104.

27. Julian and Margaret Bullard, eds., *Inside Stalin's Russia: The Diaries of Reader Bullard, 1930–1934* (Charlbury, UK: Day Books, 2000), 237.

28. André Liebich, *From the Other Shore: Russian Social Democracy after 1921* (Cambridge: Harvard University Press, 1997), 128; and biographical information on Bissenieks in RGANI, f. 6, op. 13, d. 14, ll. 14–15.

29. See Bilmanis to Prime Minister Ulmanis, Jan. 4, 1935, in RGANI, f. 6, op. 13, d. 14, ll. 96–104, and Party Control Commission report on Bissenieks case file, probably 1960–1961, authored by Klimov, in RGANI, f. 6, op. 13, d. 14, ll. 4–15.

30. RGANI, f. 6, op. 13, d. 14, l. 23.

31. See Aleksandr Sabov's interview with Zhukov, "Shestaia versiia," *Rossiiskaia gazeta nedelia,* Nov. 26, 2004, also at www.rg.ru/2004/11/26/kirov.html. Note that Zhukov gets some facts wrong in this interview. He claims that the German consul in Leningrad, Richard Sommer, left the USSR on the night of Dec. 1–2, 1934 and never returned. However, an NKID (People's Commissariat of For-

eign Affairs) intelligence report on the Leningrad consuls places Sommer in Leningrad in late December. See RGANI, f. 6, op. 13, d. 14, ll. 45–46.

32. Jonathan Haslam, *The Soviet Union and the Struggle for Collective Security in Europe, 1933–1939* (New York: St. Martin's Press, 1984), 6–51.

33. Haslam, *The Soviet Union and the Struggle for Collective Security,* 37–38, 236–238. Andrejs Plakans, *The Latvians: A Short History* (Stanford: Hoover Institution Press, 1995), 120–135, 138–140; Edgar Anderson, "The USSR Trades with Latvia: The Treaty of 1927," *Slavic Review* 21, no. 2 (June 1962): 296–321.

34. Haslam, *The Soviet Union and the Struggle for Collective Security,* 154–155; RGANI, f. 6, op. 13, d. 14, ll. 115–118 (Filholds' Jan. 2, 1935 report to Bilmanis on interview with Bissenieks).

35. On Bissenieks' attitude toward the Ulmanis government see his biographical information in RGANI, f. 6, op. 13, d. 14, ll. 14–15. On the plan to recruit him, see 1960–1961 KPK report signed by Klimov in RGANI, f. 6, op. 13, d. 14, ll. 4–15. On Lentsmanis' Comintern employment see testimony of NKVD Officer E. A. Fortunatov, Oct. 27, 1937, in RGANI, f. 6, op. 13, d. 14, ll. 36–37. On Lentsmanis' organization of a strike among Latvian sailors in Leningrad, see Moscow envoy Bilmanis to Prime Minister Ulmanis, Jan. 4, 1935, RGANI, f. 6, op. 13, d. 14, ll. 96–104.

36. RGANI, f. 6, op. 13, d. 14, ll. 8 (Klimov report, 1960–1961), 36 (Fortunatov testimony, Oct. 27, 1937), 115–118 (Filholds to Bilmanis, Jan. 2, 1935), 134–136 (report of Latvian ambassador to Finland to Foreign Minister Munters on interview with Bissenieks), 166 (Munters statement of Jan. 11, 1961 to Party Control Committee).

37. RGASPI, f. 671, op. 1, d. 271, ll. 529–545.

38. "O pis'me t. Shatunovskoi O. G. ot 5 sentiabria 1988g. Proekt," RGANI, f. 6, op. 13, d. 138, ll. 4–9; and Kirilina, *Neizvestnyi Kirov,* 363–364.

39. RGASPI, f. 671, op. 1, d. 271, l. 542.

40. APRF, f. 3, op. 24, d. 197, ll. 89–92.

41. Kirilina, *Neizvestnyi Kirov,* 287–288.

42. See Zinoviev's December 22 testimony excerpted below; Kamenev's testimony, probably from December 23, in RGASPI, f. 671, op. 1, d. 121, ll. 106–117; Robert V. Daniels, *The Conscience of the Revolution: Communist Opposition in Soviet Russia* (Cambridge: Harvard University Press, 1960), 371; and "Reply to Iakovlev," 469–471. On the "nonreturners" controversy in 1928 see Kamenev's testimony, probably on Dec. 23, 1934, in RGASPI, f. 671, op. 1, d. 121, ll. 106–117; and "Reply to Iakovlev," 469–470.

43. Kirilina, *Neizvestnyi Kirov,* 290–291; and "Plenum Verkhovnogo suda SSSR: Protest po delu L. V. Nikolaeva . . . ," Nov. 12, 1990, in RGANI, f. 6, op. 13, d. 136, ll. 28–40. On Lashevich, see commentary in L. Kosheleva et al., eds., *Pis'ma I. V. Stalina V. M. Molotovu, 1925–1936 gg.* (Moscow: "Rossiia molodaia," 1995), 50–53.

44. Kirilina, *Neizvestnyi Kirov,* 291.

45. See ibid., 288. Zvezdov interrogations cited are in RGASPI, f. 671, op. 1, d. 114, ll. 96–99, and RGASPI, f. 671, op. 1, d. 114, ll. 114–117.

46. Arthur Koestler, *Darkness at Noon* (New York: Bantam Books, 1968), 69–77.

47. Jochen Hellbeck, *Revolution on My Mind: Writing a Diary under Stalin* (Cambridge: Harvard University Press, 2006), 182–192.

48. RGASPI, f. 671, op. 1, d. 128 ("Stenogramma sudebnogo zasedaniia vyezdnoi sessii Voenkollegii verkhsuda SSSR po delu ob ubiistve S. M. Kirova"), ll. 62–63.

49. Kirilina, *Neizvestnyi Kirov,* 288–289.

50. RGASPI, f. 671, op. 1, d. 114, ll. 148–149.

51. Kirilina, *Neizvestnyi Kirov,* 289–290; TsA FSB RF, a.u.d. N-Sh44, t. 12, ll. 160–163.

52. Presumably Lavrenty Beria's efforts at around this time to inflate Stalin's importance to the early Social Democratic movement in the Caucasus were part of the same campaign. See Amy Knight, *Beria: Stalin's First Lieutenant* (Princeton: Princeton University Press, 1993), 54–62.

53. RGASPI, f. 671, op. 1, d. 114, l. 210, d. 120, ll. 1–10, 60–69.

CHAPTER 9. THE TRIALS OF THE MOSCOW AND LENINGRAD CENTERS

1. See *Leningradskaia pravda,* April 17, 1925 and Dec. 10, 1925.

2. APRF, f. 3, op. 24, d. 198, ll. 37–39.

3. See Alla Kirilina, *Neizvestnyi Kirov* (Moscow: OLMA-PRESS, 2001), 293.

4. APRF, f. 3, op. 24, d. 197, ll. 141–142 (Agranov telegram to Stalin); RGASPI, f. 671, op. 1, d. 114, ll. 187–196 (Rumiantsev interrogation).

5. Mikhail Rosliakov, *Ubiistvo Kirova: Politicheskie i ugolovnye prestupleniia v 1930-kh godakh* (Leningrad: Lenizdat, 1991), 57–58.

6. Ibid.

7. Iagoda to Stalin, Dec. 17, 1934, RGANI, f. 6, op. 13, d. 33, ll. 19, 84.

8. *Pravda,* Dec. 17, 1934, 1; *Leningradskaia pravda,* Dec. 17, 1934, 1.

9. *Leningradskaia pravda,* Dec. 18, 1934, 1, 2; Marc Jansen and Nikita Petrov, *Stalin's Loyal Executioner: People's Commissar Nikolai Yezhov, 1895–1940* (Stanford: Hoover Institution Press, 2002), 29–31.

10. APRF, f. 3, op. 24, d. 199, l. 21.

11. After the Fifteenth Party Congress expelled Zinoviev in late 1927, the authorities exiled him and Kamenev from Moscow to the province of Kaluga in European Russia. In late 1932 Zinoviev and Kamenev were again exiled, for failing to disclose the existence of the Riutin Platform (an anti-Stalin manifesto circulated in secret by the Rightist former Communist official Mikhail Riutin) to the party or police. This time they were sent to Kustanaya in Kazakhstan. They were permitted to return in 1933.

12. TsA FSB RF, a.u.d. N-Sh44, t. 34, ll. 25–34.

13. Vyshinsky and Akulov met Stalin in his office on December 17 (A. V. Korotkov et al., eds., "Posetiteli kremlevskogo kabineta I. V. Stalina," *Istoricheskii arkhiv,* no. 3 [1995]: 119–177). Vyshinsky, Akulov, and Sheinin interrogated Kotolynov in Leningrad on December 19 (prosecutor's report to Molotov commission, RGANI, f. 6, op. 13, d. 1, ll. 153–194).

14. Yuskin interrogation of Dec. 10, 1934 in RGASPI, f. 671, op. 1, d. 114, l. 100; Yuskin interrogation of Dec. 15, 1934 in RGASPI, f. 671, op. 1, d. 120, l. 15;

RGANI, f. 6, op. 13, d. 1, ll. 153–194 (1956 prosecutor's report to Molotov commission).

15. RGANI, f. 6, op. 13, d. 1, ll. 153–194.

16. William J. Chase, *Enemies within the Gates? The Comintern and Stalinist Repression, 1934–1939* (New Haven: Yale University Press, 2001), 42–95.

17. APRF, f. 3, op. 24, d. 197, ll. 141–142.

18. RGANI, f. 6, op. 13, d. 14, ll. 24–25.

19. Korotkov et al., "Posetiteli kremlevskogo kabineta I. V. Stalina."

20. On Stalin's editing of the Dec. 22, 1934 NKVD bulletin, see RGANI, f. 6, op. 13, d. 39, ll. 1–7 (Sept. 1961 Shvernik commission report). A copy of the bulletin is in RGANI, f. 6, op. 13, d. 34, ll. 33–34.

21. Agranov interrogated Zinoviev on Dec. 22, 1934 in Leningrad. Yezhov doesn't appear on visitors' register of Stalin's office on Dec. 22, 23, or 24, suggesting that he may have been in Leningrad during that period. On NKVD notification of the accused about the completion of the preliminary investigation, see RGANI, f. 6, op. 13, d. 1, ll. 153–194 (late April 1956 report of USSR prosecutor on Kirov case).

22. Korotkov et al., "Posetiteli kremlevskogo kabineta I. V. Stalina."

23. For summary of depositions of all fourteen persons accused in the "Leningrad Center" case, see RGANI, f. 6, op. 13, d. 1, ll. 153–194 (late April 1956 report of USSR prosecutor's office on Kirov murder). For relevant depositions of Antonov, Zvezdov, and Sokolov, see RGASPI, f. 671, op. 1, d. 120, ll. 90, 93–94, 138–148, 202–204.

24. This is based on depositions available in RGASPI, f. 671, op. 1, dd. 114, 120, and 121 (the Yezhov archive), as well as on all available summaries of evidence in RGANI f. 6, op. 13 and published summaries of depositions.

25. See Sheila Fitzpatrick, "Ascribing Class: The Construction of Social Identity in Soviet Russia," in Fitzpatrick, ed., *Stalinism: New Directions* (London: Routledge, 2000), 20–46.

26. RGASPI, f. 671, op. 1, d. 121, l. 153.

27. RGANI, f. 6, op. 13, d. 1, ll. 153–194.

28. J. Arch Getty and Oleg Naumov, *The Road to Terror: Stalin and the Self-Destruction of the Bolsheviks, 1932–1939* (New Haven: Yale University Press, 1999), 45–50.

29. RGANI, f. 6, op. 13, d. 39, ll. 1–7; Iu. I. Sedov, N. V. Kulish, and A. Ia. Valetov, "Spravka rabotnikov prokuratury SSSR i sledstvennogo otdela KGB SSSR po povodu zapiski A. N. Iakovleva 'Nekotorye soobrazheniia po itogam izucheniia obstoitel'stv ubiistva S. M. Kirova,'" June 14, 1990, published in A. Artizov et al., eds., *Reabilitatsiia: Kak eto bylo,* vol. 3: *Seredina 80-kh godov–1991* (Moscow: Mezhdunarodnyi fond "Demokratiia," 2004), 492 (hereafter cited as "Reply to Iakovlev"). The last time Ulrikh was in Stalin's office before the trial of the Leningrad Center was late in the afternoon of December 26. See Korotkov et al., "Posetiteli kremlevskogo kabineta I. V. Stalina."

30. RGANI, f. 6, op. 13, d. 1, ll. 153–194.

31. RGASPI, f. 671, op. 1, d. 128, l. 10.

32. "Reply to Iakovlev," 461; RGANI, f. 6, op. 13, d. 1, ll. 153–194.

33. TsA FSB RF, a.u.d. N-Sh44, t. 34, ll. 1–2.

34. RGASPI, f. 671, op. 1, d. 128, l. 20.
35. RGASPI, f. 671, op. 1, d. 128, ll. 23–30.
36. RGASPI, f. 671, op. 1, d. 128, l. 30.
37. TsA FSB RF, a.u.d. N-Sh44, l. 106. t. 34, ll. 4–6.
38. RGASPI, f. 671, op. 1, d. 128, ll. 37–45.
39. RGASPI, f. 671, op. 1, d. 128, ll. 46–51.
40. RGASPI, f. 671, op. 1, d. 128, ll. 56–61.
41. RGASPI, f. 671, op. 1, d. 128, ll. 62–66; TsA FSB RF, a.u.d. N-Sh44, t. 34, ll. 10–12.
42. RGASPI, f. 671, op. 1, d. 128, ll. 72–77.
43. RGASPI, f. 671, op. 1, d. 128, ll. 80–90. In his final plea, Kotolynov gave the last date he met with Shatsky as 1928. See transcript in Kirilina, *Neizvestnyi Kirov,* 434.
44. RGASPI, f. 671, op. 1, d. 128, ll. 90–101; TsA FSB RF, a.u.d. N-Sh44, t. 34, ll. 10–12.
45. RGASPI, f. 671, op. 1, d. 128, ll. 103–107.
46. RGASPI, f. 671, op. 1, d. 128, ll. 111–112; TsA FSB RF, a.u.d. N-Sh44, t. 34, ll. 16–18.
47. RGASPI, f. 671, op. 1, d. 128, ll. 111–112.
48. RGASPI, f. 671, op. 1, d. 128, ll. 117–119; TsA FSB RF, a.u.d. N-Sh44, t. 34, ll. 16–18.
49. RGASPI, f. 671, op. 1, d. 128, ll. 125–135; TsA FSB RF, a.u.d. N-Sh44, t. 34, ll. 22–24.
50. RGASPI, f. 671, op. 1, d. 128, ll. 136–143; TsA FSB RF, a.u.d. N-Sh44, t. 34, ll. 22–24.
51. On the declarations of loyalty, see Rumiantsev's testimony on Dec. 29 in RGASPI, f. 671, op. 1, d. 128, l. 142. On his contacts with the GPU, see his deposition of Dec. 20 in RGASPI, f. 671, op. 1, d. 121, l. 31. On his meeting with Kirov and his promotion as probable outcome of that meeting, see Alla Kirilina, *Rikoshet* (St. Petersburg: "Znanie," 1993), 123–124.
52. TsA FSB RF, a.u.d. N-Sh44, t. 34, ll. 22–24; RGASPI, f. 671, op. 1, d. 128, ll. 148–153.
53. TsA FSB RF, a.u.d. N-Sh44, t. 34, ll. 25–32.
54. TsA FSB RF, a.u.d. N-Sh44, t. 34, ll. 25–32.
55. TsA FSB RF, a.u.d. N-Sh44, t. 34, ll. 25–32.
56. Transcript of Kotolynov's testimony in Kirilina, *Neizvestnyi Kirov,* 433–437.
57. Ibid.
58. Ibid.
59. Ibid.
60. Transcript of trial in RGASPI, f. 671, op. 1, d. 128, ll. 196 and following. Kotolynov's thanks to Dmitriev do not appear in Kirilina's transcript of his last plea.
61. TsA FSB RF, a.u.d. N-Sh44, t. 34, ll. 25–32.
62. TsA FSB RF, a.u.d. N-Sh44, t. 34, ll. 25–32; Kirilina, *Neizvestnyi Kirov,* 431–433.
63. RGASPI, f. 671, op. 1, d. 128, l. 162 and following; TsA FSB RF, a.u.d. N-Sh44, t. 34, ll. 25–32. Rumiantsev quote is from RGANI, f. 6, op. 13, d. 1, ll. 153–194.

64. Katsafa was the same guard who claimed to have heard Nikolaev talking in his sleep about Kotolynov and Shatsky.

65. RGANI, f. 6, op. 13, d. 2, ll. 78–107 (August 1956 KGB report of Serov to Molotov commission).

66. RGANI, f. 6, op. 13, d. 24, ll. 51–68.

67. RGANI, f. 6, op. 13, d. 24, ll. 51–68.

68. On Rumiantsev's 1932 meeting with an OGPU resident, see his deposition in RGASPI, f. 671, op. 1, d. 121, l. 31 (Dec. 20, 1934). Rumiantsev's use of Smorodin as a reference in his Dec. 19 appeal to Stalin indicates the two had a close political relationship (RGANI, f. 6, op. 13, d. 1, ll. 112–113). On Smorodin's relationship to Kirov, see Sveshnikov interview, 1966, RGANI, f. 6, op. 13, d. 73, ll. 96–132. On the probability of Kirov's having met Rumiantsev see Kirilina, *Rikoshet,* 123–124. On Antonov's job, see Rumiantsev petition of Dec. 27 to Akulov in RGANI, f. 6, op. 13, d. 1, ll. 114–116. On his aid to Tolmazov's sister, see Tolmazov testimony of Dec. 11 in TsA FSB RF, a.u.d. N-Sh44, t. 12, l. 107. On the cafeteria passes for Kotolynov, see RGASPI, f. 671, op. 1, d. 120, l. 89 (Kotolynov deposition of Dec. 17, 1934).

69. See trial testimony of Khanik summarized by Agranov in TsA FSB RF, a.u.d. N-Sh44, t. 34, ll. 16–18, Rumiantsev letter to Akulov, Dec. 27, 1934, RGANI, f. 6, op. 13, d. 1, ll. 114–116, and Kirilina, *Neizvestnyi Kirov,* 290.

70. For surveillance files on Korol and information on his move back to Leningrad in 1933, see RGANI, f. 671, op. 1, d. 129, ll. 61–64, 86–88.

71. See trial transcript, RGASPI, f. 671, op. 1, d. 128, l. 82. For protocol of the confrontation, see RGASPI, f. 671, op. 1, d. 120, ll. 167–168. Popov had in the past (1930) informed on ex-oppositionists to the OGPU. See his evidence of Dec. 18, 1934, RGASPI, f. 671, op. 1, d. 120, l. 170.

72. For Dec. 12, 1934 testimony of Yuskin's wife, Anna Yakovlevna Yuskina, about his "anti-Soviet statements" see RGASPI, f. 671, op. 1, d. 114, ll. 152–153.

73. See Agranov report of Dec. 7 to Stalin and Iagoda, Chapter 8, Document 46.

74. For Sokolov's Dec. 19, 1934 testimony, see RGASPI, f. 671, op. 1, d. 120, ll. 202–204. For his trial testimony, see RGASPI, f. 671, op. 1, d. 128, ll. 56–61.

75. Popov was sentenced to a labor camp term in the "Leningrad Counterrevolutionary Zinovievite Group of Safarov, Zalutsky, and Others" trial in January 1935 (see below). On the surveillance of ex-Zinovievites in Leningrad from 1928, see "Reply to Iakovlev," 469–471.

76. Raikhman in *Rodina,* no. 1 (1989): 73, cited in Kirilina, *Neizvestnyi Kirov,* 276.

77. See Robert Conquest's discussion of official reports on the "Moscow Center" trial in *Stalin and the Kirov Murder* (Oxford: Oxford University Press, 1989), 59–68. See also Kirilina, *Neizvestnyi Kirov,* 365–369.

78. Kirilina, *Neizvestnyi Kirov,* 365–367; Iurii Zhukov, "Sledstvie i sledstvennye protsessy po delu ob ubiistve Kirova," *Voprosy istorii,* no. 2 (2000): 33–51.

79. For the full text of the letter, see J. Arch Getty, *The Road to Terror: Stalin and the Self-Destruction of the Bolsheviks, 1932–1939* (New Haven: Yale University Press, 1999), 147–150.

80. Ibid.

81. RGANI, f. 6, op. 13, d. 14, l. 9 (Klimov report to KPK, probably dated 1961), 41–42 (Stomoniakov log report of Dec. 29, 1934).

82. Reports of Commissariat of Foreign Affairs Leningrad agent Vainshtein to Stomoniakov, RGANI, f. 6, op. 13, d. 14, ll. 45–48.

83. RGANI, f. 6, op. 13, d. 14, ll. 47–49 (Vainshtein to Stomoniakov).

84. RGANI, f. 6, op. 13, d. 14, ll. 115–127 (Filholds' report to Bilmanis on interview with Bissenieks, plus Bissenieks' responses–Russian translation by Party Control Committee in early 1960s, hereafter "Russian translation").

85. RGANI, f. 6, op. 13, d. 14, ll. 134–136 (Russian translation).

86. RGANI, f. 6, op. 13, d. 14, ll. 9–10 (Klimov report, probably 1961).

87. RGANI, f. 6, op. 13, d. 14, ll. 96–104 (Bilmanis to Munters, Jan. 4, 1935, Russian translation).

88. RGASPI, f. 671, op. 1, d. 128, l. 26.

89. RGANI, f. 6, op. 13, d. 14, ll. 96–104 (Bilmanis to Munters, Jan. 4, 1935, Russian translation).

90. RGANI, f. 6, op. 13, d. 14, ll. 140–149 (Munters interview with Bissenieks, Jan. 7, 1935, Russian translation).

91. RGANI, f. 6, op. 13, d. 14, ll. 130–131, 140–149.

92. Stomoniakov to Brodovskii, Soviet ambassador to Latvia, Jan. 4, 1935, RGANI, f. 6, op. 13, d. 14, l. 58.

93. V. Munters circular to Latvian ambassadors, Jan. 15, 1935, RGANI, f. 6, op. 13, d. 14, ll. 150–155 (Russian translation), 156–161 (Latvian original).

94. Stomoniakov to Brodovskii, Jan. 7, 1935, RGANI, f. 6, op. 13, d. 14, ll. 62–63; Stomoniakov log of Bilmanis interview, Jan. 7, 1935, ll. 64–66.

95. See RGANI, f. 6, op. 13, d. 14, ll. 12 (in 1960–1962 Klimov report on Bissenieks to KPK), 70–71 (Litvinov telegram to Commissariat of Foreign Affairs, Jan. 22, 1935), 81 (Stomoniakov log of Feb. 1, 1935 on Bilmanis visit to protest Molotov comments of Jan. 28, 1935 at All-Union Congress of Soviets), 150–155 (Munters circular).

96. RGANI, f. 6, op. 13, d. 14, l. 14 (Klimov report).

97. RGANI, f. 6, op. 13, d. 14, ll. 12–13 (Klimov report).

CHAPTER 10. INVESTIGATING THE LENINGRAD NKVD

1. On Zaporozhets' post as head of the Special Department, see November 1963 statement of former operations secretary of the Special Department A. Annushkov excerpted in N. Petukhov and V. Khomchik, "Delo o 'Leningradskom tsentre,'" *Vestnik verkhovnogo suda SSSR*, no. 6 (1991): 19–21.

2. On Zaporozhets' leave of absence and return to Leningrad around December 7, see testimony of Medved's former aide Zavilovich, 1939, RGANI, f. 6, op. 13, d. 13, l. 55; Annushkov 1963 statement and Zaporozhets' wife's testimony excerpted in Petukhov and Khomchik, "Delo o 'Leningradskom tsentre'"; Sveshnikov interview, 1966, RGANI, f. 6, op. 13, d. 73, ll. 96–132. These cites are only a partial sample of the testimony as to Zaporozhets' absence from Leningrad in the months prior to the murder.

3. RGASPI, f. 671, op. 1, d. 114, ll. 28–29 (Draule interrogation of Dec. 3, 1934).

4. See RGANI, f. 6, op. 13, d. 13, ll. 84–87 (interrogation of Griunvald by Chertok, Dec. 6, 1934), 92–93 (interrogation of Griunvald by Sosnovsky, December 1934). See also RGANI, f. 6, op. 13, d. 13, ll. 7–45 (1961 Klimov report on detention[s] of Nikolaev).

5. RGANI, f. 6, op. 13, d. 13, ll. 118–119 (interrogation of Tereshchenko, March 2, 1939), 122–123 (interrogation of Tereshchenko, March 6, 1939).

6. RGANI, f. 6, op. 13, d. 13, ll. 98–101 (Sosnovsky interrogation of Kotomin, Dec. 5, 1934).

7. RGANI, f. 6, op. 13, d. 13, ll. 98–101.

8. RGANI, f. 6, op. 13, d. 13, ll. 98–101.

9. RGANI, f. 6, op. 13, d. 13, ll. 92–93. On Jan. 13, 1935 interrogators also asked Operations Department chief Gubin whether other "operational departments" had ever informed him about terrorism cases they were pursuing, "so that you could take measures to strengthen the guard." Gubin indicated that they had not, although he had "heard" about a "terrorist group" in the Leningrad soviet garage "liquidated" by the Special Political Department. See RGANI, f. 6, op. 13, d. 13, ll. 112–114 (Gubin interrogation of Jan. 13, 1935).

10. RGASPI, f. 671, op. 1, d. 271, ll. 529–533 (Yezhov's notebooks on Kirov investigation).

11. RGASPI, f. 671, op. 1, d. 271, ll. 529–533.

12. RGASPI, f. 671, op. 1, d. 271, ll. 529–533.

13. On the organization of Kirov's guard prior to the summer of 1933 see testimony of Ivan Ivanovich Baskakov to KPK, RGANI, f. 6, op. 13, d. 13, ll. 263–274, 279–281.

On Kirov's assistant Bukovsky see Dec. 26, 1934 interrogations of Kotomin, Gubin, and Bukovsky himself in RGASPI, f. 671, op. 1, d. 113, ll. 63–64, 69–71. In interviews with Bukovsky, Kotomin, and Gubin on that day, L. G. Mironov, head of the central NKVD's Economic Security Department, and Kosaryov, head of the Komsomol, ascertained that Bukovsky had served in the Leningrad security police since 1930, starting as an official in the supply department. In November 1931 he was attached to Kirov personally. Bukovsky accompanied Kirov on his hunting expeditions outside the city, maintained his automobile and speedboat, and had charge of housekeeping at his apartment and his "hunting lodge in Dudergof." Although he was listed as a security officer in Kirov's guard, his relations with the party secretary were informal and he received no instructions from his nominal supervisors in the Operations Department.

14. RGANI, f. 6, op. 13, d. 13, ll. 112–114 (Gubin interrogation of Jan. 13, 1934).

15. Baskakov testimony in RGANI, f. 6, op. 13, d. 13, ll. 263–274. Sveshnikov testimony in RGANI, f. 6, op. 13, d. 73, ll. 96–132.

16. For Sveshnikov interview, see RGANI, f. 6, op. 13, d. 73, ll. 96–132. On the Stalin trip to Leningrad, see A. N. Pazi, ed., *Nash Mironych* (Leningrad: Lenizdat, 1969), 447.

17. RGANI, f. 6, op. 13, d. 13, ll. 279–281. Smolny deputy commandant A. D. Mikhalchenko reported in January 1961 that Smolny commandant Nikitin, N. F. Sveshnikov, and "the Operations Department" (i.e. Gubin) took part in the decision to move Kirov from his apartment to a separate house. See RGANI, f. 6, op.

13, d. 13, ll. 288–295ob. For Rosliakov's evidence, see Mikhail Rosliakov, *Ubiistvo Kirova: Politicheskie i ugolovnye prestupleniia v 1930-kh godakh* (Leningrad: Lenizdat, 1991), 37. Sveshnikov stated in 1966 that in his 1933 visit to Leningrad Stalin first stayed at Kirov's apartment, but moved to a separate house. This tends to confirm Baskakov's account through Medved that Stalin was unhappy with security arrangements at Kirov's apartment building. See RGANI, f. 6, op. 13, d. 73, ll. 96–132.

18. RGANI, f. 6, op. 13, d. 13, ll. 112–114. On guard numbers see 1967 Pelshe report, RGANI, f. 6, op. 13, d. 117, ll. 1–18.

19. RGANI, f. 6, op. 13, d. 13, ll. 112–114.

20. RGANI, f. 6, op. 13, d. 13, ll. 252–262, 263–274, 279–281, 289–295ob (statements of Baskakov and Mikhalchenko, 1960–1961).

21. Gubin report quote is in Iu. I. Sedov, N. V. Kulish, and A. Ia. Valetov, "Spravka rabotnikov prokuratury SSSR i sledstvennogo otdela KGB SSSR po povodu zapiski A. N. Iakovleva 'Nekotorye soobrazheniia po itogam izucheniia obstoitel'stv ubiistva S. M. Kirova,'" June 14, 1990, published in A. Artizov et al., eds., *Reabilitatsiia: Kak eto bylo*, vol. 3: *Seredina 80-kh godov–1991* (Moscow: Mezhdunarodnyi fond "Demokratiia," 2004) (hereafter cited as "Reply to Iakovlev"), 494. Sveshnikov evidence is in RGANI, f. 6, op. 13, d. 73, ll. 96–132. Rosliakov evidence is from Rosliakov, *Ubiistvo*, 37.

22. RGANI, f. 6, op. 13, d. 13, ll. 263–274 (Baskakov deposition, November, 1960).

23. For documents on Nikolenko's case, see RGANI, f. 6, op. 13, d. 67, ll. 110–133.

24. Alla Kirilina, *Rikoshet* (St. Petersburg: "Znanie," 1993), 46–47. Of 1,613 people enumerated in a police list of suspected and/or former oppositionists in Leningrad, seven, or just over 0.4 percent, had the family name Nikolaev. Extrapolated to a total population of about 3 million, this would make about twelve thousand Nikolaevs in the city of Leningrad and environs. See RGASPI, f. 671, op. 1, d. 151.

25. RGASPI, f. 671, op. 1, d. 114, ll. 74–75.

26. RGASPI, f. 671, op. 1, d. 114, ll. 74–75.

27. RGASPI, f. 671, op. 1, d. 114, ll. 82–85. For Yaroslants', Ponomarenko's, and Pankratev's posts in the NKVD, see Agranov report to Stalin, Dec. 9, 1934, in APRF, f. 3, op. 24, d. 197, ll. 89–92.

28. On the arrests of Kuzin, Maly, Vinogradov, and Maksimov, see Alla Kirilina, *Neizvestnyi Kirov* (Moscow: OLMA-PRESS, 2001), 344, citing Resolution No. 29-I of the Plenary Session of the USSR Supreme Court, May 17, 1991. On Khviiuzov's testimony, see RGANI, f. 6, op. 13, d. 1, ll. 10–53.

29. For Khviiuzov's testimony, see RGANI, f. 6, op. 13, d. 1, ll. 10–53. For Raikhman quote, see Kirilina, *Neizvestnyi Kirov*, 344.

30. RGANI, f. 6, op. 13, d. 2, ll. 78–107 (August 1956 KGB/prosecutor's report to Shvernik/Molotov commission).

31. RGASPI, f. 671, op. 1, d. 271, ll. 539–540.

32. On Dec. 14, 1934 NKVD driver Aleksandr Chopovsky confirmed to investigators that one leaf in a front spring was broken when he handed his truck over to Kuzin on the morning of December 2. He said that he'd told Kuzin he'd tight-

ened down the nuts on the spring clamps and that the truck was safe to drive at moderate speeds. See TsA FSB RF, a.u.d. N-Sh44, t. 24, ll. 291–292.

33. R. W. Rivers, email communication to author, Oct. 6, 2006. Rivers' publications include *Evidence in Traffic Accident Investigation and Reconstruction: Identification, Interpretation, and Analysis of Evidence* (Springfield: Charles C. Thomas, 2006).

34. Rivers, email communication to author, Oct. 6, 2006.

35. Ibid., Oct. 6 and 11, 2006.

36. Ibid., Oct. 6, 2006.

37. Ibid.

38. Testimony of Borisov's wife and daughter to KPK, Jan. 18, 1961, RGANI, f. 6, op. 13, d. 9, ll. 132–135, 161.

39. The August 1956 KGB report, signed by KGB chief Ivan Serov, indicates that the medical commission looking into Borisov's death included six doctors– Mamushin; medical school professors Nadezhdin, Dobrotvorsky, and Rozanov; the head of a local clinic, Olshansky; and instructor in forensic medicine Izhevsky. The report also describes the commission visiting the accident site with Yezhov and Kosaryov. See RGANI, f. 6, op. 13, d. 2, ll. 78–107 (August 1956 report to Shvernik/Molotov commission).

40. RGANI, f. 6, op. 13, d. 12, ll. 16–24, 42–43.

41. Author's interview with Jennifer Prutsman-Pfeiffer on Dec. 20, 2006.

42. Report of J. A. J. Ferris on Borisov death, Feb. 9, 2007, in author's possession (emphasis in original).

43. "Reply to Iakovlev," 497.

44. RGANI, f. 6, op. 13, d. 2, ll. 78–107 (August 1956 KGB/prosecutor's report to Nikolai Shvernik, Molotov commission, on Kirov murder); RGANI, f. 6, op. 13, d. 1, ll. 10–53 (1956 USSR prosecutor's report to Molotov commission on Kirov murder); Kirilina, *Neizvestnyi Kirov,* 346–347, apparently citing Resolution No. 29-I of the Plenary Session of the USSR Supreme Court, May 17, 1991.

45. See RGANI, f. 6, op. 13, d. 116, ll. 1–65.

46. RGANI, f. 6, op. 13, d. 116, ll. 5–9.

47. According to Petrov's later petitions for rehabilitation, Volkova labeled Karlinsky a "White general" in the fall of 1934.

48. RGASPI, f. 671, op. 1, d. 116, ll. 1–4, 5–9 (1934 documents on case against Petrov, Baltsevich, and other Leningrad NKVD officers).

49. RGASPI, f. 671, op. 1, d. 116, ll. 1–4, 5–9, 32–35.

50. See Petrov statement in Kirilina, *Neizvestnyi Kirov,* 449–451.

51. RGASPI, f. 671, op. 1, d. 116, ll. 1–65 (1934 documents on case against Petrov, Baltsevich, and other Leningrad NKVD officers).

52. See interrogations of Bravo, Miasnikov, and Korshunov in RGASPI, f. 671, op. 1, d. 120, ll. 31, 34, 121–123. On Korshunov's sentence in January 1935 see *The Crime of the Zinoviev Opposition: The Assassination of S. M. Kirov* (Moscow: Cooperative Publishing Society of Foreign Workers in the USSR, 1935), 49–50. On Korshunov's position on the Central Ward soviet, see the list of former oppositionists in Leningrad dated February 1935 in RGASPI, f. 671, op. 1, d. 151, ll. 12–97.

53. For summary of Gromov and Kazansky statements, see F. R. Kozlov to Central Committee, probably late March 1956, in A. Artizov et al., eds., *Reabili-*

tatsiia: Kak eto bylo, vol. 2: *Fevral' 1956–nachalo 80-kh godov* (Moscow: Mezh-dunarodnyi fond "Demokratiia," 2003),36–38. Kirilina, *Neizvestnyi Kirov,* 449–451 reprints the Petrov petition cited, and gives the date on 271. On Mosevich's assignment to the Volkova case, see RGANI, f. 6, op. 13. d. 79, ll. 99–104 (sentencing of the Leningrad NKVD officers, Jan. 23, 1935).

54. "Reply to Iakovlev," 477–478; Kirilina, *Neizvestnyi Kirov,* 269–270.

55. See Struppe's April 2, 1926 letter to Kirov in support of keeping Komarov and Moskvin in the Leningrad organization, cited in Kirilina, *Neizvestnyi Kirov,* 148, and the September 1929 attack on Struppe's Vyborg Ward organization in *Red Gazette* ("Kak dushili samokritiku v Vyborgskom raione," *Krasnaia gazeta,* Sept. 8, 1929, 2–3).

56. RGANI, f. 6, op. 13, d. 79, ll. 99–104 (my emphasis).

57. The statements are also mutually inconsistent on many points. Volkova's interrogators in 1960, O. Shatunovskaya and A. Kuznetsov, repeatedly caught her in lies. See "Beseda s Volkovoi," Nov. 24, 1960, RGANI, f. 6, op. 13, d. 28, ll. 7–75. Volkova's 1956 statement to the party Central Committee, dated May 30, 1956, is reproduced in Kirilina, *Neizvestnyi Kirov,* 452–457. On Volkova's admission in 1956 see "Reply to Iakovlev," 481.

58. See Petrov statement in RGANI, f. 6, op. 13, d. 116, ll. 5–9, and "Beseda s Volkovoi," Nov. 24, 1960, RGANI, f. 6, op. 13, d. 28, ll. 7–75.

59. "Beseda s Volkovoi," Nov. 24, 1960, RGANI, f. 6, op. 13, d. 28, ll. 7–75; Kirilina, *Neizvestnyi Kirov,* 452–457. Petrov statement in RGANI, f. 6, op. 13, d. 116, ll. 5–9. On Leningrad NKVD Officer P. I. Malinin's 1961 testimony to the KPK, see "Reply to Iakovlev," 472.

60. APRF, f. 3, op. 24, d. 197, ll. 84–86, 89–92.

61. Volkova's 1956 statement in Kirilina, *Neizvestnyi Kirov,* 452–457.

62. "Beseda s Volkovoi," Nov. 24, 1960, RGANI, f. 6, op. 13, d. 28, ll. 7–75, Kirilina, *Neizvestnyi Kirov,* 452–457.

63. See F. R. Kozlov to Central Committee, probably late March 1956, in Artizov et al., *Reabilitatsiia,* 2:36–38.

64. Bozhichko's letter of Nov. 29, 1960 and statements by other officers in RGANI, f. 6, op. 13, d. 28, ll. 156ff.

65. See list of interrogations of Leningrad NKVD officers attached to NKVD Secret Circular Letter of Jan. 26, 1935 in APRF, f. 3, op. 24, d. 201, ll. 106–108, 114. For Rosliakov's evidence see Rosliakov, *Ubiistvo,* 47–48. For Sorokin's testimony, see his letters to Nikita Khrushchev of Jan. 25 and March 5, 1962 (RGANI, f. 6, op. 13, d. 67, ll. 4–15). See also the March 26, 1956 statement of Fomin in RGANI, f. 6, op. 13, d. 62, ll. 62–76. The list of interrogations of Leningrad NKVD officers attached to NKVD Secret Circular Letter of Jan. 26, 1935 (APRF, f. 3, op. 24, d. 201, ll. 106–108, 114) shows that Medved, Zaporozhets, and Gorin-Lundin were all formally interrogated on Jan. 13–14, 1935, which would tend to support Fomin's claim that preparations for the trial began on January 12, on which date senior officers were incarcerated.

66. A. V. Korotkov et al., eds., "Posetiteli Kremlevskogo kabineta I. V. Stalina," *Istoricheskii arkhiv,* no. 3 (1995): 119–177; RGANI, f. 6, op. 13, d. 79, ll. 49–55, 64 (Prokofev note to Iagoda with attached draft sentencing document); July 1937

testimony of the re-arrested Vinogradov to interrogators, RGANI, f. 6, op. 13, d. 96, ll. 111–114.

67. RGANI, f. 6, op. 13, d. 1, ll. 10–53, d. 79, l. 63.

68. Someone must have questioned Nikolaev, because his explanation for trying to approach Kirov (seeking work) appears in the October 1934 log report on his detention.

69. RGANI, f. 6, op. 13, d. 13, ll. 7–45 (1960–1961 KPK report on Nikolaev's detention[s]).

70. See 1956 KGB report to Molotov commission (RGANI, f. 6, op. 13, d. 1, ll. 10–53).

71. RGANI, f. 6, op. 13, d. 1, ll. 10–53 (April 1956 USSR prosecutor's report).

72. RGANI, f. 6, op. 13, d. 1, ll. 10–53.

73. RGANI, f. 6, op. 13, d. 1, ll. 10–53.

74. RGANI, f. 6, op. 13, d. 28, l. 204.

75. In her 1960 interview with Volkova, Olga Shatunovskaya also refers to Volkova spending eight days in jail prior to her commitment. RGANI, f. 6, op. 13, d. 28, ll. 7–75.

76. See 1960s testimony of officers' wives in RGANI, f. 6, op. 13, d. 82, ll. 15–132.

77. On the Korean agent incident, see R. W. Davies et al., eds., *The Stalin-Kaganovich Correspondence, 1931–36* (New Haven: Yale University Press, 2003), 151, 155–157. On the Nakhaev mutiny, see ibid., 246–249, 253–254, 258–261. OGPU officers had been executed for corruption and espionage in the 1920s and early 1930s (A. I. Kolpakidi, *Entsiklopedia sekretnyk sluzhb Rossii* [Moscow: AST, 2004], 216–217).

78. APRF, f. 3, op. 24, d. 201, ll. 106–108, 114 (secret NKVD circular, Jan. 26, 1935).

79. RGANI, f. 6, op. 13, d. 92, ll. 169–172.

CHAPTER 11. THE KIROV MURDER AND THE GREAT TERROR

1. Eugenia Ginzburg, *Into the Whirlwind* (New York: Harcourt Brace Jovanovich, 1967), 3–5; V. K. Zavalishin, "Vokrug ubiistva Kirova," unpublished ms., Boris I. Nicolaevsky Collection, Hoover Institution Archives, Series 236, Box 411, File 1, 1–55.

2. RGASPI, f. 671, op. 1, d. 122, ll. 1–35.

3. RGASPI, f. 671, op. 1, d. 117, ll. 1–5.

4. RGASPI, f. 671, op. 1, d. 117, ll. 1–5, 67–70; Mikhail Rosliakov, *Ubiistvo Kirova: Politicheskie i ugolovnye prestupleniia v 1930-kh godakh* (Leningrad: Lenizdat, 1991), 14.

5. RGASPI, f. 671, op. 1, d. 271, ll. 535–536, 544 (Yezhov's notebooks); Marc Jansen and Nikita Petrov, *Stalin's Loyal Executioner: People's Commissar Nikolai Yezhov, 1895–1940* (Stanford: Hoover Institution Press, 2002), 24–25.

6. V. N. Khaustov et al., eds., *Lubianka: Stalin i VChK-GPU-OGPU-NKVD, ianvar' 1922–dekabr' 1936* (Moscow: Mezhdunarodnyi fond "Demokratiia," 2003), 613–616.

7. Ibid., 617 (Iagoda to Stalin, Feb. 26, 1935), 654–657 (Zakovsky's final report), 670–671 (Vyshinsky's report on appeals).

8. RGASPI, f. 671, op. 1, d. 129, ll. 12, 92, 126, 168–188; Iu. I. Sedov, N. V. Kulish, and A. Ia. Valetov, "Spravka rabotnikov prokuratury SSSR i sledstvennogo otdela KGB SSSR po povodu zapiski A. N. Iakovleva 'Nekotorye soobrazheniia po itogam izucheniia obstoiatel'stv ubiistva S. M. Kirova,'" June 14, 1990, published in A. Artizov et al., eds., *Reabilitatsiia: Kak eto bylo,* vol. 3: *Seredina 80-kh godov–1991* (Moscow: Mezhdunarodnyi fond "Demokratiia," 2004), 478–479 (hereafter cited as "Reply to Iakovlev").

9. Boris I. Nicolaevsky Collection, Hoover Institution Archives, Series 212, Box 88, File 18, 2.

10. RGANI, f. 6, op. 13, d. 16, ll. 19–21; Amy Knight, *Who Killed Kirov? The Kremlin's Greatest Mystery* (New York: Hill and Wang, 1999), 243.

11. RGASPI, f. 671, op. 1, d. 271, ll. 548–548ob.

12. RGASPI, f. 671, op. 1, d. 129, ll. 61–88; f. 80, op. 17, d. 70, ll. 1–8.

13. RGASPI, f. 671, op. 1, d. 112, ll. 12–14, 27–28.

14. Khaustov et al., *Lubianka, 1922–1936,* 820 n. 155; Oleg Khlevniuk, *Politbiuro: Mekhanizmy politicheskoi vlasti v 30-e gody* (Moscow: ROSSPEN, 1996) 143.

15. Iurii Zhukov, "Tainy 'Kremlevskogo dela' 1935 goda i sud'ba Avelia Enukidze," *Voprosy istorii,* no. 9 (2000): 83–113.

16. Ibid.; Khaustov et al., *Lubianka, 1922–1936,* 599 (Iagoda report to Stalin, Jan. 20, 1935).

17. Zhukov, "Tainy 'Kremlevskogo dela'"; Khaustov et al., *Lubianka, 1922–1936,* 599–600, 602–612, 618–619, 626–637, 638–650.

18. Zhukov, "Tainy 'Kremlevskogo dela'"; Khaustov et al., *Lubianka, 1922–1936,* 648–650, 658–660, 663–669, 681.

19. On Yezhov's supervision of the Kremlin staff purge, see Zhukov, "Tainy 'Kremlevskogo dela,'" 95. On the purge of Moscow, see Strobe Talbott, ed., *Khrushchev Remembers* (Boston: Little, Brown, 1970), 78–79.

20. Iurii Zhukov, *Inoi Stalin* (Moscow: "Vagrius," 2003), 175–176.

21. Iurii Zhukov, "Tak, byl li 'zagovor' Tukhachevskogo?" *Otechestvennaia istoriia,* no. 1 (1999): 176–181 (Gagra and Sochi incidents); Simon Sebag Montefiore, *Stalin: The Court of the Red Tsar* (New York: Knopf, 2004), 156 (Stalin's security increased post–Kirov murder).

22. Yagoda seems to have initially pressed for the "foreign plot" version of Kirov's murder. In 1935 he noted on at least one memorandum that the Menshevik Party was moribund and not worth NKVD attention (see Mikhail Ilin'skii, *Narkom Yagoda: Dvadtsat' let v maske* [Moscow: "Iauza," "EKSMO," 2005], 157, based on transcripts of Yagoda interrogations in 1937). On Yezhov's speech to the plenum, see J. Arch Getty and Oleg Naumov, *The Road to Terror: Stalin and the Self-Destruction of the Bolsheviks, 1932–1939* (New Haven: Yale University Press, 1999), 161–167.

23. Getty, *Road to Terror,* 167.

24. Ibid., 156–157, 588; Khlevniuk, *Politbiuro,* 141–159.

25. Getty, *Road to Terror,* 189–193, 197–211. On Yezhov's involvement in the vetting of foreign Communists resident in the USSR see Jansen and Petrov, *Stalin's Loyal Executioner,* 41–43.

26. S. V. Sukharev, "Litsedeistvo na poprishche istorii," *Voprosy istorii KPSS,* no. 3 (1990): 103–118.

27. Getty, *Road to Terror,* 176–177; Oleg Khlevniuk, *Stalin i Kaganovich: Perepiska, 1931–1936 g.g.* (Moscow: ROSSPEN, 2001), 557–558; Robert Conquest, *The Great Terror: A Reassessment* (New York: Oxford University Press, 1990), 76–77.

28. Jansen and Petrov, *Stalin's Loyal Executioner,* 46; Conquest, *The Great Terror: A Reassessment,* 80; Getty, *Road to Terror,* 247–250; Khaustov et al., *Lubianka, 1922–1936,* 712–720.

29. Jansen and Petrov, *Stalin's Loyal Executioner,* 46–48; Getty, *Road to Terror,* 248–250.

30. Getty, *Road to Terror,* 62–63, 256–257; *Report of Court Proceedings: The Case of the Trotskyite-Zinovievite Terrorist Center* (New York: Howard Fertig, 1967), 1–11, 40–42; Jansen and Petrov, *Stalin's Loyal Executioner,* 46–48.

31. Getty, *Road to Terror,* 68.

32. Ibid., 256–257; *Report of Court Proceedings: The Case of the Trotskyite-Zinovievite Center,* 39.

33. Jansen and Petrov, *Stalin's Loyal Executioner,* 49–55; Getty, *Road to Terror,* 274–281.

34. O. V. Khlevniuk, *Stalin i Ordzhonikidze* (Moscow: "Rossiia Molodaia," 1993), 66–129.

35. People's Commissariat of Justice of the USSR, *Report of the Court Proceedings in the Case of the Anti-Soviet Trotskyite Centre* (Moscow: People's Commissariat of Justice, 1937).

36. Conquest, *The Great Terror: A Reassessment,* 165.

37. Getty, *The Road to Terror,* 326–357.

38. Jansen and Petrov, *Stalin's Loyal Executioner,* 59–60; Getty, *Road to Terror,* 364–419.

39. Jansen and Petrov, *Stalin's Loyal Executioner,* 61; Getty, *Road to Terror,* 420–435; V. N. Khaustov, V. P. Naumov, and N. S. Plotnikov, *Lubianka: Stalin i glavnoe upravlenie gosbesopasnosti NKVD, 1937–1938* (Moscow: Mezhdunarodnyi fond "Demokratiia," 2004), 640 n. 20.

40. Getty, *Road to Terror,* 437–453; Jansen and Petrov, *Stalin's Loyal Executioner,* 69–78.

41. On the mass operations, see Getty, *Road to Terror,* 468–481, and Paul Hagenloh, "'Socially Harmful Elements' and the Terror," in Sheila Fitzpatrick, ed., *Stalinism: New Directions* (London: Routledge, 2000), 286–308. On the ethnic deportations, see Terry Martin, "The Origins of Soviet Ethnic Cleansing," *Journal of Modern History* 70 (December 1998): 813–861.

42. Getty, *Road to Terror,* 588.

43. See Conquest, *The Great Terror: A Reassessment*; Robert Tucker, *Stalin in Power: The Revolution from Above, 1928–1941* (New York: Norton, 1990); J. Arch Getty, *Origins of the Great Purges: The Soviet Communist Party Reconsidered, 1933–1938* (Cambridge: Cambridge University Press, 1985), and *Road to Terror*; Hagenloh, "'Socially Harmful Elements' and the Terror"; Moshe Lewin, "Bureaucracy and the Stalinist State," in Ian Kershaw and Moshe Lewin, eds., *Stalinism and Nazism: Dictatorships in Comparison* (Cambridge: Cambridge Uni-

versity Press, 1997), 53–74; Gabor Rittersporn, "The Omnipresent Conspiracy: On Soviet Imagery of Politics and Social Relations in the 1930s," in Nick Lampert and Gabor Rittersporn, eds., *Stalinism: Its Nature and Aftermath* (Armonk: M. E. Sharpe, 1992), 101–120.

44. See Ian Kershaw, "'Working towards the Fuhrer': Reflections on the Nature of the Hitler dictatorship," in Kershaw and Lewin, *Stalinism and Nazism: Dictatorships in Comparison*, 88–106.

45. Sheila Fitzpatrick, *The Russian Revolution* (Oxford: Oxford University Press, 1990), 153–161.

46. James Harris, "Stalin's Spymania," presented at the Melbourne Conferences on Soviet and Australian History and Culture, University of Melbourne, July 4–8, 2006.

47. Hiroaki Kuromiya, *Stalin* (Harlow, UK: Pearson Longman: 2005), 115; V. N. Denisov and Iu. G. Murin, eds., *Iosif Stalin v obiiatiakh sem'i: Iz lichnogo arkhiva* (Moscow: Rodina, 1993), 168.

48. Khaustov et al., *Lubianka, 1937–1938*, 135–144.

49. KGB documentation indicates archivists destroyed a mass of Leningrad Operations Department files, including the 1934 records of Kirov's guard, in the spring and summer of 1941. This was probably due to the approach of Axis troops to Leningrad. Note that if the guard records did not support the 1937–1938 version of the Kirov murder the authorities would have had reason to destroy them. Documents on persons detained by the Operations Department in the "special duty zone" (*zona osobogo obsluzhivaniia*) were destroyed in September 1945, although it is not clear whether any of these dated from 1934. The destruction of the guard files, etc., was part of a much larger, and apparently routine, purge of documents considered unimportant. On the document purges of 1941 and 1945, see RGANI, f. 6, op. 13, d. 13, ll. 175–178.

50. For Maksimov's June 1937 testimony, see RGANI, f. 6, op. 13, d. 9, ll. 1–18 (1961 KPK report on Borisov's death).

51. Alla Kirilina, *Neizvestnyi Kirov* (Moscow: OLMA-PRESS, 2001), 348; RGANI, f. 6, op. 13, d. 9, ll. 1–18 (1960–1961 KPK report on Borisov's death).

52. RGANI, f. 6, op. 13, d. 62, ll. 62–76 (March 1956 testimony of former Leningrad NKVD deputy chief Fomin).

53. Kirilina, *Neizvestnyi Kirov*, 495. The official report states that Zaporozhets died of heart failure. August 14 was the same date as Gubin's execution, however, and Zaporozhets was almost certainly shot.

54. RGANI, f. 6, op. 13, d. 13, ll. 7–45. Tyshkevich's evidence shows the same parallel phrasing and the same "overkill" as Gubin's and Zaporozhets' testimony.

55. RGANI, f. 6, op. 13, d. 13, ll. 7–45.

56. RGANI, f. 6, op. 13, d. 2, ll. 78–107 (Aug. 31, 1956 KGB/prosecutor's report to the Molotov commission).

57. Kirilina, *Neizvestnyi Kirov*, 347–348, based on May 17, 1991 resolution of the Supreme Court of the USSR.

58. Kirilina, *Neizvestnyi Kirov*, 348–349.

59. Ibid., 349.

60. All of these men had died in 1934–1936, apparently of natural causes. Now their doctors were charged with poisoning and/or killing them with inappropriate

treatments. All four probably did die naturally (see testimony of Genrikh Liush-kov, Conclusion, Documents 126, 127).

61. See Conquest, *The Great Terror: A Reassessment*, 341–398; Getty, *Road to Terror*, 525–527; People's Commissariat of Justice of the USSR, *Report of the Court Proceedings in the Case of the Anti-Soviet Bloc of Rights and Trotskyites* (Moscow: People's Commissariat of Justice of the USSR, 1938).

62. *Case of the Anti-Soviet Bloc of Rightists and Trotskyites*, 552–553, 678.

63. Ibid., 737–741, 768–772.

64. At two points in the trial, Yagoda asked to discuss specific parts of the charges against him in camera. His requests were granted. Although it has been suggested that Yagoda might have wanted to explain to the judge that he was only following Stalin's orders in murdering Kirov, this is incorrect. The trial transcript makes it crystal clear that Yagoda wanted to discuss privately the charge that he had murdered Gorky's son Maxim Peshkov. Yagoda was having an affair with Peshkov's wife at the time Peshkov died, and the Soviet government did not want news of such "immoral" goings-on spread throughout the world.

65. "Ubiistvo v Smol'nom," *Rodina*, no. 10 (Fall 1995): 62–66.

66. See Feb. 9, 1956 report to TsK Presidium in A. Artizov et al., eds., *Reabilitatsiia: Kak eto bylo*, vol. 1: *Mart 1953–fevral' 1956* (Moscow: Mezhdunarodnyi fond "Demokratiia," 2000), 317–348.

67. A. Artizov et al., eds., *Reabilitatsiia: Kak eto bylo*, vol. 2: *Fevral' 1956–nachalo 80-kh godov* (Moscow: Mezhdunarodnyi fond "Demokratiia," 2003), 482–485.

68. Getty, *Road to Terror*, 452.

69. Artizov et al., *Reabilitatsiia*, 2:83–84.

70. Ibid., 1:323–325.

71. On NKVD consideration of using Antipov at the March 1938 show trial see ibid., 2:629 (February 1963 KPK report on the Terror). On Komarov's testimony and execution see ibid., 1:334–335. On Chudov, see RGANI, f. 6, op. 13, d. 73, l. 1. On Kodatsky's execution see Knight, *Who Killed Kirov*, 246. On Irklis' execution see RGANI, f. 6, op. 13, d. 73, l. 13.

72. Getty, *Road to Terror*, 491–529; Khaustov et al., *Lubianka, 1937–1938*, 527–537.

73. On Zakovsky's firing, see Khaustov et al., *Lubianka, 1937–1938*, 517. On A. I. Ugarov, see Artizov et al., *Reabilitatsiia*, 1:297–298. On Ugarov and Pozern, see RGANI, f. 6, op. 13, d. 73, ll. 14–19.

74. See RGANI, f. 6, op. 13, d. 13, ll. 7–45 (1960 or 1961 KPK report on Nikolaev's detentions), and RGANI, f. 6, op. 13, d. 13, ll. 133–137ob (1961 testimony of interrogating officer Krutov).

75. RGANI, f. 6, op. 13, d. 13, ll. 7–45.

76. RGANI, f. 6, op. 13, d. 13, ll. 133–137ob.

77. RGANI, f. 6, op. 13, d. 13, ll. 7–45; RGANI, f. 6, op. 13, d. 13, ll. 125–126, 133–137ob.

78. RGANI, f. 6, op. 13, d. 13, l. 130.

79. Mikhalchenko testimony of 1961, RGANI, f. 6, op. 13, d. 13, ll. 289–295ob. For Pauzer testimony of March 13, 1939, see ll. 129–129ob.

80. RGANI, f. 6, op. 13, d. 13, ll. 118–123.

81. On the end of the Terror, see Getty, *Road to Terror,* 546–550. On Krutov's case, see his 1961 testimony, RGANI, f. 6, op. 13, d. 13, ll. 131–1330b. Kotomin died of natural causes in 1943 (see 1964 testimony of his wife, RGANI, f. 6, op. 13, d. 82, ll. 29–320b). Most of the other defendants lived into the Khrushchev era.

82. See RGANI, f. 6, op. 13, d. 9, ll. 257–279 (Petrovskii deposition of Dec. 1, 1960), d. 13, ll. 283–284 (1938 data on Petrovskii), 287–288 (Petrovskii letter to Ezhov, April 23, 1938).

83. RGANI, f. 6, op. 13, d. 13, ll. 287–288.

84. RGANI, f. 6, op. 13, d. 13, ll. 287–288.

85. RGANI, f. 6, op. 13, d. 13, l. 286; RGANI, f. 6, op. 13, d. 9, ll. 257–279.

86. "Reply to Iakovlev," 468. Beria also ordered Karl Radek murdered in prison.

CHAPTER 12. RUMORS, SPECULATION, AND
THE MARTYR CULT

1. Lesley Ann Rimmel, "The Kirov Murder and Soviet Society: Propaganda and Popular Opinion in Leningrad, 1934–1935" (Ph.D. diss., University of Pennsylvania, 1995), 21, 27–28; Memoirs of V. I. Rudol'f-Iurasov in Boris I. Nicolaevsky Collection, Hoover Institution Archives, Series 212, Box 249, File 3; Benno Ennker, *Die Anfänge des Leninkults in der Sowjetunion* (Cologne: Bohlau Verlag, 1997), 69; Alla Kirilina, *Rikoshet* (St. Petersburg: "Znanie," 1993), 30–31; *Leningradskaia pravda,* Dec. 2, 1934, 3.

2. *Leningradskaia pravda,* Dec. 2, 1934, 1–3.

3. On the "positive hero" in Socialist Realist literature, see Katerina Clark, *The Soviet Novel: History as Ritual* (Chicago: University of Chicago Press, 1981), 9–10, 32–34, 48, 57–74.

4. Ennker, *Anfänge,* 1–31.

5. On the Leningrad committee for funeral arrangements and the joint commission see Kirilina, *Rikoshet,* 30–33. On the Moscow commission, see APRF, f. 3, op. 62, d. 92, l. 45. Sveshnikov testimony is in RGANI, f. 6, op. 13, d. 73, ll. 96–132.

6. APRF, f. 3, op. 62, d. 92, l. 29–300b, 45; Ennker, *Anfänge,* 143–144.

7. APRF, f. 3, op. 62, d. 92, l. 29–300b, 45. On the work of the Lenin funeral commission and the funeral itself, see Ennker, *Anfänge,* 138–154.

8. On the motive for Lenin's mummification, see ibid., 171.

9. *Leningradskaia pravda,* Dec. 2, 1934, 2–3; Rimmel, "The Kirov Murder and Soviet Society," 31–33.

10. On the role of party/workplace meetings in the fabrication of "public opinion" in the Lenin mourning campaign, see Ennker, *Anfänge,* 76–86.

11. For the child's drawing, see Alla Kirilina, "Vystrely v Smol'nom," *Rodina,* no. 1 (1989): 33, 70–78. For "We will be like Kirov!" see *Leningradskaia pravda,* Dec. 3, 1934, 3. For the renaming of Viatka, see ibid., Dec. 6, 1934, 1.

12. *Leningradskaia pravda,* Dec. 3, 1934, 3.

13. For Butiagin's piece, see *Tovarishch Kirov* (Moscow: Profizdat, 1935), 97–98. For Desov's comments, see Mikhail Rosliakov, *Ubiistvo Kirova: Politicheskie i ugolovnye prestupleniia v 1930-kh godakh* (Leningrad: Lenizdat, 1991), 109.

14. Rimmel, "The Kirov Murder and Soviet Society"; Sarah Davies, *Popular Opinion in Stalin's Russia: Terror, Propaganda, and Dissent, 1934–1941* (Cambridge: Cambridge University Press, 1997), 114–118.

15. On the problems with *svodki* as sources, see Peter Holquist's comments in "'Information is the Alpha and Omega of Our Work': Bolshevik Surveillance in Pan-European Context," *Journal of Modern History* 69 (September 1997): 415–450, and Terry Martin, "'Registration' and 'Mood': OGPU Information Reports and the Soviet Surveillance System" (unpublished ms.).

16. Rimmel, "The Kirov Murder and Soviet Society," 31–33.

17. Ibid., 42–47.

18. Ibid., 49–55.

19. Lesley Rimmel, "Another Kind of Fear: The Kirov Murder and the End of Bread Rationing in Leningrad," *Slavic Review* 56 (Autumn 1997): 481–499; Rimmel, "The Kirov Murder and Soviet Society," 114, 117, 137–139.

20. Rimmel, "The Kirov Murder and Soviet Society," 74–76, 136–137, 171; Davies, *Popular Opinion,* 116.

21. Rimmel, "The Kirov Murder and Soviet Society," 80–83, 100.

22. Ibid., 105, 109–110, 118–120.

23. RGASPI, f. 671, op. 1, d. 122, ll. 1–6.

24. RGASPI, f. 671, op. 1, d. 122, ll. 109, 121–122.

25. Adam B. Ulam, *Stalin: The Man and His Era* (New York: Viking, 1973), p. 382.

26. Davies, *Popular Opinion,* 114–118; Rimmel, "Another Kind of Fear"; Rimmel, "The Kirov Murder and Soviet Society," 58, 131–132.

27. Boris I. Nicolaevsky Collection, Hoover Institution Archives, Series 212, Box 249, File 3.

28. Rimmel, "The Kirov Murder and Soviet Society," 56; Davies, *Popular Opinion,* 116.

29. Rimmel, "The Kirov Murder and Soviet Society," 59, 62–64; Davies, *Popular Opinion,* 116.

30. Rimmel, "The Kirov Murder and Soviet Society," 51, 61–66.

31. Ibid., 59.

32. On the reproduction of political power by putting individual subjects through public rituals and getting them to reproduce state narratives, regardless of their "real" internal beliefs, see Lisa Wedeen, *Ambiguities of Domination: Politics, Rhetoric, and Symbols in Contemporary Syria* (Chicago: University of Chicago Press, 1999).

33. For the Karakhan letter, see A. V. Kvashonkin at al., eds., *Sovetskoe rukovodstvo: Perepiska, 1927–1941* (Moscow: ROSSPEN, 1999), 299. For Mikoyan quote, see Oleg Khlevniuk, *Politbiuro: Mekhanizmy politicheskoi vlasti v 30-e gody* (Moscow: ROSSPEN, 1996), 122.

34. Kvashonkin et al., *Sovetskoe rukovodstvo,* 301.

35. James C. Scott, *Domination and the Arts of Resistance* (New Haven: Yale University Press, 1990), 108–182.

36. J. Arch Getty makes a similar point forcefully in *Origins of the Great Purges: The Soviet Communist Party Reconsidered, 1933–1938* (Cambridge: Cambridge University Press, 1985).

37. RGANI, f. 6, op. 13, d. 28, ll. 224–231.

38. RGANI, f. 6, op. 13, d. 28, l. 204.

39. Kirchakov letter in RGANI, f. 6, op. 13, d. 23, ll. 2–3.

40. RGANI, f. 6, op. 13, d. 67, ll. 4–14.

41. Testimony of Noi Aronovich Zavilovich, April 20, 1939, RGANI, f. 6, op. 13, d. 13, l. 55.

42. Roy Medvedev, *Let History Judge: The Origins and Consequences of Stalinism* (New York: Knopf, 1971), 161.

43. Larina story is from Amy Knight, *Who Killed Kirov? The Kremlin's Greatest Mystery* (New York: Hill and Wang, 1999), 247. "V. Sh.'s" story is from Medvedev, *Let History Judge*, 159.

44. Boris I. Nicolaevsky Collection, Hoover Institution Archives, Series 212, Box 249, File 3.

45. *S. M. Kirov, 1886–1934: Materialy k biografii* (Moscow: Partizdat TsK VKP[b], 1934), 17, 37, 60, 73.

46. *Tovarishch Kirov* (Moscow: Profizdat, 1935), 16–17, 24, 44, 80, 122–123.

47. B. P. Pozern, ed., *Sergei Mironovich Kirov, 1886–1934* (Leningrad: Partizdat, 1937), 5–7, 15–19, 32, 52, 55, and passim.

48. M. D. Ivanova et al., eds., *Sergei Mironovich Kirov, 1886–1934* (Leningrad: Gosudarstvennoe izdatel'stvo politicheskoi literatury, 1939), 18, 48, 64, 74, 127, and passim.

49. Evgeny Dobrenko, "Shoots from the Underground: Dialectics of Conspiratorial Thinking" (unpublished ms. provided to author).

50. Ibid. Dobrenko cites Oksana Bulgakowa on the role of "scenting" the enemy in the film.

51. Georgii Kholopov, *Groznyi god* (Moscow: "Molodaia gvardiia," 1955).

52. A. M. Kostrikova and E. M. Kostrikova, *Eto bylo v Urzhume: Vospominaniia o S. M. Kirove* (Kirov: Kirovskoe knizhnoe izdatel'stvo, 1962), esp. 4–5, 40–42, 54–55, 72–73. On the shift to an emphasis on "humanitarian values" and individual problems in the press, see Thomas Cox Wolfe, "Imagining Journalism: Politics, Government, and the Person in the Press in the Soviet Union and Russia, 1953–1993" (Ph.D. diss., University of Michigan, 1997).

53. Kostrikova and Kostrikova, *Eto bylo v Urzhume*, 31, 95–96.

54. S. Sinel'nikov, *Kirov* (Moscow: Molodaia gvardiia, 1964), passim.

55. Ibid., 257–258, 265, 272, 281, 315–318.

56. Ibid., 288, 326, 333, 337.

57. A. N. Pazi, ed., *Nash Mironych* (Leningrad: Lenizdat, 1969).

58. David Brandenberger, *National Bolshevism* (Cambridge: Harvard University Press, 2002), 38–42, 60–62.

59. I am not suggesting that de-Stalinizers all chose to build up Kirov as an alternative to Stalin for consciously Machiavellian political reasons. Many no doubt came to believe that he had been a genuine alternative. However, the power and positioning of Kirov (the imagined figure) in the Soviet political imagination was part of this process of coming-to-believe.

CHAPTER 13. THE KIROV MURDER IN THE WEST, 1934–1956

1. "Novaia volna terrora v SSSR," *Sotsialisticheskii vestnik* 15, no. 1 (Jan. 10, 1935): 1.

2. L. D. Trotsky, "Stalinskaia biurokratiia i ubiistvo Kirova," *Biulleten' oppozitsii*, no. 41 (January 1935).

3. J. Arch Getty, *The Road to Terror: Stalin and the Self-Destruction of the Bolsheviks, 1932–1939* (New Haven: Yale University Press, 1999), 256–257, 300; *Report of Court Proceedings: The Case of the Trotskyite-Zinovievite Terrorist Center* (New York: Howard Fertig, 1967), 65–72.

4. See "Moskovskii protsess–protsess nad Oktiabrem," *Biulleten oppozitsii*, nos. 52–53 (October 1936): 2–49.

5. P. Garvi, "Udar nalevo i napravo," *Sotsialisticheskii vestnik*, nos. 1–2 (Jan. 17, 1937): 8–10.

6. "Kak podgotovlialsia Moskovskii protsess (Iz pis'ma starogo Bolshevika)," ibid., nos. 23–24 (Dec. 27, 1936): 20–23; nos. 1–2 (Jan. 17, 1937): 17–24.

7. See Boris Nicolaevsky, "Letter of an Old Bolshevik," in Nicolaevsky, *Power and the Soviet Elite* (New York: Praeger, 1965), 26–65.

8. J. Arch Getty, *Origins of the Great Purges* (Cambridge: Cambridge University Press, 1985). On the negotiations for the purchase of the Marx archives, see Boris Nicolaevsky, "N. I. Bukharin i moi s nim vstrechi v 1936 g.: Iz vospominanii," Boris I. Nicolaevsky Collection, Hoover Institution Archives, Series 249, Box 514, File 28; Anna Larina, *Nezabyvaemoe* (Moscow: Izdatel'stvo "APN," 1989), 245–259; Boris Sapir, ed., *Iz arkhiva L. O. Dan* (Amsterdam: Stichting Internationaal Instituut voor Sociale Geschiedenis, 1987), 106–114; André Liebich, "'I Am the Last'–Memories of Bukharin in Paris," *Slavic Review* 51, no. 4 (Winter 1992): 767–781; Liebich, *From the Other Shore: Russian Social Democracy after 1921* (Cambridge: Harvard University Press, 1997), 230–235.

9. See Nicolaevsky, *Power*, 8–9. For the footnote text from Nicolaevsky's manuscript, see Nicolaevsky Collection, Series 249, Box 522, File 16 (pages not numbered). For the published footnote see Nicolaevsky, *Power*, 92n.

10. Nicolaevsky, *Power*, 7, 14.

11. Ibid., 7.

12. It is possible that Nicolaevsky was minimizing Bukharin's revelations to protect the latter's living relatives in the Soviet Union, including his wife and son.

13. Nicolaevsky Collection, Series 249, Box 522, File 19, manuscript copy of "interviu."

14. Nicolaevsky, *Power*, 8–9. On the break with Dan, see Liebich, *From the Other Shore*, 260–270.

15. See the correspondence between Nicolaevsky and editor Janet Zagoria in Nicolaevsky Collection, Series 249, Box 522, File 16.

16. See Oleg Khlevniuk, *Politbiuro: Mekhanizmy politicheskoi vlasti v 1930-e gody* (Moscow: ROSSPEN, 1996), 74–77. On Bukharin's attendance at Politburo sessions in 1932 see O. V. Khlevniuk et al., eds., *Stalinskoe politbiuro v 30-e gody: Sbornik dokumentov* (Moscow: AIRO-XX, 1995), 211–223.

17. Khlevniuk, *Politbiuro*, 118–127. See also Alla Kirilina, *Neizvestnyi Kirov* (Moscow: OLMA-PRESS, 2001), 309–323.

18. Anna Larina, *Nezabyvaemoe* (Moscow: Izdatel'stvo APN, 1989), 243–289.

19. Liebich, "'I Am the Last,'"; Sapir, *Iz arkhiva*, 106–114.

20. Liebich, *From the Other Shore*, 142.

21. See "T" in "Po rossii," *Sotsialisticheskii vestnik,* nos. 23–24 (Dec. 20, 1934): 22–23; "P" in "Po rossii," ibid., no. 13 (July 10, 1935): 16; and "N" and "P" in "Po rossii," ibid., no. 16 (Aug. 25, 1935): 15–16.

22. Liebich, *From the Other Shore*, 141, 226.

23. Sarah Davies, *Popular Opinion in Stalin's Russia* (Cambridge: Cambridge University Press, 1997), 153–154.

24. Liebich, *From the Other Shore*, 278, 301–302, 319–320.

25. Nicolaevsky Collection, Series 248, Box 509, File 7, Nicolaevsky to Zavalishin, April 15, 1951.

26. Nicolaevsky Collection, Series 236, Box 411, File 1, V. K. Zavalishin, "Vokrug ubiistvo Kirova," 15.

27. See for example Liebich's comments in "'I am the Last.'"

28. See André Liebich's account of the negotiations for the archive in *From the Other Shore*, 231–233.

29. Ibid., 231.

30. RGASPI, f. 671, op. 1, d. 60, ll. 2–5 (Sept. 11, 1935 report to Eezhov and Adoratskii from Arosev and Tikhomirov), 6 (V. Adoratskii to Ezhov, Sept. 19, 1935). On the Soviet offer of a job to Nicolaevsky, see Liebich, *From the Other Shore,* 231–232.

31. RGASPI, f. 671, op. 1, d. 60, ll. 7–8.

32. Tikhomirov to Arosev, Jan. 9–10, 1936, RGASPI, f. 671, op. 1, d. 60, ll. 29–31. See also Liebich, *From the Other Shore,* 232.

33. Liebich, *From the Other Shore,* 232–233.

34. Ibid., 297–302. On the concealment of Nicolaevsky's socialism by the editors of *Power and the Soviet Elite,* see Nicolaevsky Collection, Series 413, Box 522, Files 16–18, which contain materials related to publication of the book. In a preface that editors scrapped, Nicolaevsky wrote that the single-party dictatorship in the USSR "stand[s] in the way of a democratic Russia. In the last analysis it is also incompatible with a genuinely socialist Russia." In another unpublished draft he referred to "the humanitarian base of Communism." Sections of George Kennan's introduction to the book that speculated about whether Nicolaevsky still hewed to the old Menshevik belief system were also cut.

35. See Robert Conquest, *The Great Terror: A Reassessment* (Oxford: Oxford University Press, 1990), 364–367.

36. G. N. Grammatikopoulos, "K zagadkam moskovskikh protsessov," *Sotsialisticheskii vestnik* 19, nos. 1–2 (Jan. 29, 1939): 5–14; no. 3 (Feb. 17, 1939): 28–32.

37. See W. G. Krivitsky, "Why Did They Confess?" *Saturday Evening Post* 211, no. 51 (June 17, 1939): 5–6, 96–103. See also Krivitsky's 1939 book, in part a reprint of his *Saturday Evening Post* series, *In Stalin's Secret Service* (New York: Harper, 1939), 181–210. Other articles in the *Saturday Evening Post* series included "Stalin's Hand in Spain," 211, no. 42 (April 15, 1939), 5–7, 115–122; "Why Stalin Shot His Generals," ibid., no. 43 (April 22, 1939), 16–17, 71–77; and "Stalin Appeases Hitler," ibid., no. 44 (April 29, 1939), 12–13, 84–89.

38. See Krivitsky, "Why Did They Confess," and *In Stalin's Secret Service,* pp. 181–85; and Nicolaevsky, "Letter of an Old Bolshevik."

39. Krivitsky, *In Stalin's Secret Service,* 184–86.

40. Orlov seems to have plagiarized this quote from Krivitsky. See Alexander Orlov, *The Secret History of Stalin's Crimes* (London: Jarrold's, 1953), 22.

41. Ibid., 186.

42. See V. Krivitsky, "Iz vospominanii sovetskogo kommunista," *Sotsialisticheskii vestnik* 18, no. 6 (1938); no. 7 (1938): 3–8.

43. Isaac Don Levine, *Eyewitness to History* (New York: Hawthorn Books, 1973), 1–20, 34–50. See also Levine's *Stalin* (New York: Cosmopolitan Book Corporation, 1931).

44. Levine, *Eyewitness,* 185–86. On Levine's work for Krivitsky as a ghost-writer, see Gary Kern, *A Death in Washington: Walter G. Krivitsky and the Stalin Terror* (New York: Enigma Books, 2003), 177–178. See also Sapir, *Iz arkhiva,* 121–124 (including note 11).

45. Sapir, *Iz arkhiva,* 121–124. According to Alexander Orlov, Max Eastman told him essentially the same story (Kern, *A Death in Washington,* 179).

46. Kern, *A Death in Washington,* 231–232, 256–257.

47. See Isaac Don Levine, *Stalin's Great Secret* (New York: Coward-McCann, 1956). On the forgery of the "Yeremin Letter," see Robert Tucker, *Stalin as Revolutionary. A Study in History and Personality* (New York: Norton, 1973), 111–112; and B. I. Kaptelov and Z. I. Peregudova, "Byl li Stalin agentom okhranki?" *Voprosy istorii KPSS,* no. 4 (1989): 90–98.

48. See Levine, *Eyewitness,* pp. 185–86; Sam Tanenhaus, *Whittaker Chambers: A Biography* (New York: Random House, 1997), pp. 286–87; and issues of *Plain Talk* from 1946 through 1948.

49. It seems well established that Alger Hiss worked with Soviet intelligence, but there remain questions about his identification as the Soviet agent "Ales." The information Hiss passed on was not particularly significant, and claims that the Roosevelt administration was "honeycombed with Communist spies" were hyperbole. See Allen Weinstein and Alexander Vassiliev, *The Haunted Wood: Soviet Espionage in America—The Stalin Era* (New York: Random House, 1999); Herbert Romerstein and Eric Breindel, *The Venona Secrets: Exposing Soviet Espionage and America's Traitors* (Washington, D.C.: Regnery, 2000); Tanenhaus, *Whittaker Chambers,* 515–520. For a compilation of analysis skeptical of Hiss's guilt, see the website "The Alger Hiss Story: Search for the Truth," http://homepages.nyu.edu/~th15/lowsoviet.html, especially articles by Eric Alterman, Victor Navasky, and John Lowenthal.

50. See George Hamilton Combs, "Must It Be War?" *Plain Talk* 3, no. 1 (October 1948): 1–6. Combs compared the American public's aversion to preemptive attacks on other nations to "measles." See also ibid., 3, no. 5 (February 1949) for caricature of "Professor Pinko" and Mitchell's letter. The reality is that the anti-Communist movement in the United States attracted both principled believers in liberal democracy and some of the most antidemocratic elements of American society, including militarists, white supremacists, segregationists, anti-Semites, opponents of women's rights, and antilabor ideologues who denied workers' right to organize. Levine seems to have treated many such people indiscriminately as allies.

"Liberals" quote is ibid., 3, no. 4 (January 1949): 37–40. "Crackpotism" is from Tanenhaus, *Whittaker Chambers,* 487.

51. Alexander Barmine, *One Who Survived* (New York: Putnam and S, 1945), 246–253, and *Memoirs of a Soviet Diplomat* (London: L. Dickson, 1938). See also J. Arch Getty's review of Robert Conquest's *Stalin and the Kirov Murder* (New York: Oxford University Press, 1989) in *Russian Review* 48, no. 3 (July 1989): 348–351.

52. See Alexander Orlov, *The Secret History of Stalin's Crimes* (New York: Random House, 1953), 9–24; and John Costello and Oleg Tsarev, *Deadly Illusions* (New York: Crown, 1993), 141–247, 280–292, 304–305, 332, 380–87. See also J. Arch Getty, *Origins of the Great Purges: The Soviet Communist Party Reconsidered, 1933–1938* (Cambridge: Cambridge University Press, 1985), 212.

53. Orlov, *Secret History,* 21–32.

54. Elizabeth Lermolo, *Face of a Victim* (New York: Harper, 1955), 117, 122–23, 229, 272.

55. Ibid., 91, 113, 236.

56. Ibid., 58, 76, 176, 225, 226–229.

57. Ibid., 112, 134, 204–205, 212, 220, 235, 289.

58. For example Conquest, *The Great Terror: Stalin's Purge of the 1930s* (Toronto: Macmillan, 1968) 43–61; and Mikhail Heller and Aleksandr Nekrich, *Utopia in Power* (New York: Summit Books, 1986), 277.

59. See Amy Knight, *Who Killed Kirov? The Kremlin's Greatest Mystery* (New York: Hill and Wang, 1999), 312 n. 63; and Aleksandr Bastrykin and Olga Gromtseva, *Teni izchezaiut v Smol'nom: Ubiistvo Kirova* (Saint Petersburg: Evropeiskii dom, 2001), 61.

60. Lermolo, *Face of a Victim,* 35. Volkova's reference to Malinin is in Kirilina, *Neizvestnyi Kirov,* 452. Malinin's 1961 interview with the Party Control Commission is in Iu. I. Sedov, N. V. Kulish, and A. Ia. Valetov, "Spravka rabotnikov prokuratury SSSR i sledstvennogo otdela KGB SSSR po povodu zapiski A. N. Iakovleva 'Nekotorye soobrazheniia po itogam izucheniia obstoiatel'stv ubiistva S. M. Kirov," June 14, 1990, in A. Artizov et al., eds., *Reabilitatsiia: Kak eto bylo,* vol. 3: *Seredina 80-kh godov–1991* (Moscow: Mezhdunarodnyi fond "Demokratiia," 2004), 472.

61. Lermolo, *Face of a Victim,* 172.

62. Ibid., passim.

63. Ibid., 15–16, 55–63.

64. *The Crime of the Zinoviev Opposition: The Assassination of S. M. Kirov* (Moscow: Cooperative Publishing Society of Foreign Workers in the USSR, 1935), 50; Lermolo, *Face of a Victim,* 71, 112. Of course the author of *Face of a Victim* could have gotten these names from a number of open Soviet sources.

65. RGASPI, f. 671, op. 1, d. 114, ll. 208–209.

66. RGASPI, f. 671, op. 1, d. 120, l. 137.

67. RGASPI, f. 671, op. 1, d. 128, l. 51.

68. RGASPI, f. 671, op. 1, d. 128, l. 52.

69. Lermolo, *Face of a Victim,* 68.

70. *Crime of the Zinovievite Opposition,* 51.

71. Lermolo, *Face of a Victim,* 1–8, 15–17.

72. Ibid., 38.

CHAPTER 14. THE POLITICS OF REHABILITATION
AND THE KIROV MURDER, 1953–1957

1. See William Taubman, *Khrushchev: The Man and His Era* (New York: Norton, 2003), 160; and documents in V. Naumov et al., eds., *Lavrentii Beria, 1953: Stenogramma iul'skogo plenuma TsK KPSS i drugie dokumenty* (Moscow: Mezhdunarodnyi fond "Demokratiia," 1999), 17–55.

2. See Alla Kirilina, *L'assassinat de Kirov: Destin d'un stalinien, 1888–1934* (Paris: Seuil, 1995), 223; and J. Arch Getty, *Origins of the Great Purges: The Soviet Communist Party Reconsidered, 1933–1938* (Cambridge: Cambridge University Press, 1985), 216–217. For summaries of the history of Soviet investigative commissions, see N. Petukhov and V. Khomchik, "Delo o 'Leningradskom tsentre,'" *Vestnik verkhovnogo suda SSSR*, no. 5 (1991): 15–18; and Pelshe report, RGANI, f. 6, op. 13, d. 117, ll. 1–18.

3. Dmitry Shepilov, *Neprimknuvshii* (Moscow: Vagrius, 2001), 26; Taubman, *Khrushchev*, 246.

4. Naumov et al., *Lavrentii Beria*, 95, 168.

5. Taubman, *Khrushchev*, 240–241, 258, 264; Shepilov, *Neprimknuvshii*, 294; Naumov et al., *Lavrentii Beria*, 216–217.

6. On Rudenko's biography, see N. S. Khrushchev, *Vremia, Liudi, Vlast': Vospominaniia*. 4 vols. (Moscow: "Moskovskie novosti," 1999), 1:144 n. 29, 185–86, 3:572; Naumov et al., *Lavrentii Beria*, 480.

7. N. V. Petrov, "Pervyi predsedatel' KGB general Ivan Serov," *Otechestvennaia istoriia* 5 (1997): 23–42. Source found through Taubman, *Khrushchev*, 741 n. 48.

8. Petrov, "Pervyi predsedatel'"; Shepilov, *Neprimknuvshii*, 159, 269, 353–354; Taubman, *Khrushchev*, 370; Anastas Mikoian, *Tak bylo: razmyshlenie o minuvshem* (Moscow: Vagrius, 1999), 607.

9. Quotations from Khrushchev, *Vremia, Liudi, Vlast'*, 2:174.

10. This observation is made by Shepilov (*Neprimknuvshii*, 397), Taubman (*Khrushchev*, 241), and Sergo Mikoyan, Anastas Mikoyan's son (*Stalinism as I Saw It* [Washington, D. C.: Kennan Institute for Advanced Russian Studies, 1991], 43).

11. A. Artizov et al., eds., *Reabilitatsiia: Kak eto bylo*, vol. 1: *Mart 1953–fevral' 1956* (Moscow: Mezhdunarodnyi fond "Demokratiia," 2000), 115–142; N. Kovaleva et al., eds., *Molotov, Malenkov, Kaganovich, 1957: Stenogramma iiun'skogo plenuma TsK KPSS i drugie dokumenty* (Moscow: Mezhdunarodnyi fond "Demokratiia," 1998), 201–203; Taubman, *Khrushchev*, 263–264.

12. Artizov et al., *Reabilitatsiia*, 1:116–117.

13. See Taubman, *Khrushchev*, 277–278, Khrushchev speech to Leningrad *aktiv* in Artizov et al., *Reabilitatsiia*, 1:133, and biographical material on Snegov in A. Artizov et al., eds., *Reabilitatsiia: Kak eto bylo*, vol. 2: *Fevral' 1956–nachalo 80-kh godov* (Moscow: Mezhdunarodnyi fond "Demokratiia," 2003), 891.

14. See biographical material on Snegov in Artizov et al., *Reabilitatsiia*, 2:891, and Sergei Khrushchev, *Khrushchev on Khrushchev: An Inside Account of the Man and His Era* (Boston: Little, Brown, 1990), 11–13.

15. See Olga Shatunovsky, "Gone Century: Memoirs Edited by Jana Kutin and Andrei Broido," www.caida.org/broido/ola/ola.html, rasskazy 1, 2, and biographical data on Shatunovskaya in Artizov et al., *Reabilitatsiia*, 2:904.

16. Shatunovsky, "Gone Century," passim; Artizov et al., *Reabilitatsiia,* 2:904.

17. Shatunovsky, "Gone Century," rasskaz 20; information on Bagirov case in Artizov et al., *Reabilitatsiia,* 1:407 n. 61.

18. Shatunovsky, "Gone Century," rasskaz 10; L. Kosheleva et al., eds., *Pis'ma I. V. Stalina V. M. Molotovu, 1925–1936 g.g.* (Moscow: "Molodaia gvardiia," 1995), 144–149.

19. The two men were Vladimir Lebedev, Khrushchev's longtime personal assistant, and Zinovy Serdiuk, a Khrushchev supporter and Central Committee member from Ukraine. See Shatunovsky, "Gone Century," rasskazy 20, 22. According to Sergei Khrushchev, both of these men maintained their loyalty to Khrushchev after his fall from power and lost their high-level jobs as a result. Not just Shatunovskaya, but also Snegov, believed Lebedev to be a "hidden Stalinist." See S. Khrushchev, *Khrushchev on Khrushchev,* 10, 160. Nikita Khrushchev reports in his memoirs on Serdiuk calling him in 1967 to congratulate him on the fiftieth anniversary of the founding of the Red Army. It took courage and personal devotion to do this—very few members of the party elite remained in touch with Khrushchev after he was ousted. See Khrushchev, *Vremia, Liudi, Vlast'*, 1:324.

20. Shatunovsky, "Gone Century," rasskaz 20; Mikoian, *Tak bylo,* 583. Throughout her memoirs, Shatunovskaya aims to differentiate Mikoyan from the Stalinist "butchers" during the Terror.

21. Shatunovsky, "Gone Century," rasskaz 9; Mikhail Rosliakov, *Ubiistvo Kirova: Politicheskie i ugolovnye prestupleniia v 1930-kh godakh* (Leningrad: Lenizdat, 1991, 91–92); B. S. Popov and V. G. Opponokov, "Berievshchina," *Voenno-istoricheskii zhurnal,* no. 1 (1990): 68–78 (last source found through Amy Knight, *Beria: Stalin's First Lieutenant* [Princeton: Princeton University Press, 1993], 18.)

22. Shatunovsky, "Gone Century," rasskaz 1; Iurii Zhukov, *Inoi Stalin* (Moscow: Vagrius, 2003), 175–176; Iu. G. Murin, ed., *Iosif Stalin v obiatiiakh semi* (Moscow: "Rodina," 1993), 154–196.

23. Shatunovsky, "Gone Century," rasskazy 9, 16.

24. Anti-Shatunovskaya comments from A. T. Rybin, *Stalin i Kirov (zapiski telokhranitelia)* (n.p., 1995). Rybin was an ex-bodyguard of Stalin's and later head of security at the Bolshoi Theater. His pamphlet presents an unreconstructed Stalinist account of the Kirov murder, naming Trotsky as the organizer.

25. On Mikoyan's "adoption" of Shaumian, see Mikoian, *Tak bylo,* 90.

26. On Beria's effective takeover of the Transcaucasian leadership from Ordzhonikidze clients in 1931–1932, see R. W. Davies et al., eds., *The Stalin-Kaganovich Correspondence, 1931–1936* (New Haven, Yale University Press, 2003), 66–67, 86–88, 89 n. 6, 140, 142–143, 182 (including note 3). For an account of Beria's efforts to promote a new history exaggerating Stalin's pre-1917 role in the Caucasian revolutionary movement, see S. V. Sukharev, "Litsedeistvo na poprishche istorii," *Voprosy istorii KPSS,* no. 3 (1990): 102–118. See also Knight, *Beria,* 42–64.

27. For Khlevniuk's argument against Beria's involvement in Ordzhonikidze's death, see Oleg Khlevniuk, *Stalin i Ordzhonikidze* (Moscow; "Rossiia Molodaia," 1993), 76–82. Petr Chagin's comments in September 1960 about Bagirov's "grudge" against Kirov (RGANI, f. 6, op. 13, d. 23, ll. 20–22) would seem to imply that Beria somehow engineered Ordzhonikidze's end.

28. Mikoian, *Tak bylo,* 589–590.

29. Ibid., 590–592; Taubman, *Khrushchev,* 266–269.

30. Artizov et al., *Reabilitatsiia,* 1:816, n. 5.

31. Rosliakov, *Ubiistvo,* 45–46.

32. Artizov et al., *Reabilitatsiia,* 1:296, 2:816 n. 5.

33. See notes on Presidium sessions of Nov. 5, 1955, Feb. 1, 1956, and Feb. 9, 1956, ibid., 275–276, 308–309, 349–351.

34. Ibid., 317–348.

35. Khrushchev, *Vremia, Liudi, Vlast'',* 2:758–759.

36. "Zapiska P. N. Pospelova ob ubiistve Kirova," *Svobodnaia mysl',* no. 8 (1992): 64–71.

37. Ibid., 66–71.

38. On the disorders in local party and professional organizations following the "Secret Speech," see Artizov et al., *Reabilitatsiia,* 2:21–65.

39. RGANI, f. 6, op. 13, d. 9, ll. 89–103; Artizov et al., *Reabilitatsiia,* 2: 36–38.

40. Ibid., 36–38.

41. Ibid., 38.

42. See RGANI, f. 6, op. 13, d. 1, ll. 10–53, 153–194, and d. 24, ll. 24–32. Pospelov and Aristov were joint authors of one draft of Khrushchev's "Secret Speech" (Taubman, *Khrushchev,* 280). They and Kozlov were working on "useable" versions of Stalinist history for Khrushchev.

43. See A. I. Mlechin, *Nikolai Shvernik: Biograficheskii ocherk* (Moscow: Politizdat, 1977), 208, 216. Shvernik was appointed on February 27, 1956, at the plenum of the Central Committee that immediately followed the Twentieth Party Congress.

44. Artizov et al., *Reabilitatsiia,* 2:70.

45. Email to author from M. Iu. Prozumenshchikov, deputy director of RGANI, Sept. 5, 2005.

46. RGANI, f. 6, op. 13, d. 1, ll. 10–53.

47. On Kuzin's motivations, see N. Petukhov and V. Khomchik, "Delo o Leningradskom tsentre," *Vestnik verkhovnogo suda SSSR,* no. 6 (1991): 19–21.

48. RGANI, f. 6, op. 13, d. 1, ll. 153–194.

49. Iu. I. Sedov, N. V. Kulish, and A. Ia. Valetov, "Spravka rabotnikov prokuratury SSSR i sledstvennogo otdela KGB SSSR po povodu zapiski A. N. Iakovleva 'Nekotorye soobrazheniia po itogam izucheniia obstoiatel'stv ubiistva S. M. Kirov," June 14, 1990, published in A. Artizov et al., eds., *Reabilitatsiia: Kak eto bylo,* vol. 3: *Seredina 80-kh godov–1991* (Moscow: Mezhdunarodnyi fond "Demokratiia," 2004) (hereafter "Reply to Iakovlev"), 462 (Nikolaev's diary mentions Kotolynov et al.), 469 (destruction of "Svoiak"); email to author from M. Iu. Prozumenshchikov, deputy director of RGANI, Sept. 5, 2005 (absence of any mention of Kotolynov et al. in 1956 document release).

50. Khrushchev, *Vremia, Liudi, Vlast'',* vol. 2, 178–179.

51. Artizov et al., *Reabilitatsiia,* 2:77–78, 83–84.

52. RGANI, f. 6, op. 13, d. 43, l. 3.

53. See Taubman, *Khrushchev,* 283–294; Artizov et al., *Reabilitatsiia,* 1:128, 132–148.

54. Artizov et al., *Reabilitatsiia,* 2:146.

55. Ibid., 162–163, 172, 181–183, 172–176.
56. RGANI, f. 6, op. 13, d. 43, ll. 1–16; Artizov et al., *Reabilitatsiia,*2:114.
57. Artizov et al., *Reabilitatsiia,*2:163–167.
58. RGANI, f. 6, op. 13, d. 13, ll. 7–45.
59. RGANI, f. 6, op. 13, d. 43, ll. 12, 13.
60. Artizov et al., *Reabilitatsiia,*2:204–207.
61. Ibid., 207–208.
62. Taubman, *Khrushchev,* 300–306; Kovaleva et al., *Molotov, Malenkov, Kaganovich,* 10–13; Shepilov, *Neprimknuvshii,* 36–38, 387–396.
63. Taubman acknowledges claims that Khrushchev knew about the June 1957 overthrow attempt against him, but concludes, "The last thing [Khruschchev] let himself believe was that the power and glory he craved were about to be taken from him," Taubman, *Khrushchev,* 316–317. Taubman also notes Demichev's belief that Khrushchev knew the coup attempt was coming. For Shepilov's belief that Khrushchev knew, see Shepilov, *Neprimknuvshii,* 393.
64. RGANI, f. 6, op. 13, d. 43, ll. 14, 15.
65. Artizov et al., *Reabilitatsiia,*2:269–270.
66. Ibid., 270–271. For Brezhnev quote, see Kovaleva et al., *Molotov, Malenkov, Kaganovich,* 245–246.
67. Artizov et al., *Reabilitatsiia,*2:271–272.
68. Taubman, *Khrushchev,* 317–320; Kovaleva et al., *Molotov, Malenkov, Kaganovich,* 14–15, 183; Shepilov, *Neprimknuvshii,* 393–396.
69. Kovaleva et al., *Molotov, Malenkov, Kaganovich,* 567.
70. Ibid., 176, 199–201, 205, 246–247, 250, 258, 417–419.
71. Ibid., 188–197.
72. Ibid., 429.
73. Ibid., 479.

CHAPTER 15. SHATUNOVSKAYA'S INVESTIGATION AND AFTER

1. See documents in A. Artizov et al., eds., *Reabilitatsiia: Kak eto bylo,* vol. 2: *Fevral' 1956–nachalo 1980-kh godov* (Moscow: Mezhdunarodnyi fond "Demokratiia," 2003),294–295 and 310–324 (report on Malenkov's participation in the Terror, May 22, 1958).
2. RGANI, f. 6, op. 13, d. 23, ll. 20–22.
3. The Jan. 28, 1961 KPK report is in RGANI, f. 6, op. 13, d. 7, ll. 1–56.
4. See Olga Shatunovsky, "Gone Century: Memoirs Edited by Jana Kutin and Andrei Broido," www.caida.org/broido/ola/ola.html, rasskaz 21 ("Peresmotr Stalinskikh protsessov: Beseda s rezhisserami Mosfil'ma, 1988").
5. For the Presidium order creating a new commission in May 1961, see Alla Kirilina, *Neizvestnyi Kirov* (Moscow: OLMA-PRESS, 2001), 338. For the September 1961 commission report, see RGANI, f. 6, op. 13, d. 117, ll. 1–18, and d. 138, ll. 4–9.
6. January 1961 report is in RGANI, f. 6, op. 13, d. 7, ll. 1–56. On Molotov's criticisms of Khrushchev, see William Taubman, *Khrushchev: The Man and His Era* (New York: Norton, 2003), 368–369.
7. Ken Jowitt, "'Moscow Centre,'" in *New World Disorder: The Leninist Ex-*

tinction (Berkeley: University of California Press, 1992), 159–219. For Khrushchev's clashes with the Albanians and the Chinese, see A. A. Fursenko et al., eds., *Prezidium TsK KPSS, 1954–1964* (Moscow: ROSSPEN, 2004), 1080–1081 (notes 2 and 3). On China's superior revolutionary charisma, note that in the summer of 1961 Castro's emissary to Moscow Ramiro Valdes compared Soviet failure to support Latin American revolutionaries unfavorably with China's sponsorship of international revolution. See Aleksandr Fursenko and Timothy Naftali, *One Hell of a Gamble: Khrushchev, Castro, and Kennedy, 1958–1964* (New York: Norton, 1997), 168.

8. For criticisms of Enver Hoxha's "cult of personality," see *XXII S"ezd Kommunisticheskoi partii Sovetskogo soiuza. 17–31 oktiabria 1961 goda" Stenograficheskii otchet* (Moscow: Gosizdat politicheskoi literatury, 3 vols., 1962), 1:342–343, 458–459, 483, 487–492, 558, 2:577–580.

9. Taubman, *Khrushchev*, 507–516.

10. See RGANI, f. 6, op. 13, d. 9, passim, for Kozlov materials used by the Shatunovskaya commission. On the promotion of Kozlov and the demotion of Kirichenko et al., see Taubman, *Khrushchev*, 758 n. 54; Fursenko et al., *Prezidium TsK KPSS*, "No. 217. Protokol No. 279 ot 4 maia," 443 n. 2, and "No. 218. Protokol No. 284 ot 2 iiunia," 1075 n. 1.

11. Petrovskii testimony in RGANI, f. 6, op. 13, d. 9, ll. 69–70.

12. Anastas Mikoian, *Tak bylo: Razmyshleniia o minuvshem* (Moscow: Vagrius, 1999), 592–593.

13. Ivanov testimony in RGANI, f. 6, op. 13, d. 13, l. 170.

14. Roy Medvedev gives 270 votes against Stalin in *Let History Judge* (New York: Knopf, 1971), 156. L. S. Shaumian, son of the Baku commissar and effectively "adopted" son of Mikoyan, gave 300 in *Pravda*, Feb. 7, 1964.

15. One early example of these stories, that Kalinin got more votes than Stalin (true), appeared in the *Socialist Herald* in early 1934 (see above, p. 128). Another was a report from an informer in February 1939 that Anastasia Plotnikova, a Leningrad party official at the "Krasnaia zaria" factory, had told her that Stalin, Voroshilov, Kirov, and Kaganovich had not been elected unanimously to the TsK at the Seventeenth Party Congress. The rumor, although true, was treated as "counterrevolutionary." It is quite likely that the state's treatment of such innocuous, and true, oral stories, led the population to perceive them as more important than they were, and to inflate them. See RGANI, f. 6, op. 13, d. 78, ll. 54–55.

16. On the flu epidemic, see RGANI, f. 6, op. 13, d. 78, ll. 150–155 ("Obzornaia spravka o materialakh OGPU 'Ob obsluzhivanii i okhrane XVII s"ezda VKP(b)'"). For results of voting at the Fifteenth and Sixteenth Party Congresses, see RGASPI, f. 56, op. 1, d. 61, l. 19; op. 2, d. 36, l. 23, and f. 58, op. 1, d. 37, ll. 31–34, 53; d. 46, l. 9. See N. Mikhailov and V. Naumov, "Skol'ko delegatov XVII s"ezda partii golosovalo protiv Stalin?" *Izvestiia TsK KPSS*, no. 7 (1989): 114–121, on the results of voting at the Seventeenth Party Congress.

17. Verkhovykh's testimony is in RGANI, f. 6, op. 13, d. 23, ll. 47–49. For KGB data on the fate of Seventeenth Party Congress Electoral Commission members, see RGANI, f. 6, op. 13, d. 23, ll. 54–63.

18. Olga Shatunovskaia, "Vospominaniia veterana partii: Fal'sifikatsiia," *Argumenty i fakty*, June 2–8, 1990, 6–7. Shatunovskaia charged that the official pro-

tocol of her commission's 1960 unsealing of the Seventeenth Party Congress had been falsified, and that they had in fact found 289 ballots missing from the record. However I have seen microfilm of the 1934 Electoral Commission documents as well as scratched calculations made in pencil, apparently from 1960 (RGANI, f. 6, op. 13, d. 23, l. 66), confirming that 166 ballots were not turned in.

19. RGANI, f. 6, op. 13, d. 23, ll. 47–49.

20. Five years later, in 1966, aged over eighty, Viksin would give contradictory testimony, claiming that Stalin's name was crossed off twenty-seven ballots in his urn. RGANI, f. 6, op. 13, d. 78, ll. 142–144.

21. RGANI, f. 6, op. 13, d. 78, ll. 96–100.

22. See Andreosian's deposition in RGANI, f. 6, op. 13, d. 23, ll. 43–430b, and Jan. 28, 1961 KPK report, RGANI, f. 6, op. 13, d. 7, l. 10.

23. Andreosian testified in November 1960 that the Electoral Commission tried to determine who had written the notes attacking Stalin. RGANI, f. 6, op. 13, d. 23, ll. 43–430b.

24. For voting results of the Fifteenth, Sixteenth, and Seventeenth party congresses see RGASPI, f. 56, op. 1, d. 61, l. 19, and op. 2, d. 36, l. 23; and f. 58, op. 1, d. 37, ll. 31–34, 53, and d. 46, l. 9; and Mikhailov and Naumov, "Skol'ko delegatov." At the Sixteenth Party Congress (1930), for example, of 1,132 votes cast, Stalin and Kirov received 9 against, while the disgraced leaders of the Right, Rykov, Tomsky and Bukharin received, respectively, 119, 128 and 407 votes against. According to the archival record of the Seventeenth Party Congress, the most "No" votes for membership in the TsK were cast against Yakov Yakovlev, recently dismissed as Commissar of Agriculture (118), and for candidate membership, against Tomsky (258).

25. Medvedev, *Let History Judge,* 155–156. Apart from testimony to the KPK in 1960–1961, another possible source for such rumors is prisoner interrogations from the Terror. According to Genrikh Liushkov's April 1939 article in the Japanese journal *Kaizo* (see Conclusion, Document 127) Aleksei Rykov testified that a coup attempt against Stalin was planned for the Seventeenth Party Congress. This is mentioned briefly also in the official transcript of the March 1938 show trial (People's Commissariat of Justice of the USSR, *Report of the Court Proceedings in the Case of the Anti-Soviet Bloc of Rights and Trotskyites* [Moscow: People's Commissariat of Justice of the USSR, 1938], 178). "Confessions" of an attempt to get rid of Stalin at the Seventeenth Party Congress during the Terror could have led to later rumors of such an attempt.

26. RGANI, f. 6, op. 13, d. 23, ll. 47–49 (Verkhovykh); d. 78, ll. 50–53 (Zemtsova); Kirilina, *Neizvestnyi Kirov,* 312. Kirilina believes that the origins of the "general secretary" rumor may have to do with Stalin's dropping of the title in correspondence and public documents after the Sixteenth Party Congress. The post was not formally abolished in the 1930s. Stalin was putting on a show of "collective leadership," similar to his frequent use of the phrase "Central Committee" in place of "I."

27. Mikhail Rosliakov, *Ubiistvo Kirova: Politicheskie i ugolovnye prestupleniia v 1930-kh godakh* (Leningrad: Lenizdat, 1991, 91–92), 122–123. RGANI, f. 6, op. 13, d. 23, ll. 110–111, and d. 78, l. 32.

28. RGANI, f. 6, op. 13, dd. 23, 78. The three post-1964 depositions were from Sidorov, Slinko, and Mart'ianov.

29. RGANI, f. 6, op. 13, dd. 23, 78.

30. RGANI, f. 6, op. 13, dd. 23, 78.

31. RGANI, f. 6, op. 13, d. 23, ll. 6–8, 13–14, 20–22.

32. Kirilina, *Neizvestnyi Kirov*, 313–315, 334–335.

33. Ibid. Shatunovskaya also claimed that Petr Smorodin's wife, Elena, told a similar story after 1956.

34. Francesco Benvenuti refers to party "lore" on the subject in "Kirov in Soviet Politics, 1933–1934," CREES Discussion Papers, Soviet Industrialisation Project Series, no. 8 (University of Birmingham, 1977), 10.

35. RGANI, f. 6, op. 13, d. 23, ll. 20–22.

36. RGANI, f. 6, op. 13, d. 7, ll. 11–12.

37. See above, p. 622, for Tyshkevich's failure to recognize Nikolaev in a photo line-up. For excerpts from Tyshkevich's testimony during the Terror and later, see the Klimov report, RGANI, f. 6, op. 13, d. 13, ll. 7–45. For Tyshkevich's false testimony to the commission that he was not interrogated in 1934–1935, see RGANI, f. 6, op. 13, d. 13, ll. 179–181.

38. RGANI, f. 6, op. 13, d. 13, ll. 138–139, 161–162, 170.

39. RGANI, f. 6, op. 13, d. 13, ll. 7–45 ("K vyiasneniiu voprosa o zaderzhanii Nikolaeva L. V. do soversheniia im ubiistva S. M. Kirova").

40. RGANI, f. 6, op. 13, d. 7, ll. 1–56.

41. RGANI, f. 6, op. 13, d. 9. March 1956 letters of Kuzin, Yanelis, Mamushin, and Iakushev to Kozlov and Khrushchev are in ll. 100–123. Shatunovskaya commission report on Borisov's death dated Feb. 10, 1961 is on ll. 1–18. Jan. 28, 1961 KPK report on Kirov murder and effort to expel Molotov from the party are in d. 7, ll. 1–56.

42. RGANI, f. 6, op. 13, d. 9, ll. 1–18, 35–39. On Kuzin's motive for continuing to repeat his Terror testimony, see N. Petukhov and V. Khomchik, "Delo o Leningradskom tsentre." *Vestnik verkhovnogo suda SSSR,* no. 5 (1991): 15–18.

43. RGANI, f. 6, op. 13, d. 9, ll. 35–39.

44. RGANI, f. 6, op. 13, d. 9, ll. 1–18, 121–123.

45. See RGANI, f. 6, op. 13, d. 9, ll. 1–18, and TsA FSB RF, a.u.d. N-Sh44, t. 24, ll. 291–292.

46. RGANI, f. 6, op. 13, d. 9, ll. 1–18.

47. RGANI, f. 6, op. 13, d. 9, ll. 1–18.

48. Iu. I. Sedov, N. V. Kulish, and A. Ia. Valetov, "Spravka rabotnikov prokuratury SSSR i sledstvennogo otdela KGB SSSR po povodu zapiski A. N. Iakovleva 'Nekotorye soobrazheniia po itogam izucheniia obstoiatel'stv ubiistva S. M. Kirov," June 14, 1990, published in A. Artizov et al., eds., *Reabilitatsiia: Kak eto bylo,* vol. 3: *Seredina 80-kh godov–1991* (Moscow: Mezhdunarodnyi fond "Demokratiia," 2004), 497 (hereafter cited as "Reply to Iakovlev").

49. RGANI, f. 6, op. 13, d. 13, ll. 287–288.

50. Medvedev, *Let History Judge,* 159–160; Robert Conquest, *Stalin and the Kirov Murder* (Oxford: Oxford University Press, 1989), 42; Robert Tucker, *Stalin in Power: The Revolution from Above, 1928–1941* (New York: Norton, 1990),

294–295; Anton Antonov-Ovseyenko, *The Time of Stalin: Portrait of a Tyranny* (New York: Harper and Row, 1981), 94. For Khrushchev's use of Kuzin's testimony, see *XXII S"ezd kommunisticheskoi partii sovetskogo soiuza*, 2:583–584.

51. RGANI, f. 6, op. 13, d. 7, ll. 1–56.

52. RGANI, f. 6, op. 13, d. 7, ll. 1–56.

53. RGANI, f. 6, op. 13, d. 7, ll. 1–56.

54. RGANI, f. 6, op. 13, d. 23, ll. 20–22.

55. RGANI, f. 6, op. 13, d. 23, l. 29.

56. RGASPI, f. 80, op. 18, d. 121, ll. 93–96, 178–179. See also Kirov note to Chagin, April 27, 1928, RGASPI, f. 80, op. 12, d. 26, l. 1, expressing irritation with the latter's publication of the journal *The Art of Dressing Well* without his or any other senior authority's permission.

57. Medvedev, *Let History Judge*, 224. For Kirov's 1926 reprimand to Chagin, see Chagin's September 1960 testimony in RGANI, f. 6, op. 13, d. 23, ll. 20–22.

58. Sorokin letter to Khrushchev, Jan. 25, 1962, RGANI, f. 6, op. 13, d. 67, ll. 4–50b, and March 5, 1962 deposition, ll. 7–15.

59. RGANI, f. 6, op. 13, d. 67, ll. 7–15.

60. For a list of the Electoral Commission members, see RGANI, f. 6, op. 13, d. 23, ll. 54–62.

61. Sorokin letter to Khrushchev, Jan. 25, 1962, RGANI, f. 6, op. 13, d. 67, ll. 4–50b, and March 5, 1962 deposition, ll. 7–15.

62. Ibid., RGANI, f. 6, op. 13, d. 67, ll. 17–29.

63. On the May 1961 establishment of a new investigative commission and the June 1961 discussion of the January 1961 Shatunovskaya report, see RGANI, f. 6, op. 13, d. 117, ll. 1–18; d. 40, ll. 36–54 (1967 Pelshe report and March 16, 1965 KPK report on the Kirov investigation). For the membership of the new commission established in May see RGANI, f. 6, op. 13, d. 39, ll. 1–7 (commission report of September 1961).

64. Fursenko et al., *Prezidium TsK KPSS*, 497. Shatunovskaya complained in a 1988 interview that most of the permanent staff at the KPK obstructed her investigation of the Kirov murder, but never refers to the documented removal of Stalinists from staff (Shatunovsky "Gone Century," rasskaz 21).

65. RGANI, f. 6, op. 13, d. 40, ll. 36–54.

66. RGANI, f. 6, op. 13, d. 40, ll. 36–54.

67. Quoted in Rosliakov, *Ubiistvo*, 91.

68. *XXII S"ezd*, 2:583–585.

69. Taubman, *Khrushchev*, 508–514.

70. Medvedev, *Let History Judge*, 156.

71. A. M. Kostrikova and E. M. Kostrikova, *Eto bylo v Urzhume: Vospominaniia o S. M. Kirove* (Kirov: Kirovskoe knizhnoe izdatel'stvo, 1962); S. Sinel'nikov, *Kirov* (Moscow: "Molodaia gvardiia," 1964).

72. Stepan Krasnikov, *Sergei Mironovich Kirov: Zhizn' i deiatel'nost'* (Moscow: Gosizdat politicheskoi literatury, 1964).

73. Shatunovsky, "Gone Century," rasskaz 22 ("Ukhod iz TsK"). On Molotov's expulsion from the party see "Reshenie KPK pri TsK ob iskliuchenii iz partii V. M. Molotova," in Artizov et al., *Reabilitatsiia*, 2:378–392. On Shatunovskaya's retirement from the KPK, see ibid., 372–374.

74. Shatunovskaia letter to Khrushchev, May 22, 1962, Artizov et al., *Reabilitatsiia*, 2:372–374.

75. On Khrushchev's "wait fifteen years," see Shatunovsky, "Gone Century," rasskaz 21. On the petitions to rehabilitate Rightist leaders and Pospelov's comments, see Artizov et al., *Reabilitatsiia*, 2:366–367, 474–475 (petition of Stasova et al. for rehabilitation of Bukharin, Jan. 20, 1965).

76. For the testimony of the wives of Kotomin, Gorin-Lundin, and Mosevich, see RGANI, f. 6, op. 13, d. 82, ll. 29–320b, 76–86, 133–145. It seems possible that Mosevich's wife misremembered "Special Department" (*Osobyi otdel*) for "Operations Department" (*Operativnyi otdel*). The latter department did have materials on Nikolaev—related to his October 15, 1934 detention. See the Conclusion, p. 678, for a discussion of the possibility that the Special Department did have materials on Nikolaev before the murder. A substantial part of Annushkov's testimony is reproduced in "Reply to Iakovlev," 490–491. Reports on the search for surviving employees of the Leningrad regional NKVD from 1934 are in RGANI, f. 6, op. 13, d. 60, ll. 41–58.

77. For the "readmissions" to the party and Serdiuk's report on the OGPU's fake counterrevolutionary organizations, see Artizov et al., *Reabilitatsiia*, 2:313–314, 408–412, 455. For the February 1963 report on the Terror, see ibid., 541–670.

78. Fursenko et al., *Prezidium TsK KPSS*, 862–872; Taubman, *Khrushchev*, 3–17, 615–619.

79. For evidence that Serdiuk was still in charge of the investigation, see note from central party archive to Serdiuk, March 29, 1965, in RGANI, f. 6, op. 13, d. 78, ll. 1–5.

80. See Aleksandr Nekrich, *Forsake Fear* (Boston: Unwin Hyman, 1991), 174–175 (January 1966 *Pravda* article), and 187–202 (Pelshe harassment of Nekrich, Petrovskii). See also Artizov et al., *Reabilitatsiia*, 2:484–488 (Semichastnyi brief to TsK on anti-Stalin writers, March 1966), 505–516 (Nov. 10, 1966 Politburo session), 523 (KPK persecution of Snegov).

81. Kutin quote from Shatunovsky, "Gone Century," introduction to rasskaz 20 ("Rabota v TsK"). On the connections between the people listed, see also Nekrich, *Forsake Fear*, 159, 191–194; Sergei Khrushchev, *Khrushchev on Khrushchev: An Inside Account of the Man and His Era* (Boston: Little, Brown, 1990), 1990, 7–10; Sergo Mikoyan, *Stalinism As I Saw It* (Washington, D.C.: Kennan Institute for Advanced Russian Studies, 1991), 26.

82. Artizov et al., *Reabilitatsiia*, 2:518–520.

83. Medvedev, *Let History Judge*, 152–166.

84. See for example Conquest, *Stalin and the Kirov Murder*, and Tucker, *Stalin in Power*.

85. Nicolaevsky's 1956 articles were republished in English in Boris Nicolaevsky, *Power and the Soviet Elite* (New York: Praeger, 1965), as "The Murder of Kirov" (69–97). On Shatunovskaya's knowledge of Nicolaevsky's writings, see Shatunovsky, "Gone Century," Rasskaz 21.

86. A. A. Kirilina and I. P. Donkov, *Kirov i vremia* (Leningrad: Lenizdat, 1986), 5, 30, 32, 52, 57, 310.

87. Artizov et al., *Reabilitatsiia*, 3:16–21, 31–44, 50–52, 74–75, 95. On the

background to Gorbachev's decision to reexamine Stalinist history, see Geoffrey Hosking, *Russia and the Russians* (Cambridge: Harvard University Press, 2001), 576–577.

88. Artizov et al., *Reabilitatsiia*, 3:122.

89. Ibid., 343.

90. Aleksandr Iakovlev, *Sumerki* (Moscow: Izdatel'stvo "Materik," 2003), 20–21.

91. After Kirov was shot, he was carried into his office and treated there until he was pronounced dead. At 9:30 P.M. on December 1 his office was sealed by N. F. Sveshnikov, Officer Gubin of the Leningrad NKVD, and the head of the regional party committee's Special Section. At this time a complete list of documents and objects found in the office was made, which is still extant. (Kirilina, *Neizvestnyi Kirov*, 230, provides complete text of the document recording the sealing.) See also "Gibel' Kirova. Fakty i versii," *Rodina*, no. 3 (2005): 57–65. The office was apparently opened on the morning of December 2 so that Stalin could use it for meetings and interrogations. That evening at 8:45 P.M. central and Leningrad NKVD officers sealed the office again (TsA FSB RF, a.u.d. N-Sh44, t. 24, l. 399).

The Politburo created a special commission to go through Kirov's documents, consisting of the latter's old comrade-in-arms from the Caucasus M. D. Orakhelashvili, Mikhail Chudov, Boris Pozern, and Andrei Zhdanov. Orakhelashvili was given the keys to Kirov's office and to his apartment, which was sealed on the morning of December 2 (Kirilina, *Neizvestnyi Kirov*, 230–231). In his 1966 interview with KPK officials, Sveshnikov recalled going through Kirov's papers with Orakhelashvili on December 2 in the offices of the Leningrad party committee's Special Section, while Stalin conducted business across the hall in Kirov's office (RGANI, f. 6, op. 13, d. 73, ll. 96–132). Sveshnikov, who cooperated with the 1960–1961 Shatunovskaya commission that sought evidence implicating Stalin in Kirov's murder, never mentioned suspicious correspondence between Stalin and Kirov. However, Orakhelashvili, when he reported to Zhdanov and Chudov on December 22 on his inventory of Kirov's documents, stated that letters "of comrades Stalin and Ordzhonikidze have been put aside separately" (Kirilina, *Neizvestnyi Kirov*, 232). This appears to be the basis for Yakovlev's statement about the disappearance of Stalin's and Ordzhonikidze's correspondence with Kirov.

92. Discussion and analysis of the testimony of these officers appears in Chapters 4, 5, 7–10, and 14–15.

93. Interviews by Kirilina with former Leningrad NKVD officer Leonid Raikhman and Leningrad soviet security officer A. P. Pachinsky confirm that the NKVD conducted a large-scale operation in Leningrad Region in the summer of 1934 aimed at capturing "White Guard terrorists" who had supposedly crossed into the Soviet Union from Finland. Documentation from the All-Russian Military Union, an anti-Soviet organization abroad, indicates that two members of the group crossed the Finnish border into the USSR that summer, and ultimately returned safely. See Kirilina, *Neizvestnyi Kirov*, 198.

94. On Maria Volkova and the case of the "Green Lamp," see Chapter above, pp. 428–434.

95. On Mamushin's evidence, see above, pp. 625–626.

96. See Chapter 10, Document 97, and pp. 413–427.

97. For discussion of the pass regime at Smolny and Kirov's guard, see Chapters 3–6 and 10.

98. "Reply to Iakovlev," 487–488.

99. RGANI, f. 6, op. 13, d. 135, ll. 1–19; "Reply to Iakovlev," 467.

100. RGANI, f. 6, op. 13, d. 135, ll. 1–19.

101. RGANI, f. 6, op. 13, d. 135, ll. 1–19.

102. Such as the destruction of the surveillance file "Svoiak" in January 1956—see above, p. 592. The complete "Reply to Yakovlev" can be found in Artizov et al., *Reabilitatsiia*, 3:459–507.

103. *Trud,* Dec. 4, 1990, 4.

104. See for example "Fal'sifikatsiia: Vospominaniia veterana partii," *Argumenty i fakty,* June 2–8, 1990, 6–7.

105. Mikoyan, *Stalinism As I Saw It,* 14, 25–26, 28–30.

CONCLUSION

1. Pavel Sudoplatov, *Special Tasks: The Memoirs of an Unwanted Witness—A Soviet Spymaster* (New York: Little, Brown, 1994); *Razvedka i Kreml': Zapiski nezhelatel'nogo svidetelia* (Moscow: "Geia," 1996); *Spetsoperatsii: Lubianka i Kreml', 1930–1950 gody* (Moscow: OLMA-PRESS, 1997).

2. For Sudoplatov's claims about the Kirov murder, see Sudoplatov, *Special Tasks,* 50–56. For Raikhman's post in 1934, see Alla Kirilina, *Neizvestnyi Kirov* (Moscow: OLMA-PRESS, 2001), 519. For functional divisions of NKVD departments, see A. I. Kokurin and N. V. Petrov, *Lubianka: Organy VChK-OGPU-NKVD-NKGB-MGB-MVD-KGB, 1917–1991. Spravochnik* (Moscow: Mezhdunarodnyi fond "Demokratiia," 2003), 182–248. For Raikhman's testimony, see Alla Kirilina, "Vystrely v Smol'nom," *Rodina,* no. 1 (1989): 33, 70–78.

3. "Gibel' Kirova: Fakty i versii," *Rodina,* no. 3 (2005): 57–65.

4. Ibid.

5. "Kirov umer so spushchennymi shtanami," *Ekspress gazeta online,* Oct. 5, 2005, at http://www.eg.ru/Publication.mhtml?PubID=7258&Menu=&Part=16&Page=20; Sukharnikova, "Gibel' Kirova." With regard to the clothing listed for the Draule sisters, clearly it was NKVD practice not to list ordinary shirts, dresses, trousers, etc., on prisoners. Probably the items inventoried were those taken away from arrestees—overcoats, for example.

6. RGANI, f. 6, op. 13, d. 78, ll. 150–155 (March 28, 1967 report on OGPU materials on Seventeenth Party Congress from KGB to KPK).

7. Adam Ulam, *Stalin: The Man and His Era* (New York: Viking Press, 1973), 385.

8. For primary source documents on Mikhoels' murder, see V. Naumov and Iu. Sigachev, eds., *Lavrentii Beriia, 1953: Stenogramma iiun'skogo plenuma TsK KPSS i drugie dokumenty* (Moscow: Mezhdunarodnyi fond "Demokratiia," 1999), 25–28.

9. A. Artizov et al., eds., *Reabilitatsiia: Kak eto bylo,* vol. 2: *Fevral' 1956–nachalo 1980-kh godov* (Moscow: Mezhdunarodnyi fond "Demokratiia," 2003), 313–314.

10. Alvin D. Coox, "L'Affaire Lyushkov: Anatomy of a Defector," *Soviet Studies* 19, no. 3 (January 1968): 405–420.

11. Ibid.; Alvin D. Coox, "An Intelligence Case Study: The Lesser of Two Hells, NKVD General G. Liushkov's Defection to Japan, 1938–1945," pts. 1 and 2, *Journal of Slavic Military Studies* 11, no. 3 (September 1998): 145–186 and no. 4 (December 1998): 72–110.

12. Coox, "L'Affaire Lyushkov," 411; Kirilina, *Neizvestnyi Kirov,* 353; Soviet intelligence translation of Liushkov's comments in RGANI, f. 6, op. 13, d. 102, ll. 54–56.

13. Coox, "An Intelligence Case Study," pt. 1, 148.

14. RGASPI, f. 671, op. 1, d. 114, ll. 23–29, 70–73, 89, 100, 112, 125–126, 132–133, 148–149, 150–151, 166–167, 187–189; TsA FSB RF, a.u.d. N-Sh44, t. 12, ll. 41–42, 45–46, 77–78, 260–261, 294–298; RGASPI, f. 671, op. 1, d. 121, ll. 166, 170; APRF, f. 3, op. 24, d. 200, ll. 163–173; RGASPI, f. 671, op. 1, d. 120, ll. 167–168, 229–233; RGANI, f. 6, op. 13, d. 34, l. 94.

15. Mustafa Kemal Atatürk, President of Turkey, died of cirrhosis of the liver on Nov. 10, 1938.

16. Coox, "An Intelligence Case Study," pt. 2, 95–101.

17. Ibid., pt. 1, 150–151; A. V. Korotkov et al., eds., "Posetiteli Kremlevskogo kabineta I. V. Stalina, 1936–1937," *Istoricheskii arkhiv,* no. 4 (1995): 15–73.

18. Coox, "An Intelligence Case Study," pt. 1, 176; J. Arch Getty and Oleg Naumov, *The Road to Terror: Stalin and the Self-Destruction of the Bolsheviks, 1932–1939* (New Haven: Yale University Press, 1999), 588.

19. Kirilina, "Vystrely v Smol'nom."

20. See Hannah Arendt, *Eichmann in Jerusalem: Report on the Banality of Evil* (New York: Penguin, 1977), esp. 276.

21. S. N. Fridinskii, "Priznan podvergshimsia politicheskoi repressii syn ubiitsa Sergeia Kirova," *Pravda-Info,* Aug. 18, 2005, at http://www.pravda.info/news/3511.html.

22. Tat'iana Sukharnikova, "My nagnali takoi velichaishii, podobaiushchii strakh revoliutsii strakh," interview by Iuliia Kantor, *Vremia,* Nov. 29, 2007. Online at www.vremya.ru/2007/219/13/1s305.html.

23. Ibid.

Index of Documents

Index

Academy of Sciences (USSR): 118, 496, 501–502

Agranov, Yakov: 262–264, 270, 272, 274, 275; manages Kirov investigation, 304, 321–322, 399–400, 434, 633–634; communications with Stalin during Kirov investigation, 279–280, 289–290, 295–296, 306, 329–334, 342, 399–400, 432; presses Nikolaev to confess Zinovievite connections, 281–287; informs Stalin on trial of Leningrad Center, 358–371 passim, 586; and Borisov's death, 427, 437, 686; attacks Yagoda at 1937 TsK plenum, 467; in "Letter of an Old Bolshevik," 530

Akulov, Ivan: 279, 334, 337, 342, 344–345, 437

Albania: 608–609

All-Union Council on the National Economy (see VSNKh)

Allilueva, Nadezhda (Stalin's wife): 139, 460, 471, 546, 549

Allilueva, Svetlana (Stalin's daughter): 140, 471

Amenitsky, A.: 88, 101, 104, 458

Andreev, A. (not TsK secretary): 616, 638

Andreev, Andrei (Central Committee secretary): 75, 83–84, 342

Andreev, Leonid (playwright): 33

Andreosian, N. V.: 613, 802n23

Andzhievsky, Grigory: 40, 42, 53, 524

Annushkov, A. F.: 390, 445, 639

Antipov, N. K.: 94, 102, 480–481; rehabilitated, 592

Antonov, Nikolai: 283, 290–291, 307, 309, 311; and Leningrad Center, 315–318, 325, 343, 345–354 passim, 634; biographical information, 306; testimony at trial of Leningrad Center, 360–361, 366; member of Fellowship of Komsomol Militants, 373; links to ex-Zinovievites, 374–376; mentioned in Nikolaev's diary, 283, 592

Anti-semitism: 275, 523

Archives, access (see also "Documents"): 15, 603, 607, 668, 740n18

Aristov, A. B.: 570, 575–576, 579, 594–595, 601, 603, 609

Armenia: 50, 54–55, 565

Arosev, A. Ya.: 534, 541–542

Astrakhan, defense of (1919): 45, 520–521

Avvakumov (member of Institute of Party History party cell): 201–205, 207, 211, 232, 238, 373

Azerbaijan: 50–51, 57–63, 520, 524, 563, 565, 744n81, 745n89

Badaev, Aleksei: 70, 77, 80, 84, 94, 104, 458

Bagirov, Mir: 564, 567

Bakaev, Ivan: 66, 296, 309, 310, 314, 318, 323–325, 329, 332, 363; continuing ties to ex-Zinovievites, 371; trial of Moscow Center, 379; and Korshunov, 430; August 1936 show trial of, 464–465, 596–597, 685; contradictions in testimony (1935–1936), 596–597

Baku: 48, 50–52, 57–61, 563; veterans of revolution, 556, 563, 566–568

Baltic republics: 302

BOOKS IN THE
ANNALS OF COMMUNISM SERIES

The Diary of Georgi Dimitrov, 1933–1949, introduced and edited by Ivo Banac

Dmitrov and Stalin, 1934–1943: Letters from the Soviet Archives, edited by Alexander Dallin and Fridrikh I. Firsov

Enemies Within the Gates? The Comintern and the Stalinist Repression, 1934–1939, by William J. Chase

The Fall of the Romanovs: Political Dreams and Personal Struggles in a Time of Revolution, by Mark D. Steinberg and Vladimir M. Khrustalëv

The History of the Gulag: From Collectivization to the Great Terror, by Oleg V. Khlevniuk

Katyn: A Crime Without Punishment, edited by Anna M. Cienciala, Natalia S. Lebedeva, and Wojciech Materski

The KGB File of Andrei Sakharov, edited by Joshua Rubenstein and Alexander Gribanov

The Kirov Murder and Soviet History, by Matthew E. Lenoe

The Last Diary of Tsaritsa Alexandra, introduction by Robert K. Massie; edited by Vladimir A. Kozlov and Vladimir M. Khrustalëv

The Road to Terror: Stalin and the Self-Destruction of the Bolsheviks, 1932–1939, by J. Arch Getty and Oleg V. Naumov

The Secret World of American Communism, by Harvey Klehr, John Earl Haynes, and Fridrikh I. Firsov

Soviet Culture and Power, by Katerina Clark and Evgeny Dobrenko, with Andrei Artizov and Oleg Naumov

The Soviet World of American Communism, by Harvey Klehr, John Earl Haynes, and Kyrill M. Anderson

Spain Betrayed: The Soviet Union in the Spanish Civil War, edited by Ronald Radosh, Mary R. Habeck, and G. N. Sevostianov

Stalinism as a Way of Life: A Narrative in Documents, edited by Lewis Siegelbaum and Andrei K. Sokolov

The Stalin-Kaganovich Correspondence, 1931–36, compiled and edited by R. W. Davies, Oleg V. Khlevniuk, E. A. Rees, Liudmila P. Kosheleva, and Larisa A. Rogovaya

Stalin's Letters to Molotov, 1925–1936, edited by Lars T. Lih, Oleg V. Naumov, and Oleg V. Khlevniuk

Stalin's Secret Pogrom: The Postwar Inquisition of the Soviet Jewish Anti-Fascist Committee, edited by Joshua Rubenstein and Vladimir P. Naumov

The Unknown Lenin: From the Secret Archive, edited by Richard Pipes

Voices of Revolution, 1917, by Mark D. Steinberg

The War Against the Peasantry, 1927–1930, edited by Lynne Viola, V. P. Danilov, N. A. Ivnitskii, and Denis Kozlov